Port Royal, and Kingston:
By Archibald Bontein.
His Majesty's chief Engineer in ye said Island during the
late War.

To his Royal Highness
William Duke of Cumberland
Captain General, and Commander in Chief of all
His Majesty's Forces, &c.
This Map of the Island of Jamaica, with
the Plans of the Towns of Port Royal & Kingston, are most
Humbly Dedicated by
His Royal Highness
Most humble and
Most Obed'. Servant
Arch'. Bontein.

Published 1st. March 1753.

The Natural, Moral, and Political
History of Jamaica

North West View of LUCK

The
Natural, Moral, and Political History of Jamaica

and the Territories thereon depending from the First Discovery of the Island by Christopher Columbus, to the Year 1746

JAMES KNIGHT

EDITED WITH ANNOTATIONS AND AN INTRODUCTION BY

JACK P. GREENE

IMAGES EDITED BY

TAYLOR STOERMER

WITH A HISTORIOGRAPHIC ESSAY BY

TREVOR BURNARD

UNIVERSITY OF VIRGINIA PRESS

CHARLOTTESVILLE AND LONDON

UNIVERSITY OF VIRGINIA PRESS

First published 2021

1 3 5 7 9 8 6 4 2

Library of Congress Cataloging-in-Publication Data
Names: Knight, James, 1745 or 1746, author. | Greene, Jack P., editor,
writer of added commentary, writer of introduction. | Stoermer,
Taylor, editor. | Burnard, Trevor G. (Trevor Graeme), author.
Title: The natural, moral, and political history of Jamaica and the territories thereon
depending : from the first discovery of the island by Christopher Columbus, to the year
1746 / James Knight ; edited with annotations and an introduction by Jack P. Greene ;
images edited by Taylor Stoermer ; with a historiographic essay by Trevor Burnard.
Description: Charlottesville : University of Virginia Press, 2020.
| Includes bibliographical references and index.
Identifiers: LCCN 2020026840 (print) | LCCN 2020026841 (ebook) |
ISBN 9780813945569 (hardcover) | ISBN 9780813945576 (epub)
Subjects: LCSH: Slavery—Jamaica—History—18th century—Early works
to 1800. | Natural history—Jamaica—History—18th century—Early works
to 1800. | Jamaica—History—To 1962—Early works to 1800. | Jamaica—
Politics and government—To 1962—Early works to 1800. | Jamaica—Social life
and customs—Early works to 1800. | Jamaica—Description and travel—Early
works to 1800. | Jamaica—Economic conditions—Early works to 1800.
Classification: LCC F1884 .K48 2020 (print) | LCC F1884 (ebook) | DDC 972.92—dc23
LC record available at https://lccn.loc.gov/2020026840
LC ebook record available at https://lccn.loc.gov/2020026841

End papers: *A New Map of the Island of Jamaica: With Exact Plans of the Towns
of Port Royal, and Kingston*, Archibald Bontein, London, 1753. (Harvard
University Map Collection, University Special Collections)

Cover art and frontispiece: From an insert on Benjamin Haynes's
Plan of Lucky Valley Estate, Clarendon, 1816. (Long Family Papers,
Additional Manuscripts 43379, item no. C, British Library)

Unless otherwise noted, images are courtesy of the John Carter Brown Library.

For

NORMAN FIERING,

scholar, advisor, editor, and friend, who during his tenure
as director of the John Carter Brown Library presided
over the creation of an important international center for
the advanced study of the early modern American world

Contents

VOLUME I

Volume II

Acknowledgments

First and foremost, the editor is grateful to the British Library for permission to publish James Knight's manuscript *History of Jamaica;* to the Reed Foundation and the University of Melbourne for the funds necessary to bring it to fruition; and to Taylor Stoermer and Trevor Burnard, both former students, for their respective contributions to this publication. Norman Fiering, to whom this volume is dedicated, not only provided editing and publishing advice but put me in touch with Jane Rubin, director of the Reed Foundation, who offered encouraging support for this project over more than a decade after I first talked to her about it, and to David Latham who shepherded that foundation's generous grant through its final stages. Mary Gwaltney Vaz and Sarah Springer transcribed Knight's manuscript; Steve Sarson made an initial, extensive, and useful pass at the annotations; and Michelle LeMaster, Emma Hart, and Ellen Person proofread the typescript. James Robertson supplied me with a copy of Knight's will. Margaret Porter translated a critical Latin passage. Bradley Dickson helped with the annotations for part 1. Taylor and Emily Stoermer aided in finding a competent digitizer for the many images I collected for this project, and Kerry Sheridan did the digitization. In collecting these images, most of them from the John Carter Brown Library, the staff, especially Susan Danforth, Ross Mulcare, Kim Nusco, and Val Andrews, were invariably helpful. Special help in the collection of images came from Charina Castillo, assistant, Department of Rights and Reproductions, New-York Historical Society; Yvonne Fraser Clarke, manager, Special Collections Department, and Keisha Myers, librarian, National Library of Jamaica; Richard Dabb, picture researcher, Museum of London; Dr. Courtney Skipton Long, acting assistant curator/prints and drawings, and Maria Singer, imaging and rights assistant, Yale Center for British Art; Anna Louise Mason, archive and documentation manager, Castle Howard Estate Ltd.; Ann McShane, digital collections archivist, the Library Company of Philadelphia; Robin Ness, senior library specialist, Special Collections Department, Rockefeller Library, Brown University; Claire Rudyj, Lennoxlove Trust; Susan Sherrit, gallery manager, the Harley Gallery, and Dr. Sophie Littlewood, curator, the Portland Collection; and Cecile van der Harten, Head Image Department, Rijksmuseum Amsterdam. Trevor Burnard, Max Edelson, Philip D.

Morgan, Brooke Newman, James Robertson, and Linda Sturtz offered much useful advice and encouragement. Amy Turner Bushnell applied her customarily excellent editorial skills to my introduction and captions and to the final version of the index. As copyeditor, Margaret A. Hogan saved me from many mistakes and did a superb job in standardizing the various elements in this complicated project. David Robertson and I collaborated on the index. And finally, Richard Holway and colleagues at the University of Virginia Press—especially Morgan Myers, who took primary responsibility for shepherding this volume through the editorial process—once again demonstrated their adventurous spirit in taking on this difficult publishing project and their excellent work in bringing it to a conclusion.

Editorial Conventions

This text—in the handwriting of an unknown professional copyist or clerk with some interlineations and revisions in James Knight's own hand—is fully legible. Like many eighteenth-century texts, it exhibits considerable variations in spelling, for which there is no way to tell whether Knight or the copyist was responsible. With a few exceptions, however, I have followed the spelling in the text. Seeking to make as little use of [*sic*] as possible, I have, first, silently corrected the spelling of all words in which *i*, rather than *e*, should follow *c*, as, for instance, in *receiving*. Second, the manuscript being inconsistent in its punctuation of possessive nouns, I have routinely added an apostrophe before a final *s*, as in *majesty's*. Third, I have silently corrected obvious copyist errors. Although Knight made free and often haphazard use of the comma, I have removed commas only when they seemed likely to confuse the reader. Added commas or semicolons are put in square brackets. Every sentence ends with a period, although Knight's copyist occasionally omitted them. Using square brackets, I have expanded contractions and abbreviations, but I have not endeavored to fill in the blank spaces that Knight left, pending further information, simply rendering them as [*blank*]. Knight himself did little annotating, marking the places to which his footnotes referred with a simple asterisk. I have numbered these notes continuously with my own editorial notes. To distinguish them, I have ended Knight's notes with "*—Author.*" In notes that contain material from both Knight and myself, my portion ends with "*— Ed.*" In the interest of cutting costs on this extensive project, I have endeavored to keep annotations relatively short and free from references to a source unless the information in the note came directly from it. To the same end, I have not annotated information from standard sources such as the *Dictionary of National Biography*. I have tried to identify as many as possible of the people Knight mentions and the sources he used, but have not annotated the many places that appear in his text.

Note on Images

Had James Knight's *History of Jamaica* been published during his lifetime, the publisher might well have commissioned an engraver to provide some illustrations, but the manuscript itself offers no indication that any were intended. From early on in our negotiations for a publishing subsidy from the Reed Foundation, however, Jane Rubin urged me to enrich the work with a generous number of visual images. Starting with a substantial body of contemporary images that I had collected over many years for various projects and adding still others recommended by Taylor Stoermer, whom I recruited to serve as visual editor, I selected and wrote the captions for the seventy-seven images in this volume and also chose the images for the dust jacket and end papers. Dr. Stoermer made sure that the digitized images were in the requisite format, obtained the permissions to publish them where necessary, and gathered them into a single digital file. Together, we edited the images, at times cropping them to sharpen and maximize their capacity to illustrate the subject depicted.

Two criteria governed my selection of images. The first was that they be essentially contemporary to Knight's own generation. Only a few images derive from the years after the early 1780s (when the rapid expansion of the antislavery movement, the French Revolution, the Haitian Revolution, and the Napoleonic Wars changed the cultural map of the Western world), and those few depict nothing that would have been unfamiliar to Knight himself.

The second was that they correspond to Knight's own mindset and objectives. A longtime settler himself, he wrote from a settler perspective that championed empire, colonization, trade, and what then passed for free governments; he was intensely anti-Catholic, anti-Spanish, and pro-British; and was deeply critical of corrupt, inept, or imperious metropolitan officials and of metropolitan ignorance of the best interests of the empire, as defined by those on the ground in the colonies.

Because the indigenous Tainos had been largely displaced during Jamaica's century and a half Spanish occupation, Knight was far more sympathetic to them than were settlers who encountered populous and resistant indigenous cultures elsewhere in the Americas. The intensely anti-Spanish views of Spanish-indigenous relations used here to depict the indigenous population of Jamaica—the only contemporary images available on that subject—all come from English or (mostly) Dutch works that, in contrast to modern scholarship, accepted and for political purposes circulated the black legend about Spanish transgressions against indigenous people in the Americas, without, again in contrast to modern scholarship, exhibiting much explicit awareness that British and other European colonizing powers also were guilty of killing off, mistreating, dispossessing, and reducing indigenous and other captured peoples to enslavement and civic emasculation. The use of such images is thus fully compatible with Knight's own views.

Because the enslavement of Africans and their descendants would not come under international attack until nearly thirty years after his death, Knight, like the overwhelming majority of British people involved in colonization, questioned neither the utility of the institution of slavery to meet the labor demands of empire nor its compatibility with metropolitan English legal and cultural values. Rather, in sharp contrast to those colonials who in the mid-1770s took the lead in formulating a proslavery argument, Knight displayed no tendency to denigrate the mental capacities of the enslaved nor the integrity of their cultures, emphasizing instead their obvious aptitude for all kinds of work and social interaction, and making a serious effort to understand and appreciate their cultural diversity. The images of Black people in this volume, all showing them at work and in subjection to or at odds with whites, are illustrative of Knight's views. A list of illustrations can be found in the back matter.

James Knight and His History

JACK P. GREENE

Jamaica, one of the four Greater Antilles in the West Indies, had been a Spanish colony for a century and a half before an English expeditionary force captured it and, during the last half of the 1650s, drove out the Spanish settlers and all but a remnant of their slaves, who established autonomous settlements in the least accessible areas of the mountainous island. Under the Spanish, the colony was an early bloomer, reaching its high point in the first third of the sixteenth century, but as Spanish emigrants bypassed and existing settlers deserted the once thriving island for more dynamic economic regions of colonial Spanish America, it underwent a slow but significant economic and demographic decline into a peripheral area of the Spanish Main, unable in 1655 to repel an invading army. Within a quarter century after the English conquest, however, Jamaica went from a Spanish backwater to England's most promising American colony.

Initially valued for its proximity to the rich colonies of the Spanish Empire and its plantation economy on the Barbadian model, it quickly became notorious for the new English port city of Port Royal, whose unabashed privateering and marauding against the Spanish in times of war and of clandestine trade with the Spanish Main at all times made it the richest English city in the Americas, overflowing with gold, silver, and ships, and the mariners, service personnel, and shopkeepers who flocked to share in the wealth. Outside of Port Royal, wealth flowed into the countryside to fuel the labor and plant demands of an expanding sugar and provision economy. Over the next century, no English American colony, not even the fabulously successful sugar colony of Barbados, got more press attention in London, as travel writers, trade analysts, chorographers, cartographers, historians, naturalists, belletricians, political combatants, social critics, moralists, and satirists, rushing to capitalize on the island's growing fame, produced an astonishing volume of literature about it.

By the turn of the seventeenth century, Jamaica was better known and more thoroughly valued in the metropolis than any other American colony. During the early decades of the eighteenth century, it surpassed Barbados as Britain's most valuable overseas settler colony, a status that it would enjoy throughout the eighteenth century, leaving the more populous continental colonies of Virginia and New England considerably behind as partners in trade and even as consumers of English manufactures. No wonder, then, that during the middle decades of the eighteenth century, a proud Jamaican would be inspired to produce a formal history of Jamaica's rapid rise and tumultuous development, or that that undertaking would result in a work of genuine intellectual distinction and extraordinary historical utility. That historian was James Knight, and that history, his *The Natural, Moral, and Political History of Jamaica and the Territories Thereon Depending: From the Earliest Time to the Year 1742.*

Inspired by a brisk interest in England in the exotic settings and economic and political results of English colonizing activities in America, enterprising participants in that process early produced works that they referred to as histories but that consisted of a blend of historical narrative and geographical, economic, and cultural description. Works by Captain John Smith on Virginia[1] and Richard Ligon on Barbados[2] were two of the more substantial examples. At the beginning of England's second century of American colonization, Robert Beverley, a prominent Virginia planter, took this historical impulse to a new level with the publication in 1705 of his *History and Present State of Virginia*,[3] a work that signaled the emergence of a new genre of historical writing about the English colonies in America, the most accurate name for which should be *provincial histories*. Over the next century, many of the more successful, populous, and richer colonies were the subjects of such studies. Written by native creoles or long-term residents during the three decades between 1750 and 1780, William Smith's two-volume *History of the Province of New-York*,[4] Thomas Hutchinson's three-volume *History of the Colony of Massachusetts Bay*,[5] Edward Long's three-volume *History of Jamaica*,[6] and Alexander Hewat's two-volume *Historical Account of the Rise and Progress of the Colonies of South Carolina and Georgia*[7] provide four excellent examples of this genre. Expressions of provincial patriotism and often including key illustrative documents,

1. Captain John Smith, *Generall History of Virginia, and New England* (London, 1626). A modern edition may be found in volume 2 of Philip L. Barbour, ed., *The Complete Works of Captain John Smith (1580–1631)*, 3 vols. (Chapel Hill, N.C., 1986).

2. Richard Ligon, *A True and Exact History of the Island of Barbadoes* (London, 1657).

3. Robert Beverley, *The History and Present State of Virginia* (London, 1705). Louis B. Wright edited and published a modern edition of this work (Chapel Hill, N.C., 1947).

4. William Smith, *The History of the Province of New-York from the First Discovery to the Year 1732* (London, 1757). A second volume, published posthumously in Canada in 1824, carried the story from 1732 to 1762. In 1972, Harvard University Press published an excellent modern edition of both volumes, edited by Michael Kammen.

5. Thomas Hutchinson, *The History of the Colony of Massachusetts Bay*, 2 vols. (Boston, 1764, 1767). The first two volumes provided a description of the colony and a history of its development until 1750. A third volume, published posthumously in London in 1828, covered the years 1749–74.

6. Edward Long, *The History of Jamaica*, 3 vols. (London, 1774).

7. Alexander Hewat, *An Historical Account of the Rise and Progress of the Colonies of South Carolina and Georgia*, 2 vols. (London, 1779).

these works, from Beverley onward, used some combination of narrative, chorography, and important documents to promote provincial historical consciousness within their respective polities, correct metropolitan misconceptions about their character and development, and enhance metropolitan appreciation of their value to Great Britain. Constructed between 1737 and the mid-1740s, Knight's imposing *History* falls squarely into and is a relatively early example of this literary tradition.

Far from paling by comparison with these well-known works, Knight's *History* represents a remarkable intellectual achievement. From the founding of Virginia in 1607 through the mid-eighteenth-century imperial wars for empire that began in 1739 with the War of Jenkins' Ear, no other historian of any colony in British America produced a historical study so substantial, so comprehensive in scope, so thoroughly researched in original sources and contemporary published literature, so grounded in close personal observation, or so penetrating in its analysis. By providing a complete history and a full and accurate description of Jamaica, Knight endeavored to raise historical consciousness among Jamaica's free population, to promote British interest in and knowledge of what many metropolitan Britons already thought of as their most important American colony, and—particularly impressive—to raise metropolitan consciousness about flaws that he systematically identified in the British imperial system. A profound expression of provincial sensibilities and attitudes about the essential foundations and larger meanings of the process of British settler colonizing activities in America, Knight's *History* provides an excellent guide to the provincial mentality—and to the aspirations, anxieties, and pride that underlay that mentality—not just of free Jamaicans but of settler colonists throughout British America.

Yet, until now, this sturdy monument to the early modern British Empire in America and national treasure for Jamaica has remained unpublished. Having finished his manuscript and reviewed and annotated sample printer's proofs for the table of contents and preface, Knight died in late 1745 or early 1746 before the project could proceed to publication. For whatever reasons, the executors of his estate never pushed it through to publication, the finished manuscript in a clerk's hand probably remaining with one of his heirs for several decades before it came to the attention and then into the hands of Edward Long (1734–1813) sometime after Long had published his own three-volume *History of Jamaica* in 1774. Although Long made extensive use of Knight's much more comprehensive work in a revision of his 1774 work,[8] he never published this revised edition, and

---

8. Long's annotated volumes for revising his *History* may be found in Additional Manuscripts 12404–12406, British Library, London. K. E. Ingram, comp., *Sources of Jamaica History, 1655–1838: A Bibliographic Survey with Particular Reference to Manuscript Sources*, 2 vols. (Zug, Switzerland, 1976), 1:200–201, provides a cogent discussion of Long's use of Knight's manuscript for his revisions.

in the early nineteenth century Knight's manuscript came into the possession and care of the British Library with the acquisition of the Long Family Papers. It has since been available only to interested scholars and readers in the library's manuscript division, where it can be found in Additional Manuscripts 12418 and 12419. With the permission of the library, it is here published for the first time in a handsome edition made possible by generous subsidies from the Reed Foundation and Melbourne University. This work includes the full text of Knight's *History* along with the editor's introduction and annotations, and Trevor Burnard's essay on the modern historiography on Jamaica before 1750. Although Knight himself provided no illustrations for his work, this addition includes seventy-seven illustrations, all drawn from contemporary sources from Knight's own era for which Taylor Stoermer served as visual editor.

Vita: Who Was James Knight?

James Knight is all over the public records of Jamaica during his residence in the colony, but we know relatively little about his private life: where and when he was born, whom he married, how many children he sired, how extensive his immediate social circle was in either Jamaica or London, or even how he looked, no portrait having come to light. By the time he himself emigrated from Great Britain to Jamaica in 1712 to take up a post in Britain's overseas imperial bureaucracy, however, Knight was already a conspicuous surname in late seventeenth- and early eighteenth-century Jamaica. A soldier named George Knight had died during the English conquest of the island, and a trio of Knights obtained seats in Jamaica's elected representative assembly, Andrew representing Vere Parish between 1677 and 1683; Ralph, sequentially, St. Andrew and Port Royal in 1688 and 1689; and Dr. Samuel, Kingston from 1698 to 1701 and St. Andrew in 1702, with the constituencies of Ralph and Samuel suggesting that they were probably merchants. Even more prominent, Colonel Charles Knight, an overseas merchant involved with the African slave trade, was a member of the provincial military establishment and occupied a seat on the Jamaica Council from 1690 until his death in late 1706. Whether any of these people was either related to another or provided a family connection and economic base on which James could build a long and notable career as a merchant, officeholder, and landholder in Jamaica remains to be established. As he inadvertently reveals in the text of his history, he had himself resided in Jamaica for at least a part of his childhood, which suggests that his father was one of the trio of Charles, Ralph, or Samuel.[9] His exact pa-

---

9. In the "History," Knight writes that he had known Sir Nicholas Lawes, who would become governor of Jamaica in 1718, "from my Infancy" (p. 290). Because Knight must have

ternity could possibly be established through a more intense investigation of the rich holdings of the Jamaica Archives and Island Record Office in Spanish Town.

Whatever such research may uncover, James Knight seems to have come from a mercantile background and, at the time of his arrival in Jamaica in 1712, to have been a mature and accomplished adult, his ability to rent the office of deputy receiver general from the longtime non-resident patentee Leonard Compere suggesting that Knight was already a person of means looking to create an estate in Jamaica. By 1716, just four years after Knight's arrival, Acting Governor Peter Heywood, impressed by Knight's handling of his official duties and perhaps also by his activities as a merchant, considered recommending him to London authorities to fill a vacancy in the Jamaica Council, whose twelve members were, at least prescriptively, the leading men in the colony. But Knight's tenure as a royal official was relatively short, lasting just six years. In June 1717, Compere sold his receiver generalship patent to Richard Mill, to whom Knight turned over his duties in 1718 when Mill arrived in Jamaica to take up the office himself. By early 1719, records refer to Knight as "the late Receiver General," and Knight was describing himself simply as "a merchant at Kingston," who, as he testified before the British Board of Trade in May 1726, "had lived several years as a factor in Jamaica," a factor being a merchant who handled shipments from British merchants in the colony.[10]

Although Knight never achieved a seat on the Jamaica Council, his loss of the deputy receiver generalship did not impede his growing public prominence in Kingston, and over the next two decades, as he continued to follow his mercantile pursuits and to acquire and manage productive land holdings, he rose to become custos rotulorum (the first among the parish magistrates) of Kingston Parish, which he also represented in the Jamaica Assembly from 1722 to 1725 and again from 1732 to 1737. During at least parts of five years of the seven-year gap in his assembly service, from 1723 to 1728, Knight was in England, perhaps living in Charton, Kent, now in east London. Whether this long trip was for reasons of health, business, or other considerations is unknown, but while he was there, he appeared before the Board of Trade at a hearing on Jamaica's African slave imports in May 1726[11] and, with other Jamaica and British West Indian merchants, pressed British ministers and Parliament for a firmer response to Spanish

---

been at least twenty years old when he migrated to Jamaica in 1712, and because Lawes resided in Jamaica for the forty years before he retired to Twickenham, near London, about 1704, Knight must have first encountered Lawes in Jamaica through his father sometime in the late 1680s or early 1690s.

10. Hearing before the Board of Trade, May 11, 1726, in *Journal of the Commissioners for Trade and Plantations*, 14 vols. (London, 1920–38), 5:251–70.

11. Ibid.

depredations on British West Indian shipping, a subject on which he published, anonymously, a substantial and well-informed pamphlet in 1726.[12]

Over the decade between his return to Jamaica in 1728 and his final departure for England in 1737, Knight resumed both his successful mercantile business and his highly visible role in the colony's public life, once again obtaining for the final six years of his residence in Jamaica election as one of Kingston's two representatives in the Jamaica Assembly. Although he never became one of the colony's great landowners and sugar planters, he managed to build an impressive estate. Retaining two substantial rental and profit-making properties on Port Royal Street in the heart of Kingston's shipping and financial district, Knight also owned, as he specified in his will in March 1743, a plantation called Molynes and two cattle pens or ranches in St. Andrew Parish, which was adjacent to Kingston, plus a financial interest in a plantation in St. Ann Parish on Jamaica's north coast. At his death in late 1747 or early 1748, Knight bequeathed these properties to his son John Knight, who had remained in Jamaica to oversee his father's St. Andrew properties. As landholdings went in Jamaica, this estate was a relatively modest one. Just before his death in late 1753 or early 1754, only five years after his father's, John was using these St. Andrew properties, two white servants, and seventy-five black slaves, as James had probably done before him, to produce sugar and provisions and raise cattle for the Kingston market. Out of a total of 368 acres, John cultivated just 134 (34.6%), with 84 acres (23%) used to produce annually 45 hogsheads of sugar and 15 puncheons of rum, and 50 acres (14%) used to raise provisions. The remaining 164 acres (64%) were in pasture.[13]

When in 1737 James Knight took up residence in Britain for what would be the last decade of his life and settled with his two daughters, Sarah and Jane, and a ward, Mary Willis, the surviving daughter of his Jamaica associate William Willis, in Stoke Newington in the parish of St. Mary, Newington in Middlesex County, now part of north London, he thus remained

---

12. [James Knight], *The State of the Island of Jamaica, Chiefly in Relation to Its Commerce, and the Conduct of the Spaniards in the West-Indies: Addressed to a Member of Parliament* (London, 1726). Signing himself A. B., the author, who on the title page described himself as a "Person who resided several Years at *Jamaica*," dated his pamphlet February 25, 1725–26, and gave his location as Charton in Kent. The attribution to Knight's authorship of this pamphlet derives from the similarity of its contents to that in his few surviving letters from this period and from contemporary attribution reported by Henry Newman, secretary of the Society for the Promotion of Christian Knowledge (SPCK), in a letter to Marquis Du Quesne, April 30, 1726, in Unofficial Letter-Books, 1718–29, 9 vols., 2:46, SPCK Library, London, as cited by Ingram, *Sources of Jamaican History*, 1:507.

13. Will of James Knight, February 28, 1747, Wills: Old Series, 26:fols. 99–100, Island Record Office, Spanish Town, Jamaica (hereafter Knight, will). On the extent and use of the property holdings of James and John Knight, see "Quantity of Land Cultivated and in What Kind of Manufacture, with the Number of White Servants Negros' and Cattle Employed in Each Settlement, Anno 1753," CO 137/28, fols. 192–96, National Archives, London. John Knight's holding are analyzed in Jack P. Greene, *Settler Jamaica in the 1750s: A Social Portrait* (Charlottesville, Va., 2016), 79, 238.

bound to Jamaica by his family estate, left in the hands of his son, and by his continuing business and property interests in Kingston and elsewhere on the island, which James Barclay, his friend and business associate in Kingston, managed for him. Although he had become a resident of Stoke Newington, he still thought of himself, as he announced in the first lines of his will, as being "of the Island of Jamaica."[14]

Far from distancing himself from the place where he had successfully sought his fortune over the previous quarter century, Knight remained intensely engaged with the island throughout his final years. Both before and during the War for Jenkins' Ear (1739–45), he busied himself with lobbying for Jamaica's interests with the ministry and other metropolitan agencies of colonial administration.[15] Most of all, however, he simultaneously filled his time and displayed his passionate and continuing emotional attachment to Jamaica by conceiving, gathering materials for, writing, and completing his substantial two-volume history of Jamaica. No previous work on the colony had been anywhere nearly so comprehensive in its conception and execution, been based on such extensive research and so much personal observation, nor exhibited such thoughtful commentary and analysis. In every possible respect, this work compared favorably with contemporary histories of other British American colonies produced up to that time and indeed for many decades thereafter. With the possible exception of Sir Hans Sloane's *Natural History of Jamaica*,[16] Knight's manuscript was the most impressive intellectual production relating to Jamaica during its first century as a British colony.

Knight's *History*

Designating himself as "A Gentleman, who resided above Twenty Years in Jamaica" (p. 2),[17] Knight entitled his ambitious two-volume work *The Natural, Moral, and Political History of Jamaica, and the Territories Thereon*

14. Knight, will.

15. Richard Pares, *War and Trade in the West Indies, 1739–1763* (Oxford, 1936), 78–79, 83–84, 180, 228, 253–54, 424, provides the context for and treats Knight's activities as a lobbyist and exponent of a hardline policy with Spain. See also the petitions signed by Knight in February 1738 in Noel Sainsbury et al., eds., *Calendar of State Papers, Colonial Series*, 45 vols. (London, 1860–), 44:112–30; in June 1739, in ibid., 45:112–30; and in November 1739, in ibid., 45:215–34; and his letters to the Duke of Newcastle and others, December 3, 1739, and August 15, 1745, Additional Manuscripts 22677, f. 32, and October 21, 1740, Additional Manuscripts 32695, f. 309.

16. Sir Hans Sloane, *A Voyage to the Island of Madera, Barbados, Nieves, St. Christopher and Jamaica with the Natural History of the Herbs and Trees, Four-Footed Beasts, Fishes, Birds, Insects, Reptiles, etc., of the Last of Those Islands*, 2 vols. (London, 1707–25).

17. This and the many subsequent quotations in this introduction come from Knight's text, the page numbers of which have been designated in parentheses immediately following each quotation.

Depending from the First Discovery of the Island by Christopher Columbus to the Year 1746. As he explains in his preface and introduction, his interest in pursuing this project principally derived from his conviction that Jamaica had long suffered from an inaccurate, undeserved, and negative reputation in metropolitan Britain, a reputation fostered by persistent "Misrepresentation and prejudice" and sustained by the absence of reliable published information about the colony. Older accounts, mostly published soon after its conquest and before the English had made "any Considerable Improvements," were, in his view, both out of date and too insubstantial, while more recent accounts, all authored by "Obscure Creatures," not only exhibited "great Ignorance" but were full of "Malice, and notorious Fals[e]hoods" (p. 5).[18]

In Knight's view, this situation had produced several deleterious effects, at once contributing to the metropolitan government's failure to provide any funds to subsidize the colony's settlement and development, discouraging metropolitan immigration and private investment, and preventing Jamaica's free inhabitants from fully appreciating the substantial achievements of their predecessors, who in less than eight decades had overcome many difficulties and turned Jamaica into an important extension of British culture overseas and a valuable component of the British Empire. Persuaded that Jamaica only wanted "to be better known, to be more Encouraged, and Countenanced" in Britain, Knight decided to take it on himself to produce an extended work that, copiously and in detail, would put Jamaica "in a just and true light," provide "a clear and Satisfactory Idea of the Country to Strangers," and be of utility "to every Person who has any Interest or Concern in that part of the World" (pp. 5–6). As the "Memoirs of this Island" (p. 200), moreover, the *History* would provide a venue for Knight to evaluate the administration of each of its royal governors and to call attention to those local personages who had rendered meritorious service to the colony's public life, defense, and development.

Initially, Knight's interest in this project seems to have been stimulated by his experience in Jamaica's public affairs. For the "most Part" of his residence, he tells his readers, his deep involvement in "the Service of the Crown and Country" had furnished him with knowledge of "some Remarkable transactions, which were unknown to every Common Observer," about which he collected information that, along "with several Observations" he "made upon the Spot," he "committed to Writing, with . . . the Design of methodizing and putting them together, whenever I had the leisure and a proper Opportunity" (pp. 6–7). Eventually, he decided to make his "Treatise" nothing short of "a faithful Register; of all the Memorable

18. Knight is here referring specifically to Charles Leslie, *A New and Exact Account of Jamaica* (Edinburgh, 1739), and Leslie's *A New History of Jamaica* (London, 1740), the same work with a few additions, both of which were highly critical of Jamaican white society.

Events; which have hap[pe]ned, and I could attain the knowledge of, from the first Discovery of Jamaica, to the present time" (pp. 6–7).

When, after he moved to London in 1737, Knight finally found time to design this expansive project, he seems early to have settled on a plan that would involve a "Treatise" (p. 7) broken down into ten parts in two volumes, each one quite different in character from the other. Consisting of a table of contents, preface, introduction, and parts 1–3, the first volume, a comprehensive history of Jamaica, would require extensive reading and research for the long period before his 1712 arrival. For parts 1–2, Knight could draw most of what he needed from contemporary published materials. For part 1, which covered indigenous culture before Columbus encountered the island in the 1590s and its development as a Spanish colony over the next century and a half, he could rely on English translations "of some of the most Eminent Spanish writers" (p. 7), including Peter Martyr, Antonio de Herrera y Tordesillas, and Gonzalo Fernández de Oviedo. For part 2, which treated the English conquest of Jamaica and its early occupation under military rule, Knight found many published sources and was also able to acquire an original manuscript of the proceedings of Colonel Daniel Doyley while he was commander in chief of English military forces and then, from 1660–62, the Crown's first governor of Jamaica.[19]

Together with the preface and introduction, part 1 and 2 accounted for just under a fourth of the total number of words in the first volume, and part 3, a narrative of Jamaican history during the eight decades after the establishment of English civil government in the early 1660s, took up the last three-quarters of the volume and required research in a much wider range of sources. Like most English historians of his day, Knight conceived of his history as a narrative of the course of successive administrations and reigns, and of the major natural events, civil disturbances, and military and naval engagements that had broad public ramifications. Following in this tradition, Knight made the "Proceedings of the several Governors, Council and Assembly" (p. 9) the central subject in part 3, while also paying systematic attention to natural disasters, including earthquakes and hurricanes; slave rebellions; defense preparations against and interactions with pirates and the forces of foreign rivals, including the French invasion of 1693; ongoing relations, both commercial and military, with the Spanish Main; and the changing naval administration in Jamaica.

On some of these subjects, such as the great Port Royal earthquake of 1692, he found printed accounts or took testimony from survivors he encountered. With regard "to the Administration of the Several Governours" (p. 12) in part 3, however, he soon realized that getting the "best Infor-

---

19. Doyley's journal can be found in Knight's surviving manuscripts in the Long Family Papers, Additional Manuscripts 12423, British Library.

mation" he could on that subject would require extensive research into "Original Minutes and other Authentick papers" (pp. 6–9) relating to the course of Jamaican provincial governance. In sharp contrast to previous Jamaica analysts, who, building "chiefly upon Tradition and hearsay," had produced accounts that were incomplete and jumbled things "together . . . in an Obscure, confused manner," Knight was determined both "to Omit no material Transaction, which hap[p]ened in their respective Governments" and "to place things in the Natural [sequential] order, in which they hap[pe]ned; and to give a Relation of Facts from Authentick Records and Tracts" (pp. 11–12).

No doubt he thought—correctly—that London would be the very best place for such research. Metropolitan authorities required colonial governors to transmit all the important executive and legislative records from their jurisdictions to London, where they were subject to review by the Privy Council's Committee on Plantation Affairs and filed away for use and safekeeping at the Board of Trade, the principal agency for colonial oversight. To Knight's surprise and annoyance, however, when he applied to the board for permission to examine and make copies of documents transmitted from Jamaica, board officials refused his request on the grounds that it only granted access to its holdings in cases involving appellate jurisdiction or actions of law or equity. Although, as Knight writes in his preface, this response considerably "retarded the finishing of" his project and "almost discouraged" his proceeding further on it, he managed, "with great Expence and trouble to my friends" (p. 11) in Jamaica, to secure the documents he sought from the originals in Jamaica.[20] Had he obtained access to the Board of Trade records, which would have included gubernatorial reports not in the original public records in Jamaica, his research might well have been even more exhaustive and publication of work during his lifetime more achievable.

As it turned out, however, the success of Knight's collecting effort was impressive, supplying him with so much information that, along with his determination to leave out no "material Transaction which came to my knowledge nor any Observation I thought proper to be incerted," and his decision to include in his text full copies of many of the most important documents, the process certainly "swelled this History beyond the bulk I at first designed" (p. 641), as he acknowledged in the concluding paragraphs of his work. Indeed, part 3 was almost seven times as long as part 2, the next longest portion of his project, and about 15 percent longer than the seven parts that constituted volume 2 combined. Knight himself made no

20. William Beckford of Somerly was one of Knight's Jamaica friends who helped him obtain documents. See Beckford to Knight, June 18, 1743, Additional Manuscripts 12431, British Library. In this letter, Beckford remarked that the sample of his work Knight had sent to Jamaica had "been well received and approved of by all gentlemen that had seen it."

apology for the disproportionate length of part 3 in relation to the other nine parts of what he regarded as the "well intended and necessary Work" (p. 12) of bringing the island's intricate political history fully into public view. Indeed, this achievement resulted in the production of what remains to this day—almost three centuries later—the fullest and most coherent narrative of Jamaica's political history as a British colony before the mid-1740s. For the convenience of modern readers, however, the present editor has broken the long text of part 3 into five roughly equal chronological units and designated them as chapters A–E.

Notwithstanding Knight's admission that, as a merchant, historical writing was "a thing that is out of my Province" (p. 5), his practice in constructing his history followed many of the same guidelines that emerged as standard procedures as professional historical studies took shape during the nineteenth century, with comprehensiveness and deep research in original sources being two of the most important. Like his successors, moreover, he carefully noted his indebtedness to "the Authors of such Pieces as I thought necessary to quote or make use of" (p. 11). Taking for his motto a quotation from Cicero, which Knight translated from the Latin as "The first law in History Writing is not to dare to Assert any thing that is false, and the next [is] not to be afraid of speaking the truth. Let there be no Appearance of Dissimulation[;] let there be none of private Malice" (p. 13), he also made every effort to achieve the elusive goal of objectivity and rarely emphasized his own role in the events he described, on the grounds that it was "difficult for a Man to speak of himself without Suspicion of prejudice or partiality" (p. 246). While his propensity to publish key documents in their entirety is uncommon in modern historical studies (though relatively common in histories written during this time period), he rarely let them speak for themselves, usually interpreting them and commenting on their significance in Jamaica's history. Nor did he, like some modern historians, reduce a complex history to the elaborate analysis of a few illustrative anecdotes or stories.

Knight's second volume was not a history but a full-blown chorography, an ancient genre designed to describe a particular place in terms of its principal characteristics. Intending to make this chorography as comprehensive as he possibly could, Knight divided it into seven separate sections, parts 4–10, each of which covered a different set of related topics: part 4, physical and human geography; part 5, climate, seasons, wind and water resources, and disease environment; part 6, inhabitants, free and slave and white and black, including the free Maroon populations in the mountains and the indigenous occupants on Jamaica's dependencies in central America; part 7, government, political and religious establishments, and revenues; part 8, soil and economic products; part 9, animals, both wild and domestic, birds, fish, and insects; and part 10, continuing problems and opportunities for further development, or, to use the popular language of

Knight's era, *improvement*. This last section also included a thoughtful discussion of specific measures by which the metropolitan government might render Jamaica even more secure and valuable to the emerging British Empire. By thus "digesting the[se] Severall matters under their proper heads" (p. 6), Knight hoped to make it easier for readers to find the information that most interested them or that would be useful in undertaking their own particular ventures in the island. Except for his descriptions in part 4 of "several parts of the island" in which he had himself little experience and therefore had to depend on residents of "Candour and Judgement" who were "much better acquainted with them" (p. 11), Knight derived the information he presented throughout his chorography "chiefly from" his "own Observation and Experience" (p. 11). And he had no doubt that the result was "a more particular Description of the Island and Inhabitants, Their Customs, manner of living, Climate, Air &c. than has been hitherto published, or is now Extant," an account that, he hoped, would provide readers with "a Natural and Artless View of the Country, and every Circumstance relating to it, that is Material or Necessary for Their information or Satisfaction" (p. 11).

Notwithstanding his aspiration to be objective, however, Knight throughout both the history and the chorography exhibited a sturdy appreciation of Jamaica's achievements and potential. As he freely acknowledged, his study was "principally Calculated" to contribute to "the Interest and well fare of Jamaica" (p. 641), and he repeatedly invoked the many "Pleasures and gratifications, which nature has bestowed on" the island for the "comfort and Happiness" of its inhabitants (p. 17). Yet, he was careful to distinguish himself from promotional writers who in both the Spanish and English worlds touted the "great Riches" (p. 15) to be obtained, the salubriousness of the climate, and the fecundity of the earth in whatever place to which they sought to entice settlers from the Old World, disclaiming any intention to suggest that Jamaica was "so agreeable a Country to live in as England, and other Parts of Europe, or that Men of Fortune, who" were "Easy and happy in other Respects" should "choose to go over and reside there" (p. 15).

Knight provided unity and coherence for his ambitious undertaking by giving special prominence to several general themes that he worked into the fabric of his work whenever they seemed appropriate or relevant. These recurring themes were neither original nor exclusive to Knight. Deeply rooted in early modern English overseas settler colonization, they were, rather, omnipresent in the writing of colonial analysts seeking to inform metropolitan readers about the character and importance of the societies and polities that Britons were then constructing on the other side of the Atlantic. Few such writers, however, managed as well as Knight to formulate these themes fully, develop them cogently, or ground them on a sturdy empirical base. Indeed, Knight's use of them can be taken as exemplary, even paradigmatic, of the attitudes and aspirations of settler populations throughout the colonial British American world and perhaps beyond it.

Celebrating Cornucopia

Despite his resolve not to turn his magnum opus into a promotional tract, Knight rarely missed an opportunity to praise Jamaica's natural beauty, its fortunate geography, its abundant natural resources, and its promising situation for trade, devoting substantial sections of four parts of his seven-part chorography to those subjects and presenting Jamaica as a bounteous natural cornucopia that could attract and sustain a large volume of people and domestic animals and awaited only the application of English industry and art to turn it into a highly productive, attractive, and congenial civil and social space.

In part 4, Knight took the reader right around the island with a parish by parish survey that, while paying substantial attention to the human geography of each parish as it had taken shape by the late 1730s, also emphasized the island's complex, varied, and attractive natural topography, ranging from accessible and cultivatable coastal lowlands to upland savannas suitable for cattle raising, fertile flat valleys fit for all sorts of agricultural enterprises, and a hilly and mountainous interior that from a distance appeared "Strange . . . and Romantick" but, even in its rockiest places, always exhibited a "beautiful verdure" from the "Leaves[,] Blossoms and Fruit" (pp. 388, 393–94) of the numerous trees and plants that adorned its slopes, and contained ample spaces for settlers and their auxiliaries to build profitable enterprises. With eighty-seven rivers that discharged into the sea, on some of whose courses could be found "divers[e] Beautifull Cataracts or Cascades" and an abundance of "Rivulets and Springs almost every where" in the island, Jamaica, Knight reported, was "plentifully furnished" with a "great Variety of Water" (pp. 451–52) and "eight fine Harbours, and severall Convenient Coves and Bays where Ships may safely ride" (p. 614). Endowed with a mineral-rich hot spring on the eastern slopes of the mountains, Jamaica, he predicted, would ultimately be found to contain large deposits of copper and possibly even smaller ones of gold that could provide the basis for a substantial mining industry.

In Knight's presentation, Jamaica's natural geographic advantages were reinforced by its beneficent climate, the subject of part 5. Except for the highest elevations of the towering mountain chain on the eastern half of the island (later known as the Blue Mountains), where, Knight reported, citing "several Affidavits," on one occasion several black men in pursuit of rebellious Maroons became "so benumbed that they died with Cold"

(p. 391), Jamaica was a place with neither cold weather nor radical changes in temperature. In an extended survey of the diseases and health problems that were "most common and incidental to the Climate" (p. 458), he devoted several pages to a prescription of a dietary regimen and modes of behavior that, he was persuaded, would be a helpful preventative. He was careful to point out that the climate in the island's higher elevations was "undoubtedly more Suitable, and Agreeable to an European Constitution, than in any other part of the Island" (p. 391). Nor did he shy away from acknowledging that "the Extreme heat of the Sun" in the lowlands could be "sometimes hot and troublesome" during the hours from 9 a.m. to 4 or 5 p.m. But he insisted that the mornings were always "fresh and cool," that the days were "generally Serene and Clear throughout the Year without any Foggy or hazy Weather," and that the nights were "for the most part fair" cool and "exceeding pleasant" (p. 437). Indeed, he called the reader's attention to the refreshing effects of the air and the prevailing winds that, in conjunction with occasional rain showers, cooled the bodies of both men and beasts and had "Wonderful Operation and Effects on . . . Vegetables, and even on Iron, which is the hardest of all Metals" (p. 437). With no pronounced changes in seasons, Jamaica actually had "two Springs," one "after the great Rains in May" and a second after similar rains in October so that the inhabitants annually enjoyed "two Crops of Corn, Pease, and other Grain, and almost all sorts of Fruit, which are Natural to the Climate." Spring vegetables appeared in all their glory in kitchen gardens, the savannas and pastures were "cloathed with Green" and the trees and "Plants with Blossums and Flowers," and the air became "fresher, cooler and Pleasanter" (p. 441).

Along with its geography and climate, Jamaica's natural abundance was conducive to both plant and animal life, and Knight surveyed the former in part 8 and the latter in part 9, both of which Knight used to emphasize the extraordinary diversity and richness of Jamaica's natural environment. Giving particular attention to those trees, plants, and creatures that were "peculiar and Natural to the Country" (p. 569), he also included the many Old World plants and animals that had been successfully transplanted to Jamaica and those commodities that settlers had been able to turn to their economic advantage. Also in part 8, Knight explained to readers the process and conventions of the production of sugar, minor staples, and other items that had been fundamental to the development of the island's export economy.

Following in the tradition of Dr. Thomas Trapham's early report in the 1670s[21] and Hans Sloane's systematic and comprehensive two-volume nat-

---

21. Thomas Trapham, *A Discourse on the State of Health in the Island of Jamaica* (London, 1679).

ural history of the island between 1707 and 1725, and foreshadowing Patrick Browne's impressive study of the same subject in 1754,[22] just a few years after Knight's death, Knight in part 8 produced, tree by tree and plant by plant, a descriptive catalogue that carefully assessed the character and utility of each, singling out the plantain for its beauty as a plant and value as a food source and closing his description of island fruits with the "Pine," or pineapple, which in his view exceeded any other fruit in the world in "its Singular beauty and delicious tast[e]" (p. 574). In part 9, he did the same for domestic and wild animals, birds, sea animals such as turtles and manatees, fish, and insects. Along with those of Sloane and Browne, Knight's detailed descriptions of early eighteenth-century Jamaica's natural plant and animal worlds provide still a third set of data evidently derived from extensive independent investigations of Jamaica's natural world and certainly invite the attention of modern scholars interested in exploring the importance of Jamaica in expanding Old World knowledge of the wider overseas world.[23] Knight strongly implied that his own descriptions were based mainly on personal observation and were not a mere repetition of entries in Sloane when he noted that his descriptive entries omitted such "Valuable Commodities" as "Drugs and Woods" because they were "not within my Province" and because Sloane had already "very particularly delineated and described" them (p. 564).

Knight was too critical a scholar not to note important qualifications to his affectionate celebration of Jamaica as a natural cornucopia. Over the course of his residency in Jamaica, the lowland parishes along the south coast had, in what Knight thought of as a failure of "the seasons" (p. 396), become too dry for reliable sugar production with the result that the centers of sugar culture shifted to the east and west. Yet the older parishes still had enough water and other resources to sustain a shift to ranching, provision farming, and minor staple cultivation. Long before, early Spanish settlers had converted the savannas that the indigenous population used to cultivate corn and other vegetables into pastures to feed their "Cattle and Horses" (p. 393), and early English settlers followed this example. As a result, Knight noted, those lands, having gone "so many years without Tillage, or Culture," had "become barren" and could no longer be cultivated. Yet, they continued to "produce great plenty of Grass" and appeared "pleasant, and Green after Rains, and feed Vast numbers of Sheep and Cattle" (pp. 393–94). Even in the face of adversity, Jamaica's extraordinary natural endowments invited and sustained such adjustments.

22. Patrick Browne, *The Civil and Natural History of Jamaica* (London, 1756).

23. On this subject as it applies to Jamaica, see especially James Delbourgo, *Collecting the World: The Life and Curiosity of Hans Sloane* (New York, 2017).

Craving Validation

Notwithstanding their colony's greater visibility in Britain, Jamaicans shared with other British colonists a widespread and peculiarly colonial anxiety about the effects of their physical separation from the parent state. As they pursued projects of society and polity building out of the immediate sight of the metropolis and in obscure places on the outer edges of the English-speaking world, they feared that they would slowly drift out of metropolitan consciousness, their achievements going unnoticed, unappreciated, and open to the distortions and slanders of malicious commentators, and their very status as English people coming under challenge. Thoroughly expressive of such anxieties, Knight's *History* pursued a strategy designed to persuade metropolitan British readers that Jamaica contributed substantially to their economic welfare and international prestige, and that Jamaicans were creating a world which, despite modifications required by differences in physical setting and economic orientation, was not only recognizably English but thoroughly compatible with its English heritage. In doing so, he, like numerous other colonial writers, sought metropolitan validation and the respect that it conferred.

In his pursuit of validation, Knight was particularly concerned to refute allegations about Jamaica's supposedly sickly climate, its association with piratical activity in the Caribbean, and the social excesses of its free inhabitants. With regard to health, Knight acknowledged that Jamaica, like England and "any other part of the world," suffered from its own "Endemicall Evils" (p. 17), but he argued that the longevity of many of the original settlers and the prevalence during his own residence of "Divers Persons, who have lived on the Island, from 20 to 50 years, and Natives, Whites as well as Blacks, who are Sixty Years of Age and upwards" (p. 18), gave the lie to charges that Jamaica was an especially unhealthy place and suggested that it was healthier than many a neighboring place on the Spanish Main. Moderation and adaptation to a hotter climate were, in his view, all that was required to stay healthy. Provided a person was "Temperate in his diet, and Exercises, and Conforms to the Nature of the Climate," Knight wrote, "a Man, with common Industry and Oeconomy, may . . . enjoy his health, and live in a decent and Comfortable manner" (p. 17).

Much more fully, Knight sought to refute allegations that Jamaica had been a den of pirates and had officially encouraged piracy or buccaneering. Carefully distinguishing between buccaneers—who made Tortuga their rendezvous, acted without a Commission or "legal authority," and preyed indiscriminately on English as well as French or Spanish shipping—and privateers, who acted "under and by Vertue of a Commission, from any Prince or State, at Enmity or War with any other Nation or Country," he argued that before Jamaica had had notice of the Treaty of Breda (1667) officially ending the war between Britain and Spain, Jamaica's governors had encouraged privateers in their attacks on Spanish shipping and settlements "on Account of the great Riches They brought in" (pp. 107, 109, 134). Indeed, those riches had brought Jamaica "to the time of its greatest prosperity, when it was not only Populous and in flourishing Circumstances, but mon[e]y so very plenty[ful] that Port Royal was Reckoned the Richest Town in America," and as "the great Resort of Privateers," attracted a large population of people willing to go "a rambling on the Seas, and Shores, of America, in Search of Prizes and other Booty" (pp. 107–8).

Acclaiming the "Gallant Exploits" of Jamaica's legally authorized privateers such as John Davis and Henry Morgan, who had "Executed Their Designs with such Intrepidity and Surprising Success" and thereby "made so much noise in the World" without any repudiation from the English government, he objected that the indiscriminate coupling of them with pirates by earlier writers had resulted in "the Inhabitants of the Island in general [being] unjustly Stigmatized for the Actions of" pirates operating without official sanction. Knight admitted "that some of the real Bucaniers, by permission or Connivance, did dispose of their prizes and Squander away their money at Port Royal, before the Treaty concluded between Great Britain and Spain in 1667" (p. 109), but he refused to excuse such complicity. Nor did he deny that some of the privateers may have been guilty of some of the same "Attrocious Actions" committed by the buccaneers, whom he denounced as "undoubtedly the most cruel and Inhuman Villains that ever Appeared in the World." But he argued that, even if some Jamaicans had connived with buccaneers, it was unreasonable to reproach "a whole society or Country . . . for the action of a Part of Them only," and protested that both at the time and subsequently, "no Country or People, ever was more assiduous, or at a greater Expence, than this Island has been at, to Suppress those who acted without a legal Authority" (pp. 109–10).

Improvements Made and to Be Made

To combat metropolitan perceptions of Jamaica's social deficiencies, Knight employed the language of improvement, perhaps the most common of the themes he used to structure his volumes. Omnipresent in the economic writings of early modern Britain, this language referred primarily to schemes, devices, or projects through which the economic position of the nation might be advanced, the estates or fortunes of individuals bettered, or existing resources made more productive. In the new and relatively undeveloped societies of colonial British America, the term *improvement* carried similar connotations but also acquired a wider meaning: it was used to describe a state of society that was far removed from that of

the indigenous inhabitants. An improved society was one defined by a series of positive and negative juxtapositions. As opposed to migratory, im-
permanent, rustic, and crude, it was settled, cultivated, civilized, orderly,
developed, and polite. The model for an improved society was the settled
society of Great Britain. Colonials aspired to create a fully developed market society with credit, commercial agriculture, a stable labor force, and a
brisk circulation of money and goods through busy urban centers. In particular, they hoped to create a social structure in which successful, independent, and affluent people would have the opportunity, in conformity with
the longstanding traditions of British and other European societies, to exploit dependent people, whether free or slave. They desired authoritative,
if unobtrusive and inexpensive, political institutions that would facilitate
their socioeconomic and cultural development and be presided over by
the most successful part of the community. They wanted vital traditional
institutions that would contribute to and stand as visible symbols of their
civility, including courts, churches, schools, and towns. Most of all, they
wanted metropolitans to regard the very process of colonization as a form
of national improvement.

Sharing this well-established colonial mindset, Knight stressed the many
changes Jamaica had undergone under English governance in expanding
settlement, collecting a labor force, producing vendable commodities, becoming a growing market for British manufactures, building and maintaining a polity along English lines, and creating a functional and increasingly
refined social environment—all of which he regarded as improvements.
At both ends of his account of English Jamaica, he inserted a document to
give the reader a clear impression of the transit of the island's development.
Illustrating the extent to which royal encouragement and "the fair Prospect
of raising . . . Fortunes, by the Fertility of the Soil and other Advantages"
(p. 102) had caused many immigrants to flock to the island, the first, a demographic table made in 1664, revealed that in just ten years, the English
had divided the island into twelve precincts occupied by more than 1,900
families or households with a total population of "upwards of 17,000 Inhabitants," including "Men, Women and Children of which not more than
One third were Negroes" (p. 106). The second, evidently made by Knight
himself, was a parish by parish survey of the number of sugar works in each
parish and the average annual quantity of sugar they produced for the three
years ending in 1737, the year of Knight's return to Britain. This survey
indicated that in 1737, Jamaica's nineteen parishes contained a total of 428
sugar works with an annual production of 33,234 hogsheads of sugar, almost 1.2 million gallons of molasses, and just over 1.5 million gallons of
rum, together valued at slightly more than £6 million. This figure did not
include the value of an unknown number of bags of cotton and ginger;
casks of pimento, coffee, and indigo; tons of logwood and fustic; and linear

feet of mahogany that the island yearly shipped to Britain and its colonial territories, for which Knight never managed to obtain precise information.

In Knight's view, these figures made it clear that, notwithstanding the many misfortunes it had suffered as a result of the earthquake of 1692; the French invasion of 1694; major hurricanes in 1712, 1722, and 1726; and serious droughts after each of those storms, Jamaica had not only "in a great measure" recovered but was also at the time of his writing in "a very flourishing condition" (p. 618). These figures were also a principal illustration of the island's extraordinary economic improvements, and he took special pride in the fact that those improvements had both contributed substantially to the "Trade, Revenues and Navigation of Great Britain" itself and had been accomplished "merely by the force of Industry, without the Assistance that other Colonies have had" (p. 617).

But, as Knight emphasized, Jamaica's improvement went well beyond the economic realm. Indeed, his second volume functioned as a veritable catalogue of the various ways settlers had altered—for the better, he believed—the physical, demographic, economic, social, and political landscape of Jamaica in an effort to persuade metropolitan readers that, so far from being a new colony that required settlers "to run the hazards, or undergo the Fatigues" commonly associated with such places, Jamaica had been for "many years Inhabited, though not fully," and had "a great Number of fine Plantations set[t]led thereon; [with] some rich inhabitants" and many "others in a prosperous way" and with "an extensive and beneficiall Commerce to Severall parts of the World" (p. 20). As a result, "large tracts of Woody lands, which never had been manured before," were "now Cleared and Cultivated to great Advantage," and "even remote and Mountainous Parts difficult of Access have been planted with great Care, Labour, and Expence," albeit "the inland" and other remote areas were "still Capable of further & very Considerable Improvements" (p. 629).

The character of the changes the English had wrought, Knight thought, were especially evident in the social landscapes of the older and best-settled parishes. From the middle of Jamaica's towering mountains, Knight enthused, one could look down over St. Andrew Parish to "one of the most Beautifull Landscapes in the World; the Sugar Works in the Low Lands, with the Planters' Houses and other buildings, together with the Negrohouses to the number of 70 or 80, or more to each Plantation laid out in Streets, make those Plantations appear like so many Villages; and the Cane pieces, which are of different greens, according to their age or Standing, are not unlike so many Meadows or Gardens, the lime-fences between them being cut like the quick set hedges in England, and green all the Year. From thence," he continued, "you have also a view of many Settlements and some Sugar-works, on the sides of the Mountains upon each hand and of the Towns of Kingston, Port Royal, [and] Passage Fort . . . below with the Ocean beyond all, where Ships and other Vessells daily coming in or going out, add greatly to the Beauty of the Prospect." At the center of St. Andrew, the "pleasant little Village" of Halfway Tree was the site of the parish church, the court, and, until it accidentally burned, a free school (pp. 397–98).

By the time Knight reached Jamaica in 1712, Port Royal—having been partially destroyed by the devastating earthquake of 1692 and then, after rebuilding, leveled by a fire in 1702—had been superseded by Kingston as "the chief Port of Trade." Over the next few decades, Kingston had developed into a thriving urban center. With broad streets and laid out in a regular pattern with a large parade at its center, it contained, by the 1740s, "above 1200 Houses and Storehouses, most of which" were "handsome Buildings, two Stories high besides Garrets" and "covered with Shingles, Sashed, and Glazed." In an adaptation designed to protect residents from midday heat, "Piazzas before every House" enabled people to "walk from one end to the other without going in the Sun, but in Crossing the Streets." In addition, it contained a "very good Town Store" that did double duty as a commercial exchange; "several Convenient Wharfs" for lading and unlading ships; the Anglican parish church, which had elegant cedar woodwork and "a very good Organ"; a Quaker meetinghouse; and a Jewish synagogue (pp. 399–401).

"Seated in a large pleasant Vale" less than twenty miles west of Kingston, Jamaica's "Seat of Government," the old Spanish capital, St. Jago de la Vega or Spanish Town, was a second prominent urban community. "Finely situate[d], with Regard to Health and other Conveniencies," and within easy reach of the most populous rural region in Jamaica, it contained around 1740 six hundred houses and storehouses, a "large and commodious" governor's house, a "Town-House" for meetings of the assembly and the general courts, a chapel, and a church built on the foundations of an old Spanish abbey and regarded by Knight as "the neatest Building in America." Surrounded on three sides by "large wide Savannas, whereon feed great numbers of Sheep and Cattle," it had become what in England would have been called a gentry town in which "Several Eminent Planters, whose Estates" were nearby, resided for much of the year, riding out to the savannas in their carriages in the morning and evening "for the benefit of the air" and frequently organizing "Horse-Racing and other Diversions" for themselves (pp. 406–7).

Although Knight considered housing in the island as "in general too slight" and too simple in plan, with the kitchen and offices always separated from the main house by about twenty or thirty feet, and noted that most rural houses in the "remote parts of the Island" were built of stone and "made Defensible" by "Musquet proof" doors and windows and gun ports for firearms, along with small carriage guns for defense against either foreign or "intestine" enemies, he further observed that during the early decades of the eighteenth century, "some of the Planters' Houses, as well as many Houses in" the towns, had been "built after the English manner with Brick, two Stories high & Garretts over them" (p. 423).

For Knight, these many improvements made clear that Jamaicans under English governance had succeeded in creating a settled society. In imitation of metropolitan Britain, it was based on a solid and highly differentiated, if necessarily distinctive, social structure of the sort that could be found all over Western Europe and that was composed of four "Ranked . . . Orders" (p. 471). At the bottom of this social order was an already vast number of enslaved people, almost entirely of African descent and numbering more than 100,000, whose labor, as Knight acknowledged, accounted for virtually all of the produce and much of the technical and management skills associated with the island's economy as well as the many other improvements that his *History* celebrated. Just above them in the social order were about two thousand free blacks and mulattoes who had gained their freedom through "their fidelity, good Services to their Masters," or "by distinguishing Themselves" during the French invasion of 1693 or during various expeditions against the Maroons in the 1720s and 1730s (p. 481). Their status as free people did not, however, entitle this group to full access to the rule of law that free whites enjoyed. In capital or criminal cases, they were, like the enslaved, tried by two justices of the peace and three freeholders. These disabilities separated them from the white servants who, few in number, also occupied an intermediate status in the Jamaican social order. At the top of that order were the "Masters," a heterodoxy of people including English, Scottish, and Irish immigrants and their creole descendants and "some Portoguese Jews" (p. 471), the common denominator of whom was their whiteness and their economic independence, *independence* meaning in contemporary English parlance freedom from subjection to the will of any other person. According to Knight, masters were divided into two principal "Classes, Merchants or Trading People, and Planters" (p. 471), the former also including free white tradesmen. This group was the one on which Knight principally focused when he was trying to increase British awareness of Jamaica's achievements and possibilities.

Jews, encouraged by promises of religious liberty and rights of land ownership, began migrating to Jamaica in the late 1680s. By the 1730s, they constituted nearly 10 percent of the island's white population and formed a special category among this group of masters. Although they could own land, very few, according to Knight, had "any Notion of Planting," altogether, he estimated, owning no more "than eight or ten Plantations, of which" fewer than half were sugar works. Although some Jews were "scattered about in the Country Villages" where they occupied an important economic niche, keeping shops and furnishing the "Planters, as well as the Negroes, with many Necessaries," they mostly resided in the colony's three major towns, each of which had a synagogue. The wealthiest of them carried on an extensive trade on their own accounts all over the Atlantic and on commission from Jewish merchants in London, eventually acquiring a "great part of the Houses and Ware houses" in Port Royal and Kingston, showing themselves to be "men of Probity, Exact and Punctual in their dealings," and exhibiting a level of "Industry, Moderation, and Oeconomy" and a degree of temperance and "regular" manner of living that was conducive to the "Preservation of their Healths" that Knight recommended "as Patterns to the other Inhabitants." But they had a limited civic role. Excluded from serving on juries or participating in "many other Publick occasions," they constituted a nation apart, a country within a country (pp. 477–78).

By far the most numerous among the masters were the mostly Christian planters, a category in which Knight included all rural proprietors, including the minority involved in sugar cultivation and the more numerous group who produced minor staples or provisions or operated cattle pens. They mostly resided in the countryside "upon their Estates," where, Knight took pains to emphasize, aside from the few who were "clear of incombrances" and could afford to live "in a genteel manner," the generality of them lived simply, in relative harmony with their neighbors, without ostentation, luxury, or extravagance except on the rare occasions when they entertained strangers and other visitors, when they put on their best clothes and displayed a generous hospitality. But "their common . . . manner of living" was much more "ordinary." "Like the Country Gentlemen in England," they had "most necessaries within themselves." Unlike many of their English counterparts, however, they had a far more strenuous regimen of life, requiring enormous "Care and Industry." Obliged "to be up Early, and ride about" their "Plantations [a] great part of the day, in the Scorching heat of the Sun," the "Crop and Planting Season" required their constant attention, and even those planters who lived in one of the nearer parishes and had houses in Spanish Town had to remain on their rural properties during those times. Moreover, Knight observed, the lives of Jamaica planters were far more anxious than those of English proprietors, because they had to keep a "constant eye over" their "Servants and Negroes." With their "Dispositions . . . being as different as their Several Countries, or Nations," he wrote, the Negroes in particular got into "many Quarrells, and Controversies" that required "great Thought, Temper, and Discretion" on the part of the masters responsible for ordering and managing them (pp. 473–75).

Although some in the merchant category, like Knight himself, had "Plantations or Country Houses," they mostly lived in one of the urban centers, carried on their "Several Professions in the same manner" as their counterparts in Britain, and constituted a valuable and respectable segment of Jamaica society. However, there were few merchants among the "Severall Gentlemen who" had "Estates in the Island, and" enough wealth to "live in an Affluent manner in any other Country, [but] think the Climate [of

Jamaica] preferable, and choose to spend Their days there." Rather, merchants frequently removed "to Great Britain, or other Parts of the British Dominions, when they have acquired Estates, or what they think sufficient to maintain Them there," so that planters typically "looked upon" merchants "as transient People, or Sojourners" with a limited commitment to the colony (pp. 15, 471).

Contrary to "the false notions" that earlier writers had circulated in Britain about Jamaicans' "Extravagance, Luxury, . . . Immorality," and "Profligate manner of living," Knight thus sought to assure his British audience that the island's "Planters and other Inhabitants" were rather a people of great "Care and Industry" who included "many Persons of great Honour and Virtue." "However they have been Represented" in Britain, he declared, "I don't know a more Industrious, usefull, and beneficial Society to the Nation, than they are" (pp. 474–75).

Confronting a Culture of Impermanence

In articulating a fourth important theme that infused his study—Jamaica's many continuing deficiencies—Knight addressed the white Jamaican establishment as well as the metropolitan British public. Exhibiting a deep veneration for the early generations of English settlers, Knight took pains in his *History* to stress the "*Difficulties* and *hardships*, the *first Set[t]lers* laboured under,*" the "*Calamities* and *misfortunes*, which attended the Island for a *Course of years*," and "the *Considerable improvements* which have been made, by the *force* of *Industry*." With no financial assistance from the British state, he stressed, those generations had "laid the foundation of the best Estates, & paved the way to the flourishing Condition the Island is now in." Knight also emphasized the extraordinary unity among those generations. Including people who had been on both sides of the English Civil War and represented a wide "diversity of Opinions, and Principles," he reported, "those Several Classes of People . . . wisely buried in oblivion all former Distinctions, and never upbraided one Another with the part, they had acted at Home." "It would have been happy for their Successors," Knight wrote, "had they always acted with the same Prudence in other Respects, and not suffered themselves to be divided, as They often have been, by little Emulations, private piques, or the Interest of Governours; from whence" the colony had "often been inflamed, and divided into Factions" to the prejudice of the general "Interest of the Country." Decrying a phenomenon that was widely known in colonial British America as creolean degeneracy, Knight encouraged Jamaica's "present & future Inhabitants" to return to the values of "Industry, Unanimity and Publick Spirit" exhibited by the ancestors "from whom many of Them" were descended (pp. 641–42, 471).

Knight traced the social behaviors that prompted him to make this atavistic appeal to a single source: the island's capacity to generate individual wealth. By the 1730s, enough planter families had acquired sufficient resources to enable them to follow the example of merchants and remove to Britain to live as absentees. In fact, such an objective became a social goal among planters. As a result, even though most had but "a very distant or slender prospect of ever being able to do so," many put all their energies into "the improvement of their Plantations," with "no other View than to raise Estates" so that they could eventually "live in England." As a result, Knight lamented, a decreasing number of planters, including "even those that were born there," looked "upon the Island as their Home," intending to remove to England as soon as they could. This mentality, Knight explained, fostered the emergence of a culture of impermanence in which planters endured "many inconveniences" and took "no thought of Posterity, or those that come after them; nor even to make things pleasant and agreeable to themselves, for the present; though it might be done without any considerable Expence or Trouble" (pp. 575–76).

This mindset, Knight complained, led directly to what modern analysts would call economic and social underdevelopment. "However bountiful Nature has been in" enabling planters to produce valuable staples, he lamented, the planters could not "be much commended with Regard to good Husbandry, in cultivating, manuring, and improving of Lands: for if a piece of Ground proves unkindly, or when it is much worn, and does not produce well, they throw it up, clear and plant another, without using any Art or Labour to improve the first." Nor did "they take any pains or Care, to raise Gardens, Orchards, Groves or Shady Walks, so necessary and useful in this part of the World; nor any conveniencies which serve to make life Easy and Comfortable, and would render the Island more Pleasant and delightful, as well as more Healthful." Nothing was "more Common," he observed, "than to See some of the finest fruits in the World, such as the best Gardens in England cannot pretend to, grow in the Hedges, and in the Fields neglected and uncultivated, vizt. Oranges, Lemons, Shadocks, Cashews, and other sorts in great Plenty" (p. 568).

If Jamaica planters were guilty of poor husbandry, they also neglected to pursue other beneficial projects, including the transplantation from the continent and cultivation of "divers Trees" that produced "Drugs, Balsams, Spices and Bark" (pp. 568–69) and the draining and improvement of Jamaica's many "Lagunes, Swamps, and boggy lands" that might both improve health and render productive rich soils that could be used to grow "Rice, Wheat and other Grain" as well as "all sorts of Garden Stuff" (p. 569) that had already been successfully planted in the mountains. Similar success "with English fruits, particularly Apples, and Strawberries," also suggested that those and others might be brought to "Perfection and Plenty" in the mountains should the "Inhabitants be at the pains of raising and Cultivating them" (p. 575). Such projects. Knight observed, could

certainly "Contribute towards raising a Publick Spirit amongst the Planters, and Consequently towards promoting the improvement and advantage
of the Island." Yet he despaired that Jamaicans "seldom thought on" any
project that required "trouble or Expence" unless it involved "the improvement of Sugar, and other common Products" that provided sure economic
returns. Unless Jamaican masters could develop a stronger public spirit, he
believed, Jamaica would continue to exhibit "that total neglect or disregard
of Gardens, Buildings, and other Amusements, which would make the Island, agreeable to them, and perhaps Equal to most other Countries in living, and all other Respects" (pp. 569, 576).

Although few planter families could yet afford to make the transition
to Britain, a great many had the resources to educate their sons there,
with several unfortunate ramifications for colonial society, which Knight
pointed out in the expectation that he might convince the planters "of
some mistakes in that Respect." Although girls were "generally bred at
home" under the tutelage of their mothers and rarely went abroad for their
education, many families sent their sons to England when they were "5 or
6 years of age, to their Agents or Factors, and placed out in some Private or
Publick School; and some of them sent afterwards to one of the Universities, or according to the Custom of their Mother Country, to France, Italy,
and other Parts; where they acquire[d] little more, than the Foppish Airs,
and Ridiculous Customs of those Countries." Although Knight acknowledged that "some of the Gentlemen Educated in this way" had "turned
out well and done Honour to their Country," he thought that it was "too
often otherwise" and that such educations "generally" alienated the "Children's Affections from Their Parents as well as from the Country," which
in itself, he was persuaded, was "a Cogent and sufficient Objection" to the
practice. "Upon Their return to the Island," he complained, many children knew "neither Their Father, nor Mother," and brought "over the
Habits, Customs, and Constitutions, of Europeans, improper for the Climate." These circumstances rendered them wholly "unfit to go through
the hardships, and fatigues of a Planter." Moreover, their long stays abroad
had given them "such a taste of the Pleasures and luxury of England" that
they could not "reconcile Themselves to any other manner of living and
when they" got "Possession of Their Paternal Estates" left them "to the
management of Their Agents, and Overseers," the "neglect or mismanagement" of whom combined with "Their Expensive way of living in England" soon brought them to financial ruin. Indeed, Knight thought, "the
Imputation of Luxury and Extravagance, [with] which the Planters, in general are loaded" in Britain was "in a great degree owing to the Conduct and
Behaviour of some of these Gentlemen in England" (pp. 475–76).

Arguing that it was "Practicable to give . . . Children a very good Education in the Island, and equal to most, or any, that have been in England,"
and professing to know of "several Instances . . . of Gentleman who never

were off the Island, and yet are as well Instructed in Grammar, and other usefull parts of Learning," and made "as good a Figure in Conversation, and in Publick Stations, as well as in the conduct and management of their private Affairs, as any in the Island," Knight sought to make "the Planters truly sensible of the prejudices, and disadvantages" of the existing system and to encourage them to devise "some other method by giving due and Reasonable Encouragement, to men of Ability and Virtue, to settle amongst them, and set up Schools and Nurseries of Learning" in what would have been Jamaica's first sustained effort to establish schools in the colony (pp. 475–76).

Knight did not blame the Jamaican establishment for "the State of Religion" in the colony, a subject to which he devoted scant attention, other than to report that it was "greatly neglected and disregarded." Except for a few Quakers and Presbyterians, most of the "Christian Inhabitants" of Jamaica were of the Anglican faith, and, lacking a church or a minister of their own, most Presbyterians attended Anglican services. With strong support from "the laity in general," the legislature had enacted "proper Laws" to provide comfortable livings for the clergy, intending to promote virtue and discourage vice and immorality. Rather, Jamaica's religion deficiencies, according to Knight, were entirely owing to "the Supineness and misbehaviour of the Clergy." Although he professed to know of some clergymen who led lives compatible "to their Doctrine and Profession" and had "not by their Conduct or Behaviour thrown any blemish on their Function or Order," he charged that, at least while he resided in the colony, "the major part of them were the most licentious set of men of any Society I was ever acquainted with," a situation he traced to the fact that the pool of ministers willing to leave their "Native Country" for overseas positions was limited to those forced to leave through "mere want or Necessities" and those whose already "corrupted" morals made it impossible for them to find a post in Britain. In his view, the "Advancement of Religion" in the colonies would only occur when the bishop of London, who had jurisdiction over colonial clergy abroad, found ways to monitor and discipline his errant clergy and to recruit more satisfactory ministers (p. 542).

Seeking Security

A pervading theme in Knight's long narrative of Jamaica's first eighty years as an English colony was its extreme vulnerability. Its situation in a cockpit of international rivalry, often complicated by the operations of predatory pirate communities, meant that shipping to and from the island was frequently at risk of capture and that its "Extensive Trade" (p. 614) depended for protection on metropolitan naval support. As Knight pointed out, all shipping to and from Britain and other Atlantic ports necessarily followed a route that was "well known" to seafaring men and passed "in Sight and even within two leagues . . . of some Parts of the French and Spanish Dominions . . . in America." For that reason, he contended, British naval cruisers were "at all times necessary, for the protection of Trade, against Pirates and Spanish Guarda Costas in time of Peace, and Privateers in time of War" (p. 615). Knight put so much emphasis on this point that he evaluated every naval commander in charge of the Jamaica station according to the level of his activity in protecting the island's shipping. Inspired by a wave of Guarda Costa peacetime captures of British vessels not engaged in any forbidden trades, his substantial seventy-nine-page 1726 London pamphlet was mostly devoted to an account of these attacks, making a case for a stronger metropolitan response.[24] With its long coastline, Jamaica was also open to hit-and-run marauders, especially on the less heavily settled north coast, and in wartime the entire island was vulnerable to invasion and possible conquest.

Especially because the Crown, itself without funds to invest in colonizing projects, had left earlier English colonies in America to their own defenses, Jamaicans had from the start made their own military preparations. "Being surrounded with Enemies," Knight recounted, the "first Set[t]lers who were Military Men, were from Their Situation . . . so well Convinced of the Absolute Necessity of having a . . . well Disciplined" militia that immediately after their discharge, they "formed Themselves into Regiments and obliged every Man to take a Commission according to His Rank or to bear Arms," an action to which the Jamaica Assembly, in the process of taking every possible measure "for the Security and preservation of the Island," quickly gave legal sanction (p. 640). When he arrived in the colony in 1712, half a century later, he recalled, "the principal Furniture of the Hall or Dining Room in every House from the Highest to the Meanest House-keeper was [still] a Rack of Fire Arms &c. in the Neatest Order," and the militia officers, composed of "Gentlemen of the greatest Abilities & Fortunes," were "at all times very diligent and Exact in Exercising and Disciplining their Militia in order to render them usefull, and fit for Service," in every parish presiding over monthly musters and seeking to "train up the Common People" in the use of firearms by sponsoring and awarding prizes in marksmanship competitions every Saturday afternoon (p. 640). When this system of self-defense barely managed to thwart the massive French invasion of 1694, however, Crown officials made an exception to its traditional policy and sent companies of English soldiers to help with the island's defense, thereby acknowledging Britain's high regard for the colony as a strategic and economic resource, albeit the provincial government took responsibility for feeding and housing the troops.

24. [Knight], *State of the Island of Jamaica.*

But there never was enough metropolitan troops in the colony to guarantee its security without help from the militia, and Knight decried the
erosion of Jamaica's militia system following the politicization of militia
offices by Crown governors during the early decades of the eighteenth century, a development that, he noted, had "brought those Commissions into
Contempt" by awarding them to people "unequal to Them, and incapable
of preserving the Authority" they required. "Time and Circumstances," he
wrote, now demanded a reinvigoration of the militia system to make it inclusive of all free whites between fifteen and sixty years old and to require
every parish to hold military exercises every Saturday and participate in a
general muster once a month (pp. 264, 640–41).

To render the colony's free population entirely secure, however, required
more far-reaching measures designed to decrease the growing racial im-
balance between enslaved and free people. "A Country . . . that is Cultivated with Negroes or Slaves & a Small Number of White People," Knight
warned in a candid analysis, "may indeed become Rich . . . but it cannot be
deemed safe or secure" (pp. 633–34). A British naval squadron might be
able to protect Jamaica against a foreign invasion but would be of little
use against an "intestine Enemy." Nor could "4 or 500 Planters, supposing Them all to be Rich or in good Circumstances, with the White Servants They commonly Employ, be able to protect [such] a large Extensive Country, and resist an Invading or Intestine Enemy." In either case,
Jamaica needed either "a sufficient Strength of White Inhabitants able to
bear Arms, who have some property to defend; or a Military Force established among Them for Their protection," the latter of which he thought
would in the long term be disagreeable and inconsistent with either "Industry or an English Constitution" (p. 633).

For nearly four decades before Knight produced his treatise, the Jamaica
Assembly had been trying to deal with this shortage in white population
through legislation that required every slaveholder either to keep at least
one white servant for every twenty to thirty enslaved blacks or to pay a
deficiency tax, but it failed to produce a rise in the servant population because landowners found it cheaper to pay the tax than to acquire and keep
servants. Besides, in the competition among colonies for labor, Jamaica,
like all colonies with a substantial population of enslaved people, was not
an especially desirable destination for free people, despite Knight's insistence that "people of all Professions" who as servants had recommended
themselves "by their Sobriety, Industry, and discreet behaviour" would in
Jamaica, "as many have happily Experienced," find "no Encouragement
wanting" and no lack of "Opportunity of Advancing themselves" after their
contracts had expired. Indeed, he professed to "know Several, that are now
Masters of Families, live in good Credit, and by their Industry have raised
Considerable Fortunes" (p. 479).

But Knight was skeptical that even the massive importation of white servants would solve the security problem for Jamaican whites. Those "whose Servitude Renders Their Liberty little more than Nominal, and such as have no Property," he observed, citing the failure of expeditions that included large numbers of servants during the Maroon War of 1730–39, "may sometimes fight" but could never "be depended on; for it cannot reasonably be supposed, that they will have the same Spirits, or Arm with the same generous Ardour, as those who Act in Defence of Their Liberty and Property, which is the Principal Motive to great and Noble Actions" (pp. 480–81).

Indeed, Knight questioned whether even Jamaica's Jewish population could be relied on "in Case of an Invasion or Insurrection." Noting that Jews had "often been suspected of holding a Correspondence [with] and of giving Intelligence to the Spaniards," and invoking English prejudices against Jews in general as a "Roguish" and "Noxious" people incapable of courageous action, he inquired, "What use or Advantage" might they be "to an Island that wants Inhabitants to Improve and defend it"? Further, he suggested that the Jamaica legislature consider ways to lessen the privileges Jews enjoyed and encourage "poor Christian Families" to supplant them and take over their businesses (p. 478). But any such measures, as Knight realized, would not resolve the security problem facing Jamaican whites. Clearly, Jamaica's very survival depended on its legislature's "taking some other [and much more extensive] measures, to People and Strengthen the Island" (p. 481).

The most promising approach, he thought, would be to devise measures designed to increase the number of white Christian property owning settlers of every variety. Estimating that "not one fifth part of the manurable lands in Jamaica" had "ever been set[t]led," he insisted that Jamaica still had plenty of land in the interior and other remote areas that was "Capable of further & very Considerable improvements." Moreover, additional land would become available if the assembly could be persuaded to act to remedy the colony's greatest defect: "suffering Persons to Patent large Tracts of land, more than They can possibly Occupy or make use of, and hold Them in Expectation of disposing of Them to great Advantage," which, notwithstanding Crown instructions forbidding governors from granting more than three hundred acres to any one person, had, in Knight's opinion, long been and still was "a principal Obstruction to the Settlement & Improvement of this Island." As a result, he lamented, "divers Gentlemen in England as well as in Jamaica" held "many Thousand Acres[,] some not less than 14 or 15000[, a] great part of which never was manured or paid one penny Quit Rent," a practice that was illegal as Jamaica law required a forfeiture of title to land remaining unimproved after a set time. As Knight reported, however, that restriction had been constantly "winked at thro[ugh] the Influence and Power of some of those Land holders" (pp. 621, 636).

To remedy this deep flaw in Jamaica society. Knight asked the Jamaica
Assembly to take effective measures to "restrain the Engrossing of lands or
any Man from holding more than He can Occupy & improve," proposing
that it "Establish something like the Agrarian Law," not for the purpose of
"levelling . . . Property, and Rightfull Possession of Lands which are Manured & Cultivated, but to restrain the Collusive taking up for the future
or holding such lands as have been taken up in that manner, because it is
a bar to the Industry of others," and to "the improvement of the Island,"
as well as the increase of Crown revenues through the collection of quit-
rents. Specifically, he called the assembly's attention to an Antigua law that
levied a prohibitively high tax on every acre of such "uncultivated Tracts"
(pp. 633, 636–37).

Even with the availability of land that might be suitable for creating a
sugar estate, however, Knight realized that "Private Persons . . . engaged
in any kind of business which will support Them in England, much less
People of Fortune," could not be expected to "engage in New Adventures,
so [that] none or very few but such as are uneasy in Their Circumstances[,]
needy or Necessitous" would "entertain any thoughts of removing &
set[t]ling with Their Families in remote & distant Parts of the World"
(p. 635). However, he did encourage "Persons of small or mid[d]ling
Fortunes," who were interested in "advancing Their Own Interest, and
providing for their Families," to "go over with Alacrity." Even for "those
Gentlemen, who have small Estates in Great Britain or Ireland or who are
so much incumbered, that they Struggle with many difficulties" and "great
Anxieties," Jamaica offered "an Opportunity of Extricating themselves, living Comfortably for the future, and providing in a decent manner for their
Families." Simply by selling their estates and paying off their debts, such
people, providing they had an "Overpluss of 800 or £1000 Sterling," could
"Settle a Plantation, which in a few years will bring in 3 or £400 per Annum and with Industry and good Husbandry improve the same and raise
a Sugar Work" and "be so Improved as to enable them to raise and make
some Figure in the World." Knight claimed to know "severall Persons who
live[d] in a Comfortable manner, and others who in my time, acquired
good Estates in Jamaica with a less Foundation, and some meerly by their
Industry, Oeconomy and Address" (pp. 19–20).

But Knight concluded that the "most likely means" to resolve the problem of white deficiency in Jamaica was to bring in "poor families," preferably from Wales, where they were "used to hard living, and a Mountainous Country," and were "unacquainted with . . . Vice and Debauchery,"
or from Scotland or Protestant Switzerland, but not from either England,
where the inhabitants were "accustomed to great Plenty" and unused to
the hardships involved in making a new settlement, or Ireland, where the
common people were "mostly Papists and naturally attached to the Spaniards" (p. 481). Declaring it unreasonable "to suppose that any Country

will encrease in people and thereby gather Strength as well as Riches unless it be made a Poor Man's Country" in which an ordinary settler could have "the necessaries of life at moderate Rates" and thereby be able both to "support Himself & His Family in a Comfortable manner" and to "lay up something yearly," in the process providing an example that would "encourage others to become set[t]lers," he proposed to push Jamaica in that direction by establishing "in this Island, something of the Nature of the Ten Acre Men, as They are called in Barbados," who produced provisions for the island market, and by encouraging "such Settlements as may be Cultivated & carried on with a few Hands and at a small Expence namely for raising live Stock[,] Ground Provisions, Coffee, Cotton, Ginger & such like Commodities." Having by previous laws already offered to pay for "the passages of all such Persons as shall go over & become Set[t]lers," to assign them up to three hundred acres of land in "proportion to the Number of White Persons in [a] Family," and to provide "an Allowance for Their Subsistence for 12 Months, & an exemption from all Taxes except Parochial for 7 years," the Jamaica Assembly, Knight proposed, should raise the ante and, following the example of the French Crown, establish an additional fund "by subscription or a publick Tax" from which immigrants without funds could borrow enough money on long-term credit at a moderate rate of interest to purchase the "Negroes, Cattle[,] Poultry[,] Seeds & Plantation Utensils" needed to establish themselves and begin to build an estate. "Unless such Encouragement be given to invite poor Families to become Set[t]lers in this Island," he warned, "it cannot be expected . . . that it ever will be populous and able to make a proper defence without the Assistance of a sufficient Military Force, which will be attended with greater Inconveniencies & Expence than those I have mentioned" (pp. 633, 635–36).

Knight suggested two additional strategies to help overcome the deficiency problem. The first was to subsidize the importation from Britain of boys and girls from "about ten or twelve Years of Age," who had "not contracted any ill habits nor entered into any kind of Debauchery," and who could be expected to be quickly "inured to the Country," with the climate becoming "as Habituall to Them, as to the Natives." The second was to restrain or limit "the Number of Negro Tradesmen" and replace them with white immigrants from Britain, because planters preferred "such Tradesmen," whom they regarded as "in general more hardy & usefull" and capable of "dispatch[ing] more business than White Men." The "Number of Negro Tradesmen such as Carpenters, Bricklayers, Wheel Wrights, Black Smiths, Taylors &c. among the Plantations," he estimated, had grown to two thousand, while those in the towns and villages included at least another thousand, and he speculated that the replacement of all three thousand by white immigrants, "or even one half," would provide "a very considerable Additional Strength" to the white population. To achieve this goal, Knight proposed that the assembly pass measures to limit severely the number of black tradesmen who could "be brought up or made use of for the future in every Plantation, or perhaps" even "to Prohibit altogether the bringing up any such Tradesmen for the future, or making use of any such after the Death of those who are already brought up to the Business." If any such tradesmen were allowed, Knight further suggested, "every Planter or other Person, who employ[ed] Them" should be obliged "to Maintain one White Man able to bear Arms for every Negro Tradesman." Although he acknowledged that "the Planters & other Inhabitants who employ[ed] Them" would "think this a great hardship, and [that] few if any" would "be able to digest it," he was hopeful that when they "consider[ed] the necessity of it, & how much the preservation of the Island, in Consequence Their own lives & Fortunes depend upon it," they would "rather submit to some Inconveniencies than run so great a Risque" (pp. 481, 633–34).

Controlling the Enslaved

Lest his British readers conclude that the great demographic superiority of the enslaved population rendered Jamaica "exceeding dangerous, and unsafe living amongst Them" (p. 482), Knight in his discussion of the in-habitants of Jamaica in part 6 constructed a substantial ethnography of slave origins and culture to emphasize the many deterrents to slave re-volt. So far, Jamaican whites had kept the enslaved majority under control through a combination of strategies that included scattering, mixing, di-viding, intimidating, and monitoring. Scattering was mostly a function of "the great Extent of the Country." Because individual land holdings were "Separated by Woods and Mountains, difficult of access," and "lying at a great distance" from one another, Knight noted, "the Negroes can have no communication together, or if they had, it would be almost impossible" that "they should join to Execute Their Designs. This Natural Security," he stressed, distinguished Jamaica "from all the other British Sugar Islands. For in the latter, notwithstanding they have every other Security" but "ex-tent of Country, general Conspiracies have been formed, and sometimes with great probability of Success. But I never heard that this Island was at any time in the like danger," even though the Maroons "in the Mountains were not wanting to promote and encourage such a design" (pp. 482–83).[25]

If Jamaica's size provided "the chief security of Jamaica against any gen-eral Insurrection of the Negroes" (p. 482), the heterogeneity of the en-slaved population, in Knight's view, was also a significant deterrent. That

25. Interestingly, Knight always used the term "wild Negroes," not "Maroons," to refer to these groups, a usage that suggests the term "Maroon" was not yet in circulation among Jamaicans at the time Knight wrote.

population included a small number of Amerindians, imported from the continent, unaccustomed to hard labor, and almost entirely employed in fishing. Overwhelmingly, however, almost all of the enslaved were African or descendants of Africans. They were drawn, he estimated, from "more than twenty different Countries or Nations," each of which was "different in language, and Customs" and frequently exhibited "as great and Natural an Antipathy to each other, as any two Nations in the World." Usually buying from eight to ten new black people at a time, plantation owners deliberately mixed into their labor force people from different and antagonistic ethnic groups, whose difficulties in communicating or conferring together and being suspicions of one another would prevent them from combining to "Shake off the Yoke of the English" (pp. 482–84).

Slave owners also pursued a strategy of dividing the enslaved community by creating an elite cadre of people from among those who, behaving "extremely well," exhibiting special aptitudes or skills or talents, and showing "great Fidelity" to their masters, enjoyed privileged status and were employed in special roles as artisans, overseers, drivers, boilers, boatmen, cooks, or house servants and exempted from fieldwork. Few masters of "Plantations or Families" in Jamaica, Knight observed, had not created a privileged group within the enslaved population to hold such "places of Trust" and to execute whatever was "committed to Their Care and management" in such a way as to justify their masters' having so "distinguished" them. These groups were often composed largely of "Creoles or those Born in the Country" who were fluent in English and thoroughly socialized into the island's economic and cultural regime. So close could attachments become between them and their masters that Knight claimed to know of "many Instances" of privileged slaves "making known to Their Masters and Mistresses the Treacherous Practices and Rebellious designs of other Negroes, by which means several Families have been preserved, and much mischief prevented." Indeed, he declared himself to be persuaded that many of these privileged people, already competent in the "use of Fire Arms" and with a "kind of property [of their own] to defend" and a deep attachment to their own plantations and neighborhoods, could "be confided in, and . . . be very Serviceable, in Case the Island should be at any time Invaded by a Foreign Enemy" (pp. 488–89). By creating and thereby coopting such groups, he suggested, slave owners effectively organized the enslaved community along hierarchical lines—and divided it, thereby contributing to a sense of white security.

Knight also remarked on how the white establishment counted on public display as a form of intimidation to keep the enslaved population quiescent. Witnessing the "White People Muster or Exercise, especially the Regular forces, and Troops of Horse," he wrote, struck newly imported blacks with "Awe and terrour," as did the spectacle of Royal Navy ships that were "constantly on the Station, and the great number of Shipping, Continually Coming and going," which impressed on the enslaved "an Idea of the Strength and Power of the English Nation." Creole blacks were less intimidated by such theater. "Far from being under the like apprehensions of a Muster," they were so "familiar with it" that "many of them" could "Exercise and make use of fire Arms as well as the Militia" (pp. 482–83).

In the final analysis, Knight thought, close monitoring and just application of "the Laws for the good Order, and Government of Slaves" represented the best "Security of the White People." Jamaican law formally placed severe restrictions on all enslaved people, forbidding them "to keep Arms, or dangerous Weapons in Their Houses" or to leave their plantation or other places of residence "without a Certificate from the Master, or Overseer, Expressing the time" and reason for the absence, although Knight acknowledged that this last prohibition, being troublesome to masters, was "sometimes winked at, and not Strictly put in Execution." By law as well, he reported, "the Several Parishes, or Precincts" into which the colony was divided were required "Constantly . . . on Sundays and Hollidays" to keep up guards and to have "Troops of Horse" to "Patrol in Their Respective Divisions, to prevent Conspiracies or disorders amongst the Negroes; who generally assemble together at those times, get drunk and quarrel among Themselves, and sometimes in Their drink grow turbulent, and even Mutinous, if they are not timely dispersed" (p. 482).

As Knight noted, however, the law left the day-to-day management of "Every Plantation" entirely in the hands of "the Master, or Owner, and in his absence the Overseer," who had "an Absolute Authority over" the enslaved with the exception of charges involving penalties of "Life and Limb." Such cases were to be heard by two magistrates and three freeholders "sworne to judge uprightly and according to Evidence." "In the management of those People," he thought that it was "absolutely Necessary" for masters "to keep a Vigilant Eye, and a Strict hand over most of Them so as to keep Them in Awe, and prevent Their doing wrong or Mischief." Yet at the same time, he also stressed that masters needed to take care "to treat" the enslaved "with Humanity, and not to Correct Them unjustly or without proof of Their having committed some fault," for, although they "never repine when They are Conscious of having deserved Correction, yet They seldom or ever forgive Injuries or Maltreatment." "Using them well," Knight emphasized, could elicit a degree of affection toward a master that, along with their attachment to their own houses, garden plots, and family, as well as "Friendship[s] and Alliances" they had "Contracted . . . in the Neighbourhood," might produce a strong and positive identification with a particular plantation and master (pp. 474, 482, 488, 491).

Knight was one of the first to suggest the use of religion as a way of reconciling the enslaved to their condition. Although he noted that the enslaved showed "no manner of inclination to be instructed or Converted," and was skeptical whether the few who had been "taught to Read, and had been Baptised, however devo[u]t and attentive They appeared to be during Divine Service," had actually acquired much if "any Notion of Religion," he thought it "possible to Instruct many Negroes, especially the Creoles, or such as are brought Young to the Island, in the Belief of a Deity . . . and of a Future State of Rewards and Punishments." Moreover, such instruction might inculcate in them "some Principles of Morality" that "would tend very much to make Them better Servants and subjects, as well as to fit them for another World." Although, in his opinion, "to Attempt any thing more" would "be in Vain and [require] a Herculean labour," "far from discouraging so laudable a design," he would "be glad to see some attempt to accomplish it" (pp. 496–98).

Knight found a final deterrent to slave revolt in the gradual emergence of a large body of creole blacks in the colony. Because the island was still importing so many people from Africa, creoles almost certainly had not yet become a majority of the enslaved population, but they were growing in number. Whereas Knight expressed fears about creolean degeneracy among island whites, he reported a kind of adjustment and socialization among the blacks. "These Creole Negroes speak very good English," he noted, "especially such as are brought up in the Towns, or in Gentlemen's Houses, and have so good and tractable a Genius, that They are easily Instructed in most Mechanical Trades, and to be usefull in many other Respects. They look upon Themselves to be as much above the Salt Water Negroes, as They call . . . those that are brought from Guinea, as the Gentry think Themselves above the Commonalty in England; and will seldom keep any of Them Company" (p. 483).

Observing the Enslaved

Knight's preoccupation with the problem of keeping Jamaica's overwhelming black majority from revolt did not deter him from giving serious attention to a description of black society as it had taken shape in the island. Indeed, his discussion of that society in part 6, on the inhabitants of Jamaica, represents the fullest and most sustained effort up to that time to produce in short compass what modern scholars would recognize as an ethnographic portrait of its origins, composition, and culture.

For modern readers, it is important to put his ethnography in its temporal context. Throughout much of the British (and Atlantic) world, black enslavement, during the decades when Knight was living in Jamaica and writing his treatise, had been for almost two centuries and remained an essential building block of empire. Within the British Empire, it was arguably the most important component in the economic development of the colonies from Maryland south to Barbados and a major contributor to the growing wealth and maritime resources of metropolitan Britain. Moreover, the entire transatlantic slave system had never functioned with more vigor.

The slave trade was enormously profitable and expanding, with the supply of slaves in Africa continually rising to meet colonial demand; the colonies were developing rapidly, and their demand for British manufactures was stimulating the growth of the domestic British economy. The colonies most valued by the British state were those in the West Indies, the Chesapeake, and the Carolinas—those with the largest numbers of enslaved workers. In the colonies north of Maryland and in Britain itself, the enslaved population was visibly growing.

Nor was there any sustained general challenge to this system. Knight wrote nearly two decades before Tacky's Revolt, in St. Mary Parish along the north coast of Jamaica in the spring and summer of 1760. The most extensive and successful such revolt in colonial British American history to that time, it gave concrete reality to white fears of general slave rebellion, nearly three decades before the sustained attack on the legitimacy of slavery mounted by Granville Sharpe and others in the late 1760s and before Lord Mansfield's decision in the Somerset Case in 1772 put American slaveholders on the defensive.

So deeply embedded was this slave system in British imperial culture by the 1730s and 1740s that Knight, perhaps surprisingly for modern readers, could write about it and Jamaica's black population with cool detachment, displaying no special need to defend it and in a way that was profoundly more measured, more appreciative and positive, and largely free of the denigrative language and virulent racism found in the proslavery literature generated in the 1760s and after in response to British antislavery writings and the Somerset Case. Edward Long's three-volume *History of Jamaica*, published in 1774, is representative of this later literature, and a comparison between Knight's and Long's histories is instructive. Knight provides a much fuller account of Jamaica's civil history, while Long's narrative effectively ended in 1679, and Knight fully anticipated Long in articulating most of the central themes discussed in this introduction. On the subject of Jamaica's black inhabitants, however, the two historians were in agreement on only one point: that they had played an extraordinarily important part in the economic and social construction of Jamaica. Driven by his determination to defend the institution of slavery, Long's descriptions of blacks were often purely polemical and designed to denigrate their intellectual capacities in comparison to those of whites. Knight, in sharp contrast, displayed a genuine interest in black life and culture and showed no disposition to question the humanity of blacks, commenting rather that "Nature" had "implanted in Them, as well as the rest of Mankind, Pride, Ambition, Dissimulation and all other passions and Vices; though They have not the same Opportunity of exerting Them" (p. 487). In his comments on the widespread employment of black artisans in all areas of the Jamaica economy and the achievements of creoles, Knight did not question the aptitude or intellectual and social competence of blacks. Nor did he treat them as an ethnically undifferentiated mass, emphasizing that the people brought from Africa came from "more than twenty different Countries or Nations" (pp. 483–84).

Knight also thought that black personal habits and practices helped to make them considerably more "hardy[,] healthy and Robust" than Jamaican whites. In particular, he suspected that their insistence on "Constantly Bath[ing] or Wash[ing] themselves every day" was the principal reason why they were rarely "Afflicted with some of the Distempers" that were "peculiar and incidental to White People" (pp. 466–67). Similarly, Knight proposed that their practice of always having "a Fire near them, when they sleep, even in the Sun and the open Air" was "not meerly on account of their being more Chilly, and of a Colder Constitution than White People, but because they find by Experience [that] it dissipates the Damps and Vapours of the Earth, and drives away the Musquitos and other Flies, which are often troublesome in all parts of the West Indies, and especially after great Rains" (p. 469).

Knight disclaimed having knowledge enough to "enter into a Particular Description of all the . . . Nations of Negroes brought to this Island," but he did try to characterize the three ethnic groups that were "most esteemed" by slave owners: "Whidah, the Gold Coast, and Angola." "Very justly preferred to all others," the Whidahs (Ouidahs) were, Knight wrote, "more manageable, accustomed to labour, and hard living in Their own Country," and "of so chearfull a disposition that They generally sing or Whistle at the hardest Work, they" could be "put to, insomuch that" when a large number were at work together in a field, they could commonly be heard "Singing in Parts or together" and audible "at a considerable distance" (pp. 484–85).

Although the "Gold Coast Negroes" generally went under the denomination of "Coromantus," according to Knight they actually came from several different areas and did not speak the same language. Because they had been "more accustomed to labour, and hard living in Their own Country; where their Common food" was "Maiz[e], or Corn, Plantains, Yams and other ground Provisions" and they ate little meat, and because "most of Them, particularly the Coromantines" were "ingenious, and when . . . Young easily taught any Science, or Mechanick Art," planters preferred those Gold Coast people called "Coromantines, Santuns, Shantus, and Achims." But Knight reported that they were also "Fractious, and in Their Nature Deceitfull, Revengefull, and blood thirsty, and require[d] a Stricter hand being kept over Them than those of any other Country; for which reason every prudent Planter" was "cautious of having too many of Them in his Plantation" and therefore commonly tried to mix them in with people from other countries. "There never was as I have heard of in this or any other Colony," he noted, "any Plot or Conspiracy, but they were at the bottom of it" (p. 484).

Even though the Angolans, who, as Knight recognized, had had some exposure to Christianity before being brought to Jamaica, and were "likewise used to Labour," planters did not value them "so much . . . as the others," because they had "been accustomed to Eat flesh in Their own Country," which the planters could not afford. For that reason, he added, they were "generally brought up to Trades or to go in Sloops, Cannoes, and Wherries, as Watermen, where a better subsistance can be allowed Them, than in Plantations" (p. 484).

In his description of the lives and culture of enslaved blacks, Knight focused primarily not on such ethnic distinctions but on the general cultural patterns that had emerged in Jamaica. Paying virtually no attention to the work regimes that structured enslaved lives, he concentrated on living arrangements, property accumulation, marriage patterns, musical expression, and leisure activities. Planters expected all the enslaved males attached to a rural plantation or pen to build their own houses, which, according to Knight, they did "after Their Country manner" in a rectangular shape of approximately twenty-four feet by eight or nine feet, supported by posts and divided into three sections, with a door to the outside in the middle of both of the longer sides, ceilings no more than six feet high, a few openings for light without windows, no chimneys, and a thatched roof. Both the exterior walls and the partitions were "lined with watles, a kind of laiths neatly plaistered with mud." In these structures, they kept their poultry and "Constant fires, both night and day," which made all enslaved houses "smell very strong of smoak," despite the occupants' endeavors to keep them "very neat and clean" (p. 486).

Because masters only promised to subsist newly imported people for six months, they also expected them to feed themselves by cultivating and improving assigned plots, where, Knight noted, an industrious person could not only "raise as many Plantains, Yams, Potatoes and other ground Provision, and also Hogs, and Dunghill Fowles . . . as will be sufficient for Himself and Family; but to Sell enough" at Sunday morning markets in towns and villages to enable him "to purchase better Cloathing, than" his master annually furnished, as well as "Salted Beef, Pork, Fish and other necessaries." Indeed, those who were "frugal as well as Industrious" could also "lay up Money beside," of which few or no masters, according to Knight, were "so unjust as to deprive" them (pp. 485–86).

According to Knight, marriage customs and family relations among the enslaved were left entirely in their own hands. Despite the absence of "form or Ceremony" in their marriages, he claimed to "have known some, that never separated or Acknowledged any other Husband or Wife during the life of the first." While "in general" they often changed mates when quarrels disturbed their relationships, even after parting, they "always" remained fond of their children and took care of them. Jamaica had no laws against polygamy among the enslaved, and as slaveholders had every reason to encourage natural reproduction among them, men were able to take as many wives as they liked. Nevertheless, as Knight pointed out, many enslaved men had "no more than one wife, and some have none. For Interest," he explained, "governs them as well as the rest of Mankind, and unless a Man can provide better Cloaths, and other necessaries, than his Master allows, He will find some difficulty in getting a Wife." Moreover, those men who were polygamous never had more than three wives: a primary wife to manage the family, a second wife who was "the Object of his Affections," and a third who was "little more than His Drudge, or Housekeeper." These multiple spouses often lived amicably, but when disputes arose among them, the husband settled it, not, Knight thought, by the "Rules of Reason of Justice" but "agreeable to His own Humour or Caprice," sometimes by dismissing one of the wives and finding another. Indeed, Knight expressed considerable dismay that some enslaved men kept "Their Wives in such awe and subjection, that They" would "not suffer Them to Dine, or Sup with Them; but make Them wait till They have done, and the Reason They give is, because it would make Them Saucy, as they express Themselves" (pp. 487–88).

What seems to have most fascinated Knight about black culture was its deep musicality. "On Sundays and Hollidays in the Evenings, as well as in Moon light nights, after They have done work," he reported, the enslaved assembled, danced, sang, and played together, keeping "very good time" and showing remarkable "Agility of Body" and "a great Variety of Steps" in their dancing. In general, and from a European perspective, Knight found their musical instruments "very Noisy," with "no manner of Harmony," but he made an exception for the "Merry Wang," a guitar-like instrument, which he pronounced as "far from being disagreeable, when it is in a good hand; and I have heard Minuits, and other English Tunes played thereon, so distinctly, and with so good time, as might serve European Dancers upon Occasion." Composing their own songs, the enslaved sang, danced, and played "on Their Musick" whenever they were "under any affliction or trouble to dissipate Melancholy thoughts, as well as to amuse and divert Themselves upon other Occasions," such musical activities being appropriate for funerals and extended bereavement ceremonies as well as for "Festivals or Publick Meetings on Holidays." "At a distance," Knight wrote, it was impossible to tell whether their music proceeded from "Mirth, or Sorrow," but he professed to have heard "very few Tunes" that were "brisk and Airy" and found "in general . . . something in them extremely Melancholy" and a perfect expression of the "Natural gloomy Countenance" he observed in "Negroes in general" (pp. 486–87). Knight did not go on to make the point obvious to all modern scholars: that the melancholy silently exhibited in the demeanor of the enslaved and explicitly expressed in their music registered a profoundly negative judgment on the Jamaican institution of slavery.

Taking Enslavement for Granted

Knight showed no inclination to defend Jamaica for its heavy dependence on the institution of enslavement. Rather, he seems to have taken it for granted, assuming, as did most of the many thousands of Britons directly involved in the system, that the trade in and employment of enslaved Africans were foundational building blocks of empire and that the Jamaica Knight sought to depict would and could not exist without them. Without any manifest moral or legal compunctions or reservations, he seems to have assumed that Jamaica's black population had been legally enslaved in Africa and that, notwithstanding their obvious humanity and mental abilities to handle every sort of work or trade required in Jamaica, their legal status as enslaved chattels condemned them to a social and civil position that would forever subordinate them to free whites, as the only road to freedom for them was heroic actions in support of the white population that they served. Indeed, although the number of free blacks seems by the 1730s and 1740s to have been increasing at an ever accelerating rate, primarily as a result of interracial sexual unions, Knight seems to have assumed that the group was too small to require much attention in his analysis of the island's inhabitants.

Where Knight became defensive was when he came to address metropolitan accusations about "the Inhumanity and Cruelty of the Planters to Their Negroes." He did not deny that there were grounds for such charges but argued that they were "very much aggravated" and that "very few" planters were "so Barbarous" as they had been "Represented to be" in Britain. "Whoever considers the Negroes' Superiority in Number, the sullen, deceitfull, Refractory Temper of Most of Them; that some are Careless, others Treacherous or Idle, and apt to Run away; and how much Their Master's Interest depends on the Care, and diligence of His Slaves," he wrote, must realize the "Absolute necessity of keeping a Vigilant Eye, and strict hand over Them." Admitting that the usual punishment inflicted on enslaved people, "a severe whipping on the bare back," might "be shocking to a tender mind," he contended that in Jamaica, treatment of the enslaved was much less "Rigid and Severe" than "the kind of Discipline" routinely "practised in English, as well as Foreign Camps and Garrisons; where I have seen the common Soldiers punished with much greater Severity than I ever saw the Negroes in Jamaica." As an additional comparison, Knight observed that, although readers would find it "very strange," it was "a matter of Fact to my own knowledge, and Observation, that the Free Negroes and Mulattos, even those who have been Slaves Themselves, were the most Rigid and Severe Masters in all Respects" (pp. 492–93).

While Knight acknowledged that in colonial British American slave systems "the Usage and treatment of the Negroes, greatly depends on the Temper and discretion of the Master," he suggested that compassion and interest combined to prevent mistreatment. Most planters, he affirmed, were "Men . . . of a more tender, humane, Compassionate disposition" who were "led by those motives and Principles, as well as Regard to Their Interest to be kind to Their Negroes, to be carefull" that the enslaved "neither want[ed] Provisions, nor proper Cloathing, and to preserve Their lives and limbs; because the death or disability of a Negro" was "a Certain loss and Their Plantations depend[ed] on keeping up the Number" of the enslaved, which a combination of low birthrate, high mortality, accidents, the high price of "good working field hands" and "good Boilers, Carpenters, Bricklayers and other Tradesmen, and [the] shallow mortgage market" rendered exceedingly difficult (p. 493).

He acknowledged that "to an Englishman, who has always enjoyed His liberty and lived in ease and plenty," the "Negroes' manner of Living in our Plantations, and above all the very name of Slavery" might "be disagreeable and shocking," but he endeavored to "remove the Prejudice, which many Persons" in Britain who were "unacquainted with our Colonies, have conceived against Them" by asking his English readers to consider the possibility that the condition of the enslaved "in general" was "much better, and that They live[d] happier" in Jamaica than they "did in Their own Country, or even than some of the working People in England, and preferably to those of some other Nations." "For every Plantation-Negroe in Jamaica," he stressed, was "allowed to build a House for Himself and Family, after His own manner; which tho[ugh] mean and low, yet is such, as They have been used to in Their own Country; They are also allowed to Fence in a small yard Contiguous, and to raise Hogs, and Poultry for Themselves, beside His little Plantation, which produces Corn, Pease &c. and all sorts of ground Provisions; some of which They dispose of, and purchase other necessaries." If, moreover, their diet was coarse, it was "the same and in some Respects much better than They were used to, which was nothing more than Maiz[e] or Corn, in some Parts Rice, Plantains, Yams and Potatoes roasted or boiled (and now and then a Goat, or a small Deer)." But in Jamaica, he continued, "They not only have those sorts of Provisions in great plenty, but Salted Beef, Pork and Fish, which many of Them prefer to fresh Meat," and in some parts of the island "plenty of fresh Fish." In addition, by selling the meat and fowls at weekly markets, they could obtain "Cloathing and many other Necessaries" to "which They were Strangers . . . before They came to the Island" (pp. 493–94).

"Notwithstanding all the objections and Cavils that are made" in Britain "against the usage and treatment the Negroes meet with" in Jamaica,

Knight concluded that in Jamaica almost every enslaved person, with the exception of those who were "so Roguish or idle, as not to take that provident care, and therefore often suffer [the] want and Extremity which They very justly deserve," had "a kind of property," and looked "upon His little Plantation as such, it being seldom taken away without giving Him an Equivolent." Enslaved people also had "stated times of Working and Recess, and several Hollidays in the Year, beside Saturdays in the Afternoon and Sundays." A slave was "allowed at those times to go upon His own Occasions, divert Himself, or Visit His friends, provided He asks leave and Obtains a Certificate." He was "taken care of in sickness and Health, and at no Expence for Rent, or an Apothecary or Surgeon," had "plenty of ground Provisions and with Care and Industry" could "furnish Himself with salted Provisions, and other Necessaries, besides what his master allowed," and in old age, infirmity, or past labor was "supported by His Master." In addition, because "in Their own Country . . . most of Them were subject to the Arbitrary Will and Pleasure of Their Kings or Chief Men, who disposed of Them as They thought proper, and had an Absolute power of life and Death," they could "justly be said to be less Slaves in our Plantations, than They were in their own Country" because colonial law restrained masters "from Maiming or dismembering Them upon any pretence whatever without a legal Trial" (pp. 494–95).

Comparing the "Condition and Manner of living of the common People in England" with that of Jamaica's enslaved, Knight called the reader's attention to the degree to which the former were often "under great difficulties in Subsisting Themselves and Their Families in Sickness or the dead of Winter; and sometimes in the Summer Season; that Their Diet in general" was "as coarse as the Negroes, few of Them being able to purchase Meat, above once a week, and that of the worst sort; that many of Them" were "as Ragged, and bare of Cloathing as the Negroes, considering the difference of the Climate, and that often in Health, as well as in sickness, Old Age, or Disability, They are reduced to very great extremity." On balance, Knight asserted, the enslaved "in our Plantations" clearly had "the Advantage," and he marveled that the English poor could "yet . . . startle," and be "Shocked at the proposition of going over to the Plantations; where They may live better and have a prospect of raising Their Fortunes" (p. 495).

Maintaining English Rights

While Knight's deeply qualified analysis of colonial systems of enslavement might not have persuaded his British readers either that slavery was far less onerous than they supposed, or that in Jamaica, as he put it, "the Planters as well as those in the Towns" lived "in greater Security . . . than

People do in England" (p. 483), he was far less equivocal when he turned to the Jamaica Assembly's long-running struggle to create a constitution that would secure the liberty of the island's free white population to enjoy the traditional English rights to consensual governance and the rule of law. No less than his celebration of the island's improvement, Knight's preoccupation with this struggle was one of the most prominent features of his grand treatise.

Indeed, he made it the central theme of his first volume and came back to it in parts 7 (on governance) and 10 (on desirable imperial reforms) of his second. Beginning public life in Jamaica as a Crown official, he might well have been expected to turn into a supporter of Crown policy, and during his six-year tenure as receiver general, he trod carefully, trying to stay neutral in all disputes between the Crown and the colony. "As I was then in the Service of the Crown . . . and in a Station which (by a late Act of the Country) disqualified me among others from being a Member of the Council or Assembly," as he told his readers, "I thought it prudent, (Especially as I was just entered on the Stage of Business) to attend the Duty of my Office, to pay a due deference and Respect to the Governour, and to avoid giving offence to the Council[,] Assembly or to Either Party" (p. 246). At heart, however, he seems to have been a classic Whig who in his political opinions was a strong adherent to the belief that consensual governance and the rule of law were the essential foundations of liberty in British polities, wherever found. Perhaps his service in the Jamaica Assembly beginning in 1722 served to confirm him in this belief. Likewise, his insertion on the title page of his second volume of a quotation from the economic writer Charles Davenant manifested Knight's firm conviction that liberty was essential to the success of new commercial enterprises and the creation of new polities in distant regions of the globe. "Industry has its first foundation in Liberty," Davenant wrote, and "they who either are Slaves, or who believe their Freedoms precarious, can neither Succeed in Trade, or Meliorate a Country."[26] However Knight came to it, his commitment to liberty infused his narrative of Jamaican political life as an English colony, which he depicted as a more or less continuous controversy between prerogative and liberty.[27]

The aggressor in these disputes, according to Knight, was always, in the first instance, the metropolitan state. Having only just in the early 1660s prescribed for Jamaica a tripartite form of government of the kind devel-

---

26. Charles Davenant, *Discourses on the Public Revenues, and on the Trade of England Which More Immediately Treat of the Foreign Traffick of This Kingdom* (London, 1698), part 2:152.

27. Of course, the Whig conception of liberty Knight advocated was highly exclusionary, applying only to adult male independent property holders of the established religious orientation. On this subject, see Jack P. Greene, ed., *Exclusionary Empire: English Liberty Overseas, 1600–1900* (New York, 2010).

oped earlier in the seventeenth century by provincial settler establishments in the older colonies—having a governor, a council, and an assembly and being accompanied by guarantees that settlers and immigrants to the colony were to be entitled to all the privileges of Englishmen, including consensual government—colonial administrators, Knight lamented, sought in the 1670s to tighten metropolitan controls over the colonies by copying the "Maxims" of the Stuart monarchs Charles II and James I and endeavoring to stretch "the prerogative of the Crown, beyond its limits . . . and . . . to make Parliaments useless by endeavouring to raise monies, without the Consent of the Representatives of the People." Jamaica's travails thus were but "a further Instance of the Arbitrary proceedings of those times, especially in our Colonies abroad" (pp. 139, 152).

In 1678, Knight recounted, Charles Howard, First Earl of Carlisle, Jamaica's new governor, brought instructions from London officials to introduce "a new Scheme of Government" for the colony, declaring the governor's commission, "(and by His Commission, all His Instructions) Law," requiring the Jamaica Assembly to pass several bills prepared in London, including an act to establish a perpetual revenue that would free royal governors from dependence on the assembly for all routine public expenses, such as the salaries of royal officials, and stipulating "that no Laws were to be enacted in Jamaica, for the future, but Such as being framed by the Governor and Council, were first transmitted for His Majestie's Approbation, and afterwards remitted to Jamaica to be passed by the Assembly, without allowing" it "a Deliberative power and Negative Voice or making any alterations or amendment" (pp. 136, 146). As Knight noted proudly, however, such a scheme, representing as it did an effort to apply the "same method in legislative matters" to Jamaica as had long been used in Ireland, "could not possibly be digested by an English Colony" (p. 152).

Fearing that this new "form of Government . . . would render the Governor *absolute*," Knight wrote, the "Inhabitants in general . . . were greatly uneasy and inflamed at the Attempt to alter the Constitution or form of Government," and successive assemblies, behaving "with a great deal of spirit," "faithfully and Strenuously" insisting "on what they thought their Natural and undoubted Rights and privileges," adamantly refused to accept it on historical, constitutional, and practical grounds. Making the king's instructions—to which the assembly had never consented—law, the assembly declared, would constitute an open invitation "to the Annulling and rendering to us ineffectual, any beneficial Laws, made in England or this Island, by which we are secured in our lives, liberties and properties, the like of which never was done, or Attempted; in any of His Majestie's Dominions, and in Effect is to make, Will to be Law." Expressing its difficulties in imagining "that the Irish Model of Government was, in principio, ever intended for Englishmen," including colonial settlers who, the Crown had repeatedly assured, would enjoy "all the Privileges of His Subjects of

the Kingdom of England," the assembly, in a petition to London authorities, pointed out that "the Major part of the Planters who" had settled in
Jamaica had been attracted by their "good liking of the form and Constitution being set[t]led after the English manner, and on Assurance of their
enjoying all their Native Rights and privileges, which They humbly apprehend and hope They have not lost by Their removall; or that They
have by any Act or deed forfeited, or provoked his Majesty, by attempting
to lessen, or to Question His Royal prerogatives; the inviolation of which
they ever deemed, the best means of preserving Their own privileges and
Estates" (pp. 118, 131, 140, 145, 147–49).

Arguing as well that the distance of Jamaica from Britain made the new
"method of passing laws impracticable," the assembly in this petition expressed its strong preference for "the old form, which was assimulated as
near as possible, to the Model of Government in England" and "must undoubtedly be more Acceptable, and be of greater Utility and Encouragement, not only to His Majestie's Natural born Subjects of England, but
others to Remove and Settle in this Island" (pp. 147, 149).

Mixing these strong objections with profuse expressions of the assembly's "Strongest assurances of their Loyalty and Obedience" to the
King's "Person and Government," the petition closed by suggesting that if
the king decided that Jamaica "must hereafter be Governed by the Governor and Council," the colony's residents were "so sensible of Their Duty
and Allegiance that Their Submission and deportment to His Majestie's
Authority should be such as They hoped in due time His Majesty would be
graciously pleased to restore them to the Ancient form of Government."
After the council supported the assembly, a frustrated Carlisle returned
to England, and the Crown, perhaps influenced by the assembly's professions of loyalty and respect, abandoned this effort at constitutional reform,
thereby leaving Jamaica in full possession of its system of consensual English governance, an outcome that Knight attributed to a combination of
the assembly's unyielding resistance and its professions of allegiance to the
king and respect for royal authority. He further celebrated it as yet another
example in which "the Spirit of liberty, inherent in Englishmen [had] prevailed," adding that he hoped it would "ever . . . prevail in all their due and
Natural Rights and privileges abroad as well as at Home" (pp. 149, 152).

However favorable the outcome in this particular case, the new metropolitan theory and the rhetoric of imperial governance that it represented
remained deeply embedded in metropolitan minds and, as Knight proceeded to show, over the next fifty years continued to serve as a bar to Jamaica's constitutional security and to provoke violent political controversies in the colony. Just a decade later, in 1688, Christopher Monck, Second
Duke of Albemarle arrived in Jamaica with a commission from James II
to be governor of Jamaica with authority over the governors of all other
English island colonies. He was also, as Knight speculated, "charged with

Instructions, agreeable to the measures of that Reign" and "Conformable to the Scheem" James II was laying "for a Change of Government, in England, and its dependencies," including the centralization of authority within several regional clusters of American colonies. Immediately showing "a Zealous Disposition" to execute his instructions, Albemarle responded to assembly resistance by trying to imprison one of its more outspoken members for words spoken in legislative debate and by dissolving the assembly when it tried to protect the speaker. By these actions, Albemarle created a "flame" that "soon spread itself all over the Country, and occasioned . . . great disorders and Confusion" and "a General Defection" from Albemarle's administration (pp. 165, 168).

Undeterred, Albemarle organized a party around those who were "strongly attached to the Principles and Interest of the Prince who was then on the throne," and taking his advice from "Father Churchill, a Roman Priest," proceeded to displace judges and other officers, rig an election to get an assembly more sympathetic with his demands, imprison and fine political opponents, deny them habeas corpus, and commit other "Acts of Power and Oppression." His appointee as chief justice, according to Knight, openly declared "in Court, that they should be ruled with Rods of Iron." Such actions, Knight wrote, "greatly inflamed the minds of the People" and drove "several of the principal Inhabitants" who were fearful of experiencing the governor's wrath to flee the island (pp. 165–66). In the end, the Glorious Revolution in England and Albemarle's sudden death rescued Jamaica from this ordeal, as William III sided with colonial petitioners, rejected the acts passed by Albemarle's rigged assembly, and restored displaced officers to their posts.

Remarking that he had "never heard of the like Extremities in this or the other British Plantations, nor of any of their Governours' having acted with so high a hand and in so Despotick a manner," Knight cited many cases in which governors had exceeded "the bounds of their Commission in Violation of the Rights, Priviledges, and Quiet of the People." Using Albemarle's administration as a prime example of "the fatal Consequences which attend the Governours of the British Colonies being vested with many large and Extraordinary Powers more than any one Man ought to be intrusted with," Knight argued that it was "highly necessary, if any regard be had to the Interest and wellfare of our Plantations to restrain & lessen the Powers usually granted to those who are sent to preside over them" (p. 168).

William's concessions on this occasion and the diminution of the Crown's prerogative powers in England in the wake of the Glorious Revolution did not, however, lead to a similar abatement in regard to the colonies, where unrestrained by the British Parliament, the Crown continued to claim extensive prerogative authority. Knight narrated at length the assembly's intense battles with Governors Thomas Handasyd and Lord Archibald Hamilton during the first decade and a half of the eighteenth century, just before and after Knight migrated to the colony, over the assembly's rights to exclude the council from amending money bills and to adjourn itself without gubernatorial approval, with the governors denying the assembly's claim to those rights on the basis of their instructions from the Crown and the assembly's defending it on the grounds that the English House of Commons exercised those rights and that it was its constitutional duty to assimilate itself "as near as possible" to that body. Knight sided with the assembly in his narrative, writing that if the English House of Commons had those rights, it then followed that it was "not only Reasonable but Necessary that the Assemblies in our Colonies, should be vested with the same Powers and Privileges there, as the Parliament have in England, because they are directed by all the Charters and Commissions to the Respective Governours, to Assimilate themselves as near as possible to that August Body, which they cannot do, if They are deprived of any of Their Rights or Priviledges" (pp. 220, 237).

In Knight's view, the assembly's exclusive right to shape all money bills without interference from either governor or council was not only "an inherent Right in" it, "as Representatives of the People," but also the essential foundation of the Jamaican and all colonial British American constitutions. Should "a future Assembly . . . on any Occasion give up this Right," he warned, it would then find itself to "be the Shadow of Power only, and nothing more than the Tools and Instruments for raising of money" (p. 236). Moreover, colonial assemblies had an even stronger case for excluding colonial councils from any role in creating money bills because, in contrast to the English House of Lords, all members of which were independent property holders, colonial councillors were royal appointees nominated by the governors and "often" had "no Property or Real Estate in the Country." Thus, he argued, it was "unreasonable" that people who had no property of their own "should have a Right to dispose of the Property of Others" (p. 236).

Throughout these controversies, the Jamaica Assembly, in relation to metropolitan objections, pursued a strategy of open rejection followed by studied efforts to ignore. Governors' efforts to enlist the aid of metropolitan officials produced reiterations of the doctrines first articulated in 1678: that the very existence of assemblies derived not, as colonials contended, from "an Inherent Right" of English people to consensual government but from nothing more than a clause in the governor's commission empowering him to call representatives of the electorate together to make local laws; that colonial assemblies were not entitled by right to all the privileges enjoyed by the English House of Commons; and that, in the particular case of Jamaica, which was a "Conquered Country," the colony's freeholders were "intitled to all the Rights, Liberties and Privileges of the People [of] England" only to the extent that Crown officials designated (pp. 236, 579). But the assembly refused to let Crown officials have the defining power in ascertaining the constitution, sharply and boldly dismissing such claims as nothing more than pretensions that had never been achieved. Even when presented with the threat from London authorities that if the assembly continued to "insist upon that Illgrounded pretence" that it enjoyed "the Right and Privileges of the House of Commons in Great Britain," they would take "such measures . . . as may be Effectual to Assert Her Majestie's undoubted Prerogative in that Island," the assembly stood firm. Knight noted approvingly that this London directive had no "Effect," and that the assembly emerged from this long round of disputes with its privileges in regard to money bills and unapproved adjournment intact, if also still under challenge (pp. 253–54).

Nevertheless, as the assembly subsequently explained in a 1725 message to then-governor Henry Bentinck, First Duke of Portland, which Knight included verbatim in his *History*, "a Survey of the Fluctuation of our Constitution for some time past" had persuaded it that Jamaica's "Welfare . . . could only be promoted by fixing our Selves upon the firm and durable Basis of the Law" (p. 303). Indeed, as early as 1718, the assembly had begun to consider negotiating an agreement with London authorities whereby metropolitan assurances of Jamaica's rights and liberties would be combined with a grant of a permanent revenue of the kind London had been seeking unsuccessfully since 1678. London authorities, as Knight noted, were intrigued by but wary of this possibility and instructed the Duke of Portland, who arrived in Jamaica in late 1722, to encourage the Jamaica Assembly either to prepare a draft of such a bill to be sent to London for approval or to pass a bill including a clause "to Suspend the Execution of it, till His Majesty's pleasure should be known" (p. 300). But the assembly had never been willing to include suspending clauses in its legislation, and for this reason, as well as because it refused to consider Portland and the council's suggestions for revisions on the traditional grounds that it could not constitutionally consider amendments to money bills, Portland reluctantly signed it only to have metropolitan authorities disallow it the following August and direct him to require the assembly to produce another that would provide more revenue, be more specific about what laws and rights would be assured to Jamaica, and contain a suspending clause.

This episode marked the first round of a six-year constitutional struggle over the details, form, and preparation of such a bill, a struggle for which Knight provides a full account. Complying with metropolitan orders, Portland laid the orders before the assembly in January 1724, assuring it that the Crown had every intention "to perpetuate their Laws" and recommending that it accept the royal terms and "not . . . be disturbed with Imaginary Fears or groundless Jealousies or Soured with any Sullen or

Stubborn Humours." But the assembly held its ground, repassing the revenue bill "in the same words, and with the same title," and at one point spelling out in an address to Portland "the Motives and Reasons" for its behavior in what Knight described as "a very decent and Respectfull manner." Praising "the Moderation and Justice" of George I's reign, the assembly suggested that it was "from so Excellent a King that the best Laws" were "to be expected," and expressed its conviction that, so far from "acting a disagreeable Part," it was merely "contending for that which distinguishes his Subjects from those of other Princes." Indeed, asserting its full confidence in "His Majesty's Goodness," it declared that it was impossible that it "should be disturbed with imaginary Fear or groundless Jealousies! Or soured with any sullen and Stubborn Humours." At the same time, however, it reminded Portland that "a sort of Jealousy" was "natural and Interwoven with every English Constitution" and was "always upon the Watch for the Preservation of the Community," and admitted that "such a Jealousy" had been excited by reports that metropolitan officials were considering drafting a bill in England to be recommended to the Jamaica legislature. Although "we confess in the fullest Extent his Majesty's Right to dissent to our Laws," yet, the assembly declared, that such legislation should take its "Rise from our selves, without being obliged to digest what is dealt to us by other Hands, Strangers in a great Measure to our Defects and Necessities. And here, my Lord, we only speak the same Language, and imitate the Spirit with which our Predecessors formerly [in 1676] asserted their Right of framing their own Bills, and in a Reign less favourable to the Liberties of the People, prevailed in the same Points; which Maxims of Government they wisely drew from their Mother Country, who can endure no Laws, but those of her own chusing" (pp. 302–4). Following the concurrence of a majority of the council, Portland after much deliberation assented to the law.

Metropolitan authorities would also reject this bill, but they had been preparing a draft of their own which they sent to Jamaica, where in the fall of 1726 the assembly, as Knight wrote, being deeply "alarmed at a Bill being drawn up in England, to be enacted Here without allowing them a Negative or to make any alteration or Amendment," both rejected it as "an Infringement on Their Rights and Privileges" and declined to pass any temporary bill that would have funded public expenses for that year, a stance it maintained for the two years immediately following. As a result, Jamaica "continued without Courts of Justice, or the Operative force of the Laws (which were perpetual) near 3 Years," until the arrival of Robert Hunter as governor in January 1728 brought news that the Crown had backed down and was willing to accept a law devised by the assembly, which, to its "great satisfaction" had thereby been "restored to" its "Natural Right and Priviledge of framing Their own Bills." It moved expeditiously to prepare a bill "for the support of the Government of this Island,

and for preserving & perpetuating the Acts & Laws thereof," to which the council and governor immediately consented (pp. 317, 319, 323).

Although London officials would not formally confirm this act until March 1729, this agreement quickly served to dissipate "the Jealousies and fears of the People, who had been . . . without Courts of Justice" for so long, and "were apprehensive of an Alteration being intended in their Constitution or form of Government, but being now restored to their rights & Previledges, as well as their Laws, their minds were quieted and made easy" (p. 323).

Indeed, as a strong Whig devoted to those English traditional rights of consensual government and rule of law that were "and ought to be inherent in Englishmen" in whatever part of the vast English world they inhabited, Knight attributed Jamaica's present "*Happiness* [as] . . . a *Free People*" to be entirely owing to the vigilance of previous generations of settlers in "Strenuously" insisting on retaining "Their Native Rights & Privileges" as Englishmen in their new polity and their repeated and steady refusal to "suffer the least innovation or Encroachment" on them. Yet, by composing the remonstrances and memorials they from time to time submitted to the Crown in justification of their opposition with "decency, strength of Reason, Submission to the Crown, and Deference to the Royal Representative," Jamaican political leaders had demonstrated the "Moderation and prudent behaviour" that, in his opinion, eventually in the late 1720s enabled them to gain their point and to work out the constitutional settlement that, with the Crown's confirmation and recognition of the perpetuity of Jamaica's existing laws, finally allayed the constitutional tensions that had disturbed metropolitan-colonial relations since the colony's beginning and enabled Jamaica's "present Inhabitants [to] enjoy all the Advantages of an English Colony" (pp. 11, 642).

Notwithstanding this settlement, Knight remained anxious about the sustainability of colonial claims to the right of consensual governance and the rule of law. Recalling that the Crown had "formerly made" several attempts to alter Jamaica's "constitution," and that it had only relented to quiet "the minds of the people," he argued that the sanctity of those claims remained "a Question of the utmost Consequence," not just to Jamaica but "to all the British Plantations," expressing his great desire "that no Question of this kind may hereafter arise, or be insisted upon, nor the Rights and Privileges of the People or their Representatives in any degree weaken[e]d, or infringed" (pp. 519–20). In part 7 he took special pains to lay out for metropolitan readers not just the substance but the logical implications of the colonial Whig constitutional case in terms that echoed earlier colonial political understandings and anticipated by thirty years the argument that colonists throughout colonial British America would make against metropolitan efforts to tighten the reins of empire after midcentury and, for those continental colonies that decided to secede from the empire in 1776, to justify their position.

Defining an Imperial Constitution for the Empire

A model of economy, Knight's explication of this case began by explaining that when a new colony was "transplanted from hence," the colonists, as had been repeatedly acknowledged by the Crown, carried the rights to the laws of England with them. Yet, he observed, "from the time of their Settlement," they necessarily became "in some measure a Seperate and Distinct Dominion and no ways bound by the Laws, that are afterwards made in England; excepting those only wherein They are particularly named." As British colonies, they were entitled "to the same Protection, and to the same benefits, and Advantages of the Laws of England, as if they had remained in England," but their great distance "from their Mother-Country" rendered it "impracticable for them to receive" that "protection and those advantages through the same Channel." They could not, he wrote, "have it from the Parliament," as both distance and their lack of representation made it "difficult and often impracticable for that August Body . . . to be well and truly informed of their wants and Necessities, or what may be proper to be enacted for their Protection or Relief." For these reasons, Knight declared, colonists could not "truly Enjoy" the "same privileges to all intents and purposes, as our free born Subjects of England . . . unless the Legislature[s] there have the same powers, as legislature has in Great Britain" (pp. 520–21).

"These arguments," Knight concluded, "plainly prove[d], that our British Colonies are, and must be considered as distinct, though subordinate Dominions"; that they could not "have Laws made for them, nor Justice administered to them, from Home"; and that "they must therefore have new Laws from a legislature of their own." That was why, he explained, the colonies all "have had Legislatures and Courts of Justice of their Own, but Analogous to the methods observed by the Legislature and Courts of Justice here. They have all their strong lines the same—Their Courts of Law are the same as ours; and their Trials are by Juries as with us—They have the same Courts of Equity, as we have, only subject to an Appeal to the King in Council, in all Causes exceeding £300 Value—And for the Exercise of Extraordinary Acts, which could not be performed by the Supreme Power here, because such acts can not, in their Nature, admit of any Delay, they have in all respects a Supreme Power there, analogous but Subordinate to that which we have here in England," a constitutional arrangement that insured Britons in the colonies, like those in the metropolis, would, insofar as their domestic governance was concerned, be exempt from any laws that were not of their own making (pp. 521–22).

Creating an Empire of Mutual Advantage

Underlying Knight's vision of what the British Empire should be constitutionally was an implicit irritation about the metropolis's privileging its own goals and interests over those of its colonies. Addressing this situation directly, Knight called for metropolitan acknowledgment of the extraordinary advantages the colonies had contributed to the strength and wealth of the British nation and for the reconstruction of the empire in ways that would transform it into an empire of mutual advantage with a mutual accommodation of interests and shared liberties. In his "Inclination and Disposition to promote the *British Plantations, particularly Jamaica*," he believed, he was also contributing to advance "the Interest of *Great Britain* to the utmost of my power and Ability." "Whatever tends to the Interest or Improvement of this Island," he explained, "must in Consequence be of Advantage to the British Trade, Navigation, and Colonies in generall— Their Interest being one and the Same, and not to be Separated without prejudice to them all. Whatever is hurtful to any of them, must in some degree, affect the rest and whatever tends to the Service of the one, will proportionably augment the Interest, and Advantage of Them all" (pp. 6, 13).

In pursuit of this project, Knight took on himself to show the many "Inconveniences, and Damages which attend the British Colonies by their present form and method of Government and to advocate a number of alterations," all of which were premised on the proposition that as long as the metropolis took care "to keep the Colonies dependant" and to "render them usefull to their Mother Country," there was no reason why it should not also endeavor to make sure that it always "preserved and in no degree violated" those "Conditions, Terms, and Privileges" that "encouraged Them at their own Expence, and the hazard of their lives, to Transport themselves" to and "to cultivate and Plant foreign Countries" to the nation's considerable benefit (pp. 522, 626).

The chief deficiency Knight identified in Britain's existing system of colonial governance involved the governors, who, as the Crown's representative in each colony, provided the main interface between colony and metropolis. "As the Welfare of all Countries, depends on good Government, without doubt," he observed, "our American Colonies would Improve and flourish more than they ever have done were they always conducted by Men of probity, Wisdom and personal Courage." But Knight questioned whether metropolitan authorities had always "duly and Constantly observed" that objective and suggested that they had entrusted many "Indigent, unskilful, and Avaritious Persons . . . with the Care and Administration" of the colonies. "It is the misfortune of our Plantations in general," he complained, "to be Governed by those who" went "over with no other View than to raise or repair a shattered Fortune." Commonly "thinking their Interest different from the Inhabitants and . . . uncertain how long" they should "Continue in the Government," such governors were frequently "intent on nothing more than how to improve and make the most of their time to their own private Advantage," which resulted in perpetual "Dissentions" between governors and assemblies and "Jarring and Jealousies among the People," who suffered themselves "to be divided on these Occasions by little Emulations, private Piques, or worse motives" between those who supported and those who opposed "the interest of such Governours" and thereby obstructed "the Peace, wellfare and Prosperity of the Country" (pp. 276, 625).

To put a stop to such pernicious controversies, Knight strongly urged that metropolitan authorities make better choices, requiring that every governor "be a Gentleman of Experience, Abilities and Virtue" who was "Easy in His Circumstances, and not under any Temptation to fleece and Injure the People or to Violate His Trust in any Degree." The necessary qualifications, Knight believed, were "Temperance, Moderation, and Justice," and "a general knowledge of men and Things" that would enable a governor to "be Active, Vigilant and Attentive to the welfare and Interest of the Territories under His Command," studying "the Temper and Genius of the People; the Nature of the Soil, and Commerce of the Country" to suggest desirable improvements, encourage industry, and "discountenance Idleness, Immorality and Profaneness." Without such qualities, no governor could expect to maintain order, cultivate allegiance to the parent state, or "reform the manners" of the "many Thousand Families" under his jurisdiction, much less to fulfill the "great . . . Trust" the Crown had "vested in Him." Knight actually expressed his preference for a governor who, as a native or resident, already had property in a colony. It was "happy for a Colony," he declared, when it was "under the Government of a Gentleman, whose Interest is blended with Theirs" (pp. 276, 625).

Moreover, because the king and his people in the colonies were "supposed to be of the same Country," he thought it little difference whether a governor was a metropolitan or a colonial. As a further reform intended to eliminate "those Jealousies and Animosities, which commonly attend the Administration of most of the Governours of the British Colonies, in America" and "undoubtedly [to] Conduce to" the "Welfare and good Government" of the colonies, Knight recommended that the English Crown follow the example of the French and pay all governors out of the royal coffers, restraining them from taking any "Perquisites, or drawing any Advantages from the People" and promoting those who acted honorably on their return home (pp. 276, 625–26). Such a step would have represented a drastic departure from British imperial practice, the Crown having, since the establishment of the first royal colony in Virginia in the mid-1620s, consistently refused to provide any remuneration for its officials in the colonies.

But Knight's recommendations for changes in the nature of colonial governors were not limited to questions of selection and the source of remuneration: he went on to object to the Crown's endowing them "with many and large Powers" that had "too often been made use of to the prejudice of the people." The most pernicious of these powers, in his view, were the unrestrained authority to dismiss officers and magistrates, an excessive influence on the composition of the council, and jurisdiction over equity cases in chancery court. "It is notorious," Knight declared, that in Jamaica, as he had repeatedly shown in his *History*, governors had removed "Gentlemen of the best Fortune and Characters . . . from Civill and Military Employments" entirely for political reasons and "without any charge of misbehaviour or disability." For similar reasons, some governors, contrary to the Crown's express prohibition of their filling council vacancies until the number of councillors had dropped below seven, had "assumed a Power" of unilaterally suspending political opponents in order to "make Vacancies" that they could then fill with men who would passively support them. By bringing royal offices and council membership "into great Contempt, insomuch that very few Gentlemen who are properly qualified" would accept them, and by having them "commonly" filled "with Persons of Inferiour Rank who" were "incapable of Executing them and preserving the Authority that is necessary," such practices had become "very prejudicial to the British Plantations." Similarly, he charged, some governors, by protracting suits involving political opponents and issuing decrees that were "not always according to the strict Rules of Justice and Equity," had made their enormous chancery powers "Subservient to purposes Foreign to the Distribution of Justice" (pp. 626, 628).

Knight acknowledged that the governor, "as the King's Representative," was undoubtedly the proper person to be entrusted with the "Nomination and disposal of all Civil and Military Employments in the Island" but proposed, as "the only Expedient" that might "restore the Credit and Reputation of those Offices, and be an inducement to Gentlemen of Fortune and Characters to accept of them," that he "be restrained from removing Officers at his Will and pleasure without cause or complaint or even being heard," and that in such cases the officer "be allowed to make his defence before his Peers," consisting of a "Judge of the Grand Court" and a bench of magistrates in civil cases or a court martial in military ones (pp. 626–27). Even if such bodies approved a dismissal, Knight thought that the officer involved should not be removed without the consent of the council.

In regard to gubernatorial manipulation of council appointments, Knight suggested that the governor's powers of suspension should require the approval of the other members of the council. An uncontrolled power of suspension, he pointed out, not only subverted "His Majesty's Nomination but in Effect" enabled a governor to "take upon himself two parts in three of the Legislative power, and act without restraint in other matters as the Councill will in such Case be little more than a Screen for his Actions," thus manifestly tending "to abolish part of the Constitution and render the Seat of a Councellor so precarious, that no man of Honour and Spirit will accept of it, since dissenting from the Opinion of a Governour may be deemed disaffection to His Person and Government or perhaps to his Majesty, and be attended with a Suspension." Indeed, Knight declared, it was "of great Concernment to the Interest and welfare of the Plantations, that the Councill should be put on some other and better footing, that no discouragement may be given to the Members in acting freely and without Restraint in a Station which may otherwise be exposed to great Contempt." Moreover, because councillors were also a "part of the Legislature as well as a Councill of State," Knight noted, in still a further plea for limiting royal colonial posts to local magnates and extending the reach of the principle of consensual governance, it seemed both "reasonable and necessary that none should be qualified to sit and vote in the passing of Laws, who" did not have "an Estate or Interest in the Country, for it cannot be thought reasonable that any Person should have a right to raise and dispose of Publick Monies, who is not any ways affected by it" (p. 628).

In the case of the governor's chancery powers, Knight advocated taking them away altogether on the grounds that chancery matters were "the most troublesome branch" of the governor's duties and that he already had "full Employment . . . in other matters." Knight reported that the Jamaica Assembly had often considered providing a "proper Salary and Fees" for "a Person duely qualified to execute that important Commission" but had given it up because of fears that "the Commission would probably be given to some favourite or Creature who perhaps may not be properly qualified" for the post. Hence, Knight proposed an alternative that would essentially have put equity proceedings entirely in provincial hands by having the assembly appoint "three Gentlemen of the best Characters and Abilities in the Island" to split chancery duties among themselves (p. 627).

Knight closed his ruminations on the defects of "the present State and form of the Constitution of the British Colonies" with a proposal for a wholesale change in the existing system of filling Crown offices in the colonies. Since the beginnings of British colonization in America, these offices had usually been granted through a well-established system of patronage by patent to "some favourites of the Ministers," and those grantees had usually rented the office out to the highest bidder. Knight himself had first come to Jamaica as an adult to take up a rented office that he may subsequently have lost to a higher bidder. The problem with this arrangement was that some of the patentees, remaining in Britain and without themselves being at any trouble about the operation of the office, or "being of the least use and Service to the Island," had demanded ever higher annual returns from rent holders, so that, according to Knight, their deputies by the 1740s were remitting to Britain every year a total of "upwards of £3000 Sterling," which Knight regarded as a "Tax or imposition on the Island." In his view, "the most Effectual way" to restrain such abuses and "be an Encouragement to the Plantations" would be to oblige "the Patentees of all the Offices . . . to Execute them in Person" and for the Crown to refrain from granting any future patents except on those terms (pp. 628–29).

But Knight's proposals for imperial reform went considerably beyond the political and constitutional realm. Throughout his volumes, he touted Jamaica as a place that both enabled individual Britons to strive for economic and social success and provided "many *Advantages*" for the British nation (p. 11). Seconding the opinion of Sir Joshua Child, the late seventeenth-century English economic analyst, "that one Man in the Southern Colonies gave Employment to five men at Home," an assertion Knight was persuaded that with regard to Jamaica could "be proved even to a Demonstration," he stressed the beneficial effects of those colonies in stimulating the British domestic economy and expanding the metropolitan workforce, as well as accelerating the trade and enhancing the navigation on which the very "Security and wellfare of Great Britain" depended (p. 19). Hence, the island's military and naval situation was much on his mind. Because the governor could not possibly "in so large and Extensive a Country as Jamaica" attend necessary military reviews in every parish, and because it was "necessary in Case of an Invasion or general Insurrection of the Negroes," Knight, again taking a cue from French colonial practice, advocated the appointment of a salaried officer of high rank who would "be ready to Command the Forces under the Governour, and to take the Chief Command" in case the governor was ill or disabled and troops needed to be sent on "any Important Service" such as preventing invasions or insurrections (p. 641).

As a merchant himself dependent on safe shipping in the Caribbean and the Atlantic, Knight throughout his *History* displayed a strong interest in shipping losses from piratical or foreign national attacks. Although he admired French ingenuity in the construction of an overseas imperial regime, he deplored treaty-violating Spanish depredations on British shipping during peacetime. As one of the many British and Jamaican merchants whose ships Spanish Guarda Costas had taken as prizes, plundered, and condemned in the wake of the War of the Spanish Succession during the late 1710s and early 1720s, Knight applauded a metropolitan decision, in response to mercantile appeals, to station a small squadron to protect "the Trade and Coasts of this Island" (pp. 615–16).

Whenever these squadrons had been commanded by a vigilant commander who paid a due regard for the "Publick Service," this arrangement worked, clearing the seas of pirates and forcing the Guarda Costas into port, with British vessels passing "unmolested" and without interruption. Whenever the commander "had more regard" for his "own Ease or private

Interest," as was the case in 1730–32 and after 1735, the Guarda Costas renewed hostilities, eventually in 1739 provoking the "just and Necessary" War for Jenkins' Ear that Knight hoped would enable the British "to obtain satisfaction for all past injuries, and a freedom of Navigation for the future." Meanwhile, Knight was convinced that imperial rivalries in the Caribbean would always require Britain to maintain a squadron of warships there in "Peace as well as War." Indeed, he advocated establishing an even larger force that could keep the inward and outward sea passages to Jamaica open and constantly monitor Jamaica's remote and exposed north coast. "In Respect to the Advantages that will Arise to the Nation" from duties payable on Jamaican products, Jamaican consumption of British manufactures, the stimulus Jamaican trade gave to British maritime resources, and the employment those trades provided for a "vast number of Artificers and Tradesmen, throughout Great Britain, Ireland, and the Northern Plantations," Knight argued, the considerable expense to the Crown for such naval protection would "be inconsiderable" (pp. 525, 616–17).

On similar grounds, Knight called for a reconsideration of metropolitan trade regulations, particularly those that affected Jamaica. "It is . . . of great importance to the Nation as well as to the Plantations," he declared, for the metropolis to take "due Care . . . not only to preserve" the colonies' "just Rights & Privileges & to discourage the Avaricious Schemes of Governours abroad or hungry Courtiers at Home" but also to refrain from laying "such heavy Duties and impositions" on the colonies "as may discourage Industry & obstruct further improvements if not ruin those that are already made" and thereby serve to "dispeople the Islands & in process of time occasion Their total desertion or falling into the hands of the French" (p. 630).

What concerned him most was that the Crown had "manifestly over loaded" sugar products "with Duties & Excises." French competition having driven down the price of sugar well below what it was when the duties were first laid during the closing decades of the seventeenth century, the duty on sugar had by the 1730s come to equal the land tax in England at its highest during wartime, which the English found a grievous burden. Along with similar charges on rum, ginger, coffee, and other Jamaica products, these duties, Knight objected, caused "great Hardships" among the planters, discouraging production, encouraging smuggling, and threatening the sugar colonies with ruin and the Crown with loss of revenue. Because revenue maintenance seemed to be "the principal if not the only Consideration with those [Crown officials] to whom such matters were referred," Knight predicted that their opposition would be difficult to surmount. But he argued, making an explicit distinction between the welfare of the Crown and that of the state, lowering duties might well be of considerable "Advantage to the Nation" by stimulating colonial production, lessening British dependence on foreign products, increasing British exports to the colonies, and contributing to the growth of the British domestic economy, all of which might actually serve to increase royal revenues from duties and excises (pp. 633, 637–38).

In addressing Spanish charges about Jamaica's extensive and allegedly "illicit" commercial intercourse with the Spanish Main, which Knight regarded as merely a screen "to colour the illegal and unwarrantable behaviour of that Perfidious Nation in America," he came close to calling for free trade (p. 623). Although he acknowledged that every state had the right to exclude foreigners from various areas of its commerce, he argued that no nation had ever discouraged a trade that was beneficial to its subjects and suggested "that no Trade" could "truly be deemed Illicit in regard to me or any other Subject of Great Britain which is not prohibited by the Laws of God or my Own Country." Given the "great Quantities of British Manufactures" that were "yearly vended" in the "Spanish Main" through Jamaica's trade with it, he observed, "I cannot think that man a Friend to His Country, who Endeavours to Prohibit or Obstruct it," especially because it met a strong demand among Spanish colonies for British goods, which no country could meet "so Easily" as Jamaica. "To Export as many of our Manufactures, as we can possibly vend, and receive in Return Bullion and other Valuable commodities, without Considering who are the Exporters or Importers," he asserted, certainly was in the best "Interest of Great Britain," and though it might "not be Consistent with Treaties, in time of Peace, for the Government to Encourage and Countenance it in a Publick Manner," it would certainly be "bad Policy in us, to give any Obstruction to that Branch of our Commerce" (pp. 623–24).

Perhaps Knight's most daring proposal was for the reform of British colonial administration in London. He had little respect for the Board of Trade, the agency that since 1696 had borne responsibility for presiding over colonial affairs and, perhaps not incidentally, had denied him access to Jamaica records when he was starting to write his *History*. To perform its duties effectively, Knight thought, the members of the board should be men of "*Experience, Publick Spirit,* and *great Abilities*," whose "*Vigilance* and *care* of the *British Trade* and *Plantations*" would be "*Conspicuous* to all the World." Instead, he complained, the Crown had often appointed men "without *Experience* or *proper Abilities*" to the board and other "*Eminent Stations* . . . of great consequence to the Nation," who in turn appointed avaricious, corrupt, incompetent, or lazy men to colonial governorships and other executive offices, and otherwise neglected their responsibilities by laying aside "*Memorialls* and *Representations,* of the utmost importance to *Trade* and *Plantations* . . . without any notice or Consideration; or perhaps ever being Read" and leaving "Acts of the [colonial] Assemblies" without attention or report "for 6 or 7 Years, and some [times] more." In Knight's opinion, such "misconducts or neglects" left no doubt that the board, as he bluntly put it, had not answered its "original Institution & Design" and needed to be put "under some other & better Regulation" and filled with "Men of Experience as well as Capacity" (pp. 12–13, 631).

But, Knight asked, given the sorts of people who sat on the board, the Privy Council, and parliamentary committees, how could it have been otherwise? It consisted entirely of "Noblemen and Gentry whose Education" and experience had never offered them "the least Occasion to inspect into, the Nature of Trade in general or of any particular Branches much less to acquire the proper Skill or Experience" in regard to "Trade, Manufactures and Plantations; to distinguish between the Clashing Interest of Universal Trade & the Interest of particular Branches." Merely "for want of a more perfect understanding," he complained, both Crown officials and Parliament had been often imposed upon, by "misrepresentation, sollicitation of Friends or some prevailing Interest," appealing for confirmation of this judgment "to those who have ever been concerned or obliged to attend either of the Assemblies I have mentioned, whether" they had "not frequently met with unnecessary delays, and had difficulties thrown in Their way for want of a proper knowledge in the respective Members with Regard to our Plantations & the several Branches of the British Commerce" (pp. 18–19).

Knight did not propose to exclude nobility and gentry from concern with imperial affairs. On the contrary, linking colonization, trade, and navigation to Britain's national well-being, he denounced those members of the "Nobility and Gentry" and other wealthy people who had no part of their fortunes "in Trade, or in Some way encouraging the manufactures of" their "Country" as "useless Member[s] of the Common wealth" and urged them to take a cue from merchants who had long ago learned that they could get more than twice the rate of interest by investing in trade or manufacturing rather than in the stock market and thereby serve "at the same time" both their "Friends and . . . Country" (pp. 18–19). However, because Britain was "a Nation, which has a very great dependance on Trade," he advocated giving merchants a much greater role in formulating and administering imperial policy at the metropolitan level. A merchant himself, Knight was unabashedly resentful that in British society, merchants were regularly "Neglected and Slighted," declaring that they should rather "be considered as one of the most usefull Societys to the Common Wealth" and deserved to be so "distinguished," as they already were "in Some Countrys," by which he probably meant the Netherlands. Trade, in Knight's view, was "a kind of Mystery," a "perfect knowledge" of which could only "be acquired by . . . Application, Experience and proper Abilities." Subject to all sorts of "interfereing Accidents," it required expert care to prevent its being "diverted into other Channells thro[ugh] neglect, mismanagement or the Artfull Schemes of our Rivals in Trade" (pp. 19, 631).

Specifically, he proposed to remedy this situation by replacing the Board of Trade with "an experienced, unbyassed Council of Trade after the Model of the Council of Commerce in France or the Council of the Indies in Spain," which would include merchants and have "proper Powers & Authority to inspect into the Laws relative to Trade & Plantations; to enquire into all hardships, Defects and Obstructions; to discuss what is necessary to be done for promoting every Colony or branch of Trade, and to lay Their Remarks and Opinions before the House of Commons [at] the beginning of every Session." Both because "the Interest of Trade in general & the Plantations" were "so Closely Connected that They cannot be separated without prejudice to both," and because no merchant was "well enough acquainted with all the British Plantations to form a true Judgment of what is proper to be done for Them Respectively," he also proposed "that every Colony have the liberty of appointing a Representative" to this new body, or at the very least that it should include a minimum of six colonial members, some representing the North American colonies and others the sugar islands (p. 630). No doubt, Knight would have been happy to have been Jamaica's representative on such a council. Within the context of the existing system of British colonial management, however, Knight's proposal to involve colonial representatives in the metropolitan supervision of empire was genuinely radical and had little chance of eliciting a favorable response.

Equally radical was Knight's call for substantial metropolitan subsidies to pay the cost of his many proposals. As he thoroughly understood and took considerable pains to emphasize, however, from the beginnings of state involvement in overseas colonization in early seventeenth-century Virginia, the Crown had insisted that the colonies pay their own way, raising and supporting "Themselves by Their own Prudence & labour to the Condition and Circumstances They are now in without any Assistance from the Crown" (p. 629). Thus, in the case of Jamaica, as Knight pointed out, the colonial government had defrayed all "Annual Charges for the Support of the Government of the Island, namely the Salaries of the Governour and other Publick Officers, the Additional Subsistance to the Soldiers, building & repairing Fortifications and other Contingencies," which annually amounted "to a very Considerable Sum" (p. 629). Although he acknowledged that Britain had been "at a great Charge" in the conquest of the island as well as in subsequently "Maintaining Ships of War as well as Land Forces to preserve our Right to this Valuable Acquisition; and the several branches of Trade that" were "dependant on it," he argued that those charges were "very inconsiderable" in comparison to the many "Duties & other Advantages arising from it," and more especially from the "gross Value" of its produce, which Knight estimated to have been at least £60 million over the ninety years since the English conquest, nearly all of which, he suggested, should be "deemed almost clear Proffit" to the British nation, besides "other Advantages arising by Trade" (pp. 629–30).

If the extraordinary improvements that Jamaica had made, described so fully in the *History*, had been entirely accomplished "by mere Indus-try or very Slender means" without royal bounties of the kind the Crown provided to the continental colonies to encourage the production of na-val stores and indigo (bounties that, Knight thought, "would have been more usefully bestowed on this Island"), he asked his readers to consider "what great things" might have been "Expected of Them, had They been furnished with Negroes and other necessaries for Planting on Publick Credit" at a moderate and easy rate of interest, "or had They been un-der such Regulations, and met with such Encouragement as the French" had provided to their colonies, "which has enabled Them to make a greater progress in Trade and Plantations than we have done, and to supplant us with regard to Sugar and other products in Foreign Markets" (p. 629).

In raising the possibility of metropolitan subsidies, Knight was no doubt encouraged by Parliament's annual subsidy to the new colony of Georgia starting in the early 1730s. Unprecedented in the history of Britain's Amer-ican empire, that subsidy suggested a growing metropolitan awareness of the importance of the empire to Britain's prosperity and national standing and, to Knight, seemed to herald a new approach to British imperial devel-opment in which the state would assist expansion in existing colonies such as Jamaica. Through the publication of his history, Knight thought, "the Importance of the Island and the Value of the Produce from The labour & Industry of the Inhabitants" would "become more & more known," and London authorities would realize "how much" Jamaica deserved "not only protection, but all the Encouragement that can be given." "When the Af-fairs of the Nation are set[t]led" following the war, he enthused, "We have great Reason to Expect" Crown officials and Parliament to take into con-sideration and remove the many "Difficulties and Obstructions" inhibit-ing trade expansion, immigration, and the full settlement of the island. "If some such Assistance was given to" Jamaica, "as hath been granted to Georgia . . . or as the French" gave to their colonies, Knight speculated, "it would in a few Years, be the means of Strengthening the Island" by at-tracting large numbers of white settlers, expanding settlement, enhancing production and trade, and rendering its white proprietors less vulnerable to domestic revolt on the part of the island's black majority, thus sparing Brit-ain the "great expence, which the Nation is now at, in Maintaining Troops for" the "protection" of those proprietors. Such state intervention, Knight was persuaded, would at the same time help Jamaica's white minority "to Strengthen and Secure their possessions" and greatly augment the wealth of both Britain and Jamaica (pp. 12, 20, 642).

In writing his *History*, James Knight's primary objective was to raise his-torical consciousness about Jamaica in the wider British world with a com-prehensive and accurate evocation of the historical events and processes that in his view had, by the late 1730s, made Jamaica such a successful and valuable contributor to the British imperial project on the one hand, yet prevented it from achieving its full potential on the other. Decidedly not written for an audience with modern sensibilities, it endorses ethnic and religious stereotypes of Spaniards, Jews, and Catholics and pays scant attention to several subjects in which modern scholars have taken a profitable interest, largely neglecting, for instance, the important roles of women, white and black, in Jamaican society, together with education, religion, family organization, child-rearing, and voluntary organizations; barely acknowledging a sizeable free black and mulatto population; and entirely finessing the subject of interracial sexual relations.

Operating within the paradigm of power that informed most historical writing until the closing decades of the twentieth century, Knight produced a study that both took for granted and implicitly justified the centrality of the propertied and the powerful in historical study and focused heavily on the civically empowered and almost entirely white settler population who laid claim to and acquired legal title to virtually all of Jamaica's available resources. Taking a friendly and unquestioning view of imperialism and colonization as positive instruments for the extension of European civilization into overseas spaces, he celebrated settler achievements in trying to transform Jamaica into a British society, thereby expanding the British world, and presented as favorable a view as possible of Jamaica's health conditions, social order, economic opportunities for prospective immigrants, and slave labor system. The overwhelming numerical superiority of black people in the Jamaica population demanded that he give them substantial attention, which he used to point out their ethnic diversity and explore the parameters of slave culture, and also to endorse slavery as a viable solution to the colony's labor demands and an institution that was neither excessively harsh nor un-English.

In his expression of these views, as well as in singling out for improvement free government and security as the central issues in Jamaican history, Knight no doubt expressed the consensus among the most successful estate-builders in Jamaica. From his position as an insider, he spoke for a provincial mentality that took great pleasure in Jamaica's economic success and was deeply anxious in the face of external attacks and internal rebellions. Defiantly devoted to English legal and constitutional traditions, Jamaican insiders had a profound desire to be—and to appear to be—civil, especially to those in the metropolis; were keenly resentful of metropolitan condescension; and had an overwhelming yearning for metropolitan validation and recognition, all of which permeate Knight's long treatise.

Of course, that treatise is much more than a narrative history and deep description of Jamaica. It is also a critical and thoughtful commentary on the island's current condition, its relationship to the parent state, and the flaws in metropolitan administration that inhibited British imperial development. A perceptive analyst and a critical observer, Knight identified and addressed issues that kept Jamaica from being more secure, more free, and more British, thus inhibiting the smooth operation of the British Empire. Endeavoring to shake Jamaicans out of the culture of impermanence that he thought had permeated and stunted the development of Jamaican society, he explored its sources and exhorted Jamaicans to many measures intended to enable the island to transcend that culture. A reformer at heart, with a profound attachment to the British Empire, he also aspired to reshape the empire into an entity that would be mutually advantageous to all of its members, calling for a variety of reforms in colonial administration that would be conducive to the quiet enjoyment of colonial rights and at the same time involve considerably more mercantile and colonial input into the operation of the empire. As we know, Knight's grand project for reform never came into public view. Subsequent history strongly suggests that the empire ought to have found a place for the voice of such an insightful analyst.

The Natural, Moral *and* Political History of Jamaica, and the Territories thereon depending;

From the first Discovery of the Island by *Christopher Columbus*, to the Year 1746.

Volume I

By J[AMES] K[NIGHT] ESQ[UIRE,]
A Gentleman, who resided above Twenty Years in Jamaica.

—*Primam esse Historiae legem, nequid falsi dicere audeat; deinde nequid veri non audeat; nequa suspicion gratia sit in Scribendo, nequa Simultatis.*[1]

Cic[ero]. De Orat[ore]. Lib. 2.

London

Printed for [blank]

---

1. "The first law of history is, that one shall not dare to speak falsehoods, the next that he shall endeavor [to speak] truths, and there shall be no suspicion of favoritism in his writing, nor of hostility."

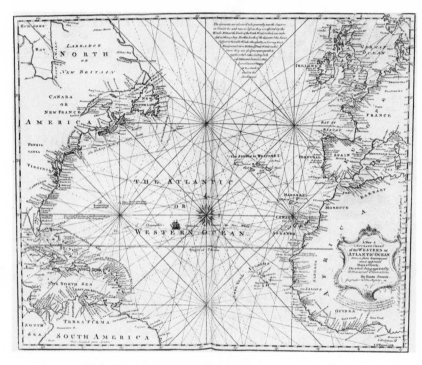

Emanuel Bowen's expansive "A New and Accurate Chart of the Western or Atlantic Ocean," published in a new edition of John Harris's 1705 *Navigantium Atque Itinerantium Bibliotheca; or, A Complete Collection of Voyages and Travels,* 2 vols. (London, 1764), provides a panoramic view of Knight's spatial transoceanic world. Bowen (1694?–1767) was an English map engraver who was "geographer to His Majesty," George II.

Vol[ume] the 1st

PART THE 1ST

Contains

The Etymology of the word Jamaica, and the Discovery of the Island by Christopher Columbus; some Account of the Native Indians, before they were Subdued, and Extirpated by the Spaniards; with such other Events, as happened, while it was in their Possession.

PART THE 2D.

Of the Expedition and miscarriage of the Design against St. Domingo. The Conquest of Jamaica by the English, with such other Occurrences, as happened, before the Restoration of King Charles the Second, or any form of Civil Government was Established.

PART THE 3D.

Of the Administration of the Severall Governors of Jamaica. The Origin and Exploits of the Privateers Commonly Called Buccaniers and all the Other Remarkable Transactions by Sea and Land, which happened during the Respective Governments.

Preface

Custom has made it Necessary to give a Prefatory Account of the following Treatise. And, I apprehend, it will likewise be expected, that, I should make an Apology, for undertaking a thing, that is out of my Province. Indeed, I should have been pleased to See the Design executed by some other Person, who has more Experience and greater Abilities: But, since nothing of the kind appeared, and I observed the difficulties and Inconveniences, which this Valuable Colony labours under, through Misrepresentation and prejudice, I thought it necessary, that the Island should be put in a just and true light, and to give my Assistance therein being persuaded that it only wants to be better known, to be more Encouraged, and Countenanced, than it has hitherto been.

The Accounts, which were formerly published are not only too Concise, but deficient in many things, being wrote soon after it was taken from the Spaniards, and before any Considerable Improvements were made by their Successors. And some late pieces are not only imperfect, and Erroneous, but discover great Ignorance, Dissappointment or something worse in the Writers, who are such Obscure Creatures, that I think it beneath me to take any further notice of them, and needless to point out their Inconsistencies, little Malice, and notorious Fals[e]hoods.[1]

1. English and British publications about Jamaica predating Knight are I. S., *A Brief and Perfect Journal of the Late Proceedings and Successe of the English Army in the West Indies* (London, 1655); *A Book of the Continuation of Foreign Passages* (London, 1657); *A True Description of Jamaica, with the Fertility, Commodities and Healthfullness of the Place* (London, 1657); Edmund Hickeringill, *Jamaica Viewed with All the Ports, Harbours, and Their Several Soundings, Towns, and Settlements Thereunto Belonging, Together with the Nature of Its Climate, Fruitfulness of the Soile, and Its Suitableness to English Complexions* (London, 1661), 2nd edition (London, 1661), 3rd edition (London, 1705); Richard Blome, *A Description of the Island of Jamaica and Other Isles and Territories in America, to Which the English Are Related . . . Taken from the Notes of Sir Thomas Lynch Knight, Governor of Jamaica, and Other Experienced Persons in the Said Places* (London, 1672); Thomas Malthus, *The Present State of Jamaica with the Life of the Great Columbus, the First Discoverer; to Which Is Added an Exact Account of Sir Henry Morgan's Voyage to, and Famous Seige and Taking of Panama from the Spaniards* (London, 1683); *The Present State of His Majesties Isles and Territories in America: viz: Jamaica* (London, 1687); Edward Ward, *A Trip to Jamaica: with a True Character of the People and Island* (London, 1698); Sir Hans Sloane, *A Voyage to the Island of Madera, Barbados, Nieves, St. Christopher and Jamaica with the Natural History of the Herbs and Trees, Four-Footed Beasts, Fishes, Birds, Insects, Reptiles, etc., of the Last of Those Islands*, 2 vols. (London, 1707–25); John Oldmixon, *British Empire in America. Containing the History of the Discovery, Settlement, Progress and Present State of All the British Colonies in the Continent and*

And though I have not the Vanity to imagine I shall escape Censure, or that I have not Committed Some mistakes; Yet I hope they will appear to be Errors in Judgment, or through Inadvertency, having inserted nothing, but what I know, or believe to be Fact, from the best Information, I was able to get.

But, notwithstanding the Piece is not Perfectly drawn, or to Advantage; Yet by Striking the Outlines, it may be allowed, that I have given it such a Likeness, as probably, will invite a more skillfull hand to finish, and render it not only Compleat, but usefull. This was my principall View, and Design: and if I am so happy as to Succeed, in any degree, I shall attain all I propose to my Self, the Satisfaction of being an Instrument of Service to my Country. For whatever tends to the Interest or Improvement of this Island, must in Consequence be of Advantage to the British Trade, Navigation, and Colonies in generall—Their Interest being one and the Same, and not to be Separated without prejudice to them all. Whatever is hurtful to any of them, must in some degree, affect the rest and whatever tends to the Service of the one, will proportionably augment the Interest, and Advantage of Them all.

In compiling this Piece, I have endeavoured to avoid Repetition and make it Easy to the Readers, by digesting the Severall matters under their proper heads; so that they may easily turn to such Parts as are most agreeable, or They, at any time, may have Occasion to look into. And though perhaps some may think, that I am too Copious and Circumstantiall; Yet when it is considered that my intention is not merely to please and Entertain, but to be of some Utility and Service, to the Publick, it will be allowed necessary to be thus particular and not too Concise, in order to give a clear and Satisfactory Idea of the Country to Strangers; and to render the piece, in all respects, usefull to every Person who has any Interest or Concern in that part of the World.

It is likewise my intention, to make it a faithful Register; of all the Memorable Events; which have hap[pe]ned, and I could attain the knowledge of, from the first Discovery of Jamaica, to the present time. My Residence in the Island above twenty Years, and the Employment I was in, most Part

---

Islands of America, 2 vols. (London, 1708), 2nd edition (London, 1741); A. B. [James Knight], *The State of the Island of Jamaica, Chiefly in Relation to Its Commerce, and the Conduct of the Spaniards in the West-Indies: Addressed to a Member of Parliament* (London, 1726); Charles Leslie, *A New and Exact Account of Jamaica* (Edinburgh, 1739); Charles Leslie, *A New History of Jamaica* (London, 1740), 2nd edition (London, 1740), 3rd edition (Edinburgh, 1740); and *The Importance of Jamaica to Great Britain Considered* (London, 1740). In his text, Knight is specifically referring to Leslie's work. See K. E. Ingram, comp., *Sources of Jamaica History, 1655–1838: A Bibliographic Survey with Particular Reference to Manuscript Sources*, 2 vols. (Zug, Switzerland, 1976), 1:197, and Frank Cundall, *Bibliographica Jamaicensis: A List of Jamaican Books and Pamphlets, Magazine Articles, Newspapers, and Maps, Most of Which Are in the Library of the Institute of Jamaica* (New York, 1902, 1971), 1–16.

of that time in the Service of the Crown and Country, having furnished me with some Remarkable transactions, which were unknown to every Common Observer; and others I collected from time to time which I committed to Writing, with several Observations I made upon the Spot, having then formed the Design of methodizing and putting them together, whenever I had the leisure and a proper Opportunity.

The first Part of this Treatise, the Reader will observe, is chiefly abstracted from some of the most Eminent Spanish Writers of America, namely Peter Martyr,[2] Herera,[3] and Hernandez Oviedo,[4] and put into a form and language, that is more Eligible and Agreeable to an English Reader.

2. Peter Martyr, *De Orbo Novo; or, The Decades of the Newe Worlde or West India*, trans. Richard Eden (London, 1555). Eden published the first three *Decades* in 1555. The remaining five were translated by M. Lok and published in London in 1612, 1625, and 1628. Knight probably used one of the three Lok editions. Also known as Pietro Martire d'Anghiera (1455–1526), Martyr was a native of Arona, Italy; apostolic protonotary; member of the Council of the Indies to Charles V; and the first abbot of Jamaica, although he never went there.

3. Antonio de Herrera y Tordesillos, *General History of the Vast Continent and Islands of America, Commonly Call'd the West Indies, from the First Discovery Thereof*, 8 vols. (Madrid, 1601–15), trans. Captain John Stevens, 6 vols. (London, 1725–26). The work covers the period 1492–1554. Some of it has been said to be plagiarized from the writings of Bartolome Las Casas. Herrera y Tordesillos (1549?–1625) was historiographer of the Indies for Philip II and Philip III of Spain, but he never visited the islands.

4. Hernandez Oviedo, also known as Gonzalo Fernández de Oviedo y Valdés (1478–1557), *Historia General y Natural de las Indias*, 19 vols. (Seville, 1535–57). Born in Madrid, a page to Prince Juan in 1490, acquainted with Columbus's sons, and present at the reception for Columbus in Barcelona in 1493, Oviedo became acquainted with the New World while accompanying Pedrarius de Avila, governor of Darien, in 1513. He subsequently acted as governor of Cartagena and alcade of the fort at St. Domingue. Returning to Europe to become chronicler to Charles V, he became historiographer of the Indies in 1533 and produced his *Historia General y Natural de las Indias* while he was serving in that capacity. In part 1 below, Knight tells his readers that he relied on English translations of Spanish works he used in constructing his work, which could not have been true with Oviedo, because Richard Eden translated only a small portion of that work to include in his 1655 translation of Martyr, *De Orbo Novo*, 173–214, and these pages contain scant reference to Jamaica. Moreover, Eden's translated pages seem to have been the only portions of Oviedo's *Historia General y Natural de las Indias* to appear in English before the nineteenth century (Samuel Purchas's *Extracts of Gonzalo Ferdinande De Oviedo His Summarie and General Historie of the West Indies*, in *Hakluytus Posthumus; or, Purchas His Pilgrims* [London, 1625], was only a republication of the Eden translation). Because the Eden translation does not include any of the extensive information Knight drew from and attributed to Oviedo, we can only conclude that Knight must have used the Spanish edition, his business relations with the Spanish Main perhaps having equipped him with a reading knowledge of Spanish. Alternatively, of course, he might also have employed a translator to produce an English translations of Oviedo's sections on Jamaica. Indeed, although Sterling A. Stoudemire, *Natural History of the Indies by Gonzalo de Oviedo e Valdê* (Chapel Hill, N.C., 1959), provides a modern edition of the sections on natural history, the general history portions seem never to have been fully translated into English. A modern Spanish edition is Gonzalo Fernández de Oviedo, *Historia General y Natural de las Indias*, 5 vols., ed. Juan Perez de Tudela Bueso (Madrid, 1959).

The second Part contains a Narrative of our Expedition to St. Domingo, which is Collected from Secretary Burchet[']s Naval History,[5] the
Journals of General Venables[6] and another Officer of Distinction;[7] Also
an Account of the proceedings from the Taking of the Island, to the Restoration,[8] abstracted from Divers letters from Commissioner Sedgewick,[9]
Vice Admiral Goodson,[10] General Brayne,[11] and Collo[nel] Doyley;[12] and

5. Josiah Burchet, *A Complete History of the Most Remarkable Transactions at Sea, from the Earliest Accounts of Time to the Conclusion of the Last War with France* (London, 1720). Of humble
origins, Burchet (1666?–October 2, 1746) was taken in by Samuel Pepys about 1680 as a body
servant and clerk, rising to joint secretary of the admiralty by February 1693–94 and sole secretary in 1698, a position he retained until 1742.

6. Robert Venables (1612?–1687), *The Narrative of General Venables, with an Appendix of Papers Relating to the Expedition to the West Indies and the Conquest of Jamaica, 1654–1655* (London,
1655). Born in Rudheath, Cheshire, Venables served in the Parliamentary Army during the
English Civil War, and in December 1654 Cromwell sent him along with William Penn and
Edward Winslow to command an expedition to capture the Spanish colony of Hispaniola.
The failure of this effort earned him and Penn imprisonment in the Tower of London, and
he became a Royalist in 1659. It is not clear what edition of Venables's *Narrative* was available
to Knight.

7. Neither the officer of distinction nor his journal have been identified. Perhaps it was
Cornelius Burroughs, *Rich Newes from Jamaica* (London, 1659), in which Burroughs describes
himself as "Steward General."

8. Knight may have found these letters in Thomas Birch, ed., *A Collection of the Papers of
John Thurloe, Secretary First to the Council of State and Afterwards to the Two Protectors*, 7 vols.
(London, 1742).

9. Robert Sedgewick (1611–May 24, 1656). Born in Woburn, Bedfordshire, Sedgewick
migrated to New England in 1635 and became a merchant in Charlestown and then Boston.
He helped found the Military Company of Massachusetts in 1638, served against the French
in Acadia in 1654, and sailed to fight the Spanish in the West Indies in July 1655, arriving on
October 1 at Jamaica, where he received a commission as military governor of the island on
May 12, 1656, but died just twelve days later. Frank Cundall, *Governors of Jamaica in the Seventeenth Century* (London, 1936), xxxi–xxxviii.

10. William Goodson (1634–1662?). Born in Yarmouth, Norfolk, to a staunch Puritan
family, Goodson was rear admiral of the blue aboard the *Rainbow* in 1653 and served as vice
admiral with Penn at Hispaniola in 1654. He helped capture Jamaica, May 11–17, 1655, and
became commander in chief of the island when Penn returned to England on June 21. Ibid.,
xxx–xxxi.

11. William Brayne (?–September 2, 1657). The earliest public record for Brayne is as
lieutenant-colonel of the foot in Scotland in 1653 and governor of Inverlochy, which he defended against Royalist attack. Sent to Jamaica in the summer of 1656 as commander of the
land forces, he became commander in chief of the island on his arrival in December 1656,
where he died within ten months. Ibid., xl–xli.

12. Edward Doyley (1617–1675). Born in Albourne, Wiltshire, into a large aristocratic
family and educated at the Inns of Court, Doyley fought for Parliament in Wiltshire in
the Civil War and served Cromwell in Ireland. In 1654, he went as a lieutenant-colonel to the
West Indies where he played a small role at Hispaniola and in the capture of Jamaica. His role
was elevated in October 1655 when he was appointed to replace the late Richard Fortescue
as one of the commissioners of the island until Brayne arrived as commander in chief in December 1656. On Brayne's death in September 1657, Doyley became sole commander in chief
and Jamaica's first civil governor on February 8, 1661. In this role he began establishing a civil

from an Original Manuscript of that Worthy Gentleman last mentioned, which I was favoured with by a friend (who had it some Years ago from a Lady of the Name of Doyley that was either Sister or Daughter to the Coll[onel]) and Contains the Resolutions of the Councils of War, His orders and Instructions to divers Officers by Sea and Land, and other Transactions, during the times He was Commander in Chief of the Island[13] and until He was Superseded by the Lord Windsor.[14]

The Reader will likewise expect to be satisfied in my Authority for the Subsequent transactions, particularly the 3d. Part, relative to the Proceedings of the several Governours, Councill and Assembly, and being desirous of removing every objection that may be made, I shall proceed to inform them that all such matters, together with the Speeches, Addresses, Memorials, &c., are transcribed from Original Minutes, and other Authentick papers. The Narrative of the Expedition to Panama in 1670 under the Command of Capt[ain] Morgan, is extracted from a Journal of that Memorable Enterprize, which with his Commission, Instructions, the Minutes of the Governour and Councill, and other papers relative to it, were printed and published in 1672, in Vindication of his Conduct,[15] and I was favoured

---

polity, including an elected advisory council, forerunner to the House of Assembly. Replaced in August 1661, he retired to St. Martin-in-the-Fields, London, where he died. Ibid., 1–9.

13. This manuscript may be found in the Long Family Papers, Additional Manuscripts 12423, British Library, London.

14. Thomas Hickman, Seventh Baron Windsor of Stanwell and First Earl of Plymouth (1627?–November 3, 1687), first appears in the public record as a Royalist captain in 1642 when he was only fifteen years old, and in May 1645 when he was a lieutenant-colonel. Charles II appointed him governor of Jamaica, July 20, 1661, where he arrived on August 2 but spent only ten weeks on the island before returning to England and leaving Charles Lyttleton in charge. The Crown revoked his commission on February 15, 1664, though he subsequently received various governorships. Briefly imprisoned in the Tower of London for challenging Lord Berkeley, lord lieutenant of Ireland, to a duel, he became Earl of Plymouth on May 19, 1685, and a Privy Council member on October 30, 1685. Cundall, *Governors of Jamaica in the Seventeenth Century*, 10–15.

15. No copy of a 1672 publication of Morgan's *Vindication* has been found. However, a decade later Thomas Malthus published it in *Present State of Jamaica*. A manuscript copy of Morgan's voyage to Panama may be found in Ms. 53, National Library of Jamaica, Kingston. Sir Henry Morgan (1635?–August 1688) was born in Pencarn, Wales, and was a nephew of Colonel Edward Morgan. Supposedly kidnapped as a child in Bristol and sold as a servant to Barbados, he moved to Jamaica and may have been in command of a privateer that attacked Campeachy and Honduras in 1663–65. Authorized by Governor Thomas Modyford in early 1668 to capture Spanish ships, he attacked Panama, Cuba, and Maracaibo for which he was reproved for exceeding his commission. Receiving a new commission, he attacked Panama again in 1669, for which he was arrested and taken to England with Modyford. However, he soon returned to favor and was made lieutenant-colonel of Jamaica under Lord Vaughan in November 1674, arriving in March 1675. Morgan twice served as acting governor, once between Vaughan's departure on March 14, 1678, and Carlisle's arrival on July 19, and again on Carlisle's departure in May 1680. When Sir Thomas Lynch arrived as governor in May 1682, Morgan went into opposition and was dismissed from the council and all commands in

with (being out of Print) by S[i]r Hans Sloan[e].[16] The description of the Earthquake in 1692, is partly collected from Letters in Lowthorp's Philosophical Transactions,[17] though the Substance of them, as well as other particulars mentioned, I have often heard related by Persons of undoubted Credit, who were on the Spot and Spectators of that dreadfull Catastrophe. The account of the Invasion of the Island, by the French the year following, is extracted from an Authentick Copy of Sir William Beeston's Journal, which was transmitted to one of their Majestie's' Secretarys of State.[18]

October 1683. He returned to the council one month before his death. Cundall, *Governors of Jamaica in the Seventeenth Century*, 56–76.

16. Sir Hans Sloane (April 16, 1660–January 11, 1753). Born in Killileagh, County Down, Ireland, Sloane received an M.D. (University of Orange) in July 1683 and became a fellow of the Royal Society in January 1685 and fellow of the Royal College of Physicians in April 1687. In 1687, he went to Jamaica as physician to the Duke of Albemarle and stayed fifteen months, from which experience he wrote his *Natural History*. Setting up practice in London in May 1689, he served as secretary to the Royal Society from 1693 to 1712 and revived publication of that body's *Philosophical Transactions*. Subsequently, he wrote the botanical *Catalogus Plantarum quae in Insula Jamaica sponte proveniunt aut vulgo coluntor* (London, 1696) and *A Voyage to the Islands of Madera, Barbados, Nieves, St. Christopher's, and Jamaica, with the Natural History of the Last* (London, 1707) with a second volume in 1725; founded the botanic garden at Chelsea in 1712; served as an advisor to Queen Ann; was knighted in 1716; was made personal physician to George II in 1727; and promoted the colony of Georgia in 1732. He was elected to the French Academy of the Sciences in 1708, then to the Imperial Academy of St. Petersburg and the Royal Academy of Madrid. From 1729 to 1735, he acted as president of the College of Physicians, and after the death of Sir Isaac Newton he served as president of the Royal Society from 1727 to November 1741. His final work was *An Account of a Medicine for Soreness, Weakness, and Other Distempers of the Eyes* (London, 1745). At his death he left his collections, which formed the basis for the collection of the British Museum, to the nation in exchange for £20,000 for his family.

17. John Lothrop, *The Philosophical Transactions and Collections, to the End of the Year 1700* was an abridgment in three volumes of the first three volumes of the *Philosophical Transactions of the Royal Society*, 2nd edition (London, 1716), including "A Letter from Hans Sloane, M.D., and F.R.S. with Several Accounts of the Earthquakes in Peru, Oct. 20, 1687; and at Jamaica, Feb. 19, 1687-8; and June 7, 1692. No. 209, p 78," in Charles Hutton, George Shaw, and Richard Pearson, eds., *The Philosophical Transactions of the Royal Society of London, from Their Commencement, in 1665, to the Year 1800*, vol. 3, *From 1683 to 1694* (London, 1809), 624–32.

18. Where Knight found this document is unclear. A copy of it may be found in Additional Manuscripts 12424, British Library. His "A Narrative by Sir William Beeston on the Descent on Jamaica by the French" may be found in ibid., 12430. Long after Knight's death, Beeston's "Narrative" was printed in *Interesting Tracts, Relating to the Island of Jamaica: Consisting of Curious State-Papers, Councils of War, Letters, Petitions, Narratives, &c. &c., Which Throw Great Light on the History of That Island, from Its Conquest Down to the Year 1702* (Jamaica, 1800), 244–47. Beeston (1636–1702) was born in Titchfield, Hampshire, and arrived in Jamaica on April 27, 1660. He was a member for Port Royal in the first House of Assembly in 1664, when the assembly imprisoned and reprimanded him for contempt of the Speaker. He became a judge of the common pleas in December 1664 and commissioner of the admiralty in 1675. As Speaker of the House, 1677–80, he opposed Carlisle's design to make Jamaica conform to the Irish model of government and to secure a permanent revenue for the Crown from the colony, for which he was sent to England to answer to Charles II, whom he persuaded to remove Carlisle.

The transactions of his Majesty[']s Ships in America are chiefly collected from Secretary Burchet[']s and Mr. Lidiard's *Naval Historys Gazettes* and other papers published by Authority.[19] And the Depradations of the Pyrates, and Spanish Guarda Costas from the year 1712 to 1737, the several Hurricanes, and other incidents within that Space of time, are to my own knowledge litterally true, being all that time on the Island except 5 years Vizt. from 1723 to 1728.

The 4th and all other parts of the Piece are chiefly from my own Observation and Experience, though I must confess that in my Description of several parts of the Island, I have been obliged to take from others who are much better acquainted with them and on whose Candour and Judgement I can depend upon, as well as some other matters which are out of my Province. The Reader will therefore do me the Justice to observe that I have from time to time pointed them out, as well as the Authors of such Pieces as I thought necessary to quote or make use of.

By means of those Papers, I have been able to place things in the Natural order, in which they hap[pe]ned; and to give a Relation of Facts from Authentick Records and Tracts which are hud[d]led together by other Writers, in an Obscure, confused manner as being Obliged to build chiefly upon Tradition and hearsay.

I have likewise given a more particular Description of the Island and Inhabitants, Their Customs, manner of living, Climate, Air &c. than has been hitherto published, or is now Extant. Hence, the Readers will have a Natural and Artless View of the Country, and every Circumstance relating to it, that is Material or Necessary for Their information or Satisfaction.

They will perceive, What *Difficulties* and *hardships*, the *first Set[t]lers* laboured under. The *Anxious* and *fatiguing* life of a *Planter*. The *Calamities* and *misfortunes*, which attended the Island for a *Course of years*. And notwithstanding all, the *Considerable improvements* which have been made, by the *force* of *Industry*, without the Assistance, some other Colonies have had from Their Mother Country.

They will See by what Laws Their distant Countrymen are Governed. The *fatal Consequences* which attend *Oppression* or *Mal-Administration*. The *Happiness* of a *Free People*. And the Advantages, which flow from *Temperance*, *Application* and *Oeconomy*.

And, upon the whole it will manifestly Appear How many *Advantages*, Accrue to *Great Britain*, from this Island. What great improvements may

---

Knighted in 1692, Beeston returned to Jamaica as lieutenant-governor in March 1693 and commanded the forces that repelled the French invasion attempt in 1694. He received a commission as governor of Jamaica on April 8, 1700, but was replaced early in 1702, after which he retired to London where he died. His daughter married Sir Thomas Modyford and then Charles Long. Cundall, *Governors of Jamaica in the Seventeenth Century*, 143–65.

19. See note 5, above.

still be made, which will proportionably Augment the Interest of both. And how much it deserves not only protection, but all the Encouragement that can be given.

Before I conclude this Preface I think my self obliged to mention (though with Regret) a Circumstance, which laid me under some difficulties, retarded the finishing of this Piece, and almost discouraged my proceeding upon it: For being desirous of making the third part, relating to the Administration of the Several Governours, as usefull and entertaining, as possible, and to Omit no material Transaction, which hap[pe]ned in their respective Governments, I applied in a Respectfull manner to the B[oar]d of T[rade] from whence alone proper and Authentick Accounts could be had in this part of the World. But, though I had great reason to expect from the Nature, Institution and Design of that Office, all the Assistance, they Could give me, in a well intended and necessary Work; Yet I was with great Civility dismissed, with an Assurance of the Refusall not being personal; for that it was not Customary to grant Copies of any Papers in that Office; unless it was in Cases of Appeals, or in Actions depending in Law or Equity.

The Readers will undoubtedly be surprized, when I assure Them, that I required nothing more than the Copy of the first Governour's Commission and Instructions (which I afterwards obtained at another Office, without any hesitation) and though I desired leave to look into and to make such Extracts from the Minutes of Council and other Papers transmitted from Jamaica, which I thought necessary, yet I took care to mention expressly that I did not desire leave so much as to look into any Paper transmitted from thence within these last twenty Years.

This Disappointment laid me under the necessity of sending over to JAMAICA, where I obtained the Papers I wanted with great Expence and trouble to my Friends, though perhaps I might have met with others, which would likewise have been proper; had I obtained the favour of looking over those *obsolete Minutes* and *Papers* which could not have discovered any of the Secrets of our present Government nor could it have any way affected the *Honourable Persons* now at that Board because my Request related to Transactions before Their time; though possibly, They were apprehensive of some *Discoveries*, which would expose certain Persons, who had been promoted to *Eminent Stations* and of great consequence to the Nation, without *Experience* or *proper Abilities*.

Memorialls and *Representations*, of the utmost importance to *Trade* and *Plantations*, might likewise have appeared which had been laid aside, without any notice or Consideration; or perhaps ever being Read. Acts of the Assemblies, laid by for 6 or 7 Years, and some more, without any Report being made upon them, &c., &c. But, whatever may be said of such misconducts or neglects, nothing of the kind can I hope be Suggested during the time of those *Honourable Gentlemen* now at that Board whose *Vigilance* and *care* of the *British Trade* and *Plantations* are *Conspicuous* to all the World; and whose *Experience, Publick Spirit*, and *great Abilities* are Equally *Approved* and Applauded.

It only remains, that I should Apologize for the liberty, I have taken in expressing myself, on some Occasions, with great freedom; which I hope will not give any Offence, since they relate to matters of a Publick nature, and no ways reflecting on private or particular Persons.

Nor, should I otherwise have been impartial, and Consistent with the Motto, I have taken, namely—The first law in History Writing is not to dare to Assert any thing that is false, and the next not to be afraid of speaking the truth. Let there be no Appearance of Dissimulation[,] let there be none of private Malice.

My Inclination and Disposition to promote the *British Plantations*, particularly *Jamaica*, and consequently the Interest of *Great Britain* to the utmost of my power and Ability, is a Reasonable Plea, for a favourable Construction, and to induce not only the Gentlemen of that Island, but every Candid Reader, to pass over, whatever may be liable to exception in other respects, and to throw a Veil over the Errors and Imperfections of the Writer. For According to the Celebrated Roman Orator, and Philosopher—*Omne Officium, quod ad conjunctionem hominum, et ad Societatem tuendam valet, anteponendum est illi Officio, quod cognitione et Scientiâ continetur*

Cic[ero] De. Off[iciis]: Lib. 1[:158].[20]

---

20. The quotation is from M. Tullius Cicero, *De Officiis*, 1:158. Walter Miller translates this passage as "Every duty that tends effectively to maintain and safeguard human society should be given the preference over that duty which arises from speculation and science alone" (Cambridge, Mass., 1913).

Introduction

It is Customary with most Writers, who have nothing more in View than their Own private Interest and Advantage, to give a partiall account of things; and to draw the most Agreeable landskip, of the Countries whose Settlement They intend to promote, in order to invite and encourage People to go over and Settle them. This hath been the *Constant* practice of the Spaniards, who have given pompous Descriptions of all their Settlements in America, and not only suggested the great Riches, which are to be acquired in Them; but that the Climate is free from the Inconvenience of heat and cold, and that the Fruits of the Earth grow Spontaneously, with very little labour or trouble. This was likewise the Conduct of Sir Walter Raleigh,[1] when He was about to plant Colonies in Virginia; and many other English Writers Since His time; and probably the same thing may be insinuated in regard to my Design. But though I confess that I am desirous of Contributing to the Interest and well fare of Jamaica; Yet I should be Extreamly Concerned to be the Cause of any man's Embarqueing in a Design, which may prove disagreeable to him, or lead Him into any thing, which is not apparently for His Interest and Advantage.

It will manifestly appear to those, who peruse and Consider the whole tenour of this Treatise, that I am very far from Suggesting or insinuating, that this Island is so agreeable a Country to live in as England, and other Parts of Europe; or that Men of Fortune, who are Easy and happy in other Respects, would choose to go over and Reside there; though Severall Gentlemen who have Estates in the Island, and can live in an Affluent manner in any other Country, think the Climate preferable, and choose to spend Their days there. This will not appear Strange, Since it is Naturall

---

1. Sir Walter Raleigh (1552?–October 29, 1618). Heavily involved in privateering, exploration, and colonization, including the failed colony at Roanoke in 1584–86, he helped to introduce tobacco and the potato to England and was involved in the defense of England from the Spanish Armada in 1588. But he fell out of favor at court after a quarrel that year with Robert Devereux, Second Earl of Essex, and was committed to the Tower of London in 1592. After he had revived his reputation, he went on missions against the Spanish in the 1590s but James I stripped him of his office and titles and committed him again to the Tower until 1616. That year he was permitted to make an expedition to Orinoco, but against his instructions he burned San Tomas and for this action was executed. He was the author of *The Discoverie of the Large, Rich, and Beautiful Epyre of Guiana* (London, 1596) and *The Historie of the World, in Five Books* (London, 1614), as well as much poetry, prose, and colonial propaganda.

This version of Jamaica's English seal is from a map entitled *Novissima et accuratissima insulae Jamaicae. Descriptio*, published in London in 1671. Based on a map by John Man, surveyor general of Jamaica from 1661 to 1671, it was the work of John Seller (1632–1697), an English compiler, publisher, and seller of maps, charts, and geographical books, who from 1671 was hydrographer to the king. The seal depicts two indigenous figures, a woman bearing a basket of fruit and a man with a hunting bow, standing below an alligator and encircled by a Latin inscription, "*Ecce alium ramos porrexit in ordem nec sterris est crux.*" Roughly translated as "Behold, in the other branches of the universe people have no cross nor other order," this inscription evokes the central themes through which Europeans justified their efforts to dispossess Native Americans and other peoples: their being without fixed settlements, intercessional religions, and a complex social order. Under the feet of the indigenous figures in the seal is a second Latin inscription, "*Indus utero serviet uni,*" which may be freely translated as "The abundance of the Indies serves all," not just the Spaniards who had presided over it for a century and a half.

to mankind, to prefer to all others the Place of their Birth, or Some like a Cold, others a hot Climate, and in generall most People prefer the place in which They have resided many Years, and w[hi]ch by that means is become habituall to Them. All that I propose or Aim at, is to Convince the World, that a Man, with common Industry and Oeconomy, may not only improve or raise a Fortune there but enjoy his health, and live in a decent and Comfortable manner; provided He is Temperate in his diet, and Exercises, and Conforms to the Nature of the Climate. It must at the same time be acknowledged; that notwithstanding all the Care and Caution, which can be taken, it doth not agree with Some Constitutions, nor Indeed doth England or any other part of the World; for it is not to be imagined that any place or Climate is Exempt from Endemicall Evils, but are all subject to Diseases of some kind or Other.

That the Climate is as healthy as any Part of South America, and not so noxious as Carthagena[,] Porto Bello, and some other Places, I may with great truth affirm. For though we often hear of Sickness and Mortality in this Island, more than in any other; yet the great resort of Strangers is to be considered, and that They die elsewhere in proportion to Their Number. Nor is it at all to be wondered at, that many of Them are taken away, particularly Soldiers and Seamen[,] and that others are rendered feeble and unfit for Service, considering Their method and manner of living, being crouded on Shipboard without Conveniences, or necessary Exercises; feeding on Salted Provisions for many months together without any Refreshments (but when they are in Port, and then but once a Week) which causes Scurvies and other Disorders; Drinking Spirituous liquors to Excess; and Their Cloathing the Same as in the Northern Climates, to which may be added that most People in that Part of the World, indulge Themselves in all kind of Pleasures and gratifications, which nature has bestowed on Them for their comfort and Happiness and not for their Destruction.

Thus I have Seen Persons Who had treated Themselves by labour or Exercise Strip off their Cloaths to Their Shirts, and expose Their open Pores to the Air. Others in the like Condition unadvisedly Drank large draughts of Cold Water, or other liquors which they supposed and are deemed to be more Cooling in their Nature.

And it is very common with Soldiers, Seamen, Servants, and others, upon those Occasions, or when they have Inflamed their blood with excessive Drinking of Spirituous liquors, to lie upon the Grass or upon the Earth under Shady Places, and there forgetting Themselves fall a sleep. And this not only in the Day, but in the Evenings, and sometimes all Night, when between the Dew from Heaven, and the Damps from the Earth, such impressions are made on Human Bodies, as occasion fatall Disorders.

Strangers or New Comers are likewise incautious in their manner of living, upon their first Arrivall, often intemperate, do not Consider the Effects of a change of diet, or Alteration of Climate; and commonly indulge Themselves with the pleasant Fruits of the Country, which by eating to excess, or such as are immature, Occasions Fluxes, and other Distempers. These Points are worthy of Notice and Consideration. And I am perswaded, will be of Singular use and Service to Persons of all Conditions in that part of the World.

Many of the first English Set[t]lers, who copied after the Spaniards in Their manner of living, Attained to great Ages; for I have Seen Severall of the Officers of the Army, which took the Island in 1655, and many of the Privateers, who took Panama in 1669. And heard them relate Divers passages and Circumstances which are mentioned in this Treatise, relating to the Settlement of the Island by the English and their Expeditions against the Spaniards in America.

As some of them lived to the Year 1708, and Others died Since 1720, they must have lived on the Island from 50 to 60 Years and been about 80 years of age, when they died, if not more. There are at this time, Divers Persons, who have lived on the Island, from 20 to 50 years, and Natives, Whites as well as Blacks, who are Sixty Years of Age and upwards: And it is probable there would be many more, did not the Island often change its Inhabitants; It being Common for Merchants, and Others, and even some Planters, to remove to Great Britain, as soon as they have acquired sufficient to maintain them there; and by that means many Persons are constantly coming from thence, as well as going over so that once in 7 Years there is almost a new Set of Inhabitants.

These Instances and the great ages of many of the Negroes, as well as the Indians of America, who are generally Vigorous and Strong, notwithstanding their hard labour and coarse diet, Evince the truth of what I have advanced. But for the further Satisfaction of the Readers, I refer them to the 5th part of this Treatise, wherein I have more particularly and amply discussed these matters, and laid down some Rules, which I think proper and necessary to be Observed in that part of the World.

Upon the whole it will manifestly appear, That this Island has been greatly misrepresented; That its product is so Considerable, and the Situation so advantagious, that it is highly Worthy of our Attention and Care; And that the Settlement of the large Tracts of lands which are uncultivated, will not only Strengthen and Secure that Valuable Acquisition; but give a further Employment to a great number of People at home; Encrease our Shipping and Seamen; promote the Consumption of British Manufactures; furnish us with Indigo, Cocoa and other Commodities which we are now obliged to purchase of the French and Spaniards; and proportionably augment His Majesty's Revenues.

The Encouraging and Improving our Plantations and Colonies, in America, particularly Jamaica, is Certainly worthy [of] the Notice and Consideration of our Nobility and Gentry; Since they are the principall support of our Trade and Navigation, on which the Security and wellfare of Great Britain depend.

It is likewise to be Considered, that the Improvement of our Colonies, will not only be attended with all the advantages I have mentioned, but give Employment to the Poor, and inrich the Nation by their labour which though paid by the Tenant, is a Charge on the Landlord, because it disables the Tenant from paying so high a Rent as He might otherways be able to do instead of being a nu[i]sance to it by their falling into Vicious Courses; and it will likewise lessen the Poor[']s Rate.

It was the Opinion of S[i]r Josiah Child, that one Man in the Southern Colonies, gave Employment to five men at Home.[2] As this is an assertion, which may be proved even to a Demonstration, it is in my Opinion, a sufficient motive, to incite Gentlemen of Fortune to Encourage and promote so usefull and Necessary a Design. And methinks that Consideration, should likewise induce Persons of small or mid[d]ling Fortunes to go over with Alacrity; Since at the same time that they are advancing Their Own Interest, and providing for their Families, they have the Satisfaction of Contributing to the Relief and Support of others.

It will not be improper to observe, that the Man who lives merely on the Interest of His money in the Funds, and employs no part of His Fortune in Trade, or in Some way encouraging the manufactures of His Country, is a useless Member of the Common wealth: But He that endeavours to advance, or is in some degree beneficiall to them, at the same time Serves Himself, His Friends, and His Country. The Merchants therefore ought to be considered as one of the most usefull Societys to the Common Wealth; and in Some Countrys are deservedly distinguished, however Neglected and Slighted in a Nation, which has a very great dependance on Trade.

It is likewise worth observing that one thousand pounds placed out in the Funds at most brings in not more than 4 p[er] Cent p[er] an[num] even supposing the principall to be well secured, and in no danger of being impaired or less[e]ned by dividends and other means, when the same sum employed in some Trade or Manufacture will bring in 10 p[er] Cent or more: or by being laid out in a Plantation in the Sugar Islands, in a few Years, would bring in 3 or £400 p[er] Annum and might with Industry and good Husbandry be so Improved as to enable them to raise and make some Figure in the World: I could instance, was it proper, severall Persons who

---

2. Sir Josiah Child (1630–June 22, 1699). Born in London, the son of merchant Richard Child, Child served as MP for Petersfield in 1659, Dartmouth from 1673 to 1678, and Ludlow from 1685 to 1687. He made a large fortune in commerce, including in the East India Company of which he was governor from 1681 to 1683 and 1686 to 1688. Knight was here referring to Child's *A New Discourse of Trade* (London, 1690), which stressed the colonial contribution to English wealth and argued for a reduction of the legal interest rate from 6 to 4 percent as a strategy to raise England's fortune in international competition.

live in a Comfortable manner, and others who in my time, acquired good Estates in Jamaica with a less Foundation, and some meerly by their Industry, Oeconomy and Address.

Would those Gentlemen, who have small Estates in Great Britain or Ireland or who are so much incumbered, that they Struggle with many difficulties; Consider, that by the Sale of them, they might not only make themselves easy in respect to Their Debts, but with an Overpluss of 800 or £1000 Sterling Settle a Plantation, which in a few years will bring in 3 or £400 per Annum and with Industry and good Husbandry improve the same and raise a Sugar Work. Certainly they would not lead a disagreeable life, attended with difficulties and great Anxieties, would they but consider that they have an Opportunity of Extricating themselves, living Comfortably for the future, and providing in a decent manner for their Families.

I am not here inviting Gentlemen and others to run the hazards, or undergo the Fatigues, which Commonly Attend new Colonies: No; Jamaica has been many years Inhabited, though not fully, and has a great Number of fine Plantations set[t]led thereon; some of the Inhabitants are Rich, others in a prosperous way, and they carry on an extensive and beneficiall Commerce to Severall parts of the World: but want more Inhabitants, to Strengthen and Secure their possessions, and to Cultivate large Tracts of land, which never yet have been manured. And here, it is worth observing, that it would tend to the advantage of Great Britain, if some such Assistance was given to them, as hath been granted to Georgia, and in other Cases of the like Nature, or as the French give to their Colonies, not only for the Reasons before mentioned, but as it would in a few Years, be the means of Strengthening the Island, and thereby Saving a great expence, which the Nation is now at, in Maintaining Troops for their protection.

The Assembly have done every thing, in their power, to attain and Accomplish so good a Design, by passing severall Laws for that purpose; which are now Confirmed by the Crown; and particularly an Act intitled *an Act for introducing of White People into this Island, for subsisting them for a Certain time, and providing them with Land that they may have become Set[t]lers.*[3]

But having treated amply of these matters in the 10th and last part of this Piece, I beg leave to refer the Reader thereto.

It is Necessary, before I conclude, to Explain Some particular words and Phrases, in this Piece, which many Readers will otherwise be at a loss to know the meaning of. And therefore I must observe that Several Places and things, in this Island, retain the Indian, or some the Spanish, Names,

---

3. The Jamaica Assembly first passed "An Act for the Introducing of White People into This Island, for Subsisting Them for a Certain Time, and Providing Them with Land That They May Become Settlers" in 1703 and often revised and renewed it thereafter. See N. A. T. Hall, "Some Aspects of the 'Deficiency' Question in the Eighteenth Century," *Caribbean Studies* 19 (1975): 5–19.

and others are derived from one of them, but corrupted or altered in the Pronounciation. St. David's Precinct, was called Yallahs, by the Aborigines, and commonly goes by that name, as well as Guanaboa, which Precinct, was called St. Juan, by the Spaniards, and from thence St. Johns by the English. But, I have not been able to find out the Etymology, or Signification of Either of those Indian Names.

Savanna is an Indian word, and Signifies a Field or Common.

Many Fruits, Roots and Herbs also retain the Indian Names, particularly Guavas, Mamees, Sapotilles, Ananas commonly called Bonanos, Yams[,] Toyers, Cassavi or Bread made out of the Root of a Shrub which they call Yuca, Callilu, which is not unlike Spinage, Curito, a sort of Aloes, and others.

St. Iago delavega, (or St. James in the Plain) was and is now the proper Name of the Town Vulgarly called Spanish Town, because it is the only one remaining which was built by the Spaniards.

St. Andrews Precinct, was named by the Spaniards Lagonia from a Place in Old Spain, and from thence corruptly called Liguinea, which name it most Commonly goes by, except in Acts of Assembly, Writs, or proceedings at Law. And, in Such Cases, the other Places, as well as this, run in their proper or English Name.

Port Antonio, [is] now Called Portland, though the former Name generally prevails; Port Maria and other Parts are called after the Spanish Names, and others transposed into English as St. Marys, St. Anns &c. Point Morant at the E[astern] end of the Island, is taken from the Spanish Name Pointo Moranto or Brown Point, because it often appears, at a Distance of that Colour. Point Nigril, at the W[est] end from Pointo Nigril or Black Point, for the same Reason. Barcadier, from the Spanish word Barcadiera, or a landing Place. Barica, is a word used in Jamaica, and is Spanish for a small Barrel, or Cask which contains about 3 or 4 Gallons.

Lagune from Laguna[,] a Lake or great Pond.

Rio Grande, or great River, Rio d'ora or Gold River, Ora Cabesa or Gold head, and some other Rivers also derive their Names from the Spanish.

Part the 1st.

The Etymology of the word Jamaica; and the Discovery of the Island by Christopher Columbus. Some account of the Native Indians, before they were Subdued and Extirpated by the Spaniards; with such other Occurrences, as happened, while it was in their possession.

Jamaica derived its Name from the Indian Language, & was so called by the Aborigines or Native Indians,[1] the word signifies a *Water Country;* and probably alludes to the great Number of Springs, Rivers, and Lagunes, that are within this Island.[2]

It was discovered by Christopher Columbus,[3] who in His second Voyage to America, after He had made a Settlement on the North side of Hispaniola, which He named St. Isabella, sailed from thence the 26th of April 1494, in order to find out, whether Cuba was an Island, or Part of a Continent; which was not Certainly known till after His Death.

He arrived at the East end of that Island the 1st of May following; where He spent three days in Searching the Bays and Harbours, in that part of the Coast; and upon the Information He had of Jamaica from the Natives of Cuba, and of there being plenty of Gold in it, He Resolved to be satisfied of the truth of what they related to Him. Accordingly, on Sunday the 4th, of May, He directed His Course thither, and came in Sight of the

---

1. See the Decades of Peter Martyr: who says it was called in His time, St. Iago, by the Spaniards; though it afterwards reassumed its former Name.—*Author.* Peter Martyr, *De Orbo Novo; or, The Decades of the Newe Worlde or West India,* trans. Richard Eden (London, 1555). Martyr's enormous compendium was published in several contemporary editions, and it is unclear which of these Knight may have used or where in the work Knight may have gotten this information.—*Ed.*

2. There are 84 Rivers in this Island, which run into the Sea, & numberless Springs & Rivulets, that run into them.—*Author.*

3. Life of Col[umbus]: Ch. 54.—*Author.* Christopher Columbus (1447–1506), the Genoese mariner who is credited with the first European encounter with the New World. Knight here refers to Ferdinand Colon, "The Life of the Admiral Christopher Columbus by His Son," which would have been available to him in English in John Churchill, *A Collection of Voyages and Travels Some Now First Printed from Original Manuscripts, Others Now First Published in English,* 6 vols. (London, 1732), 2:558–59, where Colon refers to his father's first encounter with Jamaica. A modern English translation of this work may be found in Benjamin Keen, trans. and ed., *The Life of the Admiral Christopher Columbus: By His Son Ferdinand,* rev. edition (New Brunswick, N.J., 1959).—*Ed.*

This image depicts a friendly reception for Spanish visitors on the shores of an unidentified West Indian island at which an indigenous cacique, tobacco pipe in hand, wearing an elaborate feathered cape and standing beside a Europeanized temple housing a pagan idol, invites the newcomers to partake in an all-male feast of roasted snake and iguana and bounteous quantities of fruit. The indigenous participants, many of whom are dancing, are adorned with feathered headdresses and garments and carry ceremonial clubs with Spanish sailors looking on or playing a bagpipe. In the background are the visitors' ship, sea creatures, an alligator tied to a palm tree, and several items portraying indigenous culture, including a canoe, huts, and hammocks strung between trees. Wolfgang Kilian (1581–1662), an Augsburg printmaker, is presumed to have been the artist for this engraving, which is taken from Honorius Philoponus, *Nova typis transacta navigatio* (Linz, 1621), plate following p. 36.

Island the same day; the next morning He dropped Anchor, and declared it to be the most beautifull of all the Islands, He had seen in the West Indies.

On Tuesday the 7th, He sailed towards the West end; and sent his Boats to sound and discover the Harbours: which the Natives perceived, and apprehending, that the Spaniards intended to land, came off in Canoes, in great Numbers armed, to oppose and prevent them; upon which they returned to their Ships. But, afterwards, considering that if they shewed any signs of fear, it would animate and embolden the Indians, they Sailed into a Port, which Columbus called Puerto Bueno.[4] Here the Natives came off, in like manner; upon which a Skirmish ensued, wherein several of them, being killed & wounded, the rest retreated to the Shore. Nevertheless many

---

4. Ocho Rios corruptly called Chenanas. — *Author.*

others came from the Neighbouring Parts soon after, in a peaceable manner; and brought with them Provisions, which they trucked for Toys and Trifles. At this Port, which is in the form of a Horse shoe, Columbus repaired and fitted his Ships which were leaky.

The ninth of May He Sailed again to the Westward; and kept so near the Shore, that the Indians followed Him in their Canoes. But the Wind being contrary for some days, He resolved to stand over again to Cuba, with an intention of making a full Discovery of that Coast. Upon His leaving Jamaica, an Indian Youth desired to go with them, to Spain, which He persisted on notwithstanding the Entreaties and Tears of His Friends and Relations; and to avoid their importunity He went between the Decks of the Ships, and hid Himself.

Columbus, after searching the Coast of Cuba, from the 15th of May to the 13th of June, finding it to run far Westward, and that it was a matter of the greatest difficulty, to Sail that way, by Reason of an infinite Number of small Islands, Shoals and Sands, intended to return to His Settlement on Hispaniola: but meeting with Contrary winds and Violent Rains, He was in great distress, and obliged to put into Cape Cruz on Cuba, where the Natives received Him in a friendly manner, and furnished Him with Provisions, and such other Necessaries as they had.

The Wind continuing contrary, the 22d of July, He stood over for Jamaica, and sailed Westward so near the Shore, that the Indians came off in their Canoes, and followed Him, contentedly receiving, whatever was given them in Exchange for their Provisions, which the Spaniards liked much better, than any they met with in the other Islands.

This part of the Country, is described by Columbus in His Journal, to be pleasant and fruitfull; to have many Excellent Harbours at almost every league distance, and all the Coast full of Towns, and very Populous.[5]

Columbus proceeded round the S[outh]W[est] end of the Island, which He called Point Nigril; and from thence stood to the Eastward, taking advantage of the land Breezes, or Night winds which blow from the Shore. The land on the Southside of the Island, He also describes to be green, pleasant and fruitful, abounding with Provisions, and so Populous, that He thought, none excelled it; especially near a Bay,[6] which He called de la

---

5. Churchill, *Collection of Voyages and Travels*, 2:559. Columbus first sighted Jamaica during the second voyage on April 14, 1494, and landed on May 4, 1494, probably at Dry Harbour. See Frank Cundall, *Chronological Outlines of Jamaica History, 1492–1926* (Kingston, Jamaica, 1927).

6. By the description, this part of the Country is now called Liguinea, and the nine small Islands, the Cays off of Port Royal; which were formerly much larger than they are now, and covered with Mangroves: but were *greatly* diminished by the Hurricanes in 1712 and 1722. — *Author.*

Vacas,[7] because there are nine small Islands, near the land, which, He says were as high[8] as any He had Seen, yet, all Peopled, and very fruitful.[9]

This Island, He judged to be 800 miles in Circumference, 50 leagues or 150 miles in length, and 20 leagues or 60 miles in breadth. Being much taken with it, He had an Inclination to stay there some time, and fully inform Himself of the Nature of the Place: but want of Necessaries, and His Ships being leaky prevented that design, and obliged Him to Continue on His Course. On the 18th of August He reached the S[outh]E[ast corner] of the Island, which He called Cabo de Ferrole, afterwards named Point Morante; and on the 19th He lost sight of it.[10]

Columbus in His fourth and last Voyage to America, which was in 1503, being driven from His Settlement at Veraguas, on the Main Continent, by the Indians, intended to return to St. Domingo (on the South side of Hispaniola) which was then settled by the Spaniards: but was forced by the Strong Sea Breezes, and Le[e]ward Currents, so far to the Westward as the Islands of Caimainos. From thence He sailed Northward; on the 5th of May passed by Jardin[11] de la Reignas, or the Queen[']s Garden; which are a great Number of small Islands on the South side of Cuba: and after many difficulties and great dangers, He arrived at an Indian Town on the Coast of Cuba, which was called Mataia; where having got some Refreshments, He sailed for Jamaica, finding it impossible to reach St. Domingo, the Wind continuing to blow hard, and His Ships foul, Worm Eaten, and Leaky. On Midsummer day He put into a Bay,[12] but not finding Water or any Indian Settlements there, He proceeded to a more Convenient Place to the Eastward, inclosed with Rocks, which break of the Sea, and called it Santa Gloria[13] or Holy Glory. Here He run His Ships ashore, not being able to keep them above Water, and laid them close together, fixed in such manner that they could not move. Being in this Posture and Condition, the Water came up almost to the Decks of the Ships, so that He was obliged to build Sheds over them, and on the Poops and Forecastles, to Shelter his Men from the Weather. The Indians, who were a Peaceable, well tempered People came off to them, and brought Provisions; which they trucked for such commodities, as the Spaniards had; and for prevention of differences or disputes, Columbus appointed two men to deal with them, and Equally to divide amongst His Company, the Provisions, they

---

7. Cow Bay. — *Author.*

8. The Mountains on the back or to the Northward, of Liguinea, above which the Blue Mountain appears the largest and highest in the Island. — *Author.*

9. Churchill, *Collection of Voyages and Travels,* 2:559.

10. Ibid., 2:562–63.

11. Called by the English the Jardines. — *Author.*

12. Dry Harbour. — *Author.*

13. Called by the Eng[lish] St. Anns. — *Author.*

This image, an engraving by Richard Johnson (1733?–1793), is taken from *The History of South America: Containing the Discoveries of Columbus, the Conquest of Mexico and Peru, and the Other Transactions of the Spaniards in the New World by the Rev. Mr. Cooper* (London, 1789), following p. 46. It depicts the wreck of Columbus's fleet on June 24, 1503, in a storm on the coast of Jamaica during his last trip to America.

received in Exchange, their own being Spent, or so much damaged, that they were not fit for use.[14]

In this Situation, Columbus chose to remain, rather than make any Settlement on the Shore; because it might give umbrage to the Natives, and He was better able to keep His Men, who were grown turbulent and Refractory under some Regulation. He also forbid them Rambling, or going into the Country; apprehending, that they would commit some disorders, which would give offence to those People. By those means, and His Prudent behaviour in other Respects, the Indians were no ways dissatisfied with their Guests, and freely furnished them with Provisions in great plenty.

But, it being thought necessary to find out some way of Returning to Hispaniola, Columbus consulted with the Caciques and Principal Inhabitants, the most proper means of getting out of that Confinement, and disagreeable Situation: for to stay in hopes of some Ship touching there, would be mere folly, and to think of building a Vessel, was impossible having neither Tools, [n]or Workmen for that purpose. At length it was Resolved to send advice to Hispaniola, of their disaster and unhappy Circumstances, and to desire some Assistance. Accordingly He made choice of two Persons, whom He thought fit for such an Enterprize; and two large

14. Churchill, *Collection of Voyages and Travels*, 2:620–21.

Canoes were provided, and fitted for that purpose; James Mendez de Segura His Secretary,[15] with six Spaniards and ten Indians, were to go in one, and Bartholomew Fiesco[,][16] a Portuguese, with the like Number of Men in the other. Those Canoes after great difficulties and dangers got safe to the West end of Hispaniola, where James Mendez, according to his Directions, went by land to St. Domingo.[17]

When the Messengers were gone, some of Columbus's men, who remained with Him at Jamaica, began to Sicken through hardships and Change of diet; Others grew uneasy and dissatisfied, upon a Suggestion that He intended to Settle there, and had sent those Canoes to St. Domingo, upon some private Affairs, knowing that He was under the displeasure of their Catholick Majestys,[18] through the Malicious Insinuation of His Enemies. Hence arose a Mutiny fomented and Encouraged by two Brothers, whose names were Porras;[19] which in all probability had been the destruction of them all for had it not been prevented by His Prudent and Discreet behaviour: for the Mutineers Siezed upon what necessaries they had occasion for, and some of the Indian[']s Canoes, in which they went towards the East End of the Island, Insulted and Plundered the Inhabitants, wherever they came, telling them they might go to the Admiral for Satisfaction; and in Case He refused it, they might kill Him, which was the best thing they could do, because He was hated by the Spaniards, and the cause of all the Mischiefs, that had befallen them.[20]

The Mutineers also attempted to go over to Hispaniola; but being driven back by the Violence of the Winds, they determined to Wait for a more favourable opportunity; and accordingly staid in the Town of Aoamapique above a month. They afterwards Embarqued twice, but not understanding, how to manage those Canoes without the Assistance of the Indians,

15. James Don Diego Mendez de Segura accompanied Columbus on his final voyage in 1503, arranged the attack on the native chief Quiban of Veragua, and defended his capture of Belem in February 1503. He made the canoe journey to Hispaniola to inform Spanish authorities of Columbus's marooning at St. Ann's Bay, Jamaica, June 24, 1503. Clements R. Markham, *Life of Christopher Columbus* (London, 1892), 251, 263, 264, 267, 271, 272, 280, 286–87, 290.

16. Bartholomew Fiesco also accompanied Columbus on the final voyage and Segura on the canoe journey from Jamaica to Hispaniola.

17. Churchill, *Collection of Voyages and Travels*, 2:620–21.

18. Ferdinand of Aragon (March 10, 1452–January 25, 1516) and Isabella of Castille (April 22, 1451–November 26, 1504).

19. Francis de Francisco Porras was captain of the *Santiago de Palos* during the last voyage of Columbus. Diego Porras, his brother, was royal inspector and accountant. They were both brothers-in-law of the Spanish treasurer, who particularly requested their inclusion in the expedition. They were joined in the mutiny by Juan Sanchez, Pedro de Ledesma, Juan Barba, and about fifty others on January 2, 1504, and rebelled again on May 19. Markham, *Life of Columbus*, 251, 276, 279, 297.

20. Knight drew his long account of this mutiny from Churchill, *Collection of Voyages and Travels*, 2:620–27.

who refused to go with them, they were obliged to return. Being dissappointed in their Designs, they set out by land towards the West end of the
Island, taking whatever they had Occasion for by force, being Superior
in Strength to the Caciques or Indian Princes, through whose Territories
they passed. While they were thus Roving and pillaging the Natives, Columbus carefully attended the Sick; and furnished the rest of His Men, who
remained with Him, with such Necessaries as He had: by which means He
ingratiated Himself, and engaged them in His Interest. He also assiduously
Cultivated a good understanding with the Natives, who were so pleased
with His behaviour, that they readily Supplied him with as much Provisions, as He thought necessary.

At length the Indians began to grow tired of their Guests, when they had
got all their Toys and other Commodities, insomuch that they furnished
them very sparingly with Provisions, scarcely sufficient for their Subsistance. But it pleased God to relieve them after the following manner. Columbus, understanding Astronomy, found, that there would be an Eclipse
of the Moon in three days, & in the first part of the Night, upon which He
sent an Indian of Hispaniola who was with him, that Voyage, to Summons
the Caciques or Principal Inhabitants upon a matter of great Concern,
which He had to Communicate to them. Being met the day on which the
Eclipse was to happen, according to Appointment, He directed the Interpreter to tell them, that the Spaniards were Servants of God, who dwelt in
Heaven, Rewarded the Good and Punished the Wicked. That He Perceiving the misbehaviour of the Spaniards, would not permit them to go over
to Hispaniola, but made them undergo those hardships and dangers, which
all the Island had heard of. That as for the Indians, God was also angry
with them, because they declined furnishing Him with a Sufficient quantity
of Provisions; and had decreed to punish them with Plague and Famine;
to Convince them of the truth of what He said, God was pleased to give
them a manifest token of it, in the Heavens; that they might plainly know
the Punishment was to come from Him. He therefore bid them observe,
that Night, when the Moon appeared, she would put on a bloody Hue and
look Angry, to denote the Punishment, God would inflict on them. When
He had made His Speech, some of them went away in a great fright, and
others laughed at it as an Idle Story or Invention. But the Eclipse beginning soon after the Moon was up, and encreasing as she rose, the Indians
took notice of it; and in a great fright came from all Parts, loaded with Provisions; and entreated Columbus to interceed with God, that they might
not feel the Effects of his Wrath, promising for the future to bring Him as
much Provisions as He required. Columbus Replied, that He would offer
up His Prayers to God, in their behalf, and then shutting Himself up in
His Cabin waited till the Eclipse was at the height, and ready to decrease;
when He came out, and told them, that He had prayed for them, promised
that they would be good and supply Him with Provisions; whereupon God

Taken from *Naakukange Versameling der gernkrddigate zee en land-risen* (Leiden, 1707), this image depicts a conflict between two rival groups during Columbus's third visit to Jamaica, with three indigenous people looking on from a boat in the water.

had forgiven them, and consequently they would see the Moon by degrees return to her usual Complexion. The Indians perceiving the Eclipse to decrease and in a short space of time to disappear gave the Admiral thanks, and returned to their Habitations with great Satisfaction. Nor were they unmindfull of their promise; for they afterwards furnished the Spaniards with Provisions in great plenty; and imagined that the Eclipses, they had formerly Seen, denoted [that] some mischiefs, would befall them, being ignorant of their Causes, and that they hap[pe]ned at certain times, believing it impossible for any man on Earth to know, what was to happen in the Heavens[; they] therefore concluded that God had certainly revealed it to Him.

Columbus being desirous of reducing the Mutineers by fair means, rather than by force, that they might not do any further mischief to the Natives, Sent two Persons, who were most likely to succeed; to acquaint them, that He had received advice from Hispaniola with promises of Relief; and that if they would submit themselves, no further notice should be taken of what had hap[pe]ned. Francis de Porras received the Messengers at some distance, being apprehensive, that they might prevail on some of His Men, and not only sent the Admiral a disdainfull answer, but marched with His followers towards the Ships. When He was within a quarter of a league of them, He halted at an Indian Town called Mayena, where some Years after was a Spanish Colony named Sevill. Columbus, being informed of it, Sent His Brother with Fifty men to persuade, or oblige them to return to their Duty: But they Rejected His Offers, and advanced in order to attack them; upon which a Skirmish ensued; wherein some of the Mutineers were killed, and Francis de Porras and others being taken Prisoners, the rest submitted.

In this Melancholy Situation, and under those distress[ing] Circumstances, Columbus had been a full Year, when a Ship and a Caravell freighted by His Secretary James Mendez, arrived at Jamaica; whereon He, and His Company Embarqued, sailed from Jamaica the 28th of June, and arrived at St. Domingo on Hispaniola the 13th of August following.

From that time to the Year 1509 the Natives remained undisturbed, and were not so much as Visited by the Spaniards.

Herera[21] tells us, that this Island and Puerto Rico were like Hispaniola, as to Plants, living Creatures, Customs, Religion, and Nature of the Inhabitants;[22] and that they used the same Weapons, but were Braver. Peter Martyr[23] describes them to be men of quicker Wit, and better understanding than those of the other Islands, more expert Artificers and Warlike men.[24] And Oviedo says, they were more Industrious, and Resolute, as well as better made men, and Women; and that this Island was several times Invaded by the Natives of Aiti or Haiti now called Hispaniola, who, were always defeated and driven off, the Inhabitants being more dextrous in the use of their bows and Arrows, which were their Weapons in War.[25]

In my Description of those People, their Customs and manner of liv-

---

21. vol. 1. P. 340. —*Author.*

22. Antonio de Herrera y Tordesillas, *The General History of the Vast Continent and Islands of America, Commonly Call'd the West-Indies,* trans. John Stevens, 6 vols. (London, 1725–26), 1:340.

23. Peter Martyr[']s dec. P. 20. —*Author.*

24. Martyr, *De Orbo Novo,* 20.

25. Hernandez Oviedo, also known as Gonzalo Fernández de Oviedo y Valdés (1478–1557), *Historia General y Natural de las Indias,* 19 vols. (Seville, 1535–57). On the apparent absence of any English translation of the general sections of Oviedo's work and the problem of locating any edition with page numbers matching those Knight provides for the information he drew from Oviedo in this part of his study, see note 5 in the preface, above. A modern study, Kathleen Ann Myers and Nina M. Scott, *Fernández de Oviedo's Chronicle of America* (Austin, Texas, 2007), contains English translations of selective parts of natural sections of Oviedo's study but not the general sections.

ing, I shall chiefly follow Don Hernandez de Oviedo, who was Governour of St. Domingo; because He is an Author of great Credit and Reputation among the Spaniards; had been at Jamaica, and resided above twenty years in those Parts, where He made His Observations by order of their Catholick Majesties.[26]

This Island was divided, in the time of the Native Indians, into twelve Provinces; though we cannot ascertain their particular Districts or boundaries; and they were Governed by their Respective chiefs, who were called Caciques, to whom they were very Submissive: but three of them had Superiority over the rest.

Those little Princes Presided in all their Councills, and Commanded in time of War; and were so absolute in their particular Dominions, that they not only took such Women, as they liked best, for Wives, or any thing else they had occasion for without Contradiction; But, when any of them imagined a Town too full of People, He ordered such of them, as He thought fit to remove, and settle in another Place; though He always took care to have the most able men, and best Warriors near Himself. And Notwithstanding Polygamy was not allowed among them; yet those Princes were indulged with three or four Wives; but, the Children of the first only were deemed legitimate and Capable of Succession.

The Native Indians of this Island were of a Dun Colour. They were not so tall, as Europeans, but Robust, Active, and well proportioned. The Men were beardless, and all went naked, Women, as well as the Men, except those that had Husbands; who wore a kind of a Petticoat made of Cotton down to the Calves of their legs: and the Wives or Women belonging to the Caciques, for distinction, wore them as low as their Ancles. Their heads were broad and flat; and their nostrils very large, not Naturally but made so, when they were Infants of about a Week old, by Squeezing or Pressing hard, with one hand behind the head, and the other on the face. They had long black hair, which hung down their Shoulders, and in general had very bad teeth.

The Weapons, they made use of in War, were Bows[,] Arrows and Lances; which they managed with great Dexterity, being early instructed, and constantly Exercised in the use of them.

The Women not only performed all Domestick Offices; but went with their Husbands to War, or to Fish and Hunt. Upon those occasions, when they were obliged to pass broad or deep Rivers, they swam over with their Children on their backs. This will not appear strange, since it is well known, that all the Indians in America, Females as well the Males, are in their Infancy taught to Swim and dive; so that it is in a manner natural to

26. What translated version of Oviedo's work Knight used for his extended discussion of Amerindian culture is unknown but it did not come from the Oviedo selections in Martyr, *De Orbo Novo*, 173–214.

The Dominican missionary and sugar planter Jean Baptiste Labat (1663–1738) drew a large number of illustrations for inclusion in his two-volume *Nouveau voyage aux isles de l'Amerique* (Paris, 1722), including these two images, which are some of the best representations of individual indigenous West Indians. The one on the left, entitled "Caraïbe ou Sauvage des Antisles de l'Amerique," which appears in volume 2, following p. 8, shows a warrior with an arrow, spear, knife, and a crescent-shaped ornament called a caracoli, while the one on the right, entitled "Femme Caraïbe des Antisles de l'Amerique," which appears in volume 2, following p. 74 of the 1742 edition of the same work, depicts an indigenous woman adorned with bracelets, anklets, necklace, and garment or apron. Labat identifies them as Caribs, a term that Spaniards used to apply to a militant and mobile group that raided both indigenous and Spanish settlements throughout the Antilles, including Jamaica. Jamaica having no Labat to provide similar contemporary representations of its native Tainos, Labat's drawings may provide at least a rough approximation of the physique and dress of indigenous Caribbean peoples with whom Spanish Jamaicans had contact.

them, and a common Diversion. It was likewise a Custom among them in general, as well as with their Caciques, that when any of them died, their Land and Goods were given to the Eldest Son, and after His Death, if He had no Son, they went to His Sister[']s Son, and not to the Brother's: because they thought the Consanguinity more certain, and Consequently the Sister[']s Son the Right and proper Heir.

When a Person lay very ill, and His friends had no hopes of His Recovery, they strangled him, to put him out of pain. Some they carried out of their Houses in their Hammocks, which were their Beds, and laid them in Caves, setting bread and Water by them; and never went to see, what became of them. Others, when they were sick, were carried to the Cacique; who ordered whether the Person should be strangled, or not; so great was their Submission to those Princes.

Among the common sort they only kept the heads of those that died; But their Caciques, and Principal Persons were preserved in the following manner. They opened and dried the Deceased at a Fire; and then Swathed him very hard from head to foot, with a Roller made of Cotton; that He might be kept entire. They then laid Him in a Cave or Vault, with a Table and Stool, His Arms, and such other things as He was fond of; also Provisions, Fruit and Liquor, and the Wife, He loved best, or She that would shew her love to Him above the rest, was Shut up with Him.

In some Parts of the Mountains there are Natural Caves, where they usually reposited their dead; and others w[h]ere they laid the Heads of the Common Sort: but often they made Vaults for that purpose in the following manner. They dug a large hole; and round the sides drove piles of Wood so close, that the Earth could not fall in; the tops were arched in the same manner, and then Covered with Earth.

When they interred a Cacique, or Person of Distinction, they invited all their Neighbours; and for 14 days or more, Men and Women Sung Mournfull Ditties over the Place of Interrment. The most skilfull among them dictated, and the rest Sung after Him, what He said; wherein they related the life, Works, and Actions of the Deceased; His manner of Government, the Victories, He had gained, and whatever else, He performed, that was Worthy of Remembrance.

They were of Opinion, that after Death they went to a Pleasant Valley; where they should find their Friends and Predecessors, have Wives, and Enjoy all sorts of Pleasures.

They had many Towns in this Island, which consisted of 250 or 300 Houses; and in some of them several Families Resided. Most of them were Situate near the Sea, and those in the Country near the Rivers, for the Convenience of Fishing, and Swimming, wherein they were very Expert, by reason of the Custom among them from their Infancy to plunge themselves daily in the Sea or Rivers; so that they spent great part of their time in, or upon the Water, in Swimming or Fishing, which was their greatest

Diversion. Some of those Towns were Regularly built. But in general the Houses were scattered, and not Contiguous, but made after the following manner. They put Posts into the ground at four or five feet distance, According to the bigness of the Structure; at the top they fixed other Posts, and laid upon them long Sticks, formed at the top like a Pavillion; over which they laid Canes or Reeds and Covered them with thatch, or Palm leaves. The sides and Ends were likewise closed up with Canes or Reeds, stuck in the Ground, and tied with Withs, which made them strong binding, and permanent. There was also, in the middle of the House, a long Post fixed in the ground, to which they tied the Sticks, that formed the Roof.

As to the Houses of the Caciques, and Principal Men, they were Built of the same Materials, and after the same manner, but, larger, higher, and long, not round, like the Others.

Their Beds they called Hamaca and from thence by us they are called Hammocks; which were made of Cotton, partly wove and partly Network; about two Yards and a half long, and two Yards broad; at the Ends they fixed a Cord made also of Cotton; which they fast[e]ned to the Wall plates of their Houses, or in the Fields between two Trees.

They had no Religion, Temples or Sacrifices. But a Set of Men, who acted in the Capacity of Physicians and Priests, or rather Conjurers; and by their Artifices gained such an Influence, that they led them into many Superstitious and Ridiculous Customs, pretending to Cure the Sick, by blowing on them, mumbling some words between their Teeth and such like Exterior Actions. They were called Buhiti and held in great Veneration, for by their Craft and Subtilty they persuaded those Simple People, that their *Cemis* spoke to them with great familiarity, and told them of things to Come. Their *Cemis* were Images made of Wood or Clay, of Various Figures, and painted some of them in a frightful manner. When any of them had been Sick, and Recovered, the Buhiti persuaded them, that they obtained their health, by their Intercession with those *Cemis*; and when things did not happen, as they had foretold; they made them believe their *Cemi* had changed His mind for Reasons best known to Himself.

When the Caciques enquired of them concerning their Warrs[,] increase or Scarcity of the Fruits of the Earth, Sickness or Health, they entered into the House, where their *Cemis* were reposited, and snuffed up their Nostrills the powder of a Herb, they called *Cohobba*, which had such Effect on them, that it immediately took away their Senses, and made them rage and foam like Lunatick Persons. When the Priest came to Himself, He embraced the Knees of the Cacique, holding down His head, in which posture, He continued sometime, and then raised himself astonished like one just awakened or recovered out of a deep trance, looking up to the Heavens, muttering some unintelligible words to Himself. The Cacique, and His Principal Men, (for none of the common Sort were admitted to those

Mysteries) with great joy gave notice, that He was returned to them; and had conversed with their *Cemis*, and demanded of Him, what he had Seen and heard. He then declared to them, what He said was Revealed to Him concerning the Question proposed, as to Victory or Destruction, Famine or Plenty, Sickness, or Health. They often fasted, and sometimes eat nothing but Herbs, and cleansed themselves from outward impurities, especially when they undertook the Cure of a Cacique or Great Man.

When a sick Person died, and His kindred imagined, it was through the negligence or Carelessness of the Priest or Buhiti in not fasting as He ought to have done, or administering proper Remedies, they revenged themselves by beating Him severely, and sometimes putting Him to Death.

Every Cacique had a House at some distance from the Town, where those Ceremonies were performed; and others, which they suggested, tended to the Service of their *Cemies*. They likewise gave names to them, which were those of their Fathers or some of their Ancestors, and usually shewed more Devotion and Respect to one, than Another: and suggested among the Common People, that those *Cemis* often spoke, and Conversed with them.

This had some Resemblance of Idolatry; though it was nothing more than a design or fraud in the Caciques and Priests to keep the People in Subjection, and render themselves absolute. For a hollow Cane was fixed to the Statue, that reached to the Corner of the House; where a Person lay concealed, and Spoke, whatever the Cacique had directed, by which means they drew what Tribute, and Exacted whatever they thought fit, from those Credulous People. The Secret being discovered by the Spaniards, the Cacique Earnestly entreated them not to speak of it to His Subjects, or Country men; because He kept them in order, and Obedience by those means.

Those Caciques had likewise three Stones; to which they, as well as the Common People, paid a sort of Devotion, for they said, that the One forwarded the growth of Corn and other grain the second made their Wives be delivered without Pain; and the third procured Rain, or fair Weather, as their Occasions Required.

Near every Town a large space of Ground was intrenched or fenced on all sides, only a door place or Passage to enter in. Benches or Seats were made of Stone or Earth, round the inside for the Spectators; and at the other end a wooden Stool finely wrought for the Cacique to Sit upon. Here they assembled on their Festivals, and other Publick Occasions, played at Batey, Danced and Sung their *Areytos*.

The Play of Batey consisted of an Equal Number on Each side, like our Bandy without Chaces; and they would touch the Ball in a very Active manner, with all Parts of their Body without making use of their hands. The Balls were made of a Gum, and the juice of Herbs, which they boiled into a sort of Paste, and formed round fit for the purpose. When the Balls were dried; they were somewhat spungy, and would rebound more than those made in Europe of leather, tho[ugh] they were heavier.

In Dancing they were very Active and shewed more Agility than Europeans.

It was a Custom with their Caciques and Principal men to commit their Children to the Care of their Priests, or Buhiti; who Instructed them in their Antiquities, and to rehearse the Actions of their Ancestors in Peace and War; which was the only means, they had, of transmitting any Remarkable transactions to Posterity. Those Circumstances were composed in a sort of Ballads, which they called Areytos, and were sung on all Publick Occasions, to their Musick or Instrument which was made of the Shell of a Fish, and called Mag; and another Instrument which was made of a hollow piece of Wood about two feet long, and one in breadth; the part on which they Struck was like a Smith[']s Pincers; and the other a Club, with a long Neck. This when played upon, was heard at a league's distance. The Prime Men Sung those Areytos on Publick Occasions, and played on their Musick, which they were taught in their Infancy.

The Men, as well as the Women, frequently painted themselves, with Balls made of the Kernells[27] of a Cod, that grew on a Plant called Bixa; which were mixed up and made supple with certain Gums; and painted a fine Vermillion Colour.

The Women, to adorn themselves and appear to advantage, painted therewith, when they were to be Married, or against their Feasts, Areytos or Dancing.

The Men also painted themselves therewith in the same manner upon those Occasions; but when they went to War, in different Figures, to make themselves appear terrible to their Enemies.

When they were free of Warrs and intestine Divisions, which sometimes hap[pe]ned among them, or were not ingaged in Cultivating and Planting their Lands, they went about from one Province to another, Exchanging of Commodities or Provisions.

At other times they employed themselves in Fishing, or hunting, making Bows, Arrows, and Launces; also in Planting and gathering of Cotton; which they made use of for Hammocks; and upon other Occasions, or in making of Mats, Baskets, and Pots.

The Women were not only employed in Managing their Houses but in making and Weaving their Hamocks, Cords and Petticoats. The Crime, they seemed to detest, and have in the greatest abhorrence, was Thieving, or Robbing, which they punished with the utmost Severity.

The common Manner was by impaling the Thief or Robber; or driving a Stake through Him, [or] fast[e]ning him to a Tree, and leaving Him in

27. Anatto. — *Author.*

The Taino people who occupied Jamaica when the Spaniards arrived had, during
an almost thousand-year residence, turned it into one of the more densely popu-
lated Caribbean islands, with settlements on every coast. On the more level areas,
they had fields and gardens on which they cultivated cassava, maize, sweet potato,
and several fruits, which they exchanged at local markets. Reproduced from *Naakukange Versameling der gernkrddigate zee en land-risen* (Leiden, 1707), this image of
an indigenous market illustrates the range of commercial activity in indigenous and
early Spanish Jamaica.

that miserable Condition. And it was an Established Custom among them,
that no body should interceed for the Delinquent on Penalty of the same
Punishment.

Near the Towns they commonly had their Plantations, where they
planted Maiz[e] and other Grain and Fruits of the Earth, which they Cultivated and Manured in the following manner.

They brought into the Field great quantities of dry Reeds and brush;
which they placed in heaps at 4 or 5 feet distance; and when the Field was
covered therewith, they set them on Fire, taking Care, that the whole was
well burnt. They then spread the Ashes all over the Land; and when they
had by those means cleared it of Weeds, and levelled it, they made a Hole
in the Ground with a pointed Stick, into which they put 4 or 5 grains of
Maiz[e] or other Seed, and then with their feet covered the holes with

A seafaring people, the Tainos supplemented agricultural produce with food they harvested from the sea. This image, entitled *Von seltzamer Fischeren der Indianer*, is from Wolffgang Richter, *Neundter und Letzter Theil Americae* (Frankfurt am Main, 1601), part 3, plate 1. It illustrates indigenous modes of fishing in the West Indies, with men in boats or riding on bundles of reeds catching fish in nets and whales by climbing onto their backs, hammering wooden plugs into their blowholes, and using ropes to drag them onto the beach for butchering. The artist mistakenly shows the whales with two blowholes.

Earth loosly. The grain they put into the Water some hours before they planted it.

The Maiz[e] they Eat when it was young either boiled or Roasted. But they commonly ground it, after it was full ripe, and dried, between two Stones into flour, which they dressed Several ways.

When they planted *Yuca* to make *Cazavi*, they Manured the Ground in the same manner, only with this difference, they turned the ground into heaps, about 8 or 10 feet in Circumference, flat at the top, and raised about 18 inches with a narrow passage between. In every heap they made 6 or 8 holes a Span deep, wherein they put the plant.

The Indians of this Island, as well as in Hispaniola, when they intended to go in Search of Gold, refrained from Women, and eat nothing but Cazavi or Bread and Water for twenty days; because they were so Supersti-

Tainos were also hunters. Drawn from *Naakukange Versameling der gernkrddigate zee en land-risen* (Leiden, 1707), this image shows indigenous Jamaicans hunting parrots, presumably not for food but for feathers with which to adorn their clothing.

tious to believe, they should not otherwise be fortunate in meeting with Gold, at least with any quantity. In this they seem to imitate the Custom and Manner of the Arabians, who likewise abstain from Women thirty days before they go to gather Frankincense.

They also had a Ceremony in Smoking an Herb, which is a kind of perfume, described to be something like *Henbane*, and performed in the following manner.

The Herb being dried, and set on fire, they Snuffed the Smoke up their Nostrills through a hollow Reed or Cane, until they became intoxicated and Senseless; they were then laid in their Hamocks, or left upon the Ground, until they came to themselves. This was done for the Cure of weak, and Infirm Persons, or to make those in health more Strong, and Vigorous; for when they awoke, they found themselves Refreshed, Agile and lively: and they commonly took those perfumes after any fatigue or hard labour. They carefully cultivated this Herb for that purpose; and said, it was thrown down from Heaven for their Benefit and Service.

In this Simple, inoffensive manner the Natives lived, before they were Subdued by the Spaniards. They were contented with the Gifts of Nature, and happy in the Enjoyment of their Liberty; they Seldom had any differences among themselves nor fell at Variance with their Neighbouring Provinces; being a mild, well tempered People; though they were some times disturbed, and Invaded, as I have observed, by the Inhabitants of Hispaniola, who were always defeated in their Attempts.

The Spanish Writers differ as to their Number: some computing them at 60,000, and others at 5 or 600,000 Men, Women and Children. Peter Martyr, says, that the Number of Indians on Hispaniola were 1,200,000:[28] and Bartho[lomew] De la Casas, Bishop of Chiapo, says, that there were on Puerto Rico, Hispaniola, and Jamaica, two Millions.[29] Indeed considering the Number of Whites and Blacks, which are now on the Island of Jamaica and cannot be less than 130,000, though not the twentieth part Settled, and that great part of the present Product is for Foreign Consumption; whereas

28. Martyr, *De Orbo Novo.*

29. Bartholomew de Las Casas, bishop of Chiapo (1474–1566), witnessed Columbus's return from the first voyage and saw his father go on the second voyage. Accompanying Ovando to Hispaniola, he there joined the Dominican order and became noted for his attempts to ameliorate the conditions and protest the mistreatment of Native Americans. He was well acquainted with Columbus and many of his associates, had access to records of early exploration and colonization, and is responsible for the preservation of many appertaining documents. He began writing his *History of the Indies* in Hispaniola in 1527 and completed it in 1561, having returned to Europe in 1547 and taken up residence at the monastery of San Gregorio at Valladolid in 1550. Most of Knight's references from Las Casas appear to be from his *Brief Relation of the Destruction of the Indies* of which there were several English editions. Knight may well have used the version included in *An Account of the First Voyages and Discoveries of the Spaniards in America* (London, 1699), 18. Nigel Griffin, trans. and ed., *Bartolomé de las Casas: A Short Account of the Destruction of the Indies* (New York, 1992), provides a modern translation.

the Indians planted nothing more, than Provisions necessary for *their* Subsistance, it may reasonably be imagined, that their Number was not less
than 500,000: for Columbus describes, not only the Coast all round the
Island to be full of Towns, and very Populous; but the inland parts of the
Country and even the Mountains.[30]

The Spaniards, to Colour their Barbarous and Inhuman treatment of
those Innocent People, Accuse them of many Enormous Crimes; and represent them as the most deceitfull and Treacherous People, that ever lived.
But that Worthy man Bartho[lomew] de la Cassas before mentioned, who
was an Eye Witness of their Cruelties, hath manifested the same, in what
He has published and made known to the World; for He Computes, that
they destroyed by those means, above five Millions of Indians, on the Islands and Continent of America. In the Island of Jamaica, He says, the
Spaniards distinguished themselves in the most Inhuman Actions, Committed against the Inhabitants—killing some, burning, roasting, and
throwing others to be devoured by Wild and fierce Dogs; and Oppressed
the rest, by obliging them to work in their Mines, and do such other heavy
labour, as in a few years put an end to that unhappy, though Innocent
People.[31]

Peter Martyr says, it grieved Him to relate, that those simple, Poor Men,
who were not brought up to labour, daily perished through intolerable
hardship, being Obliged to work in the Mines; and do all sorts of drudg-
ery. That they were become desperate, many killed themselves, and others
had no manner of regard to the procreation of Children insomuch that the
Women, to prevent Conception, used Medicinal Herbs; that they might
not bring forth an Offspring to be Slaves to the Spaniards. By those means,
He says, their Numbers were so diminished, that He could not relate it,
without the greatest abhorrence.[32]

In another place[33] He says—the miserable Inhabitants, whose help the
Spaniards used in gathering of Gold, are brought to a very small number;
Consumed from the beginning by Cruel means, but many more by Famine, for they destroyed the Roots of the *Jucca*, wherewith they made bread,
and Ceased to Sow Maiz[e] and other Grain: and many others died like
rotten Sheep with the foul Disease. And to speak truly the greedy desire
of Gold, was the true Cause of their Vexing those poor Wretches to such
a degree by Searching, Sifting and gathering of it that they were in a few
Years wholly Extirpated.[34]

---

30. Churchill, *Collection of Voyages and Travels*, 2:558–59, 562–63.
31. Las Casas, *Account of the First Voyages and Discoveries of the Spaniards in America*.
32. Martyr, *De Orbo Novo*.
33. Martyr dec. P. 172.—*Author*.
34. Martyr, *De Orbo Novo*, 172.

Oviedo says,[35] the Island of Jamaica was well peopled, when it was first discovered by Christopher Columbus.[36] But from the year 1530 to 1535 there were so very few, that in His Opinion, they did not exceed 200 Men, Women and Children: so that the Planters were obliged to bring Indians from the Continent and other Parts, to work their Mines. The reason of this great diminution, or rather Extirpation, He ascribes to the following Causes.

1. That abundance of them perished by the extream hard labour, the Spaniards put them to in the Mines, and upon other Occasions, without allowing them sufficient food for their Subsistence.

2. That, when the Indians by command of the Governour, were divided among the Officers, and Planters, their treatment was so cruel, that they sunk under it for upon the least fault, or misbehaviour, they were punished with such Severity, that many of them died upon the Spot. And as their Masters were Favourites or Men of Interest at Court, no notice was taken of it. The King's Farmers were also very Inhuman, in not taking care of those, that were Sick: for upon the least indisposition they were killed, thrown into the Lakes and Rivers, or burned alive.

This Barbarous usage obliged many to run away from their Masters, and to make away with themselves by Poison or other means. Though, says He, I can[no]t but say, that they were Idle naturally, Vicious, Liars, and basely inclined.

3. There was a Pestilential Pox among them, which carried off great numbers: so that whole Families were found dead in the Morning in their Beds by this Distemper. As our Physicians had no knowledge of this sort of Illness, they could not apply any Effectual Remedy for the Cure; and there being so many Carcasses in the Fields unburied, the Air was so infected, that many of the Europeans died; till at length, by Continual Application, they were all buried, or thrown into the Sea.

4. Several thousands of the most able Indians were carried to Terra Firma, to Assist the Spaniards in their Conquests: and particularly in that unfortunate Expedition of Don Francisco Garay in 1523:[37] where most or all of them perished.

These Accounts, However shocking, and almost incredible to the Pro-

---

35. Oviedo, P. 27.—*Author.*

36. Oviedo, *Historia General y Natural de las Indias*, 27. No translated edition of this work has been found that matches the pages Knight cites here and subsequently in this chapter.

37. Don Francisco de Garay (?–1527) was sent by Columbus to search for gold in the River Hayna in Hispaniola in 1495. Around 1514, he became Spanish governor of Jamaica, arriving on May 25, 1515, and began the process of settlement of the island and enslavement of native Jamaicans. In 1518, he sent an expedition to explore the Yucatan and in 1520 produced a map of Pineda's discoveries around the Gulf of Mexico. Markham, *Life of Columbus*, 177–78; Frank Cundall and Joseph L. Pieter, *Jamaica under the Spanish* (Kingston, Jamaica, 1919), 2–10.

Taken from *Naakukange Versameling der gernkrddigate zee en land-risen* (Leiden, 1707), this shows a skirmish between indigenous and Spanish forces on the shore of Jamaica, when Juan de Esquivel led the Spanish conquest of Jamaica in 1509.

fessors of Christianity, or others, who have any Sense or Compassion of the Affliction and Misery of Innocent Human Creatures, cannot be doubted; Since they are attested by men of great Credit, and Reputation, among the Spaniards; though the last mentioned Author endeavours to Soften the matter, by Representing the Indians as naturally Idle, basely inclined &c. But Supposing this to be Fact, certainly those Poor People cannot reasonably be condemned, or Reproached on that account because the Spaniards had not only unjustly deprived them of their Native Possessions, but what must be much dearer to every part of Mankind, Liberty, and imposed on them insupportable hardships, and the worst of Slavery. As to the Pestilential Pox, which He says, carried off whole Families in a Night, this could not be for want of Knowledge of the Distemper, or the method of Cure: because this Author Himself in P[ages] 21, 22, gives an Account of that Disease being among the Indians, before the Discovery of America by Columbus; and their manner of Curing it, with *Guaicum* and *Palo Santo*, and that it was first brought into Spain by some of His Officers and Seamen, from whence it spread, by degrees, all over Europe.[38]

The true Reason then seems to be, those poor Wretches were so

38. Oviedo, *Historia General y Natural de las Indias*, 21–22.

harrassed and distressed, that life was become Burthensome and painfull, which made them neglect the necessary means of preservation. For by all Accounts great numbers of them poisoned or Starved themselves, and otherwise made an end of a miserable Being.

As Cuba, Hispaniola and Jamaica, were Similar in all other matters, I think it Cannot be doubted, that there is Gold Mines in this Island; not only from thence, but from Several passages in *Oviedo* and Other Spanish Authors. Therefore what a late Writer[39] of our own Nation observes Concerning the first of these three Islands is Applicable to them all.[40]

The true Reason, in all probability, why the Spaniards destroyed with so little Pity such a Vast number of People, was a Covetous desire of possessing the whole Island, and all its real and supposed Riches. For at this time they fancied, that the Parts of the Island possessed by the Natives, were excessively Rich in Gold, of which while, they suffered them to live, the Spaniards did really receive a large Share.

But, since the Extirpation of the Indians, there has been very little; and at present there is scarce any at all to be found which some would make a Judgment on the Spaniards for their Cruelty.

For my part, I think the matter easily unriddled—the Gold, I suppose, was taken out of the Rivers, which required not only a great deal of time and Patience; but many hands and a perfect knowledge of the places, where it was to be found. This Accounts for the loosing that precious Metal; which shews how weak a point of Policy this Doctrine of Extirpations really is.

Jamaica was at first Granted by the Crown of Spain to Alonso de Ojedo[41] and James Nicuessa;[42] who had Obtained the Government of Uraba, or the

---

39. See the *Compleat History of Span[ish] Amer[ica,]* P. 159.—*Author.*

40. John Campbell, *The Compleat History of Spanish America* (London, 1742), 159.

41. Alonzo de Ojeda (1473?–1515) was born of a well-to-do family of Cueja and was a boy page to the Duke of Medina Celi. He fought to expel the Moors from Granada, accompanied Columbus on his second voyage, explored the interior of Hispaniola, and was in charge of the Fort of San Tomas, which he defended from the Indian Caonabo, whom he captured. Ojeda commanded his own voyage in 1499 (accompanied by Amerigo Vespucci), discovered the inland gulf of Maracaibo, and undertook a second voyage in 1502 to take the governorship of Coquivacoa, or Venezuela, but instead settled at Santa Cruz where his crew mutinied though he was later freed. Made Viscount of Jamaica in 1507 and governor of Nueva Andalusia in 1509, he suffered defeat by the Turbaco Indians and died in poverty in Hispaniola after Juan de Esquivel, governor of Jamaica, removed him from his posts. Markham, *Life of Columbus,* 144, 149, 151, 155, 160–61, 174–75, 230, 239–40, 244–48, 310–11.

42. Diego de Nicuesa was also appointed Viscount of Jamaica in 1507 and chosen by someone named Fonseca to colonize the mainland as governor of Castilla del Oro. He avenged Ojeda's defeat by massacring the Turbaco Indians but his settlement attempts also failed when in 1511 seventy of his complement of six hundred died at Nombre de Dios and themselves were rescued by the governor of Darien, Vasco Nunez de Balboa. Nicuesa was refused a reception at Darien and never heard of again. Markham, *Life of Columbus,* 258, 310–13; Cundall, *Chronological Outlines of Jamaica History,* 2.

As English people began to interest themselves in Spanish activities in America increasingly after 1570, they seized on Spanish reports about the mistreatment of indigenous people in the New World to justify mounting a challenge to Spanish hegemony there. In an attempt to picture an actual event, this image, entitled *Naaukeurige versameling der gedenk-waardigste zee en land-reysen na Oost en West-Indiën . . . zedert het jaar 1524 tot 1526*, shows Spanish soldiers storming a palisaded indigenous settlement named Turbaco on the Spanish mainland in present-day Colombia and setting it on fire as women and children flee for their lives. On this occasion, an expedition, led by Alonso de Ojeda, in retaliation for the death of Juan de la Cosa by poison arrow, massacred an entire village. Whether Juan de Esquivel, who conquered Jamaica, pursued similar tactics to defeat its Taino inhabitants is unclear. This image derives from the special title page for Antonio de Herrera y Tordesillas, *Aankomst van Jean d'Ezquebel, ter bevolking van Jamaica, door den ammiraal Diego Kolumbus, van Hispaniola derwaards gezonden, in den jaare 1510* (Leiden, 1706), a Dutch excerpt and translation of the author's *Historia general de los hechos de los Castellanos* (Madrid, 1601).

Continent beyond Carthagena, and this Island was given to them, that they might be able to furnish themselves with Provisions. But Don James Columbus,[43] the Son and Heir of Christopher Columbus, who was then at St.

43. Don Diego Columbus (1478–February 23, 1526) was born in Lisbon, the eldest son of Christopher. Leaving Lisbon with his father in 1484 to become page to Prince Juan of Castille and then to Queen Isabella, after his father's death he fought for and received some of his father's titles and privileges, becoming admiral of the ocean sea. He was appointed governor of the Indies on August 9, 1508. He embarked for Hispaniola in 1509 and later that year sent

Domingo, resented those Grants, especially Jamaica; obstructed their Designs as much as He could, and to dissappoint them sent John de Esquibell with 70 men in 1509, to make a Settlement.[44]

The Natives, who admitted Columbus and His Men, as Guests, when they were driven there by Extremity, and treated them with all the Hospitality in their power; Yet when the Spaniards came with a Design of fixing themselves and by force of Arms to get in their Possession great part of the Island, they disputed every inch of Ground with great Intrepidity.

At length [the natives'] being obliged to Submit[,] John de Esquibell began to settle; and when He divided the Indians among His Men, intending to make them Work, they fled to the Mountains. But He having, in the pursuit, killed many of them, among which were some of their Caciques, and Principal Men, the rest Submitted, and were Employed in planting Cotton and Provisions, which former grows better in that Island, than in any other; for there was very little Gold, whereas the Profit of the Cotton was considerable. The account, He gave of the Island, was so agreeable, that He soon had a Supply of Men, Provisions and Cattle for Breed; and He began the Foundation of a Town, which He called[45] *Melilla:* But, not liking the Situation, He soon after removed, and settled Seville, in that part of the Island, which is now called St. Anns.

Oviedo says, that the Planters could never find any Mines of Gold in Jamaica, till those in the Year 1508, which were discovered by an Indian Woman to a Spanish Captain whom She respected.[46] Upon which the said Captain sent some of the Gold to Hispaniola, and desired Don Diego Columbus, the second Admiral, to send him some more Provisions and People. He [Columbus] thereupon appointed Don Juan de Esquibell, His Lieutenant Governour of Jamaica and sent with Him Sufficient Forces to put the whole Island in Subjection to their Catholick Majesties. And, as

---

Esquivel on a successful mission to take Jamaica from Ojedo and Nicuesa, which he did in November 1509. Frequently having to return to Spain to defend his conduct after enemies conspired against him, Columbus never lost favor and Charles V bestowed on him his father's coveted title of viceroy. His estate was the scene of America's first recorded slave rebellion on December 27, 1522. Returning again to Spain to defend his actions in 1523, he died there. Frank Cundall, *Chronological Outlines of Jamaica History,* 2–3.

44. Don Juan de Esquivel was one of the earliest European settlers of Jamaica. Under Don Diego Columbus's instructions, he captured Jamaica from Ojedo and Nicuesa in November 1509 and became the island's governor. He founded the town of New Seville on the old Arawak Indian site of Maima in 1510, though it was later abandoned for St. Jago de la Vega. He also founded Oristan (Bluefields) and Puerto Esquivel (Old Harbor). An enquiry into his governorship in 1510 exonerated him, but the Crown removed him in 1514 or 1515. Markham, *Life of Columbus,* 306–7.

45. At or near Montego Bay. — *Author.*

46. Oviedo, *Historia General y Natural de las Indias.* The translated version of Oviedo's passages here and in the remainder of Knight's discussion of Spanish Jamaica down to the 1550s has not been found.

this Governour was a well disposed Gentleman, He never made use of force of Arms, but when occasion and necessity required it. He divided the Island into Provinces and Districts, and Established such Laws, as were agre[e]able to Reason, and the Spanish Institutions. He built the Town of Seville, where He Resided and all Causes were heard and determined. His Government indeed was dependant, being held by Deputation or Commission, from the Governour of Hispaniola. However, He acted with Supreme Power, and behaved in so prudent a manner, that He gained the good will and Esteem of all the Inhabitants.[47]

The Island was so well Peopled in the second Year of His Government, that He was obliged to build Oristan; and several little Villages near the Mountains. The fruitful Soil and wholesome Air of the Country, the desire of Riches, and the affable behaviour of the Governour, invited several of the Richest Planters to settle there.

Seville was built on the North side of the Island; and Oristan on the South side of it. The Principal Church was at Seville with the Title of an Abbey, and in the time of Peter Martyr was a very Rich preferment.

This Gentlemen died much Regretted in Jamaica at the beginning of the fourth Year of His Government, and was buried at Seville. But, however just His Character may be in other Respects, yet according to the best accounts, which can be collected from all the Spanish Historians of America, the first and greatest Massacre of the Indians, was in His time; whether by His Direction, permission or Connivance, is not material, and in my Opinion, He is answerable for the Blood of many thousands of those Poor, Inoffensive People, who were destroyed or made away with themselves, through Oppression and Hardships.

He was Succeeded by a Gentleman named Perca;[48] but He was soon recalled for His Cruelty, and Misbehaviour: and [James] *Camargo*,[49] a Gentleman of Burgos, was appointed Lieutenant Governour in His Stead.

At this time Jamaica was very much improved and so Rich and Populous, that they carried on a considerable Trade with Hispaniola, and the other Islands; insomuch that several Gentlemen applied, and made Interest for the Government: among them was the Chief Magistrate of St. Domingo, named Don *Francisco de Garay*, who had some Settlements there; and proposed to farm all that His Catholick Majesty had in Jamaica.

An Agreement was accordingly made at Valladolid, and a great number of Cattle, Plants &c. were sent over; also Tradesmen and a great quantity of Provisions and other Necessary Stores. His Majesty also gave Him a letter

47. A much neglected subject, Jamaica's history under the Spanish may be followed in Francisco Morales Padrón, *Spanish Jamaica*, trans. Patrick E. Bryan (Kingston, Jamaica, 2003).

48. Perca. Garay seems to have succeeded Esquivel while one Pero Cano (the closest reference found to "Perca") succeeded Manuel de Rojas in 1534, de Rojas having succeeded Gil Gonzales de Avila who had succeeded Garay.

49. Captain James Carmago was a deputy of Garay.

to the Admiral, Don Diego Columbus, recommending the Appointment of Him Lieutenant Governour of Jamaica; which was accordingly done.

Francisco Garay, soon after His Arrival, sent Captain James Camargo with two Ships to make Discoveries; and they found Panuco, which is Fifty leagues to the Westward of Villa Rica. But, though Grijalva had been there before, yet He assumed the Discovery to Himself. In the Second year of His Government, He sent His Catholick Majesty such a present of Gold, that every Body was Surprised at it, and the most Skilful in that Metal, upon an Essay, which was made, declared it to be as good, as any in the World. At the same time He offered to Conquer, and plant Colonies at Panuco at His own Cost, provided He could have a Certain tract of land, and the Title of Adelantado, with full Jurisdiction, powers and other privileges; which were granted Him the year following vizt. in 1519. Accordingly He fitted out, and sent from Jamaica, three Caravells, which carried one hundred and Fifty Sea and Landmen, seven Horses, and some Guns, under the Conduct and direction of Capt[ain] Camargo. But they unhappily miscarried, being defeated by the Natives, who killed Eighteen of His men and the Seven Horses; the rest retreated aboard their Ships in such disorder, that they were obliged to return for want of Provisions, and afterwards lost two of the Caravells, and many other Men; so that very few returned in Safety.

In the mean time, the Affairs of Jamaica were in a prosperous and flourishing Condition, insomuch that they loaded several Ships Yearly with Hydes, Sugar, Indigo, Cotton, Cocoa and other Products; also some *Gold* from the *Mines:* and brought in return from Spain, such necessaries, as they wanted.

This Gentleman [Garay], though His Government and Possessions in this Island, were so advantagious, that He grew immensely Rich, yet not Contented therewith, but desirous of making further, and greater Acquisitions, Resolved on a third Expedition to *Panuco;* and to go in Person, in order to make a Conquest and Settlement there, pursuant to the Grant, He obtained of His Catholick Majesty; which proved fatal to Him, as well as to the Island, by the loss of a great number of Inhabitants, whom He carried with Him. Accordingly in 1523, being the fourth year of His Government, He fitted out nine Ships, and two Brigantines; wherein embarked Eight hundred and fifty Spaniards, beside Indians, with a train of Artillery, two hundred fire Arms, three hundred Cross bows, one hundred and Forty four horses, a great Quantity of Provisions, and other Necessaries. Several of the most noted Commanders, went with Him; and they sailed from Jamaica the 18th of June in the same Year, and arrived at Rio de la palmao, on St. James day.[50]

50. At Xagua, en route to Panuco, he learned that Cortes was in command and returned to Jamaica.

But as that Expedition has no further relation to Jamaica, I shall only observe, that the Island must needs have been very Populous, at that time, to be able to raise so great a Number of Men on such an Occasion, and that their miscarriage was a fatal Stroke to its further Improvement and Settlement, as they were defeated, and most of the Men were killed or died, so that very few, if any, returned to Jamaica. Garay was taken Prisoner and Carried to Mexico, where He died in a miserable manner. But notwithstanding the Expence He was at, in fitting out so considerable an Armament, He left behind Him a very great Estate in lands, Cattle, and two Sugar Mills.

The Island was afterwards governed by Don Diego Columbus: Don Luis Columbus,[51] and a Relation of theirs, Successively:[52] But the latter not being properly qualified, the Governour of Hispaniola was Impowered to appoint a L[ieutenant] Governour, and a Treasurer, to manage the Affairs of the Island.[53]

In the Year 1533 there were so many abuses Committed in Jamaica by the Governour, and the Superior Officers, that His Catholick Majesty was obliged to send over a Person of Distinction in the Law, whose name was Don Gil Gonzales Davila,[54] with full Powers not only to inspect into, and redress them, but to displace the Delinquents; and Seize their Estates.

In His Passage He touched at St. Domingo, to consult the Royal Officers about such Measures as were proper and necessary, in order to be assisted and Supported in the due Execution of His orders.

51. Don Luis Columbus (1522–1572), son and heir of Diego Columbus. Like his father he did not receive the full measure of his inheritance, and his mother, Vice-Queen Maria de Toledo, fought for his succession until her death in 1549. Cardinal Garcia de Loaysa forced Luis to renounce his viceroyalty and other titles on September 8, 1536, in exchange for an annuity of ten ducats, a fiefdom in Jamaica, and the dukedom of Veragua. He did, though, retain the title "Admiral of the Ocean Sea" and in 1540 went to Hispaniola as captain-general. He returned to Spain in 1551 and in 1556 lost his Jamaica fief, had his pension reduced, and soon afterward was banished for bigamy to Oran, where he died.

52. Possibly Diego Columbus, nephew of Luis and son of Cristoval, who married his cousin, Luis's daughter Felipa, thus becoming the Second Duke of Veragua. Cundall, *Chronological Outlines of Jamaica History.*

53. The lieutenant-governor was Pero Cano (see note 48, above). The treasurer was Pedro de Mazuelo, who arrived in Jamaica in December 1514 and began organizing the king's property in advance of the arrival of Garay. Mazuela was made alderman of Seville in 1520, but he fell out of favor with successive governors and had his property seized by Manuel de Rojas in 1536. He accused Rojas and Antonio de Garay, son of the late governor, of fraud and criticized the decision of the king to give the Jamaican fiefdom to Luis Columbus. He requested removal to Mombre de Dios, but nothing is known of him after this time. Cundall, *Chronological Outlines of Jamaica History.*

54. Don Gil Gonzales de Avila (?–June 1534) was a kinsman of Pedrarias Davila, the founder of Panama and European discoverer of Lake Nicaragua. His commission, dated February 4, 1533, entitled him to appoint a lieutenant-governor if Maria of Toledo had not already done so and to inspect the accounts of all Jamaican officers.

Upon His arrival at Jamaica, many grievous Complaints were made by the Inhabitants of the Maladministration, and Tyranical proceedings of the Governour, the Extortion and other Impositions of the Alcades, and other Officers. He thereupon Summoned a Council, which Consisted of all the Magistrates and Principal Inhabitants of the Island, before whom He cited the Governour; and the charge against Him, which consisted of 21 Articles, was publickly read. But the Governour, who did not expect to be called to an account, at least in that manner, had very little to say in His own Vindication; and was not only removed from His Government, but fined 40,000 pieces of Eight which was applied to the building of an Hospital. He also released several Planters, whom the Governour had unjustly Imprisoned, and restored their Estates which were Siezed and Confiscated, on frivolous Pretences. The Alcaydes, and other Officers were likewise brought to Tryal, and punished according to their Offences. By those means and by the appointment of a new Governor the minds of the People, who had been greatly uneasy and disturbed, were quieted; and the Planters so much encouraged, that some of them formed themselves into a Company at Port Antonio; and Trade began again to revive from that time. This Reformation had so good an Effect, that abundance of People came there and Set[t]led. The new Governour, by His prudent behaviour and Address, being as *much* beloved, as His Predecessor was hated; and Jamaica, through His management became the Market of all the American Islands.

Don Gil Gonzales Davila sent so good an Account to the King of the State of the Island, and the proceedings of the new Governour, and other Officers, that His Catholick Majesty was pleased to Continue them in their Respective Employments. And at the same time Davila received His Majestie's Patent; by which He was Appointed High Judge, Superintendant General, and High Commissioner of Jamaica for life; with full Power to inspect into the Conduct and management of the Governour, and other Officers, and when occasion required, to Call them to an account.

He was, says Oviedo, a Gentleman of great Wisdom and Integrity, for by His discreet Conduct the Inhabitants of the Island were pacified, their Injuries redressed, and every man enjoyed the Fruits of His labour, with pleasure and Satisfaction. I went (says He) to Visit Him twice, from St. Domingo, and found the Island so well settled[,] planted, and Governed that it gave me no small Satisfaction. He lived there several Years, and died soon after I came from thence the last time, and was buried in the Great Church at Seville, Attended by a great Number of the Inhabitants of that prosperous Island, who justly lamented the loss of a Person, whom they looked upon as a Father and Protector.

He was a just man, and died very Poor, having in His life time distributed His Revenues, which were considerable, among the poor Planters, to Encourage them and promote the Settlement of the Island and to such like Generous and Charitable Uses.

From this period of time, the Spanish Writers have not given any particular Account of their transactions in this Island; nor Indeed, is it pertinent
and Necessary to follow them any further, than to shew their Condition,
Circumstances and form of Government they were under, when the Island
was taken. It is certain that they were for many Years, very Populous, and
in very flourishing Circumstances; for they had many Settlements in St.
Anns, Guanaboa, St. Dorothys, Liguinea, St. Thomas in the East, Black
River and Point Pedro. And three Towns, namely, Seville, Oristan, and St.
Iago delavega.

They first began to build a Town, which they named Melilla, near Montego Bay in St. James's, and from thence the Place was afterwards called
Spanish Quarters. But, before they had made any great progress they dis-
liked the Situation and removed to St. Anns where they built Seville. This
Town flourished for many years, was very Populous, and large, a pave-
ment being found two Miles from the Church. It was graced with a Stately
Monast[a]ry, and a Collegiate Church of which Peter Martyr was Abbot
and Suffragan Bishop.

Oristan was built at the head of Black River 14 leagues, South West,
from Seville, but never was Considerable, or of any great Consequence.
It was burnt by the English Forces, in 1657 and the Ruins are Still to be
Seen.

But, about the year 1540, finding the middle part of the South side of
the Island, to be more Fruitful and pleasant, they built St. Iago delavega
in a pleasant Vale near the Banks of Rio Cobre. In a few years after they
made it the Seat of Government, which (with other Advantages) drew the
Inhabitants from Seville, and Oristan. By those means it became so Considerable, that it had once no less than 2000 Houses[,] an Abbey, a Church,
two Chappels, and two Monast[a]ry's, though it was greatly diminished,
many years before the English took it.

What contributed very much to the Settlement of the Island, was the
great Number of Portoguese (a more Industrious People than the Spaniards) who flocked over to the Island after they became subject to Spain;[55]
and improved the Culture and Commerce of Jamaica. But, the Descendants of Columbus, who were Proprietors of the Island, exacted such
high Rents, that it was not only a great discouragement but, Occasioned
many of them and other Planters to remove and Settle on the Continent
of America. Indeed, few chose to Continue in Jamaica, who could avoid it,
after those Parts came to be Set[t]led; because they had not only a fairer
prospect of making their fortunes; but, of living more at Ease, and secure from the English and Dutch Privateers, who began to infest the West
Indies.

St. Iago delavega, was taken by the English four times though it cannot

55. Which hap[pe]ned not before the year 1580. — *Author.*

English observers, including both James Knight and Edward Long, very much admired early Spanish architecture because it seemed to be more resistant than English structures to earthquakes. This cutaway *View of a Spanish Building*, in a coastal scene that includes a camel and his driver, focuses on the structural dimensions of the building. It is reproduced from Edward Long, *History of Jamaica*, 3 vols. (London, 1774), 2:opposite p. 20.

be said that they Subdued the whole Island or ever Attempted it, before they failed in the Expedition to St. Domingo.

It was first taken by George Clifford[,] Earl of Cumberland, with six Ships and about 1000 men, but, He met with no other Booty than a Ransom for the Town.[56]

In 1596 S[i]r Anthony Shirley, who had been Cruising on the Continent, landed at Passage Fort, marched up to St. Iago delavega, Surprized[,] took, and plundered the Town, and then left it.[57]

56. George Clifford, Third Earl of Cumberland (August 8, 1558–October 3, 1605), succeeded to the earldom in 1570; received an M.A. at Trinity College, Cambridge, in 1576; and used the war with Spain to recover his diminished family fortune. Receiving command of the *Golden Lion* and later the *Victory* for his deeds against the Spanish Armada, he achieved some French and Spanish captures as a privateer but also suffered some disasters and died in debt.

57. Sir Anthony Shirley (1565–1635?) fought with the Earl of Leicester in the Low Countries in the 1580s and with the Earl of Essex and the Duke of Navarre in Normandy in the 1590s, and received a knighthood from Henry IV of France for which Elizabeth I imprisoned him, though he retained the title "Sir." He attacked the Portuguese off of West Africa in 1596 and then explored America from the Spanish conquests to Newfoundland. Richard Hakluyt, *Principal Navigations*, 10 vols. (Glasgow, 1904), 10:273–74, includes Shirley's account of his expedition of 1596–97. An ambassador to Persia in 1599, then a mercenary for Rudolph II against Morocco and for the Spanish against Turkey, he apparently died in poverty in Madrid.

The Spaniards to prevent such Disasters for the future, Erected a look out on Salt pond Hill, and Constantly kept a Centinel there to give Notice of the approach of any Ships. They also built a small Fort, and cast up Some intrenchments at Passage Fort; so that in 1635, when Collo[nel] Jackson,[58] with a Fleet of Privateers from the Le[e]ward Islands, came hither, on the same Design, they drew together 2000 men and were ready to oppose Him. But, notwithstanding They received Him with some Bravery and Sustained the Fury of the Onset with great Resolution[,] He landed 600 men[,] drove them from their Works, and without delay marched up to St. Iago dela Vega; which being an Open, unfortified Town, He took it with the loss of 40 men. After pillaging it of every thing that was Valuable, He received a Considerable sum for the Ransom of the Town, and to preserve it from burning. And then retreated in great order to His Ships, the Spaniards not daring to disturb His Rear; so that He safely reimbarked all His Forces.

After this the Spaniards were not disturbed by the English, for the Space of Twenty Years, nor till the arrival of Generall Venables, with the Forces under His Command, which took the Island in 1655.[59]

The Principall Planters, and other Inhabitants, lived chiefly at St. Iago dela Vega in a Sedentary way; and kept the meaner sort of People and Negros at Their Stanches, or Plantations, in the Country, which furnished Them with the Fruits of the Earth in great plenty.

Their Trade, as well as Product, was greatly diminished, in Consequence of a great Number of the Inhabitants being removed to other Parts; so that they did not load more than 7 or 8 Ships Yearly, for old Spain, whose Cargoes consisted of Cocoa (which was the principall Commodity of the Island) Hides, Tallow, Piemento, Tobacco and some Sugar.

The Principall Sea Port was old Harbour, though they had only some few Store houses there, it being little more than a Barcadier or landing Place. The Galleons in their Passage from Porto Bello, to Havanna generally touched there, which was some Advantage to the Inhabitants. Yet for this Island, and much greater Tracts of land which they made very little (and some no) use of, did they Butcher and inhumanely destroy several Millions of poor, Innof[f]ensive People who were the Natural Proprietors of them.

Hence we may perceive the fatal Consequences which attend Rapine and Oppression, and by what means this Island, which was very Populous

58. Possibly Knight is in error on Jackson's rank A Captain William Jackson attacked and landed at Passage Fort and marched on Spanish Town, sacking it on March 5, 1643. Also, Jackson cut timber at Negril from January 8–26, 1644. For a modern mention of this attack, see Carla Gardina Pestana, *The English Conquest of Jamaica: Oliver Cromwell's Bid for Empire* (Cambridge, Mass., 2017), 121.

59. The exact date of the treaty, signed at St. Jago de la Vega, was May 11, 1655. The island was officially ceded by the Spanish Crown in the Treaty of Madrid, July 8, 1670.

and for many Years in flourishing Circumstances (when it was in the hands of the Spaniards) declined and became an Easy prey to every Invader. For the Proprietors not only exacted high Rents or Taxes, but the Governours, who had no more than 2000 p[iece]s of Eight p[er] Annum salary, were Rapacious and imposed such hardships on the Inhabitants, as occasioned many of them to remove as before related; and Those who remained neglected to improve the Natural Advantages of the Place, since they could not Enjoy the Fruits of their labour.

In this unhappy Situation, They were when the Governours perceiving that their management forced great numbers of the Inhabitants to remove; and being Sensible how much this tended to the disadvantage of themselves as well of their Sovereign and the Proprietor of the Island, instead of altering their Conduct[,] They endeavoured to prevent it by restraining the Inhabitants from removing under very severe Penalties. This new Oppression occasioned a Representation of their Grievances to His Catholick Majesty, who at that time was too Attentive to His Own Projects in Europe, to regard the Complaints of a Proprietary Colony.

This Neglect encreased the dissatisfaction of the Inhabitants and Occasioned the loss of the Island, for they having no Confidence in the Administration, or Security of their Property, by degrees became so diminished that they did not exceed 5000 men, Women and Children; and being dispersed, they were not able to gather above 7 or 800 men, at St. Iago dela vega, and the Adjacent Parts, when the Forces, under the Command of Generall Venables arrived there. And having no other Fortification, than some intrenchments, and a small Fort of 18 Guns at passage Fort, they were not able to Oppose so considerable a Force as came to invade them. Nevertheless the English would have failed in this Design likewise and been obliged to abandon the Island, had it not been for the bad Policy of the Spaniards themselves, who being acquainted with Several Places of Retreat, which were difficult of Access, retired thereto, where they could have Subsisted and defended themselves, till such time as the Neighbouring Colonies Could send them Assistance to dislodge the English. But, Contrary to their Naturall dispositions, they were too unwary in Discovering themselves, by Sending out Parties not only to gain intelligence, but to harrass and distress the English. Severall Skirmishes ensued thereupon, which for the most part were to the disadvantage of the latter, because the Spaniards, when they found themselves pressed retired to those Fastnesses, and the others being unacquainted with the Country or Passes, were unable to pursue them, and often returned Sickly and dispirited.

This made them, for some time, imagine the Affair would be tedious if not impracticable, as Indeed it would have been, had the Island been in any other hands than the Spaniards.

This Instance, and the Difficulties, which afterwards attended the Reduction of the Spanish, as well as the English Negro's who were many

Years in Rebellion, Evinces the impossibility of our ever being dispossessed of the Island, by any Foreign Enemy, unless we are wanting to our selves; so that the principal Danger to be Guarded against; is what may happen within our Selves, through our own supineness, or imprudent management.

But, as these matters will appear more clearly in Severall Parts of this Treatise I shall decline making any further Animadversions thereupon.

Part the 2d

Of the Expedition and miscarriage of the Design against St. Domingo; The conquest of Jamaica by the English, and such other Occurrences as happened before the Restoration of King Charles the Second, or any form of Civil Government was Established.

Jamaica being conquered by the land and Sea Forces, which were Sent to America, by Cromwell,[1] and failed in the Design upon St. Domingo; it will be proper to give a Nar[r]ative of that Expedition and point out the Errors and mistakes which were Committed in the Conduct and management of it: Because it will naturally lead us to the Acquisition of an Island of more importance to Great Britain in regard to Situation, Convenient Harbours, and other Advantages, which will Appear when I come to give a more particular Description of it.[2]

Cromwell soon after His advancement to the Protectorship, Resolved to break with Spain, and Suggested divers matters, to Colour his Design on that occasion. But, the true Reasons, which moved Him to it, *was* to acquire some Possessions in America, which would not only lessen and restrain the power of the Spaniards, and promote the Interest of the Common Wealth, but employ Some Old Cavalier Troops, whose Swords He was apprehensive of being turned against Himself, to which may be added, His Design of furnishing His Treasury with Money that He might be able to pay the Troops He was Obliged to Maintain, and that His Government might be Established before He should have occasion to apply to a Parliament for Supplies. The Reasons Suggested were Some late Affronts and Cruelties, exercised [by the Spanish] upon the English in America, as Appears by the Manifesto which He published soon after.

As the most impartiall account I have seen of this Expedition is in Mr.

---

1. Oliver Cromwell (1599–1658). His military career during the English Civil War led to his political prominence in the English Commonwealth following the execution of Charles I and to his appointment as protector in December 1753, a post he held until his death and used to try to bring sweeping changes to English law and religion.

2. Carla Gardina Pestana, *The English Conquest of Jamaica: Oliver Cromwell's Bid for Empire* (Cambridge, Mass., 1997), provides the fullest modern treatment of the events covered in part 2 of Knight's work.

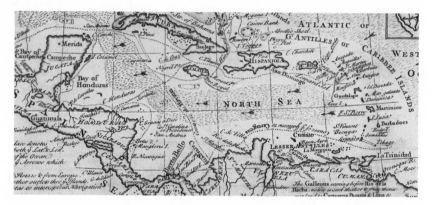

Entitled *A Map and Chart of the West Indies, Drawn from the Best Spanish Maps* and published in London in *Gentleman's Magazine,* vol. 10 (1740), frontispiece, this image illustrates Jamaica's favorable position at the very center of Spain's Caribbean colonies and the adjacent continental littoral, thus promising its English conquerors access to the region's vast resources and commercial possibilities.

Secretary Burchet[']s *Navall History,*[3] I shall follow Him chiefly, and transcribe such Remarkable Circumstances as I have met with in other Authors, and Manuscripts, particularly the Journalls of Generall Venables[4] and Another Officer of distinction under Him.

The French says Bishop Burnet[5] could not penetrate into the Secret; Cromwell had not finished his Alliance with them so that He was not bound to give them an Account of the Expedition. All He said upon it was that He Sent out the Fleet to guard the Seas and to restore England to its Dominion on that Element. And as Spain would never admit of a Peace with England between the Tropicks, so He was in a State of War with them, in those parts, even before He declared War in Europe. He therefore Equipped this Fleet which He thought was of force Sufficient to have secured St. Domingo and Cuba[,] and one Gage[6] who had been a Priest and resided Severall Years in the West Indies assured Him that Success in that Expedition, would make all the rest fall into His hands.

The land forces consisted of 3000 Cavaliers and about the same number

3. Josiah Burchet, *A Complete History of the Most Remarkable Transactions at Sea, from the Earliest Accounts of Time to the Conclusion of the Last War with France* (London, 1720).

4. Robert Venables, *The Narrative of General Venables, with an Appendix of Papers Relating to the Expedition to the West Indies and the Conquest of Jamaica, 1654–1655* (London, 1655).

5. Gilbert Burnet (1643–1715). A favorite of the Restoration Stuarts and chaplain to Charles II, he subsequently befriended William of Orange and became bishop of Salisbury. Knight probably found this information in Burnet's *History of the Reformation in England,* 3 vols. (London, 1679, 1681, 1714).

6. Thomas Gage (b. 1602) was the author of *The English-American His Travels by Sea and Land; or, A New Survey of the West-India's* (London, 1648) and chaplain to the expedition of William Penn and Robert Venables. He died soon after the conquest of Jamaica.

of men, which were draughted out of Cromwell[']s standing Army; beside Voluntiers and others who went in hopes of Acquiring some Possessions. The Command of Those Troops was Given to Generall Venables, and under Him Major Generall Haines,[7] Coll[onel]s Fortescue,[8] Buller,[9] Carter[10] and Doyley.[11]

The Fleet; which Consisted of thirty Sail of Men of War, was Commanded by Vice Admirall Pen,[12] and under Him Vice Admirall Goodson[13] and Rear Admirall Brag.[14] But the whole Design was under the direction of

7. Major General James Haines or Heine (1603–1655), an experienced officer, was second in command under Venables and fell in battle at Hispaniola on April 25, 1655. For more biographical detail, see Sir Charles Firth, *The Regimental History of Cromwell's Army*, 2 vols. (Oxford, 1940), 2:718–20.

8. Richard Fortescue (d. 1655), an officer in the Parliamentary Army, commanded the second regiment in the expedition to the West Indies. Following the capture of Jamaica and Venables's return to England, he served as commander in chief from June 24 to October 1, 1655, when Robert Sedgewick relieved him. Fortescue died three weeks later. For more biographical detail, see ibid., 2:716–17, and Frank Cundall, *Governors of Jamaica in the Seventeenth Century* (London, 1936), xxvii–xxix.

9. Anthony Buller commanded a regiment during the invasions of Hispaniola and Jamaica, and in June 1655 returned to England to provide Cromwell with an account of the expedition. For more biographical detail, see Firth, *Regimental History of Cromwell's Army*, 2:707.

10. Andrew Carter, an older soldier, commanded the fourth regiment in the expedition to the West Indies and died within a few months after the capture of Jamaica. Ibid., 2:716.

11. Edward Doyley (d. 1675) fought for Parliament during the English Civil War and was the colonel of a regiment raised in Barbados to participate in the Western Design. On the death of Colonel Richard Fortescue in October 1655, his fellow senior officers elected Doyley to be commander in chief of the forces in Jamaica, a post he continued to occupy for most of the time until the Restoration. He presided over the defeat of the various groups the Spanish sent in efforts to reconquer Jamaica and encouraged English soldiers to take up land and cultivate it. Following the Restoration, Charles II appointed him the first royal governor of the colony with instructions to establish a civil government. He served in this office until his successor, Thomas Hickman, Lord Windsor, arrived in Jamaica in the summer of 1662, returning to England shortly thereafter. For more biographical detail, see ibid., 2:712–15.

12. Sir William Penn (1621–1670) was born at Bristol into a mercantile family and became a captain on his father's Mediterranean ships at age twenty-one, a captain in the navy in the Irish fleet on the Parliamentary side in 1644, rear admiral of this fleet in 1648, and vice admiral in 1649. Sent to the Mediterranean in 1650 after Prince Rupert, he fought the Dutch in 1652–53. In 1654, he offered his services to Charles in exile, who told him to await a better moment and proceed with his mission to America commissioned by Cromwell "to assault the Spanish in the West Indies." Penn participated in the assaults on Hispaniola and Jamaica. After the capture of Jamaica on May 17, he returned to England, where for reasons unknown he was imprisoned in the Tower of London and thereafter retired to his Munster estate in Ireland. From there he kept up a correspondence with Charles II. Knighted at the Restoration, he received a new naval commission, serving with the Duke of York (later James II). His son, William Penn (1644–1718), was the Quaker founder of Pennsylvania.

13. Vice Admiral William Goddson, second in naval command during the West Indian campaign, took over the English naval squadron following the capture of Jamaica and the return of Penn to England.

14. Rear Admiral Brag, third in command of Penn, has not been specifically identified.

Commissioners, who were Generall Venables, Vice Admirall Pen[n], Edward Winslow;[15] Daniel Searl[e,] Governour of Barbadoes,[16] and Gregory Butler,[17] who were Authorized and inpowered to Consult, conclude, and Act as Commissioners in all important Affairs concerning the publick in this present Expedition.

When Venables, who had been very Serviceable to Cromwell, in the Reduction of Ireland, was first pitched upon to Command the Troops, designed for this Expedition; He made it His Request, that He might be furnished with Arms, Ammunition, and all things necessary for a Design of that nature, for otherwise very great Disappointments might happen, should He not carry them with Him from hence [England], Since they could not possibly be had abroad. He also made it His Request, that He might not be cramped with Commissions, or Instructions to other Persons; for He then knew, that Cromwell intended to send Commissioners, with large powers to inspect into, advise and Controul the Actions of Those who were to be principally employed in this Expedition: But how little Regard was had to what He thus desired, will appear, in the ensuing Relation, as also how He was Contradicted and Slighted, by Those in chief Authority.

After Venables had attended near four months, without any positive assurance, whether the Government intended to go on with the Design or not; He was sometime after sent to, and directed to hold Himself in a Readiness to proceed. And tho[ugh] He then requested, that the draughts which were to be made out of the Regiments, might be men in all Respects fitting for the intended Service; Yet the Colonels were permitted to pick and cull them as They pleased; insomuch that many of them were Raw, and Altogether undisciplined, nor had the half of them Arms in any degree Ser-

15. Edward Winslow (1595–1655). A Puritan from Worcestershire, Winslow was aboard the *Mayflower* at the founding of the Plymouth Colony; served as governor in 1633, 1636, and 1644; and occasionally represented the colony on official business in London, where he published several tracts on the settlement of New England and established his credentials as an expert on colonial affairs. He died shortly after the failure of the Hispaniola invasion.

16. Daniel Searle, a colonel, was one of three commissioners who, for Parliament, took Barbados from Royalist control under Francis, Lord Willoughby, Fifth Baron of Parham, by a treaty of January 11, 1652. Appointed governor of Barbados by military commander Sir George Ayscue, Searle had difficulties controlling the Royalists in Caribbean waters, particularly Prince Rupert, and with the Barbadian assembly. Searle's appointment as commissioner to Jamaica created confusion in the Barbadian government as Venables seemed to supersede Searle. Although Searle managed to resume his authority in 1656, he finally lost the governorship to Thomas Modyford on July 16, 1660, after the Restoration. Vincent Todd Harlow, *A History of Barbados, 1625–1685* (New York, 1926).

17. Gregory Butler served in the Civil War and moved to the West Indies to become one of three civil commissioners for the mission in 1655, Venables appointing him because of his local knowledge. Contemporary accounts portray him as an incompetent drunk. He returned to England without permission to appeal for redress of his losses and for the governorship of Tortuga. Cundall, *Governors of Jamaica in the Seventeenth Century*, xxx.

Such negative images of Spanish cruelty to indigenous peoples as depicted above gave rise to the views, widespread in England and the Netherlands, that American indigenes would welcome deliverance by Protestant arms. To forward this expectation, the engraver of this image drew on the reported experience of George Clifford, Third Earl of Cumberland, an early buccaneer who made a name for himself during Elizabeth I's reign by his short-lived capture of Fort San Felipe del Morro, the fortification protecting San Juan, Puerto Rico, in 1598. Allegedly, indigenous women welcomed his soldiers with food and dancing around a tent-like roof stretched between two trees under which sat three indistinct individuals, one of whom held a bow while another played an unidentified musical instrument. This image, entitled *Naaukeurige versameling der gedenk-waardigste zee en land-reysen na Oost en West-Indiën ... zedert het jaar 1524 tot 1526*, followed the special title page in *Vershcheyde voornaame reysen na West-Indien en andere gewesten, gedaan door den Hoogagtbaren Georg, Graaf van Cumberland* (Leiden, 1706). Round huts can be seen in the background.

viceable. And so far was the Councill from permitting Him to stay, till better could be furnished; in their Room, that They Sent Him positive orders to leave the Town, the next day, upon pain of imprisonment.

Before He came to Portsmouth, many of the Troops were Embarqued, and the Rest shipping off with the utmost Expedition; so that He had no Opportunity of viewing, much less of exercising them on Shore, and thereby informing Himself of their Condition, with Respect to Their Abilities or otherwise. And tho[ugh] He was promised that the Storeships with Arms and other necessaries, should join Him at Spithead, He was at last told, that no delay must be made, in staying for them, but that He might expect their coming to Him at Barbadoes. He was likewise assured that He should carry with Him ten months provisions for ten thousand men; But the most part thereof was sent back to London, to be Shipped off there under pretence that there was not Sufficient Room for them in the Ships at Portsmouth; though the Officers of the Fleet found passage for no inconsiderable quantities of goods, which they designed to Traffick with, when they came to the Islands.

The Fleet Sailed from Spithead the 26th day of December, and arrived at Barbadoes the 29th day of January 1655. Soon after Generall Venables wrote to the Protector, the Lord President of the Councill[18] and others, to let them know what a miserable condition the Army was in, and how destitute they were, not only of Provisions, but of Arms and other necessarys proper for carrying on the intended Design; insomuch that they were Constrained to make the hardest Shifts to supply themselves, with small quantities of one or the other, that could be had in those Parts.

The first thing they did at Barbadoes, was Seizing Some Dutch Ships and other Vessells, being Eighteen in number, which in defiance of the late Act of Navigation had presumed to Trade in Those Parts. And Admirall Pen[n] appointed His own Nephew to take an Account of their Cargoes, and all things belonging to them, without admitting of any check, as Generall Venables and Commissioner Winslow desired, and insisted in order that no Embezzlements might be made. But Pen[n] would not suffer them so much as to see the Originall Invoices, or any ways interfere in the Sales or dividend of those prizes; upon which They protested against His proceedings.

Hence arose the differance between the Generall and Admirall, who were never afterwards reconciled[,] which proved of ill consequence to the Design, Because their disagreement was the Cause of their miscarriage at St. Domingo.

At Barbadoes a Councill of War was held, the 18th of March 1655, to consider of the State of the Army; and it was there resolved to make Some proposalls to the Admirall.

1. That, as the Officers of the Army had resolved not to desert the Fleet, He with His Officers Should reciprocally resolve not to leave the Army; at least till such time, as the expected Supplies Arrived from England.

18. Henry Lawrence (1600?–1664) was from Buckinghamshire, studied at Graves Inn in 1617, and received a B.A. at Emmanuel College, Cambridge, in 1623, and an M.A. in 1627. A Puritan who spent much time in asylum in Holland, he returned to England to become MP for Westmoreland in 1646, for Hertfordshire in 1653 and 1654, and for Caernarvonshire in 1656. Elevated to a peerage in 1657, he was subsequently commissioner for plantations in 1648 and for Ireland in 1652 and became a councillor of state the following year. In January 1654, Cromwell appointed him lord president, a position he retained until July 1659. At the Restoration, he retired to his estate in Hertfordshire.

2. That it should be proposed to the Commissioners that a fitting Number of Shipping might be taken up for transporting the Forces.

3. That they might not proceed on Service, with less than twenty tons of Ball, and that they might likewise be furnished from the Fleet, with two hundred fire Arms, Six hundred Pikes, beside Pistolls, Carabines, and half Pikes. To which Venables received no Satisfactory answer from Pen[n], and the Stores not arriving from England, He again desired to know from Him, what Arms, Shot, Match and other necessaries He could furnish from the Fleet; Generall Desborow[19] having assured Him, when in England, that the Commissioners had power to dispose of what might be aboard the Ships, to the necessary use of the Army. But to this Pen[n] returned Him an Answer, that fifteen Shot a man and a few tons of match, was all He could spare. To these He at length was prevailed on to add a few half and quarter Pikes; which gave Occasion to one of the Commissioners to say, He doubted [not that] they were betrayed.

Beside these Dissapointments, the Provisions sent from England were not only bad, but Even insufficient of them[,] for the Soldiers were put to short allowance, while the Seamen were at whole [allowance], which occasioned great discontent, and rendered them Weak, and unfit for Service. And as the Commissioners were empowered and required to dispose of all prizes and Booty taken towards defraying the charge of the Expedition, and only a fortnight[']s pay was offered to the Officers and Soldiers in lieu of whatever Booty should be taken at St. Domingo, it very much encreased the Dissatisfaction of the Army, for most of them, when they set out on this Expedition, were in hopes of bettering their fortunes very considerably.

At length Generall Venables prevailed with the Officers and Men, to accept of six weeks pay, instead of their plunder; and thereupon issued out an order to restrain all Persons from pillaging without License, or from concealing any thing on pain of Death, and forfeiture of their pay. But although the Officers were willing to Submit to this, Yet the Commissioners refused to sign it; insomuch that the Soldiers publickly declared They would return to England, and never strike a Stroke, where there should be Commissioners who had power to controul the Army.

However, Upon beating up for Voluntiers they raised a Considerable number of Men in this Island [Barbados] who were formed into a Regi-

19. John Desborough (1608–1680?) was born in Cambridgeshire and in 1636 married Oliver Cromwell's sister Jane. He served successively as a captain of horse (1643), major (1645), colonel (1648), and major general (1654) in the Parliamentary Army, suppressing Royalist uprisings in the west in 1649. Taking a seat on Cromwell's Council of State in 1653, he was MP for Cambridgeshire in 1654 and for Somerset in 1656, a privy councillor in 1657, and a member of Cromwell's House of Lords in 1658. Imprisoned at the Restoration and exempted from indemnity, he was accused of conspiring to assassinate Charles II. Escaping to Holland, he returned and was imprisoned for republican conspiracy but eventually obtained his freedom and lived quietly in Hackney until 1680.

ment and the Command given to *Collo[nel] Morris;*[20] also a Troop of Sixty Horse, which were Shipped on board some of the Dutch Ships, that were Seized for Illicit Trade. And having furnished themselves with such Necessaries as were to be had, it was proposed by Generall Venables and some other Officers of the Army to proceed directly into the Harbour of St. Domingo; But, for what Reason doth not appear, that proposall was rejected and a Resolution taken to land the Troops at the River Hine, that so they might endeavour to force the Fort and Trenches.

They Sailed from Barbadoes the 31st of March and touched at St. Christophers, where they took in a Regiment raised there and in the other Islands; the command of which was given to *Collo[nel] Holdip.*[21] A Regiment of Seamen was also formed and to be Commanded by Vice Admirall Goodson.

The 7th of April a Council of War was held on board the *Swiftsure,* where the Generall and all the Colonels of the Several Regiments were present; And it was Resolved.

1. That the Regiments should cast lotts which of them should go on Shore first.

2. That two or three Regiments should be landed at once.

3. That the seconds to each Regiment should be appointed.

4. That the Ships where the Regiments were should keep near each other, for their more regular landing.

And it was further determined, that if the surge of the Sea run high, and the Enemy was prepared to defend the Fort and Trench, the Army should be landed at the Second point to leeward; and that when on Shore, one Regiment should be ordered to march Eastward of the City, provided Admirall Pen[n] would Engage to furnish the Army with all necessaries.

Accordingly Lotts being cast, pursuant to the Resolution then taken, it fell to Collo[nel] Buller[']s Regiment to land first[,] and there was one Cox[22] who had lived in those parts many Years, was to have been their Guide.

---

20. Lewis Morris was a Barbadian planter who had assisted in the Parliamentary conquest of Barbados in 1651 and took a large part in raising the regiment subsequently commanded by Daniel Doyley, Morris having decided to abandon the expedition unless his debts would be paid. See Firth, *Regimental History of Cromwell's Army,* 2:712.

21. Richard Holdep, who had previously been a lieutenant-colonel in Richard Fortescue's regiment, took command of a second colonial regiment raised in the Leeward Islands. He had been governor of the English colony in Surinam, became a trusted advisor to Robert Venables, and was one of three commissioners Venables appointed to treat with the Spaniards for the surrender of Jamaica.

22. Captain Christopher Cox of St. Christopher, an Irish Catholic who had lived twelve years in Hispaniola and served as a gunner at one of the island's forts. See Pestana, *English Conquest of Jamaica,* 58–59.

The 10th of April, They Sailed from St. Christophers; the 12th they made the high land of St. Domingo; and the day following discovered the Town, upon which preparations being made for landing, Commissioner Winslow came and informed Venables, that Pen[n] had sent away Cox and one Bounty[23] who were to be their Guides, upon pretence of gaining intelligence. This was the Second Step towards Ruining the Design; however the Generall intended to go up the River Hine before He disembarqued the Army, but Vice Admirall Goodson whose station it was to lead them in, declared that He had no orders to go up the River Hine, nor Pilots to conduct the Ships.

Monday the 14th Collo[nel] Buller[']s Regiment was landed in a Bay near a Fort, where S[i]r Francis Drake[24] landed, when He took St. Domingo in 1586; and is about 10 miles distance from the Town. Upon His approach the Enemy quitted the Fort, leaving the Guns dismounted, and the Walls as much disabled as time would permit. Collo[nel] Buller pursued His March towards the Town, through the narrow passes of the Woods; and by His Guide was lead to some Plantations, which were waterless and deserted, within 3 Miles of the Town and near a Strong Fort.

The *16th* the Main Body of the Army were landed at the Wester[n]most point, which the Generall had protested against, being Contrary to His Opinion and most of the land Officers. For by that means they were exposed to a tedious March of thirty Miles, through a Woody Country, without a Guide; insomuch that Horse and Men, by the fatigue and Extremity of Heat, fell down with Thirst; and were miserably afflicted with the Flux, by eating immature Oranges and other Fruit to quench their Thirst, so that many of them died outright, and the rest became so faint and fatigued, that they were not in a Condition to resist much less attack an Enemy.

In this Condition, after four days march, They came to the place where they might have landed the first day, and prevented not only the disasters they met with, but [also] alarming the Enemy and giving them time to put themselves in a posture of defence. At this Place a Signal was made accord-

23. Mr. Bounty was another guide with local knowledge whose first name is unknown. Ibid., 59.

24. Sir Francis Drake (1540?–1596) made three voyages from Plymouth to the West Indies in successive years from 1570. He burned Portobello in 1572, sacked Vera Cruz in 1573, and returned to serve with the Earl of Essex in Ireland. Sailing through the Magellan Strait in 1578, then to the Indian Archipelago, around the Cape of Good Hope, and north to Sierra Leone by 1680, Drake was knighted in 1581, became mayor of Plymouth in 1582, and MP for Bossiney in 1584–85 and for Plymouth in 1593. He returned to the West Indies in 1685 where he burned St. Iago and Vigo and took St. Domingue and Cartagena. He helped to repel the Spanish Armada from Gravesend in 1588 and pursued it north of Scotland. He attacked the Spanish coastline in 1589 and in 1595 commanded the unsuccessful West Indies mission on which he died, near Portobello in 1596.

ing to agreement, and Venables intended to pass over the River with the Army: But, Collo[nel] Buller who had Orders not to move from the Place where He was landed, until the Army had joined Him, was so far from complying with those Commands, that He marched away as before related, under the Guidance of Cox who was returned from the Errand He was Sent upon by Admirall Pen[n].

Soon after Collo[nel] Buller[']s departure from Drake[']s landing place, the Generall with the main Body of the Army arrived, after a tedious and tiresome March. And was informed by Rear Admirall Brag, who rode there to Secure the Fort and the Watering Place, that Collo[nel] Buller was marched to the Town; and the Tide being come in that it was impassable where He forded, the Generall was constrained to March along the River Side and to halt and lay that night, at a Sugar work without water, about seven miles from Collo[nel] Buller. Tuesday the 18th of April they marched and met with Collo[nel] Buller near the Strong Fort, in the Town Road, where the Enemy had prepared an Ambuscade, and lined the Woods, which cut off their Forlorn hope, and killed Adjutant General [Thomas] Walters, Captain Jennings, Capt[ain] Watts, Capt[ain] Cox (one of their Guides) and the Gernerall[']s Secretary. This inraged the English Forces, who Attacked the Enemy with such Vigour, that They drove them out of their Ambuscades, took their ground, and recovered their dead, and had not Extremity of Hunger, Thirst, Weariness, and the Approach of night prevented, They might have entered and taken the Town. But, necessity obliged them to Retreat at ten O'Clock at night, and knowing of no Water nearer than Drake[']s landing place, They appointed a strong Rear Guard and marched back again, to preserve their men who were by those means become very faint and Sickly.

Here they continued inactive till the 25th, during which time the Fleet was hovering in Sight of the Town, and did not come within 5 leagues of the Fort, which obliged the Generall to go on board and Consult with the Admirall and Commissioner Winslow, as nothing was to be transacted without their advice and Concurrence, which was the cause of this delay and gave the Enemy time and Opportunity to recover and Strengthen themselves, and be informed of the Weakness, and disasters our Army met with. After severall Consultations, and dis-agreements another March was Resolved upon, although they had lost Cox[,] their Guide, and feeding on bad provisions they were more and more discontented and discouraged: Accordingly a small Mortar piece[,] 10 Shells, two Drakes[,] divers blunderbusses, and some Brandy were landed, though not a sufficient Quantity. But they had neither Harness nor horses for their Artillery, so that the Soldiers were obliged to draw them, and as they made use of the ablest and Strongest men for that service, this Soon Spent and reduced them to the low condition the others were in.

Tuesday the 25th they began their March, and lay that night in the

Woods. Wednesday the 26th, Adjutant Generall Jackson[25] who commanded 400 men in the forlorn[,] advanced near the Fort. But [they] disregarded his orders, in not having two wings, on Each side, for discovering of Ambuscades, by which means Capt[ain George] Butler (a brave but unexperienced Officer) who lead them, was drawn into an Ambuscade; and after He had with great Bravery, and good order brought of[f] His Division was killed and likewise Capt[ain] Pawlet who commanded the other. Jackson upon seeing them fall faced about and basely fled, instead of supporting their men; upon which the whole forlorn Retreated in such disorder, and with such precipitation, that They fell in with the Reformadoes, in a narrow pass, and both together mixed in great confusion with the Horse. The place where the Enemy lay to flank them, being thick of Woods, and the Guns of the Fort loaded with small shot, bitts of Iron and broken Pistoll barrells, did great Execution in a long and narrow passage: by those means the front of the Army was routed, and falling in with the Generall[']s Regiment, broke and disordered them; and in this Confusion tumbled into Major Generall Haines['] Regiment and put the whole Army in the greatest disorder imaginable, insomuch that had not the Rear of the Major Generall[']s Regiment drawn into the Woods and thereby counter flanked and beat the Enemy back to the Fort, which gave the Army an Opportunity of Retreating, They had most or all of them been cut of[f]. Jackson retired into the Woods and preserved himself; But the Major Generall, who behaved with the greatest conduct and Resolution, was Slain being run through the Body with a lance; L[ieutenan]t Collo[nel John] Clark and many other Officers, were likewise killed or died of their wounds and five or 6 hundred men, with the loss of nine Colours to the great dishonour of the Nation, as well as themselves.

Thursday the 27th of April the General intended to play the Mortar piece; But, the Engineer declared it was not practicable, the Fort had Such command over those places, that They could beat them from it, whereupon considering the Weakness of the Troops, occasioned by their fatigue and the want of provisions and Water, a Retreat was concluded, and a strong Rear Guard Appointed; the ten mortar shells were neatly buried, but the Mortar, Drakes and baggage were carried of[f] and the next day They got safe to their landing place. Here sometime was Spent in Consultations and the Rains encreasing and a Supply of provisions and other necessaries not being Sent them from the Ships They were reduced to the necessity of Eating their Troopers['] horses, the Enemy depriving them of all other Relief: by these means the Forces were so weakened and distressed that the Commissioners owned in a letter they wrote to the Governour of Barbadoes, that had not the Enemy been as fearfull as their own men, they might, in a few days, have destroyed the whole Army; And withall They

25. Adjutant General Jackson's first name is unknown.

let Him know, that the Troops which had occasioned the greatest disorder, were those they brought from Barbadoes and St. Christophers.

Hereupon the Commissioners agreed to leave the place, and try what could be done against the Island of Jamaica.

The Army was accordingly embarqued; But, the sick and wounded men were left upon the Open Decks, for Eight and Forty hours, without meat, drink, or dressing, insomuch that worms bred in their Sores. Adjutant Generall Jackson was tried at a Court Martiall and not only sentenced to be cashiered, and His Sword broke over his head, but to do the Duty of a Swabber, in keeping clean the Hospitall Ship; a punishment suitable to his Notorious Cowardice, though considering the Consequence, He ought rather to have been hanged, as well as some of Collo[nel] Fortescue[']s men, who ran away, and were tried at the Same time.

Collo[nel] Fortescue was appointed Major Generall in the room of Haines; and the 1st of May They sailed from St. Domingo.

The 3d of May they appeared in Sight of Jamaica, and Generall Venables to prevent the same fate they met with at Hispaniola, issued orders that if any man Attempted to Run away, the next man to Him should put Him to Death, and if He failed to Execute this order, He should be tried for his life.

The Spaniards having no Fortifications at Cagway (now called Port Royall) the Fleet went directly into the Harbour, without any Opposition. Here, the Generall and Admirall went on board the *Martin Galley* the better to order things, and plaid upon a small Fort of 18 Guns at Passage, while the men were landing; where was little opposition; they soon took possession, and before three in the Afternoon the whole Army were safely landed. But, not having any knowledge of the Country, and fearing to be distressed again for want of Water; the Officers concluded not to begin their march to St. Iago dela vega[,] the Chief Town and Settlement, until the next morning, that They might have light to view the passes, and to take all advantages. Accordingly they proceeded at Day break, and by noon came up to the Savanna, near the Town, when the Spaniards who imagined that They were come only to plunder as S[i]r Anthony Shirley, the Earl of Cumberland, and Collo[nel] Jackson had formerly done;[26] sent divers Persons to Capitulate, which the Generall Consented to, provided they would deliver him possession of the Island, as they were come to Settle there, and not to pillage, and in the mean time, to furnish Him with a sufficient Quantity of provisions.

The Spaniards had not received any Information of the defeat of the English at Hispaniola, and were not in a condition to oppose an Army of 8000 men, for so many they Still were, so that They made use of policy more than Arms, to Save themselves and their Effects. Accordingly they

26. On these earlier attacks, see Pestana, *English Conquest of Jamaica*, 121.

Reproduced from an anonymous 1770 engraving entitled *Venables Attacks and Takes Jamaica*, this image shows General Robert Venables leading the successful English attack on Jamaica.

complyed with the Generall[']s demand of provisions, and spun out the Treaty, as long as They could, that They might in the mean time Remove their Effects, and Cattle into the Woods. After some days were Spent in treating, the following Articles were agreed upon the 15th of May by the Commissioners Appointed for that purpose.

1. That all Forts, Arms, Ammunition, and necessaries of War, and all kind of Shipping in any of the Harbours in the Island, as also all goods, wares and Merchandize should be delivered up to Generall Venables, or

whom He should Appoint, for the use of his Highness the Lord Protector and the Common Wealth of England.

2. That all and Every the Inhabitants of the Island, should have their lives granted and not be abused in their persons, and Those who were inclined to Stay; had leave so to do: and it was agreed to transport the others with their wives and children to new Spain or some of the Spanish Dominions in America, together with their Apparell, books, and papers, or writings. They providing themselves with Victualls and necessaries which they should freely be permitted to do.

3. That all Commission[ed] Officers, and no Others, should be permitted to wear their Rapiers and Poniards.

4. All Artificers, and meaner sort of People were permitted to remain on the Island, and to Enjoy their freedom[,] Goods, laws excepted, provided they submitted & Conformed themselves to the laws and Government of the English nation and such others as might be declared by authority to be put in use and exercised within this island.

Pursuant to this Agreement Don Juan Ramirez De Arellano[,][27] the Spanish Governour who was an old decrepid Man, delivered Possession of the Island to General Venables in due form. But, the Inhabitants who had been freely admitted into the Soldiers['] Quarters (during the Treaty which Continued five days) by that means became acquainted with their Defeat at St. Domingo, and other Disasters which had very much reduced and disheartened the Army; Resolved not to Comply with the Conditions stipulated by their Commissioners, in hopes of being able to dispossess the English, if Their wants were not duely Supplied from time to time. Among them was Don Christovall Arnaldo Sasi,[28] a native of the Island, who possessed a considerable property and his Interest and authority gave him a great degree of popularity and Influence. This gentleman persuaded them not to comply with the Treaty, but [to] drive off their Cattle and retire into the woods and covert places; and from them endeavour to harrass and distress the English, who, dispirited by these disruptions and want of provisions, would soon be compelled to abandon the island. Accordingly,

27. Don Juan Ramirez de Arellano, knight of the Order of Santiago, was governor of Spanish St. Domingue from 1651 until his capture during the English invasion on May 11, 1655. He was deported to Campeche. Frank Cundall, *Historic Jamaica* (London, 1915), 289.

28. Don Christovall Sasi/Ysasi/Ysassi Arnaldo. Born to an old Spanish Jamaican family, brother of Don Francisco Arnaldo Ysasi, bishop of Puerto Rico, Sasi was lieutenant to Governor Ramirez when England captured Jamaica in May 1655 and was party to the Spanish surrender. Commissioned as Spanish governor of Jamaica on October 15, 1656, he made three attempts to retake the island before being decisively defeated on May 9, 1660, at which time he fled from a place now called Runaway Point. He died in a monastery in Spain. Clinton Black, *History of Jamaica* (London, 1988), 49–54; Frank Cundall, *Jamaica under the Spanish* (London, 1919), 52, 55, 60, 64, 69, 71–75, 80, 83, 87, 92, 98, 102, 108.

they dispersed themselves to several parts that they might be better able to subsist themselves and support each other.

Accordingly they made use of that opportunity, and Conveyed away not only their most Valuable Effects, and best Horses, but drove away most or all the Cattle which was near the Town; and with their Wives and Children, retreated into the Mountains, and other Covert Places, leaving the English an Empty Town to possess; which was a great dissappointment to the Forces, who were in expectation of plunder and had been balked before.

Generall Venables, upon information of this Treacherous behaviour of the Spaniards, Ordered Collo[nel] Buller with 2000 men to pursue them and prevent their passing over to the Main, which was imagined to be their Design. But, after a tiresome and fruitless march, for Ten days, over Mountains and thick Woods, which they were unacquainted with, They were Obliged to return[;] during that time the Main Body of the Forces, were reduced to great Streights and difficulties, for want of Provisions, insomuch that they were obliged to feed on Dogs, Cats, and some strag[g]ling Horses They met with, untill Colo[nel] Buller came in and not only brought a drove of Cattle, very Seasonably, but information of great plenty in severall parts of the Country, upon which other Parties, were Sent out and likewise brought in not only great Numbers of Cattle but divers Prisoners.

The 13th of June 1655, Generall Venables wrote to Secretary Thurlo[e],[29] that the Parties He Sent out in quest of the Spaniards, had taken severall more Prisoners; the rest continued in the Mountains, without houses, in great distress, and were willing to Submit, But, were Awed and prevented by some leading men; That He had hopes of bringing them over and making them good Subjects, as there was many Portuguese amongst them. That He endeavoured to gain them by Civil and human treatment. That the Forces under his command Struggled with all manner of difficulties; above 2000 men Sick, and that They were so Short of bread and brandy,

29. John Thurloe (1616–1668). Born in Essex, Thurloe served as secretary of Parliament at the Treaty of Uxbridge in January 1645, secretary to Oliver St. John and Walter Strickland's mission to Holland in 1651, and secretary to the Council of State in 1652. A member of the council in 1654 and head of the intelligence department at home and abroad, he pushed Cromwell to take the Crown and was instrumental in the ascendance of Richard Cromwell. MP for the University of Cambridge in 1659, he was much criticized by Parliament and the army and deprived of most of his offices in May 1659. But he was reappointed secretary of state in February 1660 and worked against the Restoration, during which he was accused of high treason but released. His expertise was so esteemed that the new administration often solicited his advice. His vast correspondence was hidden after the Restoration but discovered during the reign of William III and published in seven volumes in London in 1742 as *A Collection of the State Papers of John Thurloe*.

They had not sufficient for three Weeks['] Subsistance. That there was little Cassava in the Country, of which the Enemy had by Stealth at least their Share. That the men died daily of fluxes occasioned by their Eating of roots, instead of bread, That He thought it necessary to build some block houses at the Harbour[']s mouth, but his men were so weak, and not used to hard labour, That they were not able to do it or to plant Cassava and other provisions for their own Subsistance; most of them preferring death to life, though they had Recovered their Spirits, Courage He could not say they ever had. That He was persuaded they were not men fit to carry on any Design in the Field, though They might in the Country as to planting. These, says He, with other Reasons have moved the Councill of War, to desire me to represent our Condition to His Highness and Councill, with some Expedients which are not fully resolved upon, neither am I able to Enlarge, by Generall Pe[n]n, who visited me Yesterday, and told me he was resolved to sail tomorrow morning for England[,] my Spirits being quite Spent, and having so short Warning. The inclosed[,] He adds[,] is a true account of the Island, which for Air and Commodities at least Equalizes, and in Situation exceeds Hispaniola in my Judgment.[30]

Admirall Pen[n] was very much pressed by the Officers of the Army to Continue with them; But notwithstanding their Entreaties and His own promise, He sailed from Jamaica the 25th of June, leaving twelve men of War and Some other Vessels under the Command of Vice Admirall Goodson.

And Generall Venables who had been ill sometime, was soon after reduced so low with the Flux, that His life was despaired of, whereupon He resigned His Command to Major Generall Fortescue.

The 8th of July He was by the Advice of His Physicians put on board a ship bound for England, and for 8 or 10 days it was expected that He would die, but afterwards mended and Safely arrived at Plymouth, the 10th of September 1655; where He was informed of Admirall Pen[n]'s arrivall and imprisonment, and wrote to the Protector the Occasion and Necessity of His coming Home. But, His Reasons were not sufficient to appease Cromwell[']s Anger, for upon His coming to Town, He was likewise Committed to the Tower. However, before His Commitment, He and Pen[n] were Examined before the Protector and His Councill, and both of them Severely Reprimanded for leaving the Service Committed to their charge, without permission or Authority.

Vice Admirall Pen[n] in Vindication of His Conduct alledged that He had previously consulted Generall Venables and other land Officers, who informed Him that the Forces, were so sickly and in such want of Provisions, and other Necessaries, that They were not in a Condition to proceed

---

30. This letter is reprinted in C. H. Firth, *The Narrative of General Venables* (London, 1900), 47–48.

upon any other Design. That He thereupon Called the Sea Officers together, who were of opinion, that the large ships should be sent Home and the Frigotts to remain on the Station[,] otherwise they would all, in a little time, be under the Necessity of leaving the Island for want of Provisions.

Generall Venables [was] not Conscious of having committed any Crime in coming Home, being rendered incapable by Sickness to Continue longer in those Parts, without the utmost hazard of His life, and the Protector having in such Case impowered the Commissioners to choose some other fitting Person He could not be prevailed upon to Acknowledge Himself in fault, in leaving the Army, and to throw Himself on the Protector[']s Clemency. And notwithstanding His very bad State of Health, He was not permitted to stay in His Own lodgings, but hurried away to the Tower and treated with great Severity.

But, at length through the persuasion of His Friends, He was obliged to Submit to Cromwell[']s Resolute Temper, or perish under Confinement; and not only acknowledged Himself in fault as Admirall Pen[n] had done, but Resigned His Command in Ireland, and all other Commissions under the Government, upon which He was discharged.

However blameable Generall Venables was in Other Respects, yet in regard to the miscarriage of the Design on St. Domingo, He was unjustly Censured, and did not deserve the Severe treatment He met with. It appears by all the Accounts I have seen of that Expedition, as well as His own Journall, and that of another Officer of Distinction under Him, that He was so far from being consulted or Apprized of the measures, which were necessary to be taken that most of the Troops were Shipped off before He was vested with or under any certainty that He was to be Vested with the Command, so that He had not an Opportunity of making choice of such Men as were fit for the Service, or Even of Exercising and bringing them into Order, and Discipline.

That He was not furnished with a sufficient quantity of Arms, Provisions, and other Necessaries, and even them He had, not good in their kind, though He was not wanting in Application, and representing the difficulties and inconveniences, which would attend the service unless they were well provided. That He was restrained and Cramped in the execution of His Designs by Commissioners and Instructions to other Persons, who were to inspect into, advise, and even to direct His proceedings. That so little regard was had to His Opinion, that He was Contradicted and Slighted by those who were joined in Authority with Him, and particularly Vice Admirall Pen[n], who Conceived a prejudice against Him and could never be reconciled both on account of His being first named in the Commission, and on account of His protesting against His proceedings at Barbadoes, in regard to the Dutch Captors. That the landing the Army at the West point, and not proceeding up the River Hine with the Fleet was Contrary to His Opinion and the true Cause of their Miscarriage. That the

Admirall was deficient in His Duty, in not giving Him the Aid and Assistance of His Ships against the Enemy, and in not furnishing the Troops timely with Provisions and other Necessaries. But, notwithstanding these Arguments in His favour, the Generall bore all the blame, and was the only Person punished; for though the Admirall was imprisoned and reprimanded, yet He was afterwards restored to favour, and Employed not only by Cromwell; but after the Restoration.

It must however be confessed, that Venables was greatly to blame at Jamaica, in not marching directly into the Town of St. Iago de la Vega but Suffering Himself to be amused by the Spaniards for 5 days in Treating, which gave Them an Opportunity of removing Their Families and Effects into the Country, and to settle themselves in Such a manner in divers parts, as gave the Forces a great deal of trouble before they intirely rooted them out of the Island. This will not be thought a needless Digression, since it clears up some Facts in the History of that part of the World, and it is encumbent on Every Writer to Set things in a clear and true light.

The Number of land Forces, which Generall Venables left on the Island, under the Command of Major Generall Fortescue, were Six Regiments amounting to about 5000 Men, Officers inclusive: and about 1200 men, Women and Children which came with them from England, and the Windward Islands; These underwent great hardships and their Number daily diminished, which is to be imputed to their want of Provisions, and other Necessaries, more than to the Inclemency of the Climate.

Vice Admirall Goodson sailed from Jamaica on a Cruise with Nine Ships, the 31th of July, and stood as far to the Eastward as Cape Altavela. Upon calling a Councill of War to Consider, Whether it was advisable to land on any part of the Spanish Dominions, it was Resolved to Attempt Rio de la haca, having intelligence that it was Rich and a Place of small Strength. The Town being Situated in a Bay, and the Water so Shoal that no great Ships could come near it, He ordered 350 Men to be put on board three small Ships, with an intent to land them in the Night: But, being discovered by the Spaniards, who had time to remove their Wealth into the Country, that Design was given over. They thereupon proceeded to S[an]ta Martha, and came before the Town the 24th of August, between 4 and 5, in the Afternoon.

They found two Forts[,] musket Shot one from the other Close by the Water side; in the one which was 22 feet in height were mounted 14 Guns; and between Those two Forts a Breast work: in less than an hour They were in possession of the Town and Forts, but, took only 9 or 10 Prisoners, the rest fled into Woods, and it being night and they Strangers to the Country, [they] did not think proper to pursue them.

After sometime the Spaniards proposed to Ransom the Town, which Consisted of about 200 Houses, and it was agreed, to be delivered up to them for 20,000 p[iece]s of e[ig]ht but to dispose of the Forts as They thought fit. The Agreement not being Complied with, a Party was Sent up, above 10 Miles into the Country, which burnt all their Houses and Plantations, and at Their return, they destroyed the Town and Forts after taking out the Cannon, two of which were brass pieces, great store of Ammunition and Refreshments, but their booty in other Respects was very inconsiderable. From thence the Admirall went and Cruised about Carthagena but met with no other Success than the taking of two or three small prizes of no great Value, and returned to Jamaica the 18th of September.

The 1st of October 1655, arrived twelve Ships with Provisions and other Stores, which had been long Expected, and were promised to have been Sent out of England immediately after the Sailing of the Fleet against St. Domingo. With them came Major Generall Sedgwick,[31] who was Appointed a Commissioner, jointly with the others, But They being all gone off the Island He was under some difficulty how to proceed, the Protector[']s Instructions allowing of no Act, without the Consent of Three Commissioners and in some Cases Two. But, upon a conference with the Major Generall and Vice Admiral Goodson and its appearing by the Commission and Instructions that the one was impowered to act in Case of the Death or disability of the Generall, and the other of the Admirall, after some Debates, it was agreed to Act jointly, and an Instrument in writing was drawn up Accordingly.

The 5th of November Commissioner Sedgwick wrote to the Protector, and Acquainted Him, That having some information at St. Christophers that His Forces had taken St. Domingo, He touched there in His passage, But, found the Spanish Colours flying. That He sent in a Boat which stood so near that they plainly Saw the People in Arms, and others employed in Building a new Fort, on the West side. That having intelligence of the miscarriage before that Place, He steered for Jamaica. And that He did not apprehend any difficulty in taking St. Domingo with a much less number of Forces, than had been before it.

At the same time, He Represented the Deplorable and distressed Condition He found the Forces in; That Severall of the Officers were gone to England, others Dead and Those which remained were in a very indifferent State of Health: many of the Soldiers were also Dead, their Bodies lying unburied in the High ways, and among the bushes; most of those who were living walked like Ghosts, and as He went through the Streets lay groaning and crying out Bread for the Lord[']s sake.

That when He set His foot on Shore He saw nothing but Symptoms of Necessity and desolation; the Shores filled with Casks, Butts &c. with divers sorts of Goods, Arms, Provision[s,] and other Necessaries, most of which were spoiled for want of Care, and by not making Convenient

31. Cromwell chose Major General Robert Sedgwick to supersede Edward Doyley as commander in chief of the forces in Jamaica but died not long after his selection.

Places to preserve them from the Weather; and some had been Embezled or Squandered through negligence, laying exposed to the Soldiers and Strangers. That all the Bread they had did not exceed 30,000 pounds weight, and most of it damaged, which He was the more Surprized at, Because they might in a few days have made a House, and Secured their Provisions and other Necessaries from Injuries.

That He had built a Store House at Cagway, with little or no assistance from the Army, 100 feet in length and 25 in Breadth wherein He reposited the Provisions He brought with Him.

That on the [blank] of the preceeding Month Major Generall *Fortescue died after 4 or 5 days illness*. That Vice Admirall Goodson and Himself, the Surviving Commissioners had thereupon called the Officers together to consider of the settlement and management of the Army and other Affairs. And accordingly Established a Standing Councill to Consist of the Principall Officers of the severall Regiments, which was very much to their Satisfaction, They being before Governed by One Man, without Their Advice or approbation. That the Command of the Forces, devolved on Collo[nel] Doyley, who was the Senior Officer[, and] the best fitted, and most capable of that Trust; but being ill they appointed Collo[nel] Holdipp President of the Councill, and Commander in Chief of the Forces, for seven Days. That Collo[nel] Doyley being since able to do business, They had chosen Him President and Commander in Chief, until His Highness's pleasure was known.

He also acquainted the Protector, the Soldiers had destroyed above 20,000 head of Cattle; what remained were gone into the Woods, and become so wild, it was not easy to Catch them. That the Soldiers had also destroyed all sorts of Fruits and Provisions so that nothing but Ruin attended Them whereever They went.

That some People had been of Opinion the Spaniards, Mulattos and Negroes were gone to Cuba, But they were lately Convinced to the Contrary, many struggling Soldiers, having been cut of[f] by Them, and Sometimes 3 or four in a day. That a considerable Number undoubtedly were still upon the Island, and some *imagined not less than 2000* which He apprehended would do great mischief.

That the Soldiers Expected and desired to be Employed on some Expedition, or to be sent for Home; Dig or Plant They neither were willing nor able, and had rather Starve than Work. That They might raise Provision[s] sufficient for their Subsistance, But nevertheless they would perish for want of Food, unless it was Sent them.

In this Melancholy Situation things were in at that time, and so great a disinclination the Officers and Soldiers in generall had for Planting, or even to provide Common Necessaries and Conveniences for themselves, that the Commissioners were obliged to Represent to them the Necessity of planting Provisions, in regard that there was not sufficient in the

Storehouses for four Months['] Subsistence; and that it was not Prudent in them to depend who[l]ly on Supplies from England; for though They had no Reason to doubt due Care being taken in that Respect Yet miscarriages might happen and frustrate those good intentions. And to Encourage them all to turn their thoughts to Planting, as Some of them had done, it was proposed vizt.[32]

1. To allow and lay out to every man, the particular share of land, which had formerly been allotted, and to Secureth the propriety to them, and their Heirs.

2. to Furnish them with Seed and Grain.

3. In Case the Protector should call them off the Island, upon the prosecution of the War, That then satisfaction should be made them in mon[e]y, for Their Provisions, and in recompense of Their labour and trouble.

[4.] And, it was proposed to reduce the six Regiments to four that They might be compleat in Officers and Men, and be in a better Capacity to fix themselves not only for Planting, but to attend any Military Duty as Guards, and to Settle every Regiment in the manner of a Township.

[5.] It was likewise proposed to remove the Head Quarters, it being generally Apprehended that the Air of the Town was infectious, and would destroy all the People, if not timely removed, having found by Experiences the other Quarters far more healthy.

These Propositions, however reasonable and Necessary, were not approved of by the Majority so that They did not come to any Resolutions thereupon. Nevertheless the Commissioners took all the precaution and Care in their power for the preservation and Security of the Island, and to that end were not only attentive on building a Fortification on the Extream point of Cagway, but in Sending out Frigots to Cruise against the Spaniards, and gain intelligence. One in particular was ordered round the Island, to Search every Harbour and Bay, in order to discover whether any Spaniards Still remained on the Island. On the North side they found some were Set[t]ling, upon which the frigot landed 60 men: But on their Approach the Spaniards retired into the Mountains; the Seamen however destroyed their Houses and Settlements, and brought away such Necessaries as they had.

Returning to the south side round Point Pedro, they landed, discovered two Spanish Houses which they burnt, took 17 Small Arms, and one Spanish Mullatto Prisoner. They likewise landed some men to leeward of the Cape, and encountred forty Spaniards who were Mounted but after a small Skirmish they fled into the Woods.

The Mulatto upon His Examination declared that the Spaniards lay concealed in Severall Parts of the Island, expecting that the English would

32. Thurloe, State Papers, Vol. 4. P. 389. —*Author.*

abandon the Island, and that they should again possess what was formerly their Own.

That most of the Negroes, were Separated from their Masters, and lived by themselves in Small Parties near the English Quarters.

This information was unhappily found to be true, for when the Soldiers went into the Woods to hunt and Seek for Provisions, They lay concealed and killed two or three at a time with their launces.

The Commissioners being only two in Number, thought it proper to take in Collo[nel] Doyley, who then had the Command of the Army, to Act jointly with them as a Commissioner. And perceiving things to grow worse and worse through the disinclination of Most of the Officers, and Soldiers to Planting and that some of them were inclined to quit the Island, and abandon the whole Design: They again Represented to them the Necessity of Planting, and to induce them issued out their Proposalls in writing. But on the same day vizt. the 4th of January 1656, the Army requested the Officers to propose to the President and Commissioners Their leaving the Island. And accordingly the following Instrument in writing was laid before the Commissioners.

To Colo[nel] Edward Doyley Commander in
Chief of the Army &c.
Jamaica January the 4th 1656.

Whereas we are every day importuned both by the Officers and Soldiers of this Army, representing the sadness of Their Condition, and discouraged by their Mortality and Continuall sickness, that hath utterly disabled them from performing any Service for the Commonwealth, or to plant for their Subsistence here, that we commiserate their Condition, and use Some speedy means for their removall hence, so that those remaining may be Serviceable to His Highness, and the Common Wealth of England; We therefore from the sense of the great duty lying upon Us, both towards God and our Severall Charges, have made bold to make these our humble Addresses to you That You would be pleased to represent them effectually to the Admirall and Commissioner Sedgwick that speedy Course may be taken accordingly for their Relief[.]

John Humfrey:[33] William Smith.
Samuel Barry:[34] Robert Smith.
Henry Jones.

33. Colonel John Humphrey was commander of one of the reinforcement regiments sent after the conquest of Jamaica.

34. Colonel Samuel Barry played a key role in thwarting Spanish attempts to recapture Jamaica and subsequently settled in the colony and was a member of the council from 1661 until his death around the end of the century. For more biographical details, see Firth, *Regimental History of Cromwell's Army*, 2:720–22.

The Fleet which Consisted of 23 Sail of all sorts were healthy and in a good Condition, but likewise uneasy and Murmured at their being detained in Port, and not put on Action. To Quiet them the Commissioners Summoned 12 of the Principall Officers, Six of the Fleet and Six of the land Forces. Acquainted them with the Protector's orders in relation to the Settlement of the Island; also for annoying and distressing of the Enemy: and Since they all cried out for Action, desired Their Opinions what was Necessary to be done. The Result of which Consultation was that to encourage the Soldiers and promote the settlement of the Island, every Man should have a portion of land Conveyed to Him. That 6 or 8 Ships should be left to Secure the Harbour the rest to go to Sea, under the Conduct of Vice Admirall Goodson.

But, these Resolutions were not agreeable and satisfactory to the land Forces, who insisted upon Their pay and Subsistance, if they were continued in the Service if not to be disbanded and at liberty to return to England. Hence arose a Dispute between Major Throgmorton and the Generall, who was Suspected of being privy to the Design, though He denied it before the Commissioners, which made the Major impeach Him, and to make good His Charge[.] They were both put under a Guard, in order for their Trial. Col[onel] Doyley was Acquitted but the other who was a warm, Passionate Young Gentleman, in making His Defence insisted that the Court Martial had not any power to Try Him; upon which He was rudely thrust out of the Court; and the holding up His hand to Save His Head when the Marshall offered to Strike Him with the hilt of His Sword; was deemed a Resistance. He was thereupon condemned, and Shot according to the Sentence; which quieted matters for some time.

In January the Protector's Proclamation for Encouraging the Settlement of the Island was published, the Substance of which is as follows.

Whereas, by the good providence of God, our fleet, in their late expedition into America, had possessed themselves of a certain Island, called Jamaica, spacious in its extent, commodious in its harbours and Rivers within itself, healthfull by its situation, fertile in the nature of the Soil, well stored with Horses and other Cattle, and generally fit and worthy to be planted and improved, to the advantage, honour and Interest of this Nation.

And Whereas divers persons, Merchants, and other[s] heretofore conversant in Plantations and the Trade of the like nature, are desirous to undertake and proceed upon Plantations and Settlement upon that Island: We therefore for the better encouragement of all such persons so inclined, have by the advice of our Council taken care, not only for the strengthening and securing of that Island from all Enemies, but for the constituting and settling of a civil Government, by such good Laws and Customs, as are and have been exercised in Colonies and places of the like nature, have

appointed Surveyors and other Publick Officers, for the more equal distribution of Publick right *and* justice in the said Island.

And for the further incouragement to the industry and good affection of
such persons, We have provided and given orders to the Commissioners
of our Customs, that every Planter or Adventurer to that Island shall be
exempt and free from paying any excise or Custom for any Manufactures,
provisions, or any other goods or necessaries, which he or they shall transport to the said Island of Jamaica, within the space of seven years to come
from Michaelmas next.

And also that sufficient caution and security be given by the said Commissioners, that such goods shall be delivered at Jamaica only. And, we
have also, out of our special consideration of the Welfare and prosperity of that Island, provided, that no Customs, or other Tax or impost be
laid or charged upon any commodity, which shall be the produce and
native growth of that Island, and shall be imported into any of the Dominions belonging to this common Wealth: Which favour and exemption
shall continue for the space of ten years, to begin and be accounted from
Michaelmas next.

We have also given our special orders and directions, that no imbargo
or other hinderance, upon any pretence whatsoever, be laid upon any
Ships, Seamen, or other Passengers or Adventurers, Which shall appear to
be engaged and bound for the said Island.

And we do hereby further declare, for our selves and successors, that
whatsoever other favour, or immunity, or protection shall or may conduce
to the Welfare, strength, and improvement of the said Island, shall from
time to time be continued and applied thereunto. Given under our hand at
White Hall the 10. of Oct[obe]r 1655.

In February the *Hunter* Capt[ai]n Sabada with 100 Soldiers under the
Command of Capt[ai]n Foster was sent to dispossess the Enemy who were
set[t]ling at Point Pedro. Upon landing they discovered Several Spanish
Horsemen, who immediately fled. They soon came up to a Small Town[35]
which They burned, and discovered four Spaniards who endeavoured to
draw them into an Ambuscade, but perceiving their Design they Wheeled
about a Hill from whence They came, and Discovered the Enemy, who
immediately fled and made their Escape, except Seven, who were taken.
Upon Examination they confessed their Party consisted of 20 men and the
other which fled over the River of 40. That there had been a Frigot from
Carthagena which brought them Provisions, and a letter to the Maistro
Del Campo, to gather all the People of the Island, at Paratee, for there
were two Galleons to come with 1000 men to land at Point Pedro and join
them. That the Armada from old Spain was to go into the Principall Har-

---

35. Oristan. situate near the head of Black River. — *Author.*

bour to drive the English from thence. And that They were come, upon those advices, out of the Country, and expected to be joined by their Country Men who were Set[t]led at St. Anns. They likewise confessed that They had lost above 500 Men, who were killed or perished in the Woods, Since They were dispossessed of the Town and Settlements on the South side of the Island.

The *Falmouth* returned, about the same[36] time from a Cruize, round the Island, and brought in 15 Spaniards who were taken on the North Side, and Confirmed what was related by the Other Prisoners.

In April the Enemy, and particularly the Negroes began to be very bold and troublesome for They not only cut off several Strag[g]ling Soldiers, but at one time no less than Forty men who were carelessly going about their Quarters upon which a Strong Party was Sent after them and were so lucky to discover their Settlement[,] killed severall of them and totally ruined their Quarters, in that Place.

Soon after, the Soldiers began again to be uneasy, at their allowance of Bread being short[e]ned and 30 of Colo[nel] Buller[']s Regiment actually retired with Their Arms with an intent to join the Enemy if They could find them out. But, being immediately pursued, They surrendered, upon which three of them were Executed, and the rest pardoned.

During these Transactions, Cromwell having advice of the Death of Major Gen[era]ll Fortescue and looking upon Col[one]l Doyley, as a Cavalier and not truly Attached to His Interest, Sent over a Commission of Major Generall Sedgewick to be Commander in chief of the Forces, which arrived the 12th of May. But Vice Admirall Goodson one of the Commissioners being then at Sea, He did not think fit to publish it or to take the Command upon Him. What were His Motives and Reasons doth not Appear, though it is Certain that, When He had read His letters He called Mr. Aylesbury[,] the Secretary of the Island[,][37] to Him, and Said[,] *I am utterly undone, for I have the greatest Conflict on my Spirits that ever Man had, and find I am not able to bear what is laid upon me*, upon which He gave Mr. A. the letters to read, and after He had perused them replied, *I see nothing in these letters that ought to Afflict you; His Highness hath made choice of you to command the Army, and both He and* Secretary Thurloe *have expressed so great an Esteem for you that on the Contrary you have great Cause to rejoice, your Endeavours have been so well Accepted of.* Ay Mr. Aylesbury[,] said He, *It is that which has undone me, there is so much expected, and I am Conscious of my*

36. Thurloe, State Papers, Vol. 4. P. 1711. — *Author.*

37. William Aylesbury (1615–1656), once governor to George Villiers, Second Duke of Buckingham, went into exile following the collapse of the Royalist cause and published a translation of Davila's *History of the French Civil Wars* from the Italian. Returning to England in 1650, he became in 1656 secretary to Major General Sedgewick in Jamaica, where he died after only a few months.

own dissabilities, and having beside an Untoward People to deal with, I am able to perform so little that I shall never overcome it. He never enjoyed Himself afterwards, but Appeared to have lost his usuall freedom and Cheerfullness: And without any visible Distemper only a little feverish, He died the 24th of May following which was 12 days after, the Receipt of his letters and Commission.

He was a Gentleman of a fair Character, in favour with Cromwell, and very much Esteemed by all His Acquaintance: But, he was diffident of Himself, of a desponding Nature, and under such apprehensions of dying, that the very thoughts and fear of Death *hast[e]ned* his end (as it hath done many others since of the like Temper and disposition in that part of the *World*) for it is related of him, that He Continued on board the Ship, and seldom came on Shore, but when the service required it, imagining the air of the Town and the Soldiers['] Quarters infectious, by reason of the Sickness and Mortality which hap[pe]ned amongst the Troops. It likewise Appears, by some Circumstances, that thought He was assiduous Yet He had not spirit and Resolution enough, to conduct so great an undertaking or to struggle with difficulties and to Contend with men of such Restless and Turbulent dispositions, as He had to do with, which Consideration, and the injustice that was done Colo[ne]l Doyley, in Superceeding Him, who was a Senior Officer, and twice Commander in Chief of the Forces, by Election as well as Succession, Seems to be the true Motives and Reasons of His not taking the command on Him, and the uneasiness He was under on that Occasion, perceiving the Alteration Cromwell had made in that respect, was not agreeable to the Forces, but on the Contrary they were very much dissatisfied with it; that Gentleman being very popular, and the most beloved of all the Officers who came out on this Expedition.

Vice Admirall Goodson, who sailed the 15th of April, with ten of the best Ships on a Cruise stood up as high as Cape Altavela, in hopes of meeting with some Spanish Ships, but being dissappointed in his Expectations, He stood over for the Main. The 5th of May He landed 450 men at Rio de la Hacha, but the Spaniards having descried the Ships Six hours before They could get in, had time to remove Their best Effects and fled into the Country—so that He took possession of the Fort and Town without any Opposition. He demolished the Fort after taking out the Ammunition and Stores, particularly four brass *Cannon of 4000 pounds weight each* and the Spaniards, who had sent to Ransom the Town, not complying with Their proposalls, He burnt it to the ground. He afterwards took a Spanish Ship the Master of which informed him He came from Spain, with a large Fleet; Having this Intel[l]igence, He was Apprehensive of Some design on Jamaica, immediately Stood over and arrived the *23d of May, the day before Major Generall Sedgwick* died.

The Command being again devolved on Collo[nel] Doyley He continued to Act as a Commissioner as well as Commander in Chief of the

Army. And having received letters from Collo[nel] Stokes, Governour of Nevis,[38] proposing to come down with 1000 Men[,] Women and Children and Settle on this Island on certain Conditions, which were approved of, three ships were Sent to bring them down.

In June Collo[nel] Holdipp who was most forward in planting, and had brought His Plantation into some order, was accused by *His Lieutenant Collo[nel]*[39] *of* detaining the dues of His Regiment &c., upon which Several Articles were brought against Him, and upon His trial before a Court Martiall He was not only Cashiered, but deprived of His Plantation.

The Forces having recovered their healths and Spirits some of them turned their thoughts to Planting, which Collo[nel] Doyley encouraged by assigning Them lands, and in Quartering His own Regiment at Yallah, for the Protection of New Set[t]lers.

And Vice Admirall Goodson having disposed of most of His Squadron, to cruiz[e] in proper Stations *Sailed with four Ships* the 11th of July,[40] and Cruised off the Havanna, to the 29th of August, but without any Success. It was then Resolved in a Councill of War, that it was not safe to Continue any longer on that Coast, in regard to the time of the Year; and that it was difficult; if not impracticable to turn up to Jamaica, therefore it was most advisable, and for the Publick Service, to proceed to Nevis and assist in transporting the Planters, who proposed to go down and Settle in Jamaica.

They arrived there the *9th of October,* and found the People in a readiness to imbark, and having furnished the Fleet with Wood and Water, took on board Collo[nel] Stoakes and His Family, with 1400 Men[,] Women and Children, of which 800 were able to bear Arms,[41] and Sailed directly for Port Morant where they arrived the 4th of November, and landed this Colony who having lands allotted them, according to their Proposalls, Set[t]led there Contiguously.

During these transactions, Cromwell having advice of the Death of commissioner Sedgwick and being Resolved to have a Commander in Chief who was devoted to His Interest, immediately Sent Orders to L[ieutenan]t Generall Brayne,[42] Governour of Port St. Patrick in Scotland; to imbark

38. Luke Stoakes, governor of Nevis, led 1,600 migrants to Jamaica and settled around Port Morant in December 1656 in response to Cromwell's "Proclamation Encouraging Immigration to Jamaica." Stoakes, his wife, and around 1,200 settlers died within three months in this swampy region, although the survivors developed the area into a region of more than sixty settlements by 1671. Black, *History of Jamaica,* 51–52; Cundall, *Governors of Jamaica in the Seventeenth Century,* xxxix–xl; Pestana, *English Conquest of Jamaica,* 219–20.

39. Michael Bland.

40. Thurloe[']s State Papers, Vol. 5. P. 500.—*Author.*

41. I[bi]d. Vol. 5, P. 771.—*Author.*

42. Lieutenant-General William Brayne had served in Scotland before Cromwell, in the summer of 1756, appointed him commander in chief of Jamaica, which he presided over from his arrival in December 1756 until his death the following September. For more biographical details, see Firth, *Regimental History of Cromwell's Army,* 2:704–6.

with the Regiment under His Command, and to touch at Kingsale and take in Collo[nel] Moor[43] and His Regiment. Accordingly they Sailed from thence the 20th of October, but meeting with Contrary Winds and bad Weather, did not arrive at Jamaica before the 14th of January 1656 [1657].

Upon His arrivall He took on Him, pursuant to His Commission and Instructions, the Command of the Sea, as well as of the land Forces. And Vice Admirall Goodson, soon after, returned to England with the Ships which were unfit to Continue any longer on the Station.

Generall Brayne found the State and Condition of the Island altered very much for the better; and the land Forces, which remained and were about 3000 in Number, in very good health. But, the Same Averseness and disinclination to Planting appeared (in most of them) as ever; and upon Enquiry into the Causes and Reasons he discovered that it was principally owing to the Officers, some of them Employing Their Men to work as Their Servants without allowing them any part of the Fruits of Their labour; and others, who were intent on nothing more than Returning to England, endeavoured to Obstruct and defeat the undertaking, by suggesting to the Soldiers that They would shortly be Employed on some other Expedition, and that They would then be deprived of the Benefit of Their labour. He therefore immediately Redressed the former, and Encouraged Them all to Plant, and dismissed the discontented and useless Officers. These prudent Regulations soon had a very good Effect, for some of the Soldiers who were before averse to planting, now turned Their thoughts that way, as well as the Officers and went cheerfully to work.

General Brayne finding it necessary to raise a Fortification at *Port Morant*, for the protection of the Nevis Colony, accordingly ordered a small Fort to be built at the Harbour[']s Mouth, and ten whole Culverins to be planted therein.

In March the *Selby* frigot, brought in a Spanish Periagua, with Seven Men, which was taken on the North Side of the Island. The Master being Examined declared that He belonged to St. Iago de Cuba, and was formerly an Inhabitant of this Island. That since it was taken by the English, He had made four Voyages from hence to Cuba, carried thither each time about *forty* Persons; and that He believed there had gone off, at times and in *Severall boats which were sent by the Governour of Cuba, about Three thousand Persons*. That they had advice of an Armada preparing in Old Spain for America, which was to touch at Tortugas to be joined with 800 Soldiers from St. Domingo and 500 of those, who went from this Island. That *there was about a dozen Spanish Families now upon the Island, who lived at Oristan, near the River Alvocan and Six leagues from the Sea, which was* Commodious,

43. Colonel William Moore served in Ireland before he and his Irish regiment followed Brayne to Jamaica in the spring of 1657. Unhappy and fearing for his health in Jamaica, he returned to England in August 1758. For more detail, see ibid., 2:726–27.

because it is a *private Place and cannot be discerned at Sea*. That the *Negroes, who were not of the Spanish Party, were about 200 in Number* but did not know in what Part of the Island they were in.

The Forces, who were at this time in good health, began again to be distressed for want of Provisions, most of what They had by the last Ships being Spent or decayed, no Supplies arriving in due time from England, and the New England Merchants declining to come as usual, disliking Their payment in Bills on the Government; so that They were under the Necessity of taking the Soldiers from Planting and doing Military Duty, and disperse them in the most Convenient Places to hunt for Wild Cattle and Hogs, for Their Subsistance, except such as had made some progress in planting and could maintain themselves by Their labour.

The Fleet was likewise so Short of Provisions that very few Ships could be fitted out to Sea, so that severall of them were likewise sent to the most plentifull Parts of the Island, and Their men put ashore to hunt and Subsist themselves, to make Their Provisions hold out. But, this did not answer Expectation, by reason the Seamen who were unacquainted with that kind of Exercise, went in pursuit of the Cattle with such noise and Clamour, as fright[e]ned them from the Sea Side and low lands into the Woody and Mountainous Parts, where They could not follow them, so that They were forced to return to their Ships, without any Success, greatly fatigued and half Starved. But the Officers of some of the Ships, who managed in a proper manner, made a very good Shift.

In June Cagway was laid out as a Town and the foundation of severall Houses were raised.

In July arrived Severall Ships with Provisions and other Necessaries, which was a great Relief and Satisfaction to the Forces, who had been put to hard shifts. Especially Those that were unset[t]led and expected to be maintained at the Publick charge. But, Others who were Industrious, and inclined to become Set[t]lers, the Generall thought proper to discharge, according to their own desire.

Generall Brayne having for sometime laboured under an indisposition of Body, Occasioned by His great fatigue and perplexity in the Execution of his Duty, and being Apprehensive of Death, in pursuance of the Power Vested in Him by Cromwell (in Case of imminent danger of life)[44] to name a Successor, He by Commission *dated the 27th of August 1657, Constituted and Appointed Collo[nel] Edward Doyley to be* Commander in chief of the Forces by Sea and land, in as full and Ample manner as He Himself had. And *on the 2d. of September departed this life.*

He was an able Experienced Officer, and in great Confidence with Cromwell, whose Interest He had very much at heart, particularly in pre-

---

44. Thurloe[']s State Papers Vol. 6. P. 512. —*Author.*

serving and promoting the Settlement of this Valuable acquisition, which He knew the Protector was intent and Resolved upon at all Events.

By His [Brayne's] Death Collo[nel] Doyley succeeded to the Command the 3d time, and Represented to the Protector the State and Condition of the Island and how difficult it was to command an Army without pay. He likewise desired leave to Come for England, assuring Him that as soon as He had set[t]led his private Affairs, He would return to the Island if it was His pleasure. But, this Request was not granted, nor does it appear that He was confirmed by Cromwell, or acted by any other Authority or Commission than was delegated to Him by Generall Brayne; though He was afterwards confirmed by the long Parliament.

Collo[nel] Doyley having intelligence that the Spaniards intended to make some attempts on the North side, dispatched three men of War to intercept them and prevent their Designs; the rest of the Ships he stationed in other Parts, for the Same purpose, to gain intelligence, and to Annoy the Enemy.

The 21st of February arrived the *Marston Moor*[45] with some store ships from England which were so much wanted, that the Men of War would have been in a little time, obliged to Shift for themselves, and the Soldiers reduced to very great Necessities. She also brought over £2572.17.11 in money, which was to be made use of, to Compleat the Fortifications at Cagway and Port Morant.

The same month returned two Ships which Collo[nel] Doyley sent to Bermudas to invite the Planters of the Colony to come and Settle in this Island. And in them came 250 Persons, most Women and Children who Set[t]led in several Parts, agreeable to their Own inclination.

The Cruisers, which were sent to gain intelligence[,] also returned with two or three small prizes, and confirmed the Account they had of the intentions of the Spaniards to invade this Island. On board of these Prizes they intercepted divers orders and Instructions to the Spanish Officers who were to be Employed on that Occasion. They likewise found Don Francisco de Carthagena, one of the Captains, of the Supplies from old Spain, whom they made Prisoner.

At length the Succours which had been so long promised and expected, arrived at St. Iago de Cuba, with the King of Spain[']s[46] orders to the Governours of Porto Rico, St. Domingo and the Havanna, to aid and Assist them to disposses the English and recover Jamaica. He likewise sent a Commission to Don Christovall Sasi Arnaldo to be Governour of the Island and Commander in chief of the Forces.

This Gentleman was a Native of the Island, very Popular, and had great

---

45. Thurloe's State Papers, vol. 6, 512. — *Author.*

46. Philip IV (1605?–1665) ascended to the throne in March 1621, inheriting a kingdom and empire in crisis, which his reign did not alleviate.

Possessions there before it was taken. He was the Person who persuaded the Inhabitants *not* to Comply with the Treaty, Encouraged them to retire into the Woods and Covert Places, and endeavour to harrass and distress the English in hopes by that means to oblige them to Abandon the Island. Accordingly They dispersed themselves in Severall Parts, that They might be the better able to Subsist themselves and support each other. But being often discovered and routed by the English They were reduced to the greatest extremity, insomuch that many of them perished through hardships and for want of the common necessaries of life; and the rest despairing of the promised Succours, and of recovering of their former Possessions, made their escape to St. Iago de Cuba; *except this Gentleman* and a small Party with Him. These retreated to some obscure Place where They remained undiscovered, and found means of holding a Correspondance with the Governour of St. Iago who from time to time sent them Provisions and other Necessaries, though they were frequently disappointed, by their being intercepted by our Cruisers, and were by that means put to very hard Shifts.

The 8th of May the Spaniards landed Thirty Companies of Foot, at Rio Nova, where They had been 12 days before They were discovered, at which time our Ships plying up and down descried in the Bay three Sail, which had brought over Those Forces, and immediately prepared to board Them, but being becalmed could not Effect it, and in the Night the Spanish Ships stole away.

Collo[nel] Doyley on receipt of this Intelligence called a Council of War, to Consider what was Necessary to be done on that Occasion; and it was Resolved to attack them without delay, the Officers and Soldiers being extreme[ly] desirous of Action and an Opportunity of retrieving the Honour They lost at St. Domingo.

Accordingly 750 men[,] Officers included, were Shipped of in the *Grantham, Marston Moor, Martin Galley* and Ketch; and Collo[nel] Doyley after having given the Necessary orders to Collo[nel] Moor, whom He appointed to command in His absence, the Forces which remained on the South side, Sailed from Cagway the 11th of June. On the [blank] He arrived before Rio Nova, and Attempted to land in the Bay which was defended by two Companies, and within half shot of their Cannon. The Forlorn leapt into the Water, and with great resolution marched up to Their Breast Work, which They deserted after one fire, leaving their two Captain's and 23 men more, who were Slain. In an hour all the English Forces were landed, notwithstanding the Fort continued firing at Them but did them little damage.

The next day, Collo[nel] Doyley[,] understanding the Enemy was far superior in Number to the Forces under His Command, was at a stand how to Attempt Them, as They were fortified and had six pieces of Cannon; beside he had a River to pass over, which They [Doyley's forces] were unacquainted with. But having provided Scaling ladders, and other Necessaries, He sent a Drummer, in the Evening, with the following Summons, though His principall Errand was to discover the depth of the River.

S[i]r.

Being here with the Forces of the Mighty Prince the Protector of England, and the Dominions thereunto belonging, I do in His Name, and for His use require and Summon you to deliver up the Fort of Rio Nova, with the Ordnance and Ammunition therein; assuring you of honourable terms, and transport to your Country, which if you refuse, I shall be Acquitted of the blood, which will be Shed. I expect the return of my Drummer in an hour and am

Your very humble Servant
Edward Doyley

to

Don Christopher Sasi Arnoldo
Commander in chief of the Spanish Return Forces.

The Drummer was very Civily treated[,] had 25 p[iece]s of Eight given him by the Spanish Generall and a Jarr of Sweet Meats for Collo[nel] Doyley, with the following Answer[:]

Lord Generall Don Christopher Arnoldo & Sasi, Governour for His Majesty the King of Spain, my Lord of the Island of Jamaica Answering to your letter, wherin you require me to deliver the Fort of Rio Nova, and what else is therein, I say, that His Majesty whom God preserve, hath appointed me for Governour of this Island, being his own Property, and hath remitted me unto it a Regiment of Spanish Infantry, and twenty four foot Companies to defend it. The Forts and Castles of His Majesty are not yeilded with so much facility hitherto. I have received no batteries nor have you made any advance. I want no powder, ball, Provision nor gallant men, that know how to die, before they are Overcome. God keep your Honour in those Commands you desire.

Don Christopher Sasi Arnoldo

To the Generall
Mons Doyley
Governour of the Forces
of England.

Collo[nel] Doyley upon the receipt of this Answer Resolved to march early the next morning and Ordered two Ships to war in as near as possible, and play on their Fortification, while He attacked it on the other side. Accordingly he began His march, at Day break, and when He came within a Quarter of a Mile of the Fort, He met a Party at Work on a Hill, in order to Obstruct His passing over the River; but on the Appearance of our Forces, they took to their Arms, discharged them and run away.

When Collo[nel] Doyley came in Sight of the Fort, He found it was not finished nor carried so high as it was on the other part to leeward. He thereupon ordered the Forlorn, to march with Scaling ladders, and hand Granadoes, who received their fire, and immediately run up to their Flankers, which they gained in a Quarter of an hour.

The Enemy thereupon deserted their Works, and retreated into the Mountains, our men pursuing them for 3 or 4 miles, and doing great Execution. The Seamen perceiving many of them run along the Shore, and among the Rocks, came in their boats and killed Severall of them.

In the Fort, they found ten double barrells of powder, a great quantity of shot, Six pieces of Ord[i]nance, and Eight months Store of Provisions, Wine, Brandy &c. The Number of the Spaniards who were killed, was above 300 Persons, among Them two Priests, several Captains, and their Serjeant Major. Also 100 and odd Prisoners were taken, among them Six Captains, who were Sent Home with the King of Spain[']s standard and Six Colours by Colonel [Sam] Barry[47] to the Protector, who died a few weeks before He arrived. The English Forces, in this Action, lost one Captain, two Lieutenants, one Ensign, and twenty-three private men: Severall Officers were wounded, and Thirty four private men[,] some of whom died afterwards of the wounds They had received.

Collo[nel] Doyley after pursuing and harassing the Enemy for some days, in which time He took two pair of Colours more, and between 30 and 40 private men, most of which were maimed or wounded, He thought proper to demolish the Forts and Breast work and to return to the South Side.

This Success, and a large Body of Them being afterwards defeated at Point Pedro, by Major Stevens,[48] made the desponding Spaniards resolve not to expose Themselves any longer to the Fury of the English, or the miserable Circumstances, They often were in; and at all hazards to quit and Abandon the Island for ever: After they had been in possession 146 years. Collo[nel] Doyley had notice of Their Design, but thought it prudent to overlook it, and permit them quietly to embark with their Wives and Children.

Thus was this Valuable Acquisition defended and preserved, by the Bravery and good Conduct of That Gentleman, who made its former Masters (after all Their Efforts and sustaining many and great hardships) like so many Fugitives, desert and thereby give up all their pretensions to it.

47. Colonel Sam Barry compiled a long history in the West Indies and Jamaica during the last half of the seventeenth century, becoming a member of the Jamaica Council and dying in Jamaica. For more detail, see Firth, *Regimental History of Cromwell's Army*, 2:720–22.

48. Major Richard Stevens. For more detail, see ibid., 2:713–14.

And, our Forces at Rio Nova, regained the Honour They had lost at St. Domingo; for the Spaniards were not only double Their Number, but strongly intrenched, guarded by a Fort and so Confident were They of Success, that upon The approach of our Troops They upbraided Them with Their defeat at that Place, and cried out St. Domingo[,] St. Domingo.

Collo[nel] Doyley upon His return to St. Iago de la Vega, having information of the Galleons being at Porto Bello; That They were but five in Number, and had on board 5 millions of p[iece]s of 8/8; dispatched 5 Sail of men of war and a hired Ship under the Command of Capt[ain] Mings[49] and put on board Them 300 land men. They sailed from Cagway the 2d of September, and stretched over to Carthagena where They Cruised some days and having got such intelligence as they wanted, proceeded to an Obscure Place, near Porto Bello, where They lay close for a month, and until They discovered themselves by Chasing two Ships which appeared in Sight, but having the advantage of the Wind, they run into the Harbour of Tholon, where our Ships followed Them notwithstanding the Fire from the Forts and burnt Them. They afterwards landed and burnt the Town, which was well built, and had 3 Churches in it, And, then returned to Their former Station except three Ships which wanted Water.

On the 20th of October they spied the Spanish Fleet, which Consisted of 15 Galleons, and 14 Merchant Ships, coming out of Porto Bello, but not having sufficient force to attempt Them They only exchanged Some broad sides and returned to Jamaica very much mortified.

The Affairs of the Island, at this time began to have a more promising Aspect, severall of the old Spanish Plantations, which had been neglected and gone to ruin were cultivated, and some of the Soldiers who were averse to planting; seeing the Success of others, by their Industry, likewise turned Their thoughts that way: And some employed Themselves in hunting of Wild Cattle and hogs, by which means They got a comfortable Subsistance so that They were not under the Apprehensions They had been, and were now in a Condition to Subsist themselves without Supplies from England.

The Cruisers were likewise successfull in taking Several Spanish Prizes laden with Cocoa and other Merchandize. And, 4 or 5 Sail of Ships were loaded this Year, for England and North America partly with Cocoa and other produce of the Island and partly with prize Goods.

But, though They had entirely dispossessed the Spaniards, and Things

49. Christopher Mings/Myngs (1625?–1666) was born Norfolk, served in the coastal trade as a young man, and fought against the Dutch in the 1650s. Upon the recommendation of senior officers, he received the captaincy of the *Marston Moor* in October 1655. Traveling to the West Indies, he became vice admiral of the white and fighting off Lowestoft, June 3, 1665, for which he was knighted, and then vice admiral of the blue and fighting the Dutch in the North Sea, during which conflict he was fatally wounded.

were in a prosperous way, yet They had some difficulties to Struggle with; for the Negroes, who had been for some time, Separated from Their Masters, and were very troublesome, finding the Spaniards had entirely quitted the Island, apprehended (if the English Forces should Overcome them) that They should be treated in a barbarous manner, for the mischiefs They had frequently done, were grown desperate and Resolved to maintain Their ground, to the last Extremity.

Accordingly They chose a bold Resolute fellow whom They thought a proper Person to Conduct and Govern Them; and He divided Them into Companies, and appointed Captains to Command Them. They likewise agreed to some Regulations, which They thought proper and Necessary to keep Them United. The Women and Some of the Men who were unfit for any Enterprize They Employed in building Houses and planting Maiz[e], Yams &c. in remote and unsuspected Places, where They could retire to in Case They were discovered and routed. But, all the Hail, able bodied Men went in Parties, made excursions and not only robbed and plundered, but at times cut off a great Number of Hunters, Fowlers and others who had rambled from Their Quarters.

This proved fatal to Them, and Convinced Collo[nel] Doyley of the absolute Necessity of Extirpating, or Obliging Them to Submit; and having discovered Their head Quarters the 18th of February 1659, Sent out a Strong Party commanded by L[ieutenan]t Collo[nel] Tyson,[50] who was so fortunate to meet with Their Main Body, Attacked and killed severall of Them, particularly Their head Man and some others who had Opposed and obstructed Their Submitting to the English. The Rest retreated to the Mountains, and many of them were Struck with such a Panick and so dispirited, that they despaired of being able to Support and defend themselves any longer and Sent to Collo[nel] Doyley, in the humblest manner, offering to Submit on Certain Conditions. Accordingly it was agreed that—They, their Wives, and children should be for Ever Free, subject nevertheless to the laws and Customs of England; and that They should have lands assigned Them, to possess and Enjoy for Their own use. On Their Parts it was Stipulated, that They should not only be ready on all Occasions to defend the Island, against any Foreign Enemy; but to Assist in reducing such Negroes, as should refuse to Accept of those Terms and Conditions.

In pursuance of this agreement One of their Captains named Juan de Bolas,[51] with above 100 men, Women and Children Submitted and had

---

50. Lieutenant Colonel Edward Tyson also defeated Ysasi in May 1660. For more details, see ibid., 2:724–25.

51. On Juan de Bola, the leader of the free Spanish Negro community on this occasion, see Pestana, *English Conquest of Jamaica*, 201–2, 205–7, 210–11, 231, 246.

lands allotted Them at Caimanos. Nevertheless one or two of Their Gangs obstinately refused those terms, whereupon Juan de Bolas and some others were sent out with a Party of Soldiers to pursue and reduce Them. They in hopes of the promised Rewards, and to Testify their Fidelity to the English, went out Cheerfully; and being acquainted with Their Places of Retreat, destroyed Their Settlement, killed and took severall Prisoners. By which means They were in a short time reduced to so inconsiderable a Number, that the Soldiers and other set[t]lers were not apprehensive of being any more annoyed or disturbed by Them.

It would have been happy for the Island, and Saved a vast expence, had They improved this favourable opportunity of Extirpating Them; for though They were so far reduced as to be incapable of doing any further mischief at that time yet it was easy to foresee, that while They had a Place of Retreat, and could maintain Themselves, They would in time Encrease by Procreation as they had Women amongst Them; and be joined by others who on any disgust or imagined Severity, would desert Their Masters and join Them. I have heard that Collo[nel] Doyley was not only of that Opinion but that no means should be left unattempted to Extirpate or Oblige Them to Submit; and urged the Strongest Reasons in Support of His Suggestions. Nevertheless He was opposed and obstructed in His Measures, by some Turbulent, discontented Officers, who insinuated amongst the Soldiers, that His design was only to keep Them Employed in order to deprive Them of the Fruits of Their labour By which Popular Insinuations that Worthy Gentleman was defeated in his good Intentions, and obliged to give over all thoughts of the matter, perceiving the Soldiers greatly fatigued, and uneasy at being Sent out on Such Expeditions, and inflamed at Their receiving very little, if any of Their Pay since they came out of England.

The Event has proved the Truth and Reasonableness of those Suppositions, for They in process of time encreased to such a degree, by a Rebellion which hap[pe]ned some Years after in Mr. Sutton[']s[52] Plantation in Clarendon, and another at Mr. Guy[']s[53] in Liguinea and by desertions from time to time since that They formed two Considerable Bodies, and before the Treaty made with them in 1738, indangered the Security of the Island. But, as I shall Occasionally treat of these matters, in their proper place, I will here suspend any further Remarks, on that head.

The Treaty made with the Spanish Negroes, not only prevented Their doing any further mischiefs at that time and made it safe Travelling from one Part of the Island to another, but, was attended with some other ad-

52. In part 3-B, Knight describes this revolt on Thomas Sutton's plantation on July 29, 1690.

53. Knight treats the revolt at Mrs. or Mr. Guy's plantation in 1684 in more detail in part 3-B.

vantages to the New Set[t]lers—who were not so well acquainted with the Nature of the Soil, the proper times and Seasons of Planting, or how to Cultivate and Cure Cocoa, and other Commodities, which They attained the knowledge of from those Negroes, and this enabled Them to make considerable improvements.

Collo[nel] Doyley having information of the disposition of the Inhabitants of Tortugas near the N[orth]W[est] end of Hispaniola who were of all Nations; That They were desirous of being under the English Government and That the French had been endeavouring to prevail with Them to Submit to the Crown of France; the 25th of May 1660, gave a Commission to Jeremy De Champs (who had made great professions of His Affection and Zeal to the English Nation) to take possession of that Island in the Name of the Common Wealth of England, and to be Governour and Commander in Chief; But, he proved Treacherous and unfaithfull and declared for the French, as will appear hereafter.

When the Island was free from all Apprehensions of Their Foreign and Domestick Enemies, and everything seemed to be in a prosperous way, all had like to have been undone and turned into Confusion, by a dangerous Mutiny among the Soldiers, incited and encouraged by L[ieutenan]t Collo[nel] Robert Raymond,[54] who was very Popular among the Oliverian Party, a man of great Abilities, Resolute and Ambitious. He had it seems taken a Strong prejudice to Collo[nel] Doyley whose Principles were Opposite to his, the one being an Oliverian, and the Other in his heart a Cavalier, though he had on the Change of times taken a Commission from and had been Employed by Cromwell. He was also disgusted at not being Consulted and advised with on any Occasion, nor employed in any other Office in the Army or Island, than in the Military Commission He had. And being unable to bear slights and neglects, He not only laid hold of every Occasion for Opposing and Obstructing Collo[nel] Doyley in all His measures, but Endeavoured to Subvert the Government, and take the Reins into His own Hands. By His Subtilty and Artifices He drew in most or all the Oliverian Officers into His Measures, and particularly L[ieutenan]t Col[one]l Tyson, who bore a very fair Character in other Respects, and was the Person, who Commanded the Party that defeated the Spanish Negroes, and brought about the Treaty with Them.

The kind Reception, Collo[nel] Doyley had given to many Persons, who were dissatisfied with the times in England, and others who had Suffered in the Royal Cause, and came over with a Design to Settle in this Island, Afforded an Occasion to that Artfull and intriguing Gentleman to Colour and Guild His intentions, by furnishing Him with a plausible Topick to persuade all the Oliverian Party, that Collo[nel] Doyley had some latent

54. Lieutenant Colonel Robert (or Thomas) Raymond and his role in this mutiny may be followed in Firth, *Regimental History of Cromwell's Army*, 2:724–25.

Design; And that the Encouragement He gave to the Cavaliers was with a View when He found Himself Strong enough, to expell the Republicans, and declare for the King. At the same time some Doubts and Scruples were raised concerning the Powers, and Authority, by which Collo[nel] Doyley acted, having had an Account of the Death of Cromwell, the Abdication of Richard,[55] and the long Parliament taking the Government on them.

And the Soldiers being greatly discontented and uneasy, at not receiving any Pay since their departure from England, were easily inflamed and prevailed with, to come into his Measures upon a Suggestion, that They were not Subject to a Military Authority, unless they were paid, and Consequently were not obliged to Continue any longer in the Service.

Matters were almost brought to a Crisis, when the whole Design came to light, and was discovered by the Vigilance of Collo[nel] Doyley, who used every precaution for His own, and the generall Security of the Island. And, being a man of spirit and Resolution, [he was] determined to strike at the Root that the Mutineers might be Convinced that They had to do with one, who was not to be baffled or Insulted. Accordingly on the 1st of August he Seized on Raymond and Tyson and brought them before a Court Martial (Consisting of 21 Officers) where They were tried and pursuant to their Sentence were Shot. Raymond Expressed no Concern, and with Resolution met His Fate; but the other behaved in a more becoming manner, and died with great Reluctance.

The Restless Giddy headed Soldiers, who were soon inflamed and invited to appear in Arms, being now without Their Chiefs, were confounded and knew not how to behave, but, thought it advisable to Submit on a promise of pardon to all excepting some other Officers who were cashiered. And by these means matters were quieted, and every thing Set[t]led in Their former Order.

The 15th of August arrived the *Convertine* with the Resolutions of the House of Lords and Commons to invite King Charles the second to return to His Dominions, and that He had been Accordingly proclaimed King of England, Scotland and Ireland, upon which Collo[nel] Doyley immediately ordered His Majesty to be Proclaimed in this Island, and the following Instrument in Writing to be fixed up in all Publick Places.

55. Richard Cromwell (1626–1712) served with his father and two brothers in the Parliamentary Army. He was a member of Lincoln's Inn in May 1647, MP for Hampshire in 1654 and for Cambridge in 1656, chancellor of Oxford University in 1657, and a member of the Committee of Trade and Navigation in 1655 and of the Council of State in 1657. Nominated as his father's successor on August 28, 1658, he became protector immediately on Oliver's death, and Parliament approved him on February 14, 1659. At the Restoration he retired to Paris and lived under the pseudonym John Clark, eventually returning to England, as Clark, to live out the rest of his life at Cheshunt, Hampshire.

By the L[ieutenan]t Generall and Commander in Chief
of His Majestie[']s Forces in Jamaica
Whereas in and by His Majesties Declaration dated the 14th of April
1660 from Bredah He is pleased thereby to grant a Free and Generall
Pardon to all His Subjects of what Degree or Quality soever, who shall
within 40 Days after Proclamation thereof, lay hold upon His Grace and
favour. And shall by any Publick Act declare and Testify Their return to
Their Duty, Loyalty, and Obedience of good Subjects, (Excepting only
Such Persons as shall be Excepted by Parliament) Therefore that no Per-
sons may be Excluded from His Majestie[']s Gracious Pardon for want of
knowledge of the Same and declaring Their Obedience to His Majesty by
some Publick Act or Instrument, I do hereby give Notice to all Persons,
Soldiers as well as other Inhabitants, of the Island, That there shall be an
Instrument drawn Declaring Their Submission and Obedience to His
Majesty, to which they may Subscribe Their hands at my House at Point
Cagway which is to be kept as a Record of the same Given under my hand
the 18th day of August 1660.
    Edward Doyley

Accordingly an Instrument in Writing was drawn up, and Executed the
21st of August 1660 by all the Officers, Soldiers, and other Inhabitants.
    The 5th of February 1661 Collo[nel]Doyley issued out a Proclamation,
Setting forth that he had received notice and advertisement from S[i]r
Henry Bennet[,][56] His Majestie[']s Resident at the Court of Spain; That it
was His Majestie[']s pleasure there should be a Suspension of Arms by Sea
and land, between His Majestie[']s Subjects and those belonging to His
Catholick Majesty. And commanded all Persons under His Government to
Cease and forbear all manner of Hostilities, and to treat the Spanish Subjects in all places with Civility and Friendship.
    And in March having advice that Jeremy De Champs whom He had ap-
pointed L[ieutenan]t Governour of Tortugas had taken possession of the
Island, but instead of pursuing His Instructions, Treacherously and perfid-
iously put up French Colours, (and Seized on all the English Plantations,
Ships and Effects) immediately fitted out a Party under the Command
of Collo[nel] Charles Arundell to assert the Right of the Crown of En-

56. Henry Bennett, First Earl of Arlington (1618?–1685), was a Royalist and secret Catholic who fled to France at the Regicide and was secretary to James in 1654 and Charles II's
agent in Madrid in 1658. Returning to England after the Restoration, he was made keeper of
the privy purse and secretary of state, an office he held from 1662 to 1674. Becoming Earl of
Arlington in 1663 and Viscount Thetford in 1672, he was a member of the Cabal and party to
the secret Treaty of Dover in 1670, and was impeached as a promoter of Catholicism in January 1674. Although acquitted, he resigned as secretary of state, after which he was appointed
lord chamberlain but remained an ineffective object of ridicule until his death.

gland, and to Seize the said De Champs. But, this Expedition proved un-successfull, for the Traitor being reinforced with a great Number of French Bucan[n]iers, defeated the English Forces, took Collo[nel] Arundell Prisoner, and put Him under Close confinement.

Having traced out every memorable Event in this Island from the landing of the English Forces under the Command of General Venables, to the Restoration of King Charles the second (Collected from the most Authentick Papers, particularly an Originall Manuscript of Collo[nel] Doyley[']s, by which means I have been able to place things in their Naturall order and time) it is necessary to make some Observations, which will illustrate, and set those passages in a true and just light, that have been imperfectly or partially related by other Writers.

However wisely, Cromwell had laid His Schemes for gaining some Acquisitions in America; Yet it is Obvious, that they were badly Executed by those who had the Conduct and management of the Expedition at Home, as well as by the chief Commanders and Commissioners Abroad; either for want of Money, Abilities, or some Sinister Views. For it appears that They were insufficiently provided with Arms, Ammunition, Provisions and other Necessaries for such an Enterprize; and even those They had not good in their kind. And, though Supplies were promised to be sent Them immediately, yet they did not arrive in near Six months after the Island was taken; in the mean time Admirall Pen[n] was under the Necessity of returning Home with part of the Fleet, for want of Provisions, and the land Forces were reduced to great Extremity.

We have Experienced, in Several Instances, the fatall Inconveniencies which attend Conjunct Expeditions, by the disagreement between the Principal land and Sea Officers, who, in general, seem to have a Natural prejudice and Antipathy to each other. How much more unadvised was it to Appoint Commissioners with Powers not only to inspect into but to direct the proceedings of the Sea as well as of the land Forces. For though the General and Admiral were named in the Commission, yet there were three others joined with them, two[57] of which never had been in any Military employment, and the other[58] in no higher a Rank than that of a Captain.

The Composing those Forces, of a Mixture of Cavalier and Oliverian Officers and Soldiers was likewise another imprudent Step, in regard to their different Principles, and the implacable Animosity which was between those Partisans, so that it was almost impossible there could be any Unanimity or harmony among Them which is highly Necessary in all such undertakings. The Event evinced the Truth of this Assertion, for it appears

57. Mr. Searl[e] Governour of Barbadoes who was a Planter and Mr. Winslow a private Gentleman. — *Author.*

58. Capt[ai]n Butler. — *Author.*

by the preceeding Narrative That there was a Continual Dissention and wrangling among Them from Their first setting out.

Nor was it less imprudent to Attempt set[t]ling a Foreign Colony with Soldiers; for however Vigilant and Active They may be in the Field, Yet it is Notorious that few of that Class of Men are inclined to Industry, or to Cultivate the Arts of Peace. The hardships and Miseries imposed on Them, is likewise to be Considered; for they received very little if any pay, from Their departure out of England to the Restoration, and were neither Cloathed [n]or Subsisted duly. English men cannot Submit to any kind of Injuries or Injustice, and therefore Their discontent and the Mutinies which ensued, is not to be wondered at, or that so few of them continued Obedient and turned their thoughts to Planting but rather that the whole Body did not at once desert and Abandon an Island where They met with so many Obstructions from the Enemy and so little Support from Their Native Country.

The distresses They were often under for want of the Common Necessaries of life, were, from time to time, emphatically represented by Commissioner Sedgwick, General Brayne, and Coll[onel] Doyley. That Excellent Person, last mentioned in a letter to *Secretary Thurloe* dated[59] the 6 of October 1656, says—*We are a desolate, and almost an abandoned People, deserving of Pity at least, and help from our Friends*—In his letter to the *Council of State*[60] the 27 of February 1657 [1658] He acquaints them with the *Designs* of the *Spaniards* against the Island, and says—*if They arrive before we recieve Shoes they will come to our Quarters, for we cannot go to them; and I humbly offer, how it can be thought a* private Soldier *can give* four Shillings *for* a pair of *Ammunition* Shoes, *who has not* received so *much these* three Years. And, in His letter to *Secretary Thurloe*[61] November 10: 1658, He says, *We are in Want of* Cloaths *and* Shoes, *so that we appear more like* Savages *than* English men. *And, I humbly and earnestly beg, that seeing God hath placed me in some Eminency, and hath given me a fervent desire of serving my Country, that I may not have my Endeavours* stifled, *by being made uncapable through continual wants at land and Sea, of such things as are Necessary and requisite for the undertaking; but that rather my want of Abilities for the carrying on so great a business may be made good, by your Care in Supplies.*

But, as I am now going to open a New and more agreeable Scene which commences soon after the Restoration and on Collo[nel] Doyley[']s receiving a regular Commission from King Charles the Second to be Governour, and Commander in chief, with Instructions to form and put the Island under a Civil Government, I shall wave making any further Reflections than that the last mentioned deficiencies seem to be owing to a want

---

59. Thurloe[']s State Papers Vol. 5. P. 476.—*Author.*
60. Thurloe[']s State Papers Vol. 6. P. 833.—*Author.*
61. Ibid, Vol. 7, P. 499.—*Author.*

of mon[e]y, more than to any Neglect or Design, in Cromwell, and shews the great Necessities He was under. For by all accounts He was greatly pleased with His new Acquisition, and being Sensible of the many Advantages which would arise from it, was determined to Maintain and defend it at all Events.

Indeed, nothing but that Resolute mind, which distinguished and Supported Him in many great undertakings, could overcome the difficulties and Obstructions He met with, in preserving and Set[t]ling this Island, after He had taken possession of it.

Part the 3d

Of the Administration of the Severall Governors of Jamaica. The Origin and Exploits of the Privateers Commonly Called Buccaniers and all the Other Remarkable Transactions by Sea and Land, which happened during the Respective Governments.

[Early Settlement and Travails, 1660–1684]

King Charles the Second, upon His Restoration to His Dominions, not only approved of the Conquest of Jamaica, but confirmed the Possessions and Titles of His Subjects, who were Set[t]led there. And, on the 8th of February 1660, by Patent or Commission, appointed Collo[nel] Edward Doyley to be Governour of the Island, as well as Commander in Chief of the Forces; so that this Gentleman was looked upon, as indeed He was, the first Regular Governor, the others being only Commanders in Chief of the Forces, without the Title and other Advantages of a Governor.

By His Commission, and Instructions, He was impowered and directed with the advice of the Councill (who were to be fairly and indifferently Chosen, by the Officers of the Army, Planters and other Inhabitants) or any five of Them; to raise money for the use of the Government, and to perform all other Acts, which might conduce to the Security, good Government, and Service of the Island.

Accordingly the Civil Power began to be Exercised soon after, though it was little more than nominall; for there was a Necessity at that time of Governing by Martial law, the Inhabitants being mostly Military Men; and nothing but the Strict hand of Discipline Could keep Them in order and preserve the Peace and Quiet of the Community, until the Island became better set[t]led, and Peopled by a different sort of Men. However, no Inconvenience or prejudice arose from that mixed kind of Government, through the mild and prudent Administration of the Governor; for I have often heard some of the first Set[t]lers speak of those times with great satisfaction; and highly commend His Justice, Moderation, and Discreet behaviour.

His Majesty was also pleased to Appoint by Patent, a Commissary of the Stores, who was also to be Secretary of the Island and one of the Councill,

a Provost Marshall or High Sherif[f], a Surveyor General and other Publick Officers.

And the Governor by Virtue of the Powers He was cloathed with, com-
missioned proper Persons in the severall Districts and Settlements, for the
Conservation of the Peace, to Administer Justice, and to decide matters of
Debt not exceeding Forty shillings.

The Soldiers and Inhabitants, in generall, being now convinced of the
intentions of the Crown to maintain out right of Possession, were more
assiduous in Planting and improving the Island; for many of Them had a
Notion that the Island would be restored to the Spaniards, upon a Peace
with that Nation. And, for the better Security of the Island, and to induce
all the Officers and Soldiers to become Set[t]lers, He fixed the severall
Regiments in different Parts of the Island in the manner of Townships and
allotted to every man a portion of Land vizt.

Collo[nel] Ward's[1] (late Venables) at the Angells.

The Regiment commanded by Major Wells,[2] (late Fortescue)
at Guanaboa.

Collo[nel] Barrington's[3] at Caimanos.

Collo[nel] Carter[4] and Holdip's[5] in Liguinea.

Collo[nel] Bland's[6] (late Brayne's[7]) at Morant.

His [Doyley's] own Regiment at Yallahs.

And, Collo[nel] Moore's[8] Regiment, who were most or all Irish and
would not plant or work, He Quartered at St. Iago de la vega; and in the
Fortifications at Cagway, to do Military Duty.

In August 1661, A Proclamation was Published by the Governour signifying the orders He had received from His Royall Highness James Duke of
York[9] Lord High Admiral &c, strictly to charge and Command all Persons within His Government, to forbear taking any Indians Prisoners, or
to do Them any Injury or Violence. But, that They treat Them, with all
kindness and Civility. And also to give notice to such Indians or Spanish
Prisoners who had been brought to this Island, that there was then a Ship

1. Lieutenant Colonel Philip Ward. For more biographical detail, see Sir Charles Firth,
The Regimental History of Cromwell's Army, 2 vols. (Oxford, 1940), 2:703.

2. Major Richard Wells. For more biographical detail, see ibid., 2:717.

3. Colonel Francis Barrington. For more biographical detail, see ibid., 2:707–8.

4. Colonel Andrew Carter. For more biographical detail, see ibid., 2:710.

5. Colonel Richard Holdep. For more biographical detail, see ibid., 2:702, 709, 717, 720,
727–29.

6. Major Michael Bland. For more biographical detail, see ibid., 2:708, 728.

7. Colonel William Brayne. For more biographical detail, see ibid., 2:704–6, 711, 714, 729.

8. Colonel William Moore. For more biographical detail, see ibid., 2:705, 726–27.

9. King James II (1633–1701), second son of Charles I and brother of Charles II. At the
Restoration of 1660, he became Duke of York and lord high admiral. He ascended to the
throne as James II at the death of his brother and fled England when William of Orange and
Mary (James II's daughter) invaded, instigating the Glorious Revolution in December 1688.

ready in the Harbour, to receive Them aboard, and to Transport Them to the Main Continent.

The Fortifications at Cagway being now almost compleated the largest at the Southeast Point, which was called Fort Cromwell, was named Fort Charles: and that at the Northeast end Fort Rupert.

And, the Harbour which is not only commodious for Shipping but Conveniently Situated for Trade, having drawn many Mercantile Persons and Seamen hither, the Town which now Consisted of 250 Houses and Storehouses, was called Port Royall, and began to put on the face of business, having severall small Vessells belonging to it, that were employed in Trade, beside those which came from England and other Parts.

But, Collo[nel] Doyley who had Surmounted many difficulties, and had the Satisfaction of seeing the Island, in a prosperous Condition, being desirous of retiring from business and spending the remainder of his Days in his Native Country, at His own request was recalled and embarked for England on July 1662. I shall therefore Conclude His Administration, with the following observations, which I think justly due to his merit and Memory.

It is Universally allowed that the preservation and Settlement of this Island, was owing to His Vigilance, Bravery and prudent Conduct, and in my Opinion the Conquest of it, without prejudice or partiality may likewise be Attributed to Him. For though the Island was (according to the Treaty with the Spanish Governor) delivered in Form to Generall Venables, Yet it appears by the preceeding Narrative, that the Inhabitants did not Comply with that agreement, but afterwards disputed the possession—Nor, were They intirely dispossessed, till They were defeated at Rio Nova in June 1658, which was above three Years after. It was likewise owing to His Conduct and Management that the Spanish Negroes, who were extremely mischievous and troublesome, submitted Themselves, and afterwards became usefull to the New Set[t]lers. And, to His Vigilance and Resolution, a dangerous Conspiracy and Mutiny (fomented and headed by Officers of distinction who were men of Abilities and popular in the Army) was timely Suppressed; or the whole Design would have been subverted.

Though He had an absolute Authority, unrestrained by any Civil laws, yet He did not Exact any fees, nor Extort Donatives from the People: But, Contented Himself with the Pay, and Salary, which was allowed Him by the Government, and lived on the income of His Plantation which afforded Him many Necessaries of life. He appeared in Publick as a private Gentleman, without any State or Ceremony, yet was carefull to preserve the Honour and Dignity of the Governor. He was firmly attached to the Royal Cause, which was the Reason of Cromwell's dislike to Him, and removing Him twice from the Command of the Forces, which devolved to Him by Election as well as Succession.

He incouraged and Countenanced the loyal sufferers who removed to this Island, during the troublesome times in England; Nevertheless, He did not treat the Adverse Party before or after the Restoration with any Severity or Contempt nor did They Suffer any other difficulty or hardship, than what was Common among Them all, and often happens in all new Settlements. There Cannot be a Stronger Testimony of His Merit and good Government than the Affections and Esteem of the People and the Honourable mention that is made of Him by their Posterity. Happy would it be for our Colonies, if all Governours would Copy after Him and make His Conduct and behaviour the Modell and Rule of Their Actions.

He was descended of a very Ancient Family in Oxfordshire, whose Founder was Baron Doylie or Doyley in the Dutchy of Normandy, and came over with William the Conqueror. The Collo[nel] was first bred up at one of our Inns of Court in England. and had afterwards some Preferment in Ireland, which He Quitted upon the Revolutions that happened in the Government though He was after the Death of the King[10] prevailed upon to enter into the Army and in a few years obtained the Command of a Regiment. But, Cromwell having a Jealousy of Him; as well as of severall Other Officers then in His Service, whom He looked upon as Cavaliers in their Hearts, thought proper to send Them on the Expedition to America, where He could employ Them and not be under any Apprehension of Their Swords being turned against Himself.

The 2d. of August 1661, Thomas Lord Windsor[11] was appointed to succeed Collo[nel] Doyley, and Arrived at Jamaica, in His Majestie's Ship the *Centurion*, the [blank] of June 1662: with His Lordship came over S[i]r Charles Littleton Bar[one]t,[12] who was appointed, by His Majesty, Chancellor of the Island.

And, many Persons flocking over to the Island upon the Encouragement which was given by the Crown, and the fair Prospect of raising Their Fortunes, by the Fertility of the Soil and other Advantages, His Lordship was furnished with more ample Instructions than were given to His Predecessor.

He was by His Commission impowered and directed to choose a Councill of 12 Persons, To discipline and Command the Military Forces, To inforce Martial law in Case of Necessity and imminent danger, To hold

---

10. Charles I (1600–1649).

11. Thomas, Lord Windsor (c. 1627–1687). Born Thomas Hickman, Windsor married into the Windsor family and subsequently both assumed the additional surname of Windsor and succeeded to the family's estate and impressed Charles I with his military exploits during the Civil War. After the Restoration, Charles II appointed him governor of Jamaica, a post he held from 1661 to 1663, but he actually spent only about three months in Jamaica.

12. Sir Charles Littleton (1629–1716) was a Royalist toward the end of the Civil War who accompanied Prince Charles into exile. At the Restoration, Charles II knighted him in 1662 and sent him to Jamaica as Windsor's lieutenant-governor. After Windsor left the island, Littleton assumed the governorship of Jamaica until he left the colony in May, having summoned the island's first legislative assembly.

Court Martials, And to Encourage [settlement]. And, by His Instructions He was (inter alia) empowered with the advice of His Council to settle such Judicatorios for Civil Affairs and for the Admiralty as might be proper to keep the peace of the Island, and to determine Matters of Right and Controversy. And in short all Causes Civil, Criminal, Matrimonial[,] Testamentary, and Maratime. Yet so as no man's Freehold life, or Member be taken away or harmed but by Established laws, not repugnant to the known laws of England.

To appoint and Commissionate under the broad Seal of the Island, Judges, Justices, Sheriffs and other Officers, for the more orderly Administering of Justice &c.

To Grant Commissions for Subduing His Majestie's Enemies by Sea or Land.

To appoint Markets and Fairs to be kept on such days, and in Such places, for such term or terms as should be thought Convenient.

To Call and Assemble together fit and able Persons, according to the Custom of other Plantations, to make laws and upon Imminent Necessity to levy monies, as should be most advisable for the Honour and Advantage of His Majesty's Crown and the good and Welfare of His Subjects, provided such Laws were no ways repugnant to the Laws of England, and that they should be in force for two Years, and no longer.

And lastly He was impowered to Grant[,] ratify and Confirm to all that Transport Themselves to this Island, 30 Acres of land to each Man and his Heirs for ever.

His Lordship before His departure from England having Represented in a Memorial to His Majesty in Council, That the Frenchman [Jeremy De Champs], who Commanded at Tortugas of Tortuga was sent from England by the then Council with orders to Collo[nel] Doyley Governor of Jamaica, to Commissionate the said Frenchman (if He thought fit) to be Governor of the said Island subject to such Orders as He should from time to time receive from His Majesty or the Governour of Jamaica. That in Obedience thereto Collo[nel] Doyley gave the said Frenchman (who professed great Zeal and Affection for the English Nation) a Commission which he Accepted but hath since refused to obey.

His orders, whereupon Collo[nel] Doyley appointed Collo[nel] Arundell Governor of the said Island, whom the Frenchman imprisoned. And, in regard that the Inhabitants of the said Island, were chiefly English and the Place of great Consequence to the Security of Jamaica His Lordship was thereupon ordered and impowered to use His utmost Endeavours to reduce the said Frenchman and other Inhabitants to the Obedience of the Crown of England.

Hence it appears that we had an indubitable Right and Claim to the said Island, the possession of which would have been a great Advantage to the British Nation, because it would have prevented the Settlements the French have since made on the Island of Hispaniola, at least it would be a curb and restraint on Them. By what means or for What Reason They were permitted to Enjoy the same, ever since, without any interruption; or Whether it has been Specefically yielded to Them, by Treaty, I am not able to determine, though I think it worth an Enquiry.

The Lord Windsor upon His arrival, disbanded the Army except 400 foot, and 150 Horse which He was directed to keep in pay, And, distributed the Royal Donative of £10 to Each man, which was vested in Cloath[e]s, working Tools and Instruments for planting, also 300 Negroes, which were Contracted for, and delivered by the Royal African Company.[13]

He also proceeded to Establish a Civil Government, according to the Model and form of other Colonies, as prescribed by His Majestie's Instructions. But, an Assembly was not convened during His residence on the Island, which was not above ten months, for His Lordship finding Himself unable to go through the hardships and fatigues of an Infant Colony embarqued for England the [blank] of [blank] 1663.

Upon the departure of the Lord Windsor, the Council met and assumed the Government by Virtue of a Clause in His Majestie's Commission which impowered Them (in Case of His Lordship's death or absence) or any Seven of Them, to take the Government upon Them and within one week after, to Elect a fit Person to Execute the same Commission, and the several Powers, Authorities, and Instructions until His Majestie's further pleasure was known.

Accordingly They made choice of and Elected Sir Charles Littleton Bar[ris]ter, who was Chancellor of the Island [and] Lieutenant Governor. This Gentleman convened the first Assembly who met at St. Iago de la vega, the [blank] day of [blank] 1663, and passed several Laws which were made to Continue in force for two Years only. But, having His Majestie's permission to Return to England if He thought fit, embarqued the [blank] of [blank] 1664, very much regretted by the Inhabitants, who highly approved of His Conduct and behaviour, as Chancellor as well [as] Governor of the Island.

Upon His departure the Administration devolved on Collo[nel] Thomas Lynch[14] as President of the Council.

13. The Royal African Company, chartered in 1669 and headed by James, Duke of York, initially enjoyed a monopoly over English trade with West Africa.

14. Thomas Lynch (1633–1684) served on the Jamaica expedition in 1655, and Charles II appointed him provost marshall of Jamaica for life in January 1661 and a member of the Jamaica Council in 1663. As president of the council, he acted as governor in 1663–64. Following differences with the new governor, Sir Thomas Modyford, in the late 1660s, Lynch returned to England where Charles II knighted him in 1670, and he went back to Jamaica in 1671 to replace Modyford as governor and act as commander in chief of his majesty's ships in and around Jamaica. In these positions, he, like Modyford before him, commissioned attacks on Spanish settlements and shipping, for which the English government was forced to recall him in 1674 but returned him to Jamaica in 1682 for his third stint as governor and captain-general where he died in 1684. Frank Cundall, *Governors of Jamaica in the Seventeenth Century* (London, 1936), 31–55.

During this Interval of time, nothing Remarkable happened further than that many of the Soldiers (who were disbanded and Averse to planting) and others went to Tortuga, the Inhabitants of which Place had now put Themselves under the protection of the Crown of France where They obtained Commissions to Act against the Spaniards.

Hence arose the Bucaniers, who became so Terrible to the Spaniards; and though the President did not grant Them Commissions, Yet He was far from discouraging Them. Because some of Them acted under the Authority of the Crown of France, which was then at War with Spain, and He permitted Them, in Consideration of the Treasures They brought in, to dispose of Their prizes, which occasioned many to abound, and brought over great Numbers of People, from all Parts, to this Island.

The 15th. of February 1663, S[i]r Thomas Modiford Bar[one]t[15] was appointed Governor; Collo[nel] Bledly Morgan[16] L[ieutenan]t Governor and S[i]r James Modiford[17] Major General.

They arrived at Jamaica, the [blank] of May 1664, and with Them came many Families from Barbadoes in order to Settle in this Island, upon the Encouragement which was given by the Crown; His Majesty having by His Instructions to S[i]r Thomas, Signified and declared His pleasure, That no Goods imported into or exported from the Island to any Parts should have any Duty laid on them for 21 years. Nor any Commodities brought from the Island, which were produced there should be burthened with any impost or Custom in England for five years.

And, That what Duties shall be requisite for defraying the publick charge and expence of the Government, be laid on Strong Waters and other Spirituous liquors, imported and made use of there, to restrain the

15. Sir Thomas Modyford (1620?–1679). A Royalist who switched to the Parliamentary cause, Modyford went to Barbados in 1647 and became governor of Barbados on July 16, 1660, but resigned on December 17 to become Speaker of the Assembly. Appointed governor of Jamaica in February 1664, he took seven hundred Barbadian settlers with him. To appease the Spanish court, which resented his issuing a commission to Henry Portobello that led to the capture and sacking of Portobello, Charles II revoked Modyford's commission in 1671, when he was arrested, sent home, and committed to the Tower of London. Released in 1674, he returned to Jamaica with Sir Henry Morgan in 1675 and died there in 1679. Ibid., 21–30.

16. Bledly Morgan was a kinsman of Sir Henry Morgan who fought with him in 1670, but Blair Morgan does not seem to have been lieutenant-governor of Jamaica. That was Colonel Edward Morgan, uncle of Sir Henry, who was lieutenant-governor under Thomas Lynch, arriving in Jamaica in May 1664. Frank Cundall, *Historic Jamaica* (London, 1915), xiii; Cundall, *Governors of Jamaica in the Seventeenth Century*, xiv, 19, 21, 24, 32, 38, 57, 58, 62.

17. Sir James Modyford (?–1673), younger brother of Sir Thomas Modyford, served with the Turkey Company in his youth and with the Royal Africa Company from 1663. After service in Ireland for George Monck, First Duke of Albemarle, he went to Jamaica and authored a survey and description of the island. An agent in England for Jamaica during his brother's governorship, he became lieutenant-governor of Providence Island in 1666, but the Spanish recaptured it before his arrival. Subsequently, Charles II appointed him lieutenant-general, deputy governor, and chief judge of the admiralty court at Jamaica, but his commissions were revoked at the recall of his brother, and he remained in Jamaica until he died.

excessive and Vitious use thereof, having allowed £2500 per Annum toward the publick expence of the Island.

Sir Thomas Modiford, upon his arrival, in pursuance of his Instructions (S[i]r Charles Littleton being gone to England) Consigned the Seals to three of the Council. He also Convened the Assembly, who reinacted and inlarged the Laws, which were almost expired and made to Continue in force for two Years only, being restrained to that time by His Majestie's Instructions.

At this time the Settlements were so much increased that there was up- wards of 17000 Inhabitants upon the Island,—Men, Women and Children of which not more than One third were Negroes, as appears by the follow- ing Calculation, made in the Island and transmitted to England, by order of the Government vizt.

	Families	Persons
Port Royall . . .	500	3500
St. Katherines . . .	658	6270
St. Johns . .	85	996
St. Andrews . .	194	1552
St. Davids . . .	80	960
St. Thomas in the E[ast]	59	590
Clarendon . .	143	1430
St. Elizabeths		
St. James		
St. Anns . . .	200	2000
St. Mary's		
St. Georges		
	1,919	17,298

These were all the Precincts into which the Island was at that time di- vided; and by this Account it is Surprising to observe the sudden Accession of Inhabitants, in an Island lately Conquered, in a ruinous Condition, in want of the common Necessaries of life, the Forces Mutinous and disposed to desert, and abandon the Design; Yet in a few Years became Rich, Power- full, and a Terror of the Spaniards in America. The increase of Settlements was principally owing to the Example of S[i]r Thomas Modiford, who had resided several Years in Barbadoes, where He acquired a good Estate and the Art of making Sugar, which the Inhabitants of this Island were in a manner unacquainted with, before He came among Them. He set up a Salt work in St. Katharines, and brought it to such perfection that Salt was Sold at the Barcadier or landing place at 15 p[er] Bushel. He also set[t]led a Co- coa Walk at Guanaboa (which is now known by the Name of the Angells) and a Sugar Work at sixteen Mile Walk which Estates are now Enjoyed by His Descendants in the Female line, the Male issue and Title being Ex- tinct. Indeed there could not have been a better choice made of a Gover-

This insert from a 1679 map by James Moxon, showing an African slave tending cattle and a horse, illustrates the early importance of slavery and cattle-raising and horses to the economy of English Jamaica.

nour for an Infant Colony, for He not only put the People upon Industry and Planting and was of Service to the Young Planters by His Instructions but promoted and Encouraged Trade.

But, the chief Reason of the Accession of People may be attributed to the great Resort of Privateers, commonly (though improperly) called Bucaneers, who made Port Royal Their Rendevous and as Peace was not then concluded between Great Britain and Spain, though there was a Suspension of Hostilities in Europe, between the two Nations, Yet, They were not only Encouraged, on Account of the great Riches They brought in, but the Governor even granted Commissions until the Treaty[18] was concluded in 1667.

I have now brought the History of this Island to the time of its great-

18. The Treaty of Breda (July 21, 1667) under which the Dutch ceded New York to England, and England ceded Surinam to the Dutch. Also, England secured Antigua from France but ceded St. Lucia.

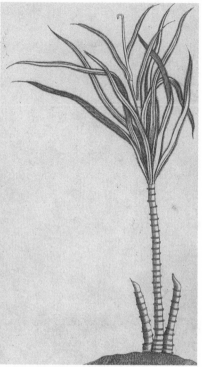

The image on the left, *Cacauifere ou arbre du Cacao*, an engraving by Johann
Hainzelman found in Nicolas de Blégny (1652–1722), *Le bon usage du thé, du caffé,
et du chocolat pour la preservation et pour la guerison des maladies* (Lyon, 1687), 203,
one of the first French books on tea, coffee, and chocolate, shows a cacao tree (*the-
obroma cacao*) with roots, branches, and pods. The image on the right is of a sugar
cane plant (*Saccharum officinarum*), a genus of tropical grasses originally native to
southeast Asia and first brought to the Caribbean by Christopher Columbus on his
second voyage in 1493. The image comes from James Grainger (1721?–1766), *The
Sugar-Cane: A Poem* (London, 1766), frontispiece. The cultivation and production
of cacao, inherited from the Spanish, and sugar, introduced by the English, were
key economic pursuits in early English Jamaica.

est prosperity, when it was not only Populous and in flourishing Circumstances, but mon[e]y so very plenty that Port Royal was Reckoned the
Richest Town in America. The success of the first Planters, and the Wealth
brought in by the Privateers, was no sooner spread abroad, but People
in low Circumstances, and those who could not endure an Unactive life
in England transported Themselves hither; some invited by the Fertility of the Soil, and the Advantageous Prospects in planting, turned their
thoughts that way; and others went a rambling on the Seas, and Shores, of
America, in Search of Prizes and other Booty.

Indeed, the latter Executed Their Designs with such Intrepidity and Surprising Success, as will perhaps Scarce gain Credit in the present, much less in Succeeding Ages. But, before I proceed to give a Narrative of Their Gallant Exploits, which have made so much Noise in the World, it will be Necessary to explain the difference between a Privateer and Bucaneer who generally are blended together without any distinction. A Privateer is one that acts under and by Vertue of a Commission, from any Prince or State, at Enmity or War with any other Nation or Country.

Bucaneer is derived from the Spanish word *Bucaniero*, which in the English language is a Pirate or Free booter, one that Acts without a Commission or legal Authority. Of this Sort was Peter Le Grand, [François] Lolonois, Bartholomew the Portoguez, Roche a Dutch Man commonly called Brazillanio and others mentioned in the *History of the Bucaneers of America*[19] who fitted out at Tortuga, and made that Island their Rendevous.

The Privateers of Jamaica, therefore, were improperly called Bucaneers, as I observed, and the Inhabitants of the Island in general unjustly Stigmatized for the Actions of those Persons aforementioned (whose Crews were a mixture of all Nations mostly French) because the former acted under Commissions from the Governors or Commanders in Chief, who we may reasonably Suppose, were Authorized to grant such Commissions, Since we never heard of any of Them being punished, or even removed from the Government on that account, except S[i]r Thomas Modiford. But, as I shall Occasionally discuss that Singular Instance, in its proper place I shall suspend any further animadversions thereon.

Nevertheless it must be confessed that some of the real Bucaniers, by permission or Connivance, did dispose of their prizes and Squander away their mon[e]y at Port Royal, before the Treaty concluded between Great Britain and Spain in 1667. How far that was justifiable or allowable, as there was not before that period of time any Peace or Friendship between the two Nations, I will not take upon me to determine. But, Supposing it otherwise, is it reasonable that a whole Society or Country should be reproached for the actions of a part of Them only? or is any City or Country Culpable for the Negligence or misbehavior of their principal Magistrate, in conniving at any Enormities within Their District? It will Evidently appear in many Instances in this History, That no Country or People, ever was more assiduous, or at a greater Expence, than this Island has been at, to Suppress those who acted without a legal Authority.

Collo[nel] Lynch who was then President and Commander in Chief of the Island, was very much Censured for Conniving at [with] those who acted without any legal Authority, although He alledged in His Defence, that there was not any Treaty of Peace and Friendship between Great Britain and Spain.

19. Alexander Exquemelin, *History of the Bucaneers of America* (London, 1678).

But, John Davis,[20] [Edward] Mansvelt,[21] [Henry] Morgan,[22] Coxen[23] and many others who are ranked among the Bucaniers; acted under legal Authority and by Vertue of Commissions from the Governour of Jamaica, or Petit Guavis. For S[i]r Thomas Modiford soon after His arrival, granted Commissions (until He was acquainted with this Treaty in 1667) by Vertue of the 7th. Art[icle] of his Instructions, which impowered Him, so to do, as should seem requisite for subduing His Majestie's Enemies by Sea and Land, within and upon our Coasts of America. But, that it should be deemed Piracy, for any Ship to lay wait for, pursue or take any of the Enemies' Ships or Goods without Commission from the Lord High Admiral, or Authority from Him.

I hope, I have expressed myself in such a manner, as to be understood not to intend or mean any thing more Than to set Things in a just and true light, as an impartial Writer, without attempting to Clear the Guilty or to justify, for nothing can justify the Attrocious Actions which some of Them were Culpable of. For it is an indubitable Fact, that the Bucaniers properly so called, and even some of the Privateers, committed great Cruelties; But, as they were a mixture of all Nations, the Commanders who were not at all times able to keep Them in strict order and discipline, were not answerable for what some of Their men had done, without Their Order or Privity. Though at the same time we must likewise distinguish Davis, Morgan, Coxon and some others from Peter Le Grand, [François] Lolonois and Brazillanio, who were undoubtedly the most cruel and Inhuman Villains that ever Appeared in the World.

The Spaniards in America were so miserably harrassed by those People, that They resolved to diminish the Number of Their Trading Vessells; in hopes, by that means, the Privateers would give over, when They found They could not get good prizes. But, this Method Proved ineffectual, for

20. John Davis, born in the West Indies and raised in Jamaica, successfully led buccaneering attacks on Nicaragua and St. Augustine, Florida. Knight recounts his exploits below.

21. Edward Mansvelt or Mansfield (fl. 1659–1666) was a seventeenth-century Dutch corsair and buccaneer who operated out of Jamaica or Tortuga with commissions from Governors Doyley and Modyford. One of the first to organize large-scale raids against Spanish settlements, he participated in the sack of Compeche in 1663 and died in 1666 during a successful raid on Spanish islands off the coast of Central America.

22. Sir Henry Morgan (1635–1660) was born in Wales, migrated as a servant to Barbados, became a famous naval and military leader, and was accused of piracy and imprisoned in the Tower as a result of his successful sacking of Panama in 1670–71 but was never formally charged. Instead, Charles II knighted him in 1674 and sent him back to Jamaica as lieutenant-governor to John, Lord Vaughan. In Jamaica, Morgan became a prominent figure in provincial politics and served as acting governor on three occasions in 1674–75, 1678, and 1680–82. Cundall, *Governors of Jamaica in the Seventeenth Century*, 56–76.

23. Captain John Coxon was a buccaneer leader who captured the Spanish Island of Santa Marie in 1677 and conducted a number of raids on Panama in the early 1680s.

when the Privateers had searched the Seas and Coasts of America, with little or no Success, They determined to land and Ravage the Country. Lewis Scot[24] was the first who undertook an Enterprize of that kind; and His first Attempt was on the Town of Campeachy, which He not only took and plundered, but received a Considerable sum of mon[e]y for the Ransom of the Town. About the same time Capt[ain] Mansvell took and plundered the Island of St. Katherines and received likewise a sum of Mon[e]y for the Ransom of the Prisoners.

John Davis was a Native of the Windward Islands and came an Infant to Jamaica, with His Parents. The Man entered among the Privateers at the age of 16, and before he was 20, was so much Esteemed and distinguished that He Obtained the Command of a small Party of 80 men, with whom He made a successfull Attempt on Nicaragua, in the following Manner. He left ten Men to take care of His Vessell, and with the Main Body, Embarqued in Canoes and rowed up the River in the Night, to prevent being discovered.

When They came near the Town, the Centinel, who kept the post of the River and imagined Them to be Fishermen, permitted Them to land, without a Challenge, They were no sooner ashore, but They Seized and dispatched Him. Animated with this Successfull beginning; They boldly entered the Town, knocked at the Doors of the Inhabitants, who not suspecting any danger let Them in By those means. They soon ransacked the Town, and retreated to their Ship, before the Inhabitants had time to Assemble and endeavour to resist or repel Them by force of Arms. And, by this Expedition They gained no less than 50000 p[iece]s [of eight] with which They sailed to Jamaica.

This Exploit increased His Fame for Courage and Conduct, insomuch that He obtained the Chief command of seven small Vessells and 250 men, who were fitted out to intercept a Fleet of Ships, which were expected from New Spain; but missing of Them, They directed Their Course to St. Augustine on Florida, where They landed[,] plundered, and burnt the Town, though there was in it, a Garrison of 200 Men.

Beside Them, there were others who made very bold and desperate attempts, wherein They succeeded, and acquired great Wealth, which They spent at Port Royal, in a riotous and profuse manner; for They would Spend 1000 p[iece]s [of] 8 or more in a Night, to Entertain Their Friends. At other times They would buy a pipe of Wine, Set it upon one end in the street and Oblige every one that passed by to Drink.

By such means They idly squandered away what They acquired with

24. Lewis Scot, an English buccaneer, was the first Englishman to raid Spanish coastal settlements in the Caribbean and West Indies during the mid-seventeenth century, most famously in the 1663 attack on and ransom of Campeche.

great fatigues, and imminent danger of Their lives; nor would many of Them go to Sea again, until They had spent all Their Stock, and poverty and Necessity compelled Them to go upon other Adventures.

But, the most Famous of Them all was Henry Morgan who some Years after was knighted by King Charles the Second. He was the Son of a Yeoman in Wales, and not liking His Father's Employment being of a Rambling disposition left him privately and went to Bristol, where he engaged Himself to a Planter of Barbadoes, whom He served four Years, according to Agreement, with great Fidelity. He then went down to Jamaica, and entered Himself among the Privateers, with whom He had such Success that in 2 or 3 years, He laid up a Considerable Sum of mon[e]y; for having greater Designs in View, He lived in a more prudent manner than the rest of His Comrades, and Saved most of what He had acquired on those Expeditions, with which He purchased and fitted out a Sloop and took the command on Himself.

The first Voyage, He cruised off the Town of Campeachy, and took several Considerable prizes which He carried into Jamaica. He then joined Capt[ai]n Mansvelt, and Assisted (as His Second) at the taking of the Island of St. Katherines, where He signalized His Courage and Conduct, insomuch that upon the demise of Capt[ai]n Mansvelt, He was chosen Commander in Chief of the Privateers, or as They called Him, Admiral.

The first Expedition, after He was chose Chief by their Unanimous Suffrage, He Equipped a Fleet of 12 Sail of Sloop and 700 men, English and French, with an intention of attacking the Havanna. But, on further Consultation, They were of Opinion Their Strength was not Sufficient, and therefore concluded to Attack Puerto Principe on Cuba. The Governor of that place having got some information of Their Design, got together 800 men, to oppose Them and made a Gallant Defence for some hours; But, being Slain among others, the Spaniards quitted the Town and retreated into the Woods. In this Expedition, the plunder amounted to 50000 p[iece]s [of eight], and a Difference afterwards arising between the English and French, They parted and the former returned to Jamaica.

In His Second Expedition He got together nine Sloops and 460 men and Sailed for Costa Rica where He imparted His intention of Attacking Porto bello; but when His Officers and Men understood that was his Design, They endeavoured to dissuade Him from such an Attempt, suggesting that They had not a sufficient Number of Men, for such an Enterprize. To which He Replied, if our Numbers are small our Hearts are great, and the fewer we are the better shares we shall have in the Spoil. His words infused such spirits into His Men, that They Overcame all Difficulties, and resolved to follow Him.

Capt[ain] Morgan was acquainted with all the Avenues to that Town, and His Attempting it without Artillery and a greater number of Men, is a manifest proof not only of His Courage, but His being capable of the

Another important source of Jamaica's wealth derived from booty and treasure extracted by force from attacks on Spanish settlements around the Caribbean. Under the leadership of Captain Henry Morgan, privateers, operating with government licenses to attack Spanish sites during wartime, successfully took Portobello in Panama in January 1668, raided settlements around Lake Maracaibo in March 1669, and sacked Panama in January 1671. This image, an engraving entitled *De Boecaniers nemen de Stat en Kastelen van Porto Velo*, completed in 1668 and published in Amsterdam by Nicolaas ten Hoorn in 1700 in a volume entitled *Historie der boecaniers, of vrybuyters van America*, shows Morgan's forces in Portobello using captured Catholic priests and nuns to shield themselves as they climbed the walls of the third fort they captured in this expedition.

greatest undertaking. It was almost Night when He came to Porto de Naos which is about 10 leagues West of Porto Bello: He landed in the Night and Marched towards the Town, and began the Assault at Day break, and before the Day was spent, They were Masters of the Town and Castle, where They hoisted English Colours notwithstanding the Governor made a gallant Resistance. He continued in possession of the place 15 days, and obliged the Spaniards to pay Him 100000 p[iece]s [of eight], for the Ransom of the Town, which with the plunder They met with amounted to 250000 p[iece]s [of eight].

The President of Panama,[25] when He had advice of this Action, being amazed to hear that 400 men, had taken a Town strongly fortified and without Cannon to raise Batteries; sent to Capt[ai]n Morgan for a pattern of the Arms, with which He had performed so gallant an Exploit. He received the Messenger with great Civility, and gave Him a Pistol with a few Bullets, to carry to the President, and assure Him that He would come to Panama within 12 months to fetch them away.

Soon after His return to Jamaica, He prepared for His Third Expedition, and having, by those Successfull Attempts, Acquired great Reputation, He raised in a very few days, 900 men which He imbarqued in 15 Vessells, great and small. But, His own ship, which mounted 30 Guns, was unfortunately blown up (by some Accident) at the West end of Hispaniola, and all her Crew except Capt[ai]n Morgan, and a few others, who happened to be aboard of another Ship.

This misfortune no ways deterred Them from prosecuting their Design although They had lost Their best Ship and many Brave men, by which means Their Strength was very much diminished. Accordingly They Stretched over for the Main Continent and Entered the lake of Maracaibo, where They found Themselves in imminent Danger; for the Spaniards had lately built a new Fort, which was Capable, with a good Garrison, of defending the Place, and at first, by a brisk fire on the Privateers put Them into some disorder. But, notwithstanding the Vigorous Opposition They made, Capt[ai]n Morgan landed His Men, under the Fire of the Ships, and a sharp Engagement ensued, which ended in the Defeat of the Spaniards. However, He would not Venture to pursue Them, because it began to grow dark and being unacquainted with those Parts, He was apprehensive of Ambuscades; but, finding them Silenced, He sent a Party of Men, to take possession of the Fort, which the Spaniards had deserted. They found therein a great quantity of powder and small Arms which was divided among the Ships, nailed up the Great Guns, and proceeded to Maracaibo, but meeting with some Shoals, and not being acquainted with the Channel, They quitted their ships and in Canoes went forward, and the day following came before the Town. Upon Their being all landed They immediately marched to Attack Fort de la Barra which They found deserted as

25. The president of Panama in the 1660s was Don Juan Perez de Guizman.

well as the Town, for the Spaniards had not Resolution to make any resistance or defend Themselves, having formerly experienced the intrepidity
and Courage of those People, therefore would not Expose Themselves, to
Their Fury, a second time. But, the Privateers finding Themselves dissappointed of the Booty They expected the Spaniards[,] having removed every
thing that was of Value into the Country[,] were very much out of humour,
and Sent a Party to make Discoveries, who returned with about 30 Prisoners and 50 Mules, laden with Goods; some of Them were Compelled
by means, which cannot be justified, to Confess where the Inhabitants had
concealed Their best Effects; and having attained all the information They
wanted, other Parties were sent out, who returned with several Prisoners,
and great booty.

From thence Capt[ai]n Morgan proceeded to another Town, called Gibralter, and Sent some of the Prisoners before to assure the Inhabitants
of good Quarter, if They would surrender. But, instead of a Capitulation,
the Privateers met with a warm reception, notwithstanding which They
landed, and with great Resolution marched up to the Town. The Spaniards
were amazed and intimidated at so bold an Attempt, and as Fear sometimes magnifys Dangers, They began to doubt the possibility of repelling
Them, and became so terrified that they quitted the Town, having taken
Care to bury or Convey their best effects into the Woods, upon the first
notice They had of the Privateers being on their Coast and in hopes They
would soon leave the Place when They found nothing to invite Their Stay.

But, Capt[ai]n Morgan having prevailed on a Spanish Negro, who was
taken, to discover where the Governor and the principal Inhabitants with
their Effects lay Concealed, immediately marched with 200 Men to Attack
Them. He likewise ordered 250 more, to march to a River, which discharges into the lake in Search of a Ship and four boats, which were Richly
laden with Goods. During Their Absence, great Cruelties were Exercised
on some Prisoners, who unhappily fell into the hands of Those Privateers,
that remained in the Town. But, as Capt[ai]n Morgan neither Authorized
nor was present, when those actions were Committed He was unjustly
branded with Countenancing the base Treatment of those Spaniards; for
I have been credibly informed by some of the Ancient Inhabitants of Jamaica that He was vindicated and acquitted even by the Privateers Themselves, of those Aspersions.

Capt[ai]n Morgan with His Division, returned without Success, the
Governor on notice of his Approach, having retired to a Mountain, where
it would have been the greatest imprudence, and Rashness to Attack Him
and His followers[,] They were so advantageously posted. But, the other
Party made amends for that Dissappointment; for They seized on the
Boats and ships, and brought them, with their Treasures, to Gibralter.

And, having agreed with the Spaniards for a Ransome of the Town,
They returned to Maracaibo where They found every thing in the same
Condition as when They left it; but, were surprized at the information of

three Spanish men of War being at the Entry into the lake, and resolved to dispute the Passage. Upon this They dispatched a Boat, which rowed and Sailed well, to gain Intelligence, and in a short time returned with a Confirmation of the Fact, and that the Spaniards had again fortified the Fort at the Entrance into the lake, which They had disabled. This made most of Them despair, imagining it was impossible for Them to Escape; and that They should be treated with the utmost Rigour and Severity, in Case They fell into the hands of the Spaniards.

Under these dreadfull Circumstances, Morgan remained unshaken and unmoved; and this Extremity furnished Him with an opportunity of manifesting a greatness of mind, capable of Surmounting difficulties and Dangers, which seemed insuperable. He therefore, boldly sent one of His Prisoners to the Commanding Officer of those Ships, and demanded not only a free passage but a Tribute, or He would set the Town of Maracaibo on fire.

The Spaniards were amazed at such a message from those, whom They looked upon as Their Prisoners. However, as They expected a desperate Engagement, They thought proper to Offer them terms, though very hard and Such as could not be digested by such People. Accordingly the Chief Officer, wrote a letter to Capt[ai]n Morgan, in which He proposed to let Him pass, provided He would deliver up His Prisoners, and all the booty he had taken at Maracaibo and Gibralter. This was almost as shocking to the Privateers, as if He had proposed to Them to Surrender at discretion, being unwilling to part with what they had acquired, with the hazard of Their lives.

But, as it appeared extreme dangerous, it not impracticable to Extricate Themselves out of the Difficulties They were under by force of Arms; Capt[ai]n Morgan thought proper to make use of Art and Stratagem. Accordingly, a Fire Ship was prepared, with such Contrivance and Ingenuity, that it was impossible for their Enemies to discover her to be one; for They filled her Decks with logs of Wood, fixed upright, with Hats or Caps on their Tops, to deceive the Sight, with a false Representation of Men, Counterfeit Cannon were placed at the portholes and English Colours displayed, And having filled the hole of the Ship with Pitch, Tar, and other Combustible matter They prepared to Sail and meet Their Enemy, Capt[ai]n Morgan having Engaged Them all by the most Solemn assurances, not to yield to the Spaniards but to defend Themselves to the last drop of Blood. Thus They advanced, with Amazing Resolution, to the three Spanish Ships and notwithstanding they made a brisk fire yet, the Privateers boarded and grapled the largest, and immediately Set her on Fire. Another of Them seeing the misfortune of the Commandant, and apprehending the same Danger, run ashore. And the third fell an Easy Prey to the Privateers.

This fortunate Event revived Their Spirits, and animated Them so much that They Unanimously Resolved to land and Attack the Fort, which They did without Success; for the Spaniards defended Themselves so well that the Privateers were obliged to retire. However, They agreed, and prepared, for a second Assault; but, before they began the Spirits of the Spaniards failed, insomuch that They sent a messenger offering to Capitulate which was accepted of, and upon the payment of 15000 p[iece]s [of eight] according to Agreement They withdrew and quietly imbarqued for Jamaica. On a Computation of the purchase They made on this Expedition, They found in all 250,000 in p[iece]s [of eight], besides plate, Jewells, Merchandize and Negroes.

I am now going to Relate the most Famous Action, that ever was performed in America, or perhaps in any other part of the World; and though it has been so far misrepresented as to Cast an Odium on the Island in general as well as the Principal Actors; Yet the following Minutes of the Council of Jamaica and other Vouchers, will set that affair in a clear light, and manifestly shew that the Spaniards were the Aggressors, That Capt[ai]n Morgan had a Commission for what He did, and That S[i]r Thomas Modyford, had Authority to grant such a Commission

At a Council held at St. Iago de la vega June
the 29. 1670
Present
His Excellency S[i]r Tho[mas] Modyford Bar[one]t Governour

S[i]r James Modyford L[ieutenan]t Gov[ernor]	Rob[er]t Byndloss
Tho[mas] Modyford Esq[uir]e	William Ivy Esq[uir]e
Collo[nel] Tho[mas] Ballard	Tho[mas] Fuller Esq[uire]
John Cope Esq[uire]	Antho[n]y Collier
Richard Hope Esq[uire]	

Whereas it Evidently Appeared to this Board by a Copy of a Commission, sent His Excellency by the Honourable William Burk Governour of Curaso, that the Queen Regent of Spain[26] by Her Schedule dated at Madrid the 20. of April 1669, Command Her respective Governours in the Indies, to make Open War against the Subjects of our Sovereign Lord the King in these Parts. And also that the Governour of St. Iago de Cuba hath executed the same, by granting Commissions of War against us; and lately, in a hostile manner, landed His Men in three Several Places on the North side of the Island, marching as far as He dared into the Country, burning all the Houses They Came at, Kil[l]ing or taking Prisoners all the Inhabitants They met with. They also appeared lately with three Ships on the South Side of the Island, at Michael's hole, within Eight leagues of our Chief Harbour, and came near the shore, but finding the Inhabitants

26. Mariana of Austria (?–1669) was the wife of Philip IV, who died in September 1665 when his son and heir, Charles II, was only four years old. Mariana and a five-member committee of government ruled until Charles reached an official majority at age fourteen.

prepared for Them, stood off again, and the next Day landed at Paratee Bay, within 18 leagues, and there burnt two Houses. Divers other Spanish Governours have likewise granted Commissions, and are levying Forces against us, and have as we are credibly informed, made St. Iago de Cuba their present Magazine and Rendevouz where Their Forces are to Unite and Embody for the Speedy Invasion of this Island, which intention, if it be Suffered to ripen so far, as that the Enemy be enabled to land Their Forces, in this Island, we shall be obliged to quit the Care of our Plan-tations, and Attend the Enemies' Motions, whereby our said Plantations will run to Ruin, our Cattle and other Stock run Wild, and though by the chance of War, we should defeat Them, yet we shall suffer so far, as in a manner to begin the World again, to our insupportable loss, and infinite damage to His Majesty's Service.

And, whereas His Majesty hath out of His most Princely foresight, and great Care of us, directed in the last Article of His Royal Instructions, which His Excellency hath been pleased on this Extraordinary Occasion to Communicate to this Board in the following Words.

As, for as much as there are many things incident to that Government there, for which it is not easy for us to prescribe such Rules and Directions for you as our service, and the benefit of that Island may require, instead of them you are with the Advice of the Council, to take care therein as fully and effectually as if you were instructed by us, of which extraordi-nary causes giving us due information, you shall receive farther satisfaction from us as our Service shall require; In discharge therefore of that great trust which is by that Instruction put in us by His Majestie's Council of this Place, and in this great and urgent necessity, we humbly advise and pray your Excellency, for the seasonable prevention of these impending Evils.

It may Ordain, and be it so Ordained by his Excellency, and His Majes-tie's Council now Assembled, and by Authority of the same, that Commis-sion be granted to Henry Morgan Esq[ui]r[e] to be Admiral and Com-mander in Chief of all the Ships of War belonging to this Harbour, and of all the Officers, Soldiers and Seamen belonging to the same, requiring him with all possible speed to draw into one Fleet; and with them to put to Sea for the security of the Coast of this Island, and of the Merchants' Ships, and other Vessels Trading to and about the same. And to Attain, Seiz[e] and Destroy all the Enemies' Vessels that shall come within his reach; and also for destroying the Stores, Magazines laid up for this War, and dis-posing such Forces as are or may be brought together for prosecuting the same. That he have power to Land in the Enemie's Country as many of his Men as he shall judge needful; and with them to march to such places as he shall be informed the said Magazines or Forces are, and them accord-ingly take, destroy and dispose of; and to do and perform all manner of Exploits which may tend to the preservation and quiet of this Island, being

His Majestie's chief Interest in the Indies. And that for the better Government of the said Fleet, Officers, Soldiers and Seamen, he have power to execute Martial Law, according to the Article of War already made, or which hereafter shall be made by his Excellency, the same having been first published unto them. And it is further Ordained, in regard there is no other pay for the encouragement of the said Fleet, That they shall have all the Goods and Merchandises that shall be gotten in this Expedition, to be divided amongst them, according to their usual Rules; and for their better encouragement to engage in this so necessary a Service. It is further Ordained, by the Authority aforesaid, That no person already belonging to the said Fleet shall be molested for his Debts, but are hereby protected until further Order, of which the Provost Marshal is to take notice of at his peril.

C. Atkinson, Cl[erk of] C[ouncil].

Pursuant to these Resolutions a Commission was granted to Capt[ain] Henry Morgan which I thought proper to incert at length, and is as follows.

S[i]r Thomas Modyford Baronet, Governour of His Majestie's Island of Jamaica, Commander in Chief of all His Majestie's Forces within the said Island, and in the Islands thereunto Adjacent, Vice Admiral to his Royal Highness James Duke of York, in the American Seas.

To Admiral Henry Morgan Esq[uir]e; Greeting:

Whereas the Queen Regent of Spain, hath by her Royal Shadula, dated at Madrid the 20th. of April 1670: Commanded her respective Governours in the Indies, to publish and make open War against our Sovereign Lord the King in these Parts. And whereas the Collo[nel] Pedro Baijonaii billa uneba Capt[ain] General of the Province of Paraguay, and Governour of the City of St. Iago de Cuba, and its Province, hath executed the same, and lately in a most Hostile and barbarous manner landed his men on the North side of this Island, and entered a small way into the Country, firing all the Houses they came at, killing or taking Prisoners all the Inhabitants they could meet with, and whereas the rest of the Governours in these Parts, have granted Commissions for executing the like Hostility against us, and are diligently gathering Forces together to be sent to St. Iago of Cuba, their General Rendezvous and place of Magazine; and from thence as the most opportune place, to be transported for a thoro[ugh] Invasion and final Conquest (as they hope) of this Island, for prevention of which their mischievous Intentions, in discharge of that great trust which His Gracious Majesty hath placed in me, I do by vertue of full Power and Authority in such Cases from his most Excellent Majesty, and his Royal Highness James Duke of York, His Majestie's Lord High Admiral, derived unto me, and out of the great confidence I have in the good conduct[,]

courage and fidelity of you the said Henry Morgan, as also of your great
Experience you have in Martial Affairs, both by Land and Sea, and by the
advice and consent of His Majestie's Council, constitute and appoint you
the said Henry Morgan to be Admiral and Commander in Chief of all the
Ships, Barques and other Vessels now fitted, or hereafter shall be fitted
for the publick Service and defence of this Island, and also of the Officers,
Soldiers and Seamen, which are or shall be put upon the same, requiring
you to use your best endeavours, to get with the Vessels into one Body or
Fleet, and cause them to be well Manned, fitted, armed and *victualled*, and
by the first Opportunity, wind and weather permitting to put to Sea for
the Guard and Defence of the Coast of this Island, and of all Vessels trading to or about the same; and in order thereunto, to use your best Endeavours to surprize, take, sink, disperse and destroy all the Enemies' Ships or
Vessels, which shall come within your view; and also for preventing the
intended Invasion against this place. You are hereby further Authorized
and required, in case you and your Officers in your Judgment find it possible or feazable to Land, and attain the said Town of St. Iago de Cuba, or
any other place belonging to the Enemies, where you shall be informed
the Magazines and Stores for this War are laid up, or where any Rendevous for their Forces to Imbody, are appointed, and there to use your best
endeavour for the Seizing the said Stores, and to take, kill and disperse
the said Forces. And all Officers, Soldiers and Seamen, which are or shall
be belonging to or Embarque upon the said Vessels, are hereby strictly
enjoyned both by Sea and Land, to obey you as their Admiral and Commander in Chief in all things as becometh them; and you your self are to
observe and follow all such Orders as you shall from time to time receive
from His most Excellent Majesty, his Royal Highness, or my self. Given
under my Hand and Seal of Arms this 22d. of July, and in the 22d. year of
our Sovereign Lord King Charles the Second, Anno Dom[ini] 1670.

By Command of
His Excellency   Thomas Modyford
Cary Helier. Regist[er] of the Admiralty

Accordingly Capt[ain] Morgan sailed from Port Royal the 14th. of August 1670, with Eleven Sail of Vessels and 600 Men; and having cruised
round this Island He arrived at the Isle of Ash the Place of Rendevouz the
2d. of September following, But not meeting with the Enemy, or any advice of their Design He dispatched Capt[ain Edward] Collier[27] with six sail
and 350 men for the Main, in order to get Prisoners and Obtain Intelligence.

27. Captain Edward Collier was second in command to Henry Morgan during his invasion
of Panama in 1670–71.

The last day of September Capt[ain John] Morris[28] arrived, and joined the Fleet. He brought with Him a Spanish Vessel He had taken, commanded by Emanuel Riveras,[29] who was one of those that landed, plundered and burnt the Settlements in the remote Parts of this Island, the last year, and had with Him three Several Original Commissions, two of which Capt[ain] Morgan Sent to the Governour.

The 7. of October They had a Violent Storm in the Harbour, which drove all the Ships ashore, Except one; three of Them Stranded, but the rest were got off and made Serviceable.

In a few Days after three French ships joined Them, and offered their Assistance in the Enterprise They were going upon, which was Accepted of [by Morgan]. And in a few days after arrived Seven Sail more from this Island; so that having now Sufficient Force to Attempt St. Iago de Cuba, some of Their Men, who had lately been Prisoners there and three Spaniards, who belonged to Emanuel Riveras, were Examined as to the Situation, Avenues and other Circumstances of the Place. But, They Declaring that there was but one landing Place which was well Fortified, and it being the Season of the North Winds, it would be dangerous if not impracticable to attempt it at that time, the Design, was laid aside.

The 20th. of the same month Capt[ain] Collier returned from the Main, with two of the Enemies' Vessels[,] one of which called the *Galerdeen*, was Assistant to Riveras, in the Depredations committed on the Island. In her was taken 39 Prisoners who were severally Examined on Oath, the Depositions of two of Them were in the following Words.

November 29, 1670

Marcus de Cuba Master Pilot of the *Galerdeen* Prize, born at the Grand Canaries, aged 47 Years of thereabouts, Deposeth and Saith

That He did see the people at Carthagena in Arms offensive against the English.

That Several Ships have had and now have Commissions from the President of Panama Don Juan Perez de Guzman and that They have taken several English Vessels. That the Spaniards have great Encouragement given them by the said President, against the Island of Jamaica, and the more by reason of a Fleet fitted out of old Spain, for those Parts, under the Command and Conduct of Don Alonso, and further saith not

---

28. Captain John Morris was an important participant in Caribbean buccaneering in the 1660s and 1670s and an associate of Henry Morgan's on the Panama expedition in 1670–71.

29. Emanuel Riveras was the Portuguese pirate Manuel Ribeiro Pardal, who had long been raiding shipping under a letter of marque from Spain. After Morris's capture of his ship, the *San Pedro y La Fama*, while sailing off the northern coast of Cuba, Ribeiro managed to escape but was soon thereafter killed by Henry Morgan.

Nov[ember] 29, 1670

Lucas Perez Mariner, born at Palma, and aged 31 Years or thereabouts, deposeth and Saith

That He did see the People in Carthagena some of Them in Arms and others listing, of Themselves; That two Ships one with 18 and the other with 12 Guns were fitted and ready to Sail for Jamaica. And that the President of Panama had granted Commissions against the English, by virtue of which several English ships had been taken and further saith not.

On the 2d. of December Capt[ain] Morgan called all the Capt[ain]s on Board His Ship, being 17 in Number[,] Himself included[,] whose Names are as follows

Capt[ain] Joseph Bradley	Capt[ain] Edward Collier
Richard Norman	Lawrence Prince
Tho[ma]s Harrison	John Morris
Rob[er]t Delander	Thomas Rogers
John Harmonson	Charles Swan
John Galoone	Henry Wills
John Pyne	Richard Ludbury
Diego Moleen	Clement Simmons

These being met, Capt[ain] Morgan demanded their Opinion and Advice, what Place was fittest to Attain, for His Majestie's Honour, the preservation of Jamaica, and to put a Stop to the Insolencies of the Enemy. And, after some deliberation They Unanimously agreed to Attack Panama, by Reason the President of that City had granted Commissions against the English, to the great prejudice and Annoyance of Jamaica, and the Trade of His Majesty's Subjects.

To which proposal Capt[ain] Morgan assented; and on the 8. of December, the Fleet weighed, and Sailed from the Isle of Ash. The 14th. They arrived at the Isle of St. Katherines, about 8 in the morning; and by two in the afternoon, were possessed of the biggest Island without opposition. The 15. He sent a Summons to the Governour to Surrender the little Island, who consented on condition of good Quarters and transportation to the Main which was granted, and the agreement Mutually performed.

Capt[ain] M organ being informed by 4 Spanish Soldiers who had listed Themselves with our People, and offered to be Their Guides, that a strong Castle defended the Entrance into Chagre River and would obstruct that pass if it was not taken; He forthwith detached 470 men under the Command of Capt[ain] Joseph Bradley, to make themselves masters of that Fortress, which would facilitate His Design on Panama, and Secure His Retreat.

The 27. Capt[ain] Bradley landed His Men within four Miles of the

Among the most spectacular exploits of Sir Henry Morgan (1635–1688), the Welsh immigrant who became a successful planter, privateer, naval captain, and three-time active governor of Jamaica, was his sack of Panama in 1671, here depicted from an engraving entitled *Capt. Henry Morgan before Panama*, in *History of the Lives and Exploits of the Most Remarkable Pirates, Highway Men, Murderers, Street Robbers, etc.* (Birmingham, 1742), frontispiece.

Castle, and about 12 at noon began the Attack, with great Resolution, and the Spaniards Defended it with equal Bravery. The Action continued all Night and until 8 in the Morning of the next Day, when in playing Their Granadoes one of them luckily set the Guard House on Fire which Caused a breach, where our men entered with great Intrepidity, and the Enemy re-fusing Quarters and to Surrender, They lost 360 men. On our side 30 men were killed, and 76 wounded, among Them the Gallant Capt[ain] Bradley, who died soon after of His wounds greatly lamented.

The 2d. of January Capt[ain] Morgan arrived with the rest of the Forces, and understanding that the Spaniards had formed a Design of retaking the Place, He gave orders for the Fleet to follow Him into the Harbour, but in going in He lost His own Ship and four more, though all the men were Saved. He then prepared to go up the River, where He was informed the Spaniards had entrenched themselves and made Breast works in Six different Places: the 9th. He embarqued 1400 men on board of Seven small Vessels, and 36 Boats; and left 300 Men under the Command of Capt[ain] Richard Norman, to Garrison the Castle.

The 12. He got up to the first Breast Work, which the Enemy had set on Fire, on Their Appearance and Deserted it; as They did the rest without discharging one Gun. They were then obliged to quit their Vessels and Boats, leaving them under a Guard of 200 men and Marched 24 Miles through the Woods, without any other path than what They made Themselves.

The 14th. They arrived within two Miles of Venta Cruz, a small Town where the Spaniards land and Embarque all goods, to and from Panama, where was a very narrow and dangerous pass, which the Enemy thought would have put a Stop to all further proceedings. But, They were soon routed by the *Forlorn*, Commanded by Capt[ain] Thomas Rogers.

The 15th. They arrived at Venta Cruz, which They also found on fire and deserted.

The 16. They marched from thence, the Enemy constantly galling Them, with Ambuscades, and small Parties. But, though the Spaniards had the advantage of so narrow a pass that no more than four men could march abreast, Yet the *Forlorn* drove the Enemy before Them and Cleared the way. About noon They got into an Open Savanna, having in the Several Skirmishes lost no more than 3 men and 7 wounded, and after Marching 3 miles further They halted, in order to refresh Themselves.

The 17. They moved forwards, without any Opposition, and about 9 in the morning discovered the S[outh] Seas: But meeting with a great Number of Cattle, Capt[ain] Morgan ordered a general halt, and as many to be killed as They had Occasion for; and having refreshed Themselves, They began their March again about 4 in the Afternoon. In an hour after They came in Sight of the Enemy who were drawn up in Batalia, in number 2100 Foot, and 600 Horse, but the Day being almost spent, Capt[ain] Morgan did not think proper to Engage, and halted within 3 miles of Them, where They remained undisturbed all the Night.

The 18th. early in the Morning, Capt[ain] Morgan drew up His Men, in order of Battle; the Van was led by Capt[ain] Lawrence Prince, being 300 men in Number. The Main Body, containing 600 men, the Right wing by

Capt[ain] Morgan and the left by Capt[ain] Collier. And the Rear Containing 300 men, was Commanded by Capt[ain] Bledry Morgan.

The Spaniards kept Their Ground, though often provoked to an Engagement, upon which Capt[ain] Morgan ordered His Men to Wheel to the left, in order to gain a Hill, which would force Them to fight to Their disadvantage. This being happily Executed, the Spaniards had not room to Wheel, by Reason of a Bog, which They designed as a Trap, but in gaining the Hill, it proved one to Themselves, for They could not, out of Their great Body, fight more men at a time than we could, who were much inferior in Number, and beside we had thereby the advantage of the Wind as well as of the Sun.

Don Francisco De [la] Tarre gave the charge, with His Horse, upon the Vanguard, with great fury but our Body not having any Pikes, orders were given to double the Ranks, to the Right and left inward to close order, which Stopped his Career with the loss of His life; upon which the Horse wheeled off to the Right and their Foot advanced to try their Fortunes. But, They met with the same Fate, for we being ready with the main Body, gave Them such a warm reception, and pursued Them so close that They began to give way, and were so closely plied by our left wing, who could not, at first, come up to Engage, by reason of the Hill, that the Enemies' retreat came up to place running.

And, Here The Spaniards attempted a stratagem, which never was made use of, or thought on before for when the Foot engaged in the Flank: They drove two herds, consisting of 1500 head of Cattle, to the Right and left Angles, of the Rear. But, those Creatures being fright[en]ed with the noise of the gun turned upon their Drivers, and put them to flight in great Confusion, doing little or no damage to the Privateers, who then advanced to the City, where the Spaniards had 200 fresh men[,] two Forts[,] one of Six the other of 8 Guns, the Streets strongly Barricaded, [and] cannon mounted in all of them to the Number of 32 all Brass. But, the President instead of defending the Place, set fire to the City and blew up the Forts, which was done in such a hurry that they blew up forty of their Own men at the same time.

The Privateers, however, met with some resistance at the market Place, where they had four men killed and 6 wounded. But about 5 in the afternoon they were in possession of the City though on Fire, which They endeavoured to Extinguish: but in Vain, for by 12 at Night every part was Consumed except the Suburbs where was two Churches and about 300 Houses.

Thus was that Famous and Ancient City of Panama destroyed, which was the greatest Mart for Silver and Gold in the World, for it receives all the Goods that comes in the Galleons from Old Spain and transmits all the Silver and Gold that Comes from the Mines of Peru, and Potozi.

The Privateers remained in possession of the Suburbs of the City 28 days, making daily Excursions upon the Enemy about twenty miles by Land, without the least disturbance. They likewise kept Barks Cruising in the South Seas, which brought Them many Spaniards, who had fled to the Islands with Their Effects; so that They had in all at least 3000 Prisoners of all Sorts.

The 14. of Feb[ruary] the Privateers began Their March in order to return to the North seas, with all Their Prisoners, and the next Day came to Venta Cruz, which is about 5 English leagues or 15 miles from Panama, where they continued to refresh Themselves till the 24th.

The 26. They came to Chagra, where the Plunder was divided, which amounted to 400,000 p[iece]s [of eight]. And, after They had Spiked up the Guns, and demolished the Fort, They released the Prisoners and Sailed the 6 of March for Jamaica, where They arrived the 12th. of the same Month.

The Reason of their not acquiring much greater Wealth in this Expedition, was because the Spaniards had other [warnings] of the great Armaments [collecting] in Jamaica, and Apprehending it was intended against Them, from the Message Capt[ain] Morgan Sent the President of Panama, about 12 months before, They reimbarqued most of their Treasury, and sent it to Lima, in two Ships, one of 700 Tons and the other 300 Tons.

The 5th. of January 1670, His Majesty was pleased to revoke the powers granted to S[i]r Thomas Modiford, and to appoint Collo[nel] Thomas Lynch (on whom He likewise conferred the Honour of Knighthood) L[ieutenan]t Governour and Commander in Chief. S[i]r Thomas arrived at Jamaica the 24th. of June following, and took upon Him the Administration, pursuant to His Commission.

His general Instructions were the same as those which were given to S[i]r Thomas Modyford, And by His Additional Instructions He was directed to Cause the late Treaty between the Crown of Great Britain and Spain for Composing of differences, restraining of depredations, and Establishing of Peace in America; Concluded at Madrid the 18th. of July 1670, to be published within 8 months to be accounted from the 20th. of October 1670, or sooner if He could agree with the Spanish Governors in those Parts, upon a day of publication thereof. To revoke all Commissions and letters of Reprisall or Mark; whether the same were given and granted to any of our Subjects or to Strangers; and to declare them to be void and of no force.

And, for the Encouragement of all Capt[ain]s, Officers and Seamen, belonging to any of the Privateer Ships in America, to come in and apply Themselves to planting or Merchandising, he was impowered and directed (immediately after the publication of the said Peace) to Proclaim a general pardon, and Indemnity to such of Them as shall come in and Submit Themselves (within Such Reasonable time, as He shall with the advice of His Councill limit) for all Crimes and Offences committed by Them Since the month of June 1660, and before the publication of the said Peace. That those who shall come in, and enter Their Submission within the time pre-scribed, and Settle as aforesaid, shall quietly enjoy all such Goods as They shall be possessed of (except the Tenth or Fifteenth part, which was left to his discretion, to Ascertain or relinquish, According to Circumstances ex-pressly mentioned) and that those who were disposed to planting should have and Enjoy 30 Acres of land each man, to them and their Heirs for ever. And, in Case He found the Encouragement before mentioned, had not the desired Effect, He was to use all other means Necessary, by force or persuasion, to prevail with Them to Submit, and Continue under Obe-dience to His Majestie's Government.

S[i]r Thomas Lynch was also impowered and directed by a private In-struction to send S[i]r Thomas Modiford and Capt[ain] Morgan Prisoners to England, upon the Complaint of the Spanish Ambassador; and to an-swer the Charge Exhibited against Them. But, perceiving the Execution of that order would be attended with some difficulty, by reason of the Popu-larity of those Gentlemen, who were Extremely beloved in the Island; He took care to conceal that part of His Instructions, until the Ship of War which brought Him over was ready to Sail.

And then (having Concerted measures with the Capt[ain]) an Invitation was given to the Governor; S[i]r Thomas Modiford, Capt[ain] Morgan and some other Gentlemen, to dine aboard the Man of War. When They came aboard the Governour took Them two aside, in the Great Cabbin, and shewed Them His Instructions relating to Themselves, Excused His Manner of doing it, assigned His Reasons and among others, that it was to prevent a disturbance which He was apprehensive of, had it been known when They were ashore.

He thereupon Called the Capt[ain], and gave Him Charge of Them. However; He detained the Man of War in Port, until They had set[t]led Their private Affairs, and Admitted not only Their particular Friends, but any of the Gentlemen of the Island, to go on board and Visit Them.

S[i]r Thomas Modiford, who was thought the most blamable (the other having acted by Virtue of His Commission and Instructions) Appeared un-der no other Concern, than for the disgrace and the damage His Affairs, might sustain by His Absence; for He assured His Friends that He had suf-ficient Authority to grant Commissions against the Spaniards, and could justify His Conduct in all Respects.

Upon Their Arrival in England, They were both Sent to the Tower, where They remained about 18 months, at a great Expence and to the prej-udice of Their Healths, without being able to obtain a hearing, although a Constant application was made by Their Friends. And, the Reason is obvi-ous, the Ministers of that Reign, were sensible, He had private Instructions which would justify those proceedings, and therefore delayed the Trial, least the disclosing of that matter, should give Offence to His Catholick Majesty, with whom the Crown of England, was then upon good Terms.

At length came an order to discharge Them both, without a hearing, and Capt[ain] Morgan was introduced to His Majesty, who not only Conferred on Him the honour of Knighthood but, in a short time after, granted Him a Dormant Commission to be L[ieutenan]t Governor of Jamaica, in Case of the Death or absence of the Governor.

These Circumstances which are not publickly known, and have been misrepresented to the World are sufficient to Expunge that load of Infamy and Reproach which the Island of Jamaica has laid under, of having been a Nest of Bucaniers or Pirates whereas it is Evident from the Instances I have given that S[i]r Henry Morgan and others had legal Commissions; and though the Goods or Effects of some, who had not Commissions, were privately brought into the Country, and could not Easily be prevented in an Island of so large an Extent; yet it is an indubitable Fact, that none were admitted into Port, with Their Prizes, Encouraged or Connived at, by the Governor, but those who had acted under His Commission or the Governor of Petit Guavis.

S[i]r Thomas Lynch sent Major [William] Buston[30] to Carthagena with the Instruments of the Treaty between Great Britain and Spain, and to Cultivate a good understanding with the Spanish Nation. He also sent to all the Coasts of Cuba, and Terra Firma, to acquaint all Sea faring Men with the Proclamation of a Free and general Pardon, and that His Majesty intended to Observe Religiously the Treaties He had made with His Catholick Majesty, and Commanded all His Subjects, not to Commit any further Hostilities on the Spaniards, many of the Privateers came in upon this Notice, though others, who could not take to any other way of living, continued their practises and not being permitted to bring their Prizes or Booty to Jamaica, carried Them to Petit Guavis.

S[i]r Thomas Lynch in February 1671, called an Assembly, who passed Several Laws particularly an Act, Ascertaining the Number of the Assembly,[31] and Another for Set[t]ling the Boundaries of the Several Parishes in the Island.[32] They also altered and enlarged the Laws, which were made in the Administration of S[i]r Thomas Modiford; and passed an Act for Raising a Revenue Indefinite for the Support of the Government of this Island:[33] But, those Laws not being approved of by His Majesty, they were Rejected, and others with proper amendments were enacted by the Assembly in 1673, and made to Continue in force for two Years, and no longer.

In the same year Martial law was put in force, for three months; it being

---

30. Major William Buston also held 878 acres in St. Andrew Parish in Jamaica.

31. An Act for the Ascertaining the Number of the Assembly, March 1673/74, in *Journals of the Jamaica Assembly*, 14 vols. (Jamaica, 1795–1824), 1:7.

32. An Act for Dividing the Island into Several Parishes, March 1673–74, in ibid., 1:1–7.

33. An Act for Raising a Public Revenue Indefinite for Support of Government in the Island, February 1672/73, in ibid., 1:5.

thought Necessary to Fortify the Island, and put it in a State of Defence against Foreign Enemies. Accordingly, Breastworks were raised and Entrenchments made, at old Harbor and other parts of the Island; a platform laid and a new line of Guns planted at Port Morant. Fort James at Port Royal was also began and afterwards Compleated by a Voluntary Subscription, of the Governor[,] Council and Assembly; and other Inhabitants of the Island.

This is a Circumstance deserving of notice and commemoration in honour to those Gentlemen, and as it may be an incitement to others, to follow so good an Example, on such like Occasions, and revive Publick spirit, which seems to be almost Extinguished in other parts of the British Dominions, as well as in Jamaica. Nor is it merely an Act of Generosity, but agreeable to Reason that They, who have the most to loose, should contribute most and be at the greatest Expence, for the Publick Security, without Burthening those, who are in low Circumstances or Struggling with Difficulties, and perhaps eating their Bread with labour and Sorrow. And, in the end it will in my Opinion turn out to Their advantage for when the lower sort of People perceive those in Power or in oppulent Circumstances tender of laying any imposition or hardship on Them, They will more readily go over and Settle in the Island which will be the means of increasing the Number of Inhabitants, and in Consequence not only Secure; but raise the Value of their Estates.

S[i]r Thomas Lynch, though He was assiduous, and no ways deficient in His Duty, yet He was not able to restrain the English Privateers from Acting against the Spaniards, for many of Them Continued out, and since They could not obtain Commissions or Encouragement at Jamaica, went to Petit Guavis and Applied to the Governor of that Colony, who granted them, the French being still at enmity with the Spaniards.

The Spanish Ambassador, not being well informed of those Circumstances, made strong Representations to our Court of the Depredations committed by the Subjects of England in America, and Suggested that they were Encouraged and Countenanced by the Governor of Jamaica, which had such Influence and Effect, that to pacify Him S[i]r Thomas Lynch was recalled, to Answer the Complaints, which were made of His Conduct; and the Right Honourable John Lord Vaughan Kn[igh]t of the noble order of the Bath,[34] was appointed to Succeed Him in the Government.

The Lord Vaughan's Commission was dated the 6th. of April 1674 and therein His Council was particularly named and which has been the method ever since, whereas they were before nominated by the Governor.

---

34. John Vaughan, Third (and last) Earl of Carbery (1640–1713), was born in Carmarthenshire; educated at Christ College, Oxford (1656); knighted in April 1661; and sat as MP for Carmarthen borough, 1661–79, and county, 1679–81, 1685–87. He was governor of Jamaica from 1675 to 1678. Cundall, *Governors of Jamaica in the Seventeenth Century*, 77–85.

His Lordship was furnished with the same powers and Instructions in other Respects as were given to his Predecessor and Arrived at Jamaica the [blank] day of [blank] following; and at the same time S[i]r Thomas Modiford and S[i]r Henry Morgan returned to the Island.

The Lord Vaughan, immediately on His Arrival issued out a Proclamation commanding all His Majestie's Subjects to Cease and forbear all manner of Violence and Injury or to Commit any Hostilities against the Spaniards; nevertheless some of them ventured to land on Cuba, where they Committed great depredations, but being taken and brought to Jamaica, were put upon Their Trial before S[i]r Henry Morgan Kn[igh]t[,] Robert Bindless[35] and William Beeston Esq[uire]s[36] (who were Appointed Judges of the Admiralty) and not producing a Commission from any Prince or State, They were, according to Their Sentence, Executed at Port Royal.

His Excellency in April 1675, called an Assembly, and the several Laws which were Enacted in S[i]r Thomas Lynch's Government and made to Continue in force for two years, and no more, were revived for two years longer, Except the Revenue Bill, which was rejected, so that the Island remained without any Revenue, almost one Year. But, upon Their meeting the next Session; the Obstructions being removed His Excellency then gave His Assent to that Bill.

At this time the Island laboured under many difficulties and hardships, by means of the Royal African Company, who having Obtained a Charter to Trade to Guinea, Binny &c. exclusive of all others, Seized upon, and Condemned all Ships which They met with, and had traded to any of those places, without Their Licence.

This Monopoly gave great uneasiness, to the Planters, and Obstructed the improvement of all the British Colonies, particularly this Island; for having but one market to go to and being now under the necessity of deal-

---

35. Robert Byndloss (?–1687) married Anna Petronella, daughter of Edward Morgan and cousin of Sir Henry, in 1665. A prominent Jamaica officeholder, he was commander of Fort Charles in 1664–65, commissioner of admiralty in 1675, and, despite Governor Vaughan's accusation in October 1677 of corresponding, like Sir Henry and Sir William Beeston, with privateers, chief justice in 1681. Ibid., 29, 38, 48, 58, 60, 87, 95, 146.

36. Sir William Beeston (1636?–?). Born in Titchfield, Hampshire, Beeston went to Jamaica in 1660, was a member of the assembly for Port Royal in the first House of Assembly in 1664, and served as a judge of common pleas also in 1664. Commissioned by Modyford to negotiate with privateers off Cuba in 1665, he took peace articles to the Spanish in 1668 and gained command of a frigate. He became commissioner of the admiralty with Morgan and Byndloss in 1675 and Speaker of the House in 1677 in opposition to Charles Howard, First Earl of Carlisle, who sent him to England, where he was cleared of charges. Knighted in 1692, he was sent back to Jamaica in 1693 as lieutenant-governor and acted as commander in chief, repelling the French in 1694. He wrote *A Narrative of the Descent on Jamaica by the French*, which was later printed in *Interesting Tracts Relating to the Island of Jamaica* (St. Jago de la Vega, Jamaica, 1780), 249–59. He served as governor from 1693 to 1702, when John Selwyn replaced him and Beeston returned to England. Ibid., 143–65.

ing with Them only, They were very Scantily Supplied with Negro's and obliged to pay Extravagant rates for such as they wanted. Many Complaints were made of the Arbitrary proceedings of that Company and their Agents abroad, who were not only Countenanced and Supported by the Duke of York, but His Royal Highness who was the Governor of the Company entered so far into their measures and Interest as to threaten S[i]r Jonathan Atkins Governor of Barbadoes,[37] to have Him removed, upon a supposition of His conniving at the Separate Traders, who were stigmatized with the name of Interloper.

The Lord Vaughan was also suspected not only of Encouraging the Separate Traders, but employing a Sloop of His own to import Negroes, without permission or licence, and being Concerned with others, particularly S[i]r Thomas Modiford; for which he was severely reprimanded, without any proof of the Facts, and although, He employed His Majestie's Ships, (According to His orders) in Searching after and siezing all such as traded to Guinea and were deemed Interlopers.

But, the Inhabitants of this Island, on this Occasion behaved with a good deal of spirit, and would not tamely Submit to all the Impositions, that were attempted to be laid on Them, for Samuel Barnard Esq[uir]e[38] prosecuted the Companie's Agents, for an unjust Seizure and Detainer of the ship *St. George*, which was consigned to Him, and not only Cast the Company but recovered near £1000, for Costs and Damages.

In [blank] 1676, Mr. [Edward] Cranfield, Duckingfield and Brent, who were appointed Commissioners, for removing the English from Surinam, according to the Treaty between King Charles the 2d. and the States General Arrived in this Island, with Collo[nel James] Banister who was Governor of that Colony or One of their Principal Magistrates, and 1200 Men, Women and Children, including Negroes. They were received with great Humanity and Complacency by the Lord Vaughan, who, According to His Instructions allotted them a tract of land in St. Elizabeths which They made choice of, on account of the pleasant Situation, and being desirous of set[t]ling Contiguously. From thence that part of the Country, obtained the name of Surinam Quarters, which it Still retains. But, in a few Years after, they removed about [blank] miles Westward of that place (finding the Soil thereabout much better) except Collo[nel] Banister who set[t]led in St. Dorothys.

Those People from time to time chose to intermarry among Themselves and being very abstemious and Frugal as well as Industrious, They

37. Sir Jonathan Atkins (1610?–?), a civil servant under Charles I and Charles II, was appointed governor of Barbados in 1673, arriving there on November 1, 1774. Frequently in conflict with London over the Navigation Acts and policies of the Lords of Trade, he was recalled in 1680 in favor of Sir Richard Dutton. Vincent T. Harlow, *A History of Barbados, 1625–1685* (New York, 1926), 213–40.

38. Samuel Bernard was Speaker of the Jamaica Assembly in the late 1670s.

Lord John Vaughan, Third Earl of
Carbery (1639–1713), governor of
Jamaica, 1675–78, whose administra-
tion was notable for its corruption.
(National Portrait Gallery)

Succeeded much better than any of the other Colonies that removed to the
Island, except some few of the Barbadians. Their Descendants now Enjoy
the fruits of their labour, being possessed of some of the finest Plantations
in that or any other part of the Island.

The Assembly met again the 9th. of April 1677, and a third time (during
this Administration) the 6th. of Sept[embe]r 1677. When They proceeded
upon Such Business, as was recommended to Them, without any disputes
or Controversies, there being not only a good harmony and agreement
amongst Themselves but with the Governor.

The Lord Vaughan after having been three Years in this Island, returned
to England the [blank] day of [blank] 1677, leaving S[i]r Henry Morgan
in the Administration, who had a Commission to Succeed as L[ieutenan]t
Governor in Case of His Lordship's Death or absence. Nevertheless, He
was very much blamed and received a severe Reprimand at Court, for coming Home without His Majestie's Special licence or permission.

This noble Lord is ranked among the best Governours of this Island;
for He was Equally careful of the Prerogative of the Crown, and tender
of the Rights and priviledges of the People, which He never attempted to
lessen, or Violate in any degree. This laudable Conduct, and His agreeable
behavior in other respects, deservedly gained Him the Affections, and Esteem of the People in general. Nevertheless, He did not Escape Calumny
and Detraction, the constant Attendants on the Merit, and Persons in distinguished Stations; for He was unjustly accused of Selling his Domestick
Servants (whom He Carried out of England with Him) before His departure from the Island; and of making too much hast to be Rich. I should not

have mentioned those Circumstances, but to do Justice to His Lordship's Character and Memory since they have been mentioned by other writers and to show the Falsity and absurdity of those Insinuations; the first of which had no other foundation than the following incident.

Soon after His return to England, a Gentleman of His Acquaintance one day in Company, among other questions Enquired what became of the Chaplain, He carried Over with Him to Jamaica. His Lordship being a man of Wit and humour and like others of the same turn, was unwilling to lose a joke Replied—That as to Him, being a loose wicked fellow like many of His Brethren, He sold Him to a Planter, for an Overseer. When, in truth, he was not only a distant Relation of His Lordship's, and a Gentleman of an Amiable Character, but he had given Him the presentation of one of the best livings in the Island.

And, as to His making too much hast to be Rich, though He acquired more than any of His Predecessors, or perhaps most that have Succeeded Him, within the same space of time, yet I have heard the Ancient Inhabitants acquit Him of all kind of Extortion or Oppression and speak of Him, with the highest Commendation, and Esteem. Indeed, the following Circumstance is a sufficient Testimony, and will Corroborate, all I have related without partiality or favour.

When he was going to imbarque at Port Royal, He was attended to the Water Side by the Gentlemen of the Council, the Principal Planters and Merchants, and a great number of others. And, before He took His leave, He addressed Himself to the Company with an Audible voice, in the following manner. ["]Gentlemen, whose Ox have I taken, or whose Ass have I stolen? Whom have I Injured or Oppressed in any respect; let him now declare it with Freedom, and I do assure You upon my honour, that I will not Stir off the Island, until I have made Satisfaction:["] a profound Silence ensuing, He repeated the words a Second time; the Company shouted thereupon 3 times, which He looked upon as it was intended an acknowledgment of their Approbation of His Conduct. Then taking S[i]r H[enry] M[organ] by the hand, wished him joy of the Government, and prosperity, to the Island Stepped into the Pinnace; and went off very much regretted, by the Inhabitants in general, who lamented being deprived of so Excellent a Governor.

This is likewise a Pattern, worthy of the imitation of all those who preside in our Colonies and which truly Copied will contribute greatly to the Utility and Satisfaction of their respective, Governments, as well as to their Own honour. But, alass! how many of them can justly make the same Declaration, or are willing to stand the Test of a Scrutiny, and Submit their Actions to a publick Censure: It is notorious, that private Views and Sordid Interest engrosses the Attention of most of them, who seem Regardless of the Wellfare and happiness of those entrusted to their Care, the Interest of their Country and the honour of the Royal Person, whom they represent.

The Lord Vaughan, who was Earl of Carbery on the demise of His Father and is better known by that Title, lived many Years after his return to England, and died without Male issue, leaving only one Daughter, who is the present Dutchess of Bolton,[39] so that the Title is Extinct.

S[i]r Henry Morgan, on the departure of the Lord Vaughan, took on Him the Administration, as L[ieutenan]t Governor, by Virtue of a dormant Commission, dated the 6th. of October 1674. This Gentleman's first Care was to Compleat the Fortifications at Port Royal in which He was very Assiduous for at this time, Fort Ruport, and Fort Carlisle were finished, and a new line built at Fort James.

And, being Sensible of the imputation He laid under of having been a Bucaneer or Pyrate, He was likewise assiduous in his endeavours to Suppress or reclaim those who acted against the Spaniards under French Commissions, or without any legal Authority, and used every other means in His power of convincing the World that He was unjustly Stigmatized on that Account. But, all His Efforts were fruitless and ineffectual, for many of Them still Continued out, and Committed great Devastations particularly [Richard] Sawkins,[40] [Bartholomew] Sharp,[41] [John] Coxen &c. who Commanded a Body of Men, landed at Darien, and with the Assistance of the Indian Chiefs or Princes [from] a Nation of Indians on the Continent of America Situate[d] between Porto bello and Carthagena took the Town and Mines of St. Maria, and marched over land to the South Seas, where they cruised near two Years[,] took Several other Towns, and prizes, the plunder of which Amounted to a very Considerable Sum of Mon[e]y. A more particular account of their Transactions may be seen in Mr. Ringrose's *Account of Capt[ain] Sharp's Expedition into the South Seas,*[42] and Capt[ain] Dampier's *Voyage round the World.*[43]

39. Anne Paulet née Vaughan (?–1751) was Carbery's daughter. She married Charles Paulet/Powlett, Third Duke of Bolton (1685–1754), in 1713, thereby becoming the duchess.

40. Richard Sawkins (?–1680) became a prominent English buccaneer captain as a result of his participation in an expedition to the isthmus of Panama in 1679–80. With his associates, he made his way to the Pacific Ocean, taking a leading role in the defeat of a numerically superior Spanish force at the Battle of Pirico and in the blockade of Panama City, though its governor ignored his demands for a ransom. Later in the same expedition, he was killed while leading an attack on Pueblo Nuero.

41. Bartholomew Sharpe (1650–1702) was another prominent buccaneer captain operating in the West Indies between 1675 and 1682 who was notable for his capture of Portobello in 1679 and his prominent role in the Panama Expedition of 1679–80, and for being the first Englishman to travel south and east around Cape Horn, taking twenty-five Spanish ships and plundering numerous Spanish towns along the way. He returned to the West Indies and then to England where, at the insistence of the Spanish ambassador, English authorities tried but acquitted him of piracy. He ended his days in prison for debt in the Danish colony of St. Thomas.

42. Basil Ringrose (?–1686) traveled to the West Indies in 1679 as a doctor with the buccaneers and met his death in a Spanish ambush. He was the author of *The Dangerous Voyage and Bold Assaults of Captain Bartholomew Sharp and Others, by Basil Ringrose* (London, 1684).

43. Captain William Dampier (1652–1715) was born in Somerset, the son of a tenant farmer, and went to sea when young. In 1673, he became assistant manager of a Jamaica plan-

It is Remarkable of all those several Classes of Men (French as well as English) that They never interrupted or molested the Traders of any other Nation except the Spaniards, but permitted them to pass the Seas freely on their Occasions, and paying them the full Value of such Necessaries which they wanted, and the others could Conveniently Spare them, without taking any thing by force or Violence.

Sawkins was killed, in the Assault of a Town in the South Seas. Capt[ain] Sharp on His Arrival in England, was taken up on the Complaint of the Spanish Ambassador, and tried for Piracy, but Acquitted on His producing a Commission from the Princes of Darien, who were then at War, and never were perfectly reconciled, or at Peace with the Spaniards. Capt[ain] Coxon returned to Jamaica, where He was likewise taken up on the Complaint of the Spaniards, and tried for Piracy, but acquitted on His producing a Commission from the Governor of Petit Guavis.

This Coxon was one of the last Commanders of the Privateers of these times, who did Wonders in Courage and Conduct, and for His Mercy shown in Victory, His great Bravery and Contempt of mon[e]y, was deservedly Applauded and distinguished. He was taken up and tried for Piracy Seven Times, but always Acquitted, on His producing fair and Regular Commissions from the Governor of this Island or of Petit Guavis. He despised, and had an implacable Enmity to the Spaniards[,] alledged that they were faithless, never to be trusted, and often declared, in a Solemn manner, Eternal War against them; for that He would at all times assist any Nation or People who were at Variance with them. He proclaimed the Prince of Orange (King of England) at Port Royal, before they had advice of His being declared King in England;[44] was very Serviceable in the War with France (particularly in the Expedition against Hispaniola), but being grown old and Infirm He retired after the Peace of Ryswick,[45] and died at Kingston in the Year 1701.

----

tation belonging to his father's ex-landlord, Colonel Cary Helyar. Back in England in 1678, he profited from West Indies trade and returned to Jamaica in 1679 where he kept an account of the doings of the buccaneers and produced the work Knight refers to: *A New Voyage Round the World* (London, 1697). Subsequent adventures took him to Virginia, Africa, Mexico, Guam, and China on piratical expeditions and on an exploratory voyage of 1698 on which he sighted the coast of Australia. He was also the author of *Voyages and Descriptions* (London, 1698) and *A Discourse on Winds* (London, 1699).

44. William III (1650–1702). Born at The Hague to William II of Orange and Mary, daughter of Charles I of England, William III was captain general of Dutch forces and later stadtholder, and secured the integration of the United Provinces by the Treaty of Nijmegen in 1678. He married Mary, daughter of the Duke of York, later James II, in 1677 but became alienated from James's Catholicism. Persuaded to take England, he landed at Brixham on the south coast on November 5, 1688. Following the flight of James II, William and Mary succeeded to the throne by decree of the Convention Parliament of the Glorious Revolution Settlement. He formed a Grand Alliance with the United Provinces and defeated James II in Ireland in the Battle of the Boyne in 1690 and quelled the Scots at Glencoe in 1692. The Peace of Ryswick ended conflict in 1697 with Louis XIV's promise not to ally with William's enemies.

45. The Peace of Ryswick of September 20, 1697, ended King William's war against France over the Spanish succession.

S[i]r Henry Morgan convened the Assembly, but they did not pass any laws, nor was there any other Material transaction, during His first Administration, for He was Superceeded by the Right Hon[ora]ble Charles[,] Earl of Carlisle.[46]

The Earl of Carlisle's Commission was dated the 1st. of March 1677, and His Lordship arrived at Port Royal, the following [blank.]

In a few days after[,] the Negroes belonging to Capt[ain] Duck[']s Plantation at Caimanos, (which is about 4 miles from Spanish Town) who were most of them drunk, as they Commonly are on Sundays, and other Festivals, and Observing the River Cobre (which runs between that Plantation and the Town) to be greatly Swelled by the Rains, and as they thought impassable, set upon the Family[,] killed their Mistress and desperately wounded Capt[ain] Duck, whom they left for dead, though He afterwards recovered. But, a Faithful Negro at the imminent danger of his life, Swam over the River, and gave the Governor an Account of this Disaster, upon which His Excellency immediately detached a Troop of Horse to quell them. It was with some difficulty, they got over the River, but, after a small skirmish wherein Some of the Negroes, were killed, and Others taken Prisoners, the rest Submitted. The Ringleaders were tried According to the laws of the Country, and in pursuance of their Sentence were Executed in Terrorem.[47]

But, the Inhabitants were at that time much more alarmed at the Report of a new Scheme of Government being proposed by the Lords of the Committee of Council, for Trade and Plantations in England. That, the Earl of Carlisle was, by His Instructions, directed to lay before the Assembly the Draught of a Bill for Establishing a perpetual Revenue, with several others, which were prepared in England, and sent over to be Enacted by Them. And, that no Laws were to be enacted in Jamaica, for the future, but Such as being framed by the Governor and Council, were first transmitted for His Majestie's Approbation, and afterwards remitted to Jamaica to be passed by the Assembly, without allowing them a Deliberative power and Negative Voice or making any alterations of amendment, so that the same method in legislative matters should be made use of there as in Ireland.

46. Charles Howard, First Earl of Carlisle of the second creation (1629?–1685), had a long record of public service in the military with the Parliamentary Army. He was MP for several constituencies, a member of Cromwell's House of Lords, privy councillor, lord lieutenant of Cumberland and Westmoreland, and ambassador to Russia, Sweden, and Denmark before Charles II appointed him governor of Jamaica, a post he held from September 1677 to April 1681. He received his earldom in 1661. See Cundall, *Governors of Jamaica in the Seventeenth Century*, 86–94.

47. Perhaps Captain Edmund Duck, a resident of St. Catherine. Amy M. Johnson, "Slavery on the Gold Coast and African Resistance to Slavery in Jamaica during the Early Colonial Period," *Limina: A Journal of Historical and Cultural Studies* 18 (2012): 1–15, puts this uprising in its Atlantic context.

These Suggestions appeared to be too well founded, for on the Meeting of the Assembly on the 2d. of Sept[ember] 1678, His Excellency Confirmed the same in his Speech, the Substance of which is as Follows.

That He could not say the Bills, which He brought over with Him, to be enacted by them, were the same that were transmitted by the Lord Vaughan, to the Lords of the Committee of Council for Trade and Plantations; and that those who were present when His Commission was read might observe that an Alteration was intended in the Model of their laws, which were for the future, to be after the form and Manner of Ireland.

That the Stile and title being changed as to the King and Assembly, they had no reason to be displeased with, it being a greater honour, than was ever done to any other Plantation.

That they were under great obligations to His Majesty for his Extraordinary Care, that He looked on this Island, as His darling Plantation, and had taken more pains to make them happy than any of His other Colonies. Therefore He hoped that those Considerations would Oblige them to make Such returns, as might be agreeable to His Majesty.

That among the Bills, which He should lay before them, and were necessary to be Enacted was an Act for raising a Revenue, which there was a necessity for being dispatched, in regard to the Officers of the Forts, and Others who were employed in building them, and were in Arrears. And that they were greatly obliged, to S[i]r Henry Morgan for his Assiduity and Care, in Supervising and Seeing the Works well performed.

That His Majesty was greatly displeased with them for having passed some Acts, without mentioning his name, which never had been practised or done in any of His Plantations or Dominions.

That in the Militia Act, there was a Clause Omitted, saving the Governor's power, but He hoped none would Attempt to derogate from the Authority with which His Majesty had been pleased to Cloath His Governors.

That He was Extremely desirous of things being Conducted in such a manner, that the King might be fully satisfied, but that the restraint they lay under, in respect to the new laws, He brought over, could not be altered, for that He had not the power to do it, which he wished He had.

That He had always been deemed a man of Probity and was in nothing more desirous than to do good to this Island, that He came over with that intent and Resolution, therefore would not by his power lead them into any Inconveniences.

The several Bills prepared by the Lords of the Committee of Council for Trade, and Plantations, were accordingly laid before the Assembly, who did not take up any time in deliberating thereupon, but, Unanimously rejected them and came to Several Resolutions in regard to their Rights and privileges, in framing their Own Bills.

They at the same time, drew up an Address to His Excellency, wherein they assigned the following Motives and Reasons of their proceedings—

1

That They were dissatisfied with the Clause in the Militia Bill, whereby it is provided that the Governor may upon all Occasions and Emergencies Act as Governor in Chief, According to and in pursuance of *all the Powers and Authorities given to Him by His Majestie's Commission.* Apprehending they shall thereby make it legal to Execute *all Instructions* which are or shall be sent to *His Majestie's Governors*

2

They Objected to the Bill for raising a Publick Revenue, because it was made perpetual and [the funds raised thereby] liable to then be diverted.

3

That the Several Bills contained divers and fundamental Errors.

4

That they were not compared with and Amended by the last laws sent over by the Lord Vaughan.

5

That the distance of place rendered that method of making laws impracticable.

6

That the Nature of all Colonies is Changeable and Consequently the laws must be adapted to the Interest of the Place.

7

That they are thereby deprived of the Satisfaction of a *deliberative power* in making of Laws.

8

That the form of Government proposed would render the Governor *absolute.*

9

And that by the former method His Majestie's prerogative was better Secured.

The Address (which contained the aforementioned Reasons)—though no ways agreeable and Satisfactory, was transmitted by His Excellency to the Lords of the Committee of Council for Trade and Plantations; and in the mean time He sent for Several of the leading Members, being in hopes by fair and gentle means, to prevail with them to come into the measures proposed.

But, all His Efforts proved ineffectual, for He was not able to bring over one Member; and the House proceeded to frame and bring in Bills as usual, upon which the Governor dissolved that Assembly.

The [former] Speaker (Samuel Long Esq[uir]e)[48] in particular gave great offence, on this Occasion, for in a private Conversation with the Governor, among other things said—That as to his part *He could Submit to wear Chains Himself, but never would Consent to make them for Posterity;* for which, and some other words of the like Nature, the Governor not only *Committed Him,* but Sent him to England *a Prisoner in Irons.*

Mr. Long upon His Arrival in England, presented a Petition, to the King and Council Setting forth His Case, and praying to be heard, in Vindication of himself. This favour was immediately granted, and upon His being Called in before the Council, the King being present, He pleaded his own Cause with Such decency, Strength of Reason and Argument, that He was not only honourably Acquitted, but His Majesty was pleased to declare that *He did not think that He had Such a Subject in that part of the World.*

This is a further Instance of the Arbitrary proceedings of those times, especially in our Colonies abroad, But, though that Gentleman, never had any recompense or Satisfaction made Him for the loss of His time[,] the fatigue and Expences He was unavoidably subject to, Yet we have now the pleasure of seeing the Governors of the Plantations, restrained from Acting with so high a hand, by good and Salutary laws, particularly an Act of Parliament in the 7 and 8 of King William intitled an Act—[blank].[49]

The year following vizt. in May 1679 the Inhabitants were likewise alarmed with the Apprehensions of a French Invasion, the Count de Estres being in the American Seas, with a strong Squadron of men of War, and as there was, at that time a mis-understanding between the English and French Courts, it was Conjectured that their Designs were against this Island. Martial law was thereupon declared, and other measures taken for the Security and defence of the Island; but those Jealousies and fears soon blew over.

In July, His Excellency received fresh Instructions in regard to their

48. Samuel Long (1638–1683) was born in Wiltshire and came to Jamaica as a lieutenant in Daniel Doyley's regiment during the capture of Jamaica. Remaining there, he obtained large grants of land in Clarendon and St. Catherine Parishes. He played a major political role in the construction of the Jamaica polity. Clerk of the first House of Assembly in 1661, he represented Cagua in that body in 1664, Clarendon in 1672, and St. Catherine in 1674, and served as its Speaker from 1772 until his appointment to the council and the chief justiceship in 1764. He was the grandfather of the historian Edward Long.

49. An Act for Preventing Frauds and Regulating Abuses in the Plantation Trade, 7 & 8 Will. 3c. 22, commonly referred to as the Navigation Act of 1696.

Laws and what had passed relating thereto, upon which Writs were issued out for choosing of a new Assembly.

The Inhabitants in general[,] who were greatly uneasy and inflamed at the Attempt to alter the Constitution or form of Government, thought they could not make a better Choice than of the same Worthy Representatives, who had so faithfully and Strenuously insisted on what they thought their Natural and undoubted Rights and privileges, so that upon the meeting of the new Assembly, there was not more than 2 or 3 new Faces Seen among them.

The 19th. of August 1679 (the day after they met and Chose a Speaker) His Excellency made a Speech as usual, wherein among other things He recommended the Expediency of Complying with His Majestie's Instructions in passing the Bills which were framed in England, and sent over to be enacted Here. And, at the same time, laid before Them the Report of the Lords of the Committee, for Trade and Plantations, to His Majesty in Council, in the following words.

At the Court of White Hall, May 28. 1679
present
The King's most Excellent Majesty

The Lord Arch Bishop of Canterbury[50]
Lord Chancellor[51]
Lord President[52]
Lord Privy Seal[53]
Duke of Lodderdale[54]
Marq[ui]s of Worcester[55]
Earl of Bath etc.[56]

Whereas this day was read at the Board a Report from the Right Hon[ora]ble the Lords of the Committee for Trade and Plantations, in the words following[:]

In Obedience to your Majestie's Command we have entered into the present State of your Majestie's Island of Jamaica, in order to propose such means as may put an end to the great discouragement your Majestie's good Subjects there are under, by the unset[t]led Condition thereof, Occasioned

50. William Sancroft (1617–1693).
51. Heneage Finch, First Earl of Nottingham (1621–1682).
52. Anthony Ashley-Cooper, First Baron Ashley and First Earl of Shaftesbury (1621–1683).
53. Arthur Annesley, First Earl of Anglesey of the second creation (1614–1686).
54. John Maitland, First Duke of Lauderdale (1616–1682).
55. Henry Somerset, Seventh Earl and Third Marquis of Worcester (1629?–1700).
56. John Grenville, First Earl of Bath (1628–1701).

by the refusal of the laws which were lately offered by the Earl of Carlisle
to the Assembly for their Consent, all which proceedings and dissatisfac-
tions appear to have arisen in the manner following[:]

By the Commissions granted by Your Majesty to the Lord Vaughan, and
other Governors it was your Royal pleasure to intrust the Assembly of Jamaica, with a power to frame and enact laws, with the advice and Consent
of the Governor and Council, which laws were to Continue in force for
the space of two Years and no longer. But, so it happened that your Majesty found the Inconveniences which did attend that power and making of
laws by Irregular, Violent, and unwarrantable proceedings of the Assembly,
was pleased with the advice of the Privy Council, to provide by the Earl
of Carlisle's Commission, that no laws should be Enacted in Jamaica, but
Such as being framed by the Governor and Council, and being transmitted to Your Majesty for your Royal Approbation, were afterwards remitted
to Jamaica, and Consented to by the Assembly there. And in pursuance
hereof, the Earl of Carlisle carried over a Body of laws, under the great
Seal of England, which laws at His Lordship's Arrival there, were Rejected
by the General Assembly, upon Grounds and Reasons Contained in their
Address to your Majestie's Governor, and in divers letters from His Lordship relating thereto.

In the first place They are dissatisfied with a Clause in the Militia bill &c.

These being the Objections and pretensions, on which the Assembly
have with so much Animosity proceeded, to reject the Bills transmitted
by Your Majesty, we cannot but Offer for your Majestie's Information and
Satisfaction, such a short Answer, as may not only give a Testimony of the
unreasonableness of those proceedings, but furnish the Governor, when
occasion shall serve; with such Arguments as may be fit to be used in Justification of your Majestie's Commission and Power granted to Him.

1. It is not without the greatest presumption that They go about to
question your Majestie's Authority Over the Militia in that Island Since
it hath been allowed and declared by the Laws of this Your Kingdoms,
that the Sole Supreme Government of the Militia, and all Forces by Sea
and Land, and all Forts and places of Strength, are vested in your Majesty
within all your Realms and Dominions.

2. The Objection made against the Bill for raising a publick Revenue,
hath as little grounds, Since its being made perpetual is no more than
what was formerly Offered by Them to your Majesty, in the Government
of S[i]r Thomas Lynch, in the Same Measure and proportion as is now
proposed, and Cannot be diverted, since provision is Expressly made, that
the same shall be for the better Support of the Government. Beside, is it
Suitable to the Duty and Modesty of Subjects, to Suspect Your Majestie's
Justice and Care, for the *Government* of that Colony whose Settlement and
preservation hath been more particularly carried on, by your Majestie's
tender regard, and with the great Expence of your Treasure.

To the 3d and 4th. Objection it may be answered that if any thing had been found material of note or importance in the last Body of laws, transmitted by the Lord Vaughan, Your Majestie's tender Care of your Subjects welfare would have been such, as would not have Sent those Bills imperfect or defective in any necessary matter.

5. As to the distance of place, which they Say, renders the present method of making laws altogether impracticable, Your Majesty having been pleased to regulate the same by the advice of your Privy Council According to the usage of Ireland, such Care was then taken that no law might be wanting which might Conduce to the well being of that Plantation, and that nothing might be Omitted which in all former Governments had been thought necessary. Nor is it likely that this Colony is liable to greater Accidents, than your Kingdom of Ireland, so as to require a more frequent or Sudden change of Laws, in other Cases than such as are already provided for upon Emergencies, or in any other manner than is directed by Your Majesty, whereby the Inhabitants have free Access to make Complaints, to your Governor and Council of any defect in any old Law, or to give reasons for any new Ones, being Modelled by the Governor and Council into form of Laws and transmitted to your Majesty; And if your Majesty and Council thought reasonable may be transmitted back to be Enacted Accordingly.

6. It was Sufficiently apparent to your Majesty, that Laws must alter with the Interest of the place, when you was Graciously pleased to lodge such a power in that Government, as might only from time to time with your Majestie's Approbation and by the advice of your Privy Council here and of your Governor and Council there Enable the Assembly to Enact new Laws Answerable to their growing Necessities but even upon Urgent Occasions to raise Mon[e]y for the Security of the Island, without Attending your Majestie's order and Consent.

7. It is not to be doubted but the Assembly have endeavoured to grasp all power as well as a deliberative Voice in making Laws, but how far they have entrenched on your Majestie's prerogative, and exceeded the bounds of Duty and Loyalty on this pretence, will Appear by their late Exorbitant and unwarrantable proceedings, during the Government of the Lord Vaughan, in ordering and Signing a Warrant, to the Marshal[l] of the Island your Majestie's Officer of Justice, for the Stopping and preventing the Execution of a Sentence, passed according to the Ordinary form of Law, upon a Notorious Pirate and a Disturber of Your Majestie's Peace. And they have further taken upon them, by Virtue of this deliberative power, to make Laws Contrary to those of England, and to imprison Your Majestie's Subjects; Nor have they forbore to raise money by publick Acts and to dispose of the same according to their Will and pleasure, without any Mention made of Your Majesty, which never hath in like Cases, been practised

in any of your Majestie's Kingdoms. How far therefore it is fit to trust them, with a power which they have thus abused, and to which they have no pretensions of Right, was the Subject of Your Royal Consideration, when you was pleased to put a restraint on those Enormities and to take the reigns of Government into Your own hands, which they in Express words (against their Duty and Allegiance) have challenged and refused to part with.

8. It cannot with truth be supposed that by the present form of Government, the Governor is rendered absolute, Since He is now become more Accountable to Your Majesty for all his most important deliberations and Actions, and is not warranted to do any thing but according to Law, and Your Majestie's Commission and Instructions, given by the advice of your Privy Council.

9. And, Whether your Majesty's prerogative is prejudiced by the present Constitution is more the Concernment of your Majesty and Your Subjects than of their Consideration. And, lastly and in general we humbly Conceive, that it would be a great Satisfaction to your Subjects, there habiting, and an Invitation to Strangers, when they shall know, what Laws they are to be governed by; and great ease, to the Planters not to be Continually attending the Assembly, to Reinact old Laws which his Majesty hath now thought fit in a proper form to Ascertain and Establish whereas the late power of making Temporary Laws, could be understood to be of no longer Continuance than until such wholesome Laws founded upon so many Years Experience, should be agreed upon, by the People and finally enacted by your Majesty, in such manner as hath been practised in Other of your Majestie's Dominions to which your English Subjects have transplanted themselves, nor can they pretend to further privileges, than have been granted to them, either by Charter or by some Solemn Act under your great Seal, so having from the beginning of that Plantation been governed by such Instructions as were given by the power your Majesty had originally over them, which you have by no Authentick Act, yet ever parted with; and having never had any other right to Assemblies than by permission of the Governour, and that only Temporary and by probation, it is to be wondered, how they should presume to provoke your Majesty by pretending to that which hath been allowed them, merely out of favour; and discourage your Majestie's further favours of that kind, when what your Majesty ordered for a Temporary Experiment, to see what form would suit best with the safety and Interest of the Island, shall be Construed to be a total Resignation of your power Inherent in your Majesty, and a devolution of it to themselves, and their Wills, without which, neither the law nor Government, the Essential incidents of their Subsistence and well being may take place, among them. Since therefore it is Evident that the Assembly of Jamaica, have without any just grounds and with so

much Animosity and undutifulness, proceeded to reject this Remarkable Instance of your Majestie's favour towards them; and that Your Majestie's Resolutions in this Case, are not like to the Measures of Respect and Obedience to your Royal Commands in other Colonies, We can only offer for a Cure of Irregularities past, and a Remedy against all further Inconveniences, that your Majesty would please to Authorize and impower your Governour, to Call another Assembly, and to represent to them the great Conveniency and expediency of accepting and Consenting to Such Laws as your Majesty under your great seal transmitted to them. And that in Case of refusal His Lordship be furnished with such powers as were formerly given to Colo[nel] Doyley the first Governour of Jamaica, and since to other Governours whereby His Lordship may be enabled to govern according to the Laws of England where the different Nature of that Constitution and Colony may conveniently limit the Same. And in other Cases, to Act with the advice of the Council, in such manner as shall be held necessary and proper, for the good Government of that Plantation, until Your Majestie's further orders. And that by all opportunities of Conveyance, Your Governour do give your Majesty, a Constant and particular account of all his proceedings in pursuance of your Majestie's Instructions herein. All which is most humbly Submitted &c.

Upon reading which report, and full debate thereupon, His Majesty was pleased to Approve of the same; and the Right Hon[ora]ble Mr. Secretary Coventry,[57] is hereby directed to prepare such suitable orders and Instructions; as may Answer the Several parts and advices Contained in this Report.

The Assembly on taking this Memorial into Consideration, drew up an Address in Answer, which They presented to His Excellency, the Substance of which I thought proper to abbreviate, in regard to some Circumstances that are unnecessary to transcribe and would make it tedious, if not tiresome to the Reader.

They Set forth that—with Infinite grief of mind, They had read and Considered the Report of the Lords of the Committee for Trade and Plantations, wherein they are Represented as a People full of Animosity, Irregular, unreasonable, exceeding the bounds of Duty and Loyalty. The bitterness of which Expressions and the load of Infamy and Reproach, that is laid on them, They were not Conscious of having in any degree deserved, or They should humble Themselves, and like Job have said, Behold, we are vile, what shall we answer? we will lay our hands on our Mouths. But, lest silence should be deemed Conviction of Guilt, we shall with all humility,

57. Henry Coventry, Second Baron Coventry (1619?–1686). A Royalist in the Civil War who attended Charles II in exile, Coventry was secretary of state from 1671 until gout forced his retirement in 1680.

endeavour to Convince His Majesty, that we have always demeaned our selves, like faithfull Subjects who are truly Sensible of His Royal favours. The truth of which depending on Facts, the false Colours will soon wear of[f], and on a proper and due Representation, we hope to regain His Majestie's most Gracious Opinion and Esteem.

It is necessary on this Occasion (They Observed) to look so far back, as the Administration of S[i]r Charles Littleton and S[i]r Thomas Modiford, when the Island really Assumed a Civil, and laid aside the Military Government. Assemblies were called, and the Government Set[t]led, According to the model of the other British Plantations and in such good form and manner that until His Excellency's being Appointed Governor it was not thought proper to make any Alteration. The Increase of People and Settlements since that period of time, Evinces the goodness and Reasonableness of that Establishment, as well as the Encouragement and Satisfaction, it was to Themselves.

I.

Their Lordship's first charge is, That we presume to question His Majestie's power over the Militia, in which They Seem to be under some mistake or misinformation, though, Indeed we did with Reason object to the following Clause in the Militia Bill, vizt. Provided always, and it is hereby Enacted and declared by the Authority aforesaid that nothing in this Act contained be Expounded, Construed or understood, to diminish, alter or Abridge, the power of the Governour or Commander in Chief for the time being but, in all things He may, upon all Occasions or Emergencies, Act as Capt[ai]n Gen[era]l and Governor in Chief, according to and in pursuance of all the powers and Authorities given to Him, by His Majestie's Commission, any thing in the Act, or in any other notwithstanding.

Their Lordship's, in their Report, take no notice that the power in that Clause, extends to the Governor, as well as Capt[ai]n General, nor, of the words,—any thing in this Act or in any other notwithstanding—which words being Clear and express, need no Inference or Explanation, and being Consented to by us, there would be no Occasion, of making any other Law; because that Clause makes all the powers given by His Majestie's Commission (and by His Commission, all His Instructions) Law, though it be to the Annulling and rendering to us ineffectual, any beneficial Laws, made in England or this Island, by which we are secured in our lives, liberties and properties, the like of which never was done, or Attempted; in any of His Majestie's Dominions, and in Effect is to make, Will to be Law.

And, had Their Lordship's considered the other Clauses of the Bill as it was transmitted from hence, They would not have Suggested, that we questioned His Majestie's power, Over the Militia, Since no Law gives His Majesty the like power in England, for upon any Apprehension of Danger, the General with the Advice and Consent of a Council of War, has power to put the law Martial in force, any limitted time They think proper, and to Command not only our Servants, Negroes, and Cattle, but even our Selves on the Publick Service and Occasions.

That this has often been put in practice, and willingly Submitted to, in several Instances which They Enumerate and Set forth at large. They add further, that They never have been Wanting in respect to His Majestie's Governors, a Troop of Horse and a Company of the Militia always attending Him to Church, and on all other Publick Occasions and that no other Militia do, the like Duty as in this Island, which can be Attested by all who have been at Port Royal, that cannot be distinguished from a Garrison, in Peace or War.

2.

Their Lordship's Object to His Majestie's name being left out of the Revenue Bill. To this They Answer, that on Enquiry of those who were Members of the former Assembly, They were assured that, that Bill was Sent down, with the amendments, from the Governor and Council, as it then passed. But, should it have arisen with them, they think themselves very unfortunate, if they must bear the Censure of all mistakes, that may happen in the passing of Laws, Since the Council as well as the Governor, has a Negative Voice, which had either of them made use of in this Case, would readily have been Assented to by the Assembly, as they had formerly done in the Government of S[i]r Tho[ma]s Lynch, before which time it had been Customary to pass Laws, without mentioning His Majestie's Name and without any check, on a Supposition that the Governor's name in the Enacting part to be in Effect the same as His Majestie's in England, since in that particular He seems rather to personate, than represent.

For which Reasons, and as the Act was Consented to by His Majestie's Governor, without any objection and the monies raised thereby was applied to the payment of the Contingencies of the Government and to no other use, they humbly hope it will take off all Impressions, to their disadvantage.

3 and 4

It is very true (They say) that the Bills contain many and great Errors, as Their Lordship's will Observe in the Journalls of the Assembly for above one half the Substance of Them, never can be reasonable, to pass or be Enacted. As a proof of this Assertion, They Instance the Act for preventing damages by Fire, wherein a Single Justice of the Peace, has power of life and Death. The Militia Act, impowers the Governor and Council, to levy a tax on the whole Island. And, in the Act, directing the Marshall's proceedings is a Clause, which makes it Felony for a Man to Conceal His own Goods, left in his possession after the Execution levied &c.

And, though Their Lordship's are pleased to say, there is nothing imperfect or defective, in those Bills, Yet we humbly Conceive, that no notice
being taken how, or in what Nature we are to make use of the Laws of
England, either as they have reference to the preservation, of His Majestie's Prerogative, or the Rights of His Subjects, we ought not in Reason,
therefore, to Consent to those Bills; for nothing Appearing to the Contrary the Governor is left, *ad libitum*, to use or refuse them as suits his
pleasure, there being no direction how to proceed, according to the Laws
of England, either in Causes criminal, Testamentary, or in other Cases
which Concern the peace and quiet of the Subject, in regard to life as well
as Estate.

5.

We likewise conceive notwithstanding their Lordship's Suggestions
to the Contrary in Answer to the distance of place (which renders this
method of passing Laws impracticable) That this last Experiment is Sufficient to Evince the truth, of that assertion; it being a Year Since this Model
first came over, and was considered, before their Lordship's Report on our
Objections was made and returned, although it was sent by an Express.
That we are more Subject to delays and Accidents than Ireland is Evident,
because Answers or Advices may be had from thence in 14 days; and that
Kingdom being fully Set[t]led, whereas this Colony may be said to be in
its Infancy.

Nor can it be imagined that the Irish Model of Government was, in
principio, ever intended for Englishmen; and being introduced by a Law
made by Themselves (consequently bound thereby) They had no Reason
to repine, it being their own Act, which was made for the preservation of
the English, against the Irish faction. But, as there is not the same Cause,
so there is not the same reason, for imposing the same on us, who are all
His Majestie's Natural born Subjects of England.

6.

His Majestie's derived power, on Urgent Occasions to raise money (the
old way only) secures the King's Officers their Salaries, which they had
otherwise been dissappointed of, the Acts of Militia which were heretofore
consented to, always providing that on an Alarm or Invasion the Commander in Chief shall have unlimitted power over all Persons, Estates and
things Necessary on such Occasions.

7.

They say—They never desired any power, but what They conceived
(and His Majestie's Governors allowed) They had a Natural Right to, and
They Supposed was the Intention and meaning of His Majestie's most

Gracious Proclamation to ratify and Confirm. Beside[s], His Majesty was pleased by letter, to the Governor S[i]r Thomas Lynch (after the double Trial of one Peter Johnson[58]) to Signify his disapprobation of any thing that should Cause a doubt in his Subjects, of this Island not Enjoying all the Privileges of His Subjects of the Kingdom of England or to that Effect. And, as to the Obstructing of Justice against Brown[59] a Pirate, what They did (though not Strictly justifiable in the manner) was on assurance that there was not any Law, which declared the power of the Chancellor here; equal to the Lord Chancellor of England, in granting Commissions, in pursuance of the Statute of H[enry] the 8,[60] which His Majesty and Council, Seem to be of the same Opinion, by preparing an Act, among others, to Supply that Defect. But, since They did not intermeddle with the merits of the Cause, and only endeavoured to preserve the Forms of Justice, and even Justice itself, and after denial of several Petitions, in Conjunction with the Council, were led beyond their Duty, for which They were severely repremanded by the Governor, They humbly entreat, and hope for His Majestie's pardon. The Act, on which He came in, did not take its rise in the Assembly, but was framed, and Sent down, by the Council for their Consent, and complied with at Their request.

And, as to Their committment of Mr. Thomas Martin,[61] One of the Members of their House, for taking out a process in Chancery, in His own private Concerns, against several other Members and one of the Council, the Assembly then Setting; and for other misdemeanours, and breaches of the Rules of Their House, They hope it is Justifiable, since they Conceive, They have the same power over Their Own Members, as the House of Commons, in England have over Theirs.

8.

That the Governor having Authority to remove a Member or Members of the Council, few if any of Them dare to advise or Act Contrary to His will and pleasure. And, as He is likewise Chancellour Vice Admiral Ordinary and Sole Judge for granting Administrations &c. joined with Military

---

58. Captain Peter Johnson, a privateer, was tried twice in 1672 and finally executed for surreptitiously taking a Spanish prize after the Treaty of Madrid in defiance of Governor Thomas Lynch's prohibition of such activities. On this incident, see Mark G. Hanna, *Pirate Nests and the Rise of the British Empire, 1570–1740* (Chapel Hill, N.C., 2015), 120–22.

59. Captain James Brown was a Scottish buccaneer who in 1677 attacked a Dutch ship and took 150 slaves from it and sold them. Brown was hanged, despite a plea from the Jamaica Assembly for his pardon. This incident may be followed in Graham A. Thomas, *The Pirate King: The Incredible Story of Captain Henry Morgan* (New York, 2014).

60. Probably statute 22, Henry VIII, c. 2.

61. Thomas Martin was a representative of St. David Parish in 1677 when this incident occurred.

Authority, He is vested with such Extraordinary powers that being united in, and Exercised by one and the same person, makes Him *Totum in Toto, et Totum Equalibit Parte.*[62]

9.

It is allowed by Them that, by the new Modell of Government, it is in Their power to Consent to and perpetuate such Laws, as may be beneficial to the Island, and to reject such as They disapproved of. But, the old form, which was assimulated as near as possible, to the Model of Government in England, must undoubtedly be more Acceptable, and be of greater Utility and Encouragement, not only to His Majestie's Natural born Subjects of England, but others to Remove and Settle in this Island.

The improvements made since the Government of the Lord Windsor and the Major part of the Planters who are Set[t]led here, was on the good liking of the form and Constitution being set[t]led after the English manner, and on Assurance of their enjoying all their Native Rights and privileges, which They humbly apprehend and hope They have not lost by Their removall; or that They have by any Act or deed forfeited, or provoked his Majesty, by attempting to lessen, or to Question His Royal prerogatives; the inviolation of which they ever deemed, the best means of preserving Their own privileges and Estates.

And, in regard to their Lordship's advice to His Majesty to furnish the Governor, with such powers as were given to Colo[nel] Doyley, They humbly hope it is not with an intention of imposing on Them a Military Government, or to empower the Governor and Council to Raise or levy mon[e]y[,] His Majesty having, divested himself and his Council, of any such powers in England, and as They are equally His Natural born Subjects, Their fate would be hard, should any Taxes be imposed on Them, without their own Consent, for Their Lordship's well know, that no derived power is greater than the primitive.

However, if His Majesty should not think proper to alter the method of Government proposed and that They must hereafter be Governed by the Governor and Council according to Their Lordship's advice Yet They humbly beseech His Majesty to believe They are so sensible of Their Duty and Allegiance that Their Submission and deportment to His Majestie's Authority should be such as They hoped in due time His Majesty would be graciously pleased to restore them to the Ancient form of Government. And, Conclude, with intreating His Majesty to pardon all Errors and Mistakes, and a gracious interpretation of this Answer in Vindication of Themselves, with the Strongest assurances of their Loyalty and Obedience, to His Person and Government.

---

62. It all depends on the whole, and the whole equals the parts.

The Council, likewise, thought it Necessary to Address His Excellency, and to assure Him of Their readiness to submit to the form of Government proposed by the Lords of the Committee of Council for Trade and Plantations, if it was His Majestie's pleasure, who is best able to determine what Government is fittest for Them in this Island. Yet, They humbly begged leave to represent the Inconveniences attending that Model or form of Government.

The Vast distance of place will of necessity Cause a great expence of time between the first framing of Bills here, transmitting them home, and afterwards returning them back again; so that before they can be passed into Laws, by the Consent of the Assembly, there will probably be as great a Cause arise to Alter, as there was at first to make them.

And, with submission They judge it impossible to Adopt Laws, to the present Constitution, so as not to admit of often and great Alterations; for by Experience they had found urgent Occasions to alter and Amend the Laws that more immediately Concerned them, at least every two Years, and They cannot perceive, but that They still lay under the same Necessities, so that They hoped His Majesty would be graciously pleased to restore the former method and power of making Such Laws as were necessary, and could only concern Themselves.

These Addresses were transmitted to England, by His Excellency, who at the same time was pleased to set the facts in a favourable light, and Even to Sollicit new Instructions, on that head. Nevertheless He was so Zealous and intent on the Execution of his orders, which He thought His Duty, that He highly resented the Opposition He had met with and not only Suspended Several of the principal Gentlemen of the Island, from the Civil and Military Employments They were in, but imprisoned Others, without any other Cause, than their Opposing those measures, and insisting upon their Rights and privileges.

But, this Conduct Served only to irritate the People, and make His Administration more uneasy to Him, for They became so Exasperated, that they drew up Several Articles of Complaint, and sent home two Gentlemen to lay them before His Majesty and to Sollicit the Affairs of the Island.

The Substance of the Articles, and the Earl of Carlisle's Answer, are as follows.

1. Ar[ticle] That He Attempted to impose a Test on the Members of the Council and Assembly which was to declare that They would Submit to and Acquiesce with, the form of Government proposed, until His Majestie's further pleasure was known, concerning the same.

Answer. The Earl saith, all He did was in regard to the difficulty made in the Assembly of Submitting to the new Model of Government.

2. Ar[ticle] That He had removed three Judges and filled their Seats with others without assigning any Cause or Reason.

Answer. To this He said He had sufficient Authority and gave reasons for what He had done.

3. Ar[ticle] That he countenanced the Publick Officers in taking Exorbitant, and illegal Fees.

Answer. He denied the Fact, and defied them to prove it.

4. Ar[ticle] That He intended and proposed a new Stamp on money.

Answer. That there was not any design of Coining, only stamping some Figures on pieces of Silver, of the weight and Value of p[iece]s [of eight], to pass in Trade, there being a great want of Currency, but this was only in discourse, and never was put in Execution.

5. That, He Encouraged the Privateers.

Answer—His Excellency denied the Fact, and acquitted himself of the charge.

The Assembly however drew up an Address to His Excellency setting forth the great dishonour done to His Majesty and the English Nation, by the Continued depredations of the Privateers against the Spaniards, as well as the prejudice and Inconveniences, which attended the Planters and fair Traders in this Island by the Encouragement it gave their Servants and unset[t]led People (in hopes of Gain) to run off the Island and join them, whereby the Number of Inhabitants was not only diminished, and the Strength of the Country impaired but their Own Commodities, the product of Industry and hard labour, were rendered of little value, by reason of the great quantities of the same manufactures being Clandestinely introduced into the Island and sold much Cheaper than They could possibly Afford them.

And to prevent the like practices for the future they prayed His Excellency That the two Frigat[e]s and the two Independant Companies His Majesty was pleased to keep in pay for the Service of the Island, might be employed to Suppress them. That He would preserve inviolable the Treaties made with the Spaniards, and other Nations in Alliance with His Majesty, And to take such other measures, for those purposes, As His Excellency with the advice of the Council, should think Convenient and proper.

Upon this Address, the Governour immediately gave Orders to the Commander of His Majestie's ship the *Success* (the *Hunter* being out on a Cruise) to sail to the Coast of Cuba and other parts of America, in quest of the Privateers, and to take, Sink[,] burn or destroy Them.

But, the Uneasiness and dissatisfaction of the People Increasing, His Excellency seemed to be Convinced, in Himself, that He had been too Violent in his Measures, and that He never should be easy in His Government, unless He obtained more Agreeable Instructions. He therefore relaxed in his behaviour, and not only wrote in favour of them as I have already observed but depending on his personal Interest Resolved to Embarque for England, and sollicit the Affairs of the Island, not doubting His Majestie's favour in Continuing him in the Government.

Charles Howard, First Earl of Carlisle (1629–1685), was an English military leader and MP who, as governor of Jamaica from 1675 to 1678, precipitated Jamaica's first major constitutional crisis by trying to implement Crown instructions to persuade Jamaicans to submit to a curtailment of the legislative authority of their elected assembly and grant the Crown a permanent revenue. (Castle Howard Collection, by kind permission of the Howard family)

Accordingly He sailed from Jamaica, with His Family in a Merchant Ship the [blank] day of July 1680, and Arrived at Plimouth the latter end of September following. But, in this Step He was likewise unfortunate for though He had so far Succeeded in His Application by letters for new Instructions, Yet His Majesty was so much displeased with His Coming home, without His licence or permission that He was soon after Suspended and S[i]r Thomas Lynch Appointed to Succeed Him.

The Character of this Noble Lord, who was Colo[nel] Howard of the Guards, before he was Created Earl of Carlisle (and Afterwards Ambassador to Turk[e]y and one of the Lords of the Bed Chamber to King Charles the Second) is so well known, that I need not Expatiate thereupon; and therefore I shall only observe that He had many Amiable Qualities, which would have rendered Him Acceptable to the People and His Administration agreeable to Himself, had He not been charged with Instructions, which could not possibly be digested by an English Colony.

It must however be allowed, that He was too Sanguine in regard to the Execution of them, and That He Copied after the Maxims of that Reign, in Stretching the prerogative of the Crown, beyond its limits; and Attempting to make Parliaments useless by endeavouring to raise monies, without the Consent of the Representatives of the People. But, the Spirit of liberty, inherent in Englishmen[,] prevailed (and I hope ever will prevail in all their due and Natural Rights and privileges) abroad as well as at Home.

On the Departure of the Earl of Carlisle S[i]r Henry Morgan, took on

Him the Administration (the 2d time) as L[ieutenant] Governour, by virtue of his dormant Commission.

And perceiving the necessity of Acting with the same Vigour and Resolution, He had done in His former Administration Agreeable to the Measures of the preceeding Governours, and the Strict orders He had from His Majesty, He was very Assiduous in calling in the Privateers, who remained, and Acted under French Commissions, as well as in Extirpating those who acted against Express Declarations, without any Commissions.

On the 1st of February 1680, He had Intelligence of two Notorious Pirates[,] a Sloop and Barcalonga (whose Crews consisted of all Nations and their Chief Commander[,] a Dutchman, named [Jacob] Evertson) being at an Anchor in Cow Bay, which is about 7 leagues to the Eastward of Port Royal; and immediately put on board a Sloop (which was in the Harbour fitted for the Sea) 50 Sailors and 50 Soldiers beside Officers, to take or destroy them. When they came within Gun shot of the Pirates, they hoisted the King's Colours, and gave them a broad side, on which a smart Engagement ensued, wherein Everson and Several of His Men being killed; the rest submitted. The Barcalonga, which was to leeward, perceiving the Fate of his Comrade, got under Sail and being a prime Sailor, Escaped being taken.

S[i]r Henry Morgan not having proof of any Injury or damage they had done to the Subjects of England, though they had been very mischievous and troublesome to the Spaniards[,] thought it adviseable to send the Prisoners to Carthagena, by His Majestie's Ship the *Norwich* Capt[ain] Heywood, where they were legally tried, Convicted, and Executed. This Action of S[i]r Henry Morgan, was very pleasing to the Spaniards, who were Convinced thereby, that the English intended Strictly to observe the Treaties of Peace and Friendship between the two Nations.

Nothing further happened during His Administration that is Remarkable and worth notice, but that He behaved in Such a manner, as gained Him Universal Esteem, and Manifested that He Equally understood the Arts of Peace as well as War.

Though His Pedigree was mean and Obscure, and He entered on the Stage of life, under great disadvantages, for want of Education, and having been in so low a Station as that of a Common Servant (under Indentures to a Planter of Barbadoes) Yet, His natural Abilities, soon distinguished and raised Him (before He was Thirty Years of Age) to the chief command of twelve Sail of Vessells and 700 men, with whom He attacked and took Puerto Principe on Cuba as before related and in less than four Years after he hoisted the British Flag at Maraciabo, Gibralter, a Town on the Continent of America, Puerto Bello, Chagre Panama, and the Island of St. Katherines; which last mentioned Place He was in possession of several Months, and proposed to settle an English Colony there, but the Governour of Jamaica disapproved of it[,] having advice of the Treaty of Peace and Friendship with Spain.

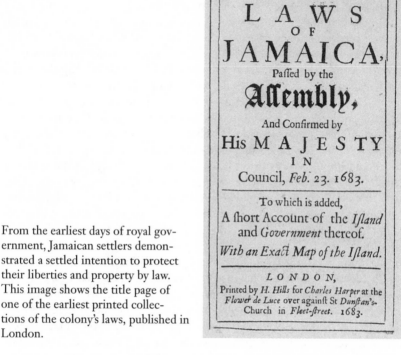

From the earliest days of royal government, Jamaican settlers demonstrated a settled intention to protect their liberties and property by law. This image shows the title page of one of the earliest printed collections of the colony's laws, published in London.

He then turned His thoughts to Planting, and Set[t]led a Sugar Work in St. Mary's Parish, though He chiefly resided at St. Iago de la vega. But, notwithstanding He had acted and performed such gallant Exploits by Commission from the Governours of Jamaica and received formal thanks from His Excellency and the Council for His Services; Yet he was Sent Home a Prisoner (confined 18 months after arrival) under the Ignominy of a Buccaneer or Pirate; and to the prejudice of His Health, which was greatly impaired thereby, as well as His Circumstances. Indeed, He was afterwards acquitted, without any Trial, it appearing that the Complaints against Him were groundless[,] He producing Regular Commissions for what He had done, and thereupon He not only had the Honour of Knighthood conferred on Him, but was appointed one of the Council, and a dormant Commission granted Him, to be L[ieutenant] Governour of the Island, in Case of the Death or absence of the Governour or Commander in Chief, for the time being.

These Circumstances are Sufficient to Corroborate all I have said in his favour, and Erase the stains, which have been made in His Character; for it would be a reflection even on the Memory of King Charles the Second to Suppose He would so far Countenance and Encourage Piracy and the

breach of the Law of Nations, as to Conferr Hounours on a Notorious Of-
fender, much less have that Confidence in Him, as to intrust Him with the
Government of so Considerable a Colony, had He not been well assured of
His Integrity and Fidelity, as well as His Abilities.

He Continued in the Council 3 or 4 Years after He was Superceeded by
S[i]r Thomas Lynch; and then retired, lived in a private manner and died
in Jamaica, the 25th. of Aprill 1688. S[i]r Thomas Lynch's Commission for
Capt[ain] General Governour and Commander in chief, was dated the 2d.
of September 1681; and He arrived at Jamaica the [blank] day of [blank]
1682.

In August following His Excellency Convened the Assembly, and in His
Speech Communicated to them, that His Majesty was pleased to revoke
the Instructions given to the late Governour Charles Earl of Carlisle, and
to Authorize and impower the Governour, Council and Assembly of Jamaica, to Constitute and Ordain Laws, which are to be in force, until His
Majestie's pleasure be signified to the Contrary.

They accordingly proceeded on business, with Indefatigable care and
Industry, and Compiled a Body of Laws, which are so well adapted to the
Nature and Circumstances of the place, that Succeeding Assemblies, have
added very little to those Excellent Regulations, which were revived from
time [to time:]

An Act, appointing the Number of the Assembly.[63]

An Act for Regulating Servants.[64]

An Act, for the Highways.[65]

An Act appointing the price of Meat.[66]

An Act against Blasphemy and for preventing disorders in Taverns, Ale
Houses, and Victualling Houses.[67]

An Act impowering Justices of the Peace to decide differences not exceeding forty shillings.[68]

And, 22 others which are printed at large, and may be seen in the new
fol[io] Edition.[69]

S[i]r Thomas Lynch on advice of the aforementioned Laws being Confirmed by His Majesty, Convened the Assembly and on the 5th. day of
Sept[ember] 1683, made the following Speech[:]

---

63. An Act Appointing the Number of the Assembly, 1683, in *Acts of Assembly Passed in the
Island of Jamaica; from 1681 to 1737, Inclusive* (London, 1738), 1–2.

64. An Act for Regulating Servants, 1682, in ibid., 2–5.

65. An Act for the Highways, 1683, in ibid., 6–7.

66. An Act for Appointing the Price of Meat, 1683, in ibid., 8.

67. An Act against Blasphemy; and for Preventing Disorder in Alehouses, Taverns, and
Victualling Houses, 1683, in ibid., 8–9.

68. An Act Impowering Justices of the Peace to Decide Differences of Forty Shillings,
1683, in ibid., 9–10.

69. Ibid.

Gentlemen of the Council

Mr. Speaker and Gentlemen

of the Assembly.

Since all Countries or People are desirous of being Governed by Certain and known Laws, and we have laboured for above twenty Years, in composing a body of them Suitable to our Circumstances, it is hoped that this session will give the finishing stroke to so great and Necessary a work, which will, undoubtedly be a Satisfaction to your selves as well as to your Constituents, and to posterity.

Former Assemblies generally met out of Temper, some prejudiced, others Jealous and the best so Anxious and dubious, that what they so much desired, was thereby rendered impracticable: But, you Gentlemen have taken more prudent measures, and in the last Session, given such Instances of your Duty to His Majesty, and Affection to your Country, that you have deservedly gained their approbation and Esteem; for by your Moderation, and Attention to the publick Utility, you have calmed the minds and Established the Quiet of the People, and given such a Sanction to the meeting of Assemblies, that I dare say, now you have paved the way and made things Easy, they will now become more frequent.

From the last Session we may date the Prosperity of this Island, for by submitting your Concerns to His Majesty's pleasure, and taking out every Offensive clause in the Act of Revenue, Your most seasonable and discreet Address, had such Effect, that even the Lords of the Committee, Seemed Concerned and became your Advocates. The happy consequences are so obvious that I need not Enumerate them and are imputed to your prudent Conduct as appears by His Majestie's most gracious letter. The Gentlemen of the Council, look upon this Transaction, as a kind of Magna Charta, and have accordingly entered the same in their Minutes, which posterity may have recourse to.

The Act, declaring the Laws of England to be in force in this Island, you will find disapproved of by His Majesty in Council. And, for my part I cannot conceive why some are so Anxious and Uneasy, since we are all Englishmen and are not denied our Native Rights; but on the Contrary His Majesty, like a wise and tender parent, only denies what will be hurtfull to us. Let us therefore, desire none but what may be usefull and beneficial to us; and Remember though England has many good Laws Yet, in Henry the 7ths.[70] time Empsome[71] and

70. Henry VII (January 28, 1457–April 21, 1509). The son of Edmund Tudor, Earl of Richmond, and Margaret Beaufort, heir of John of Gaunt, Henry was brought up in Wales by his uncle Jasper Tudor. He defeated and killed Richard III at the Battle of Bosworth Field in 1485, ending the Wars of the Roses.

71. Richard Empson (?–1510) was a lawyer, MP, and Speaker of the House of Commons, 1491–92. With Edmund Dudley, he was a chief minion of Henry VII most noted for exacting taxes and crown fines and for humbling the "overmighty" nobles. Henry VII knighted him in 1504 but at his accession, Henry VIII bowed to popular pressure and had Empson tried and executed for treason.

Dudley,[72] with other Rapacious Officers, by putting such as were penal (and become obsolete and Supernumerary) into Execution they (as my Lord Bacon[73] Says) turned Law and Justice into Wormwood and Rapine.

Laws Especially to Young Colonies may be compared to Phisick to the Body, wherein not only the Nature but the Quantity and proportion of the Medicines is considered, so that, which makes it fit, makes it operate well and with due effect.

But as Laws are restraints on bad Governours and Rules to such as mean well, you have Reason to desire such, or any other, Laws as may be of advantage, although you have not the Laws of England in general; and in this I shall heartily Concurr with you, since my Inclination and Interest, are bound up with yours, in every thing that may be for the Utility and Common good of this Island.

I cannot conclude without telling you that we are under great Obligations to our Friends in England particularly S[i]r Charles Littleton and Colo[nel] Beeston, who have been very hearty and Zealous in solliciting, your Affairs. But, I will not Anticipate or lessen the merit of any Act or deed, by my Advice, in Expressing your Duty and Gratitude to His Majesty, as well as your Obligations to those Gentlemen. God has pleased to put me under uneasy and fatal Circumstances through the Infirmities of Age, and the unhappy Voyage of my Family, so that there is nothing under Heaven I desire so much, as to See you happy, the Laws set[t]led, and the Island flourish.

This Session the Assembly passed the following Laws.

An Act requiring all Masters of Ships to give Security in the Secretaries Office.[74]

An Act for regulating Fees.[75]

An Act encouraging the Set[t]ling of the Island.[76]

An Act, for ordering of Boats and Wherries, and better Government of Seamen.[77]

And ten others printed at large in the new folio Edition.

Which Laws having, upon the perusal of the Right Honourable the Lords of the Committee for Trade and Foreign Plantations, been presented to His Majesty; He was Graciously pleased with the advice of His

72. Edmund Dudley (1462?–1510) became sheriff of Sussex and privy councillor at the accession of Henry VII and then, with Empson, a collector of the king's taxes and dues. Like Empson, he was executed for treason after Henry VII's death.

73. Francis Bacon (1561–1626), statesman, scientist, and philosopher.

74. An Act Requiring All Masters of Ships and Vessels to Give Security in the Secretary's Office, September 1683, in *Acts of Assembly*, 41–42.

75. An Act Regulating Fees, September 1683, in ibid., 43 (title of bill only).

76. An Act Encouraging the Settling of This Island, September 1683, in ibid., 43.

77. An Act for Ordering of Boats and Wherries, and Better Government of Seamen, September 1683, in ibid., 44–47.

privy Council, to Approve and Confirm the same, for the space of Twenty one Years, to Commence from the 1st. of November last, preceeding the date of the Order [blank] 1682. As also Certain other Laws confirmed by His Majesty in Council the 23d. of February 1682.

Notwithstanding all the Assiduity and Care of this Gentleman, many of the Subjects of England still, continued out and, Committed depredations on the Spaniards, some with French Commissions, and others without any Commissions. Van Horn[78] a Dutchman commanded one of the Parties, and had one of His Ships taken by the Spanish Fleet, but most of the men found means to Escape. And in December 1683, a much greater Body, which Consisted of all Nations, and were commanded by one Lawrence,[79] and Michael Tankard, intended to make some bold Attempt, which the Governour of Carthagena, having notice of, and the place of their Rende-vous; fitted out three men of War, of 40, 36, and 20 guns to take or destroy them, But, the Buccaniers were so well prepared, that after an Obstinate Engagement, wherein the Spaniards lost above 400 men, they took the three Ships, with a very inconsiderable loss on their Side.

There hap[pe]ned nothing further Remarkable in the Government of S[i]r Thomas Lynch, who died the [blank] day of [blank] 1684, very much lamented by the Inhabitants in general, and was interred in the Church at St. Iago de la vega, which was formerly a Spanish Abbey.

He was a L[ieutenan]t Collo[nel] in one of the Regiments, before the Regular Forces were disbanded, and afterwards Appointed a Colo[nel] of Militia, one of the Council and provost Marshal General, by patent, for life.

He succeeded in the Administration three times, as President of the Council, L[ieutenant] Governour, and Capt[ai]n General, in which several Stations His conduct and behaviour was Agreeable to the People, For He was Affable, Easy of Access and never assumed the Governour, or took any State or Ceremony upon Him, but when it was Necessary. He impartially administered Justice, was a steady Friend and Patron to the Island, Encouraged and promoted Trade as well as the Planting Interest and Settlement of the Island. He left large possessions there (acquired by Industry and the Several Publick Employments He had been in, without Oppression or Extortion) which descended to and are now Enjoyed by His only Daughter the Lady Cotton, Relict of S[i]r Thomas Cotton Bar[one]t.[80]

---

78. Nicholas van Hoorn (1635?–1683) was a Dutch merchant sailor and privateer.

79. Possibly Laurens de Graaf (1653–1704), a well-known Dutch pirate sometimes operating for the French against the Spanish at this time.

80. Lady Cotton (c. 1677–?) was the daughter of Thomas and Philadelphia Lynch, who married Sir Thomas Cotton and later Captain Thomas King and sold some of her Jamaica properties to Sir Thomas Beckford, a kinsman of her father. Frank Cundall, *Governors of Jamaica in the First Half of the Eighteenth Century* (London, 1937), 55.

[Slave Rebellion, Natural Disaster, and War, 1684–1702]

On the death of S[i]r Thomas Lynch the Administration devolved on, Collo[nel] Hender Molesworth,[1] who had a dormant Commission, from King Charles the Second, dated the 16th. of November 1673, to Succeed as L[ieuten an]t Governour. And, soon after He had advice of His Majestie's death, and a new Commission Sent Him from King James the second dated the 22d. of Sept[embe]r 1685.

This Year [1684] the Negroes in St. Johns commonly called Guanaboa, Rebelled and chose a negro named Cuffy, belonging to Mrs. Guy to head them. They went from Plantation to Plantation and Seized all the Arms and Ammunition they Could meet with, killed Capt[ain] Thorp and Several White Persons that could not timely join the others, who with Collo[nel] Cope, Collo[nel] Aylmer,[2] and Major Price,[3] had got together, and were only able to defend themselves and their Families, until they had some Assistance from the Town to repel them.

The Governour, on advice of this disaster, immediately dispatched the Troop, to join those who had with great Courage and Resolution defended themselves, against a much Superior Number of Negroes, who Attacked and attempted to destroy them; but the Rebells' perceiving more Forces coming to their Relief retreated to the Woods. And, apprehending further mischief, by this Rebellion becoming more general; He with the advice and Consent of a Council of War Ordered Martial law to be proclaimed throughout the Island. A Strong Party of Armed Men were fitted out and Sent after the Rebells and were so fortunate as to meet with them, to kill several[,] take others and disperse the rest, who were Reduced to so small a Number, that it was not thought worth while to follow them. Nevertheless,

---

1. Hender Molesworth (1638–1689) was of Devonshire descent and migrated in the 1660s to Jamaica, where he established himself as a merchant and later a factor of the Royal Africa Company on the island. Appointed to the council in 1670 and a close associate of Thomas Lynch, he became acting governor on Lynch's death on August 24, 1684. At the accession of James II, Crown officials replaced him as governor with Sir Phillip Howard, who died before he could take office, and Molesworth became lieutenant-governor under the Duke of Albemarle. He returned to England in October 1688 but on Albemarle's death, he went back to Jamaica and in June 1689, William I made him full governor, although he died before receiving the commission. See Frank Cundall, *Governors of Jamaica in the Seventeenth Century* (London, 1737), 95–108.

2. Whitgift Aylmer was a member of assembly for St. John, 1674–77 and 1701, and for St. Ann, 1681–84 and 1688.

3. Major Francis Price was a member of the Jamaica Assembly for St. John, 1675–84, and progenitor of the powerful Price family of eighteenth-century Jamaica. See Michael Craton and James Walvin, *A Jamaican Plantation: The History of Worthy Park, 1670–1970* (Toronto, 1970), 26–45.

From the last decades of the seventeenth century, Jamaica's increasing enslaved majority proved restive, prone to local uprisings, and difficult to repress. This image of an unspecified slave uprising derives from François Anne David's 1759 engraving entitled *Soulevement des negres à la Jamaica* (Paris, 1759).

in December following (soon after Christmas) the Rebells being joined by other Fugitives, came down and Surprised Mr. Coates'[4] Family in the same Parish, murdered 9 or 10 White People—four of which were Mr. Coate's Children, but, His Lady and Brother made their Escape. They Afterwards burnt the House[,] works, Canes &c. and would have destroyed all the Plantations in the Parish had they not been routed, by the Militia, which was raised, and prevented any further mischief being done in that part of the Country. The Rebells thereupon retreated to Mount Diablo, and from thence to St. James's destroyed several Families and Settlements in their way. But, being pursued some were killed, and others taken[;] the remain-

4. Probably Robert Coates, who was a member of the assembly for St. John in 1695–96 and 1698–99.

der made their Escape into the remote Mountains, and their Descendants are part of the Rebellious Gangs, who lately submitted.

These disturbances being happily quieted[,] the Governor put an end to Martial law, Convened the Assembly, and on the 1st. of June 1686, made the following Speech.

Gentlemen of the Council

Mr. Speaker and Gentlemen

of the Assembly

The chief occasion of my calling you together at this time, is to advise with you in a matter of the greatest importance, which is how to secure our Selves and Estates, from the Treachery, Cruelty and Ravages of our Negroes, and how to keep them in due order and Subjection. And, in Case of any sudden Insurrection, to be provided with ready means of reducing them, or discouraging all attempts of the like Nature for the future.

It is well known, what trouble and Expence a few of those desperate Villains have given us, beside the mischiefs they have done to Several poor Families, which though short of what has been reported, yet might have been Considerably more, had their Courage been Equal to their Agility and the Opportunities they had of being Injurious and Ruinous, to a much greater Number of Inhabitants. But, God was pleased to restrain their designs, and Enable us to Suppress them.

I need not tell you what measures were taken by the Government on that Occasion, under disadvantagious Circumstances, the want of Money and a Crip[p]led power Over the Militia. But, must Recommend to your immediate care, the payment of the Monies borrowed and Expended, to gratify those who were sent out on Parties; and Complying with the promised Rewards to others who behaved well in the Publick Service; to give some relief to such as were driven from their Settlements; to enlarge the power of the Officers of the Militia, and to provide a fund to Answer all such Emergencies as may happen hereafter.

I am likewise to Recommend, by His Majestie's Command, that you prepare an Act Ascertaining the servitude, of the Rebells, those who acted under the Duke of Monmouth[5] lately sent from England, for Ten years,

5. James Scott, Duke of Monmouth and Buccleuch (1649–1685), was the illegitimate son of Charles II by Lucy, daughter of Richard Walter of Haverfordwest, Pembrokeshire. He took the name James Scott and pursued a military career, serving against the Dutch in 1672–73 and the French in 1678 and becoming a privy councillor in 1670. His identification with the Protestant movement led to his being deprived of all offices in 1679, and he confessed to plotting uprisings and the murder of Charles II and the Duke of York, for which he was banished to Zealand. On Charles II's death, he began Monmouth's Rebellion, landing at Lyme Regis on June 11, 1685, and claiming the crown but was defeated at Sedgemour on July 5 and executed.

According to the Condition of their Pardon, and to prevent all Clandestine releas[e]ment, buying out their time &c.

The Act for the Government of our Slaves not having had the Royal Assent, though it is in force and we are permitted the Use of it; because His
Majesty and the Council do not think the penalties prescribed for Wanton
and Willfull effusion of Human blood is Sufficient, it is proper and Necessary for you to Consider of some expedient, and remove that Obstruction
out of the way.

As to my self, I neither require [n]or Expect any thing from you. I have
been known and resided among You, above Twenty Years; my Interest
is on the same foundation with yours, and therefore can have no View
or design, but what I shall equally be affected with in the Consequence.
Gentlemen, You have now a fair Opportunity of Serving your Selves, If
you make a proper use of it, I shall have the Satisfaction of bearing a part
with you in it.

But, if you fall into wrong measures, and frustrate my good intentions,
the bad Consequences attending it, will rise up in Judgment against You.
For, you may Expect every thing from me that is Consistent with my Duty
to His Majesty, and His Royal Prerogative.

The Rebells mentioned in the Governour's Speech were those unfortunate Persons, concerned in the Duke of Monmouth's Rebellion, and transported to this Island, pursuant to their Sentence. They served their respective Masters with great Fidelity, and most of them remained on the Island,
after the expiration of their Servitude. Several of them acquired good Plantations, by their Industry; and it is remarkable that they Annually met on
the day of their Trial, and their first Toast after dinner, was to the Memory
of Judge Jefferies,[6] who they declared was the best Friend they ever had;
for by his means they lived happier and enjoyed more, than they ever had
or could have done in their own Country.

The Jews, about this time, began to resort to this Island, and they daily
increased on the Encouragement that was given them; for as they were
skilled in Trade, the Governour thought it proper to allow them the liberty
of Erecting Synagogues; and to perform Divine Worship after their own
manner, with many other privileges. Whether this was good Policy (as well
as the nature and Dispositions of those people.) I shall discuss more particularly in its proper place.

6. George Jeffreys, First Baron Jeffreys of Wern (1648–1689), was educated at Cambridge
but left for the Inner Temple in 1663 and was received at the bar in 1668. Knighted in 1677
and made solicitor general to the Duke of York, he was noted, as recorder of London, for his
severity in Popish Plot cases. He was made lord chief justice in 1682 and privy councillor and
lord chancellor in 1685, when he also received the baronetcy of Wern in 1685. He conducted
the trials of Algeron Sidney in 1683, Titus Oates in 1685, and the "bloody assize" in the west
after Monmouth's Rebellion. After the Glorious Revolution, he was arrested and imprisoned.

King James on advice of the death of S[i]r Thomas Lynch was pleased to appoint S[i]r Phillip Howard[7] Capt[ain] General and Governour of this Island, whose Commission was dated the 28 of October 1685. But this Gentleman died in a few months after, in England and before he embarqued on which his Majesty was pleased to appoint His Grace George Duke of Albemarle[8] Kn[igh]t of the most noble order of the Garter, and one of the Privy Council, to Succeed and take on him the Government.

Colo[nel] Molesworth continued in the Administration untill his Grace arrived, and behaved to the Universal satisfaction of the Island. He was Courteous and easy of Access; given to no vice or Extravagance, and recommended himself by a Sincere and upright Conduct.

The Laws were duely Executed, The Inhabitants perfectly easy and undisturbed; and Trade flourished in his time. He was a Gentleman of great prudence and Moderation and never expressed or shewed any disregard to those who differed with him in Opinions. He remained on the Island several years after he was superseeded; was created a Bar[one]t by King William and left considerable possessions, which descended to his Son the late L[or]d Viscount Molesworth.[9]

The Duke of Albemarle by his Com[m]ission dated the 25 of November 1686, was not only Capt[ain] General and Governour of Jamaica, but the Governours of all the other British Islands, were subordinate to him. His Grace and his Dutchess embarqued on board his Majesty's Ship the *Assistance* the 12th of September 1687; but touching at Barbados and the other British Islands did not arrive at Jamaica before the 20th. of Dec[embe]r following. He brought over with him a very large retinue, for his Household Servants were the same, as Sovereign Princes, and £10,000 in Specie.

His Grace likewise brought over with him Several Miners, but they

---

7. Sir Philip Howard (?–1686) was appointed governor of Jamaica at the accession of James II but died before setting out for the colony. One of his achievements was his part in having Monmouth rebels deported to Jamaica for ten-year terms. Cundall, *Governors of Jamaica in the Seventeenth Century*, 99, 101, 110.

8. Christopher Monck, Second Duke of Albemarle (1653–1688). Knight here confuses the name of this, the second duke, with that of his father, George, the first duke famous for his role in the Restoration. Christopher succeeded to the dukedom at his father's death in January 1670. Marrying into wealth and status, he was prominent in the western counties and raised the Devon and Cornwall militias against Monmouth in 1685. James II appointed him governor of Jamaica in April 1686, although Monck did not take up his commission for a year. When he did proceed to Jamaica, he was accompanied by his personal physician, Hans Sloane. Ibid., 109–17.

9. Robert Molesworth, First Viscount Molesworth (1656–1725), supported the Glorious Revolution in Ireland, fighting at the Battle of the Boyne. Sent on missions to Denmark in 1689 and 1692, he offended his hosts with his book, *Account of Denmark* (London, 1692). His subsequent career found him as an MP in both the Irish and English Parliaments and as a commissioner for trade and plantations in 1719. Knight may well be wrong about his relationship with Hender Molesworth.

made no progress in Searching for Minerals: for instead of that some went from Plantation to Plantation, where they got drunk, and disregarded the business they went upon, and others went into the Woods and gathered Piemento, which they Sold to their own Advantage.

And soon after his Arrival: He issued out a Proclamation, for the more effectual reducing, and suppressing Pirates in America; but this was little more than mere matter of form, for they were dispersed and in a manner rooted out before and those few which remained set[t]led in the Bays of Campeachy and Honduras, where they lived undisturbed without molesting others, and maintained themselves by cutting Logwood, w[hi]ch they trucked with the Trading Sloops from Jamaica, for Cloaths Provisions and other necessaries.

The Assembly was convened the 15th of February and the day following his Grace made the following Speech.

> Gentlemen
>
> Having received from his Majesty the Honour and Trust of this Government, I think my self obliged to do all that in me lies, to promote his Service and the Public Good of this Island, which are truely consistent; for any Seperation will lessen his Majestie's intentions towards the Encouragement of this Country, and render my Endeavours ineffectual.
>
> To the End therefore that this Session may end happily as I wish it, let me advise and Command that no particular piques, or private Annamosities may hinder the general benefits of this Island, which his Majesty I believe Esteems above all others in this part of the World.
>
> And I do assure you that nothing my part shall be wanting to answer those great ends the King my Master sent me hither for; and therefore expect your ready and hearty Concurrence with me (which I do not in the least doubt)[,] otherwise the ill Consequences that may arise from the Contrary must be imputed to your fault and shall lye at your Doors.
>
> Gentlemen what at present I have to recommend to your Consideration I give you in Writing and what I have further to offer I will signifie to you at such times as I shall think Convenient.

The Assembly thereupon presented an Address to His Grace in Answer to His Speech wherein they Congratulated his safe Arrival; Expressed their Sense of the Honour of having a Person of his Grace's Eminence and Quality to be their Governour, assured him of the high esteem they had for his Person and Character; and that they should comply with whatever He thought proper to recommend for the Honour of His Majesty and the Utility of the Island.

On Sunday the 19 of February following there was an Earthquake, the greatest that ever was known before in this Island. It was preceded by a small shower of Rain, which lasted about a Minute; the Earth gave three Shocks, with a small pause between, accompanied with a small noise. It was felt all over the Island, several Houses were damaged thereby and the people every where in a very great Consternation. It was felt on board the Ships in Port Royal, and one that was Eastward of the Island, coming from Europe met with a Hurricane at the same time. Several Persons, who were in the Country, declared that the ground swelled in Waves like the Sea, and that the Earthquake seemed to pass from the North to the South.

However pleased the Inhabitants were with having a Nobleman to be their Governour, who was not only of the highest Rank, but in affluent Circumstances, and from thence they conceived He would not be under any temptation to injure or oppress them; Yet their Satisfaction did not subsist long, for it soon appeared that the head was too big for the Body; or as the Spaniards expressed themselves when they heard his Grace was appointed Governour of this Island, The Bird was too big for the Cage. He came charged with Instructions, agreeable to the measures of that Reign; and his Conduct manifested his Zealous Disposition to carry them into Execution.

The flame which broke out in the Assembly soon spread it self all over the Country, and occasioned not only great disorders and Confusion, but a General Defection from His Grace's Administration; though there was not wanting a Party who supported his measures, some through hopes of favour or Interest, there being such Sycophants and Fools in all Countrys; and others who were too strongly attached to the Principles and Interest of the Prince who was then upon the Throne. It took its rise when the House had under Consideration the Several matters His Grace had laid before them in Writing, which occasioned a Warm Debate, wherein one of the Members among other Expressions, made use of the Words [blank]. His Grace being informed of what passed on that Occasion, was so inflamed therewith, that He immediately ordered the member to be taken into Custody; but the Assembly insisted upon their previledge of Freedom of Speech in their own House, and protected their Member, upon which they were dissolved, and writs were issued for a new Election.

His Grace proceeded further, in displacing the Judges, and other principal officers of the Island, particularly the provost Marshal without assigning any Cause or Reason, and appointed such as were his Tools and Creatures to Succeed Them. One White[,] an Indigent person, was appointed Provost Marshal[l] who is the high Sherriff or returning officer of the Island, which plainly discovered his intentions in that Instance; And having appointed such persons Judges, whom he likewise thought proper and for his purpose, He ordered the aforesaid Member to be taken into Custody, and indicted at the Grand Court where He was tried and fined £600, for the said Words. Father Churchill,[10] a Romish Priest, was the Duke's Principal adviser in all these transactions, and through his instigation Colo[nel] Molesworth, late L[ieutenan]t Governour among others fell under his Grace's displeasure and was compelled to enter into a Recognizance, with seven sureties, in the Penal sum of £10,000 to appear in England, and answer to such matters as should be objected to him.

In the several Elections for Representatives in the New Assembly, the most unwarrantable and illegal methods were taken; for Servants, Seamen and others who had no Right, were carried from place to place, and permitted to give their Votes. Nor was this the only Violation of the Rights and previledges of the People, for diverse persons were imprisoned, on pretence of committing Riotts, tried at the Grand Court and fined, some of them above £2000—and two Gentlemen, who moved for the Habeas Corpus, were not only denied the benefit of that Act, but threatened to be Whipped. Dr. Rose[11] was obliged to give £10,000 Security for his good behaviour! only for Expressing his dissatisfaction at these proceedings, And, the new Chief Justice[12] openly declared in Court, that they should be ruled with Rods of Iron.

These Acts of Power and Oppression greatly inflamed the minds of the People, insomuch that several of the principal Inhabitants, went off the Island, some to complain of their injuries, and others to avoid the same treatment.

The New Assembly who were chosen by those indirect means, passed several Acts and Father Churchil was appointed Agent to Sollicit the Confirmation of them in England, not having then any notion of the Revolution, which hap[pe]ned soon after.

However unsuccessfull his Grace was in regard to the Mines through neglect and mismanagement in those who were employed about them, he was more fortunate in another Adventure, for being concerned with S[i]r James Hayes[,][13] Mr. Nicholson and others who obtained a Patent

10. Father Churchill arrived in Jamaica one month after Albemarle as chief pastor of the island's Catholics with James II's instructions to Albemarle to protect and encourage Catholics.

11. Dr. Fulke Rose, one of three brothers to migrate to Jamaica in the 1660s or early 1670s, represented St. Thomas in the Vale Parish in the assembly from 1675 to 1686 and St. John Parish from 1688 to 1693.

12. Roger Elletson, who represented St. Thomas in the Vale Parish in the Jamaica Assembly in 1688–89, was Albemarle's replacement for Samuel Barnard as chief justice. Albemarle removed Elletson because of his opposition to the governor. For more information on Barnard, see note 40 below.

13. Sir James Hayes partnered in 1686 with James II, the Duke of Albemarle, Viscount Falkland (Hayes's stepson), Sir John Narborough (commissioner of the royal navy), Isaac Foxcroft, and New York governor Francis Nicholson to fish the wreck of the Spanish vessel *Neustra Señora de la Concepcion*, which had been wrecked on November 2, 1641, off the north coast of Hispaniola. William Phips (1651–1695), a Massachusetts sea captain, led the expedition, which salvaged from 1686 to 1691 twenty-six tons of silver valued at £200,000. For find-

to search for Wrecks, accordingly fitted out two Ships under the Command of Capt[ain] Thomas [William] Phips, to search for the Wreck of a Rich Spanish Galleon which was cast away in 1659, on the Shoals near the Abrevjos, commonly called by the English Sailors, the Hankerchief Shoals, to the N[orth] E[ast] of Hispaniola. He carried out a considerable Cargo to trade likewise with the Spaniards, and while Capt[ain] Phips was disposing of his Goods. Cap[tain] Rogers[14] in the smallest Ship was sent to search for the Wreck and was so fortunate, to discover it by means of a Sea Feather, growing on the Planks of the Ship under water. On this Welcome news Capt[ain] Phips joined them, and on a further Search found great part of the Ship grown with a sort of white Coral called Lapis Astruites or Star Stone, which grows in great plenty all over America. They broke into the Ship, and every day took up Treasure more or less as the Weather permitted, and their divers held out; and upon the whole brought into Jamaica 22196 pounds weight in Bullion, and £30326 in Coined Gold beside Jewells and other Riches so that it is said the Duke's Share (which cost no more than £800 Ster[ling]) amounted to £50,000. Capt[ain] Phips was sometime after Knighted by King William and appointed Governour of new England.

Sometime in April Jeremy the King of the Musquito Indians[15] came to Jamaica and put himself and his people under the protection of the Crown of England: He was Courteously received and Entertained by his Grace, who granted him a Commission to be King of that Nation; according to his own desire; but as I shall occasionally treat more particularly of those people, in its proper place, I shall here suspend saying any thing more of them.

Having given an Account of the Arbitrary proceedings in this Island, during the Administration of the Duke of Albemarle, it will now be necessary to shew what Steps were taken in order to Redress them.

Father Churchill who as I observed was appointed Agent to Sollicit the Confirmation of the Acts which were passed by an Assembly illegally cho-

---

ing the ship and presiding over this operation, Phips became a London celebrity, and James II knighted him and appointed him provost marshall general of the Dominion of New England under Sir Edmund Andros. Quickly braking with Andros, Phips went to London, where he helped to lobby against the Dominion and for a return of the Massachusetts charter. After the fall of the Dominion, William I appointed him the first royal governor of the rechartered Massachusetts Bay colony in 1691. For more information on Phips, see Emerson W. Baker and John G. Reid, *The New England Knight: Sir William Phips, 1651–1695* (Toronto, 1998). On the treasure expedition, see Peter Earle, *Wreck of the Almiranta: Sir William Phips and the Hispaniola Treasure* (London, 1979), and Baylus C. Brooks, *The Quest for Blackbeard: The True Story of Edward Thache* (Lake City, Fla., 2017).

14. Captain Francis Rogers was second in command on Phips's expedition, and his vessel was the one that actually discovered the wreck of the *Neustra Señora de la Concepcion*.

15. King Jeremy of the Mosquito Indians. Jeremy submitted to English rule under Albemarle, 1687–88.

sen finding upon his Arrival in England, King James had abdicated the Throne, did not think proper to take that Character upon him, or even to make his appearance in Publick, but prudently withdrew and went over to France.

But, Collo[nel] Mollesworth who was bound by his Recognizance to appear in England and the other Gentlemen who went over to complain of the Oppressions I have mentioned and the hardships, particularly imposed on them, met with a favourable Reception from King William who was pleased to remit their several fines and to Create Collo[nel] Molesworth a Baronet.

The Gentlemen who were interested in this Island, also presented a Petition to his Majesty set[t]ing forth the Several Facts and praying to be heard against the passing of the Laws which were come over for the Royal Assent, upon which a Committee of the Lords in Councill were appointed to enquire into the Allegations of their Petition, before whom several Gentlemen from the Island appeared as witnesses and diverse other Authentick Vouchers were produced which clearly proved the several Irregularities, and oppressions complained of, as well as the illegality of the Assembly, who passed those Laws, and on the Report to his Majesty He was Graciously pleased not only to reject them, but to order the several officers who had been displaced by the Duke, to be restored to their Respective offices.

From hence we may perceive the fatal Consequences which attend the Governours of the British Colonies being vested with many large and Extraordinary Powers more than any one Man ought to be intrusted with; for tho[ugh] I never heard of the like Extremities in this or the other British Plantations, nor of any of their Governours having Acted with so high a hand and in so Despotick a manner, yet many of them have exceeded even the bounds of their Commission in Violation of the Rights, Priviledges, and Quiet of the People. It is probable, in the Case now before us, that the Duke of Albemarle had particular Instructions for what he did, Conformable to the Scheem that was laid for a Change of Governm[en]t, in England, and its dependancies; therefore it was thought Necessary to send over a person of His Rank, one in whom King James could confide, to carry them into execution in our Colonies, and in order to effect it all the other Governours were Subordinate to him. However that may be, it is highly necessary, if any regard be had to the Interest and wellfare of our Plantations to restrain & lessen the Powers usually granted to those who are sent to preside over them, as will hereafter be shewn in its proper place.

His Grace did not live to hear these Events, nor would he have enjoyed the Government much longer had he Survived, for I have been Credibly informed that his Suspension was determined upon, and prevented by advice of his death, which hap[pe]ned on the [blank] of October 1688. Soon

Christopher Monck, Second Duke of Albemarle (1653–1688), an English soldier and politician who was an MP from 1667 to 1670 and, following his inheritance of the dukedom in 1670, a member of the House of Lords. A favorite of James II, he served in 1687–88 as governor of Jamaica, where his efforts to enforce the Crown's restrictive colonial policy rendered him enormously unpopular. He died there in October 1688 before he could become a casualty of the Glorious Revolution. (Old Schools, Cambridge University)

after, his Majesty was pleased to appoint the Right Hon[ora]ble William Earl of Inchiquien[16] to succeed him in the Government.

His Grace during his Residence on this Island, lived in the most magnificent manner of any Governour of the British Plantations before or since his time not Excepting the late Duke of Portland;[17] He likewise took upon him much more state and was treated with greater Ceremony, though in those Respects his Dutchess exceeded him; for she assumed the Honours, which are only due to a Queen, and would not admit on her visiting days, any of the Ladies to sit in her presence, so that many of them refrained visiting her. But I think it unnecessary and needless to make any further remarks on her behaviour since she was afterwards much more known, and distinguished under another Title.

The Duke of Albemarle hast[e]ned his end, by his intemperance and manner of living for He was a man of pleasure and a very hard Drinker, and would not listen to the Advice that was given him, not to be too free

16. William O'Brien, Second Earl of Inchiquin (c. 1638–1692), was raised in London and involved early in military service with his father in France and Spain, losing an eye in combat in 1660 and held as a prisoner in Algiers. He became earl on his father's death in 1674 and also that year was made a privy councillor, captain general of the king's forces in Africa, and governor and vice admiral of Tangier. He welcomed the Glorious Revolution, was with William's forces at the Battle of the Boyne, and was appointed governor of Jamaica in 1690, arriving May 31. Cundall, *Governors of Jamaica in the Seventeenth Century*, 124–30.

17. Henry Bentinck, First Duke of Portland (1682–1726), was appointed governor of Jamaica in September 1721, arriving December 22, 1722, with great pomp and ceremony and given a double salary of £5,000. At his death, his body was carried to England and entombed in Westminster Abbey. Frank Cundall, *Governors of Jamaica in the First Half of the Eighteenth Century* (London, 1937), 104–17.

with Madeira Wine which hath a much stronger body than French Wine and not abating of the Quantity, it soon through him into a distemper which carried him to his Grave. This was foretold would happen before he embarqued from England, for an eminent Merch[an]t in London, who traded to and had been in Jamaica being offered a Policy of Insurance on the Duke's life, at a very good premium, refused it; and gave for a reason his drinking to such excess, and sitting up late would not agree with the Climate He was going to especially as he was of a Gross and Corpulent body. His bowells were buried in the Church at St. Iago de la vega, and his Body embalmed and sent to England.

His Grace was the Son of General Monk[18] who was Created Duke of Albemarle by King Charles the Second, and the Characters of both are so well known in England, that I need not enlarge upon them here; or observe, after what I have related, that he had by such Acts of Power and other Arbitrary proceedings, rendered himself obnoxious to the People, and put the whole Island into the utmost disorder and Confusion, which would have been attended with very fatal Consequences, had not a period been put to them by the Revolution and His Death which hap[pe]ned soon after.

On the Death of the Duke of Albemarle the Administration devolved on S[i]r Francis Watson[19] as President of the Council.

At this time an Agreement was made by some Portuguez Merchants to furnish the Spaniards in America with Negroes who afterwards disposed of the Contract to some Grandees of Spain for a Sum of money. Don James Del Castillo[20] was Appointed their Commissary or Agent, and sent to London to sollicit the liberty of set[t]ling a Factory in Jamaica and to purchase Negroes for the use of the Assiento Company. This being thought, as indeed it was, a very advantageous proposal to the Nation in general and more particularly to Jamaica, was not only granted but, King William was so well pleased with it that He conferred the Honour of Knighthood on the Don.

S[eno]r James Del Castillo accordingly removed to this Island, hired

18. George Monck, First Duke of Albemarle (1608–1670), played a major role in the Restoration and held many offices under Charles II.

19. Francis Watson (?–1691) was a major land owner in Jamaica who became major-general of the forces in Jamaica in January 1678 and a councillor under Carlisle and a judge on the Jamaica Supreme Court in 1680. On the death of Albemarle and in the absence of Modyford, in 1688 he was briefly deputy governor. On the arrival of Inchiquin in May 1690, he was found to be £30,000 in debt with his estates deeply mortgaged and lost his seat on the council, with Inchiquin's son, James O'Brien, replacing him. Cundall, *Governors of Jamaica in the Seventeenth Century*, 118–23.

20. Don James Del Castillo was an agent for the African Company of Portugal, which held the contract, or *assiento*, for supplying the Spanish colonies with slaves from Africa. When the Portuguese proved unequal to the task of meeting Spanish demand, he petitioned Governor William Beeston in 1698 to establish a factory in Jamaica intended to fulfill that demand by slaves imported into Jamaica by English traders. Beeston forwarded this petition to London, where William I not only granted it but conferred a knighthood on Don James.

proper Houses and Conveniences at Port Royal, and was so well Esteemed and Respected that He was likewise permitted to purchase lands, and to Erect a Fortification thereon (which is Still in being tho[ugh] the Cannon were dismounted and taken out when the War with Spain was declared in 1702[21]) it being thought Necessary, for his protection and Security against Pirates, being 5 miles to the Eastward of Kingston, above one mile beyond the Rock line, and 8 or 9 mile from Port Royal.

This was a very fortunate era of time, and the most plentiful and happy days succeeded, that ever was seen in this Island; for the Settlement of the Assiento occasioned such a flow of Riches and such a Resort of People to the Island that it abounded in Trade, Ship[p]ing and People.

And, it was attended with this further advantage, the Contracters for want of a sufficient Stock to Carry it on, were Obliged to Open Books and take in Subscriptions every Voyage and any man had liberty of Subscribing any Sum not under £100, for which He was paid 30 p[er]c[en]t on the return of the Ship. And, as the Voyage was generally made in 6 or 7 Weeks, many Considerable Estates, were made, by the Merchants and other Inhabitants though the Contracters and their Agents were ruined by the Seizures which were made on the rupture with Spain and S[eno]r James Del Castillo, died some Years after very old and Poor, but Universally Esteemed and Respected; for he was of a very Hospitable disposition generous and punctual in his dealings, insomuch that His Honour and puncto was the Ruin of Himself and Family, by Mortgaging all his Estate, to make good His Contracts which He was disabled from doing by the War and the unfair dealings of His Associate (Don Porcia)[22] who resided at Carthagena, where he raised an immense Estate.

S[i]r Francis Watson who was a Planter in this Island and a Gentleman of a fair Character did not long enjoy the Government, for the Earl of Inchiquein whose Commission was dated the 7 day of October 1689 Arrived at this Island the 31st. day of May 1690, and took on Him the Administration.

He was vested with the same Powers, which had been granted to His Predecessors, and by His Additional Instructions, He was (inter alia) directed vizt.

> To Administer the Oaths appointed by Act of Parliament, instead of the Oath of Allegiance and Supremacy, the Test &c; and to permit liberty of Conscience to all Persons, Papists only excepted.

21. The War of the Spanish Succession, or Queen Anne's War, was declared by the Grand Alliance on France on May 4, 1702. It ended with the April 11, 1713, Treaty of Utrecht, which prohibited a Bourbon succession in Spain and recognized Britain's exclusive claims to Newfoundland, Nova Scotia, Hudson Bay, Nevis, and St Kitts.

22. Don Nicholas Porcio was the official of the African Company of Portugal in charge of managing the *assiento* with Spain.

To demand of the Governors of Mexico, La vera Cruz and other Spanish Ports in America, the Subjects of England, who were kept in Slavery and Barbarously treated at those Places; and to use His Utmost endeavours that they be set at liberty.

And, Whereas great prejudice may happen to our Service, by the absence of our Governor or Commander in Chief, without a Sufficient Cause or Special leave from us, for prevention thereof, you are not upon any pretence whatever to Come to England or leave your Government, without our permission under our Signet or sign Manual or by our Order in Council. But we do Nevertheless permit you in Case of sickness to go to any of our Plantations in America, for the recovery of your health.

And, we do likewise think fit that when any Complaint shall be intended against You, that notice be immediately given you thereof by the Complainants, with the Charge against you in writing to the end, that you may make timely preparation for your Defence.

Lastly, if any thing should happen, that may be of advantage or for the Security of the said Island, and other the Territories thereon depending, which is not herein or by our Commission provided for, We do hereby allow You, with the Advice and Consent of your Council to proceed therein, but with all Convenient Speed to Acquaint our Principal Secretary of State, and our Committee for Trade and Foreign Plantations of it, that so you may receive our Confirmation, if we shall approve of the same. Provided always that you do not by Colour of any power or Authority hereby given you, commence or declare War without our knowledge and particular Commands therein.

At this time the Descendants of the Spanish Negro's who never had submitted to the English and were united with the Fugitives from Lobby's, Guy's and other Plantations, began to make excursions.[23] They came down in the Night robbed the nearest Settlements and Committed great Cruelties. They had such places of Retreat and Security that all endeavours to draw them from thence were in Vain; nor, were the several Parties who were sent out able to dislodge or drive them out. These fruitless attempts to reduce Them, and the Success They met with in robbing remote and Straggling Plantations, Encouraged others to grow turbulent and unruly, insomuch that a Universal disposition appeared among the Negroes to Rebel. However, such effectual Care was taken to prevent their getting Arms and powder, and other methods taken by keeping a Vigilant Eye and Strict hand over Them, that a general Insurrection was thereby prevented.

23. The nucleus of the first Jamaican Maroons were those Spanish slaves who ran away when the English conquered the island in 1655, but their numbers were supplemented by runaways and people who had escaped as a result of slave uprisings. See Mavis C. Campbell, *The Maroons of Jamaica, 1655–1796: A History of Resistance, Collaboration and Betrayal,* (Granby, Mass., 1988).

But, notwithstanding all the precaution that was taken on the 29. of July 1690, the Negroes belonging to Mr. Thomas Sutton's Plantation (Called St. Iago in Clarenden Mountains)[24] being 400 in Number, broke out in Rebellion, Murdered their Master and all the White Servants, Seized upon 50 Musketts; some blunderbusses, 4 Field Pieces, and a great quantity of powder. They marched from thence to the next Plantation, killed the Overseer and would have engaged the Negroes to join them, but they took an opportunity and deserted Them.

The Alarm being given to the adjacent Settlements 50 horse and Foot were immediately raised and Marched to attack them; by which means a Stop was put to their progress, and Design of joining the other Rebels in the Mountains, (which would have been of fatal Consequence had they Accomplished it): For all the Neighbouring Plantations were on their Guard, and as Terror Commonly attends Guilt, They had not the Courage and Resolution notwithstanding Their Vast Superiority in Number, to dispute Their passage; but retired to Mr. Sutton's dwelling House, and prepared to Act Defensively. They had not been long there before They were attacked by a large Body of the Militia, on which, after some Resistance, they deserted the House and fled doing all the mischief in their power; for They fired all the Houses and Cane pieces in their Way. A Party of White men pursued Came up with and engaged Them. Many of the Negroes were killed in the Action, about 200 of them Submitted, the rest were afterwards killed or taken, except 30 or 40 who escaped, set[t]led in the remote Mountains, and Some years after were incorporated with the other Rebellious Gangs.

Those who Submitted were pardoned, but most of the others who were taken Prisoners, and all the Heads or Ringleaders, met with the Fate which They deserved.

In [blank] 1690, the War was declared between Great Britain and Spain;[25] and King William being Sensible that the most effectual way of distressing the Enemy was to destroy their Trade and Plantations; the Earl of Inchiquein received Express orders how to Act on this Occasion.

Accordingly the *Guernsey* and *Swan* Men of War[,] a large Merchant Ship (which was hired) and the Quaker Ketch were fitted out, and 900 Soldiers put on board. The Hon[ora]ble Mr. Obrian,[26] His Lordship's Son,

24. Thomas Sutton was one of the earliest settlers and a large landowner who owned as many as four hundred slaves in Clarendon Parish, which he represented in the Jamaica Assembly for eight of the thirteen terms he served in that body beginning in 1677 and ending in 1707. During some of those terms he was also Speaker of the Assembly. Knight appears to be in error in his remark that the slaves killed Sutton in this uprising.

25. King William's War, or the War of the League of Augsburg, began when William III entered England into the Grand Alliance on May 12, 1689, and ended with the Peace of Ryswick of September 20, 1697.

26. James O'Brien was the third son of William, Second Earl of Inchiquin, and Lady Margaret Howard. He accompanied his father, the governor, to Jamaica in 1690 and in February

who Commanded in Chief on this Expedition behaved Extremely well, for
He destroyed many of the French Settlements on Hispaniola, and took
several valuable Ships and other Booty, which He Carried into Jamaica.
But though the Design did not fully Answer People's expectation, yet the
Enemy sustained very considerable damage thereby.

The 9th. of June 1691, the Assembly was convened and His Excellency
made the following Speech

Gentlemen of the Council

Mr. Speaker and Gentlemen

of the Assembly

Since the King was pleased to honour me with this Government, I
thought it my Duty to promote His Service and the Interest of His Subjects which are inseparable, to the Utmost of my power. Therefore finding
on my arrival some distractions among you through the practises of some
turbulent Spirits, and the laws not being duly Executed, I applied my Self,
as early as possible, to repairing the breaches they had caused, and which
laid you Open to all the Evils that could happen to a place or People, for
whom I know His Majesty hath a great Value, and whose Interest and
Wellfare shall be my Care and Study.

One of those Breaches was healed by the Laws being restored to their
due and Natural Course and in the other I have laboured as much as
I could, and I hope it will appear that I have not made an inconsiderable
progress therein, by your laying aside all private piques and Animosities,
and promoting the general good of the Island.

I find, by your Situation, that you have such dangerous Neighbours, as
may give you some Apprehensions of ruin and destruction to those who
are set[t]led in remote places or near the Sea side, which you know will in
Consequence affect the whole Community. But, when I Considered the
protection, they ought to have I found the Treasury exhausted, and the
Government greatly in Debt; insomuch that it now lies under the greatest
Exigencies, that can be imagined. Therefore, Gentlemen, since your own
preservation, as well as the honour and Interest of the Island are affected,
I will make no doubt of your taking such measures as are proper and Nec-
essary, Since no Cure for this Distemper can be had but from your Selves.

When you Consider the Circumstances of other Countries and Colonies, you will find great reason to be satisfied with your own State and
Condition. Your Mother Country and Ireland involved with Distrac-

---

1691 took Francis Watson's position on the council. He commanded the fort at Port Royal
and undertook an expedition that destroyed a French fleet at Hispaniola. He returned to
England following his father's death, dying himself shortly thereafter. Cundall, *Governors of
Jamaica in the Seventeenth Century*, 127, 129, 130, 133.

tions and Expences. New England under great difficulties in regard to the Security of their Frontiers from the Neighbouring Indians. New York, Maryland and Virginia, oppressed and distressed by Usurpations. And, the Inhabitants of St. Christophers wandering, and Seeking for New places of Abode; while you sit under your Own Vines and enjoy the Fruits of your labour without any Considerable disturbance. Do what shall be requisite on your parts and nothing shall be wanting on mine.

Gentlemen, I am Commanded by His Majesty to recommend to your Consideration the raising an Act, whereby the Creditors of Persons becoming Bankrupts in England, and having Effects in this Island, may be relieved and the Debts Satisfied out of the same. And likewise for the better management of Affairs a law may be passed for raising of £300 p[er] Ann[um] to defray the Expence in Solliciting of them in England. This is so Essentially Necessary and so much for your own Interest, that I cannot doubt your Concurrence in the manner it was done formerly.

Gentlemen, Some Grievances you were under have been removed Since I came to the Government; if any Yet remains you shall find me ready to Consent to such Laws as you shall propose for redressing them; for I know the King intends you all the kindness you can reasonably desire, and therefore I hope you will on all Occasions demean your Selves, with all the Duty and Respect that is due to a Prince whose Conduct, Wisdom and Valour hath redeemed our Religion, our Liberties and Properties by breaking the measures of those who had projected their Ruin. These Gentlemen are the means of your becoming a happy People, and whenever you are so, I shall think my self a happy Governour.

But, the Seeds of Dissention which had been sown in the Duke of Albemarle's Government not being entirely rooted out, some turbulent men who had entered into the measures of those times, having had Interest enough to be chosen into the Assembly, raised Such Divisions, as entirely frustrated the good Designs of this Noble Lord, who perceiving their perverse dispositions, and that they would not come into His proposalls and Instructions, He sent the Provost Marshall on the 30th. of July 1691 to Command their Attendance on Him in the Council Chamber and made the following Speech

Gentlemen

The Chief end of my calling you together was that you might take due Measures for your Own preservation, in this troublesome time of War and the making some Reparation to those Inhabitants who had Suffered by the Depredations of the Enemy (which you are bound to do by your Own laws) and to lay before you the Exigencies of the Government, in hopes you would have taken it into Consideration, and enabled me to do Something for your protection, as well as to discharge near £8000 debts, most of it Contracted before my Coming to the Government. You have indeed passed a bill for raising £4780, towards the Maintaining of a Sloop, and Repairing of the losses of the Sufferers, and in the same breath you Voted and passed a Bill in a matter the King had taken into Consideration which is not only disrespectfull to him but it lessens the Revenue, without giving an Equivalent, only by passing a Bill imposing a Duty on Wines imported and 40 [shillings] p[er] head on Negroes Exported, which is absolutely repugnant to my Instructions and should it pass into a law, it will, in my, Judgment, be prejudicial to Trade and Navigation (the life of this Island) which I am bound to Encourage and protect.

As to your Message desiring me to Expedite the passing of two Bills, by giving my Assent thereto, the One tending to the Destruction, of the Government, and the other to the Affronting of my self, I do not think either of them require so much haste as that for the Relief of the poor Sufferers, and preventing others falling under the same misfortunes. But, that Bill it seems you have laid aside, until you know what I propose to do with the Others; though I sent Yesterday and pressed your Expediting it which message You Vouchsafed to answer only with another And, is such a proceeding that I cannot in regard to the King, and Government, and the Interest of the Island, as well as my self, but highly Resent.

I wish you may never stand in need of that Justice and Charity, which you have by these Measures denied your Neighbours; But, God who is a God of Justice as well as Mercy will avenge the Cause of the Poor, upon them and theirs, who have been their Oppressors.

When I came to this Island, I found a Flame kindled among you, which I took some pains to Extinguish, and in a great measure I had Affected it; but since your meeting Some Turbulent spirits have added new fewell; therefore to prevent the increase of the Fire which may prove fatal to the Island though you have a Speaker and many other Members, whom I value and Esteem, and I am persuaded are well affected to the Government; But, Since I cannot say so much of the Major part of this Assembly, I think it Necessary in their Majestie's Name to dissolve You, and You are hereby Accordingly dissolved. And, since you did not think fit to Address and Congratulate so Gracious a King, it is not proper for me to receive one from You, therefore there is your Address again. And it was thrown to them with great Contempt.

Notwithstanding the dissagreement between this Noble Lord and the Assembly, He was generally Esteemed and Respected in this Island, and His Death which hap[pe]ned on the 16th. day of January 1691, greatly lamented; for He was of a Frank and Affable disposition, a lover of Justice, and firmly Attached to the Rights, and liberties of our invaluable Constitution. And, it would have been happy for the Island had He lived longer among them, since the Amiable Qualities he was Master of, would undoubtedly have Composed all differences, and His upright Conduct made his Administration Easy to them, and Agreeable to Himself.

On the Death of the Earl of Inchiquien, the Government devolved on John White Esq[ui]r[e] President of the Council.[27] But, at a time when this Island was in very prosperous and flourishing Circumstances, abounding in Wealth and People, who flocked hither from all Parts, insomuch that on a General Muster or Alarm, They could raise 3000 Effective men at Port Royal, and 1200 at Liguinea only, the most Dreadful Calamity befell them, that ever hap[pe]ned to any Country or People; the fatal Consequences of which They laboured under for many Years and have not yet entirely recovered. For though the Plantations and Settlements are greatly increased within 30 years past, and the Number of Negroes are at least twice as many as they were at that time, yet the White Inhabitants are so much diminished as to require and make it absolutely necessary to have a great number of Regular Troops, constantly there in Peace as well as in War, for their Security and protection.

But, before I proceed to give a Relation of this Catastrophe, it is Necessary to observe that Port Royal being situated at the extream point of a Peninsula or Neck of land, which is all a Sandy foundation (except that part whereon Fort Charles is built which is almost an intire Rock) sustained the greatest damage; for being low, not above a Quarter of a Mile broad in any part (and most of the land whereon the Town stood was made out of the Sea), it was liable to disasters, and for that Reason, the Spaniards never had any Buildings thereon. Nor, would the dreadfull Calamity have been so destructive and Ruinous, had the Town stood, on any part of the firm land on this Island.

On the 7th. of June 1692 one of the most terrible Earthquakes hap[pe]ned, that ever was felt in any part of the World. It began between 11 and 12 at Noon, shook down and drowned about three fourths of Port Royal in less than two Minutes time, for all the Wharfs (which were made with Piles drove into the Sea, and filled up with Stones and Earth) Sunk at once. There was soon several fathoms Water where many of the Streets and lanes Stood, and One which sustained the least damage was so Overflowed, that the Water rose as high as the uppermost Rooms of the Houses, But, the following letters (in Lowthorp's Abridgment[28]) from two Persons who were on the Spot; will give us a lively and lamentable Idea, of that amazing and dreadful Disaster.[29]

27. On John White and his administration as acting governor, see ibid., 131–39.
28. See part 1, note 17, above.
29. Lowthorps *Abridgment Philosophical Transactions.* Vol. 2d. p. 411. — *Author.*

Of several contemporary depictions of the Port Royal earthquake on June 7, 1692, perhaps an engraving entitled *In Jamaica Where the City Port Royal Is Destroyed* (Amsterdam, 1698) by the noted Dutch artist Jan Luyken (1649–1712) best captures its immediate and extensive devastation. (Rijksmuseum, Amsterdam)

> I lost all my people and Goods, my Wife and two Men, Mrs. B. and her Daughter. One White Maid escaped, who gave me an Account, that her Mistress was in her Closet, 2 Pair of Stairs high, and she was sent into the Garret, where was Mrs. B. and her Daughter, when She felt the Earthquake, and bid her take up her Child and run down, but turning about, met the Water at the Top of the Garret stairs; for the House sunk downright, and is now near 30 Foot under Water. My Son and I went that Morning to Liguinea; the Earthquake took us in the Midway between that and Port Royal, where we were near being overwhelmed by a swift rowling Sea, six Foot above the Surface, without any Wind. Being forced back to Liguinea, we found all the Houses even with the Ground, not a Place to put our Heads in, but in Negroes' Huts. The Earth continues to shake (June 20) 5 or 6 Times in 24 Hours, and often trembling: great Part of the Mountains fell down, and falls down daily.

The Other letter gives the following Account.

> Between 11 and 12, we felt the Tavern, where I then was, shake, and saw the Bricks begin to rise in the Floor: At the same time we heard a Voice in the Street cry, An Earthquake, and immediately we ran out of the House,

where we saw all People with lifted up Hands, begging God's Assistance. We continued running up the Street, while on either side of us we saw the Houses, some swallowed up, others thrown on Heaps; the Sand in the Street rising like the Waves of the Sea, lifting up all Persons that stood upon it, and immediately dropping down into Pits. At the same time a Flood of Water broke in, and rowled these poor Souls over and over; some catching hold of Beams and Rafters of Houses: Others were found in the Sand that appeared, when the Water was drained away, with their Legs and Arms out. Sixteen or eighteen of us who beheld this dismal Sight, stood on a small Piece of Ground, which, Thanks be to God, did not sink. As soon as the violent Shake was over, every Man was desirous to know, if any Part of his Family was left alive. I endeavoured to go towards my House, upon the Ruins of the Houses that were floating upon the Water, but could not. At length I got a Canoe, and rowed up the great Sea-side towards my House, where I saw several Men and Women floating upon the Wreck out at Sea, and as many of them as I could, I took into the Boat, and still rowed on, till I came where I thought my House had stood, but could hear of neither my Wife nor Family. Next Morning I went from one Ship to another till at last it pleased God I met with my Wife, and two of my Negroes. She told me, when she felt the House shake, she ran out, and called all the House to do the same. She was no sooner out, but the Sand lifted up, and her Negro Woman grasping about her, they both dropt into the Earth together, when at the very Instant the Water came in, rowled them over and over, till at length they caught hold of a Beam, where they hung, till a Boat came from a Spanish Vessel, and took them up.

The Tremblings of the Earth were so Violent, that it was a very difficult matter for People to keep on their legs, some being thrown on their knees and Others on their Faces, as they run along the Streets to provide for their Safety. Many Openings of the Earth appeared at the same time, in Some of which several Persons were absorbt; some the Earth closed and squeezed to Death, part of their Bodies or heads only appeared above Ground, Others were swallowed and never were Seen Afterwards. And some rose up again in other Streets or in the Harbour and were Saved, as I have heard from Persons of undoubted Credit. From many of those Openings of the Earth, water issued out and Spouted in the Air; accompanied with Stenches and offensive smells and the Sky which was Serene and clear, on a sudden became dull and of a dark Redish Colour.

While Nature was labouring with these Convulsions, the People ran up and down Pale and trembling with horrour like so many Ghosts thinking the Dissolution of the whole Frame of the World was at hand. And, when the first and great shake was over; the Minister of Port Royal (the Rev[erend] Mr. Heath) desired the People to join with Him in prayer, among them were several Jews, who kneeled and Answered as they did, and it was observed that they were afterwards heard to call on Jesus Christ.

Several Ships and Sloops on the Careen were Overset and lost in the Harbour; and the Swan a Sixth Rate Man of War, that lay by the Wharf to Careen (by the Violent Motion of the Sea, and sinking of the Wharf) was forced over the tops of many Houses, and passing by one which was standing, part of it fell upon her and beat in her Roundhouse. However She did not overset, but floated about the Harbour, which happy accident helped to save the lives of some hundreds of People, who were floating or swim[m]ing and found means to get on board of Her.

When the Violence of the Earthquake was over the Water men and Sailors, made no Scruple of plundering the Houses, that remained, though some of them met with the fate they deserved by one or two of those Houses falling on them, by a shake which hap[pe]ned while they were committing so horrid and Wicked an Act.

Most of the Inhabitants of Port Royal who were preserved (at least as many as could) got on board the Ships in the Harbour, where some of them continued near two months, the shakes being so frequent and Violent, during that space of time, they were afraid to Venture ashore. For the remaining Houses, were so shattered that they were not thought habitable, and Continued Empty above a Year afterwards, until they were repaired.

Several Gentlemen who were in Liguinea and near the Sea Side Reported, the Waters retired so far from the land, that the Bottom appeared dry above 300 Yards, and in two minutes or less, they returned and Overflowed great part of the adjacent Shore.

The shake was Stronger in the Country and near the Mountains, than at Port Royal and the Reason assigned is because those great Bodies contain vast Quantities of Minerals and Sulphur, to which our Modern Chymical Philosophers[30] ascribe the Cause of Earthquakes; In several parts of the Island, the Earth opened and shut again; and in many places gapings or great Cracks remained unclosed and to be seen in the low lands as well as in the Mountains.

The Salt pans, near Port Royal, were overflowed and Salt Island that lies off old Harbour, was Split in two.

The Houses at Passage Fort were all thrown down, but one left standing in Liguinea, nor any at St. Iago de la vega, Except those which were built by the wary Spaniards—most or all of which sustained that fatal shock.

Part of a Mountain near Yallahs, fell down and covered a whole Plantation, and 19 Persons—From whence the remaining part is called Judgment Cliff—not far from Port Morant, a Mountain sunk, and the place where it stood is a lake near a mile over. And, in the parish of St. Mary's a Plan-

---

30. See Lemery's *Treatise of Chymistry* P. 115. —*Author.* Louis Lémery (1677–1743) was a French botanist and chemist. His treatise, *A Course of Chymystry,* translated into English by Walter Harris, was first published in London in 1677 and went through several editions, the last in 1720. —*Ed.*

tation with the Inhabitants and 1000 Acres of land likewise sunk and were overflowed in a lake, which afterwards dried up, and there is not the least appearance of Houses, Trees or any thing else that was before.

A great and hideous noise was heard, in the Mountains, during those Convulsions of the Earth, which terrified many Negroes who had deserted their Masters some months before, insomuch that they returned home Voluntarily and submitted themselves.

Part of the Mountains on Each side Rio Cobre (between Guanaboa and Sixteen Mile Walk, which are very high and Perpendicular) fell down, about the midway, and joined together, which turned the Course of the Water, and Surprised the Inhabitants of St. Iago de la vega, who finding that part of the River which runs by the Town; to be dry, imagined that the head, or Spring was sunk. Great quantities of Fish were taken up at the same time which was a great Relief to Them, but still They were under a Concern for their usual supply of Water from that River, which did not force its way into its former Channel for 8 or 9 days. And, the Road to Sixteen Mile walk, was so Stopped by some parts of the Mountains falling down, that they were obliged to go round Guanaboa for a long time after.

Some Persons were of Opinion, that the Mountains sunk a little, but that Port Royal is at least a foot lower, is demonstrable from the Necessity the Inhabitants have since been under of building a strong Wall to prevent its being over flowed by the Sea. Others Conjectured that the whole Island sunk lower, and Assign for a Reason, that the Wells in Liguinea did not require so long a rope to draw water out of Them, by two or three feet, as they did before the Earthquake, which is an indubitable Fact I have heard attested by several of the Ancient Inhabitants; though that may be attributed to other Causes particularly the unusual Rains they had soon after this Calamitous accident, for I have often observed that in the Wells in Liguinea, the depth of Water was Owing to the rains that fall more or less, and, in a very dry Season, they have had very little Water, and Sometimes none.

The Number of People Whites and Blacks who perished on this fatal day were about 3000, of which Number above 2500, were lost at Port Royal.

A general sickness ensued which carried of[f] above 2000 more in less than 3 months, Occasioned principally by their bad Accommodations for being Obliged to live in Huts (made of boughs, not sufficient to keep out Rain, which as I have observed, followed soon after the Earthquake in an unusual manner) and lying wet, wanting Medicines and other Necessaries they died miserably. It is likewise supposed that this general Sickness proceeded from the Noxious Vapours which belched from the openings of the Earth and the lands whereon their Huts were built (afterwards called Kingston) being new cleared of the Woods. Besides, the great Number of dead Bodies, which floated about the Harbour, as the Sea and land Breezes drove them, may be thought to add to the Contagion, and unhealthiness of the place. And it is not to be doubted but that many by being dispirited and Cast down, when they reflected on the loss of their Friends, the Ruinous and deplorable Circumstances they were under, fell sick and died.

Nor were these all the bad Consequences which attended this Calamity, for many Persons were so terrified that they removed to other Countries by which means the Island was deprived of above one half of the White Inhabitants, and Strangers were so discouraged, that very few would venture over and become Set[t]lers for many Years after, although they never had the like accidents since, which have done any damage.

The French, on Notice of this Accident, Equipped three or four Sloops, and landed 300 men at the North side of this Island with an intention of robbing the distressed Inhabitants who they imagined were not in a Condition to resist or Repel Them, on which the *Guernsey* man of War and two Sloops were Sent after them, and a Party of men detached from the South side, by land. These Forces were so fortunate [as] to defeat the Enemy, to take and destroy all their Men (and Vessells) except 18 only who Escaped in one of the sloops.

The Inhabitants were at the same time Apprehensive that the Negroes would take advantage of their unfortunate Circumstances insomuch that it was thought Necessary to keep a Constant Guard day and Night in every parish throughout the Island.

And, the President and Council ordered a Search to be made for all Goods which were Stolen or found floating in the Harbour and on the Shores, in order to be laid up in Store houses for the use of those Persons who could make appear their Right or property.

The Damages sustained by the Planters as well as the Merchants was very Considerable, and much more than was pretended to be lost by the Inhabitants of the Leeward Islands, Yet they never Sollicited or obtained any Relief. The Assembly, however, Considered those who owed for the Duties of Goods, that were destroyed in the Earthquake, by an Act which remitted what was due and owing on that Account.

The President John White Esq[uir]e died the 23d of August following and was succeeded by Colo[nel] John Bourden[31] who was the Senior Councellour.

The Administration of this Gentleman was very short and nothing further Remarkable in his time than the Melancholy and deplorable Circumstances, the Inhabitants were under; Struggling with all the Difficulties and

---

31. John Bourden (1633?–1697), an Irishman, was in Jamaica by 1670 and a member of the assembly for Vere Parish in 1675 and for St. Jago de la Vega or St Catherine Parish in 1677–83. He was appointed to the council in 1683, and although Albemarle dismissed him from that body, he regained his seat in February 1689 and became president of the council and acting governor on the August 1692 death of John White. His months in office were taken up with the enormous tasks of reconstruction after the June 2, 1692, earthquake and then the French threat. Sir William Beeston replaced him as governor on March 9, 1693. Cundall, *Governors of Jamaica in the Seventeenth Century*, 140–42.

Inconveniences (through the aforementioned disaster and Sickness) that any Place or People ever were Subject to.

King William, on advice of the Death of the Earl of Inchiquien was pleased to Appoint Colo[nel] William Beeston[32] L[ieutenan]t Governour, and to Confer on Him the Honour of Knighthood.

S[i]r William Beeston's commission was dated the 20th. of September 1692. He arrived in Jamaica the 9th. of March, following, and took on Him the Administration.

His Commission and Instructions were the same as those which were granted to the Earl of Inchiquien Except the Title, of Capt[ai]n General. And, His first Care was to inquire into and redress the abuses and disorders which were committed Since the late Calamity. Accordingly the unhappy Sufferers had Restitution of their Goods and Effects which could be discovered and had been Embez[z]led.

In November the *Mordaunt* man of War[,] convoy to a Fleet of Merchant Ships bound from this Island to Great Britain[,] was lost in the Gulph of Florida, but all the men were saved.

The Assembly met in January 1693, and passed several Laws some of which were made perpetual (others Temporary) and particularly

An Act for Establishing a perpetual Anniversary Fast on the 7th of June.[33]

An Act for Raising money for and towards the Defence of this Island.[34]

An Act for making Kingston a Parish.[35]

An Act for the better Securing Port Royal.[36]

An Act for raising money to Sollicit in England the Affairs of this their Majestie's Island.[37]

And S[i]r Gilbert Heathcote,[38] S[i]r Bartholomew Graudieu[39] and Mr.

32. Sir William Beeston (1636–1702) was lieutenant governor of Jamaica from 1693 to 1699 and governor from 1699 to 1702, when he was replaced by William Selwyn. See ibid., 143–65.

33. An Act for Establishing a Perpetual Anniversary Fast on 7 June, January 1693, in *Acts of Assembly Passed in the Island of Jamaica; from 1681, to 1737, Inclusive* (London, 1738), 57–58.

34. An Act for Raising Money for and toward the Defence of Jamaica, 1693, in ibid., 58.

35. An Act for Making Kingston a Parish, 1693, in ibid., 59–60.

36. An Act for the Better Securing of Port Royal, 1693, in ibid., 60–62.

37. An Act for Raising Money to Sollicit in England the Affairs of This Their Majesties' Island, 1693, in ibid., 65.

38. Sir Gilbert Heathcote (1652–1733) was a successful British merchant and political leader who sat in the House of Commons between 1701 and 1733, often representing the city of London. A principal promoter of the new East India Company in the 1690s, he was also one of the first directors of the Bank of England and served as its governor from 1709 to 1711 and 1723 to 1725. His colonial interests included acting as one of Jamaica's agents in London with William Beeston, with Bartholomew Gracedieu and John Tutt in 1693, with Gracedieu from 1698 to 1713, with Benjamin Way and Francis Marsh from 1714 to 1716, and alone in 1717. See Cundall, *Governors of Jamaica in the Seventeenth Century*, xviii, and Cundall, *Governors of Jamaica in the First Half of Eighteenth Century*, xx, 30, 32, 33, 37, 44.

39. Sir Bartholomew Gracedieu (c. 1657–1715) was a prominent London merchant who served as one of Jamaica's London agents with Heathcote and Tutt in 1693 and with Heath-

John Tutt[40] were appointed Agents and £450 Sterl[ing] was raised and re-mitted to them for that purpose. A Committee of Correspondance was also appointed namely Samuel Barnard[41] and Nicholas Laws[42] Esq[uir]e who were Members of the Council, and James Bradshaw,[43] William Hutchin-son,[44] Thomas Clark[e],[45] James Banister[46] and Modiford Freeman[47] Esq[uire]s, who were Members of the Assembly.

---

cote from 1698 to 1713. See Cundall, *Governors of Jamaica in the Seventeenth Century*, xviii, and Cundall, *Governors of Jamaica in the First Half of the Eighteenth Century*, xv, 30, 31, 33, 44.

40. John Tutt served with Heathcote and Gracedieu as agents to England in 1693. Cundall, *Governors of Jamaica in the Seventeenth Century*, xviii.

41. Samuel Barnard (?–1693) was married to Susanna Temple, daughter of Thomas Temple of Francton, Warwickshire, and Temple Hall in St. Andrew Parish, Jamaica, and brother-in-law of Governor Charles Lyttleton. When widowed, Susanna married Nicholas Laws and died in 1707, aged forty-seven. Already in Jamaica in 1670, Barnard represented St. Catherine Parish or St. Jago de la Vega in the Jamaica Assembly from 1673 to 1688 and was its Speaker from 1680 to 1688. Appointed chief justice in 1688, he lost this post temporarily when he fell out of favor with Albemarle but was reappointed in 1692. Governor Inchiquin, in commenting on a replacement governor to the king, advised against Barnard, and also Thomas Beckford and Nicholas Lawes, on the basis that they were "incendiaries." Ibid., 29, 41, 51, 54, 101, 112, 119, 125, 131, 133, 135, 141, 153, 154; Cundall, *Governors of Jamaica in the First Half of the Eighteenth Century*, 100, 103, 119, 207.

42. Nicholas Lawes (c. 1652–1731) was born in Wiltshire, the son of Nicholas and grand-son of Henry Lawes, the composer and tutor of Alice Vaughan, Lady Carbery, third wife of the second earl and stepmother of the third earl and governor of Jamaica, 1675–78. Lawes arrived in Jamaica with his mother and stepfather, Gregory Tom, in 1663. Acquiring a large estate, he became a member of the council in 1693 and chief justice from 1698 to 1703. Returning to England in 1703 where he acted as an unofficial advocate for Jamaica, he was knighted in 1717 and on April 26, 1718, returned to Jamaica as governor. His stormy governorship ended on December 22, 1722, when the Duke of Portland replaced him. Retiring to private life, he lived to the age of seventy-nine. In retirement in 1728, he introduced coffee planting to Jamaica. He made five advantageous marriages: in 1680 to Elizabeth, widow of John Potter of Jamaica (d. 1685); in May 1685 to Frances, daughter of Paul Godwyn and widow of Caesar Carter of St. Andrew, Jamaica (d. March 1693); in July 1693 to Elizabeth, daughter of Sir Thomas Modyford (d. 1694); in 1696 to Susanna, daughter of Thomas Temple and widow of Samuel Barnard, the chief justice and Speaker of the Assembly (d. 1707); and finally to Elizabeth, daughter of Sir Thomas Lawley and widow of Thomas Cotton. His family connections even reached royalty as his granddaughter married the Duke of Cumberland, brother of George III. See Cundall, *Governors of Jamaica in the Seventeenth Century*, 20, 30, 54, 131, 133, 135, 137, 138, and Cundall, *Governors of Jamaica in the First Half of the Eighteenth Century*, 74–103.

43. James Bradshaw represented St. James Parish in the Jamaica Assembly in 1691 and Kingston in 1695–96 and 1698–99. He was a relative, probably the son, of the regicide of the same name. Cundall, *Governors of Jamaica in the Seventeenth Century*, xvii; Frank Cundall, *Historic Jamaica* (London, 1915), xvi, 149.

44. William Hutchinson, or Hutchison, represented Port Royal in the Jamaica Assembly in 1688 and 1701–4, St. George Parish in 1693, and St. Thomas Parish in 1696.

45. Thomas Clarke represented St. James Parish in the Jamaica Assembly from 1682 to 1684, St. Andrew Parish in 1686 and 1693–1703, and Kingston in 1704.

46. James Banister represented St. Dorothy Parish in the Jamaica Assembly from 1688 to 1696.

47. Modiford Freeman, a local political worthy in the parishes surrounding Port Royal and Kingston, never seems to have sat in the assembly.

In March 1694 S[i]r William Beeston received a letter from a Gentleman at Curaso, acquainting Him that the French were making preparations to invade this Island, but, as He was a Stranger and did not mention where those Armaments were making or any other particulars, very little notice was taken of His Information. However, S[i]r. William thought it Necessary to have a Vigilant Eye over His Neighbours, and Endeavour to gain Intelligence of all their Motions and proceedings.

As I have in my hands a true Copy of S[i]r William Beeston's Journal,[48] which contains the measures that were taken on that Occasion for the defence of the Island, with many other particulars relateing to the Invasion of the French under the command of Mons[ieu]r Du Cass, the following account, which is chiefly collected therefrom may be depended on as a genuine Relation of those Transactions.

S[i]r William Beeston in the aforementioned Nar[r]ative premises that He was obliged to make some short Digressions (which I shall follow Him in) because it is Necessary to mention Some Persons and Circumstances, without which the whole proceeding will not be so well understood. And, as they will likewise be a Caution and warning to the Inhabitants to have a more Watchful Eye, over Such Persons as are Suspected, on very just grounds of being disguised Papists and disaffected to the Government.

Privateering, He observed, having been for some Years past discountenanced, in this Island, and Encouraged by the French, at Hispaniola, many Persons who could not lead any other sort of lives, went over to Them and were incorporated. Others, who were Roman Catholicks, or in the Interest of King James chiefly of the Irish Nation, likewise went over to them; by which means they were Strengthened, and the Inhabitants of this Island lessened. Among them was one Grubins,[49] a Native of this Island, and born of English Parents; who being well Acquainted with all our Coasts and Settlements, had done much mischief by landing in the Night, Robbing remote Plantations near the Sea, and retreating before any Assistance could be sent to Them.

Stapleton and Lynch[,] two Irish men[,] had likewise been very inveterate and mischievous, the first came from the Windward Islands with His Family who were kindly received and Set[t]led near Port Morant. The other came passenger in a Sloop, and S[i]r William Beeston having some Reason to suspect Him as a Spy, sent for Him in order to Examine, and tender Him the Oaths, but He found means to abscond and get off the Island, with the Assistance of Major Kelly, who was sending a sloop to Curaso, on pretence of getting Sailors, who had deserted this and resorted to

---

48. On Beeston's journal, see preface, note 19, above. Most of the long narrative that follows Knight copied or paraphrased from this journal. It contains many references to people for which no further information—and in many cases not even their full names—is available beyond what Knight and Beeston provided. They are not noted in this edition.

49. William Grubbins.

that Island, for fear of being pressed to serve on board His Majestie's Ships. For that Gentleman it Seems had bought a great Dutch Ship, and probably it was partly his Design to get her manned; but He put aboard the Sloop privately £1500; worth of Indigo, Contrary to the Act of Navigation. In re-quitall for this kindness Lynch and Stapleton, who were likewise on board, and had concerted matters run away with the Sloop to the French; and Ma-jor Kelly about the same time, was killed as He was going to dispatch the Sloop at Port Morant, by a Party of French, who had landed at Cocoa Bay to plunder the Adjacent Settlements.

Those two men on their Arrival at Petit Guavis, informed Mons[ieu]r Du Casse Governour of the French Settlements on Hispaniola,[50] that the Island was in a weak and defenceless Condition by means of the late Ca-lamity, and Stapleton soon after wrote to His Wife, that He would come and fetch her away, with some other Discoveries He made, in his letter which was intercepted and Sent to the Governor.

In April Capt[ai]n Elliot,[51] whom I shall have Occasion to mention hereafter was Sent out in the *Pembrook* Sloop by some Merchants, with a Cargo of £10000 to Trade on the Coasts of Carthagena and Porto Bello; and in a Bay was taken by two French Privateers and carried into Petit Guavas about the Same time, the *Falcon* man of War Capt[ai]n Bryan was ordered to Cruise between 7 and 8 leagues to the Eastward of the Island, to prevent the Enemies' small Privateers landing and pillaging that part of the Country; and in a few days after He met with Six Sloops, which had on board 500 men who were designed to land at St. Thomas and St. Davids and rob those Districts. The chief Commander Major Beau[re]guard (as we were afterwards informed) was for engaging the *Falcon*, but the Cap-tains dissented and alledged that they should get only broken bones, and be disabled from putting their Design in Execution. They thereupon made the best of their way, and outsailing the *Falcon* Escaped; however, she re-took a New England Ship laden with Provisions, which they had taken the day before.

At this juncture arrived at Petit Guavis 3 Men of War of 50 and 54 Guns Each with a Fleet of large Merchant Ships from old France; and the Governor Mons[ieu]r Du Casse, having information of the *Falcon's* Sta-tion from those Privateers, immediately dispatched the men of War with a smaller Ship of 12 Guns to go in quest of Her. They soon met, and En-

---

50. Jean-Baptiste du Casse (1646–1715) was a French buccaneer, admiral, and colonial administrator who was the first governor of the French colony of St. Domingue from 1691 to 1702.

51. Probably Captain Stephen Elliott of Jamaica, who took news of the 1692 earthquake to England. He was captured by French privateers off the west coast of St. Domingue and kept prisoner at Petit Guavas. He then escaped to Jamaica by canoe in time to warn of the May 31 landing of Du Casse with twenty sail and three thousand men at Jamaica. Cundall, *Governors of Jamaica in the Seventeenth Century,* 149.

gaged, and being so much Superior in Force, the Falcon was obliged to Submit. But, a Sloop belonging to the Island, landing some men at the French Settlements on Hispaniola in order to get Intelligence; Accidently met with the Wife of the Renegado Grubins, and would have given her liberty to return home but she desired to go with them to Jamaica and be released from Her husband, who She said used her very ill, she being a French Woman. S[i]r William Beeston would have Sent her back again, but she Earnestly desired to Stay; and it being a Stated Agreement between S[i]r William and Mons[ieu]r Du Cass that whatever Persons should go from one Island to the other and desire protection, should not be delivered up or Obliged to go without their own Consent; He would not force her away. Nevertheless, Grubins wrote S[i]r William an Insolent letter, and told Him that if He did not send him his Wife, He would come and fetch off Island, as many Women as He could meet with; Accordingly He landed soon after at St. Elizabeth's, plundered Mrs. Barrow[,] a Minister's Widow, tortured her to make her Confess if she had any money in the House, committed many other Acts of Cruelty and Carried away her Daughter, who was about 14 Years of Age. Another Privateer landed at the North side, took Major Terry, and his Wife[,] carried them aboard, Stript her naked and whipped her, and at length compelled Him to sign a promisary Note for a Certain Sum of money for their Ransom.

S[i]r William Beeston being informed of these and many other Acts of Cruelty and Inhumanity committed by them and other French Privateers, in Violation of the law of Nations as well as Christianity; thought it Necessary to Send Mr. [Henry] Lowe a Member of the Council with a Flag of truce to represent the same to Mons[ieu]r Du Cass, and to desire some punishment might be inflicted on the Offenders. But, instead of a satisfactory answer the Sloop was Seized, and Mr. Lowe with all His Attendants were put under Confinement.

S[i]r William Beeston not having any Account of the Fate of the *Falcon* or the Flag of Truce, began to be uneasy; however, did not imagine that the French had taken the one and detained the other, much less that they had any Design on the Island, for He had not at that time any information of the Arrival of the Aforementioned Ships at Petit Guavis, or of more than one man of War, of 44 Guns being on that Station.

While He was under these inquietudes, on Thursday the last day of May, Capt[ai]n Elliot came to Him in a mean habit, and a meagre Weather beaten Countenance, and informed Him that for the preservation of the Island, He and two more English men had ventured their lives, on the Open Seas, in a small Canoe which Could not carry any more.

That, on Saturday Night last, They made their Escape from Petit Guavis, to inform Him that the Enemy had Recruits of Men and Ships of War from France and Martinico. That they had taken the *Falcon* seized the Flag of Truce and Confined Mr. Lowe and His Attendants. That they had drawn all their Ships and Forces together, which Amounted to 20 Sail and 3000 land men with a Design to take this Island, and that Mons[ieu]r Du Cass the French Governour was Comeing with them, to Command in Person.

That Stapleton, Lynch and other Renegadoes had assured Him of Success and that He would meet with little difficulty in the Enterprise, for that the Fortifications at Port Royal were thrown down in the Earthquake. That upon their landing at least 500 men, Roman Catholicks and others in the Interest of King James would join Them. That 2000 men would take the Place the People were so reduced, Sickly and dispirited with their late misfortune. And that they were ready to Sail when He Came away; might be expected in a few days; and were in hopes of surprizing the Island and making an Easy Conquest of it.

S[i]r William Beeston who was greatly surprised at this Intelligence, immediately Sent for the Speaker of the Assembly,[52] who were then Sitting and Ordered Him to adjourn the House for a Month, which was accordingly done. He also summoned a Council of War, and with their advice and Consent, proclaimed Martial Law.

At this time Fort Charles was not raised higher than the Sills of the Embrasures; but, Colo[nel] Beckford[53] who commanded that Fortress applied Himself with such Industry, that in about 10 days He had the East Bastions finished, the plat forms laid, the Guns mounted, and the Fort in as good Order as could possibly be Expected in so short a time. He also mounted 19 heavy Cannon on the East part of the Town and 5 to the West. The *Advice* man of War and the Merchant ships were drawn up in a line to the Westward of the Fort. 100 White Men and Blacks armed were sent from St. Katherines and as many from Kingston, to Strengthen Port Royal.

52. James Bradshaw, member of the Jamaica Assembly for Kingston, was Speaker of the House in 1694–95.

53. Peter Beckford (1643–1710) was of humble origins, the son of a tailor from Maidenhead, yet of noble ancestry, the Beckfords of Beckford, Gloucestershire, who had fallen on hard times after choosing the wrong side in the Wars of the Roses and later the Civil War. Beckford moved to Jamaica in 1661, settling as a merchant, and soon became a highly successful planter. He was a member of the assembly for St. Catherine Parish in 1675, for St. John Parish in 1678 and 1686, for Clarendon Parish in 1679, and for St. Dorothy Parish in 1683–84. Soon thereafter he was appointed to a seat in the Jamaica Council, becoming its president in 1702 and acting as governor in 1702–3. He became receiver general in 1691, commander of Port Royal and first custos of the new parish of Kingston in 1692, and chief justice from 1703 to 1705. His second wife was a Ballard who bore him three sons, including Peter, who was Speaker of the House frequently from 1704 to 1735 and who owned no less than twenty-four plantations. Peter's son, in turn, was William Beckford (1709–1770), the famed lord mayor of London and author of *Vathek*. Cundall, *Governors of Jamaica in the Seventeenth Century*, 55, 79, 80, 81, 98, 101, 106, 131, 134, 138, 141, 148; Cundall, *Governors of Jamaica in the First Half of the Eighteenth Century*, 12–26; Cundall, *Historic Jamaica*, xiii, xv, xvi, xvii, 33, 45, 47, 71, 98, 101, 102, 206, 247, 359, 360.

At Kingston, a Breast Work was raised and 20 heavy Cannon were mounted at the S[outh] W[est] end of the Town to defend the Harbour; an intrenchment cast up on the North side of the Town, and divers pieces of Cannon planted; and a broad Ditch dug round the Town. A Breast [work] was also raised to secure the Narrow pass, between S[eno]r James Del Castillo's Fort and the Rock River (where a strong line hath since been built) and 200 men posted there to defend it. The Forces of St. Andrews and Kingston being in Number about 700 White Men and 300 Blacks armed, under the Command of Colo[nel] [Nicholas] Law[e]s, were quartered in Kingston and in a readiness to march to any part of the Country where their Assistance was Necessary or required.

In St. Katherines Breast works were raised at Passage Fort, Black River and other places; and a deep ditch thrown up round St. Iago dela vega. Breast works were also raised at Old Harbour and Carlisle Bay, and all other preparations for the Defence of the Island which could possibly be made in so short a time. The Spirits of the People were likewise roused on this Occasion, and every one Seemed to have forgot their late misfortune and determined to defend the Country to the last Extremity. But, in regard the Island was large, and it was impossible to defend every part against so great an Armament, it was thought Necessary and adviseable to draw the Forces from remote Parts into St. Dorothy's, St. Katherine's, St. Andrew's and Port Royal, that they might be better able to assist each other and Defend the whole.

The Guns in Fort William at Port Morant were ordered to be spiked up, the shot buried and the powder and Ammunition brought away; that Fortress not being thought sufficient to defend the place, against so great a Strength as was coming against it.

On Sunday the 17th. of June 1694, in the Morning the Enemy appeared in Sight of the East end of the Island, with a fresh Gale; and it was Expected that they would have preceeded directly into Port Royal. But, on a Consultation, the Pilots being Examined (particularly Grubins) the Motion, which was made to that purpose by Mons[ieu]r Du Cass, was opposed by the French Commodore and all the Captains of the Fleet. It seems the Question proposed to the Pilots, was, Whether they would undertake to Carry the Fleet into the Harbour and to bring them out in Case they did not Succeed. The Answer given was that they could Conduct the Ships in any hour of the Day, after nine; But, that they must force their way out, which would be difficult, if they were not strong enough.

Upon which Mons[ieu]r Rollon the Commadore declared that He would not venture the King's Ships into a Harbour, where there was no Comeing out again, unless They Succeeded. On which 8 Sail remained about Port Morant and 18 Sail came down and Anchored in Cow Bay.

The Signal or Alarm being made on Sight of the Enemy, a Council of War was held at Passage Fort

Present

S[i]r William Beeston L[ieutenan]t Governour

Collo[nel] John Bourden[54]	Lieutenant Collo[nel] Richard Loyd[55]
Collo[nel] Nicholas Laws	L[ieutenan]t Collo[nel] Charles Sadler[56]
Collo[nel] Henry Low	Major James Montjoy
Collo[nel] Charles Knight[57]	Major Lancelot Talbot.[58]

Ordered, That if the Enemy endeavour to force the pass into Liguinea, then on a Signal given four Companies of Foot and the Troop of Horse be detached from Kingston to reinforce the Breast Works.

And, for a Signal 3 distinct Guns to be fired there, 3 at Kingston, and to be answered with one Gun at Port Royal.

Ordered, That if the Enemy pass Port Royal on the South side of the Cays, then four Companies of Foot and the Troop of Horse march immediately from Liguinea (without further Orders) to St. Iago dela vega. And three Companies from Port Royal, to be landed at the Salt ponds, and march directly to the said Town.

Ordered, if the Enemy attempt to land at Old Harbour, then the Major part of the Horse and Foot, March from thence to St. Dorothy's and join the Regiment of Clarendon and Vere which is likewise ordered thither, Except one Company as a Guard at Carlisle Bay.

Ordered, that on the Enemie's appearance off of Old Harbour, and steering Westward, an Express be immediately dispatched to Carlisle Bay. And, that His Majestie's Forces Horse and Foot be drawn together near Mr. Ivey's Plantation.

That, they avoid Engaging in Small Parties and until they are all joined or Reinforced. That the Forces at St. Dorothy's likewise march and join them.

Ordered, that the Troops of Horse at Clarendon and Vere do immediately March to St. Iago de la vega, Except 6 Troopers to Patroul.

It is the Unanimous Opinion of this Board that the Forces at the Windward part of the Island, be drawn down to Liguinea. And from all other parts of the Island. Except Port Royal to St. Iago de la vega and St. Dor-

54. John Bourdon was a member of the Jamaica Council, and in 1693 its president.

55. Richard Lloyd was a lieutenant colonel and council member and chief justice in 1689 and 1695–98. After the French invasion, he wrote a letter to the council criticizing Beeston's conduct of the campaign. Cundall, *Historic Jamaica*, xvii, 377, 378.

56. Charles Sadler represented St. James in the Jamaica Assembly in 1688 and Port Royal in 1688–89.

57. Charles Knight was a councillor in the 1690s and commander at Port Royal and at Fort Charles in 1696. He is not known to be a relation of James Knight. Cundall, *Governors of Jamaica in the Seventeenth Century*, 133, 135, 155; Cundall, *Historic Jamaica*, 55, 71.

58. Lancelot Talbot represented Port Royal in the assembly from 1693 to 1696.

othy's. Ordered that Collo[nel Charles] Knight take up two Ships that are proper and fit them up, for Fire Ships.

Ordered that all the Reformade Officers, inlist and do Duty in the Troops of Horse in the Respective Precincts they reside.

On the 18th. of June, the Enemy landed 500 Men at Port Morant and not meeting with any Opposition, They plundered, burnt and destroyed all before Them; killed the Cattle drove Flocks of Sheep and Poultry into Houses then Set them on Fire, Some strag[g]ling People who were left behind, and were so unfortunate as to fall into their hands, they tortured and others they murdered. They obliged the Negroes to abuse and Violate several Women, and Committed divers other Barbarous and Inhuman Actions, for such are the French, in general, when they Overcome and are Masters of a Place. The plunder they met with, and Could not carry away, they likewise burnt, and made such Devastations, that they laid Waste and destroyed the whole Parish of St. Thomas in the East. They imagined they could have done the same in other Parts of the Island, and during their Stay at Port Morant, sent 4 or 5 Vessells to the North side, and landed their Men at St. Georges and St. Mary's; but upon the Appearance of some Forces that were sent thither, They withdrew, and returned to their Fleet.

On Thursday the 21st. the Wind blowing hard Mon[sieu]r Rollon, the Commadore riding in very deep Water, His Anchors came home and was driven off, with another Ship in His Company and could not get up again with the Fleet; therefore bore away to Blewfields Bay on the S[outh] W[est] end of the Island, where He landed 60 Men. On which Major Andriess,[59] who was left there with only one Company of Foot to take Care of those Parts, marched and Attacked them. The Commadore hearing the Fire of small Arms, imagined their Men were Engaged with our People, and fired a Shot over them as a Signal to Retreat and Come off, on which they made such haste that they left their Provisions behind Them. In this Skirmish we had only one Man killed and two wounded, but the French lost several in the Action, and when they were pursued. As soon as they could get up their Anchors those two Ships sailed.

The Enemy having done all the mischief They could at Port Morant, and the adjacent Country, Rased the Walls of Fort William, burnt the Carriages of the Guns, and left nothing that could be usefull to mankind.

On Monday July 16th. the whole Fleet Sailed from Cow Bay, the next Morning some of Them were seen from Port Royal, and in the Evening they all Appeared in Sight standing in to Cow Bay where they Anchored again.

---

59. Possibly Lieutenant Colonel Barnard Andreiss, custos and member of the assembly for St. Elizabeth, who died at Lacovia, Jamaica, in 1710. Cundall, *Historic Jamaica*, 352, 353.

To Amuse the Inhabitants They landed a great Number of Men, made Fires along the Shore, and feigned a disposition to Attempt forcing the Rock line, and pass to Liguinea and Kingston. The Governor thereupon detached 100 Men to reinforce that part, though he was Suspitious it was only a Stratagem, to Cover some other Design; and so it proved, for as soon as it was dark the Enemy reimbarqued all their Men and sailed in the Night, except 3 of the largest ships which Still rode in the Bay to amuse the Inhabitants.

The 18th. early in the Morning 17 Sail were seen from our lookouts, Standing to the Westward; on which, the Governor, immediately detached two Troops of Horse, His Regiment of St. Katherines, and the Forces which had been drawn from St. Elizabeths and St. Dorothy's to Carlisle Bay, which is 36 Miles from St. Iago dela vega, judging the Enemie's Design was to Surprize that part of the Country before any Assistance could be sent to Them. The Troops of Horse, and part of the Foot, who were mounted, got thither before it was dark; and the rest made long marches and joined Them the next morning.

The Enemy came to an Anchor in the Bay, the 18th. in the Evening, where a Guinea Ship lay that happened to put in there and had landed all her Negroes. The Commander whose name was Daniel perceiving He could not Escape with His Ship, Set Her on Fire, and with His Men retired to the Breastwork where they did good Service, though Six of them were afterwards killed. The Breastwork was defended by 250 men, beside armed Negroes under the Command of Collo[nel] Sutton; but, it was ill made and worse Contrived; for on the S[outh] was the Sea, W[est] a large River, N[orth] a Village, and on the E[ast] a Wood. Nor was there any Provision made for Man or Horse.

Thursday the 19th. before Day the French Fleet made Signalls, by throwing up Balls of Wild Fire, which it Seems were for landing their Men; and by Day light they disembarqued about 1500. But, they avoided the Breast Work and landed about a mile and half to the Eastward, where Guards were placed to Watch their Motions, who, as the Enemy Approached fired and retreated. Between 9 and 10 the Enemy advanced on the Wood side, and Attacked the Breast work, on which a hot Fire on both sides, ensued for sometime; but their Officers forcing on their Men, and being greatly Superior in Number our People finding they could not maintain the Works retired and passed the River after killing many of the Enemy. In passing the River some of them were drowned and others bog[g]ed, Collo[nel] Claybourn and L[ieutenan]t Vassall of St. Elizabeths;[60] L[ieutenan]t Collo[nel] Smart[61] and L[ieutenan]t Dawkins of Clar-

60. Probably Colonel John Vassall, who represented St. Elizabeth Parish in the Jamaica Assembly in 1695–96 and 1698–99.

61. Perhaps Robert Smart, who represented Vere Parish in the Jamaica Assembly in 1686 and 1688–89.

endon were killed in this Action. Capt[ai]n Dawkins,[62] Captain Fisher and others wounded, and near 40 were killed and taken Prisoners; but, the Enemie's loss was not certainly known, though it must have been Considerable. Just as the Enemy had forced the lines, 4 Companies of the Regiment of St. Katharines, one of St. Elizabeths, and a Troop of Horse came up after a march of 30 miles rallied our Men, bravely attacked and repulsed the Enemy (who had many Men killed and wounded in this Action) otherwise most or all our Men who were at the Breast work, had been cut off. Our Troops being much Fatigued with the Action after a long March, retired to recruit, and nothing passed the 20 and 21, only one or two small Skirmishes.

The 22d. the Enemy marched to a House of Mr. Hubard's,[63] who had with Him 25 men, well provided with Arms[,] Ammunition[,] Water and Provisions and determined to defend themselves. This House was immediately attacked, but our People gave the Enemy so warm a reception, that Several were killed outright, and among them some of their Principal Officers. L[ieutenan]t Collo[nel] Loyd having advice of this Dispute, marched to their Assistance, and beat off the Enemy. The same Evening our Scouts, got Intelligence, that the Enemy were providing Cannon in order to batter and beat down the House.

At this time the principal Officer not behaving with that Spirit, Resolution, and Conduct, which was Necessary, at such a juncture; the Commission Officers held a Consultation, wherein they unanimously Suspended Him and chose L[ieutenan]t Collo[nel] Loyd to Command the Forces, which being joined, Amounted to 700 Men, and sent an Express to the Governour to Acquaint Him of their proceedings, with their Motives and Reasons for so doing; which He was pleased to Approve of, and Confirm.

Monday the 23d. L[ieutenan]t Collo[nel] Loyd lodged 50 Men in Mr. Hubbard's House, and prepared Several Ambuscades, expecting the Enemy would put their Design in Execution, which had they done few of them would have returned. But, the Enemy, finding they had lost many men, and Several of their best Officers, without gaining any advantage or making any further advance into the Country changed their Resolution and Embarqued the next day after they had burnt a small Town called Carlisle, Spiked up all the Cannon, and done all the mischief in their power.

And on the 24th. the whole Fleet sailed from thence. Mons[ieu]r Du Cass with 3 Ships more made the best of their way Home, and 17 Sail put into Port Morant to Wood and Water, which they did with all the dispatch they could. On the 28th. they landed their Prisoners and Sailed Homewards.

62. Perhaps Richard Dawkins, who represented Clarendon Parish in the Jamaica Assembly in 1681–84, 1688–89, and 1693.

63. Probably Jonathon Hubbard, who represented Vere Parish in the Jamaica Assembly in 1695–96.

At their first coming They boasted that They would Fire and destroy all the Country till they came to St. Katherines, then plunder and burn St. Iago de la vega, cut off the Water from Port Royal, oblige them by that means to Surrender, and so Secure the whole Island. They likewise declared, that whoever would Submit to the King of France[64] or acknowledge King James, should have all their Goods and Effects preserved and restored to Them. But this Scheme did not Succeed, for not one man Accepted of the Offer or went over to Them.

According to the exactest computation that could be made we lost, in the several Engagements about 60 men, and 40 wounded. 50 Sugar works were destroyed, beside other Settlements, and 1300 Negroes killed and Carried away so that the damage the Island sustained, was very Considerable, though it did not answer the Expectation and Expence the Enemy was at in this Expedition.

And, by the Report of some Prisoners, who came from Petit Guavis after the return of the Fleet, they had 350 Men killed outright, others died of their Wounds and many by Sickness, so that on the whole they lost upwards of 700 Men.

I have been more particular in this Relation, because it will not only shew the measures which were taken for the protection and Security of the Island, but discover some Errors and mistakes which are needless, and Indeed improper for me to point out here, and may be the means of their being rectified, in Case the Island should ever fall under the same Circumstances.

It must However be allowed that considering the unhappy Condition the Country was in at that juncture, all the preparations were made for Defence of it, that could possibly be expected in so short a warning, for what was done in less than 3 weeks is almost incredible, though it must be Considered the great strength and labour of the Negroes, who were taken off from Planting, and Employed in the Publick Service. Nevertheless the Conduct of S[i]r William Beeston was very much Censured for drawing off the Forces from the remote Parts to St. Iago de lavega, Port Royal and Liguinea, whereby they were exposed to the Ravages of the Enemy.

His Advocates alledge 1. That it was the Resolution of the Council of War. This His Opponents said was indeed a Screen, but not a Sufficient Justification, Since it is well known that the President in all Councils of War, influences, at least recommends such Steps as He thinks Necessary to be taken, and which are generally Observed and put in Execution.

2. That as they were not able to raise 200 Effective Men at St. Thomas in the East, such a Number was not sufficient to defend those parts; and as they might be Cut off, the Island would thereby be so much weaker and Exposed.

64. Louis XIV (1638–1715).

In Answer to this it was said that the Inhabitants in that district with Armed Negroes could have raised 300 Men fit for Service; and though such a Number Could not pretend to oppose so great a Force as the Enemy had in the Field, Yet had they been properly placed in Ambuscades, and Narrow passes they might have put a stop to and prevented the Excursions and devastations of the Enemy or a great part of Them; Whereas, drawing away the Forces from those Parts, laid them entirely open and exposed to the Fury of the Enemy.

But, whatever was or can be said in His Vindication in the aforementioned Case nothing can justify an order He afterwards sent to Collo[nel] Laws, to March with the Forces of Liguinea and Kingston under His Command to St. Iago de lavega, which would likewise have laid those Places open and Exposed to the Enemy.

This raised a further Clamour, and as He did not think proper to Suspend Collo[nel] Laws or Try Him (for not obeying that order) at a Court Martial we may reasonably Conclude He was sensible, on reflection, of His Mistake. And, Indeed, when we consider His Conduct in other Respects, and the Interest He had in the Island, particularly in Liguinea it Cannot be attributed to any thing more than an Error in Judgment, and not being Skilled in Military Affairs. For which Reason, in my Opinion this Island ought always to be under the Government of a Gentleman, who was bred in the Army, or Qualified to command and Discipline the Forces; at least there should be Such a Person in the Island not only to assist and advise the Governor, but to command where His presence is not absolutely necessary. These, I hope will not be thought needless Digressions, since they will probably point out something for the Interest and Advantage of the Island.

Capt[ain] Elliot who gave the Governor notice of the intended Expedition of the French, had a Medal and Chain of £100 Value given Him, by Command of King William, and £500 in mon[e]y. The two Seamen who escaped and came with Him from Petit Guavis on that occasion, had a Reward of £50 Each. And, His Majesty was further pleased to Order, that Capt[ai]n Elliot should be recommended to the Lords Commissioners of the Admiralty for an Employment in the Navy. Accordingly, He was promoted to the Command of a Man of War.

In October following the Governor received an Answer to the Express which He dispatched on the 24th. of June, with an Account of the Enemie's being landed on this Island, in order to make themselves Masters of it, with Assurances that Her Majesty had nothing more at Heart, than Relieving and preserving to the Crown of England a place of the greatest importance to Trade and Navigation. And, that Her Majesty had been Graciously pleased to give Express orders for preparing with all Diligence, Such strength in Ships of War and Land Forces, as may be able not only to free the Island from the Insults of the Enemy, but also to reduce the French in the Neighbourhood of Jamaica to such a Condition as may put them out of Capacity for the future, to molest the Inhabitants of this Island or to disturb the Trade and Commerce of His Majestie's Subjects.

The Council and Assembly thereupon drew up and Sent over an Address which was presented to the King, wherein They most Gratefully acknowledged His Majestie's Royal Care of Them, in ordering a speedy Relief and Assistance to be Sent thither for the Defence and Security of their Persons and Estates against a Cruel and Barbarous Enemy; who in their late Attempt had no Other Advantage over them, than what was owing to the Inequality of their Numbers, and not to the valour of their men, which shewed itself, in burning deserted Plantations, Murdering Prisoners in Cold Blood, offering Indignities to Women, and other Acts of Cruelty and Inhumanity.

The Assembly among other Acts, this Session, passed the two following.

An Act for appropriating several sums of money for the speedy Relief of the wounded and distressed Inhabitants of this Island, who have suffered by the late Invasion of the French.[65]

An Act for the Encouragement and Freedom of Servants and Slaves, who have done or shall do any Remarkable Service against the French during this present War.[66]

This last Act, was in Compliance with a Proclamation, which was made by the advice and with the Consent of the Council, at the beginning of the late French Invasion, and was punctually Executed, for many Servants had their Indentures given up[,] Negroes their Manumission, and Others Rewarded in proportion to their Services. The time the Servants had to Serve, and the Negroes were valued, by Commissioners Appointed for that purpose, and their Masters paid the Value accordingly.

The Succours, which had been promised to be Sent to Jamaica, consisted of 1200 Regular Forces, commanded by Collo[nel] Luke Lillingston[67] and one third, four fourth, one Fifth Rate and two Fireships namely the *Dunkirk; Winchester Reserve, Hampshire, Ruby* and *Swan* and 20 Sail of Transports, Storeships and other Vessels under the Command of Commadore Robert Willmot.[68]

---

65. An Act for Appropriating Several Sums of Money for the Speedy Relief of the Wounded and Distressed Inhabitants of the Island, Who Suffered by the Late Invasion of the French, 1694/95, in *Acts of Assembly*, 66.

66. An Act for Encouragement and Freedom of Servants and Slaves, Who Have Done or Shall Do Any Remarkable Service against the French during This Present War, 1694/95, in ibid., 66.

67. Luke Lillingston (1653–1713) served William III in Ireland, in the Martinique expedition of 1693, and in Jamaica in 1695. He made brigadier general in 1704 and was commissioned to go to Antigua in 1706 but was unready and had to be ordered to go in 1707, finally being deprived of command for unreadiness in 1708. Cundall, *Governors of Jamaica in the Seventeenth Century*, 154.

68. Robert Willmot (?–1695) had been an officer in the royal navy since 1658 and died of fever returning from the Jamaica expedition in 1695. Ibid.

They sailed from Plimouth the 22d. January 1694: But, having, sometime before, had advice of the retreat of the French from Jamaica, it was
thought Necessary to keep the Service, on which they were designed, a
Secret, even from the Commander in Chief of the Land and Sea Forces.
Therefore the General Instructions were Sealed up; with positive Orders
to the Commodore, not to Open Them before He came to the Lat[itude]
of 40 deg[rees] and then to do it in the presence of the Commander in
chief of the Land Forces.

They arrived at St. Christophers the 28 of March and from thence the
Swan Frigat was dispatched with a pacquet to the Governor of St. Domingo from the Spanish Ambassador in England, in which was contained
orders and Instructions from the King of Spain[69] to Concert measures with
the English Commanders, for the Execution of the intended Expedition
against the French Settlements. And, the Governour of Jamaica, was also
directed to Send what Forces He could spare to Their Assistance.

On the 5 of April They came to an Anchor with part of the Fleet, before
St. Domingo, the Remainder were ordered to the Gulph of Samana on the
North side of the Island.

The Governour of St. Domingo, though He made some shew of readiness to comply with His Instructions, yet raised some Scruples and difficulties by which means 12 days time was lost. At length matters were adjusted
and the Spanish Governor was to Assist with 1700 men and 3 small men
of War. The Spanish land Forces were to march by Land, and the English
were to disembarque at Cape Francois. And, the Rendevouz was Appointed
at the point of Land near Manchianeal Bay on the North side of the Island.

The 22d. of April the Fleet arrived in Samana Bay, where six days were
loitered away, the Commadore (according to Collo[nel] Lillingston's account) diverting Himself all that time with Women and Musick.

The 28th. they weighed and on the 4th. of May arrived at Manchinial
Bay. The 6th. the Major General of the Spanish Forces, left them in order
to Consult the English Commanders, and it was Concluded to Attack the
French Fort at Cape Francois. But the length of the march and the heat of
the Weather prevented their Comeing till the 12 when They were joined
by Major Lillingston's (the Collo[nel]'s Brother and 200 men) and, as Soon
as They were landed the whole Fleet weighed and Stood for Cape Francois, where the rest of the Men were to disembarque.

At Cape Francois the French had a small Fort which They made a shew
of Defending; but on our Men being landed, they were Apprehensive of
being cut off Their Retreat and blew up the Fort and marched away, carrying every thing They could with Them to Port de Paix, the Principal Fortification of the whole Colony.

69. Charles II of Spain (1661–1700) ascended to the throne at the death of his father,
Philip IV, on September 17, 1665.

The 27 of May the Spanish General sent an Officer to Acquaint Collo[nel] Lillingston, that having done all the damage to the Enemy, in His March, that was possible, He was now ready to join Forces, and March together, to Attack the French in their Principal Fortress.

Accordingly the English and Spanish Forces joined and Marched to Port de Paix; But, though the Spaniards informed our Men, they should get there in 4 days, Yet They made it Sixteen, being incommoded with many Violent Showers of Rain, and passing deep Rapid Rivers which They were obliged to wade through having no Horse. And the excessive Rains having spoiled all their Bread, neither Officer or Soldier, for 5 days had any Food but wild Cabages, Purcelain, Oranges, and wild Fruits to Subsist on Yet notwithstanding all these difficulties They lost no more than 12 men; but, the English Soldiers were so much incommoded with the weight of their Regimentalls, cut away the Skirts and pleats of their Coats, to make them lighter and fitter for Travelling in that hot Climate.

The 13. of June They came before the Fort, and Sent advice, to the Fleet, of their want of Provisions, and Bread in particular. In the meantime, the Principal Officers viewed the Ground, fixed upon proper places for Batteries and a place to land the Canon and Ammunition.

But, it was afterwards Resolved that the Squadron should sail to the Westward, of Port de Paix, where there was a Commodious Hill nearer than the first intended Battery.

The 15th. the Commadore landed 400 Seamen, and the four following Days were spent in putting the Cannon and Mortars ashore. But, it was with great difficulty and hard labour they got them to the Camp, being obliged by Strength of hands to draw them over a Bog. And as soon as they were planted, they began to fire upon the Fort with six pieces of Cannon, four small sakers and two Mortars. The 29 they threw Several Bombs into the Fort, one of which fell into a House where there was several Barrels of Powder which blew up, and a great many People were blown up in the Air with the House.

The 30th. the Mortars played again into the Fort and another House with powder blew up in the same manner.

The Governour expecting a General Storm and being resolved not to Surrender upon Articles packed up every thing they could carry with them, and on the 3d. of July between the Hours of 12 and one in the Night Sallied out with 300 White Men and 200 Armed Negroes. They fell in with the Body of Seamen undiscovered, poured in a Volley of shot among them, which put them in some Confusion and faced them till His whole Body Men[,] Women and Children Marched off. But, the Fort being deserted our Forces immediately took possession, and found 80 Cannon mounted, with great store of Cannon and Shot.

After this Defeat it was intended to attack Leogan and Petit Guavis, but neither the English or Spanish General thought it adviseable considering the weakness of the Troops through Sickness and Fatigue; so that the Fort was demolished and the Stores carried off.

On the 17th. of July all the Troops Artillery, Plunder, and Prisoners being sent on board, the Fleet weighed, and on the 23d. arrived at Jamaica. Where having refitted His Ships, He sailed for England the 3d. of September following, leaving the *Reserve, Hampshire* and *Ruby* to guard the Island till further Orders. And the *Swan* to Convoy the Trade.

Thus ended this Expedition and though it did not Answer Expectation, through the disagreement of the Principal land and Sea Officer (which has often been the Case before and Since, and defeated several Designs which were laid, and would have been of Infinite Service to the Nation, had they been as well Executed). Yet the damage done the Enemy, and the Booty taken from them, were not so inconsiderable as to be meanly Represented.

For in 60 days the Confederates ruined all the French Settlements for a hundred Miles; took about 1000 Negroes which were sold in Jamaica, demolished two Forts after taking 140 pieces of Cannon, a great quantity of Ammunition and Naval Stores; and the Seamen got plunder to the Value of £40000 at least. The Damage the Enemy Sustained thereby was Computed in the whole to amount to £200000 Ster[ling], beside displanting a whole Colony leaving the Inhabitants scattered in the Woods where many of them perished with Sickness and for want of Necessaries.

In 1696 the Assembly hired[,] Victualled and Manned two large Sloops, to Cruise and Guard the Coasts of the Island, from the Insults and Depredations of the French Privateers. They also raised 200 men, in order to Reduce the Rebellious Negroes, who began to make Excursions, and were become very troublesome. For which Services £4303 was laid and levied on the English and £750 on the Jews.

And, Capt[ain] John Moses[70] who Commanded His Majestie's Ship the *Reserve*, having got Information that the Renegado Grubins, was set[t]ling a Plantation among the French on Hispaniola, put 50 of His Men on board of a Sloop and went in Person to fetch Him off the Island. Accordingly he Anchored in a private place, landed 40 men well Armed and marched 7 or 8 miles up the Country, with the Assistance of a Guide He had with Him, and Surrounded the House of Grubins who hap[pe]ned to be within, and was just going to Dinner. He was immediately Seized, with all His Negroes and Effects, and Carried to Jamaica, where He was (in a few days after) tried[,] hanged and quartered on the S[outh] W[est] point of Port Royal, from thence Called Grubins Point. His Head and limbs were fixed on Poles in the same Place. This was the Fate of that Treacherous and Infamous Fellow, who met with the Punishment He highly deserved, for Aiding and Assisting His Majestie's Enemie's in Invading and plundering His Native Country and Committing many other Enormities.

70. Captain John Moses was a British naval officer who died in the West Indies in 1703.

Nor is this the only Instance of the Conduct and Gallant Behaviour of that Worthy Gentleman who did this Signal Service to the Island, for He Distinguished Himself on many other Occasions, by His Activity and Zeal in the Execution of His Duty, which justly deserved to be mentioned in the Memoirs of this Island with all the Honour that is due to His Merit and Memory. Though I shall only mention the following particular Instance with a few general Observations.

One of His Majestie's Ships, of 20 Guns, being on a Cruise met with a large French Merchant Ship of Force bound to Leogane, and after Engaging Her some short time quitted Her and returned to Port Royal. The Capt[ai]n in Vindication of Himself, alledged that she was much superior in Force to His Own ship. Capt[ai]n Moses, on this Examined more particularly into the Affair, and having got a further Information of every Circumstance relating to the French Ship as well as the Action, Manned a large Sloop that was fitted and in a readiness to Sail (His own Ship being on the Careen) and made the best of His way to Leogane, where He found the aforementioned Ship at Anchor. He boldly run close on Her Quarter and Fired into Her. The Enemy who was prepared returned the Fire with their small Arms and Such Guns as they Could bring to bear; and being surprised at the Attempt of so small a Vessel, by way of Ridicule Slung their Runners and Tackle to hoist Her in when she came along side. Nevertheless, Capt[ai]n Moses took an opportunity, laid Her on board, and soon became Master of the Ship. He then Slipped Her Cables and brought Her away, not withstanding the Fire from the Breast works ashore. On His arrival at Jamaica, He thanked the Capt[ai]n of the other Man of War, for having given Him an Opportunity of taking a very Valuable Prize.

That Gentleman commanded at times, Several of His Majestie's Ships on this Station and was so far from declining it, as many Others have done since, that He always chose it, for whenever, He returned from thence and His Ship paid off, He immediately sollicited for another to go the same Voyage. And, His Behaviour in all other Respects, was so agreeable to the Inhabitants of the Country, that He was the most Popular[,] Respected and Esteemed of any Gentleman of the same Rank in the Navy, that ever was in this Island. He was at the Invasion of Guadaloupe in 1703, and appointed Collo[nel] of a Regiment formed of the Seamen; afterwards. He came down to Jamaica Commander of His Majestie's Ship the *Anglesea* and died at Port Royal.

In February 1696, the Island was alarmed at the advice of Mons[ieu]r Pointis'[71] Arrival at Petit Guavas, with a strong Squadron and 3000 land Forces, which were to be joined with 2000 Privateers raised at Martinico and Hispaniola. An Embargo was laid, Martial law declared, and the Island

71. Bernard Desjean, Baron de Pointis (1645–1707), was a French admiral and privateer who in 1697 undertook a successful raid on Cartagena that made him extremely rich.

thereupon put in a posture of Defence. But, it afterwards appeared His Design was against Carthagena, for on the 12 of March he came in Sight of Port Royal and only made a Feint, in His way thither.

The 15th. of May arrived Vice Admiral Nevil[72] with 25 Sail of English and Dutch Men of War, who were sent after Mons[ieu]r Pointi and to Convoy Home the Galleons. He intended to Sail again, as soon as He had taken in some Wood and Water, but was unfortunately detained in Port by a strong Easterly Wind or Sea Breez[e], which blew Night and Day till the 25th., when He Sailed with a small Gale off the shore.

The 27 being half seas over, they discovered a Fleet of Ships standing westward; upon which the Admiral immediately tacked and Stood after them, with a pressed Sail. The next morning they perceived Them to be Ten French men of War and two Fly Boats; and the *Warwick* came up and Fired at one of Them, but she being a better Sailor got clear, soon after the same ship came up with one of the Fly Boats, and taking Her found, she had on board 800 Barrels of Powder, with other Ammunition and Warlike Stores, and 100 Negroes, the whole valued at £20000, Ship and Cargo.

In the afternoon, four of our Ships being near Them, Mons[ieu]r Pointi drew his Squadron into order of Battle, and fired several shot at the Bristol. But, Mons[ieu]r de Labbe[,] His Vice Admiral, and another Ship left Him, and made off; as the whole Fleet did in the Evening.

Our Squadron Continued the Chace two Days, and two Nights, but could not come up to Engage the Enemy which was occasioned chiefly by most of our Ship's Splitting their Sails and looseing their Masts. By which means we lost the great Booty Monsieur Pointi met with at Carthagena, which he had taken, plundered, and dismantled.

The 6th. of June, He [Nevill] stood over for Petit Guavas and Leogane but not being able to fetch either of those places, He bore away and Anchored again at Port Royal the 19th. of the same month.

S[i]r William Beeston having informed Vice Admiral Nevil on His return to this Island, that it would be of great Service, if Petit Guavis was destroyed, He detached Rear Admiral Meez[73] thither with nine Men of War. They sailed from Port Royal the 22d. of June, and on the 28th. at half an hour after three in the morning, the Rear Admiral with Collo[nel] Kirby[,] Capt[ain]s Lyton[,] Holmes, Julius, Elliot, and Moor, and 400 Men, landed a Mile Eastward of Petit Guavas, and then Marched directly to the Town. The Sloop with some Boats which had on board about 100 Men, not being able to keep up with Him, He thought the Place might be taken with much more Ease by Surprise, with Those Men He had, than by discov-

72. Vice Admiral John Nevell (d. 1697) was an officer in the Royal Navy. He is best known for the failed attempt to intercept the treasure-laden fleet of Pointis after its raid on Cartagena in 1697. He died later that year off the coast of Virginia from yellow fever.

73. Rear Admiral George Meez (d. 1697).

ering Themselves, which They must have done, had they waited for the Rest; and therefore at the Dawn of the Day, He marched directly to, and immediately Siezed the Main Gate. He then sent one hundred Men to Secure two Batteries of four Guns Each; and while this was doing most of the French quitted the Town.

At Sun Rise, the Seamen were no longer to be kept from plundering; and in two hours most of them were so Drunk, that the Rear Admiral was obliged to set Fire to the Town much sooner than He intended, or He could not have depended on Fifty sober and Serviceable Men. And, thus both Officers and Men were deprived of the Reward They so justly deserved for the Bravery and indefatigable Industry They shewed on this Occasion.

Vice Admiral Nevil having furnished the Fleet with Wood and Water, sailed from Port Royal the 29 of June, the next day He was joined by Rear Admiral Meez, and proceeded to the Havanna to Convoy the Galleons to Cadis. But, the Spaniards not Accepting of the Offer He sailed from thence for England; and in the Voyage both the Admirals, and several of the Captains died. The 11th. of December following, the Treaty of Ryswick was proclaimed in Jamaica, and all further Hostilities against the French prohibited.

At this time the Inhabitants began to recover their late misfortunes, occasioned by the Earthquake and the French Invasion, most of the Houses and Sugar Mills which were thrown down or destroyed being Rebuilt. Except in the District of St. Thomas in the East, which was in a manner deserted, very few choosing to Settle there again in many Years after.

Trade likewise flourished and brought in great Wealth, particularly the Assiento which was a very Beneficial Scheme, to the Nation as well as to Jamaica, and the principal Meand of the Island being in some degree Restored to its former State.

Port Royal was also Rebuilt (that is all the land which then remained above water, containing about 14 Acres) and increased in People who were invited to settle there by its Convenience for Trade.

In 1698 Fort William with a Strong Battery were ordered to be built at the N[orth] end of Port Royal, to Secure the passage between that and the Pallisadoes. Port Royal being then and for many years after a small Island, disjoined from the rest of the Island, by the land being sunk in the Great Earthquake and the Sea having a free passage between, insomuch that Sloops and small Vessells might enter the Harbour that way.

In August S[i]r William Beeston Sent his Majestie's Ship the *Ruperts Prize*, to Darien with orders to take possession for the Crown of England, and to hoist the British Flag, which was accordingly done; and as it is Supposed on Advice of the Scot's Design to make a Settlement there.

The 2d. of November following the Scots Colony arrived at Darien and began to Fortify the narrow part of the Isthmus, which might have been Easily Defended against the Spaniards and Indians, had They been enabled and Encouraged to prosecute the Design, but being in Want of Provisions and Other Necessaries and not having mon[e]y or Credit to purchase them, They were obliged to Abandon the Place and retire to Jamaica.

They arrived at Port Royal in February following, when the Commadore in the *St. Andrew* Saluting the Fort in going in the Harbour, one of the Wads of her Guns fell into some Combustible stuff, in the Fort, which took Fire, and being near the Magazine the Flame communicated it self to the Door, and in all probability would in a short time have blown up the Fort and destroyed the Town. The People were in the utmost Consternation, most of them quitted the Fortifications and Houses, Ran into the Sea, and kept only their heads above Water, Expecting the Blast every Moment. But, a Sailor who was Drunk, pulled off his Jacket and Shirt, Steeped them in a Cistern of Water which was in the Fort, and Stifled the Fire, on the Door. The Poor Fellow was Rewarded by the Inhabitants, though He had not what He deserved; and Major Charles Hobby[74] who pretended to merit of the Act, going to England soon after was Knighted for the Service though He had very little if any share in it.

The Men belonging to the Scots' ships deserting them, not more than one or two returned Home; the rest for want of Care, were sunk or destroyed in Port Royal. Many of that Colony Set[t]led on this Island, and succeeded very well, some of them are Still living.

In November 1698, Rear Admiral Bembow[75] was ordered to the West Indies and Sailed from Portsmouth the 29th. of that Month, with the *Gloucester, Falmouth, Lynn* and *Soldadoes Prize*. He arrived at Nevis in February following, from thence He proceeded to St. Martha, and Ranged the Coast to Carthagena, where He obliged the Governour to deliver up some Ships He had Seized on account of the Scots Settlement at Darien. He then stood away for Jamaica and on His Arrival, was desired by the Governour and Merchants, to Sail to Porto Bello and to demand Satisfaction of the Spaniards, for Several Depredations, they had Committed against the English.

He sailed accordingly and arrived there the 29th. of March, upon His Demand, of Satisfaction, the Admiral of the Barlovento Fleet, at whose Instigation those Depredations had been Chiefly Committed, gave him a rough Answer, and Alledged the Attempts of the Scotch, whose Interest He accounted to be the Same with that of England, as a Reason for it. But,

74. Sir Charles Hardy was a merchant in Port Royal who represented that parish in the Jamaica Assembly of 1698–99.

75. John Bembow (1653–1702) was a British naval officer and commander in chief in the West Indies in 1698–1700. In 1701, he returned to the West Indies in pursuit of Du Casse and died of wounds at Port Royal.

after several Messages, He was at length assured, if He would retire from before the Port; every thing should be restored. However, after His Departure, the faithless Spaniards, not withstanding their Solemn Promises, never made any Compliance.

In October 1699 His Majestie's ships the *South Sea Castle* Capt[ain] Stepney, and the *Biddeford* Capt[ain] Searl were lost on point Bague, near the Isle of Ash in their Passage from England to Jamaica. And, in February following Rear Admiral Bembow returned to England.

In [blank] 1701, Brigadier Selwin's[76] Regiment of Foot under the Command of L[ieutenan]t Collo[nel] Handasy'd[77] arrived in this Island; and were quartered among the Plantations and in the Towns.

And the 30th. of July, His Majesty was pleased to revoke the powers granted to S[i]r William Beeston, and to appoint William Selwin Esq[uir]e who was promoted to the Rank of a Major General of His Majestie's Forces, to be Capt[ai]n General and Commander in chief of this Island.

The 5th. of December Vice Admiral Benbow arrived at Port Royal from England with two third and Eight fourth Rate men of War.

And, the 22nd. of January 1701, Major General Selwin arrived at Port Royal, and with Him one Fourth, one Fifth Rate a Bomb Vessel, a Fire Ship, a Hulk, and three Ships laden with Naval Stores. Collo[nel] Brewer,[78] with His Regiment came over at the same time, and were Quartered in the same manner, as the other Regiment, who were Sent for the Security and Defence of this Island, a War with France being then daily Expected.

S[i]r William Beeston imbarqued for England, in April following, on board His Majestie's Ship the *Fowey*, and died there about two Years after His Arrival. This Gentleman, when He came first to Jamaica was a Merchant, Resided many Years at Port Royal, and Set[t]led a Sugar Work in Liguinea called Norbrook. He was several times chosen a Member of the As-

76. William Selwyn (1650–1702). After a successful military career under William III, Selwyn was appointed governor of Jamaica in 1701 and arrived in the colony on January 21, 1702, with instructions, devised by himself, to fortify the island. He died before being able to put them into effect. Cundall, *Governors of Jamaica in the First Half of the Eighteenth Century*, 1–12.

77. Thomas Handasyde (1645?–1729) was an army officer who served in Ireland, Flanders, and Newfoundland in the 1690s before, as a brevet colonel, he arrived in Jamaica as part of the army in January 1702 and remained regimental commander until succeeded by his son, Roger, in April 1712. In June 1702, he became lieutenant-governor and in July 1704 governor, a post he held until he was superseded by Archibald Hamilton in July 1711. Returning to England after his replacement, he bought an estate in Huntingdonshire where he died at the age of eighty-four. Ibid., 26–51.

78. Brewer (?–1702), whose first name is unknown, was commissioned as lieutenant-governor and would have succeeded Selwyn except that he died early in 1702. Thus, Peter Beckford became acting governor until Handasyde took over.

sembly, and afterwards appointed a Member of the Council and Collo[nel] of a Regiment of Militia.

He was a Gentleman of great Temperance and Moderation; for He was Contented with His Sallary and the legal Perquisites of His Government, and did not form any Schemes to augment them; nor was He ever accused of any Acts of Power or Oppression. But, He was too Easy and Relax[ed] in His Administration, Submitted to be under the Influence of some leading Men of the Country, generally liv[e]d like a Private Gentleman, and did not keep up the Part and Dignity of a Governour. For, He spent most of His time during the Intervals of the Settings of the Assembly and the Grand Court at Kingston (where He had a House of His own in the Parade) without the Guards which usually attend the Governour's Person, or even a Centinal at His Door. And when He Visited or Dined with any Gentleman in the Town or Country, He was Seldom Accompanied with more than one or two Friends, and a Single Footman. This part of His Behaviour was Commendable as well as Agreeable, because it prevented that Emulation and Expence which generally Attends Entertaining of the Governours in our Colonies.

General Selwin's first Care, like an able Experienced Soldier, was to View the Fortifications and put them in order. He also Reviewed the several Regiments of Militia, and directed them to be Instructed in Military Exercises, that they might be fit for Service in Case of Action. And Ordered Capt[ai]n Hawkins[,] the Engineer, to take a more particular Survey of all Fortified and Defensible Places and to make a Report of Them to Him in Writing.

At this time the Inhabitants were greatly divided in Parties, Occasioned by the Emulation and private Piques of some leading men of the Country, two of which were aiming at the same Ascendancy over the General, as They had over His Predecessor: But, He seeing thro[ugh] their Schemes, took an Opportunity one morning when They were both at His Levee, with many Other Gentlemen to tell Them; That He was greatly Obliged to Them, for the Information, They had from time to time given Him, of the Constitution and other matters relating to the Country, and was come to this Resolution. I will, said He Collo[nel] L—w,[79] be entirely under your Influence and direction for one Week; and the week following Collo[nel] L—d,[80] I will be under Yours: But, from thence forward, I am determined, Gentlemen, to Govern this Island my Self.

Neither of them thought proper to Reply, nor did They ever make the same Attempt during His Administration.

His Excellency having ordered Writs for choosing of a New Assembly,

79. Henry Low.
80. Richard Lloyd.

They met accordingly on the 17th. of March, when He made the following Speech.

Mr. Speaker, and Gentlemen
of the Assembly.

I have called you together with all the Dispatch I could, and I hope to find every man in a Temper Suitable to the Necessity of your Affairs.

I need not tell you the State of the Revenue, refer[r]ing that to your inspection: But, I am sorry for your own Sakes it is so far lessened, at a time, when your Defence requires it should be much greater than ever.

The Main Business I have to recommend to you is the Care of your Selves, and of those Gentlemen who are sent to Defend You. I mean Building of Fortifications and Barracks, which is the Easiest and most usefull way of Quartering of Soldiers[;] on these two Points I shall be ready to give my Advice and Assistance, and likewise in whatever else you shall think will be for the Service of the King and Country, only I must desire your immediate Application to the former least the Vigilance of our Enemies force us to Arms, while you are deliberating upon a Law.

With the Advice of the Admiral and Council I have taken up two Vessels for Fireships, which Account shall be laid before you, wherein you will See how much care has been taken to make the charge easy to the Country.

I have Reviewed the greatest part of your Regiments and Troops, who I find are, in general, good Men; and I hope you will take my Opinion and Advice, in making some Amendments to the Militia Act.

It may be Expected that I should say something of your Civil Rights, I therefore being a Stranger will unveil my Self, so that every man may See what He is to Expect from me.

When any real Grievances are duly Represented I shall readily concur with you in Redressing Them; but I hope no Imaginary ones will disturb the publick peace or Business.

Liberty and Property are the Foundation and Blessing of our Constitution, and I would no more Invade Either of them, than I would sacrifice my Son; nor will I lessen the King's Prerogative any more than I would betray my Father. And, when His Service or the Defence of the Country require it, I am ready to Expose my Self to any Fatigue or Danger.

It was in perfect Obedience to His Majestie's Command that I came hither, whose Goodness to You and Care of you was my greatest Encouragement. And during my Stay, Justice in all things shall be my Rule, and at my Return, His Majestie's Gracious Acceptance of my small Services, will be at least an Honourable Reward for the hazards of this Climate. In the mean time I shall Expect a just deference to my Authority, and as much Consideration in every other point, as has been shewn to my Predecessors.

The Assembly thereupon brought in and passed a short Bill for Continuing the two Regiments in their present Quarters,[81] until some further and better provision could be made for Them. And presented an Address to His Excellency thanking Him for His Care in preventing the Exportation of Flower and other Provisions, to the French and Spaniards, at the Dangerous juncture. And, prayed His Excellency to restrain likewise their being furnished with Arms, Ammunition and Warlike Stores, until a Bill could be brought in and had His Assent thereto for that purpose.

And a Committee of the Council and Assembly waited on His Excellency to desire His Opinion and Advice, in Building Fortifications and Barracks on which He was pleased to give the same in Writing, the Substance of which is as follows.

Port Morant I am informed is a Place of Consequence to this Island in regard to its Situation and Harbour, therefore I am of Opinion a new Fort ought to be Built there.

S[eno]r James Del Castillo's Fort is of no Consequence, but, in regard to its Situation it deserves Your Consideration, whether it ought to remain in its present Circumstances, or not. If you think fit to buy it, it may be with a small charge more be made Capable of lodging 200 Soldiers. The Rock line is at present of no Defence against Cannon, but sufficient in that pass against small Arms. It may be relieved from time to time with Soldiers from St. James's Fort. And, it wants a Guard Room, and Draw-Bridge, also the Ditch to be made broader and deeper.

Port Royal I will not advise any new Works to be made believing if those there, are kept in due order, and Guns mounted upon the new Wall, with the Assistance of the Ships drawn into a Line, that Harbour may be Secure, though we are not Masters of the Sea.

Musquito Point, may be Necessary and Advisable to Build a Fort at, if the Foundation be good. But, in regard to its unhealthy Situation, and for saving mon[e]y I imagine that a Floating Battery will be more proper, for the Place, much Cheaper, and also removeable on any Occasion.

Spanish Town I think ought to be made a Place of Retreat and Some Security for Women and Negroes though I cannot yet determine which is the best way of doing it, therefore desire other Gentlemen will Employ their thoughts about it. But, a Magazine and Storehouse will be absolutely Necessary there.

Old Harbour is a place of Dangerous Consequence for an Enemy to land at, there being nothing but Black River to make a stand, between that and Spanish Town. Therefore I am of Opinion a small Fort at West Chester, and a good Barrack for Soldiers to be Built near it, is the most that can be done there.

81. An Act for Quartering Officers and Soldiers, March 1702, in *Acts of Assembly*, 93.

Carlisle Bay the Gentlemen of Vere, I am informed have Voluntarily raised £500. for a line of Guns there, I know not Whether that sum be sufficient but I think they ought to be Encouraged by you with a Supply (if wanting) because Necessary for Their Security.

I must likewise Recommend the North side to your Consideration, for I have not Yet seen that part of the Island.

Places proper for Barracks.

At Port Morant and St. James Del Castillo's.

At Port Royal, near Fort Charles.

At Spanish Town.

At Black River Bridge, or some other Convenient place near old Harbour.

The Assembly accordingly came to the following Resolutions.

1. That Port Morant be Fortified, and a line of 12 Guns be added to the Fort. That a Barrack be Built there for 30 Officers and Soldiers. Also a Barrack at Morant and Another at Yallahs. That they be all substantially built (and Covered) with boarded Floors. That the Barracks at Morant, and Yallahs, be well stockadoed, or Pallisadoed, with Flankers to both of Them. And, that the Soldiers be provided with a good Plantain Bed, Pillows, and Blankets.

2. That S[enor]r James Del Castillo's Fort ought not to remain in its present Circumstances, and that it be Rented.

3. That the Rock line be repaired and such alterations made there as His Excellency shall think Necessary.

4. That Boarded Barracks be built at Port Royal.

5. That the Fortifying Musquito Point be left to His Excellency's discretion.

6. That Houses be rented at Spanish Town Sufficient to lodge 100 Men, and that a Fort and Magazine been erected there.

7. That a Fort and Barracks be Built at West Chester.

8. That Barracks be Built at Carlisle Bay, and the Fortification be refer[r]ed to the Generalls Discretion.

As to the North side, It was the Opinion of the Council as well as the Assembly, that two light Frigotts and two Sloops, were necessary to Cruise on that part of the Island for Their Protection.

These proceedings I thought necessary to transcribe, because they may Serve as Rules and Instructions to the Inhabitants hereafter, and probably the means of some improvements being made thereon. And in Order to it, I beg leave to Recommend to the Consideration of the Gentlemen of the Island, Whether a Battery at Plumb Point, another at Salt pond Hill, with intrenchments at Green Bay, and the passage from thence to Spanish Town, are not only Necessary, but will greatly Contribute to Their Security, if not render that part of the Country impregnable.

While the Affairs of the Island were in this agreeable Station, in Regard to the Governour and the People (between whom there was a perfect Harmony and good Agreement) He was to their inexpressible Concern taken ill the 1st. and died on the 5th. of April 1702, Universally lamented.

He was a Gentleman of strict Honour and Virtue, and by His Courteous, upright, Behaviour, He gained in the short time He lived among Them the Affections, and Confidence of all Ranks of People in this Island, as well as the Officers and Soldiers of the Regular Troops. Their loss in Him was the greater, because He was an Excellent Officer having Served under King William in all the Campai[g]ns His Majesty made in Flanders; and a War with France and Spain was daily Expected.

By His Death the Government devolved on Peter Beckford Esq[ui]r[e] the Elder, who had a Dormant Commission to Succeed as L[ieutenan]t Governour.

The Assembly, who adjourned, on account of General Selwin's indisposition, met on the 14th. of April According to Adjournment. When the L[ieutenan]t Governour made a Speech to Them, wherein He expressed the great loss the Island sustained in an Experienced General, and a Worthy Governour, on whose Character only, Their Security partly consisted. And that They could not Express, in a more Acceptable manner, Their Dutifull Acknowledgments to His Majesty in Obedience to whose Commands He came Over; Nor, the Regard They ought to have to His Memory, than to make some Return to His Remains, whose more particular loss required their Serious Thoughts and Regard.

The Assembly accordingly took this matter into Consideration, and Voted that the sum of £2500 be raised and presented to the Remains of the deceased General; which was accordingly done; and the Lady[82] with Her Son (Collo[nel] Selwin[83]) (who is still living) embarqued for England soon after.

And, upon a Representation that there was in the hands of Divers Persons great sums of money, arising by the Sale of Effects belonging to unknown Proprietors who were lost in the Earthquake. And other Publick Monies which had been received and were not applied to the intended Service nor Accounted for notwithstanding they had been Complained of by former Assemblies.

That S[i]r William, in particular, had in His Hands great sums of monies, Arising from the Sales of the Goods and Effects of Pirates; also the sum of £900, or thereabouts transmitted from England for the payment of Subscribers to Capt[ai]n Harrison's Ship sent out for the Publick Service, and

---

82. Albinia Selwyn (c. 1658–1738) married William Selwyn in 1681 and bore him three sons and three daughters. She appears never to have remarried and died at her husband's Gloucestershire estate at age eighty. Cundall, *Governors of Jamaica in the First Half of the Eighteenth Century*, 11–12.

83. Henry Selwyn was the youngest son of William. Ibid., 12.

£4000, received by order of Her late Majesty as a Benevolence to Persons distressed by the French Invasion in the late War, many of the Sufferers having complained that They had no Share thereof.

The Assembly thereupon Addressed the L[ieutenan]t Governour that S[i]r William Beeston, might not depart the Island before He and others concerned, accounted for the same.

And, a Committee of the Council and Assembly being appointed to Enquire more particularly into those Affairs, They Reported; That Colonel Low[84] informed them, by order, the L[ieutenan]t Governour, was of Opinion S[i]r William Beeston was accountable to the King only. But, in Regard to the House, He was desirous of giving Them a further answer, which He did not doubt would be to their Satisfaction. That as to the Effects of unknown Proprietors who were lost in the Earthquake, the Gentlemen of the Council who were concerned, desired that their Accounts, which They were ready to produce might be Examined, in Vindication of Themselves as well as in Regard to the Satisfaction of the House. And that S[i]r William Beeston was no ways concerned, which They affirmed to Clear His Honour in that point.

That as to Piratical monies and Effects, S[i]r William Beeston had remitted them to England, According to an Instruction from His Majesty, which Collo[nel] Low delivered a Copy of, to the Committee, and is as follows.

In Case any Goods, mon[e]y or other Effects of Pirates or Piratically taken shall be brought in or found within His Majestie's Island of Jamaica, or taken on board any Ship or Vessel, You are to Cause the same to be seized, and secured in the hands of His Majestie's Officers, until you shall have given His Majesty an Account thereof and received His pleasure concerning the disposal of the same.

Collo[nel] Knight attested to the Committee that the Sum Subscribed for fitting out Capt[ain] Harrison's Ship amounted to between £320 and £330, and not more. And that the Subscribers were to have a premium or advance of 40 P[er]Cent if she made a Voyage: But she turning Pirate, the said Sum with the advance was received by S[i]r William Beeston as Piratical Mon[e]y, by the hands of Mr. Samuel Low; and that He knows not what became of it.

And, as to the £4000 mentioned in the Address to be Her late Majestie's Benevolence money, Mr. Josiah Heathcote[85] declared that if Collo[nel] Lillingston's Regiment had not been broke the Bounty mon[e]y designed by her Majesty would have amounted to so much. But the £10000 was paid to the Soldiers, and the Exchange or advance at 15 p[er]c[en]t amounting

84. Samuel Low.

85. Josiah Heathcote was a brother of Gilbert, the merchant and agent, and resided in Jamaica for fifteen years, first at Port Royal and then, after the earthquake of 1692, in Kingston. Ibid., 30, 44; Cundall, *Historic Jamaica*, 158.

to £1500, being the Bounty was distributed among the Sufferers by the Invasion According to Her Majestie's Instructions.

The [blank] of June 1702, the War was declared with France and Spain; and His Majestie's Ships the *Falmouth*, *Ruby* and *Experiment* being Sent on a Cruise off Petit Guavas returned with 4 prizes, one of which was a very Rich ship of 24 Guns (but could mount 40), and 190 men bound to France. His Majestie's Ship the *Bristol* also took a French Man of War called the *Gloriana*, and Sent Her into Port Royal.

The Vice Admiral Benbow detached Rear Admiral Whetstone[86] with two third, three fourth Rates and a Fireship to intercept Mons[ieu]r Du Casse who as He was informed was Expected at Pourt Louis the S[outh] W[est] end of Hispaniola, to destroy the English and Dutch Trade.

The 11th. of July the Vice Admiral sailed from Port Royal with two third, Six fourth Rates, one Fire Ship, a Bomb Vessel and a Tender, designing to join the Rear Admiral, But having advice by the *Colchester* and *Pendenis* that Mons[ieu]r Du Cass was Expected at Leogane, He made for that Port. On His arrival there He saw Several Ships at Anchor near the Town, and one which was under Sail was taken by His Boats. He chased a man of War of 50 Guns which run ashore and blew up. The next morning 3 other Ships and a Sloop were taken, one of 16 Guns was sunk, another of 18 Guns which was halled in close under a Fort, the Boats were sent in and not only had the good Fortune to burn Her but brought off Several Ships laden with Wine, Brandy &c. He proceeded from thence to Cape Donna Maria on the W[est] end of Hispaniola, where He was informed that Mons[ieu]r Du Cass was gone to Carthagena, and was bound from thence to Porto Bello. He resolved therefore to Sail to that Coast in quest of Him with two third and four fourth Rates, Rear Admiral Whetstone, who had taken a French man of War of 18 Guns and two Sloops being returned to Jamaica with Instructions for the Safety of the Island.

The L[ieutenan]t Governour Collo[nel] Beckford having granted Commissions to divers Privateers, who on the declaration of the War, began to flock to this Island; the following Vessells consorted and Sailed from Port Royal, the 24th. of July Vizt.

	Guns	Men
The *Bastamenta* Capt[ain] John Rash	8	74
The *Thomas & Elizabeth* Capt[ain] Murray	8	63
The *Phenix* Capt[ain] Plowman	8	56
The Blessing Capt[ain] Brown	10	79

86. William Whetstone (?–1711) served as rear admiral in the West Indies, 1702–3, and as commander in chief in 1705–6. Knighted in 1705, he was cashiered in 1707 for allowing a convoy to be captured by de Farbin, a French privateer.

On the 28th. at 6 in the Evening they arrived at the Island of Palma. Here it was agreed that Capt[ain] Brown and Capt[ain] Murray with their Companies and Detachments from the other two Sloops should attack Toulu. They landed the 31st. at night in a Sandy Bay, about 4 miles from the Town and Orders were given to March directly. Capt[ain] Rash in the Van, Capt[ain] Brown in the Center, and Capt[ain] Murray in the Rear, being in all two hundred and Seventeen Men. They marched along the Sea Shore up to the knees in Water, and in about half an hour halted at the Walls of the Castle not a Pistol Shot off. They were all immediately challenged by the Centinel, and the Garrison fired a Volley of small Arms, which was returned by the Privateers who thereupon entered the Fort and Town finding the Spaniards had deserted them without firing a second Volley.

But, the Privateers were dissappointed in their Expectations, for the Spaniards having Intelligence of the Design, had two Days before removed their Riches into the Country. However They plundered and carried away such Goods and Effects as the Spaniards had left, the Guns were Spiked up and orders given to fire the Town, which was done accordingly.

They returned to Palmas in the afternoon and sailed from thence the 31st. for the Samblass Cays on the 9th. of August. They were joined by two other Privateers from Jamaica namely the *Dragon* Galley Capt[ain] Pilkington and the *Greyhound* Capt[ain] Golsing. The former acquainted them that His Majestie's Ships the *Gloucester* and *Sea Horse*, had attacked the Fort of Porto Bello, while they landed 300 men from the Sloops, but before they could enter the Town the Spring of the *Gloucester's* Cable gave way, which obliged them to retire.

At the Samblass Cays they were joined by the *Neptune* Capt[ain] Gandy, and two other Privateers called the *Content* and the *Edward and Sarah*. The former had on board Don Pedro[,] one of the Princes or chiefs of Darien who entered into Articles to assist them with 300 men against the Spaniards, and it was agreed to march and Attack the Town and Mines of St. Maria. Accordingly they landed on the 19th. at the mouth of a River 482 English men beside Indians, the 20th. they proceeded from thence and after an exceeding difficult march by Reason of the badness of the ways, Steepness of the Mountains, and many Rivers they had to pass Over, they came, on the 30th, within two Miles of the Town of Cana, Capt[ain] Gandy and Golding with Pedro being in the Van with 50 English and 30 Indians, made a halt, while the rest came up; and the Spaniards seeing no more made some Resistance, but discovering the rest they deserted the Town and retreated to a Hill covered with Woods. However, They were soon drove from thence, leaving behind them the Effects they had moved there, which was immediately Secured by the Privateers, and Carried into the Church, as they did the next day the Gold, Silver and other Riches they met with in the Town.

The 1st. of September, They sent out a Company of Men with Spaniards and Negroes to the Mines to wash the Gold from the Ores, and made
five pound weight nine Ounces in less than a day. The next day the Scouts
brought in more Spaniards and Negroes, whom they employed in the same
manner and made a great Quantity of Gold every day. The 4th. they made
fourteen pound weight of Gold and sixteen the day following, when they
thought of getting provisions and Mules to Carry away their Sick Men and
plunder and to return to their Sloops. The 7th. they left the Town and after a tiresome march, on the 19 got safe on board their Sloops.

The 21. the Commanders held a Consultation and it was agreed to
renew the *Consortship* for one month and that they should divide into 3
Squadrons, the *Neptune, Blessing* and *Edward and Sarah* to Cruise off Porto
Bello, the *Phenix, Thomas and Elizabeth* and the *Content* to Cruise off Car-
thagena and the *Bastimentos, Greyhound* and *Dragon* off the mouth of the
River of Jacco.

It will be too tedious and unnecessary to follow these three little Squadrons, in their Respective Stations, and therefore shall only observe that
two of Them after taking several prizes though none of any great Value,
returned to Jamaica. But, the latter whose Station was to be at the Mouth
of the River Jacco had not any Account for the Space of five months they
continued there of 201 white Men beside Negroes who landed in order to
take a Rich Town in that Country and so gave them over in a manner for
lost, nor were they heard of in some years after, or before Commodore
Wager[87] took the Rear Admiral of the Galleons and on board one Allen,
who gave a particular Account of the Fate they met with, which will be related in its proper place.

We shall now proceed to give a further Relation of the Expedition of
Vice Admiral Benbow whom we left in Donna Maria Bay, and having In-
telligence that Mons[ieu]r Du Cass was gone to Carthagena resolved to
Sail for that Coast, with the *Bredah* Capt[ain] Fog, the *Defiance* Collo[nel]
Kirby, the *Windsor* Capt[ain] Constable, the *Greenwich* Capt[ain] Wade, the
Ruby Capt[ain] Walton, the *Pendennis* Capt[ain] Hudson, and the *Falmouth*
Capt[ain] Vincent.

The 10th. of Aug[us]t He set Sail, and Stretch over to St. Maries and on
the 19th. in the afternoon He discovered ten Sail, near that Place, Steering Westward. The Vice Admiral coming up with Them about four in the
afternoon began the Engagement: But, two of His Squadron the *Defiance*
and *Windsor* did not Stand above 2 or 3 broad sides before they luffed out
of Gun shot, so that the two Sternmost Ships lay upon the Admiral and

87. Charles Wager (1666–1743) was commander in Jamaica, 1707–9, and made rear admiral in 1707. Enriched by the capture of a Spanish treasure fleet in 1708, he was knighted in
1709. An official in the Admiralty Office, 1715–33, he became a full admiral in 1733 and first
lord of the admiralty, 1733–42.

galled Him very much, nor did the Ships in the Rear come up with the Diligence they ought to have done. The Fight however lasted till Night, and
though the firing then ceased the Vice Admiral kept them Company. The
next morning at Break of Day, He was near the French Ships, but none
of His Squadron Except the *Ruby* was with Him. At two in the Afternoon
the French drew into a line, though at the same time They made what Sail
They Could to avoid Fighting. However the Vice Admiral and the *Ruby*
kept them Company the next Night. Thus the Admiral continued chasing
and Skirmishing with the Enemy five days, but was not duly Seconded by
several of the Ships in the Squadron.

The 23d. He took a small English ship Called the *Ann* Galley, which the
Enemy had taken off of Lisbon; and the *Ruby* being disabled was ordered
into Port Royal. About eight at Night the whole Squadron was up with the
Vice Admiral, and within two miles of the Enemy. There was now a prospect of doing something, and He made the best of His way after Them,
but the whole Squadron Except the *Falmouth* fell astern again. At two in
the morning the Vice Admiral came up with the Sternmost ship, and fired
a broadside into Her which was returned by the Enemy, and about 3 in the
afternoon, on the 24, His Right leg was broken to pieces by a Chain Shot.
He was carried down, but Soon after ordered His Cradle on the Quarter
Deck, and the Fight was continued. The next morning at Day break, one
of the Enemie's Ships of 70 Guns, was discovered to be very much disabled, but our Treacherous Captains Suffered them to Tow her off, which
the Vice Admiral might have prevented had they given Him any Assistance.

The Vice Admiral being very uneasy at the shamefull Conduct of several
of the Captains of His Squadron, ordered them aboard: But, not having
any Reason to hope for their behaving better[,] the Capt[ain] of the *Defiance* endeavouring to diswade Him from renewing the Engagement since
as He alledged they had tried the Enemie's Strength, with so little success
for six Days together, and most of the other Captains gave it as their Opinions it was not adviseable to Continue the Fight, though They were on
the Enemie's Broad sides and had a fair Opportunity of Succeeding, He
thought proper to return to Port Royal, and Du Cass got into Porto Bello.

The Vice Admiral on His arrival ordered the Offenders to be Confined
and granted a Commission to Rear Admiral Whetstone and other Officers to hold a Court Martial and Try them. Collo[nel] Kirby and Wade
were Sentenced to be shot for Cowardice and breach of orders, but the
Execution was Suspended till Her Majestie's pleasure should be known.
Capt[ain] Constable being acquitted of Cowardice was for breach of orders
cashiered and Condemned to be imprisoned during Her Majestie's pleasure. Capt[ain] Hudson died before the Trial. This Sentence was certainly
very just, for never did two English Officers disgrace their Country more
than Kirby and Wade by Their Cowardice and Treachery. Beside the Consequence of that Action would have been of Infinite Service to the Nation,

had we succeeded, as in all probability we should have done, had those Gentlemen discharged their Duty with honour, Since in all probability it would have defeated the Schemes of the French, and enabled us to Reduce the power of the French and Spaniards in America.

[War and Constitutional Struggle, 1702–1716]

The 4 of Sep[tembe]r Collo[nel] Thomas Handasyde received Her Majestie's Commission dated the 20 June 1702 Appointing Him L[ieutenan]t Governour of this Island, and accordingly He took on Him the Administration.

The 4th. of November the Brave Admiral Benbow, who was in a manner Sacrificed by His Captains, died of His wounds, though it was generally Conjectured that His Death was rather Occasioned by Grief, and Vexation at the Dissappointment He met with. He was buried the Day following in the Church at Kingston, greatly lamented by all Ranks of People.

On the 9. of January 1702/3, between 11 and 12 in the morning a Fire broke out at Port Royal, which before Night consumed the whole Town and did not leave one House standing. However, the Fortifications and the Ships in the Harbour did not receive any Damage except a Brigantine and one Sloop which were burnt. And the Merchants saved their money, Books, and Considerable Quantities of Merchandize through the Assistance of the Men of War and Merchant Ships with Their Boats.

The Governour on this unhappy Occasion, Convened the Assembly, Recommended to their Consideration the Case of the distressed Inhabitants of that Place, and acquainted Them, that with the advice and Consent of the Council, He had made some Disbursements for Provisions and other Necessaries for their Relief and Support.

The Assembly thereupon Resolved to reimburse the Treasury what had been or should be expended on that Occasion, and Addressed the Governour to Continue His Care of Them. And, until convenient Houses could be built, a great Number of Huts were made at the upper end of Kingston, for their Reception. The Assembly also, with the concurrence of the L[ieutenan]t Governour took such other measures as were Necessary for the safety and Wellfare of the Island. And, voted that Port Royal should not be Rebuilt, that the Inhabitants should remove to Kingston and have Lands assigned them there in lieu of what They had on Port Royal. But, the Act which They passed for that purpose, being Opposed by the Inhabitants in England, it was rejected by the Crown and They soon after Rebuilt the Town.

The Command of the Squadron, on the Death of Vice Admiral Benbow, devolved on Rear Admiral Whetstone, who sailed the 9th. of February, and cruised about 5 weeks on both sides of Hispaniola in hopes of meeting with a considerable Fleet of Merchant Ships, which, as He had been informed were expected from old France under Convoy. But missing them He looked into Port Louis and finding nothing there, or any further Intelligence He sailed to Petit Guavas and Leogane; and to prevent any Ships getting out of the Bay, He divided His Squadron, and sent Captain Vincent (who bravely Seconded Admiral Benbow in the Engagement with Mons[ieu]r Du Cass) with one half of the Ships to the Southward; and with the other half He steered Northward. As He conjectured[,] three French Privateers upon the appearance of Capt[ai]n Vincent, with His Division, immediately stood away to the Northward and Came in view of the Rear Admiral, who forced two of them[,] one of 12, the other of 14 Guns[,] ashore, and burnt Them; and the third was taken. In the meantime Capt[ai]n Vincent with His Boats rowed in the Night undiscovered into Culdesack, where lay four ships one of which was formerly taken from the English, and called the *Selwin.* She was Richly laden, having Her full Cargo, of Sugar and Indigo aboard, but all Her sails were on Shore. Capt[ain] Vincent burnt one, sunk another, towed out a third which was a Consort of the Privateers; and boarding the fourth, the Accidental Fire of a Granado shell Occasioned her blowing up.

These attempts alarmed the Enemy on Shore who were in the utmost confusion, and Consternation at this unexpected Visit; and seeing their Ships burning on both sides of the Bay, imagined we had some further Design, and prepared to defend themselves.

The Squadron sailed from thence and looked into Port de Paix on the North side of the Island, but not finding any Ships there, they returned to Port Royal the 9 of April following.

This was no unconsiderable Service, not only in regard to the damage the French Sustained, but in defeating their Design on the North side of Jamaica, the Intention of those Privateers being to make a Descent there, with 500 men to plunder and Destroy that part of the Country. Hence we may perceive, as well as in other Instances I have given, how advantageously this Island is Situated, to obstruct and Restrain the Commerce of France as well as Spain in America, especially while we are Masters of the Seas; so that it is evidently our own fault They have made so great a progress in their Plantations as to Rival us in Sugar and other Commodities, which They for many Years purchased of us. Nor is it yet too late to recover what we have lost by our Supineness, Since their Settlements on Hispaniola are so Open and Exposed, that they have not one Port which can be properly called a Harbour, except Port Louis, and that is made so only by a small Island which lays at the Bottom of a deep Bay, so that 3 or 4 Ships of the line, may force an Entrance without any great difficulty. As to the other Parts of the Island in Their Possession, we have shewn with

As Knight noted throughout his *History*, the Caribbean was a central site of contention among pirates, merchants, and rival European navies. This image, produced by
the engraver Jan Lamsvelt, entitled *Zee gevegt der Boecaniers, en 't nemen van eenige
spaansche schepen* and published by Nicolaas ten Hoorn in Amsterdam in 1700, depicts a battle between the English and Spanish fleets in the bay of Panama.

what Facility our men of War have entered and destroyed their shipping
notwithstanding all their Fortifications and Batteries on Shore. And that
Captain Moses in a Single sloop went into Petit Guavas[,] the second best
Sea Port They have[,] took and brought away a Ship of great Value.

Collo[nel] Handasyd, during these Transactions was Vigilant and carefull, in His Duty, followed the Steps of the deceased General in Regard
to the Fortifications and training the Militia; who were at this time, in
most parts of the Island as well Disciplined and fit for Service as any in the
World. And in all other Respects He behaved hitherto to the Satisfaction
of the Inhabitants, in general. But though He kept the Soldiers in good

Order Yet, the Indulgence and particular Regard He Discovered for the Officers, caused great Jealousies and uneasiness, and as He was Supported in His Measures, by Fools and Sycophants[,] the Common Attendants on Governours and Great Men[,] a Fire kindled, which was not Extinguished in His time nor in many Years after. For as the Civil offices of profit became Vacant, He filled them up with His Officers particularly the office of Attorney General He granted to Major Samuel Lovell (the Son of Sir Silathiel Lovell[1]) who had been bred to Law. And, as there was not at that time any Act for the Qualification of Members to Sit in the Assembly, He procured several of His Officers to be returned for some of the remote and smallest Parishes. This Alarmed not only the Assembly but the whole Island, and irritated them to the highest degree, for though it may be imagined from His Conduct in other Respects that He had no latent, or Sinister Design Yet it must be allowed that it was a sufficient foundation for Jealously, and Dissatisfaction.

The Assembly therefore passed a Bill intitled an Act to Disqualify the Officers of the two Regiments from Executing any Civil Office of profit in this Island or Sit in the Assembly.[2] But, the Governour refusing to give His Assent to that Bill, the Assembly became so Inflamed, that He thought it Necessary to dissolve Them.

This Year Her Majesty[3] was pleased to Appoint, the Right Honourable the Earl of Peterborough[4] (who afterwards made Himself so famous by His Conquests in Spain), to be Governour of this Island, with the same powers, which were granted to the Duke of Albermarle. His Lordship being declared Capt[ai]n General and Admiral of all Her Majestie's Dominions in America, and Vice Admiral [John] Graydon[5] was appointed to Command the Squadron, which was ordered to Convoy His Lordship and

1. Silathiel Lovell (1619–1713) was a barrister of Grays Inn from 1656; serjeant-at-law, 1688; and recorder of London, 1692–1708. Knighted in 1692, he was made fifth baron of the exchequer in 1708.

2. The Act to Disqualify Officers of the Two Regiments from Executing Any Civil Office for Profit in This Island or to Sit in Assembly, 1703, did not receive acceptance by the governor.

3. Queen Anne (1665?–1714), the second daughter of James II and younger sister of Queen Mary, acceded to the throne at the death of her brother-in-law William III on March 8, 1702.

4. Charles Mordaunt, Third Earl of Peterborough and First Earl of Monmouth of the second creation (1658–1735). Serving in the Mediterranean through much of the 1670s, he sided with the parliamentary opposition to the Stuarts from 1680 to 1686 when he traveled to Holland to conspire against James II. After the Glorious Revolution, he was a privy councillor, lord of the bedchamber, first lord of the treasury, and one of Queen Mary's Council of Nine as of 1689. He succeeded to the earldom in 1697 and declined command of a mission to Jamaica in 1702. He was joint commander of a mission to Spain in 1705, capturing Barcelona and enthroning Archduke Charles.

5. Vice Admiral John Graydon (c. 1666–1726), an English officer of the Royal Navy, participated in the Nine Years' War and the War of the Spanish Succession, was made com-

the land Forces that were to be Employed on some important Expedition. But this Project[6] was laid aside, upon an Insinuation that if we Attempted any of the Spanish Settlements in America it would Unite that Nation more firmly with the French. The Vice Admiral was thereupon ordered to proceed without the Earl and to take on Him the command of Her Majestie's Ships in the West Indies. He accordingly sailed with the *Resolution* and *Blackwall*, with the Transports having on board Brigadier [Ventris?] Columbine's Regiment.

He arrived at Nevis the 23d. of May, and having furnished Commodore Walker's[7] Squadron, with Provisions and other Necessaries, which They wanted, He sailed from thence and arrived at Jamaica the 4th. June. He immediately ordered a Survey to be taken of the Ships, which had been on the Expedition against Guadaloupe, and finding them to be very Indifferent He determined to Sail for England.

Besides, He had some Disputes with the Governour and Principal Inhabitants on account of his pressing not only Seamen and Servants, but Tradesmen and others who were Settled on the Island, insomuch that a Constant Guard was kept day and Night to prevent press Gangs coming on Them. And in other Respects He behaved in so Savage a manner as if He had been sent rather to terrify and keep in Awe than to protect the Island.

Vice Admiral Graydon, Accordingly sailed the 20th. of June 1703 from Port Royal with Rear Admiral Whetstone, leaving only three men of War, namely the *Norwich, Experiment,* and *Sea Horse,* a Fire Ship and two Sloops under the command of Commodore Douglass,[8] to attend the Island.

The 4. of April 1704, the New Assembly met and the Governour in His Speech, put them in mind of the great Confusion, occasioned by the Heat and Animosities which arose in the last Assembly which might have been of pernicious Consequence had it not been prevented by their dissolution, Therefore recommended Unanimity, and to lay aside all Controversy and Distinction. He also reminded Them of the Act for Quartering the two Regiments, being almost Expired and required not only their Speedy dis-

---

mander in chief of the English West India forces in 1703, and was subsequently cashiered for his failure to engage the French during his expedition to the West Indies.

6. Burnet.—*Author.* Gilbert Burnet (1643–1715) was a Scottish philosopher, historian, confidant of William III, and strong Whig who became bishop of Salisbury after the Glorious Revolution. The work Knight here cites is *Bishop Burnet's History of My Own Time,* 2 vols. (London, 1724, 1734), 2.—*Ed.*

7. Hovenden Walker (?–1728) was born in Ireland, joined the Royal Navy, and between 1692 and 1711 rose from captain to rear admiral. He is most famous for his failed attack on Quebec in 1711. He became commander in chief in Jamaica in 1712.

8. Probably Andrew Douglass (?–1725), who helped bust the boom at the siege of Londonderry in 1698. He was cashiered on a charge of using public resources for private ends at Port Royal in 1704 but was reinstated in 1709.

patch but that some better Provision might be made for the Officers and Soldiers. He Recommended to their Consideration the Case of Widows and Orphans; and to prevent any Injury or Injustice being done them, that all Guardians and Trustees, might be obliged by a Short Act, to Account once a Year before the Chancellor.

That as They were Englishmen They would Assimilate as near as possible to the Customs and practice of England, and to follow the Example of the Parliament, who had passed a Law to prevent Inconveniencies by privilege of Parliament, which will be attended with this good Consequence, that Necessitous Persons will not endeavour to raise and foment Factions in Elections, when They cannot be protected from payment of Debts, when They are Elected.

And, assured Them He should always concur with them, in every Measure that tended to Her Majestie's Honour, the safety wellfare and happiness of this Island.

This Assembly proceeded on Business with great Temper and Moderation, Voted an Additional Subsistance of fifteen shillings p[er] week to every Commission Officer, and passed a Bill intituled an Act for Raising money, for the Additional Subsistance of Her Majestie's Officers and Soldiers and for other Uses. They[,] However, took care to incert a Clause that no Officer in the two Regiments should be Capable of sitting in the Assembly or of Executing and Enjoying any Civil Employment in this Island. And, as They were determined not to make the usual allowance to the Officers and Soldiers, which was a Voluntary Donation, in any other manner, the Governour was under the Necessity of giving his Assent to that Act which put an end to all further Disputes on that head. But, the Fire which was kindled in the last Assembly not being intirely Extinguished broke out and began to Appear more Violently on the following Occasion.

The Planters by the last Quartering Act were left at their Option to provide for the Soldiers as Usual on their Plantations, or to allow them weekly five Shillings Each to provide for Themselves. This Regulation was made on a Representation of the Soldiers having misbehaved in some of their Quarters, which was so far from being Redressed on Application to one of the L[ieutenant] Collo[nel]s who Commanded in that part of the Country, that He ordered them to make good their Quarters. Nevertheless, the Governour did not approve of this Alternative, because the Soldiers mispent their money, and were furnished with the Means of dabauching Themselves, to the prejudice of their healths and lives, and as He imputed it to Mr. Totterdell[9] who brought in the Bill He not only

9. Hugh Totterdell/Totterdale was an Irish immigrant and lawyer and a thorn in the side of Governors Beeston through Hamilton, especially for his advocacy of the contention that the Jamaica Assembly was equivalent to the English House of Commons. He was a member of that assembly for most of the years from 1701 to 1716, representing variously St. Catherine Parish, St. George Parish, Port Royal, St. David, and Kingston, and was twice Speaker, in

Reproached Him with it, but became so heated by degrees, and to loose himself so far, among Other passionate Expressions as to Call Him Rogue and Rascal. In the Station He was in Mr. Totterdale had no other way of Redressing Himself, but when the same Bill was brought in this Session He desired to be Excused being on the Committee appointed to bring it in and among Other Reasons, Acquainted the House with the Opprobious Treatment He had met with from the Governour and in His turn was so warm, as to utter some Expressions concerning His Excellency, which gave Offence and He Complained of it to the House.

The Assembly were so desirous of pacifying the Governour, that though it was for words spoken in the House, They after having heard Mr. Totterdell in His place, Expelled Him and Refused to admit Him upon His being rechosen. Nevertheless the Governour was so far from being satisfied with what They had done, that He Ordered the Attorney General to bring an Information against Mr. Totterdell at the Ensuing Grand Court. But, He was acquitted by the Jury, after a long Trial.

The Assembly highly Resented this prosecution, which They thought an infringement on their Privileges, being for words spoken in their House, no ways penal, and Especially as they had made so great a Concession. Hence, arose a fresh Controversy, which Obstructed the good agreement that was between the Governour and the Assembly at their first meeting, and Occasioned an adjournment to the 21st. of September.

During these Transactions, the men of War brought in Several small Prizes, but none of any Considerable Value, nor was there any Remarkable Action performed at Sea during the time Commodore Douglass commanded the few Ships which were on this Station. The *Sea Horse* Capt[ain] Jones did indeed destroy a French Privateer, of 10 Guns and Eighty men which was designed to attack and plunder some of the Windward Settlements, but in Chasing was so unfortunate to lose Her Majestie's Ship, in running ashore. The French Capt[ain] and all His men were however made Prisoners, and brought to Spanish Town.

But, the Privateers began to flourish again and the success they met with, encouraged such a Resort of Seamen, that at this time, there were not less than 28 or 30 Sail fitted out of this Island, who brought in great Riches and Squandered it away after their usual manner.

The Governour[,] whatever mistakes He Committed in Civil Affairs, yet in His Military Capacity, prov'd Himself a Wary, Experience'd Officer for He not only kept a Vigilant Eye over His Neighbours, but on all Strangers

---

1708 and 1714. For his bold criticism of governors, the assembly twice expelled him, in 1704 and 1714, on the first occasion being denied seating upon his reelection and on the second being sued by Attorney General Robert Hotchkyn for words spoken in the House against Governor Hamilton and Admiral Hovenden Walker. The house treated this suit as a breach of its parliamentary privileges and imprisoned Hotchkyn, for which Governor Hamilton prorogued the house.

that came to the Island, who on the least Suspicion were taken into Custody, and Examined. This Behaviour though it was thought by some too circumspect and Rigid, Yet must be allowed by all impartial and Considerate men to be highly necessary and Commendable in Him, as we were then in the height of a Bloody War with France and Spain.

And, to His Honour it must likewise be observed, He was so Carefull of the Preservation and Security of the Remote Parts of the Island, that He obliged the Captains of all Privateers, before He granted them Commissions, to give Security that They should Cruise round the Island, and to touch at particular places where they were to put on shore, in order to be transmitted to Him, an account in Writing of such passages as They met with, before they proceeded on any other Enterprize. By this Regulation He was not only Satisfied of their having done their Duty, but, Cruisers were constantly going round the Island, and prevented the Enemy from Ravaging and plundering the remote Settlements as They had done formerly.

The 28th. of July arrived His Majestie's Ship the *Guernsey* and some Merchant ships from London, the former brought Her Majestie's Commission dated the 25th. of March 1704 Appointing Collo[nel] Thomas Handasyd (who was likewise promoted to the Rank of a Brigadier) to be Captain General Governour and Commander in chief of this Island, which was published the day following.

And on the 2d. of August a Proclamation was issued, Signifying Her Majestie's permission to all Her Subjects to Trade with the Spaniards, with an Exception to Provisions and Warlike Stores. And, Commanding them not to Molest or interrupt any Dutch Traders, but to permit them to Trade in the same manner.

The 9th. of September the *Neptune* Capt[ain] Gandy, and another Sloop which had been Trading on the Spanish Coast pursuant to Her Majestie's licence, returned in 30 days, the former brought in 20000 pieces of eight and the other 17 or 18000, having sold all their Cargoes, and met with a favourable reception and Encouragement from the Spaniards. On which Several other sloops fitted out on the same Design.

The 21st. of September the Assembly met according to Adjournment and the next day, His Excellency in His Speech, Acquainted Them with the Substance of a letter, He had received from the Lords Commissioners for Trade and Plantations Recommending that Quarters might be provided for the Soldiers belonging to the two Regiments, instead of money, which was mispent to the great Ruin of Their Healths.

At the same time He put Them in mind of what He had formerly recommended in relation to Widows and Orphans. Also the great disorders which had happened and might be expected from the Rebellious Negroes. And the great Inconvenience that might attend the Country, Especially in time of War, for want of good Roads and Bridges over Rivers of importance particularly that over the River going to Liguinea.

He informed them of Her Majestie's Indulgence, in granting liberty to all Her Subjects to Trade with the Spaniards which he hoped would be of advantage and more particularly to this Island. And, Recommended to Them a Sincere and good understanding, so that there might be no further disputes and Animosities among Them.

The Assembly on taking the Governour's Speech into Consideration came to Several Resolutions, particularly That They had made a Suitable Provision for the Two Regiments.

That the Behaviour of some Officers and Soldiers was the Cause of the Alteration in the provision which was made for Them. That the Expressions of a Collo[nel] of one of the Regiments to a Member of this House, were fit to be Spoken to a Conquer'd People only, and not to those under Her Majestie's protection. And the ordering the Soldiers to make good their Quarters, was a sufficient Reason to leave it to the Inhabitants to Entertain them or give them a Weekly allowance.

That the Laws of England had provided for Orphans and Widows, and Could not be altered without being repugnant to Them, But that the House was ready to Come into any Measures, which may be proposed for their Interest and Advantage.

That the filing a Bill of Information against Mr. Totterdell for words spoken in the House, while He was a Member, was an infringement on their priviledges, and an Arbitrary, Illegal proceeding.

They at the same time ordered the Attorney General[10] to Attend Them. But, He wrote a Letter to the Speaker wherein He excused Himself, alledging that as an Officer who was obliged to Attend the Council He could not Comply without Their permission.

Hence arose a Controversy between the Council and Assembly which occasioned the Governour to order the Speaker and the whole House to Attend Him in the Councell Chamber. And in His Speech told Them He thought it necessary to put Them in mind of Their Duty and Allegiance to Her Majesty, to lay aside all Animosities, to drop the present dispute and to proceed to Business, for that He would have no more paper War.

That Their Violent and Irregular proceedings, Exceeded forty one, except the Hatchet,[11] with other Warm and indecent Expressions of the like Nature.

The Assembly thereupon drew up a Representation in Vindication of Themselves, and Sent to know when His Excellency would be pleased to receive the same to which He Replied That if They had any thing to propose for Her Majestie's or the Countrie's Service, He was ready to Receive Them. But if their Representation related to their Disputes, He would not receive it.

10. Edward Haskins.
11. A reference to the Civil War Parliament and execution of Charles I.

And, soon after thought proper to Prorogue Them to the 8. of November following.

About the 10th. of April 1705 the Governour received an Express from Collo[nel] Parkes[12] Governour of the Leeward Islands. Acquainting Him, that Mons[ieu]r Ibberviel[13] was in those parts with 14 French men of War, and 3000 land Forces. That They had made a Descent on Nevis and St. Christophers and Expected a Strong Reinforcement in order to invade Jamaica. On this advice an Embargo was laid, Martial Law declared and the Island put into a posture of Defence.

The 17th. of May, Rear Admiral Whetstone (who had the honour of Knighthood Conferred on Him for his Services) arrived at Port Royal with His Majestie's Ships the *Suffolk, Sunderland, Mountague, Bristol, Hector* and *Folkstone*. And, having Intelligence of some Ships being ready to Sail from Carthagena, to Porto Bello, He made all the dispatch He could to sea, in order to intercept Them.

He sailed accordingly from Port Royal, the 6th. of June, and on the 17th. gave chace to a Ship which was taken after a dispute of two hours with those ships which were nearest to her, and proved to be a Ship of 46 Guns, mounted, and 150 men, with a Cargo of Negroes, plying then to the Eastward, He discovered off of the River Grande, two Sail, one of which was a Privateer belonging to Martinico and being forced ashore, was burnt by her own men. The Coast being alarmed, and no prospect of doing any immediate Service, He returned to Jamaica.

The Beginning of August the *Mountague* and *Hector*, took a French ship of 24 Guns Richly laden, soon after the former met on the Coast of Hispaniola, two French men of War, of 48 and 36 Guns, and Engaged Them both, about an hour, but was separated in the Night. They had fair Sight of Them the next day, but by the backwardness and Cowardice of the Of-

12. Daniel Parke (?–1710) was a Virginia-born adventurer whose scandalous behavior caused his expulsion from Parliament and drove him into the military. He became governor of the Leeward Islands in 1706 where he quickly wore out his welcome by seducing the wife of a local merchant and Royal Africa Company factor and got into such a profound altercation with the Antigua Assembly that an incited citizenry attacked his house and killed him. Metropolitan officials at first regarded the event as treasonous, but a crown investigation eventually concluded that Parke's extreme misconduct was to blame, pardoning all the rebels and even promoting two of them to seats on the council. Frank Cundall, *Governors of Jamaica in the First Half of the Eighteenth Century* (London, 1937), xv, 51; Richard Pares, *War and Trade in the West Indies, 1739–1763* (London, 1936), 179, 228, 248, 258; Frederick G. Spurdle, *Early West Indian Government: Showing the Progress of Government in Barbados, Jamaica, and the Leeward Islands, 1660–1783* (Palmerston North, New Zealand, 1962), 39, 74, 148, 187.

13. Pierre Le Moyne d'Iberville (1661–1706) was born in Montreal and became a soldier, ship captain, colonial administrator, and founder of the French colony of La Louisiane of New France. Early in 1706, he left France in command of twelve vessels and in April devastated the island of Nevis, taking the entire population prisoner. He died in Havana in July 1706 while planning an expedition against Charles Town, South Carolina.

ficers They were suffered to Escape. This matter being enquir'd into at a Court Martial, the Captain was acquitted, but His Officers were Cashiered.

The *Bristoll* and *Folkstone* being sent in quest of Them, soon after met with two French men of War of 30 and 24 Guns Convoying Ten Sail of Merchant ships bound from Petit Guavas to Old France. But, They were so intent on Seizing the latter, of which they took Six, that the former had an Opportunity of Escaping. Capt[ain] Anderson who was the Senior Commander, was broke at a Court Martial for His ill Conduct on that Occasion.

About this time there was a great want of Naval Stores and Provisions for the Ships of War, nor was the Island able to furnish Them, which put the Seamen to Short allowance. And, as an addition to their misfortune the *Suffolk*, where the Admiral's Flag was flying, took Fire in the Gun Room where was some powder, which blew up, Several Men were killed, and about Seventy men more so burnt that most of them died. The Ship however was preserved though much damaged, and the Admiral and His Captain received no hurt being at that time on shore.

The Assembly met according to adjournment the 8th. of November, and proceeded on Business. But a fresh dispute arose on the Council making some amendments to a mon[e]y Bill, which They would not allow of, insisting on their Sole Right of raising and disposing of all Publick monies as Representatives of the People. On which the Governour prorogued them, the 30th. of the same month to the 1st. of December and on the day following dissolved Them.

In March 1705 S[i]r William Whetston with His Squadron Stretched over and Cruised sometime on the Coast of Carthagena, where He took several small prizes; but none of any great Value. And, in June having advice of some ships being at Petit Guavas, He put to Sea with one Third, two fourth, two Fifth Rates and a Fire Ship. But, the Strong leeward Currents, and Sea Breezes obliged them to return to Port Royal, and frustrated His Design.

The 25th. of July 1706, Commodore Ker[14] arrived from England, with one Third, five Fourth, two Fifth, two Sixth Rates and a Fire ship to relieve S[i]r. William Whetstone and His Squadron.

In a few days after They had advice, that Mons[ieu]r Du Casse was gone to Carthagena, with Eight large men of War, that He designed from thence to Porto Bello, and afterwards to Lavera Cruz. They also had advice that the Ships to Windward were to join Him at the Havanna so that they would then be in all Sixteen Sail.

A Council of War being called thereupon it was Resolved, that They should proceed in Company thither[;] accordingly S[i]r William Whetstone and Commodore Ker sailed the 8th. of August, from Port Royal, and

14. Commodore William Kerr.

coming before the Harbour of Carthagena, They discovered fourteen Galleons unrigged, in the inner Harbour. But Mons[ieu]r Du Casse was not, (nor had been), there as They could learn.

The 18th. S[i]r William Whetstone wrote a Letter to the Governour of Carthagena, with an Invitation to Submit and declare for His lawfull Sovereign King Charles the 1st. In answer He wrote S[i]r William, He knew no other King but King Philip.

Nothing being, therefore, to be done, S[i]r William Whetstone returned to Jamaica, where He found Eight prizes, which His Cruisers had brought in during his Absence. One of which was a very Rich French Ship, taken by the *Experiment* and a Privateer of Jamaica. And, as Soon as the Trade was ready S[i]r William Whetstone, sailed for England, the beginning of October, leaving the Command of the Ships designed for further Service in those Parts to Commodore Ker.

In August the New Assembly was convened, but as it Consisted of most of the Members of the Former, They came with the same Temper and Dispositions. Their Disputes now turned on their having the sole Right of raising and disposing of all Publick monies; and refused a Conference with the Council, on a Bill for Subsisting the Soldiers. The Council Suggested that it was not a mon[e]y Bill, because thereby nothing was given to the Crown, and therefore made some Amendments to it, but were a last (on Considering the Necessity of the Soldiers) obliged to give their Assent without Amendments. However They entered a Protest in their Minutes wherein They declared—That They would not have passed such a pernicious Bill if the absolute Necessity of providing for the Officers and Soldiers did not Compel Them to it.

But, This did not put an end to Their dissentions for there were great Divisions and Commotions, among Themselves, insomuch that one Party was for chusing another Speaker and insisted on Peter Beckford Esq[uir]e[15] (the Eldest Son of Collo[nel] Peter Beckford, the late L[ieutenan]t Governour) Resigning the Chair, which he refused to do being supported by His Friends, who were the Majority of the House. On which several of the Members determined, at a private meeting to Compel and force Him out

15. Peter Beckford (c. 1671–1734), the son of Peter Beckford who was lieutenant governor in 1702–3, was Speaker of the Assembly in 1707–11, 1711–13, and 1716. He sat in the assembly from 1704 until his death for a total of thirty years' service. At first, he represented Port Royal and thereafter St. Elizabeth Parish, Vere Parish, and St. Catherine Parish. Governor Hamilton rejected Beckford's application for a post as deputy secretary of Jamaica on the grounds that he was "the chief actor in all the unhappy difficulties in this country," but he subsequently attained the post of comptroller of customs. His massive fortune at the time of his death included 24 plantations and 1,200 slaves. He married Bathshua, daughter of Colonel Julines Herring of Jamaica, who bore him thirteen children including Richard, MP for Bristol, and William, MP for and lord mayor of London. Cundall, *Governors of Jamaica in the First Half of the Eighteenth Century*, 12, 22, 49, 53, 60, 72, 92, 94, 145, 183; Frank Cundall, *Historic Jamaica* (London, 1915), xvi, xvii, 360–61.

of the Chair. Collo[nel] Beckford having some intimation of this, went to the Governour before the House met, Acquainted Him with the Apprehensions He was under; and desired His Excellency if He heard any bustle or disturbance (the Court House where the Assembly meet being within hearing) that He would be pleased to adjourn or prorogue Them.

The old Gentleman was under such Anxiety that He continued with the Governour, till the Assembly met, and was very Attentive to what passed; and soon after hearing a Clamour and a Noise among Them, He Acquainted His Excellency who went in Person to Command the House to adjourn. Collo[nel] Beckford who was Corpulent, and very Ancient, followed as fast as He could, and with the hurry and Fears for His Son, Stumbled and fell on His Face in the Parade, between the Governour's House and the Court House. His Excellency immediately adjourned the Assembly[,] Reproved them for the Heat and disorder They were under, which among other bad Consequences, He was Apprehensive had occasioned the Death of a very Worthy Gentleman. For seeing Him fall and not to move the Governour imagined He was dead, though all means to recover Him proved ineffectual, He died in a few Minutes after He was carried into a House, without Speaking a word or being Sensible of what passed.

He was a Gentleman of Strong Natural Parts, and of so Hail a Constitution, that He was Capable of going through great Fatigues even in the latter part of His life. He had lived upwards of forty Years in this Island; had passed through most of the Military as well as Civil Employments, and was Several Years President of the Council before and after He was L[ieutenan]t Governour. He was very Serviceable when the French Invaded the Island in 1693, and Commanded the Fortifications at Port Royal. The Year after, He Commanded the Volunteers, who went from this Island to the Assistance of Collo[nel] Lillingston and Commodore Willmot, in the Expedition against the French at Hispaniola. He left a Considerable Estate, and Vast tracts of land, which have since been greatly improved by His Descendants, particularly His Eldest Son Peter Beckford Esquire, who at His Death[16] was in possession of a greater Estate Real and Personal than any one Man ever Enjoyed in the British Dominions in America, and Equal to many Noblemen in England. But, as I shall occasionally mention this Gentleman hereafter I shall say no more of Him in this place. Collo[nel] Beckford the Elder died the [blank] of December 1706, and left only one Son more, the late Collo[nel] Thomas Beckford.[17]

16. Peter Beckford Esq[uire] died the [blank] day of August 1734 aged 63. —*Author.*

17. Thomas Beckford (?–1731) was the other son of Peter the elder. Educated at Oxford, he resided at Tom's Hall, Jamaica. He married first Mary Tolderby and second Mary Ballard, daughter and heiress of his cousin Thomas. He sat in the Jamaica Assembly continuously from 1706 to his death, representing St. Catherine Parish, St. Thomas in the Vale Parish, or Port Royal, and was Speaker of the House in 1727–28. He was killed in 1731 by a man he

Commodore Ker, on the departure of S[i]r William Whetstone sailed with the Squadron under His Command, to the Coast of Hispaniola. His Design was on Port Louis but His Pilots not being Acquainted with the Entrance into that Port, He did not think proper to Attempt it, therefore determined to proceed to Petit Guavas. The 13th. of September He dispatched the *Nonesuch* and *Experiment,* and all the Boats manned and Armed with orders to Capt[ain] Boyce who Commanded to range in the Night along the Bays of Leogane and Petit Guavas, with all possible care and Secrecy, and so to dispose of Them, that They might destroy the Enemie's Ships in those Roads. And, if He got notice at Leogane of any number of Ships at Petit Guavas, He was to come away and join the Commodore. But some of the Boats stragling from the rest, alarmed the Coast, and rendered the Design impracticable. He thereupon returned to Port Royal, and was incapable of going to Sea for Several Months, through Sickness, Mortality and desertion of His Men.

The 2d. of January 1706[/7], S[i]r John Jennings[18] arrived at this Island, with a very strong Squadron, and found the Ships under the Command of Commodore Ker refitting, but weakly manned. And, got Information that the Galleons were Still at Carthagena.

S[i]r John immediately dispatched the *Mary,* with a letter to the Governour and Admiral, with an Account of the Success of Her Majestie's Arms, and to induce them to a submission to King Charles. He offered Them Her Majestie's protection and to Convoy the Galleons to Old Spain. But, he received the same answer, which was given to S[i]r William Whetstone, with this Addition that they had fresh advices of the Scale being turned, in favour of King Philip, who was returned to Madrid. Upon this refusal it was determined in a Council of War to proceed with the whole Squadron to Carthagena. Accordingly, They sailed the 17th. of January. But the Governour and General of the Galleons, persisting in their Resolution the Fleet departed thence for Blewfields at the West end of Jamaica where They took in Wood and Water, and Sailed the 25th. of February for England.

At this time there was a very beneficial Trade carried on with the Spaniards, but in regard to the French Privateers, who infested the Coast and disturbed their Traffick, the Merchants Applied to the Commadore for a Convoy, which He absolutely refused, unless they would make Him a present of a thousand pistoles, beside a Gratuity to the Capt[ain] of the Man of War He should send with Them. This was thought so Exorbitant a de-

---

offended, probably Captain Richard Cargill, member of the assembly for Vere. Cundall, *Governors of Jamaica in the First Half of the Eighteenth Century,* 23, 37, 78, 359–60.

18. John Jennings (1664–1743), an experienced naval officer who had been present at the capture of Gibraltar in 1704, was knighted in the same year and promoted to rear admiral in 1705, his rank when he appeared in Jamaica in January 1707. Thereafter, he was lord of the admiralty, 1714–27.

mand, that the Traders sailed without, two of Them were taken, Capt[ain] Gandy and another Sloop with very Considerable Cargoes[,] being chased by two Martinico Privateers of great Force the former over set in a squal of Wind. The Captain and about twenty men were taken up by one of the Privateers, but the rest, about 50 in Number most of them Residents on the Island were drowned. The other Vessel with great difficulty Escaped.

The Merchants were so Exasperated at this fatal Stroke, the value of the Three Sloops which were lost in that manner, Amounting to upwards of Sixty thousand pounds Sterling that They Deputed Mr. Thomas Wood[19] to go for England, and lodge a Complaint against the Commadore.

The 22d. of June 1707, Commodore Wager,[20] now S[i]r. Charles Wager, late 1st. L[ieutenan]t Commissioner of His Majestie's Navy, arrived at Jamaica, with His Majestie's Ship[s] the *Expedition, Kingston, Portland, Severn, Dolphin* and *Scarbrough*. And the 26th of August following Commodore Ker sailed for England, with the *Bredah, Sunderland* and *Hawk* Fire Ship and 28 Sail of Merchant Ships.

The 28 of November, Commodore Wager with Six ships of War, sailed on a Cruise; and on the 4th. of December they were joined by the *Severn* and *Dunkirks* prize, who brought an account the Galleons were not ready to Sail. He afterwards received Intelligence of Mons[ieu]r Du Cass being in the West Indies with 8 men of War from 70 to 86 Guns, several Privateers, and Expected to be reinforced with 18 Ships more, which gave Him reason to imagine the French had some Design on Jamaica. He therefore left the Spanish Coast and arrived at Port Royal the 22d. of December.

The Governour having had the same Intelligence called a Council of War, and pursuant to their Resolutions, an Embargo was laid, Martial Law declared, and the Whole Island put into a posture of Defence.

And, for the better Security of the Harbour the Commadore drew the Squadron in a line, at the entrance into it, from Hanover line to the Salt Ponds. There was at the same time a great Number of Merchant ships, at Kingston, so that had the Enemy made an Attempt, a very good Account would have been given of Them.

The Merchants of London, on Mr. Wood's arrival, drew up an Address to the House of Lords and Commons, Representing the Conduct and Behaviour of Commodore Ker (who was likewise arrived) That He had Exacted large Sums of Money for Convoys, and put the Merchants to great Expences, in freighting Ships upon promising Them Convoy, and after-

19. Thomas Wood was almost certainly a Port Royal merchant.

20. Sir Charles Wager (1666–1743) was an experienced naval officer and soon to be promoted to rear admiral when he took up his post in Jamaica as naval commander in June 1707. In 1708, he destroyed one Spanish treasure ship and captured another. The proceeds of his capture meant that he returned to England a rich man, highly feted and knighted in 1709. He eventually became first lord of the admiralty between 1733 and 1742 during which he presided over the expansion that led to the Royal Navy's preponderance over it rivals.

wards refusing it, which was the Occasion of a Sloop, with great Wealth being lost.

The 7th. of February the House of Lords presented an Address to the Queen Representing the Allegations against Capt[ain] Ker, to have been fully proved, and beseeching Her Majesty to give such Effectual orders, as might prevent the like for the future. The House of Commons likewise Addressed Her Majesty on the same Occasion, and humbly desired Her Majesty not to Employ the said Captain Ker, in Her Service for the future. He was accordingly Cashiered and rendered incapable of serving in Her Majestie's Navy.

I thought it Necessary to incert this passage among other Remarkable Transactions in this Island, and to Refer the Reader, for a more particular account, to the *Annals of Queen Ann*,[21] and the *Compleat History of Europe*;[22] because it seems to be almost worn out of Memory, and as it may be a Caution and Warning to other Commanders, to be more Vigilant and Faithful in Their Duty, as well as to avoid treading in the same Steps.

One of the Sloops, which Commodore Wager had sent to get Intelligence of the Enemie's Design, returned with a prize she had taken off Port Louis, by which He had Information that the French Squadron consisting of Ten men of War and a Fire ship sailed from thence to the Havanna the 18 of December. Another Sloop sent in a small French Ship laden with Indigo, and some money.

On this advice it was Resolved in a Council of War, that as many Ships as could be spared, should go over to the Spanish Coast and watch the Motions of the Galleons. Accordingly the Commadore sailed the 16th. of February, with the *Expedition, Monmouth, Portland, Jersey* and a Fire ship. But, having Intelligence by the *Severn* Capt[ain] Pudnor, who was Stationed at Porto Bello that the Galleons would not Sail till May, He returned to Port Royal.

About the middle of the month, the *Scarbrough* brought in two Prizes, the one a French Ship of 300 Tuns laden with Sugar and Indigo; and the other was the *Queen Ann* Packet Boat, which had been taken from the English, and was fitting out as a Privateer. Some Days after a Jamaica Privateer brought in a French ship laden with Wine, Brandy and other Goods.

The 14th. of April the Commodore Sailed from Port Royal Cays, and gave out it was only to Cruize. About ten days after He gave Chace to Several Ships off of Boccachica, some of which got into Carthagena, and the rest Escaped in the Night.

About the middle of May the Squadron, watered in the Bay of Guira. The 17th. the Portland brought advice, that the Galleons were ready to Sail, but were inform'd of our Ships being there.

21. *The History of the Reign of Queen Anne, Digested into Annals* (London, 1710).

22. David Jones, *A Compleat History of Europe; or, A View of the Affairs Thereof, Civil and Military, for the Year 1709* (London, 1710).

The 23d. the *Ann* Sloop joined the Commadore from Bastimentos, and brought a letter from Capt[ain] Pudnor with advice, that the Galleons being thirteen Sail, were at Sea, coming from Carthagena. The 27th. the Commadore not hearing any further of the Galleons, began to Apprehend They had given Him the Slip, and were gone to the Havanna, the 28th. He discovered 17 Sail between the Baru and French Island, and Resolved to Attack them with His small Squadron namely the *Expedition, Kingston, Portland* and a Fire ship. They did not endeavour to Escape, not believing that He would dare to Engage them on such unequal terms, but drew into a line of Battle.

The Commadore being informed that the three Admirals had all the Money, thought if He could overcome Them, it would be the best Service. Accordingly he ordered the Kingston to Attack the Vice Admiral, the *Portland* the Rear Admiral while He engaged the Admiral.

The Commadore perceiving before Night, that Neither the *Kingston* [n]or the *Portland*, Complied with His Directions, made the Signal for a line of Battle. It was just Sunset, when the Commadore began to Engage the Spanish Admiral and in about an hour and half, it being then dark, she blew up, He being then along Her side and not Pistol shot from her, So that the heat of the Blast came very hot upon them, and Several Splinters of Plank and Timber came on board of Them on Fire, but they were soon thrown over or Extinquish'd. It being then dark the Enemie's ships began to Separate, so that the Commodore with all His Endeavours could keep sight but of one, which seemed to be the biggest, though it proved to be the Rear Admiral. About ten at night the Commadore came up with Her, and not seeing which was she lay with Her Head, he hap[pe]ned to fire His first Broadside into her Stern which seemingly disabled Her from making Sail, and being then to Leeward, He endeavoured to get to Windward. He had neither seen or heard anything in all this time of the *Kingston* and *Portland;* But, now by the firing of His Guns, and His lights They joined Him and assisted in taking of the Rear Admiral, who called for Quarter about two in the Morning just as the Moon was rising.

While the Commadore lay alongside of the Rear Admiral and was Engaged with Him the Vice Admiral passed by on the other Side, and was very near running Him aboard. He gave Him a broad side, as He passed, which was returned by the Commadore, who was in hopes the *Kingston* and *Portland* would have Engaged Him, but They let Him pass.

At Daylight They discovered 3 Sail on their Weather Quarter, upon which the Commadore made a Signal for the Kingston and Portland to chase. He therefore making the Signal again they continued and at Night were out of Sight. In the meantime the Commadore was forced to lye by, to put the prize in a Condition of making Sail.

The 31st. the *Kingston* and *Portland* joined the Commadore and their Captains acquainted Him, that the Ship They chased was the Vice Admiral, That they came so near as to fire their Broad Sides; But were at the same time so near the Salmadinas, that they were forced to attack and leave her. The same morning the Commadore having notice of one of the Galleons being run into the Baru; sent the *Kingston*[,] *Portland* and the Fire ship to take or burn Her. They met Her coming out, but on their Appearance she went in again, and run ashore on the Grand Bar, where they Themselves set Her on Fire and she immediately blew up with all Her Riches.

The Spanish Admiral was a Ship of 64 Brass Guns, and 600 men called the *St. Joseph*, and had on board five some say seven millions of p[iece]s [of eight] in Gold and Silver. The Vice Admiral 64 Brass Guns and 500 Men and had on board 5 millions of p[iece]s [of eight] in Gold and Silver.

The Rear Admiral [had] 44 Guns (and 11 in the Hold) and 400 men. But, it was Suggested that most of the Riches, was Shipped on board the other two, at Porto Bello, so that she did not prove so Valuable as was Expected. Though the truth of this had been Controverted, yet it was the general Opinion that the Rear Admiral had not any Registered mon[e]y aboard, but was laden with Cocoa, Vegonia Wool, Jesuits Bark and other Commodities, and some Gold and Silver belonging to private Persons.

On Board the Rear Admiral was taken one Allen a Subject of England, who gave a very particular Account of the Privateers who went up the River Jaco in 1702, and had not been heard of before. He declared, that He went from this Island with Them, and was then a Boy. That after They had got up the River, the Spaniards ordered the Indians to fall large Trees, to obstruct their Return. They afterwards fell into an Ambuscade of Spaniards and Indians, and the Privateers not returning the fire they Expected, by Reason of their Ammunition being damaged. They Sallied out with Guns and lances, and Cut them of[f]. Those that Submitted were afterwards killed in Cold Blood, Except this Allen and Another Boy, who Speaking their language, begged for Mercy, to Consider their Youths, and that being Servants They were forced to Come on this Expedition. On which they were spared, but that They might not have an Opportunity of returning or giving an Account of Their Companies' Fate, they were sent to the south Parts of America. He there met with a kind Master, who growing Rich, was desirous of Spending the Remainder of His days in Old Spain, and was going over a Passenger, in the Galleon, but in the Engagement he was killed.

The 8th. of July the Commadore returned to Port Royal and the 23d. a Court Martial was held for the Trial of Capt[ain] Bridge and Capt[ai]n Windsor, for not having performed their Duty in the late Action against the Galleons. And it appearing by Evidence, upon Oath, that They did not use their utmost Endeavours to Engage and take the Enemy; That they too Negligently chased the Vice Admiral two Days, and that They left of[f] the Chace when within Shot of Her, being near the Salmadinas Shoals, though the Pilots offered to Carry them within the Shoal: The Court thought fit, for these Offences, to dismiss them from the Service. Nor were they ever afterwards Employed in the Navy.

Though this Enterprize did not fully Answer so Glorious a Design, through the Shamefull behaviour of two of those Captains, Yet it must in Justice be observed, that the Conduct and Behaviour of the Commadore did Honour to the Nation as well as to Himself, For He sunk the Admiral with great Riches aboard, took the Rear Admiral, and destroyed another Galleon, which was a very Considerable loss and dissappointment to the Enemy. And, if we may judge by His Vigilence and Application, before the Discovery of the Galleons; His Readiness in pursuit after He had sight of Them; And, His Activity, Bravery, and Resolution in the Engagement, there is no Reason to doubt, He would have pursued, with the same Alacrity, the Vice Admiral and given a good Account of Him, if the Circumstances of Things would have admitted it. But, His Ship was very much damaged in Her Rigging and Sails, a great part of His Men on board the Prize, and not a little Confusion among Them, which rendered it impracticable for Him to pursue. But had Capt[ai]n Bridge and Windsor faithfully performed Their part and Duty, as it Appeared on Their Trial, They might have done, neither of the Admirals would have Escaped, and probably some of the other Galleons must have fallen likewise into Their hands, or been destroyed.

The same Month, Capt[ain] Pinkerman brought in a very Rich French ship of 20 Guns, bound from Nantz to Hispaniola, and the Spanish Coast, Barnet, Gething, Cook, Lyddall, Marshall[,] Quarry and Other Privateers were likewise very Successfull, for their Crews shared from £40 to £100 Each private seaman.

But the most Remarkable Action performed in America, or perhaps in Europe during the Course of the War, was by Capt[ain] Thomas Coleby, in a Privateer sloop of Jamaica, of 10 Guns and 120 Men Who after waiting some time in Expectation of Them met with 14 Sail of Bragantines and Sloops, laden with very Valuable Goods, (brought by the Galleons) and were going from Porto Bello to Chagre, under Convoy of a Sloop of the King of Spain, of 12 Guns and 80 men and bravely fought the Guard Sloop and two Others which stood by her for two Hours, and took Them with 5 more. The Spaniards Offered Capt[ain] Coleby 180,000 p[iece]s [of eight] for the Ransome of the sloops and Cargoes, which He refused, and after taking the Goods out of one of Them (which He gave to the French and Spaniards to Carry them over to Porto Bello) He returned to Port Royal with the other Six.

They proved so Valuable, that though great part of their Cargo were Wo[o]llens and other English Commodities, which sold very low, Yet the private Seamen Shared £500 Each. These Goods were afterwards carried out by the Traders, sold to the Spaniards, and taken a second time by some, English Privateers who carried them into Jamaica where they were sold again re-Exported and Sold a third time to the Spaniards. Hence arose a false and Scandalous Report that the same Men often Traded with Commissions in their pockets, were furnished with Men[,] Arms and Ammunition as if they were fitted for War, and designed for no other purpose. Insomuch that one hand played into the other, Voyages were made with prize Goods taken from the Spaniards, sold to them again, and afterwards taken and sold again, 3 or 4 times by the very same People. Whereas no other Instance can be truly Suggested, and Even in this Case, it was by different Classes, of Men, for Coleby was Actually a Privateer and not on a Trading Voyage, as well as the others who retook those Goods after They had been sold to the Spaniards a second time. But, even that procedure was loudly Complained of by the Merchants in Jamaica, to the Governour, and afterwards by their Principals to the House of Commons; and it was on their Representation, that a Clause was incerted in the Act for Encouraging the Trade to America which prescribed limits to the Cruisers and Privateers on the Main Continent Viz't not to Sail within 5 leagues of the Shore, from S[an]t[a] Martha, to the River Congo, W[est] of Porto Bello.

I thought proper to mention this Circumstance which has been Industriously propagated by those who are not in the Interest of the Island, and because I have heard this Invidious and groundless Assertion, in a Place, where nothing but Truth ought to appear and I was not permitted to disprove it, and Set the matter in a just and true light.

The 24th. of July arrived Her Majestie's Ships the *Monmouth, Jersey* and *Roebuck*, with a fleet of Merchant Ships. They brought the Commadore a Commission of Rear Admiral, and the next day He hoisted the blue Flag at the Mizen topmast head. Those Ships came to relieve the *Expedition, Windsor, Assistance, Dolphin* and *Dunkirk's Prize*. Accordingly they sailed for England the latter end of September, except the *Dunkirk's Prize*, which frigot not being in a Condition to be trusted Home in the Winter, the Rear Admiral sent Her out on a Cruiz[e], with the *Monmouth* and they brought in two French Ships from Rochell bound to Petit Guavas. But Cruising soon after on the North of Hispaniola, the *Dunkirks Prize* chased a French ship ashore near Port Francois, and following too near she struck on a ledge of Rocks, and bulged.

Capt[ain] Purvis Her Commander with His Men got on a Cay, or small Island within Shot of the Ship, and though She had 14 Guns and 60 men, and fired smartly, Yet having got His Boats with a small Canoe, He made a stage, from whence He was ready to Attack Them but the French Cried for Quarter and Surrendered the Ship.

In January the *Portland* Capt[ain] Hutchins brought in a Prize Valued at £6000 Ster[ling] the *Jersey* Capt[ain] Vernon[23] took a Spanish sloop, and

---

23. Edward Vernon (1684–1757) was the second son of Secretary of State James Vernon (1646–1727). He entered the navy in 1700 and was chiefly stationed in the Mediterranean

retook from the French a Guinea Ship with 400 Negroes. And the *Roebuck* Capt[ain] Hardy took a French Sloop laden with Indigo and other Goods. Capt[ai]n Hutchins, being sometime after Sent Convoy to Some Trading Sloops, arrived off the Bastimentos the 15th. of April; and having Intelligence of 3 Ships being at an Anchor there, He stood in the next morning upon which they drew into a line and hoisted French Colours. One of them was a Ship of 50 Guns the other two 30 Guns Each.

The 25th. Capt[ain] Hutchins sailed, from the Samblass and Anchored at the Bastimentos. The 1st. of May He had advice, that the two largest, being Guinea Ships were Sailed, the Night before, He thereupon weighed [anchor] and Stood Northward. On the 3d. about noon they both of them being to Windward bored down to Him, and as they past gave Him some Guns, and wore as if they intended to Engage Him that Evening. Between 7 and 8 in the Morning He came up with the *Mignion* a French Trader of 36 Guns and after He had been Warmly Engaged, the other ship (which was formerly the *Coventry* Man of war 50 guns and taken from us) got on His Lee Bow, and fired at His Masts very briskly. Captain Hutchins finding He had the better of the *Mignion* plied Her very Warmly, till His Main top sail Yard was shot in two, and then they got ahead of Him. But as soon as He had Repaired the Damages, He followed them with all possible Diligence, and about 3 in the Morning perceived that Boats passed very often between the two Ships. About 7 in the morning He came up with the *Coventry*, and intended to board Her, but when He came near, He found Her too well mann'd to run such a Hazard, so that He then plied her with His great Guns. Between 10 and 11 He brought the *Coventry's* Main Mast by the board, and then her Fire decreasing she struck about half an hour after 12. The first Captain was killed, the 2d. Wounded, and above Seventy Men killed in both Ships. The first Captain of the *Mignion* was on Board, the *Coventry*, having received many Wounds aboard His Own Ship, which was so disabled that they judged Her not fit to proceed to France which was the Cause of their removing with their money aboard the other Ship.

In the Action Capt[ai]n Hutchins lost no more than nine men and twelve Wounded, nor had He more than two hundred and twenty aboard. They proved very Valuable and fully rewarded so Brave and Gallant and Exploit, for every Seaman shared upwards of £50.

The Biggest Ship, after She was Condemned, was called by Her former Name the *Coventry*, and added to the Navy, and the Command given to Capt[ai]n Falkingham.

Nothing else of moment hap[pe]ned during the Command of Rear Ad-

---

until 1707 and then the West Indies until 1712. After service in the Baltic he returned to the West Indies from 1739 to 1742. A lieutenant in 1702, he was promoted to captain in 1706 and admiral in 1745. For attacking the admiralty in various pamphlets in 1745–46, he was cashiered.

miral Wager, on this Station; who having received Orders to return to England, Sailed from Port Royal about the middle of September 1709.

The Behaviour of this Gentleman was very different from His Predecessor; for He was not only very active in Annoying and distressing the Enemy, but very carefull of the Trade, in granting Convoys, whenever they were required, and in appointing Cruisers from time to time in proper Stations. He assumed much less State and Ceremony than most of His Captains, and His conduct was so agreeable in all other Respects, that the Inhabitants speak of Him with the highest commendations.

On His departure the Command of the Ships which remained devolved on Captain Tudor Trevor.

About the same time Draughts were made out of Collo[nel] Livesey's (formerly Collo[nel] Brewer's) Regiment to Compleat the Generall's, and the Coll[onel] with His Officers and the Remainder of the Men Embarqued for England pursuant to Her Majestie's Order.

In March 1709/10, the Assembly met according to Prorogation, but with the same Temper and Disposition, for They Could not digest the late proceedings nor the Behaviour of the Governour. Nevertheless, they did not delay to raise the usual and Annual Supplies, for the Subsistance of the Soldiers, and other Contingencies of the Government. But, at the same time they still insisted on the Sole Power of raising and disposing of all Publick Monies; and Their Right of adjournment for a longer time than *de Die, in Diem*. And, though I will not Attempt Either to justify or Condemn those measures, Yet, I may be allowed to observe, that the first point Seems to be not only an inherent Right in Them as Representatives of the People, but it is highly Reasonable it should be so, because the Council not only Act as a Council of State, but as part of the Legislature, and as they are Appointed by the Crown, and generally on the Recommendation of the Governours, they often Consist of Members who have no Property or Real Estate in the Country, and Therefore it cannot be thought Reasonable that they should have a Right to dispose of the Property of Others, who have none of Their own Especially considering the Influence that They are commonly under. The Assembly have hitherto maintained this Right, and Seem to have gained Their point, in Several Instances, though the Council have from time to time made a Bustle with Protest, Remonstrances &c. But, if a future Assembly should on any Occasion give up this Right, They will then be the Shadow of Power only, and nothing more than the Tools and Instruments for raising of money.

As to the Right of adjournment, in Searching the Minutes of the Assembly, from their first Institution, I met with Several Instances of this point having been Yielded to by the Governours and Sometimes by the Assembly. And, that the latter never strictly insisted or made use of it, but when the Governour persisted in His power, to tire or Compel Them to His Measures, by detaining them when their private Affairs, required

Their being at Their Respective Habitations. But, if the Parliament of England, have a Right of adjourning for a longer time than *de Die, in Diem,* as They undoubtedly have then it follows that it is not only Reasonable but Necessary that the Assemblies in our Colonies, should be vested with the same Powers and Privileges there, as the Parliament have in England, because they are directed by all the Charters and Commissions to the Respective Governours, to Assimilate themselves as near as possible to that August Body, which they cannot do, if They are deprived of any of Their Rights or Priviledges. As I shall discuss this matter more particularly, in its proper place, I shall here suspend making any further Animadversion thereon.

The Jealousy and Suspition, the Assembly had been under for sometime, of three Gentlemen, who had the Ear of the Governour and had in a manner Engrossed His Opinions and favour, seem now to be so deeply rooted, that they Attributed all their misunderstandings and Differences, to their Influence and Advice, therefore looked on Them as Incendiaries and Enemies to the Country. One of Them, Richard Rigby,[24] Came over with a Patent for the place of Provost Marshall, and in 2 or three Years insinuated Himself so far into His Excellencie's favour, that He likewise obtained the Place of Secretary of the Island, and Clerk of the Council. The Office of Secretary, He Executed in Person, and the other two by Deputy, being likewise one of the Council. Another of Those Gentlemen, Dr. John Stewart,[25] was also a Member of the Council, and the Third, W[illia]m Broderick,[26] Attorney General.

Hence arose, a fresh difference that added fuel to the Fire, which was not Extinguished, and irritated the Assembly; for as neither of those Gentlemen had any Real Estate or Property in the Country, The Inhabitants in general could not submit to Their having any share in the Conduct of Publick Affairs, and Conceived an opinion of Their playing their own Game, without any Regard to the Interest or Satisfaction of the Country. Therefore to restrain their power, the Assembly passed a Bill intituled an

24. Richard Rigby was secretary of Jamaica and provost marshall in the early 1700s under Thomas Handasyde and Archibald Hamilton though the assembly objected to his holding, contrary to law, two offices without royal assent. Admiral Hovenden Walker described him, along with William Broderick, as "men of most pernicious Principles and Practices," and Lord Hamilton's secretary wrote that he was "obnoxious to the Inhabitants of the best condition in the Island." Cundall, *Governors of Jamaica in the First Half of the Eighteenth Century,* 46, 53, 55, 56, 61, 63, 77, 78, 92.

25. Dr. John Stewart was appointed to the Jamaica Council on March 20, 1707, and was Governor Hamilton's personal physician.

26. William Broderick or Brodrick served as a member of the Jamaica Assembly from 1707 to 1714, representing several different parishes, including St. James, St. George, and St. Catherine, and serving as Speaker in 1711. He was also attorney general from 1711 until the assembly, in 1714, passed a bill barring him and Richard Rigby from holding multiple offices of profit or honor, or from practising law. When the council objected on Broderick's behalf, the assembly declared the council "unparliamentary" and itself "the grand inquest of this Island." Ibid., 53, 55, 56, 57, 59, 61, 63, 69, 70; Cundall, *Historic Jamaica,* xvii, xix.

Act to prevent any Person from holding two or more Offices of Profit in this Island. But, this Bill was rejected by the Council, through the means of the Triumvirate as They were called, and a Prorogation ensued soon after.

In March 1709/10 Commodore Span with the *Rupert* and another Ship of the fourth Rate arrived at Port Royal with orders to take on Him the command of the Squadron. But, nothing Remarkable hap[pe]ned at Sea, during His time, than the taking of a French sloop and ship off of Cape Maiz on Cuba; and afterwards forcing a ship of 30 Guns, and another of 14 ashore, near Cape Tiberon on the West end of Hispaniola. The former the Enemy blew up, and the other sunk, so that nothing but Her Guns, and furniture could be saved.

Capt[ai]n Span was superceeded in the Command of His Majestie's ships, by Commodore Littleton[27] who arrived at Port Royal the 22d. of August 1710, with the *Weymouth* Capt[ai]n Lestock, the *Jersey* Capt[ai]n Vernon, and the *Midways Prize* Capt[ai]n Fletcher.

The Assembly met in March 1710, According to Prorogation, but very much out of Temper and full of Resentment, at the Council's Rejecting the Bill sent up the last Session for Their Concurrence to prevent, Any Person from holding two or more Offices of Profit, in this Island. And, as they Thought such a Law would be of great Utility and Satisfaction to the Country, by preventing too great a Power being lodged in any Favourite or Creature of the Government, They came determined to have such a Bill Enacted, or not to Supply the Deficiency of the Revenue. But, to prevent the Bill meeting with the same Fate, the other did, after passing some few Publick and private Acts, They brought in a Bill intitled an Act to Enable the Treasury to appropriate the Sum of £2000, to Answer the Exigencies of the Government, to which They tacked a Clause, to Prevent the Provost Marshall and Secretaries office being held and Executed by one Man which answered the end of the other Bill, the Clerk of the Council being Annexed to the Secretarie's Office.

This Bill laid the Council under some Difficulties, and Occasioned Them to desire a Conference, Suggesting, that by Her Majestie's Instructions, to the Governour, He was Required to observe in passing all Laws, that different matters might be provided by different Laws without Intermixing in one and the same Act such Things as have no proper relation to Each other: But, the Assembly refused the Conference, on account of its being a Money Bill, Whereupon the Council Sent Them another Message, Signifying that They would always discourage all manner of Tacks as so many incroachments on their part of the Legislature.

After some time spent and nothing done, the Assembly sent a Message

27. Commodore James Littleton (1668–1723), who would later achieve the rank of vice admiral, was a Royal Navy officer who served as commander in chief of the Jamaica station in 1710–12.

to the Governour desiring leave to Adjourn for a month it being then the height of the Crop, and it was Necessary for Them to be on their Respective Plantations. But, instead of a Compliance His Excellency sent for Them, and after passing several Acts, which had met with the Assent of the Council, He Recommended to them to return to Their House, and finish what yet remained to be done.

At this time They insisted on the power of Adjourning Themselves, as a Right, and came to the following Resolution, That the House had an undoubted Right of adjourning Themselves, for a longer time than *de Die in Diem*. The Governour being informed thereof and that They were determined to adjourn Themselves, for a month; on the 8th. of June dissolved that Assembly[.]

The 11th. of July 1711. arrived the Right Hon[ora]ble the Lord Archibald Hamilton,[28] in His Majestie's ship the *Defiance* Capt. St. Lo,[29] with the *Salisbury* the *Salisbury's Prize*, and the Trade from Great Britain.

His Lordship's Commission for Capt[ain] General Governour and Commander in chief was dated the 15th. of August 1710. He landed the same Day and took on Him the Administration. And, General Handasyd Embarqued in August following for Great Britain, in His Majestie's ship the *Nonsuch* Capt[ain] Hardy.

He was (as I have observed) an able Experienced Officer for He went Early into the Army, had Served several Campaigns, under King William in Flanders; and by His long and Faithful Services had raised Himself by Degrees from a Cadet to a L[ieutenant] General. He had very good Natural Parts but the want of a Regular Education, and His Passionate disposition, led Him into some Indecencies in His Behaviour to Gentlemen of the best Character and Estates in the Island, which on due Reflection gave Him great uneasiness. However, He was impartial in the Administration of Justice, and whatever Mistakes He committed were Errors in Judg-

28. Lord Archibald Hamilton (1673–1754) was the seventh and youngest son of William, Third Duke of Hamilton. He went to sea in 1687, becoming a first lieutenant in 1693 and soon afterward a captain at the capture of Gibraltar. Arriving in Jamaica as governor in July 1711, he immediately ran into old problems of raising money, especially for the troop supply, but also quickly getting into trouble over his favoritism toward the unpopular Rigby and Broderick. In July 1716, he was replaced by Peter Heywood and arrested for alleged complicity in plundering Spanish wrecks off the Bahamas. That year the assembly's "Articles Exhibited against Lord Archibald Hamilton, Late Governor of Jamaica. With Sundry Depositions and Proofs Relating to the Same" appeared in London with Hamilton's reply. Although the charges against Hamilton were dropped, he was not reinstated as governor. Subsequently, he was commissioner of the office of lord high admiral, 1729–38, and governor of Greenwich Hospital from 1746 until his death. See Cundall, *Governors of Jamaica in the First Half of the Eighteenth Century*, 51–65.

29. Edward St. Lo (1682?–1729) entered the navy in 1695 and became a captain in 1703. He served in the North Sea, Baltic Sea, and West Indies and was present at the blockade of Portobello in 1727–28. He became a rear admiral in 1729.

ment, and not owing to any other Cause. For though He acquired a more Considerable Estate in the Country, than any Governour, before or Since His time, yet He was never accused by His most Virulent Opponents, of any Act of Oppression or Extortion. Indeed, He had much greater Opportunities than any other ever had, for beside the profits of His Government, He had the Command of two Regiments, and as there was a very beneficial Trade, carried on with the Spaniards in His time, He by those means made very great Advantages. The principal Objections to His Conduct was partiality to His Officers, too Strong a Biass to the Prerogative, and His Confidence in Persons, who were obnoxious to the Country, and had planted those Seeds of Dissention, which are not intirely Rooted out. However, on the whole, and, Considering His Conduct and Behaviour in other Respects, He was allowed to be an Active, Vigilant, and an Upright Governour.

In June Commodore Littleton received Intelligence by different ways of Mons[ieu]r Du Casse being in the West Indies with a Squadron of French Men of War. And, soon after the *Jersey* Capt[ain] Edw[ar]d Vernon brought in a Merchant Ship belonging to Brest of 30 Guns and 120 men. She had been Trading on the Spanish Coast and had landed her money at Port Louis from whence She sailed in Company with Monsieur Du Cass. Captain Vernon in the *Jersey* being sent over to the Coast for further Intelligence, returned the 4th. of July and Reported that having looked into Carthagena the 27th. of the preceeding month, He saw twelve ships there, Six rigged and six unrigged among the former of which He believed was the Vice Admiral of the Galleons. And beside these five sloops.

Commadore Littleton on this advice, sailed from Port Royal with one Third and four Fourth Rates, the 26th. of July He arrived on the Spanish Coast and the same Day chased five ships; but They got into Boccachica the entrance into Carthagena Harbour. He stood off to Sea that Night; and Stretching in the next morning, chased four other Ships. Between 5 and 6 the *Salisbury's Prize* Captain Robert Harland came up with and Engaged the biggest ship, which proved to be the Vice Admiral of the Galleons. The *Salisbury* Captain Hosier[30] Came up soon after, and likewise Attacked Him. And the Commadore, being within Pistol shot was just going to fire, when He Struck. She had Sixty Brass Guns, and three hundred twenty five Men. This was the same Galleon which had Escaped the *Kingston* and *Portland*, when the Admiral of the Galleons blew up and the Rear Admiral was taken by Commodore Wager, as I related before. At the same time Capt[ai]n

30. Francis Hosier (1673–1727) was a British naval officer who distinguished himself in action with the Spanish off Cartagena in 1711 and was promoted to vice admiral in 1723. He is chiefly remembered, however, for his role in the failure of the blockade of Portobello, for which poor government orders were largely responsible and during which he died of disease with thousands of his sailors.

Vernon took a Merchant ship of 400 Tons and 26 Guns, laden with Cocoa and Vigonia Wool. Capt[ai]n Hosier and Harland took another great ship, but; the fourth which was chased by the *Nonsuch* Escaped.

In October the *Jersey* brought in a French ship laiden with Sugar and Indigo, and in November the *Windsor* took the *Thetis* a French man of War of 44 Guns and 300 Men, and Sent Her into Port Royal. Capt[ain] [blank] also took a French Privateer and brought her in. Beside, these were many other Prizes taken and brought into Port Royal, by the Privateers as well as Single ships of War.

In November the Lord Hamilton Convened a New Assembly, who Conceived great Expectations, from the Character They had of His Lordship's Moderation and Dispasionate Temper, that all Their Divisions would be healed, and that They should be Easy and happy under His Administration, And Indeed there Appeared a Disposition, for sometime, in all Ranks of People, to lay aside all Animosities, and to forget Their former differences. But, this Temperament did not continue long, for in a few months They began to Entertain the same Jealousy of the Triumvirate (as They were called) as They had in the preceeding Administration, and in all appearance there was sufficient grounds to Suspect those Gentlemen, not only made use of all the Artificies They were Masters of, to ingratiate Themselves into His Lordship's favour but to make an impression to the disadvantage of all others who were not subservient to their Measures.

However, Things went on smoothly at present, and the Contending Parties met Civilly at the Governour's, and in all other Places. And, the Assembly proceeded cheerfully on Business, passed Several Acts, which were Assented to by the Governour and Council, who to prevent the Revivall of Disputes, made no Objection to the Bill, which They sent up among others intitled an Act to prevent any Person from holding two or more Offices of Profit in this Island and Carefully Avoided the old Topick of Dispute, the Sole Power the Assembly claimed of Raising and Disposing of all the Publick Monies, and their Right of Adjournment for a longer time than *de Die in Diem.* Such was the Seeming Harmony and good understanding between the several branches of the Legislature, that no less than 21 Acts, were passed this Session, and Sent to Great Britain for the Royal Assent, particularly An Act for Appropriating the Sum of £5000, for fitting out two Sloops or Brigantines, for guarding the Sea Coasts and Trade of this Island.

An Act for Regulating Fees.[31]

An Act for quieting possessions, and preventing Vexatious Suits at Law.[32]

An Act to disenable any Member of the Council or of the Assembly

31. An Act for Regulating Fees, November 1710, in *Acts of Assembly Passed in the Island of Jamaica; from 1681 to 1737, Inclusive* (London, 1738), 131–42.

32. An Act for the Further Quieting Possessions, and Preventing Vexatious Suits at Law, November 1710, in ibid., 141–45.

of this Island, from Acting as a Commissioner for receiving any Publick mon[e]y etc.[33]

An Act for the better Securing the Estates and Interest of Orphans, and Creditors; and to Oblige Executors to give Security and to return Appraisments into the Secretaries Office of this Island.[34]

An Act for preserving the publick Records of this Island.[35]

These several Laws were confirmed by the Crown Except the Act to prevent any Person from holding two or more Offices of profit in this Island, which was Suggested to be Rejected through the means or by the Instigation of the Council or some of Them the Island not having at that time an Agent, to Sollicit Their Affairs in England. The Fate of that Act was the more Surprizing, because it was not only a usefull and Necessary Law, but it was for many Years a Constant clause in the Instructions to every Governour not to Suffer any person to Execute more than one Office.

In February the *Salisbury* Capt[ain] Hosier, brought in a French ship laden with Sugar and Indigo. And, the *Jersey* Capt[ain] Vernon run a French ship of 20 Guns, ashoar, where she beat in pieces. But, the Service performed by the Squadron under Commadore Littleton, after this, Consisted only in taking some other Prizes by Single ships and providing for the Security of the Trade.

The 6th of July 1712, S[i]r Havenden Walker Rear Admiral of the *White*, with *the Monmouth*[,] *August* and *Centurion* arrived at Jamaica, with orders to take on Him the Command of the Squadron on this Station. Several Prizes, were soon after brought in by the Cruisers, one of which, taken by the *August* Capt[ain] Thompson was very Valuable.

Hurricanes, which are so frequent in other Parts of America, had not hitherto been known in this Island at least since the English had been in possession; for though they Commonly had strong Easterly Winds or Sea Breezes in the Summer Months and had often blown hard and Stormy in the Winter Months from the N[orth] or S[outh]—Yet neither the Shipping, Buildings nor the Plantations, Ever had Sustained any Damage thereby. But, on the 28. of August there hap[pe]ned a most Dreadful one, which was of very fatal Consequence to the Island, and the Trade of Great Britain. It had been Calm most part of that and the preceeding Day, only now and then a small, gentle Breez[e], which shifted round the Compass, in the space of an hour. About 7 in the Evening there was a small Rain and

33. An Act to Disenable Any Member of the Council, or of the Assembly, from Acting as Commissioner for Receiving Any Publick Money, Raised by the Governor, Council, and Assembly of This Island; and to Disable Any Such Commissioner to Be a Member of the Council, or of the Present or Any Future of This Assembly, c. 1710, in ibid., 146.

34. An Act for the Better Securing the Estates, and Interest of Orphans and Creditors, and to Oblige Executors to Give Security, and to Return Appraisements into the Secretary's Office of This Island, 1710, in ibid., 147–49.

35. An Act for Preserving the Public Records of This Island, 1711, in ibid., 152–54.

the Wind began to blow at S[outh] E[ast] it Continued Encreasing until 11 at Night and from that time until 5 in the morning, it varied from Point to Point, and blew with great Violence. It then decreased gradually and about 8 in the Morning, the Weather became moderate, but on every side there was a most melancholy and Dismal Prospect, many Houses in the Towns, as well as in the Plantations being blown down others uncovered, and none without some Damage. The Harbours which were full of shipping before none appeared after but the men of War and about 5 or 6 merchant Men (without Masts) and others with only Their Masts above Water. The Bays were full of Wrecks, ships drove so far up that several of them were dry, and never Could be got off, and great Quantities of Goods, and Dead Bodies floating from Place to Place, as the Wind blew. In the Country, great Trees were blown up by the Roots, Canes laid flat with the Ground, and other great damages Done by the Floods Occasioned by its Raining impetuously most of the time, insomuch that the Roads were scarcely passable for some Weeks after.

The 25th. of October 1712 was Published Her Majestie's order for the Cessation of Arms with France and Spain.[36] And, in March following S[i]r Havendon Walker Sailed for England, with the Squadron under His Command, leaving only the *Mary* Gally and the *Scarborough* to Attend the Island. But, notwithstanding all Enormity ceased on our side, the Spaniards Nevertheless continued their Hostilities; and though Their Privateers or Guarda Costas never dared to Appear on or near our Coasts during the War, Yet the Squadron was no Sooner gone, and the Privateers recalled but they began to Cruiz[e] about the Island and to Commit divers Depredations. For, They not only took a Coasting sloop (The Sloop *Charles* David Johnson Master) laden with Sugar and other Goods belonging to the Planters, and were intended for sale or Exportation at Kingston. But, They landed in St. James's Precinct and carried away 30 Negroes belonging to Major Cook,[37] who on Representing His Case Obtained my Lord Hamilton's letter to the Governour and Alcadies of Trinadado demanding Restitution or Satisfaction. And in hopes of the One or the Other, the Major went in Person to sollicit Justice, but though He saw several of His Negroes who had been taken from Him and informed the Spanish Governour in whose possession They were, Yet He came away after a fruitless and Expensive Attendance, tired with Delays and Evasive Answers.

The 9th. of July 1713, the Peace between Great Britain and France, was proclaimed in this Island.

The Assembly met in October following, When His Excellency Recommended Several matters to their Consideration, and to lay aside all Controversies, and Disputes.

36. Probably the preliminaries of the Treaty of Utrecht of April 14, 1713.
37. Perhaps Edward Cook, who was a member of the Jamaica Assembly in 1711–14.

Throughout his narrative, Knight gave major attention to the destructive force of the hurricanes that struck Jamaica during his tenure on the island. No known visual source records any of them, but this French engraving of an "Ouragan aux Antilles" provides a contemporary visual image of a West Indian hurricane, showing a women holding her baby and clutching another child while trying to prevent a building from falling on her and a body lying next to her under some fallen timbers. In the background, other timber flies through the air, houses are partially underwater, and several other figures stand in high water, bracing themselves against the rain and wind. This image is from the frontispiece in Abbé Guillaume-Thomas-François Raynal (1713–1796), *Histoire philosophique et politique des établissements et du commerce des Européens dans les deux Indes . . . tome sixième* (Geneva, 1783).

At the same time He laid before Them the Report of the Lords Commissioners for Trade and Plantations (in the Words following) and Her Majestie's order in Council thereupon.

To the Right Hon[ora]ble the Lords of the Council for hearing of Appeals from the Plantations.

In Obedience to your Lordship's order of Reference, of the 28th. Instant, upon the Petition of Mr. Robert Saunders[38] directing us to Report to your Lordship's, Whether priviledge has at any time been claimed by the Members of the Assembly of Jamaica, Whether the same has been allowed and in what Cases, and what hath been the Issue thereof.

We take leave to Represent to your Lordships that the Members of the Assembly, not only of Jamaica but of the other Plantations also, do assume pretended Rights and Priviledges (for which we Cannot find the least grounds) tending to an Independancy on the Crown of Great Britain, Some of Them particularly those of New York, pretending They have an Inherent Right to dispose of the mon[e]y of the Freemen of that Province.

And that such Their Rights does not proceed from any Commission, Letters Patents, or Other Grants from Her Majesty, but from the Free Choice and Election of the People, notwithstanding They had been Acquainted. They could not be Elected nor be an Assembly but by Virtue of a Clause in Her Majestie's Commission to the Governour, impowering Him to issue out Writs for Their Election. Most of the Assemblies in all the Plantations claim all the priviledges of the House of Commons and Some of Them others, that the House of Commons never pretended to.

Upon Examination of some Gentlemen of Jamaica We find that Gershom Ely[39] Esq[uir]e Complained of by the Petitioner, insists on His priviledge, as an Assembly Man, to Avoid Coming to a Trial with the Petitioner, but we do not see any Reason for it nor do we find by our Books that the Governours have any Authority by His Commission and Instructions, to allow such priviledge.

White Hall

May 28, 1713.

Her Majestie's order in Council Confirms the said Report, and it is thereby ordered that the said Robert Saunders have free liberty to proceed against the said Gershom Ely. And, the Right Hon[ora]ble the Lord Archibald Hamilton, Governour of Her Majestie's Island of Jamaica or the Governour or Commander in Chief for the time being, and all other Officers and Persons whom it may Concern, are to take Notice thereof, and pay due Obedience to Her Majestie's pleasure herein Signified.

38. A Robert Saunders represented St. James Parish from 1728 to 1735.

39. Gershom Ely represented St. Mary Parish in the Jamaica Assembly from 1711 to 1714, St. Ann Parish in 1716–17 and 1736–38, St. James Parish in 1719–21, and St. Thomas in the Vale Parish in 1721.

It does not appear that this point, was debated or that it has ever since been insisted on by any Member of the Assembly. But, the Faction increasing through Jealousy of the Power and Interest of the Triumvirate His Lordship was advised to dissolve the present, and to Convene a new Assembly, the 26th. of November following. In this Step, as well as in the Subsequent Measures thereupon, His Lordship seems to have been misadvised, because that Assembly Consisted of Gentlemen of the best Characters and Estates in the Country, who had Interest Enough to be rechosen. Some means were likewise made use of, which must be allowed to be Irregular and Served only to irritate the Inhabitants in general as Causing 3 or 4 Elections to be on one and the same day; and Dismissing divers Gentlemen from Civil and Military Employments, who were not agreeable, to the Triumvirate (on a Suggestion that They were men of Restless and Turbulent Spirits who never were pleased with any Government); and Recommending others to Succeed, who were Subservient to Their Designs. When in Reality They had not Then any personal Enmity or prejudice to His Lordship and Only aimed at removing those, who They thought Evil Councellors, Incendaries and Enemies to the Country. This was the Foundation and Cause of those Violent Animosities, which afterwards spread all over the Island, and His Lordship's attachment to those Gentlemen, brought on Him the Difficulties and Embarassments He afterwards met with, which were attended with bad Consequences to the Island as well as to Himself. Though at the same time it must be acknowledged the Opposition was carried on with great Rancour and Virulence, and that His Lordship was not deserving of the Asperity and Mal-treatment He met with.

I am now treating of Transactions, within my Own knowledge, and Memory, not taken merely from Information or Papers of any kind, being then on the Spot, and as Spectator only of what passed, without concerning my Self one way or the other. For, as I was then in the Service of the Crown as Rec[eiver] [General], and in a Station which (by a late Act of the Country) disqualified me among others from being a Member of the Council or Assembly, I thought it prudent, (Especially as I was just entered on the Stage of Business) to attend the Duty of my Office, to pay a due deference and Respect to the Governour, and to avoid giving offence to the Council Assembly or to Either Party. So that I may be allowed to be impartial though I afterwards fell under the displeasure of the Assembly. But as it is difficult for a Man to speak of Himself without Suspicion of prejudice or partiality I shall avoid any further mention of that Affair than that His late Majesty upon my humble Representation was Graciously pleased to Redress the Grievance and Penalties I was laid under.

The Assembly met according to the Writs of Election the 26th. of November 1713 but very much out of humour, not only for the aforementioned Reasons, but as it was a very unseasonable time of the Year, Christmas being near at hand, as well as the Crop, which made it Necessary for the Members to be at Their Respective Plantations. They therefore declined entering upon any other Business, than choosing a Speaker,[40] Clerk and other Officers, and Regulating the Rules of the House; And, sent two of Their Members to desire leave of His Excellency to adjourn to the 14th. of January, which was granted.

They met according to Adjournment, and passed a Bill, intituled an Act for providing an Additional Subsistence for Her Majestie's Officers and Soldiers from the 1st. of November 1713, to the 1st. of November 1714, and no longer.

This Bill met with the Governour and Council's assent and on the 19. of February His Excellency sent for the House and Recommended to their Consideration, the Exigencies of the Country and other matters he had laid before Them and to proceed thereon with Unanimity and without Delay, assuring Them of His Readiness to pass such Laws as were for the Service of the Island.

The Day following They presented an Address wherein They returned His Excellency thanks for His Speech of Yesterday [and] assured Him, that they Relied on His promise of passing such Laws, as may be for the Service of this Island, without any diffidence on Their part, And hoped no unquiet Spirit might by any Insinuations, give His Excellency the least doubt or Jealousy of the Assembly, for whatever promises They made should be punctually Complied with. That the time of Grand Court being at Hand They desired leave to adjourn for a month having several matters under Consideration which could not be dispatched before the meeting of that Court. But at Their return, They hoped every Thing would be Concluded to His Excellency's satisfaction, and the good of the Island.

His Excellency thanked Them for Their Address and said He was in Hopes They would have Complied with what He had Recommended, and was Indespensably necessary to be done without any Delay. Therefore till the Ends for which They were called together were complied with, He could not agree to any recess or adjournment, but from Day to Day. And that the due Course of Law, might not be interrupted, He offered Them the Old House belonging to the Queen, or that They might sit in the Chapel, as had been done, when the Occasion was less pressing.

The Assembly immediately took His Excellencie's Answer into Consideration Resolved That it was Their undoubted Right to adjourn, when and as often as They thought fitting; and the Question being put, Whether the House should adjourn for a month, or a lesser time, it was carried for a month. And, the Speaker adjourned the House Accordingly.

My Lord Hamilton who had hitherto endeavoured to avoid all Occasions of Contest and particularly with regard to the Rights and Priviledges, which the Assembly claimed, thought fit, with the Unanimous advice of

40. Hugh Totterdale.

the Couuncil to dissolve Them and assigned the following Reason among others for so doing—Their having Assumed a power to adjourn, when and as often as They think fit, in manifest Contempt of Her Majestie's Authority, and without His leave Actually did Adjourn Themselves for a Month.[41]

The 22d. of June, the Peace[42] between Great Britain and Spain was published in this Island. But, notwithstanding, the Spaniards did not cease Hostilities in America, but Committed them as often as it was in their power, and they were Strong enough to Overcome, even the lawful Traders belonging to the English Nation. For this Year the following Vessells were taken on the high Seas or near the Coast of this Island.

Ships' Names.	Masters.	of What Port.	Where bound
John Thomas	Charles Bags	Jamaica	Musquitos
Pearl	John Drudge	Jamaica	P[or]t. Louis
Ruby	Nat Ural	Jamaica	Curaso
John and Sarah	Fr. [?] Tarjeir	Jamaica	Curaso
Henry	St[uart?] Smith	Jamaica	Musquitos
Tho[ma]s & Elizabeth	Mat[thew] Musson	Jamaica	Musquitos
Hunter	Rich[ard] Jones	New York	Jamaica
Sarah	And[rew] Crean	Jamaica	P[or]t. Louis
Leeds Galley	John Thomas	London	Bahamas
William	Tho[mas] Fag	Jamaica	Curaso
Content	Jos[eph] Morgan	Jamaica	Coaster[43]
Westmorland	B. Schoolmaster	Jamaica	Coaster

A regular Application was made for these several unjust Captures, of the Respective Governours where They were carried to but without obtaining the least satisfaction of Redress. I shall therefore from time to time give other Instances, which will Evidently shew the Perfidy of that Nation and that They never did strictly observe the Treaties with Great Britain, and more Especially in America, where they had frequent Opportunities of breaking Them with impunity on pretences that were unreasonable and unwarrantable.

41. This quarrel with Hamilton and resentment of the continued engrossment of power by the triumvirate under his administration produced a notable pamphlet, [James Spence and Roderick MacKenzie], *The Groans of Jamaica* (London, 1714), which is reprinted in Jack P. Greene and Craig B. Yirush, eds., *Exploring the Bounds of Liberty: Political Writings of Colonial British America from the Glorious Revolution to the American Revolution*, 3 vols. (Indianapolis, 2018), 1:395–461. Other pamphlets treating this controversy are *The Representation and Memorial of the Council of the Island of Jamaica* (London, 1716), and William Wood, *A View of the Proceedings of the Assemblies of Jamaica, for Some Years Past* (London, 1716). Knight did not cite these pamphlets and may not have known about them.

42. The Treaty of Urecht, April 14, 1713.

43. A Vessel that brings Planters' Commodities to Kingston and Port Royal and taken on our Own Coast. —*Author.*

Those unfortunate Persons who went to Sollicit Justice, after a dilatory and Expensive attendance being put off in a Scandalous manner, some (who Represented their Case with Freedom) with threats and Manaces. And others with Evasive Answers or Compliments and directed to the Court of Madrid. But, how Expensive would such an Application be, and will not any Man or Company rather drop His or Their Claim, as many have done, rather than leave His Affairs in America, and to Spain to sollicit Justice, at the expence of His time and money and loss of His Business, which might end in Ruin.

The Peace with France as well as Spain being not fully concluded and Published in this Island, and other Parts of the British Dominions Draughts were made out of Gen[era]l Handasyd's Regiment, and formed into two Independent Companies, pursuant to Her Majestie's order. The Command of one of Them was given to my Lord Hamilton, and the other to L[ieutenan]t Collo[nel] Rookwood who was likewise appointed Capt[ai]n of the Fort. The Rest of the men had liberty to remain or to return to England with the Core, but most of them chose to Settle in the Island, Especially those who had been brought up to any Mechanick Art.

In October His Excellency received advice of the Death of Queen Ann, and of the Accession of the Elector of Hanover[44] to the Crown of Great Britain. Accordingly His Majesty was proclaimed with the usual Solemnity, and His Excellency invited the Gentleman of the Island to Enter into an Association, which was drawn up, and readily Subscribed to by them all Excepting About 5 or 6, who desired to be Excused but gave assurance of their Submissive and peaceable behaviour.

The new Assembly was Convened in [blank] but as very few new Members were returned, They met with the same Temper and Disposition as the last.

The Governour, with His usual Calmness, in His Speech Exhorted Them to lay aside all Animosities and Disputes, and Recommended to Their most Serious Consideration the Condition and Circumstances of the Island. That the Revenue was greatly Anticipated, and required Considerable Supplies for the Honour and Support of the Government. That the Act, for Subsisting His Majestie's Officers and Soldiers was Expired. And, Several other maters which He thought Necessary for the good and Service of the Island.

But, this Speech had very little Effect on Them, They came to Several Resolutions, that were not agreeable to the Governour, particularly in regard to their Rights and Priviledges, and, which at length ended in their Dissolution.

44. George I (1660?–1727), the great grandson of James I and elector of Hanover, acceded to the English throne at the death of Queen Anne on August 1, 1714. His siding with the Whigs and support of Robert Walpole assured the Whig ascendancy in eighteenth-century British politics.

The Assembly being dissolved without any provision made for Supplying the Deficiency of the Revenue or the Subsistence of the Soldiers, laid
His Lordship under great Difficulties and Embarassments, which in Consequence was of great prejudice to the Country. For Tradesmen and others who were Employed in the Publick Service not being duly paid, very
few would undertake any work for the Government but at Extravagant
rates, Orders of Council for Payment and other Occasions, being publickly
offered at 20 p[er]C[en]t discount; so that to gratify the Resentment of
some leading men the General Interest of the Country was Obstructed and
hurted by a load of Debts being Contracted, by those means, which were
not discharged in many Years after. And, the Soldiers became so inflamed
and unruly for want of their usual Subsistance, that They openly declared
They would not Starve, and Actually did kill Cattle[,] Sheep &c. belonging
to Gentlemen of the Assembly, particularly those in the Opposition, but
took care not to injure or molest any others. The Governour and Council to prevent any Disturbances which might arise thereupon, Raised (by
Subscription among themselves) and advanced a Sum of mon[e]y for Their
Maintenance for Six months, in Expectation of being Reimbursed by the
Assembly or the Crown.

In [blank] 1715 The S[outh] Sea Company settled a Factory in this Island, for Carrying on the Assiento Contract[45] and Mess[ieu]rs Morris[46] and
Pratter[47] were appoint[ed] Their Agents, though the principal Factory was
then and for some Years after at Barbadoes. And Commodore Balchen[48] arrived about the same time to take on Him the command of His Majestie's
Ships on this Station, which consisted only of two Fifth and one Sixth Rate.

In October a new Assembly was Convened, and His Excellency laid
before Them a more Gracious Letter, He had received from the King,
wherein His Majesty was pleased to Signify the great Regard He had for
this Island, so Valuable for its produce and Situation for Trade, and to

45. The Treaty of Utrecht of 1713 gave the South Sea Company the *assiento*, or exclusive
right to import slaves into Spanish colonies at a number up to 4,800 per annum. This arrangement greatly chagrined Jamaican slave traders because it excluded them from what had
been a lucrative trade. The factor in Jamaica was set up to facilitate trade but also cost the
island much of its maritime labor force and many ships. Cundall, *Governors of Jamaica in the
First Half of the Eighteenth Century*, 72, 79, 106, 144, 157, 194.

46. John Morris described himself and Edward Pratter as factors to the South Sea and Assiento Company in Jamaica in December 1715.

47. Edward Pratter [Prattler] (c. 1683–1735), a Kingston merchant and member of the
assembly for Hanover, 1722–27, and Kingston, 1727, 1731, and 1731–35, was also receiver
general of Jamaica and agent for the South Sea Company. Ibid., 72, 133, 148, 149; Cundall,
Historic Jamaica, 173.

48. John Balchen Esq[uir]e now Admiral of the Blue. — *Author.* John Balchen (1670–1744)
had a long and varied record of naval service before he was assigned to suppress piracy in the
West Indies in 1715. He was promoted to rear admiral in 1728, vice admiral in 1734, and admiral of the white in 1743. Knighted in 1744, he went down with a ship in the English channel that year. — *Ed.*

Express a Concern to find its Inhabitants decreased and their Trade decayed, while its Vigilant Neighbours omitted no Endeavours to increase and Strengthen themselves in both. That this Concern was the greater, as there had not been that good Agreement in the Assemblies necessary at all times for their Happiness, but more Especially at such a juncture. His Excellency was therefore required to call an Assembly if not already done and to assure Them in His Majestie's Name That as it has been His Earnest and greatest desire that all His Subjects, even the most Remote should feel the happy Influence of His Government so a particular care should be had to this Island, by Affording Them such protection from time to time, as by the Blessing of God and the Assistance of His Subjects, They may render Themselves secure. And by giving His Royal approbation, to such good Laws as might make Them happy, of which He had been Graciously pleased to give Them an Early Instance, by Confirming two most Beneficial Acts, so long and so Earnestly desired Vizt. the one for Regulating Fees. And, the other for quieting Possessions, and preventing Vexatious Suits at Law.

In return whereof His Majesty Expected from the said Island, a ready and cheerfull Compliance in making an Honourable provision for the Revenue by discharging all Publick Debts, and giving a Necessary Subsistance to the two Independent Companies, till by some good Laws which shall be made for Encouraging the increase of Inhabitants, there shall be no further Occasion for Them.

The Assembly on taking this Letter into Consideration, sent a Message to the Governour and Council, to desire They would join with Them in an Address to His Majesty, which They assented to. And accordingly an Address was drawn up in the Names of the Governour, Council, and Assembly of Jamaica: They therein returned His Majesty Their most Humble and hearty Thanks for those Extraordinary marks of Grace and Condesention with that tender Regard His Majesty in so distinguishing a manner had been pleased to declare Himself in favour of this Island, which had made the deepest impression on His Faithfull Subjects Here. They Assured Him of a cheerfull compliance, with what His Majesty had been pleased to recommend, and of Their unfeigned Attachment, Loyalty and Affection to His Majestie's Person, Family and Government.

Accordingly they Voted the Sum of £3000, to Supply the Deficiencies of the Revenue.[49] A Subsistence for His Majestie's Officers and Soldiers for 6 months to Commence from the 31 of October 1715,[50] in Case, Two

49. Possibly An Act to Impose Duties on Several Commodities to Defray the Extraordinary Charge of the Government; and Applying the Same to Several Uses, October 1715, in *Acts of Assembly*, 157.

50. An Act for Granting a Supply to His Majesty Subsistence for HM Officers and Soldiers for 6 Months, to Enable the Treasury to Discharges Its Debts, and to Answer the Other Exigencies of the Government, 1715, in ibid., 157.

hundred Men did not arrive within that time, by the Encouragement given by a Bill, Entitled an Act to Encourage the bringing Over and Set[t]ling White People in this Island.[51]

But, Voted the mon[e]y advanced by the Governour and Council for the Subsistance of the Soldiers, no Debt within the Construction of His Majestie's letter and that They were not under any Obligation to Reimburse the same. In November They sent up a Bill to the Council Entitled an Act for applying a sum of mon[e]y, for Solliciting the passing of Laws, and other Publick Affairs.[52]

But, the Committee of Council to whom it was referred Reported that They had Considered the said Bill, and found that it tended to the Subversion of the Constitution of this Island, and to the Establishing an *Ephori*,[53] to Controul the Government. That the power which was lodged by the former Act, in a joint Committee of the Council and the Assembly was by this Bill lodged in a Committee of the Assembly only, and therefore were of Opinion that the Bill ought to be rejected, which was accordingly done.

The Assembly thereupon appointed a Committee of Their House to Consider the State of the Island, who Reported among other Things, that it was absolutely Necessary to prevent the Island lying under further misrepresentation at Home, that Subscriptions should be Set on Foot, to Sollicit the Affairs of this Island, in England, and that it might be Recommended to the Several Parishes, by the Respective Members.

The House considering the Report and the Reasons given did Accordingly pass a Vote to Recommend the said Subscriptions. And the Draught of an Instrument in Writing, being prepared next Day, was Read and Agreed to. The Members of the Assembly only Subscribed thereto £1100 beside what was Collected in the several Parishes which was Remitted to S[i]r Gilbert Heathcote,[54] and Francis March Esq[uir]e[,][55] a Member of the House, was chosen among Themselves to go to Great Britain, and Sollicit Their Affairs.

The Intention of the Members of the Assembly, in sending this Gen-

51. An Act to Oblige Several Inhabitants of This Island to Provide Themselves with a Sufficient Number of White People; and to Maintain Such as Shall Come Over within a Certain Time, or Pay Certain Sums of Money in Case They Shall Be Deficient, and Applying the Same to Several Uses, 1716, in ibid., 157.

52. Act for Supply [a] Sum of Money for Solliciting the Passing of Laws, and Other Publick Affairs, 1715. Not agreed to by the governor and council, this act does not appear in the 1738 edition of *Acts of Assembly*.

53. The five elected magistrates exercising a supervisory power over the kings of Sparta.

54. Sir Gilbert Heathcote had occasionally served as London agent for Jamaica since 1698.

55. Francis March had at the time of his agency already seen extensive service in the Jamaica Assembly, representing St. James Parish in 1704, St. Mary Parish in 1705, St. George Parish in 1706–7, St. Thomas in the Vale Parish in 1707–8, and St. Catherine Parish, 1708–14. He would later sit for St. Ann Parish in 1722.

tleman to Great Britain, was not only to Sollicit the Confirmation of Their Laws, and other Affairs of the Island; but, principally to Sollicit the removall of my Lord Hamilton from the Government, as it Evidently Appeared afterward. And, an incident hap[pe]ned at the same time, which facilitated Their Design, by joining, if not spiriting up the Spanish Ambassador, in the Complaint He made of His Lordship.

The same Month They passed and Sent up to the Council for Their Concurrence, a Bill intitled an Act, to Oblige the several Inhabitants of this Island to provide Themselves, with a Sufficient Number of White People, and to Maintain such as shall come over within the Space of 3 Years, or pay certain Sums of money in Case They shall be deficient, and applying the same to Several uses.

The Council made several Amendments thereto, but it being a mon[e]y Bill, the Assembly would not agree to Them. Upon this They sent The following Message[:] That the Board was in hopes Their Right to amend mon[e]y Bills would no longer be brought into Question, the same being not only declared by His Majestie's Council of Trade, but agreeable to the almost uninterrupted proceedings of former Assemblies. They likewise conceive the Amendments They have made, are all of Them Reasonable, and some of Them of such a Nature, that They could not receed from them without Violating His Majestie's Instructions and the Constitution of the Island. They at the same time Sent Copies of several Paragraphs in His Majestie's Instructions to the Governour, relating to the Raising and issuing Publick mon[e]y; also, Extracts of two letters from the Board of Trade, the Substance of which are as follows.

We are glad to find the Council so Unanimous, in joining with your Lordship, in Supporting Her Majestie's Prerogative, against the unreasonable Attempts of the Assembly and think your Lordship did well in dissolving Them. As to Their pretence that the Council have no Right to amend mon[e]y Bills it is groundless, and will not be allowed of Here. They only Sit as an Assembly, and are part of the Legislature, as is also the Council, by Virtue of a Clause in Her Majestie's Commission to your Lordship, without which They could not be Elected and Sit in Assembly, Consequently Their assumeing a pretended Right, no ways Inherent in Them, is a Violation of the Constitution of Jamaica, and derogatory to Her Majestie's Royal Prerogative. If therefore your Lordship acquainting Them with what we now Write, They should at any time insist upon that Ill-grounded pretence, Your Lordship may inform Them, that as They must not assume to Themselves the Right and Privileges of the House of Commons in Great Britain so such measures will be taken Here, as may be Effectual to Assert Her Majestie's undoubted Prerogative in that Island.
White Hall
April 25, 1715.

But neither the message [n]or those letters from the Board of Trade had any Effect, the Assembly notwithstanding would not allow of the Council's making any Amendments, and the Councill adhereing to their Amendments the Bill dropped, and a short Prorogation insued.

In November came advice of the Spanish Flota or Galleons, Richly laden with Gold, Silver and other Merchandize, and bound to Old Spain being all Cast away and Wrecked on the Coast of Florida. On which Several sloops were fitted out, from this Island, in order to fish and save out of them what they could in hopes of getting great Riches. But, as there was at that time several Pirates cruising on the Seas and Coasts of America, it was apprehended that if They met with any of Them, They should be deprived of the Fruits of Their labour, unless They went well manned, and with some kind of Authority. The Owners therefore applied to my Lord Hamilton for Commissions to Suppress Pirates; and I am of Opinion from the personal knowledge I had of those Gentlemen, that They had not any Sinister Intention or Design, nor Indeed, was there any thing in those Commissions, which would justify or Even Countenance Hostilities, on any other People or Persons, than Pirates.

At this time there was only one man of War and one sloop on this Station, both foul and unfit to go after light Nimble Vessells, which infested our Trade and even those the Commanders had given Notice that They had received orders to return to Great Britain, as soon as their Provisions were reduced, which was very near and not more than sufficient for their Voyage Homewards.

His Lordship considering these Circumstances, and being desirous of making the best provision He could for the Security of the Trade and Navigation in these Parts; (Precedents being brought Him of the like Commissions having been granted by S[i]r William Beeston and other Governours, and not foreseeing any Inconveniences that could possibly arise, did grant Commissions, for taking and Suppressing of Pirates): But, at the same time obliged every Commander to give good Security, in the penal sum of £1500, to hinder and restrain Him from any Acts of hostility whatever against any of His Majestie's Allies, and to observe His Instructions.

As this Affair made a great Noise in the World, and has been very much misrepresented, I think it Necessary to transcribe one of those Commissions and Instructions with some abstracts of other papers relative hereto, Because they will Set things in a true light and remove any impressions, which have been made to the prejudice of the Governour, or the Island.

His Lordship very justly observed, in Vindication of Himself in granting these Commissions, that there was a real Occasion for Them, and that the Design of them had no relation to the Spanish Wrecks, But, insists that even on that supposition, it was more adviseable to grant them than not, for if the Securities given were not strong enough to hold some Men from committing Robberies, it is Ridiculous to imagine they would have been more restrained by having given none.

Jamaica Is[land]

His Excellency the Lord Archibald Hamilton, Captain General, and Governour in Chief, in and over His Majesty's Island of Jamaica, and the Territories thereon depending, in America, Chancellor and Vice Admiral of the same.

To Captain Jonathan Barnet, Commander of the *Snow Tyger*, Greeting.

Whereas since the Proclamation of the Peace, lately concluded between the Crown of Great Britain, and the Crowns of *France* and *Spain*, several *British* Ships, and other Vessels have been taken by Pirates, and frequent Depredations have been and are by them daily made and committed upon the Subjects of *Great Britain*, on the High Seas in the *West Indies;* whereby the Navigation to and from this Island, is rendered extreamly dangerous and unsafe. And whereas, for preventing of such Mischiefs for the future, it has been adjudged necessary, besides His Majesty's Ships of War, to fit out and Commission other private Men of War. And whereas you Capt[ain] Jonathan Barnet, have to that End freely offered your Self and the *Snow Tyger*, whereof you are Commander, to Act against the Pirates, wherewith these Seas are at present infested, in His Majestie's Service.

Now know ye, that by Virtue, and in pursuance of the Powers and Authorities to me granted by His Majesty, I reposing especial Trust and Confidence in your Loyalty, Courage and Capacity, have by this Commission, which is to remain in Force for the Space of six Months from the Date hereof, and no longer, authorized and appointed, and hereby do authorize and appoint you the said Jonathan Barnet, to be Commander of the said *Snow Tyger*, fitted out at the Charges of your self and Owners in a Warlike manner, therewith by Force of Arms to seize, take and apprehend all Piratical Ships and Vessels, with their Commanders, Officers, Crew and Ladings, and in general to commit, do and execute all manner of Acts of Hostilities whatsoever, against such Ships or Vessels, their Commanders, Officers and Crew, according to the Law of Arms, and the Customs of Nations; and I do hereby Command all Officers, Mariners and Soldiers in the said *Snow Tyger*, to be Obedient to you in all Things, as their Commander. And you are to observe all such Orders and Instructions as herewith delivered unto you, or you shall hereafter receive from His Majesty, my self, or other your superior Officers. Given under my Hand and Seal at Arms, at St. Iago de la Vega, the 24th. Day of November, in the Second Year of His Majesty's Reign, Anno Domini, 1715.

A. Hamilton

By his Excellency's Command,
Will Cockburn.

Jamaica Is[land]

His Excellency the Lord Archibald Hamilton, Captain General, and Governour in Chief, in and over His Majestie's Island of Jamaica, and the

Territories thereon depending, in America, Chancellor and Vice-Admiral of the same.

Instructions for Captain Jonathan Barnet, Commander of the *Snow-Tyger*, which are to remain in Force six Months, no longer.

1. You are according to your Commission to commit, do and execute all manner of Acts of Hostility against Pirates, according to the Law of Arms.
2. That you do not on any Pretence, commit any Acts of Hostility, Depredation, or other Injuries or Trespasses whatsoever, on any of His Majestie's Allies, Neuters, Friends or Subjects, but that in all Things you succour and relieve them according to your Capacity.
3. That you bring into your Commission-Port all such Pirate or Pirates as you shall take, there to be proceeded against according to Law.
4. That you keep a fair Journal of all your Proceedings, and on your Arrival, you deliver to His Majesty's Captain Gen[era]l or Commander in Chief for the Time being, a fair Transcript or Copy thereof.
5. That under Colour of your Commission, you do not carry off this Island any Person or Persons notoriously indebted, either Planter, Merchant, or others; but that you take Care to inform your self aright of each and every your Men's Conditions and Circumstances, and bring them all back again with you (Death and Danger of the Seas excepted) and that before you set Sail from the Harbour of Port Royal, you deliver to the Chief Officer of the Customs of that Port, an exact List of all your Men, belonging to your said *Snow-Tyger*, containing their Names, Ages, and Description of their Persons.
6. You are hereby required to wear no other Jack, than that worn by His Majesty's Ships, with a distinction of a white Escutcheon in the middle thereof.

Of all which Instructions you are to take due Notice, and pay Obedience thereunto. Given under my Hand at St. Iago de la Vega, the 24th of November 1715.
       A. Hamilton.

Beside that Commission, several others were granted and particularly to Capt[ain] John Wells of the *Eagle*, Capt[ain] Henry Jennings of the *Batshua*, and Capt[ain] Francis Fernando, of the Bennet, though some Vessels went on the Wrecks, without any Commission.

Capt[ains] Wells and Jennings arrived at the Wrecks some Days before the others, and found the Spaniards to the Number of 120 or 130, had fixed Tents on the Cays or little Islands, where They had got out of the Water, about 40 or 50000 p[iece]s [of eight] and were fishing for more. On Their Coming to an Anchor, the Spaniards fired several shot at Them, which They took no Notice of for sometime, nor intended any Violence or to do Them any Injury: But, several men being killed and wounded,

by the Continued fire, They were at length so far provoked, That They
landed about 100 men out of the two sloops, and after a small skirmish, the
Spaniards abandoned the Cays, with all Their money and Effects, went on
board Their own Vessells, and Sailed for the Havanna. On the return of
Wells and Jennings, to this Island, it was Suggested that the money They
brought in was fished out of the Water, nor was it Contradicted, and the
truth known, for many Days after.

The *Bennet* Capt[ain] Fernando, in the lat[itude] 24d, and about 8 leagues
from the Cape of Florida, Saw a sloop, and as He imagined she had been
on the Wrecks, He chased Her in Expectation of getting some Intelligence. She proved to be a sloop which formerly belonged to some Merchants of Kingston, and had been unjustly seized, since the Peace, and
Confiscated without a legal Trial and Condemnation. Capt[ain] Fernando,
for that Reason, and finding some English Goods on board, seized Her and
sent Her into Port Royal. But, did not think proper to come in Himself,
with His sloop, until He knew the issue of the Affair; or Whether she was a
legal Prize or not and He was justifiable in what He had done.

About the middle of January arrived Don Juan de Valle, Kn[igh]t. of the
Don Juan de Valle, Kn[igh]t e order of St. James, with a letter from the Governour of the Havanna. And on the 30th. He delivered a Memorial to His
Excellency setting forth, that notwithstanding the Peace, Amity, and Friendship between the King[s] of Great Britain and Spain, divers of His Britan-
ick Majestie's Subjects in Warlike manner, committed Hostilities upon the
Subjects of His Catholick Majesty. That two sloops belonging to this Island,
had lately in a Hostile manner, landed upon His Catholick Majestie's Dominions, in the Channel of the Bahama on the Coast of Florida, under pretence of looking for Pirates, but in reality have committed the highest Act of
Piracy, upon His said Catholick Majesty's Subjects, by forcibly taking from
Them in Value 120000 p[iece]s [of eight] contrary to the Treaties of Peace
and Commerce, and against the Laws of Christianity and of Nations.

Therefore requested His Excellency would be pleased by Proclamation to
recal[l], under pain of Their Allegiance, all His Majestie's Subjects, and
to inhibit Them to dive or Fish upon the Flota, Stranded and Cast on
shore upon or near the Bahama Islands and Coast of Florida, part of His
said Catholick Majesty's Dominions; and likewise to prevent others of
His Britannick Majesty's Subjects now preparing and fitting out at this Island to do the like.

2d. That the Effects and money Piratically taken as aforesaid, and already come into the Island be restored to the use of His said Catholick
Majesty and His Subjects, or Satisfaction made by Those who are owners
of the said Sloops.

3dly. That what money or other Effects is allready taken, or which may
hereafter be taken, and fished out of said Flota, be likewise restored as soon
as the same shall arrive, or Satisfaction made as aforesaid.

4thly. That since tis most Evident there is a Piracy Committed, and that by Persons now under His Excellency's Government, the said Deputy prays that They may be secured and brought to Justice.

His Excellency laid this Memorial and the letter He had received from the Governour of the Havanna, before the Council, for Their Opinion and Advice, and I shall transcribe Their Resolutions thereupon, taken from an Authentic Copy, that the whole Affair may appear in a just and true light to the Satisfaction of the Reader.

Minutes of the Council of Jamaica February 9th. 1715/6
Present
His Excellency L[or]d. Archibald Hamilton Capt[ai]n. Gen[era]l. &c.

Peter Heywood, Esq[uire][56]   Richard Rigby, Esq[uire]
Francis Rose, Esq[uire][57]   Thomas Bernard, Esq[uire][58]
John Stewart, Esq[uire]   James Archbould, Esq[uire][59]
John Peck, Esq[uire][60]   John Sadler, Esq[uire][61]
Valentine Mumbee, Esq[uire][62]

His Excellency and the Council taking into their Consideration the Letter to his Excellency from the Governor of the Havanna, the Extract of a Junto of the Council of Commerce at the Havanna, and the Memorial of Captain Don Juan del Valle, Deputy of the said Council of Commerce of his Catholick Majesty, and of the Flota, lately under the Command of Don Juan Estebano de Vuillia, Kn[igh]t of the Order of St. James, in the Presence of the said Don Juan del Valle, in order to his Excellency's and the Council's better understanding his Demands, where by his Excellency,

56. Peter Heywood, a longtime member of the Jamaica Council and its president by 1716, became governor following the recall of Hamilton and was twice chief justice of Jamaica, in 1703 and 1714–16. See Cundall, *Governors of Jamaica in the First Half of the Eighteenth Century*, 66–73.

57. Francis Rose was a councillor who had been a longtime member of the Jamaica Assembly, sitting for St. Thomas in the Vale Parish in 1693 and 1698–99, St. Catherine Parish in 1701–2, and St. George Parish in 1703, and was Speaker in 1703. A member of the commission investigating Lord Hamilton, he was also president of the council. Ibid., 18, 32, 69, 78; Cundall, *Historic Jamaica*, xv, xvi.

58. Thomas Bernard, a councillor, was also on the commission investigating Hamilton. Later, Nicholas Lawes appointed him lieutenant governor in the absence or death of the governor. Cundall, *Governors of Jamaica in the First Half of the Eighteenth Century*, 78, 96, 103.

59. James Archbould was a member of the Jamaica Assembly for St. Andrew Parish in 1703–4 before he became a member of the Jamaica Council.

60. John Peck, a person with a considerable estate in Jamaica, was appointed to the Jamaica Council in 1708.

61. John Sadler (d. 1725) was a longtime member of the Jamaica Council.

62. Valentine Mumbee was a Jamaican councillor who had been a representative in the assembly for Vere Parish from 1699 to 1703.

cellency and the Board offered to the Consideration of the said
l Valle, whether the prosecuting the Officers and Mariners, be-
he two Vessels complained of, or issuing such Proclamation, as
the said Memorial, may not probably deter others that are still
ay have been upon the Wrecks, from returning to this Island, and
s of putting them upon desperate Attempts of more pernicious
nce to the Crown of Spain; and whether the deferring Prosecution
return of all or most part of the Vessels, suspected to have com-
ny unlawful Act, may not upon that Account be most adviseable;
red him at the same time, he was at Liberty to take such Measures
the Subjects of his Britannick Majesty in this Island, for the Satisfac-
the King of Spain and his Subjects, for all Hostilities committed on
as by the Laws of Great Britain and this Island are prescribed.
on the whole, the said Don Juan del Valle declined insisting on any
inal Prosecution, alledging, that in Case of such Consequences happen-
as might justly be feared, the Blame thereof might be imputed to him.
nd further desired, in regard to the Amity and Friendship between
ir Catholick and Britannick Majesties, his Excellency and the Coun-
would take such Measures for the Satisfaction of his Catholick Majesty
d his Subjects, in the Premises, as to them should seem most just and
easonable; and as to the Restitution for the Damages his Britannick Maj-
stie's Subjects have sustained, from Hostilities committed by the Subjects
of his most Catholick Majesty, he knew no other way but by applying to
the Court of Spain.

It is therefore the humble Opinion and Advice of this Board, that his
Excellency be pleased to return such Answer to the Governor of the Ha-
vanna's Letter, and the Representation of the Council of Commerce, as
His Excellency shall think adviseable on these Heads.

And the Board at the same time humbly desired his Excellency, that he
would make the most pressing Instances, that Satisfaction be made to his
Britannick Majesty's Subjects, for the Damages by them sustained, from
Hostilities committed by the Subjects of the King of Spain, at a moderate Computation, amounting at least to Two Hundred thousand Pieces of
Eight, with the Assurances of the Continuance of our utmost Endeavours,
for rendering as far as in us lies, ample and impartial Justice upon all Occasions to the Spanish Nation[.]

　　　　A. Hamilton
　　S. Page,[63] Secretary.

---

63. Dr Samuel Page was deputy secretary of Jamaica under William Congreve in 1715.
He went to England to press charges against Hamilton over the Spanish wreck. Hamilton
charged that Page was unqualified and beyond his portfolio in going to England on behalf
of the assembly without the consent of the governor or council. The Council on Trade and
Plantations agreed and recommended that Page never again be given an office of trust, backed
by the king in council. Upon investigation by a Jamaica Assembly committee, however, Page
was reinstated on the council. Ibid., 60, 63, 64, 71.

with the Advice of the C.
Memorial, &c. as is agree.

260

Declare their utmost De
said to be committed by the
of the late Treaties of Peace, .
His Excellency and the Board .
sion for charging his Britannick
the least Breach of, or disregard t
their Britannick and Catholick Ma,
and this Board had an Opportunity
Sincerity and Readiness strictly to ob.
Complaint from Hispaniola, of a Desc
the Suspension of Arms, and before the
making their Descent, who carried off se
digo, and other Things of a considerable
lency caused full Satisfaction to be rend[e]r
two Days after he had Notice thereof.

And his Excellency was very much Surprize
tion some little Time after to the several Gove.
faction, in behalf of one of his Britannick Majes.
side of this Island, who was robbed and plundere.
Catholick Majesty, and no Satisfaction could be ob.
unknown to the present Governor of the Havanna,
having Personally attended the said Governor at the
ters from his Excellency on that Subject.

So that the Spaniards being the first Aggressors, his .
Council think they should be the first to give Satisfactio.
conceive it highly reasonable that the Satisfaction to be m.
Reciprocal.

That as to such part of the Flota Ship-wrecked on the C.
as remained in the Possession of the Subjects of his most Cat.
esty, of which it is pretended they were dispossessed; it is the (
his Excellency and the Council, that the Dispossessors are Rob.
ought to be treated as such; but conceive such part of the said Fl.
lying Derelict, from which the Subjects of his Catholick Majesty .
drove and forced out of Possession, belonged to the first Occupant.

That they could no ways admit, that the Bahama Islands were par.
the Dominions of the King of Spain, but looked upon the same to be
Britannick Majesty's, and had for a long time past been in the Possessi.
of his Subjects.

That his Excellency and the Board are of Opinion, that Restitution
ought to be made to the Subjects of his Catholick Majesty, for their Losses
sustained, by Hostilities committed on them by the Subjects of his Britannick Majesty, since the first Suspension of Arms.

But his Ex
Don Juan d
longing to
is desired i
out, and n
be a mean
Consequ
until the
mitted a
but ass
against
tion o
them.
U
Crin
ing,
the
cil
a
r

The Assembly, who met in January according to Prorogation, passed a Bill intituled an Act to Oblige the several Inhabitants of this Island to provide themselves with a sufficient Number of White People &c. and sent it up to the Council for Their Concurrence the 11 of February: But, having the Day before, sent as Message to the Governour and Council, charging His Excellency and others with disloyalty to His Majesty, They were the same Day, the Bill was sent up, dissolved by Proclamation.

The Assembly being dissolved without making the usual and Necessary provision for the subsistance of the Soldiers, or supplying the Deficiency of the Revenue, the Governor was now reduced to greater Streights and difficulties than ever, Especially since the Council had refused to advance anymore money, for the Subsistance of the Soldiers; so that His Excellency was under the Necessity of advancing what was Necessary, on that Account, Himself. It was thereupon moved in Council that the Ballance of the Fund which was raised by the Additional Duty Act, and amounted to near £4000., might be taken out of the hands of the Executor of Anthony Major Esq[uir]e the late Commissioner, and made use of for Support of the Revenue and the Subsistence of the Soldiers, the Act being Expired, and the monies not appropriated by any other Law. After some Debate the Executor (John Major) was directed by an Order of the Governour and Council to pay the same into the hands of the Receiver General which He refusing to Comply with, He was ordered into the Custody of the Provost Marshal[l]: But, in a few Days after His Committment He Consented to pay the Money, provided His Security Bonds were cancelled, which was accordingly done, and on payment He was discharged. This money was by a Subsequent order of the Governor and Council carried to the Credit of the Revenue, and Orders were regularly issued thereon monthly for the Subsistance of the Soldiers. But, though the Receiver General received that mon[e]y, by order of the Governor and Council, and never entered into any bond or Security to the Assembly, and the money was issued out by order of the same power and Authority which put it into His hands, yet He was, Nevertheless, obliged (after my Lord Hamilton was removed from the Government) by a Clause in the New Additional Duty Act to refund the same in 30 days or forfeit 3 times the Sum. But, on the Representation of His Case His late Majesty, was pleased to Reject that Bill and by His Sign Manual to direct the Governour or Commander in Chief for the time being to repay the same out of the first and readiest of the Revenues of this Island with Interest which met with Scruples and Delays for some time though it was afterwards Complied with.

In March the *Diamond* Capt[ain] Balchen sailed to England, and as the other two Men of War sailed sometime before, there was not now nor for some Months after one Ship of War on the Station. The Spaniards being acquainted with this Circumstance, however ready they were to Complain of Injuries[,] were as forward to Commit Depredations on the English and Evidently were the first and greatest Aggressors. For though there was at that time some English Pirates in America, who made the Island of Providence Their Rendevouz, there not being then any set[t]led Government There, Yet they did not offer any Injury, or give the least disturbance to the English Commerce, or any other Nation but the Spaniards, so that the following Vessels which were taken, within the space of Six Months by the Guarda Costa's, and carried into Port and Condemned on pretences altogether unreasonable and unwarrantable was not only a manifest Violation of the Treaties of Peace and Friendship, but the Law of Nations, as They were passing the Seas on Their lawful Occasions, and not on any Illicit Commerce.

Ships' Names	Masters	of what Port,	where bound
Newport	W. Musto	Carolina	Jamaica
John and Mary	T. Stevenson	Pensilvania	Ditto
Swan	J. Lynch	Jamaica	Providence
Rachel	W. Cook	Jamaica	Coaster
Penelope	Henry Comb	Pensilvania	Jamaica
Turtle Dove	J. Stonham	Jamaica	Carolina
Virgin Queen	[blank]	Pensilvania	Jamaica
Marlborough	Frezell	London	Saltitudas

It is to be observed, that none of these Vessells were taken and Condemned by way of Reprisal, being before They had any answer to Don Juan de Valle[']s Memorial, or could possibly know the issue or Success of His Application for Restitution or Satisfaction; but, on pretence of their being on an Illicit Trade, though they were taken on the high seas, or on the Coasts of this Island.

Mr. March, who was appointed by the Assembly to Sollicit the Affairs of this Island, on His arrival in England Exhibited several articles of Complaint against the Lord Hamilton; particularly that He had encouraged, during the time of His Government Piratical Hostilities upon the Subjects of France and Spain, in Violation of the Treaties with Those Nations, and to the great interruption and prejudice of the British Commerce. The Spanish Ambassador, at the same time, presented a Memorial to His Majesty to the same purpose through the Instigation of that Gentleman and His Associates[;] at least He was spirited up by Them as it was Commonly Suggested. On which the Powers granted to His Lordship were Revoked, and His Majesty was pleased to Appoint Collo[nel] Peter Heywood, (who was Suspended about two Months before from being one of the Council and likewise from being Chief Justice of the Island) to take the Government on Him, and to Enquire into the Conduct of the Lord Archibald Hamilton, with a discretionary power to Seize His Person, and send Him Over, with Proper Evidences for Convicting Him According to Law.

Lord Archibald Hamilton (1673–
1754), a Scottish officer of the Royal
Navy and Whig politician, was an
unusually controversial governor of
Jamaica from 1711 to 1718. (Duke of
Hamilton and Lennoxlove Trust)

This Noble Lord was one of the Brothers of the Duke of Hamilton[64]
(who was killed in a Duel with the Lord Mohun)[65] and Uncle to the present Duke.[66] As His Lordship is Living and in some Eminent Employments
under the Government, I shall avoid saying any thing which has the least
Appearance of Flattery or Dissimulation. And, therefore I shall in the next
Administration (as it will most properly come in there) only give the Substance of the Charge against Him, and the Report of the Board of Trade to
whom His examination was inferred without drawing any Inference or Remarks. However, I may be allowed to give my Testimony in such matters as
were more particularly under my Cognizance, and to Observe that though
the opposition was strong against him yet many Gentlemen of the Island,
and allmost the whole Body of Merchants (who did not interfere or concern themselves, with those points which related to the Privileges of the
Assembly) Supported and did His Lordship all the Justice in Their power.
    In order to Cramp and distress Him in His Administration (among other
Things) the Assembly neglected to Supply the Deficiency of the Revenue
although it was well known and made Appear that the Contingent charges
of the Civil list as it may properly be called exceeded the Income above
£2000 p[er] Ann[um], and in four Years granted a Supply of no more than

64. James Douglas, Fourth Duke of Hamilton (1658–1712), was the uncle of Governor
Hamilton of Jamaica and was killed by Charles, Lord Mohun, in a duel in 1712.
    65. Charles Mohun, Fifth Baron Mohun (1675?–1712), a successful duelist, killed Hamil-
ton, and he himself died as a result of a duel following a long controversy with Hamilton over
the estate of Mohun's patron, Charles Gerard, Second Earl of Macclesfield.
    66. Probably James Hamilton, Fifth Duke of Hamilton (1703–1743).

£3000. To cover this Conduct which in Consequence, was a prejudice and dishonour to the Island, it was Industriously propagated, that He was profuse and lavish of the Publick monies, in Gratuities to the Publick Officers, when in Fact to my Certain knowledge, as His Majesty's Revenues in this Island at that time passed through my hands, They never were more frugally managed, for the Gratuities given to the Publick Officers since, have been double and Some more for less Services.

It was, indeed, His Misfortune to fall in with some Gentlemen, who were Obnoxious and Suspected of having Views very different from His Lordship or the Assembly, and to prefer their private Interest to every other Consideration. Otherwise, I am persuaded, His Administration would have been Easy and agreeable to Himself, and to the Country in General. But His Attachment to those Gentlemen as I have Observed, brought on Him all the difficulties and Embarassments He met with and terminated in His Removal, in a disgraceful manner, without any other Redress or Satisfaction, than having His Adversaries afterwards removed from Their Employments, when the Merits of the Cause came to be Enquired into.

Upon the whole, among the charges brought against His Lordship I never heard Him accused by His most Violent Opponents of any Act of Injustice or oppression in His Government, Excepting what related to the Spaniards. And as to the Merits of that Affair, I shall not pass any Judgment but refer the Reader to the following Abstracts, which are taken from Authentick Minutes.[1]

[Constitutional Settlement, 1716–1728]

Collo[nel] Heywood's Commission for Capt[ain] General, Governor and Commander in chief of this Island, was dated the 26th. of May, 1716, and He entered upon the Administration the 25th. of July following. Nor was this the only alteration, which was made in the Government, Several Members of the Council being likewise removed and their places filled by some of the most Violent in the Opposition. And, Collo[nel] Heywood made almost a thorough change in the Civil and Military Commissions, which has been attended with bad Consequences, and brought those Commissions into Contempt to the great prejudice of the Island. For Gentlemen who were the most Capable of Executing Them, when They saw they were liable to be disgraced by being turned out, at the will and pleasure of a Governour, and without any misdemeanor, declined Accepting of Them, and in Consequence they commonly are given to Per-

---

1. Knight never added these abstracts to his history.

sons who are not properly qualified, and incapable of preserving such an Authority as is Necessary. And, to this Cause the Militia, in particular, is become undisciplined and not so fit for Service as They were formerly.

Collo[nel] Heywood and the New Council, immediately Entered upon an Enquiry into the Conduct of the Lord Hamilton and particularly in regard to the Spanish Wrecks. The Owners of the Sloops and others Concerned, were not only Cited before Them and Strictly Examined, but, His Lordship was likewise obliged to Appear, and in His Examination underwent a Scene of hardships, Variety of Affronts, and had many Indignities put on Him by His Adversaries, who were exalted in power, and become His Inquisitors. As the Examination and proceedings thereupon will appear in the following Abstracts, I shall wave making any further Animadversions, than that His Lordship was put under an Arrest, and sent a Prisoner to Great Britain, at a Day's warning, and all this by a Majority, in the Council, of one only, the Rest protesting against Their proceedings.

His Lordship was put on board His Majestie's ship the *Bedford* Capt[ain] Liel, and Sailed from Port Royal in September 1716. On His Arrival in Great Britain, He was obliged to give Bail to appear and Answer to His charge the Substance of which is as follows.

Ar[ticle] 1. That a Squadron or Flota of Spanish Ships or Vessels, belonging to his Catholick Majesty, and his Subjects, richly laden with Gold, Silver, Goods, and Merchandizes, of a very considerable Value, and being homeward bound for Old Spain, was, on or about the [blank] day of [blank] in the year of our Lord 1715, east away and wrecked on the Coast of Florida, within his Catholick Majesty's Dominions, tho[ugh] most of the Men on board them were saved: of which the said Archibald Hamilton having an account, and preferring his own private Ends and Interests to the Honour of our most Gracious King, and the British Nation, did grant Commissions to several of his Majesty's Subjects of this Island, for the suppressing of Pirates; under colour of which, several of his Majesty's Subjects were counselled and Instructed by the said Archibald Hamilton to go to the said Wrecks, and if stronger than the Spaniards, to beat them off, and take what Mon[e]y they could get.

2d. That the said Lord Archibald Hamilton had been concerned, an eighth part in the Voyage of each of the Sloops *Eagle* and *Bethsheba*, whom he had commissioned as aforesaid, with intent to go to the said Wrecks: And tho[ugh] he would not receive his part of the Mon[e]y they brought home; being, before the tender thereof to him made, acquainted by Don Juan del Valle, Deputy of the Council of Commerce at the Havana, that the said Sloops had robbed the Spaniards of the said Mon[e]y in the Channel of the Bahama's, on the Florida Shore, as appears by a Memorial presented to the said Archibald Hamilton, about the end of January last, by the said Don Juan del Valle, Deputy as aforesaid: In which said Memorial, the said Deputy desired Satisfaction for the Mon[e]y already come within His Government, to prevent like Practices for the future, and also to recall, by Proclamation those of His Britannick Majesty's Subjects of this Island, out on the said Wrecks, and also desiring that those who committed the Robberies and Piracies aforesaid, and that then were within the said Archibald Hamilton's Government, might be secured and brought to justice; as per the said Memorial, entered amongst the minutes of the Council held at St. Iago de la Vega aforesaid, on the 28th. day of August 1716. To which the said Deputy had had no Answer, as will appear by a Copy of another Memorial presented by the said Deputy to the said Archibald Hamilton, entered amongst the Minutes of the said day; whereas in Justice he ought to have complied with the said Memorials: But instead of doing his Duty, the Offenders were allowed all the Liberties of innocent Men, within this island; and suffered with Impunity to go where they listed. And tho[ugh] it appears by his refusing to receive his said Share of the said Mon[e]y, so tendered to him as aforesaid, That he knew, and was Sensible that it was got as aforesaid; yet he neither secured his own, or other Owners' Parts, as he ought to do, in Justice to our most Gracious Sovereign Lord the King, and his Subjects of this Island, and in performance of his Duty; nor any of the Persons committing the said Robberies.

3. That the said Archibald Hamilton was Part-Owner of the Sloop *Bennet*, under Command of Francis Fernando, to whom he gave Commission, as aforesaid, to suppress Pirates; under colour whereof, he was to go to the Wrecks in order to rob and despoil the Spaniards. That the said Francis Fernando, under colour of such Commission, on or about the 31st. day of December 1715, piratically took a trading Sloop, belonging to the Spaniards, richly laden.

4th. That the said Archibald Hamilton encouraged the said Fernando to come to him about nine of the clock at night, incognito; and that he should be admitted in at the Gate, at the North side of his Garden; And this after the Piracy aforesaid, committed by him.

5th. That afterwards the said Fernando being desirous to come in, in June last, desired him to have a little Patience, till the Spaniards had gone off, to whom he would give their Answer as soon as he could.

It was several months before His Lordship, could Obtain a hearing in his Vindication notwithstanding the constant application He made for that purpose. But, on the Memorial He presented to His Majesty, the Board of Trade was directed to Enquire into His Conduct and the proceedings of Collo[nel] Heywood the new Governour and Council thereupon, and Their Lordship's made the following Report.

Minutes of the Lords Commissioners, for Trade and Plantations, upon
hearing the Lord Archibald Hamilton on East Article of His Memorial[.]
Present

Lord Suffolk[2]	Mr. Molesworth[3]
Mr. Chetwynd[4]	Mr. Pulteney[5]
S[i]r Charles Cook[6]	Mr. Bladen.[7]

The Lord Archibald Hamilton, late Governour of Jamaica, attending as
appointed, he produced to their Lordship's several Papers, in Proof of the
Allegations of his Memorial to the King, referred to this Board, and mentioned in the Minutes of the 27th. of the last Month; his Lordship proceeded to his Proofs in Order, as the Respective Paragraphs stand Numbered in his Memorial; and begun by observing, that the Differences he
had with the Assembly of Jamaica, were chiefly upon three Points, which
his Instructions, and the Board of Trade, had recommended to him viz.
the pretended Power in the Assembly, of Adjourning themselves for what
Time they thought fit, without Leave from the Governor; their denying
the Council any Right of amending Money Bills; and refusing to make
Provision for Subsisting His Majesty's Forces there, which had been recommended by His Majesty.

1. To prove, that during the whole Administration of the said Lord Archibald Hamilton there, he endeavoured to act, in all respects, agreeable
to his Instructions, and according to the Duty of his Office, in Support of
His Majesty's Royal Authority, then manifestly struck at by a Set of violent
and ill designing Men; his Lordship referred to Mr. Secretary (now Lord)
Stanhope's[8] Letter of the 25th. of February, 1714–15, which approves the
several Steps taken by the said Lord Archibald Hamilton, in Execution
of the Orders sent him, upon the Death of Her late Majesty: And to His
Majesty's Letter of the 13th. of May, 1715, relating to the discharging of
Publick Debts, and the Subsistance of the two Independant Companies
there; wherein His Majesty was pleased to express His Royal Pleasure
in these Terms, viz. "We expect you will continue your best Endeavours
for the Advancement of these good Ends, which we hope will restore that

2. Henry Howard, Sixth Earl of Suffolk (1670–1718), was the first lord of trade from 1715
to 1718.

3. Robert Molesworth, First Viscount Molesworth (1656–1725), was the author of
An Account of Denmark as It Was in the Year 1692 (London, 1692) and a member of the Board
of Trade in 1714–15.

4. John Chetwynd (1680–1767) was a member of the Board of Trade in 1714–28.

5. Daniel Pulteney (1674–1731) was a member of the Board of Trade in 1715–21.

6. Sir Charles Cooke (?–1721) was a member of the Board of Trade in 1714–21.

7. Martin Bladen (1680–1746) was a prominent member of the Board of Trade during a
long tenure from 1717 to 1746.

8. James, First Earl Stanhope (1673–1721), was appointed secretary of state for the southern department and privy councillor in 1714.

our Island to a flourishing Condition.["] His Lordship farther appealed
to the Letter which this Board wrote to Mr. Secretary Stanhope the 17th.
of February, 1715–16, wherein it is represented, That by what appeared
by the Books in this Office, the Lord Archibald Hamilton seemed exactly
to have followed his instructions. And as to His Majesty's Authority being
struck at by violent and designing Men, his Lordship doubted not, but the
same would fully appear in his Progress through the following Articles.

2. To prove the second Article of the Memorial, where his Lordship
says, he had His Majestie's Approbation of his Conduct, by the Removal of
such Members of the Council, whose Misbehaviour and Opposition to the
King's Service, his Lordship had represented, he referred to the Report
of the 25th. of April, 1715: made by this Board; whereupon Mr. [Charles]
Chaplin[9] and Mr. [John] Blair,[10] who had encouraged the Proceedings
of the Assembly, relating to their having the sole Right of framing Money
Bills, and to a Power of Adjourning themselves at Pleasure, &c. were removed from His Majesty's Council in Jamaica. His Lordship added, that
he should give farther Instances of Mr. Chaplin and Blair's Behaviour, in
explaining the Subsequent Articles.

3. To support what is asserted in the third Article, That the Assembly
had, notwithstanding His Majesty's Recommendation, refused to make
any Provision for the Subsistance of the two Independent Companies;
the Lord Archibald Hamilton referred to the Minutes of the Assembly
of the 9th. of November 1715, and that part thereof was read; where the
aforesaid Mr. Chaplin reported from a Committee of the said Assembly,
that the Accounts of Money disbursed for the Subsistance of Colonel
Handasyd's Regiment, and the two Independent Companies, were of an
unprecedented Nature, being disbursed without a Law, or the publick
Faith given for reimbursing the same; and that the Committee could not
take upon them to determine, whether the same ought to be paid or not:
whereupon the Assembly voted the said Money to be no publick Debt,
with in the Construction of His Majesty's Letter of the 13th. of May 1715,
tho[ugh] it appears by a subsequent Letter of His Majesty, bearing Date
the 10th. of April 1716, relating to the Payment of that Money, that His
Majesty did look upon it as a publick Debt, and recommended the same
to be provided for as such, by his former Letter of the 13th. of May, 1715.
The Lord Archibald took Notice as a farther Proof of its being a publick
Debt, that Money advanced by the present Governour for the same Ser-

9. Charles Chaplin, custos and chief magistrate at Port Royal, was elected to represent
Port Royal in the Jamaica Assembly after Hamilton dismissed him from the council; he served
five terms.

10. Before his appointment to the council, John Blair had been a longtime member of the
Jamaica Assembly, representing St. Thomas in the East Parish in 1701 and 1702–9. He was
again elected following his dismissal from the council in 1715–16. He also represented Port
Royal in 1702 and St. George in 1708.

vices, was not only acknowledged as a publick Debt, but has since been re-imbursed by the Assembly, with an Allowance of 12 p[e]r Cent. Interest.

4. Upon the fourth Article his Lordship said, that contrary to his In-structions, communicated to the Council, Complaints had been sent against him to England, which had never been Communicated to him in Jamaica, as would fully appear by Proofs relating to the Subsequent Ar-ticles, and more particularly to the 11th.

5. To the fifth Article, alledging that to compass their ill Designs against his Lordship, a large Sum of Money was unwarrantably subscribed and collected by the leading Men of the Assembly, and remitted to Great Britain, on Pretence of soliciting the Affairs of that Island; his Lordship referred to the Minutes of the Assembly of the 20th. and 21st. of Decem-ber, 1715, and those Parts which relate to the said Subscription were read, as likewise the Draught of the Subscription drawn up by Captain [George] Bennet,[11] who on his Lordship's Removal, was constituted of the Coun-cil under Mr. Heywood. His Lordship observed, that the Assembly had, during his Government prepared and sent to the Council, a Bill to raise Money for soliciting the publick Affairs of the Island in this Kingdom; by which the Assembly had excluded the Governour and Council from the very Knowledge of what was intended to be transacted; the Council made several Amendments to the Bill, which the Assembly refusing to admit of, on pretence that the Council had no Right to make any Alteration to a Money Bill: upon which the Bill was dropped, and a Subscription was set on foot; and his Lordship said, he had been well informed, that about 1100£. were raised in the Assembly, besides what was collected in the sev-eral Parishes, contrary to His Majesty's Instructions. His Lordship added, that this Method of raising Money, was at first proposed to the Assembly in the Nature of an Ordinance, and read there twice as such; and as his Lordship had reason to believe, was afterwards dropped and put out of the Form of Ordinance, only upon some Observations which his Lordship made, as to the Irregularity of it. His Lordship observed, that tho[ugh] the chief Pretence for raising of this Money, was to solicit the Dispatch of several Acts, he did not know, and he appealed to the Board, if any Appli-cation had been made since that Time, for the confirming any Acts of that Island. From whence he did infer, that the forementioned Bill, for solicit-ing the publick Affairs of the Island, as well as the Subscription, were de-signed for private Ends, and not for the publick Service of that Island.

6. To the sixth Article alledging, that at the Instigation of the Party, one [Samuel] Page, Deputy Secretary of Jamaica[,] a Person unqualified, of an ill Character, and whom his Lordship had therefore refused to admit into that Office, till he received express Commands for so doing; deserted

11. Perhaps George Bennett, who was a member of the Jamaica Assembly representing several constituencies between 1701 and 1716 and again in 1718.

his Office, and left the Island, contrary to Law, without the Governour's Licence or Privity. His Lordship produced, and read a Letter under Mr. Page's own Hand, dated on Board the *Diamond* Man of War, the 6th. of March, 1715, whereof a Copy was annexed to his Memorial, desiring his Lordship's favourable Opinion and Excuse, for departing the Island without his Lordship's Leave. My Lord likewise produced a Letter from Mr. [Peter] Bernard, Chief Justice, and one of the present Council of Jamaica; wherein he says, "That turning over the Patent Book one Day, in the Secretary's Office, he was astonished to see an Entry of a Ticket from Lord Archibald Hamilton to Samuel Page, to go off the Island.["] Whereupon my Lord observed, that Mr. Page must either have forged his Lordship's Name to a Ticket, or contrary to the Trust reposed in him, and unknown to his Lordship, have filled up with his own Name, one of the Blank Tickets, which Multiplicity of Business obliged his Lordship to leave in his Hands, ready signed.

That Mr. Page had, with the Letter he wrote to his Lordship, after his leaving the Island, sent a Certificate of his Indisposition, as an Excuse for his leaving the Island; but that his Lordship could not look upon that as a just Reason for his going off so abruptly and without Leave. His Lordship farther referred to the Minutes of the Council of Jamaica, of the 9th, of March, 1715–16, upon this Subject, which was read. In relation to Mr. Page's not being qualified, his Lordship alledged, that some of the Members of the Council were always obliged to take the Minutes of what passed at that Board, where the said Page acted as Clerk. And as to his ill Character, his Lordship thought the same would more manifestly appear by the proof of the following Article of his Lordship's Memorial.

7. The seventh Article alledging, that the said Page, with one Arlington in Great Britain, defrayed out of the Subscription Money aforesaid, made Affidavits, chiefly rehearsing what they had heard the Lord Archibald Hamilton's Enemies say, concerning the Robberies committed on the Spaniards; in which Affidavits the said Persons now appear to be willfully and corruptly perjured. To prove the same, his Lordship first observed, that Mr. Page in his Affidavit of the 15th, of May, 1716, has made Oath, That the Deponent heard from Leonard Barton, a Person of a fair Character, who was dispatched to the Leeward part of Jamaica, where this Deponent was on the 9th, Day of March, that the said Spanish Sloop, with her whole Cargo, was condemned in the said Barton's Presence, the 7th. Day of March last, &c. To contradict which Affidavit, his Lordship produced an original Affidavit of the said Leonard Barton, taken before Mr. Bernard, Chief Justice of Jamaica, the 17th, of August, 1716, which was read, wherein the said Barton deposeth in the Words following, viz. And the Deponent farther saith, That he neither knoweth Dr. Samuel Page, nor ever had any Communication or Discourse with him, touching or concerning the Spanish Sloop, formerly called the *Kensington*, taken by Captain Francis Farnando, &c. Which Affidavit of Mr. Barton, his

Lordship took notice, must have been true, and consequently Page's false; because the Condemnation of the Spanish Sloop was not till the 16th. Day of March, as appears by a Copy of the Sentence under the Seal of the Island, produced by his Lordship; whereas the said Page had been several Days at Sea before that Time, and yet he pretends to have informed of this Condemnation by the said Barton so long before it hap[pe]ned, as the 7th, of that Month, His Lordship further observed, that the said Page had deposed in the Words following, viz. To which said Memorial the said Don Juan could receive no other Answer from the Governour; than that the Florida Shore was part of the King of England's Dominions; and that as the Spaniards had seized on some English Vessels since the Peace, the said Governour believed the said Spaniards were indebted to the English more than those Spanish Effects would answer. To disprove which Assertion, his Lordship produced and read a Minute of Council of the said Island, dated the 9th. of February 1715, and signed by Mr. Page himself; by which it appears, that several Answers were given to Don Juan Del Valle upon his Memorial, by his Lordship and the Council of Jamaica; who offered it to the Consideration of the said Don Juan del Valle, whether the prosecuting the Officers and Mariners of the two Vessels complained of, and the issuing such a Proclamation as desired, might not deter others, then out, from returning to Jamaica, and be a Means of putting them upon such desperate Attempts, as might be of more pernicious Consequence to the Crown of Spain, &c. Whereupon the said Don Juan del Valle declined insisting on any criminal Prosecution, lest such Consequences happening, as might justly be feared, the Blame thereof might be imputed to him. And that the said Page had been corruptly perjured, his Lordship inferred from his having received part of the forementioned Subscription Money, as his Lordship was credibly informed, as also, that upon his Return to Jamaica, he had complained of not having received enough. The Lord Hamilton farther took Notice upon this Article, of a Petition from several Merchants of Jamaica, mentioned in the Minutes of the Council of that Island of the 25th. of June, 1714, which was not read, praying, that upon the Departure of the Men of War, his Lordship would take proper Methods for the Protection of the Trade of the Island, then in Danger, from Pirates: Whereupon his Lordship said, he granted several Commissions to Commanders of Vessels, to go in quest of the said Pirates; giving them proper Instructions, and taking Security for the due Observance thereof: Which Commissions and Instructions, as his Lordship affirmed, were the same that had been formerly given by his Predecessors on like Occasions, Copies of which he promised to transmit to the Board. That upon Complaints against some of the Commanders of the Vessels, he issued a Proclamation for recalling them. His Lordship likewise observed, that Mr. Blair and Mr. Chaplin, two Persons concerned in the Complaint against him, were Security for some of the Commanders of these Vessels.

8. Upon the eighth Article, relating to his Lordship's removing Mr.

Heywood (now Commander in Chief of Jamaica) from the Place of Chief Justice, and from the Council there; his Lordship referred to the Minute of Council of the 14th. of February, 1715–16. Whereby it appeared, that his Lordship, conformable to his Instructions, had not only the Majority, but the unanimous Advice of the Council in that Proceeding.

9. As to the ninth Article, alledging, that some of the new Councillors whom the King was pleased to appoint with Mr. Heywood[,] the New Governour, were some of them the same Persons whom His Majesty had before thought fit to displace, and who had continued their Opposition to his Service; and that others of the New Councillors had been the most vi- olent Men in the Assembly, in opposing the several Matters recommended by his Majesty's Letters, and had most largely subscribed to the Sum re- mitted, as aforesaid; His Lordship named Mr. Blair and Mr. Chaplin as the former; and Mr. Rigby, Mr. Thomas Beckford[12] and Mr. Bennet as the latter.

As to the 10th, 11th, and 12th, Articles, relating to the Instruction Sent Mr. Heywood and his Council, for seizing the Lord Hamilton's Person, and sending him Prisoner to England, with proper Proofs, in case they should find him concerned in the Piracy laid to his Charge, and to the un- justifiable manner in which they put this Instruction in execution against the said Lord Hamilton, and screening Offenders; He averred, that having sent to desire a Copy of the whole Charge against him, and repeated that Message, he could obtain no Answer, as Mr. Cockburne, his Lordship's Secretary, whom he sent for such Copy, was not ready to testify upon Oath. That even Mr. Broderick and Mr. Bernard, two of the Members of that Council, were denied Copies of what passed at that Board; to prevent his Lordships knowing the full Substance of his Accusation, whereby his Lordship had not the Opportunity of cross-examining Witnesses, as afore- said. That the Majority of the said Council acted very partially, in adjourn- ing to the House of one of the Members of that Board, or their Party, who was indisposed, and refusing to adjourn to another Member's House on the like Occasion; whereas if they had done it in this last Case, the Votes for his Lordship's Commitment had been equally divided.

His Lordship being asked what Steps were taken by Colonel Hey- wood, and the Government of Jamaica to answer the Intent of his Majes- ty's aforementioned Instructions, his Lordship said he was unacquainted therewith. That he was not taken into Custody till a few Days before he was sent away; and that no Cause of Commitment was specified in the Warrant for that purpose, which was signed only by an Under Clerk of the Council. His Lordship acknowledged he was interested in the Sloop

12. Thomas Beckford represented St. Catherine Parish in the Jamaica Assembly from 1706 to 1721, St. Thomas in the Vale Parish from 1721 to 1722 and 1727, Port Royal Parish from 1722 to 1727 and 1728 to 1731, St. Marty Parish from 1722 to 1735, and Hanover Parish from 1736 to 1745. He was Speaker of the Assembly in 1727–28.

Bennet, but being sensible that the Commander thereof had exceeded his Commission, and broken his Instructions, by the Seizure he had made of Spanish Goods, his Lordship was far from intending to reap any Advantage from so unlawful a Proceeding. And he appealed to the Minutes of the Council of Jamaica of the 9th. of June, 1716, for a Proof of his Integrity upon this Occasion. His Lordship likewise farther affirmed, that above a Month before that Council was held, and before Don Juan de Valle had made any Complaint against the Ship his Lordship was concerned in, he had communicated his Intention upon this Subject to Mr. Bernard and Mr. Broderick, two of the Council, who were of Opinion, that his Lordship would do well to temporize with Bendish,[13] and receive his own Share of the Profit arising from the foresaid Capture from the Spaniards, in order to fix the Proportion of the several Owners, and thereby to discover and secure as many of the Effects as possible, for the Use of the Persons from whom the same had been illegally taken. And accordingly his Lordship did receive his Share of the Capture, and deposited the same in the Hands of the Provost Marshal, subject to His Majesty's Orders, where the same now lies.

Upon this Occasion his Lordship farther observed, that he had the rather chose to conduct himself in this Transaction by the Advice of the aforesaid Mr. Bernard and Mr. Broderick, because they were both of them Persons learned in the law; the first being Chief Justice, and the latter at that time His Majesty's Attorney General of Jamaica; and as they were perfectly informed with what Intention it was that his Lordship did receive his Share of the said Prize. When Mr. Heywood and his Council were afterwards deliberating whether they should be justified by His Majesty's Instructions, in securing the said Lord Hamilton's Person; the said Mr. Bernard and Mr. Broderick did make Oath of the Truth of the forementioned Fact, which they declared, in their Opinion, to be a sufficient Proof that the said Lord Hamilton was not concerned in the Piracy; and for that Reason they and two other Members of the Council refused to consent to the Question for his Lordship's Commitment; which was carried only by one Voice, as may appear by the Minutes of Council of the 13th. of September, 1716.

As a farther Proof of his Lordship's Intention to do Justice to the Spaniards, he referred to the Minutes of the Council of the 21st. of June, 1716, by which it appeared, how desirous he was that the Appeal offered by the Spanish Agents, from the Sentence of the Court of Admiralty, tho[ugh] not proper in Point of Form, should have its Effect.

13. As to the thirteenth Article, his Lordship alledged that Mr. Hey-

13. Thomas Bendysh was a member of the assembly for St Mary Parish in 1714 and 1718. He was chosen to travel to England as prosecutor of Hamilton and wrote one of the depositions in the "Articles Exhibited against Lord Archibald Hamilton." Cundall, *Governors of Jamaica in the First Half of the Eighteenth Century*, 68, 70, 71, 83.

wood having, contrary to his Majesty's Instructions, sent no Evidence to support the Charge against him, he had, since his Arrival here, continued many months under Bail; and not only petitioned for a Hearing, but given publick Advertisements at the Exchange in London, that he was ready to answer whatever any Persons might have to object to him; but that no body had appeared; and Mr. Bendish, who was sent over in order to be the chief Evidence against his Lordship, had declared to some of the Ministers, as his Lordship had been informed, that he had nothing to say against him. And his Lordship observed, that this Mr. Bendish was one of the Persons concerned in the Ship that had committed Piracy, and the very same that had brought him his Share of the Capture, and who by his Lordship's Order in Council, had given Security to return such Part of the Spanish Effects as had come to his Hands; notwithstanding which, the said Bendish had obtained from Mr. Heywood a *Noli Prosequi*, contrary to the Intention of His Majesty's Instructions, for discovering and punishing all Persons concerned in the Piracies complained of.

14. Upon the fourteenth Article, importing, that the present Mr. Heywood and Councillors of Jamaica had drop[pe]d their Charge on this Subject, his Lordship observed, that this Board was well acquainted what Endeavours were used to oblige Mr. Page and Arlington to appear to what they had alledged against his Lordship; so that upon the whole, his Lordship hoped his Innocence might now plainly appear, and that those of the Council, who had so notoriously misbehaved themselves, might not be continued of the Council, nor Mr. Page in the Post of Deputy Secretary.

Upon this Report being made His Lordship was acquitted and all the New Councillours were removed, as also Mr. Page the Secretary of the Island, who was rendered incapable of Serving His Majesty in any place of profit, honour or Trust.

His Majesty was also pleased to Appoint Thomas Pit[t] Esq[ui]r[e,][14] formerly Governour of Fort St. George in the East Indies, Captain General Governour and Commander in Chief of this Island. And, His Commission and Instructions were accordingly made out.

Collo[nel] Heywood convened an Assembly, who Enacted several Laws, but it is Remarkable that they were all rejected by the Crown, except two, which were Temporary and mon[e]y Bills and one which is a private Act.

At this time there was but one man of War of 40 Guns on this Station, and she being incapable of going after light Nimble Vessels, the Pirates as

14. Thomas Pitt (1653–1726) was nicknamed "Diamond Pitt" because of wealth he accrued in East Indies enterprise when he obtained the Pitt diamond from an Indian merchant in Madras in 1701. He sold it to the French regent in 1717 for £135,000. He accepted appointment as governor of Jamaica in 1716 but never took up the post. His son Thomas was governor of the Leeward Islands, 1728–29, and his grandson was William Pitt, First Earl of Chatham (1708–78). See ibid., 66.

well as the Guarda Costa's began to be very mischievous and troublesome. The first mentioned but not hitherto molested or injured any English[,] French or Dutch Traders and declared their Designs were against the Spaniards only but on a Proclamation being issued out and a large bounty offered for apprehending and making some Notorious Offenders particu-larly [Nicholas] Brown, [Christopher] Winter, Hornygow and [William] Fox, They afterwards made no distinction, for They took, destroyed or plundered Every Vessel met with, without any distinction or regard to Country or Nation. Capt[ain] Prince in the *Whidale* (a fine large new Ship, with a very Valuable Cargo abroad) bound to London, was taken in a few Days after he sailed from Port Royal by one Bellamy[,] His men refusing to fight on the Enemy putting up the bloody Flag with a Death's head; and several other Vessels some of which belonged to the Island, were also taken about the same time by other Pirates. But the following ships were actually taken by the Spanish Guarda Costa's who had Commissions from the Gov-ernours of the Havanna, St. Iago and Trinidado, on the usual pretence of Their being on an Illicit Trade, although they were not on their Coast nor designed to any part of the Spanish Dominions, but were passing the Seas on their lawfull Occasions namely

The St. Ann.	Tho[ma]s Quin,	of London	bound to this Island
Griffin	Will[ia]m Taylor	of d[itt]o	London
Betty	Ed[ward] Bridgin,	d[itt]o	Ditto
Bathshua	John Wells	of Jamaica	Coaster
Dolphin	Palmer	Pensilvania	Jamaica
Sarah	Austin	London	Carolina
Stowell	[blank]	Bristol	Jamaica

Mr. Pitt, notwithstanding He had prepared and Sent to this Island a very Costly and Magnificent Equipage, for what Reasons were not pub-lickly known[,] resigned His Commission, on which Collo[nel] Nicholas Laws, who had a Considerable Estate, had resided many Years and passed through several Offices in this Island, was thought a proper Person to Suc-ceed, as he would probably Compose and heal all differences, and was ac-cordingly Recommended by the Planters and Merchants of this Island who were in England to His Majesty, who was, thereupon, pleased to Conferr on Him the Government, and the honour of Knighthood.

As nothing further Remarkable hap[pe]ned in the Administration of Collo[nel] Heywood I shall only observe that He was of a very good Fam-ily in Devonshire, and a Grandson of S[i]r Nicholas Slaning.[15] He met with preferment in the Navy very Early, for He had the Command of a Man of War when He was not 22 Years of Age, and was sent in the *Norwich* of 50

15. Sir Nicholas Slaning of Devonshire was the grandfather of Peter Heywood.

Guns to this Island in the year [blank]. But, having the misfortune soon after to lose her on one of the Cays of Port Royal, as he was going out on a Cruise, He married and set[t]led in this Island and never returned to England.[16] He had been several Years one of the Council, and was about two months, suspended by my Lord Hamilton, but it not being known in England when His Lordship was Removed, He was appointed (for no other Reason, than His being President of the Council or first in the list and it was thought necessary in regard to the Examination of my Lord Hamilton) Capt[ain] General and Governour. He lived several Years after He was superceeded in a private Station, was of a very cheerful Temper, and of a hail Strong; Constitution though very much Afflicted with the Gout. But, as the Inhabitants did not speak favourably of Him before or since He was in the Government, I shall throw a Veil over His private as well as his Publick Conduct, in regard to that Excellent Maxim of Speaking nothing but Truth of the living, nothing but Good of the Dead.

S[i]r Nicholas Laws's Commission for Capt[ain] General, Governour and Commander in chief of this Island, was dated the 23d. of August 1717. And His Excellency arrived at Port Royal the 26th. of April following. He was received with great joy and Satisfaction, for the Inhabitants were pleased to find they were to be under the Administration of a Gentleman who had resided many Years among them, was well Acquainted with the Constitution of the Country, having passed through the most Considerable Officers of Honour and trust, with Approbation, and whose Interest was the same as theirs because he had a very Considerable Estate in the Island.

As the Interest of a King and His People who are supposed to be of the same Country is Mutual; so it is happy for a Colony, when They are under the Government of a Gentleman, whose Interest is blended with Theirs. But, it is the misfortune of our Plantations in general, to be Governed by those who have not a foot of Land there, and go over with no other View than to raise or repair a shattered Fortune. Such Governours commonly think their Interest different from the Inhabitants and as they are uncertain how long They shall Continue in the Government, they are intent on nothing more than how to improve and make the most of their time to their own private Advantage. From which different Views and Interest, are perpetually r[a]ising Dissentions between Governours and Assembly's, Jarring and Jealousies among the People, who suffer themselves to be divided on these Occasions by little Emulations, private Piques, or worse motives, in those who support the interest of such Governours which Obstruct the Peace, wellfare and Prosperity of the Country.

The Inhabitants therefore, flattered themselves with the Happiness of

16. Heywood's first wife was Grace, daughter of James Modyford, who was brother of Thomas, governor of Jamaica from 1664 to 1671, and Elizabeth Modyford née Slaning. Both Peter and Grace were grandchildren of Nicholas Slaning. They married on February 2, 1682, and had six children.

having a Governour whose Inclinations as well as Interest were united with Theirs, and that all their Feuds and Animosities would subside. Indeed They were not dissappointed in that Respect, for they never had a Governour, nor any other Person in the Island, of a more Publick spirit, nor more heartily Attached to its true Interest than S[i]r Nicholas Laws of which many Instances can be given. But, two unlucky incidents hap[pe]ned which gave some interruption, to those pleasing Expectations and disturbed the Peace and Quiet of the Island.

The One was a Letter from His Majesty, which the Governour in pursuance of His Instructions laid before the Assembly, wherein His Majesty was pleased to Recommend to Them, the payment of the money advanced by the Lord Hamilton. But They having formerly voted it no debt, and not shewing any Disposition to Comply with His Majestie's Request, His Excellency's Message and Remonstrance thereupon, gave them great disgust.

The other Circumstance, was the particular distinction and Regard the Governour discovered for the New Attorney General, Edmond Kelly Esq[ui]r[e],[17] who was one in the late opposition, and a Gentleman whose Address and Abilities qualified Him to appear in any Court in Europe. But, being now a Favourite, [he] was suspected of having an Influence over His Excellency and to have led him into some measures which were not agreeable. He was, therefore, in His turn become as obnoxious to the Assembly, as the Three Gentlemen mentioned in the former Administration.

These shelves or Rocks have often proved fatal to Princes and other Great Men as well as to the Governours of our Colonies, and on which They have generally Wrecked, not only Their own Honour, but the welfare and Interest of the Respective States, or Government, and yet we find Them still run into the Same Error notwithstanding the many destructive Precedents and Examples before their Eyes.

But these differences and Animosities, However did not rise to that height, they were under the former Governours for the Assembly cheerfully raised the Necessary Supplies for the Support of the Government, and passed among other Bills, an Act, for the Encouragement of Voluntary Parties to Suppress Rebellious and Run away Negroes.

About this time Capt[ain] Jonathan Barnet, in a Trading Sloop, met with a noted Pirate, whose name was Wrackham,[18] and not only bravely de-

17. Edmond Kelly quarreled with the assembly over the attorney general's right to arrest council members in 1721. Also, as councillor, he, his brother Dennis, Heywood, and Thomas Sutton accused the assembly of disloyalty. The Speaker signed a warrant for Kelly's arrest and appointed a committee of inquiry, which declared Kelly's activity illegal and recommended his dismissal because his words constituted "a dangerous and seditious doctrine and insinuation highly reflecting on His Majesty." One of Lowe's last acts as governor was to suspend Kelly. Ibid., 93, 95, 96; Frank Cundall, *Historic Jamaica* (London, 1915), xvii, xix.

18. John (or Calico Jack) Rackham was a Bahamian pirate who had served under Charles Vane and whose exploits included a passionate relationship with Ann Bonny but ended in his capture off Jamaica and execution in Port Royal.

fended Himself, but Overcome and took the Pirates and brought Them into Port Royal. The Assembly in Consideration of so Gallant an Action gave Him £200, and the Command of one of the sloops fitted out in the Service of the Country. He was afterwards very Active and Vigilant in the trust reposed in Him.

Wrackham and His Company were tried and Executed at Port Royal and their heads set up on Poles, on the Cays, in Terrorem.

In [blank] 1718 the War with Spain was Proclaimed[19] in this Island and at the same time was published His Majesty's Permission to His Subjects to Trade with the Spaniards with an Exception to Provisions, Naval and Warlike Stores.

S[i]r Nicholas Laws who undoubtedly had the Interest and wellfare of this Island very much at heart, was intent and Anxious not only for the suppressing the Negroes in Rebellion, but the better Settlement and Peopleing of the Island. And, being convinced that the Persons commonly employed in Parties, were incapable of the Fatigue of travelling over Rocky Mountains, crossing Rivers, and lieing in the Woods, often wet, and without any Shelter from the Weather put Him on sending to Jeremy the King of the Musquito Indians, for some of His People to be employed in that service, believing them more capable of going through hardships and Fatigues.

Accordingly an Agreement was made, and 50 able, Robust men inlisted themselves Voluntarily at 40 Sh[illings] Each per Month for 3 months, and to be provided with Arms, Ammunition and other Necessaries. On their Arrival They were properly Equipped, and some of the most hardy and Experienced Mountaineers were Sent out as Guides and to assist Them. But, though They did not Fully Answer the Governour's Expectation, not being used to such steep and Rocky Mountains, or such cold Weather as they met with on some of the highest of them, yet they did good Service, in taking and killing many of the Rebells, and destroying of their Plantations and Settlements. The Indians on their Return, had their Wages duly paid them, and a Sloop was hired to Carry them, to their own Country, it being their Custom not to be absent longer, unless detained by some Accident.

At this time Trade was at the lowest ebb that ever was known in this Island, and mon[e]y so very Scarce that it was difficult to raise sufficient for Common Occasions. This put some Evil designing men on raising the Spanish Coin the common Currency of this Island, and they so far prevailed that pistoles which usually passed at 20/. were now paid away at 22/6 p[ieces] of [eight] of an uncertain weight, which went for five Shillings,

19. War was declared on April 26 and later joined by other members of the Quadruple Alliance.

Born in Ireland, Ann Bonny (1700?–1720?), the paramour and associate of pirate leader John "Calico Jack" Rackham, was one of the more colorful of the many pirates operating in Caribbean waters in the wake of Queen Anne's War. Captured near Jamaica in 1720, Rackham and Bonny were sentenced to death, though Bonny's pregnancy provided her with a stay of execution, and she may have escaped the gallows altogether. This contemporary depiction is from an engraving entitled *Ann Bonny op Jamaica Gevangen* from the *General History of the Robbers and Murderers* (Amsterdam, 1725), following p. 220.

now passed at 6 [shillings] 3 [pence] and, Bills of Exchange were raised from 35 to 40 p[er]C[en]t. The Merchants opposed this Scheme, and Represented to the Governour the many bad Consequences, which would inevitably flow from such an alteration in their money and Exchange; for by the same Rule that P[iece]s of [eight] of an uncertain weight were raised to 6 [shillings] 3 [pence], they might in time be raised to Ten Shillings or more, and other Coin in proportion to the Infinite prejudice of Trade and the Credit of the Island. But, all their Remonstrances had no Effect, though the Struggle they made has prevented any Attempt to raise the mon[e]y higher.

In June 1719, a Remarkable Circumstance hap[pe]ned which I think worthy of notice in the Memoirs of this Island, and in Justice to the Memory of a Gentleman, who by a Stratagem did His Country a very signal Service.

About the middle of that month, sailed from Port Royal thirty odd Sail of Merchant Ships Richly laden, bound to Great Britain with no other Convoy than the *Happy* Sloop of 10 Guns and 100 Men; and in their passage through the Gulph of Florida, they met with 4 large Spanish men of War, one of which wore a Vice Admirals Flag. Capt[ain] Charles Chamberlain who Commanded the Sloop which sailed well was Sensible that He could early make His Escape, but as He was not able to protect the Fleet from such a Force, the Major part if not all of them would inevitably fall into the Enemies hands, unless He could prevent it by some Stratagem. He therefore ordered 7 Stout Ships to hoist the King's Colours, and the largest of them a broad Pennant, which was accordingly done, and the Supposed Commadore made a Signal to the Sloop to give Chace. Capt[ai]n Chamberlain on this sailed so near to the Enemy that They fired several shot at Him, and having taken a View of Them, returned to the Fleet on which a signal was made for a line of Battle. The Spaniards perceiving these passages, imagined the 7 Ships, which wore the King's Colours and one of them a distinguished Pennant, to be English Men of War, and the Sloop a Scout sent to discover their Force, They thereupon Crouded all the Sail they could make and left them. And, by this lucky Contrivance one of the Richest Fleets was preserved that ever sailed from this Island.

The Assembly met in October 1719 when His Excellency made the usual and Customary Speech and They passed Several Acts which met with the Concurrence of the Governour and Council, but not making any Provision for Supplying the Deficiency of the Revenue a Difference arose between them, which occasioned prorogation to the [blank]

In November 1719, Commodore [Edward] Vernon[20] arrived with His Majesty's Ships the *Mary* and *Mermaid*. He immediately stationed the few Ships He had under His Command in so proper a manner, that the Pirates; and Privateers did not dare to appear on or near our Coasts.

In [blank] 1720 The Assembly met according to Prorogation and His Excellency made the following Speech, which shews the Temper and Disposition they were in, and that the Dissagreement at this time cannot be

20. Commodore Edward Vernon (1684–1757).

imputed to S[i]r Nicholas who was a Gentleman of Strong Natural Parts and, great Experience and therefore it is not to be Supposed that He, whose all was embarqued in the same bottom and which was of more importance to Him than the Government[,] would Act contrary to the Interest of the Island, to ingratiate Himself with the Ministry in England. But the Temper of the Governour as well as the Assembly will appear in the following Extract, and give the Reader a better light, than a barren Journal of Facts, and the Idea of the want of Sentiments and Intentions in both at this time.

Mr. Speaker, and Gentlemen of the Assembly

I had sent for you sooner after the late Prorogation of your own begetting, but that I find by Experience you are all too wise for me to think of talking you into any thing I would have you do, though never so apparently your Interest. And I wish you were all so prudent and discreet, as not to be talked out of what you ought to do in Justice to your Country and Duty to his Majesty; and that by false Reasoning and mistaken Politicks. I am at Length convinced that there are some who would be glad to continue the old Breaches, or to see or make Divisions amongst us, and it is not to be wondered that those who obstinately refuse to serve the King and Country, will be active in doing Mischief; but I would have these Gentlemen remember, by whose Tenure they hold their Lands, and know under whose Influence and Protection they enjoy at least their well Being. But you Patriots, such as I hope you will appear to be, know how to govern your selves on such Occasions, and Wisdom will ever be justified by her Children.

Gentlemen and Brother Planters,

Let it suffice that I can say for my self, that I have been known to your Fathers, and am not unacquainted with most of you, and that my Interest and my Posterity stands upon the same Foundation with yours, and therefore I can have no Designs or Views, otherwise than what I must be equally concerned with you in the Event. I have done all Things in my Power to settle the present and future Peace and Prosperity of this Island; and I wish you had all joined with me in the same Measures. I may be allowed to say what your own Journals will say to my Honour, that I have pointed out to you many more Particulars for the Publick Welfare, Security, and Advantages of the Country, than ever any of my Predecessors did.

And now I challenge your whole Body to propose to, or lay before me any Thing that you in your Wisdom can desire or devise for your own Good, or the real Interest of this Island, consistent with my Duty and his Majesty's just Prerogative to grant, which I will not heartily concur with you in. I hope for all our Sakes you will readily fall into your Duty in the

ordinary and usual Way agreeable to our happy Constitution, otherwise it
may be easily foreseen, without the Spirit of Prophecy, that his Majesty's
wise and able Ministers will rightly counsel and inform him, how and by
what Ways and Means he may make his Government easy here, and his
People truly happy under it, and I know we are all in Love with English
Laws.

But were I capable, or might be thought worthy of advising you, it
should be not to contend with the King and Ministry, or kick against the
pricks, but to prefer Obedience before Sacrifice, which I am Confident
would be most acceptable to his most Sacred Majesty, and in Consequence
make us the happiest Subjects in all his Dominions.

The Governour having received a Petition from the Inhabitants of the
Virgin Islands, to the Number or 270 Men[,] Women and Children, who
proposed to come down and Settle in this Island, provided due and Reasonable Encouragement was given Them communicated the same to the
Assembly. His Excellency at the same time Recommended the passing of
an Act for Vesting a certain quantity of land in the Crown to be allotted among those People, with such other Encouragement, as They should
think proper.

It would have been a fortunate Event had the Assembly, immediately
complied with this proposal, because those People were inured to the Climate, as well as to labour and Hardships, and would have been of Infinite
more service, than treble their Number from Europe or North America.
But, their unreasonable feuds and Animosities occasioned Them to delay
or neglect what would apparently have been of great Utility to the Island,
for those People not receiving a Satisfactory Answer in due time, set[t]led
themselves in some other way and Could not afterwards be prevailed with
to Come down, when the Assembly came into a better disposition, and
gave very ample Encouragement to New Set[t]lers.

What contributed to, if not the chief cause of their being so much out
of humour, was an Order His Excellency received under His Majesty's sign
manuel, commanding Him to pay the monies advanced by the Lord Hamilton for the Subsistance of the Soldiers (which had been the Subject of
their former Controversy and disputes) with Interest out of the first and
readiest of the Revenues. This laid the Governour under great difficulties,
for the Revenues being in Debt and not sufficient to discharge the Contingencies of the Government He was under the Necessity of Applying to
the Assembly for a Supply. But, They were so averse to the payment of that
demand that to prevent the Governour's Compliance with His Majesty's
Order, They determined not to grant the Supplies which He required,
so that His Excellency was almost as much cramped and Embarassed in
that Respect, as the Lord Hamilton had been, for He was not able to pay
himself His own Salary, which by those means run greatly in Arrears and

was not fully satisfied in Some Years After. However, They made the usual provision for the Subsistence of the Soldiers, and for fitting out Parties to reduce the Rebellious Negroes, And passed an Act for fitting out Sloops or other Vessels, for Guarding the Sea Coasts, and better Defence of the Island.[21] But the Governour finding all His Efforts in Vain and that the Assembly had no Regard to His Moderation and dispassionate Representations so that and other Occasions or even to His Majesty's Mandamus, thought it proper, with the Advice and Consent of the Council to dissolve Them.

In June 1720 Commodore Vernon, who had been out on a Cruise, with the *Mary* of 60 Guns, and the *Ludlow Castle* of 40, returned to Port Royal. He met with 3 Spanish men of War of 70, 60, and 36 Guns, off the Havana, and had a smart Engagement with Them, for about an hour though the Spaniards endeavoured to avoid it as much as possible. But, the *Ludlow Castle* that was Engaged with the Ship of 60 Guns receiving an unlucky Shot between Wind and Water made a signal of distress, on which the Commodore bore down to Assist Her, and the Spaniards took the Opportunity of run[n]ing Away, altho[ugh] they were much Superior in the Number of Men and Guns.

And, in August came advice that the Fleet which consisted of 11 sail of Merchant Ships and Sailed from this Island the 4th, of June bound to Great Britain under Convoy of the *Milford* Capt[ain] Chamberlain were all Cast away in a Storm on the 22d. of the same month, between Cape Corientes and Cape Antonio. The Capt[ain] of the man of War and all the men, except 30, were drowned, 3 or 4 ships drove ashore the wind being at S[outh] and were left dry, by which means their Companies were preserved, the rest perished. Those men on the shore were taken off about 20 days after by another Fleet, under Convoy of the *Mermaid.* Capt[ain] Dent, who perceiving the Signalls they made as the Fleet was passing by sent His Boats and Took them in.

The 11th. of June 1721, Commodore Vernon sailed for England, with a large Fleet of Merchant ships under His Convoy. And, in regard to Truth and Justice I must Observe that He was active, and Vigilant while He was on this Station, for He constantly kept the few Ships under His command cruising in proper Stations, nor lay in Port Himself, but when the Service required it to fit His Ship or on other Occasions. Nevertheless, the Pirates and Guarda Costas did great mischief, in the Bay of Honduras and other Parts where He could not spare a ship to send after and to reduce them.

The Assembly met the 20th, of June following when His Excellency made a Speech the Substance of which is as follows.

21. An Act for Fitting Out Sloops, or Other Vessells, for Guarding the Sea-Coasts, and Better Defence of This Island, 1719, in *Acts of Assembly Passed in the Island of Jamaica; from 1681 to 1737, Inclusive* (London, 1738), 169.

That the Frequent meeting of Assemblies, actuated with Principles of serving the Publick, was very agreeable to Him; But, when they met together with a View of shewing their dislike to each other, and plant seeds of Dissention, which He was sorry to say the Soil was too Subject to, that then it was unhappy for the Governed as well as the Governour. That the last Assembly was of this Complexion, He appealed to their own Journals, and their neglect of His Majesty's Service and their own safety notwithstanding their Professions, obliged Him to part with Them and publish His Reasons for so doing. But, hoped they met with more Temper and Moderation, as well as Zeal for the Public Service.

That a Bill to Encourage the Settling a Colony from the Virgin Islands, about the N[orth] E[ast] part of the Island, was the last thing in Agitation, and of so great importance that it was Surprising it should be left to a Succeeding Assembly. But that so necessary a Work, as the better Peopling and Security of the Country was reserved for their Honour, and He hoped would be accomplished by Them. That he had often expatiated the Advantages which would accrue to the Publick by Settling that part of the Island, which has lain in the hands of about 150 Proprietors, who had neither paid the Quit Rents, nor cultivated any part of it in 45 years whereby most or all of it, is become Escheatable or forfeited to the Crown, and is in quantity not less than 60000 Acres. Therefore hoped They would Unanimously Resolve to vest that entire tract of Land in the Crown; Subject to the uses proposed by the Plan, He had laid before Them, and to give proper Encouragement, to the People of the Islands, to come with their Families and Settle among us.

That the miserable Circumstances of the Island for want of Trade and Current Cash, required their most serious attention, and Consideration, and assured them of His ready concurrence, in every thing they should propose for the general benefit of the Island, and the advantage of Posterity.

That They would find by the Publick Accounts, the Country was greatly in debt, and that the Revenue was not sufficient to discharge the Contingencies of the Government, much less the money advanced by the Lord Hamilton and the Council for their Service.

That in Obedience to His Majesty's Order, all payments must be Stopped until that Debt and the Interest is discharged; so that His Salary must be postponed, as well as all other demands unless they discharged those incumbrances, and Redeemed the Publick Credit. That, He must once more Recommend their making all orders of Council carry Interest, because it would make them Current in payment, and be a saving to the Government, more than the Interest, by having work done and materials purchased at much Easier Rates. That He hoped they would all join with Him, in pursuing the true Interest of the Country and manifesting their Duty and Affection to His Majesty, who ardently desired the Felicity and Prosperity of His Subjects.

The Assembly, accordingly passed a Bill intitled an Act to Encourage the Set[t]ling the North East Part of this Island. And, nine other Publick and Private Acts, which met with the Concurrence of the Governour and Council. But, declined granting any Supplies to the Revenue on which the Governour Prorogued Them to the 17th. of October.

At this time the Trade was very much disturbed by a Notorious Pirate, commanded by one Charles Vane,[22] who had done great mischief. The Governour having information of His Station, fitted out and Sent after Him a Sloop well manned, which had the good fortune to meet with and take him. And, in a few days after They were brought into Port, They were tried and Executed. On the Departure of Commodore Vernon, the command of His Majesty's ships devolved on Capt[ai]n Davers; But He was Superceeded by Capt[ain] Bartholomew Caudler in His Majesty's ship the *Launceston*, who arrived soon after, and hoisted a broad Pennant, being a Superior Officer, and having a proper Commission.

This Gentleman, after He had careened and fitted His ship, sailed on a Cruise to protect the Trade, from the Insults and Depredations of the Spaniards notwithstanding the late Treaty of Peace and Friendship, between Great Britain and Spain.[23] In a few Days after He saw a Sail which he Suspected to one of Their Guarda Costas, and being acquainted with their practices, He bore away as though He intended to run from Her. His design succeeded, for the Spaniards imagining Him to be a Merchant ship pursued, and on coming up laid Him on board, but was soon made Sensible to their Mistake. In searching their papers, Capt[ain] Caudler met with several, which related to a Vessel that was fitted out at Port Royal, and was bound to Curaso. She had been missing some months, and no Account could be given of Her. On which He carried the Spaniards into Port Royal, where the Masters of two Ships belonging to Boston, who had been taken by them on the high Seas, gave in their Information to the Governour on Oath, on which Thirty nine were tried, Convicted, and Executed. Some of them, after they had received Sentence, Confessed that they had taken the Vessel before mentioned and that They murdered all the men belonging to Her.

The Assembly met, according to Prorogation, the 17th. of October, when His Excellency, in His Speech, Recommended several matters to Their Consideration, particularly to lay aside all Differences, and to promote the Service of His Majesty and the Country. He acquainted Them that the Act lately passed for set[t]ling the N[orth] E[ast] part of the Island, was so defective that it would not Answer the Expectation of those People who proposed to Settle there, so that a fair Opportunity of increasing our Numbers will be lost, unless they provided some Effectual Remedy.

22. Charles Vane (1680–721) was an English pirate who preyed on English and French ships from 1716 to 1721.
23. Treaty of Madrid, June 1721.

That the sloop fitted out under the Command of Capt[ai]n Barnet, had been very Serviceable, in protecting the Coast and remote Settlements, therefore thought it Necessary, to Continue Him in that Employ. That He should with pleasure concur with them, in any thing for the publick Service that was not repugnant to His Duty and the Trust reposed in Him.

The Assembly not regarding what His Excellency Recommended to Them, and disagreeing among themselves, He prorogated them to the 10th. of February, but they not meeting at that time, He prorogated Them from time to time to the 8th. of the same Month when He dissolved them by Proclamation and assigned the following Reasons.

> That He had in the first and 2d. Sessions, Recommended to Them matters of the greatest importance, to the Island, but they had so little regard to His Advice, that most of their time at their Respective meetings, had been employed in peevish and fruitless disputes and Enquiries which at length involved them in such Difficulties, that they desired a Recess, which was granted them to the 1st. of this month. But, notwithstanding their Resolutions and promises to raise such Aids as would enable the Treasury to discharge all its Debts, yet their former and late Behaviour, fully Evinced that they never were intended to be put in Execution; for notwithstanding They were fully informed of the destitute Condition of the Treasury which is incapable of Subsisting the Servants, or providing for the Contingencies of the Government. Yet, the said Assembly failed to meet on the 1st. day of this month, According to Prorogation which Act of disobedience being willing to Excuse He prorogued Them again to the 6th. of this month and for the same Reason to the 7th. and from thence to this day, when they also failed to meet, which are such repeated Contempts and Slights to His Honour and Authority, as were become insupportable, Therefore, He thought fit by and with the advice and Consent of the Council &c. [to dissolve them.]

Whoever impartially Considers these Circumstances must allow, that the Assembly not meeting According to Prorogation, was the highest Affront They could put on the Governour and the Authority He was Cloathed with especially considering His patience and forbearance in adjourning them from time to time, in hopes of their meeting. Nevertheless it was not owing to any personal disrespect to His Excellency, but to frustrate the payment of my Lord Hamilton for they had Reason to believe that if They met and granted any Supplies to the Revenue which was the principal matter required of them, the same would be applied to that Debt in the first place, according to His Majesty's order, and therefore not only this, but the former and Succeeding Assembly, declined furnishing the Treasury, with such monies as were otherwise absolutely necessary, and which they would not have refused could they have had assurance of its not being applied to

the payment of a demand. They did not allow of, nor think themselves ob-
ligated to pay, though ways and means were afterwards found out to discharge the same with Interest, so that all the Opposition and Obstruction
they gave to it only tended to the prejudice of the Country by lessening the
Publick Credit and Contracting a load of Debts, by deficiencies and Arrears, which are not yet fully discharged.

In [blank] 1722 arrived Commodore Harris in the *Falkland* and took on
Him the command of His Majesty's ships on this Station.

The Governour considering the pressing Circumstances of the Country, thought it Necessary to issue out Writs for a new Assembly to meet
the 14th. of June, in hopes to find them in a more agreeable Temper and
Disposition. They met Accordingly and His Excellency in His Speech Acquainted Them:

> That when He parted with the last Assembly, for neglecting to meet ac-
> cording to Prorogation, He was in daily Expectation of the arrival of His
> Grace the Duke of Portland,[24] and that He did not expect to have had an
> Opportunity of meeting another, but the pressing Exigencies of the Gov-
> ernment, occasioned an absolute necessity of their Assistance and advice.
> He represented to them the distressed Condition of the Revenue, for want
> of Supplies, and how Necessary it was to preserve Publick Credit.
>
> That His Majesty had been pleased to appoint a Nobleman of the first
> Rank to be their Governour, which they must own a fresh Instance of the
> Esteem and Value He had for Them, therefore hoped they would make a
> Suitable and Honourable provision for the reception of His Grace.
>
> He likewise acquainted Them that the Rebellious Negroes had of late
> appeared in many parts of the Country, in great Numbers, and Seized on
> all Arms and Ammunition they could meet with. That He had ordered
> out Parties in pursuit of Them but money would be wanted to pay Them
> and other Parties who had ventured their lives in the Service of the Pub-
> lick, which would otherwise be Obstructed. That the Body of their Laws
> was near Expired, therefore it was necessary to Re-inact them in time.
> And, that their cheerful Compliance with what He had Recommended to
> Them, was the best means of manifesting their Zeal for His Majesty's Ser-
> vice and the Interest of their Country.

But, neither this Speech nor His Excellency's Expostulations with the
leading Members had any Effect. They differed among themselves principally on the old Topick the payment of my Lord Hamilton, there being in this, as well as in the former Assembly a party who were for dis-

24. Henry Bentinck, First Duke of Portland (1682–1726), an experienced British political
leader, accepted the post of governor of Jamaica in 1721 after losing a huge amount of money
in the South Sea Bubble the previous year. See Cundall, *Governors of Jamaica in the First Half
of the Eighteenth Century*, 104–17.

charging that demand, and Supplying the Revenue, though the Majority were against it. And, after their having sat about a month, without doing any business, several of the Members having left the House, so that they Scarcely could make a Quorum, to pass a Bill, the Governour thought proper, with the advice and Consent of the Council to dissolve them.

The 28th. of August of 1722, this Island was afflicted a second time; with a dreadful and Ruinous Hurricane. The Inhabitants had some Prognosticks of it, for a day or two before They felt its fury; for the Weather was unset[t]led[,] the Wind often shifting, though it blew gently and there was an uncommon swell of the Sea even when it was Calm. It began about 8 in the morning and Continued till ten at Night, and the height of it was from Eleven at noon till three in the afternoon, during which time it rained very hard and blew with great Violence, the Wind often shifting almost every minute or less from one Point to another round the Compass.

Port Royal and Kingston sustained very considerable damages, especially the first mentioned Place, which was again reduced to a heap of Rubbish, but the Inhabitants having time and Convenience to Escape, it being in the Day, many Persons were Saved, who would inevitably have perished had this Calamity hap[pe]ned in the Night.

But, the most melancholy account was of the shipping, for of 26 Sail of Ships and 10 Sloops in Kingston Harbour, not more than ten were Seen, after the Hurricane and few of them were got off and repaired being drove ashore and left dry. At Port Royal several ships and other Vessells were likewise lost; and three men of War namely the *Falkland*, Commodore Harris the *Swallow* Capt[ain] Ogle, the *Weymouth*, Capt[ain] Herdman, and the *Happy* sloop Cut away their Masts the *Launceston* and *Mermaid* being out on a Cruise did not meet with this Weather. In the Country the Canes, Plantain Walks, Sugar Works and other buildings were thrown down, but not more than 5 or 6 Persons lost their lives, excepting at Port Royal, and about 30 Whites and Blacks at Old Harbour.

The Governour on this occasion, ordered the Troops of Horse to Patroul round the shores of Kingston and Port Royal, to prevent Seamen and others from plundering the Goods and Wrecks drove ashore. At the same time, He issued out, a Proclamation to restrain such practices, and Commanding the Provost Marshal[l] and other Officers to Search for all Stolen or concealed Goods, in order to their being restored to their proper Owners. Another Proclamation was issued out, forbidding the Engrossing and Selling Provisions and other Necessaries of life, at any greater or higher prices, that they were sold for on the 27th. of August, being the Day before the Hurricane.

His Excellency likewise thought it Necessary to issue out Writs for chusing an Assembly, who met accordingly in October when He Recommended to their Consideration inter alia, the distressed Circumstances of the Island, by means of the late Calamity.

They met with more Temper and Moderation than the preceeding Assemblies, and passed Several Bills which met with the Concurrence of the Governour and Council particularly.

An Act for Establishing a perpetual Anniversary Fast on the 28th. of August.[25]

An Act, for fitting out a Sloop or Vessel for Guarding the Sea coasts and better Defence of this Island.[26]

And, three money Bills. But, in respect to the Revenue they followed the Steps of their Predecessors, and did not grant any Supplies to that Fund, for the same Reasons which were given.

The Spaniards this Year made several illegal Captures on the High Seas, Though I have not been able to procure the Names of any of them, except these following, namely

The Unity	Francis Plaisted Mas[te]r	of London,	from Africa
Kingsdale	[blank] England Mas[te]r	Bristol	Ireland
Betty	John Hames Mas[te]r	Bristol	Africa

The Perfidy of that Nation, and their unjustifiable conduct and behaviour in America will appear in a clearer and Stronger light, in the following letter from S[i]r Nicholas Laws to the Governour of the Havanna,[27] which the Reader may depend on to be genuine, and a true Copy.

S[i]r.

This letter will be delivered to your Excellency by Mes[sieur]s Nicholson and Calder, who are impowered by the Agents for the *Royal African Company*, of *England;* to make Application to your Excellency, for Restitution of the Ship *Unity*, with 257 Negroes, belonging to the said Company.

Your Excellency will be pleased to observe by the authentick Proofs and Certificates, which are herewith transmitted, that the said ship and Negroes were most unjustly taken off of Cape Tiberoon, on the Coast of Hispaniola, on the 28th. of July last, by a Spanish Sloop, which I am informed carried the said ship and Negroes into Trinadado, under your Excellency's Jurisdiction; and that the Alcadies of that Place have condemned them on Suggestion of the Captors, that they found her trading on that Coast: The contrary of which will evidently appear by the enclosed Depositions, as well as from the Nature of the Thing it self; therefore I cannot doubt your Excellency's ordering full and ample Satisfaction, &c.

In a former Letter I represented to your Excellency, as well as to the rest of my neighbouring Spanish Governours; but more particularly to the Governour of St. Iago, and the Alcaldies of Trinadado; the many Acts of

25. An Act for Establishing a Perpetual Anniversary Fast on 28 August, [1722–23], in *Acts of Assembly*, 179–80.

26. An Act for Fitting Out Sloops, or Other Vessells, in ibid., 179.

27. Gregorio Guazo y Calderón Fernández de la Vega was governor of Cuba from 1718 to 1724.

Pyracies and Robberies committed on the Subjects of the King my Master, by Vessells fitted out of Trinadado, and other Ports, with Commissions, as they pretend to guard their Coast from unlawful Traders: but in reality, under Colour of such Commissions, commit frequent Depredations, and are guilty of the most Enormous Crimes without (so far as I can understand) their ever being punished for them. One the contrary, they are not only admitted with their Prizes, as they call them, into the Port of Trinadado, in particular, where they are immediately condemned, the Negroes and Goods shared, and divided; but the Captors are also encouraged in their Villainy by those in Authority, who permit them to refit their Vessels, share in their Plunder, and send them out again in search of more Booty.

It must be no less surprising to his Catholick Majesty than it will be to the King my Master, when they receive an Account of such unwarrantable Proceedings in time of profound Peace; which must appear a manifest breach of that good Agreement stipulated between the two Crowns, and in our respective Capacities ought to be cultivated and improved to the utmost of our Power. As for my Part, I can with great Confidence assure your Excellency, it has been my constant Endeavour, that strict Justice should be done to such of the Spanish Nation who have had Demands here since the Cessation of Arms; and several of them have already had ample Restitution: but I am sorry that I have it to say, my Master's Subjects have not met with reciprocal Justice from the *Spanish* Governors.

> I am with great Truth and Sincerity,
> Your Excellency's most Obedient,
> And most Humble Servant.
> Nich[olas] Laws

Jamaica, Oct. 24. 1722.

As nothing further hap[pe]ned during this Administration that is remarkable, I shall Conclude with some few Observations, which will illustrate the several passages I have recited and do the Justice which is due to the merit and Memory of S[i]r Nicholas Laws.

He came over very Young, and resided above 40 Years, in this Island, before He returned to England, during which time, He acquired a very Considerable Estate, passed through the highest offices of Honour and trust with great Reputation and was always distinguished for His Publick Spirit, a Generous and Hospitable manner of living. He Resided at Twickenham about 14 Years, until He was appointed Governour, and I am persuaded from my own knowledge and observation of His Conduct and Behaviour, as I was on the Spot and had the Honour of being personally Acquainted with Him from my Infancy, that He returned to this Island with the strongest dispositions to Serve the Country and to promote its wellfare and happiness to the utmost of His power, nor did the Opposition He met with abate His Zeal and good will, though it Obstructed His measures.

It must However be confessed that He committed some mistakes, through Error in Judgment or as some imagine, the Influence and advice of His favourite, the Attorn[e]y General. But, I shall throw a Veil over them in Regard to His good Qualities and Intentions, and since He never was accused of any Schemes to fleece the People, or to advance His private Interest by any unjustifiable means therefore He may justly be Ranked among the best Governours of this Island.

Upon His being superceded, by the Duke of Portland, He retired to His Seat called Snow Hill, in Liguinea, with an Intension of Spending the Remainder of His Days there, and probably would have lived many Years longer, being of a Hail, Strong constitution, Had He not unfortunately his lip cut in Shaving, which through mismanagement turned to a Cancer and put an end to His life, the [blank] day of [blank] 1731 in the 80th. Year of His Age.

The 20th. of December 1722, arrived His Majesty's ship the *Kingston* (and 3 Merchants ships) with His Grace Henry Duke of Portland, His Dutchess,[28] and their two Daughters the Lady Ann, and the Lady Arabella Bentnick; Colo[nel] Fielding[,] His Grace's Secretary, two Chaplains[29] and a Numerous Retinue. Also Colo[nel] Charles Dubourgay,[30] whom His Majesty was pleased to appoint L[ieutenan]t Governour, the Marquis De Quesne[,][31] Capt[ain] of Fort Charles, John Aschough Esq[ui]r[e][32]

28. Lady Elizabeth Noel, daughter of Wriothesley Baptist Noel, Second Earl of Gainsborough, and Catherine Greville.

29. One of these chaplains was Reverend Charles St. John Lambe, D.D., rector of Kingston in 1729 and later dean of Ely. Cundall, *Governors of Jamaica in the First Half of the Eighteenth Century*, 115.

30. Charles Du Bourgay (?–1732), a colonel of the 32nd Foot Regiment. In his opening speech, Portland told the assembly of Du Bourgay's appointment as lieutenant-governor at a salary of £1,000 per annum. The assembly balked at paying a lieutenant-governor during the life of a governor but finally agreed to a settlement in which the assembly paid Du Bourgay £1,350 toward his expenses in returning home. Ibid., 106, 107, 108.

31. Gabriel, Marquis Du Quesne. As commander of Fort Charles, 1723–25, his own soldiers brought charges against him of ill practices and responsibility for the abominable condition of quarters at the fort. He defended himself in 1729 with *The Marquis Duquesne Vindicated: In a Letter to a Noble Lord from the Aspersions Cast on His Conduct* (London, 1728). Cundall, *Governors of Jamaica in the First Half of the Eighteenth Century*, 112, 113; Cundall, *Historic Jamaica*, 64, 71.

32. John Ayscough (?–1735) was the son of either Major Thomas Ayscough (member of the assembly for St. John, 1664–93, and member of council, 1696–1705) or William Ayscough, brother of Admiral Sir George Ayscue, of an old Lincolnshire family, a lieutenant stationed in Jamaica who died in 1658. A member of the Jamaica Assembly for St. John Parish, 1702–3 and 1706, and for St. Andrew Parish in 1704, John Ayscough was briefly expelled with six others in 1703 for leaving the house in objection against the Speaker and subsequently resisting arrest. He became a councillor in 1707 because "he has always behaved himself in the Assembly with a good deal of respect to the Queen's authority: he understands the Law, and is a man of as good substance as any in the Island." He was chief justice, 1723–24, and senior member of council from 1722. As such he became acting governor on the July 4, 1726,

Henry Bentinck, First Duke of Portland (1682–1726), was a prominent
Whig politician and member of the
House of Lords when, after losing a
huge amount of money in the South
Sea Bubble in 1720, he accepted the
post of governor of Jamaica in 1721
in the hope of retrieving his fortune.
Jamaicans widely regarded the appointment of such a prominent English nobleman as an indication of
Jamaica's growing importance within
the empire. Despite opposition over
Portland's efforts to negotiate a permanent revenue for the Crown, he
retained his popularity in the colony
from his arrival in 1722 until his death
in 1726 at Spanish Town. (Portland
Collection, Harley Gallery)

and Colo[nel] John Cam[p]bell[33] both of the Council, and several other
Gentlemen.

His Grace's Commission for Capt[ain] General[,] Governour and Commander in chief of this Island was dated the 23d. of August 1721.

He was received at Port Royal, by S[i]r Nicholas Laws (the late Governour), the Council and a great Number of Gentlemen, in as Grand a
manner as the Condition and Circumstances of the Island, would allow, at
that time, being soon after the dreadful Hurricane. His Grace landed, and
took the Oaths in Fort Charles, the same Day, and from thence proceeded
to Spanish Town, with His Family. His Affable[,] Polite and engaging Behaviour soon reconciled all Parties in Affection and Regard for His Person
and Government, and they Seem to have forgot, at least laid aside all former differences, and Animosities.

The Assembly met the 23d. of January following according to Prorogation, when His Grace made a Speech, which I thought proper to abbreviate
and to leave out some paragraphs, which are unnecessary to be repeated
in this place.

---

death of Portland until a new governor, Robert Hunter, arrived on January 29, 1728. As president of the council, he again acted as governor when Hunter died on March 31, 1734, and
then himself died in office. A progressive planter, he was the author of *Some Modern Observations upon Jamaica as to Its Natural History, Improvement in Trade, Manner of Living, etc. By an
English Merchant* (London, 1727). Cundall, *Governors of Jamaica in the First Half of the Eighteenth Century*, 78, 106, 108, 118–29, 131, 132, 145, 156, 157, 158.

33. John Campbell was appointed to the Jamaica Council in May 1722.

Gentlemen of the Council

Mr. Speaker, and Gentlemen

of the Assembly.

I have called you together, as soon as the unset[t]led State of my private Affairs, since my Arrival would permit. I wish you may not, under your present Circumstances, think I have been too hasty; the Situation I am [in], and the publick Business would not admit of such a Delay as might Reasonably have been wished for, and my Inclinations would have led me to Consent to. However I hope and promise my self, that I now meet you all well disposed, and sincerely inclined to Sacrifice all former Animosities and Resentments, to the service of your Country. Let me find you at Peace, and I believe that I shall be able to keep you so.

I could not prevail upon my self to call a new Assembly at my first entrance on the Government, though I have the Examples of almost all my Predecessors. The late dreadful Calamity, the near approach of your Crop, the Animosities and Disputes which Often attend Elections, have had a great weight with me. But what has more immediately, induced me to meet you, Gentlemen is the persuasion, that you will receive this as an Instance of an entire Confidence in You and that it will intitle me to a treatment, Answerable to it.

When the Governour and the Assembly entertain mutual Distrusts and Jealousies, nothing can be expected but uneasiness, Disaffection, Murmurs and Complaints, the Fruits whereof are Disorder and Confusion. To prevent this Evil I was willing to give the first Example by not Entertaining or Even Countenancing the least Suspicion.

I bring with me, Gentlemen, many and important Instructions from His Majesty, all tending to the honour, Security, and improvement of this Island. Though Jamaica be at a Distance from His Sacred Person, it is not out of His Thoughts and tender Care, which extends to all His Subjects.

Most of those Instructions, at proper Seasons, shall be laid before you, but some of them I am Commanded to lay immediately before You, and it is expected that they shall become the first subject of your Consideration. Among these, His Majesty has been pleased to Order that what relates to me and the support of my Government, shall have the foremost place but am unwilling to enlarge on that particular, relying wholy on you.

The Instructions I am to Communicate to You, and to Engage your entering upon without Delay, relate to those Vast tracts of land, which remain uncultivated, and are withheld from those, who would settle upon them, and increase the produce, the Revenue, and Inhabitants of this Island.

Complaints have been made to His Majesty that the Laws are Dificient for the Recovery of just Debts, occasioned by Estates not being Extendable, which reflects upon Credit, and casts a Reproach upon His Government. He therefore Recommends it to your Consideration to find out some method for removing of that Evil.

The State of the Publick Debts have also been laid before His Majesty, and it appears by the Information which gain Credit with Him, that hardly a thought has been in Earnest bestowed upon ways and means, either to discharge or even to give new life to them, so as to reduce the Discompt, which Indeed I am ashamed to mention. The Publick Faith, should always have the first Place in your most Serious considerations; for Your own Interest, as well as the Honour of the Government is affected thereby, and feel the unhappy Effects of such Remissness.

I am further to signify to you Gentlemen, that His Majesty has been pleased to appoint Colo[nel] Charles Dubourgay, a Person of great merit and Honour, to be your Lieutenant Governour. His long and Eminent Services in War, and His Sincere Attachment to His Majesty have prepared His way to this mark of the Royal Favour. And, I am commanded to let you know, that it is expected from you, that you receive Him with the Honour due to His Commission, and provide Him with the Support, which His Credentials will acquaint you with.

Gentlemen

When the King was pleased to confer on me the chief command of this Island, I immediately attended the Service of it, and though my private Affairs grew into a greater length than I expected, Yet I was not wanting in Attention to your Affairs, or in Endeavours to promote your Interest and Wellfare. And being informed that your Laws were near Expiring, I had the Honour to represent it to His Majesty, and have Commission to acquaint you, that He is willing to renew them for a term of Years, or to make them perpetual, expecting at the same time, that you make a due provision for the support of His Government of this Island.

The State of your Trade has been Represented to me, to be in a declining Condition either for want of Encouragement, in general, or by the frequent Pyracies committed. I have it much at heart to make this Island, as Flourishing as in the Days of your Forefathers, for it seems to me Extremely unfortunate, that your Commerce has hitherto been so much neglected; and while we are encompassed with the Sea, we should want the Benefits that Naturally flow from it.

Upon the whole, Gentlemen, all that you hope for from His Majesty, all that you Expect from me, and all that you Design for your selves, depend upon your Unanimity and good Agreement. It is this only that can make you usefull to your Country, and Answer the Intentions of those you Represent.

For my part I will encourage no Divisions nor give ground for any, and if possible I will discountenance the Fomenters of them, of what Denomination or Quality so ever. I will have no Favourites, but will Esteem, every one as He Concurs with me, in Supporting the Honour of His Majesty, and in promoting to the Utmost of His Power, the Peace, Safety and welfare of this Island.

The Assembly when They took His Grace's Speech into Consideration, only returned the following Answer.

To His Grace the Duke of Portland Capt[ain] Gen[era]l &c. May it please your Grace

We His Majesty's most Dutiful and Loyal Subjects, the Assembly of the Island of Jamaica, humbly beg leave to return your Grace our unfeigned and hearty thanks for Your Speech, and the assurance you are pleased to give us, of your having so much at heart, the Interest and prosperity of this Island, and your Readiness to Enter into any measures that may contribute to the advancement of it.

We are truly sensible of the many Instances of His Majesty's great Goodness, and Regard to us, particularly in appointing a Person of so Eminent a Character and Quality to be our Governour; and we do assure your Grace, we shall endeavour in all our Actions to give the highest Demonstrations of our Gratitude, Attachment and Loyalty to His Sacred Person and Government our Deference, and great Regard for your Grace, and a Sincere and Steady Love to our Country. And that we shall proceed on the Business now before us, with that Unanimity and Dispatch Recommended to us by Your Grace.

But, though the Assembly returned this short and plain Answer, Yet They were Sincere and had a greater Regard to their promises, than the two last Assemblys. For to manifest their Readiness to Comply with His Majesty's Recommendations, as well as their professions to His Grace, They Voted Him an Additional Salary of £2500 p[er] Ann[um] during His Residence in this Island as Governor which made up the set[t]led Sallary of £5000 p[er] Ann[um] although they could not, at that time, afford to lay such a Burthen on themselves, the late dreadful Calamity having almost ruined many Plantations, and done Infinite Damage to this Island in general.

However, They shewed no Inclination to Comply with that part of His Majesty's Recommendation in favour of Collo[nel] Dubourgay for though His Character and Behavior was very agreeable to Them, Yet they thought such an Extraordinary Magistrate unnecessary, Especially during Their Governor's Residence among Them, and being Apprehensive of the Consequences of admitting New Erected Officers,. They therefore dismissed Him with a present of £1000. Ster[ling], to defray the Expences of His Voyage and, He returned to England (He was soon after His Arrival, appointed His Majesty's Envoy Extraordinary to the King of Prussia[34]) in His Majesty's ship the *Kingston*. There never was a greater Disposition, than at this juncture, in the three branches of the Legislature to Avoid all manner

34. Wilhelm I (1713–1740).

of Disputes and Controversy. Nor, Indeed, did any Governour ever Recommend Himself more Effectually to the Affections and Esteem of the
People, than the Duke of Portland, by an obliging Behaviour, an Easy Access and Affable to all.

The Assembly on their part, proceeded on Business, with great Unanimity, and passed Several Bills, this Session which met with the Concurrence
of the Governour and Council, particularly.

An Act, for making His Majesty's Revenue perpetual, and Augmenting
the same; and Continuing and declaring what Laws are in Force in this Island.[35]

An Act to augment the Salary of His Grace the Duke of Portland.[36]

The Council and Assembly continued sitting till Saturday the 9th. of
February, when His Grace Commanded the Assembly in His Majesty's
Name to Attend Him in the Council Chamber and Addressed Himself to
them in the following manner.

> Gentlemen of the Council
> Mr. Speaker and Gentlemen
> of the Assembly.
>
> Being Sensible when I called you together that your Concerns at Home,
> in this Season of the Year, did require your attendance on Them, I was
> determined to make the Session as short as the Necessities of the Publick
> would allow.
>
> Those Affairs you have gone through, with such Unanimity and Dis-
> patch, that less time has been Employed, than at first could well be Ex-
> pected; which gives me the pleasing hopes that which remains undone, will
> be Attended with the same Harmony, and be carried through the House
> with the same cheerfulness and Speed.
>
> I shall, with the utmost satisfaction, Represent to His Majesty, with
> what Honour and Regard You received His Commands, and with what
> Alacrity and pleasure you Entered upon the Execution of Them.
>
> What you have done for me and the support of my Government, has
> fully answered my Expectations, and I return you my hearty Thanks for
> it. I have no Views in what I propose to you, or Require of you, than what
> I really believe will advance the honour and the Interest of the Publick.
> And if I was once persuaded that all my Endeavours to Serve you, would
> prove ineffectual I should not think my self fairly intituled to the becom-

35. An Act Making His Majesty's Revenue Perpetual and Augmenting the Same, and Continuing the Declaring What Laws Are in Force in This Island, December 1722–February
1723, in *Acts of Assembly*, 191.

36. An Act to Augment the Salary of His Grace the Duke of Portland, December
1722–February 1723, in ibid., 190.

ing Treatment I have met with, and should immediately entertain thoughts of returning Home.

In the Recess I now propose to give You, and as you are now going to disperse your Selves in Several Parts of the Country; You will Esteem it your Duty to Encourage Obedience to His Majesty and to Exhort all to a continued Unanimity and Agreement.

You will do your Utmost, as Magistrates, to Suppress all manner of Immorality, and profaneness. You will put the Laws in Execution, and inforce Them, by your own good Examples, without which your share in making Them will lose its Honour and Reputation. In full assurance therefore, that in your several Capacities you will be wanting in nothing that becomes you as Faithfull and Dutifull Subjects, as Magistrates or Christians, I do therefore in His Majesty's Name, prorogue you to Tuesday the 23d. of April next &c.

In April the Assembly was prorogued to Tuesday the first of October following.

The same month the Duke of Portland received a letter from Capt[ain John] Taylor Commander of a Pirate ship called the *Cassandra* which formerly belonged to the East India Company, wherein He and His Company offered to Surrender Themselves, and most of their Riches, upon Condition of Obtaining His Majesty's most Gracious Pardon. His Grace communicated this Offer, not only, to the Council, but to the Principal Merchants of Kingston and Port Royal and desired their Opinion and Advice. Some were for Accepting of the Offer, suggesting that if His Grace refused it, the same would be made to the French or the Spaniards, and granted. But, the Majority dissented, and Alledged that it would Countenance and Encourage such Practices, and give a handle to the Enemies of this Island for to revive their former unjust Insinuations of the Inhabitants assisting and Conniving at the Actions of the Pirates. It was therefore not only refused, but a Proclamation issued for Seizing them and their Effects, in order to be brought to Justice. Hereupon, the Captain of the *Cassandra*, made Application to the Governour of Carthagena, who not being so Scrupulous, as the Duke of Portland, received them upon Terms.

It was Reported that the Value of the Goods and Effects on board that ship amounted to One Million Sterling, one fourth of which the Pirates agreed to give to the Spanish Governour, and the rest They divided among Themselves, being 144 Men, most of Them English.

The Assembly met, according to Prorogation, the 1st. of October, when His Grace made a long Speech and Recommended several matters to their Consideration, But, I shall only transcribe the following paragraph relating to their Laws, which will shew the Steps that were taken from time to time and the Reasons of their being obstructed and not brought to an Issue sooner.

Gentlemen of the Council

Mr. Speaker and Gentlemen

of the Assembly

I meet you now with the greatest satisfaction not Questioning but that you cone with minds entirely disposed to do every thing that may conduce to the good and Service of your Country. I think, by what I have already Experienced, that I should be wanting in Justice to You, should I entertain or Harbour any Jealousy.

The chief thing which I must Recommend to your most Serious Consideration, is the Bill you passed the last Session, for the making your Laws perpetual; and at the same time a due Provision for the Expences of His Majesty's Government Here. I wish I could say I was mistaken in my Apprehensions of several Objections that would be made which you know I attempted to remove; but must acquaint you that the same have been made at Home, and are thought of such weight, that it would be deceiving you should I give you the least room to Expect that Bill will receive His Majesty's approbation.

Some Part of the Representations, which have been made against it, may be called kind ones to your selves, wherein your Situation, the nature of your Government and the Inconveniences (should that Law be confirmed) you would labour under have been duly considered. Those general words, whereby you Enact the English Laws to be perpetual, as well as your own, are expressed in such terms, as would require some further Explanation, and as they now stand in that Bill would create the greatest uncertainty and Confusion imaginable; for no man could tell what Laws or Rules should be put in Execution, and there would be too great a latitude for Discretionary Power &c.

These were cogent Reasons against passing a Bill, that was Judiciously drawn, for it cannot be supposed that the Assembly foresaw the Difficulties and Confusion in which They would thereby have been involved had that Act obtained the Royal Assent, therefore the Rejection of it was manifestly a service to the Island, though They had no Reason to be pleased with the subsequent measures, which They thought an infringement on their Rights and Privileges and would have inflamed them as much as ever, had not His Grace behaved on this, a well as on other Occasions, with the greatest prudence and Moderation. The Assembly, after They had sat about a month and passed the Annual Bills which met with the Concurrence of the Governour and Council, where at their own Request Prorogued to the 7th. of January.

About this time Jeremy the King or Chief of the Musquito Indians, who are under the protection of the Crown of Great Britain came to this Island, and paid His Duty to His Grace. He was received with all the Courtesy and good Nature peculiar to that Noble Person, and with more Ceremony than seemed to be due to an Indian Prince, who held His Sovereignty by a Commission from the Governour of this Island for the time being.

The Assembly met the 7th. of January [1724] according to Prorogation, when His grace in His Speech told them:

> That was it not their own wellfare and the set[t]ling a Foundation on which depend their own future Happiness, He should not at that time, have called them from their Respective Homes. But, when they consider, that it is to settle the Ground work upon which their Laws, their Liberties, and all that is dear to them is to be built, They won't wonder; He was glad to See them together, in order to take a matter of so great importance, to themselves and to their Posterity into their most serious Consideration. That they were apprised of what His Majesty expected from Them, and with His Commands to Himself, as fully as it was possible for Him to communicate them. That they were acquainted with His Gracious Intentions, and all that knew Him must be convinced of His Gracious Dispositions therefore it was not adviseable or decent, not to agree with their Sovereign in the manner of doing it.
>
> That the Expiration of their Laws so near approaching, brought the Publick Affairs to a sort of Crisis. That they had the Remedy in their own hands, and if they neglected to make use of it, they could not be Surprised at any effects, such unaccountable Remissness may possibly produce.
>
> That they have always been upon a different and more Advantageous foot than the rest of their Neighbours, and whoever would put them on Methods that will indanger the further Continuance of it takes an uncommon way to Convince the World of their Wisdom, or of His Affection and Zeal for the Good of this Island.

The Assembly in their Address thanked His Grace for His Speech, where in He so justly and Fully reminded them of His Majesty's constant Care and Extream goodness towards them which fitted them with the warmest Sentiments of Gratitude and Duty. That they were Unanimously disposed and unalterably determined, to proceed and Concur in such measures as will best promote the true Interest of this Island. That as His Majesty's Intentions do Evidently center in a fixed Establishment of their Rights and Privileges, no Consideration should stand in Competition with the Endeavours towards so desireable an End. That they could not find words expressive enough, of His Grace's tenderness and Generous Concern, as well for the necessity of their meeting so soon, to the neglect of their private Affairs, as for the more dreadful Condition He found the Island in. That the Calamity they were under, could only have been made tollerable, by His Grace's Conduct and behaviour which not only Composed their minds, but raised their hopes. That His Prudent Administration, His Watchfulness for the Publick good, and His distinguished Regard, not only for the Rights, but for the Ease and Contentment of even the least subject, have justified their most Sanguine Expectations; so that in this Sense it may be truly said, they were upon a different foot with our Neighbours, which they shall ever remember to the Honour of His Grace's Government.

The Assembly, this Session passed another Bill intitled an Act for making His Majesty's Revenue perpetual, and for Confirming and declaring what Laws are in force in this Island.[37] But, the Council making some amendments to that Bill, revived the former dispute in regard to the Council not having any right to Alter or amend Mon[e]y Bills. They thereupon rejected the amendments, and desired His Grace to grant them a Recess. Accordingly His Grace ordered them to Attend Him in the Council Chamber and made the following Speech, which will Explain more fully what passed on that Occasion.

> Mr. Speaker and Gentlemen
>   of the Assembly.
> In Compliance with your last message I have sent for you up to grant you a Recess, being always desirous to shew a just Regard to your private Concerns, particularly at a time when your Affairs at Home so much require your presence.
> I wish, Gentlemen, there had been no difference betwixt the Council and your House, to the Amendments proposed to the Revenue Bill, the Council's aim being chiefly to remove all Objections that might be made to it at Home. Even then to make it entirely conformable to my Instructions, His Majesty does insist that a Draught of the Bill, should be first Sent over to be approved of, or at least a Clause incerted to Suspend the Execution of it, till His Majesty's pleasure should be known.

You may depend that I shall lay your proceedings in the most favourable light, before His Majesty, and that no assistance of mine shall be wanting to forward Every thing for the Interest and Wellfare of this Island. I do therefore adjourn you to Tuesday the 28th. of July next &c.

And, in July a Proclamation was issued for adjourning them to the 30th. of September, then they met and His Grace made the following Speech, which I thought Necessary to transcribe because, it gives a lively Idea of the posture and Condition of Affairs at that juncture, as well as of the tenderness and goodness of His Grace to those who were Committed to His Care.

37. An Act for Making His Majesties Revenue Perpetual, and for Confirming the Declaring What Laws Are in Force in This Island, January 1723/24. This version of this controversial act is not found in *Acts of Assembly*.

Gentlemen of the Council
Mr. Speaker and Gentlemen
of the Assembly.

The great concern I have for your Wellfare, will not suffer me to be Silent, in this Considerable juncture of your Affairs, when notwithstanding my Earnest, and repeated Instances, You have Omitted, in proper Season, to renew your Laws in Such manner as would have been Agreeable to His Majesty's most Gracious Intentions.

If your Confidence in my Administration had any part in this your Remissness, it shall be my Care not to disappoint you in so great a Trust, but to Govern in such sort, when your Laws are Expired, as that none of you shall have any just Reason to know the want of them.

I must Gentlemen on this Occasion Recommend to you that mutual love, and Union, which, your mutual dependence on One another, were sufficient to persuade you to, and which is more especially incumbent on you, as you are fellow Country men, and Situate in so remote a part of His Majesty's Dominions. I cannot leave this head with out assuring you that this Disposition and Unanimity and your regard to the Publick service will best intitle you to the Countenance of the Government.

Gentlemen

The reason of your frequent Adjournments was the Expectations I have had of Advices from Great Britain concerning Your Laws; and as they are not yet arrived, though by the Intelligence I have received I do daily Expect His Majesty's pleasure about them, a further adjournment will be necessary, I do therefore, in His Majesty's name, adjourn you to Tuesday the 20th. of October next.

The Assembly met accordingly and passed Several Bills, particularly a Bill intitled an Act for reviving an Act for raising a Revenue to Her Majesty, Her Heirs and Successors &c. and all other Acts and Laws of Jamaica that Expired with the said Act on the first day of October 1724,[38] which met with the Concurrence of the Governour and Council. And thereupon were adjourned to the 12th. of January following.

The Assembly met on 12th. of January [1725] according to Prorogation, when His Grace in His Speech inforced the Several matters He had formerly Recommended, particularly in regard to their Laws which expired on the 1st. of October last. And Acquainted Them that, He was directed by His Instructions, to send Home the Draught of a Bill for perpetuating the Revenue and the Laws of this Island for His Majesty's Approbation,

38. An Act for Reviving an Act for Raising a Revenue to His Majesty, His Heirs and Successors, and All Other Acts and Laws of Jamaica That Expired with the Said Act on 1 October 1724 is also not found in *Acts of Assembly*.

and not to assent to the same unless a Clause was incerted to Suspend the Execution of it, until His Majesty's pleasure should be known. And in the mean time He was impowered and directed to give His Consent to a Bill to Continue their Laws for One Year to prevent the ill Consequences which may Attend the want of Laws.

The Assembly notwithstanding passed a Bill, intitled an Act for granting a Revenue to His Majesty His Heirs and Successors for the support of the Government of this Island, and for reviving and perpetuating the Laws thereof,[39] as they have been Introduced and used; which passed the Council the 27th. of the same month, and laid before His Grace for His assent.

But, His Grace was pleased to observe to the Board on their meeting the 28th. (as a Council of State) that the said Bill which He understood had lately passed their Board, as a Branch of the Legislature, and lay before Him for His Assent, was (notwithstanding His Majesty's positive Instructions by Him so often repeated) in flat contradiction to His Majesty's Commands, and having Communicated those Instructions again to the Board, and left with them for their further Satisfaction, desired they would carefully Consider them, with respect to the said Bill, and give Him their Opinion tomorrow morning, whether it would be adviseable for Him to pass it or not.

Upon their Meeting the next day, the Board acquainted His Grace that They had thoroughly Considered His Majesty's Instructions, which He was pleased to lay before them Yesterday, with the Revenue Bill now before Him for His Assent, and were of Opinion (notwithstanding the many ill consequences which might probably attend the want of their Accustomed Laws) He could by no means pass that Bill, without a manifest break of that Instruction; which positively directed a Draught of such Bill first be sent Home for His Majesty's approbation, or at least a clause incerted, suspending the Execution thereof, till His Royal pleasure should be known.

Whereupon His Grace declared He would not give His Assent to that Bill, and Prorogued the House to the 1. of February.

The Assembly met according to Prorogation, and His Grace, in His speech acquainted them with the Reasons of His rejecting the Revenue Bill, which passed the Council and was laid before Him for His assent, the last Session.

He assured them of His Majestie's Intentions to perpetuate their Laws, and therefore Recommended to Them not to be disturbed with Imaginary Fears or groundless Jealousies or Soured with any Sullen or Stubborn Humours. But, to Comply with what He had so often Recommended agree-

39. An Act for Granting a Revenue to His Majesty, His Heirs and Successors, for Support of the Government of This Island, and for Reviving and Perpetuating the Acts and Laws Thereof, as They Have Been Introduced and Used, January 1725, in ibid., 109.

able to His Majesty's Instructions, and to pass an Annual Bill to Continue their Laws.

The Assembly, Nevertheless passed the Revenue Bill, in the same words, and with the same title, and sent it up to the Council for their Concurrence, which it met with, and was likewise laid before His Grace for His Assent. And the Assembly thereupon, drew up and presented the following Remarkable Address, which I thought proper and Necessary to be incerted at length; because it sets forth the Motives and Reasons of their proceedings, in a very decent and Respectfull manner, and puts the whole Affair in a just and true light.

To his Grace Henry Duke of Portland, his Majesty's Captain-General and Governour of Jamaica.

The Address of the Assembly of Jamaica

We his Majesty's most dutiful and loyal Subjects the Assembly of Jamaica, do return your Grace our most humble Thanks for your Speech at the opening of this Session.

We have so great a Regard for your Ease and Recommendations, that you can never fail of having an Influence on the Consultations of this Assembly; nor can we apprehend that any Variation of ours, from your Grace's Sentiments, infers the least Dimunition of the Duty we owe to his Majesty, or the Regard we profess to your Grace.

We are Sharers, my Lord, in the Legislature, and therefore engaged to form some Judgment of the Means of our own Welfare, which we conceive could only be promoted by fixing our Selves upon the firm and durable Basis of the Law. This hath been the end of all our Endeavours (which how unskilfully soever we have managed them) we pursued with honest Intentions, free from all private Aims, personal Resentments and Passions whatsoever. And we humbly hope, upon a Survey of the Fluctuation of our Constitution for some time past, our Attempts to gain some sure Footing will not be counted indecent or imprudent.

The Assurances in your Grace's Speech of his Majesty's Intentions to perpetuate our Laws, and the gracious Declarations he has often made from the Throne, of His Desire to Establish the Liberties of all his People, have not a little encouraged us to petition (as we have by the Bill now before your Grace,) for such an Establishment; far, very far, from intending thereby to withdraw our Duty or Gratitude to our Sovereign!

My Lord, we can never be unmindfull of the many Blessings of his Majesty's Reign, nor shall we ever be wanting in acts of Duty and Loyalty; we are fully convinced that nothing is intended by him, to our Prejudice, the Moderation and Justice of his Government are to us certain Earnests to the contrary: But, my Lord, it is from so Excellent a King that the best Laws are to be expected, which perswade us that we are not acting a disagreeable Part, while with Duty and Submission to his Majesty, we are contending for that which distinguishes his Subjects from those of other Princes.

When we thus confide in His Majesty's Goodness, How is it possible we should be disturbed with imaginary Fear or groundless Jealousies! Or soured with any sullen and Stubborn Humours? There is indeed, my Lord, a sort of Jealousy that is natural and Interwoven with every English Constitution, and which is always upon the Watch for the Preservation of the Community; such a Jealousy might well be allarmed, at our being apprized of a Report made to His Majesty concerning a former Bill for perpetuating our Laws, wherein it was advised to have a Draught of a Bill prepared in *England*, and recommended to the Council and Assembly! For tho[ugh] we confess in the fullest Extent his Majesty's Right to dissent to our Laws, yet they ought, as we apprehend, to take their Rise from our selves, without being obliged to digest what is dealt to us by other Hands, Strangers in a great Measure to our Defects and Necessities. And here, my Lord, we only speak the same Language, and imitate the Spirit with which our Predecessors formerly asserted their Right of framing their own Bills, and in a Reign less favourable to the Liberties of the People, prevailed in the same Points; which Maxims of Government they wisely drew from their Mother Country, who can endure no Laws, but those of her own chusing.

Your Grace had, in a lively manner, imprinted many of our calamities; and we might add to the Evils, enumerated, that tho[ugh] the Law for quieting our Possessions and many others are perpetual; yet their Operative Force and Vigour are suspended by the absence of the Courts of Law, which leaves us exposed to the remediless Inlets of every Transgressor; not to mention how unsupported his Majesty's Government must be, without the means of collecting his Revenue, whereby the publick Credit is blasted almost beyond Recovery. These are certain Evils not by Consequences, but the actual Pressure of them: others may break in upon us, of which we ought to have just Apprehensions: the longer a Gap is laid open in the Law, (the only Fence between Good and Evil) the more irreparable it will grow.

We have been exceeding careful in paving the way for the perpetual Bill, now under Consideration, by providing abundantly for the Support of his Majesty's Revenue, and removing all material Objections which the former Bills were thought liable to; nor can we learn that any other Obstruction will be thrown in its way, than what is supposed to lye in his Majesty's Letter to your Grace in August 1723, whereby the Draught of an Act including the Established Revenue and your Grace's Additional Sallary, were to be sent to his Majesty for his Consideration, that he might be able to give farther Directions for the perfect Settlement thereof, before August 1724. Accordingly a draught was sent, whereto no Objection could be made, as to the Competency of the Establishment, which was the most provident part of the Letter; and as the sending a Draught at this time would be only Matter of Form, we humbly presume it ought not to stand in competition with the many Advantages arising from this Bill. The sending the former Draught before October 1724, answers the Words of the Letter, and as the Substance of the Letter hath been observed, whether another Draught shall be sent, is but a subordinate Consideration to the imminent Necessity that presses for the passing of this Bill; besides, as his Majesty may reject the Bill, he cannot be concluded by its passing here, nor can any Injury be derived to his Majesty, who had confessedly an ample Revenue raised by this Bill, which is not proposed by the Assembly to stand in the Way, to any farther Marks of our Complyance with his gracious Intentions.

We therefore humbly beseech your Grace to give life to the Bill now before you, by which you will convey Comfort and Ease to the distracted Condition of the Inhabitants of this Island; calm the Face of all publick Affairs, and secure to your self the Affections of all those whom you govern. We further intreat your Grace to become an Intercessor with his Majesty, for the Accomplishment of our most humble Desires, to whom your Grace, from our solemn and most faithfull Assurances, may be a Guarantee for our furtherance of the Publick Business now before us, and whatever his Majesty in his great Wisdom and Goodness shall think requisite for his Honour and Service, and our own Welfare.

His Grace Having taken this Address, as well as the Bill (which was laid before Him for His Assent) into Consideration, was pleased to Acquaint the Council that They could not be insensible of His having used all the means in His power with the Assembly, to Engage them to a Compliance with His Majesty's Instructions; by passing an Annual Bill to Continue the Laws. That notwithstanding what He had in so pressing a manner and so often Recommended to them more particularly in His Speech at their first meeting, they had passed and sent up another perpetual Revenue Bill, to the same purport and Effect of that which by the advice of their Board He had thought proper to reject the last Sessions. That this Second Bill, notwithstanding Such advice, had also been agreed to by the Board; and, as He could not think They had given so much Countenance to this Bill, to have the load of Inconveniences, and the ill Consequences (that might be Apprehended from any longer intermission of their Laws) laid at His Door, so He Apprehended some Weighty Considerations had prevailed with Them, to pass this Second Bill, after having advised Him, not to assent to the first, and desired He might be Acquainted with the Reasons, that induced them so to do. His Grace then laid before Them, the Assembly's Minutes of Wednesday, whereby it appeared that They had come to a Resolution, not to pass any mon[e]y Bill till the fate of the perpetual Bill was first known.

On which the Chief Justice[40] acquainted His Grace that there were several Members absent; who had joined in advising Him against passing that Bill, and as They were Expected in Town tomorrow morning desired they might be excused giving Their Reasons till then.

The day following His Grace resumed what had passed relating to the Revenue Bill, and desired Them severally to give Their Reasons, for Their passing the same.

Upon which Mr. James Laws[41] acquainted His Grace that for His own part, He was utterly for rejecting the Bill, at the time it was sent up by the Assembly as being [contrary] to His Majesty's Instructions, though at the same time He declared, that He was not Accountable for what He had acted in a Legislative Capacity.

Mr. Mill[42] informed His Grace that His Reasons for passing that Bill were reduced into writing which He was ready to produce, and to which He desired to refer Himself.

Mr. Gregory's[43] answer was to the same purpose.

Mr. Pennant[44] acquainted His Grace that Notwithstanding He had given His Consent to the passing of that Bill, as one of the Legislative Body, He humbly Apprehended He was not Obliged to give Reasons, for

40. Probably John Ayscough (?–1735). See Cundall, *Governors of Jamaica in the First Half of the Eighteenth Century*, xix, 78, 108, 126, 134, 156, 157, 158, and Cundall, *Historic Jamaica*, xviii, 32, 383, 395, 396.

41. James Lawes (c. 1697–1733) was the eldest son of ex-Governor Nicholas Lawes by Susanna Temple. On the wall of the nave in St. Andrew's parish church is what Cundall considers one of the best pieces of iconic sculpture on the island—a monument to James Lawes by John Cheere. It tells that Lawes was baptized in 1697 and married in 1720. He was a member of the Jamaica Assembly for St. Andrew Parish in 1721 and Vere Parish in 1722–25, and a councillor from 1725. He also held a commission as lieutenant-governor but never took it up. Cundall, *Governors of Jamaica in the First Half of the Eighteenth Century*, 75, 99, 101, 102, 103, 122, 127, 149; Cundall, *Historic Jamaica*, 168, 203, 390.

42. Richard Mill was a councillor and briefly, in 1733, chief justice. Cundall, *Governors of Jamaica in the First Half of the Eighteenth Century*, 159, 163; Cundall, *Historic Jamaica*, xviii.

43. John Gregory (?–c. 1764) was the son of Matthew Gregory, a long-term member of the Jamaica Assembly between 1693 and 1714, representing either St. Thomas in the Vale Parish or St. Catherine Parish. John Gregory also represented St. Thomas in the Vale in 1711–16 before his appointment to the council of which he was president from 1735 to 1751. In that capacity, he was three times acting governor: in 1735 after the death of John Ayscough, in 1736–38 after the death of Henry Cunningham, and in 1748 when Governor Edward Trelawny went on an expedition to St. Domingue and Cuba from February 14 to April 1. Cundall, *Governors of Jamaica in the First Half of the Eighteenth Century*, 78, 85, 95, 108, 126, 127, 128, 156–65, 169–208; Cundall, *Historic Jamaica*, xiv, xv, xviii, 383.

44. Edward Pennant (?–1736) was a member of the Jamaica Assembly for Clarendon Parish in 1688–89, 1705, and 1707–8; chief justice of Jamaica in 1726–28; and the senior member of the council when Ayscough died on September 30, 1735, but refused the acting governorship, an action he repeated in February 1736 when Henry Cunningham died. Cundall, *Governors of Jamaica in the First Half of the Eighteenth Century*, 78, 108, 126, 134, 156, 157, 158; Cundall, *Historic Jamaica*, xviii, 32, 383, 395, 396.

so doing; nor could He remember it had ever been a practice Here; Yet at His Grace's request, He acquainted Him, that the principal Motive He had in passing that Bill was, That he had an Interest in the Country, was one of the Community, and as Their Laws were Expired, He could not but think the Island would labour under many insupportable difficulties for want of them and therefore He had given His Consent to the Bill.

The Chief Justice was of Opinion with Mr. Pennant and Mr. Laws, that He was not Accountable for what He had done in His Legislative Capacity, and therefore did not assign any Reasons.

Then Mr. [Ezekiel] Gomersall[45] laid before His Grace, the Reasons in writing to which He, as well, as Mr. Gregory and Mr. Mill had severally referred and were in the words following.

> May it please Your Grace.
> The Board having passed a Revenue Bill and Your Grace being desirous to know the reasons that induced them to pass the same a Second time after a Majority of the Board had, as a Council of State[,] advised Your Grace to dissent to it, We humbly lay before Your Grace, Some of the Motives, that have prevailed upon Us.
> The Bill is Confessedly a good Bill, Such as his Majesty requires of Us, Else certainly, it would not have passed with our Approbation, a second time, and that after his Majestie's Instructions Communicated to Us by Your Grace. The distinction of approving in a Legislative Capacity, what as a Council of State we may advise your Grace to Dissent to is a distinction too refined, And we can never think the Interest of the Country Separate from His Majestie's.
> We acknowledge a just regard to his Majesty's Instructions and would as far as lyes in Us pay a ready Compliance to them, they are certainly intended for the good of his people, but We humbly apprehend Such Emergencies may some time Arise as may justify the not keeping Strictly to the Letter of them, when the Main purport and intent is Complied with. His Majestie's Instructions require Your Grace to take Care, that the Revenue raised for perpetuity or twenty One Years, should be Sufficient to the necessary Charges, which We apprehend is fully answered by this Bill. His Majestie's Instructions to Your Grace Seems to have foreseen some of the Calamities, that would attend our Country for want of this Law, We must beg leave to represent the same, in Some of the Words of the Instruction it self. Vizt.
> The Consequence whereof, would involve our said Island and all persons trading there in very great Difficulties, inasmuch as no Assembly

---

45. Ezekiel Gomersall, a member of the Jamaica Council since 1717, had earlier been a member of the Jamaica Assembly representing St. Andrew Parish in 1705 and St. David Parish in 1711 and 1713–14.

could be held there, the Law for Establishing Assemblies being amongst those, which Expire with the said Act, as likewise those Acts for regulating the proceedings of Courts of Judicature, So that it would be impossible to have any regular proceedings in the Court Justice there. Besides These, there are many other, not distant or Imaginary, but real and present Calamities attending our Country, which only they, that feel the Unhappy Effects can be truly Sensible of. The present ill State of the fortifications, and the want of Money to repair them, the loss of Duties, the Danger of Insurrections from Negroes, and the want of power to Suppress them, the danger of a Rupture with Our Neighbouring Countries, and Our inability of defending Our selves for want of the Militia Act (the Consequence of which, has Manifested it self by an Example but a few days Since by Some peoples refusing Obedience to the Same) call loudly for Some Present remedy. And We know none, but the passing of this Bill; The Assembly have already resolved to raise no money till they have the Benefit of it, And tho[ugh] it may be said the Resolutions of an Assembly should not Confine us, or be a rule of Our proceedings, Yet in the present Case, We must Say it is. The dissolving them and Calling a New One is only protracting time. A New Assembly would probably fall into the Same Measures, the Present Assembly are Men of the Best Capacities and Estates in the Island, We must Suppose they Speak the General Sense of the Country as well as their Own and Seem Averse to any Annual Law as will appear by their late Address. And if upon new Elections, We should have new Members they would still come possessed with the Old Sentiments.

Upon the whole, Mr Lord, the Country seems to be at Stake; their happiness or Misery depends upon Your Grace's approbation or dissent to this Bill, Your Grace has pressed as far as in You lyes, the literal Observance of his Majesty's Instructions. And we humbly hope His Majesty upon a View of the Extremitys You have been reduced to, will not insist, but be inclined to Excuse a Constrained breach, of an Instruction, which can bring no real prejudice. The Bill will still disquiet the Country, and if His Majesty should not think it Sufficient, He may Either dissent to it and put us in the same State we are in, or keep it upon the Carpet until we shall have compleated what His Majesty shall further require. But, we humbly hope from His great Goodness, that He will permit us to share, with His other Subjects, the Blessings of His Reign, by the perpetuating of us our Laws and Liberties

Ezekiel Gomersall
John Gregory
Richard Mill

His Grace having maturely considered what had been offered to Him, by the Members present, was pleased to Ask them if They had any thing further to Offer, with respect to the Bill, under Consideration, upon which

Mr. Laws acquainted His Grace, that some Reasons had occurred to Him against His passing that Bill, which He had reduced to Writing, and were read in the following words.

My Lord,

I have considered what your Grace was pleased to lay before us Yesterday, in relation to the Bill in Question, and am humbly of Opinion.

That the Bill is the very same which was passed by this Board, the last Session, and which upon a View of His Majesty's Instructions, communicate to us by your Grace, We thought by no means fit to receive your Assent, upon any Emergency of State; for as there is already a Draught of a Bill before His Majesty for His perusal, it would seem (as I humbly conceive) to Anticipate His Majesty's pleasure concerning that Bill, if your Grace should give your assent to this. And though it should in every Circumstance comply with His Majesty's terms, Yet His Majesty has in His Instructions expressly and positively reserved to Himself the sole Right and power of Considering a Bill of this Nature, which Contains a perpetual Establishment, not only of His Revenue, for the Support of His Government, but also of the Laws, Rights, Liberties and Privileges of His Subjects Here.

His Majesty has Empowered your Grace to pass a Temporary Bill to Continue our Laws for one Year, to prevent any Inconveniences that might arise from their Expiration, during the time He is pleased to take in Considering that Bill, which is a tacit implication that He will not allow your Grace to pass a Bill for a longer Continuance, and Since a general Instruction had so much weight with your Grace, as to oblige you to reject such a Temporary Bill (which in the Opinion of this Board, did not seem to be in the View of it) how much greater differance and Regard ought your Grace to pay to this, which is particularly Calculated for a Bill of this Nature, and repeated in the Strongest terms in His Majesty's letter and which He will *by no means permit to be dispensed with let the Exigency's of the Country be never so pressing.*

The whole matter, my Lord, under our Consideration, seems to me to turn upon this, the King requires your Grace to send a perpetual Bill to Him, that he may peruse it before your Grace gives a Sanction to it; Here is a perpetual Bill now before you, which the Assembly would force your Grace to consent to, by distressing the Government; *will the Obstinacy of an Assembly be a Sufficient Justification of Your Grace in disobeying His Majesty!* Will it not be urged, with Reason, that your Grace ought to have tryed Another, who, perhaps might have paid a greater difference to His Majesty's Instructions? In my humble Opinion, Your Grace ought without the least hesitation to reject the Bill, and call another Assembly, which may meet in 40 Days and revive the Laws in such a manner as may be Conformable to His Majesty's pleasure.

His Grace upon hearing the Reasons offered by Mr. Laws, acquainted the Board that they were such as He could not but highly approve of, and what He seemed to advise there in, was no more than what He had been strenuously Aiming at and Contending for, as appeared by all His Words and Actions, and wished the Council would now, advise Him (admitting the Bill rejected) what measures were immediately most proper to be taken, for the Support and Security of the Government? How to prevent the stop of public Justice, the Ruin of Trade, and the Destruction of Credit? and also how to secure the properties of those whose Affairs oblige Them Speedily to leave the Island, as of others, His Majesty's Subjects, not residing Here?

The whole Board upon a thorough Consideration thereof, and well weighing the present unhappy Circumstances of the Country found the Difficulties so great, and so many, besides all the hazards that might attend the Calling of a new Assembly whilst the Laws are expired, that They could not think of any Expedient, nor in what manner to advise His Grace. After which He was pleased to ask their Opinion, what then was most proper and Prudent to be done, upon which the Board advised His Grace, that nothing else could be done, but to give His Assent to the Bill. Accordingly His Grace ordered the House, to attend Him in the Council Chamber, and gave His Assent to the Revenue Bill.

Notwithstanding the Difficulties and Embarassments His Grace was under, in respect to that Bill, Yet it seems His conduct was disapproved of, and He was even Censured for passing it. For the Bill was not only rejected but His Majesty was advised in the Report of the Board of Trade, to order the draught of a Bill to be prepared in England, and sent over to this Island to be Enacted by the Assembly.

At this time a very considerable Trade was carried on by the British Assiento Company, with the Spaniards, and had it been skillfully and honestly managed by the Directors, and their Agents Abroad, it would have been of great advantage to the Company as well as to the Nation. But, the misconduct of the One, and the selfish Views of the other, together with Seizures, and Reprizals, defeated the Expectations of the Proprietors, who instead of being Gainers, were very Considerable sufferers by this Branch of their Commerce, which was likewise of Infinite prejudice to this Island, and almost ruined by it.

A scheme was laid to furnish, not only the Spaniards with Negroes, but the Sugar Islands and more particularly Jamaica, and with that Design large ships were chartered, and double the Cargoes were put on board of them, in proportion, to what the Separate Traders commonly sent in order to beat them out of the Trade, and to Engross it to Themselves. In Consequence of these Measures all Sorts of English Manufactures were sold very low on the Coast of Africa, and the price of Negroes raised, near double, to what they were before; nor have the Traders, been able Since to raise the value of the one, or lessen the other, to the great prejudice of the British Nation, as well as the Colonies.

The Merchants of London, as well as the Planters in this Island, were justly alarmed at this pernicious, and Destructive Design, calculated only to promote the Interest of a few Avaritious Persons, as it was Evidently made appear, and that the Company's loss thereby was not less than £100000, by that Scheem only.

There was likewise a project of introducing Spanish Sugars and Tobacco, into Europe, not only by Sending Vessells to Load at St. Iago de Cuba and the Havanna and from thence to Holland, but by way of this Island, and Accordingly an Essay was made in a Schooner called the *Esperance* laden at the first mentioned place. The Scheem was very artfully laid, and she came into Port on pretence of Stress of Weather, but on Search (which was ordered by His Grace on Suspicion of some Illicit Design) she appeared to be a Spanish Bottom navigated by Spaniards laden with Sugar, Tobacco and Snuff, and by the Bills of loading they were Ship[p]ed by the S[outh] S[ea] Company's Agents at St. Iago de Cuba, and Consigned to their Agents in Jamaica; she was accordingly Seized and Condemned, at which a great clamour was raised against His Grace by the Agents and Dependents of the Company, and an Appeal was lodged to the King and Council: But, the Company thought proper to drop the prosecution and not Expose the Affair to that August Assembly. As I shall Occationally make some further Animadversions on the proceedings of that Company, and shew the disadvantages They have been of to the Nation and to this Island in particular, I shall suspend saying any thing further in this place.

In July arrived Commodore Scot, in His Majesty's Ship the *Dragon*, who was appointed to Succeed Commodore Harris, in the Command of his Majesty's Ships at this Island.

And, the 3d. of August following Commodore Harris sailed for Great Britain with a small Fleet under His Convoy, in the Lat[itude] 34 He met with Extreme bad Weather, and received so much Damage that He was obliged to bear away for Barbadoes; and, in His Passage from thence He died. He was a Brave, Experienced Officer, and very justly Esteemed in this Island, for He was not only Vigilant and Careful of the Trade, but by keeping one of His Majesty's small Frigots constantly cruising round the Island, He saved the Country a very Considerable annual Expence, in fitting out a Sloop for that purpose. But, I cannot Express the Sentiments of the Inhabitants, and do the Justice which is due to the merit and Memory of this Gentleman more clearly, than in the following Abstract of a Letter, which the Speaker of the Assembly wrote Him by their order.

S[i]r
When the general Assembly, were engaged in the Consideration of the State and Condition of this Island, they could not overlook the Services

and Advantages, they received from your Conduct. It would have been a
satisfaction to me to have made their Acknowledgments to You in Person,
But, as I am deprived of the Opportunity by Your Absence, they have ordered me, their Speaker, to return you their most hearty thanks.

As you was Influenced by a Publick spirit which disengaged you from
any Selfish *or* Contracted Views, the Debt of Gratitude I am now offering
is well adapted to Your Sentiments, as it goes pure, unmixed, and unat-
tended with any Reward.

And, that you have Employed His Majesty's ships to His Honour in the
protection of Trade and the Planting Interest of the Island you have their
Ample (and I may say Singular) Testimony of it, from the Unanimous
Representative Body of the Inhabitants of this Island.

But, it would be Vain in me, to imagine I could Add to the Resolutions
of the House, by saying any thing which fell with in my own Observation
of the Faithful Discharge of your Trust. Therefore, I shall detain you no
longer than (in Obedience to the order I have received) to Return you,
as I do, the thanks of the Assembly, for the great Services to this Island,
during your Command of His Majesty's ships on this Station.
                William Nedham[46]

Commodore Scot, who Succeeded that Gentleman, did not live long,
for being of a Gay Disposition, and intemperate in His living, He Could
not be persuaded to conform to the Nature of the Climate, and being very
much Caressed by the Gentlemen of the Island, He was taken ill of a Fever,
which carried Him off the 15th. of September 1725.

The Assembly which met in September, passed Several Acts, which
are still in force, and among others are printed at large in the new fo[lio]
Ed[ition][47] And, the Committee of Grievances, having this Session made
a Remarkable Report to the House, I think it pertinent to give the Reader
the following Extract, which Evinces the impositions that are often laid
on Trade in our Colonies, and that the Complaints, which generally come
from those Parts, on those and other Occasions are too well grounded.

They set forth, the Ruinous Condition the Wall of Port Royal was in,
being very much undermined by the Sea, and the little care that had been
taken to Repair it, so that the whole Town was in Danger, of being destroyed the first Storm of hard Winds.

---

46. William Nedham (?–1746) was a long-term member of the Jamaica Assembly representing either St. Thomas in the Vale Parish or St. Catherine Parish from 1701 to 1721,
St. James Parish from 1722 to 1726, St. George Parish from 1731 to 1732, St. Catherine
again from 1733 to 1735, and Port Royal from 1736 to 1745. He was Speaker of the House
four times and in 1737 refused a council position, preferring to continue as Speaker. He was
chief justice first in 1716 and again in 1746. Cundall, *Governors of Jamaica in the First Half
of the Eighteenth Century* 32, 70, 114, 163, 187; Cundall, *Historic Jamaica*, xvii, xviii, 92, 173.
    47. *Acts of Assembly.*

That the Committee having seen the lodgments of His Majesty's Soldiers at Port Royal were of Opinion the Sickness and Morality among them, is in a great measure Owing to their bad Accommodation.

That it was made appear to them that Gabriel Marquis Du Quesne, Commander of His Majesty's Fortifications, levied money and laid other impositions on His Subjects Contrary to Law. And that He would not suffer the following Vessels, although cleared at the proper Offices, to pass the Fort without They paid Him mon[e]y. That he exacted £15. of Capt[ain] Alexander Murray, Commander of the *John and Sarah* of London, and divers others particularly named under the Denomination of Stone mon[e]y, and would not Accept of Stones.

They observed, that the said several Exactions are said to be by force of an order of Council, soon after the dreadful Hurricane in 1722, which order They Conceive could not be intended further than to the Speedy repairing the Fort, on that Sudden and lamentable Occasion; nor to have Continuance after the Dangerous breach or irruption made by the said Hurricane, was Repaired. That it could not be intended or understood in any Sense Contrary to Law—vizt. either the compelling People to work or to send Their Vessels against Their Consent, without a Reasonable allowance for their labours, or use; much less to give the Captain of the Fort Authority to levy mon[e]y for dispensing with that Service; it being a breach of His Duty, if the Service was Necessary to dispense therewith. If unnecessary an Unwarrantable abuse of the order, and of the Authority by which it was made, as if they could or had taken upon [them] to levy mon[e]y on the Subject without Law.

That the said Marquis Du Quesne permitted Goods of Foreign growth and Manufacture to be imported without Custom or Duty being paid for the same, by His unlawful Trade with the Dutch and other Foreigners and making the Fort a Storehouse or receptacle for the said Commodities. And it was obvious, that these practices had drawn many Aliens hither, on pretence of Refreshment, but in reality with the said Marquis's Connivance to Trace and sell Their Commodities, in such Quantities that the Goods of English Manufacture lye on the Importers' hands.

The House, according to order, taking the said Report into consideration, and the Answer or Justification of Gabriel Marquis Du Quesne came to several Resolutions, And there upon presented an Address to His Grace, praying that He would be pleased to prevent the like mischiefs and to put a Stop to the growing Dangerous Evils. They likewise desired His Grace to lay before His Majesty the said Address, Report and Resolutions in the most Effectual manner, and use His good Offices, that all these Grievances may be fully Redressed.

But, the Marquis did not think proper to Attend the issue of this Affair, for He soon after removed, privately, to Hispaniola, and from thence to Great Britain. His Grace, was thereupon pleased to Appoint Collo[nel]

Delauney (an old Officer, of a fair Character, and Capt[ain] of one of the Independent Companys) to be Capt[ain] and Commander of the Fortifications.

In May arrived the *Sea Horse* Capt[ain] Solgard with orders from Vice Admiral Hosier,[48] for all His Majesty's ships, on this Station, to join Him at Donna Maria Bay. They accordingly sailed and proceeded from thence with the Vice Admiral and His Squadron from England, Consisting of one Ship of 70 guns, 4 of 60, 1 of 50, and 1 of 20, and arrived off of Porto Bello the 6th. of June. The Governour of that Place immediately sent to know what He wanted; and the Answer was the Royal George belonging to the S[outh] S[ea] Company. She was immediately released with all the Factors, and sent under a Convoy to this Island.

The Governour of Porto Bello, sent again, to Vice Admiral Hosier desiring Him to be gone with His Squadron, but was answered by Him that He would remain there until He had further orders, and thereupon ordered a Ship of 60 guns to Anchor within reach of the Guns of the Iron Castle. However the Spaniards did not think fit to fire at Her, and the Squadron suffered no Vessells to go in or out of the Harbour without strict Examination, but did not take any thing from them, except Seamen who were not Subjects of Spain.

The Inhabitants of this Island never were more United or in a more perfect state of Tranquility than at this juncture, nor could there be a greater Harmony and good understanding between a Governour and the Representative Body of People, than there was during His Grace's Administration. For though He was charged with some Instructions which were not Agreeable, and afterwards receded from by the Government, Yet His prudent Behaviour on that Occasion, prevented any difference or Animosities, and rather Confirmed than lessened the Affection and Regard they had for His Grace. But, while They pleased Themselves with the Happiness they enjoyed in a mild and Gentle Administration, and flattered themselves with a Continuance of it for some Years, His Grace to the inexpressible Grief of the Inhabitants, was taken ill of a Fever, the 29 of June and died the 4th. of July 1726. His bowells were interred in the Church at St. Iago De la Vega and His body embalmed and Sent to England to be interred in Westminster Abby.

There never was a Governour more Universally lamented in this or any other Colony, than the late Duke of Portland, nor with greater Reason, for He manifested the Sincerity of His professions, by His readiness to promote the Interest and Wellfare of this Island [by] all that lay in His power, and had He lived to return to England, I am persuaded, He would

48. Vice Admiral Francis Hosier (1673–1727) was a British naval officer who commanded a squadron in the West Indies in 1726–27, failing in an effort to blockade Portobello and dying shortly thereafter.

have given greater Demonstrations of it. The only inconveniency which attended the Country was His manner of living for though He cheerfully spent what the Assembly set[t]led on Him, and above £5000. Ster[ling] p[er] Ann[um] out of His Revenue in England, Yet it led the Planters into an Extraordinary Expence which they could not Afford.

All the Letters from thence, were filled with Expressions of the deepest Concern, of which the following Extract is a Sufficient Specimen, and Corroborates what I have said.

> A Melancholy and Universal misfortune has befallen us Here, which had thrown us into the utmost Grief and Confusion; my Lord D[uke] of Portland is Dead!—This may be remote and unaffecting to you, at a Distance of almost half the Globe; but it is impossible for us who lived under His Mild Administration, and participated of the gentleness of His Nature, the Complacency of His Temper, the Refinement of His manners, the Generosity of His living, the lenity, Equity and Tranquility of His Government not to be sensibly touched and Afflicted at so mournful and Occasion. I could Expatiate on His Vertues, and the unspeakable loss of this unhappy Island, but I am overwhelmed with Grief. The President, Council and all the Gentlemen of the Island, went into deep mourning on this Occasion.

On the Death of the Duke of Portland the Government devolved on John Ascough Esq[uir]e as President of the Council. And two Days after, three Gentlemen of the Council waited on Her Grace the Dutchess of Portland, and in their Name presented the following Message.

> May it please your Grace
> We are directed by the Honourable the President and Council, to wait upon your Grace, to condole with You upon the late unhappy Occasion, and to assure your Grace, that as we have a very sensible share in the Loss, so likewise in the Affliction.
> The Council, may it please your Grace, will do every Thing in their Power, that may contribute to your Ease; they are informed of your Grace's Intentions of quitting speedily this Island; and as there is no Ship of War in Harbour, to convoy your Grace through these Seas, they have resolved to fit out a Vessel for that Service; and where they can be further Useful to Your Grace, they will readily embrace the Opportunity, and, upon every Occasion, endeavour to shew their Gratitude, and the Value and Regard they have for your Grace's Person and Character.

To which her Grace was pleased to return her Thanks to the Board; and soon after sent the following Answer in Writing.

To the Honourable the President, and the rest of the Gentlemen of the Council

As the Provision you are making for the Safety of my Passage Homewards, the Regard and Value you express for my Person, and the kind Assurance which you, in so mournfull a Conjuncture, have given me of your contributing to my Ease, do call for a Repetition of my hearty Thanks, and cannot but be very kindly taken by every one who has any Relation or Respect for me, or to the Memory of my deceased Lord; so I do assure, I shall not fail to represent the same in such manner as may be most for your Honour; and, as far as in me lies, for the Service of this Island.

There is none of you, I am persuaded, that is not convinced of the Necessity, in respect of my Health; that requires my immediate Departure. And, I do assure you, it is Matter of great Concern to me, that the advanced Season of the Year obliges me to leave this Place without first seeing that Part of my late Lord's Will performed, which relates to the Payment of his Debts in this Island, and without being able to judge what may be requisite for that Purpose. But, as I have given Instructions for the fulfilling thereof, with the utmost Justice and Honour to his Memory, and (lest any Deficiency should be) have subjected my own Estate to that performance; I do not in the least question, and cannot, after such kind Assurances, but desire you will give what Countenance and Assistance you can to those Gentlemen who I shall leave entrusted with my Affairs.

     Elizabeth Portland.

The 22d. of August Her Grace the Dutchess of Portland, and Her Daughters, embarqued on Board the *Essex* Capt[ain] Guering (with the Corpse of the late Duke) and Sailed, under Convoy of a Brig[an]t[ine] well Man[n]'d, and fitted out by the Country for that purpose.

The 20th. of October, the President convened the Assembly, and laid before them the Draught of a Bill for granting a Revenue to His Majesty His Heirs and Successors, and perpetuating the Acts and Laws thereof, as they now Stand and are used, which was prepared in England, and sent over to the late Duke of Portland, under His Majesty's sign Manual dated the 7th. day of July 1726. And, Recommended to them the Expediency of passing the same, agreeable to His Majesty's pleasure.

On the 26th. of the same month, hap[pe]ned another Hurricane, the 3d. that ever was known in this Island, at least since the English had been in possession of it. It began about 8 in the Morning and lasted till four in the Afternoon though it did not blow so Violent as the former. However, it did very Considerable damage, threw down many Buildings, all their Plantain Walks, and most of their Canes.

At Kingston 17 Ships and other Vessels foundered and Stranded, 12 drove ashore, but were, afterwards, got off. At Port Royal 9 ships and

Sloops foundered and 7 drove ashore. At Port Morant three ships were drove ashore, but were afterwards, got off and on the North side two sloops cast away.

The 4th. day of November the President sent a Message to the Assembly, by the Clerk of the Council, wherein He observed, that they had spent 14 days, without taking the least Notice of the King's Sign manual, or of the Draught of the Bill for perpetuating the Laws, which He by His Majesty's Express command, had Communicated to Them. That He thought Himself Obliged to remind them of it in the most pressing manner, and to Signify that it was in Vain to imagine He would give His Consent to any Bill, until They had shewn that Regard to His Majesty's Recommendation, and Zeal for the Interest of their Country, which is so indispensably incumbent on Them more Especially at this Calamitous juncture when instead of Evading the King's command and slighting His Offers, they ought with the deepest sense of Gratitude, to embrace the Gracious terms, which He was pleased to Condescend to give Them, and are calculated for the welfare and Prosperity of the Island, as well as the Honour of the Government. Therefore He Expected that they would postpone all other Business, and without Delay, to Enter on the Consideration of that Bill, as a matter of the greatest Importance to this Island.

The Assembly, who were alarmed at a Bill being drawn up in England, to be enacted Here without allowing them a Negative or to make any alteration or Amendment were much more inflamed at the President's Message. For They thought it an Infringement on Their Rights and Privileges, Especially as there was a Clause incerted for the Additional Subsistence of the Soldiers, which was making an Annual and Voluntary allowance, obligatory and perpetual.

They thereupon drew up an Answer to the President's Message, which was no ways agreeable, and on their rejecting that Bill He dissolved them, so that the Island, continued without Courts of Justice, or the Operative force of the Laws (which were perpetual) near 3 Years, and until the Arrival of Major General Hunter.[49]

And, to their Honour be it Remembered that notwithstanding the unhappy Situation they were in at that juncture, They remained Peaceable and Quiet, without Riots or Disorders, and Every one undisturbed in His Person and Property; nor was any interruption given to Trade or private Credit, only some few Necessitous Persons taking the Advantage of their Creditors. The Principal and greatest if not the only Inconveniency that attended the Island thereby was the loss of Duties and Taxes, which Oc-

---

49. Robert Hunter (c. 1668–1734), following a successful military career, obtained a series of colonial governorships, first in Virginia in 1707, a post his capture on the high seas prevented his ever taking up, then in New York from 1710 to 1719, and finally in Jamaica from 1728 until his death in 1734. Cundall, *Governors of Jamaica in the First Half of the Eighteenth Century*, 125, 130–55, 160, 172, 175, 201.

casioned the Government to run greatly in Arrears, and to Amass such a load of Debts, as are not yet fully discharged, notwithstanding the great Sums of mon[e]y that are annually raised to Supply the Exigencies of the Government.

The Squadron being disabled from Continuing any longer on the Coast of Porto Bello, by reason of the great Sickness and Mortality which hap[pe]ned among the Officers and Seamen[,] Vice Admiral Hosier Returned to Port Royal the beginning of December, and immediately ordered all His Sick men ashore, who recovered daily, and having with the cheerful assistance of the President and Council refitted His Ships and furnished them with such Necessaries as they wanted; He was ready to put to Sea by the middle of February.

It was no Small Service to the Vice Admiral in recruiting His Ships with Men, that He met with a great Number of Seamen, who belonged to the Ships which were stranded and lost in the late Hurricane.

The Squadron was now Divided, one Third[,] two fourth, three sixth Rates and a sloop (which were afterwards joined by one third[,] and two fourth Rates from Gibralter) sailed under the Command of the Vice Admiral, for the Coast of Carthagena. And, four fourth Rates, one fifth and one Sixth, under the Command of Commodore St. Loe,[50] sailed and cruised off of Lavera Cruz, to block up the Flota.

This Division was made, on the Vice Admiral receiving new Instructions from England, and advice from Porto Bello, that the Galleons were gone to Carthagena: so that the Design was to Block up the Flota, as well as the Galleons.

About the middle of June, the Vice Admiral sent into Port Royal, a Vessel laden with Hides and Tallow. And, the *Greyhound* Capt[ai]n Solgard brought in a Spanish Ship of 10 Carriage Guns, 10 Swivel Guns, and 70 men, with a great Number of Passengers. Her Cargo consisted of 70,000 p[iece]s [of eight], 70 tons of Snuff, some Hides Sugar and Tobacco. These were all the Prizes which were taken during the Rupture with Spain, for as War was not proclaimed although the King of Spain had ordered Reprisals to be made (and in Consequence the *Prince Frederick* and four other Vessels belonging to the S[outh] S[ea] Company were Seized at La vera Cruz and the Havanna) no Commissions were granted to Privateers; and His Majesty's ships were all employed in the manner I have mentioned.

Commodore St. Loe, who cruised off of La vera Cruz made a demand of the *Prince Frederick* and the Effects of the S[outh] S[ea] Company, but was denied.

The 23d. of August, Vice Admiral Hosier (who was greatly chagrined with His orders, and the unhappy Circumstances, He was under) died at

---

50. Commodore Edward St. Lo (d. 1729) was a Royal Navy officer who served as commander in chief of the Jamaica station from 1727 to 1729.

the Bastimentos after a few Days illness. His body was Embalmed and Sent Home in the Ballast of His Majesty's Sloop the *Spence*.

On the Death of the Vice Admiral, the Command of the Squadron devolved on Commodore St. Loe.

The 31st. of January 1727/8 arrived His Majesty's[51] ship the *Lark*, with Major General Hunter who was appointed Capt. General, Governour &c. of this Island, with His two Sons[52] and Diverse other Gentlemen. His Commission was dated the 12th. of September 1727.

His Excellency was joyfully received by the Inhabitants, in general, in regard to the Character They had of His being a Gentleman of great Abilities, and an Experienced Officer, as well as to the Agreeable Instructions, He brought with Him, For, He was impowered to Assent to any Act, which shall be prepared by the Assembly, for the same purposes, as to the Draught of a Bill for granting a Revenue to His Majesty, His Heirs and Successors for the support of the Government, of this Island, and ["]perpetuating the Acts and Laws thereof as they now stand and are used" which Draught was transmitted to the Duke of Portland to be laid before the Council and Assembly to be enacted, but was not complied with provided, the Substance thereof be Strictly Agreeable to the said Draught, that the proper funds be incerted in the Bill for this purpose and that the same may prove more Effectual, that such Branches of the Revenue raised in Jamaica by Annual Acts, for the Contingent Services as have been found by Experience to Answer the Sums for which they were given, may be Appropriated in this Act towards the raising a perpetual Revenue for us. And, whereas it was intended that the Sum of £2000 p[er] ann[um] for the Additional Subsistance of the two Independant Companies now serving in Jamaica should have been provided for in a Clause in the same Draught you are hereby impowered to give your assent to any Seperate Act for this purpose so that the restrictions They had been under for 3 years past, were now removed. And, the Assembly to Their great satisfaction restored to their Natural Right and Priviledge of framing Their own Bills.

The Council met, the same Day as usual, and after His Excellency had taken the Oaths prescribed by Act of Parliament, He made the following Speech to Them.

51. George II (?–1760) came to England with his father, George I, and was made Prince of Wales on the Hanoverian Succession of 1714. Unlike his father, he was popular in England but not in Hanover. His support of opposition politics caused a break with his father that deprived him of custody of his sons, but Sir Robert Walpole negotiated a reconciliation in 1720 and remained as first minister after George II's accession to the throne on June 22, 1727. Ending Walpole's pacific policy with Spain in 1739, he lost pace in domestic politics with the fall of Walpole in 1742. He oversaw the revamping of the office of secretary of state and the Board of Trade in 1748, which began a new era of metropolitan intervention in colonial affairs, particularly after the Seven Years' War (1756–63).

52. Cundall records one son, Thomas Orby Hunter (d. 1769), but also mentions three daughters: Katherine, Henrietta, and Charlotte. Ibid., 153.

Gentlemen.

I am not insensible of the Difficulties, which at this time, attend the Execution of the Trust, the King has Honoured me with; nor how unequal I am to it. I think my Self safe and Secure in my Intentions; and as to Failings or Errors in Judgment your Advice (to which I assure you I shall ever pay all due Regard) may either prevent or rectify.

You, Gentlemen, lie under the same Obligations with me, to give all Attention to the Interest and Ease of his Majesty's Government here, as you are also deeply interested in preserving the Peace and promoting the Prosperity of your Country, which are so far from being incompatible, that whoever sets about to separate them, even in his Thoughts, must do it upon the odious Supposition of lawless Power on the one Hand, or a Spirit of Sedition on the other.

There are some Instructions which I am commanded to communicate to you, which I shall do so soon as you and I have more Leisure, and shall expect and rely upon your Advice in some Matters of Consequence to his Majesty's Service, and the Interest of this Country.

The Answer of the Council
May it please your Excellency,

We thank your Excellency for this your kind Declaration, and do with the greatest Sincerity congratulate your safe Arrival to this Country. We must gratefully acknowledge his Majesty's Wisdom in his Choice of your Excellency for our Governor, at this critical Juncture which necessarily requires a Person of your Abilities and known Experience in Government. We return our most hearty Thanks to your Excellency, for the favourable Sentiments you are pleased to entertain of us; We hope our Conduct has been, and will be always such as must demonstrate, that we have no View or Inclination of running into the Extreams either of being Arbitrary on the one Hand, or of turning Liberty into Licentiousness on the other.

We beg leave to assure you, that we shall, to the utmost of our Power, both by our Advice and Assistance, endeavour to promote his Majesty's and the Country's Interest, which we take to be the only Means of rendering your Excellency easy and happy during your Administration.

His Excellency's Reply
Gent[leme]n

I am extreamly obliged to you, and give you my hearty Thanks for the good Opinion you are pleased to entertain of me, but more to find the kind Assurances you have given me of your advice and Assistance in the Execution of the Trust reposed in me. From the Confidence I have in the good Effect of that, I flatter my self with the Prospect of Ease in my Administration and Government, and Prosperity to those who are to live under it.

With the Advice of the Council the Governour issued Writs for Electing an Assembly, to meet at St. Iago de la Vega on the 28th. of March following.

They met accordingly and chose Thomas Beckford Esq[uir]e their Speaker. The day after his Excellency ordered the House to attend him in the Councill Chamber, and made the following Speech.

Gentlemen of the Councill. Mr. Speaker and Gentlemen of the Assembly.

You are by his Majestie's Command called and are now met together as soon as the nature of the thing would permit in Order to apply proper Remedies for the present and unset[t]led Condition of this Island and Government.

I think my Self Sufficiently Impowered and Instructed to Contribute my Best endeavours to yours for re-establishing order[,] Justice and Security, the true and only ends of all lawfull Government and so cannot doubt of a happy Issue to this Session.

Mr. Speaker and Gentlemen of the Assembly

What is at this time expected from you by your Sovereign and your Country is, that you prepare a Bill for reviving and perpetuating your Laws, expired by their own Limitation, and for Establishing and perpetuating a Revenue for the Support of this Governm[en]t according to the Exigencies and Dignity thereof, but I am commanded to take care that proper funds be inserted in the Bill for this purpose and that the same may prove more Effectual that such branches of the Revenue raised in Jamaica by Annual Acts for the Contingent Services as have been found by Experience to answer the Sums for which they were given may be appropriated in this Act towards the raising a perpetual Revenue. These are his own Words and the thing so reasonable and requisite to qualifie the Act for his Royal Approbation that I can make no doubt but due regard will be paid to them in the framing of the Bill.

You must be sensible of the Sufferings of the Independant Companies here under the want of that Additional Subsistance formerly granted to them to enable them to live in a Country where all necessarys of life are so dear. I earnestly recommend to you the preparing a Law for that purpose. His Majesty having given his Royal Word that he will ease you of that expence so soon as it shall appear that [the] Country's Circumstances are such as make it Sufficient for its own defence and Security.

Among the many Inconveniencies that have attended the Cessation of your Laws the present Ill State or your Militia (which I look upon to be your chief Strength) is none of the least. If your former Laws for establishing and regulating the Militia be judged Defective or not sufficient I recommend to you the preparing a Supplemental One for Rendering it more usefull with a particular View to the more Speedy and Effectual reduction of the Rebel Negroes.

The Doubtfull Prospect of a Speedy Peace and the Ill Condition of your fortifications must induce you to take them under Consideration and to make Sufficient Provision for the repairing of the old, and adding new ones where they may be thought necessary for your defence from Enemies from abroad, or preventing the Courses and Insults of the Rebell Slaves within[.] His Majesty has appointed an able and experienced Engineer for that Service whom I expect every day. He has also been graciously pleased to give his Royal Assent to two Acts, the One Entituled (an Act for Set[t]ling the North East part of the Island) the other (an Act for encouraging White people to come Over and become set[t]lers in this Island, and for the more easy and speedy set[t]ling the North East part thereof) I shall deliver to your Speaker these his Approbations together with Copies of such of his Instructions, as I am Commanded to Communicate unto you in order to their being Inserted in your Journals which contain matters recommended to be past into Laws for the benefit or better Government of this Island.

I have Ordered an Account of the Receipt and Issues of the Revenue Ordinary and Extraordinary to be prepared for your Inspection. The surprizing Arrears due on their several branches require a speedy and effectual Remedy not only in order that all may bear their due Share of the Publick burthen, but also to preserve and maintain that respect and Obedience due to Your Laws in general.

Gentlemen of the Council[,] Mr. Speaker and
You Gentlemen of the Assembly.
I am well persuaded that you are met with a View to the same ends and hope that no difficulty will fall Out about the Means; As for my part having ever since I had the Honour of being appointed Governour of this Island, applyed my Self towards obtaining what I judged might conduce to the Ease and prosperity of the Subjects thereof. I now assure you that whilst His Majesty is pleased to continue me here I shall continue to lay my Self out to the utmost reach of my Strength and Capacity, To that good purpose not barely as it is my Duty but as I take it to be the most Effectual method to recommend my Self to His Royal favour and your good Opinion.

The 3d. of April the Assembly waited on his Excellency and Presented the following Address

May it please your Exceellency.
Wee his Majestie's most Dutifull and Loyal Subjects the Assembly of this his Majesty's Island of Jamaica, Embrace this first Opportunity of Congratulating your Excell[enc]y on your safe and much longed for arrival in this Island; And do most cheerfully return your Excellency our hearty thanks for your Candid and kind Speech at the beginning of this Session and the Affection you express for us therein from w[hi]ch wee promise our

Selves that under your Administration all our fears will be prevented and even our hopes Anticipated.

Your Excellency's early appearance in England and obtaining for us many Advantages necessary to our prosperity and Quiet entirely convinces us nothing can be wanting on your part which may further Contribute to render us a flourishing and happy People.

And wee do assure your Excellency on Our part that wee shall with the utmost Alacrity and Unanimity apply our Selves to give the necessary dispatch to the many important things your Excellency has been pleased to recommend to us.

And as they tend entirely to our happieness and establishing Order, Justice and Security, Wee do promise in all our deliberations to Act with a due regard to the Exegencies and Dignity of his Majesty's Government here, the good and Interest of our Country, and the Ease and Tranquility of your Excellency's Government. And do Assure you it is our Ambition and desire, as well as our Duty to take all proper methods in our power to recommend our Selves to his Majestie's Royal favour and Gracious protection and the good Opinion of your Excellency.

The Assembly accordingly brought in and passed a Bill intituled an Act for granting a Revenue to his Majesty His Heirs & Successors, for the support of the Government of this Island, and for preserving & perpetuating the Acts & Laws thereof,[53] which met with the Concurrence of the Governour and Councill and disipated the Jealousies and fears of the People, who had been as I observed without Courts of Justice almost two years, and were apprehensive of an Alteration being intended in their Constitution or form of Government, but being now restored to their rights & Previledges, as well as their Laws, their minds were quieted and made easy. The Assembly also passed Several other Acts, which met with the Royal Assent particularly.

An Act, for the better carrying on and Securing the New Settlements at Port Antonio in the Parish of Portland.[54]

An Act for the better securing the New Settlements in the most exposed Parishes in this Island.[55]

And an Act for the better Securing this Island against any Attempts to be made by Foreign Enemies.[56]

53. An Act for Granting a Revenue to His Majesty, His Heirs and Successors, for the Support of the Government of This Island, and for Reviving and Perpetuating the Acts and Laws Thereof, April 1728, in *Acts of Assembly*, 216–24.

54. An Act for the Better Carrying on and Securing the New Settlements at Port Antonio, in the Parish of Portland, 1728, in ibid., 226–29.

55. An Act for Better Securing the Settlements in the Most Exposed Parishes in This Island, 1728, in ibid., 229.

56. An Act for the Better Securing This Island against Any Attempts to Be Made by Foreign Enemies, 1728, in ibid., 229–31.

[On the Defensive, 1728–1742]

Vice Admiral [Edward] Hobson,[1] who had been cruising with the Squadron off of Carthagena, after 5 days illness, died at the Bastimento's, on Board His Majesty's ship the *Leopard*, the 8th. of May last.

On His Death the Command devolved again on Commodore St. Loe, who continued Cruising off of that Harbour, the Galleons being there and made no preparations for sailing. But, on receiving the Preliminary Articles, (the 3d. of June) He returned to this Island, and sent Home, most of the largest Ships. Nevertheless, the Island was soon after alarmed with the apprehensions of being Invaded by the Spaniards, with a very Considerable Force. For about the [blank] day of December arrived His Majesty's ship the *Seaford* Capt[ain] Perry Main,[2] with an Express to the Governour [Robert Hunter] Acquainting Him that His Majesty had undoubted Assurances the Armaments in Old Spain, were intended against the Island of Jamaica, He was therefore commanded, immediately to put the Island into a posture of Defence. At the same time came over Collo[nel] Lilly,[3] One of His Majesty's Engineers (who was well acquainted with the Country, having been Here twice before) to Supervise the Fortifications, and to raise such new Works as should be thought Necessary.

The Governour immediately called His Council and laid before Them the Letter He received from His Majesty's Secretary of State, and with their advice, ordered an Embargo on all Shipping, and Summonsed a Council of War to meet the 7th. of January.

The Council of War met accordingly, and the Governour in His Speech Acquainted Them, that the Occasion of Their meeting was to Concert

---

1. Vice Admiral Edward Hobson or Hopson (d. 1727) was briefly in charge of the West Indian fleet.

2. Perry Mayne (1700?–1761) entered the Royal Navy in 1712, was a captain by 1725, and was present at the reduction of Portobello in 1739 and the unsuccessful attack on Cartagena in 1741. He was promoted to rear admiral in 1745 and vice admiral in 1747 and performed distinguished service in the Seven Years' War (1756–63).

3. Christian Lilly (?–1738) began his career in military engineering under the service of William III in 1688 and first appeared in the West Indies in the mid-1690s, becoming chief engineer at Jamaica in 1696 and chief engineer in the West Indies, 1704–38. In such capacities he laid out the town of Kingston in 1694, rebuilt Fort Charles in 1699, and was captain of the fort, 1734–35. He built Kingston as a parallelogram, one mile north to south and a half-mile east to west with grid pattern streets. Without the tree-lined pavements and circles of Annapolis and Williamsburg, though built at the same time as the capitals of Maryland and Virginia, Lilly's Kingston was more a precursor of American cities in the trans-Appalachian west of the late eighteenth and nineteenth centuries. See Frank Cundall, *Governors of Jamaica in the Seventeenth Century* (London, 1936), 138, 159; Frank Cundall, *Governors of Jamaica in the First Half of the Eighteenth Century* (London, 1937), 2, 30, 45, 48, 134, 144, 147, 149, 152, 160, 207; and Frank Cundall, *Historic Jamaica* (London, 1915), 48, 60, 69, 71, 150, 155, 193.

proper Measures for the Publick Security. That the preparations and Conduct of the Spaniards in Europe [and] the Continuance of the Depredations and the Interruption of our lawfull Trade by such as are Supposed to Act by orders from thence made the much desired Peace at best but dubious and laid them under an Indispensable Obligation timely to provide against Insults or Surprize, as, Indeed, He was ordered by His Majesty's Special command upon just suspicion that Their Naval Armaments and preparations pointed this way.

He then gave them some Instructions, for their Government in Case of an Invasion or Descent on any part of the Island. And by their advice and Consent proclaimed Martial Law. The Squadron, which then consisted of Eight Ships of War from 50 to 70 Guns under the Command of Commodore St. Loe were drawn into a line, at the enterance into Port Royal Harbour, between Hanover Line and the Salt, Ponds. And, the Cruisers were sent out to gain Intelligence.

Six large Merchant Ships of 20 Guns each, were properly posted at the head of Kingston Harbour, the Seamen draughted out of the other Ships to serve as occasion should require; and about 500 sensible able negroes who understood the use of Fire Arms and could be trusted, were formed into Companies and put under the Command of the Reformade Officers. And all other necessary preparations were made for the Security and Defence of the Island.

Commodore St. Loe, who had been many years in a Declining Condition, died on the 22d. of April very much lamented, for He was a Vigilant, Brave, and an Experienced Officer, and greatly Esteemed in this Island, having been, twice before on the Station. About a month after came over His Majesty's Commission appointing Him Rear Admiral of the Blue.

On the Death of Commodore St. Loe the Command of the Squadron devolved on Capt[ain] William Smith.

The Island still continued under Arms, the Governour not having had any further orders or advices from the Ministry. But, on the Representation of the Merchants, who laid before His Excellency the advices they had received from Persons of undoubted Credit in Great Britain, that the apprehensions they were under of this Island being Invaded by the Spaniards were blown over, the Armaments in old Spain being laid aside, the Embargo was taken off the 6th. of June, though Martial law was kept in Force near a month longer.

On the 10th. of June sailed from Port Royal under Convoy of two men of War, near 70 Sail of Ships and other Vessells, bound to Several Parts of the British Dominions, many of which had been laden and detained in Port above two months and some more, to the great loss and damage of the British Merchants as well as the Planters of this Island, of which great Complaints were made without Redress, the Blame being shifted from one to another, as it Commonly is on such Occasions.

The Assembly met in [blank][4] according to Prorogation and, among others, passed an Act to prevent Dangers that may arise from disguised as well as declared Papists;[5] it being Suggested with great probability of truth that there was many of that persuasion in the Island, as Indeed there are grounds to believe there is at this time.

However, this Act was afterwards found not to answer the purposes for which it was intended, but on the Contrary discouraged Protestants, well Affected to His Majesty's Government as well as Papists from coming to Settle in this Island, and for those Reasons it was afterwards repealed.

The latter end of September arrived the Honourable Charles Stuart[6] in His Majesty's Ship the *Lyon*, and took on Him the Command of the Squadron.

And, about the 1st. of October came in a Brigantine from Boston, the Master of which made Oath before the Governour, that He met 24 large ships which He took to be men of War off of Cape Francois and that one of them wore a Flag at the Fore topmast head, but was not near enough to distinguish, Whether it was French or Spanish Colours. An Embargo was immediately laid on all Shipping, the Island put under Arms, and the *Experiment* man of War, was ordered to look into St. Iago and other Ports, in order to gain Intelligence. She returned in 6 or 7 Days, with a Spanish packet Boat of 10 Guns and 90 men, who taking the man of War for a Merchant Ship, was prepared to fire Her broad side and then to board her, and without doubt had she been One, would have made no Scruple of taking, and proving Her (after their customary manner) a good Prize; but at the very Instant, the *Experiment* hoisted Her Colours, which discovered Her to be a man of War, the Spaniard submitted and was brought into Port. She had on board Dispatches for most of the Spanish Governours of America—General Hunter, the Commodore and Council were two Days debating whether they ought to be opened or not. But, the Spanish Captain and His Officers declaring that the Aforementioned Ships were the Flota from Old Spain, which sailed 6 Days before them [and] that the Differences between Great Britain and Spain was in a fair way of being Accommodated and a Ship arriving the same Day from London with advices that Confirmed their information, The Governour and Council thereupon released the Ship and delivered all the Spanish pacquets unopened; a complaisance They would not have shewn to us on the like occasion. The Embargo was also taken of[f], the same Day.

The Inhabitants of this Island now began to flatter Themselves with the

4. The assembly met again on July 24, 1729.

5. An Act to Prevent Dangers That May Arise from Disguised as Well as Declared Papists, 1729, in *Acts of Assembly Passed in the Island of Jamaica; from 1681 to 1637, Inclusive* (London, 1738), 232.

6. Rear Admiral Charles Stuart or Stewart was in command of the West India station in 1730–31.

hopes of being freed from the Insults and Depredations of the Spaniards, on advice of a new Governour being arrived at St. Iago de Cuba, who had imprisoned the former Governor, and Sent Him to Old Spain in Irons; and declared that He had Orders to live in Amity with the English. Nevertheless, this joy had short Continuance for They soon after revived Hostilities, and divers Depredations were Committed this Year, Even Contrary to the positive orders, of their own Court as may Reasonably be Supposed.

About this time a Scheme was laid for making Port Antonio, now called Titchfield Harbour, on the North East end of this Island, not only the Rendevouz of the men of War, but the chief Port of Trade, and it was so far Encouraged by the Governour and Commodore Stewart, that by Their Recommendation the Admiralty was at a very considerable Expence in building Stone Houses and other Conveniences, for fitting the Careening of His Majesty's Ships. The Principal Inhabitants of this Island, as well as the Merchants opposed this Project, in regard to the Smallness of the West Harbour, which though a very good one, can not contain twenty Sail of Ships at Moorings and the East Harbour as it is called being nothing more than an Open Bay. It was also objected to in regard to its Situation which is inconvenient for Trade at too great a Distance from the Seat of Government, and the principal Settlements of this Island. However these Reasons had no weight with those Gentlemen, who seemed determined to Accomplish what they had begun, and to Encourage and promote the Interest of the Place it was made the Rendevouz of the Parties fitted out against the Rebellious Negroes (though other parts were nearer their Quarters and more Convenient) as well as of the men of War which were sent round to fit and Careen. But, the Sickness and Mortality which afterwards happened among the Seamen, convinced them of their mistake and defeated the Design They had in View.

The beginning of May [1730] the *Dursley* Galley Capt[ain] Forrester met with a Sloop, which bore down on Her with English Colours, and coming up along side of the Man of War, the Captain bid Them lower their Sails, and come on Board, to which They answered presently, but instead of that they fired their broad side of great Guns and small Arms into the Man of War supposing Her to be a Merchant Ship, and afterwards perceiving their mistake, they hoisted all their Sails, and endeavoured to Escape. The man of War thereupon gave chase, and on coming up she struck, without making any resistance. She proved to be a Spaniard [vessel] with 76 men six Carriage Guns and four Swivells and had a Commission from the Governor of the Havanna, as a Guarda Costa. A Court of Admiralty was held to try her as a Pirate, and for firing at and boarding the King's Ship; but the Spaniards did not want assistance and Advice, for the Agents of the S[outh] S[ea] Company were as assiduous in getting her Acquitted, as they could possibly have been had their own or their Masters' Interest been immediately concerned and to the great regret and dissatisfaction of all true English men, and men of Honour, a flaw was found in the Monition (which many Persons suggested to be designed) on which she was discharged.

In April Commodore Stewart, who was Appointed Rear Admiral of the Blue, hoisted His proper Flag.

The Assembly met in October and passed 18 Acts including the Annual Laws. And, a grand Party was fitted out under the Command of Capt[ain] Brookes, Consisting of 200 Armed men, and 100 Baggage Negroes. But, this Party, through the Ignorance of the Pilots, were bewildered in the Woods, where some of them perished, others fell into the hands of the Rebellious Negroes, and great part of them lost their Arms and Ammunition. They were afterwards refitted and Sent out under the Conduct of the same Person, who unfortunately fell into an Ambuscade and was defeated. And, as many of His Men, in their flight threw down their Arms and baggage, the Rebells met with a further Supply.

The ill Success of those Parties, on whom there was a great dependance (particularly on their Commander who was a Planter in St. Marys, and had His Plantation burnt and destroyed by the Rebells, last Year) Occasioned a very great Consternation, and Encouraged not only the Rebellious Negroes, but the Negroes in the Plantations and in the Town. For the one grew more daring often came down, and continued some time near Several Plantations, which obliged the Proprietors to abandon them, so that almost all St. Georges, and part of St. James, St. Anns and St. Marys were deserted, and the Roads, in many places, were so infested that it was very unsafe Travelling. And, the others grew so turbulent and Insolent, that there was great Reason to apprehend a general Revolt.

The Governour was not wanting to represent these matters, to the Ministry, in the strongest light, and in plain terms told them, that He would not be answerable for the safety of the Island, unless some Regular Forces were Sent to Defend it. About the 1st. of September arrived at Port Royal the L[ieutenan]t of a Spanish man of War, of 50 Guns called the *Genoesa*, with an account of the said ship being Cast away, on Tuesday the 18th. of the last month, upon Point Pedro Shoals, which are about 12 leagues S[outh] of the W[est] end of this Island, and to desire assistance to Save the rest of the People and the money, she had on board, which by Computation amounted to a Million of Dollars, beside private Effects. The next day sailed two Snows belonging to the S[outh] S[ea] Company and a sloop, which arrived there about 4 in the afternoon following, and found the Ship sunk to Her upper Gun Deck, the People in the utmost distress, and despairing of Relief. A large raft capable of receiving 150 men, which they had prepared to Save themselves, in Case the ship should Stave in pieces, broke loose from the ship and drove to leeward, with Don Aldoretti[,] late President of Panama (who was sent on board that ship a Prisoner). 13 other Passengers of Note, and Effects to the Value of 100000 p[iece]s [of eight], which they had Saved out of the Wreck and were never heard of afterwards, though a Sloop was immediately sent in quest of Them.

The Captain and near 300 men, were brought in by the aforementioned Vessells, and had Separate Houses taken for their Accommodation, at the East end of Kingston and were treated not only with great humanity and Civility, but were allowed Such liberty as was Inconsistent with policy or Common prudence, for they were permitted to ramble into the Country and even to go into and View the Fortifications. But, the Governour who was then at Port Antonio with the Admiral, On His Return to the S[outh] Side, He issued out a Proclamation of the taking up any Spaniard that should be found out of the District of Kingston, and to send Him to the next Goal.

The Admiral, as soon as He had advice of the disaster of the Spanish man of War, ordered the *Experiment* and the *Trial* sloop, to attend and protect the Wreck, out of which most or all the mon[e]y and other Valuable Effects was Saved and brought into Port Royal. But, in the interim a Coasting sloop which sailed from Port Royal, with twenty Spaniards aboard having picked out of the Wreck a Considerable sum run away with it, and never were heard of afterwards. As the Master of the sloop had a very good Character, a Family and Interest on the Island, it was imagined the Spaniards, who were Superior in Number, had forced them away, and afterwards made away with them.

Notwithstanding those ship Wrecked Spaniards were thus preserved and hospitably treated, they could not help discovering their Ingratitude and the perfidy of their Nature for in about 14 Days after they came to Kingston, They committed divers disorders, offered Indecency's to Women in the streets and insulted every one They Met with[,] nor was it safe going out after 8 or 9 at Night they having assaulted several Persons and killed a Man who was a House keeper in the Town. The Offender was there upon tried and Executed, and to prevent any further mischief, the Magistrates were obliged to forbid them going out of Their Quarters after the dusk of the Evening and a Guard was afterwards kept Day and Night, during their Stay.

Every thing being fished out of the Wreck that was worth saving and could be come at, the Treasure which belonged to the King of Spain and all the Registered mon[e]y was put aboard His Majesty's Ship the *Adventure* commanded by my Lord Muskerry, and Carried to Old Spain. The Capt[ai]n, most of the Officers and Passengers, embarqued on board the same ship: But, the Major part of the People, at their own desire were sent over to Carthagena. And Mr. Paris who was appointed to go with them, at His return, Reported that He was received with great Honour and Civility. That the Spaniards made gratefull acknowledgments of the Hospitable and kind treatment they met with in this Island, and the strict Justice that was done Them. And that the Admiral of the Galleons declared that they could not have fared better, if so well, had they been Wrecked on any part of the Spanish Dominions.

Notwithstanding this and other Instances of the Amity and Friendship of the English to the Spanish Nation, divers Illegal Captures were made Soon after particularly the *Mary* Capt[ain] Benson of Liverpool, and bound to this Island. They Stripped the Master and His Men, and then turned them a drift in an Open Boat to shift for themselves, and after great difficulties, and Dangers, they got safe to this Island.

The 10th. of December, A Proclamation was issued by the Governor setting forth that He had received a letter from His Grace the Duke of New Castle[7] dated the 25th. of September 1730, Signifying His Majesty's pleasure to grant Letters of Reprisal and to use all possible means that may for the future most effectually put a stop to the Depredations of the Spaniards in the West Indies. And to that end notice was given to all Persons who had Sustained any damage by Illegal Captures, to prove the same in the Court of Admiralty, and to lay Such proof before the Governour, who was thereby directed to make a demand of the Governour of the Place, where the Ship, Goods; or other Effects were carried to, and in Case of their refusing Restitution or Satisfaction to grant letters of Reprisall.

Accordingly the aforementioned Capt[ain] Benson and others made such proof, and Obtained a letter from the Governour and Admiral, to the Governour of Port[o] Rico, which was sent by Capt[ain] Reddish in His Majesty's ship the *Experiment* who at the same time, represented the Honour and Friendship of the English, in regard to the *Genoeasa* man of War, which was Wrecked on Point Pedro Shoals. But, this and all other Applications were to no purpose for nothing more could be Obtained than Compliments and Evasive Answers; on which some of the Sufferers particularly Capt[ain] Benson did Apply for Letters of Reprisal, but such Difficulties and Obstructions were thrown in the way, as plainly discovered, that there was no intention to grant them.

The 7th. of January 1730/1 arrived Six transports with Brigadier Newton's[8] and Collo[nel] Hay's Regiments which consisted of 900 Men, under Convoy of the *Princess Louisa* Captain Dent.

Those Regiments were Sent over partly on the Representation of the Governour and the Declaration He made that He would not be Answerable for the safety of the Island, unless some Regular Troops were sent to Defend it. And, partly on the Apprehension the Ministry was under (as it

---

7. Thomas Pelham-Holles, First Duke of Newcastle-upon-Tyne and Newcastle-under-Lyme (1693–1768), was secretary of state for the southern department from 1724. He became first lord of the treasury in 1754 and in 1757 formed a coalition government with William Pitt during the Seven Years' War. The enmity of Bute forced him to retire in the early 1760s.

8. Brigadier-General William Newton (d. 1730).

was Reported) that the Spaniards had still a Design to attempt the Conquest of it.

The Inhabitants had not notice of their Coming above a month before their arrival, so that no provision was made for their Reception, and being obliged to quarter Them in the Towns where They had the opportunity of getting Rum and debauch themselves, a great Sickness and Mortality insued.

The Assembly being called on this Occasion met in March, and passed an Act for rendering the two Regiments more Serviceable, and providing an Additional Subsistence for Them.[9] But they resented the Governour's sending for those Troops without consulting them or the Council, and having their Assent. Hence arose a difference which afterwards encreased to so great a Degree that they had not the least confidence in each other, and the Country became a much inflamed as Ever.

It must, However, be confessed that though those Troops were of no Service in any other respect, yet the Appearance of Them kept the Negroes in Awe, and Struck a Terror into Them, for there was a Visible Alteration not only in their Behavior but They were afterwards more easily managed than They had been, at any time, since the defeat of the Grand Party, by the Rebellious Negroes.

On the passing the aforementioned Act, the two Regiments were quartered in different parts of the Island; and it was expected that they would have been employed in reducing the Rebells, but They were suffered to remain in their Respective Quarters without doing any Duty or being Sent on that Service.

The Coasts of this Island, were at this time, well Guarded with Cruisers nevertheless the Spanish Guarda Costa's which Cruised at a distance, in the rout[e] to this Island, took and plundered Several Vessells. The *Joseph and Anna* Capt[ain] Couples (bound to Bristol) in particular was carried into St. Iago de Cuba, but on her being demanded by Rear Admiral Steuart, She was released (the only Instance I ever heard of) though in a Scandalous manner, for the Master was at a Considerable Expence in Fees, and Rigaldos, and the Ship Stripped of her Stores, and Provisions to such a degree, that she was Obliged to return to this Island, to refit.

The Rear Admiral was at length Convinced of the Necessity of taking other measures, than He had hitherto done, and Accordingly gave orders to His Majesty's ships under His command to take and bring into Port, all the Guarda Costas They met with. And, in pursuance of that order the *Sharke* sloop Captain Crawford brought into Port Royal two sloops on Suspicion of their being Guarda Costa's or rather Pirates, for they not only

9. An Act for Rendering the Two Regiments of Soldiers More Serviceable and Providing an Additional Subsistence for Them for a Limited Time; and More Speedy Reduction of the Rebellious Negroes, March 1731, in *Acts of Assembly*, 242.

chased the *Shark*, but on Search neither of them had a Commission, and one of them, was an English bottom, and had not any Register or Condemnation. The Rear Admiral thereupon by letter, directed to the Merchants, acquainted them that those two Vessells proving to be no other than Trading Vessells, it became Necessary for Him, as Guardian of the Trade of His Majesty's subjects to desire their Opinion Whether it would be for their Interest or the Trade in general to Stop those sloops by way of Reprisalls for the Injuries that had been done or to discharge them.

The order for Granting letters of Reprisall having manifestly been evaded, the Design of the Admiral seems calculated to obtain something, under the hands of the Merchants, which would justify the Conduct of the Governour as well as Himself on that Occasion.

But, the Merchants in Answer, gave it as their Opinion, that He ought not only to detain those two Vessells, but to give orders to His Majesty's ships to Seize all other Spanish ships and Effects, they met with, in order to make Satisfaction to His Majesty's suffering Subjects, agreeable to His Grace the Duke of New Castle's letter, to the Governor dated the 25th. of September 1730, signifying His Majesty's pleasure to grant Reprisalls and to use all possible means that may for the future most effectually put a Stop to the Depredations of the Spaniards in the West Indies.

This Answer was not agreeable to the Admirall's Design, laid him under a Dilemma and put Him so much out of Temper, that He wrote a very Indecent and unhandsome Reply for He not only denied His asking their Opinion or advice, but made use of several Expressions unbecoming a Gentleman. Hence arose a paper War between Them, in which the Merchants were allowed to have much the better of the Argument.

The Assembly met in November and drew up an Address to the King, wherein they Represented to His Majesty the declining Circumstances of the Island Occasioned by the loss of their Trade[,] the continued Depredations of the Spaniards, and the lowness of their produce in Europe, and prayed Such Relief and Encouragement as His Majesty should think proper.

They also appointed a Committee to Enquire into the Conduct and management of the Parties, and to inspect into the Publick Accounts, who Reported that the Soldiers, though the Island was at a great Expence in Maintaining them, had not been of any Service. That the Parties were not duly paid or timely fitted out with Necessaries, but were suffered to mispend their time and mon[e]y at Port Antonio. And that 100 Baggage Negroes, raised for the Publick Service, were Employed on the Commissary's Plantation, with many other abuses of the like Nature.

The Governor in Vindication of Himself laid before the House Copies of His Instructions to the Officers of the Soldiers, and the orders He had Sent from time to time to Collo[nel] Ashworth, whom He had appointed Commissary and intrusted with the Disposition, and management of the

Parties at Port Antonio By which it plainly appeared that His Excellency's Instructions to the Officers of the Soldiers had been Evaded, and that He had put too great a Confidence in the Commissary. Hence arose a further cause of uneasiness and dissatisfaction, which drew on a Prorogation.

His Excellency, thereupon, being desirous of pacifying matters, and removing those complaints immediately ordered out two Parties, the one consisting of seventy Soldiers, and 30 Negro men well armed from St. Anns and the other of three Companies of Soldiers under the Command of Capt[ain] Delamulier, from Port Antonio, besides others whites and Blacks raised by the Country and Negroes to carry their Baggage.

The former returned without any Success or Disaster but, the other fell into an Ambuscade, and on the first Fire which killed Eight Soldiers and two Negroes, many of Them threw down their Arms and fled. The rest by that means would have been cut off and destroyed, had not the Officers behaved with the greatest Bravery and good Conduct.

This Disaster put the Island into a very great Consternation, and Occasioned the Governor to Call the Assembly ten Days before the time They were Prorogued to.

They accordingly met the [blank] day of January [1731/32][10] and took into Consideration the State of the Island, and among other things, Resolved to send out four Parties of 100 men Each Whites and Blacks, and to attack the Rebells in different Places, at one and the same time.

At this Juncture the Governour received orders to Send Home the two Regiments, but to discharge all that were inclined to remain and Settle on the Island, with a bounty or Gift of £10: to Each man. Between Forty and Fifty of Them listed in the Independant Companies, about 200 in the aforementioned Parties which were fitting out, and some, who were Tradesmen set[t]led in the Country and followed their respective Functions: the Rest were sent to Ireland, those two Regiments being on that Establishment.

In February arrived four Sixth Rates namely the *Experiment, Flamborough, Phoenix* and the *Deal Castle:* also two Sloops the *Wolf* and *Grampus;* such Vessells being thought Necessary to Cruise in the West Indies in order to intercept the Guarda Costas and protect our Trade.

The *Deal Castle* Captain Aubin was soon after sent to La vera Cruz to demand the *Woolball* of London, which ship was taken and Sent into that Port. The Captain did not think proper to go into the Harbour, but Sent His Lieutenant, in the Pinnace, with the Governour and Admirall's letters. But the Spaniards were so far from complying with this demand that They Seized the Lieutenant and Men, and put Them under Confinement. Capt[ain] Aubin after Waiting 10 or 14 Days without any Answer, or the return of His Boat, concluded that They were Seized upon and detained,

10. The assembly met on January 3, 1732.

and looking into His Instructions, which were abstrusely Worded, after the manner of those times, He construed them in the plain and literal sense, which was to make Reprisalls in Case the Spaniards did not comply in ordering Restitution or Satisfaction, for the *Woolball*. And, soon after meeting with a Register Ship from Cadiz, bound to La vera Cruz, He took Her and brought Her into Port Royal about the beginning of July. This proceeding embarassed the Rear Admiral, and gave Him a great deal of uneasiness, apprehending He should be blamed by the Ministry if He detained Her, and that the Merchants would Censure Him more than ever, if He should discharge Her.

While He laboured on those Difficulties, and was undetermined what to do, arrived Commodore Lestock,[11] on the 18th. of the same month, with His Majesty's ships the *Kingston* and *Rupert*, on which Rear Admiral Stewart, sailed for England two Days after, and left the decision of the Affair of the Register Ship, as well as the Command of the Squadron, to His Successor.

Commodore Lestock being Strongly sollicited by the S[outh] S[ea] Company's Agents, in a few Days after He took on Him the Command, released the Register ship Contrary to the Sentiments and Opinions of the Principal Inhabitants as well as the Merchants, who would have had her detained until Restitution or Satisfaction was made for the *Woolball* and other illegal Captures.

Commodore Lestock did not long enjoy His Command for on the 31st. of August, S[i]r Chaloner Ogle[12] arrived in a Merchant ship, with orders to take on Him the command of the Squadron. This Gentleman disposed of the Ships under His Command Vizt. two of 60 Gunns, 1 of 40, four of twenty, and two sloops, in so proper a manner, and Constantly relieved them from time to time, that our Trade passed the Seas undistrubed insomuch that not one Ship was taken or plundered, during the time He was on this Station. This the Merchants gave an Ample Testimony of, in a letter They wrote Him to thank Him for His Care and Services, which will appear in its proper place.

11. Commodore Richard Lestock (1679–1746) was appointed commander in chief of the Jamaica squadron in 1732 but recalled for unexplained reasons shortly after he got to Jamaica.

12. Chaloner Ogle (1681?–1750) was commander in chief of the Jamaica station from 1732 to 1739. Promoted to rear admiral in 1739, vice admiral in 1743, admiral in 1744, and admiral of the fleet in 1749, he was with Vernon in the attack on Cartagena in 1742 and succeeded Vernon in command. In 1742, he quarreled with Jamaica governor Edward Trelawny over Samuel Dicker, a protege of the governor whom Ogle called "a scoundrel and rascall." On July 22, Vernon prevented a likely duel between Trelawny and Ogle, and, although Ogle was tried and found guilty of assault, Trelawny prevented any punishment taking place. *A Duel and No Duel; or, The Skirmish of the West India Heroes* (London, 1743) is a twenty-four-page verse broadside describing this encounter. Cundall, *Governors of Jamaica in the First Half of the Eighteenth Century*, 148, 150, 171, 177, 180, 184, 185, 189, 204; Cundall, *Historic Jamaica*, xxi, 46, 56, 205.

The Assembly met in November, but did not sit above three Weeks, for after They had passed 3 Bills, two of Them for Continuing the Parties and Building Barracks at Manchineal and Montego Bay, and the other for the Mannumission of some Negroes, who had distinguished Themselves in the Service of the Country, They were unexpectedly dissolved and Writs issued out for choosing Members for a new Assembly to meet the 13th. of March following.

The Occasion of their Dissolution was Suggested to be owing to two Causes, namely the Appointment of a Committee to enquire into the Conduct and management of the Parties, great Complaints being made of Their being ill paid and not properly furnished with Arms[,] Ammunition, and other Necessaries. And, the other was a notion for an Address to the Governour to thank Him for His good Services, as well as His just, and prudent Administration, which was rejected by a very great Majority, as a Motion of the Same nature had been in the two former Sessions.

The new Assembly met the 13th. of March [1733] and Sat very close to Business, for they passed no less than 14 or 15 publick and private Acts this Session, which are still in force except the Annual Laws.

At this time it was considered that the ill Success of the Parties, was principally owing to their being Raw, undisciplined men and unfit for that Service, most or all of them Consisting of Endentured Servants, and Stragling Sailors; and a motion was made, for an Application to S[i]r Chaloner Ogle, for 200 Seamen to be joined with 100 Soldiers to be draughted out of the Independant Company's 50 White men and 50 Negroes armed, to be raised by the Country, and sent in three different Rout[e]s, in order to dislodge and reduce the Rebellious Negroes at the N[orth] E[ast] end of the Island.

This Request was immediately granted, and Mr. Swanton and Mr. Thompson the Commodores 1st. and 2d. L[ieutenan]t, both of them since promoted to be Captains in the Navy, generously offer'd their Service to command Them which was accepted of. They were accordingly fitted out and sent round to Port Antonio, and with them several Young Gentlemen of the Navy went as Voluntiers.

The Assembly also revived the Additional Duty Act[13] which imposed a Duty of 20. [shillings] per head, on all Negroes imported into this Island to be paid by the purchaser with a very Extraordinary clause, subjecting the Masters of every Guinea ship to Restrictions and under severe penalties, which the Council Struck out, and made some other amendments. But, it being a mon[e]y Bill, the Assembly would not agree to them on which they were Prorogued for 3 days.

13. An Act for Raising Several Sums of Money, and Applying the Same to Several Uses for the Subsisting the Officers and Soldiers of the Two Independent Companies; and Preventing the Exportation of Several Commodities, into the French and Spanish Islands, March 1733, in *Acts of Assembly*, 281.

On their meeting according to Prorogation, They brought in the same Bill, but being desirous of avoiding all Controversy, and dispute They left out that clause and such other matters as were objected to.

They also revived the Enquiry into the Conduct and Management of the Parties, as well as the application of the great Sums of money, which had been raised for those and other Occasions, and after having made some progress therein, They were unexpectedly Prorogued a 2d. time.

At Their meeting the 3d. Session, They again revived their Enquiry and in a few Days after were again Prorogued for a short time.

These short and frequent Prorogations tired the Members, and as They imagined them calculated only to obstruct Their Enquiry it put Them so much out of Temper, that They desired the Governour to grant Them Recess, for a Reasonable time, but not receiving a Satisfactory Answer, They sent the following Message to His Excellency by two of Their Members, the 15th. of August.

> May it Please Your Excellency
> This Assembly, being Convened the thirteenth of March last, have for four Months of that time, Assiduously and Zealously, applyd themselves to dispatch those things that were recommended to them by Your Excellency, for His Majesty's Service and the Publick Welfare, notwithstanding the many Obstructions given to their faithfull endeavours by frequent Prorogations, all which in Duty to His Majesty and out of regard to those whom they represent they acquiesced under, in hopes that private passions might in time give way to the publick good, but as it Evidently appears to them that such Obstructions were Calculated and are continued with an intent to Harras[s] the Members of the Assembly. And by that means bring them to betray not only themselves but those whom they represent. The House again repeat their earnest request to Your Excellency to give them a Recess for a reasonable time.

His Excellency sent for the House, two Days after and made the following Speech.

> Mr. Speaker and Gentlemen of the Assembly
> Before we part I think it necessary to say something to your last most extraordinary Message desiring a Recess, least it should have that Effect for which it seems to have been calculated, that is, to Insinuate without doors that I, or His Majesty's Council here have Obstructed business. I know of no Obstructions but what have been Occasioned by your selves or private passions but such as have arisen and have been propagated like a Post amongst your Selves.
> The Prorogations Complained of were the necessary Effects of your own proceedings in framing such Bills as the Council without breach of

duty, could not pass, or I Assent to without breach of His Majesty's Instructions, and Incurring his highest displeasure, which you have in Effect owned, by sending up a new Bill, after a short Prorogation, Conformable to His Majesty's Instructions, in lieu of one you had sent up before Expressly contrary to them.

They who betray those you represent, and you too, are such as have had the Art or luck to perswade you to Endeavour and Grasp at Powers which do not appertain to you, and which it will be for ever vain for you to attempt.

You cannot believe that your frequent Sessions give me any pleasure, and even this recess which I am about to give, and which by your repeated Messages you have extorted from me, can be but for a short time, least I also should lend a hand to the betraying or Obstructing the Publick Service, in the greatest danger, for Notwithstanding the repeated applications for prolonging the short time prescribed by the Act for Continuing the Party's now on foot for some longer time if it should be found necessary, nothing has been done for that purpose, neither has any thing been hearkened to that has been offered for Appointing some Person or Persons to Solicit the Affairs of this Island at the Court of Great Britain, so frequently recommended to you, whilst at the same time you well know that Persons Interested are determined to give all the opposition they can to your money bills.

And now Gentlemen I appeal to the world, nay to your selves. If in any one Instance I have sought my self or my Interest in what I have at any time either by Speech, Message or otherways Endeavoured at, or recommended to you, I have done Injury to no Man, tho[ugh] I have bore with much, I have been contented with the Legal Incomes of my post, tho[ugh] Scantily payed, and I have done Justice to all men without respect of Persons, my Conscience is clear, and if I have in any thing erred, for once I will be my own Judge. It has been in excess of forbearance and complaisance, which however intended I own have missed of their aims.

And now Gentlemen finding you determined to do nothing at this time, I will give you a short Recess, in hopes that at your next meeting you will do something more Effectual for the Safety of the Country in its present dangerous Situation[.] I Doe therefore in His Majesty's name Prorogue this present Assembly to the Second day of October next, and this Assembly is accordingly Prorogued to the said Second day of October.

The beginning of September came advice from Port Antonio of the unhappy miscarriage of the Seamen and Soldiers, against the Rebellious Negroes, through Treachery, Cowardice, and Mutiny.

The Seamen who led the Van under the command of L[ieutenan]t. Swanton and were to be Supported by the Soldiers, fell into an Ambuscade, and many of Them had passed it before it was Discovered for the intention of the Rebells, was to let the whole Party pass before They fired in hopes of cutting Them off, and Obstructing Their Retreat, having divided Their Gang the one half in that Ambuscade, and the other half in the Town. But, one of the Pilots who was Appointed to conduct Them perceiving the Ambuscade, fired His piece into it as a signal and fell on His Face, the other cried out we are all Cut off and fled, which struck a Panick and occasioned so much Confusion, among the Sailors, that They all deserted Their Officers, except 40 or 50, who stood by Them, and bravely drove the Rebells not only out of the Ambuscade, but out of the Town, so that had They been Supported, They might have kept possession and given the Rebells an entire defeat. In this skirmish nine Seamen were killed, and nineteen wounded[,] among Them L[ieutenan]t Swanton, who was obliged for want of Assistance to retire to Port Antonio after He had burnt the Negro Town. The Rebells, as we were afterwards informed, lost 15 men, and had many Wounded.

During this transaction the Soldiers, who were to Support the Seamen[,] mutinied and refused to March, and on the Alarm occasioned by the aforementioned Disaster, basely fled as well as the new raised Men and Armed Negroes.

The Pilots who were the Cause of this Rout and Disappointment were tried at a Court Martial, one the Them was Cashiered, and deprived of His Pay, and the other was Executed.

The Assembly on Their meeting the 2d. of October according to Prorogation, Voted Mr. Swanton £200, Mr. Thompson £100, and other Gratuities to those who behaved well.

They also passed Several Acts, for Cutting of Roads building of Barracks, and fitting out Parties for the more Speedy and Effectual Suppressing the Rebellious Negroes.

They continued Sitting to the middle of December when They were at their own Request, on Account of the ensuing Holy days, adjourned to the 14th. of February.

In January [1734] the Governour had an Account of 22 Plantation Negroes, and some others who belonged to the Parties having deserted and gone over to the Rebells. That 19 Negroes, who were purchased for the Service of the Navy, and were employed at Lynch's Island, Attempted to join Them but were intercepted. And that forty able Corromantee Negro men had likewise deserted Their Masters, at St. Thomas in the E[ast] and were supposed to have joined Them.

These accounts were magnified and Industriously propagated throughout the Country, to Justify the Measures that had been taken, in fitting out Parties and raising great Sums of mon[e]y which had been notoriously misapplied, for They were ill paid and not duly and properly fitted out, insomuch that the Certificates of their Service in order for payment were commonly sold for 15 in 20, and frequently under to the great discouragement of the Service, so that it is not Strange that the Parties behaved so ill, and were so often defeated, which not only Animated the Rebells, but spirited up the Negroes in the Plantations and Even in the Towns, who thereupon grew Insolent, unruly, and discovered a Disposition to Rise, and join the Rebells.

The Assembly on Their Meeting, immediately brought in and passed two Bills, the one for raising an Additional Duty;[14] and the other for putting the Island under Martial Law for a Certain time.[15] The first mentioned met with the Concurrence of the Governour and Council, but the other was sent down, by the Council, with some Amendments, which the House would not agree to, so that the Bill dropped. The first and principal Objection, Indeed was a very Considerable one namely the striking out the limitation, which made the Act Indefinite, and in fact Established a Perpetual Dictator.

However, the Council and Assembly joined in an Address to His Majesty, and a Representation to the Secretary of State, and the Board of Trade the last of which I think proper to transcribe, because It will not only shew the Condition and Circumstances of the Country, but the Apprehensions the Legislature were under at that juncture.

To The Right Hon[ora]ble The Lords Comm[issione]rs FOR
Trade and Plantations.

The Representation of his Majesty Councill & Assembly of the Island of Jamaica.

My Lords.

The British Plantations in America being under your Lordships more immediate Care, wee humbly beg leave to Represent the low and Distressed Condition of this Island with full Assurance from the Zeal your Lordships have always shewn for his Majesty's Service & the good of your Country that the same will be faithfully laid before our most gracious Sovereign Sup[p]orted with your Lordships' favour and Seasonable Intercession for the Aid and Assistance our present unhappy Circumstances require.

Your Lordships are undoubtedly acquainted with the Difficulties wee have laboured under for several years past, particularly in regard to the

14. An Act for Raising Several Sums of Money, and Applying the Same to Several Uses; and for Supplying the Officers and Soldiers of the Six Independent Companies Expected, January 1734, in ibid., 285.

15. An Act for Putting the Island under Martial Laws, for Any Time Not Exceeding Six Months; for Impowering the Civil Magistrates, and Other Officers of the Respective Parishes in This Island, during the Time of Martial Law, to Lay, Assess, and Collect, as Well All Publick Debts, as Parochial Taxes for Keeping the Highways in Repair, Impowering the Receiver General to Borrow Money, and for Obliging the Provost-Marshall to Sell Slaves, and Other Effects Now in His Custody in a Prefixed Time, January 1734, in ibid., 286.

Negroes in Rebellion, & the many fruitless attempts which have been made to reduce Them. The Taxes that were raised for that purpose & to defray the other Contingent Charges of the Government have been exceeding burthensome to this table thro[ugh] the deminution of our Inhabitants & the declining Circumstances of this Island.

Our misfortunes are in a great measure owing to the Cowardice & Treachery of the Parties raised from time to time which mostly consisted of Tradesmen & Indentured Servants who are unacquainted with Arms & Military Discipline and are not to be depended upon, as well as in Arming our Slaves who we are convinced have betrayed us; and the Situation of the Rebells among vast Rocky mountains covered with thick Woods and almost inaccessable furnishes them with many Advantages in forming Ambuscades and retreating to places strongly fortified by nature.

The Constant success which attends them by those means have emboldened the Rebells to that degree that they now despise our power and instead of hideing themselves as they formerly did in those Mountains and Covert places, They openly appear in Arms & are daily encreasing by the desertion of other Slaves whom They entice over to them, and have actually taken possession of three Plantations within 8 Miles of Port Antonio and the Sea whereby they may at any time cut off all Communication by Land with that Harbour and Town where the New Set[t]lers in that Neighbourhood have been obliged to retire with their families for Protection. They have also within a few days past made an Attempt on a place called the Breast Work where a Considerable number of Armed men were lodged to guard the Workmen employed in carrying on a Defensible Barrack to prevent their Incursions.

Your Lordships will from hence perceive how impracticable it will be for us to suppress them or even to defend our Selves should the Defection become more general, which wee have too great Reason to apprehend from the Encouragement They meet with; the Affinity between them, & above all the hopes of Freedom, which has shaken the fidelity of our most Trusty Slaves, insomuch that we are at a loss what measures to take, having been so often betrayed and being fully Convinced that even those who now remain in Seeming subjection to us wish well to their Cause, and only wait for an Opportunity of Joining them.

Under these Deplorable Circumstances we are necessitated to address his Majesty for Aid and Assistance without which, as wee are already under the greatest Extremity, wee must either abandon the Country or become Victims to those merciless people. As your Lordship's Affectionate care of his Majestie's Subjects has been Conspicuous throughout your Administration, Wee Have an entire Confidence in your Application for such speedy relief as his Majesty in his great Wisdom shall think proper, which will lay us under the Strongest obligations and be a farther Inducement to us to continue for ever.

The Assembly passed several other Bills this Session which met with the
Concurrence of the Governour and Council particularly an Act, for appointing John Sharp Esq[uir]e[16] Agent in Great Britain to Sollicit the passing of Laws and other Publick Affairs of this Island, and impowering Certain Members of the Council and Assembly, from time to time to give Him
Instructions for His Management[17] namely the Hon[ora]ble John Gregory and Edward Charlton[18] Esq[ui]r[e]s of the Council[,] William Nedham
Esq[uir]e or the Speaker for the time being[,] John Hudson Guy,[19] James
Knight[,] Andrew Arcedeckne[20] and Temple Laws Esq[uir]e.[21] Also an Act,
for the further Encouragement of Parties, and more speedy reduction of
Rebellious and Run away Slaves.[22]

And, in pursuance of their Resolutions two Parties were fitted out, the
one which Consisted of 250 men, under the Command of Major Mumbee (who had a Considerable Interest in this Island) was to Rendevouz at
Port Antonio, and attack the Rebells on that side of the Country; the other

16. John Sharp was the London agent for Jamaica continually from 1733 to 1754. He was
elected to the post annually until 1743 when, on the basis of his record, the council suggested
and the assembly agreed to make the office tenurable on a triennial basis. Cundall, *Governors of Jamaica in the First Half of the Eighteenth Century*, 144, 180, 186, 203; Cundall, *Historic
Jamaica*, xxiii.

17. An Act for Appointing John Sharp, of the Middle Temple, London, Esquire, Agent in
Great Britain to Sollicit the Passing of Laws etc. and Other Publick Affairs of This Island;
Impowering Certain Members of the Council and Assembly during the Intervals of Assembly,
from Time to Time, as Occasions Shall Be for Such Management, to Give Him Instructions,
1734, in *Acts of Assembly*, 281.

18. Edward Charlton was an agent to Britain in 1725–26 and a member of the council
thereafter. Cundall, *Governors of Jamaica in the First Half of the Eighteenth Century*, 159, 163;
Cundall, *Historic Jamaica*, xxiii.

19. John Hudson Guy was a member of the Jamaica Assembly for St. Andrew Parish from
1722 to 1727, for St. Thomas in the Vale Parish from 1728 to 1731, for Port Royal from
1732 to 1735 and 1746 to 1748, and for St. George Parish from 1744 to 1745. He was also
chief justice in 1744 and 1749. In 1747, the assembly complained of Guy having said, in assembly, that there was only one member of the council who could be called a gentleman. His
apology was accepted by both the assembly and the council and no further action was taken
other than to grant him leave of absence for the remainder of the session. Cundall, *Governors
of Jamaica in the First Half of the Eighteenth Century*, xix, 190, 191, 192, 194; Cundall, *Historic
Jamaica*, xviii.

20. Andrew Arcedeckne, a lawyer and planter, was a long-serving member of the Jamaica
Assembly, representing St. Catharine Parish from 1718 to 1757. As attorney general in 1716–
17, he drew up the charges against Lord Hamilton. He also represented Chaloner Ogle in his
1742 trial over the assault on Trelawny. Cundall, *Governors of Jamaica in the First Half of the
Eighteenth Century*, xix, 70, 126, 138, 186.

21. Temple Lawes (c. 1699–1754), the son of Governor Sir Nicholas Lawes and Susanna
Temple, was a member of the Jamaica Assembly for Kingston in 1729–31, Clarendon Parish
in 1731–32, and St. Andrew Parish in 1733–35, and on the council from 1735. He died in
Bath, England. Ibid., 75, 99, 101, 103, 159.

22. An Act for the Further Encouragement of Parties, and More Speedy Reduction of Rebellions and Run Away Slaves, 1734, in *Acts of Assembly*, 281.

Robert Hunter (1666–1734), a Scot
and British military officer, served as
colonial governor of New York and
New Jersey from 1710 to 1720 and of
Jamaica from 1727 to 1734. His most
notable achievement in Jamaica was
to complete negotiations between the
Crown and colony for establishing a
permanent revenue in Jamaica in return for a specific guarantee of traditional English laws and rights to free
colonial Jamaicans. He died in office.
(New-York Historical Society)

of 200 under the command of L[ieutenan]t Collo[nel George] Brooks of
Guanaboa was to march at the time appointed, from Plantain Garden
River, so that the two Parties might arrive at the same time, and Attack
the Rebells on both sides. And, to facilitate the fitting out those Parties, it
was thought Necessary by a Council of War, which was held on the 19th.
of March to put Martial Law in Force for 3 months. While the Necessary preparations were making for this Expedition, Gen[eral] Hunter who
had for some time laboured under a Complication of Distempers, though
to outward appearance He was as well and as Active as could be expected
from a Man of His Age, was taken ill the 17th. and died the 31st. of March
1734, in the 67 year of His Age, and the 6th. of His Administration.

He was a fine Gentleman, and an Experienced Officer for He went early
into the Army, served in Flanders under King William and the Duke of
Marlbourough and passed through all the degrees from a Cadet to a Major General. He was in the Year 1709 appointed Governour of *Virginia*,
but was taken in His Passage, and Carried into France where He remained
a Prisoner near two Years during which time He found means of giving
some informations to the Ministry, which were of service to His Country,
and on His being Exchanged, He was appointed Governour of New York,
where He resided above nine Years, and returned to England in 1720.

He was of a cool Dispassionate Temper, and so averse to State and Ceremony, that He never assumed more than was absolutely Necessary to Support the Honour and Dignity of the Station He was in. But, notwithstanding He had many good Qualities and great Abilities, His Administration
was uneasy to Himself, as well as to those He governed; for there was,
the most part of the time, continual Bickerings between Him and the As-

sembly, which were aggravated by frequent Prorogations, and the Dissolutions that Commonly ensued.

The first Objection to His Conduct was the long Continuance of the Embargo and Martial Law in 1729 which was of Infinite prejudice to the Trade of Great Britain as well as to the Island. His Advocates alledge that He had orders for what He did, and seem to throw the blame, of their not being discontinued sooner and in due time, On Persons in higher Stations. It is an indubitable Fact, that a manifest Blunder or mistake was Committed in that affair, though I will not presume to give my Sentiments and Opinion of the matter, more Expressly. He was likewise blamed for sending for Regular Forces, without the Approbation and Consent of the Council or Assembly, for though they were necessary at that time in the Opinion of many Persons, as well as Himself Yet He was so far from Consulting or having the Opinion and Consent of Either of Them, that it was Expressly Contrary to the Resolutions of the Representatives of the People. His Advocates disavowed the Fact to be true, and Suggested that He did not apply for those Troops but that They were sent upon another Occasion, for the Security of the Island.

The misconduct of the Parties, and the misapplication of great sums of money raised on that Occasion, more than ever was known within the same space of time, were likewise Attributed to Him. And it was Suggested that the incursions and Ravages of the Rebellious Negroes, were magnified in order to raise a Panick, and furnish an Opportunity for raising of mon[e]y, more freely.

That the Parties were not duly provided with Ammunition and other necessary's, that they were permitted to loiter and mispend their time at Port Antonio to promote the Interest of that place, and that their pay and Gratuities, were ill paid and generally disposed of at a great discount, are indubitable Facts. But, as an impartial Historian I must observe that having had an Opportunity of enquiring into those allegations, I could not discover any thing more in regard to Him than a partiality for Port Antonio, and a desire to promote the Interest of that Place. His Plans for Reducing the Rebellious Negroes, appeared to me to be well laid, but badly Executed, for being advanced in Years and Infirm He confided too much in Some Persons, who were not Equal to the trust and made unjust advantages to the great prejudice of the Island. He did Indeed Screen Them from Justice by obstructing an Enquiry into their Conduct, which gave a Suspicion and Jealousy of His having some Sinister View or Interest in it.

That He neglected Trade, notwithstanding an Express article in His Instructions to Encourage and promote it, Countenanced the heavy Duties and other Impositions that were laid thereon, from time to time are obvious and incontestable, for He seemed to have a Strong prejudice and dislike to Merchantile Persons as well as to Priests and Lawyers.

It is likewise Incontestible that He neglected the Court of Chancery, which was often not held for 3 or 4 months together, for He had such an Aversion to that Office, that it was with the greatest Reluctancy He ever sate there, and embraced the minutest occasion of adjourning that Court, so that the Dilatory proceedings therein was an Encouragement to Letigious and Vexatious Suits, which multiplied by those means, and I have been credibly informed that He never made more than 5 or 6 Decrees during His whole Administration.

It were to be wished that this was the only Instance and that no other Complaints of the same kind or any other was to be met with. But, I shall suspend any further Animadversions thereon, intending in its proper place, to shew the Inconvenience and prejudice which attends the Power of Governour and Chancellour being vested in the Same Person, in other Respects.

On the Death of General Hunter the Government devolved on John Ascough Esq[uir]e the Senior Councellour, the second time.

Soon after Collo[nel] Charlton and several other Gentlemen went to Bagnells Thicketts, to forward the Party which was to Set out from thence and to join Major Mumbe. The Captain neglecting to keep proper Centinels, and permitting His men to Straggle, the Rebells who had Intelligence of those Circumstances, Rushed out of the Woods in hopes of surprising the Gentlemen, who were in a Hutt at Dinner, and to cut off the Party, but meeting with some of the Straglers They fired at them, which had this good Effect that it alarmed the rest of the Party who had just time enough to join the Gentlemen, and to Defend themselves in the Hut, for the Rebells ventured to Attack Them, but were Repulsed.

The President on notice of this disaster, ordered a Troop of Horse, and a Company of Foot from Spanish Town to support Them, in Case They should have Occasion. In two Days after They came to a Place where They knew (by the Fires which were not Extinguished) the Negroes had lodged the Night before, and following Their tract, got sight of Them soon after. But, the Rebells had not courage to Stand an Engagement for They dispersed Themselves and fled several ways. However, in the pursuit, They killed Several, and took some Prisoners, who were tried and Executed.

The Assembly met the 4th. of August, and having advice by a letter from His Grace the Duke of New Castle, to the late Governour, that His Majesty had been pleased to order Six Independant Companys of 100 men Each, to be sent over in Compliance with Their Request for the Security, and protection of the Island, They agreed upon an Address to His Majesty suitable to the Occasion, and a letter to His Grace, returning Him thanks for His good Offices, and the assurances He was pleased to give Them in the aforementioned letter of the regard He had for the wellfare and Interest of this Island.

They also voted an Additional Subsistance to those Troops, to Commence from the day of their Arrival, and Barracks to be built in the most convenient and proper places.

The 1st. of September was a Violent Storm of Wind which began about one in the Morning and continued till one P M; it varied from N[orth] W[est] to S[outh] W[est] but was not so Violent as either of the Hurricanes. Nor had the Inhabitants those Symptoms or Notices, which usually preceed such Weather in this part of the World.

The Towns received very inconsiderable damage but the Planters suff[e]red very much, many of their Canes, and almost all their Plantain Walks being thrown down. The Men of War rode it out, and did not receive any damage, except the *Flamborough*, by three Ships driving a thwart her, by which means she lost her head, bolts Sprit and was very much Shattered. Two Merchant Ships cut away their Masts, and four others with most of the Sloops drove ashore, but were afterwards got off. The damage the Ships sustained was not so much owing to the Violence of the Weather as to the badness of some of their ground Tackle that gave way, on which they drove among the rest, and Occasioned the Mischief that would not have hap[pe]ned otherwise, though there was at that time, upwards of fifty sail at Kingston and about Twenty at Port Royal including his Majesty's Ships. This should be a warning to the Masters of our Merchant Ships, who depend too much on its being a fair weather Country, and are seldom prepared for such Casualties especially from the latter end of November, when they must expect to meet with Squalls, and sometimes storms of Wind or Hurricanes as well as in other Countrys.

The Assembly met, according to Prorogation, the 1st. of October, when the President in his Speech Acquainted them, that He should not have called them together so soon, from their private affairs, did not the Exigencies of the publick require their meeting, having received an Account that 300 Rebellious Negroes had the boldness to attack one of the Plantations in the Parish of St. Georges, carried away some of the Negroes; burnt the Mansion house and most of the Canes, and threat[e]ned to destroy several of the Neighbouring Settlements. It was therefore necessary for them, immediately to think of some more effectual Remedy, than what had hitherto been taken, to defend that part of the Country, and put a stop to the excursions of the Rebels, without waiting for the Arrival of the Forces expected, when the time of their coming was uncertain.

Upon which a Committee of the Councill, and of the Assembly were appointed to consider the Subject matter of his Honour's Speech, and made the following Report.

That it was the Opinion of both Committees since the Rebellious Negroes, had made so bold an Attempt, and more particularly on Edward's Fort[23] in St. Georges, that the only Remedy now left for the Security of the Island, was to establish Martial Law for any time not exceeding six Months; and that by a law, with power to the President and Commander in chief,

23. A Defensible House called Edwards Fort. — *Author.*

for the time being, in case the Occasion should Cease, to put an end to it, by and with the Advice and Consent of the Councill.

A Committee of the Councill and of the Assembly were also appointed to View the Fortifications, and warlike Stores, at Port Royal; and the following Report was made by the Chairman of the Committee, of the Assembly, which I think necessary to transcribe, because it discovers the great neglect and abuses, which had been committed, and may be the means of preventing the like for the future.

Mr. Speaker.

Your Committee according to order met a Committee of the Councill, and have surveyed the Fortifications and Stores at Port Royal, which They found in great disorder for want of care; the Works being very much out of Repair, many necessarys wanting, and most of the Armory unfit for Service. That the powder with respect to its quality, as well as quantity, required more time to make a proper inspection and enquiry, however, the Committee had ordered him to lay before the House, the Survey and Account taken by order of Collo[nel] Lilly His Majesty's Engineer (which was thereunto Annexed) together with their Observations thereupon.

It is the Opinion of both Committees on enquiry into the Powder, that it has been very much Neglected, and that very great abuses have been committed in respect to the Charge of Salutes, as well as the deficiency which appears to be in the quantity, according to the Account and Survey taken by order of Collo[nel] Lilly.

It appeared on the Examination of the person who has the care of the Powder, That it was always weighed when received from the Shipping and put into a store Room in the Cock Pitt, till they have a Quantity; That the Barrells are filled when delivered out of the Magazine; and That there was not any inspection into the quality or quantity when Capt[ain] Dalrymple delivered up the Fort and Stores to Mr. Fisher by order of the President, The Montrosses likewise declared to the same effect, and that the Powder had not been shifted, aired, or turned in eighteen Months, which wee humbly conceive to be a very great neglect of their Duty, and the cause that there is so great a quantity decayed and unfit for Service, it being necessary for its preservation to the turned and Aired at least ever three Months.

Your Committee think it proper to observe that when They enquired for the Master Gunners They were informed that since the death of Mr. Bouchier, which is near two years, there had not been any; and as they are of Opinion, such an Officer is absolutely necessary They humbly recommend to the House to request his Honour the President to appoint some fit and able Person for that Station, especially since the present Receiver and keeper of the Powder not only appeared to be, but has the general Character of a very stupid foolish fellow and consequently unfit for that Service.

On examination of the Powder book there appeared a charge of 11990 [lbs.] of Powder expended for Salvos from the Tenth of March 1732/3 to the 14 of April 1734, w[hi]ch is 1 year one month and four days and as the quantity charged as expended in every particular Gun seemed to be very extraordinary, They had recourse to the Rules of the Office of Ordnance, and find the same to exceed the allowance for Service, for Guns of the same Sizes; and as they were credibly informed it is not customary or necessary to expend in Salutes above half the Quantity that is allowed for Service, They made a calculation which They are ready to lay before the House, whereby it will evidently appear there is an Overcharge in that Article at least 7371½ [lb.] of Gunpowder being 73 Barrels & 66½ [lb] which at £6:5 [shillings] per Barrel amounts to £455:8 [shillings] 5½ [pence] this Currency, upon looking into the charges of Salutes the preceeding years, they observed the same Rules, and the Annual expence generally much the same, some years more.

Your Committee on comparing the several Entrys in the Powder Book with the Vouchers, and the Receiver General's acc[oun]t which is kept as a Check, find several omissions to the prejudice of the Country amounting to 417 pound weight of Gunpowder, which appeared to be received more than is Accounted for, from the 10th. of March 1732/3 to the 29 November 1733; but as They had not time to go through the examination They are of Opinion it is necessary to make a farther enquiry, it being probable many other errors, may be found. They also observe a Charge of 20 Barrels for Wastage by Rolling, triming & Shifting, which they conceive to be an imposition, since they are credibly informed, that Powder will not Wast or lessen in Weight if due care be taken of the Casks.

Your Committee likewise observe, that no Account is given of the damaged or Condemned Powder & as it will serve for Salutes as well as that which is good, and be a great saving to the Country, if applied that way, They are humbly of Opinion it will be necessary to recommend it to the Consideration of his Honour and the Board that directions may be given accordingly to the Commander of Fort Charles.

Upon the whole your Committee think themselves obliged to observe, with that just concern which becomes them, that the present State and condition of the Fortifications on Port Royal, require the immediate consideration of the Legislature, as they are the Strength and security of the Island, and more particularly at this Critical juncture.

The Assembly on taking the said Report into Consideration presented the following Address to the President.

To the Honourable John Ascough Esq[ui]r[e]

President and Commander in chief &c.

May it please your Honour

Wee his Majestie's most dutifull and loyal subjects the Assembly of
the Island of Jamaica, having taken into Consideration the Report of the
Committee ap[p]ointed to View his Majestie's Forts and Fortifications on
Port Royal, are extreamly concerned to observe them in so great disorder,
and have had so little care taken of them, that they are almost in a defenceless Condition. Wee therefore desire your Honour will be pleased to
give directions for their being forthwith repaired and furnished with such
Stores & necessarys as are immediately wanted.

Wee have hereunto Annexed a Copy of the said Report and recommend
to your Honours' Consideration such other matters as are pointed at in
the said Report, particularly the appointment of a fit and able person to be
Master Gunner of Fort Charles and the removal of one Topper a Mon-
tross, who has for some time past, had the care of the Magazine and the
Powder and is not as wee conceive qualified for that Station; the giving
directions for having all the Cannon and small Arms examined; to send
home such as are useless and unfit for Service, and to endeavour to procure others in their stead that are good and Servicable. And to give Orders
to the Commanders that for the future the damaged powder be expended
for Salutes, and the particular quantity regulated in proportion to the Size
of the Gun.

Wee likewise desire your Honour will be pleased to give directions to
the Officers Civil and Military carefully to put the Laws into execution in
relation to Negroes and that Guards be constantly kept and Patrolls ordered according to the directions of the Act of the Country.

Wee cannot doubt your Honour's care in taking such other measures
as may be necessary for the preservation of the Fortifications and Stores,
and to prevent the like abuses being committed for the future as are complained of in the abovementioned Report.

The President in his Answer assured them, that he would give directions
that the several parts of the Address should be complied with, and that he
had already done it with regard to Guards and Patrolls.

The Assembly having agreed to the Report of the Committee appointed
to confer with a Committee of the Council, on the subject matter of the
President's Speech, brought in and passed a Bill intituled an Act for putting
this Island under martial Law, for any time not exceeding Six Months, for
impowering the Civil Majestrate and other officers in the respective parishes during the time of Martial Law, to Assess, levy and Collect as well all
publick debts as Parachial taxes &c. which Bill met with the Concurrence
of the Council, and on the 17th. of October, the President gave his Consent, and made the following speech.

Gentlemen of the Council, Mr. Speaker and
Gentlemen of the Assembly

I have given my Assent to the Act for establishing of Martial law, and am heartily sorry the present state of Affairs, will oblige us to such a remedy, as the only one to preserve us. I believe you are all but too well convinced of the Necessity of it, and therefore cannot doubt that you will in your several stations give all proper countenance and encouragement to a Service upon, the Success thereof depends your lives and properties. And, that you may the better apply your selves to so necessary and important a Service, I have thought fit in his Majesty's name, by and with the consent of the Council to adjourn you to Wednesday the 6 of November, and you are hereby adjourned accordingly.

Martial Law being now declared, it was resolved in a Council of War, that 600 Men be draughted out of the several Regiments of Militia and divided into two distinct bodys, one of which to consist of 200 Men to be sent to Port Antonio and to march by way of the Breast Worke to the Negro Town, first cutting good Roads for their convenient Marching and the easier being supplied with Provisions and Amunition, and in case they get into the Town before the other 200, which are to be sent to the Breast work, then as the Rout[e] from the Town to the Breast work is difficult and dangerous by means of the many Ambuscades which the Negroes generally form, that 200 of the 400 Men be detached from the Town to the Breast Work to clear the passes and Ambuscades, in order to join the other 200, and then to march back together to the Town, Major Mumbee was appointed to command the first division and L[ieutenan]t Collo[nel] George Brooks the other.

The 27 of November arrived Six Transports under Convoy of his Majesty's Ship the *Falkland* with the Six Independant Companies, who were sent to different places. Vizt. two Companies to Morant or St. Thomas in the E[ast], two Companies to Port Antonio, one to St. Anns, and one to Westmoreland. The 22d. of December the President received advice that Collo[nel] Brooks entered and took possession of the Negro Town the 16th. of the same Month. The Rebells had laid two Ambuscades as usual, and Collo[nel] Brooks on discovery of them in his March, ordered the Party to halt, and sent to the Barracks for two Swivell Guns. In the mean time some resolute fellows offered to go and drive them out, accordingly they marched boldly up with their Pistols and Cutlasses, fired into the Ambuscade and Attacked the Rebells sword in hand, who after one fire, fled and set fire to the Town. Collo[nel] Brooks then marched forward with the Main Body, and preserved part of the Town from being burnt intending to keep possession of it, according to his Orders. The Rebels retired to an eminence which over looked, and is within Musket Shot of the Town from whence they were continually firing at our Men, for 3 or 4 days, Collo[nel]

Brooks, as soon as the Swivel Guns were brought up ordered them to be played on the Rebells, which did good Execution, for several of them fell and were seen carried off by others, and the Report made such a terrible noise among the Mountains, the Negroes were so Affrighted therewith that they never appeared afterwards in sight of that Place.

The President immediately ordered an Officer and 50 Soldiers draughted out of the two independant Companies, at Morant to march and keep possession of the Negro Town; but they had not been there above a Month before the officer grew tired of his Station and deserted the place, for which he was suspended, and another officer appointed, to command a party on the same Service, who luckily got there before the Rebels were apprized of its being Abandoned.

The Assembly who were prorogued from the 6th. of November to the 7 of April [1735], met that day, when the President made the following Speech

Gentlemen of the Council, Mr. Speaker and
Gentlemen of the Assembly
I should not especially at this time have called you together from your private concerns had not the Expiration of the Act for laying a duty on Rum, and the other Annual Laws together with the Exigency of our Affairs, made your Attendance necessary, as well to renew those as to make other Laws for the Security of this Island and the reducing the Rebellious Negroes.

Altho[ugh] Martial law may be disagreeable to a free people (which I should have been as unwilling to put in force as any person in my Station had not necessity required it) yet I am perswaded that the Country is by this time convinced, that under the Circumstances wee were then in, this was the best method that could be taken to put a stop to the excursions of the Rebels and to deliver us from the Apprehensions of their gathering into too great and powerfull a Body. The Execution of which has indeed put us to a very considerable expence and trouble, however. I can with pleasure, say, it has in a great measure answered our end, in routing and dislodging them from their strongest hold, and in distressing them so far as to force them to disperse into several Bodys, and to seek another part of the Country for their refuge and Subsistance. This success is to be farther improved if wee proceed with Vigour and Resolution.

I must therefore recommend to you the making of a Law for keeping up Partys, Cutting of Roads throughout the Island and inforcing the Barracking Act.

Mr. Speaker and Gentlemen of the
Assembly.
I have ordered the Receiver General to lay before you the publick Accounts, and particularly the Account of the Expences and other things during Martial Law.

Gentlemen of the Council, Mr. Speaker,
And Gentlemen of the Assembly.

Since your last meeting his Majesty out of his Royal Goodness has sent to us six Independant Companies, for the defence and Security of this Island whom I have placed in those parts which I thought were most in danger.

I make no doubt but at this time I shall find in you the same Zeal and Affection, for the Service of his Majesty, and the good of the Country which I have experienced through the Course of my Administration and that you will raise the necessary supplies with Cheerfullness[,] Unanimity and dispatch.

The Assembly upon taking this Speech into Consideration thought it necessary to receive the Act for putting this Island under Martial Law for any time not exceeding three Months, and to obviate any disputes which might arise, a clause was incerted, declaring the legality and consistency of the Sitting of the Assembly during the time of such martial Law, which met with the Concurrence of the President and Councill.

A Committee of the Council and Assembly was likewise appointed to prepare and draw up a Representation to the Lords Commissioners for Trade and Plantations, which was agreed to and transmitted by the President, the substance of which is as follows.

That having seen their Lordships' Representation to the Lords in Parliament, it was with particular satisfaction they observed this Island had so Considerable a share in it; That it was apparent the Sugar Colonies have long been declining, and required the Assistance of the Legislature, to put them upon an equal footing with their Neighbours the French. That the method proposed by their Lordships namely the liberty of carrying Sugars directly to foreign Markets and lowering the Duty on Rum, were the most effectual, if not the only means, of Accomplishing it.

As to what relates more particularly to this Colony They observed to their Lordships that the decrease of Their Trade and consequently of their Strength was owing to the following causes.

1. To the Establishment of the S[outh] S[ea] Company for furnishing the Spaniards with Negroes which Obstructed the further Settlement of the Island and is the principall Cause of the demunition of its Inhabitants, as that branch of Trade was formerly carried on by seperate Traders, and not only employed above 1000 Seamen, who were a considerable Security and Strength to the Island; but the means of vending large Quantities of British manufactures, and introducing about £600,000 p[er] Ann[um], which or the greatest part was reexported to our Mother Country.

2. The Farming of the Trade to Campeachy had likewise been a great and further Occasion of the decrease of our Commerce and Navigation;

as the Logwood Trade employed at least 100 Sail of Vessells and 1500
Seamen and this Island made the general Magazine of that Commodity,
which is now engrossed by some few private persons, and chiefly exported
to Holland and other foreign Parts, and their Agents have not only United
but joined with the Spaniards, As they had undoubted information, in
Attacking and destroying the British Navigation in the Bays of Honduras and Compeachy, which affects in a high degree the Honour, as well
as the Interest of the British Nation. They therefore recommended those
matters to their Lordships' consideration, in hopes some Expedient may
be thought of to preserve the Trade & Navigation of this Island, if not to
restore those valuable branches of Commerce, since their Interest was the
Interest of Great Britain, for whatever Riches and Advantages they Acquired at length Centered in her.

They likewise observed that the Soldiers his Majesty was pleased to
send over, were undoubtedly necessary; They were unable to provide an
Additional Subsistance for them, for tho[ugh] they had hitherto done it
in defferance to his Majesty's recommendation, Yet upon trial they found
themselves unequal to the Burthen, the Country was so impoverished and
dreined of Money; therefore hoped to have the benefit of their protection
without the Expence.

They further observed that those Soldiers had not been so Servicable
to the Country, as might reasonably be expected. The name and sight of
them had indeed some good Effect amongst the Negroes, but they had
been guilty of great disorders and Irregularities and seem not to be sufficiently under the power of their officers, which they imputed, in a great
measure, to their knowledge of some Instructions relating to their Tryalls,
whereby Their Officers are restrained from inflicting death, though their
Crimes be ever so notorious till his Majesty's pleasure be known, which
requires such a distance of time as emboldens them not only to have their
Officers in Contempt, and to disobey orders, but to commit Insults upon
the Inhabitants, and if suffered to go on with Impunity, will become more
dangerous to the Country, than the Negroes in Rebellion.

They concluded with returning thanks to their Lordships for Their
good Offices to this Island, which They entreated a Continuance of, and
that they should use their best endeavours to deserve them.

This Representation, though founded on Facts, and of great Consequence to the Nation as well as to this Island, never was seriously taken
into Consideration, as I have heard of, at least no measures were taken to
remedy the Evils therein mentioned, except the latter part relative to the
Soldiers, who were so disorderly and mutinous that they killed Cattle,
robed divers Settlements, and even threat[e]ned to set fire to the Plantations, upon their being restrained from purchasing and making use of
Rum to excess, but, a stop was put to those mischiefs by a power being

afterwards given to Governour Cunningham[24] and his Successors to hold Court Martials, and to try not only the Soldiers but the Officers for Capital Offences.

At this time the Island was under some Apprehensions of a Rupture with Spain, and finding upon the Survey that was taken of the Warlike Stores, that his Majesty's Fortifications on Port Royal, were very deficient, and many of the Cannon unfit for Service the following Address was drawn up and transmitted to his Grace the Duke of New Castle one of his Majesty's Principall Secretarys of State.

> To the Kings most Excellent Majesty
> The Humble Address of the President Council and Assembly of this your Majesty's Island of Jamaica
> Most Gracious Sovereign.
> We your Majestie's most Dutifull and loyal Subjects, the President Council and Assembly, of this your Majesty's Island of Jamaica, cannot but be allarmed at the Preparations of War carried on in Europe; for, though we have full confidence in the Wisdom of your Majesty's Councils and the Affection you bear towards your people, which has hitherto prevented your Majesty's ent[e]ring into a War that has proved so fatal and expensive to the Neighbouring Kingdoms, Yet as the Noblest Views pursued by the best concerted measures, cannot insure the success desired, it is uncertain how soon the Necessity of Affairs may render your Majesty's bearing a part in the present disquiet unavoidable, and in such a Case We Consider that your Majesty's Cause must engage us in Hostilities with our Neighbours the French, and Spaniards, in the West Indies, who on the least notice and slightest Occasions are ever ready to take their Advantages.
> We beg leave therefore to lay before your Majesty Our most humble Address for a supply of all Warlike Stores, but more particularly of Cannon and small Arms so requisite for our defence at this dangerous juncture, in which upon inspection, we find with some concern, our Magazine very deficient.
> The experience we have had of his Majesty's Generosity so often exerted in succouring this your Majesty's Island, emboldens us to hope for a speedy and sufficient relief in these our wants.
> We trust that your Majestie's unwaried bounty and the necessity of this Country will plead strongly to excuse our frequent Importunities, who

24. Henry Cunningham (1678–1736). A Scot and MP for Stirling burgh and county at various times between 1708 and 1734, he was injured saving First Minister Robert Walpole from a mob during the Excise Crisis of 1733. Appointed as governor of Jamaica in April 1734, he did not arrive in the colony until December 1735 and died before ever meeting the assembly after the shortest residence of any governor. He was entombed in the Spanish Town Cathedral. Cundall, *Governors of Jamaica in the First Half of the Eighteenth Century*, 157, 158, 159, 166–70.

shall pray for your Majesty's welfare, and wish the highest Success to your endeavours. A Success we mean, equal to the greatness and goodness of your Majesty's designs.

This Assembly continued sitting till the 21 of June and passed several Bills which met with the Concurrence of the President and Councill, particularly a most beneficial and necessary law intituled an Act for the better selling and securing the Island, and vesting several parcels of land in the Crown, and for building of Barracks and for fitting out Parties for the reducing the Rebellious Negroes, and cutting of Roads,[25] from whence they were continued by prorogation to the 8th. of July, and by several Prorogations to the 6 of January 1735.

The 31st. of May arrived Commodore [Digby] Dent with his Majesty's Ships the *Dunkirk*[,] *Sheerness* and *Drake* to relieve S[i]r Chaloner Ogle.

The 22 of June S[i]r Chaloner Ogle sailed for Great Britain with four Ships of War. A few days before the Merchants, in Testimony of his Vigilence and care of the Trade, wrote him the following letter.

S[i]r,

His Majesty having been pleased to recall you, and we hope with an intention of rewarding your long and faithfull Services, we beg leave to express our gratefull sense of your favours, and the constant care you have taken of the British Trade and Navigation in these parts.

It is with the highest Satisfaction we observe that not one single Vessell has been taken or Plundered nor the least Depredation committed on the Island, since you commanded his Majestie's Squadron which we justly attribute to your Vigilence and care in appointing Cruizers from time to time in proper State and in granting (with the greatest Complacency) Convoys whenever we applied for them.

These Instances of your duty to his Majesty, as well as your regard, for the Interest and welfare of his Subjects, justly claims this Acknowledgement and Testimony of our Gratitude, the only return in our power to make you, saving an inviolable regard and Esteem wherewith we have the Honour to be[.]

To Sr. Chaloner Ogle Kn[igh]t.
Commander in chief of his
Majesty's Ships in the West Indies

From this and other Instances I have mentioned we may observe that the Inhabitants of this Island, have not been wanting from time to time

25. An Act for the Better Settling and Securing the Island, and Vesting Several Parcels of Land in the Crown, and for Building of Barracks and Fitting Out of Parties for the Reduction of the Rebellious Negroes, and Cutting of Roads, June 21, 1735, in *Acts of Assembly*, 295.

to Acknowledge with the greatest Gratitude any Service that have been done them as well as to complain which is natural to all mankind, whenever they found themselves injured or Oppressed. And it were greatly to be wished, that the Gentlemen of the Navy who are sent to America, for the protection of our Trade and Colonies would set before them the Vigilence and care of S[i]r. Charles Wager[,] Commodore Harris[,] S[i]r Loe, S[i]r Chalonar Ogle and Vice Admiral Vernon whose principal Views were the publick Service, and not groveling designs or Avaritious Schemes of Trade, to the great prejudice of the Merchants, of whom they have many Advantages paying no Freight; Wages and other incidental charges or even Duties.

The 23 of September died Peter Beckford Esq[ui]r[e] of the Gout in his Stomack and in the 64 year of his Age.

He was a Native of this Island, the Eldest Son of Collo[nel] Peter Beckford, formerly L[ieutenan]t Governour, and bred at one of the Inns of Court in Westminster. He practised the Law in this Island about two or three years, but afterwards turned his thoughts to Planting in which he made the greatest progress, and left to his family the most Considerable possessions of any Planter in the British Dominions in America.

It must, however, be observed that his Father left him a Considerable Estate, and large tracts of land which He set[t]led and improved to the Degree I have mentioned.

He was a Constant Member of the Assembly, about 35 Years, and declined accepting of any other publick employment, and not only the Richest, but the most Popular Subject that ever was in this Island, for by his powerfull Interest He was not only a Check but he Controlled, whenever he thought proper the measures of most or all the Governours in his time. He was a true friend to the Island, and promoted the Settlement of it, by encouraging others to become Set[t]lers. Several Persons to my knowledge have raised Estates, and others who were unfortunate preserved from ruin, by his Friendship and Assistance; Industry[,] Sobriety and honesty, were sufficient Recommendations, and Seldom failed meeting with his Notice and Regard. Nor can I omitt observing his care and faithfull discharge of all kind of Trusts committed to him and more particularly of Orphans, whose Interest he had the regard of a friend and a Father. In fine he hath left a shining Example to all Trustees, Executors and Guardians and it would redownd to the Interest, as well as the Honour of the Island would they all tread in the same steps. He left 6 Sons and 3 Daughters, with Considerable Fortunes to them all, particularly the Eldest, now living, who has the greatest Estate in this Island or perhaps in America.[26]

The 28th. of September died after a few days illness John Ascough Esq[ui]r[e] President and Commander in chief in the 60th. year of his Age. He was a native of this Island, educated in England, and the eldest Son of

26. Peter Beckford the younger.

Thomas Ascough Esq[ui]r[e][27] of Guanaboa, who was an Officer in the Army under General Venables at the taking of the Island, and remained (without going off once) to the time of his death, which was in 1705, so that he lived here full 50 years and enjoyed a perfect state of Health.

Mr. Ascough, the Son, was many years of the Council and chief Justice during the Government of the Duke of Portland, and behaved in those important Stations to the satisfaction of the Inhabitants in general, though he did not Succeed so well in the Government, having too strong a Byass and was for extending the Prerogative of the Crown, which les[se]ned the regard they had for him; But he was universally esteemed for his generous and benevolent Temper, for he always lived in an Hospitable manner and was ready to do friendly offices, nor was he ever accused of any Act of Oppression or Injustice whatever mistakes, he committed, were imputed to Errors in Judgement, and not to any groveling or Averitious Design.

Upon the Death of the President, the Council met, and ordered his Majesty's Commission and Instructions to the late Governour Hunter to be laid before them, upon whose Death Mr. Ascough being the Eldest Councellor had Succeeded as President, by Virtue of the said Commission and Instructions. And the Commission and several Instructions relating to the Succession being read some doubts arose thereon, with regard to the present Administration, and after some debate.

It was the Opinion of the Board [that] the Goverment did devolve upon Mr. Pennant, as the Eldest Councellor and he declining to Act, for the Reasons alledged in his Answer to the Secretary (who by Letter acquainted him with the death of Mr. Ascough) That he ought to resign his Rank and Place as a Councillor and give up his right as President of the Councill, in Writing, before the Councillor or next named in the Commission could safely Act. Accordingly the following Instrument was drawn up and Executed.

To all to whom these presents shall come.

Be it known That Whereas by the death of the Honourable John Ascough Esq[ui]r[e] late President & Commander in Chief of this his Majesty's Island of Jamaica, the Administration of the Government thereof by Virtue of his Majesty's Commission and Instruction given to Major General Hunter Dec[ease]d devolves upon me Edward Pennant, of the Parish of Clarendon Esq[ui]r[e] as the Eldest and first of his Majesty's Councill after the death of the said John Ascough. And whereas I the said

27. Thomas Ayscough (?–1705). Cundall is unsure whether John Ayscough is the son of William or Thomas (see part 2, section 4, note 31, above). Here, Knight believes it was Thomas, a major of the army of occupation and commander of six troop of horse in 1655; member of the assembly for St. John and justice of the peace, 1664–93; and member of the council from 1696 to 1705. Cundall, *Governors of Jamaica in the First Half of the Eighteenth Century*, 118.

Edward Pennant find my Self so wasted with Age, and worn with Infirmities, as utterly to Incapacitate me for the exercise of the said Government, either to the Advantage of the people or the Service of his Majesty, I Do therefore by these presents in the most Solemn and humble manner, Resign to his Majesty King George the Second his Heirs and Successors, my Place or Office of Councellor and President of the Councill. And I Doe hereby renounce, refuse, release and forever, quit Claim to any Power Preeminence Rank & Authority on Acc[oun]t of the said Places, or either of them, humbly beseeching his most Sacred Majesty, Graciously to accept of this my humble Resignation, as the best Service I am capable of performing to his Majesty and the Advantage to his People since thereby the Government of this Island may fall into hands able to administer it more to the Honour of his Majesty and the Advantage of his People[,] Given under my hand and Seal the thirtieth day of September Anno Dom[ini] One Thousand Seven hundred and Thirty five.

The Board taking the same into Consideration It was their Opinion and desire that the Honourable John Gregory Esq[ui]r[e] who by the Renunciation of Mr. Pennant [was] now the Eldest Councellor, should take upon him the Administration of the Government, and Act as President of the Councill and Commander in Chief of this his Majesty's Island of Jamaica. Accordingly he took the Oaths appointed by Act of Parliament to be taken in Stead of the Oaths of Allegience and Supremacy &c. upon which the Mace and Seals were delivered up to him. During this Administration, which was very short, nothing hap[pe]ned that is remarkable, for as Mr. Cunningham who his Majesty was pleased to appoint Governour of this Island, was daily expected, Mr. Gregory did not make any Alteration in the Civil or Military Employments, and in all other Respects behaved with great prudence and Moderation.

The 18 of December 1735 Arrived his Excellency Henry Cunningham Esq[ui]r[e] on board his Majesty's Ship the *Kinsale* Capt[ain] Forrester Commander.

His Commission for Capt[ain] General, Governour &c. was published the same day at Port Royal, and is dated the [22] day of [April] 1734. He was received there by the President, Council, & a great number of Gentlemen and in the Evening went to St. Iago de la Vega the usual Residence of the Governours.

The day following the Councill met and Administ[e]red to His Excell[enc]y the Oath Acustomed to be taken by the Governours of this Island, the Oath of Allegiance.

This Gentleman was very Assiduous in making himself acquainted with every Circumstance relating to the Island, and in Order to it was determined to take a tour round it; Accordingly, in less than a Month after his Arrival, he visited St. Dorothys, Clarendon, Vere, St. Elizabeths and West-

moreland: and reviewed the Several defensible Barracks, which were building in those Precincts and greatly Approved of them. On his return he intended to View the East or Windward part, and afterwards to proceed to
the North Side of the Island; But, contrary to the Advice which was given
him to live Temperately, to make easy Journeys in the Mornings and Evenings, and in other Respects to conform to the nature of the Climate, He
depended too much on the Strength of his Constitution[,] travelled in the
heat of the day and lived in the same intemperate manner he had been
Accustomed to in England, by which means he over heated himself, was
seized on the 9th. of February [1736] with a Violent Feaver which never
intermitted, and carried him off the 12th. of the same month.

As he lived so short a time in the Island, nothing more can be said of
him, than that He appeared to be a Gentleman of Great Probity, Generosity and Complacency: And, that the Inhabitants lamented the loss of him,
believing he would have proved an upright Chancellor and a very good
Governour.

On the death of Mr. Cunningham the Administration devolved again
on John Gregory Esq[ui]r[e] but, he met with some obstruction from the
Council who would not admit him to exercise the Government untill Mr.
Pennant had resigned in form a second time so there was a vacancy for 3 or
4 days[,] that Gentleman's Residence being at some distance from the Seat
of Government, and it requiring that time to have his Answer. This dispute
was occasioned by its not being known in England, when Mr. Cunningham's Commission was made out, that Mr. Pennant had resigned by which
means he was first named in the Council, but had not qualified himself on
the New Commission; so that his Resignation the Second time seems to
be unnecessary; for though by his Majesty's Commission to his Governour
relating to the devolution of the Government in case of his death or absence in the following Words—The Eldest Councellor whose name is first
placed in our Instructions and who shall be at the time of your death or
Absence residing in the said Island of Jamaica shall take upon himself the
Government &c.

And that clause in the Governour's Commission is inforced by the 33d.
Article of his Majesty's Instructions. Yet such Eldest Councillor can only
be understood, to be an Actual Councillor and not a person who had once
Resigned. Nor was there any Occasion for a second Resignation especially
since (as I have observed) Mr. Pennant had not qualified himself, on the
New Commission or in the life time of Mr. Cunningham.

However to prevent any further disputes, Mr. Pennant sent up his Resignation in writing properly Attested, not being able through Age and Infirmities to travel to Spanish Town and do it in person. Mr. Gregory was
thereupon admitted and took the Oaths prescribed by Act of Parliament.

The day following the Council presented an Address to the President,
wherein thay thanked him for his Moderation and prudent behaviour in

his former Administration, from whence they Assured him of the pleasing prospect they had of being easy and happy under his Government.

Nevertheless a dispute arose in a few days after on the Nomination of a Chief Justice[,] the President having appointed a Gentleman of very fair Character who was on the Bench,[28] but as he did not consult the Council thereupon, and They proposed to recommend another person,[29] five of Them entered a protest in the Minutes of Council and then resigned Their Seats at that Board.

To set this Controversy in a true light, it is necessary to observe, That it has been Customary in those Cases for the Governour or Commander in Chief for the time being, to take the Opinion and Advice of the Councill: But, whether this Custom makes it a kind of a prescription, I will not take upon me to give any Opinion: Since no other Order or determination was made by his Majesty, than to refer the matter to Mr. Trelawny[30] upon his being appointed Governour, and to impower him to reinstate the five Councellors who had resigned, if he thought proper.

The New Assembly met the 10 of March according to their Summons, and the day following the President made the following Speech, which I shall incert at large because it gives some Idea of the State of the Island at that time.

Gentlemen of the Council, Mr. Speaker and Gentlemen of the Assembly.

The Unexpected loss of our late Governour has been a General misfortune to this Country. In the little time he was with us, he shewed us the prospect of a happy Administration, and his Zeal and uncommon Activity (which I fear was a means of depriving us too soon of him) gave us strong

28. The nominee was George Ellis, and he remained chief justice until his death in 1739 despite council objections. Ellis introduced guinea grass to Jamaica, initially as food for caged birds in 1744. He was also a poet. Ibid., 159, 164, 189; Cundall, *Historic Jamaica*, xviii, 266.

29. The council wrote in its objections that as Gregory declined to recommend a replacement on the council, they "thought it their duty to recommend one who they thought well qualified to discharge a Trust of so great consequence by nominating Mr Smith, who was at that time the senior Assistant Judge upon the Bench, and who on account of his Education Capacity and universally good character, seemed to them the most proper person to fill that post." Mr. Smith has not been further identified. Cundall, *Governors of Jamaica in the First Half of the Eighteenth Century*, 159.

30. Edward Trelawny (1699–1754). A Cornishman educated at Winchester School and Christ Church College, Oxford, he was an MP for West Loe, Cornwall, from 1724 until duty as a customs commissioner disqualified him in 1733. Offered the Jamaica governorship in August 1736, he did not take up the post for two years, arriving April 29, 1738. He oversaw the arrangement of peace with the Maroons and Jamaica's participation in the war with Spain. He retired for health reasons in September 1752 following the arrival of his successor, Charles Knowles, on September 19, 1752. Trelawny died in England just a year after his return. Ibid., 26, 152, 157, 164, 165, 171–207, 208, 209.

proofs of his real Inclinations to do us Service. The only returns we can
now make him, is to pay some regard to his Memory, by a becomeing Tenderness and Humanity to his unfortunate remains.

By this unhappy Accident, the Government is devolved upon me. I am
but too sensible of the difficulties which must attend it, and how unequal
I am to them; so that I can have no hopes of discharging this trust, but by
your Advice and Assistance.

There are Gentlemen many things well worthy your Consideration,
I shall point out some few which I judge most material, and most immediately necessary. The restoring of Credit, the encouraging white People to
come amongst us, the Set[t]ling the uncultivated Lands, and reducing the
Rebellious Negroes. These things have been often Attempted, but as the
Evils remain, the Measures must either have been mistaken, or unsuccessfully pursued. What now gives us most trouble are the Rebells. We have
been willing to flatter our Selves with some Success; but I fear their Numbers have been little less[e]ned by it. They begin again to be in motion in
several places, and in considerable bodys. They have lately done mischief,
and the remissness and Supineness of the Inhabitants in some Places will
too much encourage them to further Attempts, unless some immediate
care be taken to prevent them. The Building of Barracks will be a very
usefull precaution; but little Progress has been hitherto made in them, and
I believe you will think it necessary to review the Law that, directs them.

I am of Opinion it would be of singular Advantage to us, if the Mulattos and free Negroes could be made more Servicable; I am perswaded they
are the fittest for the Woods and I believe, they might be encouraged to do
their duty, if they were put under some proper establishment, formed into
Companies, and allowed a moderate and regular pay. These, being thus
made usefull, and the Barracks Compleated, and garrisoned by Soldiers,
would in my Opinion, effectually secure us against intestine Enemies, at
an easier Expence, and a much more equal and expeditious way, than by
raising of Parties. These are my thoughts Gentlemen, your own Councills
will either improve them or direct you to better.

Mr. Speaker and Gentlemen of the Assembly
The Annual Laws are now near expiring; I make no question, but you
will think it necessary to renew them. The Deficiency Law may deserve
a particular Consideration, whether upon the footing it now is, it does so
fully answer the Ends it is intended for.

I must recommend it to you Gentlemen as an Acceptable Service to
his Majesty, that you will make some further Provision for the Soldiers,
I mean for the Sick and Invalids by some proper allowances for Nurses to
attend them, and an Hospital to receive them from their several Quarters;
which as they are dispersed, makes the Attending them impracticable for
the Surgeons. His Majesty had allowed them, to give that regular Attendance which is necessary on such Occasions. This will satisfie his Majesty

of your care of them, and that you decline no reasonable expence for their Preservation and well-being amongst us.

Gentlemen of the Council Mr. Speaker and
Gentlemen of the Assembly.
Before I conclude, I think it necessary, from what has lately passed, to give you some Assurances as to my Self. I profess Gentlemen, heartily to wish well to this Country, and am desirous of giving better Proofs than by Words. I will endeavour to do my duty in this Station, without favour or prejudice; I will not attempt to Assume any powers, but such as I think do properly belong to me, by his Majesty's Commission and Instructions, and those I will endeavour always to exercise for your Security and Satisfaction. In short Gentlemen, your Interest shall be mine. I have a faithfull disposition to serve you, and a Sincere desire to be made the Instrument of procuring some Good to this Country.

The Assembly on taking this Speech into Consideration presented a Suitable Address to the President and thanked him for his Moderation and prudent behaviour, in his former Administration.

They also voted the Sum of £1000 Ster[ling] to be presented to Miss Cunningham,[31] the Sister of the late Governour in regard to the great Expences He had been at, without having had time to reap any Advantages from the Government. They also in regard to the Personal Esteem they had for the President, and His prudent behaviour in the Several Publick Stations He had been in, as well as in his former Administration set[t]led on him an Additional Salery, of £1250 per Ann[um] which made up his Sallery in the whole £2500 per Ann[um].

During this Session several necessary and beneficial Laws were passed, which are still in force except the Annual Bills, nor was there any other interruption to the Harmony and good Agreement, among the three branches of the Legislature, than the aforementioned misunderstanding, so that the Island was, at this time undisturbed at Home and abroad, though it did not long remain in those happy Circumstances, as will appear hereafter.

The Rebells who were dispossessed of Nanny Town went to Leward and proposed to incorporate with Capt[ain] Cudjo's[32] Gang, but being denied,

31. Miss Helen Cunningham was born after 1715 and was considerably younger than her brother, Governor Henry Cunningham. In 1736, the assembly is recorded as sending money to John Watkinshaw, legal guardian of Helen Cunningham until she reached her majority.

32. Cudjoe was a Coromantee (Gold Coast) African from what is now Ghana who had been enslaved and brought to Jamaica. He is thought to have escaped capture and run to the Clarendon Hills after the Sutton Estate insurrection of 1690. Instead of joining the original Maroons, he and his fellows formed small gangs raiding remote plantations and maintaining strategic communications with slaves. He emerged as a leader during the guerrilla war period between 1690 and 1720. The destruction of Nanny Town in 1734 caused many of the older Windward Maroons to join his Clarendon gangs, increasing his strength. During the

They dispersed themselves in seperate Bodies that they might be better able to Subsist, and remain undiscovered. For, being in want not only of the common Necessarys of life, but Arms and Amunition, They were not in a Condition to Act Offensively or even defensively, and at that juncture it would not have been a difficult matter to reduce them, had their places of retreat been discovered.

In the Month of May a detachment of Capt[ain] Cudjo's Gang appeared in St. James's and a party was immediately fitted out, and sent in quest of them. This Party had the good fortune to meet the Rebells, and to defeat them in two Skirmishes in which several were killed and others wounded. But, as soon as the Rebells got intelligence of that Party being returned to their Homes, they made a second Excursion[,] robbed several Plantations[,] Attacked Collo[nel] [William?] Reid[33] of St. James's Precinct who with his Servants defended themselves in his House and repulsed them on which in revenge The Rebells set fire to his Canes[,] Sugar Mill and other Buildings at some distance from the House which entirely Consumed them.

Upon this disaster another Party was raised at Saint Anns who met with greater Success than the former for they luckily discovered three of the Rebells' Settlements, which they burnt and destroyed [and] took 15 Women and Children some fire Arms and a great number of Cutlasses. Their Arms it seems were very bad, and powder grew Scarce with this Gang as well as the other, which made them retreat upon the least alarm or Appearance of a Party and being routed from these Settlements they were greatly harrassed and distressed.

The Assembly met the 2d. of November according to Prorogation, when the President made the following Speech, which I shall also transcribe at length because it contains several particulars worth Notice.

> Gentlemen of the Council Mr. Speaker and Gentlemen of the Assembly.
> I have called you together at this time, not only as the most Seasonable to you in regard to your private Affairs but likewise as necessary in regard to those of the publick.

---

later years of the war, settler parties destroyed many of his provision grounds, thereby putting him under great pressure. His main camp at Petty River Bottom in the Cockpit Country was, however, with its narrow, well-guarded passage, almost impregnable. It also allowed him to mount attacks on St. James, Hanover, Westmoreland, and St. Elizabeth Parishes, thereby creating an illusion of greater strength. Thus, both sides were ready for the peace agreement that was reached on March 1, 1739, which gave Cudjoe and his Maroons freedom in exchange for return of future runaways. Over fifty years of peace followed before the outbreak of the second Maroon War in 1795. He was, by contemporary reports, well over eighty by that time. Clinton V. Black, *History of Jamaica* (London, 1958), 84–87; Carey Robinson, *The Fighting Maroons of Jamaica* (Kingston, Jamaica, 1871), 30–52; Milton C. McFarlane, *Cudjoe of Jamaica: Pioneer for Black Freedom in the New World* (Short Hills, N.J., 1977).

33. Perhaps Colonel William Reid, who would represent St. James Parish in the Jamaica Assembly of 1758–60.

The Present state of your Country and the Evils which Attend it, require your Consideration. As these Evils are many & but too obvious,
I will only instance the loss of all valuable Trade. The extreame poverty of
the Country drain[ed] of Money, and no Channel open for a Supply, the
heavy Taxes, necessarily imposed, to preserve us from the Rebels, and, to
compleat our Misfortunes, the low Price of our principal Commodities.
These Evils are all very great, and if any one can be said to surpass the
other, this last in particular must sensibly affect us, and not only discourage the further set[t]ling the Island, but even oblige those who have made
Settlements, at a considerable Expence, to abandon them, when, after a
painful and laborious life, in the midst of Danger, they can see no other
Fruits from their Labours, than the Prospect of being in Debt and undone.
These Consequences are far from imaginary. We have already seen them
experienced in part, and have but too much Reason to fear their Increase.

I wish, Gentlemen, it was as much in my Power to ease your Misfortunes, as it is to represent them to you; that Difficulty seems too great for
this Country; our Application must be to his Majesty, from whose Goodness we may hope some Relief; and by his Influence, our Mother Country to restore us: This, I think, we have great Reason to hope, for if the
Attempt to reclaim the Desolute and Profligate has been worthy of Care,
how much more the Preservation of the Honest and Industrious, whose
Labours have been so beneficial to Great Britain.

Mr. Speaker, and Gentlemen of the Assembly;
I will order the Publick Accompts to be laid before you, and shall be
glad you may find the Funds likely to answer the Purposes intended.
I have Reason to believe the Receiver General has been under some Difficulty to subsist the Soldiers and the Parties, from the Scarcity and advanced Price of Provisions, tho[ugh] I must do him Justice, he has always
punctually complied with my Orders.

I am sorry I cannot say the Parties have succeeded to my Wishes, I have
been sometimes disappointed; and I must observe to you, there is not only
Difficulty in raising these Parties, but still greater to engage proper Persons to conduct them. Every Officer is not able to bear the Fatigues of
the Woods; and of such as are[,] little Service can be expected, if sent out
against their Inclinations. In my Opinion some Pay should be allowed to
encourage that Duty. These Difficulties will in some measure be removed,
when the Barracks are established; but hitherto that Work proceed[s]
very slowly. I have given it all the Countenance I have been able; though
it might be expected the Necessity and Usefulness of the Work would be
sufficient to recommend it self.

Gentlemen of the Council, Mr. Speaker, and Gentlemen of the Assembly,

It will be in your own Power to make this Session as short as you please; and, as it will probably be the last in which I shall have the Honour to speak to you in this Station, I shall leave it with the greater Satisfaction, if you will first give me an Opportunity of joining with you in any good Offices for you. I have hitherto used my Endeavors to serve you; and, where I have failed, or been guilty of Errors, I have this to excuse them; they must have proceeded from the Understanding, and not from the Will, which has been always truly devoted to your Interest:
Jamaica, Is[land]

To the Honourable John Gregory, Esq[ui]r[e] President of the [blank] Council, and, and Commander in Chief, in and over this His Majesty's Island of Jamaica, and the Territories thereon depending in America, and Chancellor of the same &c.

The Humble Address of the Assembly.
May it please your Honour,
We his Majesty's most dutiful and loyal Subjects, the Assembly of Jamaica, beg Leave to return you our most sincere and hearty Thanks, for your Speech at the Opening of the Sessions.

The several Matters which your Honour has so justly pointed out, and recommended to our Consideration, must be confessed to be of the utmost Importance to the Welfare of this Island, and consequently, to deserve the most serious and mature Deliberations of this House, and we assure your Honour, we shall proceed upon them with the greatest Unanimity and Dispatch.

We wish it were as much in our Power to find out Remedies for the Hardships under which the Island labours, as it is easy to point out the Sources of them.

That which more immediately presses us, and requires the particular Attention and Consideration of all the Parts of the Legislature, is the late excessive Fall of our principal Commodities, Sugar and Rum; the one of which is become of very little Value, the other of none at all.

As this Misfortune does not take its Rise, so neither can it meet with a Remedy here; and we assure your Honour, we shall readily concur and assist in any such Measures and Applications, as shall appear most likely to procure its Removal.

His Majesty's known Goodness, and the tender Regard which, upon all Occasions, he expresses for the Interests and Welfare of his Subjects in general, afford us the strongest Grounds to hope for all the Succour and Relief, which his Power and Influence can procure for us.

And as this Island is allowed to be of the utmost Importance to Great Britain, both with respect to its Trade and Manufactures, we cannot doubt, but his faithful Subjects there will chearfully concur with his Majesty, in his gracious Endeavours to retrieve its Affairs, and restore it to its prosperous and flourishing Condition.

We beg Leave, upon this Occasion, to express our entire Approbation of your Honour's Conduct, and return you our hearty Acknowledgments and Thanks, for the Integrity, Zeal, and Prudence, which your Honour has exerted upon all Occasions, during the whole Course of your impartial Administration.

Passed the Assembly
   the ninth Day of
   Novemb[er] 1736.
         William Nedham, Speak[er]

His Honour's Answer.
Mr. Speaker, and Gentlemen of the Assembly,
I Return you my hearty Thanks for this very kind Address, and for your generous Acknowledgment of my weak, though Sincere Endeavours to serve you, your favourable Opinion of my Conduct gives me great Satisfaction, and it shall be my constant Care to merit your Esteem, by giving you the best Testimonies in my Power, of my real Affection to this Country.

The Assembly then proceeded on Business, with great Unanimity revived the Annual Bills and passed Several other Beneficial Acts, which are still in force, particularly an Act intitled an Act for Introducing of white People into this Island, for subsisting them for a certain Time, and providing them with Land, that they may become Set[t]lers.

The Rebells having found means of furnishing themselves with Ammunition, in the Month of January, came down into Deans Valley in Westmoreland, and destroyed a Plantation belonging to the Heirs of Collo[nel] Foster. They also attacked one of the Barracks, where part of Capt[ain] Pope's Independant Company was lodged, having Intelligence that several of the men were absent, and others sick, therefore thought to have Surprised and cut off all that were in the Barrack. But, They bravely defended themselves and defeated the Rebells, notwithstanding their Superiority in Number, with the loss of Six Men.

It was thereupon thought absolutely Necessary to fit out a Strong Party to reduce that Gang, which was Set[t]led in that Neighbourhood, while other Parties were sent out to discover where the Windward Gang had retreated to. But, as the Avenues to Capt[ain] Cudjo's Principal Settlement were not well known, a small Party of Thirty Six Men well armed, under the Command of L[ieutenan]t Chambers, was in the mean time ordered out to make Discoveries and gain Intelligence. And, as the President, was convinced by long Experience of the Difficulties, of reducing the Rebells by force, unless a Sufficient Number of men could be procured, who were equally inured and Acquainted with the Mountains, He thought it Eligible and for the Utility of the Island, to Accommodate matters with them. Accordingly Collo[nel] Gutherie who had the Care and Direction of that Party, by the President's order gave the following Instructions to L[ieutenan]t Chambers.

> If you come up with the Settlements of any of the Negroes in Rebellion, you are if possible to take one or two alive, and when taken to use Them kindly, but in such manner as They shall be well secured in your Return.
>
> If you come to the Speech of any Negroes more Especially those under the Command of Cudjo, offer Them in the President's name terms of Accommodation, and propose a time and Place to treat, not less than 10 or 12 Days.
>
> If you come up with any Town belonging to Cudjo, on His or His People's Offering to treat, you are not to burn or destroy Such Town, or Suffer the same to be plundered, that thereby you may give the Rebells a Testimony of His Honour's good Intentions, touching the said Treaty.

These Facts, I have abstracted from an Original letter of Collo[nel] Guthrie's, which I have now in my hands, and I thought proper to mention in Justice to Mr. Gregory, with out the least Intention of lessening the Honour due to Mr. Trelawney, who perfected the Treaty with the Rebels, for though that Party returned without any other Success, than discovering the Avenues to the Rebel's principal Settlement in Westmorland, Yet it is Evident from thence the Scheem was laid, by Mr. Gregory, and that the first Step taken therein was in His Administration.

The 7th. Day of Oct[obe]r died Commodore Dent very much lamented; for having been several times on this Station He was Personally known to the Inhabitants in general, and greatly Esteemed for His Candid, and Benevolent Temper.

We are now come to a Remarkable period of time, and though the Circumstances are recent in our Memory, it is proper to take a more particular notice of them, than we have hitherto done, in order to transmit them to Posterity and Expose the perfidious practices of the Spaniards, in Manifest Violation of solemn Treaties; the Law of Nations, and even common Justice. We have from time to time taken notice of the Depredations committed by Them on the Island, as well as on the high Seas, though I have not incerted, nor have been able to procure a full and Exact list of all the Ships They have Confiscated or plundered, and only given an Account of some few which are well known, and Uncontroverted, to have been passing the Seas on Their lawful Occasions.

The Spaniards, seem at first to have made Essays, in order to see Whether the Nation would resent such Treatment, for They began—with only plundering our Ships, at Sea; then They took some and carried them into Obscure Creeks and Harbours, where they unladed the Cargoes and Sent them privately into St. Iago de Cuba and other Places. And, when Complaints were made to the Spanish Governours by the Sufferers, They disavowed the facts, and declared the Persons who Committed them to be Pyrates, and not to have Acted under any legal Commission or Authority. In process of time our Ships when taken, were not only carried into Port, and Condemned on groundless Suggestions; but Commissions were granted to those who accepted of Them on Condition of no purchase[,] no pay, and the Governours and other Royal Officers were Concerned with them. By those means our American Trade and more particularly to and from this Island, was so much disturbed, that it became unsafe for our Merchant Ships to pass the Seas on their lawful Occasions without Convoy; for no Restitution or Satisfaction could ever be obtained in any Instance, although His Catholick Majesty granted Several Schedulas for that purpose, particularly for the *Wool ball*, that was carried into La vera Cruz and three Several Men of War were Sent to demand the Execution of them, to no purpose. As those orders were Evaded, and no ways Complied with, we may Reasonably Suppose, they were only calculated to Amuse, and that the Court of Spain gave other Instructions, which were repugnant to those Schedulas.

In September came advice of the *Bath* Gally Capt[ain] Curtis, bound from Bristol and Cork to this Island with Provisions for His Majesty's Ships, being taken and Carried into Porto Rico. And soon after of the *Loyal Charles* Capt[ain] Way, the *Prince William* Capt[ain] Delamot, bound to London, and the [blank] Capt[ain] [blank] bound to Bristol (all of them laden with the Product of this Island) being taken and Carried into the Havanna, where they received the form and only the form of a Condemnation, after the following manner. The Master, and His Mate or one or two of His Men, were Carried before a Judge and Examined by an Interpreter who is a Spaniard not chosen by Himself nor one that He has any knowledge or Recommendation of and His Examination is taken in Writing, without having a Copy or being satisfied that He has Justice done Him, in that Respect. So far from it, that He is made to declare (as some of them afterwards discovered particularly Capt[ain] Jason Vaughan, who gave me this Information) things He never said, and were untrue, in order to Colour a Condemnation. An Advocate, indeed, was allowed (but He is also a Spaniard chosen by the Judge, and probably a party Concerned) who put in an Answer, in Writing to the charge founded on such Examination, on which the Judge pronounces Sentence without any other Ceremony. For the Master is not allowed even a Sight of His Papers (which were immediately Seized on His being taken) or to give any Instructions to His Advocate, much less to offer any thing in His own Vindication.

The Merchants of Kingston, on advice of those illegal Captures, drew up an Address which They presented to the President, wherein They, in a

lively and Pathetical manner, Complained of those Abuses, in the following words.[34]

The *Kinsale* man of War was thereupon sent to the Havanna, to demand the last mentioned Ships, and the Men who were under Confinement except such as had entered into the King of Spain's Service as some of
them were prevailed upon, by forcible means. The Captain sent his Lieutenant ashore for that purpose and the moment the Spaniards discovered
the Boats put[t]ing off they met her in several Boats, well man[n]ed, carried him to the Governour, who ordered the Men on board of one of the
Guarda Costas and told the Lieutenant, that as for the Ships, they had
taken they would keep them for what they did was by order from the King
of Spain[35] their Master and ordered him to be confined a close Prisoner. In
that manner they were detained three days nor would they permit our Men
to speak to the Assiento Factors or any other Englishmen.

Soon after a Spanish Sloop came into Port Royal laden with Cocoa and
Snuff, they pretended that the Sloop was leaky, therefore desired leave to
stay and repair their Vessell. The Inhabitants in general were for having
her detained, believing her to be a Spy, but the Assiento Factors prevailed
on the President and Councill to suffer her to refit, and then to dismiss her,
which was accordingly done.

I have now brought the History of this Island down to the Administration of His Excellency Edward Trelawney Esq[ui]r[e] wherein will appear
many extraordinary events which distinguishes this Island, and the great
advantages ariseing from it above all other parts of the British Dominions in America. Indeed the value and Importance of it seems to be better
known, or more truely Considered then it ever had been before, by the
signal Instances of the Care which is taken of it, particularly in keeping
constantly on the Station, ever since the Commencement of the War with
Spain, a Strong Squadron of Men of War, for its preservation and Security.

Mr. Trelawney and his Lady,[36] who had been ill all the Voyage, arrived
at Port Royal the [29] day of [April] 1738, on Board his Majesty's Ship the
Torrington Capt[ain] Knight, in a very indifferent State of health, tho[ugh]
both recovered in a very few Weeks after.

The same day arrived Commodore [Charles] Brown,[37] with His Majes-

---

34. Knight here left a blank page to provide space for this address but never transcribed
it into his text.

35. Philip V (1683–1746) was king of Spain from 1724 until his death.

36. Amoretta or Annorah, daughter of John Crawford, died in November 1741. Trelawny
remarried on February 2, 1752, Catherine, sister of Robert Penny, member of the assembly
for Portland and attorney general, 1744–49. Cundall, *Governors of Jamaica in the First Half of
the Eighteenth Century*, 171–72, 201, 205, 206.

37. Commodore Charles Brown (c. 1678–1753) was senior officer at the Jamaica station in
1737–38 and in 1739 was second in command to Admiral Edward Vernon during the attack
on Portobello.

tie's Ships, the *Hampton Court, Windsor, Falmouth* and *Sheerness;* so that the Squadron under his Command including the Ships which were on the Station before he arrived consisted on one Ship of 70 Guns, two of 60 Guns each, two of fifty, one of 40, one of 20 & and Sloop.

His Excellency's Commission, for Captain General, Governour and Commander in Chief, which bears date the 3d. of August 1737, was published on his Arrival; and the day after the Councill met and Administ[e]red to him the Oath accustomed to be taken by the Governours of this Island, the Oath of Allegiance &c.[;] soon after he endeavoured to heal the breach between the President, and the Members of the Councill, who had resigned; but tho[ugh] his Excell[enc]y did not entirely Succeed in that respect, nor would any of them accept of the offer he made to restore them to their former Stations; Yet the differences on that Occasion and all Party distinctions in this Island subsided, at least for some time.

The Assembly which stood prorogued to the [15] day of [June 1738] met accordingly, for his Excellency did not think fit to dissolve them, and call another as usually had been done by his Predecessors; and passed several Publick & private Bills, which met with the Concurrence of the Governour and Councill.

But notwithstanding all publick disputes and Animosities seemed Composed, and the Inhabitants made easy in that respect, Yet they still laboured under difficulties, and were greatly embarrassed, by the Spanish depredations, as well as the Excursions and Ravages of the Rebellious Negroes. For though there was now a Squadron of Men of War to protect their Trade, and proper Convoys and Cruizers were appointed from time to time, yet the Advanced Premiums for Insurance on the Apprehensions of a War with France as well as Spain, and their product coming late to Market by reason the Merchant Ships were obliged to wait after they were laden, to make up a Fleet, was a great inconveniency, and prejudice to them.

The Rebellious Negroes in the Windward parts of the Island after they had been dispossessed of their Town and Settlements near Port Antonio, were indeed in great distress, as I have observed for want of Powder and Amunition, as well as Provisions and other Necessarys, so that they were incapable of Acting offensively or even defensively and under the necessity of retireing to remote Parts, where they Seperated themselves into several Bodies that they might be better able to subsist and Conceal themselves.

But the Le[e]ward Gang, who were set[t]led in a part of the Country, which was very little known, and difficult of Access, animated with those Advantages and the Success they had met with made frequent Excursions which incited the Negroes in the neighbouring Plantations to such a degree, that great numbers were ready to join them, and had actually done it if the Grand party, fitted out under the Command of Collo[nel] John Guthrie, and L[ieutenan]t Sadler had not defeated and reduced them to the necessity of ent[e]ring into a Treaty. But, as I shall hereafter give a

The frontispiece to Robert C. Dallas, *History of the Marrons* (London, 1803), this image represents a later artist's conception of the agreement to peace terms between Cudjoe, leader of the Accompong Town Maroons, and Colonel John Guthrie, the representative of Governor Edward Trelawny, on March 1, 1739. The principal achievement of Trelawny's long governorship, this treaty acknowledged the Maroons' jurisdiction over the territories they inhabited in return for their ceasing hostilities against settlers and cooperating in the capture and return of runaway slaves. The following year, on March 1, 1740, Quako, chief of the Windward Maroons, agreed to and signed a similar treaty. After almost eight decades of hostilities between Maroons and settlers, these treaties ushered in a truce that lasted for most of the next six decades.

more particular Account of this Memorable Transaction, and of the Treaty which was made with those people, I shall here suspend any further Observations thereon.

In February 1738 arrived two Ships from London, with 52 Iron Cannon, all 36 Pounders, 1000 Small Arms, and all sorts of Amunition and warlike Stores, for the use of his Majesty's Fortifications, which had been long expected and were very much wanted.

And on the 1st. of March was Executed the aforementioned Treaty with the Rebellious Negroes, which not only saved a very Considerable Annual Expence, the Government was at, to little or no purpose, but promoted the further Settlement of the Island; for divers Plantations which had been deserted, and other parts that lay exposed, being now rendered safe and secure from Insults or damages, were immediately set[t]led; and are now in a flourishing Condition.

The Assembly upon their meeting the same Month, ratified the said Treaty by a Law, and in Consideration of this Signal Service, Voted Collo[nel] Guthrie £1500 and Mr. Sadler £500.

Upon the 5th. of August following arrived his Majesty's Ship the *Shoreham* Commanded by the Honourable Capt[ain] Boscowen,[38] with orders for Reprizals on the Spaniards, which were immediately published in the three principal Towns in this Island.

Commodore Brown immediately prepared for a Cruize, and on the 14 of the same Month, sailed with 5 Men of War, as He kept Secret his intentions and design great matters were expected, but it afterwards appeared that He only Cruised off the Havanna, and upon his Approach near the Moor Castle the Spaniards fired upon him, which Compliment he returned, without any damage on either side, he soon after returned to Jamaica, without making an Attempt upon any of the Spanish Settlements. Sup[p]osing himself as it was imagined not warranted by his orders, so to do; But his Conduct was Censured for appearing off the Havanna and fireing at the said Castle, because it alarmed the Spaniards who suspecting from thence a rupture between the two Crowns, immediately seized upon all S[outh] S[ea] Company's Effects in that Port, and sent Expresses to other parts of the Spanish Dominions in America, to acquaint them therewith, by which means our Men of War and Privateers were very probably, prevented from making such Advantages as they might have done, had those orders for Reprizals been privately issued, and care taken not to give the Alarm to any of the Spanish Settlements at Land.

The 23d. of October arrived Vice Admiral Vernon with His Majesty's

---

38. Edward Boscowen (1711–1761) accompanied Vernon to the West Indies in 1738 and was with him at the attacks on Portobello, 1738–40, and Cartagena. 1741. Promoted to vice admiral in 1755 and admiral of the blue in 1758, he was commander in chief of the fleet that captured Louisburg in 1758.

Ship[s] the *Burford, Worcester* and *Anglesea*, and took upon him the Command of the Squadron on this Station; having dispatched from Antegoa, the *Princess Louisa, Strafford* and *Norwich* to La Guiza, a Town & port on the Coast of Caracas, where he was informed several were taking in their Laden for old Spain.

Upon their Arrival at that Port, They discovered 17 Sail of Ships in the Harbour, which was defended by three Forts. Capt[ain] Waterhouse who Commanded his Majesty's Ships on this Enterprize drew them into a line and Battered the Town and Forts for a Considerable time, by which means they beat down a great part of the Fortifications, Churches, and Houses. The Lieutenants, and Sailors were thereupon extreamly eager for landing & would Certainly have carried the Place had they done so[,] the Spaniards being on the Point, as we have since been informed, of pu[t]ting up a white flag and Surrendering: but as the *Strafford* was very much damaged, by the fire from the Forts and the Wind blowing hard, the Commodore thought proper to give up the undertaking and returned to Jamaica, where his Conduct and behaviour was universally Condemned.

The same day as the Admiral was standing in for Port Royal they had also the pleasure to see the *Diamond* Man of War coming into the same Port, with two Spanish Prizes. One of which was a Register Ship with 130,000 p[iece]s [of eight] and Cloath's for 6000 Men &c. and the other laden with Hydes &c. was likewise a Valuable Prize.

On the 5 of November Vice Admiral Vernon who procured from Governour Trelawney 200 Soldiers, draughted out of the Independant Companies, in this Island sailed from Port Royal with his Majesty's Ships the *Burford, Hampton Court, Princes Louisa, Worcester, Strafford, Norwich* & *Sheerness* the last of which he dispached to Cruize off of Carthagena.

On the 20th. He came in sight of Porto Bellow, but being almost Calm, He Anchored within 6 Leagues of the Shore, and on the 21 the Admiral plied to Windward in line of Battle, having given the proper orders for the Attack.

Commodore Brown who led the Van in the *Hampton Court* executed his part with great Resolution, and like an experienced officer, being followed by the *Norwich* Capt[ain] Herbert and the *Worcester* Capt[ain Perry] Mayne. The Admiral Observing that some of the Spaniards fled from several parts of the Fort, made the signal for the Boats, in which the Soldiers were to land, while he was making up to the Iron Castle to batter it; and upon [coming] up as near as possible, the fire of his small Arms commanded the Enemie's lower Batteries which drove them from thence, where they could do the most harm, and by that means also secured the Soldiers at landing. This the Enemy afterwards confessed was the principall Occasion of their deserting the lower Batteries[,] the small Shot, from the other Ships not having reached them, though their Cannon had beat down some of the upper part of the Fort. The Enemy by those means being thrown into a Consternation, hoisted a White Flagg, the Signal for Capitulating, which was answered by the Admiral, though it was sometime before he could stop his own Men or those on board the *Strafford* Capt[ain] Trevor from firing.

In the mean time some of the Seamen who landed with the Soldiers, had climed up the Walls of the lower Battery and Struck the Spanish Colours, they also drew the Soldiers up after them, to whom the Spaniards who had retired to the upper part of the Fort, surrendered at discretion. Their number was only 5 Officers, and 35 Men out of 300, the rest being killed wounded and run away.

The Admiral's Ship lying open to Gloria Castle, the Spaniards kept firing one of their longest Guns at her till night, but the Shot either fell short, or went over her without doing any other damage than wounding the head of her foremast; upon w[hi]ch the Admiral ordered some of his lower Tier to be fired at them, which carried over the Castle into the Town, none of the Shot falling short, one of them went through the Governour's, and some through other Houses in the Town.

This Successfull beginning was attended with a very inconsiderable Loss only 3 men killed and 5 wounded on board the Admiral's Ship. The same number killed and wounded on board the *Worcester*, one man had both his Legs shot off on board the *Hampton Court*, and 2 Soldiers were shot going on Shore one of which died soon after of his wounds.

The 22 the Admiral went on board Com[m]odore Brown and called the Captains together in order to give the necessary directions for warping the Ships up at night, as it was not practicable to attempt it in the day time, but he was prevented by the Enemie's put[t]ing up a white flag at Gloria Castle, and sending a Boat with a Flag of Truce and the Governour's Adjutant to the Admiral. In answer to the terms proposed, the Admiral drew up the Condition on which he would admit them to Capitulation, and allow them only a few hours, for their Consideration, which they accepted of, within the time limitted, and, before night the Admiral sent Capt[ain] Newton with 120 Soldiers to take possession of Gloria Castle, and St. Jeronimo Fort.

There were in the Harbour two Spanish Men of War, of 20 Guns each, and a Snow, the Crews of which dispairing of being able to defend themselves, fell to plundering the Town in the night and committed great disorders.

The Admiral took on board his Ships forty Pieces of Brass Cannon[,] 10 Brass field pieces[,] 4 Brass Morters; and 18 Brass Pallereros; and rendered unservicable above 80 Iron Cannon. He also took on board all their Shott and Amunition except 122 Barrels of Powder that were expended in springing of Mines, by which all their Fortifications and Forts were entirely demolished and the Harbour left open and defenceless, 10,000 p[iece]s [of eight] that were arrived and designed for paying the King of

Spain's Troops, at Porto Bello, the Admiral distributed among the Soldiers and Seamen of his Squadron, for their Encouragem[en]t.

On the 6 of December the Admiral was joined at Porto Bello by the *Sheerness* Capt[ain] Stapleton who had taken and brought with him two Vessells, laden with Amunition[,] Stores and Provisions designed for Carthagena.

During Admiral Vernon's stay at Porto Bello he sent a letter to the President of Panama, demanding the Releasment of the S[outh] S[ea] Company's Factors and Servants, who were confined in that City, in Consequence of which they were immediately escorted and delivered up to him at Porto Bello. And on the 14 the Admiral with his Squadron sailed from thence to Port Royal.

The [blank] of January 1739 War against Spain was proclaimed[39] in the Three Towns in this Island to the great joy of the Inhabitants in general who were now in hopes of obtaining ample Satisfaction for the many Insults and Injuries they had sustained from the Spaniards for some years past without the least restitution or redress.

And on the 15 Arrived his Majesty's Ships the *Greenwich*, with the Fire Ships, Bomb Vessels and Store Ships which were sent to join Admiral Vernon.

Capt[ain] Cudjo, the Chief of the Rebellious Negroes, who had lately submitted, upon hearing of the declaration of War against Spain, sent one of his principall men to the Governour for Instructions, how to dispose of his People, for the defence of the Island, in case of an Invasion; and to know in what manner He and they could otherwise be of Service at that juncture.

As a further proof of his fidelity and regard to the Treaty he had entered into, I think it necessary and proper to give the following remarkable Instances, which may seem as a lesson to some European Princes, who seem to regard their Engagements no longer than it suits with their own Interest and Conveniency.

About the same time Capt[ain] Cudjo discovered that some of his head men who were dissatisfied with the Treaty entered into Caballs with the Negroes in the Neighbouring Plantations and incited them to revolt [and] immediately seized upon the Ring leaders and sent them to the Governour, they were thereupon tried according to the Laws of the Country[,] two of them rec[eive]d Sentence of Death and two were ordered to be transported; but the Governour thought proper to shew Mercy, it being the first offence, and granted them a Pardon. Nevertheless Cudjo being of a different Opinion insisted upon his own Authority and that an Example should be made of them. Accordingly upon their being returned to him he hanged the two who were condemned to die, and sent back the other two to Town,

39. War broke out on October 9, 1739.

From the mid-1720s on, James Knight was a strong advocate for British intervention to prevent Spanish Guarda Costas from interfering with colonial shipping. Entitled *Commerce Thus Guarded Spain Insults No More; But Flys Dismay'd When British Thunders Roar,* this image, an engraving by J. Talman, shows a British warship during the War for Jenkins' Ear firing on a Spanish ship in protection of a small colonial coastal trading vessel. The Latin phrase under the caption comes from Virgil's *Georgics,* book 3, line 405: "When thou has such warders of kine and sheep, / Thou shalt dread not the thief in the night, nor the wolf's swift stealthy leap, / Nor." Talman added, "the Spanish outlaw who darts unforseen from his lurking place." It appeared in *The American Traveller; Being a New Historical Collection Carefully Compiled from Original Memoirs in Several Languages* (London, 1741), frontispiece.

in order to be transported; several of the Plantation Negroes who were in the Conspiracy, were likewise taken up and tried. Some were Executed and others Transported.

This procedure struck a Terror in the Negroes, of all denominations, especially those belonging to the Plantations, who became more tractable than they had been for many years; since they met with no Encouragement to defeat, being immediately taken up and sent to their respective Masters agreeable to the Treaty.

About the middle of February several Vessells were fitted out, and sailed under Convoy of the *Sheerness*, to Trade at Porto Bello, where they sold most of their Cargoes, and made very profitable Voyages. The Spaniards discovering a disposition to Cultivate a Commerce and indeed were in great want of all kind of Merchandize and the Harbour being now open and defenseless our Vessells went in and out with the same freedom they could do into any English Port.

On the 21 the *Greenwich* Captain Windham returned from a Cruize in which he had chased ashore and destroyed to Le[e]ward of St. Iago de Cuba, a Spanish Privateer, fitted out of that Port, and would have been very pernicious to our Trade had she not been timely cut off; she had taken an English Brigantine, which Capt[ain] Wyndham retook and brought into Port Royal.

The Admiral having received an Insulting letter from Don Blass de lero since the taking of Porto Bello, in which he tells him he hoped to have the Pleasure of meeting him before he leaves these Seas, was resolved to pay him a Visit. Accordingly he hoisted his flag, on board the *Strafford*, and sailed from Port Royal on the 25 of February with the *Princess Louisa*, *Winsor*[,] *Greenwich* and *Norwich*, all the Fire Ships Bombs and Tenders; and ordered the *Burford* to follow him as soon as she could be got ready[;] the *Falmouth* was sent to Convoy a fleet of Merchant Ships thro[ugh] the Windward Passage; and Commodore Brown with the rest of the Squadron, was left at Port Royal.

The 1st. of March he got sight of St. Martha and ordered the *Greenwich* to lay off that Port for intercepting any thing that might be coming there, and with the rest of the Squadron bore away with an easy sail for Carthagena. The 3d. at Noon he was joined by the *Falmouth*, and the Evening Anchored before Carthagena, in the Open Bay called Playa Grande. The 6th. He ordered in all the Bomb Vessells with the small Ships and tenders for covering and Assisting them and Bombarded the town till 9 in the morning. The Squadron received no damage by the firing from the Batteries and Fortifications, but the Shells fell into the Town with some success, particularly into the Principal Church, the Jesuits College, and the Custom House, beat down several Houses, and a Shell that fell into the South Bastion Silenced a Batterie of 10 Guns for a long time. The 9th. the Bombs and other Ships were drawn off, and on the 10th. in the morning the whole

Squadron, weighed and Sailed in a line of Battle, towards Boca Chica. The Spaniards fired at them from the three small Castles, without that Fortress, but none of their Shot reached them and leaving the *Windsor* and *Greenwich* to Cruiz off that Port the Admiral with the other Ships sailed for Porto Bello, to repair the damages the small craft had received. From thence he detached his Cruizers to Block up Chagre, and having refitted and Watered his Ships he put to Sea on the 22d. and by 10 at Night he Anchored before that Place, the Bomb Vessells which he sent in before him with the *Norwich* began to Bombard and Cannonade that evening and continued till Monday the 24th. when the Spaniards hung out a Flag of Truce from the Fort. The Admiral thereupon sent Capt[ain] Knowl[e]s[40] on Shore, who soon returned with the Governour and Articles of Capitulation were immediately agreed upon. Accordingly Capt[ain] Knowls was sent on shore with 5 Lieutennants and 120 Men to take possession of the Fort.

In the Fort and the Custom House were found 2890 Seroons, two Butts and 5 Hogsheads of Cocoa; 1240 Seroons 4 Butts 4 Hogsheads, and 12 Puncheons of Jesuits Bark and 327 Bales of Vigonia Wool, beside other Effects, the whole valued at £70,000.

In the River were two Guarda Coastas, which the Spaniards had Sunk, and by order of the Admiral, Carpenters were ordered to break up their Decks and entirely destroy them. The Custom House being cleared, was filled with Combustible matter, and burnt to the Ground[,] the Brass Cannon and Patereros being taken out of the Fort, and embarqued. Mines were sprung under the lower Bastion which entirely demolished it. Two mines were also Sprung to blow up the upper part of the Workes, and all the inner Buildings were set on fire.

On the 30th. Vice Admiral Vernon sailed from Shagre to Porto Bello, where he was joined by the *Burford*, and soon after he returned to Jamaica.

Upon the Declaration of War with Spain several Privateers were fitted out of this Island which met with good Success in taking Prizes some of Considerable Value; but as it will be tedious to enumerate them, I shall only take notice of the gallant behaviour of Capt[ain] Stuart in the *Revenge* Show of 8 Guns and 60 Men who on the 25 of May was attacked off of Carthagena by two Sloops fitted out on purpose by the Admiral of the Galleons and Commanded by some of his best officers, who had the choosing of 200 Men out of his Squadron. Capt[ain] Stuart fought them both for a Considerable time, and finding that he could manage them Singly, endeavoured to seperate them which he did by a Run[n]ing fight, having succeeded in that design. He then brought to and engaged one of them Com-

40. Sir Charles Knowles (c. 1704–1777), a successful naval officer, subsequently became rear admiral of the white and commander in chief at the Jamaica station in 1747 and was governor of Jamaica, 1752–55.

manded by Don Joseph Piz, and after a warm dispute, wherein the Captain and the Major part of the Spaniards were killed and wounded, the Vessell struck. It hap[pe]ned unfortunately that in boarding, Stuart's Anchor fast[e]ned to the Bow of the Prize so that he could not immediately get clear or prevent the other Sloop, which was commanded by Palanco, from boarding him upon coming up, and being over powered with fresh men having all his Men Killed, in both Engagements, except 29 most of them wounded. He was obliged to Surrender. The next morning two other English Privateers Commanded by Capt[ain] Bennett and Capt[ain] Thresar came in sight, but, the Spaniards were so reduced and dispirited in the late Action that they had no thoughts of making any resistance and run the two Sloops and the Snow ashore. Capt[ain] Bennett got off the Snow, which he delivered to Capt[ain] Stuart and his People, but burnt the two Spanish Sloops, in sight of Don Blass and his Squadron.

Admiral Vernon having received an Express from my Lord Tyrawley,[41] his Majesty's Ambassador at the Court of Lisbon[,] with Advice of the Spanish Squadron being sailed from Cadiz, as supposed to Carthagena, put to Sea the 16 of June with such Ships as could be got ready, and in 6 or 7 days arrived of St. Martha, where he Cruized sometime, but having no Account of them, or any other Spanish Vessells upon that Coast and his Ships' having received great damage in their Rig[g]ing, Masts and Sails, by bad Weather, He stretched over and Arrived at Port Royal the 21 of July.

In August the *Worcester* and *Falmouth* brought in a large Dutch Ship of 28 Guns, which they took to the Westward of Cuba. The Vice Roy of Mexico was on board, and escaped in a Sloop, but through hurry and mistake left behind him his Crown Septre, and Regalia together with Jewills money and other Effects to the value £100,000.

At this time the Squadron was in great distress for want of Naval Stores, insomuch that they lay inactive at Port Royal for the Space of three months and were not able to put to sea more than two or three Ships at a time, for the protection of the Trade, and even then with great difficulty.

But on the 5 of Sep[tembe]r the Store Ships from England which they stood in such great need of, arrived under Convoy of his Majestie's Ships the *Defiance* and *Tilbury*.

The Admiral upon receiving this Supply, refitted all the great Ships as well as Cruizers and Sailed on the first of October, in order to Cruise of the West end of Hispaniola, With hopes of meeting the Reinforcement he had advice of and to proceed immediately upon some Expedition, not having then had notice of the Arrival of the Spanish and French Squadrons or

---

41. Field Marshal James O'Hara, Second Baron Tyrawley and First Baron Kilmaine (1682–1774), was an Irish officer in the British Army. After serving as a junior officer in Spain and the Low Countries during the War of the Spanish Succession, he went on to become British ambassador to Lisbon, establishing a close relationship with King John V.

that the French had any intention of sending a Fleet to the Assistance of the Spaniards in America.

On the 19 he met with 8 Sail of Transports under Convoy of his Majesty's Sloop the *Wolf*, having on board Brigadier Blakeney[42] and 3000 land forces from North America, which he conducted into Port Royal.

Soon after his return he had advice of the Spanish Squadron consisting of 12 Sail of the line, Vizt. 1 of 80 Guns 4 of 70 Guns each and 7 of 60 Guns each under the Command of Don Roderigo De Torez were arrived at Porto Rico, and the Breast and Toulon Fleets consisting of 30 Ships of the line under the Command of the Marquis D' Antin, Mons[ieu]r Roch Alard and Chevalier Nesmond, at Martinico, That an Embargo was laid upon all Ships in the last mentioned Island, and great preperations made, as if they were immediately to go upon some important Expedition.

The Admiral afterwards had information from some intercepted letters in the Prizes brought in by Cruizers, that the Spanish Squadron arrived at Carthagena the 28 of October, having suffered greatly in the Voyage by bad Weather, in which they lost two Ships. That the Breast and Toulon Squadron were also arrived at Port Louis, And, had lost a great number of Men in the Voyage by Mortality, And that the Marques D'Antin was to join Admiral Torrez in order to make an Attempt on this Island.

Thus the Scene changed and Admiral Vernon who had hitherto been Successfull, and struck a Terror throughout America was in his turn pinned up between two Squadrons, each of which was Superior to him in Ships and numbers of Men; however, the Enemy were now Masters at Sea, the Troops from North America being Arrived the Inhabitants were more easy in regard to the Apprehensions of an Invasion, and every thing was put into the best posture of Defence, that could possibly be done in so short a time. A Fire Ship was posted between Fort Charles and Gun Cay, in order to be sunk in that narrow passage, in case the Enemy should Attempt to force an Entry into Port Royal: And the Squadron was drawn into a line to the N[orth] of Musquito point, To prevent the Enemy going up to Kingston, in case they should Succeed in the other respect. The Cruisers were sent out to gain Intelligence, and soon after the *Squirrel* Capt[ain] Warren[43] performed a most acceptable piece of Service by destroying the largest and only remaining Privateer belonging to St. Iago de Cuba Commanded by a French man whose name was Valladon and had 130 Men on board. Capt[ain] Warren found him behind a Rock, cuting a Bow Sprit, and the Weather being very Favourable Anchored close to him. He defended himself from his Sloop till the Capt[ain] could clap a Spring on his Cables and

42. Brigadier General William Blakeney, First Baron Blakeney (c. 1672–1761), was an Irish soldier in command of military forces at Cartagena.

43. Peter Warren (1703–1752) was an experienced naval officer who served in North America in 1735–41 and the West Indies, 1742–45. He was promoted to vice admiral in 1747.

bring his Ship to bear on him; and then landed and kept firing from the Rocks, but Capt[ain] Warren's L[ieutenan]t and 21 Men boarded her, and the fire from the Ship and Sloop soon drove them up the Country. One of our Sailors observing a dead Spaniard lying upon an English [sailor?] went to remove him, and discovered some letters wrapped up in them, which contained an Authentick Duplicate of the Instructions, to the Marques D'Antin to Assist Admiral de Torez in making an Attempt on Jamaica, w[i]th other papers of importance, which were transmitted to his Grace the Duke of New Castle, one of his Majesty's Principal Secretarys of State.

This was afterwards confirmed by divers letters found on board a Spanish Prize, which was carried into new port and Condemned—That the French Squadrons intended to join the Spaniards in order to make an Attempt upon Admiral Vernon and the Island of Jamaica, before the Arrival of S[i]r Chalonar Ogle; But that the Execution of the design was retarded by the tediousness of Mons[ieu]r Roch Alard's Voyage who was 101 days in his passage, by the Sickness and mortallity of the men on board both Squadrons; and by several other incidents, till S[i]r Chalonars Arrival in those Seas, rendered that Scheme impracticable. These letters said further that the Scheme was well and would in all probability have been successfully Executed, if Providence had not favoured the English.

Those Circumstances were likewise confirmed by the *Publick talk at the Havanna*, which wee have had an Account of from some Gentlemen who were Prisoners there, and are since returned. For it was there said and even owned by some of their officers of Distinction, that if theirs and the French Squadrons had met with a safe and speedy Voyage, They were to have joined in Attempting the destruction of Admiral Vernon's Squadron and the Conquest of Jamaica. And in case of Success, by Agreement between the two Monarchs, this Island was to be given up to the Spaniards, and They were to have surrendered up to the French, the whole Island of Hispaniola.

Nor can the truth of these particulars be doubted, at least the junction of the two Squadrons, in order to make an Attempt on this Island, since his Majesty in the late Declaration of Warr against France among other Reasons [as]signed [the] following Viz. The French King[44] sending in the year 1741 a strong Squadron into the American Seas, in order to prevent us from prosecuting the just War, wee were carrying on against Spain in those parts. And wee have the most Authentick proof that an order was given to the Commander of the French Squadron, not only to act in a Hostile manner against our Ships either jointly with the Spaniards on Seperately; but even to concert measures with our Enemies, for attacking one of our

44. Louis XV (1710–1774) ascended to throne at age five on the death of his grandfather Louis XIV, September 1, 1715.

principal Dominions in America; a Duplicate of that Order dated the 7 of
October 1740, having fallen into the hands of the Commander in Chief
of our Squadron in the West Indies.

The 9th. of January S[i]r Chalonar Ogle Rear Admiral of the Blue with
the Squadron under his Command, which consisted of 8 Ships of 80 Guns
each, 3 of 70, 9 of 60 and 1 of 50, besides Frigots, Bombs and Fire Ships,
arrived at Port Royal, with the Transports having on board a Considerable
number of Land Forces the Command of which devolved on Major General Wentworth,[45] upon the demise of the L[ieutenan]t Cathcart[46] who
was appointed General & Commander in Chief and died at Dominica the
20th. of December.

When the Fleet were going down, off the West end of Hispaniola, they
saw 4 large Ships in the Offin, upon which S[i]r Chalonar made the Signal
for the *Prince Frederick, Orford, Lyon, Weymouth* and *Augusta* to give Chase;
At four in the Afternoon the 4 Ships hoisted French Colours, but it was 10
at night before our Ships came up with them. The *Pr[ince] Frederick* being
headmost hailed one of the Ships, first in English then in French. But they
not returning any Answer, Lord Aubrey[47] who Commanded her, Ordered
a Shot to be fired at them, and soon after another. At the Second Shot,
the French Ship in an instant opened all her Ports, and fired a Broadside,
which the *Prince Frederick* immediately returned, soon after the *Orford* and
the other three Ships came in, and Engaged the other French Ships without any Ceremony. The *Weymouth* was the last Ship that came up, and after
firing two or three Broadsides, went on board of the *Pr[ince] Frederick* and
advised Lord Aubrey to make the Signal to desist, being sure as he said,
that they were French Ships, which was accordingly done, but the French
continueing to Fire, they renewed the fight for half an hour longer, when
they discontinued firing on both sides. As soon as it was day, the Lord Aubrey sent an Officer on board the Commandant to know certainly who
they were, and the Reason they did not answer, when they were hailed.
The French Commodore replied they did Answer, and that He would Report their usage of them to the King his Master, and let him decide it, so
they parted.

Admiral Vernon having received so Considerable a Reinforcement
which put him upon equal Tunes with the Enemy, even though joined by
both the French Squadrons; and not knowing what the French might un-

45. Lieutenant-General Thomas Wentworth (c. 1693–1747) was a British Army commander who became commander of the land troops in the amphibious expedition against
Cartagena following the deaths of the original commander, Charles, Lord Cathcart, and his
second-in-command, General Alexander Spotswood.

46. Charles Cathcart, Eighth Lord Cathcart (1686–1740).

47. Lord Aubrey Beauclerk (c. 1710–1741) was an officer of the Royal Navy who was killed
at the Battle of Cartagena.

dertake, in Case he should leave Jamaica, whilst they lay so near Port Louis resolved to pay a Visit to that Place before he went upon any Expedition against the Spaniards.

Accordingly on the 22d. 24 & 26 of January [1742] the whole Fleet sailed out of Port Royal Harbour directing their Course to Port Louis, the line of Battle being appointed as follows[:][48]

48. Knight here left two blank pages, evidently never going back to conclude his account of Vernon's exploits.

The Natural, Moral, and Political History of Jamaica and The Territories thereon depending

From the Earliest account of time to the Year 1742.

By J[ames] K[night]

Vol[ume] the 2.

Industry has its first foundation in Liberty; they who either are Slaves, or who believe their Freedoms precarious, can neither Succeed in Trade, or Meliorate a Country.

Davenant.[1]

London

Printed for [blank]

---

1. Charles Davenant, *Discourses on the Public Revenues, and on the Trade of England Which More Immediately Treat of the Foreign Traffick of This Kingdom* (London, 1698), part 2:152.

Part the 4th

Contains

A Geographical Description of the Island with its Mountains, Caves, Mines, Plains, Precincts, Towns, Harbours, Bays, Fortifications, and Buildings; together with the Territories thereon depending.

Part the 5th.

Of the Climate, Air, Seasons, Winds, Weather, Currents, Waters, and Rivers; as also of the Diseases and Distempers, most frequent in the West Indies.

Part the 6th.

Of the Inhabitants; Masters, Christian Servants, and Negroes, their Number, Strength, and Manner of living: as Also an Account of the Negroes, who were many years in Rebellion and Set[t]led in the Mountains, together with the Treaty made with them in 1738, upon which They Submitted, and became Free Subjects of Great Britain.

Part the 7th

Of the Government of the Island Civil and Military; of the Laws, Courts of Justice, Publick Offices, Revenues, and Church Affairs, with some Observations thereupon.

Part the 8th.

Of the Soil and Productions, the manner of Planting Sugar Canes, and making of Sugar; as also Rum, Indigo, Ginger, Piemento, Cotton, Coffee, and other Commodities that are, or may be produced in Jamaica.

Part the 9th.

Of Beasts, Birds, Fishes, and other Animals and Insects in Jamaica.

Part the 10th.

Of the Situation and Natural Advantages of Jamaica, and the Trade thereof to and from Great Britain, Ireland, Africa, the Plantations in North America, and other Parts, with some Observations and Proposals, for their Encouragement, Improvement and Security.

Part the 4th.

A Geographical Description of the Island, with its Mountains, Mines, Plains, Towns, Precincts, Harbours, Bays, Fortifications and Buildings, together with the Territories thereone depending.

Jamaica is Situate between the Tropicks, and lies near East and West; the middle of the Island is in 18 degrees 28 minutes Northern Latitude, and the difference of Longitude from the Meridian of London, is 78 degrees 45 min. Westward. It is of an Oval form being broadest in the middle, and decreasing towards each end, and has a Continued Ridge of lofty Mountains, which run through the middle of it, almost from the one end to the other; from whence flow Numberless Springs, and Rivulets which form themselves into many larger Streams, or Rivers, and run into the Sea.

According to the Survey, which was taken in the Government of S[i]r. Thomas Lynch, by Colo[nel John] Vassell and Mr. [Mordecai] Rogers,[1] who were sent over by King Charles the Second for that purpose, it is 180 miles in length from Point Morant to Point Nigrill; But according to the Road and Common Computation it is above 80 leagues or 240 Miles; the Breadth is more Easily Ascertained and allowed to be, from Portland Point on the south side, to Rio Nova on the North side which is the middle, and the broadest part, Sixty two Miles; from Salt pond Point in St. Thomas's on the South of the East end, to Port Antonio now called Titchfeild Harbour, on the North of the East end[,] twenty Six Miles; and from Cape Bonetta on the South of the West end to Cove Harbour on the N[orth] of the West end[,] twenty two Miles and a half. And Contains 7 million 450,000 Acres of Land; whereof it is imagined, that one half is good Plantable land, one Eighth part Savanna or Pasturage, and three Eight[h]s inaccessable Mountains, barron; Rocky, and unplantable.

At some leagues distance, this Island makes a very Solemn and surprising Figure, the Mountains, being preposterously modelled and appearing

---

1. Colonel John Vassal (c. 1625–1684?), a large landholder, and Mordecai Rogers were the two surveyors the Jamaica Council designated in the summer of 1672 to work with other surveyors to draw "a most exact, large, and particular map of the whole island, perfectly describing all the mountains, rivers, valleys, settlements, creeks, and harbours," a project that seems not to have been completed until 1674. See Jamaica Council Minutes, July 2, 1672, in *Calendar of State Papers Colonial, America and West Indies*, vol. 7, *1669–1674*, ed. W. Noel Sainsbury (London, 1889), 382–83.

Painted by George Robertson and engraved and published by John Boydell in London, this 1778 *View . . . of the River Cobre near Spanish Town* provides a glimpse of the abundant fresh-water resources and the mountainous character of Jamaica's physical geography stressed by Knight in his chorography.

one above Another to a Stupendous height, with such strange Irregularity and Seeming Confusion, as if they had been thrown together by Chance, and not formed by that Great Architect, who created the rest of the World.

A Range of Clouds commonly hang about the Summit of those Mountains, the heads or tops of which sometimes appear above the Clouds; and at other times they are Covered and Seldom Clearly Seen, but when the Northerly or Land Winds blow; for in these Climates between or near the Tropicks, where the Trade Winds blow great part of the Year, the Clouds[2] which in the Vallies fly Swift over our heads, yet seem to gather, and hang about all high Land, without any Visible motion or alteration.

On a near Approach these Mountains appear more Strange, and Romantick, some of them being Covered with Woods, others bare with naked Rocks and Solid Stone up to the very Summit; Some are naked above and below, but a Wilderness about the middle, that seems stuck fast, and not growing from the sides of such Amazing Steepness: the tallest Trees ap-

---

2. See Dampier. Vol. 1. P. 283. —*Author.* Captain William Dampier, *A New Voyage Round the World* (London, 1697), 1:283. —*Ed.*

Painted by George Robertson and engraved and published by John Boydell in London, this 1778 *View . . . of Roaring River Estate Belonging to William Beckford near Savannah la Mer* shows what Knight would have regarded as an improved rural Jamaican landscape filled with a planter residence and associated buildings and a host of enslaved people occupied with various chores.

pearing as if their Arms were fastened to the Roots of their fellows above, and so suspended like a mighty Wood hanging in the Air! It is likewise Surprising to see large Timber Trees that grow amongst Piles of Solid Massy Stone, without the least appearance of Earth, yet always look flourishing full of Verdant leaves, Blossoms, or Wild Fruit.

But the Plantations in the Low Lands, which are of different Verdure, intermixed with Woods, Savannas, and other Open Lands; together with the Settlements on the Hills, Sides, and tops of some of those Mountains, make a more Agre[e]able Prospect, and the whole appears delightfull, as well as Astonishing.

Some of the Mountains are of a Regular Easy Ascent, but others inaccessible; and in general they are very Steep, so that the Inhabitants are obliged, in many parts, to cut out Roads on their Sides, which are wide enough for two Horsemen to pass abreast: on the one hand the Stupendous tops of the Mountains and dreadfull Rocks, appear hanging with impending horrour over the head of the Traveller and on the other mighty Chasms, and Vast Precipices, that are Terrible to behold, with many Cracks, and Gullies both below and above which have been Rent by the Great Earthquake, or worn by time, and the fall of Waters.

Notwithstanding the badness of the Roads, and the difficult carriage, there are many Sugar-Works beside other Plantations, for raising Ginger, Coffee, Ground Provisions, and Garden Stuff, upon Severall of those Mountains; although some of them are so Steep that they are allmost Perpendicular, so that it is Wonderfull, how the Negroes, and others, can go up and down, and much more how they are able to Work and carry Bur-

John Rome's 1767 sketch of Salt Pond Pen, a Clarendon Parish property owned
by Henry Dawkins, depicts a common type of rural establishment in the counties
surrounding Spanish Town. Originally a part of the Dawkins Family Papers at the
National Library of Jamaica, this image can no longer be found in that collection. It is here reproduced from B. W. Higman, *Jamaica Surveyed: Plantation Maps
and Plans of the Eighteenth and Nineteenth Century* (Kingston, Jamaica, 1988), 220.
(B. W. Higman)

thens. Many of them are Covered with a Rich mould, Especially the Vallies and bottoms between, and as they are often shaded, and defended from
the Violent Effects of the Sun, by the Clouds which Commonly hang over,
or near them, as well as Refreshed with Showers of Rain, even when other
parts of the Island are dry and parched up, the Air is more Temperate,
and Agreeable, than in the Low Lands. Nor doth the Sun appear in many
Places before 8 or 9 in the Morning, and disappears at three or four in the
Afternoon; and in the interval it is often clouded, and obscured; so that it
is seldom seen there, above 8 or 9 hours in the day, and in some Parts less,
all the Year. By those means the Soil is fertile, and easily produces not only
Garden Stuffs, but several sorts of European, as well as all kind of American Fruits; and with Art and Care, the Inhabitants might raise great Quantities of other Plants, Grain, Fruits and Flowers which they have not at
present, their thoughts being turned on other Improvements which Yield
greater profit They disregard pleasure and Amusement.

Whoever Considers the Climate, the different Soils, the heat in the Low
Lands, and those Parts, which are near the Sea; with the gradual increasing Temperature, and Coolness of the Air, in those Mountains, according
as they approach towards the higher Regions; must be Convinced of their
Pleasantness; and that there is a Continual Spring, in those districts: for
the Ground is always adorned with a Beautifull Verdure, the Trees and

Plants with Leaves[,] Blossoms and Fruit; so that those Persons, who In-
habit them, are fully Compensated for the difficulties and other Inconveniences they meet with in the Ascent, by the Fertility of the Soil, and by
enjoying a most agreeable Season and generally a Perfect State of Health
all the Year round[,] the Air being always fresh and Cool, even at Noon
day, and the Nights Refrigerated by the land Wind or Breezes, often render them, (especially in the Rainy Season, and about the Winter Solstice)
so cold as to require warm Cloathing or Covering; for it is a Fact, which
I would not Venture to relate, had I not seen several Affidavits, which were
made and laid before the Assembly, that on some of the highest of those
Mountains, it is so very cold, that Several able Negro-men, who went out
upon Parties in pursuit of the Rebellious Negroes, were so benumbed, that
they died with Cold.

The Inhabitants of the Low Lands, when they are indisposed, or require
a change of Air, find great benefit by removing into those Mountains, or
the Country near them; where the Climate is undoubtedly more Suitable,
and Agreeable to an European Constitution, than in any other part of the
Island. And Indeed it is Strange, they are not more frequented and used,
than they are on those Occasions, considering how beneficiall they have
been by long Experience found to Sickly, and Infirm, Persons of all Ages,
and Conditions.

In several of those Mountains, (particularly in one at the East end of Leguinea) are large Caves wherein are a great Number of Sculls and bones,
of the Native Indians, known to be so by the flatness of the back part of
the head; from whence some Persons imagine, they Reposited their dead
there, though others more probably Conjecture, (and indeed there is such
a Tradition in the Island) that those unhappy People fled thither to avoid
the Persecution and Cruelties of the Spaniards, and were Starved to Death,
or made away with themselves.

Besides the Richness of the Surface which I have already described,
many Persons are of Opinion, that there are Gold and Mines in the bowells of those Mountains, from the Steams which arise from some humid
Places, the tast[e] Waters, and the grounds being Covered with a heavy
Vitriolick Substance &c.

The first English Set[t]tlers were informed by one Juan D'Acosta, a Portoguese, who resided on the Island when the Spaniards were in Possession
of it, that they discovered a Silver Mine, in the Mountains West of Cagway, now called Port Royal; but would not open it, fearing it might Occasion the English, and Dutch Privateers, to Visit them oft[e]ner in hopes of
Richer plunder, than they had before met with.

Copper we are well assured of, not only from the Information of the
Spaniards, that the Bells which hung in the great Church at St. Iago de la
Vega, were cast of the Copper of this Island, But large Quantities of this
Ore have lately been dug up out of those Mountains in Leguinea, some of

which have been sent to London and Smelted; and though the Ore produced only 1/17 metal, yet upon the Assay it proved very fine Copper. It is
also Certain, that there are Mines of Lead, and Coals, as well as Copper,
from the several Indications I have mentioned and other Circumstances
and it is likewise probable if not Certain that there are Mines of Gold, and
Silver in this Island, as well as on Cuba, and the Main Continent, from the
severall Circumstances mentioned as well as the Testimony of the Spanish
Writings I have quoted.[3]

And though a late Project miscarried through the unskillfull management or Sinister designs of those, who were intrusted with the Execution
of it, Yet I am of opinion, that such an Enterprise might be undertaken
upon very Rational Grounds either by the Publick or a Body Corporate, if
it were prosecuted by means Suitable to so great a Design. And one would
imagine, that the Cheap labour of Negroes, plenty of Wood, and many
other Advantages, would greatly encourage such an undertaking.

The South East end of the Island is a low flat Land for 10 or 11 Miles
from the Sea to the foot of the Mountains; The North East, and most part
of the North side, is Hilly and Mountainous, and not more than two or
three Miles that is level, or gradual[l]y Rising, from the Sea to the Mountains in any Part, except in St. Ann's Precinct, where is a Plain or gradual
rising at least 25 Miles E[ast] and W[est], though the Breadth N[orth]
and S[outh] does not Exceed three Miles. The West end is also Hilly and
Mountainous; and hath very little level land, excepting the Vallies and Bottoms between them. But on the south side of the Island, the land in most
Parts rises gradually and imperceptibly 7 or 8 Miles from the Sea to the
Mountains, and in some Places 20 Miles or more, particularly St. Katherine's Precinct, which is almost all level, as well as Vere, and part of Clarendon; and from the long Mountain at the East end of Liguines, to Cape
Bonetta, Commonly called Caboritta, which is upwards of 120 Miles East
and West, is a plain level Country, and a good Coach Road; excepting over
the Devil's Race in St. Elizabeths, which is about two Miles in length. But
I am Credibly informed, there is another Road over One Eye-Savanna,
which may, and is intended to, be made passable for Carriages.

The Mountains are commonly Supplied with Rains before the Low
Lands, for they often begin there three or four Weeks, before they come to
fall in the Plain Country, or near the Sea Shore, particularly in Leguinea,
St. Katherine's, St. Dorothy's, and Vere. Sometimes Black Clouds, with
other Presages of Rain, have appeared for many Days over those Mountains; and the Clouds have seemed by their motion, to draw towards the
Sea, but have been checked in their Course and either returned towards
the Mountains again or have spent themselves, before they came from
thence, to the great disappointment and Grief of the Planters in the flat

3. See preface, note 2, above.

Country whose Product and Cattle have perished for want of Moisture, and Food. Nay the Tournadoes from the Sea, which often bring Rain, have sometimes died away, and the Clouds dissipated, before they reached the Shore, so that they Yielded no Rain to the low parched Lands.

The want of Seasonable Showers, is the greatest Inconvenience, that attends this part of the Island; for in some Years their Crops not only prove short by those Means, but their Plants are destroyed, which puts those Plantations backwards, lays the Owners under great difficulties, distresses some, and ruins others. This misfortune is the more to be lamented, because it happens to the finest and best part of the Country in all Respects; for there is not a more Beautifull Tract of Ground, in all America, nor a better Soil than Leguinea; and all St. Katherine's, great part of St. Dorothy's, and all Vere Precincts, which contain many thousand Acres, are fine levell lands or gradual[l]y rising grounds, of different Soils, productive of many Valuable Commodities, and in a pleasant healthy Situation. But the North side, and the West end of the Island, where the Mountains are bordering on or near the Sea, are Supplied with Rain almost all the Year; for they are seldom dry in those Parts, though in the Wet Seasons, the Rains are more impetuous, and Violent, which is their Inconvenience.

As to the Vallies in the Country and the bottoms between the Mountains, they are not subject to such droughts, as the Low Lands or the plain Country; but are well supplied with Rain, and Seasonable Showers; which makes those lands fertile, and very Valuable.

The Surface of the Earth seems to be different here from what it is in England; the Vallies being very level, without any Hillocks, or rising ground; and most of the Mountains, as I observed, are Steep, furrowed with Gullies, and few have any Table or flat land on the tops of them; excepting at Sixteen Mile-Walk, Clarendon, and St. Elizabeth's Precincts.

The Soil is of Various and different Coloured Earths, on the Surface, as well as several Strata of divers Sorts. The Soil which is most esteemed, is a blackish mould, mixt with Sand; which makes it porous, and very Serviceable, especially for Sugar. There is also a Reddish Earth, which produces Sugar, though Coarse, and of a Foxy Colour; but does much better for Ginger, and Provisions. And in many parts, particularly in St. Katherine's there is a grey Sandy Earth, which makes very good Bricks; also a sort of Clay, proper for making Jars, and other Earthen Vessels, of which great Quantities are made Yearly, and Vended amongst the poor People, and Negroes.

The Savannas are large Plains 9 or 10 Miles in length, and some more; intermixed with Hills, and Woods, and were formerly Fields where the Native Indians planted their Maiz[e] or Corn, and other Vegetables which, when the Spaniards became Masters of the Island, they Converted to Pastures, for feeding Cattle and Horses; and their Successors Continue them to the same use. For being so many Years without Tillage, or Culture, they are become barren, and cannot now be Cultivated. However they produce great plenty of Grass, Appear pleasant, and Green after Rains, and feed Vast numbers of Sheep and Cattle. Most of them are on the South side of the Island; and from thence it is imagined, the Native Indians had their principal Settlements in this Part of the Country. It is certainly more pleasant and levell than the North side; nor is it so Subject to heavy Rains and Violent Gusts of Wind, which probably was another Reason, that induced the Spaniards, as well as their Predecessors, to remove from the North side, where they were first set[t]led, to the South.

The Roads, in this Island, are in generall very good, that is in the Low Lands, or level part of the Country. But I cannot say any thing in favour of those in the Mountains, having already given a just tho[ugh] a terrible Description of them; nor of those from the South to the North side of the Island, which are over high Ridges, through narrow and difficult passes, and over divers[e] Rivers; so that it is dangerous Travelling those Parts in the Rainy Seasons, when the Roads are Slippery, and broken, and the Rivers high, and Rapid. But I am Credibly informed that the Road through Sixteen Mile-Walk, to St. Ann's, and St. Mary's, is lately very much improved, and made tolerable. The Roads from Morant to Cow Bay, are also very Indifferent, the one being over Mountains and Rocky Hills, and the other by the White Horses so very Terrible, that few choose to go that Way. The White Horses are two high-peaked White Cliffs, which are impending on one side of the Road, for above a mile, and the other side a sandy Bay, where the Surge of the Sea commonly breaks, and makes that Passage dangerous, when there is a strong Sea Breez[e].

By an Act of the Assembly the High ways (See an Act for the Highways, *Laws of Jamaica*, fo[lio] Ed[ition] P. 6)[4] are directed to be Sixty feet wide, in Standing Wood; Forty feet, where the Wood is only on one side, and twenty feet in open Ground. And four Surveyors are appointed to be chosen Annually, in every Precinct, by the Freeholders, with Ample Powers, for amending and keeping clear, the common high ways, and known broad Paths, within their Respective Districts; and a Penalty inflicted on them for every omission or Neglect.

The Fences on the Road sides of inclosed Grounds, are either Limes, or Penguins[?]; the former are very Beautifull, especially when they are cut as we do Quick set in England. In some places are high Trees growing in the Fences, which make those Roads shady, and pleasant; and it would be advantagious, in other Respects, were the sides of all the Roads, and Pastures, planted with Trees (which grow much sooner here than in Europe) at a proper distance; as they would undoubtedly draw Rain, and make the Lands thereabout, more fruitfull. But however usefull and Convenient,

4. An Act for the Highways, 1681, in *Acts of Assembly, Passed in the Island of Jamaica; from 1681 to 1737, Inclusive* (London, 1738), 6–7.

things of that kind would be, the People in most parts of America, as well as in this Island, are too backward not only in that Instance but in other matters that are Apparently for their own good and Service.

This Island is divided into Nineteen Parishes or Precincts vizt.

On the South Side

St. Thomas in the East; St. David's commonly Yallahs; St. Andrew's or Leguinea; Kingston; Port Royal, St. Katherine's; St. John's or Guanaboa; St. Thomas in the Vale; St. Dorothy's; Vere; Clarendon; St. Elizabeth's; and Westmoreland, being thirteen Parishes or Precincts.

And, on the North side,

Hanover, situated at the N[orth] W[est] end of the Island; St. James; St. Ann's; St. Mary's; St. George's; and Portland at the N[orth] East end; being Six Parishes or Precincts. So that the whole Island is at this time divided into 19 Parishes, or Precincts; and probably some of them will be subdivided, as others have already been, when they become more Populous, and better Set[t]led, being at present of too large an Extent.

St. Thomas in the East, presents it self first to our View and was the first New Settlement made by the English, after the Conquest of the Island; for in 1656, Collo[nel] Stokes, L[ieutenant] Governour of Nevis whose Descendants still remain in the Parish came down with 1400 hundred People of all Sorts, and Set[t]led there; so that in a short space of time, it made a better Figure than any other part of the Island, except Leguinea; and for many Years could raise one thousand able men fit for Service. The great Earthquake in 1692, which laid their Houses and Plantations in Ruins, and the Invasion by the French the Year following, was the destruction of this part of the Country; occasioned many to remove and discouraged others from set[t]ling there again, because it is open exposed to every Invader, and particularly to their Neighbours, the French at Petit Guavis, and Leogane on Hispaniola, who are within twenty four hours sail of this part of the Island. But after the Peace of Utrecht many Persons turned their thoughts that way, and raised several fine Sugar Works, Especially near Plantain Gardon River, which is about seven Miles from Port Morant and is as fine a Valley, and as fertile a Soil as any in America. And upon the Encouragement given by an Act of the Assembly in 1736,[5] many parcells of land were Patented, and divers Settlements made thereon, near Manchineal Harbour, where is a Vast tract of uncultivated levell land proper for Sugar, Indigo, Cocoa, Ginger and other Commodities, and a pleasant healthy Situation; in Clearing of those lands appeared the Ruins of Several old Spanish Plantations, many Cocoa Trees, and divers Sorts of Fruit Trees were found

---

5. An Act for the Better Settling and Securing the Island, and Vesting Several Parcels of Land in the Crown; and for Building of Barracks, and Fitting out Parties in Reducing the Rebellious Negroes; and the Cutting of Roads, 1735, in ibid., 295.

bearing, though they have been neglected, and not Cultivated, since the Conquest of the Island in 1655, if not before.

Manchineal Harbour is Situate at the East end of the Island; and has two fine Rivers, which run into it, 20 or 25 Sail of Ships may ride there Conveniently in all weathers, though none above two hundred tons can enter by reason of a Bar, which lays at its Mouth, or entrance. The Outlet is also bad by reason of a great Swell from the Eastward Occas[ione]d by the Sea Breezes, so that in Case the land Winds which carry ships out should fail, they are thrown on a Steep Rocky Shore.

Port Morant is Situated near the S[outh] E[ast] end of the Island. The Entrance is narrow, and difficult by reason of two Riefs which spits from each side of the Harbour and makes the passage not 1/4 of a mile broad. But between them is 5 & 6 fat[homs] Water, and within is good Anchorage for 50 or 60 Ships of Burthen beside small Craft in soft Ousy ground, where they may Ride Securely in all Weathers, tho[ugh] mostly exposed to the Wind at S[outh] which throws in a great swell from the Sea. This Harbour & Port Antonio are most proper for the Security of the Men of War in the Hurricane Season. Here was formerly a small Town and a Fort, which were destroyed by the Earthquake in 1692 and by the French in 1693 and have not been rebuilt since, only a few Store houses for the reception of the Planters' Goods; though a Fortification there would be very usefull in time of War, Because Single Ships and Coasters might run, in and be protected from an Enemy. There are at this time 44 Sugar Works, beside many other Settlements, so that it has a fair prospect of being more Populous, and better Set[t]led, than it ever has been, being Capable of very great improvements.

St. David's, commonly called Yallahs, which was the name the Indians gave it, is next to St. Thomas in the East; and is about 20 Miles from Port Royal; and the same distance from Kingston. The Several settlements in this Precinct, were also destroyed by the French in 1693; and as it is likewise exposed to an Enemy, the long War with France,[6] and the Seasons failing here since that time, have hitherto disco[u]raged People from resettling this part of the Island. So that there are not more than 7 or 8 sugar Works; though there are several other settlements, for raising Cotton, ground provisions, and Cattle. It was once famous for Indigo; and great Quantities were made Here formerly, the Soil being very proper for it, but this part of the Country is now become too dry, that commodity requiring a great deal of moisture or very good Seasons.

St. Andrew's commonly called Leguinea, or Ligonia (which was the name the Spaniards gave it, from a Town in old Spain) is next to St. Davids, only divided by a long narrow tract of land, which is within the Parish of Port Royal. The Spaniards were set[t]led in this Part of the Country and

6. War of the League of Augsburg (1689–98).

had two Sugar Works, now called and known by the name of Waterhouse, and Clark's Plantations. The Pleasant Situation, and the goodness of the Soil, invited their more Industrious Successors, to make it their Principal Settlement; and in 1656 Collo[nel] Doyley seated Collo[nel] Carter's, and Collo[nel] Holdip's Regiments there, and divided lands among the Officers and Soldiers; many of whom set[t]led and remained there, after they were disbanded; so that they could for a long time after raise 1500 men in this Parish only. But it is very much declined, and has lost great part of its Strength and former luster, by the Rich men buying up the Small Plantations, which lay contiguous, and by the Seasons having failed them of late Years.

This Compact Precinct is in the shape of a Bow or an Amphitheatre, crowded on the back or Northern part with lofty Mountains. That which is called the Long Mountain, extends itself Easterly to the Sea, where a Ridge of Rocks, which lie along the Shore, form so narrow a passage for a quarter of a mile, that two Horsemen cannot pass abreast. The Entrance is Fortified with a line of Guns, a Breast work, and Foot bank, with a very deep and broad Ditch; and a draw-bridge, which being drawn up cuts of[f] all Communication by Land between the Eastern parts of the Island and this Precinct of Leguinea. From hence it appears that this part of the Country is Fortified by Nature; and with a little Art and Expence, may be made so strong that 3 or 400 men will be able to defend it against 10000; the Shore for several miles to the Eastward being Rocky and Sandy, and so great a Swell or Surge from the Sea, making it impracticable to land Cannon, and even difficult to disembarque men without great danger. A little W[est] of this line is a pleasant River, which runs into Kingston Harbour and is Esteemed excellent Water. At the other end of Leguinea Westward, the Mountains run within a mile of the Harbour, which with a River that arises out of them, and likewise runs into the Harbour called the Ferry River (from a Ferry boat being formerly kept there; but now there is a bridge built over it) separates this Parish from St. Katherine's. The front of this Amphitheatre, or Bow, is the Harbour of Kingston; from whence the land rises imperceptibly to the Foot of the Mountains. On the Northmost Part, in the Mountains is Wag Water, where are 3 or 4 Sugar Works, and some Ginger Plantations. The only passage in this part of the Country, to the North side is through this place, and the Road so narrow and difficult, that 100 Men may easily defend it.

In this Parish are still 34 Sugar-works, including those at Wag Water, and many other fine settlements; some of which are in the Mountains, where they chiefly raise Ginger, Coffee, Cocoa, ground Provisions, Garden Stuff of all sorts, and some English fruits.

From the Middle of those Mountains is one of the most Beautifull Landscapes in the World; the Sugar Works in the Low Lands, with the Planters Houses and other buildings, together with the Negro-houses to the num-

This *View of Port Royal and Kingston Harbors,* reproduced from Long, *History of Jamaica,* 2: opposite p. 201, presents a view from the sea of Jamaica's largest harbor and urban center and the developed countryside to the north, east, and west of it.

ber of 70 or 80, or more to each Plantation laid out in Streets, make those Plantations appear like so many Villages; and the Cane pieces, which are of different greens, according to their age or Standing, are not unlike so many Meadows or Gardens, the lime-fences between them being cut like the quick set hedges in England, and green all the Year. From thence you have also a view of many Settlements and some Sugar-works, on the sides of the Mountains upon each hand and of the Towns of Kingston, Port Royal, Passage Fort, part of St. Katherine's, and St. Dorothy's, below with the Ocean beyond all, where Ships and other Vessells daily coming in or going out, add greatly to the Beauty of the Prospect.

In the Center of this Parish (which is in length 18 miles E[ast] and W[est] and seven from the Harbour to the foot of the Mountains) is Situated a pleasant little Village, called Half way Tree; Containing the Parochial Church, Court-House, and about Twenty Houses. Here the Quarter Sessions of the Peace, and the Court of common Pleas, are held; and formerly there was a Free School, which was Endowed by a Subscription of the Gentlemen of the Parish, who Subjected Their Estates for the Payment of what They Subscribed, and provided with a good House, for the purpose, the Gift of S[i]r Nich[ola]s Laws; but the House was accidentally burnt in 1704 and has not Since been Rebuilt.

Kingston. This Town was formerly in the Precinct of St. Andrew's, or Leguinea; the foundation was laid in 1692, soon after the dreadfull Earthquake which destroyed Port Royall, and discouraged many of the Inhabitants from Set[t]ling again, in a Place so liable to such disasters. In 1693 it was by an Act of the Assembly made a distinct Parish, impowered to hold a Court of common Pleas, and Quarter Sessions of the Peace; and to send three Members to the Assembly.[7] But, the Trading and Seafaring People being divided, and great part of them set[t]ling again at Port Royal, it made no Considerable Figure, till that Town was burnt down in 1702; when the Assembly by another Act, Obliged the Secretary, Receiver General, Naval Officer, and Collector to hold their Offices here. It has since increased very Considerably; and is now the chief Port of Trade, seldom without twenty, or Thirty, and Sometimes Sixty, or Seventy Ships & other Vessells. The Parish is bounded to the S[outh] W[est] by the lands of S[i]r William Beeston, now [belonging to] Mr. Charles Long,[8] North, by the lands of Mr. Sam[ue]ll Bradshaw, and Continued from a Calabash Tree on the North East corner in a straight line to the foot of the long Mountain, and from thence, till it meets with the bounds of Port Royal Parish. The Plan of the Town is three fourths of a mile in length N[orth] and S[outh] and half a mile in breadth, E[ast] and W[est] The Streets are broad and very Regularly laid out, with a large Parade in the Center: The South Part is built from one end to the other as high as the Parade, and many Buildings scattered on the North Part, so that there are now above 1200 Houses and Storehouses, most of which are handsome Buildings, two Stories high besides Garrets. They are covered with Shingles, Sashed, and Glazed, with Piazzas before every House; so that a man may walk from one end to the other without going in the Sun, but in Crossing the Streets. The Church, which is a handsome Building in the form of a Cross, is 120 feet in length, and Stands in the S[outh] E[ast] part of the Parade; the Pulpit, Pews and Wainscot about 8 feet in height, are all neatly made with Cedar and it has a very good Organ in it. There is also in this Town a Quakers' Meeting, and a Jews' Synagogue; but no other place of Publick Worship; though there are grounds to believe, some Roman Catholicks or disguised Papists, and Priests, privately Assemble, and meet together. There is also a very good Town Store about 80 feet in length, and 30 in Breadth, on the South side, and fronting of King street with a Piazza round it, which is made use of as an Exchange.

The Harbour will Contain 1000 Sail of Ships, land-locked by the Neck of Land, which runs from the Rock line, about 5 miles to the Eastward of the Town, to Port Royal, where all ships must pass, having no other Entrance by Sea; nor by land, but the Rock line, which is fortified by Nature. And after Ships have passed Port Royal, they must come through a very narrow Channel, not more than a quarter of a mile wide, and within less distance of Musquito Point, where a Battery is lately Built, and mounted with 12 Cannon, all four and twenty pounders. There is good riding from

7. An Act Making Kingston a Separate Parish, 1681, in *Acts of Assembly*, 59–60.

8. Probably Charles Long (1705–1778), son of Charles Long (1679–1723). In 1754, he owned 2,222 acres in St. Andrew Parish.

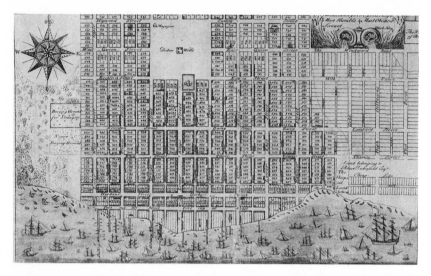

Dedicated to Governor Edward Trelawny, who was in office from 1738 to 1751, Michael Hay's mid-eighteenth-century plan of the layout of Kingston shows the town's expansion during its first half century, while the number of ships crowding the bottom panel of the map identifies it as a vigorous commercial center. (Library of Congress)

one end of the Harbour to the other, from 3 to 25 fathom[s of] Water, in soft ouzy Ground, without any Rocks or dangerous Shoals; so that Ships running ashore receive no other damage, than the charge of lightning them. On the Town side are several Convenient Wharfs, for Lading and unlading of Ships, built with Piles drove into the Sea, and covered with Plank; and opposite to the Town, on a small Island, near the Pallisade's, or narrow neck of land, are very good Conveniencies for Careening of Ships. The only fault of this Harbour is the too great length and breadth, being 9 or 10 miles E[ast] and W[est] and 2 miles over N[orth] and S[outh], and in some places more; so that in strong Sea breezes, there runs a great Swell, and Ships can seldom load or unload after 10 in the morning, and until four in the afternoon. This of itself is no great inconvenience, in regard to the preservation of the Seamen, who ought to have a Recess in that inter-val, or [be] employed in the Shade, the heat of the Sun being generally very Violent, Especially about 11, or 12 at Noon, when the wary Spaniards will not stir out of their Houses; and it is a kind of a Proverb among them, that none but Englishmen and Dogs, walk the Streets at noon.

This Town suffered very much by the Hurricane on the 28th. of August 1712; by another on the 28th. of August 1722, and by a third the 26th. of October 1726; when several Houses were blown down, others very much shattered, and few or none escaped without some damage. The Wharfs were all destroyed[,] most of the Shipping drove ashore, and some of them

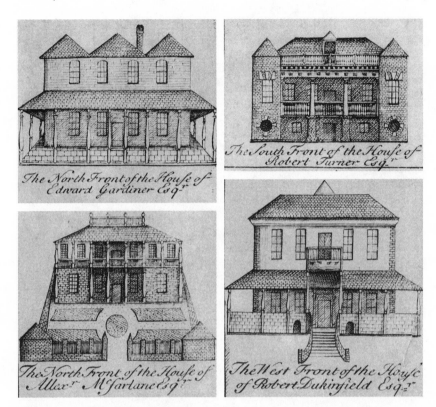

The North Front of the House of
Edward Gardiner Esqr

The South Front of the House of
Robert Turner Esqr

The North Front of the House of
Alexr McFarlane Esqr

The West Front of the House
of Robert Dukinfield Esqr

Inserts from the Hay map, above, contain drawings of four Kingston houses, illustrating the range of housing types among the independent merchants and other free inhabitants. (Library of Congress)

into such shoal Water, that it was impracticable to get them off. The greatest danger, which this Town is exposed to, is Fire, by reason the Buildings are very close, mostly of Timber and Boards, and many Coopers and other Tradesmen, who make use of fire, are Set[t]led and Scattered in the Town. The Negroes are also very Careless, and cannot sleep without a fire near them; But, the Inhabitants have taken a great deal of Precaution, in Erecting Pumps at the Corners of all the Principal Streets; and in providing several Engines, and other Instruments for Extinguishing fire; by which means the Town, or great part of it, has more than once been preserved.

Port Royall is Situate[d] at the Extreme Point of a long neck of land, or Peninsula; which runs from the Mountain 5 miles E[ast] of Kingston, near 10 miles Westward into the Sea. By the Earthquake in 1692 a part of this Neck of Land for the Space of 1/4 a mile was Sunk into the Sea, so that Boats and small Sloops had a free passage over it, and the Town was thereby quite Separated from the Main Land; but by the Seas throwing up Sand; this part began in Time to fill up which the Inhabitants' perceiv-

Born in Geneva and spending more than a decade in the West Indies before moving to New York and finally settling in Philadelphia, Pierre Eugène du Simitière (1737–1784) drew these two Kingston scenes. The first, entitled a *View of the Corner of Harbour and Duke Streets Taken near the South Sea House*, in Kingston in February 1760, and the second, entitled *A South West View of the House of Augustin Meridian in Kingston*, in March 1760, are reproduced from the Du Simitiere Papers at the Library Company of Philadelphia. (Library Company of Philadelphia)

ing, they sunk old Vessells and drove in Piles, whereby they contributed to its being intirely filled up and joined with the Main Land as formerly in which Condition it now remains. This Neck of Land is very narrow, in some places not above a hundred yards over, nor more than a quarter of a mile in any part, and covered with a loose sand without Wood (Except Mangroves) or fresh Water. It is this neck of land that forms Kingston Harbour, and being Rocky on the South side, next to the Cays and Ocean, there is always a great swell or Surge of the Sea; which make it dangerous landing in any part, and impracticable in some places; and is a Security to Port Royall, as well as to Kingston. There are two Channells leading into the Harbour: One called the East Channel lies between this neck of land and a great number of Rocky, and Sandy Cays, or small Islands; it being narrow in some places especially to the Westward of Gun Cay, where two Ships cannot conveniently pass abreast. And for that reason Pilots commonly lay off Morant Harbour to Conduct Ships in, and are obliged by an Act of Assembly, to cruise at least one league to the Eastward of Plumb point.[9] The other called the West channel cannot be Entered . . . , but with an Easterly or Southerly Wind, nor can Vessells go out, but with a North or land breez[e], and before the Sea breez[e] comes in, except Sloops or other small Vessells.

The Spaniards did not like the Situation of this place, which they thought precarious, and subject to Accidents; as the English have since unhappily Experienced; the Major part being a loose sandy foundation, and the Water brackish, therefore they had no other Settlement than a few Hutts for Fishermen who used to dry their Netts here, and called it Cagway.

In 1656, the Seaman belonging to Vice Adm[ira]ll Goodson's Squadron, built some Storehouses and a round Tower, to defend the Entrance, which they called Fort Cromwell, But it was after the Restoration improved and Enlarged, and named Fort Charles. The Year following this Point of Land was by order of Collo[nel] Doyley, who was then Governour of the Island, laid out as a Town, though not very Regular, and in 1663 it had near 500 Houses thereon and [was] named Port Royall. It was the Convenience of the Harbour which invited the English to build here, as the Shore was so bold, that Ships of 500 tons laid their Sides to the Wharfs, unloaded and loaded with little trouble and expence, but most of this land [was] sunk in the great Earthquake and some of it upon each side still Remains under Water, though great part of it is now filled up by the means aforementioned. The King's Yard and Commodious Buildings are now Erected there with very good Conveniencies for Careening of Ships of 70 or 80 Guns.

9. Possibly An Act to Prevent the Incursions of the Enemy on the Sea-Coasts, 1703, in *Acts of Assembly*, 95.

This Town before the Earthquake contained above 1500 Houses, most of them three Stories high, and built after the English manner, and beside Charles Fort, which mounted 40 Cannon, it had five others, vizt. James Fort, Carlish Fort, Morgan Fort, Whites Fort and Rupert Fort; there was also a Battery between Charles and Rupert Forts, whereon were mounted 30 Cannon, called Walker's Line, and a Breast Work at the North end from the Harbour to the Sea, which was to defend the Town from any Surprize by land.

This Town was destroyed by an Earthquake, as I have already mentioned, in 1692; great part of it still remains under Water, and in clear calm Weather the tops of the Houses are still to be seen, though small Ships ride over them. By a Survey taken of the Ground on which Port Royall stood, before that Calamity happened, it measured 51 Acres and a half; which afterwards upon a Resurvey contain[e]d no more than twelve Acres and a half. Great part of that land was made out of the Sea, by the Peoples' driving Piles into the Shoal Water, and filling it up with Stones and Sand; and on this foundation was built Brick houses two and three stories high; but the Sea recovered all again in the Space of half a minute. The Conveniency which induced People to build and settle here at first, tempted many of them to rebuild, and Encroach on the Sea, as they had done before; though that Terrible disaster seemed to forbid any future dwelling on a Place, so liable to Destruction; and in 3 or 4 Years after it was Raised again, though very short of its former Splendor; Yet by degrees they regained so much out of the Sea as made it 25 Acres, whereon stood 700 Houses and Ware Houses.

On the 9th. of January 1702 between 11 and 12 at Noon, a fire hap[pe]ned through Carelessness in a Store house, wherein was a great Quantity of Pitch and Tar; which before Night Consumed the whole Town. The Place being surrounded at that time by the Sea, the Streets narrow and thick with Houses, did not admit of that help which might otherwise have been given; so that the Inhabitants did not save so much of their Effects, as they could have done in a more open place, though they had all the Assistance the men of War and Merchant Ships could give them with their Boats. However the Fort and Fortifications did not receive any Damage; nor any of the Ships and Vessels in the Harbour, except one Sloop, and a Brigantine, which were burnt.

But notwithstanding this second disaster in less than two Years after, many of the former Inhabitants returned and Rebuilt great part of the Town, but others remained at Kingston; what contributed to its being set[t]led the third time, was the Success of the men of War and Privateers, in Queen Ann's War,[10] which were fitted out, and brought in their prizes

10. Queen Anne's War, also known as the War of the Spanish Succession (1702–13).

here, the Harbour being more Convenient for that purpose, than any other part of the Island.

The 28th. of August 1712 this Town suffered Considerably a third time, by a Hurricane, which blew down several Houses, and Shatter[e]d many others To that degree that they were irreparable.

The 28th. of August 1722 happen[e]d another Hurricane, more Violent than the former, at least it proved more fatal to Port Royal. The Evening before there was a prodigious swell of the Sea, without any Wind, which threw over the Walls to the Eastward of the Town, several hundred Tons of Stones; some of which were very large and as much as two or three men could carry. In the Morning about eight o'clock the Wind began to rise, at South East; from whence it Shifted almost every minute from one Point of the Compass to another. The Waves of the Sea flew over the Wall, which is five feet in height and 9 or 10 feet in Breadth; and broke down some part of it; by which means the Sea had a free Passage, and in two or three hours over flowed the whole Town above 5 feet Deep. At the same time by the Violence of the Wind the Houses were tumbling about the People's Ears, and Burying many of them under the Ruins, so that they could neither go into the Streets, nor Stay in their Houses with any Safety.

Under those dreadfull Circumstances, the Inhabitants continued till three in the Afternoon, when the Wind and Waters began to abate; though the Weather was Stormy all the Night, and not fully set[t]led till the Morning following. The Church and above one half the Houses were blown down, and the materialls of the former washed away, nothing remaining but the foundation; the rest of the Buildings were very much shatter[e]d, and none escaped without some damage. The East Angle of Fort Charles was undermin[e]d by the Sea, and fell down; and above 300 White men and Negroes were drowned, or Crushed to Death with the fall of Houses.

This Town and Shipping likewise suffer[e]d very much by the Hurricane in October 1726; though not so much as in other parts of the Island where the Wind was more Violent; however the Sea over flowed it above two feet and half; which put the Inhabitants again under terrible Apprehensions.

Thus, I have shewn how this once Rich, Populous and most flourishing Town in America was Ruin[e]d and destroyed four times. It doth not now Contain above 250 Houses and Storehouses, which are Chiefly Inhabited by Sea faring men, or such as depend on the Garrison and his Majestie's Ships. It is indeed an Excellent Harbour, and Ships may ride there with great security in all Weathers, except a South wind, which very seldom blows; it is likewise a Convenient Place for a Garrison, the Fortifications, on which the Security of the Island, at least of the Trade, and Navigation depend being Chiefly here. In Fort Charles, which was Rebuilt since the Earthquake, and is a Regular Fortification, are mounted Sixty five Cannon, many of them Brass; on Hannover line (which was built in 1717 near the Place, where Walker's line stood) thirty four Cannon, all two and thirty pounders; and on the Wall, which runs from the N[orth] E[ast] to the S[outh] end of the Town, forty heavy Cannon, and some Mortars. One of the Independant Companies consisting of 100 men beside Officers constantly do Duty, and there is also a Regiment of Militia, which keep a Nightly Guard, and the Publick Officers are obliged to keep under-Officers or Deputies for Ent[e]ring and Clearing of Ships. Port Royal is five miles from Kingston, four from Passage Fort, and ten miles from Spanish Town or St. Iago de la vega.

Passage Fort is a small Town, situated at the West end of Kingston Harbour, and is the Barcadier, or landing place for St. Katherine's, St. John's or Guanaboa, Caimanos, and St. Thomas in the Vale. There was formerly a Fort, which mounted Eighteen Guns, when the Spaniards were in Possession, and afterwards Rebuilt by Collo[nel] Doyley, and named Copper Fort; and the Passage Boats coming thither, which carried goods and Passengers from one Town to Another, it was from thence called Passage Fort. There are now about twenty Houses and Store houses built chiefly for the Entertainment of Passengers, and for Receiving and Shipping off Goods. It is seven Miles from Kingston by Water; and six miles from St. Iago de la vega, which is Situate[d] up the Country Westward of it; and is, as well as this Town, in the Precinct or Parish of St. Katherines.

St. Iago delavega [is] commonly called Spanish Town, [and] the Spaniards began to build, and to Settle Plantations near it, about the year 1540; tho[ugh] it made no great progress or Figure untill they removed from Sevill or St. Anns and made it the Seat of Government. The Original & proper name was Oristan, being so called in all the Spanish Historys and Writings; St. Iago delavega was only an Additional Name, it being Customary with the Spaniards to add the name of some Saint as a Patron to their Towns, therefore called it likewise St. Iago delavega that is Saint James in the Vale, being seated in a large pleasant Vale. But how it came to lose the name of Oristan and to retain the name of Iago delavega, as it is now called in all Publick and private Deeds and Writings, I have not been able to trace out. It was once as large a Town as many in England, for it Contained 2000 Houses, two Churches, an Abby, four Chappels, and two Monasteries. But it had lost very much of its lustre, before it was delivered up to the English, as it had been three times taken and plundered by the Earl of Cumberland[,] S[i]r Anthony Shirly, and Collo[nel] Jackson; so that there was no more than one Church, an Abby and two Monasteries Remaining, when it was delivered up to General Venables.

On one side of the Town is a fair though unnavigable River, called by the Spaniards Rio Cobre, or Copper River, from its being tainted by running through one or more Copper Mines; for which reason they seldom drank of it, especially in times of great Rains or Floods from the Mountains, when it is chiefly discernable. On the other sides of the Town are large wide Savannas, whereon feed great numbers of Sheep and Cattle; and in the Morning, and Evenings the Gentry ride there for the benefit of the Air, and frequently have Horse-Racing and other Diversions.

This Town is finely situate[d], with Regard to Health and other Conveniencies, being near the Center of the Island, and therefore proper for the Seat of Government; tho[ugh] it was in a manner deserted for some years, after Port Royal was Set[t]led, and until S[i]r Thomas Lynch was appointed Governour: But in the Year 1681 the Assembly, Grand Courts and the Records of the Island by a Law were directed to be held and kept there. In the great Earthquake in 1692 the Spanish Church, Abby, and most of the English Buildings were thrown down; but the Spanish Houses sustain[e]d very little damage, except some few, which had been neglected, and were out of repair; and it is observable, that they not only stood that fatal shock, but the great Hurricanes, which happen[e]d since; when most of the English Houses were blown down, or very much damaged, which may justly be attributed to their being built Stronger. They are likewise more proper in respect to Coolness, for that part of the World; though they do not make so good an Appearance as the English Buildings. None of them are more than one Story high, and 12 feet from the ground Plate to the Wall plate; the Principal Posts are fixed in the ground 6 or 7 feet deep; the Roofs are hipped and covered very snug, with Wild Canes, which are nailed to the roof close to each other, and over them Tiles laid in Mortar. The Town now contains about 600 Houses and Store houses, a Church, and a Chapel.

The King's House (as it is called) where the Governour resides, was built by the Country, and is large and Commodious, though not a very Regular Building, situate on the West side of the Parade. The Town-House, where the General Assembly, and the Grand Courts, are held, is on the North West side, and is built after the Spanish manner, though much higher, and is about 50 feet Square. The Chapel is opposite to it on the South West side. The Church stands on the Eastward part, at the Entrance into the Town; it is built on the foundation of the Spanish Abby in the form of a Cross, and is the neatest Building in America. Several Eminent Planters, whose Estates are in this part of the Country, have Houses and frequently Reside here; and one of the Independant Companies is quarter[e]d in Barracks on the Skirts of the Town, and keep[s] a Constant Guard.

St. Katherine's Precinct or Parish wherein St. Iago delavega, and Passage Fort stand, the Spaniards began to settle and Cultivate as I have observed about the Year 1540. It was their principal settlement, when the English dispossessed them; and they had 3 Sugar Works, some Cocoa Walks, and many other Plantations in this part of the Country. Great improvements were afterwards made, for raising Indigo, and Cotton, as well as Sugar, which throve very well; but the Seasons having failed for some Years past, and become precarious, they have been obliged to break up most of their Sugar, and Indigo works, which are now Converted into Pens, for raising of Cattle and Sheep. However, there are still three Sugar Works in this

Parish, besides many other Settlements, most part of it which contains many thousand Acres of Land being level, or of so easy an Ascent, that it is not discernable.

Here we must step aside to view St. John's and St. Thomas in the Vale, which are Inland Parishes; the others before described Bordering upon the Sea, on the South side and the Mountains on the North; but this being the middle and broadest part of the Island contains these two very considerable Parishes which border upon neither Sea, but lie between those upon the South and those upon the North side of the Island.

St. John's or Guanaboa, which was the name the Native Indians gave it, and it went by while the Spaniards were in Possession of the Island, was almost fully set[t]led by them after their removal from the North side. They had here one Sugar Work, many Cocoa Walks, and Provision Plantations, and some for Otta or Anatta; particularly the Angells, which afterwards belonged to S[i]r Thomas Modyford, and now to his Descendents. There are 28 Sugar Works in this Parish beside many others for Ginger and Provisions. It is six miles from St. Iago delavega, and esteemed very healthy.

St. Thomas in the Vale, commonly called Sixteen mile walk on account of it being that distance from St. Iago delavega, joins to Guanaboa; and is one of the highest and best set[t]led parts of the Country. But the Road to it, till late Years, was very inconvenient, and in some places could scarcely admit of two horsemen passing one another; which obliged the Planters to bring their Sugars to Town in Bags upon Mules. This was not only an Expensive Carriage, but the Sugars were often damaged by the Rains which they frequently met with: and beside this Road was a great way about, and round an exceeding high Mountain, which put some Gentlemen upon finding out a shorter way; and accordingly they travelled along the side of the River called Rio Cobre till they came to a very high Rock, which stood perpendicular from the Bank of the River on each side, so that with much difficulty they climbed over it; but, a Dog that was with them, finding a hole to creep through, Suggested to them that there was a Passage thro[ugh] the Rock, which being thus discover[e]d, was afterwards by Powder and other means Cleared and Enlarged till by degrees they made a way through big enough for a Horse with a Pack, and high enough for a man on Horse back. On one side of this Road Rio Cobre runs above six miles; and is generally very rapid thereabouts, being often filled with great Trees and Stones, which are rolled down from the neighbouring Mountains by the floods, or great Rains. On the other side of the Road are vast Rocks heaped up one upon another to an amazing height and among them large Trees, which look as if they were rooted upon each others tops. But this Road which at first it was thought impracticable for Horses or Mules, has lately been made passable, for all sorts of Wheel Carriages, though with great labour and Expence; yet the Convenience of it makes the Inhabitants of that Parish sufficient recompence, for the trouble and charge they have been at.

The Vale is surround[e]d with Mountains and when open[e]d to View, affords a most delightfull Landscape, being crowded with Settlements among which are no less than 48 Sugar Works; beside others for Ginger and Provisions. And notwithstanding the morning Sun screened by the mountains for some hours, so that it is generally foggy till 8 or 9, yet it is deem[e]d to be very healthy. The Road to St. Ann's on the Northside, is through this Parish; nor is there any other from the south side, to that part of the Country, but through Wagwater in Leguinea, which enters into St. Marie's and from St. Elizabeth's on the S[outh] W[est] and to St. James on the N[orth] W[est] end; and every one of them through difficult narrow passes, which renders it impracticable, for an Enemy to march from one side of the Country to the other; the Mountains in all other parts being inaccessible, and even these three Roads are often impassable, especially after great rains, when the Roads, which in some places are cut out of the sides of the Mountains, are Slippery, and sometimes washed away.

But that I may pursue the method, I proposed, in giving a Description of the several parts of the Island; I shall pass from hence to St. Dorothy's, which borders on the Sea, on the South side, and West on St. Katherine's.

St. Dorothy's, the Spaniards likewise began to set[t]le before they removed from St. Ann's on the North side; and they had here two Sugar Works, and several Cocoa Walks, at the time the English took possession of the Island. But they gave the preference to the Inland Parishes, as they thought the Air better, and their Possessors more Secure from an Invading Enemy. In the Road to the Leeward or West part of the Island we must necessarily pass over Black River, on which is built a Bridge, and near it a Breast work, to prevent an Enemy marching from that part of the Country to St. Iago delavega. From whence the River is five Miles distant and it is Remarkable for its Excellent Water, which the Spaniards chiefly made use of, rather than the River, they had so near them, for the Reason I have given. The greatest part of this Parish is low flat land, and the Soil being very good, it was well set[t]led in a few Years, after the English became Masters of the Island. It has now not more than 8 Sugar Works in it, besides other Plantations, for Ginger, Cotton, Coffee and Provisions; and Several large Savannas, whereon feed some thousand head of Sheep and Cattle. But of late Years it has suffered very much for want of the usual and necessary Seasons, by which means some of their Sugar Plantations are on the decline, and it is to be feared, must be broke up, as others have already been.

West Chester commonly called Old Harbour, is in St. Dorothy's Precinct; it was the Chief Port of Trade when the Spaniards were dispossessed of the Island, and for many years before. But they had not any other Buildings there than a few storehouses, so that it was only a Barcadier or land-

This 1750 anonymous drawing of Henry Dawkins's wharf at Salt River in Clarendon Parish offers a close look at the layout and machinery required for loading sugar onto boats to carry them down-river to ocean-going vessels. Note particularly the large crane and weigh station on the right. Originally a part of the Dawkins Family Papers at the National Library of Jamaica, this image can no longer be found in that collection. It is here reproduced from B. W. Higman, *Jamaica Surveyed: Plantation Maps and Plans of the Eighteenth and Nineteenth Century* (Kingston, Jamaica, 1988), 94. (B. W. Higman)

ing place. It is seven miles from St. Iago delavega by land, and 18 miles from Port Royal by Sea, and Esteemed a very good Harbour; for 200 Ships may conveniently ride there in all Weathers, being Shelter[e]d by several small Islands that lie before it and break off the Sea. It was latterly the only Sea Port the Spaniards had on the Island; and the Gal[l]eons in their Return to old Spain and the Flota in their passage to Lavera Cruz generally touched there for Refreshments. It doth not now contain more than 18 or 20 Houses, and Warehouses, and serves only as a Barcadier to St. Dorothy's, and some parts of Clarendon. Three or four Ships load here Yearly; but the Masters are obliged to Enter and Clear at Kingston, or Port Royal, it not being allowed Port Officers.

Clarendon is an Inland Parish and bounds E[ast] on St. Dorothy's, S[outh] on Vere, W[est] on St. Elizabeth's, and N[orth] on inaccessible Mountains which Separates it from the North side of the Island. It is partly level, but mostly Hilly and Mountainous land. The level part is about 15 miles in length E[ast] and W[est], and 11 or 12 in Breadth N[orth] and S[outh]; and Contains Severall Considerable Sugar Works, and other Settlements. But there are many more in the Mountains, and in the Vallies or bottoms between them, some of which are equal to any in America. The Mountains in this part of the Island, are different from those at the East and West end, most of them being of a gradual easy Ascent, with table or flat Land at the Tops, as well as Vallies between them. Nevertheless, the Planters in this part of the Country, are Obliged to send their Sugars in

Bags upon Mules several Miles, and some not less than 18 or 20 Miles, before they Arrive at any Road that is passable for Wheel Carriages, and from thence 11 or 12 Miles more to the Barcadiers vizt. Milk River, Carlisle Bay, and Old Harbour. But this Inconvenience is amply made up to them, by a healthy and Pleasant Situation, the fertility of the Soil, and constant Seasons, for the Inhabitants seldom have Occasion to Complain of the Want of Rain. They are likewise well furnished with Water, there being in those Mountains a great number of Springs and Rivulets from whence Several fine Rivers derives their Source. Nor, are they under any Apprehension of a Foreign Enemy, being able to Subsist and Defend themselves, as well as Sixteen Mile Walk, and Wag Water, in Case the Island should be invaded, and the Enemy become Masters of the other Parts; for all the passages are in some Places so narrow that they may be easily made Defensible, and even impregnable.

This Parish is at present in a flourishing Condition, and since the Rains have failed in Vere it, has become as Considerable a Parish as any in the Island, many Eminent Planters having removed from that part of the Country to this; so that there are now 66 Sugar Works within this District, beside many other Plantations for raising Ginger, Cotton, Coffee and Provisions.

Vere Parish is Seated along the Shore, bounding E[ast] on St. Dorothy's, North on Clarendon, and W[est] on St. Elizabeth's. It is most or all a low flat Land, of a Sandy Soil, very proper for Indigo, and Cotton. Great quantities of those Commodities were made here formerly, and it was many Years, particularly from 1700 to 1715, the Richest and the most flourishing Part of the Island. But, it has gradually declined since that period of time, by reason of the Seasons having failed, which has occasioned the breaking up of many fine Estates, or Converting them into Pens for raising Sheep and Cattle. There are now no more than 7 Sugar Mills within this Precinct.

The Principall Barcadiers are Carlisle Bay and Milk River. At the former is a small Town consisting of about thirty Houses, and Warehouses; and a small Fort of 16 Guns. Ships ride Securely within the Bay, being sheltered from the Winds and Sea, by Several Cays or small Islands.

Milk River lies open and Exposed otherwise there is good riding for Ships, and 5 or 6 load there yearly.

I should not discharge the part of a faithfull Writer, if I did not do the Inhabitants of this Parish the Justice to observe, that they distinguished themselves in the Year 1693, when the French Invaded the Island, and landed 1200 men in this part of the Country; with whom they had several Skirmishes, wherein the Enemy gained no advantage, though greatly superior in number, the Inhabitants not exceeding 500 men, until they were Reinforced from Spanish Town; when the English Forces commanded by

Collo[nel] Loyd[11] bravely attacked and drove the Invaders out of the Island. And I must Observe that in the Several engagements in this part of the Island only, the Enemy lost 370 men.

St. Elizabeth's is next to Vere, Westward, and is Separated by the Swift River; on the South is the Sea, and on the North vast high Mountains. It formerly extended as far as great River on the North West end, which now divides Hannover from St. James's Parish, but by an Act of the Assembly in 1699 Westmorland was taken out of it, and its Extent Westward limitted to Scots Cove, which now divides this Parish from Westmorland.[12]

The Spaniards were Settled in this part of the Country, and built a Town at the head of Black River, which they called S[an]ta Cruz. It was all most deserted by the Spaniards, and afterwards destroyed by the English Forces in 1656, though the Foundation and Ruins are still to be Seen. Part of the Main Road through this Parish is very bad, particularly the Devil's Race, so called from the difficulty in going over it; for about two Miles, it is cut out of the side of a Mountain bordering on the Sea, so that when the Sea breez[e] blows, the breakers and Spray of the Sea Splashes and Wets the Passengers; who would quicken Their Pace if it were possible, but the Road for this whole length besides being made Slippery by the Spray is narrow[,] Rocky and uneven, so that it is absolutely necessary to move Slowly and with Caution.

This Parish or Precinct is very large, notwithstanding the two following Considerable Parishes being taken out of it; for there are no less than 32 Sugar Works in this Division, beside other Settlements, where large numbers of Cattle, Horses, and Mules are raised, which they send up to the Towns, and other parts of the Country; and it is still Capable of Improvement, having large Quantities of uncultivated land.

Westmorland, was made a distinct Parish, as I have observed, and divided from St. Elizabeth's by an Act of the Assembly in 1699, by which Scots Cove was made its boundary to the Eastward; and in 1723 Hannover Parish was taken out of it, so that its extent Westward is now limited to Point Nigril. On the South is the Sea, and on the North Vast high Mountains; on one of the steepest and most difficult of which is Trelawney Town, built by that Gang of Wild Negroes, who were the first that submitted themselves in 1738, and were the means of bringing in the others. This Settlement is about [blank] miles from Dean's Valley and not more than [blank] miles from [blank] in St. James's Parish on the North side.

Surinam Quarters is within this Parish and was so Called from many of the Inhabitants of that Colony, coming to this Island in [blank] and according to their own desire set[t]ling contiguously in this part of the Island;

11. Richard Lloyd was a lieutenant colonel and council member who in 1689 and 1695–98 was also chief justice.

12. An Act for Dividing St. Elizabeth's into Two Distinct Parishes,1699, in ibid., 97–98.

also Cape Bonetta and Blew field Rivers; the former is not Navigable for
Boats and Canoes. But the Lands on each Side are Capable of very great
improvements were care taken to drain them for as most of them are low
and Swampy, and now overflowed by the River they must Consequently be
very Rich and well worth the labour and Expence.

Blue Field River is Navigable for Boats and Cannoes above 20 miles.
At the Mouth of it there is a Bay in which is very good Riding for Ships,
with this Convenience they may at any time of the day go in or out. The
Water is looked up on to be as good as any in the World, and ships bound
thr[ough] the Gulf of Florida, generally touch here to Wood and Water.

This Parish or Precinct made the swiftest Increase in Settlements of any
part of the Country, for before the Peace of Utrecht there was not more
than 9 or 10 Sugar Works within the present District, and now there are
no less than 64 of which 16 are Water Works. Several of them Water Mills,
there being many other Rivers beside those I have mentioned; and it is Capable of very great improvements as not one fourth part of the Manurable
land is yet Cultivated and improved.

Hanover Precinct was taken out of Westmorland, and made a distinct
Parish by an Act of Assembly, in 1723, but was formerly part of St. Elizabeth's.[13] It is now divided from Westmoreland at S[outh] Nigrill Point near
the West end of the Island, and from St. James's on the North west end by
Great River. This is one of the latest settlements in the Island; nevertheless it is a flourishing part of the Country, and has more fine Rivers and
Harbours than any other. There are now no less than 39 Sugar Works in
it, Several of them Water Mills; and Vast Tracts of rich uncultivated lands;
particularly King's Valley, which is said to Contain several thousand Acres
of Land.

In this District are the following commodious Harbours, tho[ugh] small,
[and] other convenient places for Shiping; namely Nigrill or Irish Bay, Orange Bay, Green Island, Davis's Cove, Lucia & Cove Harbour.

Nigrill or Irish Bay, is a deep Bay where is good rideing for Ships in all
Weathers, except a storm at N[orth] W[est].

Orange Bay is also a deep Bay in the form of a semicircle & expos[e]d
only to a N[orth] W[est] wind. 3 or 4 Ships load there yearly.

Green Island Harbour is commodious but very small for it will not contain more than 6 or 7 Ships at a time. Green Island which makes it a Harbour is Situate W[est] and not 1/4 of a Mile from the Bay, so that the Entrance S[outh] and N[orth] is very narrow, and it may easily be Fortified.

Davis's Cove is a Creek at the N[orth] W[est] end of the Island & runs
up the Country half a Mile or more; but the breadth is narrow[,] not a
musquet shot over and as the water is shoal except at the Mouth or Entrance, it will not contain more than 3 Ships, which must moor head &

13. An Act for Dividing Westmoreland into Two Distinct Parishes, 1723, in ibid., 192–93.

Engraved by John Spilsbury as part of a series of *Views of Jamaica* published in London in 1770, this image of *A View Looking South of the Town and Harbour of Lucea in the Parish of Hanover the North Side of Jamaica* offers a panoramic view of this lightly settled port with a bay full of ocean-going ships and with a small group of habitations on the far shore. (Yale Center for British Art, Paul Mellon Collection)

stern for there is not room for them to swing. The Shore on each side the Entrance is Rocky, whereby it may easily be made Defensible.

Lucia Harbour is about 3 leagues to the Eastward of Davis Cove; it is safe and commodious with regard to an Enemy as well as the Weather. It being land locked, the Entrance [is] not a quarter of a Mile over, and there is a Fortification on each side. It will contain 20 Ships or more, the Ground is soft and ouzy, and it is well furnished with fresh water for several Rivers discharge therein. The land round it is Hilly and Mountainous, as indeed it is about all the Harbours on the N[orth] side. Several Ships load here yearly, for Great Britain and N[orth] America, and as the lands contiguous are more & more opened yearly & now Settlements made, it will undoubtedly in a few years become more frequented and considerable than it is at present.

Cove Harbour is about 4 leagues to the Eastward of Lucia. It is the best and safest Harbour in this Island, it being land locked & the Entrance very narrow, which makes it safe riding for Ships in all weathers. And it may be easily made Defensible against an Invading Enemy, though it is not yet Fortified, nor seldom made use of, by reason that part of the Country is mostly uncultivated, and has very few Settlements in it.

Engraved by John Spilsbury as part of a series of *Views of Jamaica* and published in London in 1770, this image of *A View of the Town and Harbour of Montego Bay, in the Parish of St. James, Jamaica, Taken from the Road Leading to St. Ann's* shows a busy and rapidly developing port full of ships bordered by a road occupied by a wagon and people riding horses. The only female rider is followed by an enslaved person with his restraining hand on the tail of her horse. (Yale Center for British Art, Paul Mellon Collection)

St. James's is divided from Westmoreland to the West by Great River, and to the East from St. Ann's by Ria Bona on the North is the Sea, and on the South Vast high Mountains. It is now but thinly inhabited, though there is a great deal of good land, by Reason of the Wild Negroes, who were formally Seated in their Neighbourhood, and often came down in the Night, robbed the Planters, and sometimes Set their Houses and Canes on fire, which Occasioned Several to remove, and discouraged others from Set[t]ling here; so that here are not above [blank] or Sugar Works, and some few Plantations, for Cotton and Piemento. But as a Treaty is now made with those People, it is probable this part of the Country in a few Years, will recover itself, and become better set[t]led than it is.

In this Precinct is a very good Road and One Harbour for Shipping, Namely Montica Bay and Matabre.

Montica Bay is about 4 leagues to the Eastward of Musquito Cove. Here is safe and Convenient riding for Ships of any Draught, except when the Winds blow at N[orth] or N[orth] West which seldom happens, but from October to February. It is well furnished with fresh Water and has a Fortification to defend the Ships & Settlements from a Foreign Enemy.

Engraved by John Spilsbury as part of a series of *Views of Jamaica* and published in London in 1769, this image of *A Prospect of Rio Bona Harbour in the Parish of St. Ann's, and the Tavern, Wharf, and Stores, in the Parish of St. James's, the North Side Jamaica* provides a view of one of the many small shipping ports in Jamaica, this one in a pastoral setting. (Yale Center for British Art, Paul Mellon Collection)

Matabre is about 7 leagues to the Eastward of Montica Bay, a large & convenient Harbour for such Ships as it can receive. The Entrance is Narrow, between two Riefs, and there is depth of Water sufficient for Ships of Burthen, but within is not more than 14 or 15 Feet, so that only Sloops and small Ships load at, or frequent this place. There is a large fresh Water River, that runs from the Settlements thro[ugh] a Swamp of Mangroves, into the Harbour, and is Navigable for Cannoes and Boats, which bring down the Planters' Goods to the Ship[p]ing, and will become more usefull when Norman's Valley, which is within this Parish & 8 or 9 Miles of this River, is more opened & better Set[t]led.

St. Ann's is Separated from St. James by Rio Bona or Good River. The first settlements, the Spaniards made, were in this part of the Island; for after they had subdued the Native Indians, John De Esquibell with about Seventy Persons seated themselves in Fig Tree Bay, which is about 14 leagues to the Eastward of St. Ann's, where they built a small Town, which they called Mettilla or Melilla and settled Several Plantations near it.

But disliking the Situation & having from time to time supplies of Men, Women, Cattle, Horses, and other necessaries, they removed in a few Years to St. Ann's; where they built a much larger Town, or rather a City, and called it Sevilla. Some of the Ruins are still to be seen, and the foundations of several Houses at two miles distance from the Cathedrall Church, which was built by the famous Peter Martyr of Angleria, who was the Abbot & Suffragan to the Arch Bishop of St. Domingo on Hispaniola.

The Walls of the Cathedrall were of a sort of Free Stone, which is in great plenty in the Neighbourhood. We are uncertain as to the length and Breadth, but there were two Rows of Pillars within, and over the place, where the Altar was to be, were some Carvings under the ends of the Arches. There was also part of a large Monastry, and a House supposed to be designed for the Governour of the Island; but neither of them were finished; near them were found two Coats of Arms, the one Ducal, the other a Count's, supposed to belong to Columbus's Family, who were Proprietors of the Island. The West Gate of the Church was very fine Work, Seven feet wide, and as high under the Arch; it was intire not many Years Since, and part of it still to be seen. Over the Door in the Middle was our Saviour's head, with a Crown of Thorns, between two Angels; on the right side a small round figure of some Saint, with a knife stuck into his head; on the left the Virgin Mary, or a Madona; her Arm tied in three places after the Spanish Fashion. Over the Gate, under a Coat of Arms is this Inscription,

PETRUS MARTIR AB *Angleria, Italvs Civis. Mediolanen, Prothou, Apos, Hvivs Insulae, Abbas, Senatus Indici Consiliarivs, Ligneam Privs, Ædem Hane Bis Igne, Consvmptam, Latiricio Et Quadrato Lapide Primus A Fundamentis Extruxit.*[14]

The Ground where this Town stood, is now part of Mr. Heming's[15] Plantation, and is mostly planted with Canes; where pavements are sometimes found covered with the Earth above 3 feet, & in many places Wells, and Grave Stones finely Cut.

At some distance the Spaniards had one Sugar Mill, which went by Water, brought hither by art from some Miles Distance and also a Castle of Stone and Brick, to defend the Town.

In this Precinct are Three very Convenient & Defensible Harbours but Small, namely Dry Harbour, St. Ann's & Ochio Rios on Eight Rivers, corruptly called Chereras.

Dry Harbour, so called from its want of fresh water, having none nearer than Rio Bona, which is about 5 Miles to the Westward of it, and where is good anchoring for small vessells, but bad riding in the North Seasons.

14. This passage may be translated as "Peter Martyr, of Angleria, an Italian citizen of Milan, chief missionary and abbot of this island, member of the Council of the Indies, first raised from its foundation, with brick and square stone, this edifice, which formerly was built of wood, and twice destroyed by fire."

15. Probably Richard Hemmings, who was a member of the Jamaica Assembly for St. Ann Parish in 1727–30 and 1733–35.

Engraved by John Spilsbury as part of a series of *Views of Jamaica* and published in London in 1769, this image of *A View of Dry Harbour in the Parish of St. Ann's, Jamaica, Taken from the West End of the Tavern, with the Fort and Barracks View in Ruins* illustrates a still smaller port with scattered shoreline settlements and a close-up of a merchant house with a veranda occupied by two people. (Yale Center for British Art, Paul Mellon Collection)

The Entrance into Dry Harbour is narrow and between two Riefs but within 20 or 30 Ships may ride securely in all weathers from 2 to 16 fathom[s of] water. The deepest part is Marly ground and the Shoaly part Sandy. It is seldom made use of, by reason there are but few Settlements near it.

St. Ann's Bay is about 6 or 7 leagues to the Eastward of Dry Harbour, and is made a Harbour by a Broad Rief that runs the whole length which is about a Mile near East & West within is narrow and not above 2 Cables length, in breadth. So that it will not contain more than 10 or 12 Ships; about 1/3 of the way down, from the Entrance on the East end, there lies a Barr, and not above 14 feet water on it, which obliges Ships above that draught to take in part of their loading above it. But above & below the Bar is from 5 to 8 fath[o]m water, and good Riding. The Shiping are secured from a Foreign Enemy, by a strong Battery at the Entrance on the East end, and the West is only passable for Boats. Two fresh water Rivers run into it, & several convenient wharfs and Store houses are built on the Bay, by Neighbouring Planters for their respective uses. Also some scattered Houses for Shops & Taverns, but not enough to be called a Town, tho[ugh] it may probably increase in time and deserve the name. The Port

The work of the London engraver Isaac Taylor and published in 1774, this *View of the White River Cascade* depicts one of the most dramatic of several waterfalls spilling directly into the sea. It is reproduced from Long, *History of Jamaica*, 2:opposite p. 422.

is not allowed officers by the Crown, and is little more than a Barcadier or landing place, so that the Masters of Ships which load here yearly and do not exceed 4 or 5 in number for Great Britain, exculsive of small vessells that load with Rum & Molasses for North America[,] are obliged to Enter & clear at St. Iago delavega & Kingston.

Ocho Rios or 8 Rivers, commonly, tho[ough] corruptly called Chereras as I have observed, is a Commodious Harbour, tho[ugh] very small and is in the form of a Horse Shoe; for it will not contain more than 9 or 10 ships of Burthen; the inner part of the Harbour being filled with a Reif of Corell Rock called Pantiles, round the Southern Side, and from thence or the Breach it Shoals off from 2 to 18 fat[hom]: but the West Shoar is Steep to or deep Water. Beside these Eight Rivers, there are a giant number of Rivulets or Springs some of which run into them and the others into the Sea. It is about 4 leagues to the Eastward of St. Ann's.

St. Mary's Parish is Situate East of St. Ann's, & is divided by White River. This part of the country is Remarkable for being the last in the possession of the Spaniards, who after they had been routed out from several places, retreated and fortified themselves at Rio Nova with an intention of keeping possession, but were attacked by Collo[nel] Doyley, who drove them out of their Intrenchments, killed and took a great number of them & the rest retired to St. Iago de Cuba, where they set[t]led and never made any attempt on this Island afterwards, so that this Engagement was the last, and the decisive Battle that was fought, and the Ruins of their Fortifications are still to be seen.

This Parish is but thinly set[t]led, and has not more than 19 Sugar Works, and a few other Settlements for Cocoa, Ginger, Piemento and Cotton; by reason it lies exposed to an Invading Enemy, and has often been disturbed by the Wild Negroes who are descended from some of the Spanish Negroes, that would not submit to the English, and settled in the Mountains, between St. Maria's and St. George's, now within the Precinct of Portland.

But as they have submitted themselves, and live now in a peacable and orderly manner, it is probable the goodness of the Soil and Seasons, may invite People to Settle here.

In this Precinct are two convenient Roads or Bays, namely Ora Cabesa or Gold head, and Port Maria tho[ugh] improperly so called.

Ora Cabesa or Gold head is about 4 leagues to the Eastward of Ochio Rios, round Galena point. It is a good Road & safe Riding in all Weathers, except in the North Seasons, or when the Northerly Winds blow. Here is a salt Water River, but no fresh Water nearer than Riva Nova, which is about 2 leagues distance from it.

Port Maria is defended from the Wind at N[orth] by a small Island, or Cay, it not being above 4 or 5 Acres of Rocky land, near which the Ships that load here ride in 7, 8 & 9 feet [of] Water: the West end is open & deep Water but there is a Rief at the East end which may be filled up & make it a Harbour. There is a Chain within the Island, at the expence of the Planters, for a Ship to Moor by, there being seldom more than one at a time. It is about 3 leagues to the Eastward of Ora Cabesa.

St. George's Parish lies east of St. Mary's from which it is Divided by White River, and formerly extended to River Grande, before Portland Parish, or Precinct was taken out of it.

This part of the Island is also Exposed to an Invading Enemy; and was formerly Liable to the Incursions of the Wild Negroes; their Settlements at that time being in the Neighbourhood, from whence they often visited the Planters and were so very troublesome, as occasioned Severall Plantations to be deserted and thrown up so that there is not now above four Sugar-works, within this Division, tho[ugh] there are other Settlements insomuch that the greatest part of this district was abandoned and for some months in the possession of those Fugitives which rendered it unsafe Travelling in that part of the Country, without a proper Guard. So that there is not now above 4 Sugar Works, within this Division tho[ugh] there are other Settlements for Cotton &c, and probably further Improvements will be made in time when the Neighbouring parts are better settled.

In this Precinct are several Roads or Bays for small Vessells namely Annotta Bay, Fig Tree Bay, Orange Bay & Rio Grande; but not one Harbour that can properly be so called, nor indeed is there good Anchorage for Ships at any of them except Anotta Bay.

Anotta Bay is about 5 leagues round a point from Port Maria and divides St. Mary's from St. George's. Here are two fresh water Rivers which run into the Sea, and Ships may Ride from 3 to 9 f[oo]t water or deeper.

Fig tree Bay is about a league round a point from Anotta Bay.

Orange Bay is about 3 leagues to the Eastward of Fig Tree Bay.

And Rio Grande is about 4 leagues to the Eastward of Orange Bay, and two leagues to the Westward of Portland Harbour, or Port Antonio; it is an open Road, and vessells must Anchor near the Shore from 2 1/2 to 5 f[ee]t water. The River divides St. George's from Portland, and may be made Navigable, for Cannoes as high as the Breast Work, which is about 5 Mile above Titchfield Town & Portland Harbour.

Portland Parish or Precinct is taken out of St. George's and St. Thomas in the East, and is bounded North and North East by the Sea, from the Mouth of White River to the Westward of the Mouth of River Grand, Extending S[outh] directly fourteen Miles, then East, until it meets with Swift River; and five miles up, and from thence on a streight line, to White River.

This Division was made in the Year 1723, and named Portland in Honour of the late Duke who was at that time Governour of the Island; and a Town laid out at Patterson's Point, upon the Bay or Harbour formerly called Port Antonio, was named Titchfeild after His Graces 2d title.

Lynch's Island, which is Situate at the mouth of the Harbour, was by an Act of the Assembly Vested in his Majesty for the Use of the Navy;[16] and an Hospitall, Storehouses, and other Buildings and Conveniencies for Careening of Ships were Erected upon it at the Expence of the Government. But, the project of making it the Rendevouz of the men of War stationed at this Island, and the Chief Port of Trade, did not succeed; it being found inconvenient for those purposes, notwithstanding the Interest and Artfull Schemes of the Promoters of it, whose designs were exploded and defeated.

However the Settlement of this place, and Erecting a Fortification for the Defence of the Harbour, is Certainly of great Advantage to the Island; and will be a security to the North side, which, as I have observed, lies very much exposed to an Enemy in time of War, and to the Insults and Depredations of the Spanish Guarda Costa's, and Pyrates, in time of Peace.

These Fortifications were a curb and restraint to the Wild Negroes, before they submitted, and may be a means of keeping them orderly and Quiet, should they hereafter attempt to disturb the publick tranquility; for beside the Fort, which is built at the mouth of the Harbour, and named

16. An Act for Vesting Twenty Acres of Land in Lynch's Island in the Crown, 1730, in ibid., 232–33.

Fort George, there is a Defensible Barrack and Breast work erected about two miles distance from the Town, where one of the Companies of the Governour's Regiment consisting of 180 Men, is quartered for the Security and protection of new Set[t]lers.

The West Harbour, or rather Bason, (for it will not Contain above twenty Sail of Ships at Moorings,) is not to be excelled, for the bigness, the Channel not being a quarter of a mile broad from Lynch's Island to Patterson's Point; so that two Ships cannot conveniently go in abreast. But, after they are in they may ride Securely from all Weathers from 3 Fat[homs] 1/2 to 9 fat[homs of] Water, and in some places lay their Sides close to the Shore. And they have this further advantage, that there fine fresh water Rivers empty themselves in this Harbour.

The East Harbour, as it is called, will indeed contain above 200 Sail of Ships, but it is little more than an open Bay, and lies very much exposed to the wind at N[orth] or North West.

Here Vessells, that are homeward bound by Cape Maiz and Cape Nicholas, when chased by an Enemy, or in any other distress, may be relieved; and it will likewise be Convenient for such of His Majesty's Ships to refit; as are appointed to Cruise between those Capes, or the East end of the Island, for the protection of Trade and remote Set[t]lers.

The Soil in this Precinct is fertile and productive of any thing that grows in the West Indies; and there is great plenty of Fish, wild fowl, and Hogs. There are several Settlements made for Ginger and Cotton; also 3 or 4 Sugar-Work[s], and it is probable this part of the Island, with such advantages as they have, will in a few Years flourish, and increase greatly in Inhabitants.

Titchfeild Town, has not yet more than 25 or 30 Houses and Storehouses, but is allowed to send two Members to the Assembly, and has a Court of Sessions, and Common Pleas, with other Privileges for its Encouragement.

Nanny Town, the Grand settlement of the Wild Negroes, who submitted on the same Conditions as were granted to the Leeward Gang commanded by Capt[ai]n Cudjo, is within this Precinct; and 9 miles of Titchfeild formerly called Port Antonio. It is Situate in one of the highest Mountains, Remote and difficult of Access, for there are but two passages to it, both very narrow, and often impassable in times of great Rains, or when they were in possession and laid in Ambuscades. But they were beaten out by our Party in 1734; and we have been in possession of the place Ever Since.

They then went to Leeward, in order to join the other Gang, but disagreeing with them they returned to the Windward Parts, and Settled in the Mountains in St. George's; where they now remain and live very peacably & orderly.

Having Described the several Districks or Divisions of this Island, with their respective Towns, Harbours Bays & Barcadiers so far as is necessary for the information of my Countrymen, and proper with regard to our Enemies, it only Remains according to the method I proposed, to make some observations on their Buildings; and then I shall proceed to give an account of the Islands and other Territories which are dependant on and within the Jurisdiction of the Government of Jamaica.

I might indeed have been more full & particular in some Instances, but that I was cautious of giving any further insight into the Country, or such sights as the French or Spaniards might make use of to the disadvantage of the Inhabitants therefore [I] have carefully incerted nothing but what I thought usefull hints, which may strike out something for the benefit, improvement & security of the Island.

The Houses in this Island are in general too slight, being commonly built of Timber and Boards and only one Story, with a Hall in the middle, a chamber on each side, and a Piazza in the Front, some quite round: the Back part is shedded off, a Chamber taken out of each End, and the middle part serves for an outer or common room. Some of them have cellars for keeping liquors, and such like necessaries cool, but the Kitchen & other offices are all separate from the House, & at the distance of 20 or 30 feet, otherwise they would be very offensive in these Hot Countries.

But some of the Planters' Houses, as well as many Houses in Kingston & Port Royal are built after the English manner with Brick, two Stories high & Garretts over them, most of the Houses at St. Iago delavega are the old Spanish Buildings, and some others after the same manner: These have been found by Experience to be so well contrived, as to resist not only Hurricanes, but to have stood the great Earthquake in 1692, whereas the English Buildings in General, especially those built with Timber & boards only, are commonly damaged, some thrown down or become irreparable at those times.

Most of the Planters' Houses on the North side and the remote parts of the Island are built with stone & made Defensible with Flankers, having loop holes for Fire Arms & Ports for small Carriage Guns, the Windows and Doors being made Musquet proof; so that they are capable of making a good defence with the Assistance of their white Servants & Trusty Negroes, against a Foreign or Intestine Enemy, as wee have experienced in divers Instances. And in my Opinion they ought all to be built after that Modell, and stronger, with at least 3 or 4 three pounders in each Flanker, because they will deter the Privateers & Pyrates from making any descent to plunder those Plantations.

Upon the whole very few of them are well contrived in regard to coolness as well as strength, the Rooms being commonly low & small, and the sides not of a sufficient thickness to resist the Beams of the Sun, which laying upon them all the day, they retain the heat most part of the Night. And in my Opinion Chimneys would be of great use, not only for making a fire now and then in the Rainy Season to dissipate damps & vapours, but as they would draw down air and render the Rooms cooler at other times.

The Places dependant on Jamaica, are Lynch's Island, Pigeon Island, and Severall other little Isles or Cays, which are Contiguous but of little other use than for Catching Turtle; Fish, and Wild fowl; also the Island of Caimanbrack[,] Caimanos and Grand Caiman; the Musquitos in the Province of Jucatan in the Kingdom of Peru, the Bay of Honduras and Ratan.

The Caimanos are three small Islands, namely Caimanbrack, Little Caimanos and Grand Caimanos, Situate W[est] N[orth] W[est] and about 60 leagues distance from the W[est] end of Jamaica.

Caimanbrack is almost round and 8 or 9 leagues in Circumference.

Little Camanos is about 4 leagues in length, a league in Breadth, surrounded with Shoals and 4 leagues to the W[est] S[outh] W[est] of Caimanbrack.

Neither of these two Islands have any Inhabitants or produce anything more than Potatos, and other Ground Provisions, which are planted by the Inhabitants of the Grand Caimanos, for their subsistence when they go there to catch Turtle & Fish.

Grand Caimanos is 8 or 9 leagues in length, three leagues in Breadth, and about 4 leagues to the S[outh] W[est] of little Caimanos. On this Island grow great Numbers of Mahogany[,] Cedar & Fustick Trees which are cut and sent in Sloops to Jamaica. It is also productive of Corn, pease, potatoes and divers other sort of Ground Provisions; and contains about 200 Inhabitants, of w[hi]ch about 2/3 are whites & Mulattos, many of them born there, the rest Negroes.

The first settlement of this Island was occasioned by the following Remarkable Circumstance. A Ship on Board of which was many Passengers, bound from Jamaica to London being cast away there, The Crew built a small vessell of the wreck to transport themselves to Cuba or some other Country; but one Bawden[17] with his Family & some other Passengers chose to remain there, rather than to Expose themselves to the danger of the Seas in such a Vessell. Here They lived some years, before any Ship happened to touch there, in which time the place became so Habitual and They so well contented with their manner of living, that they chose to continue there ever since, & have been joined by others who met with the same fate, or hap[pe]ned to touch there. Old Bawden is still or was lately living, and has a Numerous Family of children & Grand Children, most of Them natives of this Island. They are within the Jurisdiction of Jamaica and are supplied from thence with Cloaths & other Necessar-

17. A Cornish man named Bodden or Bawden left Cornwall in 1654 and was one of three thousand marines who sailed from Portsmouth heading for the Caribbean as part of Oliver Cromwell's army to fight in the Anglo-Spanish War. He became the first recorded settler of the previously uninhabited Cayman Islands in 1658. His grandson Isaac Bodden was listed as an inhabitant of the island in 1700.

ies which They truck with the Trading Sloops for Turtle, Turtle Shell, Mahogany, Cedar & Fustick; but have neither Magistrates, Lawyers, nor Priests among Them. So that all matters of dispute or controversy are determined by Their Neighbours. When They Marry or Baptize Their Children, They come up to Jamaica for that purpose; and it has often hap[pe]ned that a Man & his Wife and 3 or 4 children have been married & Christened at the same time.

The Musquitos is a Nation of Indians in the Province of Jucatan, who never were conquered, or submitted to the Spaniards, nor ever would enter into any Treaty or Commerce with them.

S[i]r Hans Sloan,[18] who attended the Duke of Albemarle, as his Physician, when his Grace went Governor of Jamaica, tells us in his Natural History of this Island, that one Jeremy, who pretended to be their King or Chief (as indeed He was) came to beg His Grace's protection, and that He would send a Governour thither, with a power to make War on the Spaniards and Pyrates. This, He alledged, was due to His Country from the Crown of England, as They had in the Reign of King Charles the 1st., submitted themselves to His Majesty. The Substance of the Memorial which He had got drawn up, and presented to his Grace, was as follows.

That in the Reign of King Charles the 1st., of ever blessed Memory, the Earl of Warwick[19] (by Virtue of letters of Reprisalls, granted by His said Majesty, for damages received from the Subjects of his Catholick Majesty) did possess himself of several Islands in the West Indies, particularly that of Providence, by the Spaniards called S[an]ta Catalina, situate in 13 deg[rees] 10 m[inutes] N[orth] Lat[itude], lying East from Cape Gratios de Dios, Vulgarly called the Musquitos, between 30 and 40 leagues; which put the said Earl upon trying all ways and means of a future Correspondence with the Natives of the said Cape, and the neighbouring Country; and in some little time he was so successfull as to gain that point, and prevailed with them so far, as to persuade them to send home the King's Son, leaving one of his own People as a Hostage for Him, who was one Collo[nel] Morris[20] then living at New York. The Indian Prince going home with the said Earl, staid in England three Years, in which time the Indian King died; and the said Natives having in that time had intercourse of Friendship and Com-

18. "In S[i]r Hans Sloan's *Natural History of Jamaica* Vol. [1,] 19." —*Author.* Sir Hans Sloane, *A Voyage to the Islands Madera, Barbados, Nieves, S. Christophers and Jamaica, with the Natural History of the Herbs and Trees, Four-Footed Beasts, Fishes, Birds, etc.,* 2 vols. (London, 1707–25). —*Ed.*

19. Sir Robert Rich, Second Earl of Warwick (1587–1658), was a Puritan and extensively involved in English colonial projects during the first half of the seventeenth century. In the early 1640s, he became commander in chief of the Parliamentary Navy.

20. Colonel Morris was probably Richard Morris, who was a captain in Oliver Cromwell's army. He may have associated with the Earl of Warwick in one or more of his colonial ventures, was the first Morris to settle in New York, and was the progenitor of the Morris family in that colony, where his heirs became large landholders and achieved political prominence.

merce with those of Providence, were soon made sensible of the Grandeur of His Majesty of Great Britain; and how necessary his protection was to them. And upon the Return of the said Prince, they prevailed with him to resign up his Power, and with them Unanimously declared themselves the Subjects of His said Majesty of Great Britain.

The Duke of Albemarle, says S[i]r Hans, did nothing in this matter, apprehending it might be a trick or design in some People, to set up a Government for Buccaniers or Pyrates: and his Indian Majesty asking many Questions about the Island, and not receiving, as He thought a satisfactory account, He pulled of[f] the Cloaths, that his friends had given him, and Climbed to the top of a Tree to take a View of the Country.

However, He was Civily Entertained, and to keep him in humour, and his People in the good disposition they were in, a Commission was granted him under the Great Seal of the Island, Constituting and Appointing him in his Majesty's name, to be King of the Musquito Indians; with which He was very well pleased; and in this Opinion they have ever Since persisted, and do not own any other Supreme Command over them: for whenever their King dies, the next in blood, comes to Jamaica with two or three of the principal men of the Country to Attest the same, and in like form and manner receives a Commission from the Governour to be King over them.

As to the Country, the Soil is fertile, and it is a very great levell, free from Mountains for severall Leagues from the Sea; though in many places low and boggy, and the land covered with Pine Trees, of the Nature of New England Fir, well watered with great Rivers and Rivulets.

They have only two Harbours and both barred, and so not capable of receiving any Vessell, that draws above 11 or 12 feet Water; and all their Coast is full of Shoals, and Cays or small Islands, which makes it difficult of Access, only for Sloops and other small Vessells.

The back part of their Country is surrounded with great and inaccessible Mountains, or Morasses, which serve as Barriers against the Spaniards; and though they cannot give any Account of their Origin, yet they have by Tradition heard of the great Cruelties that were Committed by the Spaniards on the Neighbouring Nations; and 'tis not improbable, but they are descended of some, that Escaped their fury, and retired here as a proper Retreat or place of Security.

From hence arises their implacable Enmity and hatred to the Spaniards, for whenever any of that Nation are so unhappy as to fall into their hands they are sure of being put to death, or to made use of their own Expression, when they take any of their Enemys Prisoners, they hide them. Upon which Occasion, they often Reproach the English with Indescretion and Folly, in releasing the Spaniards (whom they in derision call little Breeches) when they are taken Prisoners in War, as they will say they come and disturb you again, but if you hide them, that is cut their throats or otherways destroy them, they never will trouble you more.

Nevertheless those People are naturally mild, inoffensive, and of a tender disposition, ready to relieve all persons in distress, except Spaniards, and are more particularly kind to the English Nation, having upon many Occasions been very serviceable to the Inhabitants of Jamaica, of which the following is a Remarkable Instance.

In the Year 1724 a Sloop belonging to Port Royal was taken by a Spanish Guarda Costa, and by Stress of Weather both of them were afterwards driven near the Musquitor Coast. King Jeremy having by some means got information of what had hap[pe]ned, fitted out several Periago's or large Canno's, manned them with near 200 men well Armed, went in Person, Attacked and took the Privateer; and without any Ceremony hanged every Person aboard except the English Prisoners; to whom He gave their Own Vessell and Effects, permitted them to furnish themselves with what they wanted out of the Spanish Prize; and after they had taken out what they had Occasion for themselves, burnt the Vessell.

In Return for this Service, His Grace the Duke of Portland, at the Request of the Assembly, sent his Indian Majesty, and those that accompanied him, a present of Arms, Cloaths, and such other things as were most acceptable to them.

King Jeremy being unwilling to be behind hand in Civility came up to Jamaica, personally to make his Complements to his Grace, and acknowledge the bountiful present, as he thought, was made to Him and his Country men; and was received with all the Complacency, and goodness, peculiar to that Noble Lord.

In fine He was so Caressed by People of all Ranks, and entertained for more than two months in a manner, he was unacquainted with before, in regard to living and being better Cloathed, that it was with great Reluctance He returned to his own Country, and was inclined to remain in the Island, had the least Encouragement been given to it. However he went away greatly pleased with the Reception and Entertainment He met with, and had not only more but Richer Cloaths than any of the Ancestors ever had, Several Rich Suits that his Grace had laid by, being fitted for Him.

As to the Number of the Musquito Indians no Certain Account can be given, though it is thought, they do not exceed 2000 men fit for War. Their Common Arms are Launces, which they throw very dexterously and as dexterously avoid those that are darted from the Enemy. But many of them have likewise Fire Arms, and understand the use of them; as they often come to Jamaica, and Sail in His Majesty's Ships, as well as the Vessells belonging to the Island; for they are exceeding usefull to the Company they enter with in Catching of Fish, and Turtle, and in Several Engagements, which hap[pe]ned in time of War[,] behaved Extremely well.

Their manner of living is Patriarchall; the old Women and Children doing all the Work at home, and the Master of the Family and Young men going out early every morning fishing, fowling, or hunting, without taking any Care for the morrow. Every Person pays great Duty and Respect to the Pater Familias, who is absolute Judge in all Cases in his own family; and seldom any disputes or Controversies arise between Masters, but whenever they happen, they are determined by their Friends and Neighbours.

They do not allow of Polygamy, or Concubinage, and so great respect is shewed to those that are Married, that the Elder Brother, if He is a Batchelor always gives precedence to the Younger, that is married; and they have so great a regard to truth, that they never will trust, or confide in those, that once deceive them.

All they produce from the Earth is Coconuts, Yams, Plantains, Bonano's and Potato's, and have little notion of Husbandry or Planting. But, were some Industrious Persons to settle amongst them, to instruct and Encourage them to till Plant and Sow the Richness of their Soil wou[l]d Easily and advantageously produce many Commodity's, and particularly Indigo. Capt[ai]n Tho[mas] Weir of Jamaica, had such a design, and with the Consent of the Natives, obtained of the Governour a Patent for a tract of Land there; but he was soon after Treacherously killed by the Spaniards, and thereby not only an advantageous Scheme defeated, but the Island lost a usefull Industrious, and necessary man.

They are very desirous of Englishmen set[t]ling amongst them; and indeed, they have four or five Families there, to whom they are Exceeding kind, though they are loose, Idle People, and such as ran away from Jamaica for debt, or some Crimes.

As to Religion they have very imperfect notions, tho[ugh] they believe there is a Supreme Being, and a future State; and adore the Sun as the Founder and Author of all things. When any of them die, the deceased Person is Sewed up in a Mat, and buried not length ways but upright upon his feet, with his face exactly East.

Their Government though Monarchical and Hereditary is little more than Nominal, for notwithstanding in time of War or danger the King has an Absolute Power, and great deference is paid to Him; yet in time of Peace he is obliged to fish, fowl and provide for his own family; nor is He to be distinguished from any other Person, but by having better Cloaths, which are given him by the People of Jamaica.

Two or three small Sloops go down Yearly from Jamaica to trade with those people for Turtle Shells, Sarsaparilla, Vinellos and Cocoa, which they have from their Neighbours and some times from the Spaniards in time of War; as also some Indians, whom they take Prisoners, when they are at War with any Indian Nation in their Neighbourhood and those they dispose of to the English, who seldom employ them any other way than in fishing, nor indeed are they fit for any thing else they are of mild and tender a disposition. The Commodities they take in Truck, are Oznabrigs, old Cloaths, powder, Arms, Knives, Bills, Hoes, Axes Breads, coarse Calicoes, and small looking Glasses.

The long Experience we have had of the use and Service of those People, to the English Nation, although they have no Gold, or Rich Commodities to truck with, points out the many advantages, that would arise to the British Trade and Navigation; if a Friendship and Commerce were Cultivated with others, who are known to have plenty of Gold, being situated near some of the Spanish Mines or probably have some of their own. And by the friendly disposition of the Indians in general a new branch of Commerce might be opened, and carried on in time of Peace; and by their means it would be greatly in our power to annoy and distress the Spaniards in time of War. But, However beneficial projects of this nature might be to the British Nation and Colonies we find no Steps taken to encourage or improve the Opportunities that have offered; Nay, we have even neglected the Invitations that have been made us, by some of those Nations that are always at Enmity with, and have an implacable hatred to the Spaniards; as well as by others, who are inclined and would willingly shake off the Spanish Yoke in order to put them selves under the protection of the Crown of England.

How to account for this Supineness and neglect of our own Interest, I will not take upon me, any further than to Observe, that I wish we may not Repent of it, when it is too late; as the French are so far from neglecting such opportunities that they assiduously seek them out, and omit nothing in their power to Cultivate and improve them, so that they may probably make their advantages of our Supineness in this, as well as they have done in other Respects.

I shall proceed to make some observations on the Trade to the Bays of Campeachy and Honduras; and shew not only the usefulness and Advantages of those places, to Great Britain, but our undoubted Right to them; for the asserting of which I have the Authority of the Board of Trade, and shall transcribe such parts as I think necessary, of their Report to his late Majesty the 18th Feb[ruary] and published in the *Political State of Great Britain* for the month of April 1729.[21]

The Trade to Campechy had its Rise from the decay of Privateering. For after the Treaty of Peace with Spain in 1667,[22] the Privateers, who lived upon the plunder and Booty, they acquired, by the War, were put to their Shifts, having prodigally spent, what they got; and wanting subsistance, some of them went to Petit Guaves, where a considerable Number of French and other Privateers, commonly called Bucaniers were seated, and had not then Submitted or put themselves under the protection of the Crown of France. But, the more Industrious sort of them, went and settled

21. *The Political State of Great Britain* (London, 1729), 38:337–59 is the source of this information. The Board of Trade document reprinted here is, however, dated September 25, 1717.

22. Articles of Peace, Commerce, and Alliance, between the Crowns of Great Britain and Spain: Concluded in a Treaty at Madrid the 13/23 Day of May, in the Year of Our Lord God, 1667.

in the Bay of Campeachy, for having often before cruized near Champe-
ton River, where the Spaniards cut Logwood, and having by that means
learned the Value of it, as also how to know and Distinguish the Trees, it
put them on Searching other parts of the Continent, till they found out the
Lagune of Treiste; which was sometime before the Peace in 1667. After
this Discovery whenever they were disapointed of a Prize, or other Booty,
some of them would lade their Ships with Logwood, which was then very
valuable, and Carry it to Jamaica. The Spaniards had not then frequented
that place, nor ever had any Settlement there, though they attempted it
some years after that Peace, when they dispossessed the English, who were
settled there, but they soon deserted it.

To Corroborate this I shall transcribe a passage from S[i]r Hans Sloan's
Natural History of the Island of Jamaica, Vol[ume] 1. Pag[e] 83,[23] wherein He
makes mention of this Trade to Campechy and the usage and Bahaviour of
the Spaniards to our Settlers there.

> The Spaniards, says He, who are offended at this Settlement, equipped
> some Periaguas and Hulks against them; but before they were ready, they
> were burnt by the English. They have a place Stronger than their Hutts,
> for their Provision, and when a Strength much greater than theirs come
> against them, they retire to the Woods. They have been cut off several
> times by the Spaniards in this place and yet have settled here again. This
> usage of the Spaniards is somewhat harsh, if what S[i]r Henry Morgan, has
> often told me be true, that this Logwood River was in the Possession of
> the English, at the time of the Treaties being signed at Madrid concerning
> the West Indies.

It will not be improper to Remark, that before the English set[t]led in
the Bays of Campechy and Honduras, Logwood, which of late Years has
been sold from 8 to £10 per Ton, was sold from 90 to £110 per Ton. This
will Evidently Appear upon looking into the Act of the 14. of Charles the
2d.; when a Duty was laid thereon of £5 per Ton on the Value at that time,
which was rated at £100.[24] The reduction of the price of a Commodity so
Essentially necessary to our Woollen manufactures, and which our Dyers
cannot be without, may be reckoned among other advantages arising from
the Island of Jamaica, as the Trade to those places cannot be supported or
carried on without the Aid and Assistance, they have from thence.

The Bay of Campeachy we were likewise in possession of at the time of
the Treaty of Utrecht, and as the Treaty of 1670 was therein revived and
Confirmed, I conceive, that gives us a further Right and Title to the Place.
I have also the Authority of the Board of Trade in the abovementioned Re-

23. Sloane, *Natural History of the Island of Jamaica*, 1: 83.
24. Act of Duty of £5 per Ton on Logwood. Parliament 14 of Charles II.

port in that Respect; and although we have several times been disturbed, and our Navigation there unjustly taken or destroyed, particularly in the Year 1718, 1724, 1728, and 1730; yet it is observable, that after the Spaniards drove our People from thence, they never attempted to make any Settlement, or to keep possession, until the last mentioned time.

As to the Bay of Honduras, it is a wild and uninhabited Country for above one hundred leagues, and though the Spaniards have several times disturbed our Settlers at that place likewise, yet they never attempted a Settlement, and we are at this time in possession.

It is worth considering, that the Spaniards never were allowed by the Crown of Great Britain, to have an Exclusive Right to the Continent or Islands of America, that were not actually possessed by them, any more than the Portuguese, French, or any other Nation. The words *Preeminence, Right* or *Dominion* of either Confederate in the 15th Article, having Respect only to the American Seas, Channels or Waters, which they are to have and Retain, in as full and ample, manner, as may of Right belong unto them. But what Right &c. can be pretended to be thereby yeilded to them, of uninhabited Countries or Places not in their possession? Or what Right does this Article give them, to any thing, but what belongs to them, that is, what is inhabited by them. Nor is there any thing in this Treaty, that Barrs the King of Great Britain, or his Subjects, from possessing any part of the Continent or Islands of America, where no other possessors were before them.

But these matters being more strongly urged and insisted on, in the above mentioned Report, I shall recommend the following Abstract to the further Consideration of my Readers, wherein Their Lordships insist, that the English have an unquestionable Right to the Logwood Trade, and have always been protected in it by the Kings of England, his Majestie's Predecessors.

They observe, that Logwood is the Product of *Jucaton*, a Peninsula, that extends it self an hundred Leagues into the North Sea (on each Side whereof are the Bays of Campeachy and Honduras, where this Wood is chiefly cut by the English.)

That the Spaniards are possessed only of the Town of Campechy, and two more small Places in this Part of America; and that the rest of *Jucatan* was an uninhabited Desert 'till our Logwood Cutters Settled at Cape Catoch, the North East Promontory of *Jucatan*, and at Trist or the Laguna de Terminos in the Bay of Campeachy, before or in the Year 1667, when a Treaty of Peace was concluded between Great Britain and Spain. And thereupon the Privateers of Jamaica, who used to disturb the Spanish Trade, being obliged to quit that Way of Life, became Logwood Cutters, and settled with others of their Countrymen at Trist and the Lake de Terminos aforesaid; and great Quantities of Logwood were afterwards imported from thence to Old and New England.

They observe that S[i]r Thomas Lynch, Governour of Jamaica, under whose Direction that Trade was carried on, in the Year 1671, gave his Majesty King Charles 2d. the following Reasons for his encouraging this Trade.

1. That the English had then used it for divers Years.
2. That the Logwood was cut in desolate and uninhabited Places.
3. That it was a Right confirmed by Treaty with the Spaniards.
4. That thereby we excluded the French and Dutch from that Trade.
5. That the Spaniards had not then made any Complaint of it.
6. That this Employment made the reducing our Privateers, who used to commit Hostilities against the Spaniards, more easy.

Lastly, That this Place employed 100 Sail of Ships annually, and increased his Majesty's Customs, and the Trade of the Nation, more than any of his American Colonies.

S[i]r Thomas Modyford, the succeeding Governor of Jamaica, informed the Lords of the Privy Council, in the Year 1672, That the English Logwood Cutters had used that Trade for three Years, that they had planted Corn and built Houses for their Conveniency; and though they frequently hunted Deer in the Country, they had never seen a single Spaniard or any other Man in that Part of the Country in all the Time they had been there: And concludes, That their felling of Wood, building Houses, and clearing and planting the Ground, was such a Possession as in the West-Indies gave them an undoubted Right to the Countries they thus occupied.

And S[i]r Thomas, to justify his Conduct in Encouraging this Trade, in the Year 1672 (when the Spaniards first complained of it) sent home the Copies of several Depositions, he had taken from Masters of Ships and others concerned in the Logwood Trade, with a Proclamation, he had issued for the Regulation and Security thereof, as a Confirmation of what he had asserted. And the Lords of the Council thereupon let the Governour know, that they approved of what He had done.

The Lords Commissioners of Trade further observe, That there is a Clause in the above said American Treaty, which provides, That the King of Great Britain shall keep and possess, in full Right of Sovereignty and Propriety, all Places situate in the West Indies or any Part of America, which he or his Subjects were then in possession of *Trist*, the *Lake de Terminos* and several other Places in the Province of *Jucatan*, which the *Spaniards* begun to set up a Title to about this Time, notwithstanding they enjoyed the full Benefit of what Great Britain stipulated on her Part, vizt.

1st. The securing the Trade of the Spanish West Indies to them, a Point which had never before been yielded.

2d. The obliging the Privateers to cease their Depredations, whereby the Spanish Trade had been miserably harrassed; and this had been effected chiefly by the Care of his Majesty's Governors, and the employing those People in the Logwood Trade.

That in 1680 the Spaniards proceeded in a hostile manner to dispossess the English Logwood Cutters of their Settlements of Trist, &c, and even of the Island of Providence, a British Plantation to which they had no Pretence; but these were soon repossessed by His Majestie's Subjects; and the Logwood Trade in 1682 was greater than ever, and was maintained, and carried on by the English, till the Treaty of Utrecht, 1713; when the Adjustment and Settlement thereof came again under Consideration; and it was Stipulated that (only) such Places shou[l]d be restored to the Spaniards, as had been taken during the preceding War (in the Reign of Queen Anne) among which Trist could not be reckoned one, because the English were in possession of it many Years, before that War commenced, and indeed had been in the actual possession of it from 1669 to 1713, except for two or three Months in the Year 1683, when the Spaniards surprised and expelled them by Force, as related above.

They further represented, That by a Clause in the Treaty of Commerce concluded in *November* 1713, the *American* Treaty of 1670 is confirmed and ratified; and it was thereby declared, that this should be understood to be without Prejudice to any Liberty or Power which the Subjects of *Great Britain* enjoyed before, either through *Right, Sufferance, or Indulgence;* and the *English* having long enjoyed the Liberty of cutting Logwood without interruption either through *Right, Sufferance, or Indulgence,* they are by this Treaty entitled to the same in as plain and express Words, as can be imagined.

Then the Lords Commissioners proceed to shew the Importance of the Logwood Trade *to Great Britain* by the following Account of what Logwood had been imported since the late War, viz.

	Tons	C.	Q	lb.
In 1713,	2189.	15.	3.	22
In 1714,	4878.	14.	3.	24
In 1715,	5863.	12.	1.	14
In 1716,	2032.	17.	2.	0
	14965.	0.2	3.	4

That is communibus annis 3741 Tons, which cannot be computed at less than 60,000£ per Ann[um] tho[ugh] the Price is alre[a]dy reduced from 40 £ to 16£ p[er] Ton; and before your Majestie's Subjects were settled there it was worth 100 £ the Ton.

Nor is this Trade less necessary than beneficial to your Majesty's Dominions, by reason of the great Encouragement it gives to our Seamen and Shipping, which at all Times require a particular Attention; but now especially, when it is daily observed that very many *British* Mariners, either thro[ugh] Defect of the Laws for want of Employment at home, or in hopes of greater Advantage abroad, enter themselves into foreign Service.

Upon the whole therefore we are humbly of Opinion, That the Subjects of this your Majesty's Kingdom for some Years before, as well as after the Conclusion of the *American* Treaty in 1670, did enjoy an uninterrupted Liberty of cutting Logwood in the *Laguna de Terminos*, and in other Places not inhabited by the Spaniards in the Province of *Jucatan, either through Right, Sufferance, or Indulgence.*

That the said *American Treaty* did *establish a Right* in the Crown of Great-Britain to the *Laguna de Terminos* and the Parts adjacent; those Places at the Time of the Treaty, and for some Years before, being actually *in possession* of the British Subjects. Signed

Suffolk[25]   J. Molesworth[26]
J. Chetwynd[27]   D. Pulteny[28]
Charles Cooke[29]   M. Bladen[30]

It is to be observed, that their Lordships have not included in their Calculation what was exported to Holland and other Parts, agreeable to the Act of Navigation[,] only what was imported into Great Britain. And that after the Duty was taken off there was annually exported into Europe from 8 to 10,000 Tons, which gave Employment to at least 800 men in the Bays of Campeachy and Honduras and above 2000 Seamen.

It likewise reduced the price to 8 and £9 per Ton, and enabled us to furnish other Nations with greater quantities, the Value of which may be reckoned clear profit to the Nation, Since it was the product of labour and the incidental charges Centered in our Selves. And, as that Commodity is Consumed in Great Britain by the Dyers as I have Observed and is absolutely necessary, the Reduction of the price is a Considerable advantage to the Nation as we are enabled to Sell our Woollen Manufactures considerably cheaper than we could possibly do when we purchased that Commodity of the Spaniards. But, should we entirely be deprived of those advantages, we shall be necessitated to purchase that Commodity as we did formerly of them, or other Nations, at Exorbitant prices, which will be a further obstruction if not the Ruin of that Valuable Branch of the British Commerce.

25. Henry Howard, Sixth Earl of Suffolk (1670–1718), was first lord of trade, 1715–18.
26. Sir John Molesworth, Third Baronet (1668–1723), was a member of the Board of Trade, 1714–17.
27. John Chetwynd was a member of the Board of Trade, 1714–28.
28. Daniel Pulteney (1684–1731) was a member of the Board of Trade, 1717–27.
29. Sir Charles Cooke (?–1721) was a merchant and member of the Board of Trade, 1714–21.
30. Martin Bladen (1680–1746) was a member of the Board of Trade, 1714–46.

There is indeed some Logwood growing in Jamaica and in time great Quantities will be produced in this Island, though I doubt whether it will be Sufficient for the Consumption of England. We are at this time dispossessed and deprived of Campeachy, and the demand for that Commodity as well as the imports from Honduras and Jamaica, diminished at least one third; and this I am sorry to say I believe to be principally owing to the decay of our Wo[o]llen Manufactures occasioned by the great difficulties and Embarassments it labours under at Foreign Markets. But, should that Branch of the British Commerce revive and flourish as it did formerly, we may then very sensibly feel the loss of Campeachy.

These Points are of great importance to the Trade and Navigation of Great Britain, and therefore are worthy of the Notice and Consideration of the Legislature, and of every Man who wishes well to the Interest and Prosperity of His Country.

The Island of Rattan is about 12 Leagues in length & 4 in Breadth, Situate in the Lat[itude] of [blank] and is about 150 Leagues West and by South of Jamaica, and about 8 Leagues [blank] of the Bay of Hondurus. It never was settled by the Spaniards, nor had any other Inhabitants than now & then some Pyrates who retired hither being remote, unfrequented, by any other People, and Consequently a proper Rendevouz.

The 13 August 1742 Major Cawfield[31] Sailed from Jamaica with four Transports, having on Board 300 Soldiers under Convoy of two Men of Warr to take possession of it. He arrived there the 23d and soon after disembarqued the Forces and Raised Batteries on each side of the Harbour, which He has since Fortifyed in such a manner, as to render it almost impracticable of being taken. The Mouth or Entrance into the Harbour which is called Port Royal, is so narrow that it will not admit of more than one Ship going in at a time; but within it is so Spacious that 300 Sail may ride there conveniently in all weathers.

Here is Excellent water, great Plenty of wild Hogs & Deer and the Sea abounds with all kinds of Fish that are usual and Common in America, particularly Turtle. With regard to the Product little more can be said than that here is plenty of Cocoa which grows Wild and without doubt when the Woods are Cleared and the Lands cultivated, they will be found productive of Sugar[,] Indigo, Cotton and other Commodities. It is well Situated for Trade, and will be a great Security to the Bay of Hondurus, where our Logwood Cutters are Settled, that Commodity being of great importance to the British Trade with regard to our woolen Manufactures. And, as it is likewise within a very few leagues of the River Dulce, from whence the Commerce of Guatimala and other Provinces in that neighbourhood are carried on, many other Advantages may be made by this Acquisition; there-

31. Major John Caulfield (d. 1752), a British army officer, was the first commander in chief of the island of Roatan.

fore it is to be hoped that it will not upon any Consideration be yielded up on any Treaty with Spain.

It had been as I observed the Rendevouz of Pyrates and ten were found alive there when Major Cawfield arrived. Severall English Families who were Settled in the Bay of Honduras, and among the Musquito Indians are come to the Island in Order to Settle, and others from Jamaica and North America so that there is a prospect of its being well Settled in a few years and of great use and Service to the English Nation.

It is at present under Military Goverment and Major Cawfield is appointed L[ieu]t[enant] Governour, Subordinate to the Governour of Jamaica and has a Salary allowed him by the Crown of £500 Ster[ling][per] Annum. But undoubtedly it will be thought necessary to Establish there in a little time the Civil Law and form of Government otherwise it cannot be Expected that it will be much frequented by Trading People, or that any great Advantages will arise from [it].

The Project of this New Settlement had very near proved abortive in a few months for on the 25 of December following between the hours of 12 and one at night the four American Companies Mutinied, and According to the Scheme which was laid by Corporal Badger, they sett fire to the Hutts, marched to the Water Side discharged their Fire Arms with loud Huzzas w[hi]ch allarmed the Officers who immediately Ordered the Guards to be Reinforced. But all their Efforts would have been ineffective had not two of his Majesty's Ships been in Port, and immediately landed a Captain, two Lieutenants and 50 private Men of Colo[nel] Frazier's Regiment of Marines[,] Their Sole dependance before this Reinforcement being on a Detachment of Colo[nel] Wolf's Marines. They immediately Seized the Ring leaders who were 33 in Number and several others next Morning who were tried at a Court Martial on the 27th when one of the Serjeants was admitted as an Evidence for the King and 13 others, who discovered the whole plott. Badger was Shot According to his Sentence, the other Serjeant and one private Man received 600 lashes, and were put on Board of the Ships of War. It was likewise Discovered by the Court Martiall that out of the Detachment of 200 American Soldiers, 47 were Papists who had been abetting this affair for some weeks before.

Part the 5th

Of The Climate, Air, Seasons, Winds, Weather, Currents, Water and Rivers; as also of the Diseases and Distempers Most Frequent in Jamaica, and Other Parts of the West Indies.

From the Situation of this Island, it may Reasonably be imagined to be very Hot, all the year, and especially in the Summer Solstice. Indeed the Heat would be intolerable, did not the frequent Showers of Rain, and the great Dews, which fall every Night, as well as the Easterly Winds, or Sea Breezes, that blow every day, more or less, from February to September, lessen the Influence and Effects of the Sun, and Contribute to the Temperature of the Climate. Beside, the Heat of the days are qualified by the length of the Nights, which are almost equal throughout the Year, so that the Sun has not that length of time to heat the Atmosphere and Surface of the Earth, as in those Parts, where the days are longer, and the Nights Shorter: and for the same Reason, the Evenings are much hotter than the Mornings although the Sun be equally distant, and the Rays fall equally oblique; the Heat then becoming extraordinary, because the Atmosphere and Surface of the Earth have been warmed from morning to that time by the beams of the Sun.

The other four Months of the Year vizt. from October to January, the Air is more Temperate, because the Sun is longer absent, and at a greater distance than at any other time of the Year; and the North Winds which commonly blow at that Season in the Day as well as in the Night Contribute to make the Alteration more Sensible; for at those times the Temper of the Air is much the same, as in the Months of May and June in England; and tho[ugh] in the hottest Season we sweat much yet even at that time, we do not find The faintness: nor the Air so suffocating, as it often is here in July and August.

To Enter into a particular discussion and describe all the Properties of the Air or Wind in this Region or Part of the World, I will not pretend; though I think it pertinent and Necessary to make some few observations on its Wonderful Operation and Effects on the Bodies, both of Men and Beasts as well as Vegetables, and even on Iron, which is the hardest of all Metals.

The Air is an Element,[1] in which we not only live and breathe, but which we also draw into our Entrails; and therefore it is not Strange that different Airs or Winds, and removing from one Climate or Country to another, should cause notable impressions and Alterations in the Habit of the Body, and particularly in Persons of a Sickly and Infirm Constitution; because one Wind is hot and moist, and another cold and dry; the South breeds mists and Rain, and the North dissipates them and clears the sky. The Holy Scriptures call one a Burning Wind and another a Wind full of Dew and Sweetness. And common Experience Convinces us that the Easterly Winds in Europe are sharp, penetrating and unhealthy, and the Westerly or Contrary Winds are comfortable and wholesome. Whereas in America the Easterly Winds are hot, yet deemed healthy; and the Northerly and those to the Westward of the North Cool, and Pleasant, but unhealthy.

The Air is likewise to be Considered, with regard to its general heat and Moisture; the one qualifying the other so as to render the Torrid Zone Habitable. As Heat is the Natural product of the Sun, we may Reasonably Conclude, that glorious Planet to be the Cause, or Mover, of those beneficial and necessary Breezes, which render the Air different, as I observed, from any on the other side of the Tropick; and therefore differently to be Considered as the Cause of Health; and though the Wind blows, where it listeth, yet Here it is Regular, Observes its times, and keeps its Seasons, as is well known to every common Observer; for when the Sun by its direct Rays seems to threaten to parch up the Earth, and destroy all living Creatures as well as Vegetables, then, as there is the greatest need thereof, there is generally a strong Sea-Breez[e] every day until five in the afternoon, and sometimes later. Nor can it be doubted that the Heat of the Sun[2] contributes or is the Cause of those Breezes, because when it Appears in the Horizon, it Rarifies, or clears the Air, and draws it towards the West, where it meets with another Condensed by the Coldness of the Night; and as the Sun rises in the Horizon, the Breezes freshen in proportion, and decrease upon its descending from it; so that when the Sun Sets, it seldom blows after within the land, or near the land. Though the same does not happen at Sea, because the Air being sooner Condensed upon the Sea, than on the Land, it remains longer rarified on account of the strong Exhalations from the Heat of the Earth. And this is likewise the Reason of the Inland Air, called the land Wind or Breez[e], having its tendency toward the Sea Coast, for it rises in the Evening immediately or soon after the Sea Breez[e] is laid or Ceases, and blows gently all night, until the Air at Sea begins to be rarified, the next morning, by the Heat of the Sun. As this

1. This explanation, of course, predates modern chemistry's definition of the air as a compound of elements. Other scientific taxonomies and descriptions throughout this chapter are similarly outdated.

2. See Rohault's *Nat[ural] Phil[osophy]*, Volume 1. Page 208. — *Author.* Jacques Rohault, *Natural Philosophy*, 2nd edition, 2 vols. (London, 1729). — *Ed.*

seems to be the Nature of those Winds, there is no difficulty in Assigning a Reason for their being more Constant and Stronger in America, especially in the Summer Months, than at any other Season; because the Sun has then a greater Influence and Power, on the Air.

Hence we may perceive, and have great Reason to Admit the Infinite Wisdom and Goodness of Divine Providence, in Refreshing those Parts of the Earth, which have the most occasion thereof, through such seeming Contrary Causes and Effects, for it would be impossible for Human Bodys or even many Animals to Exist, did not the heat of the Sun generate the Winds, which Ventilate the lungs, as well as cool the Body that would otherwise be inflamed and parched up.

But, those Winds not being the same and arising from different Causes, produce as Contrary Effects; for the Heat of the Sun acting all the day, with great force and Vigour upon the Ocean, must necessarily draw the Volatile and Saline parts; which floating and mixing with the Air, occasion not only a moist Atmosphere, but afford matter for the daily Sea Breez[e]; so the Stagnated Air harbouring in Mountainous Caverns and Woody Confinements, administer Sufficient matter to the land or Night Breez[e]; and as the Sea Breezes partaking of the enlivening Saline Nature, are found by Experience as well as Reason, to be healthy though not so agreeable and pleasant, resisting and defending from putrefactions, so the Stagnated Air in those Mountains and Woody Confinements impregnated by divers Minerals and Vapours cause alterative changes in respect to putrefaction and Diseases: and betwixt both, the Air is always kept in Motion, which otherwise thro[ugh] its great heat and Moisture would undoubtedly putrify, and thence arise Insects, and such like Generations, instead of more noble and perfect Animals.

It is likewise observable that the land Wind or Breezes have a more sensible chilliness than those from the Sea, and are often the Cause of Tertian and Quartan Agues; for while the pores by daily Sweating and insensible transpirations are most open, the sudden change of the land Wind or Breez[e] easily surprize the disposed Body to Aguish dispositions, and Nature being sensible of her intruding Enemy often Shuts too Close the Outlets of the Skin, and unadvisedly retains what ought to be discharged. Hence arises a sour ferment in the juices of the whole Body, first shivering and then chilling the Extreme parts, and afterwards inflaming the whole in a hot Paroxysm.

Nor is it improper to Remark, that those land Winds or Breezes, do less Injury to New Comers from Europe or Colder Climates, than to the Ancient Inhabitants, or those that are Seasoned to the Country, whose pores being moulded as it were to the bore of the Indian Air, are of a larger Size and more receptive of the Chilling breezes. Nevertheless they ought to be guarded against by all sorts of People, and of all Ages and Conditions as they are generally the foundation or Cause of most Distempers incidental to this part of the World; and the neglect thereof hath been fatal to many of the Inhabitants as well, as to the Sea and Land Forces, which have been sent from time to time to this Island, as they were tempted to partake of this Agre[e] able and pleasant Wind not Considering or regarding the Consequence; for it is a Common Custom with the Seamen on board His Majestie's Ships, as well as the Merchantmen, after they have labour[e]d hard all the day, or heated and inflamed their Bodies with drinking strong Rum Punch, to expose themselves not only to the night-Air but to the Dews, which are much heavier in these parts than in Europe, and even to Sleep upon the Deck without any Covering; so that the next morning they have not only been stiff with cold, and not able to move, but Contracted such Violent colds, and other disorders, as soon brought them to their Graves. This hath been the fate of many Stout and brave Seamen and Soldiers, and it is a matter of surprize as well as pity, that the Commanding Officers have so little regard for the healths and lives of their men, as not to prohibit, by some good orders and Rules this dangerous Custom, of suffering their men to expose themselves in that manner to the night Air and Dews.

Nor do many of the Inhabitants take that prudent Care, they ought, but frequently and unadvisedly expose themselves by Riding, Walking, and even Sitting in the times of the Nightly Winds, Damps and Dews; therefore it is not Strange that such Numbers have been carried off, as the like practice would be dangerous in Europe in the Summer Months.

And I am perswaded from my own Observation and Experience, that the Sickness, and Mortality, which often happens in this part of the World, is principally owing to Intemperance and want of Care, more than to the Inclemency of the Climate, the Truth of which may be evinced almost to a Demonstration, by observing that the Women, and Jews, as well as the Spaniards in America, who live in a Regular abstemious manner, seldom exposing themselves to the Violent heat of the Sun, or the pernicious Influence of those nightly Breezes, and Dews, are much healthier than other People, and live to a greater Age.

That the Air is moist as well as Hot is Evident from the great difficulty of preserving Iron and Steel from Rust, Brass and Copper from turning Green, and Silver from tarnishing. Flesh cannot be preserved above 24 hours without being Salted; they must bury their dead in that space of time, and Corpulent Bodies sooner. Bread becomes hard and not eatable in three days, and there is great difficulty in preserving Salted Provisions, Rice, Indian Corn and other grain for above the Space of one Year.

The Air is likewise Nitrous and may well work on Metallick Bodies and Corrode them, not much short of that which they would have suffered by being exposed to Bilge Water as the Seamen term it.[3] The great quantities

---

3. Trapham. — *Author.* Dr. Thomas Trapham, *Discourse of the State of Health in the Island of Jamaica* (London, 1679), 14. — *Ed.*

of Salt Peter brought from the East Indies into Europe evince what great store there is to be found in those hot Countries, which are every way to be equall[e]d by the West in all such Products. And from the same Cause of Nitrous parts abounding in the Air, our Rains are so fruitfull and the Dews so penetrating that they equal if not outdo Snow water.

As to the Seasons of the Year, very little distinction is to be made, there being neither Spring nor Autumn, that can be distinguished as Such; nor can we Ascertain which Months or part of the Year to call Winter and which Summer; for on the South side of the Island the Stormy Rainy Season, which makes it appear most like Winter, begins in the Month of August and ends in October; though on the North side, it is more agre[e]able to the Seasons in Europe, beginning in November and ending in February; then follows such a dry Season as Represents not only Summer, but a Summer of the Torrid Zone, for the land is deprived of its Verdant Charms, and the Savannas and Pastures appear withered and burnt up.

If the Seasons are to be reckoned from the Spring of Vegetables, the Spring will be after the great Rains in May and October; for then they shoot out, appear green and flourishing, as they do in the Months of April and May in Europe; Nature seems to revive, the Savannas, and Pastures are cloathed with Green, the Plants with Blossoms and Flowers, and the Air is fresher, cooler and Pleasanter; so that they may be said to have two Springs, as indeed they have two Crops of Corn, Pease, and other Grain, and almost all sorts of Fruit, which are Natural to the Climate.

But if we follow the nearness or distance of the Sun, they will then have the same time as in Europe; for in October the days begin to shorten, in proportion to their length the rest of the Year; so that an Alteration may be perceived tho[ugh] not much, and to lengthen in January. The Nights and Mornings in those Months are Cooler, and sometimes, especially in the Mountains, they are cold. The Plants grow but little, and the Trees shed their leaves, though they are not deprived of them all at once, or in some Weeks, the preceding Rains and warm Sun Cloathing them with New, as fast as the Old ones drop off.

The only distinction therefore, that can properly be made of the Seasons, is to consider them as they are hot and dry, or Moist and Rainy; and those wet and dry Seasons, in some parts of the Island, do follow each other as Successively as Winter and Summer do in England. If the Rains happen to fall moderately and at the usual times, the following Months prove well in Respect to Health, as well as the Product of the Earth. But when they succeed a long and intense drought, and pour down in impetuous Showers, with thunder and light[e]ning, it has not only the appearance of Winter, and great damages ensue by the Violence of the Winds and Floods, but they prove unhealthy and are attended with a train of Acute and Inflammatory diseases.

In the Months of May, August and October are the general Seasons, as they are called, which are great Rains, with Gusts of Wind, from the Sea, that continue Day and Night for 8 or 10 days together with very little intermission. But these sometimes failing[,] particularly in Leguinea, St. Dorothy's and Vere, it is greatly prejudicial to those Parts of the Island.

And it is Observable, that in this and all other Countries, under the Torrid Zone, the Rains are more frequent and impetuous as the Sun advances near the Zenith. At other times they often have showers from the Mountains, but they are not so fruitful as those Rains, which come from the Sea, in the aforementioned Months. According to the different Situation of the Places, the Rains are more or less Violent, and come at different times, though they generally begin at the New or full Moon, and fall so heavy and impetuous, that all level Places are laid under Water some Inches. And I have seen the Streets of Kingston within the Space of an hour overflowed at least a foot, and as rapid as most Rivers, which makes it quickly run off, the Town being Seated on a descent and a Gravelly Soil; insomuch that in an hour after they have ceased, a man might walk in any part of it in Slippers. The Showers from the Mountains seldom sink deep into the Earth, and only serve to moisten the Surface of the Ground, or to Sow Pease, Corn and other Grain, when they fall for three or four days together, as they sometimes do; and therefore are distinguished by the name of a Pease Season. But, in the Mountains, it Rains towards noon, almost all the Year round, though they seldom extend more than two or three miles into the Plains, and therefore the Vallies or Bottoms near or amongst the Mountains are more fertile than the Low Lands, which are further off. The Eastern, Western, and Northern Parts of the Island, are more Subject to Rainy and Windy Weather, than the Southern, But, this is Probably owing to the latter being more Open and Cleared of Woods; for it is Observable that Woods attract Rain, and as they are Cut down and destroyed, the Rains abate in proportion.

Thunder is very frequent above six months in the Year, especially in the Mountains, and when it Rains, tho[ugh] not very Violent and but faintly heard, except in the Months of July and August, when the Claps are indeed very terrible, though they seldom do any damage; nor do they Ordinarily Accompany the Rains which come from the Sea. But from November to April there is hardly any Thunder, because[,] as I conceive, the Sun does not lay long enough under the Horizon to heat, or have any Influence on the Exhalations of the Earth.

When the Sun is in the Equator, or within ten degrees of either side, no Alteration is perceivable in the length of the Days; but, when it is near the Tropick of Capricorn, we find some difference, and the perceivable Short[e]nings begin in October. The longest day from the Sun Rising to Sun Setting is 13 hours 4 minutes, the shortest 10 hours 56 minutes; and the difference of Longitude from London, being as I have observed, 78 degrees 45 minutes Westward, causes 5 hours 15 minutes difference in time;

so that when it is noon day there, it is a quarter of an hour past 5 in the afternoon in London.

The days are generally Serene and Clear, throughout the Year, without any Foggy or hazy Weather, tho[ugh] sometimes hot and troublesome, occasioned by the Extreme heat of the Sun and the Sea Wind or breezes, and especially when they blow hard. But the Nights are for the most part fair, and not a Cloud to be seen, so that by their clearness and Coolness they are exceeding pleasant. The mornings are fresh and Cool, until 8 or 9, when there is an interval between the land Wind and Sea Breez[e], and between 5 and 6 in the Evenings, which is the Reason of their being Reckon'd the hottest times of the day. Nor are the Nights at any time so dark, but that a man may travel, or see his way to go to any place: and the Reason is because the Air is more clear and fine, and the Sky is commonly filled with numberless Stars, which, on account of the Serenity of the Air, have more influence and emit a greater quantity of Rays; so that it will not appear Strange that by the light of the Stars with that of the Moon a man may sometimes be able to read papers or Manuscripts.

The Dog days, and some short time before, and after is the hottest and generally the most sickly part of the Year, and very few find themselves, in that Season perfectly well; But this is not peculiar to the Place, because it is commonly the same in Europe and other Parts of the World.

When the Rainy Seasons are over, the Dews are more heavy and frequent, especially from twelve at Night, till four in the morning. The Reason is, because the Sun in that part of the World, exhales more Vapours, than in colder Climates; and as the Nights are longer to Condense them, they must by their own Weight descend, which is a great advantage for otherwise the Plants would often Perish when they have been for some Months without Rain, nor indeed could the Vegetables subsist at such times, without the Moisture they receive from the Dews, which are sometimes so great that I have been wet through the Soals of my Shoes, by walking in the Grass before Sun-Rise; and they often drop from the leaves of the Trees, as if it had Rained.

Foggy and Hazy Weather is seldom seen in the Inland Parts except upon Rivers or in Boggy and Swampy Places; because the Sun as it rises soon dissipates all Vapours or Foggs so that there is seldom a day throughout the Year, without the Sun Shining in those parts; for whenever the Sky looks gloomy and heavy bad Weather is generally expected.

The General Winds and Weather are as follow. The Trade Winds, commonly called Sea Breezes, reign as I have Observed, from February to September, and blow from one or other of the Points between from N[orth] E[ast] and S[outh] E[ast] inclusive during which time the Weather is pleasant and Serene, excepting in the month of May or June, when one of the Rainy Seasons comes in, with Tournadoes, or Violent Gusts of Wind: The other four Months, that is from October to January, the Winds are vari-

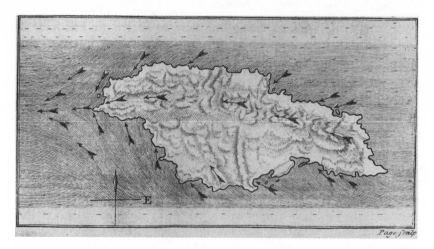

This 1774 engraving of *The Direction of the Trade Winds upon the Island* of Jamaica is reproduced from Long, *History of Jamaica*, 1:opposite p. 20.

able, sometimes Tempestuous, but, in general they blow from the N[orth] or N[orth] W[est], or some Point between these Two. The Division of the Day and Night being more equal throughout the Year than in Europe, divides the Seasons of the land Winds and Sea Breezes. The Sea Breeze comes in about 8 or 9 in the Morning, and blows till 4 or 5 in the Afternoon; when or soon after, the land Wind or Breez[e] rises and Continues till the next morning: though they sometimes borrow of each other; for in the Spring Months the Sea Breezes will sometimes blow constantly for 10 or 14 days and Nights together; and in the Winter Months the land Wind or Breeze will in like manner intrench on the times or blowings of the Sea Breeze. Beside the Season of the Norths, which blow in Dec[embe]r and January[,] alters the usual Course of the Winds and weather.

The Sea Breeze at its first coming in, make[s] at a distance a fine small black curl upon the Water, when all the Sea between it and the Shore is as smooth and even as Glass; it gently approaches with faint breathings, and sometimes makes a halt, as though it were ready to retire; in half an hour it fans briskly and Encreases gradually till about 12 o'Clock, when it is commonly strongest and after three it begins to die away and withdraw its force, till the whole is spent, sooner or later, according to the Season or time of the year.

The land Wind is as Remarkable as the other; for as the one blows direct in upon the Shore, this blows right from the Shore. And, as the Sea Breezes blow in the day, and cease in the Night, the land Wind blows in the Night and ceases in the day; so that they alternately relieve or Succeed each other. The land Wind blowing at Night, and some part of the Morning and the Sea Breeze the rest of the day, is the Reason that no Ship can come into Port Royal, but in the day, and after the Sea Breeze comes in, nor go out but soon after day break and before 8 or 9 in the Morning, while the land Wind, or Breeze Continues.

The Norths, are smart cold Winds, with unusual force and Continuance, being particular and not general Winds, either from the Mountainous tracts in Jamaica, and then only to be felt on the South side, and not far from the Shore, or else arising from Cuba, and then chiefly, if not only, on the North side of the Island; but, some times so strong as to excite the same Effort of Winds, in the Mountainous passages, where being increased and propagated to the South, it becomes a thorough and severe North to the whole Island; and sometimes extends it self almost as far as the Main Continent. The usual Seasons of these Norths are while the Sun is most remote, and in its Capricorn progress, for then the cold umbrages of the Mountains have an opportunity of Sallying, when that Over Ruling Planet is most absent.

Having treated of the Norths, I shall now give a Description of the Souths, and Hurricanes. The former seldom blow with any Violence, or to do much damage; and the latter never were known in this Island, from the time it was taken untill or before the Year 1712.

Souths blow in July or August, Months in which the Norths never blow, they are Storms of Wind which blow from that point of the Compass, and from thence they derive their Name.

Hurricanes differ from other Storms, only in this, the latter accompanied with Thunder and light[e]ning blow from one point of the Compass with very little Variation, whereas the former Shifts from one point to another, and round the Compass in the Space of a few hours.

These kind of Storms called Hurricanes, as well as Norths and Souths[4] give some Signs or presages of their Approach, before they come on, tho[ugh] they do not always give warning of their coming exactly alike.

Commonly before a North, the Weather is very Serene and fair, the Sky Clear, and but very little Wind; and that gently breathing at S[outh] and S[outh]W[est] for a day or two before, the Sea also gives notice, by an Extraordinary and long Ebb, for there will scarcely be any discernable Flood, but a Constant Ebb for a Day or two before the N[orth] begins to blow; and the Sea Fowls, will hover-over the land, which they do not at other times. But the most Remarkable sign of a North is a very black Cloud which appears above the Horizon (in the Mornings and Evenings at least it does not appear so black at any other time of the day) about 11 or 12 degrees, without any Motion; and this sometimes a day or two before, but never less than 12 or 14 hours. And tho[ugh] sometimes it may

4. See Dampier's *Discourses on Winds &c.* Vol[ume] 2.—*Author.* Knight here refers to section 3, "A Discourse of Trade-Winds, Breezes, Storms, Seasons of the Year, Tides and Currents of the Torrid Zone Throughout the World," in Captain William Dampier, *Voyages and Descriptions*, 2 vols. (London, 1700), 2:1–70.—*Ed.*

Entitled *Representation of Water Spouts at St. Jago de la Vega in Jamaica,* figure 5 in the *Gentleman's Magazine* of December 1783, vol. 54, following p. 1024, recorded this freakish weather.

happen, that such Clouds appear without any bad Effects, or very little; yet when the Winds whiffle about, to the South with fair flattering Weather, attended with the Circumstances before mentioned, a North Seldom fails to ensue.

Souths likewise give some signs of their Approach, before they come on, and are preceded by flattering small Winds, and very fair Weather, or by a great glutt of Rain, or else by Rains and Calms together.

The Clouds w[hic]h presage a Hurricane, differ from the North Banks (according to the Seaman's phrase) or the Cloud that precedes a North in this; the latter is uniform and Regular, of an equal blackness from the Horizon to the upper edge; whereas the Hurricane Clouds tower up their heads, pressing forward and seem so linked together, that they all move alike. Beside these Clouds are of various and affrighting Colours; the Edges of a pale fire Colour or dull yellow, & the Body of the Cloud appears thick and of an extraordinary black, and all together looks terrible, beyond Expression: The other warnings which precede a North, do likewise appear for a day or two before a Hurricane, when the Inhabitants, as well as the Seamen on board the Shipping, make the best provision they are able for their Security.

These Symptoms, I took particular Notice of the day before the Hurricanes in Jamaica, the 28 of August, 1712, the 28 of August 1722, and on the 1st of September 1734; at which times I was in the Island, and these three with those that hap[pe]ned in October 1726 and in October 1744 when I was in England, are the only Hurricanes I ever heard of tho[ugh] I am inclined to believe there had been some, while the Spaniards were in possession of the Island, by reason of their manner of Building which in my opinion, was designed to provide against Storms of Wind more than Earthquakes. For tho[ugh] their Houses were in all other Respects as well contrived as could be against both, yet the heavy covering which was of Large thick Tiles laid in Mortar, is a strong Argument, and evinces the truth of this position.

These kinds of Storms or Hurricanes are the more Remarkable because they seldom happen in these Climates, where the Seas are more Tranquill and moderate than in most parts of the World; so that they may be compared to a Person who is not easily inflamed and put into a Passion, but when once irritated grows furious and irresistible. For these storms or Hurricanes are so very rare, that they do not blow above once in 9 or 10 years or with any Violence, but when they do are very Terrible; tearing up Trees by the Roots, throwing down Houses & Sugar Mills, uncovering others, turning every thing into disorder and confusion. And as they are always attended with impetuous Showers of Rain, the whole Country is laid under an inundation, especially the Vallies and levell Parts of it; many Rivers raised 25 or 30 feet, and by the Overflowing Plantations have been covered with Sand and rubbish or otherwise destroyed and very considerable damages ensued.

It must likewise be observed, that the damages which the Island Sustains at those times are the greater, because they do not provide proper buildings against such Casualties, not having been accustomed to them; nor had more than 4 or 5 in 90 years, it being so long since it was taken from the Spaniards. Indeed were they more frequent, or even such storms as happen almost every Winter in Europe and other parts of the World it would be very unhappy for the Planters; because the Canes, Plantain Trees, and other Produce are of such a nature, that they would be, in such Case, more frequently if not annually blown down, and deprive them of the fruits of their labour; [and] consequently occasion them to abandon the Island.

However, as they have had four in 33 years (tho[ugh] not one before the year 1712) which did very considerable damages to the Trading as well as the Planting Int[e]rest, I think it incumbent on the Inhabitants to make the best Provision in their power against such Casualties, by Erecting stronger Buildings and having always a sufficient quantity of ground Provisions planted, to supply the deficiency of Plantains and thereby preserve their Negroes from want & Famine, as has sometimes hap[pe]ned on those Occasions.

As to the Ship[p]ing the Men of War that are obliged to be in Port, from the latter end of August to the 1st of November, ought in my Opinion to ride in Port Morant or Port Antonio, where they will be more secure from the Violence of the Winds, than in Port Royal, and in regard to the Merchant Ships, if they were at the same time, well moored under the land opposite to Kingston near Lombard's careening Place, they would in all probability ride out the most violent Storm, at any point of the Compass except a N[orth] and even then should they be parted from their anchors, it is a soft ouzy ground, and being commonly [a good] weather shore, they may afterwards be with more facility and at less Expence, got off than at any other part of the Harbour. Or whether the Men of War, as well as the Merchant Ships would not ride securely at those times, at the head of Kingston Harbour near the Rock River. However, these points are worth considering, as they may probably strike out some thing for the preservation an[d] Utility of our Navigation in that part of the World.

As to the Earthquakes, tho[ugh] there is generally a trembling in the Earth once or twice in the Year, they are so moderate, that they are over before one can well be sensible, what they are, and are often unperceived or felt by many Persons, especially such as are in motion; so that they never have been Violent to do any damage, except that on the 10th. of June 1692, of which I have given a very particular and Authentick Account, in the 3d. part Volume 1st. They always give warning near 1/2 a minute before the Shake, by a rumbling noise like that of a Coach or Cart going by, when those who hear it, immediat[e]ly quit the House.

Having treated of the Seasons of the Year, Winds and Weather; I shall now make some Observations on the Tides and Currents, collected from Capt[ain] Dampier, and the judicious Remarks of Diego Gonsalez Carranza,[5] his Catholick Majestie's principal Pilot of the Flota in New Spain Anno 1718.

5. Diego Gonsalez Carranza, *A Geographical Description of the Coasts, Harbours, and Sea Ports of the Spanish West-Indies, Particularly Porto Bello, Cartegena, and the Island of Cuba. With Observations on the Currents, and the Variations of the Compass, the Gulf of Mexico, and the North Sea of America* (London, 1740).

As Tides are known to be ebbings and flowings of the Sea, on or off any Coast; so Currents are another Motion of the Sea, which differs from Tides, in Respect to its duration, as well as to its Course.

Tides may be compared to the Sea and land Breezes, in respect to their keeping near the Shore, though indeed they alternately flow and ebb twice in 24 hours; neither are those Tides, or Land Breezes far from the land.

Currents may be compared to the Coasting Trade Wind as keeping at some greater distance from the Shore, as the Trade Winds do; and it is highly probable, they are both influenced by those Winds.

This observation I believe to be just, because it seldom ebbs and flows above 18 Inches; and as the Water rises in proportion to the Strength of the Sea Breez[e], so it ebbs upon the coming in of the land Wind or Breez[e], which blows right from the Shore.

Within the Harbours, Bays, Streights and Channels of these Parts, the Currents[6] are stronger or weaker as the Winds happen to be; for the Currents abate when there is little Wind, as we find by Experience in the Streights or Channels of Bahama, during Calm Weather. And agre[e] able to this observation in the Bay of Mexico, the Currents likewise follow the force and direction of the Winds, and the Ranging of the Coasts, that is to say, by the Easterly or Trade Winds, the Currents set N[orth] W[est]. But by the Northerly or land Winds they set S[outh]W[est] and near the Shores they run along them, according to the Winds that blow there, which likewise Occasion frequent Eddies, or Counter Currents, especially on those Coasts that lie nearly East and West.

The Currents with the Easterly or Trade Winds, run to the West along all the Coast of Carthegena and Terra Firma; but in their Course wee find some alteration occasioned by Counter Currents; and without at some distance from the said Coasts they run towards the N[orth]W[est]. On the Coast of Jamaica and Cuba they run along the Shore towards the West, and between Jamaica, Hispaniola, and Cuba, they run to the N[orth] and N[orth]E[ast] into the Entrance between Cuba and Hispaniola, and the Islands to the North of them.

With the Northerly Winds, which make a smooth Sea, the Currents set Southerly in the Windward Passage.

The Variation is Easterly in the Description that is to say between the Coasts of Cuba, Jamaica and Caimanos four, five and six degrees and rises and falls within such limits as far as Cape Cartouch.

In the Channel between Cape St. Nicholas, at the N[orth]W[est] end of Hispaniola and Cape Maysi or Maiz the S[outh]E[ast] end of Cuba, they set towards the North: Those that run by Cape Maysi, set from thence, towards the N[orth]W[est] and W[est] N[orth]W[est] and those that fall in

---

6. See the English Translation by Caleb Smith. —*Author.* Caleb Smith was the London translator of Carranza, *Geographical Description.* —*Ed.*

with the South Coast of the said Cape, run along it toward the West by the Coast of Cuba. These again that take their Course by Cape St. Nicholas, on the land side, run toward the East to fall in between the Coasts and the Island of Tortuga, from whence they take their Course towards the N[orth] and the N[orth]W[est] to fall into the Channels which are made by the Islands and Shoals, situate towards the N[orth] of the said Islands of Cuba and Hispaniola.

Notwithstanding these Remarks, which are Confirmed by other able Seamen, yet Experience has Convinced us, that the Currents are not always to be depended upon, for tho[ugh] they commonly run in the manner described, Yet it is well known to the Jamaica Traders that they sometimes set to the Eastward, when the Trade Winds or Sea Breezes blow Strongly; and at other times, when it is Calm or Moderate Weather, and even when the land Winds or Breezes Blow, they set to the Westward. Whether they are influenced by the Moon, as well as the Tides, or to what other cause this wonderful effect in Nature may be ascribed, must be left to time and an Age more diligent and Successful in such Observations than this to discover.

But, considering the Importance of our American Trade, it is certainly worth while to offer a considerable Reward to any Person who shall make so useful a discovery; for it will be a great Advantage to our Commerce in those Parts, in regard to time and Expences, and may be the means of preserving many Ships and lives.

Water being necessary for life, it is likewise proper to be taken into Consideration; with regard to its several sorts, and their Affecting in a various manner the Vegetative, as well as the Animal part of the Creation especially in those Countries and places where Water is the common & most proper drink for All.

Water is capable of receiving divers[e] forms and Mixtures, and so becomes more or less agreeable to Human life, from its great diversity of Allays and Corruptions. Therefore I shall remark the good, and point out such as are noxious and prejudicial to Human Bodies.

The most general allowed Test of Waters is their lightness, whereby all Minerall Waters, tho[ugh] ever so limpid, are first to be excepted against, at least in the way of Nourishment, though not as to Medicinal Effects. Sometimes Mountainous places such as Jamaica hide in their Bellies store of Minerals, and therefore the Waters issuing from thence, are first to be distinguished. Hence the Spanish Inhabitants of this Island named the River which passes by the Town of St. Iago delavega, Rio de Cobre or Copper River from its issuing thro[ugh] one or more Copper Mines, chiefly discernable in times of freshes or floods, when the Violent Rains wash down the Creeks and Gullies and taint the Water with a Copperish tast[e]; at which times the wary Spaniards would not drink of it; nor at other times without first set[t]ling in jars, whereby the Mineral Ocra, had time to Subside and Separate; w[hi]ch Custom their Successors continue, who generally take up the Water for the day's Expence the Evening before, and they often suffer, who neglect to do the same.

This River, after running some Miles, becomes purer and freer of taint, and is the most in use at Port Royal where it is, for this Reason, more wholesome than at St. Iago, not but that this Water brings its taint sometimes even to Port Royal, though by being Cask[e]d up, and drawn off, as occasions require, and sometimes standing a day or two before it is used, the Mineral Ocra has time to subside; otherwise the Alien Taint continues, till it be imbibed by the Drinkers, who are suddenly thrown into fluxes, especially new Comers or Strangers; nay the Country Planters and others not used to it often suffer from the like Cause; to avoid which at St. Iago as well as at Port Royal, it were much to be desired, says Doctor Trapham, that the Inhabitants of both would supply themselves with Water else where; that the one would be at the trouble as the prudent Spaniards were, to fetch their Water from the Bridge or Black River, and the other from the Rock River (above Kingston) both w[hi]ch afford Water Signally good.

These Observations are worthy of Notice, not only for the Reasons given by that Ingenious Gentleman, but because the Water, which is generally taken up at the Mouth of the River for the use of Port Royal and the Shipping, has a brackish taste, and a Mixture of Salt, for as it is Situate at the West end, or leeward part of Kingston-Harbour, and near Passage Fort, the Spray of the Sea and sometimes the Salt Water mixes with it, when the Sea Breezes Blow; and as Boats cannot pass up the River by Reason of a Bar at the Mouth or Entrance, neither the Seamen nor the Negroes will be at the trouble of rolling their Cask higher up, than the usual place of Watering, where it may be taken up purer, at least unmixed with the Salt. I have often experienced the pernicious effects of this Water at Port Royal, as well as at St. Iago, and therefore avoided drinking of it, as much as possible, at anytime or in any manner; and from this Water I am persuaded often arises those fluxes w[hi]ch are so Rife, and common among our Seamen and Strangers in general; therefore I am of Opinion the healths and lives of many would be preserved, if the Commanders of Ships and others would refrain making use of this Water, which they may easily do, because they may furnish themselves with what is good, and with very little, if any, more trouble, at the Rock River which is about five Miles to the Eastward of Kingston. And as the shore on both sides the Town, is full of exceeding good Water, they might be furnished in an easy manner, and at a small Expence, were Pumps fix[e]d in proper places with Gutters to convey the Water in to the Casks without taking them out of the Boats. Were Such Conveniencies made, they would be very usefull to the men of Warr, as well as Merchant men, and save them a great deal of time and trouble, as well as furnish them with the means of preserving their Men.

Nature hath plentifully furnished this Island w[i]th great Variety of

Water, for beside eighty four Rivers, which discharge themselves into the Sea, there are numberless Rivulets and Springs almost every where to be found, which run into them and more in the Mountains than in the Low Lands: for tho[ugh] it is with difficulty we ascend them, yet we are in some Measure recompenced with a pleasant cool Air, & excellent Water, greatly alleviating thirst; and it is further Remarkable the higher the Ascent, the purer and more wholesome the water is, for on such Eminences the Springs are generally freer from the injurious taint of Minerals, that are in the Bowels, but seldom to be met with at the Tops.

Beside the ordinary supply of Water, from the Rivers, Springs, Ponds, Wells and Rains, there grow among the Woods, the wild Pine and large Withes for so they are called, which being cut, afford a clear well tasted and wholesome Water; and is frequently used by the Hunters and Others in the Mountains, and what is more Remarkable they are chiefly to be found in dry places, where no other Water is to be met with as it were Providentially to relieve the distressed, and such as might otherwise perish, as Sometimes would have hap[pe]ned. To which may be added the Cocoa Nutt Tree well provided with all the Necessaries of Life such as Cloathing, Meat, Drink and Vessells for Use; the large branches of which produce Many Clusters containing several hundred of those Nutts, which are filled with a pleasant Milky Water, both for the alleviating of thirst and Hunger, a more particular description of this Tree and its Fruit as well as of the wild pine and Withes, I have given in the 7th. [9th] Chapter.

Most of the Rivers of this Island, take their Rise in the Mountains, and some of them sink under ground and Rise again at distant places; particularly Rio d'Oro, w[hi]ch sinks in the Earth, and rises again at Sixteen Mile Walk, in three or four different places.

In the Mountains are also divers Beautifull Cataracts or Cascades, which fall down fifty or sixty feet and some more, the water making a great noise by Rolling down in that manner from a great height, gave the name to Roaring River in Westmoreland, and to another in St. Ann's. The latter is the most Remarkable because it falls down a Mountain that is reckoned half a Mile perpendicular, and the Stream above [blank] yards in breadth. It is seen seven or eight Miles off at Sea and heard at a much greater distance, the head or Source of it, has not yet been discovered.

The Rivers in this Island, taking their Rise in the Mountains, as I observed, and running with a great Proclivity occasions most of them to be very rapid, and Especially after great Rains when the Waters commonly rise from 10 to 30 feet; particularly Dry River, so called from its being sometimes without Water; the Several Springs which run into it being thereby raised, which at other times do not reach it: But, in the Rainy Seasons, and at other times, when it rains Violently in the Mountains, the Waters not only rise to such a height as I have mentioned, but, roll down with impetuosity, and force every thing before them. Sometimes they bring down fallen Trees, which crossing one another make a Damn and turn the Stream or Current, whereby the Neighbouring Grounds at those times Sustain great damage by Inundations; and many Persons have been lost by crossing them unwarily, when it had rained Violently in the Mountains, though not in the Plains; by which means they have been deceived, the Waters being thereby raised higher, than they imagined, and so they were carried away by the Rapidity of the Stream. This should be a Caution to Strangers and others, how they Cross the great Rivers in this Island, especially after heavy Rains, when they are exceeding dangerous. Rocks of incredible bigness are likewise brought down by the impetuosity of the Waters at those times, when they frequently change their Course and form a New Channel.

None of them are Navigable, except for Canoes or small boats, by reason of a Bar which lies at the Mouths or Entrances into all of them; though were they cleared, as some of them might be, particularly Blue fields, in Westmoreland and Rio Grande which divides St. George's and Portland, they would admit of Sloops or small Vessels going up in to the Country twenty Miles or more. Nor are those, or any others, made so convenient and usefull, as they might be for Water Carriages, which would save a Considerable Expence to the Planters, particularly of St. Katherine's, St. John's and St. Thomas in the Vale, was Rio Cobre channel[le]d, and made navigable for Boats or Canoes, which may be done and without any Considerable Expence.

Milk River in the Parish of Vere, is so called from the Colour of the Water, the bottom being a white clay, which makes the Water appear Whitish; it is dangerous fording it, especially for strangers, occasioned by the Currents frequently shifting the Sands from one side to another.

Lagunes or great Ponds, made by little Springs rising and running into them, are common in the Low Lands almost in every Parish in the Island, and some of them contain 2 or three hundred Acres or more, which might be drained, and improved to great advantage.

Rio Hoa in the Parish of St. Mary's receives a great deal of Water from a River which constantly runs into it, and though it has no Visible discharge it never overflows, not even in the times of the great Rains.

But, the most Remarkable is the Blue Hole in the Parish of Westmorland, so called from the Water appearing of that Colour, though when put into a Glass or any other Vessel it is as limpid and well tasted as any Water in the World. It is about [blank] feet in breadth and though it has been often sounded with lines of 100 fathom or more, no bottom could be found. It is always full as high as the Surface of the Earth, and never runs over, and I have been credibly inform[e]d, that fine Mullets have been caught in it, and from thence it is highly probable, it has a Communication with the Sea.

There are likewise several salt Springs in the Island, which arise in level

Ground, and also in some Hills, particularly at Cabbage Tree bottom about two miles distance from the Sea, which being United make what is called Salt River that runs into the Ocean.

Salt is made here in Ponds, wherein the Sea or Saltwater flows, and by the heat of the Sun, the Moisture being exhaled, leaves the Salt, so that it may be made without any great trouble or Expence, especially at the Salt Ponds, where S[i]r Thomas Modyford had formerly proper Works and Conveniencies, and made very great Quantities. Dr. Thomas Hoy[7] and some other Gentlemen about the Year 1720 Rebuilt them, and had brought their Works to such perfection, that they made great Quantities, which they sold, at the Barcadiers for one Shilling and three pence per Bushel. But, those Works were unfortunately destroyed in the Hurricane in 1722 and put a Period to a very Useful and Beneficial Project.

I shall now give a Description of the Hot Bath in St. Thomass in the East, which I had from a Gentleman, who resided many Years in Jamaica, and made his Observations upon the Spot; for I never was in that part of the Island. To which I shall subjoin a few Remarks, which I hope may incite some Publick spirited Persons, to promote a Work, that will be of great Utility to Persons of all Ranks, Ages and Conditions.

He says, It is of the same kind with the Bath in Somersetshire, and fully possesses all the same Virtues; the only difference between them is the great Heat in the one more than in the other, for in Spouting out of the Rock, from whence it comes, it greatly exceeds the English Bath, being so Hot and Scalding, that it cannot be used in sometime after, whereas the other may immediately be drank from the Pump. And it will not only boil an Egg or a Chicken, but retain its heat so long, that it has frequently been made use of for Tea, without being put upon the Fire, after having been carried two or three miles in a Cag or Cask well Stopped up; and it is brought warm at 7 or 8 Miles distance from the Spout. It likewise Colours Silver in the same manner as the English Bath, but with a great Effect, for Silver being put near the Spout, and continued there, in less than an hour it turns Black.

To particularize the Qualities and Vertues of this Water, is unnecessary, because many learned men, have treated, and given Ample Descriptions, of the English Bath, which as I have observed is Similar to this. But it is Surprizing, Considering how many Persons have found Relief and benefit by this Bath, that the Inhabitants are not more Assiduous in rendering it more useful, by making a tolerable Road to it, with proper Accommodations for Sick and infirm Persons; which may be done without any Considerable Expence.

The Assembly indeed, have passed two Laws, and not only raised a Fund

7. Perhaps a relative of Dr. Thomas Hoy (1659–1718), Regius Professor of Physic at Oxford from 1698 and a poet.

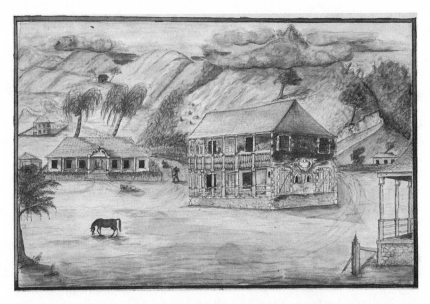

Pierre Eugène du Simitière drew this *View of the Houses at Bath in the Parish of St. Thomas in the East in the Island of Jamaica* while he was living in Jamaica during the 1760s. It shows the buildings erected to turn Jamaica's celebrated hot springs into a gentry resort in evident imitation of the English leisure and health center at Bath. It is reproduced from the Du Simitiere Papers at the Library Company of Philadelphia. (Library Company of Philadelphia)

for that purpose, but appointed Commissioners with ample Powers to enable them to Execute so good and Necessary a Work: but why these Powers have not been carried into Execution, nor any thing done, as I have heard of, is Certainly worthy of the Assembly's Notice and consideration, for should this useful work be perfected as it ought, it would probably be the means of preserving the Healths and lives of many Persons, and preventing others from being Ruined or incumb[e]red, who are under the Necessity of Removing to England, or North America, for the Recovery of their Healths, at a great Expence, and to the prejudice of their Estates, which suffer in their Absence, beside the fatigue and danger of the Seas going and returning. Hither to the badness of the Roads, and difficult Access, as well as the Remote Situation have discouraged many such Persons from making use of it, being near the Top of an Exceeding high Mountain, which is so very Steep, that there is not within a Mile and half of it so much level ground, as is Sufficient to build a House upon, except a small spot, opposite to the Spout, which is about 40 feet in length, and about 20 feet in Breadth. Though that Spot, as well as the Road may be improved and enlarged, as the Road to Sixteen mile-Walk hath been, which is now made passable for Carriages, tho[ugh] for many years it was thought impracticable. I do not mean, or intend to insinuate, that the Road to the Bath may likewise be made passable for Carriages, for that I am persuaded is impossible, up such high and Steep Mountains: but the level spot, I have mentioned, may be enlarged and improved in such a manner, that one or two Houses, with proper Conveniencies, may be built thereon; and a Sufficient Number of Houses may be raised within a Mile or two, from whence the Roads may be made convenient for Mules and Horses, as well as Litters, for Carrying sick Persons thither, or such as are not able to Ride.

Providence hath, in all Countries, provided for the Relief and Support of Mankind. According to their Wants and Necessities. Thus, we find, in this part of the World, where Poisonous Weeds grow, there is an Antidote near at hand of some Fruits, that are Astringent, the Seeds or Stones have Contrary Effects; of others that are laxative, the Seeds or Stones are of a binding Quality. And, in general, the Natural Fruits of America[8] are better adapted to a Sultry Hot Climate, which causes thirst, than the European Sorts; because they are fuller of juice, and of a more Cooling quality; and some of them are so inoffensive, as well as pleasant, that they may not only be eaten with safety at any time, and even by Sick or Infirm Persons, but, in particular Cases are allowed to be useful and of Service. Besides, those Countries which are more Subject to Endemical Diseases, than the Northern or Colder Climates, are furnished with great Variety of Drugs, and Medicinal Plants, of the Native growth, few or any of which are produced in other parts of the World. We may also observe, that the Diseases most frequent, in the West Indies, often Debilitate and enervate the Persons afflicted with them, more than most Diseases do in Europe; insomuch that those, who come to England for the Recovery of their Healths, are commonly advis[e]d by their Physicians to go to the Bath in Somersetshire, and make use of those Waters, as the most proper and Effectual Remedy. Why then may we not Reasonably imagine those Excellent Waters, at the Jamaica Bath, which are so much Neglected, not more used than they have been, were designed by the Divine Goodness, as a more immediate Relief and Remedy, for those Distempers in this part of the World?

Indeed, it is Wonderful that they have had any Effect, and much more that so many Cures have been made, Considering the difficulties and disadvantages, those People were under, who have hitherto made use of them; the Accommodations in those parts, being very inconvenient and they being obliged to send for the Water every day, 7 or 8 miles and from some places more, so that it was some hours, before they could have it, in which time the Volatile parts were Evaporated and flown off. Nor have any Persons for want of Accommodation and lodging near the Place, an Opportunity of Bathing in the Waters; which in some Cases, is as necessary, if not

8. See Fruits, Chapter the 9. — *Author.*

more than drinking them. Beside, the Negroes who are employed to fetch the Water in small Casks, which contain 5 or 6 Gallons, often impose on them, by taking up other Water nearer at hand, to save themselves trouble; for though at or near the Source, it has a pungent Chalybeate Tast[e], yet in some hours it cannot be distinguished from other Waters, that are a little Brackish, or tainted with any Mineral.

Notwithstanding those difficulties and disadvantages, many Persons who were so weak and feeble, that they could not keep themselves or move their limbs; in a short time have been Restored to Strength and Vigour, only by drinking the Water; Whereas could they have had the Convenience of Bathing, we may Reasonably suppose, they would have found the good Effects much sooner.

I cannot inform my Self Whether the Spaniards made any use [of] this Bath, or their Successors before the Year 1695, though the Hot Spring was discover[e]d before the Island was taken from them. But the distance and difficulty of get[t]ing to the Place discouraged People from making trials of it, until the month of March in the aforemention[e]d Year; when two Persons who were very much Macerated, one by the Belly Ach, and the other with the French Disease, went thither and had a Hut built to Shelter them from the Weather, and by Bathing, and Drinking the Waters, were perfectly cured in less than a Month. This Caused others to make trial of it for pains in the Bowels, limbs, and in many other Cases, which were attended with Success, and it has ever since been in great Repute, though not all the use and Advantages made of it, which might be made.

The Situation of this Bath, is between two Exceeding high and steep Mountains; the Separation is so narrow that they seem to be Cleft and only divided by a River, which is so large and Rapid, that it Occupies the whole space between them. The Road from Plantain Garden-River, into which the Bath River falls, is above two Miles up the Course of the latter, and is often impassable when the Rains fall with Violence, as they commonly do in those Mountains, and at best it is difficult and dangerous, being full of great and Slippery Stones, over which those Persons must unavoidably pass, who go that way. So that they often plunge into great holes where the Waters reach as high as the Belly of a Mule, for very few horses can travel that Road, and only such as have been bred, or used to Rocky and Mountainous Places. The nearer you approach the Mountains their height and the great Trees growing on them make the Road more and more dark and gloomy so that the Aspect added to the Apprehension of the Mules falling, or Stumbling, renders the Road dismal and affrighting beyond description. All the way on the sides of those Mountains, are innumerable Springs and Rivulets, which form many Beautiful Cascades that amuse and divert the Eye, though their hoarse murmuring Noise, multiplied by Echos, add greatly to the Awful dread which Passengers are under.

Thus travelling, in about two hours, an odd Sulphurious Smell, gives Notice of your near Approach to the Bath, and in a short time you arrive at the flat before mentioned. But the River must be waded through, to go to the Spot or head of the Hot Stream. At the Entrance it is Exceeding cold, but, on the opposite side where it is blended with the Water which comes out of the Spouts, there is a Sensible difference, so that a Person may Bathe himself, in Water of any Degree of Heat or Cold.

Out of a Stupendous Rock, almost perpendicular, and about eight feet from the Surface of the River, gushes out with great Violence, a Column of Water of 4 or 5 inches Diameter, it comes out of a hole which looks as if it had been designedly been made for that purpose.

The Gentleman, from whom I had this Relation, Says, that He tried the different Degrees of Heat in the Water, and that He climbed up the Side of the Rock, to examine the Hole or Funnel through which this Extraordinary boiling Stream Spews out two or three feet from the Rock, and makes a Cataract, that falls into the River below it, but, that the Rock of 5 or 6 feet distance from the Spout was so heated, that He could not stand on it. That the Grass and Plants, which grew near the Place, looked scorched and of a Yellowish Colour, though at some small distance, they were of an uncommon Verdure. That in his Return He chose to walk most part of the Way, and in some places perceiving a faint weak Resemblance of the Smell of the Bath, He Stopp[e]d to Examine the little Cataracts adjoining which tumble down; and found two or three of them less cold than the common Water of the River; on which He climbed up the Rocks, as far as He was able, and in one of them He found the Heat of the Water to encrease Considerably, from whence we may Reasonably conclude, that near the Source or head of that Stream it is of the same kind with the other, and being a mile lower down the River, were it opened, wou[l]d save so much of the way, and some trouble.

From hence we may Naturally proceed to the Consideration of the Customs, and manner of living in this part of the World, and to lay down some Rules necessary to be observed for the preservation of that invaluable Blessing Health, which is not truly considered or Regarded, as it ought to be; and then I shall make some Observations on the Diseases, that are most common and incidental to the Climate.

Here I am sensible of my inability to treat of those matters, and to set them in so full and clear a light, as they ought to be, being more particularly out of my Province; But, as I have not met with any Essays on those Subjects (though several Regular Physicians and other ingenious Gentlemen have resided and practis[e]d Physick in Jamaica) except a small treatise published by Dr. Thomas Trapham in 1679; intituled a *Discourse of the State of Health in Jamaica*, I am desirous of Contributing my Mite to the Service of mankind; and in order to it shall transcribe such parts as

Often serving as breeding places for larvae of *A. aegypti*, the vector of yellow fever, one of the major diseases in Jamaica, the sugar pots and jars on sugar plantations here depicted in an engraving of a scene, not of Jamaica but most likely of a French plantation in St. Domingue, is taken from Denis Diderot, *Encyclopédie; ou, Dictionnaire raisonné des sciences, des arts et des metiers . . . recueil de planches, sur les sciences,* 2 vols. (Paris, 1762), 1:plate 6. (John Hay Library, Brown University)

I think may be useful and necessary, to which I shall subjoin some few Extracts from Dr. [Richard] Town's *Treatise of the Diseases most frequent in the West Indies.*[9]

S[i]r Hans Sloan[e], has indeed curiously described a great Variety of Medicinal and other Plants and Simples in his *Natural History* of this Island;[10] but, having only made some few Cursory observations on other matters, I shall take the liberty of quoting and following him in such points as Seem to be His principal End and design.

The Consideration of the Custom and manner of living in this Island is a Reasonable and necessary Speculation, as a disregard thereto leads to intemperance, which is the foundation or Cause of most Distempers. I Confess, it is hard to shake off the Habits and Inclinations of our Native Country, or such as were early implanted in us; and though we change our place of Residence and even Climate, yet we Seem loth to change our Method of living or what from early Custom may be called our Natural Disposition,

9. Richard Towne, *A Treatise of the Diseases Most Frequent in the West-Indies, and Herein More Particularly of Those Which Occur in Barbadoes* (London, 1726).

10. Sir Hans Sloane, *A Voyage to the Islands Madera, Barbados, Nieves, S. Christophers and Jamaica, with the Natural History of the Herbs and Trees, Four-Footed Beasts, Fishes, Birds, etc.,* 2 vols. (London, 1707–25).

but carry with us Northern Propensities and Customs, which in Southern
Climates are Highly Improper and destructive of Health or Long Life.

We retain particularly our English Customs in Cloathing, Eating,
Drinking and Sleeping, very few making those alterations and Regulations,
that are indispensably necessary, although we see the necessity of it in England, and how Necessary and advisable it is to Cloath and live in a different manner in Summer from what we do in Winter; by putting on thinner
Garments, eating little flesh, and making choice of such liquors and food as
are Cooling and easy of digestion, but more particularly in abstaining from
every thing that is hot and Inflamatory. And this Regulation, or method of
living, which is practised by all Prudent Persons in England, who have any
Regard to their Health, is Certainly more advisable, and in my Opinion,
indispensably necessary in a sultry, hot Climate.

The quality, quantity, and times of our English food and Drink ought,
according to the best of my Reason, to be wholly chang[e]d for others
more Natural and agreeable to the Climate, and Circumstances of living.
As for the quantity, we neither ought to eat so much, nor so little as may
agree well enough with us in England, for excess in either cannot so suddenly threaten and endanger life here as in Jamaica because Nature is not
so impetuous and hasty with her Delinquents in cold Northern tracts as
between the Tropicks, where all motions begin more quick [and] the Punishment of all Intemperances affords less time for Repentance. The quantity therefore ought to be lessened one way, and encreased another, that is,
we may eat oft[e]ner but less at each time, when good Supplies administer
Choice and Plenty. It must contribute to Health as well as Strength, to eat
four times in twenty four-hours, and in the following manner, Chocolate
at Six in the Morning, at Ten dine more Sparingly than in England, at four
repeat Chocolate, and at Seven a plentiful Supper may be admitted. To
drink between Meals may not be forbidden in a hot Country like Jamaica,
and a draught of cold Water is usual and proper before a Cup of Chocolate, but by no means after, as Strictly forbidden by the Observing Spaniard. However, at other times a draught of pure Water may refresh and
Contribute to render our blood thin and make it Circulate the better, but
least it should sometimes chill the Stomach too much, the Spanish Custom
of eating Candid warm Fruits or Marmalades, after such draughts may be
reasonable and necessary, provided they be taken in small quantities, as
we do Cheese for Concoction. When the Sun declines, the warm spirit of
the Grape may most properly be admitted, in order to add to the Natural
warmth; for if it be not taken to excess, it will before Supper serve to whet
the Appetite, and will afterwards help the Stomach to perform the Digestion of the Greater meal as well as to fortify the Body against the Coldness
of the Night Air, and the Moisture of the Heavy Dews. And it may not be
improper to remark, that there are no Wines better adjusted to the wants,
or more proper for refreshing the Drinker than those of Madeira, they

being as it were a Medium between French Wines and Rum or Brandy, not so Hot as either of the latter, nor so mild as the former; but of a lively warming Nature, proper for Supplying the largest Expence of Moisture by Heat and Sweating adapted to Circulate our thick Blood, (for such we are liable to in Jamaica) and Suitable to the Brisk animal Motions natural to this part of the Globe.

Beside such Wines afford a good pleasant mixture with Water, and thereby become more useful where Water is our most Natural and Common Drink. Again, Contrary to other Wines, which are best preserved in Cold Places and Cellars, these as it were complying with the Place they were designed for, are best preserved in a warm Repository and grow eager and Sour in Cold Places. Having therefore so good and Agre[e]able Qualities in our Madeira Wines, we may dispence with French Clarets and White Wines, as also Canary and Sack, which are too heavy, and more especially these and all other Wines brought from England, which are generally Corrupted.

However just and Reasonable the Doctor's Observations are with Regard to Madeira Wine, yet I think it proper to Remark, that of late Years they are very much degenerated, and what is Commonly Sent to the West Indies, is not so good as was formerly produc[e]d, most of it now being a thin, eager Wine, and would soon turn sour, did they not strongly fortify it with Brandy made in that Island; which is more unwholesome than the lowest and the worst Malt Spirits made in England. To Evince the truth of this, and that I am not Singular in my Opinion, it is necessary to observe, that the Consumption in the Island by that means is diminished at least one third; most People who have any Judgment or tast[e], preferring small Rum Punch, a little upon the Acid, to the Wines, that are now brought from thence, unless they are of the best sort, such as are pick[e]d out and sent to England and Portugal; and as Madeira Wines grow more and more in use, in those and other parts, we have the less of that which is good sent to America, Especially what is Shipp[e]d for the use of His Majesty's Ships; most of which is so thick and eager that it would turn sour, was it expos[e]d forty eight hours to the Open Air, especially in the Condition in which it is drank by the Seamen with all the Dregs and Lees, and without being fined down; I take this to be another Reason of our Seamens' being so Subject to the Gripes and Fluxes in the West Indies. The best Wines drank in this Manner, without being Racked off, or forced down, is allowed to be unwholesome. How much more prejudicial to Human Bodies must such Wines be in the Condition I have mentioned? This is Worthy of the Notice of those, who have the Direction of such matters, and I am persuaded, are unacquainted with this and other Circumstances, which Regard [to] the preservation of the Healths and lives of so Valuable a Branch of the Community; or some Remedies would before now have been applied.

But, to return to the orderly and proper Supplies of the day, which I began with Chocolate; it may Serve in both Capacities as Meat and Drink, for that such it is, being Moderately hot, the agre[e]able bitterness evinces, as well as the Cool Oyl doth of its refreshing Moisture, and that thereby it most fitly nourisheth and Slacketh thirst at the same time. If any thirst ensues after the Drinking thereof, or when it disagrees with the Stomach, as sometimes it may, it is a sign that such [a] Person is not, at least then, of a Constitution fit for a West Indian Climate, or that the Place where he then happens to be is not agreeable to his Constitution, for as all Natives, so far as I have Observed; Covet and desire Chocolate from their Infance, whenever they refuse it, it is a sure Indication of their being an ill habit of Body, which stands in need of being rectifyed; therefore Chocolate is not only a food, but a Natural test of Health, for which the Stomach hath too much Choler, and a distaste to Chocolate, it indicates evacuation to be expedient and necessary, or some other Prescription for restoring a Disorderly Habit of Body. But, as luxury is too apt to Vitiate the Gifts of Nature, by Corrupting her Simplicity, I ought to Caution against Aromatick Mixtures and perfumes, which are apt to Burthen the Stomach. Eggs likewise enrich and raise it too high for a Constant usage, and therefore I recommend the Simple well ground Nut, and Water, with so little Sugar as to preserve somewhat of its Natural bitterness, which is most grateful to the Stomach. *The* better Composition, yet still as near Nature as may be, I would have the Regular living Jamaica Man, institute one half his Sustenance, it being not only very easy of Digestion, but affording solid and lasting Nourishment against the excessive heat of the Sun; for the Oily parts supply with genuine Moisture the parched Body, render the Muscular Fibres apt to Motion, leaving the Stomach with renovated ferment, and preventing Corroding defluxions. For the Kidney nothing is more genuine than Chocolate, moving a more plentiful Urine, and also administ[e]ring a Balsamick quality to the Ulcers, often incident to those Parts, provided Spices &c. be Omitted.

At the Second Meal, about ten in the Morning, the Doctor Recommends good Broths made of Mutton, Kid or Fowl well Cooled with Purslain, Lettuce &c. Fish, of which there is great plenty of divers sorts, Turtle, and such like Food, that is easy of Digestion, and the Fruits of the Country, which are then most proper to be eaten. However care ought to be taken to restrain the Appetite, the better to preserve and quicken digestion, whereby the Stomach may crave Chocolate at four, and so furnishing Nature with a gradual supply, chiefly to be Compleated at the greater Meal about Seven; When Veal, Mutton, Lamb &c. may be admitted; and now if at any time, says the Doctor, Nature may be gratified tho[ugh] not so as to Satiate or overburthen her.

And for the further and greater preservation of that invaluable blessing health, it is also necessary to observe, what I have found by long Experience to Contribute very much thereto, which is, to rise with or rather before the Sun, that is about five in the Morning; to avoid as much as possible the Violent heat of the Sun, by refraining from walking, Travelling, or any way exposing your self thereto, from Eleven in the Morning until four in the afternoon, and to avoid by any other Means overheating the Blood; for which Reason all Violent Exercises ought to be avoided; and it is also necessary to retire with the Sun, and to betake your self to your nightly Repose before Eleven, in order thereby to avoid the Night Winds and Dews, which are penetrating and greatly prejudicial to Human Bodies, as hath been before observed.

As to the Diseases of the Island, they are short of the long Bead Roll, which Afflict European and Northern Climates, though it must be Confess[e]d they are in general more Acute and Violent.

The small Pox is not a Natural Distemper of the Country but generally brought there from Guinea. The Plague never was heard of there. Consumptions are uncommon and when they do happen not so piningly tedious.

Venereal Effects are lessen[e]d, and their discharge and Cure more easy than in Colder Climates. The Stone is a Stranger here, as Hopp[e]d Beer and French Wines are not much in use.

But I shall not, says the Doctor, multiply our happy negation or Absence of Afflicting Evils any further than to excite our thankful Acknowledgments of the Divine Goodness, and that with more Courage and Contentedness we may be better able to Sustain the Maladies and Distempers incident to this Island, for it is not to be imagin[e]d that Human frailties are excluded from any Place or Climate, but that the West Indies and all other parts are Subject to endemical Evils. Let us therefore, says He, consider the Number of our Enemies, their Nature, manner of Assault, with the Reasons of all, in order to obviate or prevent, Cure and Relieve, or Manfully to Comply with the Necessities of Fate, when nothing else shall remain.

The first Indisposition that generally attends the New Comer is a Diarrhea or flux, a friendly rather than an injurious Motion of Nature, caused either by a new Sort of Drink or Diet; which falls out in most Places, more or less, and which sometimes ceaseth without prejudice or any other Remedy than a little time and Patience.

The Generous open Hospitality of the Inhabitants frequently meets with as free a Compliance from Strangers, and their liberal reception often degenerates into Intemperance and Excess. Hence proceed Diarrheas[,] Surfeits, Fevers &c, which are Commonly though unjustly attributed to Causes, that are Remote and Innocent of their production. These are sometimes Relieved or Cease by Abstinence as I have Observed. But if the fermented juices Stir up excrementitious matters and blend them with the Blood, they hurry the whole into a Chasing fret, and raging fever, if not discharged by the Crises of a plentiful sweat, which is the usual prevention, as well as the natural termination of Distempers, that are Common in a Hot Climate. Hitherto Nature is the Sole Physician, and afterwards the truest Indicator, of what is proper and necessary to be done; but while She sometimes labours in Vain and Sometimes in an excited Rage, She is gently to be Assisted and Reduced, into her first Regular Motions. Thus if the Flux continues, it indicates somewhat to be discharged in Order to the Quieting of Nature, least She spend her Strength in Vain, and then expire for want of the same, as sometimes happens.

A Diarrhea, is a frequent and plentiful discharge of thin Wat[e]ry, Mucous, Slimy, frothy, greasy, bilous or blackish matter from the intestines, sometimes with and sometimes without a mixture of Excrements.

It is frequently attended with Gripings; but they are not essential to it. The Patient is weak, makes little Urine, has a depressed Pulse, impatient Appetite and is sometimes feverish.

All these sorts of Fluxes are Endemick in the West Indies, but more especially in the Rainy Seasons, and may be imputed chiefly to the negligence of those who too unwarily expose themselves to the injuries of wet Weather, by which means Perspiration being interrupted, the thin part of the Blood, which should have been exhaled thro[ugh] the Pores of the Skin, is thrown upon the Bowels, and thence discharg[e]d in loose Stools. This appears plainly from the great number of Negroes, and the poorer sort of white People, who in these Seasons are much more afflicted with this Distemper, than such whose Conditions of life, do not Subject them to the like inconveniencies. Beside catching cold, there are other Antecedent Causes of a Diarrhea, the principal of which are an immoderate use of crude, fugacious Fruits, unwholesome Food and meats of difficult digestion; all which by Stimulating the Guts, will likewise Occasion a Diarrhea.

A Dysentery is a frequent discharge from the Bowels of Blood mixed with Slime, ichorous matter, liquid excrements, skinny Slough, and sometimes of a fleshy Substance resembling the inner Coat of the intestines. This Bloody flux is constantly accompanied with a Severe griping pain in the Guts.

The Causes of a Dysentery mention[e]d by Hippocrates are chiefly these. [blank] a Diarrhea, 2d. Sultry Weather, and 3d. hot Spirituous liquors. These as well as acrid pungent food, are capable of producing a Diarrhea, and as they greatly rarify the blood, this Rarification super added to the loos[e]ness, gives us a Satisfactory Idea of their being the Cause of a Dysentery. This is Confirmed by Observing how much this Disease rages among the Soldiers, Seamen and White Servants as well as the Negroes in our Plantations, which sort of People are much addicted to debauch in Spirits and Punch made exceeding Strong with new Rum, very acid with juice of limes, perhaps mixed with such as are green or not full ripe, or decayed and Rotten, and very fermentive with Coarse Sugar.

The Judicious Doctor Sydenham[11] hath Remarked that Fevers may be accounted equal to two thirds of the Chronical Diseases, with which mankind are afflicted: but in the West Indies, especially with Regard to Strangers, the proportion runs much higher. There are very few upon their first Arrival, who Escape the Attacks of this furious Invader. For altho[ugh] Temperance and Moderation, together with the use of the Non-Naturals, may in a great measure alleviate the Symptoms and Obviate the ill consequences; most People how wary soever they may be in their Conduct are obliged to undergo, what the Inhabitants call a Seasoning.

The Dropsy is so frequent in the West Indies, that it likewise demands notice to be taken of it, as the next ensuing Epidemicks, and Commonly Call[e]d the Country Distemper: to which Servants, and neglected or Intemperate Persons, are most subject and Obnoxious.

It is divided into three Species the Anasarca, Ascites, and the Tympany.

The first is Water betwixt the Skin, and that generally throughout the Body, and is near the same with a Leucophlesmacy. The second named Ascites being the most proper Dropsy as appearing in the Belly and Legs. The third is call[e]d Typany from the great tension in the Skin like to a Drum, is most rare though the most cruel and Afflictive. All which seem little more than Distinct Degrees of one and the same Disease, or at least I will take leave to Suppose them so, having Reason from my Experience and Practice.

The usual times of Dropsies is after Fluxes, Fevers and other disorders, whereby the discharge through the Habit of the Body is lessen[e]d and interrupted; hence what is usually carried of[f] by Sweating, and a more Silent, daily, breathing through the whole Skin, redounds inwards; thence condensed into an ichorous Water, and Aggravates more and more the first Cause through encreas[e]d Weaknesses and hinderances of the necessary transpiration; the which According to the *Statica Medicina*, is demonstrated to be very Considerable, it being some pounds Weight: and when that, in part, or in the whole, shall be retained sometime, such as the Dropsies usually take to come to their height, it may well Accumulate the greatest quantities of Water treasured up for the Destruction of the Patient.

The Antecedent Causes of a Dropsy are Cold, moist, Acrid, fermenting, tenacious and indigestible food; an immoderate use of Spirituous liquors, a moist dampy Air, Suppression of the Urine, Perspiration &c. Obstructions and Cold or Schirous tumours of the Viscora; Acute burning Fevers; long and Sever[e] Quartans; Jaundice; Diarrhea; Dysentery &c; all which occasion the Blood to become Viscid, and the Fibres lax.

As this Distemper is more frequent in the West Indies than in Europe,

11. Dr. Thomas Sydenham (1624–1689) studied medicine at Oxford and Montpellier and became one of England's most internationally renowned physicians, authoring major contributions on the treatment of epidemic diseases, smallpox, and the use of bark (quinine) in the treatment of agues.

so likewise generally Speaking it more easily admits of a Cure; though there is not any Disease more Subject to return, if the Patient be not very Cautious in his way of living after Recovery.

It is Certain that in the beginning of a Dropsy nothing conduceth more towards a Recovery than Exercise and change of Air; no kind of Exercise more than Sailing, and no Air more than Sea Air; let me therefore, says Doctor Town, exhort all such, whose Circumstances will admit of it, to leave the Island upon the first approach of this Distemper, and Remove for some time to England.

I come now to the last and most fatal Distemper, peculiar and incidental to the West Indies, and that is the Nervous or Convulsive Cholick, Commonly call[e]d the dry Belly Ach. This, though reckon[e]d a Popular Disease, and endemick in those Parts, yet it is not so frequent and Common in Jamaica, as it was formerly.

There is not in the whole Compass of Infirmities, which flesh is Subject to, any one that afflicts Human Nature in a more exquisite degree than this unmerciful Torture. The Belly is seiz[e]d with an intolerable piercing pain, sometimes in one Point only, and sometimes in several parts of the Intestines: in a short time the Affliction becomes more diffusive, and Stretches itself from the Point, where it was first felt, to a greater distance, which is done in such a manner, that the Fibres of the Bowels seem to be Contracted, and drawn up from the Anus, and the Pilorus towards the Part primarily Affected as into the Center of Misery: during this Scene of the Distemper which sometimes continues Eight, ten, or fourteen days, the Patient is upon a perpetual Rack with scarce any Remission from Pain.

The Chief causes concurring to the Production of this Cholick are immature, Austere and Astringent Fruits, eaten in too great quantities; debauching in Strong Punch, Acidulated with the juice of limes; and travelling in the Night after a debauch; or too free a use of Spirituous liquors.

Doctor Trapham Observes, that the West Indies, though of the same temperament with the East, may Sustain Infirmities, which their Customs wisely prevent and preserve them from; for they are very little, if at all, Afflicted with this Distemper, which He attributes to their use of Baths and Unctions, by which the Cutaneous and Muscular Fibres are Secured from Contracted Spasms, and kept open for the Constant discharge of transpiring Particles; the Original of the Belly Ach is cut off as also the Crowd of ensuing Symptoms. Wherefore let those (He says) who would avoid so great an Evil be provided with Convenient Bathing Tubs, or Places adapted to so necessary an Office in a Sweating Country.

It is proper to Remark, as a Confirmation of the Doctor's observations, that the Indians as well as the Negroes in America, who Constantly Bath or Wash themselves every day, are seldom or never, as I have heard of, Afflicted with this and some other Distempers peculiar and incidental to White People, and to that Custom I attribute in a great measure their being so hardy[,] healthy and Robust. The Doctor therefore Recommends it as necessary for the preservation of Health, where Nature shall want due Assistance, or Vigorous fortifying, as she may sometimes in others as well as the forementioned Cas[e]s. Because those Baths will keep free and open the Pores to Healthful transpirations and more copious Sweatings: the want of which assistances, He says, may some time or other cause Belly-achs, Tertians and other Fevers, Dropsies &c. [are] rationally to be prevented by due and Regular Bathing: the Reasons whereof are obviously two, the One is Cleansing from relicts of Obstructing Sweat, whereby the porous passages being opened easily admit a thorough fair to Nature's Ejectments, the other is the preservation of the Tone and Spring of the fibrous Skin, for the better Support of her necessary Functions; both which are secured by Bathing and proper Anointings. Let those therefore who desire the Continuance of Health, frequently make use of Baths and Unctions, especially after Travelling, as also upon all lassitudes and listless indispositions, not presently after, but rather before eating, and four hours after, at the time of distribution of nourishment into the extreme outward parts; then may such most properly be exercised with Cuppings in a warm Bath, the regard must be had as to the time and manner, that it may not extend to faintness, but Refreshment and Relief from Nature's oppressive Burthens.

Thus I have, with the Assistance of the two Gentlemen, I mention[e]d, described the Nature, Symptoms and Causes of the Distempers most frequent and endemical in other parts of the West Indies as well as in Jamaica; and by what means they may sometimes, or in some degree, be alleviated if not prevented, for surely it is in any man's power to be temperate, to refrain from eating or drinking any thing, that is unwholesome, indigestible or Inflamatory; and to guard against the Inclemencies of the Air, damps and Dews. And, it is owing to such like Rules, or Regimen, that the Spaniards are healthier and live to greater Ages than the English; and not that the Havanna, or any other part of South America is really healthier than Jamaica, as is Commonly, though untruly, Suggested. This may be evinced almost to a Demonstration from the Instances I have already given, of the Women, and Jews in this Island, who are healthy and live to great Ages; that the Ancient Inhabitants who Copied after the Spaniards, in this manner of living, lived many Years in full Vigour and Strength; and that the Negroes who fare hard and have not the free use of Spirituous liquors, are Robust, Strong and healthy.

It is also observable, that those who have lived many Years and resided in the Island, are not Subject to that train of Infirmities, which commonly attend Old Age in other Countries.

The Seasoning as it is called, (which is common and Natural on change of Climates) and sometimes a Relapse thro[ugh] neglect or want of Care, are the greatest difficulties that attend Strangers. But if they overcome them and Survive one Year, which may be Effected with temperance and a prudent management, the Climate afterwards becomes habitual, and they may then Venture to live more freely; though in all Countries, as well as in this, He that lives in an orderly, Regular way, has the best chance for Health and long life.

It must however be confessed, that all hot Countries are more Subject to Endemical Diseases, and other disorders than the more Northern and Colder Climates. Because the Extreme and Constant heat gradually, and insensibly penetrates, and Affects the Strongest People, and the hailest Constitutions by drying up or destroying in them, what the Physicians call the Radical Moistures; there being no Winter in which Nature may recover that She lost by a Constant, uninterrupted transpiration, in the Hot or Summer Season. Hence it is the Face looses its Vivacity and fresh Colour, and the Stomach its dew and Natural heat; that the Blood, which a Person is often obliged to Diminish through Precaution, and on many other accounts is Livid, To which I shall add that frequent bleeding or Indiscreetly, causes Dropsical humours; and that all Human Bodies inflamed by Heat, do not feel that Activity and Refreshment which proceeds from a Cold Air. But, when a Person is inur[e]d or Accustomed to the Climate, he is not so Subject to those incommodities as Strangers or those newly come from Europe and the Northern Climates.

And here, I think it proper to remark, tho[ugh] perhaps it may raise a Smile or Sneer in many Persons, that a Fire is frequently necessary even in Jamaica, and Other parts of the West Indies, especially in the Rainy Seasons; not for Warmth, but to rarify the Air, and dissipate the damps, and Vapours of the Earth; which are much Stronger at those time than at any other, and are commonly the Cause of the Diseases which rage every Year, after those Seasons; therefore, I am of Opinion, that every House in the Towns, as well as in the Country, ought to have One or more Chimneys in it, and a fire made therein for an hour or more every Morning and Evening in the Rainy Seasons, and at all other times in such as are Built in a low, dampy Situation or near Rivers and other Wat[e]ry Places. Dr. Freind,[12] I am credibly informed, was so strongly of this Opinion, that in the hottest Summer in England, during the time of hard Rains, or when the Weather was Cloudy and misty, He caused a Fire to be made and would set by it. And, it will Appear more Reasonable and necessary in Jamaica, when it is Considered, the Houses in the Island, are mostly no more than one Story; the Groundsil[l]s not raised above a foot from the ground; and the floors of their Stalls and dining Rooms, laid with Terras, Brick or broad flat Stones, which are indeed Cool and pleasant great part of the Year, but in those

12. John Freind (1675–1728), Fellow of the Royal Society, was a prominent English physician. Knight was probably referring to passages in his *The History of Physick; from the Time of Galen, to the Beginning of the Sixteenth Century*, 2 vols. (London, 1727).

Seasons are moist and damp, Consequently pernicious, and destructive to the Inhabitants.

It is likewise Observable, that the Negroes, who are Commonly strong, Robust and healthy, always have a Fire near them, when they Sleep, even in the Sun and the open Air; not meerly on account of their being more Chilly, and of a Colder Constitution than White People; but because they find by Experience, it dissipates the Damps and Vapours of the Earth, and drives away the Musquitos and other Flies, which are often troublesome in all parts of the West Indies, and especially after great Rains.

Part the 6th.

Of the Inhabitants, Masters, Servants, and Negroes; Their Number, Strength and Manner of living; as Also an Account of the Negroes, who were many Years in Rebellion, and Settled in the Mountains, together with the Treaty made with Them in 1738, upon which They submitted, and became Free Subjects of Great Britain.

The First English Inhabitants of Jamaica were Military men who some Years after They had taken the Island, and intirely dispossessed the Spaniards, were disbanded, and having Lands divided amongst them set[t]led there; and from them are descended several of the Oldest Families now in the Island.

In 1657 Colo[nel] Stokes w[i]th 1400 White and Blacks came down from Nevis: And many Persons, who were uneasy at home in Oliver's time, and during the Rump Parliament, thought it a proper place to Retire to; as well as others who were Busy and Active in those distracted times, and went over after the Restoration of King Charles the Second, particularly the Sons of President Bradshaw,[1] Commissioner Axtell,[2] whose Families are now Extinct.

In 1664 many Planters and others removed from Barbadoes, and Bermudas, upon the Encouragement, that was given by the Crown to Persons to go over and settle there; and when Surinam was Exchanged for New York, most of the English Inhabitants likewise removed from that Country to Jamaica, and settled Contiguously, according to their own desire, in St. Elizabeth's.

Monmouth's Rebellion furnished this Island with a great Number of those deluded People, who were engaged in his Interest: and the unhappy Reign of King James the Second, as well as the Revolution, brought

---

1. John Bradshaw (1602–1659), an English judge, was president of the High Court of Justice for the trial of Charles I and the first lord president of the Council of State of the English Commonwealth. Perhaps James Bradshaw, who represented either St. James Parish or Kingston in the Jamaica Assembly between 1691 and 1699 was his son or descendant.

2. Colonel Daniel Axtell (1622–1660), captain of the Parliamentary Guard at the trial of King Charles I at Westminster Hall in 1649, was hanged, drawn, and quartered as a regicide during the Restoration. William Axtell, who represented Port Royal and several other constituencies in the Jamaica Assembly between 1695 and 1707, and Daniel Axtell, who did the same from 1713 to 1721, may have been his sons or grandsons.

over many others, who thought themselves not safe at Home upon those changes in the Government.

But Felons, and Convicts, were always prohibited, as far as lay in Their Power, by imposing a heavy Duty on them; so that I never heard of above two hundred that were ever imported there; and in less than twelve months not twenty of them remained on the Island. Some of them followed their old Practices and were Executed, others returned to England, many went and joined the Pyrates, and some escaped to Cuba; where the Spaniards openly received them, with the Negroes and other Effects, which They had Stolen and carried with them, and permitted them to settle there with impunity.

Notwithstanding the diversity of Opinions, and Principles, of those Several Classes of People, They wisely buried in oblivion all former Distinctions, and never upbraided one Another with the part, they had acted at Home; though they seemed to be more particularly attached to those, who were engaged in the same Interest.

It would have been happy for their Successors, had they always acted with the same Prudence in other Respects, and not suffered themselves to be divided, as They often have been, by little Emulations, private piques, or the Interest of Governours; from whence have flowed numberless Evils, and the general Interest of the Country has been greatly prejudiced and Obstructed; for by those means the Island has often been inflamed, and divided into Factions, Artfull and designing Men have made advantages, and Their Enemies had an opportunity of misrepresenting them to the Government at Home. And Indeed it is not strange, that the Ministry have often been perplexed and under great difficulties, how to Reconcile and Compose those differences, considering the distance of the Place, and the Contradictory Representations, made to Them by the Contending Parties.

The Inhabitants of this Island are Ranked in these four Orders, Vizt. Masters, who are English, Scots, and Irish, and some Portoguese Jews; White Servants; Free Negroes, and Mulattos; and Negro Slaves. And the Masters may be divided into these two Classes, Merchants or Trading People, and Planters.

The Merchants and Tradesmen, reside in the Towns, and carry on Their Several Professions in the same manner, they do in England; some of them have Plantations or Country Houses, but in general they are looked upon as transient People, or Sojourners; because they remove to Great Britain, or other Parts of the British Dominions, when they have acquired Estates, or what they think sufficient to maintain Them there.

The Method, and manner of carrying on business Here, is much easier, in some Respects than in London, and other Parts of Great Britain, especially with regard to Ent[e]ring and Clearing of Ships and goods, which is attended with much less trouble and Expence. But some Innovations, and bad Customs have lately been introduced and tolerated, notwithstanding

Progenitor of one of Jamaica's oldest
white families and Jamaica's most successful estate builder, Peter Beckford
(1643–1710) migrated to Jamaica in
1662 where he eventually became an
important political figure, serving in
the assembly, as acting governor of
Jamaica in 1702, and as chief justice
from 1703. (Museum of London)

the Laws for Regulating the Publick Offices, and for Ascertaining and Establishing their Fees.

These Innovations require the Speedy Notice and Consideration of the
Legislature, or they will become grievous and Burthensome to the Planting, as well as to the Trading Interest.

The Port Officers are obliged, under the Penalty of Twenty pounds for
every default, to give their Attendance in their Respective Offices from
nine to eleven in the forenoon, and from two to four in the Afternoon,
Sundays and Holidays excepted; and their Books are open to all Persons;
who have the liberty of Searching or inspecting the same, paying fifteen
pence fee, which is about ten pence Sterling.

And all Persons keeping Publick Wharfs, are obliged under the Penalty of ten Pounds for every default, to keep a Book, wherein is fairly entered the marks and Numbers of all such Goods, as are landed on his or
their Wharf; also the Weights of Sugars, and other Produce of the Island,
bought and Sold, or Shipped off; with the names of the Person, or Persons,
by whom such Goods were landed, bought and Sold, or Shipped off and
also to take a Receipt of the Person, to whom the Said Goods are delivered.

The greatest inconvenience, that attends the Trade of this Island, and is
often the Cause of great Reproach, is the difficulty of recovering of Debts;
which in a great measure may be attributed to the unfair Practices of the
Deputy Marshalls, and other Officers belonging to the Provost Marshall or
High Sheriff: for there is often as much trouble to get a Debt from them,
after they have received it, as there was to recover it from the Debtor. This
and some other abuses of the like Nature, also require the notice and Con-

Peter Beckford, Jr. (1673–1735), inherited a large estate from his father
and expanded it substantially. At the
time of his death, he owned seventeen sugar plantations, five livestock
pens, a provision farm and storehouse,
a house in Spanish Town, nearly two
thousand enslaved Africans, a large
sum of money on loan, and a considerable amount of personal property in
Jamaica. He may well have been the
wealthiest person in the whole of colonial British America. He also had a
long and distinguished political career,
serving as a member of the Jamaica
Assembly for most of the time from
1701 to 1731. Between 1707–13 and
in 1716, that body chose him as its
Speaker. (Brooklyn Museum)

sideration of the Legislature; for nothing will tend more to the Interest,
as well as the Honour of the Island, than to Establish Publick and private
Credit, and put them on a proper Basis or foundation.

The Planters live upon their Estates; and seldom come to Town; except
those, that are near St. Iago delavega; where many of them have Houses,
and often reside, when the Crop or Planting Season is over; for at those
times the Master's Eye is highly necessary.

It must in justice and Honour to Them be observed, there is not more
Hospitality, nor a more generous freedom Shewn to Strangers in any part
of the World; for any Person, who appears like a Gentleman, and behaves
himself well, is Sure of a Wellcome to their Houses, and the best Entertainment they can afford. Those, who go over with a wounded or Ruined
fortune, are received with great humanity and good manners, without any
Scorn or insult from the Rich to the Poor, but on the Contrary a Generous
Friendship, and a ready disposition to Assist them in retrieving their Circumstances, and more Especially those, who are Soberly inclined, Industrious, and deserving of Notice. A man may Travell from one Part of the
Country to another, and even round the Island, with very little or any Expence: for there being very few Publick Houses, but in the Towns, He may
with freedom go and dine, or lodge, at the next Planter's House; and Persons of low rank and Condition, are as cheerfully received and entertained
by their Servants. In fine, however they have been Represented, I don't
know a more Industrious, usefull, and beneficial Society to the Nation,
than they are; which will appear by the advantages arising from this Island
through their Care, and Industry, and are more particularly set forth in the

8 and 10 Chap[ters] as well as the Opinion, and Testimony of Sir. Josiah Child,[3] who declared, that one person in the Plantations gave Employment to five at home, Which will not appear improbable, when it's Considered what a great number of Seamen, Manufactures[,] Labourers &c. are daily Employed by means of the Trade to and from the Plantations. It therefore only Remains, to shew the Care, Frugality, and painfull manner of living of the Planters; which will remove the false notions that have been instilled, of their Extravagance, Luxury, and Immorality.

The Life of a Planter, is attended with great Anxiety, Care, and trouble for he is Obliged not only to be up Early, and ride about his Plantation great part of the day, in the Scorching heat of the Sun; but to have a Constant Eye over his Servants and Negroes. And it requires great Thought, Temper, and Discretion to order and manage them, their dispositions being as different as their Several Countries, or Nations; and many Quarrells, and Controversies, often arise amongst them, which are heard and determined in Every Plantation, by the Master, or Owner, and in his absence the Overseer, who has an Absolute Authority over them, Life and Limb Excepted.

The Planter's Dress is generally a Waistcoat, and breeches, made of Oznabrigs, which is a Coarse German linnen; a Frock made of the same, or of Fustain, light Duroy, or some other English Manufacture. They have indeed a Dress suit, that is better and Genteeler, to appear in, when they go to Town, or upon extraordinary Occasions: but very few have more than one such suit at a time, and that commonly serves them three or four years. They are, as I have observed, Hospitable to Strangers; and upon such Occasions, or when they Expect their Friends and Neighbours to Visit them, they make the best appearance they can; and sometimes perhaps exceed what is necessary, or may Reasonably be expected; from whence in some measure arises the Notion of their Luxury, and Extravagance, without considering their common, and ordinary manner of living, which is generally upon Irish Provisions, or such as they raise within themselves; and their drink small Rum punch, made of their own Sugar unrefined; for though most of them keep Madeira Wine by them, and some of them other sorts of Liquors, yet these they seldom use, but upon the occasions before mentioned.

Nevertheless some of Them constantly live in a generous, genteel manner: and as they are clear of incumbrances and can afford it, They are rather to be commended than Reproached on that account. Nor is the Expence of Housekeeping to any of them, so great as is imagined, having most necessaries within themselves, like the Country Gentlemen in England; and with a Provident Care, they might raise all Sorts of Provisions for their Servants, as well as themselves, and not be under the neces-

3. Sir Josiah Child, *A New Discourse on Trade* (London, 1692).

sity of purchasing salted Provisions from Ireland and North America. But I cannot commend their good Husbandry in that Respect, because they are therein wanting to Their own Interest, as a great Expence might thereby be saved.

As to the Immorality, and Profligate manner of living, the Planters and other Inhabitants are charged with, I know no just Reason to distinguish them from the rest of mankind, nor did I ever See, or hear of such abandoned lewdness, as is commonly practiced in London, and other Sea Port Towns. I would not from hence be thought to insinuate, that none of them are Vitious, profligate, or Extravagant, nor to justify those that are; but I can with truth Affirm, that in general I have impartially delineated them, and without favour or Affection. In all Countries, and in all Societies, there are undoubtedly Good as well as Bad men, and though it must be Confessed, that there are loose and Wicked Persons, in Jamaica, yet I may venture to assert, from my own knowledge, and Experience, there are amongst them many Persons of great Honour and Virtue.

Their common and Ordinary Diversions, are Dancing, Horse-Racing, Fishing, Fowling, Cards, back Gammon, and Billiards. The former may perhaps be thought too Violent an Exercise in a hot Country, but as they choose the coolest part of the day, from 7 in the Evening to 11 or 12 at Night, and are Carefull in not going too Soon into the Open Air, very Seldom any inconvenience, or prejudice to their health arises from thence.

And here it may not be improper to observe the manner and method of the Planters Educating their Children; as it will naturally point out, and probably Convince them of some mistakes in that Respect. The Boys are sent to England at 5 or 6 years of age, to their Agents or Factors, and placed out in some Private or Publick School; and some of them sent afterwards to one of the Universities, or according to the Custom of their Mother Country, to France, Italy, and other Parts; where they acquire little more, than the Foppish Airs, and Ridiculous Customs of those Countries. The Girls are generally bred at Home, and brought up under their Mothers, who are Carefull to Instruct them very early, in needle work, and good Housewifery, as soon, if not before they are taught Musick, Dancing, and other Accomplishments.

Were the Planters truly sensible of the prejudices, and disadvantages, that attend the sending Their Children over to be Educated and to pass so much of their Time here and in other Parts of Europe, I am persuaded, they would take some other method by giving due and Reasonable Encouragement, to men of Ability and Virtue, to settle amongst them, and set up Schools and Nurseries of Learning. And that it is Practicable to give Their Children a very good Education in the Island, and equal to most, or any, that have been in England, several Instances may be given of Gentleman who never were off the Island, and yet are as well Instructed in Grammar, and other usefull parts of Learning, make as good a Figure in Conversation, and in Publick Stations, as well as in the conduct and management of their private Affairs, as any in the Island.

To point out all the Objections which may be made to this Custom, may, however Reasonable and just, be thought invidious; therefore [I] shall leave it to Themselves to consider and Improve what I have hinted at; and shall only observe, that this Custom generally Alienates the Children's Affections from Their Parents as well as from the Country; and this in my Opinion, was there no other, is a Cogent and sufficient Objection. Many of them, upon Their return to the Island know neither Their Father, nor Mother, and bring over the Habits, Customs, and Constitutions, of Europeans, improper for the Climate; and w[hi]ch renders Them unfit to go through the hardships, and fatigues of a Planter. Besides, they Contract such a taste of the Pleasures and luxury of England, that They cannot reconcile Themselves to any other manner of living and when they get Possession of Their Paternal Estates, leave Them to the management of Their Agents, and Overseers; and thro[ugh] Their neglect or mismanagement (for how can it be Expected that a Plantation can be so well managed and improved, as by the owner or Proprietor) and Their Expensive way of living in England, they become involved and in a few Years, are Ruined and undone. This, however is not always the Case, for some of the Gentlemen Educated in this way have turned out well and done Honour to their Country; but it is too often otherwise, and the Imputation of Luxury and Extravagance, which the Planters, in general are loaded with, is I conceive in a great degree owing to the Conduct and Behaviour of some of these Gentlemen in England.

In Regard to Truth and Justice I must likewise observe, that the Women Born and Educated in the Island, generally prove Good and make Discreet frugal Wives and Tender Mothers. They are Abstemious, living chiefly upon Chocolate, Tea, Fruits, and ground Provisions; and few of them, from the highest to the lowest, will touch any Spirituous liquors; Their common Drink being Water, or a little Madeira Wine mixed; and they are generally extreamly neat. They are mostly Tall, Straight, and well Shaped; for I never saw above two, or three, that were awry; and they are also well featured, but pale; though some of Them have the advantage of Colour. The Principal if not the only objection to Their Conduct, is in some measure excusable; because it is a Natural foible; and that is an over fondness for Their Children, which makes it absolutely Necessary, for the Boys to be removed at some distance from Them; tho[ugh] even this may be done in the Island.

Seamen were formerly very numerous, Especially in War time, and when They had a flourishing Trade. In my Memory there were not less than 3000 such men on the Island; but Their number is very much diminished, since the Settlement of the Assiento Contract, and the South Sea Company; which deprived them of all, or the greatest part of a very beneficial Commerce; and hath been of infinite prejudice to the Island; a loss to the Proprietors, and all things considered, of no manner of Advantage to the Nation.

Nevertheless the Advantageous Situation of this Island, will constantly draw a Concourse of those People from all Parts in time of War with France or Spain, particularly for the Service of our Privateers, as we have Experienced in the present War, notwithstanding the discouragement They are under by being some times pressed by His Majesty's Ships; or They would be more Numerous and Serviceable than They have lately been.

As to the Jews They are mostly Portoguese; and among themselves Speak no other Language. They chiefly reside in three great Towns, and have a Synagogue in each of them; though many of them are scattered about in the Country Villages, where They keep Shops, and furnish the Planters, as well as the Negroes, with many Necessaries. They are at least Eight or Nine hundred in Number, Men, Women, and Children. But notwithstanding They are allowed to purchase Lands, and other great Priviledges, yet very few have any Notion of Planting; so that they have not amongst Them all more than eight or ten Plantations, of which three or four are Sugar Works; though great part of the Houses and Ware houses at Port Royal, and Kingston belong to Them. Several of Them are Rich, and Trade considerably upon Their own Acc[oun]ts, as well as on Commission for the Merchants of Their own Nation, in London; and like some of Them, are men of Probity, Exact and Punctual in their dealings; Their Industry, Moderation, and Oeconomy, may serve as Patterns to the other Inhabitants and Others; And it would conduce to the Preservation of their Healths, as well as their Interest if They would likewise Imitate them in Temperance, and their regular manner of living.

I have often considered the Advantages, and disadvantages, which accrue to the Island, from that Nation or People in general; and upon the whole I cannot perceive the Policy of our Ancestors, in giving them so much Encouragement, or our own in the Continuance of it, or Even in permitting them to remain on the Island; some of Them as I have observed, are indeed men of Probity, and Virtue, as well as Substance, but the generallity of Them Trade and subsist on Credit, and have so many little Roguish tricks, as are detrimental to the Country, they live in, and a Scandall and Reproach to their own Nation. It is well known, that they Corrupt the Negroes, and Encourage them to steal, by Receiving[,] concealing and purchasing stolen goods of Them; and it is a common Custom amongst Them to purchase Houses, which are not subject to the payment of debts (to the great discredit of the Island) to screen Them from Ar[r]ests, and to make a Provision for their Family, so that when they die, Their Creditors are generally defrauded of great part, if not all, Their Debts.

The Negroes who are under the necessity of dealing with Them, often detect Them (as well as others) in false weights, and measures; and as they are frequently imposed upon by these, and other vile Practices, They have conceived so implacable a prejudice to the Jews, that were They not protected by our Laws, the Negroes would soon Root Them out of the Island. It is an Observation among the Negroes, that all other People Even Themselves, have a King or a Country or both, but that the Jews have neither; which puts Them often on enquiring from whence They came, and who they are? And the Information, that is given Them, seems not only to puzzle and Surprise Them, but to raise their Indignation and Contempt.

It is likewise to be considered, that those People deprive many poor Christian Families of Subsistance, by supplanting Them in Business, who would be much more usefull to the Community than they are: the Jews do not serve on Juries, nor upon many other Publick occasions, nor indeed is it reasonable that they should; and very little Service can be expected of Them in Case of an Invasion or Insurrection as Twenty Resolute fellows will drive five hundred before them. What use or Advantage are They then of, to an Island that wants Inhabitants to Improve and defend it? They earn the Bread of others, who would be more usefull and of more service, upon those Emergent occasions, when these People will rather be a prejudice; as a Dastardly few may, and sometimes do Strike a damp Even on Men of Courage and Resolution.

Nor are these all the objections, that are commonly made to Them for They have often been suspected of holding a Correspondence and of giving Intelligence to the Spaniards. These Circumstances are worth the Notice, and Consideration of the Legislature, that some Effectual measures may be taken to Remedy those Inconveniencies, and to render these People more usefull and less Noxious.

Servants are generally Indentured, as Carpenters[,] Bricklayers[,] Coopers[,] Smiths, &c. and many are of no Trade or Profession or meer Country Fellows. The latter are imployed as Drivers, as They are called, that is in looking after the Negroes at work or in Overseeing the Boiling of Sugars; which is no hard Service, and much less trouble and fatigue, than the day Labourers in England undergo.

When Indentured Servants go over, it is Customary for the Masters to pay Their passages, to provide Them with Tools, to advance one Quarter's wages, and to find Them with Lodging, and Board, during the Contract. Tradesmen are allowed from 15 to £30 per annum according to their abilities; those that have no Trades from 5 to £10 per Ann[um] and many nothing but Board Lodging, and Cloaths.

The generality of them take to drinking strong Rum Punch, or Rum unmixed which destroys many of Them, or impairs Their Healths. Some desert Their Master's Service, and make Their Escape out of the Island, without Serving Their time; and others Combine with the Negroes, who often Ensnare and draw Them in to betray Their trust. Those that are

Stupid, Roguish or Sottish, are Severely treated; and, what is Their great misfortune, few will Employ Them, when Their Contract is Expired; so that They generally remain in a low Abject State all the remainder of Their lives.

But such as are Sober, Honest, and Industrious, meet with due Encouragement, are well used, and find the Benefit of such behaviour, when Their Contract is expired. I know Several, that are now Masters of Families, live in good Credit, and by their Industry have raised Considerable Fortunes. This ought to warn and Admonish all, that go over in those Circumstances, how they demean themselves, and to behave in such a manner, as will most Effectually Recommend them, to the good Graces of their Masters, and the notice of the World.

Indeed there is no Encouragement wanting to People of all Professions, who are carefull to recommend Themselves by their Sobriety, Industry, and discreet behaviour; as many have happily Experienced. Nor need any apprehend want or an Opportunity of Advancing themselves, but the Slothfull, and intemperate, or such as have no Regard to their own Private Character, and Interest. I don't Remember to have seen in all the time, I resided in the Island, which was upwards of Twenty Years, one Person begging in the Streets, except some Prisoners in time of War, and now and then a poor old or decrepit free Negro; which is a sufficient proof of what I have asserted.

There are severall Municipall Laws relating to Servants; and it will not be improper to transcribe a few heads of some of Them. Because it will manifest the Justice and Care of the Legislature, tho[ugh] as an impartial Writer, I must observe, that those and many other Excellent Laws, are not always duely and truely Executed.

By a Law intituled, an Act for Regulating Servants;[4] it is Enacted as follows:

All Servants are to serve according to their Contract, and Indenture, and where there is no Contract, or Indenture, Servants under Eighteen Years of Age, at Their arrival in the Island shall serve seven years; and above Eighteen Years shall Serve four years.

All suits between Servants, and Their Masters or Mistresses, relating to Their freedom, shall be heard and Determined by any two Justices of the Peace without appeal; and if any Servants absent Themselves from their Master's or Mistresses Service, without leave, They shall for every day's absence serve one Week, and so in proportion for a longer or shorter time, the whole time not to exceed three years.

If any Person shall turn away a sick or Infirm Servant, under pretence of Freedom, or otherwise; and such Servant shall die for want of Relief, or

4. An Act for Regulating Servants, 1681, in *Acts of Assembly, Passed in the Island of Jamaica; from 1681 to 1737, Inclusive* (London, 1738), 1–2.

become chargeable to any Parish, the Offender shall forfeit Twenty Pounds to the use of the Parish, where such Death, or charge shall happen.

That no Servant be whipped naked without order of a Justice of the Peace, on Penalty of five pounds.

Whosoever shall not give to each White Servant, weekly, four Pounds of good Flesh, or four pounds of good Fish, together with such Convenient Plantation Provisions, as may be sufficient, shall forfeit to the Party injured ten Shillings for Every Offence.

And Whosoever shall not Yearly give to each Servant man three Shirts, three pair of Drawers, three pair of Shoes, three pair of Stockings, and One Hat or Cap; and to the Women proportionably, shall forfeit to the Party injured forty Shillings.

And, by a Subsequent Act, it is Enacted that all differences hereafter to arise, between Master and Servants, hired, Contracted or Indentured (Overseers of Sugar Works, or Sugar Planters Excepted) shall be fully heard, and determined, before any two Justices of the Parish, or Precinct, where any such difference shall happen to Arise, without Appeal; although the Sum determined or adjudged shall exceed Twenty pounds, or any other Sum whatever.[5]

This last Clause is more particularly, and Evidently in favour of Servants, who it cannot be supposed are able to Contest or go to Law, with their Masters for Wages, or upon any other occasion, where They are injured, or aggrieved, and therefore the easy Remedy is provided, and to save Them that Expence and trouble.

And here it will not be improper to observe that it is a mistaken Notion in the Planters to imagine, They will ever be able to Settle, and Strengthen the Island, with such Persons, as are obliged to leave Their own Country for Debt, or some misbehaviour, tho[ugh] neither Convicts nor Fellons. Many of them as I have observed, Run away from their Masters, soon after their Arrival, and return to England; Others take to drinking, and by that means impair their healths, and Shorten their days; and very few Serve out their Time, or have any notion or thought of advancing themselves, notwithstanding the great Encouragement given them.

They whose Servitude Renders Their Liberty little more than Nominal, and such as have no Property, may sometimes fight, though they are not always to be depended on; for it cannot reasonably be supposed, that they will have the same Spirits, or Arm with the same generous Ardour, as those who Act in Defence of Their Liberty and Property, which is the Principal Motive to great and Noble Actions. I need not give the Gentlemen of the Island any Instances to Evince the truth of this Position; let them only reflect on the Conduct and behaviour of the Parties, that were fitted out

5. An Act for Impowering Justices of the Peace to Decide Differences Not Exceeding Forty Shillings, 1681, in ibid., 9–10.

from time to time, to pursue and Reduce the Negroes in the Mountains, before They Submitted; and this will convince them, that such Persons are not to be depended on upon the like Occasions, and that there is a necessity of taking some other measures, to People and Strengthen the Island.

The most likely means will be to introduce poor Families, and give Them due and reasonable Encouragement. And for this purpose, the first step to be taken, in my Opinion will be to Reduce the price of Provisions, by taking proper measures to make Them plenty and Cheap; for unless this be done it will be in vain to think of Peopleing the Island. And another proper Method, will be to import Boys and Girls that are about ten or twelve Years of Age, who have not contracted any ill habits nor entered into any kind of Debauchery; for they will Soon be inured to the Country, and the Climate become as Habituall to Them, as to the Natives.

But of all Countries, England is the most improper to furnish Colonies or Infant Settlements, with Inhabitants, the People being accustomed to great Plenty, and not inured to the hardships many other Parts are Subject to, and which They must expect to Encounter, when They go abroad.

The Welch are certainly the properest, and the most unexceptionable, especially in our Sugar Islands; because They are used to hard living, and a Mountainous Country, and are unacquainted with the Vice and Debauchery of other Nations: and next to Them Scotch, and Protestant Swiss Families.

But the Irish are by all means to be avoided, as the common people are mostly Papists, and Naturally Attached to the Spaniards.

There are indeed Several good and sufficient Laws, in force, to Encourage People to go over, and Settle in the Island, tho[ugh] I am sorry to observe that They are not always regarded as They ought to be nor duly put in Execution, according to the meaning and intention of the Legislature, but often Evaded and perverted, private Interest, and Advantage, being Considered, and preferred to the Generall good of the Country, by those who are intrusted with the Execution of Them.

The other Inhabitants of Jamaica, are Mulat[t]os, Indians, and Negroes, of which near two thousand are Free, besides those in the Mountains; some Obtained Their freedom by Their fidelity, and good Services to their Masters, and others by distinguishing Themselves when the Island was Invaded by the French in 1693, or in some Expeditions against the Rebellious Negroes, Their liberty having been granted Them by their Masters, or purchased at the Publick Expence for Their good Service; and some are descended from those who were active and usefull on those Occasions.

The Mulattos are a mixed Breed, between Whites and Blacks, and are a very unhappy Race of People, being despised by the one and hated by the other: They are hardy but in general very slow and Idle.

The Indians are brought from the Continent, and not Natives of the Island; none of them remaining when the Island was taken from the Spaniards. They are of a Meek, mild Temper, and must be gently treated, or they will pine away and die, as They are not accustomed to hard labour. There are very few in the Island, and those Seldom employed in any other way, than in Fishing in which They delight, and are very Expert, which makes them usefull to the Planters, who are near the Sea Coast or large Rivers.

By the laws of the Island, Free Negroes and Mulatos for all offences Capitall or Criminal are to be tried and adjudged after the same method and manner that Negroe Slaves are directed to be tried; that is by two Justices and three freeholders, who are sworne to Judge uprightly and according to Evidence; and the Evidence of a Slave against them shall be good and Valid.

That every free Negroe, Mulatto or Indian, not having a settlement of ten Negroes therein, shall furnish Him or Herself with a Certificate of his or her being Free, under the hand and Seal of any Justice of the Peace and shall wear a Publick Badge of a Blue Cross upon the Right Shoulder to denote the same.

The Negro Slaves are very numerous, there being at least One hundred thousand in the Island, Men, Women and Children which being far Superior to the White People, the Planters are by Law Obliged to keep one White Man, to thirty Negroes, or in Case of a Deficiency to pay the Penal Sum of £13:6:8 p[er] Annum, and in proportion for a greater or lesser number. So great a Superiority one would think should render it exceeding dangerous, and unsafe living amongst Them.[6] But the Security of the White People is under Providence owing to the Laws for the good Order, and Government of Slaves, and their being brought from Several parts of Guinea, which are different in language, and Customs, consequently They cannot Converse freely, nor confide in each other. And those of different Countries, have as great and Natural an Antipathy to each other, as any two Nations in the World; so that They are under mutual apprehensions of falling into Subjection one of the other, should They Shake off the Yoke of the English, which makes Them Easy, and have no thoughts of Attempting it. Beside the men of War that are constantly on the Station, and the great number of Shipping, Continually Coming and going gives them an Idea of the Strength and Power of the English Nation, and Strikes an Awe and Terrour into Them.

But the chief security of Jamaica against any general Insurrection of the Negroes, is the great Extent of the Country. Separated by Woods and Mountains, difficult of access; the Plantations lying at a great distance from each other, so that the Negroes can have no communication together, or if they had, it would be almost impossible, They should join to Execute

6. An Act to Encourage the Importation of White Men, 1703, in ibid., 99–101.

Their Designs. This Natural Security distinguishes this Island from all the other British Sugar Islands. For in the latter, notwithstanding they have every other Security, I have mentioned, but extent of Country, general Conspiracies have been formed, and sometimes with great probability of Success. But I never heard that this Island was at any time in the like danger; tho[ugh] their friends in the Mountains were not wanting to promote and encourage such a design.

None of the Negroe Slaves are allowed to keep Arms, or dangerous Weapons in Their Houses; nor suffered to go out of the Plantation they belong to, without a Certificate from the Master, or Overseer, Expressing the time He has leave to be absent, and upon what Occasion: nevertheless this is sometimes winked at, and not Strictly put in Execution.

However Guards are Constantly kept on Sundays, and Hollidays; and the Troops of Horse in the Several Parishes, or Precincts, are Obliged to Patrol in Their Respective Divisions, to prevent Conspiracies or disorders amongst the Negroes; who generally assemble together at those times, get drunk and quarrel among Themselves, and sometimes in Their drink grow turbulent, and even Mutinous, if they are not timely dispersed.

When they See the White People Muster or Exercise, especially the Regular forces, and Troops of Horse, it strikes an Awe and terrour into Them; and They will shun a Person cloathed in Red either on foot or on Horseback; for which Reason some Gentlemen put on a Coat of that Colour, when They Travell: tho[ugh] the Negroes seldom Rob or disturb any Person on the Highway, nor attempt to Steal any thing, but Money, Provisions, or ordinary Cloathing such as they usually wear, being sensible that their having any thing else in their Possession would betray Them.

And for this Reason the Planters as well as those in the Towns, live in greater Security in that Respect, than People do in England; for it is very Common to leave their Windows, even on the ground Floor open all Night.

But the Creole Negroes or those born in the Country are so far from being under the like apprehensions of a Muster, that They are familiar with it; and many of them can Exercise and make use of fire Arms as well as the Militia, which is as good as any in the World, tho[ugh] not so well Disciplined as formerly.

These Creole Negroes speak very good English, especially such as are brought up in the Towns, or in Gentlemen's Houses, and have so good and tractable a Genius, that They are easily Instructed in most Mechanical Trades, and to be usefull in many other Respects. They look upon Themselves to be as much above the Salt Water Negroes, as They call Them or those that are brought from Guinea, as the Gentry think Themselves above the Commonalty in England; and will seldom keep any of Them Company.

The Negroes brought from Guinea are of more than twenty different

Countries or Nations; but those that are most esteemed are from Whidah, the Gold Coast, and Angola.

The Whidahs are very justly preferred to all others, because They are more manageable, accustomed to labour, and hard living in Their own Country; and They are of so chearfull a disposition that They generally sing or Whistle at the hardest Work, they are put to, insomuch that it is Common amongst them, when twenty or more are at Work in the Field, to be Singing in Parts or together so that they are often heard at a considerable distance.

The Gold Coast Negroes, tho[ugh] They generally go under the denomination of Coromantus, are of different Provinces or Clans; and not under the same Prince or Chief, nor do They Speak the same language. Of these the Coromantines, Santuns, Shantus, and Achims, are mostly Esteemed; the others which are generally brought from the Windward part of the Coast, or the Inland Countries, are not equal to Them in any Respect; because the former are more accustomed to labour, and hard living in Their own Country; where their Common food is Maiz[e], or Corn, Plantains, Yams and other ground Provisions. They have indeed some Cattle, Sheep and Horses, which they dispose of to the Europeans, who come There to Trade, and to the Factories, but seldom kill any for Their own use; and seem very much surprized upon their first Arrival, when They See those Creatures at Work in the Mills, Coaches or Carts.

They are most of Them, particularly the Coromantines ingenious, and when They are Young easily taught any Science, or Mechanick Art; Remarkable for White Teeth of which They are Extreme carefull, and so neat and cleanly in other respects, that the first thing They do, after they have done work is to wash Themselves all over.

But They are Fractious, and in Their Nature Deceitfull, Revengefull, and blood thirsty, and require a Stricter hand being kept over Them than those of any other Country; for which reason every prudent Planter, is cautious of having too many of Them in his Plantation, and therefore the common Custom is to Mix other Countries with them; for there never was as I have heard of in this or any other Colony, any Plot or Conspiracy, but they were at the bottom of it.

The Angolas are likewise used to Labour, but the Reason of their not being so much esteemed by the Planters, as the others, is Their having been accustomed to Eat flesh in Their own Country, which They cannot afford Them, tho[ugh] They are not very delicate or nice in Their Choice, for a Dog is as acceptable to them as a Pig, provided He is fat.

This Country['s] Negroes are therefore generally brought up to Trades or to go in Sloops, Cannoes, and Wherries, as Watermen, where a better subsistance can be allowed Them, than in Plantations.

To enter into a Particular Description of all the other Nations of Negroes brought to this Island, would be tedious and unnecessary; nor indeed

This image showing enslaved people of African descent by the seaside engaged in a wide variety of tasks related to the production of sugar with a detailed landscape of Jamaica in the background is taken from the detailed cartouche of a map entitled *Nova Designatio Insulae Jamaicae ex Antillanis Americae Septentrion*. The work of the German printer George Matthäus Seutter (1678–1757), it was published around 1730.

will I pretend to it there being so many and some of Them[,] especially those brought from the Inland Parts of Guinea, are so strangely stupid and Ignorant, that They cannot give any Account of Themselves. They seem to have no thought or Notion of any thing more, than satisfying the present wants of Nature; and would spend the rest of Their time if They were indulged, in sleeping. Some are so senseless as to imagine, the White People have no other intention in bringing Them from Their Own Country, than to Eat Them; and this notion causes Them to Pine, and take to eating of Dirt, or using other means to make away with Themselves.

The Planter generally buys Eight or Ten at a time according as He is furnished with Provisions, or His Occasions require, and the Custom is to give to Each Man and His Wife a piece of Ground; which They are told, They must Cultivate and improve for themselves as fast as They can; because Their Master is to subsist Them for Six months only; but after the Expiration of that term They must provide for Themselves: an Industrious Negro out of the land allotted Him, will not only be able to raise as many Plantains, Yams, Potatoes and other ground Provision, and also Hogs, and Dunghill Fowles, (w[hi]ch he is allowed to keep) as will be sufficient for Himself and Family; but to Sell enough to purchase better Cloathing, than He is Annually furnished with by His Master; and likewise Salted Beef, Pork, Fish and other necessaries; nay some of Them that are frugal as well as Industrious, will lay up Money beside; which They are carefull to keep from the knowledge of Their Masters, tho[ugh] few or none of Them,

I believe, would be so unjust as to deprive Them of it. However They generally hide Their Wealth in some private place in the Earth, so that if They happen to die suddenly, or insensible, the Money is often lost, They being extreame carefull to conceal the Place even from those of Their own Family.

Their Houses are built low and snug covered with Thatch after Their Country manner, the principall Posts being fixed in the ground three feet or more, the sides, ends, and partitions lined with Watles, a kind of laths neatly plaistered with Mud, and a little lime mixed, some without. They are commonly about twenty-four feet in length eight or nine feet in breadth and five and a half or six feet in height. They have no Windows, only small loop Holes on each side to distinguish the day from the Night, and to look out when They apprehend any danger, and Their doors are made so low that a middle size man must stoop to go in. This Building is divided into Three apartments, at one end is His Chamber, the middle part is His Hall or dineing Room at the other end, He keeps His Poultry, and it is likewise a kind of Store Room. They have all of Them a Door in the Front, and another in the back part, in order to escape any danger[;] many of Them are kept very neat and clean, but They all smell very strong of smoak by reason of the Constant fires They keep in the day as well as in the Night and not having Chimneys to carry it off.

They are extremely fond of Dogs, by reason of Their Watchfullness, and giving notice of any disturbance or Danger so that very few of Them are without one or two if They can procure them.

On Sunday mornings, They are allowed to bring their Provisions to Town, and sell Them in the market, but They are obliged to remove at nine a Clock, or before Divine Service begins: and on Sundays and Hollidays in the Evenings, as well as in Moon light nights, after They have done work, They Assemble, Dance, Sing or Play together.

In Dancing the Men as well as the Women, keep very good time, tho[ugh] in other respects Their Parts Consist of little more, than shewing Postures and an Agility of Body. But the Women have a great Variety of Steps, and are more decent and Modest in their Manner and behaviour.

Their Instruments of Musick are very Noisy, and have no manner of Harmony, except the Merry Wang; which has a Bridge with four Strings, and is played upon in the same manner, as the Guittar. It is far from being disagreeable, when it is in a good hand; and I have heard Minuits, and other English Tunes played thereon, so distinctly, and with so good time, as might serve European Dancers upon Occasion.

The Negroes in general have a Natural gloomy Countenance, and seldom look cheerfull or pleased; so that it is difficult for a Person, who is unacquainted with Their language or Custom, to distinguish when They sing and play on Their Musick, whether it proceeds from Mirth, or Sorrow; unless they Cry at the same time, as They often do, when They are very much grieved; for They sing and play on Their Musick, when They are under any affliction or trouble to dissipate Melancholy thoughts, as well as to amuse and divert Themselves upon other Occasions.

Most of Them compose their own Songs, which as to the sense and substance of the Words, are after the Italian Manner; tho[ugh] Their Notes are not so agreeable and Harmonious. Thus when any of Their Friends dye; when They have been severely, or unduly Corrected, or when their favourite Wife or Mistress gives Them any Cause of uneasiness, They put together some Words bemoaning Themselves, and complaining of Their Loss, or Injuries, and sing Them to some of Their Country Tunes. And in like manner when any Event pleases Them They Sing some particular Circumstance or Passage, that Strikes Them, and perhaps to the same Tune, or some other very like it; for They have very few Tunes, which I ever heard, that are brisk or Airy; but in general there is something in them extremely Melancholly. So that when many of Them at a distance, are singing and playing on Their Musick in parts or together, no body can be certain, not even Their Countrymen, who are unacquainted with the Occasion, whether They are at a Funeral or a Festival; for all of Them except the Angolas, and the Creole Negroes, sing, play on their Musick, and Dance round the Graves of Their Dead at Funerals, and for a Month after, as well as at Festivals or Publick Meetings on Hollidays.

Their Entertainments are likewise Remarkable; and particularly a Coromantee Feast, which is become a kind of a Proverb, in the Island; because the Person who entertaines is always a gainer. Their Custom is to invite Their Friends on some Holliday; When They kill a Hog, and dress it several ways, and every one of the Guests contributes something; one sends Fowls, others Rum, Sugar, &c. or Money, so that upon the whole They are gainers instead of being at any Expence.

Nature has implanted in Them, as well as the rest of Mankind, Pride, Ambition, Dissimulation and all other passions and Vices; though They have not the same Opportunity of exerting Them; But They are particularly Remarkable for the Art of Concealing Their passions, or any Compact or Agreement amongst Themselves; for when They are detected or Convicted of any Crime, They will not only persist in denying the fact, but assume such a Countenance, as would almost perswade one of Their Innocency; and they will suffer any Punishment, even Death it self, rather than make a Discovery, or reveal any Engagement, or Confidence reposed in Them. Tho[ugh] they are not easily or often dashed, yet I have sometimes seen Them out of Countenance or what we call Blush, which may be perceived in Them, as well as in other People, for as White Persons on such Occasions turn Red, They change to a Pale or Whitish Black.

In their Marriages They have no form or Ceremony, but take one another's words; and I have known some, that never separated or Acknowledged any other Husband or Wife during the life of the first. But in general They often change, when any quarrel arises between Them, through Jealousy or upon other Occasions. However, they are always fond of, and take care of Their Children, even in those Cases.

And notwithstanding Polygamy is allowed amongst the Negroes, yet many of Them have no more than one Wife, and some have none. For Interest governs Them as well as the rest of Mankind, and unless a Man can provide better Cloaths, and other necessaries, than His Master allows, He will find some difficulty in getting a Wife. Nor have any of Them more than Three, which go under the Denomination of Wives, and these are generally Politically chosen; One in regard to Interest, that is a House Wench, or One who has Money Relations or Friends, who can be usefull or Servicable to Him; Another is the Object of His Affections; and the Third to dress His Victuals, and manage his House, and in short is little more than his Drudge, or House-keeper. The first mentioned has always the Precedence; and tho[ugh] They often meet at the Husband's House, and in other Places, yet They converse freely, and in an Amicable manner. Nevertheless disputes and Controversies sometimes arise amongst them, which are determined by the Husband agreeable to His own Humour or Caprice and not according to the Rules of Reason or Justice; and if He happens to be displeased with or has taken a dislike to any of them, He makes use of that dispute, or takes some other Occasion, for turning Her off without any Ceremony; and takes another. Nay, some of Them keep Their Wives in such awe and subjection, that They will not suffer Them to Dine, or Sup with Them; but make Them wait till They have done, and the Reason They give is, because it would make Them Saucy, as they express Themselves.

In the management of those People, tho[ugh] it is absolutely Necessary to keep a Vigilant Eye, and a Strict hand over most of Them so as to keep Them in Awe, and prevent Their doing wrong or Mischief; yet care must be taken to treat Them with Humanity, and not to Correct Them unjustly or without proof of Their having committed some fault, for tho[ugh] They never repine when They are Conscious of having deserved Correction, yet They seldom or ever forgive Injuries or Maltreatment.

And here I must in Regard to Truth and Justice observe, that there are many Instances of great Fidelity in some Negroes, and particularly the Creoles or those Born in the Country; not only as to what is committed to Their Care and management, but in making known to Their Masters and Mistresses the Treacherous Practices and Rebellious designs of other Negroes, by which means several Families have been preserved, and much mischief prevented.

Nor have They failed of a due Reward on such and upon other Occasions, for Their Faithfull Services, as is Evident from the great number of Free Negroes now in the Island, not less than two thousand, beside those

Derived from a 1758 engraving of Henry Dawkins's Parnassus Estate in Clarendon Parish, reworked from a plate in Diderot's *Encyclopédie*, and published in Livorno in 1763, G. M. Terrenise's engraving *Canna da zucchero/Plantazione di zucchero* provides an unusually detailed image of a Jamaican sugar plantation. On the left-hand side is the planter's dwelling with two rows of slave dwellings beneath it. In the center is a pasture with a few cows and a small array of enslaved workers with several large fields planted in sugar cane above them. On the right-hand side are a stream, a water mill, and three other buildings used for processing sugar cane.

that were set[t]led in the Mountains, and obtained Their Freedom by the Treaty made with Them in 1738.

There are very few Plantations or Families but have some Negroes more or less, who behave extremely well and are therefore distinguished by Their Masters, and employed as Drivers or under Overseers, Boylers, and in other places of Trust; and I am perswaded, that many of Them, who understand the use of Fire Arms, may be confided in, and will be very Serviceable, in Case the Island should be at any time Invaded by a Foreign Enemy: not only for the Reason given, but because They have a kind of property to defend; and can't endure a change of Masters, even among the English; for They are greatly disturbed on such occasions, and are with difficulty removed from one Plantation, or part of the Island, to another. And the Reason of it is Evident, They have new Settlements to make for Themselves; and as They think, are to begin the World again, according to the common Phrase.

Besides they are acquainted with the Temper and Customs of Their first Master, and perhaps Contracted an Affection for Him, especially if He uses Them well; or They are doubtfull of the Treatment They shall meet with from the New, even though They have some knowledge, and are acquainted with Him, and have no prejudice or dislike to His Character among Themselves.

But the Strongest Objection is the Friendship and Alliances They have Contracted; or perhaps They have Children, and other Relations, in the Neighbourhood. They have likewise Terrible Notions of the Inhumanity and Cruelty of the French as well as the Spaniards, from the Accounts they received from some Negroes who had been transported, and sold to the French at Hispaniola; and made their Escape from thence at a very great Hazard of Their lives on the Seas. So that the Negroes in general think the greatest Punishment that can be inflicted on Them is to be transported and Sold to either of those Nations.

The Laws for the better order and Government of Slaves among other things Enact;

That if a Slave strike a White man, or offer any Violence to Him, such Slave shall be punished by two Justices of the Peace, and three Freeholders, who may inflict Death or any other Punishment, According to Their discretion; provided such Striking, or Assault, be not by command of His Owner, Overseer or Person having Power over Him, or in the lawfull Defence of His Owner's Person or Goods.

That all Slaves shall have Cloaths, that is Men, Jackets and Drawers, and Women, Jackets and Petticoats, once, every Year, on or before the 25 day of December, upon the Penalty of five Shillings for every Slave's wanting the same.

That all Masters and Owners of Plantations are required to have at all times hereafter one Acre of Ground well planted with Provision, for every five Negroes He has in His Plantation, under the Penalty of forty Shillings for every Acre so wanting.

That every Master, or Mistress, or Overseer shall cause all Slave's Houses to be searched every fourteen days for Clubs, wooden Swords, or other mischievous Weapons, and finding any shall cause Them to be burnt, and also upon Request, to search for stolen goods, and any Slave or Slaves in whose Custody such stolen Goods shall be found, shall suffer death, Transportation[,] Dismemb[e]ring, or any other Punishment at the descretion of two Justices, and three Freeholders, or the Major part of Them, one of which to be a Justice.

That no Person shall attempt, or endeavour to Steal or Carry off the Island, Hide, Conceal, or Employ any Slave on Penalty of £100. But whosoever shall Actually steal any Slave, or deface His, Her, or Their mark, shall be guilty of Felony, and shall be excluded the benefit of the Clergy.

That all and every Slave or Slaves, that shall run away and continue for the space of twelve months, except such Slave or Slaves, as shall not have been three years in this Island, shall be deemed Rebellious; and Their taking shall be paid for accordingly, which Slave or Slaves so taken, as a Punishment for Their Crimes, shall be Transported by order of two Justices and three Freeholders, or the Major part of Them, one of which to be a Justice, tho[ugh] no other Crime shall appear against Them: which Order the Owner or Trustee shall see duely Executed, under the Penalty of Fifty pounds for each Offence.

That if any Slave or Slaves Transported by order of two Justices and three Freeholders, willfully return; upon complaint made to any Justice of the Peace, He upon View of the Record is impowered and directed on Penalty of Fifty pounds, immediately to issue out a Warrant under His Hand and Seal, to any Marshall or Constable to Apprehend and Execute the Slave or Slaves so returning.

That upon Complaint made to any Justice of the Peace of any Fellony, Burglary, Robbery, burning of Houses or Canes, Rebellious Conspiracies, or any other Capital Offence, the said Justice shall Issue out His Warrant for the Apprehending the Offender or Offenders; and for all Persons to come before Him that can give Evidence: (and the Evidence of one Slave against another, in this and all other Cases, shall be deemed good and sufficient proof) and if upon Examination, it appears, that the Apprehended are guilty, He shall commit Him, Her or Them to Prison, and Certifie to the next Justice the Cause, and require Him to Associate Himself, which Such Justice is thereby required to do: and They, so associated, shall Issue out Their Warrant to Summon three Freeholders setting forth the matter, and Requiring Them to attend at a Certain day and hour, and at Such a place, as is Appointed by the Justices, and Vestry of the Parish, for such Trialls; and if They on hearing the matter (The Freeholders being first sworne to judge uprightly, and according to Evidence) shall judge the Person or Persons guilty, They or the Major part of Them, of w[hi]ch one shall be a justice, shall give sentence of Death, Transportation or any other Punishment, as They shall think meet to inflict; and forthwith by Their Warrant cause immediate Execution to be done, Women with Child only Excepted, who are hereby Reprieved till after Their Delivery.

And if any Slave, or Slaves, compass or imagine the death of a White Person: and thereof be attainted by open deed (or Overt Act) before two Justices, and three Freeholders, such Slave or Slaves shall suffer Death, and all Petit Crimes, Trespasses, and Injuries, committed by any Slave or Slaves, shall be heard and determined by any Justice of the Peace.

And for Prevention of the Meeting of Slaves in great numbers on Sundays and Hollidays, whereby They Contrive and bring to pass many Bloody and Inhuman transactions, it is ordered and directed;

That no Master, Mistress or Overseer shall suffer any meeting of Slaves not belonging to Their own Plantation, to Rendevouz, Feast, Revell, beat Drums or Cause any other disturbance, but shall forthwith disperse Them.

That no Slave shall be free by becoming a Christian; and for payment of Debts and Legacies, all Slaves shall be deemed and taken as Goods and

Chattles, in the hands of Executors; and where other Goods and Chattles are not Sufficient to satisfie such Debts and Legacies, then so many as are necessary shall be sold, and the Remaining Slaves after the payment of Debts and Legacies, shall be judged, deemed and taken as Inheritance, and shall descend accordingly. And all Children of Slaves shall remain, or Revert as Their Parents do.

That all Masters, Mistress[es], or Owners, and in Their absence Overseers shall as much as in Them lies, endeavour the Instruction of Their Slaves, in the Principles of the Christian Religion, whereby to facilitate Their Conversion; and shall do Their utmost to fitt Them for Baptism; and as soon as They conveniently can, shall cause to be Baptised all such, as They can make sensible of a Deity, and the Christian Faith.

That the Justices within the several and Respective Parishes and Precincts, shall at the first Session in every year, limit and appoint the number of Hollidays at the usual Festivals of Christmas, Easter, and Whitsuntide.

That no Slave or Slaves be dismemb[e]red at the Will and pleasure of His Master, Owner or Employer, and under the penalty of £100.

That if any Person shall willingly, wantonly or bloody mindedly kill a Negro, or other Slave, He, She or They so offending, being Convicted thereof by a Verdict or Confession in the Supreme Court of Judicature shall be adjudged guilty of Felony, for the first Offence, and have the benefit of the Clergy. But the Second offence shall be deemed Murder, and the Offender suffer Death, according to the Laws of England; but is not to forfeit lands, and Tenements[,] Good and Chattles.

Beside these, there are many other Excellent Laws relating to the Negroes, too tedious and indeed unnecessary to transcribe, the aforementioned Abstracts or Clauses, being sufficient to shew the Care, Justice, and tenderness of the Legislature with regard to Them, as well as to the Interest and Preservation of the Island; and I could wish They were at all times duly observed, and strictly put in Execution.

As to the Inhumanity and Cruelty of the Planters to Their Negroes, tho[ugh] I will not pretend to say, there is not any ground for that Charge, yet in general it is very much aggravated; and very few are so Barbarous as They are Represented to be. But Whoever considers the Negroes' Superiority in Number, the sullen, deceitfull, Refractory Temper of Most of Them; that some are Careless, others Treacherous or Idle, and apt to Run away; and how much Their Master's Interest depends on the Care, and diligence of His Slaves, must needs be convinced, that there is an Absolute necessity of keeping a Vigilant Eye, and strict hand over Them.

The Punishment usually inflicted on Them, unless by order of two Justices, and three Freeholders, is a severe whipping on the bare back, and though such a Correction may be shocking to a tender mind, yet it is indispensably necessary for the Reasons, I have mentioned.

Nor is that kind of Discipline so Rigid and Severe as is practised in English, as well as Foreign Camps and Garrisons; where I have seen the common Soldiers punished with much greater Severity than I ever saw the Negroes in Jamaica. However it must be confessed that the Usage and treatment of the Negroes, greatly depends on the Temper and discretion of the Master; for such Men [as] are of a more tender, humane, Compassionate disposition, than others; and are led by those motives and Principles, as well as Regard to Their Interest to be kind to Their Negroes, to be carefull that They neither want Provisions, nor proper Cloathing, and to preserve Their lives and limbs; because the death or disability of a Negro is a Certain loss and Their Plantations depend on keeping up the Number, which is not so easy as some imagine, for though Polygamy is practised amongst the Negroes, it rather hinders than promotes Their multiplying, so that when Mortality or any other Accident happens, a Planter is undone, or falls behind hand unless He has Money or Credit to purchase others; a good working field Negro being worth from 30 to £50, and good Boilers, Carpenters, Bricklayers and other Tradesmen from £60 to £150, Each according to His Skill and Ability. And tho[ugh] it will appear very strange, yet it is a matter of Fact to my own knowledge, and Observation, that the Free Negroes and Mulattos, even those who have been Slaves Themselves, are the most Rigid and Severe Masters in all Respects.

The Negroes' manner of Living in our Plantations, and above all the very name of Slavery, may be disagreeable and shocking to an Englishman, who has always enjoyed His liberty and lived in ease and plenty; But when it is considered that Their Condition in general is much better, and that They live happier than They did in Their own Country, or even than some of the working People in England, and preferably to those of some other Nations; those Circumstances will remove the Prejudice, which many Persons unacquainted with our Colonies, have conceived against Them. For every Plantation-Negroe in Jamaica is allowed to build a House for Himself and Family, after His own manner; which tho[ugh] mean and low, yet is such, as They have been used to in Their own Country; They are also allowed to Fence in a small yard Contiguous, and to raise Hogs, and Poultry for Themselves, beside His little Plantation, which produces Corn, Pease &c. and all sorts of ground Provisions; some of which They dispose of, and purchase other necessaries.

Their Diet is indeed Course, yet They are very well contented with it, as it is the same and in some Respects much better than They were used to, which was nothing more than Maiz[e] or Corn, in some Parts Rice, Plantains, Yams and Potatoes roasted or boiled (and now and then a Goat, or a small Deer)[.] But in Jamaica, They not only have those sorts of Provisions in great plenty, but Salted Beef, Pork and Fish, which many of Them prefer to fresh Meat. In some parts of the Island, They have also plenty of fresh Fish, and most of Them, as I observed, are allowed to keep Hogs and Fowls; by which means They are able to purchase a better allowance of

Throughout the Americas, masters resorted to extreme measures to punish and discipline enslaved laborers. Entitled *Wrede strasse van een Planter aan zyn knegt*, this engraving, published in Nicolaas ten Hoorn, *Historie der boecaniers, of vrybuyters van America* (Amsterdam, 1700), shows a white master whipping a man, probably a slave, who is tied to a tree, with a servant holding a tray and three other male figures standing by, at least one of whom seems to be protesting.

those things, Than They have from Their Masters, which is only at Christmas and in Croptime. They have likewise Cloathing and many other Necessaries which They were Strangers to, and never knew the use of before They came to the Island.

Nor was Their liberty in Their own Country any more than Nominal or imaginary; for as most of Them were subject to the Arbitrary Will and Pleasure of Their Kings or Chief Men, who disposed of Them as They thought proper, and had an Absolute power of life and Death, They may justly be said to be less Slaves in our Plantations, than They were in their own Country. Because in our Plantations Their Masters are allowed no power of life and death over Their Slaves, and are even restrained from Maiming or dismembering Them upon any pretence whatever without a legal Trial.

Whoever considers the condition of the common People in most other Countries, and Compares it with the Condition of the Negroes in our Plantations, must allow that the latter has the Advantage, notwithstanding all the objections and Cavils that are made against the usage and treatment the Negroes meet with. A Negro has a kind of property, and looks upon His little Plantation as such, it being seldom taken away without giving Him an Equivolent. He has stated times of Working and Recess, and several Hollidays in the Year, beside Saturdays in the Afternoon and Sundays. He is allowed at those times to go upon His own Occasions, divert Himself, or Visit His friends, provided He asks leave and Obtains a Certificate. He is taken care of in sickness and Health, and at no Expence for Rent, or an Apothecary or Surgeon. He has plenty of ground Provisions and with Care and Industry may furnish Himself with salted Provisions, and other Necessaries, beside what He is allowed by His Master. And when He is grown old, infirm or past labour, He is supported by His Master. This is the Circumstance or Condition of most, tho[ugh] not all of Them, as some of Them are so Roguish or idle, as not to take that provident care, and therefore often suffer want and Extremity which They very justly deserve.

The Condition and Manner of living of the common People in England, and other parts is very well known and therefore I shall only observe, that many of Them are under great difficulties in Subsisting Themselves and Their Families in Sickness or the dead of Winter; and sometimes in the Summer Season; that Their Diet in general is as coarse as the Negroes, few of Them being able to purchase Meat, above once a week, and that of the worst sort; that many of Them are as Ragged, and bare of Cloathing as the Negroes, considering the difference of the Climate, and that often in Health, as well as in sickness, Old Age, or Disability, They are reduced to very great extremity; yet these people startle, and are Shocked at the proposition of going over to the Plantations; where They may live better and have a prospect of raising Their Fortunes.

The Negroes are not only subject to the common Diseases, but are likewise troubled with some Distempers, peculiar to Themselves, and probably owing to Their manner of living, as They feed much on Salted Provisions, or such as They Season so Excessive high with salt and Pepper, that no body can touch it but Themselves; even the very tasting of it will inflame the Mouth to such a degree that it cannot be cooled for sometime after.

The most terrible Distemper amongst Them is the Yaws; which is very seldom known among the White People, tho[ugh] some of the poorer sort who converse and Cohabit with Them are sometimes troubled with it.

It breaks out in Blotches and sores full of Ulcerous matter, and when it spreads, and is thick over the body, it is more offensive and frightfull than the small Pox: it is seldom cured in less than two years, and very few but Their own Doctors, (for such They have amongst Them) have the Art of making a perfect Cure. For though our Physicians and Surgeons undertake it, and do seemingly make a Cure, yet it generally breaks out again.

As I have mentioned the Negro Doctors, it will not be improper to take notice that some of Them have made very Surprising Cures and particularly one belonging to Mr. Dawkins of Clarendon.[7] Their method of Practice is generally by making a hot Bath with several sorts of Herbs and Simples; or by Fomentations, which are attended with wonderfull Success, and more particularly in the small Pox. They very seldom prescribe any thing to be taken inwardly, which probably is one Reason that attaches Their own Colour so much to Them, and makes Them have so little Confidence in our Physicians and Surgeons. For tho[ugh] every Plantation has one that constantly attends Them every day, yet it is with great difficulty that many of the Negroes are prevailed upon to take Their Medicines.

The Negro Doctors very seldom discover Their Nostrums, or method of Practice; tho[ugh] some of our Practitioners have now and then got out of Them the use and Virtue of many Simples, that were unknown to Them or any Physician in England. And I am of Opinion, that many Secrets in the Art of Physick may be obtained from those Negro Doctors, were proper Methods taken; which I think is not below our Physicians to enquire into, as it may be of great Service to Themselves, as well as mankind.

There Remains one objection to the Conduct of the Planters, which I wish I could as easily answer, as those I have already mentioned; and that is the little care They take to instruct Their Negroes in the belief of a Deity, and the Principles of the Christian Religion. The Legislature indeed have by law directed, that every Master, Mistress, or Overseer shall, as much as in Them lies, endeavour to instruct Their Slaves, and to fit Them for Baptism; but it must be observed, that there is no Penalty on those who omit or neglect it; nor would it be to any purpose if there was[,] as many other Penal Laws which affect Themselves are very seldom put in Execution. The Reason commonly assigned for Their neglect of this, vizt. that the Conversion of Their Slaves to Christianity would Set Them free is Entirely groundless; because there is an Express law of the Country to the Contrary, nor do I conceive any foundation for such a suggestion if there was not.

It must be confessed, that those People shew no manner of inclination to be instructed or Converted; nor could I ever perceive it had any good

7. The Dawkins family was an old one in Clarendon Parish, Richard Dawkins having represented that parish in the Jamaica Assembly in the 1680s and 1690s and Henry Dawkins in the 1750s.

Effect on those that were taught to Read, and had been Baptised, however devo[u]t and attentive They appeared to be during Divine Service: and many of Them are so very dull and Stupid that it is impracticable to instill into Them any Notion of Religion or a future state of Rewards and Punishments. The most sensible among Them, and especially the Creole Negroes, do indeed believe in a Deity, and that there is a future State; tho[ugh] Their own Notions and Opinions are very dark and Obscure.

As to Their being Idolators, and that They Worship Snakes and other Animals, I never met with any such, or who really were of Opinion, that when They die They shall return again to Their own Country, as is commonly related of Them; and if there be any such it must be only the most Stupid and Ignorant amongst Them.

It is true, that all of Them, except the Angolas, put Meat and Drink into the Graves with Their Dead, and for some weeks after sing, Dance, and pour liquor over Them, but this proceeds from the general Opinion amongst Them of removing after Death to some other Country, where They shall Enjoy Their Freedom and live happily; and therefore they must have Provisions for Supporting Them.

It is that hope or Expectation, which makes Them so fearless of Death, and in Their last moments seem to be under no other concern, than that of parting with Their Friends; and it is so strongly imprinted on some Negroes, particularly the Eboes, that upon the least disgust or uneasiness, and sometimes to avoid Punishment, They will hang Themselves.

Nor has any means been found effectual to deter Them from that abominable Practice, but to dismember and burn the bodies of such Negroes, for as They have not any Idea of a Resurrection, it strikes the greatest terrour into Them, because they Think it Annihilates or disables such Persons from pursuing Their Journey to that other Country. Nay many of Them have discovered the greatest uneasiness, when They have seen, or heard of any of Their Friends or Countrymen being opened or dissected; and the Surgeons sometimes have been obliged to desist in order to pacify Them, altho[ugh] They were acquainted with the Motives and Reasons, and many Arguments made use of to convince Them of their absurd and Ridiculous Notions, tho[ugh] to very little purpose.

As to the Angolas, many of Them have been Baptized in Their Own Country, and have some notions of Christianity, tho[ugh] very dark and obscure. For about two hundred Years ago Their King and many of Them were converted by the Portoguese who continue to send Missionaries among Them. They have also some black Priests of Their own Country, who are Slaves as well as Themselves, and tell their Beads and perform the Offices at Funerals after the Romish manner in broken Portoguese: though I never could inform my self that they had any other Publick or private Meetings for the performing Divine Worship; or that They were better than other Negroes in any Respect.

Upon the whole, I am of Opinion, that it is possible to Instruct many Negroes, especially the Creoles, or such as are brought Young to the Island, in the Belief of a Deity which They seem Naturally inclined to, and of a Future State of Rewards and Punishments. These and some Principles of Morality which might likewise be inculcated would tend very much to make Them better Servants and subjects, as well as to fit them for another World; But to Attempt any thing more, will be in Vain and a Herculean labour, tho[ugh] I am far from discouraging so laudable a design and should be glad to see some attempt to accomplish it.

As the Negroes who are set[t]led in the Mountains, and for many years gave great disturbance and uneasiness to the Inhabitants, more particularly to the Planters in the remote Parts of the Island, Their Origin is very dark and obscure; and all that can be collected of Them is chiefly by Tradition from some of the old Standers and Themselves particularly Capt[ain] Cudjo, who is Their Chief or Head man, and a very sensible Fellow.

The Government was at a vast Expence in Building Defensible Barracks in the Mountains to prevent Their Excursions, as well as in raising Parties, to pursue and reduce Them. But all to very little purpose; for having many Fastnesses and Places of Retreat, when They were discovered and routed from one Settlement, They retired to another, where our People could not follow not being well acquainted with the Mountainous Parts, nor Capable of ascending Them, but with the greatest difficulties. By those means They were not only able to support and defend Themselves, but to be very mischievous and troublesome; and as They encreased and gathered Strength, by the Fugitives (from time to time) from the Plantations, they became formidable and threat[e]ned the Subversion of the Island.

According to the best Information I have been able to get, They are partly descended from some Spanish Negroes, who refused the Terms and Conditions which were offered by Collo[nel] Doyley, and had been accepted of by many others; but chiefly from the Negroes who some years after Rebelled at Major Lobby's Plantation in St. Ann's, Mr. Sutton's in Clarendon, and Mr. Guy's at Guanaboa and never were subdued.

When the English Forces had routed the Spaniards who were settling themselves at St. Ann's, (after the Island was surrendered by Treaty to General Venables) They left behind Them a considerable number of Negroes and Mulattos whom They were not able to carry with Them, for want of Embarkation. To encourage Them to continue Their Fidelity to harrass and distress the English, They promised Them great Rewards, and that They would soon return with sufficient Forces to recover the Island. At the same time to Exasperate and prevent Their making any Agreement, They insinuated that the English were a Bloody minded People, and never gave any quarter.

These Negroes finding Themselves at liberty, and that Their Masters did not return according to Their promise, killed the Mulattos and others who were appointed to conduct Them; Erected a kind of Government among Themselves, and Chose a Person, whom they thought fit to Govern Them. But, having already given a Relation of their Transactions, from time to time, I shall now proceed to give an account of those who continued Obstinate and refused to accept of the Terms and Conditions which were granted to the others.

When They found Their Numbers so reduced that They were not able to make any Resistance[,] They resolved to retire and settle in the most remote Parts of the Island; And if possible to avoid being discovered or giving any offence. Accordingly They divided Themselves in[to] two Bodies, that They might be better able to subsist Themselves, and remain undiscovered; the one of Them set[t]led among the Mountains between St. James's and Hannover Parishes, and the other at the Eastermost part of St. George's near Port Antonio. There they lived in an inoffensive manner many years; carefully avoiding the English, when They came to Settle in those Parts, or of doing Them any Injury, insomuch that it was generally thought they had found means of getting over to Cuba, or perished in the Woods, so that They were almost forgot; and the New Set[t]lers in those Parts scarcely ever heard of, much less imagined They had any such Neighbours, or [were] under any Apprehensions of Them.

In process of time the Hunters fell in with Theirs, who at first were very shy, but afterwards They became acquainted, grew familiar, and held a Correspondance with the English Negroes; however They did not encourage Them to desert, and those that did were treated with great severity, obliged to do all Servile Offices, They put Them to, which prevented many others from joining Them.

In 1673, the Negroes belonging to Major Lobby, who were mostly Coromantines, a Factious, Turbulent, bloody minded People, mutinied, killed Their Master and twelve white men, seized all Their Arms and Ammunition They could meet with, and retreated to the Mountains where They set[t]led and remained undiscovered many years.

The same accident hap[pe]ned, some years after at Mr. Sutton's Plantation in Clarendon, and Mr. Guy's at Guanaboa. And many of Their Negroes who escaped also set[t]led in the Mountains separately and under distinct Commanders, who were chosen among Themselves. These three Gangs lived some years in Their respective Retreats without any knowledge of each other, or of the Spanish Negroes and were contented to hide Themselves in those Parts where They could subsist without doing any Injury to the Planters or giving Them the least umbrage; But, the want of Cloaths, ammunition, and other necessaries made Them afterwards venture out in the Night, surprize and Rob the Remote Settlements. Their Success not only animated Them, but encouraged several small Bodies of Negroes to desert from the Plantations, who likewise set[t]led Separately; and particularly a parcel of New Negroes belonging to Capt[ain] Herring in St. Elizabeth's,[8] who not being at Home, they mutinied, kill[e]d His Lady and two children and retired into the Mountains, where They hap[pe]ned to meet with and joined one of those Gangs.

And in 1718 another Body of Negroes belonging to Mr. Downs of St. Elizabeth's, went away and put Themselves under the Command of a Madagascar Negroe, who was a Resolute, Cunning Fellow and set[t]led near Dean's Valley. These inveigled many discontented Negroes from the Neighbouring Plantations, and became considerable about the Year 1720. When by means of Their Hunters the severall Gangs became acquainted with each other['s] settlements, and most of Them incorporated in two great Bodies the one under the Command of the Madagascar Negro, and the others who were mostly Coromantines, under the Command of a Negro belonging to Mr. Sutton.

These, two Parties, after many disputes, and bloody Battles wherein a great number were slain on both sides, and among others the Madagascar Captain[,] joined and incorporated Themselves.

Hence arose that Great Body of Negroes near Dean's Valley in St. Elizabeth's, now under the Command of Capt[ain] Cudjo, who afterwards encreased by the desertion of other Negroes from time to time.

But However inoffensively the Spanish Negroes lived, for many years, yet when Their Posterity became acquainted with some of the small Bodies, of Rebellious Negroes and observed that They supported Themselves by Robbery and Violence; They made use of the same means to furnish Themselves with Arms, Ammunition and Women which They were in great want of. They likewise Associated Themselves with some of those small Bodies, followed the same Customs and abated of Their Severity to those who deserted and came to join Them.

Hence arose the other great Gang, which consisted of the Descendants of the Spanish Negroes, who had seated Themselves in St. James's and St. George's, were joined by divers small Bodies, and after many disputes and Battles with some other Gangs, incorporated and set[t]led together in the Mountains near Port Antonio, where They made a considerable settlement, which They called Nanny Town.

Hitherto, those Gangs only came down in the Night, and Robbed the Out Settlements, without committing any Murder, which was the principal Cause of the great neglect of the Government in not taking Vigorous measures earlier than They did to subdue or Extirpate Them, untill Their Strength and Number began to appear, which was about the year 1730. For having been overlook[e]d and disregarded so many years, They began to grow Formidable by continual desertions; and many hundred stout able Negroes being born in the Woods, who were trained up to Arms, and being from Their Infancy accustomed to Steep Rocky Mountains, it was

8. Julines Hering represented St. Elizabeth Parish in the Jamaica Assembly in 1686.

exceeding difficult, and almost impracticable for white Persons to follow Them.

The North East Part of the Island being uninhabited by the English was for many years, entirely possessed or Over run by this Windward Gang; and St. James's by the leeward Gang. And They had not only a Communication from the Mountains to the Sea (where They frequently came down to catch Turtle, and make Salt) But, from one end of the Island, (over the Mountains) to the Other, by which means they held a Correspondance with each other.

I am Credibly inform[e]d that before They had an intercourse with the Plantations or a passage to the Sea, Their want of Salt was one of the greatest inconveniences they were Subject to (being Naturely fond of it and accustomed to use great quantities) and They found Their Healths impaired by the disuse. Nor, could they without it preserve their Wild Hog and other Game, which they met with in the Mountains and on the Sea Coasts. But, this They afterwards supplied by making a strong lixivium of Wood Ashes, which They accidentally discovered to be salt; and by dipping Their Hog and other Game in the pickle which They made of it, and afterwards smoking Them, They were able to preserve Their Hog and other Game a Considerable time.

But for several years past They not only came to Manchianeal Bay, and other Parts near the Sea where They supplied themselves with Salt, Turtle and Fish; but They also had an Opportunity of furnishing Themselves with whatever They had occasion for.

The Government used all the precautions in Their power to prevent those Practices and Inconveniences; and the Assembly passed an Act which not only confined the Sale of Powder to a very few hands, but imposed a heavy penalty on those who should dispose of or deliver any quantity, to a Negro, Mulatto or other Person, who was not a House keeper or of known Residence. Notwithstanding which the Rebells found means to supply themselves, for upon Computing the Quantities which They met with in the Plantations, They robbed from time to time, and what was taken by Them from some of our Parties, whom They defeated, it was found vastly short of what They must have expended in Several Engagements, and upon other Occasions.

I have already observed, that the Ring leaders of these Rebells, (who were bold, Resolute Fellows) were by the Suffrage of the whole invested with an absolute Power, which out of fear or necessity was continued to Their Heirs; and particularly the leeward Gang; for Capt[ain] Cudjo who commands Them, is the son of one of Mr. Sutton's Negroes who was at the head of that Conspiracy and Governed the Gang to the time of His Death.

The Chief Commanders of these Gangs appointed occasionally as many Captains as were necessary whom He chose out of the ablest Men under Him; and divided the rest into Companies: And to each Capt[ain] He gave such a Number of Men, as He thought proportionable to His Merit and Services. This Distinction made those Captains ambitious to Excell in whatever might Contribute to the good of the whole. Their chief Employment was to Exercise Their respective Men; to Instruct Them in the use of the lance and small Arms, after the manner of the Negroes on the Coast of Guiney; and to conduct the Bold[,] Resolute, and Active [efforts] in Robbing Plantations &c. Others He employed in Hunting and Catching Wild Hogs, making salt and Catching Turtle, or with the Women, in Planting Provisions, and such like Offices.

And having Experienced that the Divisions and Quarrells which had hap[pe]ned amongst Themselves were owing to Their different Countries and Customs, which Created Jealousies and uneasiness; He prohibited any other language being spoken among Them, but English. This wise Institution prevented all further Distinctions and Animosities on that Acc[oun] t and kept Them united, so that all of Them, even those who were born in the Mountains, speak very good English.

When either of the Settlements of those Gangs were discovered and They were routed by our Parties, They were not at a loss for subsistance or a place of Retreat. For foreseeing such accidents might happen, They prudently made other settlements to retire to; the Inland Parts of Jamaica affording Them many such Places, which were not only difficult of access, but the Soil very good and yielded Them plenty of Corn, Yams &c.[;] nor were They otherwise at a loss for Provisions to subsist Them, there being abundance of Wild Yams and other Roots in the Woods, which They knew how to dress and make tollerable food in any Extremity.

Their Settlements were made in places commonly called Cock Pitts, being Surrounded with Mountains which are almost inaccessible and difficult of Access, having not more than one or two Avenues, leading to Them, and so narrow or rocky that only one or two Men can pass abreast, not without great difficulty, especially to those who are not used to such Parts.

At the Entrance into those Avenues, They kept a Continual Watch or Centinel, to prevent being Surprized; and upon the least appearance of danger, He made the best of His way to the Town or gave a signal or alarm upon which every Man who was able to manage a lance, or use Fire Arms immediately repaired to His Post under His respective Captain, which was in some Ambuscade or Place that was easy to be defended. In the mean time the Women and Children who commonly had their Cloaths, and best Moveables ready for a flight, made Their Escape to some other Place or Settlement, appointed for a Rendevouz in Case of an Attack, or being defeated by our Party.

When They Engaged They constantly kept blowing Horns, Conch Shells, and other Instruments, which made a hideous and terrible Noise among the Mountains in hopes of terrifying our Parties, by making Them imagine Their Number and Strength much greater than it really was.

And when They robbed any of the Plantations, the first things They looked for, was powder, and lead or Pewter to make balls. They were likewise Industrious in finding out Negro Women and Girls to carry with Them.

But when any Negro men deserted from the Plantations and went among Them, They would not Confide in Them untill They had served a time prefixed for Their Probation; which made some of Them return to Their Masters not liking the usage or treatment They met with.

In this Situation They were in, when two Strong Parties were fitted out to suppress Them, and were so successfull as to drive Them out of Nanny Town which was one of Their strongest holds, and being dispossessed of that place they were reduced to very great Extremities. But, having already given a particular Acc[oun]t of this and other passages relating to our Parties, and the several Skirmishes They had with the Rebells in the Third Part of this Treatise. I shall proceed to give an Acc[oun]t of what passed among Them afterwards, and untill They came to an agreement and submitted Themselves.

When the Windward Gang was dislodged from Nanny Town They hovered near the place in small Bodies, in hopes of distressing our people and obliging Them to desert it. But finding Them determined to keep Possession, and that They were not only duly supplied with Necessaries but had cut a Road of Communication to Port Antonio, and frequently sent out Parties w[hi]ch greatly harrassed and annoyed Them; They marched to Leeward, in hopes of being received and entertained by the other Gang near Deans Valley. But They did not meet with the Reception which They expected, for Capt[ain] Cudjo refused to admit Their Continuing with Them for the following Reasons.

1. He was apprehensive that He had not sufficient Provisions to Maintain Them, and His own People.

2. He blamed Them for Their indiscretion and imprudent Conduct before those Parties were sent against Them. For He said, it was always a Rule with Him, not to Molest or injure the White People unless He was provoked to it. And shewed Them several Graves, where He said were buried some of His Men whom He had Executed for Murdering of White People contrary to His orders.

3. He upbraided Them with Their Insolence, and Barbarity to the White People, which was the Cause of Their Sending out Parties, who in time would destroy Them all. And

Lastly, as He had an absolute command over His People, He was unwilling to receive another Body, who were Independ[en]t of Him, and subject only to Their own Chiefs, who would not submit to Him; so that He received and Entertained Them as Guests but would not allow Them to settle in that part of the Country. And as soon as they had information that our Parties in the Windward Part of the Island were retired to Nanny

Town and Port Antonio, upon the desertion of the Rebells; The Windward Gang were drove away or refused any further Entertainment of Capt[ain] Cudjo and His People

Upon their return to the Windward or Eastward part of the Island, They made a settlement on the Mountains in St. Georges Parish, where They remained undiscovered and contented Themselves with Their Circumstances, rather than give any further umbrage or uneasiness to the White People by their Excursions and Depredations.

In this Situation the Affairs of this Island was in with regard to Them, when Mr. Trelawny[9] came to the Government, in 1738, and tho[ugh] They had been quiet for some time yet He was convinced of the necessity of reducing Them or the Island would be in a few years in danger of being over run by Them. He likewise thought it necessary not only to send out strong Parties, but persons of more Consequence and Distinction to Command Them than had hitherto been sent out. And Accordingly proposed to Collo[nel] John Gutherie[10] of Westmoreland to fit out and Command a Party to Attack Capt[ain] Cudjo and His Gang.

Collo[nel] Gutherie who had resided many years (and had a Considerable Interest) in the Island, Observed with Concern all the Efforts which had been made to reduce the Rebells by Force, were Fruitless and ineffectuall, and that it was necessary to think of some other expedient. For as They were certain of being executed if They were taken, being proscribed by the Laws of the Country (and Their Children not suffered to live on the Island but Transported to other Parts)[;] Their chiefs took care to remind Them of what was to be Their Fate, in Case They were taken and which made Them desperate[,] despairing of any accommodation or agreement with the White People. He therefore thought the only method would be to grant Them a full and general pardon, on Certain Conditions, and that the same should be ratified and Confirmed by an Act of the Assembly. Accordingly He proposed the same to the Governour, who approved of it, and promised to endeavour to procure a law for ratifying whatever terms He should grant the Rebells. Upon this Collo[nel] Gutherie accepted of the Command which was offered Him, and being a Gentleman who was greatly Esteemed and approved of He soon raised 200 able Men fit for the Service beside several of the Neighbouring Planters who went with Him as Volunteers, and L[ieutenan]t Sadler[11] with 40 Soldiers draughted out

9. Edward Trelawny (1699–1754) was governor of Jamaica from 1738 to 1752.

10. Colonel John Guthrie (1687–1739) was custos rotulorum and colonel of the militia of Westmoreland Parish at the time of his appointment to lead the campaign against the Maroons during which he lost his life. For his part in negotiating a settlement with the Maroons, the Jamaica Assembly granted his widow, Mary Guthrie, a lifetime pension of one hundred pounds per annum.

11. Lieutenant Francis Sadler (d. 1753) was the son of John Sadler and his wife, Mary Hals, née Rose. For his role in negotiating the Maroon War settlement of 1739, Francis Sadler was

of the Independ[an]t Companies, were also ordered to join Them and be under His Command.

Colo[nel] Gutherie who had duly considered this Affair, and attained by good intelligence the Situation and strength of the Rebells, marched with this Party without much inconvenience untill They came to one of Their Ambuscades, from whence, after a warm dispute and the loss of several Men, They drove Them out and continued Their march towards Their chief Settlement. They afterwards passed through deep and narrow Vallies, bound with Rocks on each side, from whence the Negroes continually kept Firing at Them, and as some of Them personally knew severall of the Gentlemen who went Volunteers, They called to Them by Their Names, and with much abusive language, asked Them why They came out against Them, who never had done Them any Injury? Collo[nel] Gutherie thereupon desired to speak with Their Commander, in the mean time promised Them a Truce and that He should return, without any hurt or injury. This They would not consent to but upbraided our People with perfidiousness, and told Them that They were not to be confided in. In this manner two days were spent, in small Skirmishes and bitter Reproaches untill They were drove near the Town; When by degrees They became more Familiar, began to listen to the Offer that was made; and agreed to send one of Their Gang to meet one of our Men unarmed and to hear what He had to propose.

Accordingly a discreet sensible Person was sent to treat with one of Their Captains, who after some discourse together, and an Indemnity proposed on Certain Conditions, He departed with the presents which were made to Him and the other Commanders, and an invitation to Capt[ain] Cudjo who is Their Chief or head Man, to meet Collo[nel] Gutherie in the same place and manner in order to bring this matter to an issue upon which a Truce was agreed on, Hostages exchanged and their Apprehensions removed, by the reception and Entertainment They met with. They cheerfully accepted of our Proposals and agreed to the following Articles.

Jamaica

Copy of the Treaty made with Capt[ain] Cudjoe, and the other rebellious Negroes, &c.

By Order of Edward Trelawney, Esq[ui]r[e], Governour of the said Island

At the Camp near Trelawney, March the 1st, 1738–9

In the Name of God, Amen

Whereas Capt[ain] Cudjoe, Capt[ain] Acompong, Capt[ain] Johny, Capt[ain] Cuffoe, and Capt[ain] Quacow, and several other Negroes their

---

awarded £600 and 1,200 acres of land; the land formed the basis of Montpelier estate in St. James, to which he added through two marriages more properties to become a large Jamaica landowner who represented St. James Parish in the Jamaica Assembly from 1746 to 1751.

Defendants and Adherents, have been in a State of War and Hostility for several Years past, against our Sovereign the King, and the Inhabitants of this Island; and whereas Peace and friendship among mankind, and the preventing the Effusion of Blood is agreeable to God, consonant to Reason, and desired by every good Man. And Whereas his Majesty George the Second, King of Great Britain France and Ireland and of Jamaica, Lords &c. has by His Letters Patent, February the 24th 1738, in the 12th year of His Reign, granted full Power and Authority to John Guttery and Francis Sadler, Esq[ui]r[e]; to negotiate and finally conclude a Treaty of peace and Friendship with the aforesaid Capt[ain] Cudjoe, the rest of His Captains, Adherents and others His Men; they mutually sincerely, and amicably have agreed to the following Articles.

1. That Hostillity shall cease on both sides for ever.

2. That the said Capt[ain] Cudjoe, the rest of His Captains, Adherents and Men, shall be for ever hereafter in a perfect state of freedom and Liberty, excepting those who have been taken by or fled to Them within two years last past, if such are willing to return to Their said Masters and Owners, with full pardon and Indemnity from Their said Masters or Owners for what is past; provided always that if They are not willing to return, They shall remain in subjection to Capt[ain] Cudjoe, and in Friendship with us according to the form and Tenor of this Treaty.

3. That They shall enjoy and possess for Themselves and Posterity for ever, all the lands situate and lying between Trelawney Town and the Cock pitts to the amount of 1500 Acres bearing North West from the said Trelawney Town.

4. That They shall have liberty to plant the said land with Coffee, Cocoa, Ginger, Tobacco and Cotton, and to breed Cattle, Hogs, Goats, or any other Stock, and dispose of the produce or Increase of the said Commodities to the Inhabitants of this Island; provided always, that when They bring the said Commodities to Market, they shall apply first to the Custos, or any other Magistrate of the respective Parishes where they expose their Goods to Sale, for a Licence to vend the same.

5. That Capt[ain] Cudjoe, and all the Captains, Adherents, and People now in subjection to Him, shall all live together within the Bounds of Trelawney Town, and that They have Liberty to hunt where They shall think fit, except within three Miles of any Settlement, Crawl, or Pen; provided always, that in Case the Hunters of Captain Cudjoe, and those of other Settlements meet, then the Hogs to be equally divided between both Parties.

6. That the said Capt[ain] Cudjoe and His Successors do use Their Endeavours to take, kill, suppress, or destroy either by Themselves, or jointly with any other Number of Men, commanded on that Service by His Excellency the Governour or Commander in Chief for the Time being all Rebells wheresoever They be throughout this Island, unless They submit

to the same Terms of Accommodation granted to Capt[ain] Cudjoe and His Successors.

7. That in Case this Island be invaded by any foreign Enemy, the said Capt[ain] Cudjoe and His Successors herein after named, or to be appointed, shall then upon Notice given immediately repair to any Place the Governour for the Time being shall appoint, in order to repel the said Invaders with His or Their utmost Force, and to submit to the Orders of the Commander in Chief on that Occasion.

8. That if any White Man shall do any manner of Injury to Capt[ain] Cudjoe, his Successors, or any of His or Their People, they shall apply to any commanding Officer or Magistrate in the Neighbourhood for Justice, and in case Capt[ain] Cudjoe, or any of His People shall do any Injury to any White Person, He shall submit Himself, or deliver such offenders to Justice.

9. That if any Negroes shall hereafter run away from Their Masters or Owners, and fall into Captain Cudjoe's Hands They shall immediately be sent back to the chief Magistrates of the next Parish where They are taken, and those that bring Them are to be satisfied for Their trouble, as the Legislature shall appoint.

10. That all Negroes taken since the raising of this Party by Capt[ain] Cudjoe's People shall immediately be returned.

11. That Capt[ain] Cudjoe and His Successors shall wait on His Excellency, or the Commanders in Chief for the time being once every year if thereunto required.

12. That Capt[ain] Cudjoe during His Life, and the Captains succeeding Him, shall have full Power to inflict any Punishment They think proper for Crimes committed by Their Men among Themselves. Death only Excepted in which Case if the Capt[ain] thinks They deserve Death, He shall be obliged to bring Them before a Justice of Peace, who shall order proceedings on Their Trial equal to those of Free Negroes.

13. That Capt[ain] Cudjoe with His People shall cut, cleave, and keep open large and convenient Roads from Trelawney Town to Westmoreland and St. James, and if possible to St. Elizabeth's.

14. That two white Men, to be nominated by His Excellency or the Commander in Chief for the Time being, shall constantly live and Reside with Capt[ain] Cudjoe and his Successors, in order to maintain a friendly Correspondence with the Inhabitants of this Island.

15. That Capt[ain] Cudjoe, during His Life, shall be chief Commander in Trelawney Town, after His Decease the Command to devolve on His Brother Acompong, and in Case of His Decease, on His next Brother Capt[ain] Johny, and failing Him Capt[ain] Cuffoe shall succeed, who is to be succeeded by Capt[ain] Quacow; and after all Their Demises, the Governour or Commander in Chief for the time being shall appoint from that time whom He shall think fit for that Command.

In Testimony of the above Presents, they hereunto set Their Hands and Seals, the Day and Date above written.

Collo[nel] Guttery immediately dispatched an Express to acquaint the Governour with these transactions who thereupon set out, and went to Collo[nel] Barnetts in St. Anns, whose Plantation was within 20 miles of the Negroe Town; where Capt[ain] Cudjoe and the other Commanders of the Rebells came to Him and made Their Submission, and at the same time received the ratification of the Articles, which were Executed by Collo[nel] Guttery and L[ieutenan]t. Sadler.

Capt[ain] Cudjoe thereupon called in Several Parties He had sent out to plunder the remote Plantations and acquainted the other Towns which were subordinate to Him of the agreement He had made and required Their Acquiescence, whereupon an extraordinary satisfaction appeared among Them, especially when They found the Governour and all the White People sincere, and resolved to comply with the Agreement. For the continual apprehensions They were under, the Fatigues They underwent, and the Tyranny of the Government They had Established, made their lives miserable and almost insupportable.

Capt[ain] Cudjoe is a Resolute sensible Fellow; and as His Power is absolute, He punishes Them severely for the least Transgression against the Laws and Customs among Themselves, one of which is that They shall not often Converse together in Companies or Bodies, to prevent Jealousies, which might tend to disunite Them.

They have hitherto strictly observed the Terms and Conditions prescribed by Them, and seem not only contented but pleased with Their present Circumstances. And as They have Convenanted not to harbour or Entertain any Fugitive for the future, but also to search for, apprehend and send Them to Their respective Masters, the Advantage of Their submission soon began to appear; for many Negroes who frequently deserted and Concealed Themselves in the Mountains were immediately taken up by Them who were well acquainted with Their lurking Places. This proceeding, and the Terms granted to the Rebells, greatly discontented the Plantation and House Negroes. They repined that Freedom and other advantages should be granted to those Negroes who had first deserted Their Masters and Committed Numberless Crimes, when They who had retained Their fidelity and had done great Services should Continue all Their lives in a state of Servitude. Their Murmuring and dissatisfaction encreased to such a height, that They openly and insolently met several Nights, formed Themselves into Companies, named Commanders, and when any White Persons went among Them to reprove Their behaviour, They were insulted, and obliged to retire, apprehending something worse might otherwise attend Them. But the Governour upon the first information He had of Their Caballs, sent a Troop of Horse one Night when They were Assembled as usual and before They had perfected Their Scheme and Siezed most of Them. Some of the Ring leaders were executed, and many of the others Transported to other Countries.

A Treaty being thus happily concluded with the Leeward Rebells and the other Negroes timely Suppressed it was considered what measures were proper to be taken to induce the other Gang in St. Georges who were more considerable in Number, to accept of the same Conditions or to reduce Them by force, and Collo[nel] Guttery who had succeeded so well in the last Expedition was thought the properest Person to Conduct the same. But it was with some Reluctance He accepted of this Commission, because those Rebells were seated in a distant part of the Country which He was not acquainted with, nor with the Neighbours and others who were to be employed on that Service. However, as He was desirous of Manifesting on all occasions, His Zeal for the Publick Utility, He was prevailed on to accept of it, and L[ieutenan]t Collo[nel] Bennet[12] of St. Katherine was appointed to command under Him.

Capt[ain] Cudjoe being obliged by the Treaty to engage Them to accept of The Terms and Conditions which were granted to Him and His followers, or to assist in reducing Them, sent one of His Brothers, who is a Captain with fifty men for that purpose. And, some others of Their Chief Men were prevailed with to go with Collo[nel] Guttery as Guides, and to be Sent with proposals to the Rebells. But, the day after His departure from Spanish Town He was seized with a griping pain in His bowells; however He continued His Journey and reached D[octo]r Stuart's Plantation in St. George's, where the several detachments which were to compose the Grand Party, was to Rendevous. There His disorder Encreased and terminated in a Bloody flux, which baf[f]led all the Endeavours that were used for His Relief, and Carried Him of[f] in 3 or 4 days.

This was the End of That Worthy Gentleman who fell a Sacrifice to the resentment of the discontented Negroes, for the signal Service He had done the Island; since it cannot be doubted but They found means to poison Him. For when They found He was going to reduce the Windward Rebells, as He had done those to Leeward They were in the utmost despair, especially those who deserted and had been brought to Their Masters by Capt[ain] Cudjoe's Gang, pursuant to Their Agreement. He had this Affair so much at Heart that in the intervalls of His pain, He sent out some of Capt[ain] Cudjoe's Men, who were acquainted with the Rebells, and where They were settled, to Acquaint Them with the Terms They had Accepted of, and to invite Them to submit on the same Conditions. They at the same time assured Them of strict Justice, and a punctual Compliance with the Articles; upon which some of Their Chiefs came down to

---

12. Lieutenant Colonel Bennett was perhaps Robert Bennett, who represented the neighboring parish of St. John in the Jamaica Assembly from 1736 to 1749.

L[ieutenan]t Collo[nel] Bennett on whom the Command devolved, submitted Themselves and agreed to the same Conditions which were granted to the others.

Thus was this Island delivered from the danger which was impending so many Years from an intestine Enemy, who threatened no less than the extirpation of the White Inhabitants (had not this Treaty been happily Concluded with Them) especially at so Critical a juncture when wee were on the brink of a War with Spain. For it has been lately discovered (as I am credibly informed) that the Inhabitants of Cuba, held a Correspondence with Them, supplied Them with Ammunition and other necessaries, and were to have joined Them in order to reduce the Island, and disposses the English. And had that been done it is not to be supposed They would have Submitted to be under the Spanish Government, but preserved the Independancy and possession of the Island without receiving Laws or impositions from any other Country or People.

The Settlement of Them in distinct Bodies, in distant parts of the Country, and under their proper Chiefs, was Certainly more adviseable than to have brought Them all under the subjection of Capt[ain] Cudjoe, or any other of Their Chief Men. Because They cannot now so readily Consult or Combine together upon any disagreement with the White People; nor so easily Unite in Case the Spirit of Rebellion should ever arise and spread among Them. On the Contrary, it will probably cause an Emulation between the two Societies which shall be the most usefull and Faithfull to the White People, to engage Their favour and Encouragement.

However, it is necessary to have a strict Eye over Them to restrain as much as possible Their having any intercourse and Correspondence with the Plantation Negroes or permitting Them to have any quantity of Powder and Arms. Care ought also to be taken that all just grievances be redressed without delay. That the Treaty be as faithfully observed on our Parts, as it has hitherto been by Them; and that no Injury be done Them, nor any Cause given Them of umbrage, or offence upon any Occasion.

But, as it will be dangerous to allow Them to continue and Multiply as a distinct People, from the rest of the Island, all just and proper methods ought to be taken to induce Them and Their Posterity to incorporate and mix with the other Inhabitants; to render Them usefull upon all occasions; and prevent Their being noxious in any degree whatever. This may be done by allowing and giving Them Encouragement to bring up Their Children to some laborious handicraft Trades, which will conduce towards Their incorporating Themselves and becoming at least, one and the same People with the rest of the Inhabitants of the Island. But, this or such like Encouragement can be done only by Publick Law, which is well worth the Notice and Consideration of the Legislature.

Part the 7th.

Of the Government of the Island, Civil and Military, of the Laws; Courts of Justice; Publick Offices; Revenues, and Church Affairs; with some Observations thereupon.

This Island, for some Years after the English possess[e]d themselves of it, was under a Military Government, and Commissioners; the Commander in Chief of the Forces, presided at all their Consultations, as well as in the Councils of War, and Acted as Governour; though nothing of moment was transacted, or put in Execution, without their advice and Concurrence.

Indeed, it would not, within that period of time, admit of any other form or Constitution, Because they were not Established in their Possession, by Treaty or otherwise; and being often threaten[e]d, by the Spaniards, with an Invasion, they did not know, how soon they might be Obliged to be on the defensive, and fight in Support of what they had Acquired, by Conquest. Beside the Inhabitants being mostly Officers and Soldiers, who were unacquainted with the Civil and Common Law, They could not, by any other means, nor without strict Discipline be kept in due order and Regulation, considering those Circumstances, and the distressed Condition they were in, for want of Necessaries, which occasioned great uneasiness and dissatisfaction; insomuch that they several times mutinyd and threat[e]ned to Abandon the Island.

But, King Charles the Second, soon after his Restoration, sent over a Commission to Collo[nel] Edward Doyley dated the 2d. of February 1660, to be Governour and Commander in Chief of the Island, as well as of the Forces; and impowered him and a Council of 12 Persons (which were to be chosen by the Officers of the Army, Planters and other Inhabitants) or any five of them; to Execute and perform all such Acts of Government, as might Conduce to the Security and good Government of the Island. Accordingly the Governour issued out Writs, dated the 6 June 1661, which were directed to the Commanding Officers of the several Settlements and Districts, to Summon's the Officers and other Inhabitants Respectively to make choice of and Elect proper and fit Persons, to be of the said Council, and to return their Names to him, with all Convenient Speed.

Upon which the Following Gentlemen, were returned, duly Elected:
[blank] for the Red Hills, Guanaboa and the Places adjacent
[blank] for Liguina

[blank] for St. Jago de la Vega, and the Angels.

[blank] for the Quarters between St. Jago and Passage Fort.

It is Observable, that notwithstanding those Gentlemen were called a Council, and with the Consent of the Governour, had a power of making such Rules and Ordinances, as were necessary for the Security and good Government of the Island, and even of raising Money; Yet they were, in Fact, Representatives of the People; because they were chosen by them, and without their Consent no Taxes, or other Impositions were laid on the Inhabitants.

He also Commisioned divers Officers in those Several Districts for the Conservation of the Peace, to decide matters of Variance and to Administer Justice.

Hence it appears, that the Civil Law in this Island commenced in the Government of Colonel Doyley, though Exercised in a weak and feeble manner; for the first Planters understood the Use of Arms, and the Military Law, better than the Proceedings of the Courts of Justice, as they were unacquainted with Civil and Common Law, or Acts of Parliament. However, the Persons, who were Authorized, made plain, good, Sense, and what they thought Reason, and Justice the Rule of their decisions: and when any difficulty Arose, or they were diffident of their own Opinions, they referred the Cause to the Governour, who determined the matter according to His Judgment.

In this Situation the Publick Affairs of this Island remained 7 or 8 Years; yet those times are extolled by the Antient Inhabitants, and preferred to the present, when they have every Plea Considered according to the Civil or Common Law of England, and their own Municipal Laws. Indeed when it is Considered that their disputes and Controversies were determined in a Summary way; and that they were not encumbered with Lawyers, Marshals or Sheriff's Officers, and other Leeches or Attendants of the Law; nor perplexed with dilatory, Expensive, and Vexatious Suits, it must be Confessed they were much happier, than they are now in that respect, though their Suits at Law and Equity are not so troublesome and expensive as they are in England, and I wish I could likewise say, not so tedious and dilatory.

The 2d. of August 1661 Thomas Lord Windsor was appointed Governour, and many Persons resorting to the Island, in order to settle and Plant, upon the Encouragement which was given by the Crown; He was furnished with more ample Powers and Instructions, than were given to Collo[nel] Doyley; and directed to disband the Forces, except 400 foot, and a Troop of Horse. His Majesty was likewise pleased to appoint S[ir] Charles Lyttleton Baronet, Chancellor, and to Honour the Island with a Broad Seal.

On one side of the Seal is a Representation of His Majesty in His Royal Robes: and an Indian presenting Him with a Pine. The Motto *Duro de Cortice Fructus, Quam Dulces!*[1]

---

1. The hard rind of the fruit. How sweet!

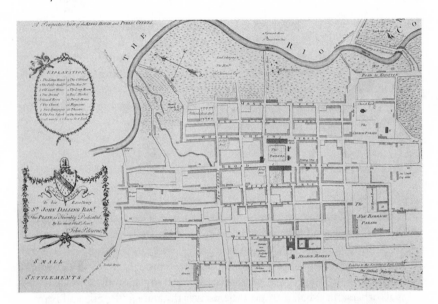

John Pitcairne's *A Plan of the Town of St Jago de la Vega, in the Island of Jamaica*, published in London in 1786, seems to be the only detailed map of Jamaica's capital city produced before the nineteenth century. Showing the town's street plan with a numbered key to indicate the sites of its public buildings and other places of consort, this image is here reproduced from a copy in the Prints, Drawings, and Paintings Collection at the Victoria and Albert Museum in London. (Victoria and Albert Museum)

The Inscription round it, *Carolus Secundus Dei Gratia Magna Britania, et Hibernage Rex Dominus Jamaica.*[2]

On the side is Quartered An Escutcheon bearing a Cross charged with five Pines, two Indians for the Supporters, and an Aligator for the Crest. The Inscription in the Orle, inclosing all is,

Ecce Alium Ramos Porrexit in Orbem
  Nec sterilis Crux est.[3]

The Motto underneath the Escutcheon

Indus Uturq[ue] Serviet Uni.[4]

With this Seal all Grants, Patents, and Civil Commissions are stamped. But though it was at first designed to be kept by a Particular Person, and

2. By the grace of Charles the Second, king of Great Britain and Ireland and lord of Jamaica.

3. Here another branch is brought into an orbit in which religion will not be ignored.

4. From both Indians, only service.

Independant of the Governour, yet it was afterwards incerted in all the Governour's Commissions.

His Majesty also, as a Signal mark of His favour honoured the Island with a large gilt Mace, which is carried before the Governour upon all Solemn Occasions.

And on the 14th. of December 1661, His Majesty was pleased to issue out the following Proclamation.

By the King.

A Proclamation for the Encouragement of Planters in His Majestie's Island of Jamaica in the West Indies.

Charles R.

We being fully satisfied, that our Island of Jamaica being a most pleasant and fertile Soil, and Situated Commodiously for Trade and Commerce, is likely through God's blessing, to be a great benefit and advantage to this and other our Kingdoms and Dominions, have thought fit for the Encouragement of our Subjects, as well such as are already upon the said Island, as all others, that shall transport themselves thither, and Reside and plant there, to Declare and Publish, and We do hereby declare and Publish, that Thirty Acres of improveable Lands, shall be granted and Allotted to every such Person, Male or Female, being twelve Years old or upwards, who now reside, or within two Years next ensuing shall reside, upon the said Island; and that the same shall be assigned, and set out by the Governour and Council, within six weeks, next after Notice shall be given in Writing, subscribed by such Planter or Planters, or some of them, in behalf of the rest, to the Governour, or such Officer as He shall appoint in that behalf, signifying their Resolutions to plant there and when they intend to be on the place; and in Case they do not go thither within Six months then ensuing, the said Allotment to be void, and free to be Assigned to any other Planter; and that every Person and Persons, to whom such Assignment shall be made, shall hold and enjoy the said Lands so to be assigned, & Houses, Edeficies, Buildings, and Enclosures thereupon to be built or made, to them and their Heirs for ever, by and under such Tenure, as is usual in other Plantations Subject unto us. Nevertheless they are to be obliged to serve in Arms upon any Insurrection, Mutiny, or Foreign Invasion, and the said Assignments and Allotments shall be made and Confirmed under the Publick Seal of the said Island, with Power to Create any Mannor or Mannors, and with such convenient and suitable privileges and Immunities, as the Grantee shall reasonably devise and require; and a draught of such assignment shall be prepared by our learned Council in the Law, and delivered to the Governour to that purpose, and that all Fishings and piscaries, and all Copper, Lead, Tin, Iron, Coals, and all other Mines (Except Gold and Silver) within Such respective allotments shall be enjoyed by the Grantees thereof; reserving only a twentieth part of the Product of the said Mines to our use.

And we do further publish and Declare, that all Children of our Natural-born Subjects of England to be born in Jamaica, shall from their respective Births be reputed to be, and shall be free Denizons of England, and shall have the same Privileges, to all intents and purposes, as our Free-born Subjects of England; And that all Free Persons shall have liberty without interruption to transport themselves, and their Families and any of their Goods, except Coin and Bullion, from any of our Dominions & Territories to the said Island of Jamaica. And We do strictly Charge and Command all Planters[,] Soldiers, and others upon the said Island to yield Obedience to the lawful Commands of our Right Trusty and well beloved Thomas Lord Windsor now our Governour of the said Island, and to every other Governour thereof for the time being under pain of our Displeasure and such Penalties as may be inflicted thereupon.

Given at our Court at White Hall, the

14th. day of December 1661, in the 13th year of our Reign.

My Lord Windsor, by His Instructions, dated the 1st. of March 1661/2 was impowered, and directed, to Choose a Council of twelve Persons.

And with the Advice and Consent of five or more of them, to settle such Indicatories, and Laws for the Admiralty, as may be proper to keep the Peace of the said Island, to determine matters of Right and Controversy, and all Causes Civil, Criminal, Matrimonial, Testamentary, and Maritime; Yet so as no man's Freehold, Life, or Member be taken away or harmed, but by Established Laws, not repugnant to the Laws of England.

To Appoint and Commissionate under the Broad Seal of the Island, Judges, Justices, Sheriffs and other Officers, for the more orderly administ[e]ring of Justice; to allow and order them, or such of them as He thought fit, meet and Convenient Sallaries, with power to Administer Oaths, &c.

To order and appoint Fairs, to be kept on such days, and in such places, for such time or times, as He thought Convenient.

To call Assemblies together, according to the Custom of our Plantations, to make Laws, and upon Eminent Necessities, to levy mon[e]y; as shall be most Conducible to the Honour and advantage of our Crown, and the good and welfare of our Subjects, Provided they be not repugnant to any of our Laws of England; and that such Laws shall be in force for two Years and no longer; unless they shall be approv[e]d and Confirmed by us.

To Ratify and Confirm to all, that transport themselves to the Island, thirty Acres of Land, to them and their heirs for ever.

Thus was the Government of this Island Set[t]led upon the same Plan, and after the Model of the other British Colonies, by a Governour, Council, and Assembly.

The Governour is appointed by Patent under the Broad Seal of England: and is likewise Capt[ain] General, Chancellor, Vice Admiral of the

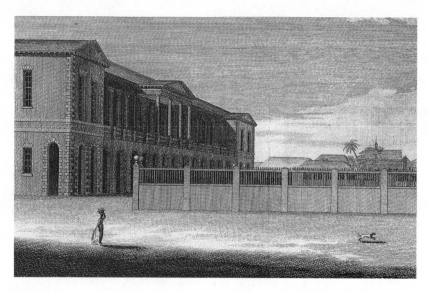

This 1774 engraving is of the King's House in Spanish Town, the most expensive and impressive public building in colonial British America. It was not completed until the late 1750s. It is here reproduced from Long, *History of Jamaica*, 2:opposite p. 10.

Island, Ordinary and sole Judge for the Probate of Wills, and granting of letters of Administration.

As Governour, He is impowered to appoint and Commissionate Judges, Justices, Sheriffs and other Civil Officers, and to remove them at his discretion, to summon, prorogue and dissolve Assemblies; to pardon Crimes, Murder and Treason excepted, and even in those Cases to grant Reprieves; to issue Commissions to Privateers in time of War, and to apprehend, or take Pirates in time of Peace; and in fine to Act with Sovereign Authority, with the Advice and Consent of the Council, According to the Laws of England, and the Municipal Laws of this Island; for He has a negative Voice in the passing of all Acts of the Assembly.

As Capt[ain] General, He appoints and Removes at pleasure all Officers of the Militia; Reviews and Commands them in Person, or Otherwise, as He thinks proper and Necessary.

As Chancellor, He hears and determines all Causes in the Court of Equity, not exceeding £300, without Appeal. But, in all Suits above that Sum, the Party against whom the Decree is made, has the liberty of appealing to the King and Council.

And as Ordinary and sole Judge for the Probate of Wills, and granting Letters of Administration, He has the presentation of all Church-Livings within the Island; is impowered to grant marriage Licences, and Administration of the Estates of Persons, who die intestate.

Whoever considers those Powers, which the Governors of all the British Colonies in America (except the Charter Governments [of] New England, Maryland, Philadelphia and Rhode Island) are cloathed with, will not be surprized at the uneasiness and dissatisfaction they are often under nor at the Complaints which in Consequence comes from thence. For, Certainly it is inconsistent with the true Interest and happiness of a Country, that one Man should be vested with too much Authority: because it is Commonly made use of to the prejudice of the People, This we have unhappily experienced at Home, as well as in the Plantations, and therefore are justly Apprehensive and Jealous of Such Persons; how much more Reason then have those People to be so, who are remote and at a great distance from the Crown! Hence we may Reasonably expect, If ever the Welfare and Prosperity of the Plantations comes to be seriously taken into Consideration, that those Powers will be abridged, and Care taken to ascertain the Rights and Liberties of the People, and to put them on a better foundation and Establishment, than they are at present, that it may not be in the Power of a Governor, to harrass and distress them at His will and pleasure, to gratify his Resentment, or perhaps His boundless Avarice and Ambition.

The Established Sallary of the Governour or Captain General is £2500 per Ann[um]; a L[ieutenan]t Governour £1500 per Ann[um]; and the President of the Council, when He is vested with the Administration, £1250 per Ann[um]: the Perquisites are computed at £1500 per Ann[um], some times more, But, this depends very much on the Number and Value of Escheats, which happen, tho[ugh] they are not so profitable to the Governour, as formerly they were.

The Assembly at the Instance and Recommendation of His Late Majesty, settled on the late Duke of Portland an Additional Sallary of £2500 p[er] Ann[um] during His Grace's Government, and residence on the Island as Governour. But, apprehending it might become a kind of Prescription, they declined making the same Settlement on Major General Hunter; who succeeded him; however in lieu thereof they presented him with £6000.

Upon the Administration devolving on John Gregory Esq[uir]e the second time, as President of the Council, the Assembly, in Consideration of His Prudent and Discreet Behaviour, when He formerly Presided, as well as the personal regard they had for him, augmented His Sallary to £2500 p[er] Ann[um] during His Administration.

And they have since set[t]led an Additional Sallary of £2500 p[er] Ann[um] on the present Governour, and assigned in the Preamble of the Act, that was passed for that purpose, their Reasons and Motives for doing it. Whether these Instances will be deemed precedents, and expected by all future Governours, as a matter of Right, I cannot pretend to determine. But, in my private Opinion the whole Sallary of £5000 p[er] Ann[um], is necessary for the Honour and Support of the dignity of the Government, and not more, than the Circumstances of the Island, at the time, will admit of; therefore such an Augmentation is not only reasonable, but well bestowed, provided it is an Encouragement to Men of Virtue and Ability to Accept of the Government, and no part of the Incomes is devoured by some Hungary or Avaritious Courtiers at Home; otherwise it will be in a manner, so much mon[e]y thrown away.

The Council are twelve in Number, and are generally Men of the best Estates and Abilities in the Island. They are either nominated in the Governour's Patent, or Appointed by Letters of Mandamus from the King or Queen Regent. On the Death, or dismission of any of them, the Governour is impowered to nominate others, provided there be not seven on the Island; and they Act in a double Capacity as a Council of State, and a Part of the Legislature.

As a Council of State, they are to advise and Assist the Governour, and to be a Check upon him, in Case he exceeds the bounds of his Commission; to Examine all Accounts for Work or Service done for the Government; and no orders for money are issued on the Revenue, without their Approbation and Consent, for the Receiver General is by Law restrained, on the penalty of £500 from payment of any of the Publick Money, even for the Governour's Sallary, without an Express order in writing, signifying the names of the Councilors present & the uses and purposes, for which the order was granted. It must likewise be Signed by the Governour, sealed with his private Seal, and testified by the Secretary of the Council, that it was by and with their Advice and Consent.

They meet every first Monday in the Month without any Summons, and as often otherwise as occasions require.

In the Assembly they make the upper House, and have a Negative voice; as the House of Peers in England, and all Bills pass through the same Form and Ceremony, they do there.

The Members of the Assembly are chosen by the suffrage of the Freeholders, in the same manner that the Members of Parliament in England are Elected. St. Katherines, Port Royal, and Kingston choose three Representatives each, and the other sixteen Parishes two a peice; so that the whole Number at present is forty one Members, and probably will be augmented, when the large Parishes become better set[t]led, and subdivided, as undoubtedly they will be.

And for preventing abuses and indirect practices in Elections, it is by an Act of the Country provided, that there shall be forty days between the Test and Return of the Writ of Summons; and that every Freeholder shall have at least five days notice of the time and place of Election.

That there shall be a Seperate day, for Elections, in every Parish, so that there may not be two or more Elections on one and the same day.

That every Freeholder before He is admitted to Poll at an Election shall, if required by the Candidates or any of them, first take an Oath that He is a Freeholder in Law or Equity, in his own or his Wive's Right, by title provided or acknowledged, and Recorded in the office of Enrollments, three Months at least; and that His Freehold consists of a Tenement of the real Value of Ten pounds p[er] Ann[um], a Pen with six head of Cattle of the like or Equal Value; or a Plantation with five Acres at least, planted; also the Situation, buttings and boundings, in whose name it was pattented; and that it was not given or granted fraudulently, or on purpose to qualify him to Vote at that Election; and that he had not before been polled, or given any Vote at that Election.

That the Poll of Each Parish be kept open until five a Clock in the Afternoon, and no longer.

That every Custos Rotulorum, Justice of the Peace, Provost Marshal, or His Deputy, neglecting His Duty shall forfeit two hundred pounds; and every Constable twenty pounds.

That no Person shall be prevented from giving his Vote, by keeping him in Arms on the day of Election, nor sent out on a Party; that no Regiment, or any Company or Troop of Horse, of any Parish or Precinct, where any Election is to be, shall be in Arms on the day of Election.

And that no Person shall be Capable of sitting in any Assembly, who shall not make Oath that He hath an Estate in his own, or His Wive's Right, in Law or Equity, or of in Lands, Tenements, Negroes or other Heridataments, over and above, what is Sufficient to pay all his just and proper debts, of the Value of Three hundred pounds p[er] Ann[um] or Three thousand pounds in gross.

Which Oath is to be taken and administer[e]d at the same time, and in the same manner, that the Oaths of Allegiance and Supremacy are to taken by, and to be administered to the several Members.

The Assembly assimulate themselves, as near as possible, to the House of Commons in England. They choose a Speaker, Appoint Committies, and their Bills are brought in the same manner, and pass through the same Ceremony, they do there. They also assume the like Powers and Privileges; and will not admit the Council to Frame, alter, or amend any money Bill, deeming the raising and disposition of all Publick mon[e]y, their Sole an undoubted Right as Representatives.

It has Indeed been pretended, that the Assembly have no Right to Exercise a Legislative Power, only by Virtue of that Authority, which they derive from the Crown; that by the Governour's Commission, they can only pass such Laws, as are not repugnant to the Laws of Great Britain; so that they can only pass Local Laws; and that Jamaica being a Conquered Country; the People are not intitled to all the Rights, Liberties and Privileges of the People [of] England.

The first is a Question of the utmost Consequence to all the British Plantations, as well as to Jamaica, and though some Attempts were formerly made, to alter their Constitution or form of Government, and the

Facing the King's House was Jamaica's equally impressive and expensive Government Office building, which housed the assembly chambers, courtrooms, and administrative offices and was completed in the late 1750s. This 1774 engraving is taken from Long, *History of Jamaica*, 2:opposite p. 10.

Crown, upon the humble Representations of the Inhabitants was graciously pleased to make some Concessions, which quieted the minds of the People; yet it is greatly to be wished and desired, that no Question of this kind may hereafter arise, or be insisted upon, nor the Rights and Privileges of the People or their Representatives in any degree weaken[e]d, or infringed.

It is to be considered that when a Colony is transplanted from hence, though they are allowed to carry with them the Laws of England; yet from the time of their Settlement, they become in some measure a Seperate and Distinct Dominion and no ways bound by the Laws, that are afterwards made in England; excepting those only wherein They are particularly named. And as British Colonies, They are intitled to the same Protection, and to the same benefits, and Advantages of the Laws of England, as if they had remained in England. But, the distance, They are at from their Mother-Country, renders it impracticable for them to receive it thro[ugh] the same Channel; They can't have it from the Parliament, by Reason of Their great Distance, and Their having no Representation there whereby it is difficult and often impracticable for that August Body, to be well and truly informed of their wants and Necessities, or what may be proper to be enacted for their Protection or Relief.

And as to Jamaica, in particular, though it was a Conquered Country, yet They are not a Conquered People, But descended from the Conquerors, who were Englishmen, and in the service of their Country; and such others as Voluntarily Transported themselves, and settled there, upon the Invitation and Encouragement given them by King Charles the second, in his Proclamation before recited; wherein it is expressly declared, that all Children of our Natural born Subjects of England, to be born in Jamaica, shall from their Respective Births, be reputed to be, and shall be, Free Denizens of England; and shall have the same privileges to all intents and purposes, as our free born Subjects of England; which privileges and advantages They cannot have, and truly Enjoy: unless the Legislature there have the same powers, as legislature has in in Great Britain.

It is Observable, that no mention is made of the Natural born Subjects of England, who were at that time in Jamaica, or should afterwards Voluntarily transport themselves, and settle there; which clearly shows, that it was not thought necessary, or that any doubts could possibly Arise, with regard to them; only the Children born of such Parents: and therefore to Obviate any difficulty, or dispute concerning them, that Declaration seems to have been made.

These arguments plainly prove, that our British Colonies are, and must be considered as distinct, though subordinate Dominions and that they cannot have Laws made for them, nor Justice administered to them, from Home, they must therefore have new Laws from a legislature of their own, and Accordingly all of them have had Legislatures and Courts of Justice of their Own, but Analogous to the methods observed by the Legislature and Courts of Justice here. They have all their strong lines the same—Their Courts of Law are the same as ours; and their Trials are by Juries as with us—They have the same Courts of Equity, as we have, only subject to an Appeal to the King in Council, in all Causes exceeding £300 Value—And for the Exercise of Extraordinary Acts, which could not be performed by the Supreme Power here, because such acts can not, in their Nature, admit of any Delay, they have in all respects a Supreme Power there, analogous but Subordinate to that which we have here in England.

What may be done by the Courts of Law or Equity here, may be done by their Courts of Law and Equity there; their powers and Jurisdictions being the same. And what may be done by the Legislature Here, may be done by the Legislature there, Subordinately indeed in this Respect, that they may not enact any thing contrary, to what has been Enacted by an Act of Parliament here, which in Express words extends to them. They have in Fact Exercised a Legislative Power in almost every Instance, wherein it is possible to be Exercised.—They have Enacted high Treason, and made

that so there, which would not be so here; particularly in such Person or
Persons as shall falsify, forge, or Counterfeit the Broad seal of the Island.—
They have created new Felonies.—They have laid Duties both on Imports
and Exports.—They have passed Acts of Naturalization.—Acts to bar En-
tails, Acts to Confirm titles of Land.—And in fine—They have suspended
the whole Law, for a limited time, by passing Acts to establish Martial
Laws for a certain time. So that by these, and many other instances, which
are to be met with in the new folio Edition of their Laws;[5] it appears, They
have exercised a Legislative power in its full Extent nor can there be any
Reasonable Objection to the Legislature in Jamaica, or any other of the
British Colonies, Exercising this Power within their own Jurisdiction since
it can only affect themselves, and can have no Effect any where else. Besides their Laws must be Confirmed by the Crown, before they are Established, and it is in His Majestie's power to reject them, if he disapproves
of them, or if any Inconvenience be in the meantime discovered; but within
the Island they are in force till expressly rejected by the Crown, unless
there be in the Act a suspending Clause, which has seldom or ever been
incerted, without it has been done lately.

Upon the whole, as care is justly taken to keep the Colonies dependant,
and render them usefull to their Mother Country, so those Conditions,
Terms, and Privileges should be preserved and in no degree violated, which
encouraged Them at their own Expence, and the hazard of their lives, to
Transport themselves; and to cultivate and Plant foreign Countries. Where
in truth they labour for us, as much as for themselves, for here at last all
that They acquire by their Industry, is remitted and Reposited; nothing
more being sent back, than Necessaries and Utensils for themselves and
their Plantations; which are wholly the Product and Manufactures of Great
Britain, or such Commodities as are brought hither, by our Commerce in
Exchange for British Commodities.

The Military Affairs of this Island, are under the sole direction of the
Governour, who appoints and removes the Officers of the Militia, at his
will and pleasure.

This is a Point which likewise deserves Consideration, because it is a
Power, that has been very much misused and of Infinite prejudice to the
Island. The Officers formerly were men of the best Fortune and Figure in
every Parish, and it is proper they should be so, to preserve the Authority, and Discipline, that is requisite and Necessary to be kept up, and in
those times the Militia in this Island, were as good, as any in the World,
for I have seen them go through all Military Exercises as well as I ever saw
them performed by the King's Guards. But they have declined ever since

---

5. *Acts of Assembly, Passed in the Island of Jamaica; from 1681 to 1737, Inclusive* (London,
1738).

the unhappy Administration of one Gentleman, who made a change almost throughout the Island, for no other Reason as I ever heard of, but because some of the Principal Officers, who were Members of the Assembly, voted on some Occasions, contrary to his Inclination, and others for voting at Elections for such Members; as were not agre[e]able to him. This gave so general a disgust, that very few Persons of distinction would accept of those Commissions; by which means they became despised, and many of them fell into the hands of People of low Rank, and Condition.

The Militia of this Island consists of one Regiment of Horse, and Eight Regiments of Foot, vizt. The Regiment of Horse, Commanded by the Governor of the Island for the time being, and under Him Lieutenant Collo[nel].

The Regiment of St. Katherine's, St. John's, St. Thomas in the Vale, and St. Dorothy's.

The Regiment of St. Andrew's or Liguinea.

The Regiment of St. Thomas in the East

The Regiment of Kingston.

The Regiment of Port Royal.

The Regiment of Clarendon and Vere.

The Regiment of St. Elizabeth's, Westmorland, & Hanover.

The Regiment of St. James's, St. Ann's, St. George's and Portland.

By an Act of the Assembly for settling the Militia,[6] it is Enacted.

That no Person from 15 to 60 years of Age, shall remain unlisted, in the Horse or Foot, above 6 weeks, on penalty of 40 Sh[illings] and so for every Six Weeks such Person shall remain unlisted.

That every Foot Soldier shall be well provided with a well fixed Musket or a Fuzee, or a good Pike, and Sword, or Launce and Pistol; and each Musketeer shall have, when he appears at a Muster, six charges of Powder and one Cartouch Box; penalty for not appearing 10 S[hillings] and for want of any of the Accoutrements 4 [shillings].

And by a subsequent Act[7] for the prevention of Confusion, by ill training and different sizes of Arms, it is ordered and directed.

That every White man, or Negro, that shall be fitted out or Armed in Defence of the Country, shall be provided with a good Musket, Bayonet, Cutlass and Cartouch Box, filled with twelve Cartridges at least, ready made up, with a proportionable quantity of spare powder and Ball; which said Muskets shall be of the same Culliber and Bore, with the Muskets usually made use of in His Majestie's Ordnance.

That every Trooper shall be provided with a good Horse of £10 Value

6. An Act for Settling the Militia, 1681, in ibid., 29–35.

7. An Act for the Strengthening and Securing the Island against Any Attempts to Be Made by Foreign Enemies, 1728, in ibid., 229–31.

at least, with good Furniture, a Case of Pistols, Sword or Hanger, and half a pound of Powder, penalty 6 Shillings for want of Accoutrements, and 10 Shillings for each Time absent at a Muster.

That every Foot Soldier shall have at His Habitation, two pounds of good powder, and six pound[s] of Ball: and every Trooper a well fixed Carbine, four pounds of fine powder, and twelve pounds of Sizeable ball, penalty 10 [shillings] for each default.

That a Commission Officer shall not be obliged to serve in any Capacity beneath his former Commission; unless such Person hath been degraded by a Court Martial.

That if any Person upon an Invasion, or other Publick Service, be wounded or disabled, He shall be cured, and maintained out of the Publick Revenue.

That one Company in every Regiment be Mustered and Exercised each week Successively, and the whole Regiment once in three months.

That no Person presume to fire any small Arms, after eight a Clock at night, unless in Case of an Alarm, Insurrection, or other lawful occasion; and in such Cases four muskets or Guns distinctly fired shall be taken for an Alarm from Quarter to Quarter; and any Person convicted before a Court Martial of neglecting his Duty, in taking and giving forward the Alarm, by firing four Guns or Muskets, or shall fire any Guns or small Arms after Eight a Clock at night upon any other occasion shall be fined or punished at the discretion of a Court Martial, not extending to life or limb.

That no Master or Commander of any Ship or Vessel Riding in any Bay, or Harbour of this Island, or any other Person, fire any Gun after Sun set: penalty 40 Shillings for every Gun so fired.

That the Justices and Vestry, or Major part of them, in all Parishes of this Island, adjacent to the Sea, shall raise, or cause to be levied, such Sums of Money, as shall seem necessary for maintaining night Watches, Guards, and Look outs in such places, as shall seem most proper for serving the Inhabitants, and discovering & preventing the Approach of an Enemy.

That upon every Apprehension and appearance of any Publick danger, or Invasion, the Commander in Chief do forthwith Call a Council of War, and with their Advice and Consent, Cause the Articles of War to be proclaimed at Port Royal, St. Jago de la vega, and Kingston, from which said Publication the Martial Law is to be in force; and then it shall and may be Lawful for the Commander in Chief, to command the Persons of any of His Majestie's leige subjects, as also their Negroes, Horses and Cattle, for all such services as may be for the publick defence, and to pull down Houses, cut down Timber command Ships and Boats, and generally to Act and do with full power and Authority, all such things as He and the Council of War shall think Necessary and expedient for His Majestie's Service and the Defense of this Island.

This is a great and extensive Power not unlike that with which the Dictators of Rome were vested, and therefore limited in the same manner, for one month, or more, as occasions require; and at the expiration revived, if it be found necessary.

Nevertheless, it is a Power not to be granted without an absolute Necessity, or upon very Extraordinary Occasions, vizt. upon Certain and undoubted Information of an Invasion, or General Insurrection of the Negroes.

The Council of War consists of the Governour or Commander in chief, the members of the Council, and the Field Officers of the Militia.

This Act, though of use and service, yet some alterations and Amendments, are necessary for rendering it beneficial; and indeed Considering the Consequences with regard to the Security and defence of the Island in Case of an Invasion or Insurrection, and how sensible the People are of them it is not a little surprizing those alterations and amendments should be neglected or delayed.

Beside the Militia, there were Eight Independant Companies, of Regular Troops, Consisting of 100 men each, beside Officers wh[ich] were lately formed into a Regiment of 10 Companies and the Command given to His Excell[anc]y Ed[ward] Trelawny Esq[uir]e the present Governour. They are maintained by the Crown, but the Assembly, in Consideration of Provisions and other Necessary's, being dearer in Jamaica than in England, allow them an Additional Subsistance vizt. twenty Shillings to every Commiss[io]n[ed] Officer and 3 [shillings] 9 [pence] to every other man, to be paid them weekly. And such Care is taken that neither the Country, nor the men be imposed on, that an Officer of each Company is obliged to make Oath to the Muster Roll monthly, and that none of the men are absent upon furlo. The mon[e]y is likewise paid into the hands of each respective Officer or Soldier, and every such Officer of Soldier is obliged to Sign his Name to the Receipt, or Voucher on the Roll.

Two Companies are Constantly kept in Garrison at Port Royal.

One Company at St. Iago de lavega, or Spanish Town, as Guards to the Governour.

One Company Quartered at Morant.

One Company in St. Elizabeth's.

One Company in St. James and St. Ann's.

One Company in St. Mary's.

One Company at Port Antonio.

One Company at Sixteen Mile Walk.

One Company at Nanny Town, which was one of the Settlements of the Wild Negroes, before they Submitted.

These Companies, in my opinion, are absolutely necessary for the Protection and Security of the Island, and their Number, at least, ought Constantly to be kept up in time of Peace, as well as War, for many Reasons, not proper to be given in this place. But, the Regulation and Disposition of those Troops, deserve a more particular discussion, and some further Consideration; which may not only be the means of preserving many Brave Men and making their lives Comfortable, but be of Public Utility, in rendering them healthier and more fit for Service.

1. The manner of Cloathing them, however Convenient and necessary in Europe, is highly improper for a hot Climate, for their Regimentals are at all times intolerably heavy and burthensome, [and] Consequently must render them unfit to March from Place to Place, or even to do Common Duty.

It would therefore be more agreeable to the men, and a less expence to the Government if their Cloathing was thin[n]er and lighter.

Their Coats made of the same Cloth and Colour, but to answer the end proposed to have neither pleats of full Sleeves, only a small Cuff, or in the manner of Frocks; and that their Waistcoats and Breeches be made of Oznaburgs, or Coarse Linnen, two of each will be less expensive than one of Cloth; and as they will wash, the Men will be kept Sweeter and Cleanlier, which may be one means of preserving their healths.

2. As we have Experienced the great Inconvenience and danger of Quartering Soldiers in or near the Towns, with regard to their Healths and Lives, it is proper, that they should be Quartered in Barracks in the inland part of the Country; except such a number as are absolutely necessary to be kept in Garrison, and to attend the Governour's Person; that these be relieved every three months; that a district of land round the respective Barracks be assigned them Sufficient to raise Corn, Peas, and ground Provision for their own use; and that they be obliged to manure and cultivate the same at proper times and Seasons. This will not only be the means of furnishing them with plenty of good and wholesome provisions, but also Contribute to their healths; which sometimes suffer through inactivity, for want of due and proper Exercise. It is likewise necessary, that due Care be taken to prevent their having to[o] free a use of Rum, and other Spirituous liquors; which in fact has destroyed more lives, than ever the Climate hath done. To evince the truth of this, I shall only give the following Instance, which is well known, and can be well attested. In the Year 1732 when Six of the Eight Independant Companies arrived from Gibralter, one of the Companies was quartered at [blank] and one at Spanish Town; the former which was in the Country, where it not only was cooler, and they could not so easily come at Rum and other liquors to debauch with, but, had Fish, wild fowl, and other Provisions at an easy and cheap rate, lost no more than 5 or 6 men in 6 months; whereas the other buried at least 30 men within the same space of time.

3. The Soldiers by being Quartered in Barracks in the Inland Part of the Country will undoubtedly be much healthier, for the Air there being more temperate than in the low lands, or near the Sea, the Climate, by degrees, will become more agre[e]able, and Habitual: which will not only inure them to the Country, but render them Robust and fit for Service.

4. The Quartering of the Soldiers in Barracks in the inland Part of the Country will be attended with these further advantages, that they will not only be readier to suppress any Insurrection or Rebellion, and be a Curb or Restraint on the Negroes in general; but, in Case of an Invasion, will be sooner able to assist any part of the Island, which may be attacked, or in danger.

5. It is necessary that a proper Apartment, or Infirmary be made at a small distance from every Barrack for the reception of Sick and Infirm Soldiers. Because the Diseases and Distempers incidental to the West Indies, being mostly Epidemical, One distempered Person will infect the rest, who are in the same Apartment, or under the same Roof; which may be prevented by their being removed, as soon as any of them find themselves indisposed.

6. It will also be proper, and of great Utility, if there was one or more Chimneys in every Barrack, and Infirmary, and a fire made therein in the Rainy Seasons, for the Reasons given in Part the 5th.; that care be taken, to restrain the Men from Sleeping in the Open Air, or being out after nine a Clock at Night.

These or such like Rules and Regulations, I am persuaded, would be the preservation of the healths and lives of a great number of Men, and render them upon Occasion fit for Service, whereas many of them are often incapable through Weakness or disability.

The Expense would be inconsiderable with regard to the Advantages arising from it, and especially considering a sufficient Number of convenient and defensible Barracks are already Built at Bagnals[,] Thickets, Clarendon, St. Elizabeth's, and other Parts; which require but a little more trouble, or charge to Compleat and render them fit for the end proposed.

The Laws of this Island are well adapted to the Circumstances of the People: and manifest, that the first Legislators were men of plain good Sense, and strong Natural Parts. For whoever has read, and considered the Old Laws, which were compiled by them, and are now made perpetual, must allow, that they have not Enacted any thing, but what is Just, Reasonable and Necessary. And to their Eternal Honour be it Rememb[e]red, that in the Infancy of the Colony, They, like true English men, asserted and insisted on their Native Rights and Privileges, with the greatest Moderation and Prudence. For in 1677, when, Their Laws, which were made to continue in force no longer than seven Years being almost expired, and a new Scheme of Government was proposed by the Committee of Trade in England, as necessary to be Established in Jamaica and the Earl of Carlisle by his Instructions was directed to lay before the Assembly the draught of a Law, for Establishing a perpetual Revenue, and several others, which were prepared, and Sent over, in order to be Enacted by them; so that the same method in legislative matters was intended to be made use of there, as in

Ireland, According to the form prescribed by Poynings law;[8] But, the Assembly, upon their meeting, were greatly dissatisfied with the alterations, which were intended to be made, and Unanimously rejected the Several Bills, that were offered them: upon which His Excellency dissolved the Assembly.

In May 1679, His Lordship was directed to Call another Assembly, and to Represent the Expediency of such Laws, as were transmitted, and in Case of their Refusal, He was furnished with such Powers as Collo[nel] Doyley had; whereby He was to govern according to the Laws of England; where the Constitution of the Colony would permit, and in other matters to Act with the advice of the Council, until his Majestie's further orders.

But, the new Assembly, which was convened in August following, and composed of the same Members, with very little, if any, Variation, showed the same, averseness to any alteration in their Constitution; insisted on their Right of framing their own Bills; and declared, that they would submit to wear, but never would Consent to make Chains for their Posterity; (for so they termed the method of Government proposed) and his Lordship finding all his Efforts ineffectual, and that the Council shewed the same disinclination to such an alteration in their Constitution, Consented to a Revenue Bill, Passed by the Assembly, for twelve months.

The 28th. of October 1680, a Petition of the Planters and Inhabitants of Jamaica was presented to His Majesty, praying to be restored to the Ancient Form of Government. Upon which, and the Earl of Carlisle representing, that the method proposed by the Committee of Trade in England, considering the distance of place was impracticable, and very distast[e]ful to the People of the Island, His Majesty was pleased, the 3d. of November following, to grant a new Commission, and Instructions to the Earl of Carlisle, impowering him to call Assemblies, and that such general Assemblies, or the Major part of them, have full power and Authority, with the Consent of the Council, to make Laws, Statutes,. and Ordinances; which were to be agre[e]able *to the Laws of England*, and to be transmitted under the publick Seal, within three months after passing the same, for His Majestie's approbation; and in Case any of them should be disapproved of' Such Laws to be void.

The Earl of Carlisle Embarking for England before the said Instructions reached him, the like powers were given to S[i]r Thomas Lynch, who was appointed to Succeed him, the 6th. Aug[ust] 1681. And soon after his Arrival in Jamaica, a Revenue Bill, and a Body of Laws were Enacted for seven Years; the greatest part of which were Confirmed by his Majesty in

8. Poyning's Law (1495) established crucial constitutional restrictions on the Irish Parliament, requiring that bills could only be initiated in the English Privy Council, leaving the Irish Parliament solely the power to consent or reject.

Council, the 28th. of Feb[ruary] 1682, and the others were transmitted to S[i]r Thomas Lynch for to be Amended by the Assembly.

In November 1683 the Assembly passed a new Revenue Bill,[9] the other being one of those that was not approved of, and several other Laws, which were transmitted with an Address to His Majesty, praying, that they might be Confirmed for twenty One Years. Accordingly that Act, with the others transmitted at the same time, as also the Body of Laws Enacted in 1682, were confirmed for twenty one years.

The term of twenty one Years expiring in 1703, an Act passed the Assembly in Jamaica, to Continue them 21 Years longer; which Act was approved of by Her Majesty Queen Ann in Council, and Confirmed.[10] And in 1722, an Act passed the Assembly intitled an Act for granting a Revenue to His Majesty, his Heirs and Successors, for the Support of the Government of this Island, and for preserving and perpetuating the Laws thereof; which being disapproved of, by his late Majesty in Council, and rejected, His Grace the late Duke of Portland, was directed to lay before them the draught of a Bill framed in England, to the same uses and purposes, and to recommend its being Enacted by them. But having already given an Account of what passed in relation to this Bill, in Part the 5th [part 3-d], I shall only observe that after vigorously Asserting their Right of framing their own Bills for above four Years, two of which they held their Laws by an annual tenure, and the remainder of the time they were without Laws, the Assembly were permitted to pass an Act, under the same Title in 1728;[11] which being drawn with great care, and rendered incapable of any Objections, it was approved of, and Confirmed by His present Majesty in Council.

This Act in the Preamble recites, that the greatest part of His Majestie's Revenue in this Island, as it was Established, did expire on the first day of October 1724. And being desirous to distinguish His Majesty's most auspicious Reign, have freely and Unanimously resolved, not only to Revive, and Continue the said Revenue, but to augment it to a degree Suitable to the dignity and State, as well as the Support of His Government; and also to give it such a Duration as, they hoped was designed by the Divine Providence, for the Succession of the Crown in His Royal Line. And therefore

9. An Act for Raising a Publick Revenue, for the Support of the Government of This His Majesty's Island, 1683, in ibid., 17.

10. An Act for Raising a Revenue to Her Majesty, Her Heirs and Successors, for Supporting the Government of This Island, and for Maintaining and Repairing Her Majesty's Forts and Fortifications, November 4, 1703, in *Journals of the Jamaica Assembly*, 14 vols. (Jamaica, 1795–1824), 1:323.

11. An Act for Granting a Revenue to His Majesty, His Heirs and Successors, for the Support of the Government of This Island and for Reviving and Perpetuating the Acts and Laws Thereof, 1728, in *Acts of Assembly*, 216–24.

they pray His Majesty, that it might be Enacted, that the following Goods, Wares, and Merchandize, afterwards to be Imported, should pay the following Impost, or Duty to his Majesty his Heirs and Successors.

For all Spanish and Madeira Wine £6 p[er] Ton.

Wines of the Western Islands or mixed therewith £12 p[er] Ton.

French, Rhenish, or Portoguese £5 p[er] Ton.

Brandy, Arrack and other Spirits 1/6 p[er] Galle[o]n.

Cask and bot[t]led beer, Ale or Cyder 40/ p[er] Tun.

Refined Sugar six pence p[er] lb.

Muscovado Sugar 3/ p[er] hundred Weight.

Tobacco three pence p[er] pound.

Ginger 15/ p[er] hundred Weight.

Indigo or Cotton three pence p[er] pound.

Cocoa in Jamaica Vessells 15/ p[er] hundred, and in other Vessels 20/ p[er] hundred w[eigh]t and so in proportion for a greater or lesser quantity.

And, that all Vessels Trading to the Northward of the Tropick of Cancer, should pay one pound of Gun powder for every Ton, they measure, Every Voyage; and all Vessels Trading to the Southward of the Tropick of Cancer, to pay only once a Year, after the same Rate.

These Duties, together with all Quit Rents, Fines, Forfeitures, and Escheats, are appropriated by this Act to the Support of the Government, and to defray the Contingent charges thereof, or what may properly be called the Civil list, and is Set[t]led in the following manner vizt.

Estimate of the present Branches of His Majestie's Revenue, and the several heads of the present Expences chargeable on the said Revenue.

Charges on the Revenue.

	£	S[hillings]	P[ence]
To the Capt[ai]n General's Salary	2500	0	0
To the Forts and Fortifications	1250	0	0
To the Chief Justice's Salary	120	0	0
To the Officers and Gunners of Fort Charles, viz,			
To the Capt[ai]n £6 per Diem	109	10	0
The Lieutenant, 4s..6d	82	2	6
Twelve Montrosses in actual Service, a 2 S[hillings] 6d [pence] per Diem, to be Inhabitants of Port Royal, and continually resident there, and not to be inlisted in either of the independant Companies	547	10	0
The Armourer	40	00	0
The Wa[i]ter	24	00	0
	803	2	6

To the Capt[ai]n of the Train in Spanish Town	45	12	6
To the Auditor Gen[era]l £150 Sterling at 35 p[er]C[ent] Exch[ange]	202	10	0
To Waiters Salary	120	00	0
To several ordinary Charges, viz. Publick Buildings, Attorney-General's Fees, Clerk of the Council, Provost Marshal, Clerk of the Crown, Clerk of the Chancery, for issuing Writs of election, Deputy-Marshals, for Prisoners, executing Writs of Election, Receiver General's Commission, Kings Evidence, and other small Expences, computed at a Medium for Nine Years past, per Annum	2390	00	00
To contingent Charges per Annum	568	15	00
	8000	00	00

Branches of the Revenue.

By Impost, at a Medium of Nine years past	2966	00	00
By Quit Rents	1460	00	00
By Fines, Forteitures and Escheats	437	13	3
By Wine Licences	200	00	00
By Gun Powder	257	2	11
By a new Impost, including Indico at 3 s[hillings] p[er] lb and Sugar at 3 p[er] Hundred, at a moderate Computation	3000	00	00
	8371	12	06

It is provided by this Act, that in Case the Several Funds or Duties should hereafter fall short of eight thousand pounds p[er] Annum, the same shall be made good by any future Assembly; and if there be any Surplusage, over and above the said Eight thousand pounds, the same shall be applied to the use of Parties to be raised for the Reduction of the Rebellious Negroes, or to or for such other use or uses as the Governour, Council, and Assembly for the time being, shall think proper, and to and for no other use, Intent, or purpose whatever.

It is also Enacted, that all the Acts and Laws of this Island, which determined and Expired on the first day of October 1724, and not by this or by any other Act of the Governour, Council and Assembly of this Island now in force, altered or Repealed, shall be and are thereby revived, and declared to be perpetual.

And that all such Laws, and Statutes of England, as have been at any time Esteemed, introduced, used, Accepted or received as Laws in this Island, shall, and are thereby declared to be, and Continue Laws of this His Majestie's Island for Ever.

The Quit Rents payable to His Majesty, and by this Act also appropriated, and applied to the use of the Revenue, are as follows.

All Land granted before the 25th. June 1671, shall pay for 30 Acres one Shilling Yearly, and so proportionally for every parcel under 100 Acres, and for every 100 Acres 2 [shillings]/6 [pence], and proportionably for a greater Quantity; and for all Lands granted from the aforesaid time; to the 12 of March in the Year 1674, or that shall hereafter be granted, shall pay one halfpenny p[er] acre; And foot land, one p[enny] per Foot for two sides of the Square added together, and so proportionably for a greater or lesser quantity.

And by a Subsequent Act passed in 1733,[12] all Owners, and Proprietors of Land within this Island, who for the future shall neglect, or refuse to account with the Receiver General or his Deputy, within every three Years after the passing this Act; and pay the same, or if exceeding the Sum of Twenty Pounds, to give Bond to pay the same in 6 months after, shall be chargeable and answerable for the same at and after the rate of twelve Pounds p[er] Centum p[er] Annum.

The other Acts for raising of mon[e]y are Temporary, and passed only from Year to Year, vizt. The Deficiency and Additional Duty Acts, and upon extraordinary Occasions, or when those Funds prove insufficient a Poll Tax is laid on all Negroes, Cattle, Horses, and Mules.

The Deficiency Act,[13] obliges all Planters to provide one Able man, fit to bear Arms, to every thirty Negroes, or one hundred and Twenty head of Cattle, Horses, and Mules included or in default to pay £13..6..8 p[er] Ann[um], and so in proportion for a greater of lesser Number; And all Absentees or Owners of Estates residing in other Parts of the World, are Assessed one third more.

This Fund produces annually at a Medium above £7000 p[er] Ann[um], and is applied to the payment of the Additional Subsistance allowed to His Majestie's Forces in this Island.

The Additional Duty Act,[14] Imposes a further Impost or Duty, on all Wines, and other Goods Imported into this Island; 10 Shillings per head on all Negroes Imported, and to be paid by the Purchaser. An Assess-

12. An Act for Securing and Collecting His Majesty's Quit-Rents, Fines, Forfeitures and Amerciaments and for Regulating the Manner of Escheats; and for Securing the Possessors of Lands Already Forfeited and Settled and Further the Discovery of Such Forfeited Lands, and Encouraging the Settling Thereof, 1733, in ibid., 262.

13. An Act to Oblige the Several Inhabitants of This Island to Provide Themselves with a Sufficient Number of White People; and to Pay Certain Sums of Money in Case They Shall Be Deficient, and Applying the Same to Several Uses, 1733, in ibid., 258.

14. An Act for Raising an Additional Duty Act was passed at virtually every session of the assembly. Ibid.

ment from £500 to £1000 laid on the Jews, According to the Necessities of Government. A Tax on all Negro Tradesmen hired out, which amounts to about £700. A Tax on the Trading Inhabitants of St. Katherine's and Kingston £500. A Tax on the Publick Offices £135; and a Duty on all Rum retailed in the Island 7 1/2d p[er] Gallon, to be paid by the Retailer, and amounts to about £3000; Which Duties, and Assessments are not always the same, but more or less, as the publick Occasions require, and produces annually at a Medium [of] £10000.

This Fund is applied to the payment of the Governour's Additional Salary of £2500 p[er] Ann[um]; the Chaplain, Clerk, and other Officers of the Assembly; whose Stipends amount to about £600, according to the time and business of the Session; also Donatives and Rewards, for Services done to the Country; which are uncertain and cannot be estimated; the Residue was formerly applied to the use of Parties, fitted out to Reduce the Rebellious Negroes; but since they have Submitted, to make good the Deficiency of other funds, if any, and to other Occasions of the Government.

Hence it appears, that the Contingent charges of the Government of this Island, in time of Peace, including the Additional Subsistance allowed to the Eight Independant Companies (which with other Expences Attending them amount to near Ten thousand pounds p[er] Ann[um]) cannot be less than Twenty five thousand pounds p[er] Ann[um]; and in time of War must needs be more in building and repairing Fortifications, and other Expences that are Necessary and unavoidable for their defence.

All which must be allowed to be exceeding burthensome, and a heavy load on the Inhabitants, considering the Small number of White men in the Island, and especially considering the Great Duties and Excises their Commodities are Subject to in England; so that unless some means are found out to Ease and Relieve them, I can't devise how it is possible for young Planters to Succeed, or those who are in debt to recover and Extricate themselves, which will undoubtedly obstruct the further Settlement of the Island, if not be the ruin and destruction of many Plantations, which are already settled.

There are many other Acts of the Assembly, which are of great Utility, particularly those relating to a Publick Register, so necessary, and so much wanted in England, and for Securing Titles to Estates, quieting possessions and preventing Vexatious Suits at Law.

Deeds[15] acknowledged or proved before the Governour, or one of the Judges of this Island, and Recorded in the Office of Enrollments at St. Iago de la vega within three months after date, shall be valid and pass an Estate without livery, Seizen, or any other Ceremony at Law; and no deed without such proof and Enrollment, shall pass away any Estate for above three years.

15. See an Act for Registering Deeds and Patents No. 14. —*Author.* An Act for Registering Deeds and Patents, 1681, in *Acts of Assembly,* 17–19. —*Ed.*

Provided Nevertheless that any Deeds made heretofore, and Omitted to be proved and Recorded, shall upon being proved and Recorded, be Valid and of force.

But, if a Second Sale or Conveyance be made for a Valuable Consideration, duly proved and Recorded before the first, the second Sale shall be good, and the other Void.

If a Purchaser omit[s] to Record in due time, and no second Sale be made, He may Record it at any time, and it shall be good against the Vender and his Heirs.

Deeds made out of the Island, proved before the Lord Mayor of London, and attested under the City Seal, or transmitted and proved before the Governour, or any Judge of the Island, and the same, with the Attestation or Proof, Recorded within Six months after the Arrival of the Ship, that brought it, shall be good. Lands sold by Attorneys, and duly Recorded, before any Sale of the same by the Proprietor be produced, and Recorded, as aforesaid shall be good and Valid in Law.

Mortgages when satisfied shall be acknowledged and Entered in the Margin of the Mortgage, Recorded, or to be Recorded in the Office as aforesaid, at the Charge of the Mortgager on penalty of £50.

All Sales and Conveyances made or to be made by Husband and Wife, acknowledged before any Judge in this Island, and duly Recorded shall be good and Valid in Law, against all Persons whatsoever that can or may pretend to claim any Estate in Lands or Tenements so Conveyed to all Intents and Purposes whatsoever, as if the same had passed by Fine and Recovery in any of His Majestie's Courts at Westminster.

All and every Person[16] who hold any Lands, Tenements, Negroes, or Hereditaments, by Vertue of any Deed, Will or Conveyance, and hath been in quiet possession for Seven Years before the making of this Act, or shall Continue in such possession of the same for the Space of seven Years from the 1 day of May 1732, or shall at any time hereafter be, and Continue in such possession for the Space of Seven Years, shall have and enjoy the same to them and their Heirs for ever. The Right and Title of any Person under 21, Women under Coverture, and Persons of unsound Memory, always excepted and foreprised.

Provided such Persons shall bring their Actions in 3 years after, such Person hath attained the age of 21: Women under Coverture become sole, or Persons of unsound Memory become Compos Mentis.

This Act not to extend to Persons seized of Lands, Negroes and Hereditaments, devised to Charitable uses, Mortgages, Lessees or any Executor Attorney Guardian or other Persons in Trust.

---

16. See an Act for Quieting Possession &c. no. 311. — *Author.* An Act for the Further Quieting Possession and Regulating Resurbeys &c., 1731, in *Acts of Assembly*, 246–48. — *Ed.*

The Record,[17] or a Copy of the Record, attested by the Secretary of the Island, of any Patent, Deed or Will lost or mislaid to be deemed good Evidence, and allowed in Court the same as if the Original had been produced.

The Exemplification of all Wills made in Great Britain[,] Ireland or other British Dominions, duly proved and attested under a proper Seal, and transmitted to Jamaica, shall be allowed in Court as good Evidence of the Title to the Estate, or Interest Claimed thereby.

All Deeds made before, or to be made after this Act, and duly acknowledged before the Governour, or a Judge, and Recorded, are to be held good and Valid, no Second Sale appearing to have been proved and Recorded, as aforesaid.

Deeds Executed in the Island are to be recorded in Ninety days after date, otherwise of no Effect against second purchasers; or Mortgages for Valuable Consideration, who shall duly prove and Record their Deeds in due time.

Vendees or Mortgages omitting to Record their deed in the time limitted, and that afterwards do it, the same shall be good; against the first Vendor or Mortgager or his Heirs.

Deeds Executed out of the Island, and Recorded six Calender months after the date, and within ninety days after their Arrival in the Island, shall be good, but, if neglected, they shall only be good against the Vendor, and not against a Second Purchaser, who has Recorded his Deed.

Vendor, or Mortgager, executing a second Deed of Sale, or Mortgage, without taking due notice of the first, shall be tried, and punished, as for like frauds committed in England.

The Secretary shall record Original Wills formerly Omitted.

And for the Easier, and more Orderly distribution of Justice, here is duly held a Court of Chancery; a Supreme Court, or Court of King's Bench, and a Court of Common Pleas; a Court of Errors; an Inferior Court of Common Pleas, Quarter Sessions of the Peace, A Court of Admiralty, and Justices of the Peace appointed in Every Parish in the Island.

The Governour, as I observed, Sets, and determines all Causes in the Court of Chancery and two Gentlemen of the Island Assist as Masters.

The first Monday in Every month is appointed for Settings; and the 3d. Monday in Every month for Motions. But this is often varied or adjourned, so that sometimes a Court of Chancery has not been held for five or Six Weeks, and sometimes 2 or three Months, to the great obstruction of Justice, and Encouragement of litigious and Vexatious Suits.

17. See an Act for preserving the Records &c. no. 312. — *Author.* An Act for the Better Preserving of the Records in the Several Publick Offices of the Island, Supplying and Remedying Defects in Several Former Laws for Preventing Fraudulent Deeds and Conveyances, and Recording Old Wills in a Prefixed Time, 1731, in *Acts of Assembly*, 249–52. — *Ed.*

The Supreme Court of Judicature commonly called the Grand Court; hath the same Jurisdiction with the King's Bench, Common Pleas, and Exchequer at Westminster, and is held four times in the Year, Vizt. the last Tuesday in February, May, August and November. The Pleas of the Crown are first tried, afterwards the Common Pleas; and the Court continues Sitting until they have gone thro[ugh] all the Trials.

The Judges are commissioned by the Governour, and are seven in Number, Vizt. a Chief Justice, and Six Assistants, whereof no less than three can try any Cause. The Chief Justice is generally one of the Council, and the rest Gentlemen of the Island. And tho[ugh] none of them are bred to the laws, yet as they are men of Sense, and Reason, whereon all Law is, or ought to be grounded, their Judgments are generally Approved and seldom reversed on any Appeal to the Court of Errors.

The Court of Errors consists of the Governour.

The Judges of the Grand Court determine all Pleas according to the Laws of England, whereby the Island is Governed, excepting some few Variations, that are Necessary for the Ease and benefit of a New Colony; as all proceedings at Law being by English Bill; by their pleading general issues, and giving Special matters in Evidence, their Suits are more Concise, and less chargeable, than in England, and the Practice of their Courts more plain and Less expensive.

The Supreme, or Grand Court. is not Burthened with many Officers for one called the Clerk of the Grand Court is Prothonotary, Custos brevium &c. Nor do they trouble themselves with many Sorts of Writs, or Originals, the arresting of any Person of known Residence; being very Rare only a Summons is Served on his Person or Left at his House to appear at the next Supreme or Grand Court; and that He may come provided, a Copy of the Declaration is always left with the Summons; which being served 14 days at least, before the Court, the Defendant is bound to appear, plead, join issue, and Come to Trial the very next Court, or Judgment will pass by Default; no Imparlance being allowed without special Cause, or an Oath made, that He hath Material Witnesses and hath endeavoured, but Cannot Subpoena them.

In Trials they have not several Veniris, nor a particular Jury, unless in Some Special matter or Cause, but by a general Venire, the Marshal prepares sufficient for four or five Sets of Jurors, who know not what issues they are to Try (which prevents packing or partial Juries) being impanelled in Court, and put upon the Crown side or Common Pleas, as the Judges think proper and just. And the same Jury commonly try six or more Causes at a time, as the Court think their Memory will bear; though they are allowed to take Minutes, and to have the Record it self, with all papers or Deeds proved in Court. Most of their Suits are plain matter of Debt or Account, some few Writs of Dower, Partition &c. The Jurors endorse their

Verdict on each Record, which is delivered in Court to the Clerk, who enters Judgment, unless it be Arrested; which every Party, against whom Judgment is given, may move for the last day of the Court; but is seldom granted without Special Cause, or Reasonable objections be Assigned. Nor are such motions favoured or allowed, except in Cases, where Excessive damages are given. In Actions of Slander, or frivolous Trespasses, they are seldom troubled with dilatory Writs of Enquiry, but when Judgment is obtained or Confessed by *nil dicit*[18] in the Case &c. the next Jury, which happens to be Trying issues in Court, take the Record, and Assess Damages immediately.

For the Ease of Persons concerned, and to prevent unnecessary Attendance and Expences, all Causes depending are every Court or Term, called and Tryed Alphebetically, and the list of the old and New Causes, are not only given to every Pleader and Attorney, but fixed up in Court, so that Witnesses and others may often guess on what day such a letter will come on, and accordingly give their Attendance.

There are also Inferior Courts of Common Pleas in Several Precincts of this Island, which have the same Jurisdiction over all Causes, wherein any Freehold is not concerned, to the Value of Twenty pounds with Costs and no more, and are held once in every three months. But, in regard to Grade and the dispatch of Maritime Affairs, the Judge or Judges of the Inferior Courts of Common Pleas, at Port Royal and Kingston, are impowered to hold and keep the Courts once every two months. In there inferior Courts of Common Pleas all not exceeding ten pounds Value, are tried and determined without appeal, and all above that Value are Returnable to the Supreme or Grand Court.

But that these matters may Appear in a clear and stronger light, I shall abstract some Clauses from an Act, for Establishing Courts and directing [the] Marshal's proceedings,[19] wherein it is Enacted.

That the Judges of the Supreme Court of Judicature shall have Cognizance of all Pleas, Civil, Criminal, and mixt, as fully, as the King's Bench, Common Pleas, and Exchequer have in England, and the same Court shall be constantly kept at St. Iago de la Vega, and not elsewhere, once every three Months, of which at least there shall be five Judges, three whereof to be a Quorum.

None shall execute the Office of a Judge in any of the aforesaid Courts, till he has taken the Oaths of Allegiance and Supremacy in open Court, and no Judge shall receive any profit, Benefit or Advantage, but what is allowed them by the Acts of this Island, under the Penalty of £500.

---

18. To say nothing.

19. An Act, for the Establishing Courts and Directing the Marshal's Proceedings, 1681, in ibid., 34–39.

The Judges of the several Courts shall order and establish Rules and Orders, for regulating the Proceedings in their respective Courts, as fully, to all Intents, as the Judges in the several Courts in England may legally do.

No Counsellor or Attorney shall be admitted to practise in any of the said Courts, till he hath taken the Oaths of Allegiance and Supremacy, &c. under Penalty of £20. And whatsoever Counsellor or Attorney shall by Negligence or Ignorance, mistake his Client's Cause or shall suffer a Non suit; he, or they, so offending, shall by Rule of Court, without any further Process, be obliged to pay the Party aggrieved full Costs of Suit.

The Judges may at all Times, upon Motion in Court, order Amendments in Matter of Form only, and shall not, upon a Writ of Error or Motion in Arrest, reverse any Judgment for Matter of Form only.

No Action of Waste shall be brought in any Court of this Island, nor any Freeholder of known Residence arrested by any Process out of the said Courts, Penalty £20. to be paid by the Plaintiff to the Party so arrested, & all Proceedings thereupon shall be void.

No Suit shall be commenced in the Supreme Court of Judicature, for any Matter or Cause, under the Value of £20, under the Penalty of £20: to be paid by the Plaintiff: but such Causes shall be tried in the inferior Courts; provided the Inhabitants of St. Katharine's, St. Dorothy's, St. Thomas in the Vale, and St. John's, may sue in the Supreme Court for any Sum, till they shall have petty Courts erected in their own Parishes.

In all inferior Courts if upon Summons, the Defendant doth not appear, Judgment shall go by Default, as in the supreme Court, the Provost-Marshal making Oath in open Court, that the Party was legally summoned 14 Days before.

Upon a Declarator exhibited in Debt, upon Speciality, or a *concessit solvere*,[20] and disclosing the Special Matter to the Chief Judge of the Supreme Court, that the Debtor is either gone off the Island, or a *non est inventus*[21] returned, an Attachment shall issue against the Goods and Chattels, etc. of the Debtor, in whose Hands soever, and upon Conviction, and the Plaintiff swearing the Debt due, and no Part paid, and giving Security to restore the same with triple Damages; if disproved, he shall have Judgment, to recover his Debt out of the said Goods, Chattels, Monies, &c. but if any Attorney appear, and put in Bail, the Attachment shall be dissolved, if the Parties in whose Hands the Goods, &c. are attached, shall part with the same before the Attachment be satisfied or dissolved, they shall make Satisfaction to the Plaintiff out of their proper Estates.

All Summons from any Court shall be delivered to the Party, or left at his Dwelling-House 14 Days, before the Sitting of the Court in which the

20. Agreement to pay.

21. The return of a sheriff on a writ or process when the defendant or person to be served or arrested is not found in the jurisdiction.

Action is brought by a sworn Marshal; except at Port-Royal, and there it shall be delivered 10 Days before the sitting of the Court, otherwise the Defendant shall not be bound to appear. Replevins, foreign Attachments at the supreme Court, and Warrants of Arrest, may be served at any Time.

No Execution shall be taken out, or Executed, till 28 days after Judgment, except at Port-Royal, and there Execution shall issue 10 Days after Judgment. No Negroes, nor any Manner of Utensils belonging to a Plantation and Works, shall be taken in Execution, where the Defendant shall offer other Goods to satisfy the Debt and Costs.

The Defendant shall have Liberty to carry his Goods, taken in Execution, to Market, and there sell them, first acquainting the Marshal who took them upon the Execution; that so he may receive the Produce thereof. If the Defendant neglect[s] to sell them, till 10 Days before, the next Court, the Marshal shall take the Goods and sell them by Auction.

If Negroes and Utensils belonging to a Plantation be taken in Execution, for want of other Goods, they shall not be removed, till a *venditioni exponas*[22] issue, impowering the Provost-Marshal to sell them; or, in case they be made away, to levy and sell any other Goods, or in Default of Goods, to take the Defendant's Body, &c.

After the Goods shall be sold by Auction, the Money shall be paid to the Plaintiff, or his Order, within 10 Days, under the Penalty of Half the Debt, to be received by the Plaintiff to his own Use.

The Marshall shall not take in Execution Negroes, or Utensils, *ut supra*,[23] if the Defendant shews him any Stock or Cattle, in a Penn, which may be sold by Auction, as aforesaid.

All Accidents that happen, while Goods taken in Execution remain in the Defendant's Possession, shall be born, and made good by the Defendant.

Where the Body of the Defendant shall be taken in Execution; yet, if any Effects afterwards appear, the Plaintiff may take out another Execution, and levy his Debt upon the same.

Where Prisoners in Execution have nothing to maintain themselves, upon Oath thereof before two neighbouring Justices of Peace, and Notice to all their Creditors ten Days before the Supreme Court, they shall be publickly let to Hire at the said Court; and the Money arising from the Hire shall be paid to such Persons, as the Court shall appoint, to be equally divided among the Creditors. If any Creditor shall refuse to consent, that the Prisoner shall be let to Hire, such Creditor shall pay the Prisoner 3 [shillings]/6 [pence] weekly.

If the Prisoner so let to Hire shall, at any Time after, come to have an

---

22. The name of a writ of execution, directed to the sheriff, commanding him to sell goods, chattels, or lands, which he has taken in execution of a court order and which remain unsold.

23. As above.

Estate, not having satisfied his Debts, another Execution upon the former Judgment shall be taken out against his Goods and Chattles.
Justices of the Peace.

All Debts, Trespasses, and other Matters not exceeding 40 S[hillings] (where the Titles of Lands are not concerned) shall be heard and determined, without Appeal, by any Justice of Peace of this Island; who, upon Complaint made, shall grant a Warrant or Summons; and in Case of Non-appearance, shall issue out a Warrant of Contempt to the Constable, to bring the Person . . . before him, and may, if he see Cause, fine the Person, but not more the 10 S[hillings] for the Use of the Parish.

After Judgment given, the Justice may grant a Warrant of Distress directed to the Constable, to levy the Fine, Debt, Damages and Charges upon the Defendant's Goods, exposing them to Sale, and to return the Overplus, if any be; and for want of Effects, to take the Defendant's Body in Execution.

The Justice may receive for each Warrant 1 S[hilling]/3d [pence], and no more. The Constable as much, with 6d [pence] for each Mile he travels, provided the whole exceeds not 5 S[hillings].

The Justice is obliged to keep a Record of all such Proceedings, under the Penalty of 10 S[hillings], Half to the Poor, and Half to the Informer.

Here is also a Court of Admiralty held, as often as occasions require, for hearing and determining all Maritime Causes. The Judge and other Officers of this Court are appointed by the Lords Commissioners for Executing the Office of L[or]d High Admiral of England. And all Appeals from thence are returnable to the King and Councill.

* * * *

The Publick Officers of this Island, are as follows. The Register, Commonly called Secretary of the Island, the Receiver General, Provost Marshal, Attorney General, Surveyor of the Customs, Collector, Naval Officer, Register in Chancery, Clerk of the Grand Court, and Clerk of the Markets.

The Register is appointed by Patent from the Crown, to be held by himself or Deputy, during life. In this Office all Deeds, Wills and other Conveyances are Registered; and any Person, during Office-hours, may demand a Sight, or take a Copy of any Deed, Will or Conveyance, paying the fees prescribed by an Act of the Assembly. He is also Commissary, and Steward General of all the Provisions, and Publick Stores of the Island; and Clerk of the Council. This Office was first granted by King Charles the Second, in January 1661, to Richard Povey Gentleman![24]

The Receiver General is also appointed by Patent from the Crown, to be held by himself or his Deputy during life. He has the Receipts, and Dis-

24. Richard Povey was the brother of merchant Thomas Povey (1614–c. 1705), who was active in colonial affairs from the 1650s and a powerful figure in the early English overseas empire.

bursments of all Publick mon[e]ys, Arising by Duties, Quit Rents, Fines[,] Forfeitures and Escheats.

This Office was for some Years in the Gift of the Governour of the Island; but in March 1673, it was granted to Thomas Martin Esq[uir]e and Leonard Compere of London Citizen,[25] and to the longest liver.

The Provost Marshal is also appointed by Patent from the Crown, to be held by himself or his Deputy, during life. This Officer is of the same Nature of a High Sheriff of a Country, and has Deputies under him, in every Parish in the Island. He also attends the Council when they sit, either as a Council of State, or in a Legislative Capacity, and Officiates as Gentleman Usher of the Black Rod.

The Patent was first granted in January 1661, to Coll[onel] Thomas Lynch, afterwards S[i]r Thomas.

The Attorney General, is appointed by Patent, during pleasure.

The Surveyor of the Customs is appointed by the Commissioners of the Customs of Great Britain with a Sallary of £150 Sterling p[er] Ann[um].

The Collector of the Customs was, till very lately, also held by Commission from the Commissioners of the Customs; and the present Patentee Bacon Morris Esq[uir]e was the first that obtained a Patent for the same to be held by himself or Deputy during life.

The Naval Officer is held by Patent *durante bene placito*.[26]

The Register in Chancery is held by Patent during life, and to be Executed by himself or Deputy.

The Clerk of the Grand Court is held by Patent during life and to be executed by himself or Deputy. He is Prothonotary, Custos Brevium &c. for He signs all Writs[,] enters Judgment obtained at the Supreme or Grand Court, and keeps the Records.

The Clerk of the Markets is also held by Patent from the Crown, and to be executed by himself or Deputy. He Superintends the markets, and Examines at least once a Year, all weights and measures.

Those several Officers are obliged by law to give attendance in their Respective Offices, from nine to Eleven in the Morning and from two to four in the Afternoon, under the Penalty of twenty Pounds for every default, the Fees of the Several Offices are also Ascertained by an Act for Regulating Fees;[27] and if any of them demand, or take any more, than is allowed by the said Act, and be duly Convicted thereof, he forfeits One hundred pounds for every Offence.

But, notwithstanding the care of the Legislature to prevent impositions, or Exorbitant fees being taken, some innovations and bad Practices have

25. Leonard Compere held the office of receiver general jointly with Thomas Martin until Martin's death in 1699, at which time Compere alone held the office and which he subsequently rented to James Knight.

26. During good behavior.

27. An Act for Regulating Fees, 1711, in *Acts of Assembly*, 131–42.

been introduced and tollerated, which require a Publick Enquiry, or they will become grievous and Burthensome. For most, or all of these offices being held by Deputation, at Rack Rents, they are under the necessity of raising their Fees, although contrary to Law, to make them worth their Attending. Hence it is that most of them pay the Patentee double what was done 20 or 25 years ago; of which I could give some Instances, but it is unnecessary, being well known in the Island. It is true that the business in most or all the Publick Offices in this Island is encreased, since the Peace of Utrecht, and Consequently the legal Income, which gives the Patentee a just right or pretence to raise his Rent, though in no Degree to such a height as they have done.

I come now to give some account of Spiritual Matters, and the State of Religion in this Island: which I wish, I could say, was not greatly neglected, and disregarded; not so much through the default of the Laity in general, much less the Legislature, who have not been wanting to Enact proper Laws, for promoting Vertue and discouraging Vice and Immorality, as to the Supiness, and misbehaviour of the Clergy. I do not from hence mean or intend wholly to acquit the former, or to make no exceptions as to the latter; for doubtless there are many loose and Wicked Persons in Jamaica, as well as in other Countries, tho[ugh] they are not all, or in general such Persons, as they are commonly Represented to be; and I should be unjust, if I did not likewise observe, that there are some of the Clergy, who have not by their Conduct or Behaviour thrown any blemish on their Function or Order, and whose Lives and Conversations are agre[e]able to their Doctrine and Profession. But the major part of them, when I resided in the Island, were the most licentious set of men, of any Society I was ever acquainted with. However, for the sake of a few deserving men, I shall throw a Veil over the Infirmities of their Brethren in hopes, that these hints may come before that Worthy Prelate, who has Power to inspect into the manners of the Clergy, in all the British Colonies, and not only be the means of an Enquiry into their Conduct, but may tend to the Advancement of Religion in those Parts.

I have often thought, it would be a great Encouragement to good and able Ministers to go over, if some Provision was made for them, in England, after they had resided for seven years or more, in any of our plantations, and demeaned themselves well; for though the livings in Jamaica will support them, or a Family in a decent and Comfortable manner yet they cannot pretend to lay up and raise Fortunes for Children, much Less to enable them to spend their latter days with their Friends in England, as it is Common and Natural for most men to wish and desire. This, I conceive, is the principal Cause, why the Plantations are generally furnished with such Clergy men, as are obliged to leave their Native Country through mere want or Necessities, or Young men, who come over as Chaplains to His Majesty's Ships, where their Morals are often Corrupted, if they were not so before.

The Christian Inhabitants of this Island are mostly of the Church of England, some few Quakers and Presbyterians; but, as the latter have not any Meeting or Pastors, they most or all of them go to [the established] Church.

And for the Maintenance of Ministers,[28] relieving the Poor, & erecting and Repairing Churches, it is by the laws of the Island Enacted and Provided,

That the Justices in Each Parish, shall, in January every Year, Summon the Freeholders to choose Church Wardens and Vestry men, to lay a Reasonable tax on the said Parish, as to them shall seem Convenient, for the Maintenance, of the Minister and Poor, Erecting Churches, Repairing such as are already Built, and making Convenient Seats in them.

Justices or Vestry men not appearing to lay taxes shall forfeit five pounds each.

A Roll of the Tax shall be delivered to the Constable with a Warrant to levy the same, and to pay it to the Church Wardens, retaining twelve pence in the pound for his trouble and charges.

Church Wardens shall keep a regular account, and issue no money without an order of the Justices and Vestry, on penalty of five pounds.

A Minister shall Demand no fee in his own Parish for Christenings, Marriages, or Burials, but what are allowed by the Justices and Vestry under the Penalty of 5£.

Church Wardens shall provide a Book, wherein the Minister, or the Church Warden or Clerk of the Vestry where there happens to be no Minister, shall Register the times of the Births, Christ[e]nings, Marriages and Burials, within the said Parish, under the penalty of five pounds for every default.

That all such Entries duly made and kept, as aforesaid, shall at all times hereafter be deemed, judged, and taken, as an Authentick Record; in all and every Court of Record in this Island. And if any Person shall make a false Entry, or erase or Embezzle any Entry or Book of Entry, He, or They, so offending shall be proceeded against, and punished in manner and form, as the Laws of England provide against such as Steal, erase or Embezzle Records.

That no Minister shall be capable of being presented to any Benefice in this Island, or of receiving the profits of the same, unless he produce due and proper Testimonials, that he is qualified according to the Canons of the Church of England, by having taken Deacon's and Priest's Orders, and the said Testimonials, be recorded in the Secretary's Office.

That no Minister, though duly qualifyed, as aforesaid, presume to Marry any Person or Persons whatsoever, under the Penalty of one hundred

28. See the Act No. 2, fol. Ed. p. 24.—*Author.* Act for the Maintenance of Ministers, and Erecting and Repairing Churches, 1681, in *Acts of Assembly*, 24–27.—*Ed.*

Entitled *Representation of Water Spouts at St. Jago de la Vega in Jamaica*, figure 6 in the *Gentleman's Magazine* of December 1783, vol. 54, following p. 1024, furnishes one of the fullest representations of the Anglican church in Spanish Town as British settlers over the decades had remodeled it from an already impressive Spanish structure. Contemporaries regarded it as Jamaica's most impressive ecclesiastical building.

pounds current mon[e]y of this Island, whose Bans have not been published three times in their Parish Church unless They have a License from the Governour or Commander in Chief for the time being.

That no Ecclesiastical Law or Jurisdiction shall have Power to inforce, confirm or Establish any penal mulcts or Punishments in any Case whatever.

That the Minister of each Parish be constantly one of the Vestry; and that no Vestry make any Order without having first given timely notice to the Minister to be there. And for the Encouragement of good and able Ministers, duly qualified as the Law Directs, that now reside in, or shall hereafter come to this Island, for the promotion of Piety, Religion and Vertue, it is Enacted and ordained, that the Ministers of Each Respective

Parish shall receive of the Church Warden or Church Wardens, as is there-inafter directed, Every Six months by Equal Portions, viz.

That the Minister of St. Catherine's shall be allowed and paid, One hundred and fifty pounds p[er] Ann[um], but if the Justices and Vestry think fit, for the Encouragement of an Able Divine, it shall and may be lawful for them to add One hundred pounds p[er] Ann[um] more to his Sallary so that the whole do not exceed two hundred and fifty pounds p[er] Ann[um].

That the Ministers of St. Thomas in the Vale, St. Dorothy's, Kingston, Vere, and Clarendon, shall be allowed each One hundred and Fifty pounds p[er] Ann[um]; Provided nevertheless, if the Justices and Vestry shall think fit, it shall, and may be lawful for them, to add Fifty pounds p[er] Ann[um], to each of their Salaries, so that the whole do not exceed two hundred pounds p[er] Ann[um].

And to the Ministers of St. Andrew's, St. John's, St. Thomas in the East, St. David's, St. George's, St. Mary's, St. Ann's, St. James, St. Elizabeth's, Westmorland, and Hanover shall be allowed each One hundred pounds p[er] Ann[um]; Provided nevertheless, if the Justices and Vestry shall think fit, it shall, and may be lawful for them to add Fifty pounds p[er] Ann[um] more to each of their Salaries, so that the whole exceed not one hundred and fifty pounds p[er] Ann[um].

And it is further enacted that no Person whatsoever, though duly Qualified, and Obtaining the ordinary Presentation, for any Parish within the Island, shall ask, demand, or take any Sum, or Sums of mon[e]y, for any further or longer time, than he shall Actually Officiate, as Minister of the said Parish (sickness only excepted) any Law, Custom, or usage to the Contrary notwithstanding.

Beside those Stipends, which are Established by Law, and the Fees set[t]led by the Justices and Vestry of every Parish, the Ministers are commonly allowed from 30 to £50 p[er] Ann[um], for a House, where there is no Parish House. St. Katherine's has not only a good Parish House in St. Jago de la vega, but a Pen or Farm belonging to it, within two Miles of the Town; and the Minister is generally chosen Chaplain to the Assembly, which makes that living worth about Five hundred pounds p[er] Ann[um], Currency.

And Kingston being the most Populous Parish in the Island, and a great number of Strangers resorting to it Yearly, the Benefice is Estimated at Six hundred pounds p[er] Ann[um], or more Currency.

Hence it appears that no Encouragement or Regard is wanting to the Clergy, who are in general treated with great decency and Civility, especially those, that demean themselves well, and no ways disgrace their Function or Order.

I have already Observed, that the Governour or Commander in Chief for the time being, is Ordinary, and has the induction or Presentation of all Church livings in this Island, by Vertue of His Commission from the King who is the head of the Church. Nevertheless the Bishop of London, and His Predecessors, have claimed the Jurisdiction, in this and all the British Colonies in Spirituals; though by the Common or Statute law of England, He has not any such Right or Authority.

This the present Bishop Dr. Gibson,[29] seemed to be fully convinced of, and therefore in the Year 1727 he Sollicited and Obtained a Commission from the Crown, to Exercise very large Ecclesiastical Powers, in all the British Plantations in America: but meeting with an Opposition, from some Gentlemen belonging to them, who entered a Caveat, before it passed the Seals, the Commission was so qualified, altered, and Amended, that He has nothing left but a bare power to inspect into the Manners of the Clergy; and when He has done that, He has done all; for His Power extends no further, not to the least degree of Punishment; so that they are at Liberty to shew just as much deference to His Lordship's Commissary, or Surrogate, as they think proper.

By Vertue of an Order of Councill, supposed to be made in King Charles the Second's Reign (and which I am credibly informed could never be found, and believed to have been burnt with White Hall, if ever there was one) the Bishops of London, and particularly Dr. Robinson,[30] always claimed Ecclesiastical Jurisdiction in the British Colonies Ex Officio, and without an Express Patent from the Crown. But by the present Bishop's Solliciting and accepting a particular Commission, He has given up that claim. He has also given up His Claim to any Authority over the Laity by Accepting it is the form, in which this Shadow of a Commission is now passed; for He can't *inspect* into the manners of a *Parish Clerk*, His inspection being confined to the Clergy, and extending to no other Person whatever. Beside, the Commission is granted during pleasure only, so that if it should be found inconvenient, or Vexatious, His Majesty can always revoke it: And as it is not annexed to any particular See, He may hereafter give it to any other Bishop, or Clergyman, or even to a Layman.

Nor, Indeed, would the Commission, as it was at first granted to Dr. Gibson, the present Bishop, had it passed the Seals, or any other that can now be granted, be of any force or Validity in respect to the Laity: because such Commissions are repugnant to the Charters granted by the Crown to Several of the Plantations, and to Express laws confirmed by the Crown in others, particularly Jamaica, viz, that no *Ecclesiastical Law* or *Jurisdiction*

29. Bishop Dr. Edmund Gibson (1669–1748) graduated from Queens College, Oxford, with an M.A. in 1694 and held a variety of ecclesiastical positions before becoming bishop of Lincoln, 1716–20, and bishop of London, 1723–48.

30. Bishop Dr. John Robinson (1650–1723) was a fellow at Oriel College, Oxford, 1675–86, and received an M.A. from Brasenose College, Oxford, in 1684. He subsequently held a variety of ecclesiastical posts, including the chaplaincy to the English embassy in Sweden for twenty-five years. He became a privy councillor and bishop of London in 1714 and held the latter office until his death.

shall have power to inforce any Penal *Mulcts* or *Punishments* in any Case whatever.

However it is highly necessary, that His Lordship should be impowered not only to inspect into the Manners and Behaviour of the Clergy, but to inflict such Punishment, as may be proper, even to deprive them, *ab Officio et Beneficio:*[31] or rather that the Governour & Council should be vested with that Power, because it may reasonably be supposed, that His Lordship cannot so well judge of matters at such a distance, as those, who are upon the spot, and may personally examine Evidences, and make such Enquiries as are requisite to form a Judgment and pass Sentence, on those that are Delinquent.

31. Without the benefits of office.

Part the 8th.

Of the Soil and Productions, the Manner of Planting Sugar Canes, and Making of Sugar, Rum, and Indigo; Also Cocoa, Coffee, Ginger, Piemento, Cotton, and other Commodities, that are or May be Produced in Jamaica.

Jamaica is not, in general, so proper for Sugar as Barbadoes and some of the other Islands in the West Indies; the Soil in many parts differing: for in some places the Earth is black, and Rich, others stiff Clay, or Sandy; some Reddish, and others Boggy, or Swampy. The Settlements are therefore distinct, Mountainous and unplantable Land interposing, which makes them appear like so many different Colonies. But this difference of the Soil in the manurable lands, is rather an advantage to them, than otherwise, as those Countries are certainly the most Valuable, that are productive of divers sorts of Commodities. Sugar is indeed the principal Product, and what they chiefly go upon, yet they do not wholly depend upon it, Considerable Quantities of other Valuable Commodities being Yearly produced, and Exported from thence, which it could not naturally produce, were the Soil and Seasons the same, throughout the Island. For though some lands are Capable of raising several sorts of Commodities with Art and Labour; yet they are not equally proper for them all, but much more for One than another. Sugar Canes and Ginger thrive best in a Rich fat mould; Indigo and Cotton in Clay or light Sandy ground; Cocoa and Coffee, require not only a rich Mould, and Moisture, but shade and shelter from high Winds, and therefore thrive best in Vallies near Rivers, or in the Bottoms, or Spaces between the Mountains. Nor is it in this alone, this Island differs from the other British Sugar Colonies, but more eminently in the Various Seasons; for whereas in the Summer Months, or the more direct neighbourhood of the Sun, it is generally observed to be very dry on the South side, it is quite Contrary on the North; for then the Violent gusts of Wind, and heavy Rains make it appear more like Winter. And this occasions the difference in the time of their Crops; for as they begin to plant Canes, whereof Sugar is made, in September on the South Side, they are three months later in the North, and begin to grind accordingly; Canes requiring at least sixteen or eighteen Months growth before they come to Maturity.

Sugar Canes, are a long Stalk about five or six feet in length, and an inch Diameter more or less, according to the goodness of the Soil, and Seasons; they are full of joints, two or three inches asunder, and therefore called

Canes. The Sprouts or flags, when full grown, are at least 8 or 9 feet in height; the Colour of the Cane top is grass green, and so is the Cane, until it ripens; and then it turns to a Straw or bright Yellow. It is covered with a Bark, and is somewhat hard in the inside, which is of a Spungy substance full of juices, and of a pleasant delicious flavour.

In Planting them, they are cut into pieces *of about 3 feet long*, and 4 or 5 of them laid in holes, of about 6 inches deep, in a straight line; and then covered very loosely with the Earth. Each joint produces many Sprouts: in good Seasons they appear in 14 days, and in three or four months, they are three feet high; though the Cane does not appear in less than [blank] months.

When the Canes are young, the care of the Planter is then to keep them clear of Weeds, which otherwise will grow among them, and Spoil their growth or destroy them, and the Roots must be examined, to see if any have failed, that they may be supplied in time. The Planter must also be mindfull to destroy the Rats, which breed in great numbers, and by gnawing and sucking the Canes render them unfit for making of Sugar; therefore they are picked out, when they are brought to the Mill, and thrown away, or they will taint the rest, and spoil the goodness of the Sugar. The Mundinga Negroes are very expert, and usefull in Catching and destroying of those Vermin; and therefore every Plantation has two or more of them, who have no other Employment when the Canes begin to ripen, for the Rats will not touch them when they are green; and for their Encouragement they have a Reward in Money or Rum for every Dozen heads they bring in, which makes them very assiduous; and thereby they prevent a great deal of damage.

When the Canes are ripe, which is known by the flags appearing above them, and their Colour, which is then the same with that of ripe Wheat, they are cut up by hand, with a Bill and after the tops and flags are chopped of[f] they are tied up in Bundles and carried to the Mill, in Carts or upon Horses or Mules; the latter is best, because the weight of the Carts often destroy, or hurt the roots of those, that are cut, and occasion the trouble of supplying them. The Cane tops and flags are saved and thrown to the Cattle, and is a very great support to them in Crop time[,] being very nourishing.

The Mills in this Island are generally wrought by Cattle, Horses or Mules, the latter are esteemed the best; Because they are hardy, of a quicker draught, and much easier Supported, than Cattle: for they will feed upon some bushes, and other Shrubs, which Cattle will not touch. There are also several Water-Mills, which are made after the English manner, but very few, if any, Wind-Mills; the Winds here, not being so Constant as in the Leeward Islands, where they generally blow night and day.

In the Cattle Mills, the Oxen, Mules or Horses are put into tackle, and turn by Sweeps or poles the middle Rowler, which is made of Wood and

Between 1756 and 1761, Thomas Craskell, chief engineer of Jamaica, and James Simpson, chief surveyor, conducted a detailed survey of Jamaica that resulted in the publication by Daniel Fournier in London in 1763 of three large maps, one for each of the colony's three counties. Each map was embellished with a finely drawn cartouche illustrating an important activity on the island. Shown here, the cartouche for the map of the County of Cornwall at the west end of the island depicts a windmill for grinding sugar with an ox-driven cart on the road next to it and an enslaved black man drawing water from a cistern with a white supervisor, whip in hand, presiding over him. Windmills were relatively rare in Jamaica, being restricted to the windier parishes on the north side of the island. (Library of Congress)

Cased with Iron; and being Cogg[e]d to others, at the upper end, turns them about. They all turn upon the same Center, made of brass or Steal. They are so easy; that a man taking hold of one of the poles or Sweeps, with one hand, may turn all the Rowlers about, but when the Canes are in, it is a good draught for Six Oxen, Mules or Horses. A Negro puts the Canes in on one side, and the Rowler draws them through on the other, where another Negro Stands to receive, and return them through the other side of the middle Rowler, which draws the other way. The bruised Cane is dried in the Sun, and made use of [as] a fuel under the Coppers; but it is [a] remarkably fierce and uncertain fire, much inferior to Wood, or Coals; nevertheless it is generally used, being a very great saving, Especially in those Plantations, that have not Wood in plenty, as in Liguinea and other places, and even where Wood is plenty it saves labour.

Under the Rowlers is a hollow place, which receives the juice, that is Squeezed from the Cane, and by leaden pipes or Gutters is conveyed into a Cistern, where it must not remain above 2 or 3 hours, least it turns Sower;

In 1749, the *Universal Magazine of Knowledge and Pleasure* published in London John Hinton's engraving, *A Representation of the Sugar-Cane and the Art of Making Sugar*, which provides a detailed look at the process of extracting and refining sugar in the West Indies with a white overseer directing three enslaved black people at a sugar mill and a boiling house. (Library of Congress)

from thence it is Conveyed through a Gutter into the Clarifier, and there boiled, until all the filth or gross matter rising at the top, is Skimmed off, from those Skimmings Rum is made, as will be shewn in its proper place. The Clarifier is the largest Copper, and as the liquor refines, it is taken out and put into a second Copper, and so into a 3, 4 and 5, and some into a 6 and 7th., all of different Sizes, and the last, being the least, is called the Tach, where it boils longest. It is continually kept boiling and stirring, till it comes to a Consistency. But after all, it would only be a Clammy Substance, without turning to a Grain, were it not for the Temper, which is thrown into it. The Ordinary Temper is unslacked lime, which the Boiler, as the Manager is called, proportions it to the bigness of the Copper, it is thrown into, and the nature of the liquor. Nor can any Sort of Muscovado Sugar be made without temper of some sort or other—for without it the juice of the Cane would never Coagulate and form itself into a Solid Body, nor acquire a Consistence, but remain a dull thick Syrup, of a gross heavy nature, neither pleasant nor wholesome. When the liquor rises up with a turbulent body, occasioned by the fermentation of the temper, and the heat of the fire, they throw in tallow, grease or Oyl, the quantity in proportion to the nature of the liquor, and its boiling or rising; this will immediately make it fall, though the Copper contains 250 or 300 gallons. From the tack, which is the last and least Copper, it is Conveyed into the cooling Cistern, made of Wood, and generally lined with Copper or Tin; here it remains till it thickens and is Cooled; When it is put into Pots, and removed to the Curing house, and set upon Pans called Drips, which receive the Molasses that drops from them. The Molasses is Conveyed into the Distilling House, and put into a Cistern; Sometimes it is boiled over again, and a Coarser sort of Sugar made of it, which is called Panulls. In 5 or 6 weeks the Sugar is commonly cured, but that in some measure depends on the Weather, for if it happens to be rainy, when they are at Work, it will not Cure kindly, and sometimes it occasions it to be moist and heavy. From the Curing House the Pots are carried to the Barbierees, as they are called; that is a Stage erected near it about 4 feet in height, and 12 feet square, where the Sugar is turned out, and the tops and bottoms chopped off, these are of a different Colour and quality; the top is of a light frothy Substance, and the bottom moist and heavy, they are therefore separated and mixed by themselves.

The difference in Muscovado Sugar as to the goodness of the Colour, and largeness of the grain, is owing to the nature of the Soil, the Art or Experience of the Boiler, and sometimes to the Seasons. The best sort, and the most Esteemed in England, is of a lively Whitish, or of a bright Straw Colour, with a large sparkling Grain: of this sort Jamaica has always been famous, very little being produced in the rest of the British or French Islands, which comes up to their first sort of Muscovado Sugar. Very little of this Commodity is Clayed, or refined in the Island, not even enough for their own Consumption; though I am informed there is a Sugar Baker lately set up, and has built proper Conveniencies at Kingston, and meets with Encouragement.

I have been the more particular in the manner of Raising and Manufacturing this Plant, as it is the principal Commodity of the British Commerce in America; and indeed, if we Consider the immense Value of what is annually Imported from this Island only; that it is the product of Labour, the Employment, it gives to our Navigation, Seamen and others; and the great Sums paid to his Majesty for Dutys; the Sugar Colonies, and more particularly this Island, may very justly be deemed equal to as many Gold or Silver Mines. It appears from hence, how Expensively and with what care and labour the Planters work up this Commodity; the Several Buildings, that are necessary, being raised and preserved at a great Expence, Subject to many Accidents, and especially from the great and Constant fires, they are obliged to keep during the Crop, for when they begin to work or grind their Canes, they Continue at it night and day, Sundays excepted, relieving their Servants, Negroes and Beasts every four hours.

The Skimings of the Coppers, and the drippings of the Pots, are pre-

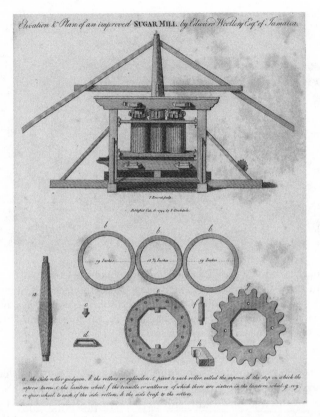

This image, entitled *An Elevation and Plan of an Improved Sugar Mill, by Edward Woolery, Esq. of Jamaica,* is here reproduced from Bryan Edwards, *The History, Civil and Commercial, of the British Colonies in the West Indies* (London, 1793), following p. 228.

served and improved, being Conveyed into Cisterns, as I have observed, where they ferment, and are then drawn by Pipes into Stills, in a House adjoining to the other Works, and is from thence called the Distilling House. Here they are distilled and rectifyed into a Spirit, well known by the name of Rum, which grows more and more into Use, is generally preferred to French brandy, and by many to Arrack. It is Certainly more wholesome than the former, and has many medicinal Virtues in it, which will make it more valued, as they come to be known, particularly in Ulcerous Cases, Colds, and Rheumatick pains; and the following Experiment will in some measure Evince, what I have asserted. Put a piece of Raw flesh into Rum, and it will be found to preserve it, whereas Brandy will by degrees waste and impair it.

A Sugar-Work is a great and Expensive thing; and cannot be settled un-

The cartouche for the 1763 Craskell-Simpson map of the County of Surry at the
east end of the island depicts many merchants and both black and white laborers
at a wharf loading sugar and other products onto ships. The buildings on the left
were probably commercial and storage buildings in which merchants also resided,
while that on the right seems to have been a tavern. (Library of Congress)

der 5 or £6000 Sterling, as there must be a great Strength of Negroes to
carry it on, beside Cattle, Horses, Mules, Wains, and very Costly buildings.
Whoever Settles one on Credit, and pays Eight p[er]C[ent] p[er] Annum,
the legal interest of the Island, must be a Slave during life, and his Son after him; unless Sugars bear a better price than they did from 1725 to 1736,
when they commonly sold from 14 to 25 [shillings] per [blank] which is
not 20 [shillings] at an Average, or unless some Encouragement be given
to it, by lessening the Duty. He must therefore be a man of Substance that
attempts to settle a Sugar work at once, and bring it to perfection in 3 or 4
Years, which is the shortest time necessary to bring it to Perfection though
some have made, and they may begin to make Sugar in 18 months or two
Years. But, the general method is to begin with 15 or 20 Negroes, who are
first employed to clear a piece of land, to build themselves houses, and to
plant provisions for their Subsistance; the Planter then opens more land,
and plants Ginger, Cotton or some other Commodity, that is raised with a
few hands; as he thrives he purchases more Negroes, clears more land; and
when he finds himself in a Condition, or able to attempt it by his Credit,
and the Assistance of Friends, he then goes upon settling a Sugar Work;
though some of them, in my time would have been much Richer men,
had they never attempted it, but Continued in the way in which they first
Set out, vizt. in raising Provisions and Garden Stuff for Sale, Ginger and
other Commodities. But, seeing the prosperous Condition of some of their

Neighbours, they were tempted to take the same measures, without considering their Ability, or the difference of their Soil, and other Advantages; for want of which they involved themselves in debt, and paying such high Interest, have not been able to Extricate themselves: nay some have had their Estates eaten up by that means, and the lowness of their produce in Europe. This ought to be a Caution to all Young Planters, how they proceed, and not to attempt things, that are not within their power and Ability.

Indigo comes next under consideration, as there was formerly great quantities made in this Island, and might still be made, was Encouragement given to it; for tho[ugh] Yallahs or St. David's, and Vere commonly Called Withy Wood, will not produce so well, as formerly, for want of the usual and necessary Seasons, yet there are many other parts of the Island very proper, and would yield as good, as any that is made in Hispaniola. It is, indeed Subject to many Accidents, which was some discouragement to the Planters; the most common is blasting, or a sort of Worm that will destroy the young Plants in one night, or in a few hours; also too much or too little Rain, for it is a very tender plant. But, the principal Reason which induced Several Planters to throw up their Indigo-Works, and go upon Sugar, was the high Duties that were laid upon that Commodity in England, which was in [blank] when that Commodity sold for [blank] and could bear such a high Duty, but the Case was quite altered when it began to be sold for 3 [shillings] and 3 [shillings] 6 [pence] p[er] [blank]. This was frequently Represented to the Government without obtaining any Relief, and tho[ugh] it was afterwards granted, by taking off the whole Duty, yet it was too late, most of our Indigo Planters having before thrown up their Works, as I observ[e]d; and the French only now Enjoy the benefit. This is not the single Instance, as many others can be given, of great advantages being lost to the Nation, by not giving timely Redress to such Branches of our Trade, as were under difficulties; and, I wish, it may not be the Case of some at this present time, which we are in danger of being supplanted in, as well as the others, by the French, who are become our greatest Rivals in Trade.

The Seed, from whence Indigo is raised, is round, of a yellowish Colour, not unlike a Tare without the husk, but somewhat larger. They are planted in holes at about a foot distance, in straight lines, between which they commonly plant Indian Corn. In good land and in proper Seasons, it will spring up, about 3 feet in height, and grow ripe in two months after it is planted. The Stalk is full of leaves, of a deep green colour, and will from its first sowing yield 5 or 6 Crops in a Year; but, this is dependant on, and according to, the goodness of the Land and Seasons.

When the Plant is ripe which is known by the leaf being full grown and ready to fall with its own Weight it is cut and Steeped in fats, made for that purpose, 24 hours, or more according to the Weather; the Water is then let out by taps, and Conveyed into Cisterns, where it is carefully beaten

Indigo was another minor staple that had been cultivated and processed in Jamaica since the last decades of the seventeenth century but became less common during the years of Knight's residence in the colony. Entitled *Indigoterie*, this French engraving, from a drawing by the author himself, comes from Jean Baptiste Du Tertre, *Nouveau voyage aux isles de l'Amerique*, 4 vols. (Paris, 1742), fold-out plate, vol. 1, following p. 268. It depicts an indigo-processing unit with a white overseer or planter presiding over six enslaved black men working at various stages of indigo production, including fields for the cultivation of the plant, the various descending processing pools, the drying sheds, and the site for draining the indigo. It also shows examples of the indigo plant and other vegetation. Items in the image are numbered for identification through a key at the top.

with boxes of a three Corner form, made tapering like a Sugar Pott without a bottom, & fixed to poles of 12 or 14 Feet long, untill it comes to a Consistency. In about 18 hours after, when it is fully set[t]led the Water that remains is drawn off by taps. The Cisterns are about nine feet square and three feet deep, with several taps to let out the Water. The Substance or Settlement at the bottom is put into bags, which are generally made of Oznaburgs about 3 feet in length, and a foot wide, and are hung up until all the liquid part has dripp[e]d out: it is then put into Boxes, 3 feet long and 15 inches wide, and a foot and half deep; these boxes are placed in the Sun but remov[e]d when it Rains and about 12 at noon, until the Extreme heat is over. The same is done every day, until it is Sufficiently dried or cured.

Cotton is likewise produced from the Seed, which is round and black, the Size of a small Pea, and is planted in the Months of October, and November. The Plants soon spring up, and with a good Season, will, in about 4 months be 5 or 6 feet high, and full of blossoms, which are of a bright yellow Colour and afterwards turn into Cods. These Cods, when they are ripe, open, and are full of Cotton, which is picked out by the hand. The Shrub or brush, (for it cannot be called a Tree) is then Cut down, within two inches of the ground, but shoots up again, spreads and flowers, in a greater degree, than at first; and will yield a Second Crop in October or November following, that is two Crops within the Year, for three Years or more; though they are generally Stocked up every third Year, because the Cotton then grows Coarser.

When the Shrub has done blooming, it is Cut down, as I Observed, not only to make the Root or Stock spread, which occasions it to Yield the more, but, that it might not grow too tall, and make it difficult to gather; for tho[ugh] it will fall on the ground, and it may be much easier picked up from thence, yet that is not so well; as it gathers dirt and Rubbish, and makes it difficult to be cleaned. The Seeds are worked out by what is called a Gin, which is a small Machine with two Wheels, set at Work by the foot, like a Turner's Wheel, and between the two Wheels are two Rollers, which are about two feet long, and an Inch diameter, These are turned round by Springs, draw in the Cotton which is put by hand, and throw out the Seeds.

This Commodity is subject to many Accidents, too much or too little Rain, a Worm that makes a kind of Web on it, and the Wind, which sometimes will blast and destroy it in one Night. It is a Common thing to see a whole Field of Cotton look fair and promising one day, and the next morning to find it all blasted by the Wind, or destroyed by the Worm.

Piemento, commonly called All-spice, or Jamaica Pepper, is a natural production of this Island, for it was found by the Spaniards in the Woods. The Trees are from 20 to 30 feet from the Ground to the tops of the uppermost branches. It is Straight and about 7 or 8 Inches diameter, covered with a Smooth bark of a grey Colour; The leaves are about 4 inches long and 2 inches broad in the middle, decreasing at both ends to a point, smooth, and of a shining deep green colour; the ends of the twigs are branched into bunches of flowers; these afterwards become berries, which are greenish when small, but, when full grown and ripe are black, and Contain two Seeds, in a green Aromatick pulp. The trees generally grow, or are transplanted on hilly ground on the North side, of the Island, where they thrive best, and most of this Commodity is produc[e]d. It flowers in June and July, earlier or later according to their Situation and the Seasons. They grow ripe much sooner in clear open ground, than in Woody land; and there is no difficulty in curing the fruit, or preserving the Trees. When

Cotton was yet another minor staple of importance in the Jamaican economy. Entitled *Raccolta del cotone*, this engraving by Giuseppe Maria Terreni illustrates the process of cotton production in the West Indies, showing enslaved black people picking, sorting, spinning, and storing cotton in bales ready to be packed onto the ship in the harbor. The image comes from *Il gazzettiere Americano* (Leghorn, 1763), 2:following p. 234. This work, an Italian translation of an English translation of Diderot's *Encyclopédie*, was the first comprehensive geographical dictionary of America in Italian.

they are ripe the twigs are pulled of[f] with the fruit, and are Separated, tho[ugh] they often fall of[f], and are picked up from the ground. They are then for many days spread upon Mats and expos[e]d to the Sun, often turning them, by which means they become wrinkled, and from a green change to a very dark brown Colour, when they are perfectly cured, and fit to send to market.

These Trees, as I observed, are not difficult to be preserved, nor Subject to any other accident than great Winds; and they often spring from the Seed, which falls from the trees, and takes Root; from whence they are transplanted to other places. They produce in two Years from the Planting of the Seed, though no great quantity, but increase every Year until they are 7 or 8 Years old, without care or trouble. The smallest sort, and most fragrant are esteemed the best.

It is deservedly reckon[e]d, says S[i]r Hans Sloan, the best and most temperate, mild and Innocent of all Spices, fit to come into great use and to gain more ground, than it has of the East India Commodities of this kind, almost all of which it surpasses by promoting the digestion of meat, attenuating tough humours, moderately heating and strength[e]ning the Stomach, expelling Wind, and doing those friendly Offices to the Bowels, which we Expect from Spices.[1]

Cocoa, was formerly the principal Commodity of Jamaica, and for many Years after it was taken by the Spaniards, but, the high Duty and Excise laid thereon, and Sugar at that time yielding more profit, Occasioned the Planters to throw up their Cocoa Walks, and turn them into Sugar Works. Notwithstanding which, many of them Continued to plant some for their own use, Others for Sale, and many are now going upon it, in hopes of Encouragement from the Legislature, by a Bounty or lessening the Duty and Excise; and very Considerable Quantities will be made in a few Years, if they are not disappointed in their Reasonable Expectations. It is Certainly the Interest of Great Britain to give them such Encouragement, as is usual in the like Cases, because it may be reckon[e]d a Native Product, and will yearly save a Considerable Sum, which is now laid out with the French and Spaniards.

It is indeed a tender Plant, Subject to many Accidents, and doth not produce in less than 4 or 5 years, or come to perfection under Seven Years. But, then it yields great profit, and continues bearing many Years, unless some Accident happens to it. However, these are discouragements, and it is not by any means a proper Commodity for Young Planters, who have not something else to depend upon, and to Support them in the mean time.

The Cocoa Trees are regularly planted in Walks about four feet distance, and Carefully kept Clear of Weeds. The Trunks of them, when they are full grown, are commonly about 5 feet high and 4 inches diameter, and 15 feet from the ground to the tops of the uppermost Branches: the Bark is almost smooth, and of a grey Colour. It is a Tree of singular Beauty, and delightful to look upon. Its large, broad, Oblong leaf falls back, and hangs with a kind of Native fondness to its Original, and like so many Shields defend the tender Plant from injuries. The Colour is a deep green, and looks Solemn and grave. It delights in Shade, and requires a great deal of Mois-

---

1. Sir Hans Sloane, *A Voyage to the Islands Madera, Barbados, Nieves, S. Christophers and Jamaica, with the Natural History of the Herbs and Trees, Four-Footed Beasts, Fishes, Birds, etc.*, 2 vols. (London, 1707–25). In his description of native plants, drugs, trees, and bushes throughout this part, Knight draws heavily on Sloane's first volume of this work and pp. 1–187 of the second volume.

ture, as well as to be preserved from the Winds, for which Reason they are generally planted in Valleys, or bottoms, between the Mountains, and near the sides of Rivers, with a Plantain Tree, by the side of it, so that the Rows Consist of one of each Sort planted Alternately. These Attendant Trees, as they may be called, or as the Spaniards call them Madre de Cocoa, that is the Mother of Cocoa, are different from any of the kind in Colder Countries, and will be more particularly describ[e]d hereafter, having a larger and broader leaf than any other Tree in the World, for they not only by that means give a Shade, and prevent too great an Exhalation in the day time, but in the night they lodge the enriching Dews, and retail the same to the neighbouring Plant.

Out of the branches of the Tree, grows a very small flower, of a very pale purple Colour, and from thence arises the Fruit; which is about the bigness of a man's fist when full grown, and ripe, biggest in the middle, and pointed at both ends.

The Nuts grow in the fruit or pods, of greenish, Red and yellow Colours, and about thirty in each Pod; they are orderly Set in a sweet slimy Substance, to preserve, as well as to Nourish them when they are young and tender.

The Nut or Seed is planted the latter end of March. In November following the Plant appears, and within the Year will be three feet high, but does not begin to bear in less than 4 or 5 years, after they are planted, the Tree then encreases every Year, till it is 7 or 8 Years old, and Continues bearing for 25 or 30 Years or more. Each Tree generally bears from two to ten pounds of Nuts; and Every Acre will produce 1000 lb weight yearly, or more, and as the Charges of gathering and housing the Fruit are small, the profit of a Cocoa Walk must be considerable.

When they are ripe they are laid in heaps to Sweat for 3 or 4 days, in order to Cure them, the Cods are then open[e]d, the Nuts taken out, and put into a trough cover[e]d with a Plantain leaf, where they sweat again about 20 days. They are then set out in the Sun to dry, for 3 or 4 Weeks together, until they become of a dark Reddish Colour; when they are perfectly cured.

Ginger is planted in trenches about 4 or 5 inches deep and about 6 inches asunder and in 12 months after, it covers the whole ground.

When the Stalks and leaves are withered 'tis fit to dig up, which is done with a hough, and the Stalks or Strings cleared with a knife, then it is washed and boiled in a Kettle, for a Quarter of an hour, and afterwards expos[e]d to the Sun and dried. This is, what is Called, the black Ginger: the White Sort is made so only by Scraping its Outward Membrane. There is also a white sort prepared as the black, only it is boiled in lime Water, which makes it, as I have been informed, not so whol[e]some.

Ginger is preserved, by drawing when it is 3 or 4 Months old, and after

Gingembre

Well before coffee, ginger had been and would continue to be an important staple crop for Jamaica planters with limited resources. Entitled *Gingembre*, this French engraving shows a ginger plant with its rhizomes and is taken from Jean Baptiste Labat (1663–1738), *Nouveau voyage aux isles de l'Amerique*, 4 vols. (Paris, 1742), 3:following p. 92.

'tis cleaned, it is Soak[e]d in fair Water, 24 hours, then shifted and boiled 5 or 6 times; the outward Membrane is then pared off, soaked in fair Water and put into a Syrup made of refined Sugar; it is also Shifted 3 or 4 times into other Syrups; for the Ginger draws the Sugar and leaves the Water, which is thrown away; the last time it is boiled over again, and then it is fit for use: the dry preserved Ginger is done the same way, only expos[e]d to the Sun, until it is dry.

Coffee is but a late production of Jamaica, the first Seeds for Planting being brought there in 1728, and for some years only planted for amusement in Gardens, People not imagining, it would thrive and produce in the manner it has done, insomuch that it will become a very Considerable Article, when they fall into the right Method of curing it, which, it is to be hop[e]d, they will soon do, as some lately brought from thence proves very good.

The Seeds are at first planted in beds, afterwards transplanted in Rows, four feet distance and 5 feet in breadth between each Row. The Tree or Shrub, (for few exceed Seven feet in height) produces in eighteen months, from the Seed, in small quantities; and continues bearing 7 or 8 Years. The leaves are about 4 Inches in length and 2 in breadth, pointing at each end and of a deep green Colour. The Blossom is like that of an Orange, which afterwards turns into a fruit the bigness of a black Cherry; It is at first green, but when ripe it turns to a dark red, and is of a very Sweet luscious tast[e], which makes the Rats fond of them and destroy great quantities. The fruit afterwards dries, grows wrinkled, and changes to a dark Colour; when they drop, or are gently shaked off, and opened; each Contains two Seeds.

Nothing can be more delightful than a Coffee Plantation; the Trees, as

In the 1720s, Governor Nicholas Lawes experimented with coffee cultivation, which proved to be especially suitable for growing in higher altitudes, and within a decade coffee had become an important minor staple crop and a significant export. This image is taken from John Ellis, *An Historical Account of Coffee with an Engraving and Botanica* (London, 1774), frontispiece.

I observed, being regularly planted, and generally about the same height, the leaves always green and the branches regularly set on *Each* Side alternately above each other; and Especially when they are in blossom, and full of ripe green fruit as they often are. It is Computed, that an Acre contains 1106 Trees or Shrubs, and that they produce, at a medium, after the first bearing, two pound weight Yearly one with another. After the land is cleared, and planted, six or eight Negroes, who are incapable of any laborious Employment are Sufficient to manage 10 or 12 Acres, and to raise Provisions sufficient for their own Subsistance; and as the charges in raising, gathering, and carrying to their Domestick Market is inconsiderable, a Poor man with 5 or 6 Negroes, and a small tract of Land, may, with Industry, be able to support himself, and his family. And it is of this further advantage, that it grows best in Mountainous places, where the difficulty and Expence of Carriage render it impracticable, at least the Profits will not answer in Raising Sugar Works, or Planting Ginger, Cotton, or such like weighty or bulky Commodity's.

Fustick is a natural production of Jamaica and grows in Common with other Trees, but Chiefly on the north side of the Island, where there is still great quantities growing.

The Tree is Commonly very Straight, and from 30 to 40 feet in height from the ground, to the top of the uppermost branches, according to the age or Standing. It has many long great Roots, by which it is firmly fixed in the ground, and not easily blown down. The bark is of a light brown, and the leaves of a rough dark green Colour, largest towards the Stalk, and ending in a point. It bears a kind of a fruit or berry about the bigness of a nutmeg, and Contains Several small flat Seeds, of a brown Colour. They are milky and unpleasant before they are Ripe, but of a luscious tast[e], when they come to Maturity. They are Coveted by the Negroes, but the White Inhabitants never touch them unless out of Curiosity.

This Tree is of a quick growth, for in 7 or 8 Years they will be 20 Feet high or more, and will rise to that height from the Roots if they are not dug up, after the Trees are Cut down.

Logwood is a knotted, Crooked Wood, and the bark which is Chipped off is of a dull Colour. It thrives in Sandy ground, but grows best in Lagunos or boggy Land. It hath a small leaf of a deep green Colour, and not unlike a Box. The Branches are covered with a smooth Ash coloured thin Bark, and have near the leaves sharp prickles almost an inch long. It bears a flower of a yellowish brown Colour, which becomes a kind of a husk, of a light green Colour, and Shaped like the end of a Spear; from whence comes the Seeds, which are small and flat, and being blown off the Trees takes Root, will soon spread and Cover the ground round about.

The Seeds were brought from Campeachy in 1714, and were first planted by Mr. George Goodwin in Caboritta where it throve well, and induced many others Since to plant it; so that in a few Years, they will probably produce great quantities if not sufficient for the Consumption of England. Some make hedges of it, as it will cut in Shapes like quick set, when it is young. Divers parcels have been imported into England, and it proves as well, and is not known from Campeachy wood.

Tobacco likewise grows in this Island, which was famous for it in the time of the Spaniards. But, as the Planters are not allowed to import it into England, they do not plant more than is Sufficient for their own Consumption; And it is thought, the best seed is lost or degenerated, as they do not make so good as they did formerly. They have two Sorts, the Oronoque, and Spanish; the Seeds of which are Sown in Beds; and when the leaves are two inches long, they are drawn, and transplanted at four feet distance one way, and three and half the other. They must be kept clear of Weeds; and when grown about a foot high, and ready to shoot out the Stalks, or tops, they are snipt of[f], that the leaves may grow the better. When they are full grown and in Vigour, they are gathered and hung up in the Shade to dry.

The Wild Cinnamon, commonly called *Cortet Winteranus*, also grows in this Island. The Tree is from 20 to 30 feet in height, and from 6 to 8 inches diameter. The branches and twigs hanging downwards make a very Com[e]ly top. The Bark consists of two parts, one outward, and another inward; the outward Bark is about the thickness of a Shilling, of an Ash or Grey Colour, with some white Spots upon it; the inward Bark is thicker than Cinnamon, and about the thickness of a Crown piece, of a more biting Aromatick tast[e], something like that of Cloves, and not glutinous like Cinnamon, but dry and crumbling between the Teeth. All the parts of this

Tree, when fresh are hot, Aromatick, and biting to the tast[e]; but no other part is used but the Bark, which is cured, without any difficulty, only by letting it dry in the Shade.

The *Lignum Vitae* Tree is generally about 15 or 16 feet in height and 6 or 8 inches diameter, with a round beautiful top; the leaves being always green, even in the driest time that ever was known. It has a smal[l] thick leaf, of a light green Colour: the flowers or blossoms blue, and the berry Yellow, flat and shaped like a small bean.

The Gum of this Tree, which is well known by the name of *Gum Guiai-cum*, often comes out of itself, but more abundantly, when the Tree is cut and slashed.

The Hog Gum Tree, is a tall high Tree, which grows only in the Mountains; the wood of it is soft and white, with a fine grain; so that it is easily work[e]d up. The Gum of this Tree, works out of itself but more abundantly, when the Tree is cut and Slashed.

It is like Bees Wax, but afterwards softer; and changes the Colour to a light Yellow. The Virtues of it are very little known in England, but it is in great use among the Negroes, who apply it to green wounds, Bruises, Swellings, Rheumatick pains, and even in the Gout; and though it does not make an absolute Cure in the last mentioned Case, yet it gives great ease and Relief.

It is said that the Virtues of it were first discovered by the Wild Hogs, who rolled themselves upon it, when they were wounded and by that means were healed or Cured.

Beside these, there are many other Valuable Commodities, Drugs and Woods, which are very particularly delineated and described by S[i]r Hans Sloan, in His *Natural History of Jamaica*; and many others might still be discover[e]d, some of which are only known to the Negroes; But as they are not within my Province, I shall not pretend to give any further detail of them, not having made any Experiment, for want of Skil[l] and knowledge in Simples, which is an Art or Science very little known, except by those, who make it their profession.

And therefore I shall proceed to give a Description of the principal Fruits and Roots of this Island; which are commonly made use of instead of Bread.

The Plantain is different from any thing of the kind in Europe, and far exceeds Potatoes in Nourishment, and Salubrity; for when green it is good food, boiled or Roasted, commonly eat instead of Bread, and is astringent and useful in ordinary Fluxes: but when ripe, it is a delicious Fruit Eaten Raw, boiled, Roasted or fried; and makes very good Tarts. It is very much Esteemed by all Europeans, as well as the Natives of America, and the Spaniards give it the preferance of all other Fruits except Avocato Pears, as being more Nourishing and conducive to Health. The Negroes, when they have neither Flesh nor Fish to eat with it, make Sauce with bell or Cod pepper, Salt and lime juice, which takes of[f] the Sweetness, gives it a relish and makes it more Savory. Sometimes by way of change, they eat a green plantain roasted, and one that is Raw and full ripe together, which Serves instead of Bread and Butter; at other times they take 5 or 6 full ripe Plantains, mash them together into a lump, and boil them in a bag, like Pudding; which they call Buffjacket. The green Plantains sliced thin, dried in the Sun, and grated makes a Sort of Flour, which eats well made into Puddings, and a Ripe Plantain sliced and dried in the Sun, may be preserved a great while, and eats sweet and pleasant not unlike a Fig. The Negroes in Guinea, as well as the Indians in America, preserve both sorts in that manner; or by mashing those that are ripe, moulding them into lumps, and gently drying them over a Fire. The Musquito Indians make a drink of them, which they call Muislaw and is sweet, pleasant and Nourishing, not unlike lambs wool; and is made after this manner. They take 10 or 12 full ripe Plantains, and mash them well in a Trough; then they pour in two gallons of Water, which in two hours will ferment and froth like Wort: in four hours it is fit to drink, and may be bottled off, but it will not keep above 24 or 30 hours, without turning sharp, and being put into the Sun, will make good Vinegar. This Drink is cool and pleasant, as I observed, but Windy; and so is the ripe Fruit, when it is Eaten Raw; but not when it is roasted or Boiled.

The Tree at its full growth is about 14 or 15 feet high, and about two feet round. The leaves, when they first shoot out, are about a foot in length, and half a foot in Breadth, and the Stem, that bears it is no thicker than a man's Finger; but when they are full grown, they are 6 or 7 feet in length, from 18 Inches to two feet in breadth, and the Stem as big as a man's Arm. These Trees are not raised from Seed; for they have not any, but from the Suckers which Spring out of the Roots in great Numbers; for they bear but once, and when they have done bearing and the Fruit begins to ripen, the Tree decays; and then it is cut down. Those Suckers being drawn and transplanted, as they generally are, bear in 14 or 15 months, but when they stand in their own Native Soil, they produce Fruit in 12 months. As the Young leaves shoot out on the inside, the old leaves spread off, and their tops hang rounding with the ends or points downwards, till they decay or rot off, but young leaves, at the same time, springing out at the top, make the Tree always look green, and flourishing.

The Trunk of this Tree seems to be made up of many thick Skins, Rinds or Coats growing one over another; and when it is full grown, there springs out of the top a strong stem, harder in Substance than any other part of the Body. This Stem shoots forth out of the heart of the Tree, is as big, and as long as a man's Arm; and full of Blossoms, which are of a purple Colour, and hang downwards till they fall of[f], and then the fruit appears. They turn up, as they grow in Rows from the Stalk like the grapple of a Boat, and in that manner 3 or 4 Rows on each Stalk, containing 15 or 20 Plantains, and in the whole 60 or more upon the Stalk or Bunch.

The Fruit is inclosed in a thick rind or Cod, it is from 5 to 9 or 10 Inches in length round and of a proportionable thickness, the largest being as thick as a man's Wrist, for there are several sorts and Sizes. It is of a deep green Colour, but when full ripe soft and of a bright Yellow: the inclos[e]d fruit is not harder than Butter in Winter, and much of the same Colour. It is of a delicate tast[e], all pure pulp, without Seed, Kernel or Stone.

The Planter, when he intends to settle a Sugar Work, or any other Plantation, after he has raised houses for himself and his Negroes, commonly begins with a good Plantain Walk, as they call it; where the Trees are planted in Rows and make very Pleasant, cool and Shady Groves: as His Family or Number of Negroes increases, He enlarges the Plantain Walk; and keeps one Negro, or more Constantly there as Watches, and to prune the Trees, and gather the Fruit, as He sees convenient, or is directed; for the Trees continue bearing, one under another all the Year. They thrive only in a rich fat mould, for they will not grow in a poor, sandy or gravelly Soil. They must also be Shelter[e]d from the Winds; for their Trunks or Bodies are not sufficient to Support their large tops or heads, with such long and broad leaves as I have described, and are often blown down in high Winds. In the Mountainous Parts of the Island they are therefore planted near Rivers, or in the Valleys or Spaces that lie between the Mountains.

This Tree, is not only of great use as the Fruit is good for food, But, the Body is very serviceable for Cloaths; being as Capt[ai]n Dampier[2] Informs us made use of and Manufactured at Mindanao, and other Parts of the West Indies; Where, He says, when they intend to make Cloath of it, they cut it close to the ground, then they cut off the top, leaving the Trunk 8 or 10 feet long, from which they Strip off 3 or 4 of the outer Rinds or Coats, and as these are all thickest towards the Lower End, the Trunk becomes then in a Manner all of one Bigness, and of a whitish Colour. Having done this they split the Trunk in two as near as they can, and leave them in the Sun for two or three days; in which time part of the juicy Substance of the Tree evaporates, and the ends appear full of threads. The Women, whose employment it is to make the Cloath, take hold of those threads one by one, which rend away easily from one end of the Trunk to the other, in bigness like whited brown thread; for the Threads, are Naturally all of one and the same determinate bigness, and consequently the Cloths made of them are all of one Substance or fineness. They are made in Pieces of 7 or 8 yards long each but the Cloth is Stubborn when New, wears out soon, and when wet grows a little Slimy.

It is not improbable, but time and Experience may make some Improvements, in this manufacture; and it is with that View and Expectation, that I have been the more particular in this description.

---

2. See Capt[ain] Dampier's *Voyage round the World.* P. 315. —*Author.* William Dampier, *A New Voyage Round the World* (London, 1697). —*Ed.*

The Bonano Trees are like the Plantain Trees in shape, and not easily distinguishable from them; only the leaves are something less, and the Bodies here and there have some blackish spots. The Blossom [is] no bigger than a large Rose Bud, of a fine purple and Ash colour mixed; and the Fruit is in shape much like a Plantain but less, none exceeding 5 or 6 inches in length; they likewise grow in the same manner in bunches; but stand outright and do not turn up as the others do. The fruit is much sweeter than the Plantain, and therefore the Negroes seldom eat it, nor any, or but few other fruits that are Sweet. It is Remarkable of this fruit, that when it is Cut sideways there plainly appears the figure of a Cross within the inside, for which Reason the Spaniards never suffer it to be cut downwards. They have a pleasant and delicious Taste, and make exceeding good Frittars, the Flavour being much beyond that of an Apple.

The Papa Tree has a very Slender trunk and is twenty feet or more in height, with a small Beautiful round top of branches. The fruit is much larger than an Orange. They are of a light green Colour, but when ripe, it is yellow on the out as well as the inside and Contains many black seeds. When young and green, it is boiled with Pork, or salted Meats, as we do turnips; but when ripe, it is eaten as fruit, and much coveted by the Negroes. There are two or three sorts, and one of them is in Shape and Size much like a Mango; these are pickled in the same manner as the East India Mango, and are not inferior to them, nor unlike in Tast[e].

The Cassava Tree or Shrub, is about four feet high, full of leaves, 5 or 6 inches long and an Inch broad, not unlike an Ash leaf, and of a dark green Colour. The Roots of which the Bread is made are large and round. They are cut into pieces, and 20 pound weight, more or less, put into a bag made of Oznaburghs or Coarse linnen, and laid between two boards with great weights or Stones upon them, to Squeeze the juice out of them. The juice so Squeezed out is Certain Poison, for if any Animal whatever drinks of it, (as many have done, when no other water was near) they are suddenly seized with Strong tremblings and Shiverings, and in a short time they fall into a mortal Lethargy; it having much the same effect as Hemlock; for they seldom live above eight hours after. I am credibly informed, that Hogs and some other Creatures eat the plant or Root, even before its being Squeezed, without any prejudice; and yet the juice by itself is mortal even to them. But no Man, I ever heard of dare try the Experiment in Regard to Mankind. When it has been well squeezed or pressed in the manner I mentioned they Soak it sometime in Water, to free it entirely of the juice, and spread it upon a Cloth in the Sun, for some days, until it is perfectly dried: they then grate and sift it; the meal is baked upon a Stone, or piece of Iron, pressed and formed into the size and Shape, they would have it; when one side has been Sufficiently baked, they turn it, and so alternately until they think it sufficient. The finest sort is generally of the size, shape and thickness of a pancake; but the common sort much larger, thicker and

Coarser. It is eaten with meat instead of Bread, makes very good puddings, and is esteemed wholesome and Nourishing.

There is also another Sort, the Root of which is not so large, nor its juice poisonous; this, Called the sweet Cassava, is frequently eaten, and esteem[e]d delicious, nourishing, and wholesome; but I never tasted of it.

Yams is a Provision, of the nature of a Potato, dug out of the ground, but much larger; for they weigh from one to eight pound weight, and some more, and before they are washed, and the Skin or rind is pared off, is not unlike the Stumps or pieces of the Roots of Trees. There are two Sorts, the White, and purple; the latter is the most esteemed; they are boiled or Roasted and Eaten with Meats, instead of Bread, but Relish best, and are most proper with Salted Meats, being in themselves very fresh.

They also make very good puddings, and eat well with Butter, and are generally dressed one of these two ways for sick People and Children, being very nourishing, light and Easy of digestion, and therefore proper for Suppers, for People of all sorts and Conditions.

When they are planted, they cut off the heads or tops, and plant them about 6 inches in the ground. They have small black seed, but the producing them from the Seed is seldom made use of, because they are not of so quick a Growth in this as in the other way. They soon shoot out, and spring up into a Vine, which runs upon Sticks; and when that Withers, which it does in about 12 months, after it is planted, it is known, they are come to Maturity, and are fit to dig up; and under every Vine is one large Yam, and generally three or four small ones.

Potatoes they have likewise of several sorts, and in great plenty, vizt. the Spanish Potatoes, the White, and the Yellow. The latter is very Sweet, and when boiled or Roasted, may more properly be eaten as a sort of Fruit, than Bread. The English, or Irish sort of Potatoes are also produced in the Mountains.

But, however bountiful Nature has been in those various Soils, and valuable Products, the Planters cannot be much commended with Regard to good Husbandry, in cultivating, manuring, and improving of Lands: for if a piece of Ground proves unkindly, or when it is much worn, and does not produce well, they throw it up, clear and plant another, without using any Art or Labour to improve the first. Nor do they take any pains or Care, to raise Gardens, Orchards, Groves or Shady Walks, so necessary and useful in this part of the World; nor any conveniencies which serve to make life Easy and Comfortable, and would render the Island more Pleasant and delightful, as well as more Healthful. For nothing is more Common, than to See some of the finest fruits in the World, such as the best Gardens in England cannot pretend to, grow in the Hedges, and in the Fields neglected and uncultivated, vizt. Oranges, Lemons, Shadocks, Cashews, and other sorts in great Plenty, and divers Trees, which grow on the Continent and produce Drugs, Balsams, Spices and Bark, might be transplanted from thence and other parts, and Cultivated here; but I am sorry to say, things of this kind are seldom thought on, or any thing more, than merely the improvement of Sugar, and other common Products. Nor is it improbable, that the Lagunes, Swamps, and boggy lands, might be drained and improved to very great advantage as the Soil must undoubtedly be very fat, Rich, and productive of Rice, Wheat and other Grain, and of all sorts of Garden Stuff, which have been planted in divers places in the Mountains, with Success. Collo[nel] Charles Price[3] has lately shewn, what may be done, by Art and Labour, in draining 300 Acres or Morass or boggy land, at Sixteen Mile-walk, which was useless, and is now in Canes, the best and most profitable part of his Plantation; and in promoting not only by a generous Subscription, but giving his Assistance in Person, in making a Coach or Cart Road to Sixteen mile Walk, which was thought impracticable, having been many Years scarcely passable for two Horsemen abreast, and in some places exceeding dangerous.

The draining of such Lands, would be exceeding advantageous in many Respects; and more particularly in regard to health; for I am not singular in opinion, that the Noisom[e] Smells, and Vapours arising out of those Lagunes, and boggy Lands, are very noxious, and prejudicial to human Bodies, and often the Cause of many diseases and disorders. This will not be thought a needless digression, since such hints or Observations, may Contribute towards raising a Publick Spirit amongst the Planters, and Consequently towards promoting the improvement and advantage of the Island.

Beside the Fruits, which are natural to this part of the World, they have some European Sorts, particularly Apples, Mulberries, and Strawberries, and the Mountains are productive of others, would they Cultivate and promote the Art of Gardening, and Agriculture. Those which are more peculiar and Natural to the Country, I shall give a particular description, of; and are as follow

Oranges thrive exceedingly in this Island, and are in very great plenty. They were first brought into this Island by the Spaniards, and are planted from the Seeds, and generally transplanted; they produce fruit in two or three Years, and when full grown, are from 20, to 25 feet in height.

Some Planters, that are curious, set them regularly in Walks, or Avenues to their Houses; which are exceeding pleasant being always covered with Leaves, and either in blossom or loaded with green and ripe fruit. There is properly but two Sorts, China, and Seville, for the Sour is only a degenerate kind by being planted or fallen into bad ground, but always in 3 or four

---

3. Sir Charles Price (1708–1772), born in Jamaica, studied at Trinity College, Oxford, and was a prominent member of the Jamaica Assembly from 1732 to 1770 and often its Speaker after 1743. One of Jamaica's largest landowners, he was knighted in 1768. For a detailed portrait of his life, see Michael Cration and James Walvin, *A Jamaica Plantation: The History of Worthy Park, 1670–1970* (Toronto, 1970), 72–94.

times planting turns sweet. All of them are larger, and have a thicker Coat or rind, than those, which are brought to England from Spain; the China, are also Sweeter, and not so apt to Surfeit.

The Lemon is a small Tree, or rather a Shrub, and seldom above 5 or 6 feet in height. The Fruit is also larger and the rind or Coat thicker, than those, that are brought from Spain, and Portugal, to England.

The Citron is also a small Tree, and the Fruit so large and Weighty, that the branches are not able to Support them, when they are full grown, but bend them down almost to the ground. Of the rind of this fruit, the famous Cordial Water is made, & also Succads or Sweetmeats.

The Shadock [grapefruits], is likewise a small Tree; but the branches are stronger than the other. The fruit is larger than a man's head, and shaped within, as well as without, like an Orange. The rind is a light yellow Colour, and half an inch thick. There are two sorts, the one red within and the other white: the former is the best; and they are deservedly esteemed one of the finest fruits in the World. The Seeds were had first from Barbadoes; and tis said, they were brought to that Island from India (where they are called purple noses) by one Capt[ain] Shadock, who happened to touch there in his passage home, and in Compliment to him were called after his name.[4]

The Avocato Tree, is as big as a large baking Pear Tree, the bark is of a dark, blackish Colour, and Smooth; the leaves are large, and of an Oval shape. The fruit, or rather food, for it is extremely nourishing, is shaped like a Lemon, but much larger, and of a light green Colour, but turns to a dull, disagreeable red when it is full ripe. They are seldom fit to Eat, until they have been gathered two or three days, when they become soft, and the Skin or rind is easily peeled of[f]. The Substance is of a Yellowish green Colour (soft as butter and may not improperly be called Vegetable Marrow) within which is one large Stone, as big as a Horse-plumb. The tast[e] of this fruit, is pleasant, but when mixed with Sugar, and a little lime or lemon juice, is exceeding delicious; though some eat it with Salt, and a Roasted Plantain; of which the Common People and the Negroes, make a good Meal. They are every way wholesome, as well as nourishing, and in very great esteem among the Spaniards, more particularly the Friars, for those Reasons, and as tis said, because they are a great provocative; tho[ugh] this perhaps [is] only an Imaginary Effect.

The Cashue Tree is as large as a Mulberry Tree, with a thick Substantial body; the branches spreading out on every side; the leaves broad round and thick; so that 50 persons or more may set under the shade of one, that is full grown, and be covered from a very great Shower of Rain. The Seed or Stone must be set in a particular manner (or it will not grow) that is to say

---

4. Allegedly, Captain Philip Chaddock from the East India Company left seeds for the plant in Barbados, probably sometime after 1649.

in a hole about 5 or 6 inches deep, and the thick end downwards they often produce fruit in 12 months, though no great Quantity; but in 4 or 5 years they will yield several bushels; and Continue bearing two or three months; for it is common to see blossoms, green, and ripe fruit on them at the same time. It is also Remarkable of this Fruit, that the Seed or Stone shoots out of the blossoms at the ends of the branches; it appears some time before the Fruit, and is shaped like a bean, about the same bigness, but fuller, rounder, and of a dark Olive Colour.

The Fruit is about the bigness of a Quince, but of a different shape and Colour, being fuller and rounder at the end where the Stone or Seed grows, than at the Stem. It grows Tapering, and is about 5 Inches long, tho[ugh] some are shorter and of a Rounder shape. The Stone grows on the outside of the further end of the Fruit instead of being in the Heart, as other Seeds and Fruit Stones are, so that the Fruit is placed between the Stone and the Branch. The rind or Coat is exceeding thin; before they are ripe, they are all of a deep green, but they then turn to a Red, or a Straw Colour; for there are two sorts, the latter most esteemed, particularly the small round sort. The inside is white soft and Spungy, full of juice, which is often Squeezed into Punch (the fruit being first Roasted) and gives it a very agre[e]able flavour. The fruit itself is delicious, having a tart pleasant tast[e], and leaves an agre[e]able roughness on the tongue. They are no ways surfeiting, but so cooling and wholesome in their nature, that they are allow[e]d by the Physicians to be eaten in the highest fevers. They are also esteemed to be very good in dropsical Cases. The Kernel of the Stone is full of an Oil, which will blister the mouth upon biting it, when it is Raw, but when Roasted it broils out, and the inside eats much like a Chesnut.

The Mamme Tree is very large, and streight bodied, without Knots, or even limbs for 20 or 25 feet; The head spreads into many small limbs and branches, which grow thick and close together. The Bark is of a dark grey Colour rough and appears chopped.

The Fruit is round, and as big as a Child's head, covered with a thin rind or Coat of a disagreeable grey Colour; but when ripe, the rind is of a deep Yellow, tough, and will peal of[f] like leather. It is brittle before it be full ripe, and the juice white and clammy; but then it changes Yellow, or the Colour of Carrots; and in the middle are two or more large rough flat Stones, of the bigness of an Almond, and of a dark disagreeable Colour. The Fruit has an agre[e]able, pleasant smell, as well as taste. It is a wild fruit which generally grows in the Mountains; and is seldom raised or Cultivated in Gardens or the Low Lands. When this Fruit ripens, and falls off the Trees, the Wild Hogs are fattest, and most in Season; and their feeding upon such like fruits, is the Reason of their flesh being so much preferred to the tame Sort.

The Mamme Sapota, is different from the other, the Tree not being so large and tall, the fruit not so round, nor bigger than a small Orange. The rind is thin and brittle; the inside or Substance of a deep red, and the Stone is of the Shape and bigness of a Pidgeon's Egg and of a shining blackish Colour. The Kernell has a pleasant bitter taste not unlike an Appricock Stone. This is also a Wild fruit, which grows in the Mountains, and is a common food for the Wild Hogs.

The Naseberry, or Sapotilla Tree is generally straight bodied, and from 20 to 30 feet to the branches; covered with a dark brown bark. The leaves thick set, of a dull green Colour and about 3 or 4 inches long.

The Fruit is round, the bigness and Colour of a Russeting Pear; When it is green, or first gathered, it is hard, and the juice white, clammy, and will stick like Glue; but in 3 or 4 days it ripens like a Burgomy Pear, and is the same in tast[e], but more delicious. It hath two small flat seeds or Stones of a shining deep black Colour; with a white slit on one Edge; and within is a hard white Kernel.

The Star Apple Tree is about 25 feet in height, and the Trunk a foot diameter, with branches and twigs that hang downwards. The leaves are about 5 inches in length, half as much in breadth, of a shining deep green Colour and very beautiful on the Inside and on the other side a fine bright Russet. The Fruit is round and about the bigness of a small China Orange; the rind smooth and of a purple Colour. the inside is like a thick jelly, and glutinous, having a purple pulp with several milky Veins running thro[ugh] it, sweet and pleasant. It hath 3 or 4 seeds of a shining deep black Colour, with a white slit on one side of the edge.

When the fruit is cut athwart, in the middle, there plainly appears the figure of a Star and from thence it derives its name.

The Sour Sop Tree is near 20 feet in height, but the Trunk not bigger than a man's thigh, covered with a dirty colour[e]d bark, which is smooth, and has some white spots on it. It does not spread much, and the branches on every side grow Straight out. The twigs are full of leaves, which are about three inches in length, and of an Oval shape, smooth, thin, and very green.

The Fruit is about the bigness of a Child's head and of an irregular shape, it is largest about the Stalk, and ending in a point. The Skin or rind is of a light green Colour, and full of small pointed knobs. When it is ripe it turns to a Yellowish green, the inside white, pulpy, full of juice, and stringy; the tast[e] a mixture of Sweet and Sour. They contain several oblong seeds, of a dark brown or blackish Colour and Shining.

The Sweet Sop Tree, is also about twenty feet high, and Covered with a smooth grey colour[e]d bark, on the outside, but redish within. The twigs are thick set with leaves, which are of an Oval shape, very smooth and of a Yellowish green Colour, of a pleasant smell. The fruit is as big as a man's fist, biggest at the stalk and decreasing towards the other end, having several round knobs growing like Scales, and is of a dirty green colour. It contains a sweetish pulp, and Several Seeds in it, but not so much esteemed as the others.

The Custard-Apple Tree is not unlike that of a Soursop, but larger, and spreads more. The leaves are about 5 inches long, and one inch broad in the middle, where it is broadest and hollow. The Fruit is of a deep yellow, or Orange Colour, the Consistance and tast[e] is not unlike a Custard, from whence it takes its name. The Seeds are black and Shining.

The Guaver Tree, or rather Shrub, hath long small branches; the leaf somewhat like a hazel leaf. The fruit is about the bigness of a large apple, though they are not all of a Size or Colour; for some are yellow, when ripe, and another sort white without, but red within. The rind is as thick, as a lemon[,] soft and of an agre[e]able tast[e]. The Substance is pulpy, and full of Seeds. They are often bak[e]d, or Stued, and Eaten with Milk. They also make Excellent jellies and Marmalade. They are binding when they are eaten green, but of a Contrary effect, when they are ripe.

The Lemon Tree, or Shrub is generally about seven feet high; the branches long and bend downwards, especially when they are loaded with Fruit, which are much larger, and the rind much thicker, than what comes to England from Spain and Portugal.

The Lime Tree, or Bastard Lemon, has a much better body; and will grow to 20 feet, or more in height, but they are generally planted as fences, and Cut as we do quick set hedges in England; though they grow thicker and much more beautiful; the leaves being larger[,] thicker, always green, and so full of prickles, that no beast will venture to penetrate through them.

The fruit is Small, and round, full of seeds; and the rind or Coat, when full ripe, of a bright yellow. The juice is something different from a Lemon, being a sharper Acid, and much fitter for Sauce, but, not for Punch; though great quantities are used that way, and yearly brought to England.

When they are full ripe, and fresh, they are in my Opinion, little inferior to Lemon[s]; but those that are green, rotten ripe, or Stale, are pernicious and unwholesom[e]; and for that Reason I do not approve of the Common lime juice, which comes over for Sale; as they are not careful to pick out such as are bad, but squeeze and mix all together.

Grapes thrive well in this Island, especially in Liginea, and in Stony, or Sandy places, where they have plenty of Water. They have three sorts, the black, white, and Muscodine, all of them larger, and more agreeable in tast[e], than any, that grow in England, and for eating not inferior to any that grow in Spain, or Portugal. I never heard of any Attempt to make Wine of them, tho[ugh] I believe, it is practicable, but they have other Products and manufactures which answer much better.

The Pomegranate Tree, or Shrub is small, and beautiful, none exceeding Six or Seven feet in height. The Leaves are small, with a green mixed with olive Colour, the blossoms are large, and of a pure Scarlet Colour. They are sometimes planted in Rows, and so thick, that they are clipt on the tops with Sheers; in which manner they make a beautiful hedge, though not sufficient to keep out a Beast.

As to the Fruit it is so well known in England, that it needs no further description, than that there are two sorts; one of which is very small, and so Crabbed that it is not eatable, and therefore is planted only as Ornaments in borders of Gardens.

There are also several sorts of Plumb Trees, peculiar to the West Indies, and unknown in Europe, vizt. Spanish plumb, Topnot Plumb, and Hog plumb.

The Spanish and Topnot Plumbs are not unlike, only the latter has a small knob at one end. They are different in tast[e], the former having a more Agreeable flavour; but neither of them have much substance, being little more than a large stone, covered with a Skin; they are somewhat bigger than a Damson, and have a small leaf thinly set. It is Remarkable of both of them, that they are covered with green fruit, before any leaves appear; for the Tree in the Season of bearing is quite naked; a small red blossom then shoots out, which turns to a small green plumb, and when the Tree is covered with them, and before they ripen, the Tree is covered with leaves, as usual. They are of a greenish Yellow, when full ripe.

The Hog plumb Tree is very large, at least 40 or 50 feet in height to the branches; which shoot out to a great length, and are full of leaves. The fruit is in bigness and shape much like an Egg plumb; and is of a bright yellow Colour, when full ripe. They have an agre[e]able smell, even at a distance; and the tast[e] would be pleasant, if it was not so very tart. They have less substance, than the others, being little more than a Skin and a very large stone. The Negroes Eat them, but they are not regarded by the White people; and as they grow Wild, and the Hogs feed much on them, they from thence derive their name.

These are all the Remarkable Fruits, which grow on Trees; though there are some others, which I omit mentioning, as they are not regarded, and Commonly grow wild.

They have also Water, and Musk-Melons in perfection, and in great plenty, much larger than any I ever saw in England; for many of the former sort, are so bulky, as to weigh from 30 to 40 pounds; and I have been credibly informed that some have Weighed fifty pounds.

But, what exceeds them all, or indeed any fruit in the World, for its Singular beauty and delicious tast[e] is the Pine, with which I shall close my description of the fruits of this Island.

At one end the leaves grow almost in the shape of a Crown; which Crown is Cut off and planted, being of the quickest growth, though the Slips or Suckers, which grow on the sides, are likewise taken off and planted, but do not produce so soon, nor any way in less than a Year. In about 3 or 4 months they will be a foot high; and the leaves 7 or 8 inches long, and 2 inches broad, hollow, pointed like a Sword, and upon the edges teeth like a Saw. They grow close together in Rows, there being 3 or 4 Rows above one another in the shape of a Crown, and the points of the lowest Row touching the ground. In about 3 or 4 months likewise appear on the top of the Stem a blossom, larger than a Carnation flower, and of different Colours; so that it may be said to contain as many Varieties to the sight as the fruit does to the tast[e]. These continue about ten days, then wither, and fall away, and a little bunch appears about the bigness of a Walnut, which has on it those various Colours mixed, and does not shew its perfect shape in less than two Months, nor does it arrive at its full growth under 7 or 8 months.

It is then round, about a foot long, and 4 inches diameter, blunt at each end, and smaller at the top where the Crown grows, than at the bottom part or foot Stalk. The fruit is inclosed in a rind covered with a kind of Scales which are as thick as a sixpence, and each about the same bigness, of a green Colour and the edges of various Colours; but, when full ripe, it turns to a lively Yellow, except the edges, which continue the same. There are two Sorts, the King and Queen Pine. The latter is smaller, and has little black seeds in it, which the other has not; and is esteemed to be much better and more delicious. The rind is pared off, and the fruit cut into Slices in a dish, and sometimes Rose Water poured on it; though in my Opinion, that is altogether Superfluous, as it wants no kind of improvement, being in its self delicious; and in the Smell, and Sight, as well as the tast[e], far excelling any thing of the kind in the World, having the flavour and relish of several Excellent fruits, mixed in one. Of this, as well as of Sorrel, Ginger, and other fruits of this Island, are made different sorts of liquors, which are very pleasant, and Cooling, therefore proper for the Country, as they are not unwholesome if used with moderation; for every thing with Excess, is undoubtedly pernicious, and dangerous, in respect to health.

This Island also produces some English fruits, particularly Apples, and Strawberries as I have observed: and might have many others in Perfection and Plenty, from the Mountains would the Inhabitants be at the pains of raising and Cultivating them, but they regard nothing of the kind, that requires trouble or Expence, most of them being intent on the improvement of their Plantations; and seem to have no other View than to raise Estates in order to live in England; to attain which end they suffer many inconveniencies, and take no thought of Posterity, or those that come after them; nor even to make things pleasant and agreeable to themselves, for the present; though it might be done without any considerable Expence or Trouble.

But, the truth of the matter is, none of them look upon the Island as their Home, not even those that were born there; but intend to remove, as soon as they can conveniently, as I have hinted; even although they have a very distant or slender prospect of ever being able to do so; and from hence arises that total neglect or disregard of Gardens, Buildings, and other Amusements, which would make the Island, agreeable to them, and perhaps Equal to most other Countries in living, and all other Respects.

However, they have most sorts of Garden Stuff, all the Year round; and might have it in much greater plenty; particularly turnips, Carrots, Asparagus, french or Kidney Beans, Leeks, Horse Radish, and Salleting of all sorts. The Cabbages are much sweeter and finer than what grow in England, nor doth the Water, it is boil[e]d in, Stink as that doth; But, their Asparagus is very small; though I am of opinion they might have much better, were they properly Skilled, and would be at more pains in raising them.

They have likewise the English Garden Peas and Beans, but in no great perfection or plenty, for the Reasons I have given; and divers other Sorts of Peas and Beans, that are peculiar to the West Indies; as the Bonavist, Callavanas, black eyed Peas, and Red Peas, the Broad Bean, and Sugar Bean; the latter, when gathered Young, and fresh, excel any thing of the kind.

As to Herbs, they have Sage, Rosemary, Mint, Thyme, Scallions, Parsly, Celery, and other Sorts; also Spinage though in no great plenty, but this Want is supplyed by the Calliloo, which is much the same, and when picked and well dressed cannot be distinguished. It grows every where wild, and there are two or three sorts of it; but that which is called the Spanish Calliloo, is the most Esteemed. It is with this Herb, the Negroes make their pepper pot, which is a Sort of Olio, having Meat, Fowl, pepper and other Roots, and Herbage mixed, and boiled together.

Beside, Piemento or Jamaica Pepper, they have in this Island several other Sorts, which grow upon Shrubs or small bushes; as Bell-pepper from its being shaped like a Bell, which is at first Green, and when full ripe, turns Red. It is this sort that is generally pickled; though the other sorts are sometimes preserved that way, but are not so much Esteemed; because they are hotter, and more inflaming. There is another, which is red, when ripe, and is not unlike a child's Coral. The Goat pepper is smaller and rounder and when full ripe, turns yellow, deriving its name from the Smell which is rank like a Goat. Hen pepper, or Negro pepper, is round, and about an Inch in length, and the Bird pepper is small and round, being so called because the Birds frequently feed on it. The Goat pepper, which is the rankest and hottest, the Negroes prefer, though very few white People will touch it; but considering its strength and Heat, the quantities made use of by the Negroes in their Pepper Pots, Sauces, and upon other Occasions, are almost Incredible.

As I do not pretend to be properly qualified to write a Compleat natural History of the Island, so I have ventured to touch only on those things, that are in general and Common use, referring those who are Curious and desirous of being better informed in Matters of that nature, to S[i]r Hans Sloan's *Natural History of Jamaica;* wherein will be found most things, more particularly described and delineated; and shall conclude this Chapter, with a description of some plants, that are not only uncommon, but surprizing in their nature and Effects.

The Cabbage Tree has a Slender Trunk, but is very Straight and Tall, being from 60 to 90 feet in height, and some more when full grown. It is full of joints, about 4 or 5 inches asunder, and without any limbs or boughs, but at the head many branches, which are bigger than a man's Arm. The Branches are commonly about 12 feet long; and about two feet from the Trunk of the Tree, they shoot forth leaves about four feet long, and an Inch and half broad, which grow so regularly on both sides of the branch, that the whole seems but one leaf.

The Cabbage Fruit is cut out of those branches, and when Stripped of the rind or Coat it is folded in, is about a foot long, and the thickness of a man's Arm. It is white as Milk, and sweet as a Nut, when eaten Raw; and when boiled not unlike common Cabbage, but much sweeter. Between the Cabbage part and the branches grow small twigs, about two feet long, at the end of which hang bunches of berries, which are hard and round, not unlike a black Cherry, and the tast[e] like English Haws. These fall from the Trees yearly; and are very good, and fat[te]ning for Hogs.

This Tree is very difficult to climb up, either for Man or Boy, being straight and high, and not having any thing to hold by; they are therefore cut down when the Cabbage is wanted. Besides, should they gather the fruit off the Tree, as it stands, it soon dies away, when the heads of the Branches are gone. The Trees are very usefull to the Planters, who make boards of them by Splitting them into four parts, and there are so many Planks.

The Trunk of the Physick Nut Tree is commonly 18 or 20 feet high and of the bigness of a man's wrist. It has many Sprigs or branches, from 4 to 6 feet long; which being cut off and planted, will grow; and are often made use of for hedges or fences, as they intermix themselves, and become strong and useful, so as to keep out hogs, Sheep or Horses. The leaves are large and shaped much like a Grape leaf, smooth and of a deep green Colour. It is Remarkable that neither Cattle, nor any other Brute Animal[s] will brouse or feed on the leaves, nor willingly come near the Shade.

The Nut, as it grows on the Tree, is like a white Pear Plumb and of the same bigness; but when ripe, it is of a yellowish Colour, then Withers, turns black and drops off the Tree. These being planted will like wise spring up, and sometimes without, when they are full ripe and fall off the Tree. It has a pulp on it like a Plumb, but thicker, and when taken off, there appears a Stone of a blackish Colour, and within that a Kernel, which may be parted in two, like Hazle nuts; and between is a thin film of a faint Carnation Colour; but the rest of the Kernel is a perfect white. The film being taken off, the Nut may be safely eaten without causing any Operation, or bad Effects; and is as sweet as an Almond: But otherwise they will purge and Vomit in proportion to the Number that is Eaten; insomuch that Strangers who tasted them and were unacquainted with their Nature and quality, have often suffered thereby. Two or three of them eaten with the Films, in a morning Fasting, will purge and Vomit any Man. And, He must have a very strong Constitution, who can eat 5 or 6 of the Kernels; as that number will work upwards 10 or 12 times, and much oftener downwards.

The *Cassia Fistula* is Remarkable for its quick growth, as it will in 12 months from the Seed, grow to be 8 feet high, and as thick as a very large walking Cane. The leaf is shaped like that of an Ash, but of darker Colour. The Fruit is 7 or 8 inches long, some more; and in shape and Colour like a black pudding. The pulp of it is Purgative, and a great Cooler of the Reins.

The Callibash Tree is commonly from 10 to 14 feet high, 6 or 7 inches diameter and full of leaves.

The Fruit or Nut springs out, and seems rather to cleave to than grow out of the branches, by their firm and close touching, with very little, if any, appearance of Stalk; and sometimes they shoot out from the upper part of the Trunks of the Trees. There are two sorts, the one round, and somewhat larger than a China Orange, smooth, shining, and of a light green Colour; the other is much larger than a Man's head, and the inside of both is Slimy, full of Seeds and very bitter, therefore no Animals will touch them except Cattle. But the Shells of the first are useful to Poor people and Negroes, who convert them into Cups and Spoons; and the other into Basons or Bowls, to carry Water, and for such like uses.

The Pinguin is a Shrub about 4 feet high. The Fruit shoots out of a Stem of about 3 or 4 Inches Circumference, and a foot and half in length, Surrounded with leaves, which shoot upwards from the foot of the Stem, and are from 2 to 4 feet in length, and two inches broad, the edges full of sharp prickles.

The Fruit is of the bigness and shape of a pullet's Egg; and has a thick skin or rind, which is of a bright Yellow Colour; the inside full of small black Seeds, mixt among the Fruit. Sixty or Seventy of them grow close together in Rows round the Stem, one above another. They are sharp, pleasant, and wholesome, a great cleanser of the mouth, and very good in the Scurvy. There is also a Red sort, the Shrub of which is like the other; though there is some differences in the shape, as well as the Colour.

It is a hardy Plant, grows even in gravel or Sandy ground, may be transplanted at any time, and in the driest part of the Year. They shoot out Suckers from their Roots, which are Slipt and transplanted; for they are not raised from the Seed. They are made use of for fences, growing thick and close together; but if care is not taken, they will in a few Years over spread a piece of Ground. They soon take fire, and cannot easily be Extinguished, when it has once got to a head; nor by any other means than is commonly made use of in such Cases in a Cane piece, by cutting a Vacancy at a little distance to prevent its Spreading, which it will soon do, if not timely stopped in that manner.

The Cotton Tree grows like an Oak, and is as Strong and Sturdy, but much bigger and Taller, many of them being from 50 to 80 feet high, some more, and from 3 to 7 feet diameter. The Trunk is generally Straight and clear of Boughs or Branches to the very head, and there spreads forth many great limbs like an Oak. The Bark is full of little knobs, and of a dirty grey Colour. The leaves are about two Inches long, and jagged at the edge: they fall off in April, and as they fall, young ones spring out; so that in ten or fourteen days the Tree casts off its old Robes, and is cloathed with new. They bear a cod about the bigness of a Pullet's Egg; about December it opens, and from thence flows the Cotton, which hath a very small black seed. The Cotton is white and soft as Silk, but the Staple short, and cannot be work[e]d up, as I conjecture; though I never heard of any Experiment, having been made, by itself, or mixed with any other. It may however be made use of for Stuffing Matrasses or Pillows.

These Trees grow near the Sea, in Salt ma[r]shy ground, and are made use of throughout America for Dories or Canoes. A Dory is a small Boat from 6 to 8 feet in length, and will carry two or three men or more; but the Canoes are much larger and will carry from one to twenty hogsheads of Sugar, and some more.

The Tree, when it is cut down for that use, is Sawed into a proper length According to the bigness; the inside dug out, and shaped within, as well as without like a Boat; so that, it is all of a Piece; but the Canoe is Strength[e]ned with knees and timbers, cut in proportionable lengths and Dimensions, whereas the Dories are all of one piece, without any knees or Timbers. They make no other use of this Tree, as I ever heard, the Timber being soft and Spungy; therefore the Canoe or Dories made of it are soon destroyed by the Worm and Water, unless they are often Scrubbed, well Tarred and Tallowed; for which Reason they are commonly drawn ashore and covered with boughs, to preserve them from the heat of the Sun, when they are not in use.

I saw one in this Island, in the year 1720, so very large, that she had a Deck built on her, and was fitted out for a Privateer with 40 men, Commanded by Capt[ain] Sam[ue]l Lyddall,[5] who was Commissioned by the Governour against the Spaniards, with whom we were then at War. These large Canoes are called by the Spaniards Periaguas, and often made use of by them, as well as the English, not only in transporting of Goods, but for Privateers, having two Masts, which can be struck as well as the Sails,

5. Samuel Lyddall was a transient merchant and ship captain of Scottish origins who commanded the *Cocoa Nut* in an expedition to the Spanish wrecks authorized by Governor Lord Archibald Hamilton in 1716. Perhaps the *Cocoa Nut* was the ship to which Knight refers here.

therefore lie near the Shores undiscovered, and being well fitted with Oars, they often surprize small Vessels, Cano[e]s and other like Craft.

The Dumb Cane is a large and Remarkable Plant that grows almost every where in Moist and boggy places, and is so called, because of its likeness to a Sugar Cane, scarcely to be distinguished by the Eye, without its leaf, though it is of a deeper Verdure, and the leaf something like the leaf of a Water Plantain, but much longer. The Epithet of Dumb is not improperly added, by reason that any Person, who touches it with his tongue becomes dumb, and unable to speak for two or three hours after. But then without any prejudice the Tongue returns to its former use and Volubility; and from thence we may reasonably conclude, there is nothing in it of a poisonous nature; so far from it, that Dr. Trapham in his *Discourse of the State of Health in Jamaica*, Acquaints us with many Virtues in it, particularly in the Dropsy.[6]

The Reason is from the Power the Tongue has of drawing Moisture from any thing it touches, and the Moisture drawn from this Plant comes in such Plenty, or is of such a Nature that it swells the Vessels of the Tongue to an immoderate Size whereby it becomes immoveable, till such Moisture is drawn of[f] or wasted; and then it . . . returns to its former State without any Injury thereto.

Was this Plant to be had in Europe, with the same Properties, it would be of singular use and Service to some unhappy Men, who might safely and Easily apply it on certain Occasions; and remain at home undisturbed, without being under the necessity of going abroad, for a little Peace and Quietness.

The Bastard Cedar, and Bread Nut Trees are of such singular use and Service, that I am surprized, the Planters are not Carefull to preserve and propagate them, their fruit being nourishing and fat[te]ning for Cattle, Horses, Sheep, and Hogs, and it is Remarkable, that the fruit of the former are in the greatest plenty, from January to March, which is the driest part of the Year, when the Grass is short, scorched up, and affords very little Sustenance to those Beasts, or any other Animals. And the leaves of the Trees are also much coveted by them; therefore the tops of the limbs and branches are commonly cut down, after they have done bearing, and are very Serviceable.

The Trunk of the Bastard Cedar Tree is from 15 to 25 feet high, and hath many branches, which spread out, are full of leaves, and consequently very shady, so that the Cattle commonly retire under them in the heat of the day.

The Fruit or Berry is very like a Mulberry, in Shape and Colour, and when full ripe, it dries and turns to a dirty black, when it falls of[f] the Tree.

---

6. Dr. Thomas Trapham, *Discourse of the State of Health in the Island of Jamaica* (London, 1679), 97–101.

It has a sweet tast[e], the Trees are covered with them in the Season, and every Tree produces Several bushels, which daily drop off more or less; and the Cattle and Horses are very diligent in going from Tree to Tree, to seek after, and Eat them up; though they will not touch any, that happen to fall off when they are green.

The Bread-Nut Tree is as big, and as high, as a very large Apple Tree, with a spreading head full of branches and leaves, which are of a dark brown Colour, and likewise make a very good shade for the Cattle and Horses, in the hot part of the day.

The Fruit shoots out of the boughs like Apples, is of a round shape, about the bigness of a Damson, and hath a thick tough rind. When ripe it is soft and yellow; the tast[e] sweet and pleasant; but grows dry and hard before it falls off the Tree, and tast[e]s not unlike a Chesnut.

The Cocoa Plumb Bush grows wild, and only in Sandy ground near the Sea, it is about 7 or 8 feet high, spreads into many twigs, and branches; the leaves [are] Oval in form, and of a deep green colour.

The Fruit is round, the bigness and shape of a Peach, with a very thin wrinkled skin; the Colour a pale red; though there is another sort which is White, when it is ripe: the inside of both sorts is soft, juicy and Wooly; the tast[e] tart and not disagreeable, or unwholesome. It hath a very large soft stone, which contains a white Kernel and tast[e]s not unlike an Almond.

The Wild Grape Bush, or Shrub is about 5 or 6 feet high, some more; and 18 or 20 inches Circumference; it shoots forth many branches, with thick twigs; and leaves Shaped like an Ivy leaf, but broader and Coarser.

The Fruit is about the bigness of a large Grape, but Oval, and not round as the other. They grow in Clusters among the Twigs all round the Tree; it is of a redish black, when ripe, and having a large Stone in the middle, it hath very little Substance; but the taste is agreeable, and the Fruit deemed wholesome.

I have already mentioned the Withies, or Water Withe, which is a very Remarkable Plant, grows Wild, and is to be found only in Rocky, barren places, where no other Water is to be had, but in this and the Water Pine.

It is a Spungy With, much like the biggest part of a Grape Vine, and twists round the Trunks and limbs of Trees, twenty feet high and more, which being Cut, and held upright, there flows from it a clear, well tasted, and wholesome Water.

The Wild Pine leaf likewise contains very good Water. The Shrub or Bush in Shape and Colour resembles the Pine, and therefore it is called the Wild Pine: but is much larger, the leaves broader, and does not bear any Fruit: nor do they grow in the same manner; for the one only grows in a good Soil, and with proper Seasons; whereas these spring up, and grow in any Soil, and with any Season upon the limbs or forky part of Trees, where the limbs shoot out. Each leaf Contains from a pint, to two Quarts of Water, according to the Age or Standing, and are Supplied by the Rains, which so frequently fall in the Mountains.

The Coco Nut Tree commonly grows near the Sea, and thrives best in Moist, Sandy Ground; though they will grow in any Soil, that is well watered, and especially near Rivers. It is shaped like the Cabbage Tree and at a distance cannot easily be distinguish[e]d, only from its being fuller of branches, which are larger, and some of the lowest hanging downward; whereas all the Branches of the other Tree shoot upright. They are in some Places planted in Rows and Walks, which are shady and pleasant, the Branches being from 10 to 15 feet in length; the leaves 3 or 4 feet in length, and 6 or 7 inches broad at the Stalk, but tapering towards the end. The wind among the leaves and branches makes an Agreeable noise, not unlike small Rain. The outside Rind of the Nuts, when they are full ripe, and fall off the Trees, or have been gathered sometime becomes dry, and of a rusty Colour so that one would imagine, they were dead. But these, after they have been carried from place to place and thrown about, sprout and grow like Onions out of their own Substance, until they are two or three feet high; and then planted in proper places, will grow and flourish without Care or trouble. In some Places they grow 5 or 6 feet high in 12 or 15 months, tho[ugh] they seldom produce Fruit in less than 6 or 7 years; but then they bear great numbers, and are continually shooting out Blossoms; so that they have commonly young and old Fruit upon them all the Year round. The Nuts grow in Clusters or Bunches which spring out from among the Branches; at the head of the Trunk of the Tree, and upon each Bunch 30 Nuts, more or less, and ten or more of those Clusters of young and old Nuts upon a good bearing Tree: so that they commonly have 4 or 500 upon them at a time and some many more: and in that manner they continue bearing 50 or 60 Years or more: for I have seen some which, I was credibly informed, were much older.

The Nut is round, and about the bigness of a Child's head; but with the outer rind which is tough and two inches thick, it is much larger than a Man's head, and of an Oval Figure. The Shell is thick, hard, and of a very dark colour, with small light spots and Veins, and the Cavity full of pleasant, wholesome, and refreshing Water.

When the Nut is young, it is full of such Water; which is best, when it begins to ripen, for then it is sweetest, brisk and more agreeable; and as the Nut ripens the Kernel gathers and settles round the inside of the Shell like thick Cream or Pap, and is Scrap[e]d out and Eaten with a Spoon. But, when it is Mature it becomes a firm hard Substance, eats like Almonds, though much sweeter, and harder to digest: however, it is Excellent in Puddings, Cakes and such like uses as Almonds, are generally applied to.

The shell of the Nut is commonly Converted into Cups and Spoons; and the Tree, as well as the Nut, might be made more serviceable for the Conveniencies as well as the Necessities of life, especially in Jamaica where they are very plenty and vast Numbers may Easily be rais[e]d. But, though they are of great use and very much Esteem[e]d in the East Indies, yet for want of the knowledge of the Benefits, which may be made of them, they are very little regarded in that Island, or any other part of America. And therefore I shall be more particular in my Description of this Plant and the use and profits, which may be made of it, in hopes it will incite Curious Persons to make Experiments, and probably some Improvements, which may be of singular use and Service.

Beside the liquor or Water in the Fruit, there is also a sort of Wine drawn from the Tree called Toddy, which looks like Whey; It is sweet and pleasant, but must be us[e]d in 24 hours, after it is drawn, for afterwards it grows sour. Those that have a great many Trees, draw a spirit from the Sour Wine, called Arrack, which is also distill[e]d from Rice, and other things in the East Indies; but none is so much esteem[e]d for making Punch as this sort made of Toddy, or the Sap of the Coco Nut Tree: for it makes most delicious Punch; though it must have a dash of Brandy or Rum, because this Sort of Arrack is not strong enough of itself to make good Punch. This Liquor is chiefly used about Goa, and therefore called Goa Arrack.

The way of drawing the Toddy from the Tree, is by Cutting the top of a Branch that bears Nuts, before it has any Fruit; and from thence the liquor which was to feed the Fruit, distil[l]s into the hole of a Calabash, that is hung upon it. This Branch continues running almost as long as the Fruit would have been growing; and then it dries away. The Tree hath usually three fruitful Branches which if they be all tapped thus, then it bears no Fruit that Year; but if one or two only be tapped, the other will bear Fruit all the while. The liquor which is thus drawn, is emptied out of the Callibash duly every Morning and Evening, while it Continues running, and is sold in the Markets in most Towns in the East Indies; and great Gain arises from it, even this Way; but they that distil[l] it, and make Arrack reap the greatest profit.

The Kernel[7] is much used in making Broths. When the Nut is dry, they take off the Husk, and split the Shell into two parts, letting the Water out, and with a small Iron Rasp, made for that purpose, the Kernel is Rasped out clean, which being put into a little fresh Water, makes it become white as Milk. In this milky Water they boil a Fowl, or any other sort of Flesh, and it makes very Savory Broth; Dampier says, English Seamen put boiled Rice into this Water, which whey eat instead of Rice Milk, carrying Nuts purposely to Sea with them, and that they learnt this from the Natives.

But the greatest use of the Kernel is to make Oil, both for Burning and frying. The way to make the Oil is to grate or rasp the Kernel, and Steep it in fresh Water; then boil it, and Scum off the Oil at the top, as it rises. But the Nuts that make the Oil, ought to be a long time gathered, so that the Kernel may be turning soft and Oily.

7. See Dampier's *Voyage round the World.* P. 293, 294. — *Author.*

The Husk of the Shell is of great use to make Cables, for the dry Husk is full of small Strings, and threads, which being beaten become soft, and the other Substance which was mixed among it falls away like saw-dust leaving only the Strings. These are afterwards spun into long yarns, and twisted up into Balls for Convenience. And many of these Rope Yarns joined together make good Cables. This Manufacture is chiefly used at the Maldive Islands, and the Threads sent in Balls into all places, that Trade thither on purpose for to make Cables.

In the South Seas[8] the Spaniards make Oakum to Calk their Ships, with the Husk of the Coco Nut, which is more Serviceable than that made of Hemp; and they say it will never rot. And in some parts of India they make a Sort of Coarse Cloth, which is used for Sails.

This Tree is Straight and from 20 to 30 feet high, and has a Bark almost like an Ash, with several large white Spots on it. The wood is white, and has a disagreeable smell. They have many Branches and Twigs, which are bare about the month of December, and in January or February they are covered over with Blossoms of a dirty white Colour, with an Eye of purple, to Each of them Succeeds a Pod or Fruit, which is about two Inches long, and within 5 or 6 Seeds, whitish, quadrangular and Oblong. When the Fruit is ripe, the leaves appear, winged like those of an Ash and are about two inches long and one broad.

This Tree grows only in the Savannas and low lands, the Bark steeped in Water cures Dogs of the Mange. And being thrown into Ponds and Rivers, it intoxicates Fish for some time. They will then Appear above water with their Bellies up, but if they are not presently caught they will recover themselves.

The Indians and Negroes make use of this Bark in that manner to Catch Fish, especially in Ponds, lagunes, and Inland Rivers, when there is no Current, and mostly Dry as many of them are some part of the Year only some deep holes or Pools where the Fish retire, at those times. The Fish caught after this manner, are not in any degree prejudicial or unwholesome.

The Mangroves are of two sorts, Black and Red, and both grow in boggy land, which has salt springs, or where the Sea flows, when it is high water.

The Black Mangrove when full grown are 40 or 50 feet high and as thick as a man's Body. The leaves are about 4 Inches long and two Inches broad, thick and of a dark green colour.

The Bark is made use of in Tanning of leather, and does very well for the Soals of Shoes (though it changes the Colour of the Stockings) and for other uses; but not proper for the upper leather or insides, because it heats and burns the Feet.

The Red Mangroves grow near the Sea; the Trunks are commonly about

8. See Dampier P. 295. — *Author.*

the bigness of a Man's Arm; the leaves of the same size, shape and Colour of the other Sort; but the Branches grow Pendulous, and those that
are undermost when they come near the mud or Ouzy land in Salt Water
strikes Root. From their Tops Spring other Branches, which propogate
themselves in the same manner; so that whatever Branches are on the under Parts of the Tree take Root and appear like so many Arches.

In this manner they propogate themselves for many Miles in length
along the shores or Coasts which are Boggy or Morassy, and where the
Water is salt or Brackish.

On the Branches which hang in the Water, Oisters stick and grow upon
them, so that on cutting off a Sprig or part of a Branch 30 or 40 Oisters
are taken at a time. Nor are they to be met with in any other manner, in
this Island.

There is another Sort, of the Mus[c]le kind which are flat, & to be met
with on all Banks within the Harbours and Bays of this Island in great
Quantities, but are not much Esteemed.

The Prickle Pear is a Shrub that grows from 3 to 4 feet high, above
Ground appears no Stalk, but leaves growing out of the sides and tops of
one another, about the bigness of the palm of a man's hand, thicker than a
Crown piece and full of prickles about the size of a small Needle.

The Blossom is of a light yellow Colour; from whence the Fruit appears,
and grows till it is almost as big as an Egg, but bigger at one end than the
other, and more tapering, and turns from a Green to a purple Colour; it
has a Cavity at the largest end, where the Blossom stands till the Fruit is
full grown and begins to ripen, when it falls off, it is all over beset with
many small Tufts of prickles which are scarcely perceivable and run into
the hands of those who unwarily touch them. The inside is of a Rose Colour, and well tasted, but full of Seeds, and under the Skin, where the hole
on the Top of the Fruit, is a small round Substance shaped like the Rowell
of a Spur, which must be taken out or Carefully avoided when the Fruit is
Eaten.

It has many Virtues and good qualities, but when Eaten Causes such alteration in the Urine, that Persons who are unacquainted with the Nature
of them, commonly are frighten[e]d after Eating them, and imagine that
they are loosing all the Blood in their Body. But, the Urine, by degrees and
in less than 24 hours changes and turns to its Natural Colour. It is of an
Astringent quality, though it purges by Urine; and the Spaniards Esteem
it a wholesome Fruit, which makes the Body Strong and Vigorous. They
make a kind of preserve of Them; as also an Emplaister which Strengthens the Weak parts of the limbs and Body. The juices dyes the hands and
lips of a Beautifull Red, which is not Easily, washed off; and they would be
very Valuable to the Dyers Could any thing be contrived that will make the
juice retain its Colour, which soon fades on linnen and paper.

The Otta or Anatto is a small Tree about 8 or 9 feet high, the Trunk is covered with an Ash Grey bark, and has such odd boughs and branches as are not easily described[.] The leaves shoot out of a foot stalk, without any order, about 6 Inches long and five broad ending in a point, shaped like a heart, and are of a dark green colour.

The Fruit is of the Shape and Size of a pullet's Egg, full of short bristles standing out, like those of Burs, the Pods Contain from 30 to 40 seeds, covered with a moist pulp or paste which Colours the hands of those who touch them. When the Fruit is full ripe, and fit to be gathered, the pods open of themselves; and the Balls of this Dye are made in the following manner.

The Seeds are taken out and thrown into a Cistern of Water, which dis[s]olves the Substance, and then the Water is drained from the Seeds, Continues 3 or 4 days to Settle and till it becomes thick; the mud which remains is made into Balls or Cakes and dried in the Sun. They are made use of by the Spaniards as well as the Indians, in Medicinal Cases and in painting.

The Colour is a beautiful Crimson, and lasting, for they will look lively some Years without being mixed with Oil, Gum, or any thing but Water. They are greatly Esteemed for their good Effects in the Stone or gravel, and in many other Cases; for which reason they are commonly put into pepper pots, Soops, Chocolate and plumb porridge, and are no ways dissagreeable, or unpleasant.

Some Onions with a little of this Paste,[9] are thought very powerful against the Difficulty of Urine. And 3 or 4 small Pills, made out of the Balls, are often taken in a Flux, it purges Easily and usually cures.

The Paste mixed with Water, gives it a Tincture, and is good against Poisons being bitter and Spicy.

It formerly grew wild[10] but they are now planted in Gardens and Plantations. It is mixed in New Spain with Chocolate, as well to hinder it from being hurtfull, as for its Colour and Taste. They give some of the Seeds *cumpulte ex Tipio ca quae Carima dicitur,* to an Indefinite Quantity to all sick Persons either poisoned or Others. It strengthens the Stomach[,] Stops Fluxes, and with Water, takes off the heat of Fevers. The Roots and Seeds have no great Taste, are Easier to be taken being cooling in the third degree, drieing and Astringent. If boiled with Broth, it gives a saffron Colour and a good Taste: The Roots have been longer in use, and are thought better. The Spaniards make an Extract of Them with burnt Wine.

---

9. Sloan. Id. —*Author.*

10. Piso. —*Author.* Willem Piso was a Dutch naturalist who in 1648 published the first scientific work on the natural history of Brazil, entitled *Historia Naturalis Brasiliae.* See Neil Safier, "Beyond Brazilian Nature: The Editorial Itineraries of Marcgraf and Piso's *Historia Naturalis Brasiliae,*" in *The Legacy of Dutch Brazil,* ed. Michiel Van Grosen (New York, 2014), 168–186. —*Ed.*

Part the 9th.

Of Beasts, Birds, Fishes, and Other Animals, and Insects in Jamaica.

All the Spanish Writers agree, that when America was first discover[e]d by Christopher Columbus, there was not in any of the Islands or upon the Continent, either Horses, Cattle, Asses, Sheep, Goats, Hogs, Cats, or Dogs of the European kind; but that those Animals were transported from Old Spain, to St. Isabella on the Island of Hispaniola, where they multiplied so fast, that in a few Years they were able to furnish Jamaica, and Cuba with some for breed.

Hernandez Oviedo, whom I have often quoted, and more particularly in the 1st. Part, as an Author of great Credit and to be depended on, having been at Jamaica not many Years after it was Set[t]led by the Spaniards, Says, there was but five Sorts of four footed Animals in any of the Islands, vizt. the Mohay, Hutia, Quams, Cori, and a sort of Mongrel Dogs.[1]

The Mohay was something like a Rabbet, but the Ears shorter; the hair was hard, stiff, streight and of a light grey Colour; the tail like that of a Mole.

The Hutia was as big as a Rabbet; their tail like that of a Mohay, and the Colour of their hair a dark brown.

The Quams were like a Hutia but bigger, and almost the size of a Blood hound.

The Spaniards, as well as the Indians, fed on those Animals, and Esteemed them good Eating; but gave the preference to the Mohay. The Spanish Dogs soon clear[e]d the Island of them; for Oviedo says there were but few remaining when he was in the Island; so that they were all destroyed many Years, before the English became Masters of it.

The Cori, known in Jamaica by the name of an Indian Cony; (for there are some remaining on the Island and I have seen several of them tho[ugh] they are seldom to be met with but in the Mountains, and other Uninhabited places) are very like a Rabbet, only their Snout is like that of a Rat;

---

1. Hernandez Oviedo, also known as Gonzalo Fernández de Oviedo y Valdés (1478–1557), *Historia General y Natural de las Indias*, 19 vols. (Seville, 1535–57). Unable to identify the English version that Knight used, no precise reference is available for this and the following references to this work in this part of Knight's manuscript. For a full discussion of the problem, see Knight's preface, note 5, above.

An engraving taken from Nathaniel Crouch, *The English Empire in America; or, A View of the Dominions of the Crown of England in the West Indies* (London, 1685), following p. 164, is entitled *Strange Creatures in America* and shows fauna common in Jamaica and elsewhere in the West Indies, including an alligator and iguana; a hawk, flamingo, pelican, and hummingbird; an insect that may be a tiger beetle; and a hermit crab.

and their Ears so close, that they almost join and seem but one. Some are White, others Black, Reddish or mixed; their feet and Legs small, but they have no Tail. They never squeak, or make any noise, and feed on Grass; though the Indians sometimes fed and fat[te]ned them with Cassava. They are said to be better tasted than Rabbets; because the flesh is not so dry, but I never had the Curiosity to tast[e] them.

The Dogs the Indians bred tame in their Houses to Catch those Animals, and they are described to be much the same in Shape and Colour, as the Dogs in Europe, but their hair harder and Coarser, and their Ears like those of a Wolf. They never barked or made any noise altho[ugh] they were beaten. Oviedo says, he brought one to Europe and endeavoured to make him bark or growl, by sitting other Dogs at him, but all to no purpose. The Spaniards when they first came to this Island, and were straight[e]ned for Provisions, fed on them, and declared them to be good Eating; though perhaps their hunger & Necessities, made them think so.

These were all the Animals, which the Spaniards found in this Island, or Hispaniola. But, when they began to settle there in 1509, they brought Horses, Cattle, Goats, and Hogs, and received Supplies from time to time from Old Spain, which multiplied exceedingly, insomuch that Oviedo says, when he was at Jamaica, which was about the year 1530, there was such

Painted by George Robertson and engraved and published by John Boydell in London, this 1778 *View . . . of the Spring-Head of Roaring River on the Estate of William Beckford* shows two enslaved people washing clothes at the spring and another tending cattle with a canine helper, thereby calling attention to the importance of cattle and cattle-raising in Jamaica.

plenty, that Don Francisco Garay only had four thousand head of Cattle of all Sorts; that He and other Planters often killed them for their Skins or Hides, and knew not what to do with their Flesh; which was so plenty, that thirty Ounces were sold for one farthing; and that they sent several thousands of their hides to Old Spain Yearly. It is Certain, that before the English took the Island, a Cow was sold for a piece of Eight, which is about 4 [shillings] 6 [pence] Sterling; and a horse half as much. But after that period of time, and before any Property was Set[t]led, the Soldiers destroyed many of them, and by hunting and Shooting them, great numbers run wild; for which they afterwards suffer[e]d very great hardships.

When S[i]r Thomas Lynch came to the Government in the Year 1671, Cows were sold from 12 to £15 p[er] head, but by Encouraging the Importation of them from Cuba, and the goodness of the Pastures, they Encreased so fast, that in four years they Currently sold at four and five pounds p[er] head.

They are of a mid[d]ling breed and Calve much about the same time they do in England. Most of the Bulls are cut, before they are twelve months old; and when they are about 3 or 4 years old, they are broke for draught in Mills, and Carts; and it is owing to the great numbers, which are by those means used and destroyed, that they are not now so cheap as formerly, notwithstanding the great Numbers which are raised Yearly. But as the Planters fall more and more into the use of Mules in their Sugar Mills, and upon many other occasions, wherein Cattle were wholly Employ[e]d, it is probable, that the price will be reduced in a few Years, and that their markets will be much better supplied with Beef; though there is no want at present. The Beef in this Island is good and well tasted (though not so large and fat as ours in England) unless the Cattle are killed soon after they have eaten Guiney Hen Weed or Callibashes, which gives the Beef as well as the Milk of the Cows, a very disagreeable tast[e]; to Remedy which, as well as to fatten the Cattle, they are commonly put into pastures, which have not either of those distastfull Weeds or Fruit.

The Oxen which have drawn in Mills, and are afterwards fattened in a good pasture are reckon[e]d the best Meat, if not very old.

Veal is also very common; though I cannot say much in favour of it, as very little care is taken to fatten the Calves, and whiten the Flesh by the same methods that are practised in England, otherwise they might have much better, though I now and then met with some, which was very good.

Cows are now sold from 4 to Seven pounds each, being cheaper in some parts of the Country than others, and dearest near the Towns; young Steirs from 6 to nine pounds, and such as are broke and fit to be used in a Mill or Cart, from 9 to £12 each.

The Horses being also of the Spanish breed are Small, very few exceeding 14 hands; but they are full of spirit, well shap[e]d, and make very good Pads. Some of them are good Coursers for a Mile or two; and it is observable, that tho[ugh] none of them are shod, they will gallop and Travel in Stony Roads without receiving any damage: Nor are they troubled with so many Distempers as the Horses in England, being so hardy that they frequently are, after a Journey or being hard rid, turned into a Pasture, without any further Care or trouble.

Likely young Horses generally sell from 7 to £12, and after they are broke to a Saddle or Coach from £15 to £40, and some more, according as they prove. Many are imported yearly from New England, and R[h]ode Island; but they are not here so much used as in the Windward Islands, where they have not Conveniency or lands for breeding any of their own. Several Planters have lately sent for large stone Horses out of England, to mend the Breed; which undoubtedly will be done in time. But, they would do better, if they would likewise send for Mares, as their breed will undoubtedly become as hardy and Natural to the Country, as the others now are.

Asses and Mules are very usefull in this Island, especially in Sugar Works, and for Carrying of Burthens, up and down the Mountains, being strong, hardy & sure footed; for these Creatures will run with their

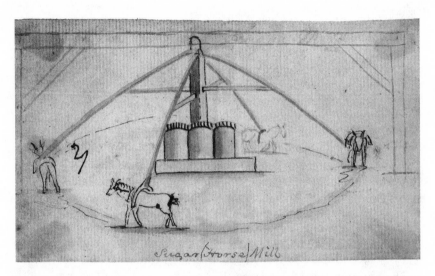

Sugar (Horse) Mill

This early nineteenth-century drawing of a *Sugar (Horse) Mill* comes from the National Library of Jamaica Print Collection IN: Quizem: Sketches of West Indian Life, 1810–1814. Used to pull wagons, carts, and carriages and to carry riders from place to place, horses were ubiquitous in early modern Jamaica. They may also have been used to power sugar mills, but the figures here labeled as horses could well have been one of the vast number of mules annually imported from mainland South America. (National Library of Jamaica)

loads, in places where Horses are scarcely able to pass. The former are mostly Imported from the Cape de verdi Islands; some from England; and the others from Rio de la Hacha, Sta. Martha, Cuba and Curiosa. But the Planters have within these twenty years past fallen into the way of breeding them in the Island, and probably will have no Occasion, in a few Years, of any Supplies from their Neighbours, at least it will be their own fault, they having such large tracts of Savanna, and other pasturage. Mules are certainly preferable to Cattle and Horses for Service, not only because they are hardy, and will go thro[ugh] more labour, but are maintained easier and at a much less expence, for they will browse on Trees and Shrubs, and eat many things that Cattle and Horses will not touch.

The Spaniards also make use of them for Coaches, Chaises, and to Ride on, and some of them are taught to pace or Amble; but, they generally walk or run a Shambling pace between a trot and gallop, as they please, for they have very little regard to a Whip and are very difficult to be put out of their own way. They are undoubtedly much better for long Journeys, in this part of the World, or to travel in the Mountains, for the Reasons I have given, and because they are cautious of danger, and very carefull in chusing their way; insomuch that in narrow or difficult passes, in the Mountains or Roads, particularly in that going to Sixteen mile-Walk, before it was improv[e]d and enlarged, they will secure the safest side and maintain it against Man or Beast; and for that reason Gentlemen, who had Occasion to go that way in Crop time, chose to travel on Sundays, when they were sure not to meet any of them on the Road.

The Attachment of those Creatures to a White Horse or Mare is likewise Remarkable, and a truth well known though I never could meet with any Person who could assign any Cause or Reason of it. But if a Number of them are in a Field, and a white Horse or Mare is rode or led amongst them, they will all gather about and follow, wherever they go; so that they are easily transported from one place to another with very little care or trouble. Because two Negroes with a White horse or Mare, the one to lead or Ride the Horse or Mare, and the other to follow in the Rear, are sufficient to go to any part of the Country with 40 or more of them. They are commonly sold from 15 or £25 p[er] head, tho[ugh] a large riding Mule, Young and well broke is worth 30 or £35, and some have been sold at £40, and Jack Asses from 5 to £20, each as in goodness.

The Sheep in this Island are of the Guiney breed, and I have been informed, were brought hither from the Windward Islands. They are a very profitable Stock: for the Ew[e]s breed twice in fifteen months, without regard to the time of the Year; and they commonly bring two at a time, sometimes three; but it is with difficulty they raise them, and for that Reason the Pen keepers destroy one of them. They are small, and well tasted exceeding the common Mutton in England, and equal to those rais[e]d upon Banstead Downs, especially when they are fed with Corn, as they commonly are by many Planters for their own Table.

They are not so large; but their heads and Bodies, are like the English Sheep, only a hairy or Shaggy Coat without any Wool.

It is observable, that the English Sheep, or those that are brought from North America, which are much the same, do not thrive so well, by degrees grow less Wooly, though not wholly deprived of their Natural Cloathing, and breed in the usual manner, at the usual Seasons, only one at a time: for which reason they are not Coveted, nor any Care taken to propogate them.

Goats also thrive here exceedingly, are fine and well tasted as any in the World; for the flesh of the kids is equal to house-lamb, and much beyond Grass lamb in England. But they are Valued chiefly for their Milk, which is almost as thick as Cream, therefore preferred to Cow's. A good Goat commonly gives two or three pints of milk a day, and rears three or four Kids, with very little Care or trouble.

The Hogs are of the Spanish breed, not so large as ours in England, but much sweeter meat, especially the Wild sort; which are killed or caught in the Mountains; for they feeding chiefly on Wild Fruits, which fall from the Trees, make their Flesh delicious, and preferable to any thing of the kind.

The Spaniards make Broth of the Flesh of both sorts, and Esteem it equal to, if not better than, any which is made of Mutton, Veal or Fowl;

The cartouche for the Craskell-Simpson map of the County of Middlesex in the center of the island depicts a single white hunter with a pack of dogs running down a wild boar, one of the many wild animals on the island.

and the Physicians allow their Patients to eat young Pork preferably to any white meat or fish; because they look upon it [as] more Nourishing and Easier of digestion.

The tame Hogs are bred in Crawles, and Multiply exceedingly. In some Remote parts of the Country particularly at the North side, and West end of the Island, many Persons, have 2 or 300 and more in Crawles; which are turned out in the Mornings into the Woods, to search for food, Attended by a Negro to watch and prevent any of them from being Stolen, and being Constantly fed with Corn in the Evening, they orderly return home at the usual time, or upon their Driver or feeder blowing a Conch-Shell. On the first sound of the Shell, which makes a loud, inarticulate noise, they prick up their Ears and immediately run homewards; and in this manner they are called home every night, or when they have Occasion for them, seldom losing any; but on the Contrary the Wild sort some times mix, and come to the Crawles with them, where the keeper easily distinguishes them, by their not being marked, as the others are, that every man may know his own from his Neighbour's. These are immediately taken out, and Secured, and others drawn from time to time which are fit for Sale, and sent to Market, where they are sold at a groat a pound alive and [blank] pence their Currency, which is about five pence Sterling, in Quarters.

The Wild sort are taken in Traps laid for them, or hunted with Dogs; and are chiefly to be met with in the Mountains or uninhabited parts of the Island. After they have been pursued sometime, and Wearied by the Dogs, and come to a bay, they are shot or pierced through with a Lance. When they are killed in that manner at a distance from any Settlement or Town, they are preserved thus; the hair is Scalded off, and after the Entrails are taken out, and the Inside well washed, it is then divided in two, the bones taken out, the Flesh cut and gashed on the inside to the Skin, after which it is filled with Salt, and then exposed to the Sun, which is called Jerking. It may be kept this way some Months, and eats as well, if not better than any Bacon, either boil[e]d or broil[e]d.

These Hunters are mostly Negroes; though sometimes White men go out with them, and taking Dogs, Salt and Bread along with them remain several days in the Mountains and other Woody unsettled parts; where the Hogs frequent, and then return with their Game preserv[e]d in the manner I have described; or if they are near any Town or Settlement, send what Hogs they have taken alive, or killed, and [blank][.]

There are Several good Laws relating to Cattle and Farms commonly call[e]d Pens, of which it will not be improper to insert the following Extracts.[2]

> All Plantations bounding on Savanna's, High-ways, &c and Pastures made out of Wood-Lands, shall be sufficiently fenced in.
>
> If any Damage shall be done by any Stock in any Plantation so fenced, the Damage and the Sufficiency of the Fence shall be determined by the Oath of three Free-holders, and the Owner of the Stock shall pay double the Damage done, to be recover[e]d before any Justice of Peace, if not exceeding 40 s[hillings] if more in any Court of Record.
>
> No Person whatsoever shall kill any Cattle, Horse, Mare, Mule, or Assinego [Asses] under the Penalty of £15. to be recovered in any Court of Record, by the Owner or Proprietor of the said Beast.
>
> All Owners of Neat Cattle shall keep one white Man at each Pen, and two white Men at every Pen, whereunto belongs above 200 head of Cattle, Penalty £10 for every white Man wanting for the Space of three Months, Half to the Poor of the Parish, Half to the Informer.
>
> All Owners of Cattle shall pen them once in three nights at least, or pay the Damage double which such Cattle shall do.

2. An Act for Preventing Damages in Plantations, Preserving of Cattle, and Regulating Hunting, 1681, in *Acts of Assembly, Passed in the Island of Jamaica; from 1681 to 1737, Inclusive* (London, 1738), 13–16.

Strays shall belong to the Proprietor of the Ground where taken up, provided he cries the Stray three Court Days with proper Descriptions, and turns the same loose in the feeding Grounds, with a Withe about the Neck for an Year; and if not claimed in that Time, the Property shall be his. Ear-mark[e]d, or burnt mark[e]d Cattle shall belong to the right Owners, if claim[e]d any Time after the Expiration of the Year.

The Clerk of each respective Court of Record in this Island shall make Entry, and toll all sorts of Cattle, that shall be sold from one Person to another; which are to be vouched by two sufficient and known Persons; which Entry and Toll shall be good against all former Sales, or any other Title, except where the Provost-Marshal has levied the same in Execution. The Clerk's Fee for such Entry [is] 1s[hilling].

No Person whatsoever shall carry Fire, or smoke Tobacco in any Savannah Plantation or Highway, under Penalty of 10s[hillings] for every Offence to him that shall sue; and further, to pay all Damages, that may happen; and, in case of Inability to be whipt at the Discretion of any one Justice of Peace; provided Owners of Land may carry Fire in their own Plantations, but liable to satisfy the Damage that may happen to others.

None shall drive or ride in any Savannah as a common Horse catcher, without first giving Security for their Honesty, and obtaining Leave from the Proprietors of the Savannah, or the major Part of them, under the Penalty of £20.

No common Driver or Horse-Catcher shall sell, or Barter any Horse, Mare or other Cattle, without bringing two sufficient Evidences to vouch for him before the Clerk of some Court, that he bred, or otherwise came lawfully by them, under the Penalty of £50. to be disposed as before, and the Buyer, without such Vouchment, shall forfeit £20.

If any Driver or Horse-catcher shall fraudulently and designedly put any false Mark, or deface any old Mark, he shall for such Offence be guilty of Felony.

If any Keeper or Owner of Goats, shall suffer his Goat to feed upon another Man's Land, the Owner of the Land shall recover his Damage for such Trespass, as the Jury shall give in any Court of Record, and full Costs of Suit in the said Action.

No common Horse-catcher shall ride or drive in any Savannah, without giving £100. Bond, with sufficient Security to the Justices in open Sessions, under Penalty of £10. for every Offence; and having so done, he shall obtain an Order from the Justices then sitting to ride and drive, &c.

No such common Horse-catcher shall mark any Cattle, without giving Notice in the Parish Church the Sabbath Day before, under Penalty of £20.

The tame Fowl are most of them the same kind as ours in England; the Geese indeed are not so large and fine as ours, but the Turkeys far exceed any we have in goodness as well as in Size; for it is common for the Hens to weigh 7 or 8 pound; and the Cocks from 15 to 18 pounds and some more, without their feathers.

Their Ducks are of the Muscovy breed; and thrive much better than any other Sort; for though the English Ducks will lay and hatch their young, yet they are not so Easily raised: the breed between both are most Esteem[e]d, and tast[e] better than any of the other kind.

Pigeons of the same sort, are larger, fatter and better tasted than any Dove House-Pigeons in England; and breed almost all the Year round. They have likewise Dunghil Fowls, and might have them in much greater plenty, which are at least equal to, if they do not exceed those of the same kind in England.

These Poultry are chiefly fed on Indian or Guiney Corn which is more hearty and Nourishing than Oats or Barley, and for that Reason, I take it, those Several sorts, I have mentioned, are fatter and better tasted when well fed, than ours in England.

They have likewise several sorts of Wild Fowl, which in general exceed any thing of the kind in England, vizt. Duck, and Teal, Pigeons, Turtle Doves, Snipe, Plovers, Guiney Hens, and October Birds.[3]

Wild Ducks are of two sorts, the one like ours in England, in bigness and Colour, but not so well tasted: the other something less than our Common Ducks, but not different from them in Shape and Colour. In flying the Wings of the Latter sort make a whistling noise, and from thence are called whistling Ducks. These sometimes perch on old dry Trees, or such as have no leaves, and seldom light on the ground, only to feed; but the others never do.

The Teal are of the same kind with ours in England, and exactly resemble them in Shape, Size, and Colour; but are much better tasted. They come in, and are in the greatest perfection in the Rainy Seasons; for at other times they are not so fleshy, and tast[e] fishy.

The Wild Pigeons are much larger than our Dove House-Pigeons in England: they are of a Dun Colour, feed on Berries and Wild Fruits; and sometimes are so fat, that when they are shot, they split in the fall. When they are in Season, they are generally allow[e]d to exceed any thing of the kind, in the World.

Of Turtle Doves there are three sorts in this Island, vizt. the white breasted, bald pate, and ground Doves.

The White breasted are plump, round and bigger than a wild Pigeon in England. They are of a bluish grey Colour, & their breasts white; from whence they derive their Name.

---

3. In his treatment of wild beasts, birds, fish, and other animals, Knight draws on his own observations and the descriptions in Sir Hans Sloane, *A Voyage to the Islands Madera, Barbados, Nieves, S. Christophers and Jamaica, with the Natural History of the Herbs and Trees, Four-Footed Beasts, Fishes, Birds, etc.*, 2 vols. (London, 1707–25), 2:189–340, and Dr. Thomas Trapham, *Discourse of the State of Health in the Island of Jamaica* (London, 1679).

The Bald Pates are so called, because they have no feathers on the top or Crown of their heads. They are something less than the other, not so plump, and their feathers all of a Dun colour. These, as well as the others, commonly feed on berries, which they pick from the Trees, where they grow; and are as good as the Wild Pigeons in England.

The Ground Doves are something bigger than a Larke, and are the most fleshy Birds of their bigness in the World, especially when the Guiney Corn begins to ripen and be gathered. They are round, plump, and better tasted than a Lark; of a dull grey Colour speckled with little white spots, and Commonly run on the Ground in pairs.

Snipes and Plovers are the same as ours in England, only there is some small difference in the Colour of the Feathers in the first mentioned, so that they need not any further description.

The Guiney Hen by the Spaniards called *Galena Pintado* or painted Hen, is of the bigness of a large Pullet. The feathers of these Birds are of a dark Grey, speckled with little white Spots, which are so regular and Uniform, that they look more beautiful than many Birds, which have gayer feathers. They have long legs, and run very fast, but cannot fly far, their Bodies being heavy and their Wings short, their heads are small and their Necks long. The Cocks are the same as to size and Colour, only to be distinquished by a small rising on their Crown like a Comb, w[hi]ch is hard and of a nut brown Colour: they have also small red gills strutting out downwards, on each side of their heads. They tast[e] like Partridge, and being also very dry eat best, when they are larded.

The October Birds, are the same as Ortelans, and call[e]d by the other Name, because they are only to be met with in that Month, when the Rains set in from the South, and come earlier or later as they do. They are then fat and equal to any in Europe.

The Parrots in this Island are different from those, which come from Guiney or the Main Continent; those from the Continent being a large green bird with yellow feathers on the top or Crown of their heads, and a mixture of Red and yellow feathers on the Edges of their Wings and noted for talking more than whistling. Those from Guinea are all blue, except a few red or white feathers about their heads, wings or tails. The former have the best voices and speak plainer than any Bird in the World: whereas the Breed in Jamaica, are very small, mostly all green or with some few red and white feathers. They have a shrill, squeaking voice, and do not talk so plain as the others do. They fly in flocks, and are very mischievous when the Corn ripens, for they destroy ten times as much as they eat.

They are at those times well tasted, if they are young, otherwise tough; and when their heads and feet are cut off, and dressed, cannot be distinguished from a Pigeon, only their skins are thicker. They are generally boiled with Bacon and Greens, or made into Soop; and are most esteem[e]d that way.

Pelicans, are almost as big as a Goose, and their feathers of the same Colour. They have short legs, flat feet, and long Necks. Their Bills are about two inches broad, & sixteen or seventeen Inches long. Their breasts are bare and covered with a smooth loose skin, like the Necks of Turkies: Their Skin is of a white Colour, mixed with a dark, light grey. They are a very heavy Bird, and cannot fly far, or very high above the Water.

They commonly perch alone, on some Rock near the Shore, or sit on the Water, as if they were asleep, holding their heads upright and resting their Bills on their Breasts.

The Flamingo, commonly call[e]d a Galding, is a large Fowl. Their feathers are Reddish or the Colour of a new brick and their legs very long; insomuch that when they hold up their heads, they are near five feet in height. They make their nests in shallow ponds; where there is much mud, which they scrape together in Hillocks, leaving a hollow space in the middle to lay their Eggs in. When they lay their Eggs, or hatch them, they cannot sit on their Nests as other Fowl and Birds do, their legs being so long that they cannot draw them into their nest nor sit down upon them; but stand all the while with their feet on the Ground or in the Water, resting themselves on the hillock, and Covering their Nests with their Rumps. They Constantly lay two Eggs, never more or less; and their young ones cannot fly until they are full grown, yet will run very fast. They feed in Ponds and muddy places, are very shy, and generally in great Companies; so that a Person unseen by them may easily kill several of them at a Shoot. The Seamen frequently eat them, and say, that their flesh is good though lean and black, neither fishy or unsavory; and that their tongues are fat about the Root, and delicious; but I never heard that either Whites or Blacks eat them in Jamaica.

Beside those, there are Gulls the same sorts as ours in England, Boobies, Noddies, Men of War-Birds, and divers other Sorts of Wild fowl and Birds, which I think unnecessary to give a particular description of, as they are of no use or service as I ever heard of, except the Carrion Crow.

The Carrion Crow is of the Size of an ordinary Hen Turkey. They are of a dirty black Colour, their heads and Necks bald and Reddish, which often leads Strangers to mistake them for Wild Turkies. They are a dull heavy lazy Bird; for they will perch and sit long in one place, unless they are hungry, and then they are quick enough to find out their prey and are very Ravenous. They live wholly on flesh, and soon devour a dead Horse or any other Beast, which makes them exceeding useful in such hot Countries, by removing what might Cause an Infection, especially in dry times, when many Beasts perish for want of Food; and for that reason there is an Act of Assembly in this Island, which prohibits any of them being killed, or destroyed under the penalty of £5.[4]

4. Perhaps An Act to Regulate Fowling and Fishing, 1711, in *Acts of Assembly*, 146–47.

There are some few of them, which are all over White, but look very much sullied; though in other Respects they are like the rest; and seldom more than one or two of them are seen at a time. These are called King Carrion Crows; and I have often heard it said, though I cannot affirm it from my own knowledge, that when a great number of them are assembled, near a dead Carcass, if a King Carrion Crow is among them, the rest will perch on Trees about it, and will not Approach, or touch it, until he has done and flies away; but then they immediately fall to, and soon dispatch it, and it is Remarkable that they pick the Eyes out first. They Constantly stink and are smelt at some distance.

There are several other sorts of Birds in this Island; but none of them are distinguished for Singing, except the Nightingale and Bonano Bird; and even those cannot be tamed, or kept any time alive in Cages, but grow Sullen, pine away, and die.

The Nightingale is much the same in all Respects as ours in England, therefore needs no further description.

The Bonano Bird is about the bigness of a Bull-finch, the Feathers upon the head black; their Wings strip[e]d black and yellow; and the rest of their Feathers a bright Yellow. They are beautiful Birds and their notes very Agreeable.

There are three sorts of Humming Birds, some of them bigger than others, but all of them very small; nor are they alike in Colour, the Feathers of some being very beautiful, and the largest Size of a deep Black. The smallest sort is not bigger than a large Wasp, with a black bill, the size of a small needle; the legs and feet in proportion to the Body. Their Nest is Curiously wrought with silk Cotton; and so small, that I have cover[e]d one with a young Bird in it, which was fledg[e]d with an English Shilling. This Creature is in Continual Motion, and seldom seen perching, but never for any time: nor do they wave their Wings like other Birds, when they fly, but keep a continued motion like Bees and other Insects, making a humming noise; and from thence they are called Humming Birds. They are Commonly seen hovering about Flowers and Fruit like a Bee, and from thence suck their Sustenance, sometimes on one side and sometimes on the other always in motion frequently rebounding a foot or two, and then swiftly returning to its delightfull Object.

The Black Bird is somewhat bigger than ours in England, only it has a longer tail. They are commonly called chattering Crows, because they often chatter and make a noise, especially if they are disturbed, or see any Person.

The Man of War-Bird is not unlike a Kite, and is about the same bigness. They feed on fish, and Soar aloft; but when they see any prey, they fly swiftly with their head downward and take their prey out of the Sea with their Bill, and immediately mount aloft in the Air. Their Wings are long, and their feet like land Fowls. They generally build their Nests on Trees, but sometimes on the Ground.

The Crab Catchers are something like a Pelican, with long Necks and legs, but not so large. They feed on small Crabs, which are not bigger than a man's thumb; of which there are great numbers on all the Coast or Shores of this Island.

Beside these, there are many other Sorts; but as they are not much regarded, I do not think them worth describing.

This Island is likewise furnished with great Variety of Fish, which is the most suitable Nutriment to the Nature of the place, being Easier of Digestion, and more wholesome than Flesh; and therefore we ought to admire, and thankfully acknowledge the Divine Bounty in Storing the Rivers in this Island, as well as the Ocean, in so plentiful a manner with what is most proper and Necessary for the Sustenance of life.

The principal sorts, which are most Esteemed, and I propose to describe, are the Manati, Turtle, Jew Fish, Rock-Fish, Mullets, Callipeavers[,] Mountain Mullets[,] Snapper Snook, Hog Fish, Cavallies[,] Grooper[,] Tarpum, Spanish Mackrell[,] Mud Fish[,] Silver Fish, Old Wives, Stone bass[,] Baracootas, Plaice, Crawfish, Shrimps[,] Crabs[,] and Lobsters. Beside these, there are Jacks, Grunts, Porgate, Gar-fish, Grass-Fish, Catfish, Pilchers, Sprats, Drummers, Parrot fish, Bonetos, Thornbacks, Stingrays, Sea Crabs, with many others which have no other Names, than the Negroes distinguish them by, and seldom are eaten by the White People; therefore I think it needless to delineate them.

The Manatee or Sea Cow, has generally the preference though she seldom Visits this Island, nor is to be met with in great plenty, in any Place, or so common as Turtle and other fish or Sea Animals. It is certainly the most Remarkable Creature in the World, no where to be met with but in America, and its form and Composition so very Extraordinary, that it is not easy to be described. They are in Circumference about the bigness of a Horse, and from 10 to 14 feet long, when full grown, for some are bigger than others. Their head in bigness and shape is like a Cow's, having a large mouth, and great thick lips like theirs and from thence called the Sea Cow: The Eyes are very small in proportion to the head, and Body, being no bigger than a Pea. They have no Ears; only two small holes on each side of the head, not far from their Eyes: The Neck, is short and thick. The biggest part of this Creature is at the Shoulders, where it hath a large Stump, or fin on each side [of] the Belly[,] very thick, and high placed near the head, with which it Swims. Under each of those fins the Female hath a small Dug to suckle her Young. From the Shoulders downwards it retains its bigness for about a foot, and from thence it grows tapering and smaller to the Tail, which is flat, about 20 inches long, and 12 or 14 inches broad; it hath not any Scales, nor hairs; but the Skin is smooth, of a dark grey colour, tough and half an Inch thick or more. I have heard of some, that weighed above 1000 pound weight, but I never saw any so large.

Their Flesh is very white, both fat and lean, tender, Sweet, and equal to

any Veal in the World, and not easily distinguished, when it's dressed. The
Tail of a young Cow is the most Esteem[e]d, but a Calf that Sucks is the
most delicious meat. The Skin or Hide is put to divers uses; for they make
good Horse whips, by Cutting them about 3 feet long; at the handle they
have the full substance, of the Skin, and from thence they cut it tapering,
but very even and Square; while they are green they twist them; and hang
them to dry; and in a week's time they become hard, & fit for use, and last
many Years. The Sailors and Negroes make use of the Hides for Straps,
which they make fast on the sides of their Canoes, through which they put
in their Oars instead of Tholes in rowing. They are also made use of for
the Soles of Shoes, and upon other Occasions.

The Manatee has two Stones among the Brains, which are as large as a
Tennis Ball, more or less according to their bigness, but not round, and a
most Excellent Remedy for the Pleurisy[5] and Stone; this Medicine is prescribed in a Common way; and is Esteemed the most effectual Remedy
among the Spaniards, though little known or used, by the English and
other Nations. Therefore I shall transcribe, from Oviedo, the manner of
preparing this Remedy.

["]They burn the Stones well, break and pulverize them; then put a Tea
spoon full of the powder into a glass of white Wine, and drink the like
quantity for some morning's fasting; which takes away the Pleurisy, and
dissolves the Stone in such a manner, that it comes out by Urine, and without any pain.["] Oviedo Affirms, that he has seen the Cure Effected in that
manner, and known Gentlemen of note enquire after the Stones, and give
an Extraordinary price for them on that Account.

He likewise tells us, that the Tail of the Manatee, which seems to be all
Sinews, being cut to pieces, dried in the Sun for several days, and afterwards fried in a Pan, the whole is Converted into a kind of butter; which is
fit to fry any thing, to burn in lamps, and has some Medicinal qualities in it.

These Creatures are not of a fierce Nature, but tamer than any thing
of the kind; for they come near the Shore, and into Rivers to feed on the
grass, which grows on the Banks, in deep Water. They are taken in Nets
made very strong with lead or great Stones at the end thereof; which by
means of a small Cord close together; and then they draw it to the Shore,
and kill it. But, they are often shot or Struck with a Harpoon or Spear, for
they commonly Swim on the Surface of the Water.

The Muskito and other Indians of America, when they seek for Manatee, paddle gently in their Canoes, that they may make no noise; because
it is a Creature that hears very well, notwithstanding it has only very small
holes or Ears. One of the Indians, (for they go but two in a Canoe) sits
in the Stern, and the other kneels down at the head, and both paddle, till

5. See Oviedo and Trapham. — *Author.* Trapham, *Discourse of the State of Health in the Island of Jamaica,* 64–65. — *Ed.*

they come to the place, where they expect their Game. He that is at the head, then lays down his paddle, and stands up with his striking Staff in his hand: this Staff is about 7 feet long, as thick as a man's wrist at the biggest end, where is a hole to fix his Harpoon in; and at the other end of the Staff, there is a piece of light Wood with a hole in it, through which the small end of the Staff comes; & on this there is a line of 10 or 12 fat[homs]: wound neatly about, and one end made fast to it. When he strikes, the Manatee swims away, the line runs of[f] the bob, and they paddle after to get hold of the bob; then they gather it in, but are often forc[e]d to let all go to the very end, until the Creature's Strength is spent, and then they hall it to the side of the Canoe, and knock it on the head, then tow it to the nearest Shore. When they strike a Cow they seldom miss the Calf, for she commonly takes her Young under one of her fins. But, if the Calf is so big that she cannot carry it, or she so frightened, that she only minds to save her own life, yet the young never leaves her; and is afterwards easily taken.

The Turtle comes next under consideration, and is also a strange and useful Creature. The Flesh is truly Solid, white and equal in goodness to fine Young Veal, yet easy of digestion, pleasant as well as Nourishing, & a compleat Restorative food. It is dressed several ways. The Callapee or back part makes an Excellent dish baked, and will suit the palate of the Curious, or even the greatest Epicure. The Flesh is sometimes fried, or dress[e]d in the same manner, we do Veal in Cutlets, or Scotch Collops. When boiled it equals Jellies, and the fins make Excellent Broth.

There are three sorts of Sea Turtle vizt. the Loggerhead, the Hawk's bill, and the green Turtle.

The Loggerhead is so call[e]d, because it hath a large head much bigger than the other Sorts. Their Flesh being Coarse and rank, few chuse to eat them, but in Case of Necessity.

The Hawk's bill Turtle is so called, because the Mouth has some resemblance of a Hawk's Bill, being long and small. They are not much coveted, and seldom eaten, the flesh being rank and coarse. In some places, especially near Porto bello, and Carthagena, they are of a Milignant nature, for they Operate Violently upwards and downwards. The Officers and men belonging to the Squadron commanded by Vice Admiral Hosier,[6] when they lay at the Bastimentos in 1727, fed much on Turtle, and their not distinguishing this sort from the others, I am of opinion, was in a great measure the Cause of the great Sickness and Mortality, which hap[pe]ned amongst them, throwing them into Fluxes, Surfeits &c which brought many of them to their End. And for that reason it is to be wished, that the Officers of our Men of War, and all others, wou[l]d be more carefull for the future, and restrain, if not prohibit their men, from that kind of food. However they are preferable to the other Sort in tast[e], and are better or

6. Vice Admiral Francis Hosier (1673–1727).

worse according to their feeding; for in some parts they feed on Grass or moss and Sea Weeds, as the Green Turtle do; and therefore it must be owing to some particular food, they eat at those places, which Causes them to have those bad Effects. But they are naturally of a purging quality, more or less, according to their feed; therefore very few care to eat them in Jamaica, though caught upon their own Coasts. It is the Shell of this Sort of Turtle, which is brought to Europe, and is so much Esteemed for making Boxes, Combs and other Utensils. They are said to have Islands and parts peculiar to themselves, where they lay their Eggs, particularly the Samblass, many places along the Coast of the main Continent, and the North side of Jamaica; and seldom come among other [kinds of] Turtle[s].

The Green Turtles are so called because their Shell is greener than either of the other Sorts. These are most Esteemed, being of a different Nature and Quality; and not only sweet tender meat, but, whol[e]some, nourishing and a great Restorative; insomuch that sickly and distempered Persons, frequently go from Jamaica to the Islands of Caimanos, which are about 25 leagues distance, and live whol[l]y on that diet, which has, in many Cases, perfectly restored them, so that they have returned hail and well. Their Backs are flatter than the Hawk's bill, their Heads round and small, and when full grown they weigh from 250 to 300 pound weight; though there are degrees even in this sort, in respect to their size; as well as the goodness of their flesh, which is exceeding sweet, and the fat of a dark green. They live who[l]ly on Grass, which grows in the Sea, and is different from the Manatee grass; for that is a small blade, but the other is 5 or 6 inches long and an inch broad.

It is Remarkable in all these Creatures, that at the Breeding time, they have their Common haunts, where they usually feed for two or three Months, & resort to other Places, to lay their Eggs. During that Season both the Male and Female are very lean, especially the former; that no body chuses to Eat them. The most Remarkable places, I ever heard of, in South America, are the Isles of Vacca or Ash, the Caimanos, and the South Cays near Cuba, tho[ugh] there are many other places, where they lay their Eggs, but not in so great numbers. They all lay their Eggs in the Sand at three different times, in May, June and July, some sooner[,] others later, and 80 or 90 at a time. Their Eggs are about the bigness of a Pullet's Egg, but perfectly round, covered with a thin yellow Skin, but it turns to a white, soft Shell, before they lay them.

When they go ashore to lay, it is above an hour, before they return into the Sea, because they are heavy and crawl very slowly; and if it happens to be low Water, they must rest once or twice; for they always lay above high Water mark. Sometimes they come ashore the night before, to take a View, and having found a proper place, return the next day; She makes a great hole with her fins, about two feet deep, wherein She lays her Eggs, and covers them with the sand that came out of the hole; and by the heat of the

Sun they are hatched. When the Female goes to those places, to lay, the Male always attends her, tho[ugh] he does not go ashore, and never leaves her till they return to their common haunt. It is affirm[e]d by the Jamaica Turtlers, that they are nine days engend[e]ring, that they are many Years, before they come to their full growth, and live to great ages.

They are taken different ways, sometimes when they are fast asleep upon the Water; and sometimes by striking them with a Harpoon. But the most common way is with Nets, or when they come ashore to lay, for then they are easily turn[e]d, and when they are laid on their backs, they cannot move. I have often seen them in that posture, emitting tears, and fetching deep Sighs and Groans, which shews that this Creature is endued with Sense, and great passions.

It is a mistaken notion, that the Turtle hath three hearts; for it has only one, and two Auricles, which has led many Persons into that Error.

But certainly it retains its Vital motion many hours after its head, heart, and other parts have been separated; for, I have often seen it move after it has been cut, slashed, and pepper[e]d, in order to be bak[e]d.

It is also Remarkable, that these creatures, will live 2 or three months without any Sustenance, though they pine and wast[e] very much; Consequently are very seldom brought in any tolerable Condition from America. But, they are commonly kept two or three weeks on Board of Sloops, without any nourishment or refreshment, than throwing now and then some buckets of Salt Water among them. When they are brought to Jamaica, they are put into Crawles, which are made with Piles drove into the Sea, in about 3 fathom Water, and about 20 feet square; where they pick up Sea weeds, and other refreshment; by which means they are preserved in good order, and taken out as occasions require or the Markets demand them.

The Heccatee or land Turtle is shaped like the Sea Tortoise but very small. The flesh is also white, tender, and sweet as any Pullet; and commonly Weigh from 10 to 15 pound weight. They have small legs, flat feet and long necks. They live in fresh water ponds, and seldom come on the land, but to lay their Eggs.

There is another sort, which the Spaniards call Tenapen; which is less than the Heccatee, and the Backs rounder. The Shells of these are naturally Carved, finely wrought, and clouded. They delight in Wet Swampy places, or on the land near such places, and are also sweet tender Meat.

The Jew Fish is so called, because it hath Scales or fins, therefore is a clean fish according to the Levitacal Law, and for that reason they are much coveted by the Jews, who eat them freely. It is shaped like a Cod, and about their bigness; for they weigh from ten to sixty pound weight, or more according to their Age. It hath a great head, with fins & Scales, according to the size: the last of which are almost as large as an English half Crown: They are sweet, firm, and fat, are preferr[e]d to all other Fish in America, and are not inferior to any sort in Europe. They feed among Rocks, and are in great plenty, in all the Bays, and Harbours of this Island.

The Rock-Fish, is often taken for a Grooper, there being a resemblance between them and by the Spaniards is called Bacalao, or Cod, because it hath a great head much like a Cod but not so large. It is a round Fish, of a dark brown Colour, and hath small scales about the bigness of a Silver pen[n]y. They are also good sweet meat, and very much Esteem[e]d.

Mullets are the same, as to shape and Colour, as ours in England, but much larger, firmer and better tasted; for they are commonly from 18 inches to two feet, and half in length, when full grown, some being larger than others. The largest size are called Callipeavers, and Eat exceeding well, when they are barbiccud, that is, open[e]d, pepper[e]d, salted and broiled over a slow fire.

There is also another sort, which is call[e]d Mountain Mullet, because they are no where to be met with but in fresh Water Rivers, and chiefly in the Mountains; these are about the bigness of a Mullet in England, but have the preference of every sort of the same kind.

The Snapper, is shaped much like an English Roach, but much larger; for they are commonly from 10 to 15 inches in length, and some more, when full grown. It hath a large head and mouth, great Gills; and the scales are about the bigness of an English Shilling. There are two sorts, the Red and black Snapper; though there is no other difference in them, than the Colour of their Scales; the one being a bright Red, and the other a very dark brown, which in the Water appears black. But the Bellies of both sorts are of a Silver Colour. They are a firm, well tasted Fish, so plentifull and cheap, that the poorer sort of people and Free Negroes in the Towns, are chiefly subsisted by them; and so much esteem[e]d, that they are often brought to the best Tables, in the Island.

The Snook, hath a long head; the Body round, the size of the small part of a Man's Leg, and from 15 to 20 feet in length. The Scales are of a light Colour. They are also good Meat, and very much Esteem[e]d.

The Hog-fish is so called, because the head has a resemblance of that Creatures, but in Shape and Colour, the body is not unlike a large Sna[p]per, only a brighter red. The flesh is very white and equally divided through every flake which is larger than in the Sna[p]per. They are es-teemed equal in goodness to any fish in these Seas.

The Cavallies are of 4 or 5 dif[f]erent sorts some from 6 to 15 Inches in length, and in proportion to Seven or Eight Inches round, with a small scale. They are Course and Seldom eaten, but by the Negroes. Some of them are upon the blue, others a green Colour, except their Bellies, which are all white[;] that sort which are called Jacks, are the best, and most es-teemed, but are small.

The Grooper is lake a Rock-fish, but larger and Courser, it is said that at some Seasons, they are full of Maggots for which reason very few choose to eat them.

The Tarpum is a large Fish and not unlike a Salmon in Shape, but flatter. They are full of Scales, which are near as big as an English half Crown, and of a Silver Colour. The flesh is Solid and firm, and within the Belly are commonly found two large Scalops of fat. They weigh from Ten to twenty pound weight, and some more.

Spanish Mackrill, are in Shape and Colour like English Mackrill, but much larger; for they are commonly from 18 inches to two feet in length, and four or five inches round, and some more.

The Mud fish hath a round head, and body, is commonly about a foot long, and of a dark brown Colour. They are neither Salt nor fresh Water Fish, but feed in Lagunes, Swampy ground, or in brackish Water. They are sometimes good Eating, but are often unpleasant, because they tast[e] of Mud.

The Silver Fish is so call[e]d bacause of its Colour. They are of the size and shape of an Anchovy, and generally thought to be the very same fish; but the Inhabitants have not the Art of curing and preserving them; however they make an Excellent dish, dressed in the manner we do smelts, in England.

Plaice and Flounders are the same as ours in England, But not so large.

Crawfish and Shrimps are likewise the same in shape and Colour, but in tast[e] far exceed any thing of the kind in England; and the latter are commonly as large as Prawns. But the Lobsters are not so good, and are generally rank.

Land Crabs are of two sorts, the one Red but when boil[e]d turns black, and therefore are call[e]d black Crabs; the other White. They both borough in the ground like Rabbets, where they Shelter themselves, and seldome appear in the day time; but in the night come out to feed, and Eat Grass, Herbs or such Fruit as they find, under Trees. It is Remarkable, that the Manchieneal Apple, which neither Bird nor Beast will touch, is greedily devour[e]d by them, without doing them any Injury; and yet they are hurtfull both to Man and Beast that Eat them soon after they have been feeding on that pernicious Fruit. They are seldom, and not easily, taken but in the Night. The common and best way is to make a fire, or carry a light to the place, where they borough, round which they will immediately gather, and are then easily taken, by laying the end of a Stick upon them, and seizing them behind the two great Claws, otherwise they will pinch very hard, and not easily let go their hold.

The black Crabs delight in dry Sandy ground, near the Sea, though they never go into it. They are generally esteemed, especially about October, when they are fat, and full of Eggs; and make Soup far Exceeding Crawfish. They are every way so delicious, that Epicures would set a great Value on them, were they to be had in perfection in England.

The White Crabs are much larger and shap[e]d like a Sea Crab, having one Claw Considerably bigger than the other. These delight in Wet, Swampy ground, and borough so near the Sea, that it often washes into their holes at high Water. The Negroes feed much on them, but they are seldom Eaten by the White Inhabitants, except poor People.

The Al[l]igator is the most terrible Creature, in the Island, and is only to be met with in lagunes or lakes, and other Boggy places. They are made like a lizard, and are from 3 to 20 feet long, according to their Age. As these Creatures are often brought to England, stuffed, and some alive, I need not give any further description. They are very swift, but it is difficult for them to turn, so that they are easily avoided, by watching their motions and turning a different way. They make no noise, commonly lie on the banks of Rivers, Ponds and Lagunes, watching for Beasts that come there to drink which they Seize on as soon as they are within Reach, and devour.

They resemble, till very near, a long piece of Old dry Wood, which deceive not only Beasts but Human Creatures, so that a Person who frequents or approaches those Places, ought to be cautious or Carefull for they devour Men as well as Beasts.

The mischief done by these Creatures, is in some degree recompensed by the advantage of their Fat, which makes an Ointment, that is good for any pains or aches in the bones or joints. And, they have bags of musks Stronger and more Odorous than what we have from the East Indies; so that They are smelt at some distance, by which means they are avoided even by the Cattle. They breed like Toads, by laying their Eggs which are no bigger than a Turkey's, in the sand near Rivers and other Wat[e]ry Places, They cover them and the Sun beams hatch Them; the Shel[l] is firm, and in Shape like to a Turkey's, but not Spotted. As soon as the Young come out of the Shell they take immediately to the Water.

Among the Insects and other Reptiles in this Island are several kind of Snakes, which are so far from being Venomous or hurtfull that they Crawl or run away on the sight of a Person unless they are interrupted or disturbed, and then they only hiss, menace and make the best defence they are able. These Creatures in the Mountains and woody Places make a disagreeable, and even a frightfull noise to Strangers most part of the Night.

They have also Scorpions, Lizards, Ants, Gras[s]hoppers[,] Flies and other Insects, which are in Europe, and some that are peculiar and only to be met with in America.

The Common Flies are more numerous and troublesome than in Europe, especially in the Plantations at the time of making of Sugar or Indigo, when they are intollerable, insomuch that at Meals People are obliged to keep a Negro with a small branch or twig of a Tree, to brush Them away.

The Fire flies contract and expand their light as they fly, and are only to be seen or met with in the Night, when great numbers of them, are Constantly floating in the Air and emitting light, which appear[s] in the dark

Engraved by Jan Lamsvelt and entitled *Geregt van een Boecanier met een Crocodil*, this image depicts a crocodile with its teeth clamped on the leg of a buccaneer who, as his indigenous companion flees into the woods, pulls his knives to kill his attacker. According to accompanying text, this attack took place on the Isla de los Pinos, the largest of the islands off the coast of Cuba and a rendezvous for buccaneers. Found in Nicolaas ten Hoorn, *Historie der boecaniers, of vrybuyters van America* (Amsterdam, 1700), following p. 138.

like so many sparks of Fire. They resemble Cantharides so much that they are generally looked upon to be the same Species.

The Musquitoes are very troublesome, Especially to Strangers, who are apt to Scratch the part that is bit, which makes it to itch, and the scratching commonly causes a humour to fall there. The only remedy to prevent this, and to asswage the itching is to rub the part effected, with the lime or bastard lemon. They need no description being the very same creature, which is well known in England, by the name of a gnat.

The merry wing or Sand fly is so small, that it is scarcely discernable with the naked Eye, and their bite or Sting is more painfull than that of the Musquito, for it burns like a spark of fire, falling on a Person's hand or Face, but they cannot pierce through a Stocking, nor is it attended with any other Consequence.

The Chego is very troublesome and mischievous to Negroes, and poor People, who are not very cleanly and Carefull of Themselves. They commonly get into the Feet, or hands in the Nervous, and Membranous Parts, itch burn and are very painfull, when they have been some days in the Flesh. They appear at first like a very small black Speck and are taken out with a needle, the hole is then filled with Tobacco Ashes, which perfects the Cure in a day or two. They breed in great numbers, in bags which must be carefully taken out, otherwise some part of the Brood will be left behind, and by degrees spread over the Feet or hands, so as to indanger them. They are incident only to Such as are uncleanly, or go into Negroes' Houses, and Places where poultry are kept. The Negroes, who neglect to make use of proper means, in time have often been obliged to have their Toes or feet cut off.

Cock-roaches are about the bigness of a beetle and are a nasty, stinking Creature. If they happen on Sound Sleepers, they bite till they fetch blood, and are so nimble that tis not easy to Catch them. They Commonly frequent, and breed in great numbers in Boiling Houses, and other Places where Sugars and other Eatables that are sweet, are kept.

An Old Wife is a flat Fish something bigger than a large Flounder and are of a Silver Colour. They are different from those of the same sort in England, because they have Scales on both sides which are so large, and lye so close together that they seem to have none. They have long heads not unlike a Snook's.

Stone Bass is also a flat Fish, and not unlike an old Wife, only not so broad nor the fins so large but are about the bigness of a Well grown Plaice. They are very much Esteemed by People in General, being firm[,] well tasted and Equal in Goodness to most or any other sort of Fish in America. They are likewise more Common and Plenty there being great Quantities in all the Harbours and Bays of this Island.

The Baracoota or Paracooda is a long round Fish about the bigness of a Well grown Pike, but Commonly longer. They are very good Meat, but few Choose to Eat them, because they are sometimes poisonous or Occasion the Hair and Nails of the Person who Eat them to come off which is Attributed to some feed they meet with in particular places. The Antidote for this it is said to be the back bone of the Fish palverized and given in any liquor. I cannot affirm the truth or Success of it, but I have heard divers Seafearing Men and others say, that when They found themselves Sick or disordered by Eating of this Fish, They made use of that Remedy and found no other ill Effect than a Numbedness or weakness in their Limbs for some short time after; some pretend to distinguish a poisonous Baracoota from a wholesome one by their liver, which as soon as they have taken the Fish, they pull out and Taste: If it taste[s] Sweet they dress and eat the Fish without fear; but if the Liver be bitter or bite the Tongue, like pepper, They conclude the Fish to be nought and throw it away.

Beside these there are divers other sorts of Shell Fish in this Island, tho[ugh] many of them are of no other use than for their Shells some of which are very Beautifull, and made into Snuff Boxes or such like uses, but chiefly to adorn Gentlemen's Grottos.

The Oysters are of the same kind with what we have in England; they are smaller but better Tasted; though I am of Opinion They might be improved was the same Art and Care taken of them for that purpose. There is another sort of the Musell kind, which are flatt and to be met with in all the Harbours and Bays of this Island, in great Quantities but are not much Esteemed.

Musel[,] Cockels and Perriwinckles are of the same kind with ours in England, therefore need no Description.

Wilks are also the same as ours, but are much larger and better tasted.

The Conch is the largest Shell Fish I ever saw of the Sort; for when they are taken out They are bigger than a Man's fist. The fleshy part is Course, rugged and Slimy, Especially the Out parts; therefore it must be Scoured w[i]th Sand, before it is dressed for Eating: and within the Substance is hard and tough, for which Reason they beat them as we do Beef Steaks to make them tender; but when They are thus managed and well dressed, They are Esteemed by some of the better sort of people, as well as the Sailors and Common sort. Their shells are Remarkably made large and winding like a Snail Shell; the Mouth is flat[,] large and very wide in proportion to the bigness of the Shell. The Outsides are rough and full of small knobs but within very smooth, and not unlike Mother of Pearl, tho[ugh] some of them are of a Vermillion Colour. They are made use of in many Plantations, which have no Bells, for Calling the Negroes into or out of the Field, as Occasions require, or in Case of an Alarm or Fire; for being put to the Mouth and blown into very strongly, it makes a loud inarticulate Noise, which may be heard at a great distance, according to the stillness of the Weather.

But the Soldier is the most Remarkable of the kind and derive their Name from the French who call them Soldats, because they Accommodate themselves in the Habitations of others, having none of their own; for as they have not any proper Shells to themselves to Secur[e] their little Bodies from Injuries, they take possession of the Shell of any other Animal, commonly a Periwinckle of which there are great Numbers of all sorts on most of the Coasts and Bays of this Island. As they grow they shift their Shells and get into others that are larger which is the Reason of their being of different forms or shape, According to the Shell they p[ick].

Their Bodies are very weak, tender and Slimy like a Snail, but they move much faster and do not[,] like them[,] foul the place they pass; near one third of this little Animal, and about the Head is in shape and Colour like a boiled Shrimp with little Claws and two larger like a Crab. The latter serves not only for Offensive and defensive Weapons, but to close the Entrance of their Shells and Secure their whole Body, so that they appear when taken up like an Entire Shell without any Cavity or Substance within. When it is put so near a fire as to heat the Shell it will immediately forsake its Quarters; but when it becomes Cool they will Enter again and Crawl in backwards. They are of the Size of a prawn, Eatable, and much Esteemed by many persons, Especially the Tail, which is well Tasted and delicious, but the fore part is bony and useless. They are thrust upon a Skuer and many of them roasted in that manner, in a row. They feed upon the Ground, and Eat what falls from Trees, and have under the Chin a little bag, into which they put a reserve of Food, beside this they have in them a little Sand bag which is commonly full of Sand, and must be taken out before they are dressed and Eaten, otherwise they would be gritty. If these Animals eat any of the Manchineal Apples, which drop from the Trees, their flesh becomes so infected with that Virulent juice, as to poison those who Eat them; tho[ugh] some have only been made very sick, and in a short time it has gone off again without any further damage.

The Oil of these Insects is a Sovereign Remedy for any Sprain or Contusion and is not only used by the Indians of America, but the Seamen and Inhabitants of Jamaica with great Success; therefore [they] are sought after for that purpose as well as to Eat. The Oil is of a yellow Colour like wax but of the Consistency of palm Oil.

Part the 10th.

Of the Situation and Natural Advantages of Jamaica, and the Trade thereof to and from Great Britain, Ireland, Africa, the Plantations in North America, and other Parts, with some Observations and Proposals, for their Encouragement, Improvement and Security.

The Situation of this Island makes it of great importance to the British Nation and may make it much more usefull than it has been hitherto, in regard to its Produce, as well as for Trade, and annoying our Enemies in time of War. But this like other Naturall advantages, Seems to have been neglected, or not truly valued or Regarded.

It is Certain that no Place can be more Commodious in all Respects, as will appear on the first View, of the Map of America considering its Vicinity or Neighbourhood, to the most Valuable possessions of the Spaniards in that part of the World; for it lies 30 leagues distance W[est] and by S[outh] of the West end of Hispaniola; 161 leagues N[orth]W[est] by N[orth] of Carthagena; 172 leagues N[orth] by E[ast] of Porto Bello; 136 leagues S[outh]E[ast] by E[ast] of Cape Antonio, 200 leagues S[outh]E[ast] of the Havanna; 352 leagues E[ast] 1/2 S[outh] of La vera Cruz; and 20 leagues S[outh] of the Easternmost part of Cuba.

Hence it appears that all Ships bound from Europe, S[an]ta Martha, Carthagena, or Porto Bello, to Havanna, or the Bay of Mexico, must necessarily pass in Sight of the North side, or the S[outh]W[est] end of Jamaica unless they go through the old Straights of Bahama which is a very difficult and dangerous passage. And even there they may be intercepted by our Ships of War on that Station, cruising in the Windward passage; so that while we are Masters of the Seas, and in Possession of this Island we are enabled to restrain the Trade, and Consequently the Power of the Spaniards, and even to prescribe laws to them in America.

Generall Venables, and Commissioner Butler in their letter to Cromwell, dated June 4. 1655 say:

> As for this Island of Jamaica (that we may acquaint your Highness with every thing that is Materiall) by its Situation lieth more Advantagiously for annoying the Spaniards on every side than Hispaniola; neither is it inferior in itself, for we find it to abound with store of Fish, Fowls, Cattle, Fruits of all sorts usuall in these Parts; and we are informed further by one of the

Chiefest and oldest Inhabitants, of the Country, that there is a Silver Mine
Here, as also one of Copper lately discovered; besides some Grains of
Gold have been found likewise. The Climate is more Temperate, than that
of Hispaniola, by Reason of its being more Open to the Eastern Breezes;
nor is it less fruitfull in any Respect.

Collo[nel] Thomas Muddiford who was Governour of Barbadoes, and
some years after the Restoration created a Baronet and appointed Governour of Jamaica, in His letter to Secretary Thurloe dated June the 20th,
1655 says

And though I am much troubled at the unexpected defeat at Hispaniola,
Yet I am not at all sorry they are gone to Jamaica. But heartily wish it had
been their first Attempt that it might have seemed rather Choice than Necessity. It is apparently far more proper for their purpose, than the other
Island or Porto Rico, as the Situation in the Maps will make more Visible.
It hath an Excellent Harbour, and is Accounted the most healthfull and
plentifull of them all. It will be sooner Peopled, and is far more Convenient for Attempts on the Spanish Fleets, and more especially the Carthagena Fleet which must pass within sight of it as they go to the Havanna.
I believe it will give the Court of Spain more trouble than ten of the other
would have done, and therefore it must be expected, that some Attempts
will be made by the Spaniards to Supplant them &c.

In the same letter He adds:

I hope our Nation will not draw back, having thus far entered for I am
most confident that if this place be fully Peopled, which in a few Years may
be done, His Highness may do what He will in the West Indies; truly if
the Men on Shore be well Armed, and a proper Number of Ships be kept
at Sea, with God's blessing there is no fear of Success. I had got near one
hundred Families that would have gone from hence to Hispaniola, and do
still hope to induce them for the other place &c.

And, Major Generall Fortescue who Commanded the Forces, upon the
departure of General Venables from Jamaica, in His letter to Secretary
Thurloe dated the 20th. of July 1655. Says:

I am only sorry that we landed on Hispaniola in regard to the loss and
disgrace we received there; it doth not repent me that we sate not down
there, being Confident that we could not subsist and that this Island is to
all intents and purposes more advantageous than that: not a Ship can Stir
from Carthagena or to Cuba but must come in View of this Island.

Experience hath confirmed the Opinions and observations of those Gentlemen, which are the more Remarkable, as they had only a transient view, and neither of them had time or Opportunity, to be more particular. This makes it necessary to explain and Set forth those advantages, and to draw a Comparison between the two Islands.

Jamaica hath eight fine Harbours, and severall Convenient Coves and Bays where Ships may safely ride; Whereas in all the Island of Hispaniola though of a much larger extent there are but two, that can properly be Called Harbours viz. St. Domingo, and Port Louis. The former is Still in the possession of the Spaniards, and is Situated on the W[est] side of the Entrance into the River Hine which is Navigable, and near the middle part of the S[outh] Side of the Island. The other is in the possession of the French, and situated near the S[outh]W[est] end of the Island; it is made a Harbour by a Cay or small Island, laying before a Bay, and without that the Isle of Ash; it is Commodious and Defensible, but small. As to the other Parts though there are Several places, where Ships may ride conveniently Yet they are all open Bays, and lay exposed to an Enemy.

But though Hispaniola has many fine Rivers in it, yet considering the extent it is not so well watered as Jamaica, where there are Eighty four Rivers, which run into the Sea, and innumerable Rivulets and Springs, that run into them.

The Situation of Jamaica is very Commodi[o]us, as I have Observed either for Annoying or carrying on an intercourse with all the Rich Trading Ports in the North Sea from St. Martha to the Gulph of Mexico. It Enjoy's this Singular Advantage, not only in being Situate near the Centre of this Tract, but also by the favour of the Winds which blow from a few Points namely from the N[orth]E[ast] to the S[outh]E[ast] w[i]th little other Variation, above three fourths of the year. In both these Respects this Island may Justly be prefer[r]ed to all the other Islands in America as well as Hispaniola; for Ships Cannot turn up from Carthagena, and Porto Bello to *St. Domingo*, in less than 4 or 5 weeks; nor from Havanna and Lavera Cruz, in twice that space of time. Whereas Ships are seldom more than three or four days, in their passage from *Jamaica* to Carthagena, and Porto Bello; and return in about the Same space of time; and to the other Places Ships Commonly Sail in 10 or 14 days, and return in three or four weeks, sometimes less. These Circumstances when Compared together with skill & Attention, will sufficiently point out the Advantages that may be drawn from this Island both in Peace and War.

But, However convenient or usefull the Situation of this Island is, or may be made, it is at all times necessary to keep a Squadron of men of War there, because of the Extensive Trade, and because the Course of Navigation to and from Great Britain, and other Parts, is surrounded with Envious and potent Neighbours; otherwise what is now an Advantage; or may be made so, may prove a misfortune to the Inhabitants as well as the Trade.

This Consideration lays the Inhabitants under the Necessity of being more than ordinar[il]y Vigilant for by their Laws, they are oblig[e]d to Appear in Arms, and to Cause Signalls or Alarms to be made throughout the Island, upon the appearance of four Sail of Ships on any part of their Coast; and They are at all times very diligent and Exact in Exercising and Disciplining their Militia in order to render them usefull, and fit for Service, in Case of an Invasion or Insurrection. As to the Course of the Navigation it is improper, and cannot be expected, that I should be more particular in this place than to observe, that all Ships out and Home, must necessarily, and unavoidably, pass in Sight and even within two leagues, of some Parts of the French and Spanish Dominions, in America. And the Rout[e] is so well known to seafaring men, French and Spanish as well as English, that Cruisers are at all times necessary, for the protection of Trade, against Pirates, and Spanish Guarda Costas in time of Peace, and Privateers in time of War. Many Instances may be produc[e]d to Evince the truth of this Position, from my own Experience and observation, though I shall only make the following Remarks, which will Evidently shew the Reasonableness, and even the Necessity of what I here Suggest.

Whenever a Squadron of Six or Eight Ships of War were stationed at Jamaica, and Commanded by an Active, Vigilant Officer, the Navigation has been Safe and Secure: But, as often as this has been neglected the Trade and Riches of that Island has constantly drawn that way Wicked and abandoned men, or all Nations, who live upon Rapine and plunder. America, Swarmed with them, soon after the Peace of Utrecht, and as no more than two Small ships of War, were on the Station from that time to Nove[mbe]r 1719[,] the Trade and Navigation of this Island sustained very considerable damages by those People, and the Spaniards perceiving how much the Island was neglected and Exposed were also encouraged thereby, and in 1715 began to fit out Vessells under Colour of Guarding their own Coasts, and preventing an Illicit Commerce, but in reality to plunder and disturb our lawfull Trade; for some of them not only Visited and searched our Ships upon the open Seas, which were bound directly from or to Great Britain or the Northern Colonies, But even landed on the Island, in the remote parts, plundered the Inhabitants and at times carried away above three hundred Negroes, for which the unhappy Sufferers never obtained any Satisfaction or Redress.

This Conduct of the, Spaniards laid the Island under the necessity of fitting out two armed Sloops at a great Expence for the protection of their own Coasts until his late Majesty, upon the application of the Merchants[,] was pleased to Order a small Squadron Consisting of four men of War, and two Sloops, for the protection of the Trade and Coasts of this Island, commanded by Commodore Vernon; through whose Vigilance and care those Seas were not only cleared of Pirates; But the Spanish Guarda Costas, never dared to appear out of their proper Stations, and our Merchants'

Ships passed the Seas, unmolested and were not in any degree interrupted on their lawfull Occasions. They were likewise quiet, in Port and our Navigation suffered very little damage from them or common Pyrates, from 1727 to July 1729, when the Squadron was Commanded by Commodore St. Lo; nor was one Vessell taken or plundered from August 1732 to July 1735, through the Activity and Vigilance of S[i]r. Chaloner Ogle, who then Commanded on that Station.

But, before and after those periods, when they had no more than two or three Ships of War whose Commanders had more regard to Their own Ease or private Interest, than the Publick Service, our Ships were daily taken, some of them plundered, and others carried into Port and Condemned on pretences alltogether unreasonable and unwarrantable, and even Contrary to Solemn Treaties subsisting between the two Crowns. This brought on a just and Necessary War which it is to be hoped will enable us to obtain satisfaction for all past injuries, and a freedom of Navigation for the future.[1]

But, However it is indispensably necessary to maintain a Squadron of men of War there in Peace as well as in War, for the Reasons I have given. And though I do not presume to advise, or lay down Rules to my Superiors, Yet I hope, I may without offence, be allowed to give my Opinion, that not less than ten sail of the line, and some small frigots, with a Flag Officer, ought to be on that Station, in time of War; and in time of Peace two Ships of the line, three or four frigots or Twenty Gun Ships and two Sloops, with an Officer of Distinction to command them.

That the Commanding Officer should have orders to keep a Ship cruising between Cape Altavela and Cape Tiberoon, or the West end of Hispaniola, for the protection of the outward bound Trade; Another between Cape Antonio, and Havanna; and one between Cape Maiz and Cape Nichola, Commonly called the Windward Passage, for the protection of our Homeward bound Trade. That one of the Sloops be Employed in Cruising round the Island, and particularly on the North side, for the Security of the Remote Settlements, which lay open and Exposed, and probably will be thrown up and deserted, unless protected. And that those Ships be duly relieved from time to time in Such manner, that Cruisers may be constantly on those Stations. The Expence of the Crown will be inconsiderable in Respect to the Advantages that will Arise to the Nation, by the Duties that are payable on their product; their Consumption of British manufactures; and the Employment they give to our Navigation and Seamen, beside a

1. The War for Jenkins' Ear began on October 23, 1737, in retaliation for the removal of the ear of Captain Robert Jenkins by Spanish customs officials for suspected smuggling. By December 1740, this war had been subsumed by the war to which Knight here refers, the War of the Austrian Succession, or King George's War, against France and Spain. It concluded with the Treaty of Aix-la-Chapelle in which France rescinded its claims to the Austrian throne and regained its military losses in the American theater of war.

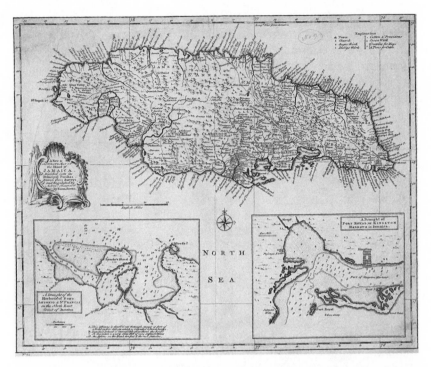

In 1747, the London cartographer Emanuel Bowen (1693–1767) published *A New and Accurate Map of the Island of Jamaica. Divided into Its Principal Parishes*, which offers a cartographic portrait of Jamaica's development close to the time of James Knight's demise. Of particular interest are the two inset maps of Kingston and Port Antonio, intended to emphasize the colony's growing urbanization and commercial resources.

vast number of Artificers and Tradesmen, throughout Great Britain, Ireland, and the Northern Plantations, who are absolutely supported and are dependant on them.

To Evince the truth of these observations, it is necessary to Shew the improvements, which have been made in this Island, merely by the force of Industry, without the Assistance that other Colonies have had; and the Advantages which arise thereby to the Trade, Revenues and Navigation of Great Britain, notwithstanding the difficulties and misfortunes they have from time to time met with viz. the dreadfull Earthquake in 1692, which laid their Houses and Plantations in Ruins, the Invasion by the French in the year 1694, who though they were repulsed with great loss, yet destroyed many fine Estates, and did other Considerable waste and damage, to the Island. Three Hurricanes, in 1712, 1722, and 1726, which likewise did an infinite deal of prejudice, and Especially as they were attended with long and Severe droughts. But, [from] these misfortunes the Planters have in a great measure recovered, and the Island is at this time in a very flourishing Condition as will appear from the following Calculation, of the Number of Sugar Works in Every Parish and the Quantity of Sugar which they produce at a medium, and upon a reasonable and Moderate computation.

	Sugar Works	N[umber] of Hogsheads
In St. Thomas in the E[ast]	44	4120
St. David's	8	455
St. Andrew's	31	1450
Kingston	0	
Port Royal	0	
St. Katherine's	3	210
St. John's	28	2000
St. Thomas in the Vale	48	3315
St. Dorothy's	8	370
Vere	7	405
Clarendon	66	5480
St. Elizabeth's	32	2745
Hannover	39	2620
Westmorland	64	5450
St. James	8	660
St. Ann's	19	2050
St. Mary's	19	1525
St. George's	4	380
Portland		
	428	33,235

This Calculation was made in 1737, and the produce of the several Plantations taken at a medium for 3 years. At that time ten of those Plantations, did not make Sugar, being newly Set[t]led, and several others have Since been raised, so that although some of the Old ones, are declined, Yet upon the whole the Annual Product must have encreased greatly, and will still encrease with due and Reasonable Encouragement from Their Mother Country, which will hereafter be pointed Out.

To illustrate the Advantages of this Island to Great Britain and to Set them in a Stronger light, I shall Estimate the Annual produce, in as exact a manner as the Nature of the thing will admit. For though a computation may be made of Sugars; with some Certainty, Yet it Cannot be done so well in Respect to other Commodities, and therefore I have had recourse to the imports into Great Britain at a Medium for 3 Years.

This 1780 *View of Virgin Valley Estate Jamaica* in Trelawny Parish provides a close-up look at a portion of a plantation, showing and identifying by numbers the wide variety of structures necessary for plantation life: the fowl house, pigeon house, overseer's house, cook room, wash house, stables, sheep pen, hospital or hot house, mill house with mules at work, a curing house, and trash house. (National Library of Jamaica)

33,150 Hogshead of Sugar, commputing them at 14 [?] each at 20/ Ster[ling] p[ercent] at a medium is   £4,641,000

It is generally computed that 60 pound [weigh]t of Sugar, produces 4 Gallons of Molasses, and makes that article 3,536,532 Gallons, whereof 1/3 or 1,178,844 Gallons is commonly sold and Shipped off to North America, at 6 [pence] Ster[ling] p[er] gallon . . .   29470,10 [shillings]

The other 2/3 or 2,357,688 Gallons of Molasses is distilled into Rum, 3 gallons to make 2 gallons of Rum including the Skimmings is 1571792 gallons of Rum at 18 [pence]   1,17884—
          ─────────────
          601454–10 [shillings]

Bags of Cotton qt. [blank] at [blank] p[ercen]t

Casks of Piemento qt. [blank] at [blank] p[ercen]t

Bags of Ginger qt. [blank] at [blank] p[ercen]t

Casks of Coffee qt. [blank] at [blank] p[ercen]t

of Indigo qt [blank] at [blank]

Tons of Logwood [blank]

Tons of Fustick [blank]

feet of Mohogany [blank]

The Major part if not the whole value of those Manufactures, may be deemed clear profit to the Nation, since they are the product of labour, and the Duties and incidental Charges Center in our Selves. It is also to be considered that the other British Colonies, produce very little or any of those Commodities except Sugar, so that we must be obliged to purchase them of other Nations, were they not produced in this Island. Cotton is necessary to work up with our Wool, in many of our Manufactures, Ginger is chiefly Exported, though great quantities are consumed at Home, Especially among the poor People. Piemento lessens the Consumption of Spice, which is only to be had of the Dutch at their own rates. Indigo, Logwood, and Fustick, are Consumed by the Dyers, and are absolutely necessary in many of our Manufactures.

To which may be added that before we had those commodities of our own, we paid five times the price for them, we do now, and for some of them more; and it is probable we should do the same again, were we deprived of having them in the Same manner. To Explain this more particularly I must observe that before the British Sugar Islands, were set[t]led, we paid the Portuguese from 4 to £5 per [cen]t weight for Muscovado or unrefined Sugar, which of late years hath been sold from 15 to 34 shillings per weight sometimes under according to the goodness; and £5 per weight for Ginger which is commonly sold from 20 [shillings] to 22 [shillings] 6 [pence] per [cen]t weight. Our Dyer's wares were bought of the Spaniards to whom we paid from 100 or £130 p[er] ton, for Logwood, which is now sold from 7 to £10 per ton, and other goods in proportion. So that by having this and other Plantations of our own we not only save so much as we paid formerly for those Commodities but we are able to furnish other Nations, our Navigation and Seamen are considerably encreased; and our Manufacturers are enabled to sell their Commodities proportionably cheaper, which is undoubtedly another very great advantage to the Nation.

It is also worth observing that not one fifth part of the manurable lands in Jamaica have ever been set[t]led, and one Reason of their not being Cultivated is owing to our false maxims of suffering People to possess greater tracts of land than they can plant, and hold them in hopes of making great advantages by the Sale of them.

This is not only an Obstruction to the Encrease of Settlements and Strengthening the Island but, to His Majestie's Revenues in Great Britain as well as in Jamaica Because, the improvement of those lands would greatly Augment the annual Product and Consequently the Duties payable to His Majesty; and enable the Receiver General to Collect the Quit Rents, great part of them having never paid One Shilling to the Crown since the first grant, or Contributed in any degree to the support of the Government. For, as many of the Proprietors are in England, and have no Effects upon those uncultivated Lands[,] no levy or distress can be made for want of a proper Law, to Subject the Lands. But, considering the Reasonableness and even the Necessity of such a law, or some other measures being taken to Remove this Grievance, it Cannot be doubted but that the Legislature, will take the same into Consideration, and Apply a Proper Remedy, without any longer Delay. The Advantages are so great and Obvious that no arguments are wanting to inforce them; for were those Lands duly Cultivated, the Annual produce might be raised to three Millions or more p[er] An[num] instead of one. The Duties to His Majesty, the Consumption of British Manufactures and the Number of Shipping Seamen and others, who are Employed by the Trade would be proportionally encreased. And we might also be furnished with Indigo, Cocoa and other Commodities, which we now purchase of the French and Spaniards; those Lands are Capable of producing such Commodities and with proper Encouragement great Quantities would be made sufficient not only for our own Consumption and to the Saving of £300000 p[er] An[num] which is now laid out with those Nations but a surplusage for the Supply of our Neighbours, who have not any of those Commodities of Their Own, and the Exportation whereof would be a further Benefit to the Nation.

I come now to treat of the Trade of this Island, which in general, has greatly encreased in my time, though some particular Branches are declined. For in 1711 the Exports of Sugars did not exceed 14,000 h[ogs]h[ea]ds though there was not any Complaint of the want of Seasons, or any other Disaster, nor did They weigh more than 11 weight each, so that considering the difference of the weights of the h[ogs]h[ea]ds, the Quantity now Exported annually is more than double what was made, any one Year, before that period of time.

Nor did the Number of Shipping of all Sorts Exceed 170 or 180 Sail which now at a medium for 3 Years, are upwards of 300.

Of these I compute about 50 Sail belonging to the City of London which are Constant Traders; and 30 more which are Transient ships Guinea men &c in all.

To the Port of Bristol, including the Ships they send to	80
Africa & this Island	50
To the Port of Liverpool, including the Ships they send to Africa . . .	25
To the Out Ports	10
To Scotland . . .	10
To Boston, New York, Philadelphia, Carolina, and R[h]ode Island . . .	100
To the Island [colonies]	30
	———
	305

If we compute the Number of men each Ship Carrys at 20, one with another, the whole number will Appear to be 6100 men. Beside those employed in the Logwood Trade, who are not less than 1000 more, there being 7 or 800 men Set[t]led in the Bay of Honduras before the War with Spain. And, though many of Them, are now among the Privateers, yet it is probable upon a Peace They will return to their former Employment.

London, Bristol, Liverpool and the Out Ports furnish this Island with the Manufactures of Great Britain, East India Goods, and other Commodities which are received in Exchange for the Manufactures of Great Britain. Such as Wines from Madeira and Negroes from Africa.

The Quantity of Wines imported Annually from Madeira for some Years past are Considerably lessened, not being in such repute as They were formerly, by reason they are not so good in Quality, and Small Rum punch a little upon the Acid, being found by Experience to be more wholesome, so that the imports do not Exceed 2000 pipes annually at a Medium.

But, the following account of the Number of Negroes, imported into and Exported from this Island for 10 Years, which I had out of the Books of the Receiver General will clearly shew the Value of that Branch of Trade (which is now in a declining way) and how necessary it is to preserve and Support it; least we should be entirely Supplanted by other Nations.

1725. 10,061 . . .	5916
1726. 8,635 . . .	3862
1727. 3,532 . . .	1591
1728. 7,110 . . .	2146
1729. 9,277 . . .	4157
1730. 11,572 . . .	5510
1731. 9,933 . . .	5331
1732. 11,090 . . .	4605
———————	———
72,210	33,318

It must be observed that the Assiento Company did export great part of those Negroes, except in the years 1727, 1728, 1729, when there was an interruption to their Commerce, by the Rupture with Spain, so that the Exports as well as the imports were chiefly, if not wholly part of that time carried on by the Private Traders. But, had that Company never Subsisted, the advantages arising to the Nation would not have been less in that Branch of Trade, and much greater in other Respects.

Ireland, Supplys the Island with salted Provisions, namely Beef, Pork, Herrings, and Butter.

Scotland with Woolens, Linnens, and Herrings.

Boston with Boards, Shingles, Staves, Lamp Oil, salted Cod, and Mackarell.

New York with Flower, Biscuit, Hams, Peas, Staves, some salted Beef and Pork, which is good for present use, but those People not having Yet fallen into a right way of salting and preserving their meat it will not keep above 5 or 6 months.

Philadelphia also furnishes the Island, with the same Commodities as are imported from New York.

Carolina with Rice, Pitch, Tar, and some salted Beef and Pork.

And, R[h]ode Island with Boards, Shingles, Staves and Horses.

These Northern Traders load with Mollasses[,] Rum and other Commodities. But, some of them will receive nothing but mon[e]y, in payment, and in defiance of several Acts of Parliament sail to the French Islands where they purchase Rum and Mollasses to the great Benefit of that Nation, and to the Prejudice of Great Britain, as well as our American Colonies, by promoting the Trade of our most Dangerous Rivalls and Natural Enemy, and depriving the Crown of its just Dues; for as those Commodities, purchased of the French cannot be legally imported, they are landed at North America in a private and Clandestine way.

It may perhaps be Expected that I should likewise mention another Branch of Trade, which is deemed by many, to be Illicit, and tho[ugh] this Opinion has been Exploded: yet the Inhabitants of this Island, are still unjustly Stigmatized by the Emissaries, and Advocates of Spain to colour the illegal and unwarrantable behaviour of that Perfidious Nation in America. That the Spaniards have a right, as well as other States, to train Their Commerce, and prohibit Strangers, or other Nations from Trading within any part of their Dominions; And, that by the 8th. Article of the Treaty with Spain in 1670, it is Stipulated that the Subjects of the King of Great Britain shall abstain and forbear to Sail and Trade in the Ports and Havens which have Fortifications, Castles, Magazines or Ware Houses and in all other Places whatsoever possessed by the other Party in the West Indies; I will readily admit. Also that the Goods and Effects of such Traders, are justly liable to Seizure and a legal Condemnation. Nor have I heard of any Complaint being made in such Cases notwithstanding the Clamour that was raised or whatever may have been suggested to the Contrary; though

I think the usage and treatment our men meet with, even in those Cases cannot be justified, But, I conceive that no Trade can truly be deemed Illicit in regard to me or any other Subject of Great Britain which is not prohibited by the Laws of God or my Own Country tho[ugh] I am subject to the Forfeitures and Penalties of the Laws of other Countries, on a proper and legal Conviction. And, as it is Certainly the Interest of Great Britain, to Export as many of our Manufactures, as we can possibly vend, and receive in Return Bullion and other Valuable commodities, without Considering who are the Exporters or Importers it would be bad Policy in us, to give any Obstruction to that Branch of our Commerce, though it may not be Consistent with Treaties, in time of Peace, for the Government to Encourage and Countenance it in a Publick Manner.

This we find to be the Practice, in all Ages of the French, Dutch and other Nations. And, though the Laws of England are as restrictive as possible, in regard to the Exportation of Wool, yet the late King of France, Lewis the 14, was so far from Discouraging a Trade so Beneficial to His Subjects, and pernicious to Great Britain, that He even advanced large Sums of money to enable them to carry it on[,] particularly to some who were ruined by Seizures, which had been made. Nor do we find the French or the Dutch restrain their Subjects from Trading with the Spaniards in America; though they have Constantly carried on a more Extensive Commerce and in a more Publick manner, than the Subjects of Great Britain without any noise or Clamour.

It cannot be expected, as it is highly improper, that I should state the manner and method of carrying on this Trade; But considering the practice of other Nations, and the great Quantities of British Manufactures, which are yearly vended by that means, I cannot think that man a Friend to His Country, who Endeavours to Prohibit or Obstruct it. And should so pernicious a Scheme ever prevail, the Spaniards themselves in America, would often be put to very great Streights, and Difficulties because no other Country can so Easily relieve them under any Exigency or Distress, as this Island. For it is well known that the Galleons, in time of Peace, have been furnished with Naval Stores and Provisions, without which They could not have proceeded on Their Voyage to Old Spain.

And that when Panama was burnt in 1737, They sent to this Island in the most supplicating manner for relief and Assistance which was granted Them[;] Otherwise They could not have raised new Buildings for want of proper Materials, and many Persons would have perished for want of Food. In return for the timely assistance given them, They soon after fitted out ships and interrupted even our lawful Trade in that part of the World.

From Hence it appears, Great Britain Derives many Considerable Advantages from this Island, and that they may be greatly improved with due and Reasonable Encouragement. This leads me to Consider what is proper and necessary to be done, in order to promote so good and Beneficial a Design.

As the Welfare of all Countries, depends on good Government, without doubt our American Colonies would Improve and flourish more than they ever have done were they always conducted by Men of probity, Wisdom and personal Courage. Whether this part of Policy has been duly and Constantly observed or Neglected? And Whether there has not been formerly, Indigent, unskilful, and Avaritious Persons sent Over and entrusted with the Care and Administration of them are Questions, worthy of notice and Enquiry, though not proper for me to Expatiate upon? However, I may without offence declare my Sentiments and Opinion of the qualifications Necessary in such a Principal Magistrate.

A Governour ought to be a Gentleman of Experience, Abilities and Virtue. Who is Easy in His Circumstances, and not under any Temptation to fleece and Injure the People or to Violate His Trust in any Degree. He should be a man of Temperance, Moderation, and Justice, for He that is not possessed of those Qualities, can never Expect order or be able to reform the manners of others. He should be qualified to look into the Temper and Genius of the People; the Nature of the Soil, and Commerce of the Country, in order to form a Judgment what improvements they are Capable of, and will be most Advantagious. One that will Encourage Industry, discountenance Idleness, Immorality and Profaneness; And be Active, Vigilant and Attentive to the welfare and Interest of the Territories under His Command.

It is Certainly Necessary, and of great importance to the Nation, as well as to the Colonies, that He, who is to command many Thousand Families, and has so great a Trust vested in Him, should be endowed with those Qualities and a general knowledge of men and Things.

And it would undoubtedly Conduce to their Welfare and good Government, if the same method was taken which the King of France Observes strictly in His Plantations not only in giving large appointments to all His Governours out of His own Coffers, Restraining Them from Perquisites, or drawing any Advantages from the People; but in promoting Them upon Their Return, if They behave well. Whereas the Governours in general of other Nations, having no other hopes or expectations, and being uncertain how long They shall enjoy Their Stations make the most of Their time, to the prejudice of the People, who perceiving an Interest seperate from Their own, carried on[,] constantly oppose such measures and from thence arise those Jealousies and Animosities, which commonly attend the Administration of most of the Governours of the British Colonies, in America.

To such wise Regulations, as I have mentioned, is owing the great improvement the French have made in Trade and Plantations within the space of 40 years. For it appears by a memorial of the Deputies of Commerce in France, presented to the Royal Council in 1701, that the English then Employed 5 Ships to Their one, whereas it is Evident their Trade and Navigation to America at this time, is Equal if not Superior to ours and that Their Colonies do produce more Commodities in Quantity and

Value, than we do in ours, so that instead of purchasing Sugars and other Manufactures of us, as the French did formerly, they are now become our greatest Rivalls in Trade, and have been able, by the great Encouragement given to Their Colonies, to Supplant us in Foreign Markets.

Whether these matters will ever be seriously taken into Consideration, and any Regulations made thereupon, must be left to time to discover. However; I shall proceed to shew the Inconveniences, and Damages which attend the British Colonies by their present form and method of Government in hopes some alterations, or Amendm[en]ts may be thought of, for their benefit and Advantage.

I have in a former part of this History observed that the Governours of the British Colonies are cloathed with many and large Powers which have too often been made use of to the prejudice of the people. It is notorious that Gentlemen of the best Fortune and Characters there, have been removed from Civill and Military Employments without any charge of misbehaviour or disability; and as no causes were assigned, we may reasonably suppose, that [the] true and only motive was their Voting in the Assembly or acting in other respects, contrary to the Sentiments or Inclinations of the Governour. And will any Man of Honour or Spirit accept of an employment, which is attended with great trouble and expence, without any lucrative advantages, when he must either give up his native Right and Privileges or subject himself to be disgraced for acting according to the dictates of his Reason and Conscience? Such practises have been very prejudicial to the British Plantations, by bringing those offices into great Contempt, insomuch that very few Gentlemen who are properly qualified, will now accept of them, so that they are commonly filled up with Persons of Inferiour Rank who are incapable of Executing them and preserving the Authority that is necessary.

The Power of a Chancellor with which the Governour is Cloathed, well deserves a particular Remark because there is Reason to suspect it has been made Subservient to purposes Foreign to the Distribution of Justice. This Power is a great check and awe on those who have suits depending in that Court, which have been in some Instances protracted or length[e]ned according to the behaviour of the Parties concerned. And, the frequent appeals from the Plantations, to the King in Councill, give grounds of suspicion, that their Determinations or Decrees are not always according to the strict Rules of Justice and Equity, however inclined I may be to impute them to Errors in Judgement.

The Governour as the King's Representative, is undoubtedly the most proper person to be intrusted with the Nomination and disposal of all Civil and Military Employments in the Island. But then he ought to be restrained from removing Officers at his Will and pleasure without cause or complaint or even being heard. In such cases an officer should be allowed to make his defence before his Peers, namely a Judge of the Grand

Court, before the rest of the bench[,] a Magistrate by the Custos Rotulorum and his Associates and a Military officer before a Court Martial and
their Report made thereupon to the Governor and Councill, before he is
removed and even then not without the advice and Consent of the Councill. This is the only Expedient that can be thought of in my Opinion to
restore the Credit and Reputation of those Offices, and be an inducement
to Gentlemen of Fortune and Characters to accept of them.

As to the Chancellorship, it is to be considered whether it would not be
for the Utility of the Colonies if it was seperate and Independant of the
Governour, not only for the Reasons I have given, but because the Persons
most commonly appointed, are Military Men, or others, who have little
knowledge in the practice of the Courts of Law or Equity. And, as it is the
most troublesome branch of their office without any Emoluments worth
their Notice[,] it is not surprising that so very few of them give that Attention that is necessary. Beside, as they have full Employment, especially the
Governour of this Island, in other matters, this shews the Reasonableness,
and even the necessity of putting that Commission into other hands, that
there may be no Obstruction in regard to the Government or the Court of
Equity, which sometimes unavoidably happens as matters now stand.

These Points have often been under the Consideration of the Assembly
who were inclined to settle a proper Salary and Fees on a Person duely
qualified to execute that important Commission, but in their Debates some
Objections were started which could not be reconciled and Obstructed so
good a design, particularly that the Commission would probably be given
to some favourite or Creature who perhaps may not be properly qualified,
altho[ugh] bred up in the Court of Law or Chancery, and therefore I beg
leave to propose an Expedient, which if not wholly approved of, yet may
strike out something that will remove many obstructions and grievances,
and put the Court of Equity on a much better footing than it stands at
present. Namely That the Office of Chancellor be put into Commission,
with a Salary of £1000 p[er] Annum, which together with the Usual &
Customary Fees to be equally Divided among the Commissioners.

That three Gentlemen of the best Characters and Abilities in the Island
be nominated. That any one have power to hold a Court to hear motions,
but that no less than two shall sit to hear causes. And in case of a disagreement between them the Cause to be heard and determined by them all.

That the first Monday in every Month be appointed to hear motions,
and the third Monday in every Month be appointed to hear Causes. That
in case they cannot go through either the Motions or hearings on their
respective days the Court shall sit the day following and in Case any Extraordinary matter should happen so as to make it necessary to Adjourn
the Court without going through the business. Then and in such Case the
Court shall sit on some day the same Week or as soon after as may be convenient.

The usual method of nominating and appointing Members of the Councill, is likewise worth considering as it is a matter of great Consequence to the Plantations.

The Governour has not indeed the Power to appoint any Gentleman to be of the Councill unless the number be under Seven, but he recommends such Persons as He thinks proper, which is much the same because his Recommendation generally prevails, and it is to be supposed that he takes care to have none but such as will be passive and submit to all His measures. For Such Sycophants and Tools are to be met with in all Countries who will come into any Scheme or proposal, provided they are gratified in their own way.

The Governour as I observed, has not power to fill up any Vacancy in the Councill, unless the number be under Seven, and that expressly by death or absence. Nevertheless some of them, have assumed a Power of suspending without the Opinion or Consent of the rest of the Board. And if such a liberty is tolerated, He may make Vacancies, that will reduce them below Seven, and fill up those Vacancys at his own pleasure, and in Consequence not only subvert His Majesty's Nomination but in Effect take upon himself two parts in three of the Legislative power, and act without restraint in other matters as the Councill will in such Case be little more than a Screen for his Actions. This manifestly tends to abolish part of the Constitution and render the Seat of a Councellor so precarious, that no man of Honour and Spirit will accept of it, since dissenting from the Opinion of a Governour may be deemed disaffection to His Person and Government or perhaps to his Majesty, and be attended with a Suspension.

It is therefore of great Concernment to the Interest and welfare of the Plantations, that the Councill should be put on some other and better footing, that no discouragement may be given to the Members in acting freely and without Restraint in a Station which may otherwise be exposed to great Contempt. And, as they are part of the Legislature as well as a Councill of State, it is reasonable and necessary that none should be qualified to sit and vote in the passing of Laws, who has not an Estate or Interest in the Country, for it cannot be thought reasonable that any Person should have a right to raise and dispose of Publick Monies, who is not any ways affected by it.

The Publick Offices likewise require some further notice and Consideration, for as I have observed, most or all of them being Executed by Persons, who hold them by Deputation at Rack Rents, they are under the necessity of raising their Fees, contrary to Law, and to the great prejudice of Trade as well as of the Island. These offices are generally granted to some favourites of the Ministers, who farm them out to those who will give the most for them, and as there are not wanting Indigent and Avaricious Persons who are constantly hunting after such jobs, and know how to find their account in them, some of the Patentees have been able to raise their

Rent near double what it was about 20 years ago, and enjoy five or Six hundred Pounds p[er] Annum without any trouble or being of the least use and Service to the Island. This will appear the more grievous & burthensome when it is considered, that the Fees of the Publick offices are not only become Exhorbitant by those means, but the several Rents which amount to upwards of £3000 Sterling p[er] Annum, may be deemed a Tax or imposition on the Island. It would therefore be an Encouragement to the Plantations & the most Effectual way of restraining those Abuses, if the Patentees of all the Offices were obliged to Execute them in Person and no doubt if this matter was properly Represented, the Crown might be prevailed upon, not to grant any Patents for the future, but on those Conditions.

Having considered the present State and form of the Constitution of the British Colonies, and more particularly this Island, I shall now proceed to enquire into some other matters complained of and propose such Remedies, as may be necessary for their Relief, and tend to the further Improvement of the Island, and consequently to the Trade and Navigation of Great Britain.

If ever any thing be done for the Real Service and Utility of the British Plantations, Industry must be Encouraged by removing every Obstruction to the improvement of those Countries which have Raised and Support Themselves by Their own Prudence & labour to the Condition and Circumstances They are now in without any Assistance from the Crown, or very inconsiderable in respect to the many Advantages the Nation Annually derives from Them.

This Island must be distinguished in that particular Instance for not only large Tracts of Woody lands, which never had been manured before, are now Cleared & Cultivated to great Advantage; but even remote and Mountainous Parts difficult of Access have been planted with great Care, labour, and Expence. And the inland as well as the remote Parts are still Capable of further & very Considerable improvements.

The Nation indeed was at a great Charge in the Conquest of it, and in Maintaining Ships of War as well as Land Forces to preserve our Right to this Valuable Acquisition; and the several branches of Trade that are dependant on it: But all other Annual Charges for the Support of the Government of the Island, namely the Salaries of the Governour and other Publick Officers, the Additional Subsistance to the Soldiers, building & repairing Fortifications and other Contingencies, which am[oun]t to a very Considerable Sum Annual[l]y are defrayed by the People Themselves, as I have observed, without any other Assistance from the Crown (except Warlike Stores for the Use of the Fortifications) and without such Bounties as have been granted to other Settlements which would have been more usefully bestowed on this Island. For if such Improvements as I have mentioned, were made by mere Industry or very Slender means, what great things might have been Expected of Them, had They been furnished with

Negroes and other necessaries for Planting on Publick Credit at an easy rate & moderate Interest, or had They been put under such Regulations, and met with such Encouragement as the French have in Their Colonies, which has enabled Them to make a greater progress in Trade and Plantations than we have done, and to supplant us with regard to Sugar and other products in Foreign Markets.

As to the Expence of the Nation, in the Conquest of this Island and in maintaining Ships of War & Troops for the defence of it and the Trade, that will appear to be Amply made up, by the Duties & other Advantages arising from it; but much more by the gross Value of the Product which may be deemed almost clear Proffit, when it is considered that the incidental Charges Center in our selves; so that on a Moderate Computation the Nation cannot have gained less by this Island only, than Sixty Millions since we have been in the possession of it, supposing the Product for 60 years to amount to no more than £500,000 p[er] *Annum Communibus Annis* and the last 30 years at a Million p[er] Ann[um] it being now 90 years since it was first Conquered & possessed by us; beside other Advantages arising by Trade.

It is therefore of great importance to the Nation as well as to the Plantations, that due Care should be taken not only to preserve Their just Rights & Privileges & to discourage the Avaricious Schemes of Governours abroad or hungry Courtiers at Home; but also not to lay such heavy Duties and impositions upon Them, as may discourage Industry & obstruct further improvements if not ruin those that are already made, Consequently dispeople the Islands & in process of time occasion Their total desertion or falling into the hands of the French.

The Remedy I shall propose for these Inconveniencies is what we are Certainly very defective in; I mean an experienced, unbyassed Council of Trade after the Model of the Council of Commerce in France or the Council of the Indies in Spain, with proper Powers & Authority to inspect into the Laws relative to Trade & Plantations; to enquire into all hardships, Defects and Obstructions; to discuss what is necessary to be done for promoting every Colony or branch of Trade, and to lay Their Remarks and Opinions before the House of Commons the beginning of every Session.

Now as the Interest of Trade in general & the Plantations are so Closely Connected that They cannot be separated without prejudice to both; and as every Merch[an]t is not well enough acquainted with all the British Plantations to form a true Judgment of what is proper to be done for Them Respectively, I shall leave it to be Considered, whether it is not advisable & necessary that every Colony have the liberty of appointing a Representative, at least that a Certain Number may be Chosen by the Northern Colonies, and a Certain Number by the Sugar Islands; not less than Six for the whole.

It may perhaps be said, that we have already a Board of Trade Established for those purposes; to which I beg leave to observe, and I hope without Offence, as I intend & mean nothing more than to promote the Interest of my Country, that it is impos[s]ible for Them, the Privy Council or Committees of Parliament, in the usual methods They proceed by, to inform Themselves truely & Consequently to form a right Judgment of any one difficult matter that comes before Them.

It is to be Considered, that Trade is a kind of Mystery, and that a perfect knowledge of it, is not to be acquired but by Application, Experience and proper Abilities. It is subject to Various interfereing Accidents and liable to be diverted into other Channells thro[ugh] neglect, mismanagement or the Artfull Schemes of our Rivals in Trade, unless due Care be taken to prevent it. How then is it possible for the two Houses of Parliament or the Board of Trade which Consist of Noblemen and Gentlemen whose Education has been quite different from the Study of such improvements, as might be made in Trade, Manufactures and Plantations; to distinquish between the Clashing Interest of Universal Trade & the Interest of particular Branches; when few or none of Them ever had the least Occasion to inspect into, the Nature of Trade in general or of any particular Branches much less to acquire the proper Skill or Experience. Consequently for want of a more perfect understanding They are often imposed upon, by misrepresentation, sollicitation of Friends or some prevailing Interest.

I appeal to those who have ever been concerned or obliged to attend either of the Assemblies I have mentioned, whether I have not fairly stated the Case, tho[ugh] great Attention is given to all such matters as come before Them; and whether the Suiters have not frequently met with unnecessary delays, and had difficulties thrown in Their way for want of a proper knowledge in the respective Members with Regard to our Plantations & the several Branches of the British Commerce some of which by those means have declined or met with Embarassments & others are in a manner lost to the Nation.

It is manifest that the flourishing Condition of the Trade & Colonies of France, is owing to Their Council of Commerce as well as to the great Care & Application of Their Ministers to assist and encourage Their subjects in both, which has enabled Them to make such improvements as They have done within 30 years past; and if They continue to exert Their Policy that way, whilst we continue supine and Negligent the Consequence must needs be that They will increase in Riches & Power & we shall decline in both.

It is therefore of the last Concernment to Great Britain which has so Absolute a Dependance on Trade & Navigation that something like what I have hinted at be Established and a Method taken to fill the Board of Trade with Men of Experience as well as Capacity; or to put that Board under some other & better Regulation for at present They do not seem to answer the Original Institution & Design.

And as Numbers of Industrious People are the Riches and Strength of a Country, it is highly necessary to Consider all possible ways and means for Encouraging People to go over & Settle in our Colonies, and thereby not only preserve and improve Them, but in Consequence the National Stock. For tho[ugh] it is the Opinion of some Persons, who have not well considered the Matter, that the Plantations drain the Kingdom of People & that the Nation is at a great Expence in supporting Them; yet upon a thorough Examination, it will evidently appear even to a Demonstration, that They not only employ a great Number of People, who were useless at Home, but They are indisputably for Their Number, the most proffitable Subjects of Great Britain, as They promote by Their product & Trade the Wealth & Power of the Nation in a greater degree and support an Infinite Number of Merch[an]ts[,] Shopkeepers, Mechanicks, Seamen &c. who could not otherwise support Themselves & Their Families. For as I have already observed, it was the Opinion of S[i]r. Josiah Child, that one Man in the Plantations gave Employment to five Men at Home, and in the Opinion of others as well as my self the proportion runs much higher.

To illustrate this position it is necessary to observe that I have Estimated the Gross Produce of this Island, exclusive of the Rents of Houses and the Advantages arising by Trade to amount at this time, on a Medium to a Million p[er] Annum: which supposing the Number of White People, Free Mulattos and Negroes to be 20,000 Men[,] Women & Children, They Acquire one with another £50 p[er] Ann[um] each; And if we include the Negro Slaves as the Product of the Plantations arises from Their labour which in such Case must be allowed a Considerable Acquisition of Subjects, as well as Riches, the gain will then be £8 6 [shillings] 8 [pence] per Ann[um] each. Whereas by S[i]r William Petty's Computation,[2] which we will take for granted, as there has not appeared a better since, the Number of People in this Kingdom are supposed to be Eight Millions, and the general Rental or Income of Houses and Lands is Computed at 10 Millions which bear no manner of Proportion to the Proffits of the Plantations; and manifest how much it is the Interest of the Nation to Encourage the further Settlement & improvement of Them.

For the Accomplishment of so beneficial a Design particularly with regard to this Island which is the most Capable of Improvement, it is highly necessary in my Opinion & I beg leave to recommend to the Publick Consideration.

1st. That such measures may be taken as are necessary for Reducing the price of Provisions.

2. Sir William Petty (1623–1687), *Political Arithmetick; or, A Discourse Concerning the Extent and Value of Lands, People, Buildings* (London, 1690). In this treatise, Petty denounced "prohibitory" mercantilism and the use of precious metals as standards of value, arguing that labor and land were the real sources of wealth.

2. To restrain the Number of Negro Tradesmen.

3. To Establish a proper Coin to pass in this Island only.

4. To give the same or such like Encouragement as the French have done, which has occasioned such Surprizing Improvements as They have made in Their American Plantations.

5. To promote the Planting of such Commodities as are raised & Cultivated with a few hands.

6. To Establish in this Island, something of the Nature of the Ten Acre Men, as They are called in Barbados.

7. To restrain the Engrossing of lands or any Man from holding more than He can Occupy & improve.

8. To ease such Commodities as are manifestly over loaded with Duties & Excises.

9. To Regulate & put the Militia of this Island under a more proper and better Establishment than it is at present.

These several matters I propose to discuss more particularly & I hope in such a manner as will not only shew the reasonableness, but even the necessity of Their being carried into Execution; and how much it will tend to the Utility of Great Britain, as well as the Plantations.

1[.] The Reducing the price of Provisions, and rend[e]ring Them plenty & cheap, is absolutely necessary in this and all other Countries, because every labourer or Manufacturer will Estimate His Work in proportion to His Expence in living. And in Consequence the reduction of the price of Provisions will reduce the price of Wages & labour; enable the Planter to sell His Commodities proportionably Cheaper which will be one means of regaining the Sugar Trade in Foreign Markets, where the French have supplanted us by selling that Commodity Cheaper than we can.

Nor is it reasonable to suppose that any Country will encrease in people and thereby gather Strength as well as Riches unless it be made a Poor Man's Country, by having the necessaries of life at moderate Rates whereby He may not only support Himself & His Family in a Comfortable manner, but lay up something yearly, which will add to the National Stock & encourage others to become set[t]lers.

A Country may indeed become Rich that is Cultivated with Negroes or Slaves & a Small Number of White People; but it cannot be deemed safe or secure from an intestine or a Foreign Enemy. For will 4 or 500 Planters, supposing Them all to be Rich or in good Circumstances, with the White Servants They commonly Employ, be able to protect a large Extensive Country, and resist an Invading or Intestine Enemy? No, there must be a sufficient Strength of White Inhabitants able to bear Arms, who have some property to defend; or a Military Force established among Them for Their protection. And how agreeable or Consistent that will be to Industry or an English Constitution I need not Examine; yet one or the other is indispensably necessary, as there is no other Alternative; for tho[ugh] ships of War may protect the Island against a Foreign, yet They can't be any defence against an intestine Enemy.

These Circumstances will Evince how necessary it is to promote the raising of Ground Provisions & live Stock in such manner that They may become Plenty & Cheap, which will be attended with this further good Consequence; it will lessen the Consumption of Salted Provisions and not only be a great saving to the Planters, but contribute to make the Island more healthy. For undoubtedly those Salted Provisions is the Principal Cause of Scurvys, and as They occasion thirst & promote drinking, often throw such Persons as feed much on Them into Acute & Inflam[m]atory disorders.

It is therefore recomme[n]ded to the Consideration of the Gentlemen of this Island, whether it is not advisable for the Attaining those desirable ends to give all possible Encouragement to poor Families, to plant ground Provisions & raise live Stock, by exempting Them from all Taxes, except Parochial or by such other ways and means, as may be thought more Convenient & proper.

2[.] The restraining or limiting the Number of Negro Tradesmen. I am sensible the Planters & other Inhabitants who employ Them will think this a great hardship, and few if any will be able to digest it; because such Tradesmen are in general more hardy & usefull, and dispatch more business than White Men; but when They consider the necessity of it, & how much the preservation of the Island, in Consequence Their own lives & Fortunes depend upon it, We may reasonably imagine They will rather submit to some Inconveniencies than run so great a Risque.

It is to be considered that the Number of Negro Tradesmen such as Carpenters, Bricklayers, Wheel Wrights, Black Smiths, Taylors &c. among the Plantations, cannot be less than 2000; and in the Towns & Vil[l]ages 1000, in the whole about 3000; which Number of White Men or even one half, would be a very considerable Additional Strength.

It is likewise to be Considered that the Negro Tradesmen in general are the most sensible, Robust, Active Negroes, and have great Opportunities by Conversing[,] & dealing with the Common People & Jews, of doing Mischief.

To Remedy this Evil it is proposed that an Acc[oun]t of all the Negro Tradesmen in the Island be taken & to limit under severe Penalties, the number that shall be allowed to be brought up or made use of for the future in every Plantation, or perhaps it may be found necessary to Prohibit altogether the bringing up any such Tradesmen for the future, or making use of any such after the Death of those who are already brought up to the Business. And if any such Tradesmen be allowed, to oblige every Planter or other Person, who employ Them to Maintain one White Man able to bear Arms for every Negro Tradesman, or under such other Regulations as may be more Convenient & necessary.

3[.] The Extablishing a proper Coin to pass in this Island only, is so essentially necessary, that nothing more need to be said to Evince the Usefullness & Necessity of it, than to observe that They have no other Coin at present than Spanish Money of an uncertain weight & often not sufficient of that for Common Occasions, for such as is of due weight, is shipped for Great Britain as fast as it is brought in, and the Traders from North America, Carry away such as is light, which in time of Peace They lay out with the French for Sugar & Molasses.

To Remedy this Evil it is necessary in my Opinion that not less than 40 or £50,000 be Coined for this Island only, in pieces from 3 [pence] to 5 [shillings] Value; the Allay [Alloy]to be in proportion to the present Exchange of Money which is 40 p[er]C[en]t or less if it be thought proper, as every Commodity will bear a price in proportion; the King's head to be stamped on the one side, and the Arms of the Island on the other, & to prohibit under Severe penalties, the Exportation of it to any other Country.

The French were so fully Convinced of the Necessity & Advantages of having a proper Coin to pass in Their Colonies, that among other Encouragements They some years ago Coined such pieces as I have mentioned & have Experienced the use & benefit arising from it.

4[.] As it cannot be expected that Private Persons who are engaged in any kind of business which will support Them in England, much less People of Fortune will engage in New Adventures, so none or very few but such as are uneasy in Their Circumstances[,] needy or Necessitous, will entertain any thoughts of removing & set[t]ling with Their Families in remote & distant Parts of the World. It is therefore necessary to take the same or such like Methods, as are practised by the French, who give all manner of Encouragem[en]t to Poor Families, to go over and Settle in Their Plantations. For their passages are paid by the King[, and] Lands are Assigned Them without any Expence, provided They are set[t]led in a limitted time. They have an allowance of Provisions to support Them for one whole Year. They have *Credit* given Them for *Negroes* and all *necessary Utensils* for Clearing and Cultivating of lands with many privileges and Advantages, which They were not allowed in France. By such Wise measures Their Plantations in America are become Populous[,] well Set[t]led, & thereby enabled to make such improvements that unless due care is taken to strengthen & promote our Colonies by giving the same Encouragement to poor Industrious Families to go over & settle there, we shall hereafter reap no other Advantage from Them than supplying our own Consumption with Their produce, if They do not decline more & more, & become so feeble, as to fall a prey to an intestine or Foreign Enemy.

5. And as Sugar Works cannot be raised without a very Considerable Stock, it is necessary to encourage such Settlements as may be Cultivated & carried on with a few Hands and at a small Expence namely for raising

live Stock[,] Ground Provisions, Coffee, Cotton, Ginger & such like Commodities.

The Laws of the Country have already provided for the payment of the passages of all such Persons as shall go over & become Set[t]lers, assigned Them lands in proportion to the Number of White Persons in [a] Family, so that the Number of Acres do not exceed 300, also an Allowance for Their Subsistence for 12 Months, & an exemption from all Taxes except Parochial for 7 years. But this has been found by Experience, not to be sufficient or to Answer effectually the intention & design of the Legislature. It is therefore proposed that another Fund be raised by subscription or a publick Tax, for purchasing Negroes, Cattle[,] Poultry[,] Seeds & Plantation Utensils & to furnish those Persons with Them, who are not able to purchase on Credit for 3 years or more, & at a Moderate Interest. For unless such Encouragement be given to invite poor Families to become Set[t] lers in this Island, it cannot be expected, as I have already observed, that it ever will be populous and able to make a proper defence without the Assistance of a sufficient Military Force, which will be attended with greater Inconveniencies & Expence than those I have mentioned.

6[.] [blank]

7[.] Our false Maxims of suffering Persons to Patent large Tracts of land, more than They can possibly Occupy or make use of, and hold Them in Expectation of disposing of Them to great Advantage or such like Motives is highly deserving of Notice and Consideration, because it has been and is still a principal Obstruction to the Settlement & Improvement of this Island. It has indeed, been a Constant Article, in every Governour's Instruction not to grant more than 300 Acres to any one Person: Nevertheless it has been Notoriously Evaded & perverted, even by some of the Governours Themselves, by causing lands to be run out in the Names of other Persons and after They had Patents granted to reconvey Them. By those means divers Gentlemen in England as well as in Jamaica hold many Thousand Acres some not less than 14 or 15000 [acres,] great part of which never was manured or paid one penny Quit Rent, which is not only a further Abuse, but in fact They have Thereby forfeited Their Tenure, tho[ugh] it has hitherto been winked at thro[ugh] the Influence and Power of some of those Land holders. It is therefore necessary to Establish something like the Agrarian Law, by which I do not mean or intend to propose a levelling of Property, and Rightfull Possession of Lands which are Manured & Cultivated, but to restrain the Collusive taking up for the future or holding such lands as have been taken up in that manner, because it is a bar to the Industry of others[,] the improvement of the Island, the encrease of His Majesty's Revenues and the National Stock.

In the Infancy of Antigua I am inform[e]d the Legislature of that Island, thought the most Effectual way to settle it was to lay an Annual Tax of 2 [shillings] 6 [pence] p[er] Acre, upon such Lands as I have described, and in case of Non paym[en]t to seize them without Redemption, for the use of the Publick; upon which several uncultivated Tracts were thrown up, for no Man could Afford to hold more than He Actually Occupied or made use of. And I am of Opinion that some thing like this will be found Necessary to be done in Jamaica, if it be thought Expedient or for the Publick Utility to promote & Extend the Improvem[en]ts in that Island.

8th. To Evince the Reasonableness & even the Necessity of easing such Commodities as are manifestly over loaded with Duties & Excises, it is necessary to shew in what particular Instances They are over burthened, and the Obstruction it gives to the improvement of our Colonies, if it do[e]s not so far discourage those Manufactures, as to endanger Their being lost to the Nation, which is now our Case with regard to the Article of Indigo.

In Regard to Sugar, it has been manifestly made appear that the Duties now payable to the Crown, is equal to the Land Tax in England of 4 [shillings] in 20 [shillings or £1] which is so grievously Complained of, tho[ugh] raised only in time of War, or upon Emergent Occasions; whereas the other is payable in Peace as well as War and without any Regard to the price of that Commodity which is no ways equal to what it was when the Duties were laid; nor is there so ready a Vent for it as formerly by reason we have only our own Market to go to, the French having supplanted us, by being able to undersell us, at all others.

The lessening the Duties & Excises on Rum, Ginger & Coffee may be objected to with regard to His Majesty's Revenue, which is the great difficulty we have to surmount, because it seems to be the principal if not the only Consideration with those to whom such matters are commonly referred. Though in such Cases, it ought likewise to be Considered, whether the less[e]ning the Duty or Excise on particular Commodities, will not be of Advantage to the Nation, Notwithstanding the loss it may occasion to the Revenue; because it will save a Considerable Sum Yearly w[hi]ch we now lay out w[i]th Foreigners; for the purchase of those Com[m]odities whereas we might with proper Encouragement have Them raised and imported from our own Plantations. It ought likewise to be Considered whether the Continuance of the Duty & Excise, will not be so great a discouragement as to prevent the raising and importing of such Commodities, as are subject to Them, from our own Plantations; and if it should what will then become of that branch of the Revenue?

But I do not apprehend that the Revenue will suffer any thing Considerable if at all, by an Abatement or allowance in the Duties or Excise, because it will occasion a great Consumption; & the Duties & Excise on the increase of our Imports will make ample amends for any deficiency wh[i]ch may be Occasioned by such Abatement or Allowance.

It is likewise to be Considered that an Abatement of the Excise, will in Consequence not only promote the importation of Rum in particular, but lessen the Consumption of Brandy & Arrack, which are Foreign-

Manufactures, often Clandestinely imported by Smug[g]lers, and Annually drain the Nation of very Considerable Sums of Money. But to sett this matter in a fuller and stronger light, and to shew the great hardships of the Planters with Regard to the Duties and Excise which bear no manner of proportion to the Value or Cost, and are manifestly a discouragement to such Manufactures; it is necessary to shew how much a Puncheon of Rum[,] a hundred Weight of Ginger and a hundred weight of Coffee pays to the King & how much They clear to the Planter. This will Evidently shew the Encouragement thereby given to Smug[g]ling, and the Evil is so great & Burthensome in other respects that no other Arguments need be offered to Convince every impartial Person of the Absolute Necessity of easing the Planters, or that They will inevitably sink under the Weight. And if the Planters are Ruined and undone or discouraged from going upon those Commodities, will not the Revenue as I have observed suffer more Considerably, as well as the Nation, by the Diminution of our Imports?

To illustrate this Position it is necessary to shew what the Duties, Excises & other Charges amount to; and how much a Puncheon of Rum, a hundred Weight of Ginger and a hundred Weight of Coffee produce to the Planter or Importer.

For Instance supposing a Puncheon of Rum to run 98 Gallons at 6 [shillings] p[er] Gallon at a Medium (for it is seldom higher in time of Peace) it amounts to £29 8 [shillings].

Out of which the following Charges are to be Deducted.

Cask &c. in Shipping	£1 10 [s.]
Freight 6 [pence] p[er] Gallon	[£]2 9. [s.]
Excise	£17 19 [s.] 3 [p.]
Custom	[£]1 11 [s.]:3 [p.]
[Subtotal:]	[£]19 10 [s.] 6 [p.]
Factor at. 2 ½ p[er]C[en]t	[£]04 10 [s.] ¾ [p.]
Broker at	11 ¾ [p.]
Water a. Waiters Fees &	15 [s.] 4 [p.]
[Subtotal:]	[£]1 1 [s.] 2½ [p.]
[Total:]	[£]24 10 [s.] 8½ [p.]
[Subtracted from £29.8 shilling Return to Producer:]	[£]4 17 [s.] 3½ [p.]

By this Estimate it manifestly appears that a Puncheon of Rum at the Common Rate, exclusive of leakage and Insurance, will not in general clear more that £4:17 [shillings]:3½ [pence] & pays to the King £19:10 [shillings]:6 [pence] which is some thing more than 2/3 of the Gross Produce and four times the Value of what it Neats to the Planter or Importer.

Secondly with regard to Ginger to shew the Produce of that Commodity to the Planter or Importer I shall give a genuine Acc[oun]t of Sales of

Sixty Bags of Ginger which were sold before the Commencement of the War, since which the price is indeed advanced but as the Freight and Insurance is as much if not more advanced in proportion that will make little Alteration if any.

60 Bags of Ginger w[eigh]t. [£]53 6 [s.]

[£] 1 3 [s.] 16 [p.] Fare
[£]51 18 [s.] Neat at 20 [s.]/6
[p.] £52:8 [s.] 9 [p.]

Charges Vizt.	
Custom on [£]51 1 [s.]:1[p.]	£19 5 [s.]6 [p.]
Fees & Land w[i]th Bill Money.	6 [s.]
Freight on [£]51 1 [s.] 1 [p.]	[£]10 5 [s.]
Primage 1d[p.]. Peer a[t] 1/4 Trade 1d[p.] P[er]	
20 Bags	6 [s.] 6 [p.]
Wharfage & Lighterage 2d[p.]	10 [s.]
Warehouse Rent 5 Weeks	15 [s.]
Porterage 3 d[p.]	15 [s.]
Brokerage ½ p[er] C[en]t	5 [s.] 3 [p.]
Com[missio]n. 2½ p[er]C[en]t	[£]1 6 [s.] 2 [p.]
[Total]	[£]33 14 [s.] 5 [p.]
Neat Proceeds	£18 14 [s.] 4 [p.]

But the hardship is still greater with regard to Plantation Coffee which is seldom sold for more than £12 per hund[r]e[d] weight by reason of the great Quantities of French Coffee which is Clandestinely imported into great Britain & Ireland and Vended at so low a rate as to enable the Purchasers to retail it at 2 [shillings]/4 [pence] p[er] in the Country; or to mix it with India & Mocho to great Advantage to Themselves & to the Prejudice of the India Company, as well as to the Nation in General.

1 hund[r]e[d] Weight of Coffee	£12
Freight Wharfage Fees &c	£ 0 13 [s.] 6 [p.]
Custom .	[£] 1 6[s.] 6 [p.]
Excise . . .	[£] 8 8 [s.]
[Total:]	[£]10:8 [s.]:–
[Return to Producer:]	[£] 1 12 [s.]

To that 1 Weight of Coffee pays to the King, £9:14 [shillings]:6 [pence] & clears to the Planter, or Importer. £1:12 [shillings,] out of which the Charges abroad & the Insurance is to be deducted, and then it will appear very little if any thing at all & what is a further hardship, it must remain in the King's Warehouse till the Excise as well as the Duty is paid, at a greater

Expence than They can otherwise lay it up; and by those means They are deprived of the Opportunity of Airing & Drying it, which is Absolutely necessary, after having been stowed among other Commodities that give it an ill smell, which chiefly Occasioned its having been formerly in so great disrepute & often rendered it unsaleable.

These Examples sufficiently manifest the great hardship on the Planter or Importer, with regard to the Duty & Excise on those Commodities, and the absolute Necessity of easing Them; not only to prevent Their being lost to the Nation, but as They are most proper for young Planters and Poor Families to go upon, Consequently the Continuance of the Duty & Excise will discourage the Encrease of People, and the further Improvement of the Plantations.

To which may be added, that as young Planters and poor Families are under the Necessity of selling Their produce in the Islands, because They cannot afford to Export Them on Their own Accounts and Risque, They must Consequently allow a Proffit to the Purchaser or Importer, which lessons Their own.

I shall now proceed to the Ninth & last head. I proposed to treat of, Namely; to Regulate and put the Militia of this Island, under a proper & better Establishment than it is at present.

The first Set[t]lers who were Military Men, were from Their Situation and being surrounded with Enemies so well Convinced of the Absolute Necessity of having a Militia well Disciplined, that upon Their being disbanded from the Service, and paid off by Their Mother Country, They immediately formed Themselves into Regiments and obliged every Man to take a Commission according to His Rank or to bear Arms.

The Assembly for that purpose enacted proper Laws, & took every other Method in Their power for the Security and preservation of the Island, and had it not been for Their precaution, and such wise Measures it is to be doubted whether we should have enjoyed it so long as we have done.

In my Memory the principal Furniture of the Hall or Dining Room in every House from the Highest to the Meanest House-keeper was a Rack of Fire Arms &c. in the Neatest Order.

And it was made a Diversion in order to train up the Common People, to form Companies to shoot at a Target or other mark every Saturday afternoon for Wagers, Donatives or Subscriptions. A Target was made of lead about half an Inch in thickness 2 feet and 1/2 in Circumference and painted; the middle & least Circle white, the 2d. Blue and the 3d. Red, and set at about 40 or 50 yards distance. He that made the best Shot or nearest to the Center was intituled to the highest Reward, and in proportion to the 2d. & 3d. By such methods They were in general good Marks Men and Excelled in that branch of Military Exercise.

Time and Circumstances (but more particularly the Conduct of some Governours in displacing Officers for no other Reason than to gratify

Their Resentment or to promote some private View) have brought those Commissions into Contempt & Consequently have made it necessary to Revise the Militia Act in Order to Establish Them on some other & better footing than They are at present.

All proper means should therefore be made use of to induce Gentlemen of the greatest Abilities & Fortunes in every Parish, to accept of Commissions, to prevent Their falling into hands that are unequal to Them, and incapable of preserving the Authority that is necessary. And that none should be Exempted from doing Military Duty from 15 to 60 years of Age, under pretence of being Reformade Officers, or any other except Clergyman, Physical Men, & Publick Officers. And it would be of great Utility if every Parish or District gave proper Encouragem[en]t to an Experienced half pay Officer, or Veteran Sergeant by allowing Them a set[t]led Salary to instruct a Company every Saturday in Military Exercises & to be present at a General Muster every Month.

It is likewise Expedient in my Opinion to Establish an Officer who has served in the Army, not under the Degree of a Colonel and is well acquainted with Military affairs, with the Title & power of L[ieutenan]t General, and to allow Him a Salary Suitable to the Post & Character. Such an Officer is highly necessary in so large and Extensive a Country as Jamaica, not only because the Governour cannot give that Attention which is required to such matters or be present at Reviews in distant parts of the Country, but also because it is necessary in Case of an Invasion or general Insurrection of the Negroes. Such an Officer should be ready to Command the Forces under the Governour, and to take the Chief Command in Case of illness, Disability, or of a Body of Forces which may be detached on any Important Service on those Occasions.

The French whose Policy is well known in the Arts of Peace & War, have an Establishment something like this, of an Officer at Martinico and Hispaniola for Military Affairs, as well as a Governour who presides in Civil Affairs and has the Supreme Command of those Islands. And it is greatly to be wished, that we would not only imitate Them in that Respect, but in Their Conduct in general, relative to the management of Their Colonies, whereby They have acquired many Advantages over us, which has encreased Their Trade & Navigation to a very great degree.

Having swelled this History beyond the bulk I at first designed & having omitted no material Transaction which came to my knowledge nor any Observation I thought proper to be incerted, I shall think the trouble and Expence I have been at in Compiling it amply Recompenced if it meets with the Approbation of the Publick; and promotes the Improvement, Security and Welfare of Jamaica, for which purpose it was principally Calculated. And shall Conclude with Recommending to the Imitation of the present & future Inhabitants the Industry, Unanimity and Publick Spirit of the first English Set[t]lers, from whom many of Them are Descended:

For They laid the foundation of the best Estates, & paved the way to the flourishing Condition the Island is now in.

It is likewise Owing to Their Moderation and prudent behaviour that the present Inhabitants enjoy all the Advantages of an English Colony. That Their Constitution was set[t]led on a proper Basis and is now happily Established by Their Laws being Confirmed and made perpetual. For tho[ugh] They had a jealousy of most of Their Governours they Strenuously insisted on Their Native Rights & Privileges and would not suffer the least innovation or Encroachment, yet Their Remonstrances, and Memorials from time to time, were drawn with that decency, strength of Reason, Submission to the Crown, and Deference to the Royal Representative, that They at length gained Their point, w[hi]ch Dissipated the Fears and uneasiness They were under having never been any other than what are and ought to be inherent in Englishmen. And as the Importance of the Island and the Value of the Produce from The labour & Industry of the Inhabitants become more & more known, We have great Reason to Expect that They will not only be duly protected, but that when the Affairs of the Nation are set[t]led They will be taken into Consideration & relieved of the Difficulties and Obstructions which They have now to struggle with. Let Them therefore imprint on Their minds the Fable of the Father & His Sons. He called for a bundle of Rods and bad[e] Them take it and try one after another with all Their Force if They could break it. They accordingly tried but could not, upon which He Ordered Them to unbind it, and try every twig apart and see what They could do that way. They did so, and with great ease one by one They snapped it all to pieces. This said He, is the true Emblem of your Condition, keep together and you are safe, Divide & you are undone.

Those Other English Colonies

The Historiography of Jamaica in the Time of James Knight

Trevor Burnard

One curiosity about the historiography of Jamaica is that relatively few modern historians have concentrated on when Jamaica established itself as the richest and most important colony in British America. James Knight's unpublished history of Jamaica was composed right in the middle of this distinct period of Jamaican history (roughly 1720–70) and provides a welcome summary of a long span of Jamaican history up to around 1740 from a well-informed and patriotic but not uncritical elite white Jamaican man. As Jack Greene notes in his introduction to this much anticipated and extremely useful edition, Knight wrote his two-volume history in the early 1740s, several decades after Jamaica had surpassed Barbados as Britain's most valuable overseas settler colony. Jamaica was so central to imperial imagining in the long rule of Robert Walpole that it attracted an "astonishing volume of literature," though sadly much of what was written in Jamaica itself, notably in its flourishing newspapers from 1717 onward, has not survived. The writers of this literature, including Knight himself, were anxious to understand both Jamaica's peculiar political, social, and economic culture and its role within Britain's imperial system.

These writers wrote copiously about Jamaica because Jamaica was believed to be central to Britain's imperial prosperity at a time when pro-imperialist Britons were arguing that the empire was "the principal cornucopia of Great-Britain's Wealth."[1] They insisted that wealth from the colonies underlined Britain's growing commercial strength, maritime power, and self-appointed role as the upholder of liberty in a world that had too little freedom (the irony that such freedom rested on the enslavement of Africans was usually lost on contemporary observers).[2] "It is universally allowed," insisted one government-paid author, "that our sugar colonies are of the greatest consequence and advantage to the trade and

---

1. G. B., Esq., *The Advantages of the Revolution Illustrated by a View of the Present State of Great Britain* (London: W. Owen, 1753).

2. Outlined in Jack P. Greene, *Evaluating Empire and Confronting Colonialism in Eighteenth-Century Britain* (New York, 2013), chap. 1.

navigation of Great-Britain . . . [the] equal to the mines of the Spanish West Indies."[3]

Jamaica's role in shaping a growing and increasingly integrated imperial system was celebrated at the time by other writers besides James Knight. In 1756, the British naturalist Patrick Browne described Jamaica as a "necessary appendage to our present refined manner of living," making an oblique reference to Jamaica's principal product shipped to Britain (sugar), the consumption of which was transforming British culture, as Nuala Zahedieh details in the most recent and best update on the history of Jamaica's contribution to the late seventeenth-century English economy.[4] Profits from sugar and other tropical commodities made Jamaica "not only the richest, but the most considerable colony at this time under the government of Great Britain." It surpassed "all the other *English* sugar colonies, both in quantity of land and the conveniences of life." Like Knight, Browne used Enlightenment vocabulary, notably the ubiquitous term of "improvement," to celebrate Jamaica's growing wealth, usefulness to empire, and strong attachment to efficacious British forms of government, the last allowing "for the more easy and orderly management of both the public and private affairs of the community."[5]

Modern historians have affirmed the accuracy of these accounts. Kenneth Morgan has shown how contemporaries of Knight gave Jamaica first

3. [Anon.], *The Importance of the Sugar Colonies to Great-Britain Stated* (London, 1731), 4, 7, 35–36.

4. Nuala Zahedieh, *The Capital and the Colonies: London and the Atlantic Economy, 1660–1700* (Cambridge, 2010), 221–25. Sugar was the only consistently deflationary commodity in the cost of living of Londoners in the early modern period. Its price fell 56 percent between 1574 and 1700 and fell further in the eighteenth century as British sugar producers were outcompeted in Europe by French sugar producers. Jeremy Boulton, "Food Prices and the Standard of Living in London in the 'Century of Revolution,'" *Economic History Review* 53 (2000): 455–92. The fall in the price of sugar and the development of a very sweet tooth among Britons and North Americans are the most important facts shaping early Jamaican history. This essay looks only at the historiography of Jamaica in the first half of the eighteenth century but it is worth noting that there has been an efflorescence of books and articles on the period between 1655 and 1700 which places Jamaica firmly within a developing literature about how the empire became integrated around slave-based economies from 1655 and especially after the Glorious Revolution. Besides Zahedieh, important contributions to seventeenth-century Jamaican history are Carla Gardana Pestana, *The English Conquest of Jamaica* (Cambridge, Mass., 2017); James Robertson, "Making Jamaica English People: Priorities and Processes," in *The Torrid Zone: Caribbean Colonization and Cultural Interaction in the Long Seventeenth Century*, ed. L. H. Roper (Columbia, S.C., 2018), 105–17; David Eltis, *The Rise of African Slavery in the Americas* (Cambridge, 2002); Abigail L. Swingen, *Competing Visions of Empire: Labor, Slavery, and the Origins of the British Atlantic Empire* (New Haven, Conn., 2015); and Mark G. Hanna, *Pirate Nests and the Rise of the British Empire, 1570–1640* (Chapel Hill, N.C., 2015). The best work seeing Jamaica as part of a changing seventeenth-century English world encompassing settler colonies is Susan Dwyer Amussen, *Caribbean Exchanges: Slavery and the Transformation of English Society, 1640–1700* (Chapel Hill, N.C., 2007).

5. Patrick Browne, *The Civil and Natural History of Jamaica* (London, 1756), 9–25.

place among colonies most valuable to Britain by reprinting reports by Robert Dinwiddie, surveyor general of customs for the southern department, made between 1741 and 1748. These reports assessed Jamaica's contributions to empire as nearly a quarter of the value of all colonies to Britain with only Massachusetts, a repository of soldiers and shipping, being slightly more important.[6] No colony, however, contributed nearly as many exports to Britain as did Jamaica. Dinwiddie's conclusions were confirmed by Richard B. Sheridan in extensive work on West Indian and Jamaican economic history compiled in the 1960s and 1970s, complemented by additional empirical information on the Jamaican economy provided by J. R. Ward, Jack P. Greene, David Ryden, and Trevor Burnard.[7] Sheridan's confirmation of Browne and Knight's assertions about the economic value of Jamaica to Britain gave empirical heft to the famous but largely empirically unsupported contentions of Eric Williams in 1944 that in the first half of the eighteenth century, the British government and "all classes in English society" were uniformly consistent in their unwavering encouragement of the slave trade as a means to keep colonies like Jamaica economically strong and geopolitically vital to imperial interests.[8] As William Wood succinctly put it in 1719: "The labour of Negroes is the principal foundation of our riches from the plantations."[9]

Nevertheless, the economic and geopolitical importance of Jamaica in Knight's lifetime is not matched by an abundance of writing on this period. Modern historians have concentrated on Jamaican history after 1770, especially on the years between the abolition of the slave trade in 1807 and full slave emancipation in 1838.[10] To an extent, the relatively limited his-

6. Kenneth Morgan, ed., "Robert Dinwiddie's Reports on the British American Colonies," *William and Mary Quarterly*, 3rd ser., 65 (2008): 305–46.

7. Richard B. Sheridan, *Sugar and Slavery: An Economic History of the British West Indies* (Baltimore, 1974). Jack P. Greene and Trevor Burnard have written extensively about mid-eighteenth-century Jamaica. Greene provides references to their work in Greene, *Settler Jamaica in the 1750s: A Social Portrait* (Charlottesville, Va., 2016), itself a vital addition to the empirical literature on Knight's period. See also Burnard, *Planters, Merchants, and Slaves: Plantation Societies in British America, 1650–1820* (Chicago, 2015); Burnard and John Garrigus, *The Plantation Machine: Atlantic Capitalism in French Saint-Domingue and British Jamaica* (Philadelphia, 2016); and Burnard, *Jamaica in the Age of Revolution* (Philadelphia, 2019). Despite the temporal limits noted in its titles, there is excellent empirical material on Jamaica's economy before 1750 in David Ryden, *West Indian Slavery and British Abolition, 1783–1807* (Cambridge, 2009). The data on plantation productivity in J. R. Ward, "The Profitability of Sugar Planting in the British West Indies, 1650–1834," *Economic History Review* 31 (1978): 197–213, remains authoritative.

8. Eric Williams, *Capitalism and Slavery* (Chapel Hill, N.C., 1944).

9. William Wood, *Survey of Trade, in Four Parts*, 2nd edition (London, 1722), 179.

10. Bibliographies on Jamaican history are dated but see Howard Johnson, "Historiography of Jamaica," in B. W. Higman, *Methodology and Historiography of the Caribbean*, vol. 6, *General History of the Caribbean* (London, 1999), 478–530; Higman, *Writing West Indian Histories* (London, 1999); and, for the most recent survey, James Robertson, "The Caribbean Islands:

toriography on this period arises from a paucity of contemporary histories written in the mid-eighteenth century. Knight's history is a welcome addition to a small number of key Jamaican historical texts. It bridges the gap between Hans Sloane's natural history of seventeenth-century Jamaica, excellently mined in James Delbourgo's penetrating account of the entanglements of global scientific discovery with early eighteenth-century British imperialism, and Edward Long's panoramic sociohistorical survey of Jamaica on the eve of the American Revolution, about which Catherine Hall is currently completing a major study.[11] This edition of Knight's history should lead to greater concentration on Jamaica in a largely forgotten period of its fascinating history.

What is immediately apparent, however, on reading Knight is that his view of Jamaican history is almost completely at odds with today's historical orthodoxy. Knight was not uncritical of Jamaica, but his account is mostly affirming, as Greene notes in his introduction to this edition. Jamaica had a proud history, in Knight's view; was immensely valuable to Britain; and was daily improving so that "however they have been represented" in Britain, "I don't know a more Industrious, usefull, and beneficial Society to the Nation" (p. 473). Knight's view of Jamaica is not one that prevails in modern historical scholarship. Indeed, the view that historians have of eighteenth-century Jamaica is exactly the image that Knight wanted to dispel. It is seen as a place of "Extravagance, Luxury . . . Immorality," and "Profligate manner of living" (pp. 474, 475). Indeed, the modern view of Jamaica is close to the slight productions on Jamaica and its people that Knight wanted to counter in his writing. Seventeenth-century writers, some of whom, like the tabloid journalist Ned Ward, were unlikely to have visited

---

British Trade, Settlement and Colonization, 1540s–1780s," in *Converging Worlds: Communities and Cultures in Colonial America*, ed. Louise Breen, 2 vols. (New York, 2011), 2:176–248. Few Jamaica-based scholars have worked recently on this period—James Robertson being the most significant exception. Sir Hilary Beckles writes extensively about seventeenth- and eighteenth-century Caribbean history, but his focus is usually on Barbados. See Beckles, *The First Black Slave Society: Britain's Barbados, 1636–1876* (Kingston, Jamaica, 2016). For an illuminating historiographical perspective by a Jamaican historian on neighboring Haiti, which outlines current historiographical issues seen as vital by Caribbean scholars, see Matthew J. Smith, "Footprints on the Sea: Finding Haiti in Caribbean Historiography," *Small Axe* 18 (2014): 55–71.

11. James Delbourgo, *Collecting the World: Hans Sloane and the Origins of the British Museum* (Cambridge, Mass., 2017). I have neglected natural history in this essay but this area has inspired some of the best scholarship on the British West Indies, including Londa Schiebinger, *Secret Cures of Slaves: People, Plants, and Medicine in the Eighteenth-Century Atlantic World* (Stanford, Calif., 2017); Matthew Mulcahy, *Hurricanes and Society in the British Greater Caribbean, 1624–1783* (Baltimore, 2006); and Jefferson Dillman, *Colonizing Paradise: Landscape and Empire in the British West Indies* (Tuscaloosa, Ala., 2015). One of the very best contributions to eighteenth- and nineteenth-century Jamaican history is a study of Jamaica's built landscape by Louis P. Nelson, *Architecture and Empire in Jamaica* (New Haven, Conn., 2016). Catherine Hall provides a taste of her study of Edward Long in Hall and Daniel Pick, "Thinking about Denial," *History Workshop Journal* 84 (2017): 1–23.

Jamaica, and others like John Taylor who were in Jamaica only briefly, had seen Jamaica as so contentious, conflict-ridden, and sinful that they had termed it the "Dunghill of the Universe," a perfect "Sodom," and "as Hot as Hell, and as Wicked as the Devil."[12] Those negative perceptions continued into the eighteenth century, usually asserted by people like Charles Leslie, who wrote a quick history of Jamaica published in 1740 that longtime settlers disparaged as written by someone with no knowledge of the island and its people. Leslie admitted that Jamaica was a "Constant Mine whence Britain draws prodigious riches" but argued that it was a deadly place in which so many people died that "no doubt the Multitude that dies would soon leave the Place a Desert, did not daily Recruits come over from Great Britain." It was a place with no "Beauties of Architecture" and mostly distinguished by the cruelty of the planters to their slaves, where every white man had "something of a Haughty Disposition" and "required Submission" from all around them. When slaves displeased them, Leslie believed that "No Country excels them . . . in the cruel Methods they put them to death."[13]

It is Leslie, not Knight, whose views on Jamaica have dominated recent scholarship. Jamaica is variously described as "a catastrophe," a "landscape of violence," and a "place of dislocation, alienation and death."[14] Sarah Yeh, in an especially insightful article on white West Indian identity before the Seven Years' War, draws on descriptions of Jamaica as a "sink of all filthiness" to describe the worthy gentleman planter Knight lionizes as being "a hideous parody of the benevolent English lord of the manor" and a "disturbingly extreme version of the new 'improving' landlords in rural Britain who callously hired and fired tenants and laborers according to their needs without any sense of obligation or responsibility to those beneath them."[15] Knight was incredibly anxious that Jamaica be seen as an Anglicizing place, but modern historians like Yeh note that even in an age where few people doubted the necessity of slavery in the plantations, it was hard to see white Jamaicans as comparable to English aristocrats when they "maintained their estates with violence and chains rather than through the bonds of loyalty, tradition, and proverbial mutual respect."[16]

12. Dillman, *Colonizing Paradise*, 97–98.

13. [Charles Leslie], *A True and Exact Account of Jamaica* (Edinburgh, 1740), 41, 50–51; Trevor Burnard, "'Prodigious Riches': The Wealth of Jamaica before the American Revolution," *Economic History Review* 54 (2001): 506.

14. Vincent Brown, *The Reaper's Garden: Death and Power in the World of Atlantic Slavery* (Cambridge, Mass., 2008), 12, 29; Nelson, *Architecture and Empire*, 6.

15. *A True and Perfect Relation of That Most Sad and Terrible Earthquake, at Port Royal in Jamaica* (London, 1692); Sarah Yeh, "'A Sink of All Filthiness': Gender, Family, and Identity in the British Atlantic, 1688–1763," *The Historian* 68 (2006): 66–88.

16. Sarah Yeh, "Colonial Identity and Revolutionary Loyalty: The Case of the West Indies," in *British North America in the Seventeenth and Eighteenth Centuries*, ed. Stephen Foster (Oxford, 2013), 202, 204.

In short, modern historians depict Jamaica as the nightmare vision of British colonization in the Americas. The "contested and barbarous marchland" landscape that Bernard Bailyn has memorably described as characterizing seventeenth-century British North America, historians think, contra Knight, best describes eighteenth-century Jamaica.[17] Even those aspects of Jamaican life that might seem somewhat praiseworthy—its precocious modernity, its indifference to social hierarchy and religious cant, its remarkable and unprecedented economic success based on a highly productive and ever improving agricultural economy presided over by planters attuned to the latest scientific and labor management strategies, and its racially and gender-determined but still forward-thinking white egalitarianism—are castigated in the historical literature as emblematic of a society unmoored from morality.[18] This unrelenting negativity is probably enhanced by the fact that, unlike in North America, the descendants of the ruling class of the eighteenth century have vanished from modern Jamaican life. Few Jamaicans today, most of whom are descended from the people whom planters oppressed rather than from planters themselves, have felt much urge to commemorate their beautiful landscape with any sort of remembrance of the days when slave masters ruled and enslaved people obeyed. The twenty-first-century Jamaican landscape thus shows little sign that people like Knight and the world he celebrated ever existed.[19]

Vincent Brown, in the most compelling recent meditation on the cultural history of Jamaica in Knight's time, attempts initially a positive view of Jamaica, arguing that we ought to build on the work of Richard D. E. Burton (still the best work on slave culture in Jamaica in the early eighteenth century) and the theoretical exhortations of Sidney W. Mintz and Richard Price to explore the cultural creativity of enslaved Africans in de-

17. Bernard Bailyn, *The Barbarous Years: The Peopling of North America — The Conflict of Civilizations, 1600–1675* (New York, 2012).

18. These are themes I have stressed in books and articles on eighteenth-century Jamaica though this interpretation needs to be balanced against what Vincent Brown calls my "unflinching examination" of the brutal slave owner Thomas Thistlewood, who came to Jamaica in 1750. Brown criticizes this "indispensable" account by arguing it is associated too closely with Orlando Patterson's nihilistic vision of Jamaican slavery as a form of social death. He argues that I pathologize slaves by "allowing the condition of social death to stand for the experience of life in slavery." His own work, however, tends to see the lives of enslaved people in Jamaica before 1760 as being the nadir of black experience in the Americas. Trevor Burnard, *Mastery, Tyranny, and Desire: Thomas Thistlewood and His Slaves in the Anglo-Jamaican World* (Chapel Hill, N.C., 2004); Brown, "Social Death and Political Life in the Study of Slavery," *American Historical Review* 114 (2009): 1236.

19. For a poignant reminder of how little remembered even the wealthiest Jamaican planters are compared to their North American counterparts, see Christer Petley, *White Fury: A Jamaican Slaveholder in the Age of Revolution* (Oxford, 2018). It may not be coincidental that the contemporary West Indian artists who most incisively, and in often troubling ways, interrogate the visual legacy of eighteenth-century slavery for contemporary Jamaica—Joscelyn Gardner and Laura Facey—are each descendants of eighteenth-century planters.

veloping vibrant cultures marked by what these authors call creolization.[20] Yet Brown's work soon turns grim, which is hardly surprising seeing that his theme is how death was the center of social experience in the island and that this ghost-filled land echoed with acts of violence by whites against blacks amounting to an unrelenting campaign of spiritual terror by the strong against the weak. Even the greatest triumph of the planters—the creation of a flourishing plantation system—and Jamaica's considerable economic diversity, cultural heterogeneity, and extensive urban commercial life—Kingston was the richest and most important town in British America in Knight's period, thus belying the idea that Jamaica was just a plantation colony—are seen by Brown as essentially negative. He argues that "in one of history's greatest episodes of creative destruction, Jamaica's dynamic and profitable economy consumed its inhabitants." The island, he asserts, was "much more than a failed settler society, it was an abundant garden of power and terror." While it was "the indispensable locus of British imperial ambition," standing "at the pinnacle of colonial wealth creation," it was a social "catastrophe" where death was "the landscape of culture itself, the ground that produced Atlantic slavery's most meaningful idioms."[21]

It is not hard to find the foundational historical text from which Brown's vision of a dark and nightmarish eighteenth-century Jamaica emerges. Most historians of Jamaica in Knight's time acknowledge their debt to Richard S. Dunn's classic 1972 book, *Sugar and Slaves*. Brown is explicit about his debt, citing Dunn's summary of life in the tropics as a starting point for his analysis: "The specter of death helps us explain the frenetic tempo and mirage-like quality of West Indian life. . . . It was impossible to think of the sugar islands as home when they were such a demographic disaster zone." So too Yeh anchors her analysis of Caribbean identity around Dunn's evocative description of a Jamaican planter class that around 1700 "lived fast, spent recklessly, played desperately, and died young." Dunn's contempt for the morals of his subjects shines out among his recognition of the material achievements that white Jamaicans made in the late seventeenth-century transformation of their island. Thus, he noted that "the colorful trappings and lurid events of early Jamaican history mask a social development of considerable significance: the emergence, in England's largest Caribbean island, of the sugar and slave systems in its starkest and most exploitative form." These were Englishmen who "made their beautiful islands almost uninhabitable."[22]

Dunn concentrated on the "shabby" but "illuminating" task of telling

20. Richard D. E. Burton, *Afro-Creole: Power, Opposition and Play in the Caribbean* (Ithaca, N.Y., 1997); Sidney W. Mintz and Richard Price, *The Birth of African-American Culture: An Anthropological Perspective* (1976; reprint Boston, 1992).

21. Brown, *Reaper's Garden*, 12, 57, 59.

22. Richard S. Dunn, *Sugar and Slaves: The Rise of the Planter Class in the English West Indies, 1624–1713* (Chapel Hill, N.C., 1972), xiii, xv, 151.

"what these English sons of Adam did to the Garden of Eden islands they discovered and what the islands did to them." It is an intensely human story. J. R. McNeill extends the criticism of these intruders into paradise to examine their role in the environmental degradation of the tropics. McNeill's *Mosquito Empires* is the twenty-first-century follow-up to Dunn, a history in which the humble female mosquito is the hero, or more precisely the villain. Knight's enthusiasm for how Europeans had transformed the physical and human geography of Jamaica to take advantage of the island's "natural abundance" is outlined differently by McNeill. He describes the European alterations of the tropical landscape as a great tragedy. And McNeill dwells on the ironies resulting from settlers' environmental vandalism by showing how such activity facilitated the mosquito's ability to destroy white migrant populations through the yellow fever vector. He demonstrates that it was during the period in which Knight lived that demographic decline arising from yellow fever was most acute. Yellow fever devastated white settler populations, starting from the dire decade of the 1690s and continuing unabated until the 1750s, after which Jamaica experienced some mild demographic improvement for its settler population. The rule of the mosquito over humans culminated in disastrous military expeditions undertaken by the British in Spanish America, where nonimmune soldiers from Britain and New England were cut down in droves by an enemy (the mosquito) more pernicious and deadlier than any Spanish weapon. In another irony, the very success of the implementation of the large plantation regime from the late seventeenth century heightened European susceptibility to disease. Planters brought in Africans from West Africa to satisfy their insatiable need for labor, but mosquitoes arrived along with the enslaved. These insects found the plantation landscape very much to their liking. In McNeill's reading, Jamaica could never become a settler colony on the British North American model for epidemiological even more than for sociocultural reasons.[23]

The only recently published book that escapes Dunn's compelling but highly moralistic vision of a society in which there was "a stark dichotomy between the all-powerful sugar magnate and his abject army of black bondsmen," showing man's capacity to do evil to other men (and women), is Adrian Finucane's interrogation of the *assiento* trade in slaves between Jamaica and Spanish America from 1713 to 1748.[24] Her Jamaica is derived from another foundational text for this period, Richard Pares's 1936 his-

23. J. R. McNeill, *Mosquito Empires: Ecology and War in the Greater Caribbean, 1620–1914* (Cambridge, 2010). McNeill was mostly influenced not by Dunn but by another book originally published in 1972, later reprinted with a foreword by McNeill: Alfred Crosby, *The Columbian Exchange: Biological and Cultural Consequences of 1492: 30th Anniversary Edition* (Westport, Conn., 2003).

24. For white women, see Kathleen Wilson, "Rethinking the Colonial State: Family, Gender, and Governmentality in Eighteenth-Century British Frontiers," *American Historical Re-*

tory of wars among France, Spain, and Britain in the Caribbean between the War for Jenkins' Ear in 1739 and the end of the Seven Years' War in 1763. For Finucane, Jamaica was a place of great commercial opportunity and a successful example of how European empires became entangled productively through commerce. She emphasizes Jamaica as being a heterogenous place and an island economy "integrated closely into the multi-imperial Caribbean system of commerce, exporting the produce of its plantations and importing manufactured goods and European foods." Jamaica was thus illustrative of how the British Empire became integrated in the early eighteenth century but where tensions between an empire built mainly on territorial expansion and an empire based on trade and the interests of private enterprise were seldom resolved.[25]

Other historians have avoided writing histories of Jamaica that are relentlessly negative by examining the one group in the island that was not only clearly native to the island but demographically successful and growing in importance: free mixed-race people. Free people of color occupied an ambivalent place in Jamaica's complicated racial hierarchy. They achieved a position of power and influence (at least for the wealthiest of their number) in the decade when Knight was writing his history. That power and influence disappeared after reorganization of the settler social order following the trauma of a nearly successful slave revolt in 1760. Daniel Livesay has analyzed the tiny numbers of wealthy British-educated free people of color whose places in very rich and politically well-connected Jamaican families from 1733 onward were contentious in the urgent definition of what comprised race in a racially divided plantation society. The numbers of people involved in this redefinition of racial classification might be small, but figuring out the extent to which wealth and family connections could overwhelm the tendency of white Jamaicans, especially the poorer sort, to insist on whiteness being a social reality that trumped all other political, social, and familial considerations reveals the racial tensions that animated Jamaican society in Knight's time. Livesay argues that between 1733 and 1760, Jamaica experimented with empowering mixed-race elites so that these "whitened" people might form the seedbed for a new population of free people who could form a demographic counter to a growing enslaved population. Tacky's Revolt of 1760 put an end to these idealistic notions of racial "improvement," but Livesay insists that it was in Knight's period, for probably the only time in the history of Jamaican slavery, during which a small gap opened in the edifice of white supremacy

view 116 (2011): 1294–1322, and Christine M. Walker, "Pursuing Her Profits: Women in Jamaica, Atlantic Slavery and a Globalising Market," *Gender and History* 26 (2014): 478–501.

25. Dunn, *Sugar and Slaves*, 341; Adrian Finucane, *The Temptations of Trade: Britain, Spain and the Struggle for Empire* (Philadelphia, 2016), 39; Richard Pares, *War and Trade in the West Indies* (Oxford, 1936).

and into which wealthy mixed-race people might move and "pass" themselves off as whites.[26]

Similarly, in a broad reinterpretation of the intersection of ideas about race with a developing literature on subjecthood, as complicated by understandings of gender and interracial sexual relations, Brooke Newman has explored changing notions of racial classifications in Jamaica beginning in the early eighteenth century. She stresses the ways in which Jamaica conformed to Iberian and French understandings of race. She notes that white Jamaicans insisted that "blood heredity" or their lineal connections to Britain through birth of ancestral descent justified their claims to Britishness as people with rights to British subjecthood. The racial debates of the period involved longstanding discourses whereby hereditary rights and privileges and physical, moral, and intellectual characteristics were transmitted through biological inheritance. She argues that by "enumerating whiteness as a matter of blood heredity," white Jamaicans could maintain "the continuance of white control over property and power despite deeply unfavorable demographic conditions and the potential to augment the white settler population through selective intermixture."[27] It did not matter so much that these attempts proved in the end unsuccessful, so that Jamaica could never become a settler society. That was impossible in such a racially divided society, even if Jamaican politicians had taken a further step in the 1740s toward a looser racial classification than most whites were willing to do, by accepting the most presentable mixed-race people as full members of the Jamaican polity. What Newman's research shows is that the time in which Knight's history was composed was one of singular possibility for transformative change in how race was conceptualized. It was a time of racial experimentation unprecedented in Jamaican history and might have resulted, if events had proceeded differently after 1760, in a more racially tolerant and diverse society emerging, rather than Jamaican history becoming a relentless march toward gross inequality, extraordinary exploitation, and the ritual debasement of Africans and people of African descent, whether enslaved or free. Race was not a fixed idea, either ideologically or in practice, in the second quarter of the eighteenth century. While the trend in the seventeenth century was for Jamaicans to adopt race as the principal way to divide its community over other forms of categorization, such as being Christian, as Edward B. Rugemer notes in an important article on the politics of slavery and the law in South Carolina and Jamaica, there was a moment in the 1740s, when Knight was finishing his work, that

26. Daniel Livesay, *Children of Uncertain Fortune: Mixed-Race Jamaicans in Britain and the Atlantic Family, 1733–1833* (Chapel Hill, N.C., 2018). For poor white opposition to any loosening of racial boundaries, see James Robertson, "A 1748 'Petition of Negro Slaves' and the Local Politics of Slavery in Jamaica," *William and Mary Quarterly*, 3rd ser., 67 (2010): 319–46.

27. Brooke Newman, *A Dark Inheritance: Blood, Race, and Sex in Colonial Jamaica* (New Haven, Conn., 2018), 21–22.

the rigid race relations that characterized late eighteenth-century Jamaica could have developed in a looser fashion.[28]

This brief survey of a portion of the principal works in the historiography of Jamaica in the period between the Treaty of Utrecht in 1713 and the start of the Seven Years' War in 1756 shows that some interesting angles of historical interpretation have recently developed within a relatively underpopulated historiography. Yet there is one glaring lacuna that needs to be addressed before Knight's work can be put fully in context. There are several acclaimed histories of slavery in the Americas which have made us conscious that slavery is spatially and temporally specific, reflecting the obvious but often overlooked point that every colonial British American society had its own peculiarities and complexities. Scholars of Atlantic slavery, however, have seldom addressed the nature of enslaved experience when black life was at its nadir in the British American world and especially in the place where being enslaved was more miserable than probably anywhere else in the British Empire.[29] We know much less about enslaved people in Knight's Jamaica of the 1730s and 1740s than we do about all the other sectors of Jamaica's population in this period. We could know more about women, mixed-race people, Maroons, Jews, planters, and merchants, but we have lots more studies about these groups—who comprised perhaps 14,500 people or just over 10 percent of Jamaica's 1755 population of 144,500—than we do about the approximately 130,000 enslaved people, of whom probably 80 percent or more were born in Africa and of whom most of the rest were just one generation away from residence in Africa.[30] Without understanding the demography of the enslaved population, the cultural patterns that they established in the face of vicious op-

28. Edward B. Rugemer, "The Development of Mastery and Race in the Comprehensive Slave Codes of the Greater Caribbean during the Seventeenth Century," *William and Mary Quarterly*, 3rd ser., 70 (2013): 429–58.

29. The fine-grained and contextually rich exploration of slave life in eighteenth-century Virginia and South Carolina made in Philip D. Morgan, *Slave Counterpoint: Black Culture in the Eighteenth-Century Chesapeake and Lowcountry* (Chapel Hill, N.C., 1998), has not been replicated for any other British American slave society. Jamaica would be ideal for an empirically grounded exploration of slavery and the lives of the enslaved on the model provided by Morgan.

30. Newman, *Dark Inheritance*, 17. For Jews, see Holly Snyder, "Rules, Rights, and Redemption: The Negotiation of Jewish Status in British Atlantic Port Towns, 1740–1831," *Jewish History* 20 (2006): 147–70. For Maroons, see Kathleen Wilson, "The Performance of Freedom: Maroons in the Colonial Order in Eighteenth-Century Jamaica and the Atlantic Sound," *William and Mary Quarterly*, 3rd ser., 66 (2009): 43–86. The literature on Jamaica in the early eighteenth century is growing. The following recently published books on this place and period were published too late for incorporation into this essay: Edward B. Rugemer, *Slave Law and the Politics of Resistance in the Early Atlantic World* (Cambridge, Mass., 2018); Katherine Gerbner, *Christian Slavery Conversion and Race in the Protestant Atlantic World* (Philadelphia, 2019); Vincent Brown, *Tacky's Revolt: The Story of an Atlantic Slave War* (Cambridge, Mass., 2020); Christine Walker, *Jamaica Ladies: Female Slaveholders and the Creation of Britain's*

pression from white masters and overseers, the varieties of ways in which enslaved people were held in bondage in urban and rural areas, and most of all how enslaved people were worked so that Britain's sweet tooth for sugar could be satisfied, our knowledge of this crucial but understudied period of Jamaican history will be limited and incomplete. It will be incomplete despite this historical period being the time when the large, integrated sugar plantation became established as the principal place where enslaved people lived, worked, and died. It was also the time during which the urban center of Kingston flourished economically but where blacks and whites suffered demographically in ways that seldom occurred elsewhere in the Atlantic world. The materials exist in Jamaican and British archives for a study of slavery in the African period. Recapturing the lives of the enslaved in Knight's time is the urgent next step in the continuing evolution of historiography on Britain's most important colony. Jack Greene argues in his introduction that James Knight was the first historian of Jamaica or of any British plantation society to give serious attention to the origins, composition, and culture of enslaved Africans to such an extent that he might be considered almost an ethnographer. Future historians will find Knight a useful, if not unbiased, guide to recovering the texture of black culture in Jamaica in a period when the island was more an offshoot of Africa than of Europe. One doubts that these efforts would please Knight, given his unthinking acceptance of white supremacy and his firm belief that Jamaica and white Jamaicans were part of an expanding and ever more successful British imperial world. We do not need to agree with Knight's ethnographic and political assumptions to find what he writes about eighteenth-century Jamaica immensely interesting and a spur for fresh historical investigations.

Atlantic Empire (Chapel Hill, N.C., 2020); and Jason T. Sharples, *The World That Fear Made: Slave Revolts and Conspiracy Scares in Early America* (Philadelphia, 2020).

Illustrations

Index

Page numbers in italics refer to illustrations.

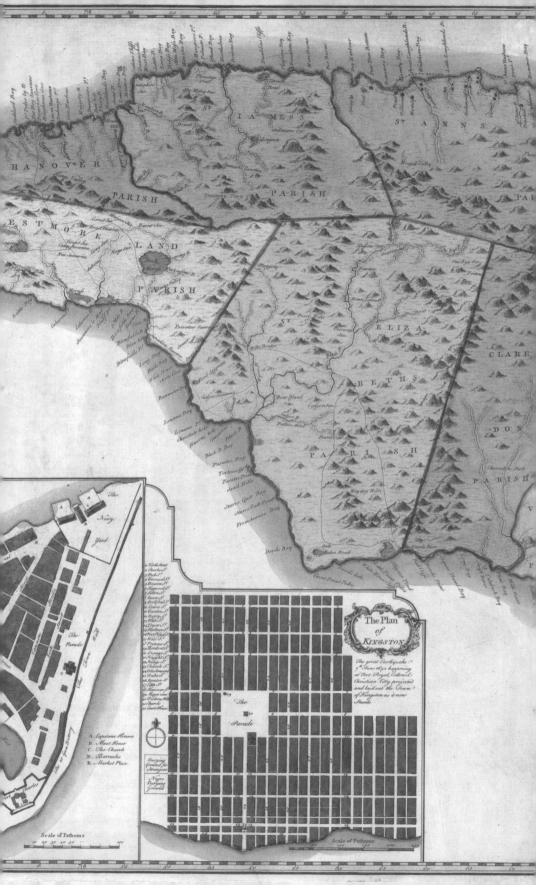